CHILD DEVELOPMENT

An Introduction

CHILD DEVELOPMENT

An Introduction

FIFTH EDITION

John W. Santrock
University of Texas at Dallas

Steven R. Yussen
University of Wisconsin at Madison

 Wm. C. Brown Publishers

Book Team

Editor *Michael Lange*
Developmental Editor *Sheralee Connors*
Production Editor *Debra DeBord*
Art Editor *Carla Heathcote*
Photo Editor *Laura Fuller*
Permissions Editor *Vicki Krug*
Visuals Processor *Kenneth E. Ley*

 Wm. C. Brown Publishers

President *G. Franklin Lewis*
Vice President, Publisher *Thomas E. Doran*
Vice President, Operations and Production *Beverly Kolz*
National Sales Manager *Virginia S. Moffat*
Group Sales Manager *Eric Ziegler*
Executive Editor *Edgar J. Laube*
Director of Marketing *Kathy Law Laube*
Marketing Manager *Carla J. Aspelmeier*
Managing Editor, Production *Colleen A. Yonda*
Manager of Visuals and Design *Faye M. Schilling*
Production Editorial Manager *Julie A. Kennedy*
Production Editorial Manager *Ann Fuerste*
Publishing Services Manager *Karen J. Slaght*

WCB Group

President and Chief Executive Officer *Mark C. Falb*
Chairman of the Board *Wm. C. Brown*

Cover photo © Maria Taglienti/The Image Bank

The credits section for this book begins on page C1, and is considered an extension of the copyright page.

Copyright © 1978, 1982, 1987, 1989, 1992 by Wm. C. Brown Publishers. All rights reserved

Library of Congress Catalog Card Number: 90–84773

ISBN 0–697–11597–6 (cloth)
     0–697–11598–4 (paper)

Printed in the United States of America by Wm. C. Brown Publishers, 2460 Kerper Boulevard, Dubuque, IA 52001

10 9 8 7 6 5 4 3 2 1

With special appreciation to our wives Mary Jo and Suzann and to our children Jennifer and Tracy, David and Elayna

BRIEF CONTENTS

SECTION
1

THE NATURE OF CHILD DEVELOPMENT

1   History, Issues, and Methods   5
2   Theories of Child Development   45

SECTION
2

BIOLOGICAL PROCESSES, PHYSICAL DEVELOPMENT, AND PERCEPTUAL DEVELOPMENT

3   Biological Beginnings   83
4   Prenatal Development and Birth   107
5   Physical, Motor, and Perceptual Development in Infancy   137
6   Physical Development in Childhood and Puberty   165

SECTION
3

LEARNING, COGNITION, AND LANGUAGE DEVELOPMENT

7   Learning and Motivation   217
8   Cognitive Development and Piaget's Theory   255
9   Information Processing   297
10   Language Development   333
11   Intelligence   363

SECTION
4

SOCIAL AND PERSONALITY DEVELOPMENT

12   Families   401
13   Peers, Play, and the Media   441
14   Schools   475
15   The Self, Social Competence, and Identity   517
16   Gender   549
17   Moral Development   583

CONTENTS
■ ■ ■ ■ ■

Concept Tables   xvii
Perspective on Child Development Boxes   xviii
Cultural Worlds of Development Boxes   xix
Preface   xxi

SECTION

1

THE NATURE OF CHILD DEVELOPMENT   3
■ ■ ■ ■ ■

1   History, Issues, and Methods   5

Child Development—Today and Yesterday   7
Some Contemporary Concerns   7
Historical Accounts of Childhood   9
The Modern Study of Child Development   10
Social Policy and Children's Development   13
*Cultural Worlds of Development: Caring for
Children—Cross-cultural Comparisons   14*

The Nature of Development   17
Biological, Cognitive, and Social Processes   17
Periods of Development   18

Developmental Issues   19
Maturation and Experience (Nature
and Nurture)   20
Continuity and Discontinuity   20
*Cultural Worlds of Development 1.2: The
Heterogeneity of Ethnic and Cultural Groups   21*

Stability and Change   22
Evaluating the Developmental Issues   22

The Science Base of Child Development   23
Theory and the Scientific Method   24
Collecting Information About Children's
Development   25
Strategies for Setting Up Research Studies   30
Time Span of Inquiry   32
Cohort Effects   34
Basic Versus Applied Research in Child
Development   35
Reducing Sexist Research   35
*Perspective on Child Development 1.1: Cohort
Effects and Children's Computer Skills   36*
Ethics in Research on Child Development   38

Careers in Child Development   38
Summary   40
Key Terms   42
Suggested Readings   43

2 Theories of Child Development 45

Psychoanalytic Theories 47
  Freud's Theory 47
  Erikson's Theory 51
  Perspective on Child Development 2.1:
    Gender-Based Criticisms of Freud's Theory 52
  Evaluating the Psychoanalytic Theories 55

Cognitive Theories 55
  Piaget's Theory 58
  Information-Processing Theory 59
  Evaluating the Cognitive Theories 62

Behavioral and Social Learning Theories 63
  Skinner's Behaviorism 63
  Social Learning Theory 65
  Evaluating the Behavioral and Social Learning
    Theories 66

Phenomenological and Humanistic Theories 67
  Rogers' Humanistic Approach 68
  Evaluating the Phenomenological and Humanistic
    Theories 68

Ethological Theories 70
  Lorenz's Classical Ethological Theory 70
  Hinde's Neo-Ethological Theory 71
  Evaluating the Ethological Theories 71

Ecological Theory 72
  Environmental Systems 72
  Cultural Worlds of Development 2.1: Culture and
    Personality: Individualistic and Collectivistic
    Orientations 74
  Evaluating Ecological Theory 75

An Eclectic Theoretical Orientation 75

Summary 78
Key Terms 79
Suggested Readings 79

SECTION

2

BIOLOGICAL PROCESSES, PHYSICAL DEVELOPMENT, AND PERCEPTUAL DEVELOPMENT 81

■ ■ ■ ■ ■

3 Biological Beginnings 83

The Evolutionary Perspective 85

Genetics 86
  What Are Genes? 87
  Reproduction 88
  Abnormalities in Genes and Chromosomes 90
  Some Genetic Principles 91
  Perspective on Child Development 3.1:
    Genetic Counseling 92
  Methods Used by Behavior Geneticists 95

Heredity's Influence on Development 97
  Intelligence 97
  Perspective on Child Development 3.2: Doran,
    Dr. Graham, and the Repository for Germinal
    Choice 98
  Temperament 97
  Perspective on Child Development 3.3:
    Born to Be Shy? 101
  Cultural Worlds of Development 3.1:
    Imperturbability in European American, Chinese
    American, and Navaho Indian Newborns 102

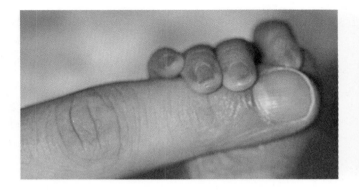
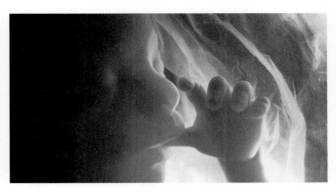

Heredity-Environment Interaction and
Development 102

Summary 104
Key Terms 105
Suggested Readings 105

4 Prenatal Development and Birth 107

Prenatal Development 108
    The Course of Prenatal Development 108
    Miscarriage and Abortion 112
    Cultural Worlds of Development 4.1:
    An International Perspective on Abortion
    Trends 113
    Teratology and Hazards to Prenatal
    Development 113
    Perspective on Child Development 4.1: Ethics and
    the Medical Use of Fetal Tissue 114
    Perspective on Child Development 4.2: Cocaine
    Babies 120

The Birth Process 120
    Childbirth Strategies 122
    Stages of Birth and Delivery Complications 123
    Use of Drugs During Childbirth 125
    Preterm Infants and Age-Weight
    Considerations 125
    Some Conclusions About Preterm Infants 126
    Stimulation of Preterm Infants 127
    Cultural Worlds of Development 4.2: Prenatal Care
    in the United States and Around the World 128
    Perspective on Child Development 4.3: Massaging
    and Exercising Preemies 129
    Measures of Neonatal Health and
    Responsiveness 129
    Bonding 132

Summary 134
Key Terms 135
Suggested Readings 135

5 Physical, Motor, and Perceptual
Development in Infancy 137

Physical Growth and Development in Infancy 138
    Reflexes 138
    Emotions 142
    States 144
    Physical Growth and Motor Development 145
    The Brain 148
    Perspective on Child Development 5.1: Babies Don't
    Need Exercise Classes 149
    Nutrition 149
    Perspective on Child Development 5.2: What's
    Good Food for an Adult Can Be Bad Food for
    a Baby 152
    Cultural Worlds of Development 5.1: Children
    Living Hungry in America 153

Sensory and Perceptual Development 155
    What Are Sensation and Perception? 155
    Visual Perception 155
    Hearing 157
    Smell 157
    Taste 158
    Touch 158
    Pain 158
    Perspective on Child Development 5.3: The Fetus
    and The Cat in the Hat *159*
    Perspective on Child Development 5.4: Yellow
    Kangaroos, Gray Donkeys, Thumps, Gongs, and
    4-Month-Old Infants 160
    Intermodal Perception 160

Summary 162
Key Terms 163
Suggested Readings 163

6 Physical Development in Childhood and
Puberty 165

Physical Development in Early Childhood 167
    Body Growth and Change 167
    The Brain 168
    Motor Development 169

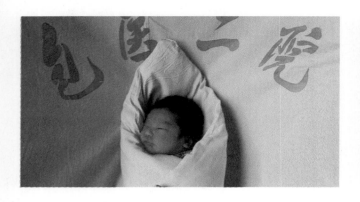

**Physical Development in Middle and Late
Childhood** 172
The Skeletal and Muscular Systems 172
Motor Skills 172

Health, Nutrition, and Exercise 174
A Developmental Perspective on Children's
Health 174
The State of Illness and Health in the World's
Children 176
Nutrition 177
Exercise 178
*Perspective on Child Development 6.1:
Heart Smart 180*

Puberty 181
Pubertal Change 183
Psychological Accompaniments of Pubertal
Change 185
Pubertal Timing and Health Care 186

Sexuality 187
Sexual Attitudes and Behavior 188
Sexually Transmitted Diseases 192
Adolescent Pregnancy 195

Some Adolescent Problems and Disturbances 197
Drugs 197
*Cultural Worlds of Development 6.1: Adolescent
Sexual Orientation in Holland and Sweden 198*
Suicide 201
Eating Disorders 201
The Interrelation of Problems and Programs That
Prevent or Reduce Adolescent Problems 203

Stereotyping Adolescents and Today's Youth 204
Stereotyping Adolescents 204
Today's Youth 206

Summary 210
Key Terms 212
Suggested Readings 212

LEARNING, COGNITION, AND LANGUAGE DEVELOPMENT 215

■ ■ ■ ■ ■

7 Learning and Motivation 217

The Nature of Learning and Motivation 219

Learning 220

Classical Conditioning 221
How Classical Conditioning Works 221
Classical Conditioning with Children 222
Evaluating Classical Conditioning 224
*Perspective on Child Development 7.1: Fear,
Excitement, and Salivation 225*

Operant Conditioning 225
What Is Operant Conditioning? 225
The Flow of Events 226
Arrangements of Reinforcements - 228
*Perspective on Child Development 7.2: The Role of
Immediate and Delayed Consequences in
Developing Self-control 229*
Punishment 231
Applications of Operant Conditioning 233
*Perspective on Child Development 7.3:
Assertive Discipline in Classrooms: Panacea
or Problem? 234*

Habituation 234

Imitation and Cognitive Learning 237
Bandura's Concept of Imitation 237
Infant's Imitation 239
Behavior, Person (Cognition), and
Environment 241

Motivation 241
Some Ideas About the "Whys" of Children's
Behavior 241
Achievement 243
***Cultural Worlds of Development 7.1: Comparisons
of Children's Math Achievement in Japan, China,
and the United States 248***

Summary 250
Key Terms 251
Suggested Readings 252

8 Cognitive Development and Piaget's
Theory 255

**Jean Piaget and His Place in Developmental
Psychology 257**

Cognitive Developmental Theory and Processes 257
Cognitive Developmental Theory 258
Cognitive Processes 258

Sensorimotor Thought 259
The Substages of Sensorimotor Thought 260
Object Permanence 262
A New Perspective on Cognitive Development in
Infancy 264

Preoperational Thought 266
The Nature of Preoperational Thought 266
The Substages of Preoperational Thought 266
***Perspective on Child Development 8.1: Where
Pelicans Kiss Seals, Cars Float on Clouds, and
Humans Are Tadpoles 268***

Concrete Operational Thought 274

***Perspective on Child Development 8.2: Piglet,
Pooh, and Piaget 275***
Conservation 276
Classification 277
Application of Piaget's Ideas to Education 278

Formal Operational Thought 278
Characteristics of Formal Operational
Thought 278
Formal Operational Thought and Language 280
Adolescent Egocentrism 282
Early and Late Formal Operational Thought 282
Variations in Adolescent Cognition 283
Beyond Formal Operational Thought 284

Piagetian Contributions and Criticisms 285

Vygotsky's Theory of Cognitive Development 286
Zone of Proximal Development 286
Language and Thought 287
Culture and Society 289
***Cultural Worlds of Development 8.1: Culture,
Schooling, and Cognitive Development 288***
***Cultural Worlds of Development 8.2: Cultural
Similarities and Variations Among Thinking
Apprenticeships 290***

Summary 293
Key Terms 294
Suggested Readings 295

9 Information Processing 297

The Nature of Information Processing 299
Framework 299
Developmental Change 301
***Perspective on Child Development 9.1: "Ask If the
Computer Ever Eats Breakfast" 302***

**Elementary Cognitive Processes Necessary to Process
Information 303**
Attention 303
Memory 306

Higher-Order Cognitive Processes 310
Problem Solving 310
Cognitive Monitoring 311
Critical Thinking 312

Knowledge and Expertise 313
Perspective on Child Development 9.2: Information Processing, the Information Age, and Children's Education 314
Knowledge 315
Expertise 320
Cultural Worlds of Development 9.1: Cultural Literacy 321

Individual Differences in Information Processing 323

Summary 327
Key Terms 328
Suggested Readings 328
Answer to Inoperable Tumor Problem 328

10 Language Development 331

What Is Language? 333

Language's Rule Systems 333
Phonology 334
Morphology 334
Syntax 335
Semantics 335
Pragmatics 335

Language's Biological and Sociocultural/Environmental Heritages 336
Biological Influences 336
Perspective on Child Development 10.1: Genie, Modern-Day Wild Child 340
Sociocultural and Environmental Influences 340
Cultural Worlds of Development 10.1: Mother-Child Interaction in an Inner-City Housing Project 342
Perspective on Child Development 10.2: Picture Books, First Words, and Labeling 344

The Role of Cognition in Language 345

How Language Develops 347
Language Development in Infancy 347

Language Development in Early Childhood 349
Language Development in Middle and Late Childhood 353

Summary 358
Key Terms 360
Suggested Readings 360

11 Intelligence 363

What Is Intelligence? 364

How Tests Are Constructed and Evaluated 365
Reliability 365
Validity 366
Standardization 367

The Measurement and Nature of Children's Intelligence 368
Alfred Binet and the Binet Tests 368
The Wechsler Scales 370
Does Intelligence Have a Single Nature? 370

Infant Intelligence and the Stability of Intelligence 374
Infant Intelligence Tests 375
The Stability of Intelligence 376
Use of Information-Processing Tasks in Infancy to Predict Intelligence 378

Controversies and Issues in Intelligence 378
The Heredity-Environment Controversy 380
Culture and Ethnicity 381
Cultural Worlds of Development 11.1: Larry P., Intelligent but Not on Intelligence Tests 384
Knowledge Versus Process in Intelligence 386
The Use and Misuse of Intelligence Tests 387

The Extremes of Intelligence 388
Mental Retardation 388
Giftedness 389
Creativity 390
Perspective on Child Development 11.1: The Snowflake Model of Creativity and Its Application to Education 392

Summary 395
Key Terms 396
Suggested Readings 396

SOCIAL AND PERSONALITY DEVELOPMENT 399

■ ■ ■ ■ ■

12   Families   401

Family Processes   402
Transition to Parenthood   402
Reciprocal Socialization   404
The Family As a System   405

Attachment   405
What Is Attachment?   406
Individual Differences   407
Attachment, Temperament, and the Wider Social
World   408

The Father's Role   409

Day Care   410
*Cultural Worlds of Development 12.1: Child-Care
Policies Around the World   411*
*Perspective on Child Development 12.1: What Is
Quality Day Care?   414*

Parenting Styles   416
The Nature of Parenting Styles   416
Adapting Parenting to Developmental Changes in
the Child   417
*Perspective on Child Development 12.2: A Primer
for Competent Parenting   419*
Cultural, Social Class, and Ethnic Variations in
Families   420
Child Abuse   421
*Cultural Worlds of Development 12.2:
Black American and Mexican Family
Orientations   422*

Sibling Relationships and Birth Order   424

Family Processes in Adolescence   426
Autonomy and Attachment   426
Parent-Adolescent Conflict   428
The Maturation of the Adolescent and
Parents   429

The Changing Family in a Changing Society   430
Working Parents   430
The Effects of Divorce on Children   433
Stepfamilies   434

Summary   438
Key Terms   439
Suggested Readings   439

13   Peers, Play, and the Media   441

Peers   443
Peer Group Functions   443
The Distinct but Coordinated Worlds of Parent-
Child and Peer Relations   444
The Developmental Course of Peer Relations in
Childhood   445
Peer Popularity, Rejection, and Neglect   445
Social Cognition   446
Friends   448
Peer Relations in Adolescence   450
*Cultural Worlds of Development 13.1: Ethnic
Minority Adolescents' Peer Relations   453*

Contents   xiii

Play   454
   Play's Functions   454
   Parten's Classic Study of Play   456
   Types of Play   457
   ***Perspective on Child Development 13.1: Superhero
      Play   460***
   The Sociocultural Contexts of Play   462

Media Influences   464
   Television   464
   ***Cultural Worlds of Development 13.2: Sesame
      Street Around the World   466***
   Computers and Children   468

Summary   472
Key Terms   473
Suggested Readings   473

14   Schools   475

The Nature of Children's Schooling   476
   Do Schools Make a Difference?   477
   Functions of Children's Schools   478
   Schools' Changing Social Developmental
      Contexts   479

Early Childhood Education   480
   Child-Centered Kindergarten   480
   Developmentally Appropriate and Inappropriate
      Practices in the Education of Young Children
      481
   Does It Matter If Children Attend Preschool Before
      Kindergarten?   482
   ***Cultural Worlds of Development 14.1: Early
      Childhood Education in Japan   487***

   The Effects of Early Childhood Education   486
   Education for Disadvantaged Young Children   488

The Transition to Elementary School   489

Schools, Classrooms, and Teachers   491
   School Size and Classroom Size   491
   Classroom Structure and Climate   492
   Teachers   493

Social Class and Ethnicity in Schools   494
   Social Class   494
   Ethnicity   494
   ***Cultural Worlds of Development 14.2:
      The Jigsaw Classroom   497***

The Nature of Adolescents' Schooling   497
   The Transition to Middle or Junior High
      School   497
   High School Dropouts   500
   ***Perspective on Child Development 14.1:
      Beyond the Zoo   501***
   ***Cultural Worlds of Development 14.3: Helping
      Hispanic Youths Stay in School and Go to
      College   503***
   Part-Time Work and School   504

Educating Children with Special Needs   504
   Handicapped Children   505
   Learning Disabilities   508

Summary   512
Key Terms   514
Suggested Readings   514

15   The Self, Social Competence,
     and Identity   517

The Self   518
    Self-understanding   519
    Self-esteem   525
    ***Cultural Worlds of Development 15.1: Ethnicity,
        Self, and Self-esteem   529***

Social Competence   529
    What Is Social Competence?   529
    Measuring Social Competence   533

Identity   535
    Erikson's Ideas on Identity   535
    Some Contemporary Thoughts on Identity   536
    The Four Statuses of Identity   536
    Developmental Changes   537
    ***Perspective on Child Development 15.1: Hitler,
        Luther, and Gandhi—the Development of Their
        Identities   538***
    Family Influences on Identity   539
    Cultural and Ethnic Aspects of Identity   540
    ***Cultural Worlds of Development 15.2: The
        Development of Identity in Native American
        Adolescents   542***
    Gender and Identity   542

Summary   545
Key Terms   547
Suggested Readings   547

16   Gender   549

What Is Gender?   551

**What Are the Biological, Social, and Cognitive
    Influences on Gender?   551**
    Biological Influences   551
    Social Influences   552
    Cognitive Influences   557
    ***Perspective on Child Development 16.1: How Good
        Are Girls at Wudgemaking If the Wudgemaker Is
        He?   560***

**Gender Stereotypes, Similarities and Differences, and
    Achievement   560**
    Gender Role Stereotyping   562
    Gender Similarities and Differences   563
    Achievement   564

**Gender Role Classification—Masculinity, Femininity,
    and Androgyny   567**
    ***Cultural Worlds of Development 16.1:
        Gender Roles in Egypt, China, and the Soviet
        Union   570***

The Feminist Perspective on Gender   571

Gender and Social Policy   572
    Gender Role Stereotypes and the Media   572
    Gender and Education   573
    Gender and Child Care   573

Ethnicity and Gender   573
    Ethnic Minority Females   574
    Ethnic Minority Males   575

Summary   578
Key Terms   580
Suggested Readings   580

17 Moral Development 583

What Is Moral Development? 585

Moral Thoughts 585
Piaget's Ideas About Moral Development 585
Kohlberg's Ideas About Moral Development 586
Influences on the Kohlberg Stages 589
Kohlberg's Critics 590
Perspective on Child Development 17.1: Amy Says They Should Just Talk It Out and Find Some Other Way to Make Money 593
Cultural Worlds of Development 17.1: Cultural Variations in Children's Moral Development 595

Moral Behavior 595
Reinforcement, Punishment, and Imitation 596
Resistance to Temptation and Self-control 597
Cognitive Social Learning Theory 598

Moral Feelings 600
Psychoanalytic Theory 600
Childrearing Techniques and Moral Development 600
Empathy 601
The Contemporary Perspective on the Role of Emotions in Moral Development 604

Altruism 604

Moral Education 606
The Hidden Curriculum 606
Direct and Indirect Moral Education 606
Damon's Comprehensive Approach to Moral Education 608

Juvenile Delinquency 610
Perspective on Child Development 17.2: Frog and Dolores 613

Summary 616
Key Terms 617
Suggested Readings 617

Epilogue: The Odyssey of Childhood 619
Glossary G1
References R1
Credits C1
Name Index N1
Subject Index S1

CONCEPT TABLES

1.1 The History of and Issues in Children's Development 23

1.2 The Science Base of and Careers in Child Development 40

2.1 The Psychoanalytic and Cognitive Theories 64

2.2 The Behavioral and Social Learning Theories and the Phenomenological and Humanistic Theories 69

2.3 The Ethological Theories, Ecological Theory, and an Eclectic Theoretical Orientation 77

3.1 The Evolutionary Perspective and Genetics 96

3.2 Heredity's Influence on Development and Heredity-Environment Interaction 104

4.1 Prenatal Development 122

4.2 The Birth Process 133

5.1 Physical Growth and Development in Infancy 154

5.2 Perceptual Development in Infancy 161

6.1 Physical Development, Health, Nutrition, and Exercise 182

6.2 Puberty, Sexuality, Adolescent Problems and Disturbances, Stereotyping Adolescents, and Today's Youth 208

7.1 The Nature of Learning and Motivation, Classical Conditioning, and Operant Conditioning 236

7.2 Habituation, Imitation and Cognitive Learning, Motivation, and Achievement 249

8.1 Piaget's Place in Developmental Psychology, Cognitive Developmental Theory, Cognitive Processes, Sensorimotor Development, and Preoperational Development 276

8.2 Concrete Operational Thought, Formal Operational Thought, Piagetian Contributions and Criticisms, and Vygotsky's Theory of Cognitive Development 292

9.1 The Nature of Information Processing and the Elementary Cognitive Processes Necessary to Process Information 309

9.2 Higher-Order Cognitive Processes, Knowledge and Expertise, and Individual Differences in Information Processing 326

10.1 What Is Language, Language's Rule Systems, and Language's Biological and Sociocultural/Environmental Heritages 346

10.2 The Role of Cognition in Language and How Language Develops 358

11.1 Intelligence, Test Construction, and Intelligence Tests 379

11.2 Controversies and Issues in Intelligence and the Extremes of Intelligence 394

12.1 Family Processes, Attachment, the Father's Role, and Day Care 415

12.2 Parenting Styles, Sibling Relationships and Birth Order, Family Processes in Adolescence, and the Changing Family in a Changing Society 436

13.1 Peers 455

13.2 Play and Media Influences 471

14.1 The Nature of Children's Schooling and Early Childhood Education 490

14.2 The Transition to Elementary School; Schools, Classrooms, and Teachers; Social Class and Ethnicity in Schools; the Nature of Adolescents' Schooling; and the Education of Children with Special Needs 510

15.1 The Self 530

15.2 Social Competence and Identity 544

16.1 The Nature of Gender and Biological, Cognitive, and Social Influences on Gender 561

16.2 Gender Stereotyping, Similarities and Differences, and Achievement; Gender Role Classification; the Feminist Perspective on Gender; Gender and Social Policy with Children; and Ethnicity and Gender 577

17.1 The Nature of Moral Development, Moral Thought, and Moral Behavior 599

17.2 Moral Feelings, Altruism, Moral Education, and Juvenile Delinquency 614

PERSPECTIVE ON CHILD DEVELOPMENT BOXES

1.1 Cohort Effects and Children's Computer Skills 36

2.1 Gender-Based Criticisms of Freud's Theory 52

3.1 Genetic Counseling 92

3.2 Doran, Dr. Graham, and the Repository for Germinal Choice 98

3.3 Born to Be Shy? 101

4.1 Ethics and the Medical Use of Fetal Tissue 114

4.2 Cocaine Babies 120

4.3 Massaging and Exercising Preemies 129

5.1 Babies Don't Need Exercise Classes 149

5.2 What's Good Food for an Adult Can Be Bad Food for a Baby 152

5.3 The Fetus and *The Cat in the Hat* 159

5.4 Yellow Kangaroos, Gray Donkeys, Thumps, Gongs, and 4-Month-Old Infants 160

6.1 Heart Smart 180

7.1 Fear, Excitement, and Salivation 225

7.2 The Role of Immediate and Delayed Consequences in Developing Self-control 229

7.3 Assertive Discipline in Classrooms: Panacea or Problem? 234

8.1 Where Pelicans Kiss Seals, Cars Float on Clouds, and Humans Are Tadpoles 268

8.2 Piglet, Pooh, and Piaget 275

9.1 "Ask If the Computer Ever Eats Breakfast" 302

9.2 Information Processing, the Information Age, and Children's Education 314

10.1 Genie, Modern-Day Wild Child 340

10.2 Picture Books, First Words, and Labeling 344

11.1 The Snowflake Model of Creativity and Its Application to Education 392

12.1 What Is Quality Day Care? 414

12.2 A Primer for Competent Parenting 419

13.1 Superhero Play 460

14.1 Beyond the Zoo 501

15.1 Hitler, Luther, and Gandhi—the Development of Their Identities 538

16.1 How Good Are Girls at Wudgemaking If the Wudgemaker Is *He?* 560

17.1 Amy Says They Should Just Talk It Out and Find Some Other Way to Make Money 593

17.2 Frog and Dolores 613

CULTURAL WORLDS OF DEVELOPMENT BOXES

■ ■ ■ ■ ■

1.1 Caring for Children—Cross-Cultural Comparisons   14

1.2 The Heterogeneity of Ethnic and Cultural Groups   21

2.1 Culture and Personality: Individualistic and Collectivistic Orientations   74

3.1 Imperturbability in European American, Chinese American, and Navaho Indian Newborns   102

4.1 An International Perspective on Abortion Trends   113

4.2 Prenatal Care in the United States and Around the World   128

5.1 Children Living Hungry in America   153

6.1 Adolescent Sexual Orientation in Holland and Sweden   198

7.1 Comparisons of Children's Math Achievement in Japan, China, and the United States   248

8.1 Culture, Schooling, and Cognitive Development   288

8.2 Cultural Similarities and Variations Among Thinking Apprenticeships   290

9.1 Cultural Literacy   321

10.1 Mother-Child Interaction in an Inner-City Housing Project   342

11.1 Larry P., Intelligent but Not on Intelligence Tests   384

12.1 Child-Care Policies Around the World   411

12.2 Black American and Mexican Family Orientations   422

13.1 Ethnic Minority Adolescents' Peer Relations   453

13.2 *Sesame Street* Around the World   466

14.1 Early Childhood Education in Japan   487

14.2 The Jigsaw Classroom   497

14.3 Helping Hispanic Youths Stay in School and Go to College   503

15.1 Ethnicity, Self, and Self-esteem   529

15.2 The Development of Identity in Native American Adolescents   542

16.1 Gender Roles in Egypt, China, and the Soviet Union   570

17.1 Cultural Variations in Children's Moral Development   595

PREFACE

■ ■ ■ ■ ■

This book is the fifth edition of *Child Development*. We have presented the basic knowledge about children's development and chronicled the changes in the field that have taken place over almost 2 decades in subsequent editions of the book. As we approach the twenty-first century, the field of child development continues to be a lively research enterprise, with many scholars seeking new information about the nature of children. In the fifth edition of *Child Development,* we have kept the core knowledge of the field. At the same time, we have extensively modified this edition to include the major new research developments and emerging issues in the field.

Highlights of Changes in the Fifth Edition of *Child Development*

The fifth edition of *Child Development* continues to follow a topical format. However, as a result of our thorough, painstaking analysis of the current nature of the field of child development, we have done considerable adding, subtracting, simplifying, and integrating of chapters and sections of the book.

Chapter and Section Changes

The fourth edition of *Child Development* had 5 sections and 18 chapters. The fifth edition has 4 sections and 17 chapters. At the request of a number of reviewers and adopters of the book, we have deleted its final section— Abnormal Behavior, Stress, and Health—and integrated that information into appropriate chapters. For example, a discussion of child abuse now appears in chapter 12 on families, and an examination of juvenile delinquency now appears in chapter 17 on moral development. The first four major sections of *Child Development* have remained the same: (1) The Nature of Child Development;

(2) Biological Processes, Physical Development, and Perceptual Development; (3) Learning, Cognition, and Language Development; and (4) Social and Personality Development.

We have made several chapter changes in *Child Development*. In previous editions of the book, theories were touched on briefly in chapter 1 and then extensively discussed in a chapter in the second half of the book. In the fifth edition of *Child Development,* we have placed the theories chapter second, just after the student has learned about the history, main issues, and methods of the field. In addition to the traditionally discussed theories—psychoanalytic, cognitive, behavioral/social learning, and humanistic—we also extensively examine two other important theories in chapter 2—ethological and ecological. This chapter provides students with a firm grounding in the theories of child development before they read about the research base of the field. Appropriately, since theories are now discussed in chapter 2, the previous edition's chapter on the theories of socialization has been deleted.

Another chapter change in the fifth edition is the devotion of a full chapter (chapter 5) to infant physical, motor, and perceptual development. In the fourth edition, children's and infants' physical development were combined in this chapter. In the fifth edition, children's physical development is discussed in the same chapter as puberty (chapter 6). These changes allowed us to devote more attention to the expanding knowledge about infant development and to present more information about physical development in childhood as well.

Yet another important change is the devotion of an entire chapter to schools (chapter 14). In previous editions, the discussion of schools was embedded in the chapter on peers, schools, and the media. Schools are extremely important contexts in children's development, and a number of important issues in children's schooling merit extensive discussion. By giving schools a separate chapter, more space has been freed up to expand our discussion of peers, play, and the media. For example, you will find a completely new section on the positive and negative aspects of children's use of computers in chapter 13.

Content Changes

In addition to major section and chapter changes in the fifth edition of *Child Development,* our extensive examination of the research taking place in the field has led to a number of content modifications. These modifications include an increased emphasis on ethnicity and culture, gender, education and schools, social policy, and prenatal development and infancy.

Ethnicity and Culture

Special attention is given to the roles of ethnicity and culture in children's development. This increased coverage reflects the growing interest in ethnic minority and cross-cultural research. A special new feature in the fifth edition of *Child Development* is the *Cultural Worlds of Development* boxes in every chapter. A look through any chapter of the book reveals their special appeal. Reviewers of the fifth edition of *Child Development* have consistently commented that this book now has far more discussion of ethnicity than any other child development text and more discussion of cultural issues than any other topical child development text.

Gender

An equally important change in the fifth edition of *Child Development* is the increased coverage of gender issues and female development. The chapter on gender (16) has been expanded to include a discussion of social policy issues and gender, as well as the feminist perspective on gender issues. Chapter 16 also includes an extensively revised discussion of gender stereotypes, similarities, and differences, as well as a completely new section on ethnicity and gender. Gender issues also are discussed in a number of other places in the text, such as the gender-based criticism of Freud's theory (chapter 2), gender issues and schools (chapter 14), and Gilligan's recent ideas on the care perspective (chapter 17).

Education and Schools

In addition to appearing in the new chapter on schools, education issues are discussed in a number of other places. This expanded coverage of education issues includes the new, updated, or improved presentation of material on the quality of child care, assertive discipline in classrooms,

ethnic diversity and achievement, math achievement across cultures, Vygotsky's theory of cognitive development and its application to education, Rogoff's concept of apprenticeship thinking, the application of the information-processing perspective to education, reciprocal teaching, individual differences and information processing, literacy and early childhood education, the Snowflake Model of creativity and its application to education, constructive play and education, the positive and negative aspects of children's use of computers, and Damon's comprehensive moral education approach.

Social Policy

Another important feature of the fifth edition of *Child Development* is increased coverage of social policy issues. The importance of social policy issues in children's development is highlighted in chapter 1; social policy issues are discussed in a number of other chapters as well.

Prenatal Development and Infancy

Research has extensively increased at the beginning of children's development. Issues that have been given more attention include: cocaine babies, the stimulation of preterm infants, prenatal care around the world, high-quality child care, and the stepped-up challenge to Piaget's ideas on sensorimotor development.

Increased Coverage of Other Topics

In addition to increased coverage of the topics already mentioned, the following areas have been given more attention in *Child Development,* fifth edition: AIDS in children and adolescents, developmentally appropriate and inappropriate practice in preschools, Damon's views on empathy and altruism, health and nutrition, careers in child development, critical thinking, metacognitive knowledge, Bruner's Language Acquisition Support System, divorce and stepfamilies, the types of play, the development of self-understanding, and self-esteem.

Pedagogical Changes

One of the main features of the fourth edition of *Child Development* was its extensive attention to pedagogy. The core of this well-received pedagogical system has been retained—such as the useful concept tables, high-interest introductions to chapters, outlines at the beginnings of chapters, and chapter summaries. However, to make *Child Development*'s learning system more effective and challenging, we have incorporated a number of new features that include: key term definitions in text, critical thinking questions, and visual figures and tables.

A very important aspect of *Child Development*'s improved learning system is the new way KEY TERMS are presented. Key terms appear in the text in **boldfaced type,** with their definitions following immediately in *italics*. This provides students with a clear understanding of important concepts in child development. The key terms also are listed, with page references, at the end of each chapter and are defined in a page-referenced GLOSSARY at the end of the book.

To encourage CRITICAL THINKING, topics are explored in sufficient depth to challenge students, and the complex nature of child development is presented in such a way as to encourage the development of critical thinking skills. In each chapter, three or four critical thinking questions appear in the margin.

The presentation of figures and tables has also been dramatically improved in the fifth edition of *Child Development*. Every chapter has a number of VISUAL FIGURES AND TABLES, which include both a description of important content information and photographs to illustrate the content. In many instances, the visual figures and tables represent summaries or reviews of important concepts. For example, in chapter 8, four visual figures summarize the key themes of each of Piaget's stages after they are discussed in the text. In chapter 10, a visual figure shows the interaction of Chomsky's and Bruner's ideas. In chapter 13, a visual figure summarizes the types of play, and, in chapter 14, a visual table summarizes developmentally appropriate and inappropriate practice in early childhood education. The combination of summary descriptions and carefully selected photographs in the form of visual figures and tables presented periodically within each chapter enhances students' retention and makes *Child Development* an attractive book to study.

Overview of Basic Features in *Child Development*

In addition to the important changes that have been made in the fifth edition of *Child Development,* a number of basic features from previous editions have been continued. These features include the book's research system, writing system, learning system, and supplementary materials.

The Research System

The present edition of *Child Development* is, above all else, an extremely up-to-date presentation of research in the three primary domains of development: biological processes, cognitive processes, and social processes. Research on biological, cognitive, and social processes continues to represent the core of *Child Development*. This core includes both classic and cutting edge research. More than 40 percent of the references in *Child Development* are new, with more than 500 of these coming from 1990, 1991, and *in press* sources. Scientific knowledge about child development is expanding on many frontiers, and we have tried to capture the excitement of these discoveries, while presenting the classic studies that are the foundation of the discipline.

The Writing System

With the entire field of child development to cover, it was important that this book be written clearly and efficiently. We added, subtracted, integrated, and simplified as we wrote the fifth edition of *Child Development*. Why spend so much time rewriting the book? Because, when material is simply added without extensive rewriting, later editions become long and choppy. With the continued expansion of the research on many frontiers of child development, we found it necessary not only to add material but to start with page one and write the fifth edition as if we were beginning a new book. This strategy has the important benefit of allowing us to eliminate ideas and references that have become dated; to retain the theories, concepts, and research that are the core of the discipline; to add newly developed theories, concepts, and research ideas; and to integrate these changes so the presentation of the material is clear, efficient, and easy to read. The reviewers of the manuscript for the fifth edition of *Child Development* have consistently commented on the significant improvements in the writing and presentation of the material.

The Learning System

Child Development incorporates an extremely effective and challenging learning system. This text has been designed to enhance student comprehension and to encourage critical thinking. We wanted to challenge students with the latest knowledge in the field of child development. We wanted them to think about, to analyze, and to understand this information. Topics are explored in sufficient detail to challenge students, and the complex nature of child development is presented in such a way as to encourage critical thinking. Also, three or four times in each chapter, critical thinking questions appear in the margin.

However, we not only wanted to encourage thinking skills, but we also wanted to use textbook pedagogy to help students learn. Thus, an extensive, carefully designed pedagogical system has been built into *Child Development*. Critical to this pedagogical system are the CONCEPT TABLES that appear two or three times in every chapter. They are designed to activate students' memory and comprehension of major topics or key concepts that have been discussed to that point. This allows students to get a handle on complex concepts and ideas and to understand how they are interrelated. Concept tables provide a visual picture, or cognitive framework, of the most important information in each section.

A very important aspect of *Child Development*'s learning system is the new way key terms are presented. As mentioned previously, key terms appear in the text in **boldfaced type** with their definition following immediately in *italics*. This provides students with a clear understanding of important concepts in child development. The key terms are also listed, with page references, at the end of each chapter and are defined in a page-referenced glossary at the end of the book.

The new visual figures and tables are also an important addition to the learning system of *Child Development*. Every chapter has a number of visual figures and tables, which include both a description of important content information and photographs to illustrate the content. The combination of summary descriptions and carefully selected photographs enhances students' retention and makes the book a more attractive one to study.

In addition, an outline at the beginning of each chapter shows the overall hierarchical organization of the material. Then, an imaginative, high-interest piece follows—focusing on a topic related to the chapter's content. *Perspective on Child Development* boxes appear in every chapter, and a second type of box has been added to the fifth edition of *Child Development; Cultural Worlds of Development* boxes highlight ethnic and cultural issues in child development. At the end of each chapter, a detailed Summary in outline form provides a helpful review. An annotated list of Suggested Readings also appears at the end of every chapter. These elements should help students understand the field of child development.

Supplementary Materials

The publisher and ancillary team have worked together to produce an outstanding integrated teaching package to accompany *Child Development*. The authors of the ancillaries are all experienced teachers of the child development course. The ancillaries have been designed to make it as easy as possible to customize the entire package to meet the unique needs of professors and students.

The key to this teaching package, the *Instructor's Course Planner,* was created by Janet A. Simons. This flexible planner provides a variety of useful tools to enhance teaching efforts, reduce workload, and increase enjoyment. For each chapter of the text, the Planner provides a summary outline, learning objectives, key terms, research projects, classroom activities, discussion topics, mini-lecture topics, essay questions, and a transparency guide. The Planner also contains a section on "Ethical Practices in Research with Human Subjects" and a chapter-by-chapter film and videotape list. The *Instructor's Course Planner* is conveniently housed within an attractive $11'' \times 13'' \times 9''$ carrying case. This case is designed to accommodate the complete ancillary package by containing each chapter's material within a separate hanging file, allowing instructors to keep all their class materials organized at their fingertips.

The *Test Item File* was constructed by Lynne Blesz-Vestal and Janet A. Simons, Central Iowa Psychological Services. This comprehensive test book includes over 3,000 new multiple-choice test questions that are keyed to the text and learning objectives. Each item is designated as factual, conceptual, or applied.

The *Student Study Guide* was also prepared by Janet Simons. For each chapter of the text, students are provided a summary outline, learning objectives, a fill-in-the-blank guided review, key terms, a "This 'N That" section consisting of crossword puzzles and anagrams, two sets of twenty multiple-choice items for self-testing, and questions to encourage critical thinking. The guide also contains a section on "How to Study Effectively and Efficiently" and another on "Ethical Practices in Research with Human Subjects." The students are also provided the list of research projects that appears in the *Instructor's Course Planner.*

The *WCB Developmental Psychology Transparency/ Slide Set* consists of 100 newly developed acetate transparencies or slides. These full-color illustrations include graphics from various outside sources. Created by Lynne Blesz-Vestal, these transparencies were expressly designed to provide comprehensive coverage of all major topic areas generally covered in developmental psychology. A comprehensive annotated guide provides a brief description for each transparency and helpful suggestions for use in the classroom.

The *WCB Customized Reader* allows instructors to select up to 80 journal or magazine articles from a menu provided by WCB sales representatives. These readings will be custom printed for students and bound into an attractive $8¼'' \times 11''$ book, giving instructors the opportunity to create their own student reader.

WCB TestPak 3.0 is an integrated computer program designed to print test masters; to permit on-line computerized testing; to help students review text material through an interactive self-testing, self-scoring quiz program; and to provide instructors with a gradebook program for classroom management. Test questions can be found in the *Test Item File,* or instructors may create their own. Professors may choose to use Testbank A for exam questions and Testbank B in conjunction with the quiz program. Printing the exam requires access to a personal computer—an IBM that uses 5.25- or 3.5-inch diskettes, an Apple IIe or IIc, or a Macintosh. TestPak requires two disk drives and will work with any printer. Diskettes are available through a local WCB sales representative or by phoning Educational Services at 319–588–1451. The package contains complete instructions for making up an exam.

A large selection of videotapes is also available to adopters based on the number of textbooks ordered directly from Wm. C. Brown Publishers.

Acknowledgments

A project of this magnitude requires the efforts of many people. We owe special thanks to Acquisitions Editor Michael Lange, who has intelligently and cheerfully guided us through the fifth edition of the book. We also thank Developmental Editor Carla Aspelmeier, who showed a special enthusiasm in monitoring the revision process. Production Editor Debra DeBord copyedited the manuscript with care and competence and spent long hours overseeing the production of *Child Development.* Designer Elise Burckhardt provided creative touches that make the book more attractive and appealing. Laura Fuller went the extra mile in tracking down elusive and effective photographs, and Vicki Krug efficiently obtained permissions. Art editor Carla Heathcote and Visuals Processor Ken Ley contributed insightful aesthetic touches to the book and handled the production of the art. Thanks also go to Lynne Blesz-Vestal and Janet Simons, who prepared an excellent *Test Item File,* and to Janet Simons, who created a very useful *Instructor's Course Planner* and *Student Study Guide.*

The fifth edition of this book has benefited from a carefully selected board of reviewers, who provided in-depth reviews of chapters dealing with their areas of expertise and/or a page-by-page analysis of the entire manuscript. For their generous help and countless good ideas, we would like to thank:

David Bernhardt
Carelton University

Elaine Blakemore
Indiana University

Theodore Chandler
Kent State University

Denise M. DeZolt
Kent State University

Claire Etaugh
Bradley University

Saul Feinman
University of Wyoming

Jane Goins Flanagan
Lamar University

Janet Fuller
Mansfield University

Colleen Gift
Highland Community College

Donald E. Guenther
Kent State University

Elizabeth Hasson
Westchester University

Rebecca Heikkinen
Kent State University

Dottie McCrossen
Ottawa University

Sherry J. Neal
Oklahoma City Community College

Cosby Steele Rogers
Virginia Polytechnic Institute & State University

Cherie Valeithian
Kent State University

We also remain indebted to the following individuals, who reviewed previous editions and whose helpful guidance has been carried forward into the current edition of this text:

Ruth L. Ault
Davidson College

Michael Bergmire
Jefferson College

Susan Bland
Niagara County Community College

Maureen Callahan
Webster University

Debra E. Clark
SUNY–Cortland

Audrey E. Clark
California State University, Northridge

Robert C. Coon
Louisiana State University

Roger W. Coulson
Iowa State University

Daniel R. DiSalvi
Kean College

Diane C. Draper
Iowa State University

Dennis T. Farrell
Luzerne County Community College

Irma Galejs
Iowa State University

Margaret S. Gill
Kutztown State College

Robert A. Haaf
University of Toledo

Stanley Hensen
Arkansas Technical University

Seth Kalichman
Loyola University

Kenneth Kallio
SUNY–Geneseo

Daniel W. Kee
California State University, Fullerton

Melvyn B. King
SUNY–Cortland

John W. Kulig
Northern Illinois University

Daniel K. Lapsley
University of Notre Dame

Carolyn Meyer
Lake Sumter Community College

Dalton Miller-Jones
NE Foundation for Children

Jose E. Nanes
University of Minnesota

Daniel J. O'Neil
Bristol Community College

Robert Pasnak
George Mason University

Douglas B. Sawin
University of Texas, Austin

Matthew J. Sharps
University of Colorado

Ed Scholwinski
Southwest Texas State University

Marilyn Shea
University of Maine, Farmington

Bill M. Seay
Louisiana State University

Mark S. Strauss
University of Pittsburgh

The quality of this text is greatly due to the ideas and insights of many other colleagues. We would like to thank the following individuals for sharing their thoughts and beneficial suggestions for improving *Child Development:*

Stewart R. Beasley
Central State University

Chloe Merrill
Weber State College

Phil Brown
College of Eastern Utah

Elizabeth Pemberton
University of Iowa

William J. Cumes
University of Calgary

Bridgett Perry
Framingham State College

Philip S. Dale
University of Washington

Ann A. Rhodes
Arkansas College

Coralie Dietrich
University of Wisconsin

Amy Tolson
Delta College

John Durkin
University of Victoria

Hope Underwood
University of Wisconsin

Francene Evans
Worthington Community College

Marcia Weinstein
Salem State College

Nancie Lobb
Alvin Community College

Eileen Wood
Wilfrid Laurier University

Daniel Lynch
University of Wisconsin

A final note of thanks goes to our families. Mary Jo Santrock and Suzann Yussen have lived through five editions of *Child Development*. We appreciate the support and encouragement they have given to our writing. Our children, Tracy and Jennifer Santrock and Elayna and David Yussen, have provided us with firsthand experiences at watching children develop. Tracy was 7, Jennifer was 5, Elayna was about to be born, and David had not yet been born when the first edition of *Child Development* was published. Now Tracy is 25, Jennifer is 22, Elayna is 17, and David is 13. Through these 17 years, they have helped us render a treatment of children's development that captures its complexity, its subtlety, and its humanity.

CHILD DEVELOPMENT

An Introduction

THE NATURE OF CHILD DEVELOPMENT

IN EVERY CHILD WHO IS

BORN, UNDER NO MATTER

WHAT CIRCUMSTANCES,

AND OF NO MATTER WHAT

PARENTS, THE

POTENTIALITY OF THE

HUMAN RACE IS BORN

AGAIN.

—James Agee

CHAPTER

1

■

HISTORY, ISSUES, AND METHODS

Child Development—Today and Yesterday
    Some Contemporary Concerns
    Historical Accounts of Childhood
    The Modern Study of Child Development
    Social Policy and Children's Development
    Cultural Worlds of Development 1.1: Caring for
        Children—Cross-cultural Comparisons
The Nature of Development
    Biological, Cognitive, and Social Processes
    Periods of Development
Developmental Issues
    Maturation and Experience (Nature and Nurture)
    Continuity and Discontinuity
    Cultural Worlds of Development 1.2: The
        Heterogeneity of Ethnic and Cultural
        Groups
    Stability and Change
    Evaluating the Developmental Issues
The Science Base of Child Development
    Theory and the Scientific Method
    Collecting Information About Children's
        Development
    Strategies for Setting Up Research Studies
    Time Span of Inquiry
    Cohort Effects
    Basic Versus Applied Research in Child
        Development
    Reducing Sexist Research
    Perspective on Child Development 1.1: Cohort
        Effects and Children's Computer Skills
    Ethics in Research on Child Development
Careers in Child Development
Summary
Key Terms
Suggested Readings

WE REACH BACKWARD TO OUR PARENTS AND FORWARD TO OUR CHILDREN AND THROUGH THEIR CHILDREN TO A FUTURE WE WILL NEVER SEE, BUT ABOUT WHICH WE NEED TO CARE.

—Carl Jung

Why study children? Perhaps you are or will be a parent or teacher. Responsibility for children is or will be a part of your everyday life. The more you learn about children, the better you can deal with them. Perhaps you hope to gain some insight into your own history—as an infant, as a child, and as an adolescent. Perhaps you just stumbled onto this course thinking that it sounded interesting and that the topic of child development would raise some provocative and intriguing issues about how human beings grow and develop. Whatever your reasons, you will discover that the study of child development *is* provocative, *is* intriguing, and *is* filled with information about who we are and how we grew to be this way.

As you might imagine, understanding children's development, and our own personal journey through childhood, is a rich and complicated undertaking. You will discover that various experts approach the study of children in many different ways and ask many different questions. Amid this richness and complexity we seek a simple answer: to understand how children change as they grow up and the forces that contribute to this change.

What are some of these changes? Children grow in size and weight. They learn to stand, walk, and run. They learn language, picking up words as pigeons pick up peas. They learn to read, to write, and to solve math problems. They learn behaviors and roles that society considers acceptable for "boys," "girls," "men," and "women." They learn the necessity of curbing their will and develop an understanding of what is morally acceptable or unacceptable. They learn how to communicate and to get along with many different people. Their families—parents and siblings—are very important influences in their lives, but their growth also is shaped by successive choirs of friends, teachers, and strangers. In their most pimply and awkward moments as adolescents, they become acquainted with sex and try on one face after another, searching for an identity they can call their own. These are but a few of the fascinating changes that take place as children develop—many more await you in this text.

In a sense, then, the modern study of child development is concerned with the same matters that we, as ordinary people might want to understand if and when we raise our own sons and daughters; teach children in school; or try to get along with children as brothers or sisters, aunts or uncles. Whatever the context, though, it will help us immensely to understand precisely how children change.

In this chapter, you will be introduced to some contemporary concerns about child development and to a historical perspective. You will learn what development is, what issues are raised by a developmental perspective on children, and what methods are used to study child development.

Child Development—Today and Yesterday

Everywhere an individual turns in contemporary society, the development and well-being of children capture public attention, the interest of scientists, and the concern of policymakers. Through history, though, interest in the development of children has been uneven.

Some Contemporary Concerns

Consider some of the topics you read about in newspapers and magazines every day: educational reform, contemporary changes in family structure and work, the impact of computers on children, ethnic issues, and changing gender roles, for example. What the experts are discovering in each of these areas has direct and significant consequences for understanding children and for our decisions as a society on how children are treated. Let's examine these issues further.

During the past several years, the American educational system has come under attack (Glasser, 1990; Kearns, 1988). A national commission appointed by the Office of Education concluded that our children are poorly prepared for the increasingly complex future they will be asked to face in our society. The problems are legion—declining skills of those entering the teaching profession, adolescents graduating from high school with primary-grade-level reading and mathematics skills, a shortage of qualified mathematics and science teachers, less time being spent by students in engaging academic work in their classrooms, an absence of any real signs of challenge and thinking required by school curricula, and a high dropout rate over the 4 years of high school. Solutions to these problems are not easy. However, in searching for solutions, policymakers repeatedly turn to experts in the field of child development, because, to design an engaging curriculum, a planner must know what engages and motivates children. To improve our national effort in teaching thinking skills, planners must understand what thinking is and how it changes across the school years (Belmont, 1989; Haywood & Brooks, 1991; Kagan, 1991; Kuhn, 1991). To understand the roots of the social difficulties encountered by so many of today's adolescents—difficulties that lead them to drop out of school in droves—planners need to understand the nature of the socialization processes involved in the transition to adolescence and the ways in which schools fail to address them (Entwisle, 1990; William T. Grant Foundation, 1989).

We hear a great deal from experts and popular writers about pressures on contemporary families. The number of families in which both parents work is increasing; at the same time, the number of one-parent families has risen over the past 2 decades as a result of a climbing divorce rate. With more children being raised by single parents or by parents who are both working, the time parents have to spend with their children is being squeezed and the quality of child care is of concern to many. Are working parents better using the decreased time with their children? Do day-care arrangements provide high-quality alternatives for parents? How troubled should we be about the increasing number of latchkey children—those at home alone after school, waiting for their parents to return from work? Answers to these questions can be formed by several different kinds of information obtained by experts in

As our educational system has come under attack, one proposed solution has been to provide more extensive early childhood education. The children shown here are attending a Head Start program for young children from disadvantaged families.

Our most basic link is that we all inhabit the same planet. We all breathe the same air. We all cherish our children's future.

—John F. Kennedy

■ *Critical Thinking*
Genetic research, child abuse, homosexuality, mental retardation, parenting, intelligence, the role of computers, divorce, and the increasing ethnic minority population are concerns in children's development. What other contemporary concerns related to children's development can you generate?

Although there may remain towns in which only a few ethnic minority families live, they are the exception. This changing demographic tapestry promises not only the richness that diversity produces but also difficult challenges in extending the American dream to children of all ethnic groups.

child development. This information comes from studies of the way working parents use the time with their children and the nature of their parenting approaches and behaviors, studies of the way various day-care arrangements influence children's social and intellectual growth in relation to home care, and the examination of the consequences of a child being without supervision for hours after school (Belsky, 1989; Galambos & Maggs, 1990; Hoffman, 1991; Hoffereth & Brayfield, 1991; Scarr, Lande, & McCartney, 1989).

We are now and, for the foreseeable future, will be in the information age. Increasingly, our economy and our lives depend on the quality, speed, and availability of information. Advances in the field of computing have brought this about, and nowhere is the trend more apparent than in the explosion of the use of computers in business, at home, and in schools. Computing power, available only to large corporations in the 1960s, is now in the hands of 4- and 5-year-olds. How will this change the nature of children's learning and development in the future? Futurists have many ideas about this, but no one really knows. The nature of the change, however, must be reckoned with on several different fronts. From the perspective of developmentalists, one must ask a number of questions. How do family members interact when extensive time is spent with computers? How are television time and school work influenced? How do children's social interaction patterns with other children change because of exposure to computers; the tendency to associate with other "hackers"; and the discovery of the computer as companion, baby-sitter, or mentor? Finally, how will exposure to computers and programming alter the nature of thinking, learning, and reasoning, the way these activities must surely have been altered forever when humans learned to read, write, and use mathematics to understand the world many years ago? Psychologists are addressing these questions, but, as you might expect, the evidence is still quite sketchy (Lepper & Gurtner, 1989; Nix & Spiro, 1991; Valsinar, 1991).

The tapestry of American culture has changed dramatically in recent years. Nowhere is the change more noticeable than in the increasing ethnic diversity of America's citizens. Ethnic minority groups made up 20 percent of all children and adolescents under the age of 17 in 1989. Projections indicate that, by the year 2000, one third of all school-aged children will fall into this category. This changing demographic tapestry promises not only the richness that diversity produces but also difficult challenges in extending the American dream to individuals of all ethnic groups. Historically, ethnic minorities have found themselves at the bottom of the economic and social order. They have been disproportionately represented among the poor and the inadequately educated. Half of all Black American children and one third of all Hispanic children live in poverty. School dropout rates for minority youths reach the alarming rate of 60 percent in some urban areas. These population trends and our nation's inability to prepare ethnic minority individuals for full participation in American life have produced an imperative for the social institutions that serve ethnic minorities (Allen & Santrock, in press; Gibbs & Huang, 1989; Gordon, 1991; Jones, 1990; Marín & Marín, 1991; Olmedo & Walker, 1991; Sue, 1990). Schools, social services, health and mental health agencies, juvenile probation services, and other programs need to become more sensitive to ethnic issues and to provide improved services to ethnic minority and low-income individuals (Ramirez, 1990; Spencer & Dornbusch, 1990).

The changing tapestry of American culture also encompasses gender roles (Bronstein & Quina, 1988; Doyle & Paludi, 1991). A special concern is that girls historically have grown up in a male-dominated society and that much of psychology portrays human development with a "male dominant theme"

(a)

(b)

Figure 1.1
An Artist's Renditions of Children As Miniature Adults
These artistic impressions by Francisco Goya—(a) Maria Teresa de Borbon and (b) Don Manuel Osorio de Zuniga—show how children were viewed as miniature adults earlier in history. Artists' renditions of children as miniature adults may have been too stereotypical, however.

(DeFour & Paludi, in press). Feminist scholars are developing perspectives that focus on girls' life experiences and development. These perspectives include an emphasis on girls and women as authorities on their own experiences or, as Harvard psychologist Carol Gilligan (1990, 1991; Gilligan, Brown, & Rogers, 1990) advocates, a focus on listening to females' voices. These perspectives also emphasize females' competence in relationships, emotional development, and development of the self. Chapter 16 of this book is devoted exclusively to gender issues, and throughout the book you will find discussions of the increasing interest in gender issues.

Historical Accounts of Childhood

Childhood has become such a distinct period that it is hard to imagine that it was not always thought of in that way. However, in medieval times, laws generally did not distinguish between childhood and adult offenses. After analyzing samples of art along with available publications, historian Philippe Ariès (1962) concluded that European societies did not accord any special status to children prior to 1600. In the paintings, children were often dressed in smaller versions of adult clothing (see figure 1.1).

Were children actually treated as miniature adults with no special status in medieval Europe? Ariès' interpretation has been criticized. He primarily sampled aristocratic, idealized subjects, which led to the overdrawn conclusion that children were treated as miniature adults and not accorded any special status (Borstelmann, 1983). In medieval times, children did often work and their emotional bond with parents may not have been as strong as it is for many children today. However, in medieval times, childhood probably was recognized as a distinct phase of life more than Ariès believed. Also, we know that, in ancient Egypt, Greece, and Rome, rich conceptions of children's development were held.

Through history, philosophers have speculated at length about the nature of children and how they should be reared. Three such philosophical views are original sin, *tabula rasa,* and innate goodness. In the **original sin view,** *especially advocated during the Middle Ages, children were perceived as basically bad, being born into the world as evil beings.* The goal of childrearing was to provide salvation, to remove sin from the child's life. Toward the end of the seventeenth century, the **tabula rasa** view *was proposed by English philosopher John Locke. He argued that children are not innately bad but instead are like a "blank tablet," a* tabula rasa. Locke believed that childhood experiences are important in determining adult characteristics. He advised parents to spend time with their children and to help them become contributing members of society. In the eighteenth century, the **innate goodness view** *was presented by Swiss-born philosopher Jean-Jacques Rousseau, who stressed that children are inherently good.* Because children are basically good, said Rousseau, they should be permitted to grow naturally, with little parental monitoring or constraint.

In the past century and a half, our view of children has changed dramatically. We now conceive of childhood as a highly eventful and unique period of life that lays an important foundation for the adult years and is highly differentiated from them. In most approaches to childhood, distinct periods are identified, in which children master special skills and confront new life tasks. Childhood is no longer seen as an inconvenient "waiting" period during which adults must suffer the incompetencies of the young. We now value childhood as a special time of growth and change, and we invest great resources in caring for and educating our children. We protect them from the excesses of the adult work world through tough child labor laws; we treat their crimes against society under a special system of juvenile justice; and we have governmental provisions for helping children when ordinary family support systems fail or when families seriously interfere with children's well-being.

The Modern Study of Child Development

The modern era of studying children has a history that spans only a little more than a century (Cairns, 1983). This era began with some important developments in the late 1800s and extends to the current period of the 1990s. Why is this past century so special? During the past 100 years, the study of child development has evolved into a sophisticated science. A number of major theories, along with elegant techniques and methods of study, help organize our thinking about children's development. New knowledge about children—based on direct observation and testing—is accumulating at a breathtaking pace.

During the last quarter of the nineteenth century, a major shift took place—from viewing human psychology from a strictly philosophical perspective to one that includes direct observation and experimentation. Most of the influential early psychologists were trained either in the natural sciences (such as biology or medicine) or in philosophy. In the field of child development, this was true of such influential thinkers as Charles Darwin, G. Stanley Hall, James Mark Baldwin, and Sigmund Freud. The natural scientists, even then, underscored the importance of conducting experiments and collecting reliable observations of what they studied. This approach had advanced the state of knowledge in physics, chemistry, and biology; however, these scientists were not at all sure that people, much less children or infants, could be profitably studied in this way. Their hesitation was due, in part, to a lack of examples to follow in studying children. In addition, philosophers of the time debated, on both intellectual and ethical grounds, whether the methods of science were appropriate for studying people.

The deadlock was broken when some daring and entrepreneurial thinkers began to study infants, children, and adolescents, trying new methods of study. For example, near the turn of the century, French psychologist Alfred Binet invented many tasks to study attention and memory. He used them to study his own daughters, normal children, retarded children, extremely gifted chil-

Figure 1.2
Gesell's Photographic Dome
Gesell is shown inside his photographic
dome with an infant. Cameras rode on
metal tracks at the top of the dome and
were moved as needed to record the child's
activities. Others could observe from
outside the dome without being seen by the
child.

dren, and adults. Eventually, he collaborated in the development of the first
modern test of intelligence, which is named after him (the Binet). At about
the same time, G. Stanley Hall pioneered the use of questionnaires with large
groups of children and popularized the findings of earlier psychologists, whom
he encouraged to do likewise. In one investigation, Hall tested 400 children in
the Boston schools to find out how much they "knew" about themselves and
the world, asking them such questions as "Where are your ribs?"

Later, during the 1920s, a large number of child development research
centers were created (Cairns, 1983; Senn, 1975), and their professional staffs
began to observe and chart a myriad of behaviors in infants and children. The
centers at the Universities of Minnesota, Iowa, California at Berkeley, Columbia, and Toronto became famous for their investigations of children's play,
friendship patterns, fears, aggression and conflict, and sociability. This work
became closely associated with the so-called child study movement, and a new
organization, The Society for Research in Child Development, was formed at
about the same time.

Another ardent observer of children was Arnold Gesell. With his photographic dome, Gesell (1928) could systematically observe children's behavior without interrupting them (see figure 1.2). The direct study of children,
in which investigators directly observe children's behavior, conduct experiments, or obtain information about children by questioning their parents and
teachers, had an auspicious start in the work of these child study experts. The
flow of information about children, based on direct study, has not slowed since
that time.

History, Issues, and Methods

Gesell not only developed sophisticated observational strategies for studying children, but he also had some provocative views on the nature of children's development. He theorized that certain characteristics of children simply "bloom" with age because of a biological, maturational blueprint. Gesell strived for precision in charting what a child is like at a specific age. Gesell's views, as well as G. Stanley Hall's, were strongly influenced by Charles Darwin's evolutionary theory (Darwin had made the scientific study of children respectable when he developed a baby journal for recording systematic observations of children). Hall (1904) believed that child development follows a natural evolutionary course that can be revealed by child study. He also theorized that child development unfolds in a stagelike fashion, with distinct motives and capabilities at each stage. Hall had much to say about adolescence, arguing that it is full of "storm and stress."

Sigmund Freud's psychoanalytic theory was prominent in the early part of the twentieth century. Freud believed that children are rarely aware of the motives and reasons for their behavior and that the bulk of their mental life is unconscious. His ideas were compatible with Hall's, emphasizing conflict and biological influences on development, although Freud did stress that a child's experiences with parents in the first 5 years of life are important determinants of later personality development. Freud envisioned the child moving through a series of psychosexual stages, filled with conflict between biological urges and the environmental demands placed on the child by society. Freud's theory has had a profound influence on the study of children's personality development and socialization, especially in the areas of gender, morality, family processes, and problems and disturbances.

During the 1920s and 1930s, John Watson's (1928) theory of behaviorism influenced thinking about children. Watson proposed a view of children very different from Freud's, arguing that children can be shaped into whatever society wishes by examining and changing the environment. One element of Watson's view, and behaviorism in general, was a strong belief in the systematic observation of children's behavior under controlled conditions. Watson had some provocative views about childrearing as well. He stressed that parents are too soft on children; quit cuddling and smiling at babies so much, he told parents.

Whereas John Watson was observing the environment's influence on children's behavior and Sigmund Freud was probing the depths of the unconscious mind to discover clues about our early experiences with our parents, others were more concerned about the development of children's conscious thoughts—that is, the thoughts of which they are aware. James Mark Baldwin was a pioneer in the study of children's thought. **Genetic epistemology** *was the term Baldwin gave to the study of how children's knowledge changes over the course of their development.* (The term "genetic" at that time was a synonym for "development," and the term "epistemology" means the nature or study of knowledge.) Baldwin's ideas were initially proposed in the 1880s. Later, in the twentieth century, Swiss psychologist Jean Piaget adopted and elaborated on many of Baldwin's themes, keenly observing the development of thoughts in his own children and devising clever experiments to investigate how children think. Piaget became a giant in developmental psychology. Many of you, perhaps, are already familiar with his view that children pass through a series of cognitive, or thought, stages from infancy through adolescence. According to Piaget, children think in a qualitatively different manner than do adults.

TABLE 1.1
One Day in the Lives of Children in the United States

17,051	women get pregnant.
2,795	of them are teenagers.
1,106	teenagers have abortions.
372	teenagers miscarry.
1,295	teenagers give birth.
689	babies are born to women who have had inadequate prenatal care.
719	babies are born at low birth weight (less than 5 pounds 8 ounces).
129	babies are born at very low birth weight (less than 3 pounds 5 ounces).
67	babies die before 1 month of life.
105	babies die before their first birthday.
27	children die from poverty.
10	children die from guns.
30	children are wounded by guns.
6	teenagers commit suicide.
135,000	children bring a gun to school.
7,742	teens become sexually active.
623	teenagers get syphilis or gonorrhea.
211	children are arrested for drug abuse.
437	children are arrested for drinking or drunken driving.
1,512	teenagers drop out of school.
1,849	children are abused or neglected.
3,288	children run away from home.
1,629	children are in adult jails.
2,556	children are born out of wedlock.
2,989	see their parents divorced.
34,285	people lose jobs.

Children's Defense Fund, Copyright 1990.

Our introduction to several influential and diverse theories of children's development has been brief, designed to give you a glimpse of some of the different ways children have been viewed as the study of child development unfolded. You will read more about the three main theoretical perspectives later in the text—psychoanalytic theory (Freud's view) in chapter 2, behaviorism (Watson's view) in chapters 2 and 7, and cognitive developmental theory (Piaget's view) in chapters 2 and 8.

Social Policy and Children's Development

Social policy *is a national government's course of action designed to influence the welfare of its citizens.* A current trend is to conduct child development research that produces knowledge that will lead to wise and effective decision making in the area of social policy (Gallagher, 1989; Wilcox & Naimark, 1991). When more than 25 percent of all children and more than half of all ethnic minority children are being raised in poverty, when between 40 and 50 percent of all children born in a particular era can expect to spend at least 5 years in a single-parent home, when children and young adolescents are giving birth, when the use and abuse of drugs is widespread, and when the spectre and spread of AIDS is present, our nation needs revised social policy related to children (Horowitz & O'Brien, 1989). Table 1.1 vividly portrays 1 day in

Caring for Children—Cross-cultural Comparisons

According to a recent report by the Children's Defense Fund (1990), the United States does not fare well in caring for children when compared with other nations. In this report, the Children's Defense Fund gave the United States an *A* for capacity to care for children but an *F* for performance on many key markers of children's well-being. Consider the following cross-cultural comparisons:

- One-year-olds in the United States have lower immunization rates against polio than 1-year-olds in 14 other countries. Polio immunization rates for non-White infants in the United States rank behind 48 other countries, including Albania, Colombia, and Jamaica.
- The United States overall infant mortality rate is higher than 18 other countries. Our non-White infant mortality rate ranks 13th compared to other nations' overall rates. A Black American child born in inner-city Boston has less chance of surviving the first year of life than a child born in Panama, North or South Korea, or Uruguay.
- In a study of eight industrialized nations (the United States, Switzerland, Sweden, Norway, West Germany, Canada, England, and Australia), the United States had the highest poverty rate.

- The United States has the highest adolescent pregnancy rate of any industrialized Western nation.
- The United States and South Africa are the only industrialized countries that do not provide universal health coverage to families, child care, and parental leave when a child is born.
- American school children know less geography than school children in Iran, less math than school children in Japan, and less science information than school children in Spain.
- The United States invests a smaller portion of its Gross National Product (GNP) in child health than 18 other industrialized nations. It invests a smaller portion of its GNP in education than 6 other industrialized countries.

In sum, the United States needs to devote more attention to caring for its children. Too many American children from every socioeconomic and ethnic group are neglected and are not given the opportunity to reach their full potential.

the lives of children in the United States. To read about how our nation's social policy has not adequately addressed the needs of children, turn to Cultural Worlds of Development 1.1.

The shape and scope of social policy related to children are heavily influenced by our political system, which is based on negotiation and compromise (Garwood & others, 1989). The values held by individual lawmakers, the nation's economic strengths and weaknesses, and partisan politics all influence the policy agenda and whether the welfare of children will be improved (Spencer, 1990). Periods of comprehensive social policy are often the outgrowth of concern over broad social issues. Child labor laws protected children and jobs for adults as well; federal day-care funding during World War II was justified by the need for women laborers in factories; and Head Start and other War on Poverty programs in the 1960s were implemented to decrease intergenerational poverty (McLoyd, 1990; Zigler, 1991c).

Among the groups that have worked to improve the lives of the world's children are UNICEF in New York and the Children's Defense Fund in Washington, DC. At a recent United Nations convention, a number of children's rights were declared; a sampling of these rights appears in table 1.2. (Cohen & Naimark, 1991; Hart, 1991; Melton, 1991). Marian Wright Edelman (1987), president of the Children's Defense Fund, has been a tireless

TABLE 1.2
A Partial Listing of the Declaration of Children's Rights Presented to the United Nations

Abuse and neglect
The need to protect children from all forms of maltreatment by parents and others: In cases of abuse and neglect, the government is obligated to undertake preventive and treatment programs

Best interests of the child
The need for the best interests of children to prevail in all legal and administrative decisions, taking into account children's opinions

Child labor
The need to protect children from economic exploitation and from engaging in work that is a threat to their health, education, and development

Children of ethnic minorities
The right of children from ethnic minority backgrounds to enjoy their own culture and to practice their own religion and language

Children without families
The right to receive special protection and assistance from the government when deprived of family support and to be provided with alternative care

Drug abuse
The need of children to be protected from illegal drugs, including their production or distribution

Education
The right to education: The government should be obligated to provide free and compulsory education and to ensure that school discipline reflects children's human dignity

Aims of education
Education that develops a child's personality and talents and fosters respect for human rights and for children's and others' cultural and national values

Sexual exploitation
The right of children to be protected from sexual exploitation and abuse, including prostitution and pornography

Freedom from discrimination
The need to protect children without exception from any form of discrimination

Handicapped children
The right of handicapped children to special care and training designed to help them achieve self-reliance and a full, active life in society

Health and health services
The right to the highest standard of health and access to medical services: The government should be obligated to ensure preventive health care, health care for expectant mothers, health education, and the reduction of infant and child mortality

Leisure and recreation
The right to leisure, play, and participation in cultural and artistic activities

Standard of living
The right to an adequate standard of living: The government should have a responsibility to assist parents who cannot meet this responsibility

(a)

(b)

(a) Marian Wright Edelman, president of the Children's Defense Fund (shown here interacting with a young child) has been a tireless advocate of children's rights and has been instrumental in calling attention to the needs of children. (b) Edward Zigler, professor of psychology at Yale University, has been a pioneer in influencing social policy on children in the United States.

15

(a) With over 25 percent of all American children being raised in poverty, our nation needs to revise its social policy related to children. (b) Public concern over the provision of day care is mounting as more women enter the workforce. Child developmentalists hope that a revised social policy will improve children's well-being and give more children the opportunity to reach their potential.

(a)

(b)

advocate of children's rights and has been instrumental in calling attention to the needs of children. Edward Zigler (1988, 1991c) has also worked extensively as a champion of children's rights, initially to urge government funding of Project Head Start and to improve the lives of mentally retarded and handicapped children, and more recently to encourage the formation of a national policy on day care.

We may be facing a new era of comprehensive change in federal child-care policy (Garwood & others, 1989). Public concern over the provision of day care is mounting, as an increasing number of women enter the workforce. In a recent poll, 34 percent of the respondents said they would support higher taxes to fund better early childhood education programs and to improve programs that affect children's health (Hart, 1987). Seventy percent of the respondents said the next president of the United States should give children's health issues more attention, and 52 percent said preschool education deserves more presidential attention. Similarly, the Committee for Economic Development (1987), a nonprofit organization of business leaders and higher education officials, recently underscored the need for comprehensive reform in several areas of child care, including early childhood education aimed at disadvantaged young children.

Several comprehensive child-care bills have recently been proposed in Congress but have not yet been made law. One proposal places public schools at the hub of a new national system of child-care services. Before-school and after-school programs would be housed in available classrooms, with a network of family day-care providers caring for younger children. Traditional child-care services would be augmented by a home visitation program for new parents, parent education, and training for child-care staff. Another proposal, the Comprehensive Child Care bill, addresses issues that range from the licensing standards of child-care services to the upgrading of the quality and status of child-care providers.

The Nature of Child Development

Child developmentalists can play an important role in social policy related to children by helping develop more positive public opinion for comprehensive child welfare legislation, by contributing to and promoting research that will benefit children's welfare, and by helping provide legislators with information that will influence their support of comprehensive child welfare legislation (Garwood & others, 1989).

As the twenty-first century approaches, the well-being of children is one of America's foremost concerns. We all cherish the future of our children, because they are the future of any society. Children who do not reach their potential, who are destined to make fewer contributions to society than it needs, and who do not take their place as productive adults diminish the power of society's future (Horowitz & O'Brien, 1989).

The Nature of Development

Each of us develops in certain ways like all other individuals, like some other individuals, and like no other individuals. Most of the time, our attention is directed to a person's uniqueness, but psychologists who study development are drawn to our shared as well as our unique characteristics. As humans, each of us has traveled some common paths. Each of us—Leonardo da Vinci, Joan of Arc, George Washington, Martin Luther King, Jr., and you—walked at about the age of 1, talked at about the age of 2, engaged in fantasy play as a young child, and became more independent as a youth.

What do psychologists mean when they speak of an individual's development? **Development** *is the pattern of movement or change that begins at conception and continues through the life cycle.* Most development involves growth, although it includes decay (as in death and dying). The pattern of movement is complex because it is the product of several processes—biological, cognitive, and social.

Biological, Cognitive, and Social Processes

Biological processes *involve changes in an individual's physical nature.* Genes inherited from parents, the development of the brain, height and weight gains, motor skills, and the hormonal changes of puberty all reflect the role of biological processes in development.

Cognitive processes *involve changes in an individual's thought, intelligence, and language.* The tasks of watching a colorful mobile swinging above a crib, putting together a two-word sentence, memorizing a poem, solving a math problem, and imagining what it would be like to be a movie star all reflect the role of cognitive processes in children's development.

Social processes *involve changes in an individual's relationships with other people, changes in emotions, and changes in personality.* An infant's smile in response to her mother's touch, a young boy's aggressive attack on a playmate, a girl's development of assertiveness, and an adolescent's joy at the senior prom all reflect the role of social processes in children's development.

Remember as you read about biological, cognitive, and social processes that they are intricately interwoven. You will read about how social processes shape cognitive processes, how cognitive processes promote or restrict social

■ *Critical Thinking*
What do you believe is the most important social policy issue involving children today? How would you persuade the government to improve children's lives related to this particular issue?

Each of you, individually, walkest with the tread of a fox, but collectively ye are geese.

—Solon

The chess-board is the world. The pieces are the phenomena of the universe. The rules of the game are what we call laws of nature.

—Thomas Henry Huxley

I think, therefore I am.

—René Descartes

Man is by nature a social animal.

—Aristotle

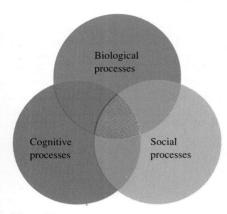

Figure 1.3
Biological, Cognitive, and Social Processes in Development
Changes in development are the result of biological, cognitive, and social processes. These processes are interwoven in human development through the life cycle.

processes, and how biological processes influence cognitive processes. Although it is helpful to study the various processes involved in children's development in separate sections of the book, keep in mind that you are studying the development of an integrated human child who has only one interdependent mind and body (see figure 1.3).

Periods of Development

For the purposes of organization and understanding, we commonly describe development in terms of periods. The most widely used classification of developmental periods involves the following sequence: the prenatal period, infancy, early childhood, middle and late childhood, and adolescence. Approximate age bands are placed on the periods to provide a general idea of when a period first appears and when it ends.

The **prenatal period** *is the time from conception to birth.* It is a time of tremendous growth—from a single cell to an organism complete with a brain and behavioral capabilities, produced in approximately a 9-month period.

Infancy *is the developmental period that extends from birth to 18 or 24 months.* Infancy is a time of extreme dependence on adults. Many psychological activities are just beginning—language, symbolic thought, sensorimotor coordination, and social learning, for example.

Early childhood *is the developmental period that extends from the end of infancy to about 5 or 6 years; sometimes the period is called the preschool years.* During this time, young children learn to become more self-sufficient and to care for themselves, develop school readiness skills (following instructions, identifying letters), and spend many hours in play and with peers. First grade typically marks the end of this period.

Middle and late childhood *is the developmental period that extends from about 6 to 11 years of age, approximately corresponding to the elementary school years; sometimes the period is called the elementary school years.* Children master the fundamental skills of reading, writing, and arithmetic, and they are formally exposed to the larger world and its culture. Achievement becomes a more central theme of the child's world, and self-control increases.

Adolescence *is the developmental period of transition from childhood to early adulthood, entered approximately at 10 to 12 years of age and ending at 18 to 22 years of age.* Adolescence begins with rapid physical changes—dramatic gains in height and weight; changes in body contour; and the development of sexual characteristics such as enlargement of the breasts, development of pubic and facial hair, and deepening of the voice. At this point in development, the pursuit of independence and an identity are prominent. Thought is more logical, abstract, and idealistic. More and more time is spent outside of the family during this period.

Today, developmentalists do not believe that change ends with adolescence (Hetherington & Baltes, 1989; Santrock, 1992). They describe development as a lifelong process. However, the purpose of this textbook is to describe the changes in development that take place from conception through adolescence.

The Nature of Child Development

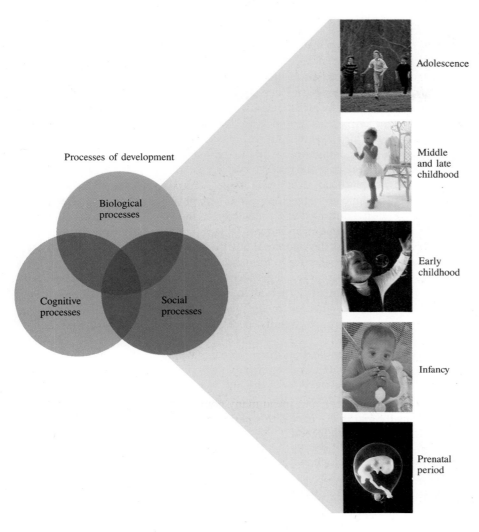

Figure 1.4
Processes and Periods of Development
Development moves through the prenatal, infancy, early childhood, middle and late childhood, and adolescence periods. These periods of development are the result of biological, cognitive, and social processes. Development is the creation of increasingly complex forms.

Processes of development

Biological processes

Cognitive processes

Social processes

Adolescence

Middle and late childhood

Early childhood

Infancy

Prenatal period

The periods of development from conception through adolescence are shown in figure 1.4, along with the processes of development—biological, cognitive, and social. As figure 1.4 shows, the interplay of biological, cognitive, and social processes produces the periods of development.

Developmental Issues

A number of issues generate spirited debate among developmentalists: To what extent is development influenced by maturation and experience (nature and nurture)? To what extent is it characterized by continuity and discontinuity? To what degree does it involve stability and change? We will consider each of these issues in turn.

Maturation and Experience (Nature and Nurture)

We can think of development as produced not only by the interplay of biological, cognitive, and social processes but also by the interplay of maturation and experience. **Maturation** *is the orderly sequence of changes dictated by the genetic blueprint we each have.* Just as a sunflower grows in an orderly way—unless flattened by an unfriendly environment—so does a human being grow in an orderly way, according to the maturational view. The range of environments can be vast, but the maturational approach argues that the genetic blueprint produces communalities in our growth and development. We walk before we talk, speak one word before two words, grow rapidly in infancy and less so in early childhood, experience a rush of sexual hormones in puberty after a lull in childhood, reach the peak of our physical strength in late adolescence and early adulthood and then decline, and so on. The maturationists acknowledge that extreme environments—those that are psychologically barren or hostile—can depress development, but they believe that basic growth tendencies are genetically wired into human beings.

By contrast, other psychologists emphasize the importance of experiences in child development. Experiences run the gamut from individuals' biological environment—nutrition, medical care, drugs, and physical accidents—to their social environment—family, peers, schools, community, media, and culture.

The debate about whether development is primarily influenced by maturation or by experience has been a part of psychology since its beginning. This debate is often referred to as the **nature-nurture controversy.** *"Nature" refers to an organism's biological inheritance, "nurture" to environmental experiences. The "nature" proponents claim biological inheritance is the most important influence on development, the "nurture" proponents that environmental experiences are the most important.*

Ideas about development have been like a pendulum, swinging between nature and nurture. In the 1980s, we witnessed a surge of interest in the biological underpinnings of development, probably because the pendulum previously had swung too far in the direction of thinking that development was exclusively due to environmental experiences (Hinde & Gorebel, 1989). As we enter the 1990s, a heightened interest in sociocultural influences on development is emerging, again probably because the pendulum in the 1980s had swung so strongly toward the biological side (Bruner, 1989, 1991; Ceci, 1991; Gibbs & Huang, 1989; Nicolopoulou & Cole, 1991; Rogoff & Morelli, 1989). As indicated earlier in the chapter, an important dimension of development is the changing cultural tapestry of America, which is especially apparent in the increasing ethnic diversity of America's citizens. More on this subject appears in Cultural Worlds of Development 1.2.

Continuity and Discontinuity

Think about your development for a moment. Did you gradually grow to become the person you are, like the slow, cumulative growth of a seedling into a giant oak, or did you experience sudden, distinct changes in your growth,

The Heterogeneity of Ethnic and Cultural Groups

An especially important idea in considering the nature of cultural and ethnic groups is that not only is there ethnic diversity within a culture—our American culture includes Black Americans, Caucasian Americans, Hispanic Americans, Native Americans, Asian Americans, and so on—but there is diversity within each ethnic group. For example, no cultural characteristic is common to all or nearly all Black Americans and absent in Caucasian Americans, unless it is the experience of being Black American and the beliefs that develop from that experience (Havighurst, 1987).

Black Americans make up the largest ethnic minority group in the United States. They are distributed throughout the social class structure, although they constitute a larger proportion of low-income individuals than does the majority Caucasian American group (Bell-Scott & Taylor, 1989; Gibbs, 1989). The majority of Black American youths stay in school, do not take drugs, do not get married prematurely, and grow up to lead productive lives in spite of social and economic disadvantage.

Hispanic Americans also are a diverse group of individuals. Not all Hispanic Americans are Catholic, although many are. Neither do all Hispanic Americans have a Mexican heritage. Many do, but many others have cultural ties with South American countries, with Puerto Rico or other Caribbean countries, or with Spain (Laval & others, 1989).

Native Americans also make up an extremely diverse and complicated ethnic group (Trimble, 1989, in press). There are more than 450 identifiable tribal units. Asian Americans are also a complex group, with more than 30 distinct divisions listed under this designation (Wong, 1982).

Not only is it important to consider ethnic diversity in a culture, but it also is important to recognize the diversity that exists within each ethnic group.

America has embraced new ingredients from many cultures, which often mix their beliefs and identities. Some aspects of the culture of origin are retained, some are lost, and some are mixed with the American culture. As ethnic minority groups continue to expand at a rapidly increasing rate, an important agenda for child developmentalists is to increase their attention to the role of culture and ethnicity in understanding development (Coll, 1990; Harrison & others, 1990; McLoyd & Wilson, in press; Spencer & Dornbusch, 1990).

like the way a caterpillar changes into a butterfly? (See figure 1.5.) For the most part, developmentalists who emphasize experience have described development as a gradual, continuous process; those who emphasize maturation have described development as a series of distinct stages (Bornstein & Krasnegor, 1989).

Some developmentalists emphasize the **continuity of development,** *the view that development involves gradual, cumulative change from conception to death.* A child's first word, while seemingly an abrupt, discontinuous event, is actually the result of months of growth and practice. Puberty, while also seemingly an abrupt, discontinuous occurrence, is actually a gradual process occurring over several years.

Figure 1.5
Continuity and Discontinuity in Development
Is development more like a seedling
gradually growing into a giant oak or a
caterpillar suddenly becoming a butterfly?

Other developmentalists focus on the **discontinuity of development,** *the view that development involves distinct stages in the life span.* Each of us is described as passing through a sequence of stages in which change is qualitatively rather than quantitatively different. As an oak moves from seedling to giant tree, it becomes *more* oak—its development is continuous. As a caterpillar changes into a butterfly, it becomes not just more caterpillar but a *different kind* of organism—its development is discontinuous. For example, at a certain point, a child moves from not being able to think abstractly about the world to being able to do so. This is a qualitative, discontinuous change in development, not a quantitative, continuous change.

Stability and Change

Another important developmental topic is the **stability-change issue,** *which addresses whether development is best described by stability or by change. The stability-change issue involves the degree to which we become older renditions of our early experience or whether we can develop into someone different from who we were at an earlier point in development.* Will a shy child who hides behind the sofa when visitors arrive be a wallflower at college dances, or will the child become a sociable, talkative individual? Will a fun-loving, carefree adolescent have difficulty holding down a 9-to-5 job as an adult or become a straight-laced, serious conformist?

Evaluating the Developmental Issues

As we consider further these three salient developmental issues—nature and nurture, continuity and discontinuity, and stability and change—it is important to realize that most developmentalists recognize that it is unwise to take an extreme position on these issues. Development is not all nature or all nurture, not all continuity or all discontinuity, and not all stability or all change. Both nature and nurture, continuity and discontinuity, stability and change characterize our development through the human life cycle. For example, in considering the nature-nurture issue, the key to development is the *interaction* of nature and nurture rather than either factor alone (Plomin, 1989, 1991; Scarr, 1991a). For example, an individual's cognitive development is the result of heredity-environment interaction, not heredity or environment alone. More about the role of heredity-environment interaction appears in chapter 3.

Nonetheless, although most developmentalists do not take extreme positions on these three important issues, this consensus has not meant the absence of spirited debate about how strongly development is influenced by each of these factors. Are girls less likely to do well in math because of their "feminine" nature or because of society's masculine bias? How extensively can the elderly be trained to reason more effectively? How much, if at all, does our memory decline in middle age? Can techniques be used to prevent or reduce the decline? If, as children, adolescents experienced a world of poverty, neglect by parents, and poor schooling, can enriched experiences in adolescence remove the "deficits" they encountered earlier in their development? The answers developmentalists give to such questions depends on their stance on the issue of nature and nurture, continuity and discontinuity, and stability and change. The answers to these questions also influence public policy decisions about children, adolescents, and adults, and they influence how each of us lives through the human life cycle.

At this point, we have discussed a number of ideas about the contemporary and historical perspectives on development and the nature of development. A summary of these ideas is presented in concept table 1.1.

Concept	Processes/related ideas	Characteristics/description
Child development— today and yesterday	Contemporary concerns	Today, the well-being of children is a prominent concern in our culture—such concerns are educational reform, changes in family structure and work, the impact of computers on children, ethnic issues, and changing gender roles.
	Child development and history	The history of interest in children is long and rich. In the Renaissance, philosophical views were important, including original sin, *tabula rasa*, and innate goodness. We now conceive of childhood as highly eventful. The modern era of studying children spans a little more than a century, an era in which the study of child development has developed into a sophisticated science. Methodological advances in observation and theoretical views—among them psychoanalytic, behavioral, and cognitive-developmental— characterized this scientific theme.
	Social policy research	A current trend is to conduct child development research that is relevant to the welfare of children. The shape and scope of social policy are influenced by our political system. Child developmentalists can play an important role in social policy. Improved social policy related to children is needed to help all children reach their potential.
The nature of development	What is development?	Development is the pattern of movement or change that occurs throughout the life span.
	Biological, cognitive, and social processes	Development is influenced by an interplay of biological, cognitive, and social processes.
	Periods of development	Development is commonly divided into the following periods from conception through adolescence: the prenatal period, infancy, early childhood, middle and late childhood, and adolescence.
Developmental issues	Maturation and experience (nature and nurture)	The debate over whether development is due primarily to maturation or to experience is another version of the nature-nurture controversy.
	Continuity and discontinuity	Some developmentalists describe development as continuous (gradual, cumulative change), others as discontinuous (abrupt, sequence of stages).
	Stability and change	Is development best described as stable or changing? The stability-change issue focuses on the degree to which we become older renditions of our early experience or develop into someone different from who we were earlier in development.
	Evaluating the developmental issues	Most developmentalists recognize that extreme positions on the nature-nurture, continuity-discontinuity, and stability-change issues are unwise. Despite this consensus, spirited debate still occurs on these issues.

The Science Base of Child Development

Some individuals have difficulty thinking of child development as a science in the same way physics, chemistry, and biology are sciences. Can a discipline that studies how babies develop, how parents nurture children, how peers interact, and how children think be equated with disciplines that investigate how

Truth is arrived at by the painstaking process of eliminating the untrue.

—Arthur Conan Doyle

gravity works and the molecular structure of a compound? Science is not defined by *what* it investigates but by *how* it investigates. Whether you are studying photosynthesis, butterflies, Saturn's moons, or human development, it is the way you study that makes the approach scientific or not.

Theory and the Scientific Method

According to nineteenth-century French mathematician Henri Poincaré, "Science is built of facts the way a house is built of bricks, but an accumulation of facts is no more science than a pile of bricks a house." Science *does* depend on the raw material of facts or data, but, as Poincaré indicated, child development's theories are more than just facts.

A **theory** *is a coherent set of ideas that help explain data and make predictions.* A theory contains **hypotheses,** *assumptions that can be tested to determine their accuracy.* For example, a theory about children's aggression would explain our observations of aggressive children and predict why children become aggressive. We might predict that children become aggressive because of the coercive interchanges they experience and observe in their families. This prediction would help direct our observations by telling us to look for coercive interchanges in families.

The **scientific method** *is an approach that can be used to discover accurate information about behavior and development which includes the following steps: identify and analyze the problem, collect data, draw conclusions, and revise theories.* For example, you decide that you want to help aggressive children control their aggression. You *identify a problem,* which does not seem like a difficult task. However, as part of the first step, you need to go beyond a general description of the problem by isolating, analyzing, narrowing, and focusing on what you hope to investigate. What specific strategies do you want to use to reduce children's aggression? Do you want to look at only one strategy, or several strategies? What aspect of aggression do you want to study—its biological, cognitive, or social characteristics? Gerald Patterson and his colleagues (Patterson, 1986, 1991; Patterson, Capaldi, & Bank, 1991; Patterson, DeBaryshe, & Ramsey, 1989) argue that parents' failure to teach reasonable levels of compliance sets in motion coercive interchanges with family members. In this first step in the scientific method, a problem is identified and analyzed.

After you have identified and analyzed the problem, the next step is to *collect information (data).* Psychologists observe behavior and draw inferences about thoughts and emotions. For example, in the investigation of children's aggression, you might observe how effectively parents teach reasonable compliance levels to their children and the extent to which coercive exchanges take place among family members.

Once data have been collected, psychologists use *statistical procedures* to understand the meaning of quantitative data. They then try to *draw conclusions.* In the investigation of children's aggression, statistics would help you determine whether or not your observations were due to chance. After data have been collected, psychologists compare their findings with what others have discovered about the same issue.

The final step in the scientific method is *revising theory.* Psychologists have generated a number of theories about children's development; they also have theorized about why children become aggressive. Data such as those collected by Patterson and his colleagues force us to study existing theories of aggression to see if they are accurate. Over the years, some theories of children's development have been discarded and others revised. Theories are an

■ *Critical Thinking*
Theories help us make predictions about how we develop and how we behave. Do you believe we can predict an individual's behavior and development? Explain your answer.

The Nature of Child Development

integral part of understanding the nature of children's development. They will be weaved through our discussion of children's development throughout the remainder of the text.

Collecting Information About Children's Development

Systematic observations can be conducted in a number of ways. For example, we can watch behavior in a laboratory or in a more natural setting such as a school, home, or neighborhood playground. We can question children using interviews and surveys, develop and administer standardized tests, conduct case studies, examine behavior cross-culturally, or carry out physiological research. To help you understand how developmentalists use these methods, we will continue to draw examples from the study of children's aggression.

Observation

Sherlock Holmes chided Watson, "You see but you do not observe." We look at things all the time; however, casually watching a mother and her infant is not scientific observation. Unless you are a trained observer and practice your skills regularly, you may not know what to look for, you may not remember what you saw, what you are looking for may change from one moment to the next, and you may not communicate your observations effectively.

For observations to be effective, we have to know what we are looking for, whom we are observing, when and where we will observe, how the observations will be made, and in what form they will be recorded. That is, our observations have to be made in a *systematic* way. Consider aggression. Do we want to study verbal or physical aggression, or both? Do we want to study younger or older children, or both? Do we want to evaluate them in a university laboratory, at school, at home, at a playground, or at all of these locations? A common way to record observations is to write them down, using shorthand or symbols. However, tape recorders, video cameras, special coding sheets, and one-way mirrors are increasingly used to make observations more efficient.

Frequently, when we observe, it is necessary to control certain factors that determine behavior but that are not the focus of our inquiry. For this reason, much psychological research is conducted in a **laboratory,** *a controlled setting in which many of the complex factors of the "real world" are removed.* For example, Albert Bandura (1965) brought children into a laboratory and had them observe an adult repeatedly hit an inflated plastic Bobo doll about 3 feet tall. Bandura wondered to what extent the children would copy the adult's behavior. After the children saw the adult attack the Bobo doll, they, too, aggressively hit the inflated toy. By conducting his experiment in a laboratory with adults the children did not know as models, Bandura had complete control over when the children witnessed aggression, how much aggression the children saw, and what form the aggression took. Bandura could not have had as much control in his experiment if other factors, such as parents, siblings, friends, television, and a familiar room, had been present.

Laboratory research, however, has some drawbacks. First, it is almost impossible to conduct the research without the participants knowing they are being studied. Second, the laboratory setting may be *unnatural* and, therefore, elicit unnatural behavior from the participants. Subjects usually show less aggressive behavior in a laboratory than in a more familiar natural setting, such as in a park or at home. They also show less aggression when they are unaware they are being observed than when they are aware that an observer is studying

(a)

(b)

Figure 1.6
Observing Children's Aggression in a Laboratory and in Naturalistic Conditions
(a) A child's aggressive behavior is being observed in a laboratory through a one-way mirror, which allows the observer to exercise control over the observation of aggression. (b) A child's aggressive behavior is being observed in a naturalistic situation. This allows the observer to obtain information about the everyday occurrence of behavior.

them. Third, some aspects of child development are difficult if not impossible to examine in a laboratory. Certain types of stress are difficult (and unethical) to study in the laboratory, such as recreating the circumstances that stimulate family conflict.

Although laboratory research is a valuable tool for developmentalists, naturalistic observation provides insight we sometimes cannot achieve in a laboratory. In **naturalistic observation,** *scientists observe behavior in real-world settings and make no effort to manipulate or control the situation.* Developmentalists conduct naturalistic observations at day-care centers, hospitals, schools, parks, homes, malls, dances, and other places where people live and frequent. In contrast to Bandura's observations of aggression in a laboratory, developmentalists observe the aggression of children in nursery schools, of adolescents on street corners, and of marital partners at home (Bronfenbrenner, 1989; Cairns & Cairns, in press). Figure 1.6 compares aggression in a laboratory with that in a naturalistic situation.

Interviews and Questionnaires

Sometimes the best and quickest way to get information from children is to ask them for it. Psychologists use interviews and questionnaires to find out about children's experiences and attitudes. Most interviews occur face-to-face, although they can take place over the telephone.

The types of interviews range from highly unstructured to highly structured. Examples of unstructured interview questions include: How aggressive do you see yourself? and How aggressive is your child? Examples of structured interview questions include: In the last week how often did you yell at your spouse? and How often in the last year was your child involved in fights at school? Structure is imposed by the questions themselves, or the interviewer can categorize answers by asking respondents to choose from several options. For example, in the question about your level of aggressiveness, you might be asked to choose from "highly aggressive," "moderately aggressive," "moderately unaggressive," and "highly unaggressive." In the question about how often you yelled at your spouse in the last week, you might be asked to choose "0," "1–2," "3–5," "6–10," or "more than 10 times."

An experienced interviewer knows how to put respondents at ease and encourage them to open up. A competent interviewer is sensitive to the way people respond to questions and often probes for more information. A person may respond with fuzzy statements to questions about the nature of marital conflict—for example, "Well, I don't know whether we have a lot of conflict or not." A skilled interviewer pushes for more specific, concrete answers, possibly asking, "If you had it to do over, would you get married?" or "Tell me the worst things you and your husband said to each other in the last week." Using these interviewing strategies forces researchers to be involved with, rather than detached from, their subjects, which yields a better understanding of children's development.

Interviews are not without drawbacks. Perhaps the most critical is the response set of "social desirability," in which individuals tell the interviewer what they think is most socially acceptable or desirable rather than what they truly think or feel. When asked about her marital conflict, Jane may not want to disclose that arguments have been painfully tense in the past month. Her 10-year-old son may not want to divulge that he often gets into fights with his peers. Skilled interviewing techniques and questions to help eliminate such defenses are critical in obtaining accurate information.

The Nature of Child Development

Child developmentalists also question children and adults using questionnaires or surveys. A **questionnaire** *is similar to a highly structured interview except that respondents read the questions and mark their answers on paper rather than respond verbally to the interviewer.* One major advantage of surveys and questionnaires is that they can be given to a large number of people easily. Good surveys have concrete, specific, and unambiguous questions and assessment of the authenticity of the replies.

Case Studies

A **case study** *is an in-depth look at an individual; it is used mainly by clinical psychologists when the unique aspects of a person's life cannot be duplicated, either for practical or ethical reasons.* A case study provides information about an individual's fears, hopes, fantasies, traumatic experiences, upbringing, family relationships, health, or anything that helps a psychologist understand that person's development. Some vivid case studies appear at different points in this text, among them one about a modern-day wild child named Genie, who lived in near isolation during her childhood (chapter 9).

Although case studies provide dramatic, in-depth portrayals of people's lives, we need to exercise caution when generalizing from this information. The subject of a case study is unique, with a genetic makeup and experiences no one else shares. In addition, case studies involve judgments of unknown reliability, in that usually no check is made to see if other psychologists agree with the observations.

Standardized Tests

Standardized tests *require people to answer a series of written or oral questions. They have two distinct features. First, psychologists usually total an individual's score to yield a single score, or set of scores, that reflects something about the individual. Second, psychologists compare the individual's score to the scores of a large group of similar people to determine how the individual responded* relative *to others.* Scores are often described in percentiles. For example, perhaps a child scored in the 92nd percentile of the Stanford-Binet Intelligence Test. This method informs us how much lower or higher the child scored than the large group of children who had taken the test previously.

To continue our look at how different measures are used to evaluate aggression, consider the Minnesota Multiphasic Personality Inventory (MMPI), which includes a scale to assess delinquency or antisocial tendencies. The items on this scale ask you to respond whether or not you are rebellious, impulsive, and have trouble with authority figures. This part of the MMPI might be given to adolescents to determine their delinquent and antisocial tendencies.

The main advantage of standardized tests is that they provide information about *individual differences* among people. However, information obtained from standardized tests does not always predict behavior in nontest situations. Standardized tests are based on the belief that an individual's behavior is consistent and stable. Although personality and intelligence, two of the primary targets of standardized tests, have some stability, they *can* vary, depending on the situation in which a person is evaluated. Someone may perform poorly on a standardized test of intelligence but display a much higher level of intelligence when observed in a less anxious context such as at home.

Standardized tests require individuals to answer a series of written or oral questions. The individual on the right is being given a standardized test of intelligence.

Systematic observations in natural settings provide valuable information about behavior across cultures. For example, in one investigation, observations in different cultures revealed that American children often engage in less work and more play than children in many other cultures (Whiting & Whiting, 1975). However, conducting cross-cultural research using such methods as systematic observation in natural settings is difficult and requires attention to a number of methodological issues (Berry & others, in press; Longabaugh, 1980).

This criticism is especially relevant for members of minority groups, some of whom have been inappropriately classified as mentally retarded on the basis of their scores on standardized intelligence tests. For example, one Black American child from a low-income family scored in the mentally retarded range on a standardized intelligence test, yet he was bright enough to plan an elaborate escape from the institution in which he lived. Cross-cultural psychologists also caution that, although many psychological tests may work reasonably well in Western cultures, they may not always be appropriate in cultures where they were not developed (Lonner, 1990). Next, we will further examine cross-cultural research strategies and research with ethnic minority children.

Cross-cultural Research and Research with Ethnic Minority Groups

When researchers examine the behavior and mental processes of children in different cultures and different ethnic minority groups, they must follow certain strategies. When measures are used with cultural and ethnic groups with whom the researchers are unfamiliar, it is vital that they construct the measures so that they are meaningful for all of the cultural or ethnic minority groups being studied. To accomplish this objective, cross-cultural researchers do not use one culture as the sole source for developing a measure. Rather, informants from all cultures in the investigation provide information to the researchers so they can develop a meaningful measure (Berry, 1980; Berry & others, in press).

In conducting developmental research on cultural and ethnic minority issues, investigators distinguish between the emic approach and the etic approach. In the **emic approach,** *the goal is to describe behavior in one culture or ethnic group in terms that are meaningful and important to the people in that culture or ethnic group, without regard to other cultures or ethnic groups.* In the **etic approach,** *the goal is to describe behavior so that generalizations can be made across cultures.* That is, the emic approach is culture-specific; the etic approach is more culture-universal. If researchers construct a questionnaire in an emic fashion, the concern is only that the questions are meaningful to the particular culture or ethnic group being studied. If, however, the researchers construct a questionnaire in an etic fashion, they want to include questions that reflect concepts familiar to all the cultures involved (Brislin, 1990; Sue, 1990).

How might the emic and etic approaches be reflected in the study of family processes? In the emic approach, the researchers might choose to focus only on White middle-class families, without regard for whether the information obtained in the study generalizes or is appropriate for ethnic minority groups. In a subsequent study, the researchers may decide to adopt an etic approach by studying not only White middle-class families, but also White lower-income families, Black American families, Hispanic American families, and Asian American families. In studying ethnic minority families, the researchers discover that the extended family is more frequently a support system in ethnic minority families than in White American families. Thus, the emic approach revealed a different patterning of family interaction than the etic approach, documenting that research with White middle-class families cannot always be generalized to all ethnic groups.

Joseph Trimble (1989, in press) is especially concerned about the tendency of researchers to use *ethnic gloss* in their selection and description of ethnic groups when studying various dimensions of children's development. By ethnic gloss, Trimble means the superficial use of an ethnic category, such as Black, Hispanic, Asian, or Native American, that is often more homogeneous than the ethnic group actually is. For example, an unsuitable description of an investigation of ethnic groups would say: The subjects included 28 Black children, 22 Hispanic children, and 24 White children. An acceptable description of each of the groups requires much more detail about the country of origin, socioeconomic status, language, and ethnic self-identification of the children. Thus, the description of each of the groups might follow this example for the Hispanic children: The subjects were 22 10-to-12-year-old Mexican American children from low-income neighborhoods in the southwestern area of Los Angeles. Twelve spoke Spanish in the home, whereas 10 spoke English; 11 were born in the United States, 11 in Mexico; 16 described themselves as Mexican, 3 as Chicano, 2 as American, and 1 as Latino. Trimble believes that ethnic gloss can lead researchers to obtain samples of ethnic groups or cultures that are not truly representative of the ethnic and cultural diversity within each group. In this way, ethnic gloss can produce overgeneralizations and stereotypes about an ethnic group or a culture.

In keeping with our theme of applying different ways of obtaining information about children to aggression, what have cross-cultural psychologists discovered about aggression in different cultures? They have found that aggression is a cultural universal, appearing in all cultures studied. Therefore, we can say that aggression is an etic behavior; however, the ways in which aggression is expressed may be culture-specific, which means that aggression is also an emic behavior (Segall & others, 1990). For example, in the !Kung culture of southern Africa, the members actively try to dissuade individuals from behaving aggressively, whereas, in the Yanomamo Indian culture of South America, the members promote aggression. Yanomamo youths are told that they cannot achieve adult status unless they are capable of killing, fighting, and pummeling others.

(a)

(b)

Aggression occurs in both the !Kung and Yanomamo cultures. However, (a) the !Kung of southern Africa discourage aggression, whereas (b) the Yanomamo of South America actively promote aggression.

Physiological Research

Researchers also can use physiological methods to obtain information about children's development. Increased research into the biological basis of children's development has produced remarkable insights. For example, researchers discovered that higher concentrations of some hormones are associated with delinquent behavior in male adolescents (Nottelman & others, 1990; Susman & Dorn, 1991).

Multimeasure, Multisource, Multicontext Approach

The various methods have their strengths and weaknesses. Direct observations are extremely valuable tools for obtaining information about children, but there are some things we cannot observe in children—their moral thoughts, their inner feelings, the arguments of their parents, how they acquire information about sex, and so on. In such instances, other measures, such as interviews, questionnaires, and case studies may be valuable. Because virtually every method has limitations, many investigators use multiple measures in assessing children's development. For example, a researcher might ask children about their aggressive behavior, check with their friends, observe them carefully at home and in their neighborhood, interview their parents, observe the children at school during recess, and ask teachers to rate the children's aggression. Researchers hope that the convergence of multimeasure, multisource, and multicontext information provides a comprehensive and valid assessment of children's development.

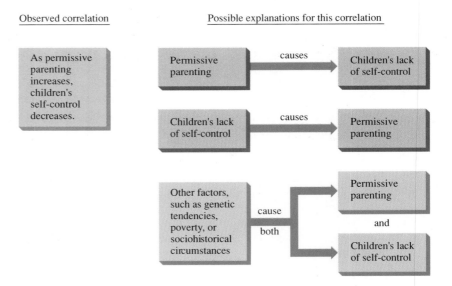

Figure 1.7

Possible Explanations for Correlational Data
An observed correlation between two events cannot be used to conclude that one event caused the other. Some possibilities are that the second event caused the first event or that a third, unknown event caused the correlation between the first two events.

Observed correlation

Possible explanations for this correlation

Strategies for Setting Up Research Studies

How can we determine if a pregnant woman's cigarette smoking affects her offspring's attentional skills? How can we determine if responding nurturantly to an infant's cries increases attachment to the caregiver? How can we determine if day care is damaging to a child's development? How can we determine if listening to rock music lowers an adolescent's grades in school? When designing a research study to answer such questions, investigators must decide whether to use a correlational or an experimental strategy.

Correlational Strategy

In the **correlational strategy,** *the goal is to describe the strength of the relation between two or more events or characteristics. This is a useful strategy because, the more strongly events are correlated (related, or associated), the more we can predict one from the other.* For example, if we find that as parents use more permissive ways to deal with their children the children's self-control decreases, this does not mean that the parenting style caused the lack of self-control. It could mean that, but it could also mean that the children's lack of self-control stimulated the parents to simply throw up their arms in despair and give up trying to control the obstreperous children's behavior, or it could mean that other factors might cause this correlation, such as genetic background, poverty, and sociohistorical conditions. (Several decades ago a permissive parenting strategy was widely advocated but today it no longer is in vogue.) Figure 1.7 portrays these possible interpretations of correlational data.

The **correlation coefficient** *is a number based on statistical analysis that is used to describe the degree of association between two variables. The correlation coefficient ranges from −1.00 to +1.00.* A negative number means an inverse relation. For example, today we often find a *negative* correlation between permissive parenting and children's self-control, and we often find a *positive* correlation between a parent's involvement in and monitoring of a child's life and the child's self-control. The higher the correlation coefficient (whether positive or negative), the stronger the association between the two

The Nature of Child Development

variables. A correlation of 0 means that there is no association between the variables. A correlation of $-.40$ is a stronger correlation than $+.20$ because we disregard the negative or positive nature of the correlation in determining the correlation's magnitude.

Experimental Strategy

Whereas the correlational strategy allows us to say only that two events are related, **experimental strategy** *allows us to precisely determine behavior's causes. Psychologists accomplish this task by performing an* experiment, *which is a study done in a carefully regulated setting in which one or more of the factors believed to influence the behavior being studied is manipulated and all others are held constant.* If the behavior under study changes when a factor is manipulated, we say that the manipulated factor causes the behavior to change. Experiments establish cause and effect between events, something correlational studies cannot do. *Cause* is the event being manipulated and *effect* is the behavior that changes because of the manipulation. Remember that, in testing correlation, nothing is manipulated; in an experiment, a researcher actively changes an event to see its effect on behavior.

The following example illustrates the nature of an experiment. The problem to be studied is whether aerobic exercise during pregnancy affects the development of infants. We need to have one group of pregnant women engage in aerobic exercise and the other not engage in aerobic exercise. We randomly assign our subjects to these two groups. **Random assignment** *occurs when researchers assign subjects to experimental and control conditions by chance, thus reducing the likelihood the results of the experiment will be due to preexisting differences in the two groups.* For example, random assignment greatly reduces the probability the two groups will differ on such factors as age, social class, prior aerobic exercise, intelligence, health problems, and alertness.

The **independent variable** *is the manipulated, influential, experimental factor in an experiment. The label* independent *is used because this variable can be changed independently of other factors.* In the aerobic exercise experiment, the amount of aerobic exercise is the independent variable. We manipulate the amount of the aerobic exercise by having the pregnant women exercise four times a week under the direction of a trained instructor. The **dependent variable** *is the factor that is measured in an experiment; it may change because of the manipulation of the independent variable. The label* dependent *is used because this variable depends on what happens to the subjects in the experiment.* In the aerobic exercise experiment, the dependent variable is represented by two infant measures—breathing and sleeping patterns. The subjects' responses on these measures depend on the influence of the independent variable (whether or not pregnant women engaged in aerobic exercise). An illustration of the nature of the experimental strategy, applied to the aerobic exercise study, is presented in figure 1.8. In our experiment, we test the two sets of offspring in the first week of life. We find that the experimental group infants have more regular breathing and sleeping patterns than their control group counterparts; thus, we conclude that aerobic exercise by pregnant women promotes more regular breathing and sleeping patterns in newborn infants.

It might seem as if we should always choose an experimental strategy over a correlational strategy, since the experimental strategy gives us a better sense of the influence of one variable on another. Are there instances when a

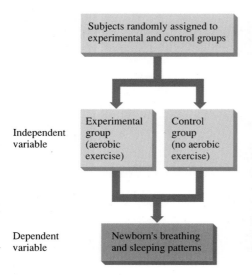

Independent variable

Experimental group (aerobic exercise)

Control group (no aerobic exercise)

Dependent variable

 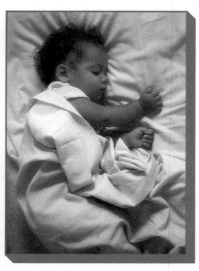

Figure 1.8
Principles of Experimental Strategy: The Effects of Aerobic Exercise by Pregnant Women on Their Newborns' Breathing and Sleeping Patterns

correlational strategy might be preferred? Three such instances are (1) when the focus of the investigation is so new that we have little knowledge of which variables to manipulate (as when AIDS first appeared), (2) when it is physically impossible to manipulate the variables (such as factors involved in suicide), and (3) when it is unethical to manipulate the variables (for example, in determining the association between illness and exposure to dangerous chemicals).

Time Span of Inquiry

A special concern of developmentalists is the time span of a research investigation. Studies that focus on the relation of age to another variable are common in the field of child development. We have several options—we can study different children of different ages and compare them, we can study the same individuals as they grow older, or we can combine these two approaches. We will consider each of these in turn.

Cross-sectional Approach

The **cross-sectional approach** *is a research strategy in which individuals of different ages are compared all at one time.* A typical cross-sectional study might include a group of 5-year-olds, 8-year-olds, and 11-year-olds. The different groups can be compared with respect to a variety of dependent variables—IQ, memory, peer relations, attachment to parents, hormonal changes, and so on. All of this can be accomplished in a short time. In some studies, data are collected in a single day. Even large-scale cross-sectional studies with hundreds of subjects usually do not take longer than several months to complete data collection.

The main advantage of a cross-sectional study is that researchers do not have to wait for subjects to grow up. Despite its time efficiency, the cross-sectional approach has its drawbacks: It gives no information about how individuals change or about the stability of their characteristics. The increases

The Nature of Child Development

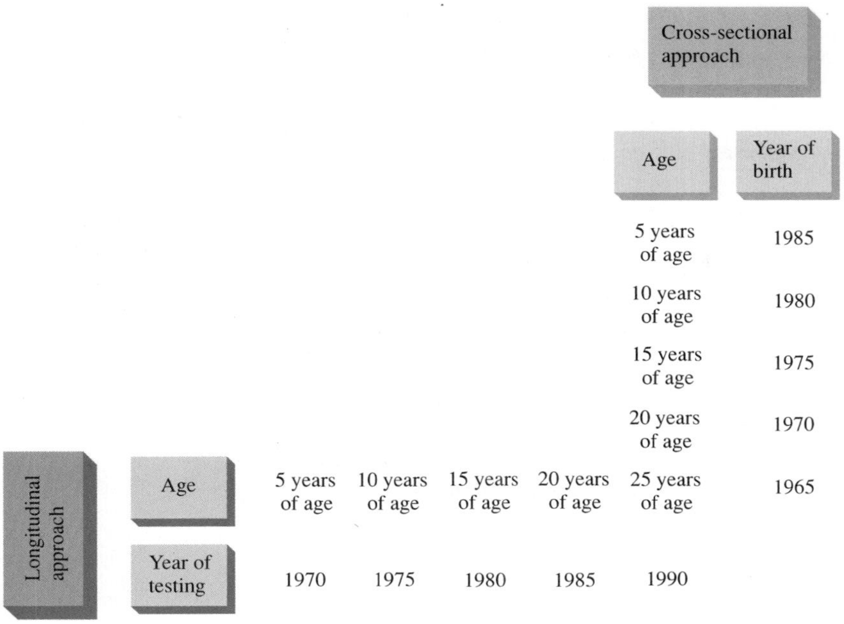

Figure 1.9
A Comparison of Cross-sectional and Longitudinal Approaches

Cross-sectional approach

Age	Year of birth
5 years of age	1985
10 years of age	1980
15 years of age	1975
20 years of age	1970
25 years of age	1965

Longitudinal approach

Age	5 years of age	10 years of age	15 years of age	20 years of age	25 years of age
Year of testing	1970	1975	1980	1985	1990

and decreases—the hills and valleys—of growth and development can become obscured in the cross-sectional approach. Also, because the children studied are of different ages and different groups, they were born at different times; they may have experienced different types of parenting and schooling; and they may have been influenced by different trends in dress, television, and play materials.

Longitudinal Approach

The **longitudinal approach** *is a research strategy in which the same individuals are studied over a period of time, usually several years or more.* In a typical longitudinal study of the same topics we discussed with the cross-sectional approach, we might structure a test to administer to children once a year when they are 4, 8, and 12 years old. In this example, the same children would be studied over an 8-year time span, allowing us to examine patterns of change within each child. One of the great values of the longitudinal approach is that we can evaluate how individual children change as they grow up.

Fewer longitudinal than cross-sectional studies are conducted because they are time consuming and costly. A close examination of the longitudinal approach reveals some additional problems: (1) When children are examined over a long period of time, some drop out because they lose interest or move away and cannot be recontacted by the investigator. A fairly common finding is that the remaining children represent a slightly biased sample, in that they tend to be psychologically superior to those who dropped out on almost every dimension (intelligence, motivation, and cooperativeness, for example) that the investigator checks. (2) With repeated testing, some children may become more "testwise," which may increase their ability to perform "better" or "more maturely" the next time the investigator interacts with them. For a comparison of longitudinal and cross-sectional research designs, see figure 1.9.

Sequential Approach

Developmentalists also sometimes combine the cross-sectional and longitudinal approaches to learn about development (Schaie, 1973, 1989). The **sequential approach** *is the term used to describe the combined cross-sectional, longitudinal design. In most instances, this approach starts with a cross-sectional study that includes individuals of different ages. A number of months or years after the initial assessment, the same individuals are tested again—this is the longitudinal aspect of the design. At this later time, a new group of subjects is assessed at each age level.* The new groups at each level are added at the later time to control for changes that might have taken place in the original group of subjects—some may have dropped out of the study or retesting might improve their performance, for example. The sequential approach is complex, expensive, and time consuming, but it provides information that is impossible to obtain from the cross-sectional or longitudinal approach alone. The sequential approach has been especially helpful in examining cohort effects in child development, which we will discuss next.

Cohort Effects

Cohort effects *are those due to a subject's time of birth or generation but not actually to age.* Today's children are living a childhood of firsts (Louv, 1990). They are the first day-care generation; the first truly multicultural generation; the first generation to grow up in the electronic bubble of an environment defined by computers and new forms of media; the first post–sexual revolution generation; the first generation to grow up in new kinds of dispersed, deconcentrated cities, not quite urban, rural, or suburban.

Cohort effects are important because they can powerfully affect the dependent measures in a study ostensibly concerned with age. Researchers have shown that cohort effects are especially important to investigate in the assessment of intelligence (Willis, 1989; Willis & Schaie, 1986). For example,

The mark of the historic is the nonchalance with which it picks up an individual and deposits him in a trend, like a house playfully moved in a tornado.

—Mary McCarthy

BY BILL HOEST

"That's my dad when he was 10...He was in some sort of cult."

© 1986; Reprinted courtesy of Bill Hoest and Parade Magazine.

The Nature of Child Development

individuals born at different points in time—such as 1920, 1940, and 1960—have had varying opportunities for education, with the individuals born in earlier years having less access. Perspective on Child Development 1.1 provides further information about the role of cohort effects in children's development.

Basic Versus Applied Research in Child Development

In discussing children's development and social policy issues earlier in the chapter, we indicated that a current trend is an increase in research that is relevant to social policy. The question of whether child developmentalists should conduct research that is relevant to social policy touches on a long-standing issue: Should researchers who study children conduct research that is basic or applied? **Basic research,** *sometimes called pure research, is the study of issues to obtain knowledge for its own sake rather than for practical application.* Basic research is often conducted to test a theory or to follow up on other research. Rarely is basic research a response to a pressing practical problem. Basic research may or may not eventually be applied to social policy or practical problems. By contrast, **applied research** *is the study of issues that have direct practical significance, often with the intent of changing human behavior.* Thus, social policy research is applied research rather than basic research.

A developmentalist who conducts basic research might ask: How is the cognitive development of children different from that of adolescents? By contrast, a developmentalist who conducts applied research might ask: How can knowledge about children's and adolescents' cognitive development be used to educate them more effectively or to help them cope more effectively with stress? A basic researcher also might ask: Can a nonhuman primate, such as a chimpanzee, learn to use sign language? An applied researcher might ask: Can strategies used to teach language to chimpanzees be applied to improve the language capabilities of retarded or disturbed children who do not speak (Wade & Tavris, 1990)?

Most developmentalists believe that both basic and applied research are important. Although basic research can sometimes produce information that can be applied to improve the welfare of children, it does not guarantee this application. By contrast, insisting that research always be relevant is like trying to grow flowers by focusing only on the blossoms and not tending to the roots (Walker, 1970). Basic research is root research. Without the discovery of basic scientific principles, we would have little knowledge to apply (Wade & Tavris, 1990).

Now that we have considered the main ways that child developmentalists conduct research, it is also important to examine whether research on child development is value free, how child development research can become less sexist, and some ethical considerations in child development research.

Reducing Sexist Research

Traditional science is presented as being value free and, thus, a valid way of studying mental processes and behavior. However, there is a growing consensus that science in general, and psychology in particular, are not value free (Doyle & Paludi, 1991). A special concern is that the vast majority of psychological research has been male oriented and male dominated. Some researchers believe that male-dominated sciences, such as psychology, need to be challenged to examine the world in a new way, one that incorporates girls'

Cohort Effects and Children's Computer Skills

For some time, educators have been interested in teaching school-age children basic information about computers. The programming language BASIC, which was invented in the 1960s, is one of the tools many experts feel they can teach young children. Imagine a study of a group of elementary school children, designed to determine just how much of this language children can learn. Following is a brief summary of this hypothetical investigation.

In 1975, a large group of children in grades one through five (roughly 6 to 10 years of age) is randomly selected from two schools in the same school district of a small city. The children are given 10 hours of instruction about the BASIC programming language, including the definition and usage rules of elementary programming commands (such as PRINT, HOME, REMARK, =, LET, FOR, NEXT, ":", GO TO, and END) and the rules for writing and sequencing simple lines of code, such as:

```
10 PRINT "HELLO, STUDENTS"
20 PRINT "DO YOU LIKE THIS CLASS"
30 END
```

At the end of their instruction, they are given a standard test to determine how many commands they know and how well they can correct errors in simple programs. Table 1.A shows how many of 30 questions children at each grade correctly answer.

Fifteen years later, in 1990, the same instructional study is repeated with children randomly sampled from the same schools. The researchers check the backgrounds of this new sample of children and discover that they are equivalent to the 1975 sample in terms of their average ability levels, their achievement in school, and their socioeconomic backgrounds. Table 1.A shows how this new sample of children performs on the same test given to the children in 1975. Take a careful look at the results for these two samples. What do you see?

In 1975, the youngest children were able to correctly answer five to six questions, with a modest increase in average performance of fifth graders to eight to nine correct answers. In 1990, however, the youngest children correctly answered more than twice as many questions as their earlier counterparts and actually outperformed the fifth graders tested a decade and a half earlier. Again, in 1990, we see an increase in children's average level of performance across the elementary school grades.

This hypothetical study is a classic example of a cohort effect. Children born in one era perform differently than do children born in another era. It does not take much imagination to arrive at a plausible explanation of the cohort effect. An elementary analysis of major historical events between

TABLE 1.A
Children's Knowledge of BASIC

	Grade				
	1	*2*	*3*	*4*	*5*
Correct answers, 1975	5.5	5.3	6.8	7.0	8.8
Correct answers, 1990	12.5	13.0	15.2	18.5	20.0

Today's children are experiencing a computer revolution. What are some ways developmentalists could study the effects of computers on children?

1975 and 1990 would show that millions of homeowners purchased computers during this time. Most of those homeowners used their computers for word processing and for playing skill and adventure games. They also made modest efforts to learn simple programming with the BASIC language.

The children tested in 1990 were not necessarily better learners than those tested in 1975. They simply knew more to begin with—before instruction began—than the children from a decade and a half earlier. We are not aware of any investigation of children's development that documents such a dramatic cohort effect, although, if someone had had the foresight to envision the modern computer revolution, results such as these would be easily found.

and women's perspectives and respects their ethnicity, sexual orientation, age, and socioeconomic status (Denmark & others, 1988; McHugh, Koeske, & Frieze, 1986; Quina, 1986). For example, Florence Denmark and her colleagues (1988) provided the following three recommendations as guidelines for nonsexist research:

1. *Research methods*
   Problem: The selection of research participants is based on stereotypic assumptions and does not allow for generalizations to other groups.
   Example: On the basis of stereotypes about who should be responsible for contraception, only females are studied.
   Correction: Both sexes should be studied before conclusions are drawn about the factors that determine contraception use.

2. *Data analysis*
   Problem: Gender differences are inaccurately magnified.
   Example: Whereas only 24 percent of the girls were found to . . . fully 28 percent of the boys were . . .
   Correction: The results should include extensive descriptions of the data so that differences are not exaggerated.

3. *Conclusions*
   Problem: The title or abstract (summary) of an article makes no reference to the limitations of the study participants and implies a broader scope of the study than is warranted.
   Example: A study purporting to be about "perceptions of the disabled" examines only blind White boys.
   Correction: Use more precise titles and clearly describe the sample and its selection criteria in the abstract or summary.

Ethics in Research on Child Development

Increasingly, child developmentalists recognize that considerable caution must be taken to ensure the well-being of children when they are involved in a research study. Today, colleges and universities have review boards that evaluate the ethical nature of research conducted at their institutions. Proposed research plans must pass the scrutiny of an ethics research committee before the research can be initiated. In addition, the American Psychological Association (APA) has developed guidelines for its members' ethics.

The code of ethics adopted by the APA instructs researchers to protect their subjects from mental and physical harm. The best interests of the subjects must be kept foremost in the researcher's mind. All subjects, if they are old enough, must give their informed consent to participate in a research study. This requires that subjects know what their participation will entail and any risks that might develop. For example, subjects in an investigation of the effects of divorce on children should be told beforehand that interview questions might stimulate thought about issues they might not anticipate. The subjects should also be informed that in some instances a discussion of the family's experiences might improve family relationships, but in other instances it might bring up issues that bring the children unwanted stress. After informed consent is given, the subjects reserve the right to withdraw from the study at any time.

Special ethical concerns govern the conduct of research with children. First, if children are to be studied, informed consent from their parents or legal guardians must be obtained. Parents have the right to a complete and accurate description of what will be done with their children and may refuse to let them participate. Second, children have rights too. Psychologists are obliged to explain precisely what the children will experience. The children may refuse to participate, even after parental permission has been given. Also, if a child becomes upset during the research study, it is the psychologist's obligation to calm the child. Third, psychologists must always weigh the potential for harming children against the prospects of contributing some clear benefits to them. If there is the chance of harm—as when drugs are used, social deception takes place, or children are treated aversively (that is, punished or reprimanded)—psychologists must convince a group of peers that the benefits of the experience clearly outweigh any chance of harm. Fourth, since children are in a vulnerable position and lack power and control when facing adults, psychologists should always strive to make a professional encounter a positive and supportive experience.

Careers in Child Development

A career in child development is one of the most rewarding vocational opportunities one can pursue. By choosing a career in child development, you will be able to help children who might not reach their potential as productive contributors to society develop into physically, cognitively, and socially mature individuals. Adults who work professionally with children invariably feel a sense of pride in their ability to contribute in meaningful ways to the next generation of human beings.

If you decide to pursue a career related to children's development, a number of options are available to you. College and university professors teach courses in child development, education, family development, and nursing; counselors, clinical psychologists, pediatricians, psychiatrists, school psychologists, pediatric nurses, psychiatric nurses, and social workers see children with problems and disturbances or illnesses; teachers instruct children in kindergartens, elementary schools, and secondary schools. In pursuing a career related to child development, you can expand your opportunities (and income) considerably by obtaining a graduate degree, although an advanced degree is not absolutely necessary.

Most college professors in child development and its related areas of psychology, education, home economics, nursing, and social work have a master's degree and/or doctorate degree that required 2 to 5 years of academic work beyond their undergraduate degree. Becoming a child clinical psychologist or counseling psychologist requires 5 to 6 years of graduate work to obtain the necessary Ph.D.; this includes both clinical and research training. School and career counselors pursue a master's or doctorate degree in counseling, often in graduate programs in education departments; these degrees require 2 to 6 years to complete. Becoming a pediatrician or psychiatrist requires 4 years of medical school, plus an internship and a residency in pediatrics or psychiatry, respectively; this career path takes 7 to 9 years beyond a bachelor's degree. School psychologists obtain either a master's degree (approximately 2 years) or a D.Ed. degree (approximately 4 to 5 years) in school psychology. School psychologists counsel children and parents when children have problems in school, often giving psychological tests to assess children's personality and intelligence. Social work positions may be obtained with an undergraduate degree in social work or related fields, but opportunities are expanded with an M.S.W. (master's of social work) or Ph.D., which require 2 and 4 to 5 years, respectively. Pediatric and psychiatric nursing positions can also be attained with an undergraduate R.N. degree; M.A. and Ph.D. degrees in nursing, which require 2 and 4 to 5 years of graduate training respectively, are also available.

Although a B.A. or B.S. in child development, psychology, or education does not automatically lead to fame and fortune, they are marketable degrees in a wide range of job settings. Such jobs as parent or family life educator, drug abuse counselor, mental health aide, teacher of mentally retarded children, school teacher, child care director, and staff member of a crisis hotline center often require only an undergraduate degree. Majoring in child development or its related fields also provides students with a sound preparation for adult life.

At this point, we have discussed a number of ideas about the science base of child development and careers in that field. A summary of these ideas is presented in concept table 1.2. In this chapter, we discovered that, as a science, the developmental perspective stresses the importance of theories and methods. In the next chapter, we will turn our attention exclusively to theories of children's development.

Concept	Processes/related ideas	Characteristics/description
Theory and the scientific method	Theory	Theories are general beliefs that help us explain what we observe and make predictions. A good theory has hypotheses, which are assumptions that can be tested.
	Scientific method	Scientific method involves a series of procedures (identifying and analyzing a problem, collecting data, drawing conclusions, and revising theory) to obtain accurate information.
Ways of collecting information—measures	Observation	It is a key ingredient in research that includes laboratory and naturalistic observation.
	Interviews and questionnaires	They are used to assess perceptions and attitudes. Social desirability and lying are problems with their use.
	Case studies	They provide an in-depth look at an individual. Caution in generalizing is warranted.
	Standardized tests	They are designed to assess an individual's characteristics relative to those of a large group of similar individuals.
	Cross-cultural research and research with ethnic minority groups	This research focuses on the cultural-universal and culture-specific nature of children's development. A special concern in research on ethnic minorities is ethnic gloss.
	Physiological research	In physiological research, focus is on the biological dimensions of an organism.
Strategies for setting up research studies	Correlational strategy	It describes how strongly two or more events or characteristics are related. It does not allow causal statements.
	Experimental strategy	It involves manipulation of influential factors—independent variables—and measurement of their effect on the dependent variables. Subjects are randomly assigned to experimental and control groups in many studies. The experimental strategy can reveal the causes of behavior and tell us how one event influenced another.
Time span of inquiry	Cross-sectional approach	Individuals of different ages are compared all at one time.
	Longitudinal approach	The same individuals are studied over a period of time, usually several years or more.

Summary

I. Child Development—Today and Yesterday

Today, the well-being of children is a prominent concern in our culture—five such concerns are educational reform, changes in family structure and work, the impact of computers on children, ethnic issues, and changing gender roles. The history of interest in children is long and rich. In the Renaissance, philosophical views were important, including original sin, *tabula rasa,* and innate goodness. We now conceive of childhood as highly eventful. The modern era of studying children spans a little more than a century, an era in which the study of child development has developed into a sophisticated science. Methodological advances in observation and theoretical views—among them psychoanalytic, behavioral, and cognitive-developmental—characterized this scientific theme.

II. Social Policy Research

A current trend is to conduct child development research that is relevant to the welfare of children. The shape and scope of social policy are influenced by our political system. Child developmentalists can play an important role in social policy. Improved social policy related to children is needed to help all children reach their potential.

III. The Nature of Development

Development is the pattern of movement or change that occurs throughout the life span. It is influenced by an interplay of biological, cognitive, and social processes. Development is commonly divided into the following periods from conception through adolescence: the prenatal period, infancy, early childhood, middle and late childhood, and adolescence.

Concept	Processes/related ideas	Characteristics/description
Cohort effects	Their nature	Cohort effects are due to a subject's time of birth or generation but not actually to age. The study of cohort effects underscores the importance of considering the historical dimensions of development.
Basic versus applied research	Their nature	Basic research, sometimes called pure research, is the study of issues to obtain knowledge for its own sake rather than for practical application. Applied research is the study of issues that have direct practical significance, often with the intent of changing human behavior. Most developmentalists believe that both basic and applied research are important.
Reducing sexism	Its nature	A special concern is that the vast majority of psychological research has been male oriented and male dominated. Some researchers believe that developmentalists need to be challenged to examine children's worlds in a new way, one that incorporates girls' and women's perspectives. Recommendations have been made for conducting nonsexist research.
Ethics in research on child development	Their nature	Researchers must ensure the well-being of subjects in research. The risk of mental and physical harm must be reduced, and informal consent should be obtained. Special ethical considerations are involved when children are research subjects.
Careers in child development	Their nature	A wide range of opportunities is available to individuals who want to pursue a career related to child development. These opportunities include jobs in college and university teaching, child clinical psychology and counseling, school teaching and school psychology, nursing, pediatrics, psychiatry, and social work.

IV. Developmental Issues

Three important developmental issues are the extent to which development is influenced by maturation and experience (or nature and nurture), the extent to which it is characterized by continuity and discontinuity, and the degree to which it involves stability and change. The debate of whether development is due primarily to maturation or to environment is another version of the nature-nurture controversy. Some developmentalists describe development as continuous (gradual, cumulative change), others as discontinuous (abrupt, sequence of stages). The stability-change issue focuses on the degree to which we become older renditions of our early experience or develop into someone different from who we were earlier in development. Most developmentalists recognize that extreme positions on these issues are unwise. Despite this consensus, spirited debate characterizes the issues.

V. Theory and the Scientific Method

Theories are general beliefs that help us explain what we observe and make predictions. A good theory has hypotheses, which are assumptions that can be tested. A series of procedures (identifying and analyzing a problem, collecting data, drawing conclusions, and revising theory) called the scientific method is followed to obtain accurate information about development.

VI. Ways of Collecting Information—Measures

Observation is a key ingredient in developmental research that includes laboratory and naturalistic observation. Interviews and questionnaires are used to assess perceptions and attitudes. Social desirability and lying are problems with their use. Case studies provide an in-depth look at an individual. Caution in generalizing is warranted. Standardized tests are designed to assess an individual's characteristics relative to those of a large group of similar individuals.

Cross-cultural research focuses on the culture-universal and culture-specific nature of children's development. A special concern in research on ethnic minorities is ethnic gloss. Physiological research focuses on the biological dimensions of organisms.

VII. Strategies for Setting Up Research Studies

The correlational strategy describes how strongly two or more events or characteristics are related. It does not allow causal statements. The experimental strategy involves the manipulation of influential factors—the independent variables—and the measurement of their effect on the dependent variables. Subjects are randomly assigned to experimental and control groups in many studies. The experimental strategy can reveal the causes of behavior and tell us how one event influenced another.

VIII. Time Span of Inquiry

In the cross-sectional approach, individuals of different ages are compared all at one time. In the longitudinal approach, the same individuals are studied over a period of time, usually several years or more. In the sequential approach, a combination of the cross-sectional and longitudinal approaches are used. The sequential approach highlights cohort effects.

IX. Cohort Effects

Cohort effects are those due to a subject's time of birth or generation but not actually to age. The study of cohort effects underscores the importance of considering the historical dimensions of development.

X. Basic Versus Applied Research

Basic research, sometimes called pure research, is the study of issues to obtain knowledge for its own sake rather than for practical application. Applied research is the study of issues that have direct practical significance, often with the intent of changing human behavior. Most developmentalists believe that both basic and applied research are important.

XI. Reducing Sexism

A special concern is that the vast majority of psychological research has been male oriented and male dominated. Some researchers believe that developmentalists need to be challenged to examine children's worlds in a new way, one that incorporates girls' and women's perspectives. Recommendations have been made for conducting nonsexist research.

XII. Ethics in Research on Child Development

Researchers must ensure the well-being of subjects in research. The risk of mental and physical harm must be reduced, and informed consent should be sought. Special ethical considerations are involved when research with children is conducted.

XIII. Careers in Child Development

A wide range of opportunities is available to individuals who want to pursue a career related to child development. These opportunities include jobs in college and university teaching, child clinical psychology and counseling, school teaching and school psychology, nursing, pediatrics, psychiatry, and social work.

Key Terms

original sin view 9
tabula rasa view 10
innate goodness view 10
genetic epistemology 12
social policy 13
development 17
biological processes 17
cognitive processes 17
social processes 17
prenatal period 18
infancy 18
early childhood 18
middle and late
  childhood 18
adolescence 18
maturation 20
nature-nurture
  controversy 20
continuity of
  development 21
discontinuity of
  development 22
stability-change issue 22

theory 24
hypotheses 24
scientific method 24
laboratory 25
naturalistic observation 26
questionnaire 27
case study 27
standardized tests 27
emic approach 28
etic approach 28
correlational strategy 30
correlation coefficient 30
experimental strategy 31
random assignment 31
independent variable 31
dependent variable 31
cross-sectional approach 32
longitudinal approach 33
sequential approach 34
cohort effects 34
basic research 35
applied research 35

Suggested Readings

Borstelmann, L. J. (1983). Children before psychology: Ideas about children from antiquity to the late 1800s. In P. H. Mussen (Ed.), *Handbook of child psychology* (4th ed., Vol. 1). New York: Wiley. This is a comprehensive treatment of the historical perception of children from ancient times to the twentieth century.

Brim, O. G., & Kagan, J. (Eds.). (1980). *Constancy and change in human development.* Cambridge, MA: Harvard University Press. Several developmental experts contributed articles to this book, which focuses on how stable or changeable children's lives are.

Child Development and *Developmental Psychology.* These are two of the leading research journals in the field of children's development. Go to your library and leaf through issues from the past several years to get a feel for the research interests of developmentalists.

Children's Defense Fund (1990). *Children 1990.* Washington, DC: Children's Defense Fund. The Children's Defense Fund is an important advocate of children's rights. This book charts how our nation's social policy toward children does not provide adequate care for them.

Kessen, W. (1979). The American child and other cultural inventions. *American Psychologist, 34,* 815–820. This intriguing essay describes how childhood has come to be understood and viewed in contemporary America, contrasting this with perceptions of children at other times in history.

Louv, R. (1990). *Childhood's future.* Boston: Houghton Mifflin. Social commentator Richard Louv criss-crossed the United States for 3 years and conducted interviews with parents and children. Louv describes the vast reduction in family time, the growing conflict between home and work, and a pervasive concern about how our culture is reshaping childhood. He then describes how families can face these challenges.

CHAPTER

2

∎

THEORIES OF CHILD DEVELOPMENT

Psychoanalytic Theories
    Freud's Theory
    Erikson's Theory
    *Perspective on Child Development 2.1: Gender-
        Based Criticisms of Freud's Theory*
    Evaluating the Psychoanalytic Theories
Cognitive Theories
    Piaget's Theory
    Information-Processing Theory
    Evaluating the Cognitive Theories
Behavioral and Social Learning Theories
    Skinner's Behaviorism
    Social Learning Theory
    Evaluating the Behavioral and Social Learning
        Theories
Phenomenological and Humanistic Theories
    Rogers' Humanistic Approach
    Evaluating the Phenomenological and Humanistic
        Theories
Ethological Theories
    Lorenz's Classical Ethological Theory
    Hinde's Neo-Ethological Theory
    Evaluating the Ethological Theories
Ecological Theory
    Environmental Systems
    *Cultural Worlds of Development 2.1: Culture and
        Personality: Individualistic and Collectivistic
        Orientations*
    Evaluating Ecological Theory
An Eclectic Theoretical Orientation
Summary
Key Terms
Suggested Readings

THERE IS NOTHING QUITE SO PRACTICAL AS A GOOD THEORY.

—Kurt Lewin

I magine that you have developed a major theory of child development. What would influence someone like you to construct this theory? A person interested in developing such a theory usually goes through a long university training program that culminates in a doctoral degree. As part of the training, the future theorist is exposed to many ideas about a particular area of child development, such as biological, cognitive, or social development. Another factor that could explain why someone develops a particular theory is that person's life experiences. Two important developmental theorists, whose views we will describe later in the chapter, are Erik Erikson and Jean Piaget. Let's examine a portion of their lives as they were growing up to discover how their experiences might have contributed to the theories they developed.

Erik Homberger Erikson was born in 1902 near Frankfurt, Germany, to Danish parents. Before Erik was born, his parents separated and his mother left Denmark to live in Germany. At age 3, Erik became ill, and his mother took him to see a pediatrician named Homberger. Young Erik's mother fell in love with the pediatrician, married him, and named Erik after his new stepfather.

Erik attended primary school from the ages of 6 to 10 and then the gymnasium (high school) from 11 to 18. He studied art and a number of languages rather than science courses such as biology and chemistry. Erik did not like the atmosphere of formal schooling, and this was reflected in his grades. Rather than go to college at age 18, the adolescent Erikson wandered around Europe, keeping a diary about his experiences. After a year of travel through Europe, he returned to Germany and enrolled in art school, became dissatisfied, and enrolled in another. Later he traveled to Florence, Italy. Psychiatrist Robert Coles described Erikson at this time:

> To the Italians he was . . . the young, tall, thin Nordic expatriate with long, blond hair. He wore a corduroy suit and was seen by his family and friends as not odd or "sick" but as a wandering artist who was trying to come to grips with himself, a not unnatural or unusual struggle. (Coles, 1970, p. 15)

The second major theorist whose life we will examine is Jean Piaget. Piaget (1896–1980) was born in Neuchâtel, Switzerland. Jean's father was an intellectual who taught young Jean to think systematically. Jean's mother was also very bright. His father had an air of detachment from his mother, whom Piaget described as prone to frequent outbursts of neurotic behavior.

In his autobiography, Piaget detailed why he chose to study cognitive development rather than social or abnormal development:

> I started to forego playing for serious work very early. Indeed, I have always detested any departure from reality, an attitude which I relate to . . . my mother's poor health. It was this disturbing factor which at the beginning of my studies in psychology made me keenly interested in psychoanalytic and pathological psychology. Though this interest helped me to achieve independence and widen my cultural background, I have never since felt any desire to involve myself deeper in that particular direction, always much preferring the study of normalcy and of the workings of the intellect to that of the tricks of the unconscious. (Piaget, 1952a, p. 238)

The Nature of Child Development

These excerpts from Erikson's and Piaget's lives illustrate how personal experiences might influence the direction in which a particular theorist goes. Erikson's own wanderings and search for self contributed to his theory of identity development, and perhaps Piaget's intellectual experiences with his parents and schooling contributed to his emphasis on cognitive development.

Erikson's and Piaget's theories are but two of the many theories you will read about in this chapter. The diversity of theories makes understanding children's development a challenging undertaking. Just when you think one theory correctly explains children's development, another theory crops up and makes you rethink your earlier conclusion. To keep from getting frustrated, remember that children's development is a complex, multifaceted topic, and no single theory has been able to account for all its aspects. Each theory has contributed an important piece to the child development puzzle. Although the theories sometimes disagree about certain aspects of children's development, much of their information is *complementary* rather than contradictory. Together the various theories let us see the total landscape of children's development in all its richness.

■ *Critical Thinking*
What personal experiences in your own life might influence the kind of developmental theory you would construct?

Psychoanalytic Theories

For psychoanalytic theorists, development is primarily unconscious—that is, beyond awareness—and is heavily colored by emotion. Psychoanalytic theorists believe that behavior is merely a surface characteristic and that to truly understand development, we have to analyze the symbolic meanings of behavior and the deep inner workings of the mind. Psychoanalytic theorists also stress that early experiences with parents extensively shape our development. These characteristics are highlighted in the main psychoanalytic theory, that of Sigmund Freud (Looney & Blotcky, 1989; Nichtern, 1989).

Freud's Theory

Loved and hated, respected and despised, for some the master and for others misdirected—Sigmund Freud, whether right or wrong in his views, has been one of the most influential thinkers of the twentieth century. Freud was a medical doctor who specialized in neurology. He developed his ideas about psychoanalytic theory from his work with patients with mental problems. He was born in 1856 in Austria and he died in London at the age of 83. He spent most of his years in Vienna, though he left the city near the end of his career because of the Nazis' anti-Semitism.

The Structure of Personality

Freud (1917) believed that personality has three structures: the id, the ego, and the superego. One way to understand the three structures is to consider them as three rulers of a country (Singer, 1984). The id is king or queen, the ego is prime minister, and the superego is high priest. The id is an absolute monarch, owed complete obedience; it is spoiled, willful, and self-centered. The id wants what it wants right now, not later. The ego as prime minister has the job of getting things done right; it is tuned into reality and is responsive to society's demands. The superego as high priest is concerned with right and wrong; the id may be greedy and needs to be told that nobler purposes should be pursued.

Sigmund Freud was the founder of psychoanalytic theory.

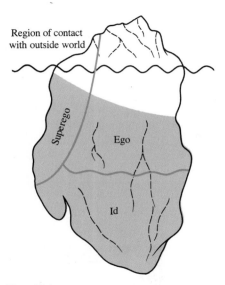

Region of contact
with outside world

Superego

Ego

Id

Figure 2.1
Conscious and Unconscious Processes:
The Iceberg Analogy
This odd-looking diagram illustrates Freud's
belief that most of the important personality
processes occur below the level of
conscious awareness. In examining
people's conscious thoughts and their
behaviors, we can see some reflections of
the ego and the superego. Whereas the
ego and superego are partly conscious and
partly unconscious, the primitive id is the
unconscious, totally submerged part of the
"iceberg."

The **id** *is the Freudian structure of personality that consists of instincts, which are an individual's reservoir of psychic energy.* In Freud's view, the id is unconscious; it has no contact with reality. The id works according to the **pleasure principle,** *the Freudian concept that the id always seeks pleasure and avoids pain.*

It would be a dangerous and scary world if our personalities were all id. As young children develop, they learn, for example, that they cannot slug other children in the face. They also learn they have to use the toilet instead of their diaper. As children experience the demands and constraints of reality, a new structure of personality is formed—the **ego,** *the Freudian structure of personality that deals with the demands of reality. The ego is called the executive branch of personality because it makes rational decisions.* The ego abides by the **reality principle,** *the Freudian concept by which the ego tries to bring individuals pleasure within the boundaries of reality.* Few of us are cold-blooded killers or wild-wheeler-dealers; we take into account obstacles to our satisfaction that exist in our world. We recognize that our sexual and aggressive impulses cannot go unrestrained. The ego helps us test reality—to see how far we can go without getting into trouble and hurting ourselves.

Whereas the id is completely unconscious, the ego is partly conscious. It houses our higher mental functions—reasoning, problem solving, and decision making, for example. For this reason, the ego is referred to as the executive branch of the personality; like an executive in a company, it makes the rational decisions that help the company succeed.

The id and ego have no morality. They do not take into account whether something is right or wrong. The **superego** *is the Freudian structure of personality that is the moral branch of personality. The superego takes into account whether something is right or wrong.* Think of the superego as what we often refer to as our "conscience." Like the id, the superego does not consider reality; it doesn't deal with what is realistic, only with whether the id's sexual and aggressive impulses can be satisfied in moral terms. You probably are beginning to sense that both the id and the superego make life rough for the ego. Your ego might say, "I will have sex only occasionally and be sure to take the proper precautions because I don't want the intrusion of a child in the development of my career." However, your id is saying, "I want to be satisfied; sex is pleasurable." Your superego is at work too: "I feel guilty about having sex."

Remember that Freud considered personality to be like an iceberg; most of personality exists below our level of awareness, just as the massive part of an iceberg is beneath the surface of the water. Figure 2.1 illustrates this analogy.

Defense Mechanisms

How does the ego resolve the conflict between its demands for reality, the wishes of the id, and the constraints of the superego? Through **defense mechanisms,** *the psychoanalytic term for unconscious methods, the ego distorts reality, thereby protecting it from anxiety.* In Freud's view, the conflicting demands of the personality structures produce anxiety. For example, when the ego blocks the pleasurable pursuits of the id, inner anxiety is felt. This diffuse, distressed state develops when the ego senses that the id is going to cause harm to the individual. The anxiety alerts the ego to resolve the conflict by means of defense mechanisms.

Repression *is the most powerful and pervasive defense mechanism, according to Freud; it works to push unacceptable id impulses out of awareness and back into the unconscious mind.* Repression is the foundation from which all other defense mechanisms work; the goal of every defense mechanism is to *repress* or push threatening impulses out of awareness. Freud said that our early childhood experiences, many of which he believed were sexually laden, are too threatening and stressful for us to deal with consciously. We reduce the anxiety of this conflict through the defense mechanism of repression.

Displacement *is the psychoanalytic defense mechanism that occurs when an individual shifts unacceptable feelings from one object to another, more acceptable object.* For example, an 8-year-old boy gets reprimanded by his teacher for disrupting the class. He can't harass the teacher because he knows he would get in even more trouble. Later, during recess, he says some nasty things to a smaller boy on the playground, thus transferring his feelings toward his teacher to the smaller boy.

Projection *is the psychoanalytic defense mechanism we use to attribute our own shortcomings, problems, and faults to others.* For example, an adolescent who manipulates others tells her friend, "The students at our school are so manipulative. They never consider my feelings." When children and adolescents can't face their own unwanted feelings, they *project* them onto others and see others as having those traits.

Sublimation *is the psychoanalytic defense mechanism that occurs when an individual replaces a socially distasteful course of action with a socially useful one.* For example, an adolescent with strong sexual urges may turn them into socially approved behavior by painting nudes.

Reaction formation *is the psychoanalytic defense mechanism that occurs when an individual expresses an unacceptable impulse by transforming it into its opposite.* For example, a boy who likes a particular girl but doesn't want to acknowledge it might say that he can't stand the girl when he actually loves her.

Regression *is the psychoanalytic defense mechanism that occurs when individuals behave in a way that characterizes a previous developmental level.* When anxiety becomes too great, the person may revert to an earlier behavior that provided pleasurable feelings. For example, a woman may run home to her mother every time she and her husband have a big argument.

Two final points about defense mechanisms need to be understood. First, they are unconscious. Children and adolescents are not aware they are using them to protect their ego and reduce anxiety. Second, when used in moderation or on a temporary basis, defense mechanisms are not necessarily unhealthy. For example, such defense mechanisms as denial (protecting oneself from unpleasant aspects of reality by refusing to accept them) can help an individual cope with impending death. For the most part, though, defense mechanisms should not be allowed to dominate behavior and prevent people from facing reality.

"So, Mr. Fenton . . . Let's begin with your mother."

The FAR SIDE cartoon by Gary Larson is reprinted by permission of Chronicle Features, San Francisco, CA.

The Development of Personality

As Freud listened to, probed, and analyzed his patients, he became convinced that their problems were the result of experiences early in life. Freud believed that we go through five stages of psychosexual development and that, at each stage of development, we experience pleasure in one part of the body more than in others. **Erogenous zones** *refer to Freud's concept of the parts of the body that have especially strong pleasure-giving qualities at each stage of development.*

Freud thought that the adult personality is determined by the way conflicts between the early sources of pleasure—the mouth, the anus, and then the genitals—and the demands of reality are resolved. When these conflicts are not resolved, the individual may become fixated at a particular stage of development. **Fixation** *is the psychoanalytic defense mechanism that occurs when an individual remains locked into an earlier developmental stage because needs are under- or overgratified.* For example, a parent may wean a child too early, be too strict in toilet training, punish the child for masturbation, or smother the child with warmth. We will return to the idea of fixation and how it may show up in an adult's personality, but first we need to learn more about the early stages of personality development.

The **oral stage** *is the first Freudian stage of development, occurring during the first 18 months of life, in which the infant's pleasure centers around the mouth.* Chewing, sucking, and biting are the chief sources of pleasure. These actions reduce tension in the infant.

The **anal stage** *is the second Freudian stage of development, occurring between 1½ and 3 years of age, in which the child's greatest pleasure involves the anus or the eliminative functions associated with it.* In Freud's view, the exercise of anal muscles reduces tension.

The **phallic stage** *is the third Freudian stage of development, which occurs between the ages of 3 and 6; its name comes from the Latin word* phallus, *which means "penis." During the phallic stage, pleasure focuses on the genitals as the child discovers that self-manipulation is enjoyable.*

In Freud's view, the phallic stage has a special importance in personality development because it is during this period that the Oedipus complex appears. This name comes from Greek mythology, in which Oedipus, the son of the King of Thebes, unwittingly kills his father and marries his mother. The **Oedipus complex,** *is the Freudian concept in which the young child develops an intense desire to replace the parent of the same sex and enjoy the affections of the opposite-sexed parent.* Freud's concept of the Oedipus complex has been criticized by some psychoanalysts and writers. To learn more about the gender-based criticisms of Freud's theory, turn to Perspective on Child Development 2.1.

How is the Oedipus complex resolved? At about 5 to 6 years of age, children recognize that their same-sex parent might punish them for their incestuous wishes. To reduce this conflict, the child identifies with the same-sex parent, striving to be like him or her. If the conflict is not resolved, though, the individual may become fixated at the phallic stage. Table 2.1 reveals some possible links between adult personality characteristics and fixation, sublimation, and reaction formation involving the phallic stage, as well as the oral and anal stages.

TABLE 2.1
Possible Links Between Adult Personality Characteristics and Fixation at Oral, Anal, and Phallic Stages

Stage	Adult extensions	Sublimations	Reaction formations
Oral	Smoking, eating, kissing, oral hygiene, drinking, chewing gum	Seeking knowledge, humor, wit, sarcasm, being a food or wine expert	Speech purist, food faddist, prohibitionist, dislike of milk
Anal	Notable interest in one's bowel movements, love of bathroom humor, extreme messiness	Interest in painting or sculpture, being overly giving, great interest in statistics	Extreme disgust with feces, fear of dirt, prudishness, irritability
Phallic	Heavy reliance on masturbation, flirtatiousness, expressions of virility	Interest in poetry, love of love, interest in acting, striving for success	Puritanical attitude toward sex, excessive modesty

From *Introduction to Personality* by E. J. Phares. Copyright © 1984 by Scott, Foresman and Company. Reprinted by permission of HarperCollins Publishers.

The **latency stage** *is the fourth Freudian stage of development, which occurs between approximately 6 years of age and puberty; the child represses all interest in sexuality and develops social and intellectual skills.* This activity channel's much of the child's energy into emotionally safe areas and helps the child forget the highly stressful conflicts of the phallic stage.

The **genital stage** *is the fifth and final Freudian stage of development, occurring from puberty on. The genital stage is a time of sexual reawakening; the source of sexual pleasure now becomes someone outside of the family.* Freud believed that unresolved conflicts with parents reemerge during adolescence. When they are resolved, the individual is capable of developing a mature love relationship and functioning independently as an adult.

Erikson's Theory

Erik Erikson spent his childhood and adolescence in Europe. After working as a young adult under Freud's direction, Erikson came to the United States in 1933. He became a U.S. citizen and taught at Harvard University.

Erikson recognized Freud's contributions but he believed that Freud misjudged some important dimensions of human development. For one, Erikson (1950, 1968) says we develop in *psychosocial stages,* in contrast to Freud's psychosexual stages. For another, Erikson emphasized developmental change throughout the human life cycle, whereas Freud argued that our basic

Gender-Based Criticisms of Freud's Theory

The Oedipus complex is one of Freud's most influential concepts pertaining to the importance of early psychosexual relationships for later personality development. Freud developed his theory in the Victorian era of the late 1800s, when males were dominant and females were passive, and when sexual interests, especially females', were repressed. According to Freud, the sequence of events in the phallic stage for a girl begins when she realizes she has no penis. According to Freud, she recognizes that the penis is superior to her own anatomy; thus, she develops *penis envy.* Since her desire for having a penis can never be satisfied directly, Freud said, the young girl develops a wish to become impregnated by her father. Holding her mother responsible for her lack of a penis, she renounces her love for her mother and becomes intensely attached to her father, thus forming her own version of the Oedipus complex, sometimes referred to as the Electra complex. The sequence of events becomes reversed: for boys, the Oedipal complex produces castration anxiety; for girls, the parallel to castration anxiety—penis envy—occurs first and leads to the formation of the Oedipus complex (Hyde, 1985).

Many psychologists believe that Freud overemphasized behavior's biological determinants and that he did not give adequate attention to sociocultural influences and learning. In particular, his view on the differences between males and females, including their personality development, has a strong biological flavor, relying mainly on anatomical differences. That is, because they have a penis, boys are likely to develop a dominant, powerful personality, girls a submissive, weak personality. In basing his view of male/female differences in personality development on anatomical differences, Freud ignored the enormous impact of culture and experience in determining personality.

In the Trobriand Islands, the authoritarian figure in a young boy's life is his maternal uncle, not his father. Young boys in this culture fear their maternal uncles, not their fathers. Thus, it is not sexual relations in a family that create conflict and fear—a damaging finding for Freud's Oedipus complex theory.

More than half a century ago, English anthropologist Bronislaw Malinowski (1927) observed the behavior of the Trobriand Islanders of the Western Pacific. He found that the Oedipus complex is not universal but depends on cultural variations in families. The family pattern of the Trobriand Islanders is different from those found in many cultures. In the Trobriand Islands, the biological father is not the head of

Erik Erikson developed a theory that consists of eight psychosocial stages of human development.

personality is shaped in the first 5 years of life. The **epigenetic principle** *is Erikson's term for the process that guides development through the life cycle. The epigenetic principle states that anything which grows has a blueprint, each part having a special time of ascendency, until all of the parts have arisen to form a functioning whole.* In Erikson's theory, eight stages of development unfold as we go through the life cycle. Each stage consists of a unique developmental task that confronts individuals with a crisis that must be faced. For Erikson, this crisis is not a catastrophe but a turning point of increased vulnerability and enhanced potential. The more an individual resolves the crises successfully the healthier development will be.

Trust versus mistrust *is Erikson's first psychosocial stage, which is experienced in the first year of life. A sense of trust requires a feeling of physical comfort and a minimal amount of fear and apprehension about the future.*

(a)

(b)

(a) Karen Horney developed the first feminist-based criticism of Freud's theory, creating a model of women with positive qualities and self-valuation. (b) Nancy Chodorow has

developed an important contemporary feminist revision of psychoanalysis theory that emphasizes the meaningfulness of emotions for women.

the household, a role reserved for the mother's brother, who acts as a disciplinarian. Thus, the Trobriand Islanders tease apart the roles played by the same person in Freud's Vienna and in many other cultures. In Freud's view, this different family constellation should make no difference: the Oedipus complex still should emerge, in which the father is the young boy's hated rival for the mother's love. However, Malinowski found no indication of conflict between fathers and sons in the Trobriand Islanders, though he did observe some negative feelings directed by the boy toward the maternal uncle. Thus, the young boy fears the man who is the authoritarian figure in his life, which in the Trobriand Island culture is the maternal uncle, not the father. In sum, Malinowski's study documented that it is not the sexual relations within the family

that create conflict and fear for a child, a damaging finding for Freud's Oedipus complex theory.

The first feminist-based criticism of Freud's theory was proposed by Karen Horney (1967). She developed a model of women with positive feminine qualities and self-valuation. Her critique of Freud's theory included reference to a male-dominant society and culture. Rectification of the male bias in psychoanalytic theory continues today. For example, Nancy Chodorow (1978, 1989) emphasizes that many more women than men define themselves in terms of their relationships and connections to others. Her feminist revision of psychoanalytic theory also emphasizes the meaningfulness of emotions for women, as well as her belief that many men use the defense mechanism of denial in self-other connections.

Trust in infancy sets the stage for a lifelong expectation that the world will be a good and pleasant place to live.

Autonomy versus shame and doubt *is Erikson's second stage of development, occurring in late infancy and toddlerhood (1–3 years).* After gaining trust in a caregiver(s), infants begin to discover that their behavior is their own. They start to assert their sense of independence or autonomy. They realize their *will*. If infants are restrained too much or punished too harshly, they are likely to develop a sense of shame and doubt.

Initiative versus guilt *is Erikson's third stage of development, occurring during the preschool years.* As preschool children encounter a widening social world, they are challenged more than when they were infants. Active, purposeful behavior is needed to cope with these challenges. Children are asked to assume responsibility for their bodies, their behavior, their toys, and their pets. Developing a sense of responsibility increases initiative. Uncomfortable guilt feelings may arise, though, if the child is irresponsible and is made to feel too anxious. Erikson has a positive outlook on this stage. He believes that most guilt is quickly compensated for by a sense of accomplishment.

Industry versus inferiority *is Erikson's fourth developmental stage, occurring approximately in the elementary school years.* Children's initiative brings them in contact with a wealth of new experiences. As they move into middle and late childhood, they direct their energy toward mastering knowledge and intellectual skills. At no other time is the child more enthusiastic about learning than at the end of early childhood's expansive imagination. The danger in the elementary school years is the development of a sense of inferiority—of feeling incompetent and unproductive. Erikson believes that teachers have a special responsibility for children's development of industry. Teachers should "mildly but firmly coerce children into the adventure of finding out that one can learn to accomplish things which one would never have thought of by oneself" (Erikson, 1968, p. 127).

Identity versus identity confusion *is Erikson's fifth developmental stage, which individuals experience during the adolescent years. At this time, individuals are faced with finding out who they are, what they are all about, and where they are going in life.* Adolescents are confronted with many new roles and adult statuses—vocational and romantic, for example. Parents need to allow adolescents to explore many different roles and different paths within a particular role. If the adolescent explores such roles in a healthy manner and arrives at a positive path to follow in life, then a positive identity will be achieved. If an identity is pushed on the adolescent by parents, if the adolescent does not adequately explore many roles, and if a positive future path is not defined, then identity confusion reigns.

Intimacy versus isolation *is Erikson's sixth developmental stage, which individuals experience during the early adulthood years. At this time, individuals face the developmental task of forming intimate relationships with others.* Erikson describes intimacy as finding oneself yet losing oneself in another. If the young adult forms healthy friendships and an intimate close relationship with another individual, intimacy will be achieved; if not, isolation will result.

Generativity versus stagnation *is Erikson's seventh developmental stage, which individuals experience during middle adulthood.* A chief concern is to assist the younger generation in developing and leading useful lives—this is what Erikson meant by *generativity*. The feeling of having done nothing to help the next generation is *stagnation*.

Integrity versus despair *is Erikson's eighth and final developmental stage, which individuals experience during late adulthood.* In the later years of life, we look back and evaluate what we have done with our lives. Through many different routes, the older person may have developed a positive outlook in most or all of the previous stages of development. If so, the retrospective glances will reveal a picture of a life well spent, and the person will feel a sense of satisfaction—integrity will be achieved. If the older adult resolved many of the earlier stages negatively, the retrospective glances likely will yield doubt or gloom—the despair Erikson talks about.

Know thyself, for once we know ourselves, we may learn how to care for ourselves, otherwise we never shall.

—Socrates

You come to a place in your life when what you've been is going to form what you will be. If you've wasted what you have in you, it's too late to do much about it. If you've invested yourself in life, you're pretty certain to get a return. If you are inwardly a serious person, in the middle years it will pay off.

—Lillian Hellman

Erikson does not believe the proper solution to a stage crisis is always completely positive in nature. Some exposure or commitment to the negative end of the person's bipolar conflict is sometimes inevitable—you cannot trust all people under all circumstances and survive, for example. Nonetheless, in the healthy solution to a stage crisis, the positive resolution dominates. A summary of Erikson's stages is presented in figure 2.2.

Evaluating the Psychoanalytic Theories

Although psychoanalytic theories have become heterogeneous, they share some core principles. Our development is determined not only by current experiences but by those from early in life as well. The principles that early experiences are important determinants of personality and that we can better understand personality by examining it developmentally have withstood the test of time. The belief that environmental experiences are mentally transformed and represented in the mind likewise continues to receive considerable attention. Psychoanalytic theorists forced psychologists to recognize that the mind is not all consciousness; our minds have an unconscious portion that influences our behavior. Psychoanalytic theorists' emphasis on the importance of conflict and anxiety requires us to consider the dark side of our existence, not just its bright side. Adjustment is not always easy, and one's inner world often conflicts with the outer demands of reality.

However, the main concepts of psychoanalytic theories have been difficult to test. Inference and interpretation are required to determine whether psychoanalytic ideas are accurate. Researchers have not successfully investigated such key concepts as repression in the laboratory. Much of the data used to support psychoanalytic theories come from patients' reconstruction of the past, often the distant past, and are of doubtful accuracy. Other data come from clinicians' subjective evaluations of clients; in such cases, it is easy for clinicians to see what they expect because of the theory they hold. Some psychologists object that Freud overemphasized sexuality and the unconscious mind. The psychoanalytic theories also provide a model of people that is too negative and pessimistic. We are not born into the world with only a bundle of sexual and aggressive impulses; our compliance with the external demands of reality does not always conflict with our biological needs.

Cognitive Theories

Exploring the human mind has been regarded with a kind of mystical awe throughout most of human history. Now, 10,000 years after the dawn of civilization, a new understanding of the mind is flourishing. "Mind" is a complex term, but primarily it is our cognitive activity—perception, attention, memory, language, reasoning, thinking, and the like. Whereas psychoanalytic theories emphasize unconscious thoughts, cognitive theories emphasize conscious thoughts. Developing individuals are perceived as rational and logical, capable of using the mind to effectively interact with and control the environment. The cognitive theory that has dominated the study of development is the Swiss psychologist Jean Piaget's. A second important cognitive approach is information processing.

Man is a reed, the weakest in nature; but he is a thinking reed.

—Pascal

Figure 2.2
Erikson's Eight Stages of the Human Life Cycle

Erikson's stages	Developmental period	Characteristics
Trust versus mistrust	Infancy (first year)	A sense of trust requires a feeling of physical comfort and a minimal amount of fear about the future. The infant's basic needs are met by responsive, sensitive caregivers.
Autonomy versus shame and doubt	Late infancy - toddlerhood (1 to 3 years)	After gaining trust in caregivers, infants start to discover that they have a will of their own. They assert their sense of autonomy or independence. They realize their will. If infants are restrained too much or punishment is too harsh, they are likely to develop a sense of shame and doubt.
Initiative versus guilt	Early childhood (preschool years, ages 3 to 5)	As preschool children encounter a widening social world, they are challenged more and need to develop more purposeful behavior to cope with these challenges. Children are now asked to assume more responsibility. Imaginative play develops. Uncomfortable guilt feelings may arise, though, if the child is irresponsible and is made to feel too anxious.
Industry versus inferiority	Middle and late childhood (elementary school years, 6 to puberty)	At no other time is the child more enthusiastic than at the end of early childhood's expansive imagination. As children move into the elementary school years, they direct their energy toward mastering knowledge and intellectual skills. The danger at this stage involves feeling incompetent and unproductive.

Erikson's stages	Developmental period	Characteristics
Identity versus identity confusion	Adolescence (10 to 20 years)	Individuals are faced with finding out who they are, what they are all about, and where they are going in life. An important dimension is the exploration of alternative solutions to roles. Career exploration is important.
Intimacy versus isolation	Early adulthood (20s, 30s)	Individuals face the developmental task of forming intimate relationships with others. Erikson described intimacy as finding oneself yet losing oneself in another person.
Generativity versus stagnation	Middle adulthood (40s, 50s)	A chief concern is to assist the younger generation in developing and leading useful lives.
Integrity versus despair	Late adulthood (60s -)	Individuals look back and evaluate what they have done with their lives. The retrospective glances can either be positive (integrity) or negative (despair).

Jean Piaget, the famous Swiss developmental psychologist, changed forever the way we think about the development of children's minds. For Piaget, a child's mental development is a continuous creation of increasingly complex forms.

■ *Critical Thinking*
What experiences in your own life provide examples of Piaget's concepts of assimilation and accommodation?

Piaget's Theory

At the age of 10, Jean Piaget wrote an article about a rare albino sparrow, which was published in the *Journal of the Natural History of Neuchâtel*. The article was so brilliant that the curators of the Geneva Museum of Natural History, who had no idea the article had been written by a 10-year-old, offered young Piaget the job of museum curator. The museum heads quickly rescinded their offer when they realized Piaget was only a child. Piaget continued to live in Switzerland as an adult and became one of the most influential forces in child development in the twentieth century. In a eulogy to Piaget following his death at the age of 84 in 1980, it was said that we owe him the present field of cognitive development. What was the theory of this giant in developmental psychology like?

Piaget's theory will be covered in greater detail as we discuss cognitive development in chapter 8. Here we will briefly present the main ideas in his theory. Piaget stressed that children actively construct their own cognitive worlds; information is not just poured into their minds from the environment. Two processes underlie an individual's construction of the world: organization and adaptation. To make sense of our world, we organize our experiences. For example, we separate important ideas from less important ideas. We connect one idea to another. We not only organize our observations and experiences, however; we also *adapt* our thinking to include new ideas because additional information furthers understanding. Piaget (1954) believed that we adapt in two ways: assimilation and accommodation.

Assimilation *occurs when children incorporate new information into their existing knowledge.* **Accommodation** *occurs when children adjust to new information.* Consider a circumstance in which a 5-year-old girl is given a hammer and nails to hang a picture on the wall. She has never used a hammer, but from experience and observation she realizes that a hammer is an object to be held, that it is swung by the handle to hit the nail, and that it is usually swung a number of times. Recognizing each of these things, she fits her behavior into information she already has (assimilation). However, the hammer is heavy, so she holds it near the top. She swings too hard and the nail bends, so she adjusts the pressure of her strikes. These adjustments reveal her ability to alter her conception of the world slightly (accommodation).

Piaget thought that assimilation and accommodation operate even in a very young infant's life. Newborns reflexively suck everything that touches their lips (assimilation), but, after several months of experience, they construct their understanding of the world differently. Some objects, such as fingers and the mother's breast, can be sucked, and others, such as fuzzy blankets, should not be sucked (accommodation).

Piaget also believed that we go through four stages in understanding the world. Each of the stages is age-related and consists of distinct ways of thinking. Remember, it is the *different* way of understanding the world that makes one stage more advanced than another; knowing *more* information does not make a child's thinking more advanced in the Piagetian view. This is what Piaget meant when he said a child's cognition is *qualitatively* different in one stage compared with another. What are Piaget's four stages of cognitive development like?

The **sensorimotor stage,** *which lasts from birth to about 2 years of age, is the first Piagetian stage. In this stage, infants construct an understanding of the world by coordinating sensory experiences (such as seeing and hearing) with physical, motoric actions—hence the term* sensorimotor. At the beginning of this stage, newborns have little more than reflexive patterns with which to work. At the end of the stage, 2-year-olds have complex sensorimotor patterns and are beginning to operate with primitive symbols.

The **preoperational stage,** *which lasts from approximately 2 to 7 years of age, is the second Piagetian stage. In this stage, children begin to represent the world with words, images, and drawings.* Symbolic thought goes beyond simple connections of sensory information and physical action. However, although preschool children can symbolically represent the world, according to Piaget, they still lack the ability to perform operations, the Piagetian term for internalized mental actions that allow children to do mentally what they previously did physically.

The **concrete operational stage,** *which lasts from approximately 7 to 11 years of age, is the third Piagetian stage. In this stage, children can perform operations, and logical reasoning replaces intuitive thought as long as reasoning can be applied to specific or concrete examples.* For instance, concrete operational thinkers cannot imagine the steps necessary to complete an algebraic equation, which is too abstract for thinking at this stage of development.

The **formal operational stage,** *which appears between the ages of 11 and 15, is the fourth and final Piagetian stage. In this stage, individuals move beyond the world of actual, concrete experiences and think in abstract and more logical terms.* As part of thinking more abstractly, adolescents develop images of ideal circumstances. They may think about what an ideal parent is like and compare their parents with this ideal standard. They begin to entertain possibilities for the future and are fascinated with what they can be. In solving problems, formal operational thinkers are more systematic, developing hypotheses about why something is happening the way it is, then testing these hypotheses in a deductive fashion.

Piaget's stages are summarized in figure 2.3, and a comparison of Piaget's stages with Freud's and Erikson's stages is presented in figure 2.4. Notice that only Erikson describes changes in the adulthood years. Remember also that Piaget's theory stresses conscious thought, whereas Freud's and Erikson's theories stress unconscious thought.

Information-Processing Theory

Information processing *is concerned with how individuals process information about their world—how information enters the mind, how it is stored and transformed, and how it is retrieved to perform such complex activities as problem solving and reasoning.* A simple model of cognition is shown in figure 2.5.

Cognition begins when children detect information from the world through their sensory and perceptual processes. Then children store, transform, and retrieve the information through the processes of memory. Notice in our model that information can flow back and forth between memory and

Figure 2.3
Piaget's Stages of Cognitive Development

Stage	Sensorimotor	Preoperational	Concrete operational	Formal operational
Ages	Birth to 2	2 to 7	7 to 11	11 to 15
Description	The infant constructs an understanding of the world by coordinating sensory experiences with physical actions.	The child begins to represent the world with images and words, which reflect symbolic thinking.	The child can now perform operations and can logically reason about concrete circumstances.	The adolescent reasons in more abstract, logical, and idealistic ways.

Figure 2.4
A Comparison of Piaget's, Freud's, and Erikson's Stage Theories

The life cycle	Piaget's cognitive stages	Freud's psychosexual stages	Erikson's psychosocial stages	
Late adulthood			Ego integrity vs. despair	
Middle adulthood			Generativity vs. stagnation	Adolescent and adult stages
Early adulthood			Intimacy vs. isolation	
Adolescence	Formal operational	Genital	Identity vs. identity confusion	
Middle and late childhood	Concrete operational	Latency	Industry vs. inferiority	Middle and late childhood stages
Early childhood	Preoperational	Phallic	Initiative vs. guilt	Early childhood stages
Infancy	Sensorimotor	Anal / Oral	Autonomy vs. shame, doubt / Trust vs. mistrust	Infant stages

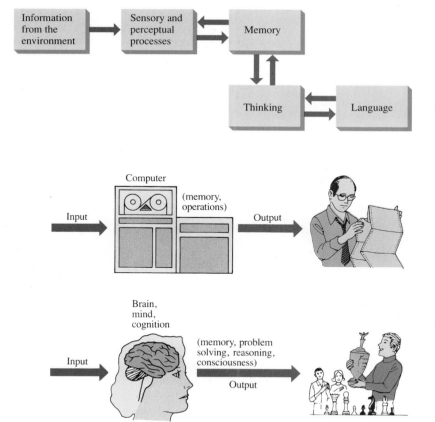

Figure 2.5
A Model of Information Processing
In this simplified model of how individuals process information, sensory and perceptual processes, memory, thinking, and language are described as important cognitive processes. Notice the flow of information back and forth between these cognitive processes.

Figure 2.6
Computers and Cognition: An Analogy
The computer revolution has influenced the way cognitive psychologists view cognition. Cognitive psychologists have often used a computer analogy to help explain the relation between cognition and the brain. The physical brain is described as the computer's hardware, cognition as its software.

perceptual processes. For example, children are good at remembering the faces they see, yet their memory of a person's face may differ from the way the person actually looks. Keep in mind that our information-processing model is a simple one, designed to illustrate the main cognitive processes and their interrelations. We could have drawn other arrows—between memory and language, between thinking and sensory and perceptual processes, and between language and sensory and perceptual processes, for example. Also, it is important to know that the boxes in figure 2.5 do not represent sharp, distinct stages in processing information. There is continuity and flow between the cognitive processes, as well as overlap.

In the 1940s, the behaviorists' claim that children learn primarily through environment-behavior connections was being challenged. The first success with computers suggested that machines could perform logical operations. This indicated that some mental operations might be modeled by computers, and possibly computers could tell us something about how cognition works. Cognitive psychologists often compare the brain to a computer to help explain the relation between cognition and the brain. The physical brain is described as the computer's hardware and cognition as its software (see figure 2.6). The ability to process information has highlighted psychology's cognitive revolution since the 1950s.

■ *Critical Thinking*
What things can a computer do that a human mind cannot? What things can a human mind do that a computer cannot?

"I Feel Pretty Silly Putting Pegs In Holes When I Have A Personal Computer At Home."

The information-processing approach raises important questions about changes in cognition during children's development. Does processing speed increase as children grow older? The idea of speed of processing is an important aspect of the information-processing approach. Many cognitive tasks are performed under real time pressure. For example, at school, children have a limited amount of time to add and subtract and take tests; they also have deadlines for completing projects. There is a good deal of evidence that processing speed is slower in younger children than in older children, but the cause of this difference has not been determined. Although some of the difference might be biological in origin, the faster information-processing speed of older children might reflect differences in knowledge about a task or practice on the task (Santrock & Bartlett, 1986).

Evaluating the Cognitive Theories

Piaget's cognitive-developmental theory and the information-processing theory both contribute in important ways to our knowledge about children's development. Today, researchers enthusiastically evaluate the accuracy of Piaget's theory, with the result that some of his ideas remain unscathed, whereas others require extensive modification (Beilin, 1989). The information-processing approach has opened up many avenues of research, offering detailed descriptions of cognitive processes and sophisticated methods for studying cognition (Klahr, 1989). The cognitive theories provide an optimistic view of human development, ascribing to children the ability and motivation to know their world and to cope with it in constructive ways.

Like all theories, the cognitive theories have their weaknesses. There is skepticism about the purity of Piaget's stages, and his concepts are somewhat loosely defined, and the information-processing approach has not yet produced an overall perspective on development. Both the Piagetian and information-processing approaches may have underestimated the importance of the unconscious mind and environmental experiences—especially those involving families—in determining behavior.

So far, we have discussed two main theories of children's development: psychoanalytic and cognitive. A summary of the main ideas in these two theories is presented in concept table 2.1. The psychoanalytic and cognitive-developmental theories are stage theories, each highlighting the ascendance of certain characteristics at particular points in development. The other theories we will discuss do not specify stages in child development.

Behavioral and Social Learning Theories

Fifteen-year-old Tom is going steady with 14-year-old Ann. Both have warm, friendly personalities, and they enjoy being together. Psychoanalytic theorists would say that their warm, friendly personalities are derived from longstanding relationships with their parents, especially their early child experiences. They also would argue that the reason for their attraction to each other is unconscious; they are unaware of how their biological heritage and early life experiences have been carried forward to influence their personalities in adolescence.

Behaviorists and social learning theorists would observe Tom and Ann and see something quite different. They would examine their experiences, especially their most recent ones, to understand the reason for their attraction. Tom would be described as rewarding Ann's behavior, and vice versa, for example. No reference would be made to unconscious thoughts, the Oedipus complex, defense mechanisms, and so on.

Behaviorists believe we should examine only what can be directly observed and measured (Baer, 1989; Bijou, 1989). At approximately the same time that Freud was interpreting his patients' unconscious minds through early childhood experiences, behaviorists such as Ivan Pavlov and John B. Watson were conducting detailed observations of behavior in controlled laboratory circumstances. Out of the behavioral tradition grew the belief that development is observable behavior, learned through experience with the environment. The two versions of the behavioral approach that are prominent today are the view of B. F. Skinner and social learning theory.

Skinner's Behaviorism

During World War II, B. F. Skinner constructed a rather strange project— a pigeon-guided missile. A pigeon in the warhead of a missile operated the flaps on the missile and guided it home by pecking at an image of a target on a screen.

This produced corrective signals to keep the missile on its course. The pigeons did their job well in trial runs, but top Navy officials just could not accept pigeons piloting their missiles during a war. Skinner, however, congratulated himself on the degree of control he was able to exercise over the pigeons.

Following the pigeon experiment, Skinner (1948) wrote *Walden Two,* a novel in which he presented his ideas about building a scientifically managed society. Skinner envisioned a utopia that could be engineered through behavioral control. Skinner viewed existing societies as poorly managed because individuals believe in such myths as free will. He pointed out that humans are

CONCEPT TABLE 2.1
The Psychoanalytic and Cognitive Theories

Concept	Processes/related ideas	Characteristics/description
Psychoanalytic theories	Freud's theory	Freud said personality is made up of three structures—id, ego, and superego—which conflict with each other. In Freud's view, most of children's thoughts are unconscious, and the id is completely unconscious. The conflicting demands of children's personality structures produce anxiety. Defense mechanisms, especially repression, protect the child's ego and reduce anxiety. Freud was convinced that problems develop because of early childhood experiences. He said individuals go through five psychosexual stages: oral, anal, phallic, latency, and genital. During the phallic stage, the Oedipus complex is a major source of conflict.
	Erikson's theory	Erikson developed a theory that emphasizes eight psychosocial stages of development: trust vs. mistrust, autonomy vs. shame and doubt, initiative vs. guilt, industry vs. inferiority, identity vs. identity confusion, intimacy vs. isolation, generativity vs. stagnation, and integrity vs. despair.
	Evaluating the psychoanalytic theories	Strengths of the theories are an emphasis on the past, the developmental course of personality, mental representation of the environment, focus on the unconscious mind, and emphasis on conflict. Weaknesses are the difficulty in testing main concepts, lack of an empirical data base, overreliance on reports of the past, too much emphasis on sexuality and the unconscious mind, and a negative view of human nature.
Cognitive theories	Piaget's theory	Piaget's theory is responsible for the field of cognitive development. He believed that children are motivated to understand their world and use the processes of organization and adaptation (assimilation, accommodation) to do so. Piaget said children go through four cognitive stages: sensorimotor, preoperational, concrete operational, and formal operational.
	Information-processing theory	This theory is concerned with how individuals process information about their world. It includes how information gets into the child's mind, how it is stored and transformed, and how it is retrieved to allow people to think and solve problems. The development of the computer promoted this approach. The mind as an information-processing system is compared to how a computer processes information. The information-processing approach raises questions about the nature of development, among them the increased speed of processing information as children grow older.
	Evaluating the cognitive theories	Both the Piagetian and information-processing approaches have made important contributions to our understanding of children's development. They have provided a positive, rational portrayal of how children develop, although they may have underestimated the importance of unconscious thought and environmental experiences, especially in the family. The purity of Piaget's stages has been questioned, and the information-processing approach has not yet produced an overall perspective on development.

no more free than pigeons; denying that our behavior is controlled by environmental forces is to ignore science and reality, he argued. In the long run, Skinner said, we would be much happier if we recognized such truths, especially his concept that we could live a prosperous life under the control of positive reinforcement.

Behaviorism *emphasizes the scientific study of observable behavioral responses and their environmental determinants.* In Skinner's behaviorism, the mind, conscious or unconscious, is not needed to explain behavior and development. For him, development is behavior. For example, observations of Sam reveal that his behavior is shy, achievement-oriented, and caring. Why is Sam's behavior this way? For Skinner, rewards and punishments in Sam's environment have shaped him into a shy, achievement-oriented, and caring person. Because of interactions with family members, friends, teachers, and others, Sam has *learned* to behave in this fashion.

B. F. Skinner was a prominent American behaviorist.

Since behaviorists believe that development is learned and often changes according to environmental experiences, it follows that rearranging experiences can change development. For behaviorists, shy behavior can be changed into outgoing behavior; aggressive behavior can be shaped into docile behavior; lethargic, boring behavior can be turned into enthusiastic, interesting behavior.

Skinner described the way in which behavior is controlled in the following way. The individual *operates* on the environment to produce a change that will lead to a reward (Skinner, 1938). Skinner chose the term *operants* to describe the responses that are actively emitted because of the consequences for the individual. The consequences—rewards and punishments—are *contingent,* or dependent, on the behavior. For example, an operant might press a lever on a machine that delivers a candy bar; the delivery of the candy bar is contingent on pressing the lever. In sum, **operant conditioning** *is a form of learning in which the consequences of behavior lead to changes in the probability of that behavior's occurrence.*

More needs to be said about rewards and punishments. **Reinforcement (or reward)** *is a consequence that increases the probability a behavior will occur.* By contrast, **punishment** *is a consequence that decreases the probability a behavior will occur.* For example, consider the situation in which a boy starts talking with a girl and she then smiles. Later, he strikes up a conversation with another girl, who frowns at him. He subsequently approaches the first girl and talks to her again but doesn't approach the second girl. The first girl's smile has reinforced the boy's talking; the second girl's frown has punished it.

■ *Critical Thinking*
Think about your life during the past 24 hours. How did rewards and punishments influence the way you behaved during this time frame?

Social Learning Theory

Some psychologists believe that the behaviorists basically are right when they say development is learned and is influenced strongly by environmental experiences. However, they believe that Skinner went too far in declaring that cognition is unimportant in understanding development. **Social learning theory** *is the view of psychologists who emphasize behavior, environment,* and *cognition as the key factors in development.*

The social learning theorists say we are not like mindless robots, responding mechanically to others in our environment. Neither are we like weathervanes, behaving like a Communist in the presence of a Communist or like a John Bircher in the presence of a John Bircher. Rather, we think, reason, imagine, plan, expect, interpret, believe, value, and compare. When others try to control us, our values and beliefs allow us to resist their control.

Theories of Child Development

(a) Albert Bandura and (b) Walter Mischel crafted social learning theory's contemporary version, which Mischel labeled cognitive social learning theory.

(a)

(b)

American psychologists Albert Bandura (1977, 1986, 1989) and Walter Mischel (1973, 1984) are the main architects of social learning theory's contemporary version, which Mischel (1973) labeled *cognitive* social learning theory. Both Bandura and Mischel believe that cognitive processes are important mediators of environment-behavior connections. Bandura's research program has focused heavily on observational learning, learning that occurs through observing what others do. Observational learning is also referred to as imitation or modeling. What is *cognitive* about observational learning in Bandura's view? Bandura believes that people cognitively represent the behavior of others and then sometimes adopt this behavior themselves. For example, a young boy may observe his father's aggressive outbursts and hostile interchanges with people; when observed with his peers, the young boy's style of interaction is highly aggressive, showing the same characteristics as his father's behavior. A girl may adopt the dominant and sarcastic style of her teacher. When observed interacting with her younger brother, she says, "You are so slow. How can you do this work so slow?" Social learning theorists believe that children acquire a wide range of such behaviors, thoughts, and feelings through observing others' behavior. These observations form an important part of children's development.

Social learning theories also differ from Skinner's behavioral view by emphasizing that children can regulate and control their own behavior. For example, another girl who observes her teacher behaving in a dominant and sarcastic way toward her students finds the behavior distasteful and goes out of her way to be encouraging and supportive toward her younger brother. Someone tries to persuade an adolescent to join a particular club at school. The adolescent thinks about the offer to join the club, considers her own interests and beliefs, and makes the decision not to join. The adolescent's *cognition* (thoughts) led her to control her own behavior and resist environmental influence in this instance.

Like the behavioral approach of Skinner, the social learning approach emphasizes the importance of empirical research in studying children's development. This research focuses on the processes that explain children's development—the social and cognitive factors that influence what children are like.

Evaluating the Behavioral and Social Learning Theories

The behavioral and social learning theories emphasize that environmental experiences determine children's development. These approaches have fostered

The Nature of Child Development

a scientific climate that highlights the observations of children's behavior. Social learning theory emphasizes that both environmental influences and cognitive processes are involved in understanding children's development. This view also suggests that, as children develop, they acquire the ability to control their own behavior and exercise control over their social world.

The criticisms of the behavioral and social learning theories sometimes are directed at the behavioral view alone and, at other times, are directed toward both approaches. The behavioral view has been criticized for ignoring the importance of cognition in children's development and placing too much importance on environmental experiences. Both approaches have been described as being too concerned with change and situational influences on children's development, and as not paying tribute to the enduring qualities of children. Both views are said to ignore the biological determinants of children's development. Both are labeled reductionistic, which means that they look at only one or two components of children's development instead of how all of the pieces fit together. Critics have also charged that the behavioral and social learning theorists are too mechanical. By being overly concerned with several minute pieces of children's development, they miss the most exciting and rich dimensions of development, say the detractors. This criticism—that the creative, spontaneous, human characteristics of children's development are missing from the behavioral and social learning theories—has been made on numerous occasions by adherents of the humanistic approach, which we will consider next.

Phenomenological and Humanistic Theories

Recall the adolescent couple, Tom and Ann, who were described as having warm, friendly personalities. Phenomenological and humanistic psychologists would describe their warm, friendly personalities as reflecting their inner selves. They would emphasize that the key to understanding their attraction is their positive perception of each other. Tom and Ann are not viewed as controlling each other's behavior. Instead, each has determined a course of action, and each has freely chosen to like the other. No recourse to biological instincts or unconscious thoughts as determinants of their attraction occurs in phenomenological and humanistic theories.

Phenomenological theories *stress the importance of children's perceptions of themselves and their environment in understanding personality.* For every child, reality is what is perceived. **Humanistic theories** *are the most widely known phenomenological approaches to personality. Humanistic theories stress children's capacity for personal growth, freedom to choose one's own destiny, and positive qualities.* Humanistic psychologists believe that all children have the ability to cope with stress, to control their lives, and to achieve what they desire. Each child can burst the cocoon and become a butterfly, say the humanists.

You may sense that the phenomenological and humanistic approaches provide stark contrasts to the psychoanalytic approach to development, which is based on conflict and has little faith in children's ability to understand their development, and to the behavioral view, which emphasizes that behavior is determined by rewards and punishments from others. The leading architect of the phenomenological and humanistic approaches in children's development is Carl Rogers (1902–1987).

Carl Rogers is one of the architects of the humanistic approach.

Figure 2.7
Picasso's Portrait Reflecting Rogers' Ideal and Real Selves
Half-clothed, Picasso's 1932 portrayal of a *Girl Before a Mirror* reflects the twin images of Carl Rogers' ideal and real selves.

Oil on canvas, 64 × 51¼ in. Collection, The Museum of Modern Art, New York. Gift of Mrs. Simon Guggenheim.

Rogers' Humanistic Approach

In the knotted, anxious, defensive verbal stream of his clients, Rogers (1961, 1974) examined the conditioned, controlling world that individuals experienced as they were growing up, a world that kept them from having positive self-concepts and reaching their full potential as human beings. In Rogers' view, the child's self develops through experiences with the world. The self is the "I" or "me" of the child's existence. The self is a whole, consisting of self-perceptions (how attractive I am, how well I get along with others, and how good an athlete I am, for example) and the values children attach to these perceptions (good-bad, worthy-unworthy, for example). **Self-concept** *is a central theme in Rogers' and others' humanistic views; self-concept refers to individuals' overall perceptions of their abilities, behavior, and personality.* In Rogers' view, a child who has a positive self-concept is likely to think, feel, and act positively; a child who has a negative self-concept is likely to think, feel, and act negatively.

In discussing self-concept, Rogers distinguished between the real self—that is, the self as it really is as a result of our experiences—and the ideal self, which is the self we would like to be (figure 2.7 shows a portrait that reflects the ideal and real selves). The greater the discrepancy between the real self and the ideal self, the more maladjusted children will be, said Rogers.

How can adults help children develop a more positive self-concept? Rogers stressed three factors: unconditional positive regard, empathy, and genuineness. Rogers said children need to be accepted by others, regardless of what they do or say. **Unconditional positive regard** *is Rogers' concept of accepting, valuing, and being positive toward another person regardless of that person's behavior.* Rogers recognized that, when a child's behavior is below acceptable standards, is inappropriate, or even is obnoxious, the child needs the respect, comfort, and love of others. Rogers strongly believed that unconditional positive regard elevates the child's self-worth; however, Rogers (1974) distinguished between unconditional positive regard directed at the child as a person of worth and dignity and unconditional positive regard directed at the child's behavior. Thus, a Rogerian counselor might say, "I don't like your behavior, but I accept you, value you, and like you as a person."

Rogers also said we can help children develop a more positive self-concept if we are *empathic* and *genuine*. Being empathic means being a sensitive listener and understanding another's feelings. Being genuine means being open with our feelings and dropping our pretenses and facades. For Rogers, unconditional positive regard, empathy, and genuineness are the three key ingredients of human relations. We can use these techniques to help children feel good about themselves, and the techniques can also help us get along better with others.

Evaluating the Phenomenological and Humanistic Theories

Children's perceptions of themselves and their world are key ingredients of their development. The emphasis on consciousness likewise has had a significant impact on how developmentalists view children's perceptions of their world. The humanistic psychologists remind us that we need to consider the whole child and the child's positive nature. The contribution of these approaches has been felt in human relationships. Many people believe that the humanistic approach has helped them understand both themselves and others. The approaches also have facilitated the ability to communicate effectively with others.

The Nature of Child Development

The Behavioral and Social Learning Theories and the Phenomenological and Humanistic Theories

Concept	Processes/related ideas	Characteristics/description
The behavioral and social learning theories	Skinner's behaviorism	Behaviorism emphasizes that cognition is not important in understanding children's behavior. Development is observed behavior, which is determined by rewards and punishments in the environment. Behavior varies according to the situation.
	Social learning theory	The environment is an important determinant of children's behavior, but so are cognitive processes. Children have the ability to control their own behavior through thoughts, beliefs, and values. Bandura's emphasis on observational learning highlights the cognitive aspects of social learning theory.
	Evaluating the behavioral and social learning theories	The strengths of both theories include emphases on environmental determinants and on a scientific climate for investigating children's behavior, as well as on cognitive processes and self-control in social learning theory. The behavioral view has been criticized for taking the person out of development and for ignoring cognition. These approaches have not given adequate attention to enduring individual differences, to biological factors, and to development as a whole.
The phenomenological and humanistic theories	Their nature	Phenomenological theories emphasize children's perceptions of themselves and the world. Reality is what is perceived. Humanistic theories are the most widely known phenomenological theories.
	Rogers' humanistic theory	In Rogers' view, the self is the core of development. Self-concept refers to individuals' overall perceptions of their abilities, behavior, and personality. Rogers distinguishes between the ideal self and real self. Rogers said adults can help children improve their self-concept by giving them unconditional positive regard, by being empathic, and by being genuine.
	Evaluating the phenomenological and humanistic theories	These theories sensitized us to the importance of subjective experience, consciousness, self-conception, the whole person, and children's innate positive nature. Their weaknesses are the absence of an empirical orientation, a tendency to be too optimistic, and an inclination to encourage self-love.

One weakness of these approaches is that they are very hard to test scientifically. Some humanistic psychologists even scorn the scientific approach, preferring clinical interpretation as a data base. Verification of humanistic concepts has come mainly from clinical experiences rather than from controlled scientific efforts. Some critics also believe that these approaches are too optimistic about human nature. They possibly overestimate the freedom and rationality of humans, and some critics say these approaches encourage self-love and narcissism.

We have seen that the behavioral, social learning, phenomenological, and humanistic approaches take different paths to understanding development. A summary of the main ideas in each of these approaches is presented in concept table 2.2.

The tide of evolution carries everything before it, thoughts no less than bodies, and persons no less than nations.

—George Santayana

Ethological Theories

Sensitivity to different kinds of experience varies over the life cycle. The presence or absence of certain experiences at particular times in the life span influences individuals well beyond the time they first occur. Ethologists believe that most psychologists underestimate the importance of these special time frames in early development and the powerful roles that evolution and biological foundations play in development.

Lorenz's Classical Ethological Theory

Ethology emerged as an important view because of the work of European zoologists, especially Konrad Lorenz. **Ethology** *stresses that behavior is strongly influenced by biology, is tied to evolution, and is characterized by critical or sensitive periods.*

Working mostly with graylag geese, Lorenz (1965) studied a behavior pattern that was considered to be programmed within the birds' genes. A newly hatched gosling seemed to be born with the instinct to follow its mother. Observations showed that the gosling was capable of such behavior as soon as it hatched. Lorenz proved that it was incorrect to assume that such behavior was programmed in the animal. In a remarkable set of experiments, Lorenz separated the eggs laid by one goose into two groups. One group he returned to the goose to be hatched by her; the other group was hatched in an incubator. The goslings in the first group performed as predicted; they followed their mother as soon as they hatched. However, those in the second group, which saw Lorenz when they first hatched, followed him everywhere, as though he were their mother. Lorenz marked the goslings and then placed both groups under a box. Mother goose and "mother" Lorenz stood aside as the box was lifted. Each group of goslings went directly to its "mother" (see figure 2.8). Lorenz called this process **imprinting,** *the ethological concept of rapid, innate learning within a limited critical period of time that involves attachment to the first moving object seen.*

The ethological view of Lorenz and the European zoologists forced American developmental psychologists to recognize the importance of the biological basis of behavior. However, the research and theorizing of ethology

Figure 2.8
Lorenz and Imprinted Graylag Geese
Ethologist Konrad Lorenz, a pioneering student of animal behavior, is followed through the water by three imprinted graylag geese.

The Nature of Child Development

still seemed to lack some ingredients that would elevate it to the ranks of the other theories discussed so far in this chapter. In particular, there was little or nothing in the classical ethological view about the nature of social relationships across the human life cycle, something that any major theory of development must explain. Also, its concept of **critical period,** *a fixed time period very early in development during which certain behaviors optimally emerge,* seemed to be overdrawn. Classical ethological theory was weak in stimulating studies with humans. Recent expansion of the ethological view has improved its status as a viable developmental perspective.

Hinde's Neo-Ethological Theory

British ethologist Robert Hinde (1983, 1989b) developed a view that goes beyond classical ethological theory. **Neo-ethological theory** *is Hinde's view that emphasizes sensitive rather than critical periods of development, social development and relationships, and the application of ethological theory to human development.* The following discussion presents Hinde's description of the issues that are important to ethologists.

British ethologist Robert Hinde developed the neo-ethological theory of development.

Like behaviorists, ethologists are careful observers of behavior. Unlike behaviorists, ethologists believe that laboratories are not good settings for observing behavior; rather, they meticulously observe behavior in its natural surroundings, in homes, playgrounds, schools, hospitals, and so on.

Ethologists also point out that children's development is studied by adults, who consider the end point of development to be mature adulthood. However, ethologists believe that an infant's or a child's behavior should not always be considered in terms of its importance for mature adulthood. Rather, a behavior may be only adaptive at an early stage of development. For example, caterpillars are excellent leaf eaters, but they do not pretend to be butterflies. Ethologists believe that the word *development* too often diverts attention away from viewing each stage of development in its own right.

Ethologists emphasize sensitive periods. Hinde distinguishes between critical and sensitive periods. Classical ethologists, such as Lorenz, argued for the importance of critical periods in development. A **sensitive period** *is the ethological concept that describes a more flexible band of time for behavior to emerge than does the concept of a critical period.* Sensitive periods occur on the order of months or years rather than weeks or days. For children, sensitive periods for language, vision, and attachment have been proposed (Bornstein, 1987; Bowlby, 1989).

Ethologists also are becoming interested in social relationships and personality. Hinde argues that certain properties of relationships, such as synchrony and competitiveness, do not describe individuals in isolation. Relationships have properties that emerge from the frequency and patterning of interactions over time. For example, if the mother-infant relationship is studied at one point in development, researchers may not be able to describe it as rejecting, controlling, or permissive, but such categorization may be possible through detailed observations over a period of time.

Evaluating the Ethological Theories

Ethological theories emphasize the biological and evolutionary basis of behavior, giving biology an appropriate, prominent role in development. Ethologists use careful observations in naturalistic surroundings to obtain information about development, and ethologists believe development involves sensitive periods.

However, like other theories we have discussed, ethology has its weaknesses. At times, even its emphasis on sensitive periods seems to be too rigid; the critical period concept is too rigid for human development. The emphasis still slants more toward biological-evolutionary explanations of development rather than a biological-environmental mix. Another criticism of the ethological theories is the virtual absence of attention to cognitive processes and development. The theories have been slow in generating research about human development, and they are better at explaining behavior retrospectively than prospectively. That is, ethology is better at explaining what caused a child's behavior after it has happened than it is at predicting the behavior's occurrence in the future.

Ecological Theory

At approximately the same time Robert Hinde was developing his biology-based neo-ethological theory, Cornell University developmental psychologist Urie Bronfenbrenner (1979, 1986, 1989) was proposing a sociocultural view of development. **Ecological theory** *is Bronfenbrenner's sociocultural view of development, which consists of five environmental systems ranging from the fine-grained inputs of direct interactions with social agents to the broad-based inputs of culture. The five systems in Bronfenbrenner's ecological theory are the microsystem, mesosystem, exosystem, macrosystem, and chronosystem.* Bronfenbrenner's ecological model is shown in figure 2.9.

Environmental Systems

The **microsystem** *in Bronfenbrenner's ecological theory is the setting in which an individual lives. This context includes the person's family, peers, school, and neighborhood.* It is in the microsystem that most of the direct interactions with social agents take place—with parents, peers, and teachers, for example. The individual is not viewed as a passive recipient of experiences in these settings, but as someone who helps construct the settings. Bronfenbrenner points out that most of the research on sociocultural influences has focused on microsystems.

The **mesosystem** *in Bronfenbrenner's ecological theory involves relations between microsystems or connections between contexts.* Examples are the relation of family experiences to school experiences, school experiences to church experiences, and family experiences to peer experiences. For instance, a child whose parents have rejected him may have difficulty developing positive relations with teachers. Developmentalists increasingly believe it is important to observe behavior in multiple settings—such as in family, peer, and school contexts—to obtain a more complete picture of development.

The **exosystem** *in Bronfenbrenner's ecological theory is involved when experiences in a social setting in which an individual does not have an active role influence what that person experiences in an immediate context.* For example, work experiences may affect a woman's relationship with her husband and their adolescent. The woman may receive a promotion that requires more travel, which might increase marital conflict and change patterns of parent-adolescent interaction. Another example of an exosystem is a city government, which is responsible for the quality of parks, recreation centers, and library facilities for children and adolescents.

The **macrosystem** *in Bronfenbrenner's ecological theory involves the culture in which individuals live.* **Culture** *refers to the behavior patterns, beliefs, and all other products of a group of people that are passed on from*

Urie Bronfenbrenner developed an ecological theory, a sociocultural approach that emphasizes five environmental systems.

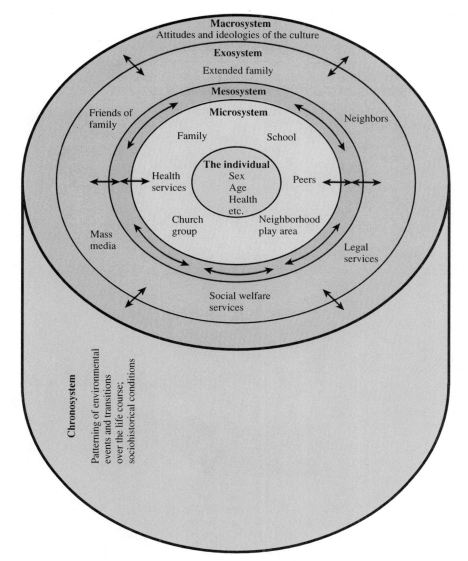

Figure 2.9
Bronfenbrenner's Ecological Theory of Development
Bronfenbrenner's ecological theory consists of five environmental systems: microsystem, mesosystem, exosystem, macrosystem, and chronosystem.

generation to generation. A cultural group can be as large and complex as the United States or it can be as small as an African hunter-gatherer group. Whatever its size, the group's culture influences the identity, learning, and social behavior of its members (Whiting, 1989). For example, the United States is a very achievement-oriented culture with a strong work ethic, but recent comparisons of American and Japanese children have revealed that Japanese children are better at math, they spend more time working on math in school, and they spend much more time doing math homework than American children (Corser, Stevenson, & Lee, 1989). Cross-cultural studies, the comparison of one culture with one or more other cultures, provide information about the generality of development. More information about the role of culture in personality and development is presented in Cultural Worlds of Development 2.1. Another important dimension of culture is **ethnicity** *(the word* ethnic *comes from the Greek word for "nation"), which is based on cultural heritage, nationality characteristics, religion, and language.* Each of you is a member of one or more ethnic groups, and so is every human being. As we discussed in chapter 1, nowhere are sociocultural changes in American life more profound

73

Culture and Personality: Individualistic and Collectivistic Orientations

Because the concept of personality, or self—like other concepts—is socially constructed, it is likely to involve at least some cross-cultural variation (Kagitcibasi & Berry, 1989). Many of the assumptions about personality have been developed in Western cultures, which emphasize the individual, or self. Self-oriented terms dominate thinking about personality in such Western cultures as that of the United States—self-actualization, self-awareness, self-concept, self-efficacy, self-reinforcement, self-criticism, self-serving, selfishness, self-doubt, and so on (Lonner, 1988).

Many non-Western cultures, including Communist countries such as Russia and Eastern countries such as Japan, China, and India, are collectivistic rather than individualistic (Hui & Villareal, 1989; Kagitcibasi, 1988; Triandis, 1985). *Individualistic* describes an individual, or self, orientation that involves separating the self from others. *Collectivistic* refers to a group orientation that involves relating the self to others. In one investigation of 40 nations, an individualistic versus collectivistic orientation was found to be a basic dimension of national culture (Hofstede, 1980).

The individualistic/collectivistic dichotomy has not gone uncriticized. Describing entire nations of children and adults as having a basic personality obscures the extensive diversity and individual variation that characterizes a nation's people. Critics of the individualistic, self orientation of Western personality conceptions point out that human beings have always lived in groups, communities, and societies, mutually needing one another. However, the individualistic orientation of many Western cultures, especially of the United States, may undermine our species' basic need for relatedness (Kagitcibasi, 1988). Some social scientists believe that many of our problems, such as anxiety, depression, and shyness, would not be as intense if the American cultural emphasis on the self and independence were not so strong (Munroe & Munroe, 1975). The pendulum may have swung too far in the individualistic direction in Western cultures. To develop a healthy, optimal personality, all people in all cultures need to develop a positive sense of self *and* a positive connectedness with others.

For American children, the development of autonomy, or independence, is believed to be a prerequisite for an ideal personality. Many American parents train their children to be self-sufficient at an early age. In many non-Western cultures, however, parents and other adults train children to be more other- or group-oriented. These non-Western cultures include Russia, China, Japan, and Israel. In North America, many Mexican parents also train their children to be more group-oriented than do American parents (Holtzmann, 1982). In Russia, from the earliest years in school, adult authorities enlist the help of peer groups to teach and enforce the culture's social values (Bronfenbrenner, 1970). Behavior is pri-

(a)

(b)

(a) These school children are on a holiday in Red Square in Moscow. In the Soviet Union's schools, the group is emphasized, rather than the individual. (b) In Japan, schools emphasize a group orientation and connectedness to others rather than individualism.

marily evaluated in terms of how well it matches the collective's goals and aims. To encourage group identification and pride, interclass and interschool competitions are frequently held. In school, the social unit may be the rows of pupils in a classroom; later it may be a "cell" of the Communist Youth Organization. In Japan, beginning in kindergarten, children wear the same type of uniform, including caps of different colors to indicate the classrooms to which the children belong. The students have identical sets of equipment kept in identical drawers and shelves. This is not intended to turn the Japanese children into robots, as some Americans have observed, but to impress on them that other people just like them have needs and rights that are equally as important as their own (Hendry, 1986). In sum, our American culture needs to emphasize a stronger sense of connectedness in addition to a positive development of self.

than in the rapidly increasing ethnic diversity of its citizens (Miller, 1989). An important goal of this textbook is to provide a wide-ranging portrait of cultural and ethnic diversity in children's development.

The **chronosystem** *in Bronfenbrenner's ecological theory involves the patterning of environmental events and transitions over the life course.* For example, in one research investigation, Mavis Hetherington and her colleagues (Hetherington, 1989; Hetherington, Cox, & Cox, 1982) found that the disruptive effects of divorce peak 1 year after the divorce, with the effects being more negative for sons than for daughters. By 2 years after the divorce, family interaction has become less chaotic and more stable. In another example of the chronosystem, Glenn Elder and his colleagues (Elder & Caspi, in press; Elder, Caspi, & Downey, 1986) have found that the presence of an irritable father or an irritable child increases the probability that unemployment will have long-range negative consequences for development. Also critical is the presence of marital conflict, which often arises, or becomes exacerbated, following the father's loss of a job.

Evaluating Ecological Theory

Bronfenbrenner's ecological model is one of the few comprehensive frameworks for understanding the environment's role in development. The model includes both micro (molecular) and macro (molar) aspects of environmental, sociocultural influences on development. Bronfenbrenner's most recent addition to the model—the chronosystem—takes into account development over time and sociohistorical influences on development. The main weaknesses of the ecological model are its failure to adequately account for the influence of both biological and cognitive processes.

An Eclectic Theoretical Orientation

No single indomitable theory is capable of explaining the rich complexity of child development. Each of the theories described in this chapter has made important contributions to our understanding of children's development, but none provides a complete description and explanation. Psychoanalytic theory best explains the unconscious mind. Erikson's theory best describes the changes that occur in adult development. Piaget's theory is the most complete description of children's cognitive development. The behavioral and social learning and ecological theories have been the most adept at examining the environmental determinants of development. The phenomenological and humanistic theories have given us the most insight about self-conception, and the ethological theories have made us aware of biology's role and the importance of sensitive periods in development. It is important to recognize that, although theories are helpful guides, relying on a single theory to explain child development probably is a mistake.

An attempt was made in this chapter to present six theoretical perspectives objectively. The same eclectic orientation will be maintained throughout the book. In this way, you can view the study of children's development as it actually exists—with different theorists making different assumptions, stressing different empirical problems, and using different strategies to discover information.

These theoretical perspectives, along with the research issues and methods described in chapter 1, provide a sense of development's scientific nature. Table 2.2 compares the main theoretical perspectives in terms of how they view some

A Comparison of Theories and the Issues and Methods in Child Development

Theory	Issues and Methods			
	Continuity/discontinuity, stability/change	*Biological and environmental factors*	*Importance of cognition*	*Research methods*
Psychoanalytic	Discontinuity between stages—continuity between early experiences and later development; later changes in development emphasized in Erikson's theory	Freud's biological determination interacting with early family experiences; Erikson's more balanced biological-cultural interaction perspective	Emphasized, but in the form of uncon-scious thought	Clinical interviews, unstructured personality tests, psychohistorical analyses of lives
Cognitive	Discontinuity between stages—continuity between early experiences and later development in Piaget's theory; has not been important to information-processing psychologists	Piaget's emphasis on interaction and adaptation; environment provides the setting for cognitive structures to develop; information-processing view has not addressed this issue extensively, but hardware-software metaphor emphasizes biological-environmental interaction	The primary determinant of behavior	Interviews and observations
Behavioral and social learning	Continuity (no stages); experience at all points of development important	Environment viewed as the cause of behavior in both views	Strongly deempha-sized in the behavioral approach but an im-portant mediator in social learning	Observation, especially laboratory observation
Phenomenological and humanistic	Continuity (no stages); experience at all points in development important, especially immediate experience	Environmental influences empha-sized, especially warmth and nurturance	Important, especially in the form of self-perception	Scientific approach deemphasized; self-report measures and interviews
Ethological	Discontinuity but no stages; critical or sensitive periods emphasized	Strong biological view	Not emphasized	Observation in natural settings
Ecological	Little attention to continuity/discontinuity; change emphasized more than stability	Strong environmental view	Not emphasized	Varied methods; especially stresses importance of collecting data in different social contexts

The Ethological Theories, Ecological Theory, and an Eclectic Theoretical Orientation

Concept	Processes/related ideas	Characteristics/description
Ethological theories	Lorenz's classical ethological theory	The biological and evolutionary basis of development needs to be emphasized. Critical periods, at which time a characteristic has an optimal time of emergence, occur in development.
	Hinde's neo-ethological theory	Hinde's theory emphasizes sensitive rather than critical periods. It places a premium on naturalistic observation and biological/evolutionary ties but also focuses on social relationships and personality.
	Evaluating the ethological theories	Their strengths include an emphasis on the biological and evolutionary basis of behavior, naturalistic observation, and sensitive periods. Their weaknesses include the rigidity of the critical period concept, an overemphasis on biology and evolution, a failure to generate studies of human development, and an inability to predict behavior prospectively.
Ecological theory	Bronfenbrenner's model	In Bronfenbrenner's ecological theory, five environmental systems are described: the microsystem, mesosystem, exosystem, macrosystem, and chronosystem.
	Evaluation	Bronfenbrenner's theory provides one of the few comprehensive models of environmental influences on development. Both macro and micro aspects of environmental influence are included. Criticisms focus on the lack of emphasis on biological and cognitive processes.
Eclectic theoretical orientation	Its nature	No single theory can explain the rich, awesome complexity of children's development. Each of the theories has made a different contribution, and it probably is a wise strategy to adopt an eclectic theoretical perspective as we attempt to understand children's development.

of the issues we have discussed thus far. By studying table 2.2, you should be able to integrate some of the most important ideas about issues and methods described in chapter 1 with the main theories described in chapter 2.

At this point, we have discussed a number of ideas about ethological theories, Bronfenbrenner's ecological theory, and an eclectic theoretical orientation. A summary of these ideas is presented in concept table 2.3. In the next section of the book, Biological Processes, Physical Development, and Perceptual Development, we will begin the child's odyssey of development by studying biological beginnings.

Summary

I. Freud's Theory

Freud said that personality has three structures—id, ego, and superego—which conflict with each other. In Freud's view, most thoughts are unconscious, and the id is completely unconscious. The conflicting demands of personality structures produce anxiety; defense mechanisms (especially repression) protect the ego and reduce anxiety. Freud was convinced that problems develop because of childhood experiences. He said we go through five psychosexual stages: oral, anal, phallic, latency, and genital. During the phallic stage, the Oedipus complex is a main source of conflict.

II. Erikson's Theory and Evaluation of the Psychoanalytic Theories

Erikson developed a theory that emphasizes eight psychosocial stages of development: trust versus mistrust, autonomy versus shame and doubt, initiative versus guilt, industry versus inferiority, identity versus identity confusion, intimacy versus isolation, generativity versus stagnation, and integrity versus despair. Strengths of the psychoanalytic theories are an emphasis on the past, the developmental course of personality, a mental representation of the environment, a focus on the unconscious mind, and an emphasis on conflict. Weaknesses are the difficulty in testing main concepts, a lack of an empirical data base and an overreliance on past reports, too much emphasis on sexuality and the unconscious mind, and a negative view of human nature.

III. Piaget's Theory

Piaget's theory is responsible for the field of cognitive development. He believed that children are motivated to understand their world and use the processes of organization and adaptation (assimilation and accommodation) to do so. Piaget said that children go through four cognitive stages: sensorimotor, preoperational, concrete operational, and formal operational.

IV. Information-Processing Theory and Evaluation of the Cognitive Theories

The information-processing approach is concerned with how people process information about the world. It includes how information gets into the mind, how it is stored and transformed, and how it is retrieved for thinking and solving problems. The development of the computer promoted this approach; the mind as an information-processing system has been compared to the way a computer processes information. The information-processing approach raises questions about children's development, among them developmental changes in the speed of processing information. Both the Piagetian and information-processing approaches have made important contributions to children's development. They have provided a positive, rational portrayal of children as they develop, although they may have underestimated the importance of unconscious thought and environmental experiences, especially family processes. The purity of Piaget's stages has been questioned, and the information-processing approach has not yet produced an overall perspective on development.

V. The Behavioral and Social Learning Theories

Skinner's behaviorism emphasizes that cognition is unimportant in development; development is observed behavior, which is influenced by the rewards and punishments in the environment. In social learning theory, the environment is an important determinant of development, but so are cognitive processes. Children develop the ability to control their own behavior through thoughts, beliefs, values, and social skills. Bandura's emphasis on observational learning and his model of the reciprocal influences of behavior, person (cognition), and environment exemplify social learning theory. The contemporary version of social learning theory is called cognitive social learning theory.

VI. Evaluating the Behavioral and Social Learning Theories

The strengths of both theories include emphases on environmental determinants and on a scientific climate for investigating development, as well as a focus on cognitive processes and self-control in social learning theory. The behavioral view has been criticized for taking the person out of development and for ignoring cognition. These approaches have not adequately considered biological factors and development as a whole.

VII. The Phenomenological and Humanistic Theories

Phenomenological theories emphasize children's perceptions of themselves and their world. Reality is what is perceived. Humanistic theories are the most widely known phenomenological theories. In Rogers' view, the self is the core of development. Self-concept refers to individuals' overall perceptions of their abilities, behavior, and personality. Rogers distinguishes between the ideal self and the real self. Rogers said adults can help children improve their self-concept by giving them unconditional positive regard, by being empathic, and by being genuine. The phenomenological and humanistic theories sensitized us to the importance of subjective experience, consciousness, self-conception, the whole person, and the child's innate positive nature. Weaknesses focus on the absence of an empirical orientation, a tendency to be too optimistic, and an inclination to encourage self-love.

VIII. The Ethological Theories

Ethological theories emphasize the biological and evolutionary basis of development. In Lorenz's classical ethological theory, critical periods—at which time a characteristic has an optimal time of emergence—are emphasized. In Hinde's neo-ethological theory, sensitive periods rather than critical periods are stressed, along with naturalistic observation, and social relationships and personality. Strengths include an emphasis on biological and evolutionary bases of behavior, naturalistic observation, and sensitive periods. Weaknesses include the rigidity of critical periods, an overemphasis on biology and evolution, a failure to generate studies of human development, and the inability to predict behavior prospectively.

IX. Ecological Theory

In Bronfenbrenner's ecological theory, five environmental systems are described: the microsystem, mesosystem, exosystem, macrosystem, and chronosystem. Bronfenbrenner's theory provides one of the few comprehensive models of environmental influences on development. Both macro and micro aspects of environmental influence are included. Criticisms focus on the lack of attention to biological and cognitive processes.

X. An Eclectic Theoretical Orientation

No single theory can explain the rich, awesome complexity of children's development. Each of the theories has made a different contribution, and it is probably a wise strategy to adopt an eclectic theoretical orientation as we attempt to understand children's development. The different theoretical perspectives often take different stands on the main issues in children's development.

Key Terms

id 48
pleasure principle 48
ego 48
reality principle 48
superego 48
defense mechanisms 48
repression 49
displacement 49
projection 49
sublimation 49
reaction formation 49
regression 49
erogenous zones 50
fixation 50
oral stage 50
anal stage 50
phallic stage 50
Oedipus complex 50
latency stage 51
genital stage 51
epigenetic principle 52
trust versus mistrust 52
autonomy versus shame and doubt 53
initiative versus guilt 53
industry versus inferiority 54
identity versus identity confusion 54
intimacy versus isolation 54
generativity versus stagnation 54
integrity versus despair 54
assimilation 58
accommodation 58
sensorimotor stage 59
preoperational stage 59
concrete operational stage 59
formal operational stage 59
information processing 59
behaviorism 65
operant conditioning 65
reinforcement 65
punishment 65
social learning theory 65
phenomenological theories 67
humanistic theories 67
self-concept 68
unconditional positive regard 68
ethology 70
imprinting 70
critical period 71
neo-ethological theory 71
sensitive period 71
ecological theory 72
microsystem 72
mesosystem 72
exosystem 72
macrosystem 72
culture 72
ethnicity 73
chronosystem 75

Suggested Readings

Bandura, A. (1986). *Social foundations of thought and action.* Englewood Cliffs, NJ: Prentice-Hall. This book presents Bandura's cognitive social learning view of development, including an emphasis on reciprocal connections between behavior, the environment, and people.

Bronfenbrenner, U. (1986). Ecology of the family as a context for human development: Research perspectives. *Developmental Psychology, 22,* 723–742. In this article, Bronfenbrenner adds the chronosystem to his other four environmental systems. It includes a discussion of a number of research studies involving various environmental systems.

Cowan, P. (1978). *Piaget with feeling.* New York: Holt, Rinehart & Winston. This text provides a well-written overview of Piaget's theory and draws implications for understanding children's emotional development.

Erikson, E. H. (1968). *Identity: Youth and crisis.* New York: W. W. Norton. Erikson's book is must reading for anyone interested in developmental psychology. Erikson outlines his eight stages of the life cycle and talks extensively about identity.

Hinde, R. (1983). Ethology and child development. In P. H. Mussen (Ed.), *Handbook of child psychology* (4th ed., Vol. 2). New York: Wiley. Hinde's views are strongly influencing thinking about child development. Here he outlines the questions ethologists ask and the issues they research.

Miller, P. H. (1989). *Theories of developmental psychology* (2nd ed.). New York: W. H. Freeman. An excellent presentation and evaluation of a number of the developmental theories discussed in this chapter are presented in this book.

Shostrum, E. (1967). *Man, the manipulator.* New York: Bantam. Shostrum presents an intriguing humanistic perspective on development, including many helpful ideas about adjustment and self-evaluation.

SECTION
2

BIOLOGICAL PROCESSES, PHYSICAL DEVELOPMENT, AND PERCEPTUAL DEVELOPMENT

WHAT ENDLESS QUESTIONS

VEX THE THOUGHT, OF

WHENCE AND WHITHER,

WHEN AND HOW.

—Sir Richard Burton

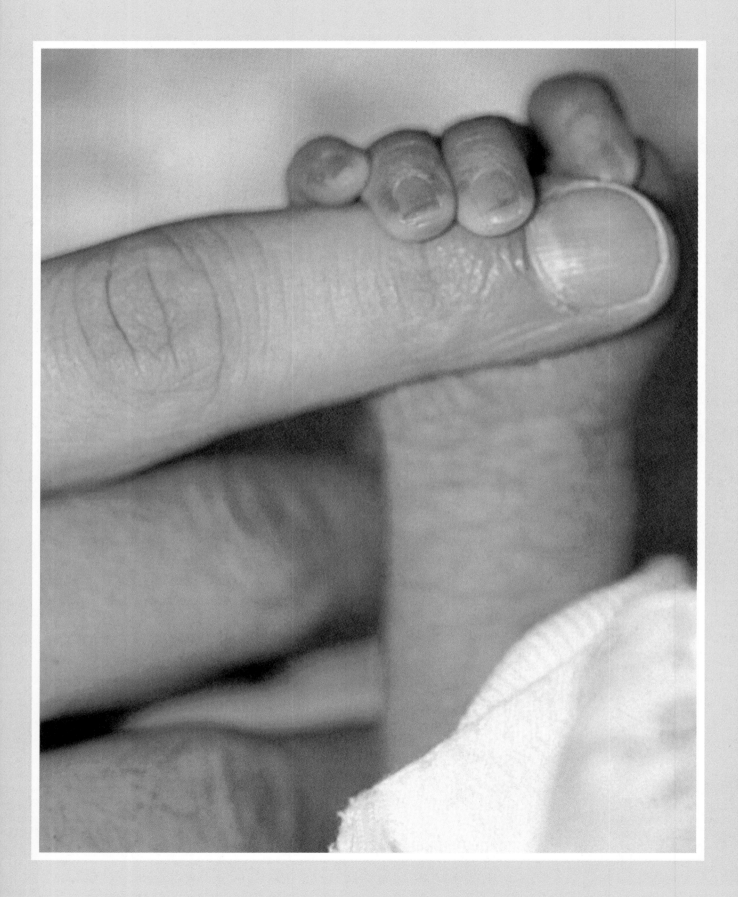

BIOLOGICAL
BEGINNINGS

The Evolutionary Perspective
Genetics
    What Are Genes?
    Reproduction
    Abnormalities in Genes and Chromosomes
    Some Genetic Principles
    Perspective on Child Development 3.1:
        Genetic Counseling
    Methods Used by Behavior Geneticists
Heredity's Influence on Development
    Intelligence
    Temperament
    Perspective on Child Development 3.2: Doran,
        Dr. Graham, and the Repository for
        Germinal Choice
    Perspective on Child Development 3.3: Born to
        Be Shy?
    Cultural Worlds of Development 3.1:
        Imperturbability in European American,
        Chinese American, and Navaho Indian
        Newborns
Heredity-Environment Interaction and Development
Summary
Key Terms
Suggested Readings

Jim Springer and Jim Lewis are identical twins. They were separated at the age of 4 weeks and did not see each other again until they were 39 years old. Both worked as part-time deputy sheriffs, both vacationed in Florida, both drove Chevrolets, both had dogs named Toy, and both married and divorced women named Betty. One twin named his son James Allan, and the other named his son James Alan. Both liked math but not spelling, enjoyed carpentry and mechanical drawing, chewed their fingernails down to the nubs, had almost identical drinking and smoking habits, had hemorrhoids, put on 10 pounds at about the same point in development, first suffered headaches at the age of 18, and had similar sleep patterns. However, Jim and Jim had some differences. One wore his hair over his forehead; the other, slicked back with sideburns. One expressed himself best orally; the other was more proficient in writing. For the most part, however, their profiles were remarkably similar.

Another pair, Daphne and Barbara, were called the "giggle sisters" because they were always making each other laugh. A thorough search of their adoptive families' histories revealed no gigglers. The identical sisters handled stress by ignoring it, avoided conflict and controversy whenever possible, and showed no interest in politics.

Two other identical twin sisters were separated at 6 weeks and reunited in their fifties. Both had nightmares, which they described in hauntingly similar ways: Both dreamed of doorknobs and fishhooks in their mouths as they

The Jim and Jim twins, (a) Springer and (b) Lewis, are identical twins who were separated at the age of 4 weeks and didn't see each other again until they were 39 years old. As adults, they show remarkably similar behavior patterns.

(a)   (b)

smothered to death. The nightmares began during early adolescence and had stopped in the past 10 to 12 years. Both women were bed wetters until about 12 or 13 years of age, and they reported remarkably similar educational and marital histories.

These sets of twins were part of the Minnesota Study of Twins Reared Apart, directed by Thomas Bouchard and his colleagues. They bring identical twins (identical genetically because they come from the same egg) and fraternal twins (dissimilar genetically because they come from two eggs) from all over the world to Minneapolis to investigate their lives. The twins are given a number of personality tests; detailed medical histories are obtained, including information about diet, smoking, and exercise habits; and chest X rays are taken; and heart stress tests and EEGs (brain-wave tests) are given. The twins are interviewed and asked more than 15,000 questions about their family and childhood environment, personal interests, vocational orientation, values, and aesthetic judgments. They also are given ability and intelligence tests (Bouchard & others, 1981; McGue & Bouchard, 1989).

Critics of the Minnesota identical twins study point out that some of the separated twins were together several months prior to their adoption, that some of the twins had been reunited prior to their testing (in some cases, a number of years earlier), that adoption agencies often place twins in similar homes, and that even strangers who spend several hours together and start comparing their lives are likely to come up with some coincidental similarities (Adler, 1991). Still, even in the face of such criticism, the Minnesota study of identical twins indicates how scientists have recently shown an increased interest in the genetic basis of human development and that we need further research on genetic and environmental factors.

The examples of Jim and Jim, the giggle sisters, and the identical twins who had the same nightmares stimulate us to think about our genetic heritage and the biological foundations of our existence. Organisms are not like billiard balls, moved by simple, external forces to predictable positions on life's pool table. Environmental experiences *and* biological foundations work together to make us who we are. Our coverage of life's biological beginnings focuses on evolution, genetics, heredity's influence on development, and the nature of heredity-environment interaction.

The Evolutionary Perspective

In evolutionary time, humans are relative newcomers to Earth, yet we have established ourselves as the most successful and dominant species. If we consider evolutionary time in terms of a calendar year, humans appeared on the planet late in December (Sagan, 1980). As our earliest ancestors left the forest to feed on the savannahs, and finally to form hunting societies on the open plains, their minds and behaviors changed. How did this evolution come about?

Natural selection *is the evolutionary process that favors individuals within a species that are best adapted to survive and reproduce.* To understand natural selection, let's go back in time to the middle of the nineteenth century. Charles Darwin traveled around the world to observe many different species of animals in their natural surroundings. Darwin (1859) published his observations and thoughts in *On the Origin of Species*. He observed that most

What seest thou else
in the dark backward and abysm of time.
—William Shakespeare

(a) (b) (c)

Figure 3.1

Adaptation

The better an animal adapts, the more successful it becomes. Humans, more than any other mammal, adapt to and control most types of environments. (a) Technological advances give greater freedom of movement and independence; (b) greater intelligence is tied to the use of complex objects that enhance life; and (c) because of longer parental care, humans learn more complex behavior patterns, which contribute to adaptation.

I am a brother to dragons,
and a companion to owls.

—Job 30:29

There are one hundred and ninety-three
living species of monkeys and apes. One
hundred and ninety-two of them are
covered with hair. The exception is the
naked ape self-named, homo-sapiens.

—Desmond Morris

organisms reproduce at rates that would cause enormous increases in the population of most species, yet populations remain nearly constant. Darwin reasoned that a constant, intense struggle for food, water, and resources must occur among the many young born each generation. Because of this struggle, many young do not survive. Those that do survive pass on their genes to the next generation, and, as Darwin believed, those that survive to reproduce probably are superior in a number of ways to those that do not. In other words, the survivors are better adapted to their world than are the nonsurvivors. Over the course of many generations, organisms with the characteristics needed for survival constitute a larger percentage of the population. Over many, many generations, this could produce a gradual modification of the whole population. If environmental conditions change, however, other characteristics might develop and this process could move in a different direction.

Over a million species have been classified, from bacteria to blue whales with many varieties of beetles in between. The work of natural selection produced the disappearing acts of moths and the quills of porcupines, and the effects of evolution produced the technological advances, intelligence, and longer parental care of human beings (see figure 3.1).

Generally, evolution proceeds at a very slow pace. The lines that led to the emergence of human beings and the great apes diverged about 14 million years ago. Modern humans, *Homo sapiens,* came into existence only about 50,000 years ago, and the beginning of civilization as we know it began about 10,000 years ago. No sweeping evolutionary changes in humans have occurred since then—for example, our brains have not grown 10 times bigger, we have not developed a third eye in the back of our heads, and we haven't learned to fly. Although there have been no dramatic evolutionary changes in the 50,000 years since *Homo sapiens* appeared on the fossil record, there have been sweeping cultural changes. Biological evolution has shaped human beings into a culture-making species.

Genetics

Every species must have a mechanism for transmitting characteristics from one generation to the next. This mechanism is explained by the principle of genetics. Each of us carries a genetic code that we inherited from our parents. This code is located within every cell in our bodies. Our genetic codes are alike in one important way—they all contain the *human* genetic code. Because of the human genetic code, a fertilized human egg cannot grow into an egret, eagle, or elephant.

Biological Processes, Physical Development, and Perceptual Development

What Are Genes?

Each of us began life as a single cell weighing about one twenty millionth of an ounce. This tiny piece of matter housed our entire genetic code—the information about who we would become. These instructions orchestrated growth from that single cell to a person made of trillions of cells, each containing a perfect replica of the original genetic code.

The nucleus of each human cell contains 46 **chromosomes,** *which are threadlike structures arranged in 23 pairs, one member of each pair coming from each parent.* Chromosomes contain the remarkable genetic substance deoxyribonucleic acid, or DNA. **DNA** *is a complex molecule that contains genetic information;* DNA's "double helix" shape looks like a circular staircase (see figure 3.2). **Genes,** *the units of hereditary information, are short segments of the DNA "staircase."* Genes act as a blueprint for cells to reproduce themselves and manufacture the proteins that maintain life. Chromosomes, DNA, and genes can be mysterious. To turn mystery into understanding, take a look at figure 3.3.

Gametes *are human reproduction cells, which are created in the testes of males and the ovaries of females.* **Meiosis** *is the process of cell division, in which each pair of chromosomes in a cell separates, with one member of each pair going into each gamete, or daughter cell.* Thus, each human gamete

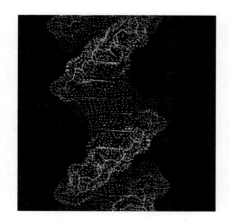

Figure 3.2
The Remarkable Substance DNA
Notice that the DNA molecule is shaped like a spiral staircase. Genes are short segments of the DNA molecule. The horizontal bars that look like the rungs of a ladder play a key role in locating the identity of a gene.

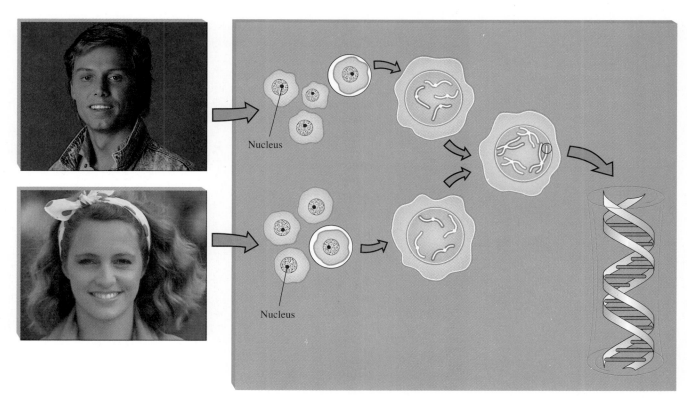

Figure 3.3
Facts About Chromosomes, DNA, and Genes
The body contains billions of cells that are organized into tissue and organs. Each cell contains a central structure, the nucleus, which controls reproduction. Chromosomes reside in the nucleus of each cell. The male's sperm and the female's egg are specialized reproductive cells that contain chromosomes. At conception, the offspring receives matching chromosomes from the mother's egg and the father's sperm. The chromosomes contain DNA, a chemical substance. Genes are short segments of the DNA molecule; they are the units of hereditary information that act as a blueprint for cells to reproduce themselves and manufacture the proteins that sustain life. The rungs in the DNA ladder are an important location of genes.

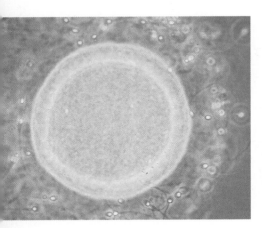

Figure 3.4
Ovum and Sperm
An ovum ready for release has been extracted and put into a nutritive solution with a drop of specially treated seminal fluid. The sperm are eagerly striving toward the ovum. Notice the difference in size between the ovum and the sperm.

The turtle lives twixt plated decks
Which practically conceal its sex.
I think it clever of the turtle
In such a fix to be so fertile.

—Ogden Nash

has 23 unpaired chromosomes. **Reproduction** *takes place when a female gamete (ovum) is fertilized by a male gamete (sperm)* (see figure 3.4). A **zygote** *is a single cell formed through fertilization.* In a zygote, two sets of unpaired chromosomes combine to form one set of paired chromosomes—one member of each pair from the mother and the other member from the father. In this manner, each parent contributes 50 percent of the offspring's heredity.

Reproduction

An ovum is about 90,000 times as large as a sperm. Thousands of sperm must combine to break down the ovum's membrane barrier to allow even a single sperm to penetrate it. Ordinarily, females have two X chromosomes and males have one X and one Y chromosome. Because the Y chromosome is smaller and lighter than the X chromosome, Y-bearing sperm can be separated from X-bearing sperm in a centrifuge. This raises the possibility that the offspring's sex can be controlled. Not only are the Y-bearing sperm lighter, but they are more likely to coat the ovum than are the X-bearing sperm. This results in 120 to 150 males being conceived for every 100 females. However, males are more likely to die (spontaneously abort) at every stage in prenatal development, so only about 106 are born for every 100 females.

Reproduction's fascinating moments have been made even more intriguing in recent years. **In vitro fertilization** *is conception outside of the body.* Consider the following situation. The year is 1978. One of the most dazzling occurrences of the 1970s is about to unfold. Mrs. Brown is infertile, but her physician informs her of a new procedure that could enable her to have a baby. The procedure involves surgically removing the mother's ovum, fertilizing it in a laboratory medium with live sperm cells obtained from the father or another male donor (figure 3.5), storing the fertilized egg in a laboratory solution that substitutes for the uterine environment, and implanting the egg in the mother's uterus. For Mrs. Brown, the procedure is successful, and 9 months later her daughter Louise is born.

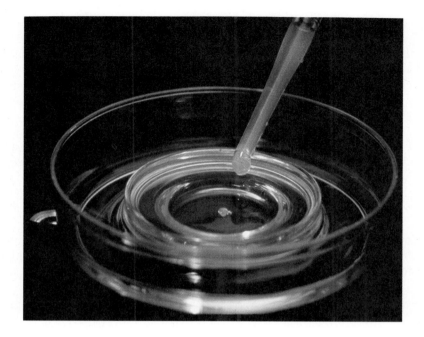

Figure 3.5
In Vitro Fertilization
In vitro fertilization is conception outside of
the womb. Here sperm meet egg in a
laboratory dish.

Since the first in vitro fertilization in the 1970s, variations of the procedure have brought hope to childless couples. A woman's egg can be fertilized with the husband's sperm, or the husband and wife may contribute their sperm and egg with the resulting embryo carried by a third party, who essentially is donating the use of her womb. Researchers have not found any developmental deficiencies in children conceived through in vitro fertilization.

Approximately 10 to 15 percent of all couples in the United States experience **infertility,** *the inability to conceive a child after 12 months of regular intercourse without contraception.* The cause of infertility may rest with the woman or the man. The woman may not be ovulating, she may be producing abnormal ova, her fallopian tubes may be blocked, or she may have a disease that prevents implantation of the ova. The man may produce too few sperm, the sperm may lack motility (the ability to move adequately), or he may have a blocked passageway. In one recent investigation, the long-term use of cocaine by men was related to low sperm count, low motility, and a high number of abnormally formed sperm (Bracken & others, 1990). Cocaine-related infertility appears to be reversible if users stop taking the drug for at least 1 year. In some cases of infertility, surgery may correct the problem; in others, hormonal-based drugs may improve the probability of having a child. However, in some instances, fertility drugs have caused superovulation, producing as many as three or more babies at a time.

Although surgery and fertility drugs can solve the infertility problem in some cases, another choice is to adopt a child. At the time of the adoption, most adoptive parents receive little information about the child's family history, and, in turn, the child's biological parents are given little information about the adoptive parents. Although most adoption agencies have followed this policy as being in the child's best interests, it is currently being challenged by a number of activist groups, who argue that the sealing of records at the time of adoption violates individuals' basic rights to know about themselves.

Researchers have found that adopted children are often more at risk for psychological and school-related problems than are nonadopted children (Brodzinsky & others, 1984), although some adopted children adapt well to their circumstances (Marquis & Detweiler, 1985). In adolescence, some adopted children show difficulties, when, as part of their search for identity, they feel a void and incompleteness because they do not know their biological family's history.

A question that virtually every adoptive parent wants answered is "Should I tell my adopted child that he or she is adopted? If so, when?" Most psychologists believe that adopted children should be told that they are adopted, because they will eventually find out anyway. Many children begin to ask where they came from when they are 4 to 6 years old. This is a natural time to begin to respond in simple ways to children about their adopted status. Clinical psychologists report that one problem that sometimes surfaces is the adoptive parents' desire to make life perfect for the adoptive child and to present perfect images of themselves to the child. The result often is that adopted children feel they cannot release angry feelings and openly discuss problems in such a climate of perfection (Warshak, 1991).

Abnormalities in Genes and Chromosomes

Geneticists and psychologists have identified a range of problems caused by major gene or chromosome defects. **Phenylketonuria (PKU)** *is a genetic disorder in which an individual cannot properly metabolize protein.* Phenylketonuria is now easily detected but, if left untreated, mental retardation and hyperactivity result. The disorder is treated by diet to keep poisonous substances from entering the nervous system. Phenylketonuria involves a recessive gene and occurs about once in every 10,000 to 20,000 live births. Phenylketonuria accounts for about 1 percent of institutionalized mentally retarded people and it occurs primarily in White individuals.

Down syndrome, *the most common genetically transmitted form of mental retardation, is caused by the presence of an extra (47th) chromosome.* An individual with Down syndrome has a round face, a flattened skull, an extra fold of skin over the eyelids, a protruding tongue, short limbs, and a retardation of both motor and mental abilities. It is not known why the extra chromosome is present, but the health of the male sperm or female ovum may be involved. Women in the age range of 18 to 38 are less likely to give birth to a Down syndrome child than are younger or older women. Down syndrome appears approximately once in every 700 live births. Black children are rarely born with Down syndrome.

Sickle-cell anemia, *which occurs most often in Black individuals, is a genetic disorder that affects the red blood cells.* A red blood cell is usually shaped like a disk but, in sickle-cell anemia, a change in a recessive gene modifies the cell's shape to a hook-shaped "sickle." These cells fail to carry oxygen to the body's cells and they die quickly, causing anemia in the afflicted person and early death. About 1 in 400 Black babies is affected. One in 10 Black Americans is a carrier, as is 1 in 20 Latin Americans (Whaley & Wong, 1989).

Other disorders are associated with sex-chromosome abnormalities. Remember that normal males have an X chromosome and a Y chromosome, and normal females have two X chromosomes. **Klinefelter syndrome** *is a genetic disorder in which males have an extra X chromosome, making them XXY* *instead of just XY.* Males with this disorder have undeveloped testes, and they usually have enlarged breasts and become tall. Klinefelter syndrome occurs in approximately 1 in every 3,000 live male births.

Turner syndrome *is a genetic disorder in which females are missing an X chromosome, making them XO instead of XX.* These females are short in stature and have a webbed neck. They may be mentally retarded and sexually underdeveloped. Turner syndrome occurs in approximately 1 in every 3,000 live female births.

The **XYY syndrome** *is a genetic disorder in which males have an extra Y chromosome.* Early interest in this syndrome involved the belief that the Y chromosome found in males contributed to male aggression and violence; thus, it was reasoned that, if a male had an extra Y chromosome, he likely would be extremely aggressive and possibly develop a violent personality. However, researchers subsequently found that XYY males are no more likely to commit crimes than are XY males (Witkin & others, 1976).

Each year in the United States, approximately 100,000 to 150,000 infants with a genetic disorder or malformation are born. These infants make up about 3 to 5 percent of a total of 3 million births and account for at least 20 percent of infant deaths. Prospective parents increasingly are turning to genetic counseling for assistance, wanting to know their risk of having a child born with a genetic defect or malformation. To learn more about genetic counseling, turn to Perspective on Child Development 3.1.

Some Genetic Principles

Genetic determination is a complex affair, and much is unknown about the way genes work. However, a number of genetic principles have been discovered, among them dominant-recessive genes, sex-linked genes, polygenically inherited characteristics, genotype-phenotype distinction, reaction range, and canalization.

According to the **dominant-recessive genes principle,** *if one gene of the pair is dominant and one is recessive (goes back or recedes), the dominant gene exerts its effect, overriding the potential influence of the other, recessive gene. A recessive gene exerts its influence only if the two genes of a pair are both recessive.* If you inherit a recessive gene for a trait from both of your parents, you will show the trait. If you inherit a recessive gene from only one parent, you may never know you carry the gene. Brown eyes, far-sightedness, and dimples rule over blue eyes, near-sightedness, and freckles in the world of dominant-recessive genes. Can two brown-eyed parents have a blue-eyed child? Yes, they can. In each parent, the gene pair that governs eye color includes a dominant gene for brown eyes and a recessive gene for blue eyes. Because dominant genes override recessive genes, the parents have brown eyes; however, both may be carriers of blueness and pass on their recessive genes for blue eyes. With no dominant gene to override them, the recessive genes can make the child's eyes blue.

For thousands of years, people wondered what determined whether we become male or female. Aristotle believed that the father's arousal during intercourse determined the offspring's sex. The more excited the father was, the more likely it would be a son, he reasoned. Of course, he was wrong, but it was not until the 1920s that researchers confirmed the existence of human

When prospective parents visit a genetics counselor, they are asked about the incidence of genetic disorders in their family history. In this situation, the genetics counselor has drawn a chart to display how close in genetic relatedness a disorder has appeared.

■ *Critical Thinking*
Imagine that you want to start a family. Probe your family background. What questions would you want to ask a genetic counselor?

Genetic Counseling

Bob and Mary Sims have been married for several years. They would like to start a family, but they are frightened. The newspapers and popular magazines are full of stories about infants born prematurely who don't survive, infants with debilitating physical defects, and babies found to have congenital mental retardation. The Simses feel that to have such a child would put a social, economic, and psychological strain on them and on society.

Accordingly, the Simses turn to a genetic counselor for help. Genetic counselors are usually physicians or biologists who are well versed in the field of medical genetics. They are familiar with the kinds of problems that can be inherited, the odds of encountering them, and the helpful measures for offsetting some of their effects. The Simses tell their counselor that there has been a history of mental retardation in Bob's family. Bob's younger sister was born with Down's syndrome, a form of mental retardation. Mary's older brother has hemophilia, a condition in which bleeding is difficult to stop. They wonder what the chances are that a child of theirs might also be retarded or have hemophilia and what measures they can take to reduce their chances of having a mentally or physically defective child.

The counselor probes more deeply, because these facts in isolation do not give her a complete picture of the possibilities. She learns that no other relatives in Bob's family are retarded and that Bob's mother was in her late forties when his younger sister was born. She concludes that the retardation was due to the age of Bob's mother and not to a general tendency for his family members to inherit retardation. It is well known that women over 40 have a much higher probability of giving birth to retarded children than younger women have. Apparently, in women over 40, the ova are not as healthy as in women under 40.

In Mary's case, the counselor determines that there is a small but clear possibility that Mary may be a carrier of hemophilia and may transmit that condition to a son. Otherwise, the counselor can find no evidence from the family history to indicate genetic problems.

The decision then is up to the Simses. In this case, the genetic problem will probably not occur, so the choice is fairly easy. However, what should parents do if they face the strong probability of having a child with a major birth defect? Ultimately, the decision depends on the couple's ethical and religious beliefs. They must decide how to balance these against the quality of their child's life.

The decision is even more acute, of course, once pregnancy has begun. **Amniocentesis** *is a prenatal medical procedure in which a sample of amniotic fluid is withdrawn by syringe and tested to discover if the fetus is suffering from any chromosomal or metabolic disorders. Amniocentesis is performed in the 12th to 16th weeks of pregnancy.* The later amniocentesis is performed, the better is its diagnostic po-

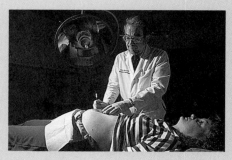

Amniocentesis is being performed on a pregnant woman.

A 6-month-old infant poses with its ultrasound sonography record taken at 4 months into prenatal development.

tential. The earlier it is performed, the more useful it is in indicating whether a pregnancy should be terminated.

Ultrasound sonography *is a prenatal medical procedure in which high-frequency sound waves are directed into a pregnant woman's abdomen.* The echo from the sounds is transformed into a visual representation of the fetus's inner structures. This technique has been able to detect such disorders as microencephaly, a form of mental retardation involving an abnormally small brain. Ultrasound sonography is often used in conjunction with amniocentesis to determine the precise location of the fetus in the mother's abdomen.

As scientists have searched for more accurate, safe assessments of high-risk prenatal conditions, they have developed a new test. The **chorionic villus test** *is a prenatal medical procedure in which a small sample of the placenta is removed at a certain point in the pregnancy from the 8th through the 11th week.* Diagnosis takes approximately 10 days. The chorionic villus test allows a decision about abortion to be made near the end of the first trimester of pregnancy, a point when abortion is safer and less traumatic than after amniocentesis in the second trimester. These techniques provide valuable information about the presence of birth defects, but they also raise issues pertaining to whether an abortion should be obtained if birth defects are present.

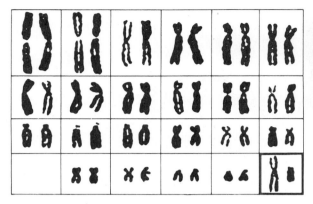

(a)

(b)

Figure 3.6

Genetic Difference Between Males and Females
Set (a) shows the chromosome structure of a male, and set (b) shows the chromosome structure of a female. The 23rd pair is shown in the bottom right box of each set. Notice that the Y chromosome of the male is smaller than that of the female. To obtain this kind of chromosomal picture, a cell is removed from a person's body, usually from the inside of the mouth. The chromosomes are magnified extensively and then photographed.

sex chromosomes, 2 of the 46 chromosomes human beings normally carry. As we saw earlier, ordinarily females have two X chromosomes and men have an X and a Y. (Figure 3.6 shows the chromosome makeup of a male and a female.)

Genetic transmission is usually more complex than the simple examples we have examined so far. **Polygenic inheritance** *is a genetic principle that describes the interaction of many genes to produce a particular characteristic.* Few psychological characteristics are the result of single pairs. Most are determined by the interaction of many different genes. There are more than 50,000 genes, so you can imagine that the number of possible combinations of these is staggering. Traits produced by this mixing of genes are said to be polygenically determined.

No one possesses all the characteristics that our genetic structure makes possible. A **genotype** *is a person's genetic heritage, the actual genetic material.* However, not all of this genetic material is apparent in our observed and measurable characteristics. A **phenotype** *is the way an individual's genotype is expressed in observed and measurable characteristics.* Phenotypes include physical traits—such as height, weight, eye color, and skin pigmentation—and psychological characteristics such as intelligence, creativity, personality, and social tendencies. For each genotype, a range of phenotypes can be expressed. Imagine that we could identify all the genes that would make a child introverted or extraverted. Would measured introversion-extraversion be predictable from knowledge of the specific genes? The answer is no because, even if our genetic model were adequate, introversion-extraversion is a characteristic shaped by experience throughout life. For example, parents may push an introverted child into social situations and encourage the child to become more gregarious.

That which comes of a cat will catch mice.

—English proverb

93

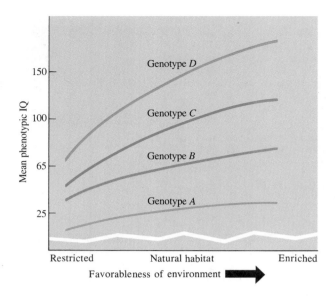

Figure 3.7

Some Possible Reaction Ranges for the Development of Intelligence Under Poor-to-Good Environmental Conditions
Although each genotype responds favorably to improved environments, some are more responsive to environmental deprivation and enrichment than are others.

To understand how introversion is measured, think about a series of genetic codes that predisposes a child to develop in a particular way, and imagine environments that are responsive or unresponsive to this development. For example, the genotype of some persons may predispose them to be introverted in an environment that promotes a turning inward of personality yet, in an environment that encourages social interaction and outgoingness, these individuals may become more extroverted. However, it would be unlikely for an individual with this introverted genotype to become a strong extrovert.

The term **reaction range** *is used to describe the range of phenotypes for each genotype, suggesting the importance of an environment's restrictiveness or enrichment* (figure 3.7). Sandra Scarr (1984b) explains reaction range this way: Each of us has a range of potential. For example, an individual with "medium-tall" genes for height who grows up in a poor environment may be shorter than average, but, in an excellent nutritional environment, the individual may grow up taller than average. No matter how well fed the person is, however, someone with "short" genes will never be taller than average. Scarr believes that such characteristics as intelligence and introversion work the same way. That is, there is a range within which the environment can modify intelligence, but intelligence is not completely malleable. Reaction range gives us an estimate of how modifiable intelligence is.

Genotypes, in addition to producing many phenotypes, may show the opposite track for some characteristics—those that are somewhat immune to extensive changes in the environment. These characteristics seem to stay on a particular developmental course regardless of the environmental assaults on them (Waddington, 1957). **Canalization** *describes the process by which characteristics take a narrow path or developmental course. Apparently, preservative forces help protect, or buffer, a person from environmental extremes.* For example, American developmental psychologist Jerome Kagan (1984) points to his research on Guatemalan infants who had experienced extreme malnutrition as infants yet showed normal social and cognitive development later in childhood.

However, it is important to recognize that, although the genetic influence of canalization exerts its power by keeping organisms on a particular developmental path, genes alone do not directly determine human behavior

Identical twins develop from a single fertilized egg that splits into two genetically identical organisms. In a twin study, identical twins are compared with fraternal twins, who develop from separate eggs, making them genetically less similar than identical twins.

(Cairns, 1991; Gottlieb, 1991a,b; Lerner, 1991). Gilbert Gottlieb (1991b) points out that genes are an integral part of an organism but that their activity (genetic expression) can be affected by the organism's environment. For example, hormones that circulate in the blood make their way into cells, where they influence the cells' activity. The hormonal flow itself can be affected by environmental events such as light, day length, nutrition, and behavior.

Methods Used by Behavior Geneticists

Behavior genetics *is concerned with the degree and nature of behavior's hereditary basis.* Behavior geneticists assume that behaviors are jointly determined by the interaction of heredity and environment. To study heredity's influence on behavior, behavior geneticists often use either twin studies or adoption studies.

In a **twin study,** *the behavior of identical twins is compared with the behavior of fraternal twins.* **Identical twins** *(called monozygotic twins) develop from a single fertilized egg that splits into two genetically identical replicas, each of which becomes a person.* **Fraternal twins** *(called dyzygotic twins) develop from separate eggs, making them genetically less similar than identical twins.* Although fraternal twins share the same womb, they are no more alike genetically than are nontwin brothers and sisters, and they may be of different sexes. By comparing groups of identical and fraternal twins, behavior geneticists capitalize on the basic knowledge that identical twins are more similar genetically than are fraternal twins. In one recent twin study, 7,000 pairs of Finnish identical and fraternal twins were compared on the personality traits of extraversion (outgoingness) and neuroticism (psychological instability) (Rose & others, 1988). On both of these personality traits, identical twins were much more similar than fraternal twins, suggesting the role of heredity in both traits. However, several issues crop up as a result of twin studies. Adults may stress the similarities of identical twins more than those of fraternal twins, and identical twins may perceive themselves as a "set" and play together more than fraternal twins. If so, observed similarities in identical twins could be environmentally influenced.

In an **adoption study,** *investigators seek to discover whether the behavior and psychological characteristics of adopted children are more like their adoptive parents, who provided a home environment, or their biological parents, who contributed their heredity.* In one investigation, the educational

The Evolutionary Perspective and Genetics

Concept	Processes/related ideas	Characteristics/description
The evolutionary perspective	Its nature	Natural selection is the evolutionary process that favors individuals within a species that are best adapted to survive and reproduce. This concept was developed by Darwin. Evolution generally proceeds at a slow pace. Biological evolution shaped human beings into a culture-making species.
Genes, chromosomes, and reproduction	Genes and chromosomes	The nucleus of each human cell contains 46 chromosomes, which are composed of DNA. Genes are short segments of DNA and act as a blueprint for cells to reproduce and manufacture proteins that maintain life.
	Reproduction	Genes are transmitted from parents to offspring by gametes, or sex cells. Gametes are formed by the splitting of cells, a process called meiosis. Reproduction takes place when a female gamete (ovum) is fertilized by a male gamete (sperm) to create a single-celled ovum. In vitro fertilization has helped solve some infertility problems. Approximately 10 to 15 percent of couples in the United States experience infertility problems, some of which can be corrected through surgery or fertility drugs. Another choice for infertile couples is adoption.
Abnormalities in genes and chromosomes	The range of problems	A range of problems is caused by major gene or chromosome defects, among them PKU, Down syndrome, sickle-cell anemia, Klinefelter syndrome, Turner syndrome, and the XYY syndrome.
	Genetic counseling and tests	Genetic counseling has increased in popularity as couples desire information about their risk of having a defective child. Amniocentesis, ultrasound sonography, and the chorionic villus test are used to determine the presence of defects after pregnancy has begun.
Genetic principles	Their nature	Genetic transmission is complex, but some principles have been worked out, among them dominant-recessive genes, sex-linked genes, polygenic inheritance, genotype-phenotype distinction, reaction range, and canalization.
	Methods used by behavior geneticists	Behavior genetics is the field concerned with the degree and nature of behavior's hereditary basis. Among the most important methods used by behavior geneticists are twin studies and adoption studies.

levels attained by biological parents were better predictors of adopted children's IQ scores than were the IQs of the children's adopted parents (Scarr & Weinberg, 1983). Because of the genetic relation between the adopted children and their biological parents, the implication is that heredity influences children's IQ scores.

So far, our coverage of the biological beginnings of the life cycle has taken us through some important aspects of heredity. A summary of these ideas is presented in concept table 3.1. Now let's turn our attention to some aspects of development that are influenced by heredity.

Heredity's Influence on Development

What aspects of development are influenced by genetic factors? They all are. However, behavior geneticists are interested in more precise estimates of a characteristic's variation that can be accounted for by genetic factors. Intelligence and temperament are among the most widely investigated aspects of heredity's influence on development.

Intelligence

Arthur Jensen (1969) sparked a lively and, at times, hostile debate when he presented his thesis that intelligence is primarily inherited. Jensen believes that environment and culture play only a minimal role in intelligence. He examined several studies of intelligence, some of which involved comparisons of identical and fraternal twins. Remember that identical twins have identical genetic endowments, so their IQs should be similar. Fraternal twins and ordinary siblings are less similar genetically, so their IQs should be less similar. Jensen found support for his argument in these studies. Studies with identical twins produced an average correlation of .82; studies with ordinary siblings produced an average correlation of .50. Note the difference of .32. To show that genetic factors are more important than environmental factors, Jensen compared identical twins reared together with those reared apart; the correlation for those reared together was .89 and for those reared apart it was .78 (a difference of .11). Jensen argued that, if environmental influences were more important than genetic influences, then siblings reared apart, who experienced different environments, should have IQs much further apart.

Many scholars have criticized Jensen's work. One criticism concerns the definition of intelligence itself. Jensen believes that IQ as measured by standardized intelligence tests is a good indicator of intelligence. Critics argue that IQ tests tap only a narrow range of intelligence. Everyday problem solving, work, and social adaptability, say the critics, are important aspects of intelligence not measured by the traditional intelligence tests used in Jensen's sources. A second criticism is that most investigations of heredity and environment do not include environments that differ radically. Thus, it is not surprising that many genetic studies show environment to be a fairly weak influence of intelligence.

Jensen places the importance of heredity's influence on intelligence at about 80 percent (Jensen, 1969). Jensen is such a strong advocate of genetic influences on intelligence that he believes we can breed for intelligence. Just such an effort—the Repository for Germinal Choice—is in progress. To read more about this Nobel Prize sperm bank for breeding geniuses, turn to Perspective on Child Development 3.2. Intelligence is influenced by heredity, but most developmentalists do not put the figure nearly as high as Jensen does. Other experts estimate heredity's influence on intelligence to be in the 50 percent range (Plomin, 1989; Plomin, DeFries, & McClearn, in press).

Temperament

Temperament *is an individual's behavioral style and characteristic way of responding.* Developmentalists are especially interested in the temperament of infants. Some infants are extremely active, moving their arms, legs, and

Doran, Dr. Graham, and the Repository for Germinal Choice

Doran (a name from the Greek word meaning "gift") learned all the elements of speech by 2 years of age. An intelligence test showed that, at the age of 1, his mental age was 4. Doran was the second child born through the Nobel Prize sperm bank, which came into existence in 1980. The sperm bank was founded by Robert Graham in Escondido, California, with the intent of producing geniuses. Graham collected the sperm of Nobel Prize–winning scientists and offered it free of charge to intelligent women of good stock whose husbands were infertile.

One of the contributors to the sperm bank is physicist William Shockley, who shared the Nobel Prize in 1956 for inventing the transistor. Shockley has received his share of criticism for preaching the genetic basis of intelligence. Two other Nobel Prize winners have donated their sperm to the bank, but Shockley is the only one who has been identified.

More than 20 children have been sired through the sperm bank. Are the progeny prodigies? It may be too early to tell. Except for Doran, little has been revealed about the children. Doran's genetic father was labeled "28 Red" in the sperm bank (the color apparently has no meaning). He is listed in the sperm bank's catalog as handsome, blond, and athletic, with a math SAT score of 800 and several prizes for his classical music performances. One of his few drawbacks is that he passed along to Doran an almost one-in-three chance of developing hemorrhoids. Doran's mother says that her genetic contribution goes back to the royal court of Norway and to poet William Blake.

The odds are not high that a sperm bank will yield that special combination of factors required to produce a creative genius. George Bernard Shaw, who believed that heredity's influence on intelligence is strong, once told a story about a beautiful woman who wrote to him that, with her body and his brain, they could produce marvelous offspring. Shaw responded that, unfortunately, the offspring might get his body and her brain.

Not surprisingly, the Nobel Prize sperm bank is heavily criticized. Some say that brighter does not mean better. They also say that IQ is not a good indicator of social competence or human contribution to the world. Other critics say that intelligence is an elusive concept to measure and that it cannot reliably be reproduced, as the sperm bank is trying to do. Visions of the German gene program of the 1930s and 1940s are created. The German Nazis believed that certain traits are superior; they tried to breed children with such traits and killed people without them.

Doran is one of the offspring born through the Repository for Germinal Choice.

Robert Graham, the founder of the Repository for Germinal Choice, holds a container of frozen sperm.

Although Graham's Repository for Germinal Choice (as the Nobel Prize sperm bank is formally called) is strongly criticized, consider its possible contributions. The repository provides a social service for couples who cannot conceive a child, and individuals who go to the sperm bank probably provide an enriched environment for the offspring. To once-childless parents, the offspring produced by the sperm bank, or any of the other new methods of conception available, are invariably described as miracles (Garelik, 1985).

mouths incessantly. Others are tranquil. Some children explore their environment eagerly for great lengths of time. Others do not. Some infants respond warmly to people. Others fuss and fret. All of these behavioral styles represent a person's temperament (Goldsmith & others, 1991).

A widely debated issue in temperament research is just what the key dimensions of temperament are. Psychiatrists Alexander Chess and Stella Thomas (Chess & Thomas, 1977; Thomas & Chess, 1987, 1991) believe there are three basic types, or clusters, of temperament—easy, difficult, and slow-to-warm-up.

1. An **easy child** *is generally in a positive mood, quickly establishes regular routines in infancy, and adapts easily to new experiences.*

2. A **difficult child** *tends to react negatively and cry frequently, engages in irregular daily routines, and is slow to accept new experiences.*

3. A **slow-to-warm-up child** *has a low activity level, is somewhat negative, shows low adaptability, and displays a low intensity of mood.*

Different dimensions make up these three basic clusters of temperament. The three basic clusters and their dimensions are shown in table 3.1. In their longitudinal investigation, Chess and Thomas found that 40 percent of the children they studied could be classified as "easy," 10 percent as "difficult," and 15 percent as "slow-to-warm-up." Researchers have found that these three basic clusters of temperament are moderately stable across the childhood years.

Other researchers suggest that temperament is composed of different basic components. Personality psychologist Arnold Buss and behavior geneticist Robert Plomin (1984, 1987) believe that infants' temperament falls into three basic categories: emotionality, sociability, and activity level.

1. **Emotionality** *is the tendency to be distressed.* It reflects the arousal of a person's sympathetic nervous system. During infancy, distress develops into two separate emotional responses: fear and anger. Fearful infants try to escape something that is unpleasant; angry ones protest it. Buss and Plomin argue that children are labeled "easy" or "difficult" on the basis of their emotionality.

2. **Sociability** *is the tendency to prefer the company of others to being alone.* It matches a tendency to respond warmly to others.

3. **Activity level** *involves tempo and vigor of movement.* Some children walk fast, are attracted to high-energy games, and jump or bounce around a lot; others are more placid.

A number of scholars, including Chess and Thomas, conceive of temperament as a stable characteristic of newborns that comes to be shaped and modified by the child's later experiences (Thomas & Chess, 1987; Goldsmith, 1988). This raises the question of heredity's role in temperament. Twin and adoption studies have been conducted to answer this question (Plomin, 1989; Matheny, Dolan, & Wilson, 1976). The researchers found a heritability index in the range of .50 to .60, suggesting a moderate influence of heredity on temperament. However, the strength of the association usually declines as infants become older (Goldsmith & Gottesman, 1981). This finding supports the belief

■ *Critical Thinking*
Consider your own temperament. Does it fit into one of the clusters described by Chess and Thomas? How stable has your temperament been in the course of your development? What factors contributed to this stability or lack of stability?

TABLE 3.1
Chess and Thomas' Dimensions and Basic Clusters of Temperament

Temperament Dimension	Description	Temperament Cluster		
		Easy child	*Difficult child*	*Slow-to-warm-up child*
Rhythmicity	Regularity of eating, sleeping, toileting	Regular	Irregular	
Activity level	Degree of energy movement		High	Low
Approach-withdrawal	Ease of approaching new people and situations	Positive	Negative	Negative
Adaptability	Ease of tolerating change in routine plans	Positive	Negative	Negative
Sensory threshold	Amount of stimulation required for responding			
Predominant quality of mood	Degree of positive or negative affect	Positive	Negative	
Intensity of mood expression	Degree of affect when pleased, displeased, happy, sad	Low to moderate	High	Low
Distractibility/attention span/persistence	Ease of being distracted			

Note: This table shows which of the dimensions are critical in spotting a basic cluster of temperament and what the level of responsiveness is for a critical feature. A blank space indicates that the dimension is not strongly related to a basic cluster of temperament.

that temperament becomes more malleable with experience. Alternatively, it may be that, as a child becomes older, behavioral indicators of temperament may be more difficult to spot. The biological basis of the temperament of inhibition or shyness and its developmental course is currently the interest of Jerome Kagan (1988b, 1989, in press) and Stephen Suomi (1987). To learn about how stable our tendency to be shy is and how much it can be modified, turn to Perspective on Child Development 3.3. To read about likely biologically based ethnic differences in temperament, turn to Cultural Worlds of Development 3.1.

The consistency of temperament depends, in part, on the "match" or "fit" between the child's nature and the parent's (Nitz & Lerner, 1991; Plomin & Thompson, 1987; Rothbart, in press). Imagine a high-strung parent with a child who is difficult and sometimes slow to respond to the parent's affection. The parent may begin to feel angry or rejected. A father who does not need much face-to-face social interaction will find it easy to manage a similarly

Biological Processes, Physical Development, and Perceptual Development

Born to Be Shy?

Everyone has seen a shy toddler—one who clings to a parent and only reluctantly ventures into an unfamiliar place. Faced with a stranger, the shy toddler freezes, becomes silent, and stares fearfully. The shy toddler seems visibly tense in social situations; parents of such children often report that they always seem to have been that way.

Despite parents' comments that shy children seem to have been shy from birth, psychologists have resisted the notion that such characteristics are inborn, focusing instead on the importance of early experiences. Both the research of Jerome Kagan with extremely shy children and the research of Stephen Suomi with "uptight" monkeys support the belief that shyness is a part of a person's basic temperament.

Kagan (1987b, 1989; Snidman & Kagan, 1989), collaborating with Nancy Snidman, Steven Resnick, and Jane Gibbons, followed the development of extremely inhibited and uninhibited 2-to 3-year-old children for 6 years. They evaluated the children's heart rates and other physiological measures, as well as observed their behavior in novel circumstances. After 6 years, the very inhibited children no longer behaved exactly as they did when they were 2, but they still revealed the pattern of very inhibited behavior combined with intense physiological responsiveness to mild stress. Very uninhibited children typically speak within the first minute in a social situation, but very inhibited children sometimes wait as long as 20 minutes before they say anything.

Suomi (1987) has discovered that uptight monkeys, like Kagan's inhibited children, do not easily outgrow their intense physiological response to stress and their frozen behavioral responses to social situations. Even as late as adolescence—which is 4 to 5 years of age in monkeys—those who were uptight at birth continued to respond in intense ways to stress, but at this point they became hyperactive. As adults, they seemed to regress in the face of stress, revealing the shy, inhibited behavior seen in infancy.

Kagan says that the proper environmental context can change the tendency to be shy, but, if parents let their child remain fearful for a long time, it becomes harder to modify the shyness. Kagan reported that 40 percent of the originally inhibited children—mainly boys—became much less inhibited by 5½ years, whereas less than 10 percent became more timid. Based on parent interviews, parents helped their children overcome their shyness by bringing other children into the home and by encouraging the children to cope with stressful circumstances.

Extremely shy children at the age of 2 or 3 usually show similar inhibited behavior 6 years later, although environmental experiences can modify shyness to a degree.

"Uptight" infant monkeys show some of the same shy, inhibited behaviors as their human counterparts.

Modification of shyness in some cases can be extreme. Some shy individuals even become performers. Such celebrities as Johnny Carson, Carol Burnett, Barbara Walters, and Michael Jackson have strong tendencies toward shyness, but, even with the biological underpinnings loaded against them, they turned the tables on heredity's influence (Asher, 1987).

Imperturbability in European American, Chinese American, and Navaho Indian Newborns

Do newborns from different cultures have different biological predispositions of temperament? In one investigation, researchers observed 24 Chinese American and 24 European American 2-day-old babies (Freedman & Freedman, 1969). The Chinese American infants had a less rapid buildup to an excited state of arousal, showed less facial and body reddening, and showed fewer state changes. When placed in the prone position, the Chinese Americans tended to remain inactive, face flat against the bed. By contrast, the European Americans were more likely to lift their head or turn their face to one side. The Chinese American babies were easier to control when crying and were able to stop by themselves without being consoled. The researchers suggested that these behaviors reflect the temperament of "imperturbability," which affects the way adults care for infants. Further comparison of this temperament indicated that newborn Navaho Indians are more perturbable than newborn Chinese Americans (Freedman, 1971).

Researchers have found that Chinese American newborns are calmer than European American and Navaho Indian newborns.

introverted baby, but he may not be able to provide an extraverted baby with sufficient stimulation. Parents influence infants, but infants also influence parents. Parents may withdraw from difficult children, or they may become critical and punish them; these responses may make the difficult child even more difficult. A more easygoing parent may have a calming effect on a difficult child or may continue to show affection even when the child withdraws or is hostile, eventually encouraging more competent behavior.

In sum, heredity does seem to influence temperament. However, the degree of influence depends on parents' responsiveness to their children and on other environmental childhood experiences.

Heredity-Environment Interaction and Development

Both genes and environment are necessary for an organism to exist. Heredity and environment operate together—or cooperate—to produce an individual's intelligence, temperament, height, weight, ability to pitch a baseball, career interests, and so on. Without genes, there is no organism; without environment, there is no organism (Scarr & Weinberg, 1980). If an attractive, popular, intelligent girl is elected as president of the student body, would we conclude that her success is due to environment or to heredity? Of course, it is due to both. Because the environment's influence depends on genetically endowed characteristics, we say that the two factors *interact* (Plomin, 1991; Scarr, 1989, 1991; Scarr & Weinberg, 1980; Wahlsten, 1991; Weinberg, 1989).

As we have seen, however, developmental psychologists probe further to determine more precisely heredity's and environment's influence on development. What do we know about heredity-environment interaction? According to Sandra Scarr and Kenneth Kidd (1983), hundreds of disorders appear because of miscodings in DNA. We know that abnormalities in chromosomal number adversely influence the development of physical, intellectual, and behavioral features. We also know that genotypes and phenotypes do not map onto each other in a one-to-one fashion, and it is very difficult to distinguish between genetic and cultural transmission. There usually is a familial concentration of a particular disorder, but familial patterns are considerably different from what would be precisely predicted from simple modes of inheritance. When we consider the normal range of variation, the stronger the genetic resemblance, the stronger the behavioral resemblance. This holds more strongly for intelligence than for personality or interests. The influence of genes on intelligence is present early in children's development and continues through the late adulthood years. We also know that being raised in the same family accounts for a portion of the intellectual differences among individuals, but common rearing accounts for little of the variation in personality or interests. One reason for this discrepancy may be that families place similar pressures on their children for intellectual development in the sense that the push is clearly toward the highest level, although they do not direct their children toward similar personalities or interests, in which extremes are not especially desirable. That is, most parents would like their children to have above-average intellect, but there is much less agreement about whether or not a child should be highly extraverted.

What do we need to know about the role of heredity-environment interaction in development? Scarr and Kidd (1983) commented that we need to know the pathways by which genetic abnormalities influence development. The PKU success story is but one such example. Scientists discovered the genetic linkage of the disorder and, subsequently, how the environment could be changed to reduce the damage to development. We need to know more about genetic-environment interaction in the normal range of development. For example, what accounts for the difference in one person's IQ of 95 and another person's IQ of 125? The answer requires a polygenic perspective and information about cultural and genetic influences. We also need to know about heredity's influence across the entire life cycle. For instance, puberty is not an environmentally produced accident (Hopwood & others, 1990; Rowe & Rodgers, 1989); neither is menopause. Although puberty and menopause can be influenced by such environmental factors as nutrition, weight, drugs, and health, the basic evolutionary and genetic program is wired into the species. It cannot be eliminated; nor should it be ignored. This evolutionary and genetic perspective gives biology its appropriate role in our quest to better understand human development through the life cycle.

A summary of the main ideas in our discussion of heredity's influence on development and heredity-environment interaction is presented in concept table 3.2. In the next chapter, we will continue our discussion of biological beginnings, turning to information about prenatal development and birth.

■ *Critical Thinking*
Beyond the fact that heredity and environment always interact to produce development, first argue for heredity's dominance in this interaction, and, second, argue for environment's dominance.

Concept	Processes/related ideas	Characteristics/description
Heredity's influence on development	Its scope	All aspects of development are influenced by heredity.
	Intelligence	Jensen's argument that intelligence is due primarily to heredity sparked a lively and, at times, bitter debate. Intelligence is influenced by heredity, but not as strongly as Jensen envisioned.
	Temperament	Temperament refers to behavioral style; temperament has been studied extensively. Chess and Thomas described three temperamental clusters—"easy," "difficult," and "slow-to-warm-up." Temperament is influenced strongly by biological factors in early infancy but becomes more malleable with experience. An important consideration is the fit of the infant's temperament with the parents' temperament.
Heredity-environment interaction and development	Its nature	Without genes, there is no organism; without environment, there is no organism. Because the environment's influence depends on genetically endowed characteristics, we say that the two factors interact.

Summary

I. The Evolutionary Perspective

Natural selection is the evolutionary process that favors individuals within a species that are best adapted to survive and reproduce. This concept was developed by Darwin. Evolution generally proceeds at a slow pace. Biological evolution shaped human beings into a culture-making species.

II. Chromosomes, DNA, and Genes

The nucleus of each human cell contains 46 chromosomes, which are composed of DNA. Genes are short segments of DNA that act as a blueprint for cells to reproduce and manufacture protein that maintains life.

III. Reproduction

Genes are transmitted from parents to offspring by gametes, or sex cells. Gametes are formed by the splitting of cells, a process called meiosis. Reproduction takes place when a female gamete (ovum) is fertilized by a male gamete (sperm) to create a single-celled zygote. In vitro fertilization has helped solve some infertility problems. Approximately 10 to 15 percent of couples in the United States experience fertility problems, some of which can be corrected through surgery or fertility drugs. Another choice for infertile couples is adoption.

IV. Abnormalities in Genes and Chromosomes

A range of problems is caused by major gene or chromosome defects, among them PKU, Down syndrome, sickle-cell anemia, Klinefelter syndrome, Turner syndrome, and the XYY syndrome. Genetic counseling has increased in popularity, as couples desire information about their risk of having a defective child. Amniocentesis and the chorionic villus test are used to determine the presence of defects after pregnancy has begun.

V. Some Genetic Principles

Genetic transmission is complex, but some principles have been worked out, among them dominant-recessive genes, sex-linked genes, polygenic inheritance, genotype-phenotype distinction, reaction range, and canalization.

VI. Methods Used by Behavior Geneticists

Behavior genetics is the field concerned with the degree and nature of behavior's heredity basis. Among the most important methods used by behavior geneticists are twin studies and adoption studies. The concept of heritability is used in many of the twin and adoption studies. The heritability index is not without flaws.

VII. Heredity's Influence on Development

All aspects of development are influenced by heredity. Jensen's argument that intelligence is influenced primarily by heredity sparked a lively and, at times, bitter debate. Intelligence is influenced by heredity, but not as strongly as Jensen envisioned. Temperament refers to behavioral style; temperament has been studied extensively in infancy. Chess and Thomas developed three temperament clusters—"easy," "difficult," and "slow-to-warm-up." Temperament is strongly influenced by biological factors in early infancy but becomes more malleable with experience. An important consideration is the fit of the infant's temperament with the parents' temperament.

VIII. Heredity-Environment Interaction and Development

Without genes, there is no organism; without environment, there is no organism. Because the environment's influence depends on genetically endowed characteristics, we say that the two factors interact.

Key Terms

natural selection 85
chromosomes 87
DNA 87
genes 87
gametes 87
meiosis 87
reproduction 88
zygote 88
in vitro fertilization 88
infertility 89
phenylketonuria (PKU) 90
Down syndrome 90
sickle-cell anemia 90
Klinefelter syndrome 90
Turner syndrome 91
XYY syndrome 91
dominant-recessive genes
  principle 91
amniocentesis 92

ultrasound sonography 92
chorionic villus test 92
polygenic inheritance 93
genotype 93
phenotype 93
reaction range 94
canalization 94
behavior genetics 95
twin study 95
identical twins 95
fraternal twins 95
adoption study 95
temperament 97
easy child 99
difficult child 99
slow-to-warm-up child 99
emotionality 99
sociability 99
activity level 99

Suggested Readings

Chess, S., & Thomas, A. (1986). *Temperament in clinical practice.* New York: Guilford. Details of Chess and Thomas' classical longitudinal study of temperament are provided; applications to clinical problems are described.

Gould, S. (1983). *Hen's teeth and horse's toes: Reflections on natural history.* New York: W. W. Norton. This book is a collection of fascinating articles by a biologist interested in evolution. The essays originally were published in the magazine *Natural History.*

Lewontin, R. C., Rose, S., & Kamin, L. J. (1984). *Not in our genes.* New York: Pantheon. *Not in Our Genes* argues for an environmental view of development and provides many reasons as to why heredity's role is overestimated.

Plomin, R., DeFries, J. C., & McClearn, G. E. (1990). *Behavioral genetics: A primer.* New York: W. H. Freeman. This text is a good introduction to research on genes and behavior by leading behavior geneticists.

Watson, J. D. (1968). *The double helix.* New York: New American Library. This is a personalized account of the research leading up to one of the most provocative discoveries of the twentieth century—the DNA molecule. Reading like a mystery novel, it illustrates the exciting discovery process in science.

CHAPTER

4

PRENATAL DEVELOPMENT AND BIRTH

Prenatal Development
  The Course of Prenatal Development
  Miscarriage and Abortion
  *Cultural Worlds of Development 4.1: An
      International Perspective on Abortion Trends*
  Teratology and Hazards to Prenatal Development
  *Perspective on Child Development 4.1: Ethics and
      the Medical Use of Fetal Tissue*
  *Perspective on Child Development 4.2:
      Cocaine Babies*
The Birth Process
  Childbirth Strategies
  Stages of Birth and Delivery Complications
  Use of Drugs During Childbirth
  Preterm Infants and Age-Weight Considerations
  Some Conclusions About Preterm Infants
  Stimulation of Preterm Infants
  *Cultural Worlds of Development 4.2: Prenatal
      Care in the United States and Around the
      World*
  *Perspective on Child Development 4.3: Massaging
      and Exercising Preemies*
  Measures of Neonatal Health and Responsiveness
  Bonding
Summary
Key Terms
Suggested Readings

THE HISTORY OF MAN FOR NINE MONTHS PRECEDING HIS BIRTH WOULD, PROBABLY, BE FAR MORE INTERESTING, AND CONTAIN EVENTS OF GREATER MOMENT THAN ALL THREE SCORE AND TEN YEARS THAT FOLLOW IT.

—Samuel Taylor Coleridge

Teresa Block's second pregnancy was difficult. Her amniotic sac ruptured, she contracted an infection that sent her temperature skyrocketing, and she had an exhausting breech delivery. Her son Robert weighed just less than 2 pounds at birth. Teresa said she had never imagined a baby looking so tiny. The first time she saw Robert, he was lying on his back attached to a respirator, and wires were connected all over his body. Robert stayed at the hospital until 2 weeks before his originally projected birth date, at which time he weighed 4 pounds, 8 ounces. Teresa and her husband lived in a small town 60 miles from the hospital; they commuted each day to spend time with Robert and brought their other child with them whenever it was practical. Considering his circumstances, Robert had a relatively uncomplicated stay at the hospital. Not all children born so frail survive, and sometimes those who do show the consequences many years in the future.

A decade later, Robert is still at the bottom of the weight chart, but he is about average in height, and the only physical residue of his early birth difficulties is a "lazy eye." He is 20/20 in his good eye but 20/200 in the other. He is doing special exercises for the bad eye, and his doctor thinks he is not far from the day he can go without glasses. Robert is on the soccer team and the swim team (Fincher, 1982).

At one time, you were an organism floating around in a sea of fluid inside your mother's womb. From the moment you were conceived until the moment you were born, some astonishing developments occurred. This chapter chronicles the truly remarkable developments from conception to birth and the nature of the birth process itself.

Prenatal Development

Imagine how you came to be. Out of thousands of eggs and millions of sperm, one egg and one sperm united to produce you. Had the union of sperm and egg come a day or even an hour earlier or later, you might have been very different—maybe even of the opposite sex.

The Course of Prenatal Development

Remember from chapter 3 that conception occurs when a single sperm cell from the male unites with an ovum (egg) in the female's fallopian tube in a process called fertilization. Remember also that the fertilized egg is called a zygote. By the time the zygote ends its 3-to-4-day journey through the fallopian tube and reaches the uterus, it has divided into approximately 12 to 16 cells.

The **germinal period** *is the period of prenatal development that takes place in the first 2 weeks after conception. It includes the creation of the zygote, continued cell division, and the attachment of the zygote to the uterine*

What web is this
Of will be, is, and was?

—Jorge Luis Borges

Biological Processes, Physical Development, and Perceptual Development

wall. By approximately 1 week after conception, the zygote is composed of 100 to 150 cells. The differentiation of cells has already commenced as inner and outer layers of the organism are formed. The **blastocyst** *is the inner layer of cells that develops during the germinal period.* These cells later develop into the embryo. The **trophoblast** *is the outer layer of cells that develops during the germinal period.* It later provides nutrition and support for the embryo. **Implantation,** *the attachment of the zygote to the uterine wall, takes place about 10 days after conception.*

The **embryonic period** *is the period of prenatal development that occurs from 2 to 8 weeks after conception. During the embryonic period, the rate of cell differentiation intensifies, support systems for the cells form, and organs appear.* As the zygote attaches to the uterine wall, its cells form two layers. At this time, the mass of cells changes its name from *zygote* to *embryo.* The embryo's **endoderm** *is the inner layer of cells, which will develop into the digestive and respiratory systems.* The outer layer of cells is divided into two parts. The **ectoderm** *is the outermost layer, which will become the nervous system, sensory receptors (ear, nose, and eyes, for example), and skin parts (hair and nails, for example).* The **mesoderm** *is the middle layer, which will become the circulatory system, bones, muscle, excretory system, and reproductive system.* Every body part eventually develops from these three layers. The endoderm primarily produces internal body parts, the mesoderm primarily produces parts that surround the internal areas, and the ectoderm primarily produces surface parts.

DENNIS THE MENACE

"MY MOM SAYS I COME FROM HEAVEN. MY DAD SAYS HE CAN'T REMEMBER AN' MR. WILSON IS POSITIVE I CAME FROM MARS!"

Figure 4.1
Embryo at 4 Weeks
At about 4 weeks, the embryo is about .2 inches long. The head, eyes, and ears begin to show. The head and neck are half the body length; the shoulders will be located where the whitish arm buds are attached.

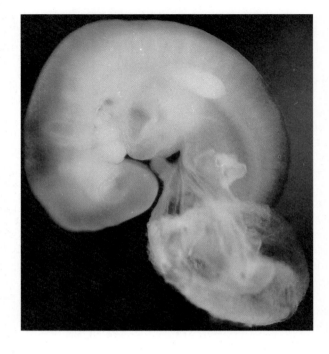

If I could have watched you grow
As a magical mother might,
If I could have seen through my magical
*   transparent belly,*
There would have been such ripening
*   within . . .*

—Anne Sexton

As the embryo's three layers form, life-support systems for the embryo mature and develop rapidly. These life-support systems include the placenta, the umbilical cord, and the amnion. The **placenta** *is a life-support system that consists of a disk-shaped group of tissues in which small blood vessels from the mother and the offspring intertwine but do not join.* The **umbilical cord** *is a life-support system, containing two arteries and one vein, that connects the baby to the placenta.* Very small molecules—oxygen, water, salt, food from the mother's blood, and carbon dioxide and digestive wastes from the embryo's blood—pass back and forth between the mother and infant. Large molecules cannot pass through the placental wall; these include red blood cells and harmful substances such as most bacteria, maternal wastes, and hormones. The mechanisms that govern the transfer of substances across the placental barrier are complex and are still not entirely understood (Rosenblith and Sims-Knight, 1985). The **amnion,** *a bag or envelope that contains a clear fluid in which the developing embryo floats, is another important life-support system. It provides an environment that is temperature and humidity controlled, as well as shock proof.*

Before most women even know they are pregnant, some important embryonic developments take place. In the third week, the neural tube that eventually becomes the spinal cord forms. At about 21 days, eyes begin to appear and, at about 24 days, the cells for the heart begin to differentiate. During the fourth week, the first appearance of the urogenital system is apparent, and arm and leg buds emerge. Four chambers of the heart take shape, and blood vessels surface. (Figure 4.1 shows a 4-week-old embryo.) From the fifth to the eighth week, arms and legs differentiate further; at this time, the face starts to form but still is not very recognizable. The intestinal tract develops and the facial structures fuse. At 8 weeks, the developing organism weighs about one thirtieth of an ounce and is just over 1 inch long. **Organogenesis** *is the process of organ formation that takes place during the first 2 months of prenatal development.* When organs are being formed, they are especially vulnerable to environmental changes. Later in the chapter, we will describe the environmental hazards that are harmful during organogenesis.

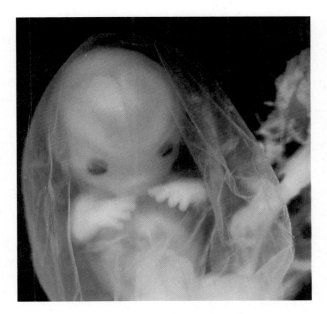

Figure 4.2
Embryo at 8 Weeks
At 8 weeks and 4 centimeters (1.6 inches), the developing individual is no longer an embryo, but a fetus. Everything that will be found in the fully developed human being has now been formed; the fetal stage is a period of growth and perfection of detail. The heart has been beating for a month, and the muscles have just begun their first exercises. Two of the mother's menstrual periods have now been skipped. Ideally, at about this time, the mother goes to a doctor or clinic for prenatal care.

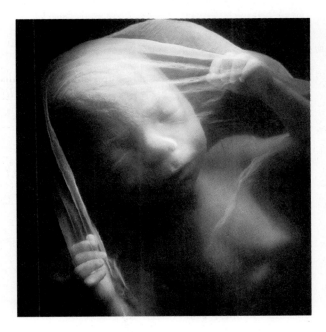

Figure 4.3
Fetus at 4 Months
At this point, the fetus has grown to approximately 6 inches in length and weighs 4 to 7 ounces. The mother can feel arm and leg movements for the first time.

The **fetal period** *is the prenatal period of development that begins 2 months after conception and lasts for 7 months on the average.* Growth and development continue their dramatic course during this time (figure 4.2 shows a fetus at 8 weeks after conception). Three months after conception, the fetus is about 3 inches long and weighs about 1 ounce. It has become active, moving its arms and legs, opening and closing its mouth, and moving its head. The face, forehead, eyelids, nose, and chin are distinguishable, as are the upper arms, lower arms, hands, and lower limbs, and the genitals can be identified as male or female. By the end of the fourth month, the fetus has grown to 6 inches in length and weighs 4 to 7 ounces. At this time, a growth spurt occurs in the body's lower parts. Prenatal reflexes are stronger; arm and leg movements can be felt for the first time by the mother. (Figure 4.3 shows the fetus at 4 months of age.)

So the riders of the darkness pass on their circuits: the luminous island of the self trembles and waits, waits for us all, my friends, where the sea's big brush recolors the dying lives, and the unborn smiles.

—Lawrence Durrell

By the end of the fifth month, the fetus is about 12 inches long and weighs close to a pound. Structures of the skin have formed—toenails and fingernails, for example. The fetus is more active, showing a preference for a particular position in the womb. By the end of the sixth month, the fetus is about 14 inches long and already has gained another pound. The eyes and eyelids are completely formed, and a fine layer of hair covers the head. A grasping reflex is present and irregular breathing occurs. By the end of the seventh month, the fetus is about 16 inches long and has gained another pound, now weighing about 3 pounds. During the eighth and ninth months, the fetus grows longer and gains substantial weight—about another 4 pounds. At birth, the average American baby weighs 7 pounds and is 20 inches long. In these last 2 months, fatty tissues develop and the functioning of various organ systems—heart and kidneys, for example—steps up.

Miscarriage and Abortion

A miscarriage, or spontaneous abortion, happens when pregnancy ends before the developing organism is mature enough to survive outside the womb. The embryo separates from the uterine wall and is expelled by the uterus. About 15 to 20 percent of all pregnancies end in a spontaneous abortion, most in the first 2 to 3 months. Many spontaneous abortions occur without the mother's knowledge, and many involve an embryo or fetus that was not developing normally.

Early in history, it was believed that a woman could be frightened into a miscarriage by loud thunder or a jolt in a carriage. Today, we recognize that this occurrence is highly unlikely; the developing organism is well protected. Abnormalities of the reproductive tract and viral or bacterial infections are more likely to cause spontaneous abortions. In some cases, severe traumas may be at fault.

Deliberate termination of pregnancy is a complex issue, medically, psychologically, and socially. Carrying a baby to term may affect a woman's health, the woman's pregnancy may have resulted from rape or incest, the woman may not be married, or perhaps she is poor and wants to continue her education. Abortion is legal in the United States; in 1973, the Supreme Court ruled that any woman can obtain an abortion during the first 6 months of pregnancy, a decision that continues to generate ethical objections from antiabortion forces. The Supreme Court also has ruled that abortion in the first trimester is solely the decision of the mother and her doctor. Court cases also have added the point that the baby's father and the parents of minor girls do not have any say during this time frame. In the second trimester, states can legislate the time and method of abortion for protection of the mother's health. In the third trimester, the fetus' right to live is the primary concern. To learn about abortion trends around the world, turn to Cultural Worlds of Development 4.1.

What are the psychological effects of having an abortion? In 1989, a research review panel appointed by the American Psychological Association examined more than 100 investigations of the psychological effects of abortion. The panel's conclusions follow. Unwanted pregnancies are stressful for most women. However, it is common for women to report feelings of relief as well as feelings of guilt after an abortion. These feelings are usually mild and tend to diminish rapidly over time without adversely affecting the woman's ability to function. Abortion is more stressful for women who have a history of serious

An International Perspective on Abortion Trends

An estimated 40 million abortions are legally performed each year in the world; for every two births, one pregnancy is terminated. In most countries, laws permit induced abortion, but conditions regulating the practice range from limited prohibition to an elective abortion at the request of a pregnant woman. Under limited prohibition, abortion is usually permitted on the grounds that it will save the woman's life. Most countries of Islamic faith (for instance, Indonesia and Bangladesh), half of the countries of Africa (for example, Nigeria and the Republic of South Africa), about two thirds of the countries of Latin America, and three countries in Western Europe (Belgium, Ireland, and Malta) fall under these prohibitive statutes. These countries make up about one fourth of the world's population.

Thirty-nine percent of the world's population live in countries that have statutes broad enough to permit termination of pregnancy on request, usually during the first trimester. The time limit does not apply to abortions performed on med-ical grounds, however, which may be carried out even up to and beyond the 20th week. A wide range of countries follow this policy, including the United States, Denmark, Singapore, Cuba, and Yugoslavia.

Nearly one fourth of the world's population is governed by laws that authorize abortion on sociomedical grounds—that is, where such factors as inadequate income, poor housing, and unmarried status are considered risks to the mother's health if her pregnancy is allowed to continue. Such countries as India, Japan, most of the countries of Eastern Europe, and the United Kingdom fall into this category.

Access to legal abortion is relatively easy in most Asian countries because there are few regulations and administrative requirements. In several countries, such as China and Korea, governments have introduced a variety of incentives, such as paid leave and subsidies for nourishment, to encourage women to use abortion as a means of fertility regulation (Sachdev, 1988).

emotional problems and who are not given support by family or friends. According to the American Psychological Association report, only a small percentage of women fall into these high-risk categories. If an abortion is performed, it should not only involve competent medical care but the woman's psychological needs as well. Yet another ethical issue related to abortion has appeared recently—the medical use of tissues from aborted fetuses. To learn more about this ethical issue in abortion, turn to Perspective on Child Development 4.1.

Teratology and Hazards to Prenatal Development

Some expectant mothers carefully tiptoe about in the belief that everything they do and feel has a direct effect on their unborn child. Others behave casually, assuming that their experiences will have little effect. The truth lies somewhere between these two extremes. Although living in a protected, comfortable environment, the fetus is not totally immune to the larger world surrounding the mother. The environment can affect the child in many, well-documented ways. Thousands of babies born deformed or mentally retarded every year are the result of events that occurred in the mother's life, as early as 1 or 2 months before conception.

Teratology

A **teratogen,** *which comes from the Greek word* tera *meaning "monster," is any agent that causes a birth defect. The field of study that investigates the causes of birth defects is called teratology.* A specific teratogen (such as a

■ *Critical Thinking*
What are the arguments for and against abortion? Where do you stand on this sensitive issue? Why?

Ethics and the Medical Use of Fetal Tissue

The increased interest in medical uses for tissue from aborted fetuses opens up a new debate about medical technology and the beginnings of life, adding a new dimension to the long-standing controversy over abortion. Evidence is increasing that the special properties of fetal tissue make it ideal for tissue transplants to treat Parkinson's disease, Alzheimer's disease, and other disorders. Most medical researchers believe it is only a matter of time until fetal tissue is used routinely. Scientists expect fetal tissue to be especially valuable in implant treatments because it grows faster than adult tissue, is more adaptable, and causes less immunological rejection. One of the most troubling possibilities is that some women will conceive children with the intent of aborting them, either to aid a family member or to sell them for their tissue.

The laws governing organ donations require the consent of the donor, or the donor's next of kin. In the case of fetuses, tissue may be donated with the consent of the pregnant woman. Many states have laws restricting experiments on fetuses, and this may interfere with the new medical uses of fetal tissue. A recent panel on biomedical ethics at Case Western Reserve University in Cleveland made recommendations about the use of fetal tissue. First, the doctors involved in decisions regarding an abortion should conduct the procedures using fetal tissue. Second, anonymity should be maintained between the donor and the recipient, and donors and recipients should not be related. Almost everyone concerned with the use of fetal tissue agrees that it is morally wrong, although not illegal, to become pregnant for the sole purpose of aborting a fetus to obtain certain tissues. The U.S.

Department of Health and Human Services has placed a moratorium on certain fetal tissue research until the ethical issues are resolved (U.S. Public Health Service, 1988). Specifically, research on induced abortions, but not spontaneous abortions or stillbirths, is banned. Prior to the announcement by the Department of Health and Human Services, some ethics committees had already shut down this type of fetal research until the ethical issues could be evaluated further (Burtchaell, in press).

Biomedical ethicists say there is a big difference between taking advantage of a death to harvest tissue and creating a life just to abort it. When an abortion is planned anyway, some ethicists say, donating the fetal tissue may help relieve some of the sadness surrounding the decision. Donating tissue to help someone else can aid in the process of grieving or bereavement, say some ethicists. The National Right-to-Life Committee, however, says the idea is morally repulsive. They assert that people who kill tiny, developing babies lose any moral right to use those tissues. They also believe that the medical use of fetal tissue offers an additional rationale to some individuals who defend abortion. As can be seen, the use of fetal tissue is a debate that probably will be with us for some time (Lewin, 1987).

For the first time, in 1991, the American College of Obstetricians and Gynecologists and the American Fertility Society established a board to examine ethics and the medical use of fetal tissue. The board will develop standards to ensure that fetal research is ethically sound.

---

drug) usually does not cause a specific birth defect (such as malformation of the legs). So many teratogens exist that practically every fetus is exposed to at least some teratogens. For this reason, it is difficult to determine which teratogen causes which birth defect. In addition, it may take a long time for the effects of a teratogen to show up; only about half of all potential effects appear at birth.

Despite the many unknowns about teratogens, scientists have discovered the identity of some of these hazards to prenatal development and the particular point of fetal development at which they do their greatest damage. As figure 4.4 shows, sensitivity to teratogens begins about 3 weeks after conception. The probability of a structural defect is greatest early in the embryonic period, because this is when organs are being formed. After organogenesis is complete, teratogens are less likely to cause anatomical defects. Exposure later, during the fetal period, is more likely to stunt growth or to create problems in the way organs function. The precision of organogenesis is evident; teratologists point out that vulnerability of the brain is greatest at 15 to 25 days

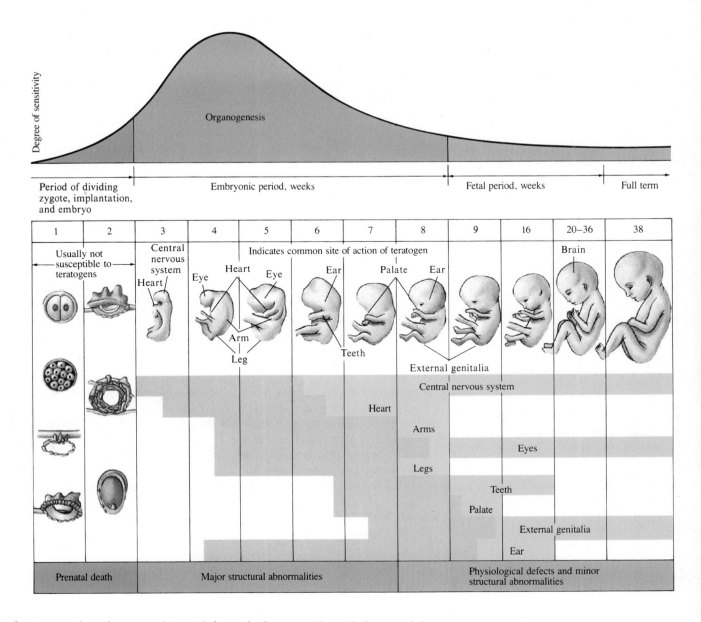

after conception, the eye at 24 to 40 days, the heart at 20 to 40 days, and the legs at 24 to 36 days.

In the following sections, we will explore how certain environmental agents influence prenatal development. That is, we will examine how maternal diseases and conditions, drugs, and environmental hazards affect the fetus.

Maternal Diseases and Conditions

Maternal diseases or infections can produce defects by crossing the placental barrier, or they can cause damage during the birth process itself. Rubella (German measles) is a maternal disease that can damage prenatal development. A rubella outbreak in 1964–1965 resulted in 30,000 prenatal and neonatal (newborn) deaths, and more than 20,000 infants were born with malformations, including mental retardation, blindness, deafness, and heart problems. The greatest damage occurs when mothers contract rubella in the

Figure 4.4

Teratogens and the Timing of Their Effects on Prenatal Development
The danger of structural defects caused by teratogens is greatest early in embryonic development. This is the period of organogenesis, and it lasts for several months. Later assaults by teratogens typically occur during the fetal period and, instead of doing structural damage, are more likely to stunt growth or cause problems in organ function.

third and fourth weeks of pregnancy, although infection during the second month is also damaging. Elaborate efforts ensure that rubella will never again have the disastrous effects it had in the mid-1960s. A vaccine that prevents German measles is routinely administered to children, and women who plan to have children should have a blood test before they become pregnant to determine if they are immune to the disease.

Syphilis (a sexually transmitted disease) is more damaging later in prenatal development—4 months or more after conception. Rather than affecting organogenesis, as rubella does, syphilis damages organs after they have formed. Damage includes eye lesions, which can cause blindness, and skin lesions. When syphilis is present at birth, other problems involving the central nervous system and gastrointestinal tract can develop. Most states require that pregnant women be given a blood test to detect the presence of syphilis.

Another infection that has received widespread attention recently is genital herpes. Newborns contract this virus when they are delivered through the birth canal of a mother with genital herpes. About one third of babies delivered through an infected birth canal die; another one fourth become brain damaged. If a pregnant woman detects an active case of genital herpes close to her delivery date, a cesarean section can be performed (in which the infant is delivered through the mother's abdomen) to keep the virus from infecting the newborn (Byer & Shainberg, 1991).

Mothers can also transmit AIDS to their offspring (Peterson & others, 1991; Seibert & Olson, 1989). The first infant case of AIDS appeared in this country in 1979. By the end of 1991, 3,000 cumulative cases of AIDS are expected (Task Force on Pediatric AIDS, 1989). In the majority of cases, the mother's infection is linked to her own or her sexual partner's use of intravenous drugs. Most children develop symptoms in the first year of life, including bacterial infections, neurological impairment, and delayed development. Early recognition and treatment of AIDS symptoms may prolong life (Novick, 1989), although treatment is still in the trial stages.

The Mother's Age

When the mother's age is considered in terms of possible harmful effects on the fetus and infant, two time periods are of special interest: adolescence and the thirties and beyond. Approximately one of every five births is to an adolescent; in some urban areas, the figure reaches as high as one in every two births. Infants born to adolescents are often premature. The mortality rate of infants born to adolescent mothers is double that of infants born to mothers in their twenties. Although such figures probably reflect the mother's immature reproductive system, they also may involve poor nutrition, lack of prenatal care, and low socioeconomic status. Prenatal care decreases the probability that a child born to an adolescent girl will have physical problems. However, of women in all age groups, adolescents are the least likely to obtain prenatal assistance from clinics, pediatricians, and health services (Osofsky, 1990; Timberlake & others, 1987).

Increasingly, women are seeking to establish their careers before beginning a family, delaying childbearing until their thirties. Down syndrome, a form of mental retardation, is related to the mother's age. A baby with Down syndrome rarely is born to a mother under the age of 30, but the risk increases after the mother reaches 30. By age 40, the probability is slightly over 1 in 100 and, by age 50, it is almost 1 in 10. The risk also is higher before age 18.

Women also have more difficulty becoming pregnant after the age of 30 (Toth, 1991). In one investigation, the clients of a French fertility clinic all had husbands who were sterile (Schwartz & Mayaux, 1982). To increase their chances of having a child, they were artificially inseminated once a month for 1 year. Each woman had 12 chances to become pregnant. Seventy-five percent of the women in their twenties became pregnant, 62 percent of the women 31 to 35 years old became pregnant, and only 54 percent of the women over 35 years old became pregnant.

We still have much to learn about the role of the mother's age in pregnancy and childbirth. As women remain active, exercise regularly, and are careful about their nutrition, their reproductive systems may remain healthier at older ages than was thought possible in the past. Indeed, as we will see next, the mother's nutrition influences prenatal development.

Nutrition

A developing fetus depends completely on its mother for nutrition, which comes from the mother's blood. Nutritional state is not determined by any specific aspect of diet; among the important factors are the total number of calories and the appropriate levels of protein, vitamins, and minerals. The mother's nutrition even influences her ability to reproduce. In extreme instances of malnutrition, women stop menstruating, thus precluding conception, and children born to malnourished mothers are more likely to be malformed.

One investigation of Iowa mothers documents the important role of nutrition in prenatal development and birth (Jeans, Smith, & Stearns, 1955). The diets of 400 pregnant women were studied and the status of their newborns was assessed. The mothers with the poorest diets were more likely to have offspring who weighed the least, had the least vitality, were born prematurely, or died. In another investigation, diet supplements given to malnourished mothers during pregnancy improved the performance of their offspring during the first 3 years of life (Werner, 1979).

Emotional State and Stress

Tales abound about the way a mother's emotional state affects the fetus. For centuries, it was thought that frightening experiences—a severe thunderstorm or a family member's death—would leave birthmarks on the child or affect the child in more serious ways. Today, we believe that the mother's stress can be transmitted to the fetus, but we have gone beyond thinking that these happenings are somehow magically produced. We now know that, when a pregnant woman experiences intense fears, anxieties, and other emotions, physiological changes occur—in heart rate, respiration, and glandular secretions among them. For example, producing adrenaline in response to fear restricts blood flow to the uterine area and may deprive the fetus of adequate oxygen.

The mother's emotional state during pregnancy can influence the birth process too. An emotionally distraught mother might have irregular contractions and a more difficult labor, which can cause irregularities in the baby's

Nothing vivifies, and nothing kills, like the emotions.

—Joseph Roux

Figure 4.5
Fetal Alcohol Syndrome
This child has fetal alcohol syndrome.
Notice the wide-set eyes, flat bones, and
thin upper lip. This child also is mentally
retarded.

oxygen supply or lead to irregularities after birth. Babies born after extended labor also may adjust more slowly to their world and be more irritable. One investigation revealed a connection between the mother's anxiety during pregnancy and the newborn's condition (Ottinger & Simmons, 1964). In this study, mothers answered a questionnaire about their anxiety every 3 months during pregnancy. When the babies were born, the babies' weights, activity levels, and crying were assessed. The babies of the more anxious mothers cried more before feedings and were more active than the babies born to the less anxious mothers.

Drugs

How do drugs affect prenatal development? Some pregnant women take drugs, smoke tobacco, and drink alcohol without thinking about the possible effects on the fetus. Occasionally, a rash of deformed babies are born, bringing to light the damage drugs can have on a developing fetus. This happened in 1961, when many pregnant women took a popular tranquilizer, called thalidomide, to alleviate their morning sickness. In adults, the effects of thalidomide are mild; in embryos, however, they are devastating. Not all infants were affected in the same way. If the mother took thalidomide on day 26 (probably before she knew she was pregnant), an arm might not grow. If she took the drug 2 days later, the arm might not grow past the elbow. The thalidomide tragedy shocked the medical community and parents into the stark realization that the mother does not have to be a chronic drug user for the fetus to be harmed. Taking the wrong drug at the wrong time is enough to physically handicap the offspring for life.

Heavy drinking by pregnant women can also be devastating to offspring (Coles, Platzman, & Smith, 1991). **Fetal alcohol syndrome (FAS)** *is a cluster of abnormalities that appear in the offspring of mothers who drink alcohol heavily during pregnancy.* The abnormalities include facial deformities and defective limbs, face, and heart. Most of these children are below average in intelligence and some are mentally retarded. Figure 4.5 shows a child with fetal alcohol syndrome. In a recent study, the effects of fetal alcohol syndrome were still apparent in adolescence and adulthood (Streissguth & others, 1991). Adolescents and adults with FAS had an average IQ of 68 (normal is about 100), learning levels equal to second-to-fourth grade, and an abnormally small head and below-average height, and they showed maladaptive behaviors such as poor judgment, distractibility, and social interaction problems. Although no serious malformations such as those produced by FAS are found in infants born to mothers who are moderate drinkers, in one investigation, infants whose mothers drank moderately during pregnancy (for example, one to two drinks a day) were less attentive and alert, with the effects still present at 4 years of age (Streissguth & others, 1984).

Cigarette smoking by pregnant women can also adversely influence prenatal development, birth, and postnatal development (Chasnoff, 1991; Fried & O'Connell, 1991; Streissguth & others, 1991). Fetal and neonatal deaths are higher among smoking mothers; also prevalent are a higher incidence of preterm births and lower birthweights. In one recent investigation, prenatal exposure to cigarette smoking was related to poorer language and cognitive development at 4 years of age (Fried & Watkinson, 1990). In another study, mothers who smoked during pregnancy had infants who were awake more on a consistent basis—a finding one might expect, since the active ingredient in cigarettes is the stimulant nicotine (Landesman-Dwyer, 1983). Respiratory problems and sudden infant death syndrome (also known as crib death) are

Biological Processes, Physical Development, and Perceptual Development

also more common among the offspring of mothers who smoked during pregnancy. Intervention programs designed to get pregnant women to stop smoking are successful in reducing some of smoking's negative effects on offspring, especially in raising their birth weights (Sexton & Hebel, 1984; Vorhees & Mollnow, 1987).

Marijuana use by pregnant women also has detrimental effects on a developing child (Day, 1991). Marijuana use by pregnant mothers is associated with increased tremors and startles among newborns (Fried, Watkinson, & Dillon, 1987) and poorer verbal and memory development at 4 years of age (Fried & Watkinson, 1990).

It is well documented that infants whose mothers are addicted to heroin show several behavioral difficulties (Hans, 1989; Hutchings & Fifer, 1986). The young infants of these mothers are addicted and show withdrawal symptoms characteristic of opiate abstinence, such as tremors, irritability, abnormal crying, disturbed sleep, and impaired motor control. Behavioral problems are often still present at the first birthday, and attention deficits may appear later in the child's development.

With the increased use of cocaine in the United States, there is growing concern about its effects on the embryos, fetuses, and infants of pregnant cocaine users (see figure 4.6). To learn more about researchers' efforts to study the effects of cocaine use by pregnant women, turn to Perspective on Child Development 4.2. A list of the effects of cocaine, and of various other drugs, on offspring and some guidelines for safe use of the drugs are presented in table 4.1.

Environmental Hazards

Radiation, chemicals, and other hazards in our modern industrial world can endanger the fetus. For instance, radiation can cause a gene mutation, an abrupt but permanent change in genetic material. Chromosomal abnormalities are higher among the offspring of fathers exposed to high levels of radiation in their occupations (Schrag & Dixon, 1985). Radiation from X rays also can affect the developing embryo and fetus, with the most dangerous time being the first several weeks after conception, when women do not yet know they are pregnant. It is important for women and their physicians to weigh the risk of an X ray when an actual or potential pregnancy is involved.

Environmental pollutants and toxic wastes are also sources of danger to unborn children. Researchers have found that various hazardous wastes and pesticides cause defects in animals exposed to high doses. Among the dangerous pollutants and wastes are carbon monoxide, mercury, and lead. Some children are exposed to lead because they live in houses where lead-based paint flakes off the walls or near busy highways, where there are heavy automobile emissions from leaded gasoline. Researchers believe that early exposure to lead affects children's mental development. For example, in one investigation, 2-year-old infants who prenatally had high levels of lead in their umbilical cord blood performed poorly on a test of mental development (Bellinger & others, 1987).

Researchers also have found that the manufacturing chemicals known as PCBs are harmful to prenatal development. In one investigation, the extent to which pregnant women ate PCB-polluted fish from Lake Michigan was examined, and subsequently their newborns were observed (Jacobson & others, 1984). Women who had eaten more PCB-polluted fish were more likely to have smaller, preterm infants, who were more likely to react slowly to stimuli.

■ *Critical Thinking*
How can we reduce the number of offspring born to drug-dependent mothers? If you had $100 million to spend to help remedy this problem, what would you do?

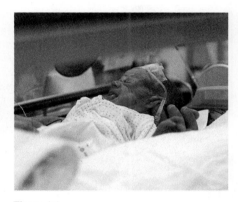

Figure 4.6
A Cocaine Baby
This baby was born addicted to cocaine, because its mother was a cocaine addict. Researchers have found that the offspring of women who take cocaine during pregnancy often have hypertension and heart damage. Many of these infants face a childhood full of medical problems.

Cocaine Babies

Cocaine use during pregnancy has recently attracted considerable attention because of concerns about possible harm to the developing embryo and fetus. Surprisingly little is known about the potential adverse health outcomes associated with cocaine abuse during pregnancy, although a number of research studies are beginning to be conducted (Beckwith & Howard, 1991; Behnke & Eyler, 1991; Dixon, 1991; Lester, 1991). The most consistent finding is that infants born to cocaine abusers have reduced birthweight and length (Chasnoff & others, 1989). There are increased frequencies of congenital abnormalities in the offspring of cocaine users during pregnancy, but other factors in the drug addict's life-style, such as malnutrition and other substance abuse, may be responsible for the congenital abnormalities (Eyler, Behnke, & Stewart, 1990; Little & others, 1989; Stewart, 1990). For example, cocaine users are more likely to smoke cigarettes and marijuana, drink alcohol, and take amphetamines than are non-cocaine users (Little & others, 1989). Teasing apart these potential influences from the effects of cocaine use itself has not yet been adequately accomplished. Obtaining valid information about the frequency and type of drug use by mothers is also complicated because many mothers fear prosecution or loss of custody because of their drug use.

In one recent investigation, 172 mothers who used cocaine prenatally and their offspring were compared with 155 mothers who had not used cocaine prenatally and their offspring (Eyler, Behnke, & Stewart, 1990). Cocaine users were more likely to have more children, to be slightly older, to enter the prenatal care system later, and to use more alcohol and tobacco. Also, in the cocaine-exposed group there were generally lower birthweights, more instances of preterm labor, a greater need for resuscitation, and a larger number of infants who remained hospitalized after birth.

In another investigation, 75 cocaine-using women enrolled in a comprehensive perinatal care program were divided into two groups: those who used cocaine in only the first trimester of pregnancy (23 mothers and their offspring) and those who used cocaine throughout pregnancy (52 mothers and their offspring) (Chasnoff & others, 1989). The outcomes of these pregnancies were compared with the outcomes of a group of pregnant women with no history or evidence of substance abuse (40 mothers and their offspring). Both groups of cocaine-exposed infants had significantly impaired orientation and motor behaviors on the Brazelton Neonatal Behavior Assessment Scale. The mothers who used cocaine throughout their pregnancy were more likely to have a preterm delivery and a low-birthweight infant than were the other two groups of mothers.

Each year, 375,000 babies are born to women who used drugs during pregnancy; in recent years, an increasing number have been cocaine babies. Although some of the babies born to mothers who take drugs during pregnancy will suffer little or no long-term effects, many of the drug-affected infants will require extra attention. One intervention effort aimed at helping drug-abusing mothers and their young children is Operation PAR (Parental Awareness and Responsibility), which serves 28,000 people a year in Florida. Operation PAR includes a day-care center, which in St. Petersburg serves 31 2-to-6-year-old children. Much of what goes on in the day care is indistinguishable from any good day-care center. For example, the staff-to-child ratio is low, teachers are warm and friendly to the children, and there is an abundance of attractive and interesting toys and play areas. What is different are the antidrug cartoons that start early in the children's entrance to the center. Also, the parents whose children are in the center must seek drug treatment and attend parenting-skill groups.

A recent environmental hazard involves women who spend long hours in front of a video display terminal. The fear is that the low level of electromagnetic radiation from the video display terminal adversely affects their offspring. As yet, there is little research about this potential hazard.

At this point, we have discussed a number of ideas about prenatal development. A summary of these ideas is presented in concept table 4.1. Next, we will turn to the study of the birth process.

There was a star danced, and under that I was born.

—William Shakespeare

The Birth Process

Delivery can be as difficult for the baby as for the mother, lasting anywhere from 4 to 24 hours, from which the newborn emerges covered with a thick, greasy, white material called vernix, which eases movement through the birth

TABLE 4.1
Drug Use During Pregnancy

Drug	Effects on fetus and offspring	Safe use of the drug
Alcohol	Small amounts increase risk of spontaneous abortion. Moderate amounts (1-2 drinks a day) are associated with poor attention in infancy. Heavy drinking can lead to fetal alcohol syndrome. Some experts believe that even low-to-moderate amounts, especially in the first 3 months of pregnancy, increase the risk of FAS.	Avoid use.
Nicotine	Heavy smoking is associated with low-birth-weight babies, which means the babies may have more health problems than other infants. Smoking may be especially harmful in the second half of pregnancy.	Avoid use.
Tranquilizers	Taken during the first 3 months of pregnancy, they may cause cleft palate or other congenital malformations.	Avoid use if you might become pregnant and during early pregnancy. Use only under a doctor's supervision.
Barbiturates	Mothers who take large doses may have babies who are addicted. Babies may have tremors, restlessness, and irritability.	Use only under a doctor's supervision.
Amphetamines	They may cause birth defects.	Use only under a doctor's supervision.
Cocaine	Cocaine may cause drug dependency and withdrawal symptoms at birth, as well as physical and mental problems, especially if the mother uses cocaine in the first 3 months of pregnancy. There is a higher risk of hypertension, heart problems, developmental retardation, and learning difficulties.	Avoid use.
Marijuana	It may cause a variety of birth defects and is associated with low birth weight and height.	Avoid use.

Source: Modified from The National Institute on Drug Abuse.

canal. The newborn's head may be swollen at the top because of pressure against the pelvic outlet during the last hours of labor. The baby's face may be puffy and bluish; her ears may be pressed against her head in a bizarre position—matted forward on her cheeks, for example. Her nose may be flattened and skewed to one side by the squeeze through the pelvis. The baby may be bowlegged, and her feet may be cocked pigeon-toed from being up beside her head for so long in the mother's womb; however, they can be flexed and put in a normal position at birth. How stunning it must be to be thrust suddenly into a new, bright, airy world so totally different from the dark, moist warmth of the womb. Despite the drama of human birth, newborns who have had a comfortable stay in the womb and are born when due are well equipped by nature to withstand the birth process.

There are many intriguing questions about the birth process. What kinds of childbirth strategies are available? What are the stages of birth, and what delivery complications can arise? What are preterm infants like? How can we measure the newborn's health and social responsiveness? How crucial is bonding? We will consider each of these in turn.

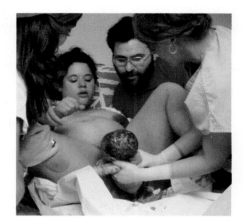

Birth is a time of dramatic transition for a fetus; the baby is on a threshold between two worlds.

Prenatal Development and Birth

121

Concept	Processes/related ideas	Characteristics/description
The course of prenatal development	Germinal period	This period is from conception to about 10 to 14 days later. A fertilized egg is called a zygote. The period ends when the zygote attaches to the uterine wall.
	Embryonic period	The embryonic period lasts from about 2 to 8 weeks after conception. The embryo differentiates into three layers, life-support systems develop, and organ systems form (organogenesis).
	Fetal period	The fetal period lasts from about 2 months after conception until 9 months or when the infant is born. Growth and development continue their dramatic course and organ systems mature to the point where life can be sustained outside the womb.
Miscarriage and abortion	Their nature and ethical issues	A miscarriage, or spontaneous abortion, happens when pregnancy ends before the developing organism is mature enough to survive outside the womb. Estimates indicate that about 15 to 20 percent of all pregnancies end this way, many without the mother's knowledge. Induced abortion is a complex issue medically, psychologically, and socially. An unwanted pregnancy is stressful for the woman regardless of how it is resolved. A recent ethical issue focuses on the use of fetal tissue in transplant operations.
Teratology and hazards to prenatal development	Teratology	This field investigates the causes of congenital (birth) defects. Any agent that causes birth defects is called a teratogen.
	Maternal diseases and conditions	Maternal diseases and infections can cause damage by crossing the placental barrier, or they can be destructive during the birth process. Among the maternal diseases and conditions believed to be involved in possible birth defects are rubella, syphilis, genital herpes, AIDS, the mother's age, nutrition, and emotional state and stress.
	Drugs	Thalidomide was a tranquilizer given to pregnant women to alleviate their morning sickness. In the early 1960s, thousands of babies were malformed as a consequence of their mothers having taken this drug. Alcohol, tobacco, marijuana, heroin, and cocaine are other drugs that can adversely affect prenatal and infant development.
	Environmental hazards	Among the environmental hazards that can endanger the fetus are radiation in occupations and X rays, environmental pollutants, and toxic wastes.

Childbirth Strategies

Controversy swirls over how childbirth should proceed. Some critics argue that the standard delivery practices of most hospitals and physicians need to be overhauled. Others suggest that the entire family—especially the father—should be more involved in childbirth. Others argue that procedures that ensure mother-infant bonding should be followed.

In the standard childbirth procedure that has been practiced for many years—and the way you probably were delivered—the expectant mother is taken to a hospital, where a doctor is responsible for the baby's delivery. The pregnant woman is prepared for labor by having her pubic hair shaved and by having an enema. She then is placed in a labor room often filled with other pregnant women, some of whom are screaming. When she is ready to deliver,

*Birth is not one act
It is a process.*

—Erich Fromm

Biological Processes, Physical Development, and Perceptual Development

she is taken to the delivery room, which looks like an operating room. She is laid on the table with her legs in the air, and the physician, along with an anesthetist and a nurse, delivers the baby.

What could be wrong with this procedure? Critics list three things: (1) Important individuals related to the mother are excluded from the birth process. (2) The mother is separated from her infant in the first minutes and hours after birth. (3) Giving birth is treated like a disease, and a woman is thought of as a sick patient (Rosenblith & Sims-Knight, 1985). As we will see next, some alternatives differ radically from this standard procedure.

The **Leboyer method,** *developed by French obstetrician Frederick Leboyer, intends to make the birth process less stressful for infants. Leboyer's procedure is referred to as "birth without violence."* He describes standard childbirth as torture (Leboyer, 1975). He vehemently objects to holding newborns upside down and slapping or spanking them, putting silver nitrite into their eyes, separating them immediately from their mothers, and scaring them with bright lights and harsh noises in the delivery room. Leboyer also criticizes the traditional habit of cutting the umbilical cord as soon as the infant is born, a situation that forces the infant to immediately take in oxygen from the air to breathe. Leboyer believes that the umbilical cord should be left intact for several minutes to allow the newborn a chance to adjust to a world of breathing air. In the Leboyer method, the baby is placed on the mother's stomach immediately after birth so the mother can caress the infant. Then the infant is placed in a bath of warm water to relax. Although most hospitals do not use the soft lights and warm baths that Leboyer suggests, they sometimes do place the newborn on the mother's stomach immediately after birth, believing that it will stimulate mother-infant bonding.

Another well-known birth procedure that deviates markedly from the standard practice is the **Lamaze method,** *a form of prepared or natural childbirth developed by Fernand Lamaze, a pioneering French obstetrician. It has become widely accepted in the medical profession and involves helping pregnant women cope actively with the pain of childbirth to avoid or reduce medication.* Lamaze training for parents is available on a widespread basis in the United States and usually consists of six weekly classes. In these classes, pregnant women learn about the birth process and are trained in breathing and relaxation exercises. As the Lamaze method has grown in popularity, it has become more common for fathers to participate in the exercises and to assist in the birth process.

We must respect this instant of birth, this fragile moment. The baby is between two worlds, on a threshold, hesitating . . .
—Frederick Leboyer

As the Lamaze method has become popular, it has become common for fathers to assist in the birth process.

Stages of Birth and Delivery Complications

The birth process occurs in three stages. For a woman having her first child, the first stage lasts an average of 12 to 24 hours; it is the longest of the three stages. In the first stage, uterine contractions are 15 to 20 minutes apart at the beginning and last up to a minute. These contractions cause the woman's cervix to stretch and open. As the first stage progresses, the contractions come closer together, appearing every 2 to 5 minutes. Their intensity increases too. By the end of the first birth stage, contractions dilate the cervix to an opening of about 4 inches so that the baby can move from the uterus to the birth canal.

The second birth stage begins when the baby's head starts to move through the cervix and the birth canal. It terminates when the baby completely emerges from the mother's body. This stage lasts approximately 1½ hours. With each contraction, the mother bears down hard to push the baby out of her body. By the time the baby's head is out of the mother's body, the contractions come almost every minute and last for about a minute.

Afterbirth *is the third birth stage, at which time the placenta, umbilical cord, and other membranes are detached and expelled.* This final stage is the shortest of the three birth stages, lasting only minutes.

Complications can accompany the baby's delivery. **Precipitate** *is a form of delivery that takes place too rapidly. A precipitate delivery is one in which the baby takes less than 10 minutes to be squeezed through the birth canal.* This deviation in delivery can disturb the infant's normal flow of blood, and the pressure on the infant's head can cause hemorrhaging. On the other hand, **anoxia,** *the insufficient availability of oxygen to the infant,* can develop if the delivery takes too long. Anoxia can cause brain damage.

The **breech position** *is the baby's position in the uterus that causes the buttocks to be the first part to emerge from the vagina.* Normally, the crown of the baby's head comes through the vagina first, but, in 1 of every 25 babies, the head does not come through first. Breech babies' heads are still in the uterus when the rest of their bodies are out, which can cause respiratory problems. Some breech babies cannot be passed through the cervix and must be delivered by cesarean section.

A **cesarean section** *is the surgical removal of the baby from the uterus.* A cesarean section is usually performed if the baby is in a breech position, if it is lying crosswise in the uterus, if the baby's head is too large to pass through the mother's pelvis, if the baby develops complications, or if the mother is bleeding vaginally. The benefits and risks of cesarean section delivery are debated. Cesarean section deliveries are safer than breech deliveries, but a higher infection rate, a longer hospital stay, greater expense, and the stress that accompanies any surgery characterize cesarean section deliveries. Some critics believe that, in the United States, too many babies are delivered by cesarean section. More cesarean sections are performed in the United States than in any other industrialized nation. From 1979 to 1987, the cesarean section rate increased almost 50 percent in the United States alone, to an annual rate of 24 percent (Marieskind, 1989). However, a growing use of vaginal birth after a previous cesarean, greater public awareness, and peer pressure in the medical community are beginning to slow the rate of increase (Enkin, 1989; Marieskind, 1989).

Biological Processes, Physical Development, and Perceptual Development

Use of Drugs During Childbirth

Drugs can be used to relieve pain and anxiety and to speed delivery during the birth process. The widest use of drugs during delivery is to relieve the expectant mother's pain or anxiety. A wide variety of tranquilizers, sedatives, and analgesics are used for this purpose. Researchers are interested in the effects of these drugs because their use is so widespread and because they can cross the placental barrier. One survey of hospitals found that only 5 percent of deliveries involved no anesthesia (Brackbill, 1979).

Oxytocin, *a hormone that stimulates and regulates the rhythmicity of uterine contractions, has been widely used as a drug to speed delivery.* Controversy surrounds the use of this drug. Some physicians argue that it can save the mother's life or keep the infant from being damaged. They also stress that using the drug allows the mother to be well rested and prepared for the birth process. Critics argue that babies born to mothers who have taken oxytocin are more likely to have jaundice; that induced labor requires more pain-killing drugs; and that greater medical care is required after the birth, resulting in the separation of the infant and mother.

The following conclusions can be reached, based on research about the influence of drugs during delivery (Rosenblith & Sims-Knight, 1985):

1. Few research studies have been done, and many that have been completed have had methodological problems. However, not all drugs have similar effects. Some—tranquilizers, sedatives, and analgesics, for example—do not seem to have long-term effects. Other drugs—oxytocin, for example—are suspected of having long-term effects.
2. The degree to which a drug influences the infant is usually small. Birthweight and social class, for instance, are more powerful predictors of infant difficulties than are drugs.
3. A specific drug may affect some infants but not others. In some cases, the drug may have a beneficial effect, whereas in others it may be harmful.
4. The overall amount of medication may be an important factor in understanding drug effects on delivery.

■ *Critical Thinking*
After reading the information on the use of drugs during childbirth, what considerations would be foremost in your mind if your offspring is about to be born? What questions about the use of drugs during delivery would you want to ask the individuals responsible for delivering the baby?

Preterm Infants and Age-Weight Considerations

A full-term infant is one who has grown in the womb for the full 38 to 42 weeks between conception and delivery. A **preterm infant** *(also called a premature infant) is one who is born prior to 38 weeks after conception.* **Low-birthweight infants** *are infants born after a regular period of gestation (the length of time between conception and birth) of 38 to 42 weeks, but who weigh less than 5½ pounds.* Both preterm and low-birthweight infants are considered high-risk infants (Crisafi & Driscoll, 1991; Dedrick & others, 1991; Holmes, Reich, & Gyurke, 1989; Hunt & Cooper, 1989). In one recent study, an intervention program was implemented to improve the developmental outcomes of low-birthweight infants (Achenbach & others, 1990). The program was designed to enhance the mother's adjustment to the care of a low-birthweight infant by (a) enabling the mother to appreciate her baby's specific behavioral and temperamental characteristics; (b) sensitizing her to the baby's cues, especially those that signal stimulus overload, distress, and readiness for interaction; and (c) teaching her to respond appropriately to those cues to facilitate mutually satisfying interactions. The intervention involved seven hospital sessions and four home sessions, in which a nurse helped mothers adapt

Some infants are born very early and have a precariously low birthweight. Shown here is a "kilogram kid," who weighs less than 2.3 pounds. In neonatal care units, banks of flashing lights, blinking numbers, and beeping alarms stand guard over extremely premature infants. Their vital signs, such as brain waves, heartbeat, and respiratory rate, are monitored constantly.

to their low-birthweight babies. At age 7, the low-birthweight babies whose mothers had participated in the intervention program scored higher than a control group of low-birthweight babies on information-processing measures. The researchers commented that the intervention prevented cognitive lags among low-birthweight children and that long-term follow-ups are needed to overcome major biological and environmental risks.

A short gestation period does not necessarily harm an infant. It is distinguished from retarded prenatal growth, in which the fetus has been damaged (Kopp, 1983, 1987). The neurological development of a short-gestation infant continues after birth on approximately the same timetable as if the infant still were in the womb. For example, consider an infant born after a gestation period of 30 weeks. At 38 weeks, approximately 2 months after birth, this infant shows the same level of brain development as a 38-week fetus who is yet to be born.

Some infants are born very early and have a precariously low birthweight. "Kilogram kids" weigh less than 2.3 pounds (which is 1 kilogram, or 1,000 grams) and are very premature. The task of saving such a baby is not easy. At the Stanford University Medical Center in Palo Alto, California, 98 percent of the preterm babies survive; however, 32 percent of those between 750 and 1,000 grams do not, and 76 percent of those below 750 grams do not. Approximately 250,000 preterm babies are born in the United States each year and more than 15,000 of these weigh less than 1,000 grams.

Preterm infants have a different profile from that of full-term infants. For instance, Tiffany Field (1979) found that 4-month-old preterm infants vocalize less, fuss more, and avoid eye contact more than their full-term counterparts. Other researchers have found differences in the information-processing skills of preterm and full-term infants. In one investigation, Susan Rose and her colleagues (1988) found that 7-month-old high-risk preterm infants are less visually attentive to novelty and show deficits in visual recognition memory when compared with full-term infants.

Some Conclusions About Preterm Infants

What conclusions can we draw from the results of research about preterm infants? Four such conclusions seem appropriate (Kopp, 1983, 1987; Kopp & Kaler, 1989):

1. As intensive care technology has improved, there have been fewer serious consequences of preterm births. For instance, from 1961 to 1965, the manner of feeding preterm infants changed and intravenous fluid therapy came into use. From 1966 to 1968, better control of hypoxemia (oxygen deficiency) was gained. In 1971, artificial ventilation was introduced. In the mid-1970s, neonatal support systems became less intrusive and damaging to infants.
2. Infants born with a problem that is identifiable at birth are likely to have a poorer developmental future than infants born without a recognizable problem (Cohen & others, 1989). For instance, extremely sick or extremely tiny babies are less likely to survive than healthy or normal-weight babies.
3. Social class differences are associated with preterm infants' development. The higher the socioeconomic status, the more favorable is the developmental outcome for a newborn. Social class differences also are tied to many other differences. For

Biological Processes, Physical Development, and Perceptual Development

example, the quality of the environment, cigarette and alcohol consumption, IQ, and knowledge of competent parenting strategies are associated with social class; less positive characteristics are associated with lower-class families.

4. We do not have solid evidence that preterm infants, as a rule, have difficulty later in school. Nor is there good evidence that preterm children perform poorly on IQ and information-processing tests.

Despite the advances made in prenatal care and technology in the United States, the availability of high-quality medical and educational services still needs much improvement. In some countries, especially in Scandinavia and western Europe, more consistent, higher-quality prenatal care is provided than in the United States. To read further about the nature of prenatal care in different countries, turn to Cultural Worlds of Development 4.2.

Stimulation of Preterm Infants

Just 3 decades ago, preterm infants were perceived to be too fragile to cope well with environmental stimulation, and the recommendation was to handle such infants as little as possible. The climate of opinion changed when the adverse effects of maternal deprivation (mothers' neglect of their infants) became known and was interpreted to include a lack of stimulation. A number of research studies followed that indicated a "more is better" approach in the stimulation of preterm infants. Today, however, experts on infant development argue that preterm infant care is far too complex to be described only in terms of amount of stimulation (Field, 1990; Korner, 1990; Lester & Tronick, 1990b).

Recently, experts on the stimulation of preterm infants held a roundtable discussion and offered the following recommendations (Lester & Tronick, 1990a):

1. Preterm infants' responses to stimulation vary with their conceptual age, illness, and individual makeup. The immature brain of the preterm infant may be more vulnerable to excessive, inappropriate, or mistimed stimulation. The very immature infant should probably be protected from stimulation that could destabilize its homeostatic condition.

2. As the healthy preterm infant becomes less fragile and approaches term, the issue of what is appropriate stimulation should be considered. Infants' behavioral cues can be used to determine appropriate interventions. An infant's signs of stress or avoidance behaviors indicate that stimulation should be terminated. Positive behaviors indicate that stimulation is appropriate. To read about the stimulation strategies of massage and exercise used with preterm infants, turn to Perspective on Child Development 4.3.

3. Intervention with the preterm infant should be organized in the form of an individualized developmental plan. This plan should be constructed as a psychosocial intervention to include the parents and other immediate family members and to acknowledge the socioeconomic, cultural, and home environmental factors that will determine the social context in which the infant will be reared. The developmental plan should also include assessing the infant's behavior, working with the

Prenatal Care in the United States and Around the World

As advanced a nation as the United States has become economically and technologically, it still has more low-birthweight infants than a number of other countries (Grant, 1986). As indicated in table 4.A, only 4 percent of the infants born in Sweden, Finland, the Netherlands, and Norway are low-birthweight, and only 5 percent of those born in New Zealand, Australia, France, and Japan are low-birthweight. In the United States, 7 percent of all infants are low-birthweight. Also, as indicated in table 4.A, in some developing countries, such as Bangladesh, where poverty is rampant and the health and nutrition of mothers are poor, the percentage of low-birthweight infants reaches as high as 50 percent of all infants.

In the United States, there also are discrepancies between the nature of prenatal development and the birth of Black infants and White infants. Black infants are twice as likely to be born prematurely, have low birthweight, and have mothers who received late or no prenatal care; are three times as likely to have their mothers die in childbirth; and are five times as likely to be born to unmarried teenage mothers (Edelman, 1987).

In many of the countries with a lower percentage of low-birthweight infants than the United States, either free or very-low-cost prenatal and postnatal care is available to mothers. This care includes paid maternity leave from work that ranges from 9 to 40 weeks (Miller, 1987). In Norway and the Netherlands, prenatal care is coordinated with a general practitioner, an obstetrician, and a midwife.

Pregnant women in the United States do not receive the uniform prenatal care that women in many Scandinavian and western European countries receive. The United States does not have a national policy of health care that assures high-quality assistance for pregnant women. The cost of giving birth is approximately $4,000 in the United States (more than $5,000 for a cesarean birth), and more than 25 percent of all American women of prime childbearing age do not have insurance that will pay for hospital costs. More than one fifth of all White mothers and one third of all Black mothers do not receive prenatal care in the first trimester of their pregnancy. Five percent of White mothers and 10 percent of Black mothers receive no prenatal care at all (Wegman, 1986). Many infant-development researchers believe that the United States needs more comprehensive medical and educational services to improve the quality of prenatal care and reduce the percentage of low-birthweight infants.

TABLE 4.A
Percentage of Low-Birthweight Infants

Country	Low-Birthweight Infants %
Bangladesh	50
India	30
Guatemala	18
Iran	14
Mexico	12
USSR	9
United States, Great Britain, Israel, Egypt	7
Canada, China	6
New Zealand, Australia, France, Japan	5
Sweden, Finland, the Netherlands, Norway	4

Massaging and Exercising Preemies

In one investigation, 40 preterm infants who had just been released from an intensive-care unit and placed in a transitional nursery were studied (Field, Scafidi, & Schanberg, 1987). Twenty of the preterm babies were given special stimulation with massage and exercise techniques for three 15-minute periods at the beginning of 3 consecutive hours every morning for 10 weekdays. For example, each infant was placed on its stomach and gently stroked. The massage began with the head and neck and moved downward to the feet. It also moved from the shoulders down to the hands. The infant was then rolled over. Each arm and leg was flexed and extended; then both legs together were flexed and extended. Next, the massage was repeated.

The massaged and exercised preterm babies gained 47 percent more weight than their preterm counterparts who were not massaged and exercised, even though both groups had the same number of feedings per day and averaged the same intake of formula. The increased activity of the massaged, exercised infants would seem to work against weight gain. However, similar findings have been found with animals. The increased activity may increase gastrointestinal and metabolic efficiency. The massaged infants were also more active and alert, and they performed better on developmental tests. Also, their hospital stay was about 6 days shorter than the nonmassaged, nonexercised group's. This saved about $3,000 per preterm infant.

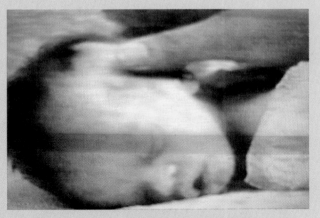

This preterm baby is being massaged as part of Tiffany Field's investigation of the effects of massage and exercise on infant development. The massaged and exercised infants were more active and more alert and performed better on developmental tests than their preterm counterparts who were not massaged and exercised.

The massaged, exercised infants also were more socially interactive than the other infants. This may happen because massage stimulates intimacy between infants and the social figures in their world (Field, 1991).

parents to help them understand the infant's medical and behavioral status, and helping the parents deal with their own feelings (Lester & others, 1990).

Measures of Neonatal Health and Responsiveness

The **Apgar scale** *is a method widely used to assess the health of newborns at 1 and 5 minutes after birth. The Apgar scale evaluates infants' heart rate, respiratory effort, muscle tone, body color, and reflex irritability.* An obstetrician or nurse does the evaluation and gives the newborn a score, or reading, of 0, 1, or 2 on each of these five health signs (see table 4.2). A total score of 7 to 10 indicates that the newborn's condition is good, a score of 5 indicates there may be developmental difficulties, and a score of 3 or below signals an emergency and indicates that the baby's survival may be in doubt.

TABLE 4.2
The Apgar Scale

Health sign	Score		
	0	*1*	*2*
Heart rate	Absent	Slow—fewer than 100 beats per minute	Fast—100-140 beats per minute
Respiratory effort	No breathing for more than 1 minute	Irregular and slow	Good breathing with normal crying
Muscle tone	Limp and flaccid	Weak and inactive, but some flexion of extremities	Strong, active motion
Body color	Blue and pale	Body pink but extremeties blue	Entire body pink
Reflex irritability	No response	Grimace	Coughing, sneezing, and crying

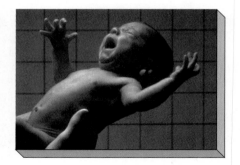

From V. A. Apgar, "A Proposal for a New Method of Evaluation of a Newborn Infant" in *Anesthesia and Analgesia: Current Researches*, 32:260–267, 1953. Copyright © 1953 International Anesthesia Research Society, Cleveland, OH. Reprinted by permission.

Whereas the Apgar scale is used immediately after birth to identify high-risk infants who need resuscitation, the **Brazelton Neonatal Behavioral Assessment Scale** *is given several days after birth to assess the newborn's neurological development, reflexes, and reactions to people* (Brazelton, 1973, 1984; Brazelton, Nugent, & Lester, 1987). The Brazelton scale is usually given on the third day of life and then repeated several days later. Twenty reflexes are assessed, along with reactions to circumstances such as the infant's reaction to a rattle. The examiner rates the newborn, or neonate, on each of 26 categories (see table 4.3). As an indication of how detailed the ratings are, consider item 14 in table 4.3: "cuddliness." As shown in table 4.4, nine categories are involved in assessing this item, with infant behavior scored on a continuum that ranges from the infant being very resistant to being held to the infant being extremely cuddly and clinging. The Brazelton scale not only is used as a sensitive index of neurological competence in the week after birth, but it also is used widely as a measure in many research studies on infant development. In recent versions of scoring the Brazelton scale, Brazelton and his colleagues (1987) categorize the 26 items into four categories—physiological, motoric, state, and interaction. They also classify the baby in global terms, such as "worrisome," "normal," or "superior," based on these categories.

A very low Brazelton score can indicate brain damage. However, if an infant merely seems sluggish in responding to social circumstances, parents are encouraged to give the infant attention and to undergo **Brazelton training,** *which involves using the Brazelton scale to show parents how their newborn*

TABLE 4.3
The Categories on the Brazelton Neonatal Behavioral Assessment Scale

1. Response decrement to repeated visual stimuli
2. Response decrement to rattle
3. Response decrement to bell
4. Response decrement to pinprick
5. Orienting response to inanimate visual stimuli
6. Orienting response to inanimate auditory stimuli
7. Orienting response to animate visual stimuli—examiner's face
8. Orienting response to animate auditory stimuli—examiner's voice
9. Orienting responses to animate visual and auditory stimuli
10. Quality and duration of alert periods
11. General muscle tone—in resting and in response to being handled, passive, and active
12. Motor activity
13. Traction responses as he or she is pulled to sit
14. Cuddliness—responses to being cuddled by examiner
15. Defensive movements—reactions to a cloth over his or her face
16. Consolability with intervention by examiner
17. Peak of excitement and capacity to control self
18. Rapidity of buildup to crying state
19. Irritability during the examination
20. General assessment of kind and degree of activity
21. Tremulousness
22. Amount of startling
23. Lability of skin color—measuring autonomic lability
24. Lability of states during entire examination
25. Self-quieting activity—attempts to console self and control state
26. Hand-to-mouth activity

From *Cultural Perspectives on Child Development* by Daniel A. Wagner and Harold W. Stevenson. Copyright 1982 W. H. Freeman and Company. Reprinted with permission.

TABLE 4.4
The Assessment of Cuddliness on the Brazelton Neonatal Behavioral Assessment Scale

Score	Infant behavior
1	The infant resists being held and continually pushes away, thrashes, and stiffens.
2	The infant resists being held most of the time.
3	The infant does not resist but does not participate either, acting like a rag doll.
4	The infant eventually molds into the examiner's arms after considerable nestling and cuddling efforts by the examiner.
5	The infant usually molds and relaxes when initially held, nestling into the examiner's neck or crook of the elbow. The infant leans forward when held on the examiner's shoulder.
6	The infant always molds at the beginning, as described above.
7	The infant always molds initially with nestling and turns toward body and leans forward.
8	The infant molds and relaxes, nestles and turns head, leans forward on the shoulder, fits feet into cavity of other arm, and all of the body participates.
9	All of the above take place and, in addition, the infant grasps the examiner and clings.

From *In the Beginning: Development in the First Two Years,* by J. F. Rosenblith and J. E. Sims Knight. Copyright © 1985 by Wadsworth, Inc. Reprinted by permission of Brooks/Cole Publishing Company, Pacific Grove, CA 93950.

How critical is bonding for the development of social competence later in childhood?

responds to people (Brazelton, 1987, 1989). As part of the training, parents are shown how the neonate can respond positively to people and how such responses can be stimulated. Brazelton training has improved the social interaction of high-risk infants as well as the social skills of healthy, responsive infants (Widmayer & Field, 1980; Worobey & Belsky, 1982).

Bonding

Bonding *is the occurrence of close contact, especially physical, between parents and newborn in the period shortly after birth.* Some physicians believe that this period shortly after birth is critical in development; during this time, the parents and child need to form an important emotional attachment that provides a foundation for optimal development in years to come. Special interest in bonding came about when some pediatricians argued that the circumstances surrounding delivery often separate mothers and their infants, preventing or making difficult the development of a bond. The pediatricians further argued that giving the mother drugs to make her delivery less painful may contribute to the lack of bonding. The drugs may make the mother drowsy, thus interfering with her ability to respond to and stimulate the newborn. Advocates of bonding also assert that preterm infants are isolated from their mothers to an even greater degree than full-term infants, thereby increasing their difficulty in bonding.

Is there evidence that such close contact between mothers and newborns is absolutely critical for optimal development later in life? Although some research supports the bonding hypothesis (Klaus & Kennell, 1976), a growing body of research challenges the significance of the first few days of life as a critical period (Bakeman & Brown, 1980; Rode & others, 1981). Indeed, the extreme form of the bonding hypothesis—that the newborn must have close contact with the mother in the first few days of life to develop optimally—simply is not true.

Nonetheless, the weakness of the maternal-infant bonding research should not be used as an excuse to keep motivated mothers from interacting with their infants in the postpartum period, because such contact brings pleasure to many mothers. In some mother-infant pairs—including preterm infants, adolescent mothers, or mothers from disadvantaged circumstances—the practice of bonding may set in motion a climate for improved interaction after the mother and infant leave the hospital (Maccoby & Martin, 1983).

We have discussed many dimensions of the birth process. For a summary of the main points of this discussion, turn to concept table 4.2. This concludes our discussion of biological beginnings. In the next chapter, we will turn our attention to the nature of infant development.

Biological Processes, Physical Development, and Perceptual Development

The Birth Process

Concept	Processes/related ideas	Characteristics/description
Childbirth strategies	Their nature	A controversy currently exists over how childbirth should proceed. Standard childbirth has been criticized, and the Leboyer and Lamaze methods have been developed as alternatives. Medical doctors deliver most babies in the United States.
Stages of birth and complications	Stages	Three stages of birth have been defined. The first lasts about 12 to 24 hours for a woman having her first child. The cervix dilates to about 4 inches. The second stage begins when the baby's head moves through the cervix and ends with the baby's complete emergence. The third stage is afterbirth.
	Complications	A baby can move through the birth canal too rapidly or too slowly. A delivery that is too fast is called precipitate; when delivery is too slow, anoxia may result. A cesarean section is the surgical removal of the baby from the uterus.
Use of drugs during childbirth	Drugs used to relieve pain and anxiety and to speed up delivery	A wide variety of tranquilizers, sedatives, and analgesics are used to relieve the expectant mother's pain and anxiety, and oxytocin is used to speed delivery. Birthweight and social class are more powerful predictors of problems than are drugs. A drug can have mixed effects and the overall amount of medication needs to be considered.
Preterm infants and age-weight considerations	Types	Preterm infants are those born after an abnormally short time period in the womb. Infants who are born after a regular gestation period of 38 to 42 weeks but who weigh less than 5½ pounds are called low-birthweight infants.
	Conclusions	As intensive-care technology has improved, preterm babies have benefited considerably. Infants born with an identifiable problem have a poorer developmental future than those born without a recognizable problem. Social class differences are associated with development. There is no solid evidence that preterm infants perform more poorly than full-term infants when they are assessed years later in school.
	Stimulation	Preterm infant care is much too complex to be described only in terms of amount of stimulation. Preterm infants' responses vary according to their conceptual age, illness, and individual makeup. Infant behavioral cues can be used to indicate the appropriate stimulation. Intervention should be organized in the form of an individualized developmental plan.
Measures of neonatal health and responsiveness	Types	For many years, the Apgar scale has been used to assess the newborn's health. A more recently developed test—the Brazelton Neonatal Behavioral Assessment Scale—is used for long-term neurological assessment. It assesses not only the newborn's neurological integrity but also social responsiveness. If the newborn is sluggish, Brazelton training is recommended.
Bonding	Its nature	There is evidence that bonding—establishment of a close parent-infant relationship in the first hours or days after birth—is not critical for optimal development, although for some mother-infant pairs it may stimulate interaction after they leave the hospital.

Summary

I. The Course of Prenatal Development

Prenatal development is divided into three periods. The germinal period lasts from conception to about 10 to 14 days. The fertilized egg is called a zygote. This period ends when the zygote attaches to the uterine wall. The embryonic period lasts from 2 to 8 weeks after conception. The embryo differentiates into three layers, life-support systems develop, and organ systems form (organogenesis). The fetal period lasts from 2 months after conception until 9 months or birth. Growth and development continue their dramatic course, and organ systems mature to the point that life can be sustained outside the womb.

II. Miscarriage and Abortion

A miscarriage, or spontaneous abortion, happens when pregnancy ends before the developing organism is mature enough to survive outside the womb. Estimates indicate that about 15 to 20 percent of all pregnancies end this way, many without the mother's knowledge. Induced abortion is a complex issue medically, psychologically, and socially. An unwanted pregnancy is stressful for the woman regardless of how it is resolved. A recent ethical issue focuses on the use of fetal tissue in transplant operations.

III. Teratology and the Hazards to Prenatal Development

Teratology is the field that investigates the causes of congenital (birth) defects. Any agent that causes birth defects is called a teratogen. Maternal diseases and infections can cause damage by crossing the placental barrier, or they can be destructive during the birth process itself. Among the maternal diseases and conditions believed to be involved in possible birth defects are rubella; syphilis; genital herpes; and the mother's age, nutrition, and emotional state and stress. Thalidomide is a tranquilizer that was given to pregnant women to reduce their morning sickness. In the early 1960s, thousands of babies were malformed as a consequence of their mother taking this drug. Alcohol, tobacco, marijuana, heroin, and cocaine are other drugs that can adversely affect prenatal and infant development. Among the environmental hazards that can endanger the fetus are radiation in occupations and X rays, environmental pollutants, and toxic wastes.

IV. Childbirth Strategies

A controversy exists over how childbirth should proceed. Standard childbirth has been criticized, and the Leboyer and Lamaze methods have been developed as alternatives. Medical doctors deliver most babies in the United States.

V. Stages of Birth and Complications

Three stages of birth have been defined. The first lasts about 12 to 24 hours for a woman having her first child. The cervix dilates to about 4 inches. The second stage begins when the baby's head moves through the cervix and ends with the baby's complete emergence. The third stage is afterbirth. A baby can move through the birth canal too quickly or too slowly. A delivery that is too fast is called precipitate; when delivery is too slow, anoxia may result. A cesarean section is the surgical removal of the baby from the uterus.

VI. Use of Drugs During Childbirth

A wide variety of tranquilizers, sedatives, and analgesics are used to relieve the expectant mother's pain and anxiety, and oxytocin is used to speed delivery. Birthweight and social class are more powerful predictors of problems than are drugs. A specific drug can have mixed effects, and the overall amount of medication needs to be considered.

VII. Preterm Infants and Age-Weight Considerations

Preterm infants are those born after an abnormally short time period in the womb. Infants who are born after a regular gestation period of 38 to 42 weeks but who weigh less than 5½ pounds are called low-birth-weight infants. As intensive-care technology has improved, preterm babies have benefited considerably. Infants born with an identifiable problem have a poorer developmental future than those born without a recognizable problem. Social class differences are associated with development. There is no solid evidence that preterm infants perform more poorly than full-term infants when they are assessed years later in school. Preterm infant care is much too complex to be described only in terms of the amount of stimulation. Preterm infants' responses vary according to their conceptual age, illness, and individual makeup. Infant behavioral cues can be used to indicate appropriate stimulation. Intervention should be organized in the form of an individualized developmental plan.

VIII. Measures of Neonatal Health and Responsiveness

For many years, the Apgar scale has been used to assess the newborn's health. A more recently developed test—the Brazelton Neonatal Behavioral Assessment Scale—is used for long-term neurological assessment. It assesses not only the newborn's neurological integrity but also its social responsiveness. If the newborn is sluggish, Brazelton training is recommended.

IX. Bonding

There is evidence that bonding—establishment of a close parent-infant relationship in the first hours or days after birth—is not critical for optimal development, although for some mother-infant pairs it may stimulate interaction after they leave the hospital.

Key Terms

germinal period 108
blastocyst 109
trophoblast 109
implantation 109
embryonic period 109
endoderm 109
ectoderm 109
mesoderm 109
placenta 110
umbilical cord 110
amnion 110
organogenesis 110
fetal period 111
teratogen 113
fetal alcohol syndrome
  (FAS) 118

Leboyer method 123
Lamaze method 123
afterbirth 124
precipitate 124
anoxia 124
breech position 124
cesarean section 124
oxytocin 125
preterm infant 125
low-birthweight infants 125
Apgar scale 129
Brazelton Neonatal
  Behavioral Assessment
  Scale 130
Brazelton training 130
bonding 132

Suggested Readings

Brazelton, T. B., & Lester, B. M. (1982). *New approaches to developmental screenings of infants.* New York: Elsevier. A group of experts on infant development relate new developments in the assessment of newborns.

Falkner, F., & Macy, C. (1980). *Pregnancy and birth.* New York: Harper & Row. This is an easy-to-read description of experiences during pregnancy and the nature of childbearing.

Lester, B. M., & Tronick, E. Z. (Eds.). (1990). *Stimulation and the preterm infant: The limits of plasticity.* Philadelphia, PA: W. B. Saunders. This book is based on a roundtable discussion by a number of leading experts in the field of prenatal development and birth. The result is a provocative set of chapters that addresses important issues in intervention with preterm infants.

Nilsson, L. (1966). *A child is born.* New York: Delacourt. An abundance of breathtaking photographs take you inside the womb to see the developmental unfolding of a zygote, an embryo, and a fetus.

5

PHYSICAL, MOTOR, AND PERCEPTUAL DEVELOPMENT IN INFANCY

Physical Growth and Development in Infancy
  Reflexes
  Emotions
  States
  Physical Growth and Motor Development
  The Brain
  Perspective on Child Development 5.1: Babies Don't Need Exercise Classes
  Nutrition
  Perspective on Child Development 5.2: What's Good Food for an Adult Can Be Bad Food for a Baby
  Cultural Worlds of Development 5.1: Children Living Hungry in America
Sensory and Perceptual Development
  What Are Sensation and Perception?
  Visual Perception
  Hearing
  Smell
  Taste
  Touch
  Pain
  Perspective on Child Development 5.3: The Fetus and The Cat in the Hat
  Perspective on Child Development 5.4: Yellow Kangaroos, Gray Donkeys, Thumps, Gongs, and 4-Month-Old Infants
  Intermodal Perception
Summary
Key Terms
Suggested Readings

A BABY IS THE MOST COMPLICATED OBJECT MADE BY UNSKILLED LABOR.

—Anonymous

The creature has poor motor coordination and can move itself only with great difficulty. Its general behavior appears to be disorganized, and, although it cries when uncomfortable, it uses few other vocalizations. In fact, it sleeps most of the time, about 16 to 17 hours a day. You are curious about this creature and want to know more about what it can do. You think to yourself, "I wonder if it can see. How could I find out?"

You obviously have a communication problem with the creature. You must devise a way that will allow the creature to "tell" you that it can see. While examining the creature one day, you make an interesting discovery. When you move a large object toward it, it moves its head backward, as if to avoid a collision with the object. The creature's head movement suggests that it has at least some vision.

In case you haven't already guessed, the creature you have been reading about is the human infant, and the role you played is that of a developmentalist interested in devising techniques to learn about the infant's visual perception. After years of work, scientists have developed research tools and methods sophisticated enough to examine the subtle abilities of infants and to interpret their complex actions. Videotape equipment allows researchers to investigate elusive behaviors, and high-speed computers make it possible to perform complex data analysis in minutes instead of months and years. Other sophisticated equipment is used to closely monitor respiration, heart rate, body movement, visual fixation, and sucking behavior, which provide clues to what is going on inside the infant.

Among the first things developmentalists were able to demonstrate was that infants have highly developed perceptual motor systems. Until recently, even some nurses in maternity hospitals believed that newborns are blind at birth, and they told this to mothers. Most parents were also told that their newborns could not taste, smell, or feel pain. As you will discover later in this chapter, we now know that newborns can see (albeit fuzzily), taste, smell, and feel pain. Before we turn to the fascinating world of the infant's perception, however, we will discuss a number of ideas about infants' and children's physical development.

Physical Growth and Development in Infancy

How do infants respond to their world? Can infants express emotion? What are an infant's states like? What is the nature of the infant's nutritional world? We will consider each of these questions in turn.

Reflexes

The newborn is not an empty-headed organism. Among other things, it has some basic reflexes that are genetically carried survival mechanisms. For example, the newborn has no fear of water; it will naturally hold its breath and contract its throat to keep water out.

■ *Critical Thinking*
Other than moving a large object toward a newborn's head to see if the newborn responds to it, can you think of other techniques that could be used to determine whether a newborn can see?

Reflexes govern the newborn's movements, which are automatic and beyond the newborn's control. They are built-in reactions to certain stimuli. They provide young infants with adaptive responses to their environment before they have had the opportunity to learn. The **sucking reflex** *occurs when newborns automatically suck an object placed in their mouth. The sucking reflex enables newborns to get nourishment before they have associated a nipple with food.* The sucking reflex is an example of a reflex that is present at birth but later disappears. The **rooting reflex** *occurs when the infant's cheek is stroked or the side of its mouth is touched. In response, the infant turns its head toward the side that was touched in an apparent effort to find something to suck.* The sucking and rooting reflexes disappear when the infant is about 3 to 4 months old. They are replaced by the infant's voluntary eating. The sucking and rooting reflexes have survival value for newborn mammals, who must find the mother's breast to obtain nourishment.

The **Moro reflex** *is a neonatal startle response that occurs in reaction to a sudden, intense noise or movement. When startled, the newborn arches its back, throws its head back, and flings out its arms and legs. Then, the newborn rapidly closes its arms and legs to the center of its body.* The Moro reflex is a vestige from our primate ancestory and it, too, has survival value. This reflex—normal in all newborns—also tends to disappear at 3 to 4 months of age. Steady pressure on any part of the infant's body calms the infant after it has been startled, as will holding the infant's arm flexed at the shoulder.

Some reflexes present in the newborn—coughing, blinking, and yawning, for example—persist throughout life. They are as important for adults as they are for infants. Other reflexes, though, disappear several months following birth as the infant's brain functions mature, and voluntary control over many behaviors develops. The movements of some reflexes eventually become incorporated into more complex, voluntary actions. One important example is the **grasping reflex,** *which occurs when something touches the infant's palms. The infant responds by grasping tightly.* By the end of the third month, the grasping reflex diminishes and the infant shows a more voluntary grasp, which is often produced by visual stimuli. For example, when an infant sees a mobile whirling above its crib, it may reach out and try to grasp it. As its motor development becomes smoother, the infant will grasp objects, carefully manipulate them, and explore their qualities.

An overview of the main reflexes we have discussed, along with others, is given in table 5.1. Let's look now at three important reflexes in greater detail—sucking, crying, and smiling.

Sucking

Sucking is the infant's route to nourishment. The sucking capabilities of newborns vary considerably. Some newborns are efficient at forceful sucking and obtaining milk; others are not so adept and get tired before they are full. Most newborns take several weeks to establish a sucking style that is coordinated with the way the mother is holding the infant, the way milk is coming out of the bottle or breast, and the infant's sucking speed and temperament.

An investigation by pediatric researcher T. Berry Brazelton (1956) involved observations of infants for more than 1 year to determine the incidence of their sucking when they were nursing and how their sucking changed as they grew older. More than 85 percent of the infants engaged in considerable sucking behavior unrelated to feeding. They sucked their fingers, their fists, and pacifiers. By the age of 1 year, most had stopped the sucking behavior.

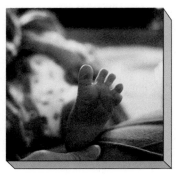

Babinski reflex

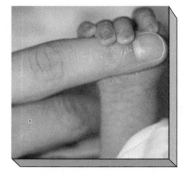

Grasping reflex

Moro reflex

Reflex	Stimulation	Infant's response	Developmental pattern
Blinking	Flash of light, puff of air	Closes both eyes	Permanent
Babinski	Sole of foot stroked	Fans out toes, twists foot in	Disappears 9 months to 1 year
Grasping	Palms touched	Grasps tightly	Weakens after 3 months, disappears after 1 year
Moro (startle)	Sudden stimulation, such as hearing a loud noise or being dropped	Startles, arches back, throws head back, flings out arms and legs and then rapidly closes them to center of body	Disappears 3 to 4 months
Rooting	Cheek stroked or side of mouth touched	Turns head, opens mouth, begins sucking	Disappears 3 to 4 months
Stepping	Infant held above surface and feet lowered to touch surface	Moves feet as if to walk	Disappears 3 to 4 months
Sucking	Object touching mouth	Sucks automatically	Disappears 3 to 4 months
Swimming	Infant put face down in water	Makes coordinated swimming movements	Disappears 6 to 7 months
Tonic neck	Infant placed on back	Forms fists with both hands and usually turns head to the right (sometimes called the "fencer's pose" because the infant looks like it is assuming a fencer's position)	Disappears 2 months

Rooting reflex

Stepping reflex

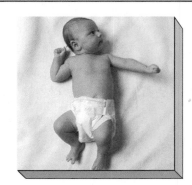

Tonic neck reflex

Parents should not worry when infants suck their thumb, fist, or even a pacifier. Many parents, though, do begin to worry when thumb sucking persists into the preschool and elementary school years. As much as 40 percent of all children continue to suck their thumbs after they have started school (Kessen, Haith, & Salapatek, 1970). Most developmentalists do not attach a great deal of significance to this behavior and are not aware of parenting strategies that might contribute to it. Individual differences in children's biological makeup may be involved to a degree in the late continuation of sucking behavior.

Nonnutritive sucking, *sucking behavior unrelated to the infant's feeding,* is used as measure in a large number of research studies with young infants because young infants quit sucking when they attend to something, such as a picture or a vocalization. Nonnutritive sucking, then, is one of the ingenious ways developmentalists study the young infant's attention and learning.

Crying and Smiling

Crying and smiling are emotional behaviors that are important in the infant's communication with the world. Crying is the infant's first emotional, or affective, behavior. Newborns spend 6 to 7 percent of their day crying, although some infants cry more and others less (Gotowiec & Ames, 1989). An infant's earliest cries are reflexive reactions to discomfort. The cries may signify information about the infant's biological state and possibly indicate distress. Infants' cries may have different patterns of frequency, intensity, and pause (Gustafson & Green, 1989, 1991).

Most adults can determine whether an infant's cries signify anger or pain (Barr, Desilets, & Rotman, 1991; St. James-Roberts, Bower, & Hurry, 1991). In one investigation, even when the crying segments were brief, adults could distinguish between aversive, arousing cries (more distressful) and those indicating hunger (less distressful). Even shortly after birth, infants' cries communicate information (Lester & Boukydis, 1991; Zeskind & Marshall, 1988).

Should a crying infant be given attention and soothed, or does this spoil the infant? Many years ago, behaviorist John Watson (1928) argued that parents spend too much time responding to infants' crying and, as a consequence, reward the crying and increase its incidence. By contrast, recent arguments by ethologists and attachment theorists, such as Mary Ainsworth (1979), stress that it is difficult to respond too much to an infant's crying. Ainsworth views caregivers' responsiveness to infant crying as contributing to the formation of a secure attachment between the infant and the caregiver. One investigation found that mothers who responded quickly to their infants' crying at 3 months of age had infants who cried less later in the first year of life (Bell & Ainsworth, 1972). In contrast, other research by behaviorists suggests that a caregiver's quick, soothing response to crying increases the infant's subsequent crying (Gewirtz, 1977). Controversy, then, still surrounds the issue of when and how caregivers should respond to infant crying.

Smiling is another important communicative behavior of the infant. Two kinds of smiling can be distinguished in infants—one reflexive, the other social. A **reflexive smile** *does not occur in response to external stimuli. It happens during the first month after birth, usually during irregular patterns of sleep, not when the infant is in an alert state.* On the other hand, a **social smile** *occurs in response to an external stimulus, which early in development typically is in response to a face.* Social smiling usually does not occur until 2 to 3 months of age (Emde, Gaensbauer, & Harmon, 1976), although some researchers believe that infants grin in response to voices as early as 3 weeks of

He who binds himself to joy
Does the winged life destroy;
But he who kisses the joy as it
Flies lives in eternity's sun rise.
—William Blake

age (Sroufe & Waters, 1976). The power of the infant's smiles was appropriately summed up by British attachment theorist John Bowlby (1969): "Can we doubt that the more and better an infant smiles the better is he loved and cared for? It is fortunate for their survival that babies are so designed by nature that they beguile and enslave mothers." More information about Bowlby's ideas on attachment appears in chapter 12, as well as further discussion of the infant's emotional world.

Blossoms are scattered by the wind
And the wind cares nothing, but
The blossoms of the heart
No wind can touch.

—Youshida Kenko

Emotions

If you cannot name an emotion, it does not exist. That was the dominant view of infant emotions for much of this century. However, now a different picture has emerged, one that recognizes the infant's repertoire of emotions. Just as you will discover later in the chapter that seeing and hearing are more highly developed in infancy than was originally believed, we now know that interest, distress, and disgust are present early in infancy and can be communicated to parents. Much earlier than the arrival of language, infants add the expression of emotions, such as joy, anger, surprise, shyness, and fear, to their capabilities.

What are the functions of emotions in infancy? Emotions are adaptive and promote survival, serve as a form of communication, and provide regulation (Barrett & Campos, 1987; Bretherton & others, 1986; Izard & Malatesta, 1987; Lewis, 1989). For example, various fears—such as fear of the dark and fear of sudden changes in the environment—are adaptive because there are clear links between such events and possible danger. Infants also use emotions to inform others about their feelings and needs. The infant who smiles probably is telling others that she is feeling pleasant; the infant who cries probably is communicating that something is unpleasant. Infants also use emotions to increase or decrease the distance between themselves and others. The infant who smiles may be encouraging someone to come closer; the infant who displays anger may be suggesting that an intruder should go away. Emotions also influence the information the infant selects from the perceptual world and the behaviors the infant displays. For example, an infant who is feeling pleasant may attend more efficiently to a mobile than would an infant who is crying uncontrollably.

How can we find out if the infant is displaying emotion? Carroll Izard (1982) developed a system for decoding the emotional expressions on infants' faces. Izard wanted to discover which emotions were inborn, which emerged later, and under which conditions they were displayed. The conditions included being given an ice cube, having tape put on the backs of their hands, being handed a favorite toy and then having it taken away, being separated from and reunited with their mothers, being approached by a stranger, having their heads gently restrained, having a ticking clock held next to their ears, having a balloon pop in front of their faces, and being given camphor to sniff and lemon rind and orange juice to taste. The **Maximally Discriminative Facial Movement Coding System,** *called MAX for short, is Izard's system of coding infants' facial expressions related to emotion. Using MAX, coders watch slow-motion and stop-action videotapes of infants' facial reactions to stimuli,* such as the circumstances described earlier. For example, anger is indicated when the brows are sharply lowered and drawn together, the eyes are narrowed or squinted, and the mouth is open in an angular, square shape. The key elements of emotional facial codes are shown in figure 5.1, and the developmental timetable of their emergence in infancy appears in table 5.2.

Joy: Mouth forms smile, cheeks lifted, twinkle in eyes

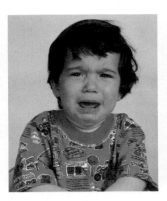

Anger: Brows drawn together and downward, eyes fixed, mouth squarish

Interest: Brows raised or knit, mouth softly rounded, lips pursed

Disgust: Nose wrinkled, upper lip raised, tongue pushed outward

Surprise: Brows raised, eyes widened, mouth rounded in oval shape

Distress: Eyes tightly closed; as in anger, mouth squared and angular

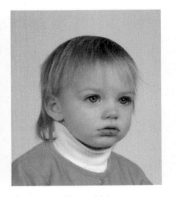

Sadness: Brows' inner corners raised, drawn out and down

Fear: Brows level, drawn in and up; eyelids lifted; mouth retracted

Figure 5.1
Facial Expressions of Emotion and Their Characteristics

TABLE 5.2
The Developmental Course of Infant Emotions

Emotional expression	Approximate time of emergence
Interest, neonatal smile (a sort of half smile that appears spontaneously for no apparent reason),* startled response,* distress,* disgust	Present at birth
Social smile	4 to 6 weeks
Anger, surprise, sadness	3 to 4 months
Fear	5 to 7 months
Shame/shyness	6 to 8 months
Contempt, guilt	2 years

*These expressions are precursors of the social smile and the emotions of surprise and sadness, which appear later. No evidence exists to suggest that they are related to inner feelings when they are observed in the first few weeks of life.

States

To chart and understand the infant's development, developmentalists have constructed classification schemes of the infant's states (Berg & Berg, 1987; Brown, 1964; Colombo, Moss, & Horowitz, in press). One classification scheme (Brown, 1964) describes seven infant states:

1. *Deep sleep.* The infant lies motionless with eyes closed, has regular breathing, makes no vocalization, and does not respond to outside stimulation.
2. *Regular sleep.* The infant moves very little, breathing might be raspy or involve wheezing, and respirations may be normal or move from normal to irregular.
3. *Disturbed sleep.* There is a variable amount of movement; the infant's eyelids are closed but might flutter; breathing is irregular; and there may be some squawks, sobs, and sighs.
4. *Drowsy.* The infant's eyes are open or partly open and appear glassy, there is little movement (although startles and free movement may occur), vocalizations are more regular than in disturbed sleep, and some transitional sounds may be made.
5. *Alert activity.* This is the state most often viewed by parents as being awake. The infant's eyes are open and bright, a variety of free movements are shown, fretting may occur, skin may redden, and there may be irregular breathing when the infant feels tension.
6. *Alert and focused.* This kind of attention is often seen in older children but is unusual in the neonate. The child's eyes are open and bright. Some motor activity may occur, but it is integrated around a specific activity. This state may occur when focusing on a sound or visual stimulus.
7. *Inflexibly focused.* In this state, the infant is awake but does not react to external stimuli; two examples are sucking and wild crying. During wild crying, the infant may thrash about, but the eyes are closed as screams pour out.

Using classification schemes such as the one just described, researchers have identified many different aspects of infant development. One such aspect is the sleeping-waking cycle. Each night, something lures us from our work, our play, our loved ones; sleep claims more of our time than any other pursuit. When we were infants, sleep consumed even more of our time than it does now. Newborns sleep for 16 to 17 hours a day, although some sleep more, and others less. The range is from a low of about 10 hours to a high of about 21 hours (Parmalee, Wenner, & Schulz, 1964). The longest period of sleep is not always between 11 P.M. and 7 A.M. Although total sleep remains somewhat consistent for young infants, their sleep during the day does not always follow a rhythmic pattern. An infant might change from sleeping several long bouts of 7 or 8 hours to three or four shorter sessions only several hours in duration. By about 1 month of age, most infants have begun to sleep longer at night, and, by about 4 months of age, they usually have moved closer to adultlike sleep patterns, spending their longest span of sleep at night and their longest span of waking during the day (Coons & Guilleminault, 1984).

Sleep that knits up the ravelled sleave of care . . .
Balm of hurt minds, nature's second course,
Chief nourisher in life's feast.

—William Shakespeare

Biological Processes, Physical Development, and Perceptual Development

However, it is common for 9-to-10-month-old infants to wake up in the middle of the night and start crying. Sometimes the crying results from illness or other physically based distress (Ferber, 1989; Thorpy & Glovinsky, 1989). Most of the time, though, middle-of-the-night crying occurs because the infant is alone usually in a dark or dimly lit room, is not very sleepy, and does not have much to do. At this point, infants use the one tool that eliminated their boredom in the past—crying. Middle-of-the-night crying is usually motivated by the infant's desire to have the company of others rather than to be alone, awake, and bored. This can become a serious inconvenience to many parents. Some couples spend long hours awake in the wee hours trying to cope with a wide-awake baby. Infancy expert Burton White (1988) described one such encounter. A dentist in Georgia called him long-distance. Mildly embarrassed, the dentist said that he and his wife were taking a minimum of two automobile rides after midnight and before 6 A.M. each night in an attempt to lull their baby to sleep. Like others in the same situation, they could not believe they had gotten themselves into this predicament. They finally went to a pediatrician who checked the baby's health, which was fine. He told the parents the baby was not crying at night because it was hurt or in pain. The pediatrician told them simply to let the baby cry it out at this age. This wasn't easy for the parents to do, but ignoring their 10-month-old's crying in the middle of the night quickly led to much quieter nights for the parents and the infant.

Researchers are intrigued by the various forms of infant sleep. They are especially interested in **REM (rapid eye movement) sleep,** *a recurring sleep stage during which vivid dreams commonly occur among children and adults* (Carskadon & Dement, 1989; McCarley, 1989). Most adults spend about one fifth of their night in REM sleep, and REM sleep usually appears about 1 hour after nonREM sleep. However, about one half of an infant's sleep is REM sleep, and infants often begin their sleep cycle with REM sleep rather than nonREM sleep. By the time infants reach 3 months of age, the percentage of time spent in REM sleep falls to about 40 percent and no longer does REM sleep begin the sleep cycle. The extensive amount of REM sleep in infancy is shown in figure 5.2. The large amount of REM sleep may provide infants with added self-stimulation, since they spend less time awake than do older children. REM sleep also may promote the brain's development.

Physical Growth and Motor Development

Physically, newborns are limited. They are tiny; from head to heels, they are only about 20 inches long and weigh 7 pounds. They are bound by where they are put, and they are at the mercy of their bodily needs. Their heart beats twice as fast as an adult's—120 beats a minute—and they breathe twice as fast as an adult—about 33 times a minute. They urinate as many as 18 times and move their bowels from 4 to 7 times in 24 hours. On the average, they are alert and comfortable for only about 30 minutes in a 4-hour period.

The infant's pattern of physical development in the first 2 years of life is exciting. At birth, the neonate has a gigantic head (relative to the rest of the body) that flops around in uncontrollable fashion; she possesses reflexes that are dominated by evolutionary movements. In the span of 12 months, the infant becomes capable of sitting anywhere, standing, stooping, climbing, and usually walking. During the second year, growth decelerates, but rapid increases in such activities as running and climbing take place.

Growth is the only evidence of life.
—John Henry, Cardinal Newman

Figure 5.2

REM Sleep

The graph shows changes (with age) in total amounts of daily sleep, in daily REM sleep, and in percentage of REM sleep. Note the sharp diminution of REM sleep in the early years. REM sleep falls from 8 hours at birth to less than 1 hour in old age. The amount of NREM sleep throughout life remains more constant, falling from 8 hours to 5 hours. In contrast to the steep decline of REM sleep, the quantity of NREM sleep is undiminished for many years. Although total daily REM sleep falls steadily during life, the percentage rises slightly in adolescence and early adulthood. This rise does not reflect an increase in amount; it is due to the fact that REM sleep does not diminish as quickly as total sleep. Data for the 33 to 45- and 50 to 90-year groups are taken from Kales et al. (1967), Feinberg et al. (1967), and Kahn and Fisher (1969), respectively (revised by the authors [Roffwarg, et al. 1967] since publication in *Science,* 152:604–619, 1966). The photo on the right shows the rapid eye movement that gives REM sleep its name. In children and adults, dreams are most likely to occur in REM sleep. The function of REM sleep in infancy is debated.

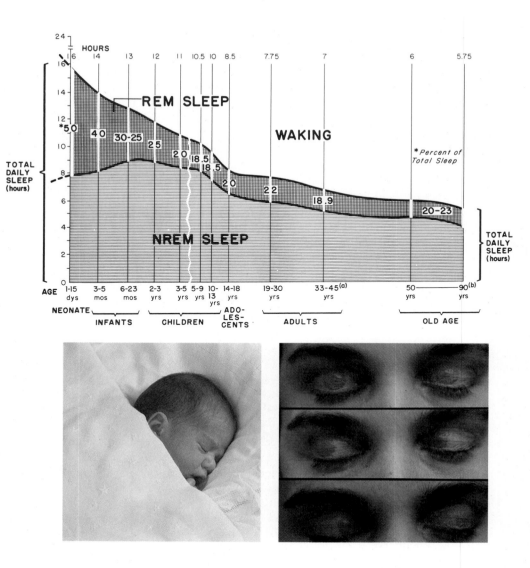

Among the important changes in growth are those involving the cephalocaudal and proximodistal sequences, gross and fine motor skills, and the brain. We will examine each of these, as well as nutrition, in turn.

Cephalocaudal and Proximodistal Sequences

The **cephalocaudal pattern** *is the sequence in which the greatest growth always occurs at the top—the head—with physical growth in size, weight, and feature differentiation gradually working its way down from top to bottom (for example, neck, shoulders, middle trunk, and so on).* This same pattern occurs in the head area because the top parts of the head—the eyes and brain—grow faster than the lower parts—such as the jaw. As illustrated in figure 5.3, an extraordinary proportion of the total body is occupied by the head during prenatal development and early infancy.

The **proximodistal pattern** *is the sequence in which growth starts at the center of the body and moves toward the extremities.* An example of this is the early maturation of muscular control of the trunk and arms as compared with that of the hands and fingers.

Biological Processes, Physical Development, and Perceptual Development

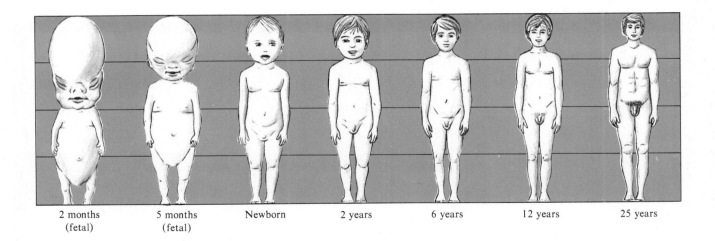

| 2 months (fetal) | 5 months (fetal) | Newborn | 2 years | 6 years | 12 years | 25 years |

Gross and Fine Motor Skills

In addition to cephalocaudal and proximodistal growth patterns, we also can describe growth in **gross motor skills**, *those involving large muscle activities such as moving one's arms and walking,* and **fine motor skills**, *those involving more finely tuned movements, such as finger dexterity.*

At birth, the infant has no appreciable coordination of the chest or arms. By about 4 months of age, however, two striking accomplishments occur. The first is the infant's ability to hold its chest up in a face-down position (at about 2 months). The other is the ability to reach for objects placed within the infant's direct line of vision, without making any consistent contact with the objects (because the two hands don't work together and the coordination of vision and grasping is not yet possible). A little later, at about 3 to 4 months of age, there is further progress in motor control. By 5 months, the infant can sit up with some support and grasp objects. By 6 months, the infant can roll over when lying down in a prone position.

At birth, the newborn is capable of supporting some weight on its legs. This is proven by formal tests of muscular strength. These tests use a specially constructed apparatus to measure the infant's leg resistance as the foot is pulled away by a calibrated spring device. This ability is also evidenced by the infant's partial support of its own weight when held upright by an adult. If an adult gives an infant enough support, some forward movement is seen in a built-in stepping reflex, which disappears in a few months. Each leg is lifted, moved forward, and placed down, as if the infant were taking a series of steps. However, the sequence lasts only two to three steps, and, of course, the infant does not have sufficient balance or strength to execute the movement independently.

By about 6 months of age, infants can sit unaided. By about 7 months, they can pull to sit unaided and crawl or scoot. By about 8 months, they can pull to a stand. By about 11 months, they can walk unaided. By about 13 months, they can ride four-wheel wagons, and, by about 26 months, they can ride a tricycle (White, 1988). The average age of infant motor accomplishments in the first year of life are shown in figure 5.4. The actual month at which the milestones occur varies as much as 2 to 4 months, especially among older infants. What remains fairly uniform, however, is the sequence of accomplishments. An important implication of these infant motor accomplishments is the increasing degree of independence they bring. Infants can explore their environment more extensively and initiate social interaction with caregivers and peers.

Figure 5.3
Changes in Body Form and Proportion During Prenatal and Postnatal Growth

A traditional practice among many Hopi and Navaho Indians is to wrap babies in cloth and strap them to a cradleboard until they are about 6 months old. Infants in the Hopi and Navaho cultures learn to walk at about the same time as babies who are not constrained in this way. Even though there are often substantial differences across cultures among infants' opportunities to practice their motor movements, infants in every culture walk at about the same age.

A baby is an angel whose wings decrease as his legs increase.

—French proverb

Figure 5.4

The Development of Posture and Locomotion in Infants
The time periods shown are averages for American infants. The actual times at which such milestones occur vary by as much as 4 months.

Not content with their infants reaching the motor development milestones at an average rate, many American parents want to accelerate their infants' physical skills. Is this a wise practice? To learn more about this intriguing question, turn to Perspective on Child Development 5.1.

The Brain

As an infant walks, talks, runs, shakes a rattle, smiles, and frowns, changes in its brain are occurring. Consider that the infant began life as a single cell and, in 9 months, was born with a brain and nervous system that contained approximately 100 billion nerve cells. Indeed, at birth, the infant probably had all of the nerve cells—called neurons—it is going to have in its entire life. At birth and in early infancy, the connectedness of all these neurons, however, is impoverished. As shown in figure 5.5 on page 150, as the infant moves from birth to 2 years of age, the interconnections of neurons increase dramatically as the dendrites (the receiving part) of the neuron branch out.

Neurotransmitters also change through the prenatal period and during the infant years. Neurotransmitters are the tiny chemical substances that carry information across gaps from one neuron to the next. Little is known about neurotransmitter changes in infancy, although changes in one important neu-

Babies Don't Need Exercise Classes

Six-month-old Andrew doesn't walk yet, but his mother wants him to develop his physical skills optimally. Three times a week, she takes him to a recreation center, where he participates with other infants in swimming and gymnastics classes. With the increased interest of today's adults in aerobic exercise and fitness, some parents have tried to give their infants a head start on becoming physically fit and physically talented. However, the American Academy of Pediatricians recently issued a statement that recommends against structured exercise classes for babies. Pediatricians are seeing more bone fractures and dislocations and more muscle strains in babies now than in the past. They point out that, when an adult is stretching and moving an infant's limbs, it is easy to go beyond the infant's physical limits without knowing it.

The physical fitness classes for infants range from passive fare—with adults putting infants through the paces—to programs called "aerobic" because they demand crawling, tumbling, and ball skills. However, exercise for infants is not aerobic. They cannot adequately stretch their bodies to achieve aerobic benefits. Even swimming classes before early childhood have a down side. Children cannot cognitively learn to swim until they are 3 or 4 years of age. It is not uncommon for 4-year-olds who have had swim classes since infancy to become suddenly terrified of the water because, for the first time, they understand that they could drown.

Pediatricians and child psychologists advise that exercise classes for infants are not needed and may have more negative than positive outcomes.

For optimal physical development, babies simply need touch, face-to-face contact, and brightly colored toys they can manipulate. If infants are not couch potatoes who are babysat extensively by a television set, their normal play will provide them with all the fitness training they need.

rotransmitter—dopamine—has been documented in monkeys (Goldman-Rakic & others, 1983). The concentration of dopamine in the prefrontal lobe—the area of the brain involved in higher cognitive functions such as problem solving—peaks at 5 months of age, declines until about 18 to 24 months, and then increases again at 2 to 3 years of age. These changes in dopamine concentration may reflect a switch from growth and nutritional functions to neurotransmitter function for this substance. Such speculation only begins to scratch the surface of the important role neurotransmitter substances might play in the brain's early development.

Nutrition

Four-month-old Robert lives in Bloomington, Indiana, with his middle-class parents. He is well nourished and healthy. By contrast, 4-month-old Nikita lives in Ethiopia. Nikita and his parents live in impoverished conditions. Nikita is so poorly nourished that he has become emaciated and lies near death. The lives of Robert and Nikita reveal the vast diversity of nutritional status among today's children. Our coverage of infant nutrition begins with information about nutritional needs and eating behavior, then turns to malnutrition.

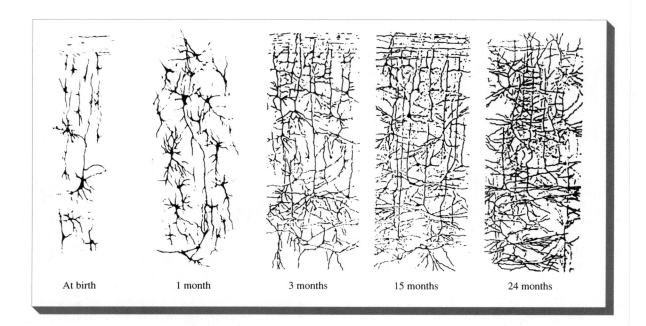

| At birth | 1 month | 3 months | 15 months | 24 months |

Figure 5.5
Development of Dendritic Spreading
Note the increase in connectedness among neurons over the course of the first 2 years of life.

Nutritional Needs and Eating Behavior

The importance of adequate energy and nutrient intake consumed in a loving and supportive environment during the infant years cannot be overstated (Pipes, 1988a). From birth to 1 year of age, human infants triple their weight and increase their length by 50 percent. Individual differences of infants in terms of their nutrient reserves, body composition, growth rates, and activity patterns make defining actual nutrient needs difficult. However, because parents need guidelines, nutritionists recommend that infants consume approximately 50 calories per day for each pound they weigh—more than twice an adult's requirement per pound.

Human milk, or an alternative formula if needed, is the baby's source of nutrients and energy for the first 4 to 6 months. For years, developmentalists and nutritionists have debated whether breast-feeding of an infant has substantial benefits over bottle-feeding. The growing consensus is that breast-feeding is better for the baby's health (Lozoff, 1989; Walton & Vallelunga, 1989; Worthington-Roberts, 1988). Breast-feeding provides milk that is clean and digestible and helps immunize the newborn from disease. Breast-fed babies gain weight more rapidly than do bottle-fed babies. However, only about one half of mothers nurse newborns, and even fewer continue to nurse their infants after several months. Mothers who work outside the home find it impossible to breast-feed their young infants for many months. Even though breast-feeding provides more ideal nutrition, some researchers argue that there is no long-term evidence of physiological or psychological harm to American infants when they are bottle-fed (Caldwell, 1964; Ferguson, Harwood, & Shannon, 1987; Forsyth, Leventhal, & McCarthy, 1985). Despite these researchers' claims that no long-term negative consequences of bottle-feeding have been documented in American children, the American Academy of Pediatrics, the majority of physicians and nurses, and two leading publications for parents—the

Infant Care Manual and *Parents* magazine—endorse breast-feeding as having physiological and psychological benefits (Young, 1990). There is a consensus among experts that breast-feeding is the preferred practice in developing countries where inadequate nutrition and poverty are common. In the United States, the majority of experts favor breast-feeding, although the issue of breast- versus bottle-feeding continues to be hotly debated.

Some years ago, controversy also surrounded the issue of whether a baby should be fed on demand or on a regular schedule. The famous behaviorist John Watson (1928) argued that scheduled feeding was superior because it increased the child's orderliness. An example of a recommended schedule for newborns was 4 ounces of formula every 6 hours. In recent years, demand feeding—in which the timing and amount of feeding are determined by the infant—has become more popular.

The maturation of oral and fine motor skills indicates the appropriate ages for the introduction of semisolid and solid foods. Current recommendations are to introduce semisolid foods at 4 to 6 months of age and finger foods when infants reach out, grasp, and bring items to their mouths. When munching and rotary chewing begin, the use of soft-cooked foods is appropriate. Infants can begin to drink from a cup with help between 9 and 12 months of age.

There has been speculation that formula feeding and the early introduction of semisolid foods might contribute to excessive intakes of energy and the development of infant obesity. It also has been speculated that obese infants often become obese adults. However, neither breast- nor bottle-feeding, nor the age of introduction of semisolid foods, are causes of obesity. Obesity in infancy also has not been a very good predictor of obesity in adulthood (Stunkard, 1989).

In the 1990s, we have become extremely nutrition conscious. Does the same type of nutrition that makes us healthy adults also make young infants healthy? For the answer to this question, turn to Perspective on Child Development 5.2.

Arguments continue to swirl about whether breast-feeding or bottle-feeding is best for an infant. Experts argue that breast-feeding is more likely to ensure that an infant's nutritional requirements are met, but no long-term negative effects of bottle-feeding have been documented in American children.

What's Good Food for an Adult Can Be Bad Food for a Baby

Some yuppie parents may not know the recipe for a healthy baby: whole milk and an occasional cookie, along with fruits, vegetables, and other foods. Some affluent, well-educated parents almost starve their babies by feeding them the lowfat, low-calorie diet they eat themselves. Diets designed for adult weight loss and prevention of heart disease may actually retard growth and development in babies. Fat is very important for babies. Nature's food—the mother's breast milk—is not low in fat or calories. No child under the age of 2 should be consuming skim milk.

In a recent investigation, seven cases were documented in which babies 7 to 22 months of age were unwittingly undernourished by their health-conscious parents (Lifshitz & others, 1987). In some instances, the parents had been fat themselves and were determined that their child was not going to be. The well-meaning parents substituted vegetables, skim milk, and other lowfat foods for what they called junk food. However, for infants, broccoli is not always a good substitute for a cookie. For growing infants, high-calorie, high-energy foods are part of a balanced diet.

What hazards might there be in the current trends toward diet foods and parental health preoccupation when it comes to choosing foods for infants?

■ *Critical Thinking*

If and when you become a parent, what considerations would you have about the nutrition your infant gets? How important do you believe breast-feeding is for infant development? Explain.

Malnutrition in Infancy

Marasmus *is a wasting away of body tissues in the infant's first year, caused by severe protein-calorie deficiency.* The infant becomes grossly underweight and its muscles atrophy. The main cause of marasmus is early weaning from breast milk to inadequate nutrients such as unsuitable and unsanitary cow's milk formula. Something that looks like milk, but is not, usually a form of tapioca or rice, also may be used. In many of the world's developing countries, mothers used to breast-feed their infants for at least 2 years. To become more modern, they stopped breast-feeding much earlier and replaced it with bottle-feeding. Comparisons of breast-fed and bottle-fed infants in such countries as Afghanistan, Haiti, Ghana, and Chile document that the rate of infant death is much greater among bottle-fed than breast-fed infants, with bottle-fed infants sometimes dying at a rate five times higher than breast-fed infants (Grant, 1990).

Even if not fatal, severe and lengthy malnutrition is detrimental to physical, cognitive, and social development (Super, Herrera, & Mora, 1990). In some cases, even moderate malnutrition can produce subtle difficulties in development. In one investigation, two groups of extremely malnourished 1-year-

Children Living Hungry in America

Harlingen, Texas, is a heavily Chicano city of approximately 40,000 near the Rio Grande. At Su Clinica ("Your Clinic"), which serves many Chicano residents, poverty and unemployment are evident in the waiting list of 800 families needing low-cost care. Many of the Chicanos working in Texas agriculture receive no health-care benefits, and few make even the minimum wage. Farm workers usually get less than $1.50 an hour for working long days in the pesticide-infected fields. The infant mortality rate for the region is listed as good by the U.S. government, but this description is wrong. Many of the deaths are not counted. A baby dies and is buried. People outside the family seldom know. Many infants and young children here experience growth problems because they do not get enough to eat. This is not unique to Harlingen, Texas; many other locations in the United States have their share of impoverished families who have difficulty making ends meet and putting food on the table. Hunger and poverty are seen in the children of poor Mississippi tenant farmers, in the children of laid-off coal miners in West Virginia, in neglected children in the ghettos of New York and Chicago, and in the increasing number of homeless families across the nation. In many instances, these children are the victims of silent undernutrition, less dramatic than in Africa or Bangladesh, but no less real (Brown & Pizer, 1987).

Many Mexican American children, such as these in Harlingen, Texas, do not get adequate nutrition and live in poverty conditions.

old South African infants were studied (Bayley, 1970). The children in one group were given adequate nourishment during the next 6 years; no intervention took place in the lives of the other group. After the seventh year, the poorly nourished group of children performed much worse on tests of intelligence than did the adequately nourished group. In yet another investigation, the diets of rural Guatemalan infants were associated with their social development at the time they entered elementary school (Barrett, Radke-Yarrow, & Klein, 1982). Children whose mothers had been given nutritional supplements during pregnancy and who themselves had been given more nutritious, high-calorie foods in their first 2 years of life were more active, more involved, more helpful with their peers, less anxious, and happier than their counterparts, who were not given nutritional supplements. The undernourished Guatemalan infants were only mildly undernourished in infancy, suggesting how important it is for parents to be attentive to the nutritional needs of their infants. Other researchers have demonstrated that nutritional supplements can improve the cognitive development of malnourished children (Engle, 1991; Gorman & Pollitt, 1991; Super, Herrera, & Mora, 1991). Much of our discussion of malnutrition has focused on developing countries, but hunger is also a problem in some areas of the United States. To read about children living hungry in America, turn to Cultural Worlds of Development 5.1.

Physical, Motor, and Perceptual Development in Infancy

Physical Growth and Development in Infancy

Concept	Processes/related ideas	Characteristics/description
Reflexes	Their nature	The newborn is no longer viewed as a passive, empty-headed organism. Newborns are limited physically, though, and reflexes—automatic movements—govern the newborn's behavior.
	Sucking	For infants, sucking is an important means of obtaining nutrition, as well as a pleasurable, soothing activity. Nonnutritive sucking is of interest to researchers because it provides a means of evaluating attention.
	Crying and smiling	Crying and smiling are affective behaviors that are important in the infant's communication with the world.
Emotions	Their nature	Emotions in infancy are adaptive and promote survival, serve as a form of communication, and provide regulation. Izard developed the MAX system for coding infant facial expressions of emotion. Using this system, interest and disgust were present in the newborn; a social smile, anger, and surprise developed in the first year; and contempt and guilt appeared in the second year.
States	Classification	Researchers have put together different classification systems; one involved seven infant state categories, including deep sleep, drowsy, alert and focused, and inflexibly focused.
	The sleeping-waking cycle	Newborns usually sleep 16 to 17 hours a day. By 4 months, they approach adultlike sleeping patterns. REM sleep, during which children and adults are most likely to dream, occurs much more in early infancy than in childhood and adulthood. The high percentage of REM sleep—about half of neonatal sleep—may be a self-stimulatory device, or it may promote brain development.
Physical growth and motor development	Cephalocaudal and proximodistal sequences	The cephalocaudal pattern is growth from the top down; the proximodistal pattern is growth from the center out.
	Gross motor and fine motor skills	Gross motor skills involve large muscle activity, as in walking. Fine motor skills involve more fine-grained activities such as manual dexterity. Both gross and fine motor skills undergo extensive change in the first 2 years of development.
	The brain	There is a great deal of brain growth in infancy as well as in prenatal development. Dendritic spreading is dramatic in the first 2 years. Some important changes in neurotransmitters probably also take place, although these changes are just beginning to be charted.
Nutrition	Nutritional needs and eating behavior	Infants need to consume approximately 50 calories per day for each pound they weigh. Human milk, or an alternative formula, is the baby's source of nutrients for the first 6 months. The growing consensus is that breast-feeding is superior to bottle-feeding, but the increase in working mothers has meant fewer breast-fed babies. Parents are increasingly using a demand feeding schedule. The maturation of oral and fine motor skills indicates appropriate ages for introducing semisolid and solid foods. Obesity in infancy has not been a good predictor of obesity in adulthood. Infants should not be placed on lowfat, low-calorie diets.
	Malnutrition in infancy	Severe infant malnutrition is still prevalent in many parts of the world. Severe protein-calorie deficiency can cause marasmus, a wasting away of body tissues. It is mainly caused by early weaning from breast milk. Even if not fatal, severe and lengthy malnutrition is detrimental to physical, cognitive, and social development.

At this point, we have discussed a number of ideas about physical growth and development in infancy. A summary of these ideas is presented in concept table 5.1. Now we will turn our attention to the infant's sensory and perceptual worlds.

Sensory and Perceptual Development

At the beginning of this chapter, you read about how newborns come into the world equipped with sensory capacities. What are sensation and perception? Can a newborn see and, if so, what can it perceive? What about the other senses—hearing, smell, taste, touch, and pain? What are they like in the newborn? These are among the intriguing questions we will now explore.

What Are Sensation and Perception?

How does a newborn know that her mother's skin is soft rather than rough? How does a 5-year-old know what color his hair is? How does an 8-year-old know that summer is warmer than winter? How does a 10-year-old know that a firecracker is louder than a cat's meow? Infants and children "know" these things because of their senses. All information comes to the infant through the senses. Without vision, hearing, touch, taste, smell, and other senses, the infant's brain would be isolated from the world; the infant would live in dark silence, a tasteless, colorless, feelingless void.

Sensation *occurs when information contacts sensory receptors—the eyes, ears, tongue, nostrils, and skin.* The sensation of hearing occurs when waves of pulsating air are collected by the outer ear and transmitted through the bones of the inner ear to the auditory nerve. The sensation of vision occurs as rays of light contact the two eyes and become focused on the retina. **Perception** *is the interpretation of what is sensed.* The information about physical events that contacts the ears may be interpreted as musical sounds, for example. The physical energy transmitted to the retina may be interpreted as a particular color, pattern, or shape.

Visual Perception

How do we see? Anyone who has ever taken pictures while on vacation appreciates the miracle of perception. The camera is no match for it. Consider a favorite scenic spot that you visited and photographed some time in the past. Compare your memory of this spot to your snapshot. Although your memory may be faulty, there is little doubt that the richness of your perceptual experience is not captured in the picture. The sense of depth that you felt at this spot probably is not conveyed by the snapshot. Neither is the subtlety of the colors you perceived nor the intricacies of textures and shapes. Human vision is complex, and its development is complex too.

Psychologist William James (1890) called the newborn's perceptual world a blooming, buzzing confusion. Was James right? A century later we can safely say that he was wrong. Infants' perception of visual information is *much* more advanced than previously thought (Bower, 1989, 1990).

Our tour of visual perception begins with the pioneering work of Robert Fantz (1963). Fantz placed infants in a "looking chamber," which has two visual displays on the ceiling above the infant's head. An experimenter viewed the infant's eyes by looking through a peephole. If the infant was fixating on one of the displays, the experimenter could see the display's reflection in the infant's eyes. This allowed the experimenter to determine how long the infant

Systematic reasoning is something we could not, as a species of individuals, do without. But neither, if we are to remain sane, can we do without direct perception . . . of the inner and outer world into which we have been born.

—Aldous Huxley

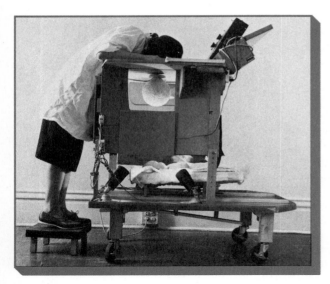

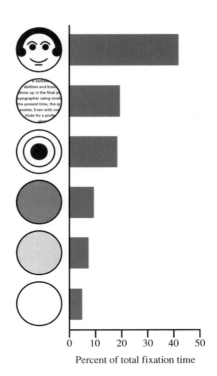

Percent of total fixation time

Figure 5.6
Fantz's Experiment on Infants' Visual Perception
Fantz used a ''looking chamber'' to study infants' perception of stimuli. As shown in the graph, 2-to-3-month-old infants preferred to look at some stimuli more than others. In Fantz's experiment, infants preferred to look at patterns rather than at color or brightness. For example, they looked longer at a face, a piece of printed matter, or a bull's eye than at red, yellow, or white discs.

looked at each display. In figure 5.6, you can see Fantz's looking chamber and the results of his experiment. The infants preferred to look at patterns rather than at color or brightness. For example, they preferred to look at a face, a piece of printed matter, or a bull's eye longer than at red, yellow, or white discs. In another experiment, Fantz found that younger infants—only 2 days old—looked longer at patterned stimuli, such as faces and concentric circles, than at red, white, or yellow discs. Based on these results, pattern perception likely has an innate basis, or at least is acquired after only minimal environmental experience. The newborn's visual world is not the blooming, buzzing confusion William James imagined.

Just how well can infants see? The newborn's vision is estimated to be 20/200 to 20/600 on the well-known Snellen chart that you are tested with when you have your eyes examined (Haith, 1991). This is about 10 to 30 times lower than normal adult vision (20/20). By 6 months of age, however, vision is 20/100 or better (Banks & Salapatek, 1983).

The human face is perhaps the most important visual pattern for the newborn to perceive. The infant masters a sequence of steps in progressing toward full perceptual appreciation of the face (Gibson, 1969). At about 3½ weeks, the infant is fascinated with the eyes, perhaps because the infant notices simple perceptual features such as dots, angles, and circles. At 1 to 2 months of age, the infant notices and perceives contour. At 2 months and older, the infant begins to differentiate facial features; the eyes are distinguished from other parts of the face, the mouth is noticed, and movements of the mouth draw attention to it. By 5 months of age, the infant has detected other facial features—its plasticity, its solid, three-dimensional surface, the oval shape of the head, and the orientation of the eyes and the mouth. Beyond 6 months of age, the infant distinguishes familiar faces from unfamiliar faces—mother from stranger, masks from real faces, and so on.

Biological Processes, Physical Development, and Perceptual Development

How early can infants perceive depth? To investigate this question, infant perception researchers Eleanor Gibson and Richard Walk (1960) conducted a classic experiment. They constructed a miniature cliff with a drop-off covered by glass. The motivation for this experiment happened when Gibson was eating a picnic lunch on the edge of the Grand Canyon. She wondered whether an infant looking over the canyon's rim would perceive the dangerous drop-off and back up. In their laboratory, Gibson and Walk placed infants on the edge of a visual cliff and had their mothers coax them to crawl out onto the glass (see figure 5.7). Most infants would not crawl out on the glass, choosing instead to remain on the shallow side, indicating that they could perceive depth. However, because the 6-to-14-month-old infants had extensive visual experience, this research did not answer the question of whether depth perception is innate.

Exactly how early in life does depth perception develop? Since younger infants do not crawl, this question is difficult to answer. Research with 2-to-4-month-old infants shows differences in heart rate when they are placed directly on the deep side of the visual cliff instead of on the shallow side (Campos, Langer, & Krowitz, 1970). However, an alternative interpretation is that young infants respond to differences in some visual characteristics of the deep and shallow cliffs, with no actual knowledge of depth.

What can we conclude about infants' visual perception? Many fundamental aspects of vision are in working order by birth, and many aspects of visual perception are present early in the infant's first year of life. Objects are seen as bounded, unitary, solid, and separate from the background, possibly from birth, but certainly by 3 to 4 months of age (Mandler, 1990). With further development there still is a great deal to learn about objects, but the world must appear both stable and orderly even to very young infants.

Hearing

Immediately after birth, infants can hear, although their sensory thresholds are somewhat higher than those of adults (Trehub & others, 1991). That is, a stimulus must be louder to be heard by a newborn than by an adult. Not only can a newborn hear, but the possibility has been raised that the fetus can hear as it nestles within its mother's womb. To learn more about this possibility, turn to Perspective on Child Development 5.3. Also, in a recent study, as infants aged from 8 to 28 weeks, they became much more proficient at localizing sounds (Morrongiello, Fenwick, & Chance, 1990).

Smell

Newborn infants can differentiate odors. For example, by the expressions on their faces, they seem to indicate that they like the way vanilla and strawberry smell but do not like the way rotten eggs and fish smell (Steiner, 1979). In one investigation, young infants who were breast-fed showed a clear preference for smelling their mother's breast pad when they were 6 days old (MacFarlane, 1975) (see figure 5.8). However, when they were 2 days old, they did not show this preference (compared to a clean breast pad), indicating that they require several days of experience to recognize this odor.

Figure 5.7
Examining Infants' Depth Perception on the Visual Cliff
The apparatus consists of a board laid across a sheet of heavy glass, with a patterned material directly beneath the glass on one side and several feet below it on the other. Placed on the center board, the child crawls to its mother across the "shallow" side. Called from the "deep" side, the child pats the glass but, despite this tactual evidence that the cliff is a solid surface, the child refuses to cross over to the mother.

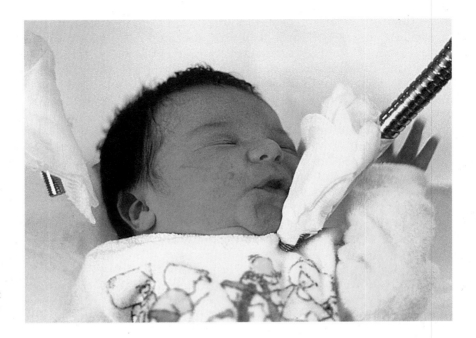

Figure 5.8
Newborns' Preference for the Smell of Their Mother's Breast Pad
In the experiment by MacFarlane (1975), 6-day-old infants preferred to smell their mother's breast pad over a clean one that had never been used, but 2-day-old infants did not show this preference, indicating that this odor preference requires several days of experience to develop.

Taste

Sensitivity to taste may be present before birth. When saccharin was added to the amniotic fluid of a near-term fetus, increased swallowing was observed (Windle, 1940). Sensitivity to sweetness is clearly present in the newborn. When sucks on a nipple are rewarded with a sweetened solution, the amount of sucking increases (Lipsitt & others, 1976). In another investigation, newborns showed a smilelike expression after being given a sweetened solution but pursed their lips after being given a sour solution (Steiner, 1979). In a recent study, 1-to-3-day-old infants cried much less when they were given sucrose through a pacifier (Smith, Fillion, and Blass, 1990).

Touch

Just as newborns respond to taste, they also respond to touch. A touch to the cheek produces a turning of the head, whereas a touch to the lips produces sucking movements. An important ability that develops in infancy is to connect information about vision with information about touch. One-year-olds clearly can do this and it appears that 6-month-olds can too (Acredolo & Hake, 1982). Whether still younger infants can coordinate vision and touch is yet to be determined.

Pain

If and when you have a son and need to consider whether he should be circumcised, the issue of an infant's pain perception probably will become important to you. Circumcision is usually performed on young boys about the third day after birth. Will your young son experience pain if he is circumcised when he is 3 days old? Increased crying and fussing occur during the circumcision procedure, suggesting that 3-day-old infants experience pain (Gunnar, Malone, & Fisch, 1987; Porter, Porges, & Marshall, 1988).

The Fetus and *The Cat in the Hat*

The fetus can hear sounds in the last few months of pregnancy: the mother's voice, music, and so on. Given that the fetus can hear sounds, two psychologists wanted to find out if listening to Dr. Seuss' classic story *The Cat in the Hat*, while still in the mother's womb, would produce a preference for hearing the story after birth (DeCasper & Spence, 1986). Sixteen pregnant women read *The Cat in the Hat* or a story with a different rhyme and pace, *The King, the Mice, and the Cheese*, to their fetuses twice a day over the last 6 weeks of their pregnancies. When the babies were born, they were given a choice of listening to each story by varying their sucking rate. Sucking at one rate (slowly, for example) resulted in their hearing a recording of one story. Sucking at another rate resulted in a recording of the other story. The newborns preferred listening to *The Cat in the Hat*, which they had heard frequently as a fetus.

Two important conclusions can be drawn from this investigation. First, it reveals how ingenious scientists have become at assessing the development not only of infants but of fetuses as well, in this case discovering a way to "interview" newborn babies who cannot yet talk. Second, it reveals the remarkable ability of an infant's brain to learn even before birth.

(a)

(b)

(a) Pregnant women read The Cat in the Hat *to their fetuses in the last few months of pregnancy. (b) When the babies were born, they preferred listening to a recording of their mothers reading* The Cat in the Hat, *as evidenced by their sucking on a nipple that produced this recording.*

In the recent investigation by Megan Gunnar and her colleagues (1987), the healthy newborn's ability to cope with stress was evaluated. The newborn males cried intensely during the circumcision, indicating that it was stressful. The researchers pointed out that it is rather remarkable that the newborn does not suffer serious consequences from the surgery. Rather, the circumcised infant displays amazing resiliency and ability to cope. Within several minutes after the surgery, the infant can nurse and interact in a normal manner with his mother, and, if allowed, the newly circumcised newborn drifts into a deep sleep that seems to serve as a coping mechanism. In this experiment, the time spent in deep sleep was greater in the 60 to 240 minutes after the circumcision than before it.

For many years, doctors have performed operations on newborns without anesthesia. This accepted medical practice was followed because of the dangers of anesthesia and the supposition that newborns do not feel pain. Recently, as researchers have convincingly demonstrated that newborns feel pain, the longstanding practice of operating on newborns without anesthesia is being challenged.

Yellow Kangaroos, Gray Donkeys, Thumps, Gongs, and 4-Month-Old Infants

Imagine yourself playing basketball or tennis. There are obviously many visual inputs: the ball coming and going, other players moving around, and so on. However, there also are many auditory inputs: the sound of the ball bouncing or being hit and the grunts, groans, and curses emitted by you and others. There is also good correspondence between much of the visual and auditory information: When you see the ball bounce, you hear a bouncing sound; when a player leaps, you hear a groan.

We live in a world of objects and events that can be seen, heard, and felt. When mature observers look at and listen to an event simultaneously, they experience a unitary episode. All of this is so commonplace that it scarcely seems worth mentioning, but consider the task of a very young infant with little practice at perceiving. Can she put vision and sound together as precisely as adults?

To test intermodal perception, Elizabeth Spelke (1979) performed three experiments with the following structure. Two simple films were shown side-by-side in front of a 4-month-old infant. One film showed a yellow kangaroo bouncing up and down, and the other showed a gray donkey bouncing up and down. There also was an auditory sound track—a repeating thump or gong sound. A number of measures assessed the infant's tendency to look at one film instead of the other.

In Experiment 1, the animal in one of the films bounced at a slower rate than the animal in the other. The sound track was synchronized either with the film of the slow-bouncing animal or with the film of the fast-bouncing animal. Infants' first looks were toward the film that was specified by the sound track. Experiments 2 and 3 explored two components of the relation between the sound track and the matching film: common tempo and simultaneity of sounds and bounces. The findings indicated that the infants were sensitive to both of these components.

Spelke's clever demonstration suggests that infants only 4 months old do not experience a world of unrelated visual and auditory dimensions; they can perceive them as unified.

Intermodal Perception

Are young infants so competent that they can relate and integrate information through several senses? **Intermodal perception** *is the ability to relate and integrate information about two or more sensory modalities, such as vision and hearing.* An increasing number of developmentalists believe that young infants experience related visual and auditory worlds (Bahrick, 1988; Gibson & Spelke, 1983; Rose & Ruff, 1987). To learn more about intermodal perception, turn to Perspective on Child Development 5.4. Keep in mind, though, that intermodal perception in young infants remains a controversial concept. For example, in one recent investigation of 6-month-old infants, the auditory sense dominated the visual sense, restricting intermodal perception (Lewkowicz, 1988).

The claim that the young infant can relate information from several senses has been addressed by two important theoretical perspectives. The **direct perception view** *states that infants are born with intermodal perception abilities that enable them to display intermodal perception early in infancy.* In this view, infants only have to attend to the appropriate sensory information; they do not have to build up an internal representation of the information through months of sensorimotor experiences. In contrast, the **constructivist view** *advocated by Piaget states that the main perceptual abilities—visual, auditory, and tactile, for example—are completely uncoordinated at birth*

CONCEPT TABLE 5.2
Perceptual Development in Infancy

Concept	Processes/related ideas	Characteristics/description
What are sensation and perception?	Sensation	When information contacts sensory receptors—eyes, ears, tongue, nostrils, and skin—sensation occurs.
	Perception	Perception is the interpretation of what is sensed.
Visual perception	The newborn's visual world	William James said it is a blooming, buzzing confusion; he was wrong. The newborn's perception is more advanced than we previously thought.
	Visual preferences	Fantz's research—showing how infants prefer striped to solid patches—demonstrated that newborns can see.
	Quality of vision	The newborn is about 20/600 on the Snellen chart; by 6 months, vision has improved to at least 20/100.
	The human face	It is an important visual pattern for the newborn. The infant gradually masters a sequence of steps in perceiving the human face.
	Depth perception	A classic study by Gibson and Walk (1960) demonstrated, through the use of a visual cliff, that 6-month-old infants can perceive depth.
Other senses	Hearing	The fetus can hear several weeks before birth; immediately after birth, newborns can hear, although their sensory threshold is higher than adults'.
	Smell, taste, touch, and pain	Each of these senses is present in the newborn. Research on circumcision shows that 3-day-old males experience pain and can adapt to stress.
Intermodal perception	Its nature	Considerable interest focuses on the infant's ability to relate information across perceptual modalities; the coordination and integration of perceptual information across two or more modalities—such as the visual and auditory senses—is called intermodal perception. Research indicates that infants as young as 4 months of age have intermodal perception. The direct perception and constructivist views are two important views of perception that make predictions about intermodal perception.

and that young infants do not have intermodal perception. According to Piaget, only through months of sensorimotor interaction with the world is intermodal perception possible. For Piaget, infant perception involves a representation of the world that builds up as the infant constructs an image of experiences.

Although the intermodal perception and direct perception/constructivist arguments have not completely been settled, we now know that young infants know a lot more than we used to think they did (Bower, 1989, 1991; Mandler, 1990). They see and hear more than we used to think was possible.

At this point, we have discussed a number of ideas about perceptual development in infancy. A summary of these ideas is presented in concept table 5.2. In the next chapter, we will discuss the nature of physical development in childhood and puberty.

■ *Critical Thinking*
Increasingly, developmentalists have been surprised by the early competencies of newborns and young infants. Are we going too far in believing that newborns and young infants are competent in dealing with their world, or are they really as sophisticated as the new wave of research seems to suggest?

Summary

I. Reflexes

The newborn is no longer viewed as a passive, empty-headed organism. Physically, newborns are limited, however, and reflexes (automatic movements) govern the newborn's behavior. Sucking is an important means of obtaining nutrition, as well as a pleasurable, soothing activity for infants. Nonnutritive sucking interests researchers because it provides a means of evaluating attention. Crying and smiling are affective behaviors that are important in the infant's communication with the world.

II. Emotions

Emotions in infancy are adaptive and promote survival, they serve as a form of communication, and they provide regulation. Izard developed the MAX system for coding infant facial expressions of emotion. Using this system, Izard found that interest and disgust are present in newborns; a social smile, anger, and surprise develop in the first year; and contempt and guilt appear in the second year.

III. States

Researchers have put together several classification systems; one classification involves seven infant state categories, including deep sleep, drowsy, alert and focused, and inflexibly focused. Newborns usually sleep 16 to 17 hours a day. By 4 months, they approach adultlike sleeping patterns. REM sleep, during which children and adults are most likely to dream, occurs much more often in early infancy than in childhood or adulthood. The high percentage of REM sleep—about half of neonatal sleep—may be a self-stimulatory device, or it may promote brain development.

IV. Physical Growth and Development in Infancy

The cephalocaudal pattern is growth from the top down; the proximodistal pattern is growth from the center out. Gross motor skills involve large muscle activity, as in walking; fine motor skills involve more fine-grained activities, such as manual dexterity. Both gross and fine motor skills undergo extensive change in the first 2 years of a child's development. During the first year, rhythmic motor behavior—involving rapid, repetitive movement of the limbs, torso, and head—is common; this type of movement seems to represent an important adaptive transition in development. A great deal of brain growth occurs in infancy, as well as in prenatal development. Dendritic spreading is dramatic in the first 2 years of life. Some important changes in neurotransmitters probably also occur, although these changes are just beginning to be charted.

V. Nutritional Needs and Eating Behavior

Infants need to consume about 50 calories per day for each pound they weigh. Human milk, or alternative formula, is the baby's source of nutrients for the first 6 months. The growing consensus is that breast-feeding is superior to bottle-feeding, but the increase in working mothers has meant fewer breast-fed babies. Increasingly, parents are using a demand feeding schedule. The maturation of infants' oral and fine motor skills indicates appropriate ages for introducing semisolid and solid foods. Obesity in infancy has not been a good predictor of obesity in adulthood. Infants should not be placed on lowfat, low-calorie diets.

VI. Malnutrition in Infancy

Severe infant malnutrition is still prevalent in many parts of the world. Severe protein-calorie deficiency can cause marasmus, a wasting away of body tissues. It is caused mainly by early weaning from breast milk. Even if not fatal, severe and lengthy malnutrition is detrimental to physical, cognitive, and social development.

VII. Sensation and Perception

Sensation is when information contacts sensory receptors—eyes, ears, tongue, nostrils, and skin. Perception is the interpretation of what is sensed.

VIII. Visual Perception

William James said that the newborn's world is a blooming, buzzing confusion. He was wrong. The newborn's perception is more advanced than previously thought. Fantz's research demonstrated—by showing that infants prefer stripes to solids—that newborns can see. The human face is an important visual pattern for the newborn. The infant gradually masters a sequence of steps in perceiving the human face. A classic study by Gibson and Walk demonstrated, through the use of a visual cliff, that 6-month-old infants can perceive depth.

IX. Other Senses

The fetus can hear several weeks before birth; immediately after birth, newborns can hear, although their sensory threshold is higher than adults'. Smell, taste, touch, and pain are present in the newborn. Research on circumcision shows that 3-day-old males experience pain and can cope with stress.

X. Intermodal Perception

Considerable interest focuses on the infant's ability to relate information across perceptual modalities; the coordination and integration of perceptual information across two or more modalities—such as the visual and auditory senses—is called intermodal perception. Research suggests that infants as young as 4 months of age have intermodal perception. The direct perception and constructivist views are two important views of perception that make predictions about intermodal perception.

Key Terms

sucking reflex 139
rooting reflex 139
Moro reflex 139
grasping reflex 139
nonnutritive sucking 141
reflexive smile 141
social smile 141
Maximally Discriminative
  Facial Movement Coding
  System 142
REM (rapid eye
  movement) sleep 145

cephalocaudal pattern 146
proximodistal pattern 146
gross motor skills 147
fine motor skills 147
marasmus 152
sensation 155
perception 155
intermodal perception 160
direct perception view 160
constructivist view 160

Suggested Readings

Banks, M. S., & Salapatek, P. (1983). Infant visual perception. In P. E. Mussen (Ed.), *Handbook of child psychology* (4th ed., Vol. 2). New York: Wiley. This authoritative version of research on infant perception covers in great detail the topics discussed in this chapter.

Caplan, F. (1981). *The first twelve months of life.* New York: Bantam. This easy-to-read, well-written account of each of the first 12 months of life includes extensive information about motor milestones.

Lamb, M. E., & Bornstein, M. C. (1987). *Development in infancy.* New York: Random House. This portrayal of the infant by two leading researchers includes chapters on perceptual development, as well as the ecology of the infant's development.

Osofsky, J. D. (1987). *Handbook of infant development* (2nd ed.). New York: Wiley. Leading experts in the field of infant development have contributed chapters on a far-ranging set of topics about infants.

Williams, S. R., & Worthington-Roberts, B. S. (1988). *Nutrition through the life cycle.* St. Louis: Times Mirror/Mosby. This up-to-date, authoritative examination of nutrition in development has separate chapters on breast-feeding and nutrition in infancy.

PHYSICAL DEVELOPMENT IN CHILDHOOD AND PUBERTY

Physical Development in Early Childhood
    Body Growth and Change
    The Brain
    Motor Development
Physical Development in Middle and Late Childhood
    The Skeletal and Muscular Systems
    Motor Skills
Health, Nutrition, and Exercise
    A Developmental Perspective on Children's
        Health
    The State of Illness and Health in the World's
        Children
    Nutrition
    Exercise
    Perspective on Child Development 6.1:
        Heart Smart
Puberty
    Pubertal Change
    Psychological Accompaniments of Pubertal
        Change
    Pubertal Timing and Health Care
Sexuality
    Sexual Attitudes and Behavior
    Sexually Transmitted Diseases
    Adolescent Pregnancy
Some Adolescent Problems and Disturbances
    Drugs
    Cultural Worlds of Development 6.1: Adolescent
        Sexual Orientation in Holland and Sweden
    Suicide
    Eating Disorders
    The Interrelation of Problems and Programs That
        Prevent or Reduce Adolescent Problems
Stereotyping Adolescents and Today's Youth
    Stereotyping Adolescents
    Today's Youth
Summary
Key Terms
Suggested Readings

IN NO ORDER OF THINGS IS ADOLESCENCE THE SIMPLE TIME OF LIFE.

—Jean Erskine Stewart

Standing on the balance beam at a sports school in Beijing, China, 6-year-old Zhang Liyin stretches her arms outward as she gets ready to perform a backflip. She wears an elite, bright red gymnastic suit given to only the best 10 girls in her class of 6-to-8-year-olds (see figure 6.1). Her face wears a dreadful expression, however; she can't drum up enough confidence to do the flip. Maybe it is because she has had a rough week; a purple bruise decorates one leg, and a nasty gash disfigures the other. Her coach, a woman in her twenties, makes Zhang jump from the beam and escorts her to the high bar, where she is instructed to hang for 3 minutes. If Zhang falls, she must pick herself up and try again. However, she does not fall, and she is escorted back to the beam, where her coach puts her through another tedious routine.

Attending the sports school is a privilege given to only 260,000 of China's 200 million students of elementary to college age. The Communist party has decided that sports is one avenue through which China can prove it has arrived in the modern world. The sports schools designed to produce Olympic champions were the reason for China's success in the 1984 and 1988 Olympics. These schools are the only road to Olympic stardom in China. There are precious few neighborhood playgrounds, and, for every 3.5 million people, there is only one gymnasium.

Many of the students who attend the sports schools in the afternoon live and study at the schools as well. Only a few attend a normal school and then go to a sports school in the afternoon. Because of her young age, Zhang stays at home during the mornings and goes to the sports school from noon until 6 P.M. A part-timer like Zhang can stay enrolled until she no longer shows potential to move up to the next step. Any child who seems to lack potential is asked to leave.

Zhang was playing in a nursery school class when a coach from a sports school spotted her. She was selected because she has broad shoulders, narrow hips, straight legs, symmetrical limbs, an open-minded attitude, vivaciousness, and an outgoing personality. If Zhang continues to show progress, she could be asked to move to full time next year. At age 7, she would then go to school there and live in a dorm 6 days a week. If she becomes extremely competent at gymnastics, Zhang could be moved over to Shishahai, where the elite gymnasts train and compete.

At Shishahai, the day begins at 6 A.M. with breakfast, followed by 4 hours of academic classes and study until 11:30 A.M. Then follows lunch and a nap until 2:30, 4 grueling hours of athletic training, dinner at 7, more studies from 7 to 9, and lights out at 9:30. No TVs are allowed in the school, no in-room phones are permitted, and dating is prohibited. Coca-Cola, VCRs, and Colonel Sanders may have arrived in Beijing, but they won't be found at the Shishahai sports school.

Possibly someday Zhang will be one of the special ones, achieving a good education, a good salary, and perhaps an Olympic medal. For now, however, she is just one of many aspirants. Every day she is tested to see if she is on schedule for stardom (Reilly, 1988).

■ *Critical Thinking*
Is the policy of China and other countries that use massive efforts to discover and train potential Olympic athletes at very young ages a wise one? What needs and concerns of children are involved?

Biological Processes, Physical Development, and Perceptual Development

By American standards, Zhang's life sounds rigid and punitive. Although achievement in sports has a lofty status in American society, children are not trained with the intensity now being witnessed in China, some Eastern European nations, and the Soviet Union.

Later in the chapter, we will discuss further information about children's sports and physical fitness in middle and late childhood. Our coverage of children's development in this chapter will also focus on physical development in early childhood; physical development in middle and late childhood; children's health, nutrition, and exercise; puberty; adolescent sexuality; some adolescent problems and disturbances; stereotypes of adolescents; and what youths today are like.

Figure 6.1
Training Future Olympians in the Sports Schools of China
Six-year-old Zhang Liyin is the third from the left. She hopes someday to become an Olympic gymnastics champion. Attending the sports school is considered an outstanding privilege; it is given to only 260,000 of China's 200 million children.

Physical Development in Early Childhood

Remember from chapter 5 that an infant's growth in the first year is extremely rapid and follows cephalocaudal and proximodistal patterns. At a point around their first birthday, most infants begin to walk. During an infant's second year, the growth rate begins to slow down, but both gross and fine motor skills progress rapidly. The infant develops a sense of mastery through increased proficiency in walking and running. Improvement in fine motor skills—such as being able to turn the pages of a book one at a time—also contributes to the infant's sense of mastery in the second year. The growth rate continues to slow down in early childhood; otherwise, we would be a species of giants.

Body Growth and Change

An average child grows 2½ inches in height and gains between 5 and 7 pounds a year during early childhood. As the preschool child grows older, the percentage of increase in height and weight decreases with each additional year. The average height and weight of children as they age from 3 to 6 is shown in figure 6.2. Girls are only slightly smaller and lighter than boys during these

Figure 6.2
**Average Height and Weight of Children As
They Age from 3 to 6**

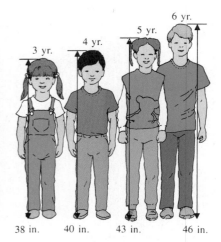

Physical growth, ages 3 to 6 (50th percentile)				
	Height (inches)		Weight (pounds)	
Age	Boys	Girls	Boys	Girls
3	38	37¾	32¼	31¾
3½	39¼	39¼	34¼	34
4	40¼	40½	36½	36¼
4½	42	42	38½	38½
5	43¼	43	41½	41
5½	45	44½	45½	44
6	46	46	48	47

years, a difference that continues until puberty. During the preschool years, both boys and girls slim down as the trunk of their bodies lengthens. Although their heads are still somewhat large for their bodies, by the end of the preschool years, most children have lost their top-heavy look. Body fat also shows a slow, steady decline during the preschool years, so that chubby babies often look much leaner by the end of early childhood. Girls have more fatty tissue than boys, and boys have more muscle tissue.

Growth patterns vary individually. Think back to your preschool years. This was probably the first time you noticed that some children were taller than you, some shorter; some were fatter, some thinner; some were stronger, some weaker. Much of the variation is due to heredity, but environmental experiences are involved, to an extent. A review of the heights and weights of children around the world concluded that the two most important contributors to height differences are ethnic origin and nutrition (Meredith, 1978). Urban, middle-class, and firstborn children are taller than rural, lower-class, and later-born children. Children whose mothers smoked during pregnancy are ½ inch shorter than children whose mothers did not smoke during pregnancy. In the United States, Black children are taller than White children.

The Brain

One of the most important physical developments during early childhood is the continuing development of the brain and nervous system. Although the brain continues to grow in early childhood, it does not grow as rapidly as in infancy. By the time children have reached 3 years of age, the brain is three quarters of its adult size. By age 5, the brain has reached about nine tenths its adult size.

The brain and the head grow more rapidly than any other parts of the body. The top parts of the head, the eyes, and the brain grow faster than the lower portions, such as the jaw. Figure 6.3 reveals how the growth curve for the head and brain advances more rapidly than the growth curve for height and weight. At 5 years of age, when the brain has attained approximately 90 percent of its adult weight, the 5-year-old's total body weight is only about one third of what it will be when the child reaches adulthood.

Some of the brain's increase in size is due to the increase in the number and size of nerve endings within and between areas of the brain. These nerve

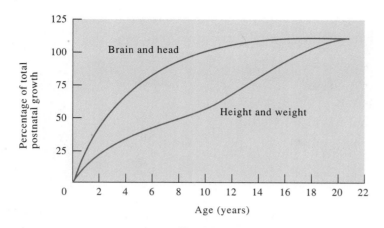

Figure 6.3
Growth Curves for the Brain and Head, Height and Weight
The more rapid growth of the brain and head can be seen. Height and weight advance more gradually over the first 2 decades of life (After Damon, 1977).

endings continue to grow at least until adolescence. Some of the brain's increase in size also is due to the increase in **myelination,** *a process in which nerve cells are covered and insulated with a layer of fat cells. This process has the effect of increasing the speed of information traveling through the nervous system.* Some developmentalists believe myelination is important in the maturation of a number of children's abilities. For example, myelination in the areas of the brain related to hand-eye coordination is not complete until about 4 years of age. Myelination in the areas of the brain related to focusing attention is not complete until the end of middle and late childhood (Tanner, 1978).

The increasing maturation of the brain, combined with opportunities to experience a widening world, contributes enormously to children's emerging cognitive abilities. Consider a child who is learning to read and is asked by her teacher to read aloud to the class. Input from the child's eyes is transmitted to her brain and then passed through many brain systems, which translate (process) the patterns of black and white into codes for letters, words, and associations. The output occurs in the form of messages to the child's lips and tongue. Her gift of speech is possible because brain systems are organized in ways that permit language processing.

Motor Development

Running as fast as you can, falling down, getting right back up and running just as fast as you can . . . building towers with blocks . . . scribbling, scribbling, and more scribbling . . . cutting paper with scissors—during your preschool years, you probably developed the ability to perform all of these activities.

Gross Motor Skills

The preschool child no longer has to make an effort simply to stay upright and move around. As children move their legs with more confidence and carry themselves more purposefully, the process of moving around in the environment becomes more automatic.

At 3 years of age, children are still enjoying simple movements, such as hopping, jumping, and running back and forth, just for the sheer delight of performing them. They take considerable pride in showing how they can run across a room and jump all of 6 inches. The run-and-jump will win no Olympic gold medals, but, for the 3-year-old, the activity is a source of considerable pride and accomplishment.

That energy which makes a child hard to manage is the energy which afterward makes him a manager of life.

—Henry Ward Beecher

Preschool children are very active. Three-year-olds have the highest energy level of any age in the human life span. Because of their activity level and the development of their large muscles, especially in the arms and legs, preschool children need daily exercise.

At 4 years of age, children are still enjoying the same kind of activities, but they have become more adventurous. They scramble over low jungle gyms as they display their athletic prowess. Although they have been able to climb stairs with one foot on each step for some time now, they are just beginning to be able to come down the same way. They still often revert to marking time on each step.

By 5 years of age, children have become even more adventuresome than when they were 4. It is not unusual for self-assured 5-year-olds to perform hair-raising stunts on practically any climbing object. Five-year-olds run hard and enjoy races with each other and their parents.

You probably have arrived at an important conclusion about preschool children: They are very, very active. Indeed, researchers have found that 3-year-old children have the highest activity level of any age in the human life span. They fidget when they watch television. They fidget when they sit at the dinner table. Even when they sleep, they move around quite a bit. Because of their activity level and the development of their large muscles, especially in the arms and legs, preschool children need daily exercise.

Fine Motor Skills

At 3 years of age, children are still emerging from the infant ability to place and handle things. Although they have had the ability to pick up the tiniest objects between their thumb and forefinger for some time now, they are still somewhat clumsy at it. Three-year-olds can build surprisingly high block towers, placing each block with intense concentration but often not in a completely straight line. When 3-year-olds play with a form board or simple jigsaw puzzle, they are rather rough in placing the pieces. Even when they recognize the hole a piece fits into, they are not very precise in positioning the piece. They often try to force the piece in the hole or pat it vigorously.

By 4 years of age, children's fine motor coordination has improved substantially and has become much more precise. Sometimes 4-year-old children have trouble building high towers with blocks because, in their desire to place each of the blocks perfectly, they may upset those already stacked. By age 5, children's fine motor coordination has improved further. Hand, arm, and body all move together under better command of the eye. Mere towers no longer interest the 5-year-old, who now wants to build a house or a church complete with steeple, though adults may still need to be told what each finished project is meant to be.

How do developmentalists measure motor development? The **Denver Developmental Screening Test** *is a widely used test to measure young children's motor development. It is especially helpful in assessing developmental delay in motor skills and can be used with children from birth through 6 years of age.* The test is individually administered and includes an evaluation of language and personal-social ability, in addition to separate assessments of gross and fine motor skills. Among the gross motor skills that are measured are the child's ability to sit, walk, long jump, pedal a tricycle, throw a ball overhand, catch a bounced ball, hop on one foot, and balance on one foot. Fine motor skills that are measured include the child's ability to stack cubes, reach for objects, and draw a person.

Young children's developing ability to hold a pencil or crayon reveals growth in fine motor coordination. Toddlers tend to grasp a pencil or crayon in the palm of their hand and make rough, crude movements with it. During early childhood, children become more proficient, learning to use their fingers and wrist to manipulate the tip rather than the whole pencil or crayon.

Handedness

For centuries, left-handers have suffered discrimination in a world designed for right-handers. Even the devil was portrayed as a left-hander. For many years, teachers forced all children to write with their right hand even if they had a left-hand tendency. Fortunately, today, most teachers let children write with the hand they favor.

Some children are still discouraged from using their left hand, even though many left-handed individuals have become very successful. Their ranks include Leonardo da Vinci, Benjamin Franklin, and Pablo Picasso. Each of these famous men was known for his imagination of spatial layouts, which may be stronger in left-handed individuals. Left-handed athletes also are often successful; since there are fewer left-handed athletes, the opposition is not as accustomed to the style and approach of "lefties." Their serve in tennis spins in the opposite direction from right-handers', their curve ball in baseball swerves the opposite way, and their left foot in soccer is not the one children are used to defending against. Left-handed individuals also do well intellectually. In an analysis of the Scholastic Aptitude Test (SAT) scores of more than 100,000 students, 20 percent of the top scoring group was left-handed, which is twice the rate of left-handedness found in the general population (Bower, 1985). Quite clearly, many left-handed people are competent in a wide variety of human activities ranging from athletic skills to intellectual accomplishments.

Today, most teachers let children write with the hand they favor.

When does hand preference develop? Adults usually notice a child's hand preference during early childhood, but researchers have found handedness tendencies in the infant years. Even newborns prefer one side of their body over the other. In one research investigation, 65 percent of the infants turned their head to the right when they were lying on their stomachs in the crib. Fifteen percent preferred to face toward the left. These preferences for the right or left were related to later handedness (Michel, 1981). By about 7 months of age, infants prefer grabbing with one hand or the other, and this is also related to later handedness (Ramsay, 1980). At 2 years of age, about 10 percent of children favor their left hand (Hardyck & Petrinovich, 1977). Many preschool children, though, use both hands, with a clear hand preference not completely distinguishable until later in development. Some children use one hand for writing and drawing, and the other hand for throwing a ball.

What is the origin of hand preference? Genetic inheritance and environmental experiences have been proposed as causes. In one investigation, a genetic interpretation was favored. The handedness of adopted children was not related to the handedness of their adopted parents but was related to the handedness of their biological parents (Carter-Saltzman, 1980).

Physical Development in Middle and Late Childhood

The period of middle and late childhood involves slow, consistent growth. This is a period of calm before the rapid growth spurt of adolescence. Among the important aspects of body change in this developmental period are those involving the skeletal system, the muscular system, and motor skills.

The Skeletal and Muscular Systems

During the elementary school years, children grow an average of 2 to 3 inches a year until, at the age of 11, the average girl is 4 feet 10 inches tall and the average boy is 4 feet 9½ inches tall. Children's legs become longer and their trunks slimmer. During the middle and late childhood years, children gain about 5 to 7 pounds a year. The weight increase is due mainly to increases in the size of the skeletal and muscular systems, as well as the size of some body organs. Muscle mass and strength gradually increase as "baby fat" decreases. The loose movements and knock knees of early childhood give way to improved muscle tone. The increase in muscular strength is due to heredity and exercise. Children double their strength capabilities during these years. Because of their greater number of muscle cells, boys are usually stronger than girls (Whaley & Wong, 1988).

Motor Skills

During middle and late childhood, children's motor development becomes much smoother and more coordinated than it was in early childhood. For example, only one child in a thousand can hit a tennis ball over the net at the age of 3, yet, by the age of 10 or 11, most children can learn to play the sport. Running, climbing, skipping rope, swimming, bicycle riding, and skating are just a few of the many physical skills elementary school children can master. When mastered, these physical skills are a source of great pleasure and accomplishment for children. In gross motor skills involving large muscle activity, boys usually outperform girls.

As children move through the elementary school years, children gain greater control over their bodies and can sit and attend for longer periods of time. However, elementary school children are far from having physical maturity, and they need to be active. Elementary school children become more fatigued by long periods of sitting than by running, jumping, or bicycling. Physical action is essential for these children to refine their developing skills, such as batting a ball, skipping rope, or balancing on a beam. An important principle of practice for elementary school children, therefore, is that they should be engaged in *active,* rather than passive, activities (Katz & Chard, 1989).

Little league baseball, soccer, basketball, tennis, dance—as children's motor development becomes smoother and more coordinated, they are able to master these activities more competently in middle and late childhood than in early childhood.

Increased myelinization of the central nervous system is reflected in the improvement of fine motor skills during middle and late childhood. Children use their hands more adroitly as tools. Six-year-olds can hammer, paste, tie shoes, and fasten clothes. By 7 years of age, children's hands have become steadier. At this age, children prefer a pencil to a crayon for printing, and reversal of letters is less common. Their printing becomes smaller. Between 8 to 10 years of age, the hands can be used independently with more ease and precision. Fine motor coordination develops to the point where children can write rather than print words. Letter size becomes smaller and more even. At 10 to 12 years of age, children begin to show manipulative skills similar to the abilities of adults. The complex, intricate, and rapid movements needed to produce fine-quality crafts or to play a difficult piece on a musical instrument can be mastered. Girls usually outperform boys in fine motor skills.

Health, Nutrition, and Exercise

Although we have become a health-conscious nation, aware of the importance of nutrition and exercise in our lives, many of us still eat junk food, have extra flab hanging around our middles, and spend too much time as couch potatoes. All too often, this description fits children as well as adults.

A Developmental Perspective on Children's Health

Although there has been great national interest in the psychological aspects of adult health, only recently has a developmental perspective on the psychological aspects of children's health been proposed. The uniqueness of young children's health care needs is evident when we consider their motor, cognitive, and social development (Maddux & others, 1986). For example, think about the infant's and preschool child's motor development—it is inadequate to ensure personal safety while riding in an automobile. Adults must take preventive measures to restrain infants and young children in car seats. Young children may lack the intellectual skills—including reading ability—to discriminate between safe and unsafe household substances, and they may lack the impulse control to keep them from running out into a busy street while chasing after a ball or toy.

Playgrounds for young children need to be designed with their safety in mind (Frost & Wortham, 1988). The initial steps in ensuring children's safety is to walk with children through the existing playground or the site where the playground is to be developed, talking with them about possible safety hazards, letting them assist in identifying hazards, and indicating how they can use the playground safely. The outdoor play environment should enhance children's motor, cognitive, and social development.

Health education programs for preschool children need to be cognitively simple. There are three simple but important goals for health education programs for preschool children (Parcel & others, 1979): (1) to help children identify feelings of wellness and illness and be able to express them to adults, (2) to help children identify appropriate sources of assistance for health-related problems, and (3) to help children independently initiate the use of sources of assistance for health problems.

Caregivers have an important health role for young children (Farmer, Peterson, & Kashani, 1989). For example, by controlling the speed of the vehicles they drive, by decreasing their drinking, and by not smoking around children, caregivers enhance children's health. In one recent investigation, it was found that, if a mother smokes, her children are twice as likely to have respiratory ailments (Etzel, 1988). The young children of single, unemployed, smoking mothers are also three times more likely to be injured. Smoking may serve as a marker to identify mothers less able to supervise young children. In sum, caregivers can actively affect young children's health and safety by training them and monitoring their recreational safety, self-protection skills, proper nutrition, and dental hygiene.

Illnesses, especially those that are not life threatening, provide an excellent opportunity for young children to expand their development. The preschool period is a peak time for such illnesses as respiratory infections (colds, flu) and gastrointestinal upsets (nausea, diarrhea). The illnesses usually are of short duration and are often handled outside the medical community, through the family, day care, or school. Such minor illnesses can increase the young child's knowledge of health and illness and sense of empathy (Parmalee, 1986).

Young children may confuse such terms as "feel bad" with bad behavior and "feel good" with good behavior. Examples include:

"I feel bad. I want aspirin."
"I feel bad. My tummy hurts."
"Bobby hurt me."
"I bad girl. I wet my pants."
"Me can do it. Me good girl."
"I'm hurting your feeling, 'cause I was mean to you."
"Stop; it doesn't feel good."

Young children often attribute their illness to what they view as a transgression, such as having eaten the wrong food or playing outdoors in the cold when told not to. In illness and wellness situations, adults have the potential to help children sort out distressed feelings resulting from emotional upsets from those caused by physical illness. For example, a mother might say to her young daughter, "I know you feel bad because you are sick like your sister was last week, but you will be well soon, just as she is now," or a father might comment, "I know you feel bad because I am going on a trip and I can't take you with me, but I will be back in a few days" (Parmalee, 1986).

Physical Development in Childhood and Puberty

Although oral rehydration therapy is being used in Bangladesh, 10 percent of all children born there die before the age of 5 from dehydration and malnutrition brought about by diarrhea.

A simple child,
That lightly draws its breath,
What should it know of death?

—William Wordsworth

■ *Critical Thinking*

What responsibility do the wealthier nations of the world have for fostering and financially supporting health and nutrition services for children in developing countries? Explain.

The State of Illness and Health in the World's Children

A special concern is the state of children's illness and health in developing countries around the world. One death of every three in the world is the death of a child under the age of 5 (Grant, 1990). Every week, more than a quarter of a million children die in developing countries in a quiet carnage of infection and undernutrition. The leading cause of childhood death in the world is dehydration and malnutrition as a result of diarrhea. Approximately 70 percent of the more than 40 million children killed by diarrhea in 1989 could have been saved if parents had available a low-cost breakthrough known as **oral rehydration therapy (ORT),** *a treatment involving a range of techniques designed to prevent dehydration during episodes of diarrhea by giving the child fluids by mouth.*

Most child malnutrition and deaths could now be prevented by parental actions that are almost universally affordable and based on knowledge that is already available. Making sure that parents know they can improve their children's health by adequate birth spacing, care during pregnancy, breast-feeding, immunization, special feeding before and after illness, and regular check-ups of the children's weight can overcome many causes of malnutrition and poor growth.

Among the nations with the highest mortality rate under age 5 are Asian nations, such as Afghanistan, and African nations, such as Ethiopia (Grant, 1990). In Afghanistan, in 1986, for every 1,000 children born alive, 325 died before the age of 5; in Ethiopia, the figure was 255 per 1,000. Among the countries with the lowest mortality rate under age 5 are Scandinavian countries, such as Sweden and Finland, where only 7 of every 1,000 children born died before the age of 5 in 1986. The United States mortality rate under age 5 is better than that of most countries, but, of 131 countries for which figures were available in 1986, 20 countries had better rates than the United States. In 1986, for every 1,000 children born alive in the United States, 13 died before the age of 5.

Biological Processes, Physical Development, and Perceptual Development

Fortunately, in the United States, the dangers of many diseases, such as measles, rubella (German measles), mumps, whooping cough, diphtheria, and polio, are no longer as severe as they once were. The vast majority of children in the United States have been immunized against such major childhood diseases. It is important, though, for parents to recognize that these diseases, although no longer afflicting most of our nation's children, do require a sequence of vaccinations. Without the vaccinations, children can still get the diseases.

The disorders most likely to be fatal during the preschool years are birth defects, cancer, and heart disease. Death rates from these problems have been reduced in recent years because of improved treatments and health care (Garrison and McQuiston, 1989).

Nutrition

Four-year-old Bobby is on a steady diet of double cheeseburgers, french fries, and chocolate milkshakes. Between meals, he gobbles up candy bars and marshmallows. He hates green vegetables. Only a preschooler, Bobby already has developed poor nutrition habits.

Energy Needs

Eating habits are important aspects of development during early childhood. The food children eat affects their skeletal growth, body shape, and susceptibility to disease. Recognizing that nutrition is important for children's growth and development, the federal government provides money for school lunch programs. An average preschool child requires 1,700 calories per day. Table 6.1 shows the increasing energy needs of children as they move from infancy through the childhood years. Energy requirements for individual children are influenced by their **basal metabolism rate (BMR),** *which is the minimum amount of energy a person uses in a resting state.* The energy needs of children of the same age, sex, and size vary. These differences remain unexplained. Variances in physical activity, basal metabolism rate, and the efficiency with which children use energy are among the candidates for explanation (Pipes, 1988b).

Eating Behavior

A special concern in our culture is the amount of fat in our diets. Whereas some health-conscious mothers may be providing too little fat in their infants' and children's diets, other parents are raising their children on diets in which the percentage of fat is far too high. Our changing life-styles, in which we often eat on the run and pick up fast-food meals, probably contribute to the increased fat levels in children's diets. Most fast-food meals are high in protein, especially meat and dairy products, but the average American child does not need to be concerned about getting enough protein. What must be of concern is the vast number of young children who are being weaned on fast foods that are not only high in protein but also high in fat. Eating habits become ingrained very early in life, and, unfortunately, it is during the preschool years that many people get their first taste of fast foods. The American Heart Association recommends that the daily limit for calories from fat should be approximately 35 percent. Compare this figure with the figures in table 6.2. Clearly, many fast-food meals contribute to excess fat intake by children.

TABLE 6.1
The Recommended Energy Intakes for Children

Age	Weight (kg)	Height (cm)	Energy needs (calories)	Calorie range
1 to 3	13	90	1,300	900 to 1,800
4 to 6	20	112	1,700	1,300 to 2,300
7 to 10	28	132	2,400	1,650 to 3,300

Source: Food and Nutrition Board, National Research Council: *Recommended Dietary Allowance*, Revised Ed. 9, Washington, DC, 1980, National Academy of Sciences.

TABLE 6.2
The Fat and Calorie Content of Selected Fast Foods

Food	Calories	% of calories from fat
Burger King Whopper, fries, vanilla shake	1,250	43
Big Mac, fries, chocolate shake	1,100	41
McDonald's Quarter-Pounder with cheese	418	52
Pizza Hut 10-inch pizza with sausage, mushrooms, pepperoni, and green pepper	1,035	35
Arby's roast beef sandwich, two potato patties, coleslaw, chocolate shake	1,200	30
Kentucky Fried Chicken dinner (three pieces chicken, mashed potatoes and gravy, coleslaw, roll)	830	50
Arthur Treacher's fish and chips (two pieces breaded and fried fish, french fries, cola drink)	900	42
Typical restaurant "diet plate" (hamburger patty, cottage cheese, etc.)	638	63

From Virginia Demoss, "Good, the Bad and the Edible" in *Runner's World*, June 1980. Copyright Virginia Demoss. Reprinted with permission.

Being overweight can be a serious problem in early childhood. Consider Ramon, a kindergartner who always begged to stay inside to help his teacher during recess. His teacher noticed that Ramon never joined the running games the small "superheroes" played as they propelled themselves around the playground. Ramon is an overweight 4-year-old. Except in extreme cases of obesity, physicians usually do not encourage overweight preschool children to lose a great deal of weight, but to slow their rate of weight gain so that they will grow into a more normal weight for their height by thinning out as they grow taller. The prevention of obesity in children includes helping children and parents see food as a way to satisfy hunger and nutritional needs, not as proof of love or as a reward for good behavior. Snack foods should be low in fat, simple sugars, and salt and high in fiber. Physical activity should be a daily routine. The child's life should be centered around activities, not meals (Javernik, 1988).

In sum, although there is individual variation in appropriate nutrition for children, their diets should be well balanced and should include fats, carbohydrates, protein, vitamins, and minerals. An occasional candy bar does not hurt and can even benefit a growing body, but a steady diet of hamburgers, french fries, milkshakes, and candy bars should be avoided.

Exercise

Many of our patterns of health and illness are longstanding. Our experiences as children contribute to our health practices as adults. Did your parents seek medical help at your first sniffle, or did they wait until your temperature reached 104 degrees? Did they feed you heavy doses of red meat and sugar or a more rounded diet with vegetables and fruit? Did they get you involved in sports or exercise programs, or did you lie around watching television all the time?

Are children getting enough exercise? The 1985 School Fitness Survey tested 18,857 children aged 6 to 17 on nine fitness tasks. Compared to a similar survey in 1975, there was virtually no improvement on the tasks. For example, 40 percent of the boys 6 to 12 years of age could do no more than one pull-up, and a full 25 percent could not do any. Fifty percent of the girls aged 6 to 17 and 30 percent of the boys aged 6 to 12 could not run a mile in less than 10 minutes. In the 50-yard dash, the adolescent girls in 1975 were faster than the adolescent girls in 1985.

Some experts suggest that television is at least partially to blame for the poor physical condition of our nation's children. In one investigation, children who watched little television were significantly more physically fit than their heavy-television-viewing counterparts (Tucker, 1987). The more children watch television, the more they are likely to be overweight. No one is quite sure whether this is because children spend their leisure time in front of the television set instead of chasing each other around the neighborhood or whether they tend to eat a lot of junk food they see advertised on television.

Some of the blame also falls on the nation's schools, many of which fail to provide physical education classes on a daily basis. In the 1985 School Fitness Survey, 37 percent of the children in the first through the fourth grades took gym classes only once or twice a week. The investigation also revealed that parents are poor role models when it comes to physical fitness. Less than 30 percent of the parents of children in grades 1 through 4 exercised 3 days a week. Roughly half said they never get any vigorous exercise. In another study, observations of children's behavior in physical education classes at four elementary schools revealed how little vigorous exercise is done in these classes (Parcel & others, 1987). Children moved through space only 50 percent of the time they were in the class, and they moved continuously an average of only 2.2 minutes. In summary, not only do children's school weeks not include adequate physical education classes, but the majority of children do not exercise vigorously even when they are in such classes. Furthermore, most children's parents are poor role models for vigorous physical exercise.

Does it make a difference if we push children to exercise more vigorously in elementary school? One recent investigation says yes (Tuckman & Hinkle, 1988). One hundred fifty-four elementary school children were randomly assigned either to three 30-minute running programs per week or to regular attendance in physical education classes. Although the results sometimes varied according to sex, for the most part, the cardiovascular health as well as the creativity of children in the running program were enhanced. For example, the boys in this program had less body fat and the girls had more creative involvement in their classrooms. Exercise is also an important component in a large-scale investigation of children's health called the Bogalusa Heart Study, which involves an ongoing evaluation of 8,000 boys and girls in Bogalusa, Louisiana (Berensen, 1989; Downey & others, 1987). Observations show that the precursors of heart disease begin at a young age, with many children already possessing one or more clinical risk factors, such as hypertension or obesity. Based on the Bogalusa Heart Study, a cardiovascular health intervention model for children has been developed. The model is called Heart Smart, which you can read about in Perspective on Child Development 6.1.

The quality of life is determined by its activities.

—Aristotle

Heart Smart

The school is the focus of the Heart Smart intervention. Since 95 percent of children and adolescents aged 5 to 18 are in school, schools are an efficient context in which to educate individuals about health. Special attention is given to teachers, who serve as role models. Teachers who value the role of health in life and who engage in health-enhancing behavior present children and adolescents with positive models for health. Teacher in-service education is conducted by an interdisciplinary team of specialists, including physicians, psychologists, nutritionists, physical educators, and exercise physiologists. The school's staff is introduced to heart health education, the nature of cardiovascular disease, and risk factors for heart disease. Coping behavior, exercise behavior, and eating behavior are discussed with the staff, and a Heart Smart curriculum is explained. For example, the Heart Smart curriculum for grade 5 includes the content areas of cardiovascular health (such as risk factors associated with heart disease), behavior skills (for example, self-assessment and monitoring), eating behavior (for example, the effects of food on health), and exercise behavior (for example, the effects of exercise on the heart).

The physical education component of Heart Smart involves two to four class periods each week to incorporate a "Superkids-Superfit" exercise program. The physical education instructor teaches skills required by the school system plus aerobic activities aimed at cardiovascular conditioning including jogging, race walking, interval workouts, rope skipping, circuit training, aerobic dance, and games. Classes begin and end with 5 minutes of walking and stretching.

The school lunch program serves as an intervention site, where sodium, fat, and sugar levels are decreased. Children and adolescents are given reasons they should eat healthy foods, such as a tuna sandwich, and why they should not eat unhealthy foods, such as a hot dog with chili. The school lunch program includes a salad bar, where children and adolescents can serve themselves. The amount and type of snack foods sold on the school premises are monitored.

High-risk children—those with elevated blood pressure, cholesterol, and weight—are identified as part of Heart Smart. A multidisciplinary team of physicians, nutritionists, nurses, and behavioral counselors work with the high-risk boys and girls and their parents through group-oriented activities and individual-based family counseling. High-risk boys and girls and their parents receive diet, exercise, and relaxation prescriptions in an intensive 12-session program, followed by long-term monthly evaluations.

Extensive assessment is a part of this ongoing program. Short-term and long-term changes in children's knowledge about cardiovascular disease and changes in their behavior are being assessed.

One of the most important components of heart disease prevention programs is a regular, vigorous exercise workout.

In addition to the school, the family plays an important role in a child's exercise program. A wise strategy is for the family to take up activities involving vigorous physical exercise that parents and children can enjoy together. Running, swimming, cycling, and hiking are especially recommended. In encouraging children to exercise more, parents should not push them beyond their physical limits or expose them to competitive pressures that take the fun out of sports and exercise. For example, long-distance running may be too strenuous for young children and could result in bone injuries. Recently, there has been an increase in the number of children competing in strenuous athletic events such as marathons and triathalons. Doctors are beginning to see some injuries in children that they previously saw only in adults. Some injuries, such as stress fractures and tendonitis, stem from the overuse of young, still-growing bodies (Risser, 1989). If left to their own devices, how many 8-year-old children would want to prepare for a marathon? It is recommended that parents downplay cutthroat striving and encourage healthy sports that children can enjoy (Puffer, 1987).

At this point, we have discussed a number of ideas about children's physical growth, health, nutrition, and exercise. A summary of these ideas is presented in concept table 6.1. Now we will turn our attention to the nature of pubertal changes.

Puberty

Imagine a toddler displaying all the features of puberty. Think about a 3-year-old girl with fully developed breasts or a boy just slightly older with a deep male voice. That is what we would see by the year 2250 if the age at which puberty arrives were to continue to decrease at its present pace (Petersen, 1979).

In Norway, **menarche,** *first menstruation,* occurs at just over 13 years of age, as opposed to 17 years of age in the 1840s. In the United States—where children mature up to a year earlier than children in European countries—the average age of menarche has declined from 14.2 in 1900 to about 12.45 today. The age of menarche has been declining at an average of about 4 months per decade for the past century (see figure 6.4).

I think that what is happening to me is so wonderful and not only what can be seen on my body, but all that is taking place inside. I never discuss myself with anybody; that is why I have to talk to myself about them.

—Anne Frank

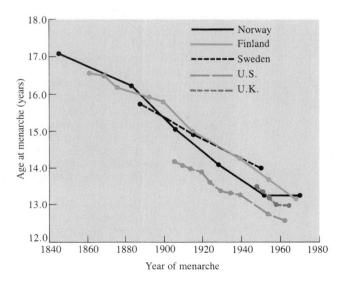

Figure 6.4
Age at Menarche, 1845–1969

Physical Development, Health, Nutrition, and Exercise

Concept	Processes/related ideas	Characteristics/description
Physical development in early childhood	Body growth and change	The average child grows 2½ inches in height and gains between 5 and 7 pounds a year during early childhood. Growth patterns vary individually.
	The brain	The brain is a key aspect of growth. By age 5, the brain has reached nine tenths of its final size. Some of its increased size is due to increases in the number and size of nerve endings, some to myelination. Increasing brain maturation contributes to improved cognitive abilities.
	Motor development	Both gross and fine motor skills improve considerably in early childhood. Young children's lives are extremely active, more active than at any point in the human life cycle. At one point, all children were taught to be right-handed. In today's world, the strategy is to let children use the hand they favor. Both genetic and environmental explanations of handedness have been given.
Physical development in middle and late childhood	The skeletal and muscular systems	During the elementary school years, children grow an average of 2 to 3 inches a year. Muscle mass and strength gradually increase. Legs lengthen and trunks slim down as "baby fat" decreases. Growth is slow and consistent.
	Motor skills	During the middle and late childhood years, children's motor development becomes much smoother and more coordinated. Children gain greater control over their bodies and can sit and attend for longer frames of time. However, their lives should be activity oriented and very active. Increased myelinization of the central nervous system is reflected in improved fine motor skills. Boys are usually better at gross motor skills, girls at fine motor skills.
Health, nutrition, and exercise	A developmental perspective on children's health	Only recently have researchers applied a developmental perspective to children's health. Children's health care needs involve their motor, cognitive, and social development.
	The state of illness and health in the world's children	One death of every three in the world is the death of a child under 5. Every week, more than a quarter of a million children die in developing countries. The most frequent cause of children's death is diarrhea. Oral rehydration therapy can be used to prevent diarrhea from leading to death. Most child malnutrition and death could be prevented by parental actions that are affordable and based on knowledge available today. The United States has a relatively low rate of child deaths compared to other countries, although the Scandinavian countries have the lowest rates. The disorders most likely to be fatal for American children in the preschool years are birth defects, cancer, and heart disease.
	Nutrition	Energy needs increase as children go through the childhood years. Energy requirements vary according to basal metabolism, rate of growth, and activity. Many parents are raising children on diets that are too high in fat and sugar content. Children's diets should include well-balanced proportions of fats, carbohydrates, protein, vitamins, and minerals.
	Exercise	Every indication suggests that our nation's children are not getting enough exercise. Television viewing, parents being poor role models for children's exercise, and the lack of adequate physical education classes in schools may be to blame.

Puberty involves a dramatic upheaval in bodily change. Young adolescents develop an acute concern about their bodies. Columnist Bob Greene (1988) dialed a party line in Chicago, called Connections, to discover what young adolescents were saying to each other. The first things the boys and girls asked for—after first names—were physical descriptions. The idealism of the callers was apparent. Most of the girls described themselves as having long blond hair, being 5 feet 5 inches tall, and weighing about 110 pounds. Most of the boys said they had brown hair, lifted weights, were 6 feet tall, and weighed about 170 pounds.

Fortunately, however, we are unlikely to see pubescent toddlers, since what has characterized the past century is special—most likely, a higher level of nutrition and health. The available information suggests that menarche began to occur earlier at about the time of the Industrial Revolution, a period associated with increased standards of living and advances in medical science.

Menarche is one event that characterizes puberty, but there are others. What are puberty's markers? What are the psychological accompaniments of puberty's changes? What health care issues are raised by early and late maturation?

Pubertal Change

Puberty *is a period of rapid skeletal and sexual maturation that occurs mainly in early adolescence.* However, puberty is not a single, sudden event. It is part of a gradual process. We know when a young person is going through puberty, but pinpointing its beginning and its end is difficult. Except for menarche, which occurs rather late in puberty, no single marker heralds puberty (Brooks-Gunn, 1991; Brooks-Gunn & Reiter, 1990; Malina, 1990). For boys, the first whisker or first wet dream are events that could mark its appearance, but both may go unnoticed.

Behind the first whisker in boys and widening of hips in girls is a flood of hormones, powerful chemical substances secreted by the endocrine glands and carried through the body by the bloodstream (Kulin, 1991; Rabin, 1991). The concentrations of certain hormones increase dramatically during adolescence. **Testosterone** *is a hormone associated with the development of genitals, an increase in height, and a change in voice in boys.* **Estradiol** *is a hormone associated with breast, uterine, and skeletal development in girls.* In one investigation, testosterone levels increased 18-fold in boys but only 2-fold in girls during puberty; estradiol increased 8-fold in girls but only 2-fold in boys (Nottelmann & others, 1987).

The same influx of hormones that puts hair on a male's chest and imparts curvature to a female's breast may contribute to psychological development in adolescence (Susman & Dorn, 1991). In one study of 108 normal boys and girls ranging in age from 9 to 14, a higher concentration of testosterone was present in boys who rated themselves more socially competent

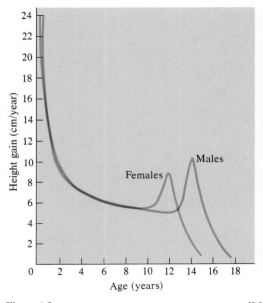

Figure 6.5
Pubertal Growth Spurt
On the average, the growth spurt that characterizes pubertal change occurs 2 years earlier for girls (age 10½) than for boys (age 12½).

(Nottelmann & others, 1987). In another investigation of 60 normal boys and girls in the same age range, girls with higher estradiol levels expressed more anger and aggression (Inoff-Germain & others, 1988). However, hormonal effects, by themselves, may account for only a small portion of the variance in adolescent development. For example, in one recent study, social factors accounted for two to four times as much variance as hormonal factors in young adolescent girls' depression and anger (Brooks-Gunn & Warren, 1989b).

These hormonal and body changes occur, on the average, about 2 years earlier in females (10½ years of age) than in males (12½ years of age) (see figure 6.5). Four of the most noticeable areas of body change in females are a height spurt, menarche, breast growth, and growth of pubic hair (Malina, 1991; Tanner, 1991); four of the most noticeable areas of body change in males are a height spurt, penile growth, testes growth, and growth of pubic hair. The normal range and average age of these characteristics are shown in figures 6.6 and 6.7. Among the most remarkable normal variations is that two boys (or two girls) may be the same chronological age, yet one may complete the pubertal sequence before the other has begun it. For most girls, the first menstrual period may occur as early as the age of 10 or as late as the age of 15½ and still be considered normal, for example (Brooks-Gunn, 1988; Hood, 1991; Paikoff, Buchanan, & Brooks-Gunn, 1991).

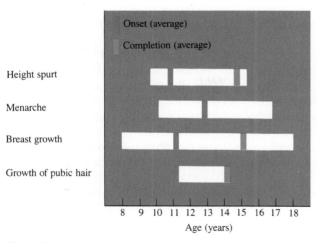

Figure 6.6
**Normal Range and Average Age of Female
Sexual Development**

"Adapted from 'Growing Up' by J. M. Tanner.
Copyright © 1973 by Scientific American, Inc. All
rights reserved."

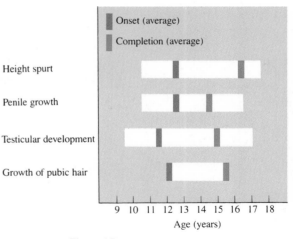

Figure 6.7
**Normal Range and Average Age of Male
Sexual Development**

"Adapted from 'Growing Up' by J. M. Tanner.
Copyright © 1973 by Scientific American, Inc. All
rights reserved."

Puberty is not simply an environmental accident; genetic factors are also involved. As indicated earlier, although nutrition, health, and other factors affect puberty's timing and variations in its makeup, the basic genetic program is wired into the nature of the species (Scarr & Kidd, 1983).

Another key factor in puberty's occurrence is body mass. For example, menarche occurs at a relatively consistent weight in girls. A body weight of approximately 106 ± 3 pounds signals menarche and the end of the adolescent growth spurt. For menarche to begin and continue, fat must make up 17 percent of a girl's total body weight (Frisch, 1991).

Psychological Accompaniments of Pubertal Change

A host of psychological changes accompany an adolescent's physical development. Imagine yourself as you were beginning puberty. Not only did you probably think about yourself differently, but your parents and peers probably began acting differently toward you. Maybe you were proud of your changing body, even though you were perplexed about what was happening. Perhaps your parents no longer perceived you as someone with whom they could sit in bed and watch television or as someone who should be kissed goodnight.

One thing is certain about the psychological aspects of physical change in adolescence: Adolescents are preoccupied with their bodies and develop individual images of what their bodies are like (Adams, 1991; Koff & Riordan, 1991). Perhaps you looked in the mirror daily or even hourly to see if you could detect anything different about your changing body. Preoccupation with one's body image is strong throughout adolescence, but it is especially acute during puberty, a time when adolescents are more dissatisfied with their bodies than in late adolescence (Wright, 1989).

Being physically attractive and having a positive body image are associated with an overall positive conception of one's self. In one investigation, girls who were judged as being physically attractive and who generally had a positive body image had higher opinions of themselves in general (Lerner & Karabenick, 1974). In another investigation, breast growth in girls 9 to 11 years old was associated with a positive body image, positive peer relationships, and superior adjustment (Brooks-Gunn & Warren, in press).

185

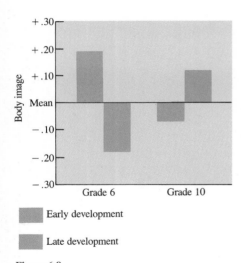

Figure 6.8
Early- and Late-Maturing Adolescent Girls' Body Image, Grades 6 and 10

■ *Critical Thinking*
Do you think puberty's effects are exaggerated? Has too much credit been given to early and late maturation? Do these changes possibly balance out over the long course of life's development?

Some of you entered puberty early, others late, and yet others on time. When adolescents mature earlier or later than their peers, might they perceive themselves differently? Some years ago, in the California Longitudinal Study, early-maturing boys perceived themselves more positively and had more successful peer relations than did their late-maturing counterparts (Jones, 1965). The findings for early-maturing girls were similar but not as strong as for boys. When the late-maturing boys were in their thirties, however, they had developed a stronger sense of identity than the early-maturing boys (Peskin, 1967). Possibly this occurred because the late-maturing boys had more time to explore life's options or because the early-maturing boys continued to focus on their advantageous physical status instead of on career development and achievement.

More recent research confirms, though, that at least during adolescence it is advantageous to be an early-maturing rather than a late-maturing boy (Blyth, Bulcroft, & Simmons, 1981; Simmons & Blyth, 1987). The more recent findings for girls suggest that early maturation is a mixed blessing: These girls experience more problems in school but also more independence and popularity with boys. The time that maturation is assessed also is a factor. In the sixth grade, early-maturing girls showed greater satisfaction with their figures than late-maturing girls, but, by the tenth grade, late-maturing girls were more satisfied (see figure 6.8). The reason for this is that, by late adolescence, early-maturing girls are shorter and stockier, whereas late-maturing girls are taller and thinner. Late-maturing girls in late adolescence have bodies that more closely approximate the current American ideal of feminine beauty—tall and thin.

Some researchers now question whether the effects of puberty are as strong as once believed (Brooks-Gunn & Warren, 1989a; Lerner, Petersen, & Brooks-Gunn, 1990; Montemayor, Adams, & Gulotta, 1990; Paikoff & Brooks-Gunn, 1990). Puberty affects some adolescents more strongly than others and some behaviors more strongly than others. Body image, dating interest, and sexual behavior are affected by pubertal change. The recent questioning of puberty's effects suggests that, if we look at overall development and adjustment in the human life cycle, pubertal variations (such as early and late maturation) are less dramatic than is commonly thought. In thinking about puberty's effects, keep in mind that an adolescent's world involves cognitive and social changes as well as physical changes. As with all periods of development, these processes work in concert to produce who we are in adolescence.

Pubertal Timing and Health Care

What can be done to identify off-time maturers who are at risk for health problems? Many adolescents whose development is extremely early or extremely late are likely to come to the attention of a physician—such as a boy who has not had a spurt in height by the age of 16 or a girl who has not menstruated by the age of 15. Girls and boys who are early or late maturers but are well within the normal range are less likely to be taken to a physician because of their maturational status. Nonetheless, these boys and girls may have fears and doubts about being normal that they do not raise unless a physician, counselor, or other health-care provider takes the initiative. A brief discussion outlining the sequence and timing of events and the large individual variations in them may be all that is required to reassure many adolescents who are maturing very early or very late.

Health-care providers may want to discuss the adolescent's off-time development with the adolescent's parents as well. Information about the peer pressures of off-time development can be beneficial. Especially helpful to early-maturing girls is a discussion of peer pressures to date and to engage in adult-like behavior at an early age. The transition to middle school, junior high school, or high school may be more stressful for girls and boys who are in the midst of puberty than for those who are not (Brooks-Gunn, 1988; Brooks-Gunn & Reiter, 1990).

If pubertal development is extremely late, a physician may recommend hormonal treatment. In one investigation of extended pubertal delay in boys, hormonal treatment worked to increase the height, dating interest, and peer relations in several boys but resulted in little or no improvement in other boys (Lewis, Money, & Bobrow, 1977).

In sum, most early- and late-maturing individuals weather puberty's challenges and stresses competently. For those who do not, discussions with sensitive and knowledgeable health-care providers and parents can improve the off-time maturing adolescent's coping abilities.

Sexuality

> I am 16 years old and I really like this one girl. She wants to be a virgin until she marries. We went out last night and she let me go pretty far, but not all the way. I know she really likes me too, but she always stops me when things start getting hot and heavy. It is getting hard for me to handle. She doesn't know it but I'm a virgin too. I feel I am ready to have sex. I have to admit I think about having sex with other girls too. Maybe I should be dating other girls.
>
> —Frank C.

> I'm 14 years old. I have a lot of sexy thoughts. Sometimes just before I drift off to sleep at night I think about this hunk who is 16 years old and plays on the football team. He is so gorgeous and I can feel him holding me in his arms and kissing and hugging me. When I'm walking down the hall between classes at school, I sometimes start daydreaming about guys I have met, and wonder what it would be like to have sex with them. Last year I had this crush on the men's track coach. I'm on the girls' track team so I saw him a lot during the year. He hardly knew I thought about him the way I did, although I tried to flirt with him several times.
>
> —Amy S.

During adolescence, the lives of males and females become wrapped in sexuality. Adolescence is a time of sexual exploration and experimentation, of sexual fantasies and sexual realities, of incorporating sexuality into one's identity. At a time when sexual identity is an important developmental task of adolescence, the adolescent is confronted with conflicting sexual values and messages. The majority of adolescents eventually manage to develop a mature sexual identity, but most have periods of vulnerability and confusion along life's sexual journey. Our coverage of adolescent sexuality will focus on sexual attitudes and behavior, sexually transmitted diseases, and adolescent pregnancy.

Puberty: The time of life in which the two sexes begin first to become acquainted.

—Samuel Johnson

Adolescence is a time of sexual exploration and experimentation, of sexual fantasies and realities, of incorporating sexuality into one's identity.

"Don't encourage him, Sylvia."

The FAR SIDE cartoon by Gary Larson is reprinted by permission of Chronicle Features, San Francisco, CA.

Sexual Attitudes and Behavior

How extensively have heterosexual attitudes and behaviors changed in the twentieth century? What sexual scripts do adolescents follow? How extensive is homosexual behavior in adolescence? We will consider each of these questions in turn.

Adolescent Heterosexual Behavior—Trends and Incidence

Had you been in high school or college in 1940, you probably would have had a different attitude toward many aspects of sexuality than you do today, especially if you are a female. A review of students' sexual practices and attitudes from 1900 to 1980 revealed two important trends (Darling, Kallen, & Van Dusen, 1984). First, the percentage of youth reporting that they had had sexual intercourse increased dramatically. Second, the percentage of females reporting that they had had sexual intercourse increased more rapidly than for males, although the initial base for males was greater (see figure 6.9). These changes suggest movement away from a double standard that says it is more appropriate for males than females to have sexual intercourse.

Large numbers of American adolescents are sexually active. Table 6.3 shows that, by age 18, 44 percent of adolescent females and 64 percent of adolescent males are sexually experienced (National Research Council, 1987). Other surveys indicate that almost four of five adolescents from 17 to 19 years old have experienced sexual intercourse at least once (Zelnik & Kantner, 1980). Although the gap is closing, males still are more sexually experienced at an earlier age than females (Forrest, 1990). Black adolescent females are more sexually active than their White counterparts, with approximately two of three Black adolescent females, but slightly less than one of two White adolescent females, reporting having had sexual intercourse at least once (Hofferth & Hayes, 1987).

Among younger adolescents, surveys indicate that between 5 and 17 percent of girls 15 years old and younger have had sexual intercourse. Among

Biological Processes, Physical Development, and Perceptual Development

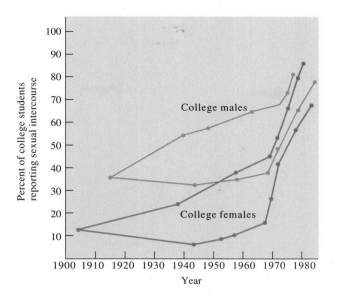

Figure 6.9
**Percentage of College Students Reporting
Having Sexual Intercourse, 1900–1980**
Two lines are drawn for males and two for
females. The lines represent the best two
fits through the data for males and the data
for females of the many studies surveyed
(Darling, Kallen, & Van Dusen, 1984).

TABLE 6.3
Percentages of Sexually Active Young People

Age	Females (%)	Males (%)
15	5.4	16.6
16	12.6	28.7
17	27.1	47.9
18	44.0	64.0
19	62.9	77.6
20	73.6	83.0

Reprinted with permission from *Risking the Future: Adolescent Sexuality, Pregnancy, and
Childbearing,* c. 1987 by The National Academy of Sciences. Published by National Academy
Press.

boys the same age, the range is 16 to 38 percent (Gilgun, 1984; Jessor &
Jessor, 1975; National Research Council, 1987; Ostrov & others, 1985). At
age 13, boys also show earlier experience with sexual intercourse than girls—
12 percent versus 5 percent (Dreyer, 1982). The pressure on adolescent males
to have sexual intercourse is reflected in these figures, even though, on the
average, males enter puberty 2 years later than females.

Recent data indicate that, in some areas of the country, sexual experiences of young adolescents may be even greater than these figures indicate.
In inner-city Baltimore, 81 percent of 14-year-old males said they had already
engaged in sexual intercourse. Other surveys in inner-city, low-income areas
also reveal a high incidence of early sexual intercourse (Clark, Zabin, & Hardy,
1984).

Clearly, large numbers of America's adolescents are sexually active, but
there is a positive note in the most recent data collected about adolescent sexual
behavior. Although the rate of sexual activity among adolescents increased
dramatically in the 1970s, it appears to be stabilizing or decreasing as we enter
the last decade of the twentieth century (National Research Council, 1987).

More female adolescents than male adolescents report being in love as the main reason for being sexually active.

Adolescent Sexual Scripts

As adolescents explore their sexual identities, they engage in sexual scripts (Bancroft, 1990; Gagnon & Simon, 1973; Gordon & Gilgun, 1987). A **sexual script** *is a stereotyped pattern of role prescriptions for how individuals should behave sexually.* Differences in the way females and males are socialized are wrapped up in the sexual scripts adolescents follow. Discrepancies in male-female scripting can cause problems and confusion for adolescents as they work out their sexual identities. Adolescent girls have learned to link sexual intercourse with love. Female adolescents often rationalize their sexual behavior by telling themselves that they were swept away by love. A number of investigators have reported that adolescent females, more than adolescent males, report being in love as the main reason for being sexually active (Cassell, 1984). Far more females than males have intercourse with partners they love and would like to marry. Other reasons for females having sexual intercourse include giving in to male pressure, gambling that sex is a way to get a boyfriend, curiosity, and sexual desire unrelated to loving and caring. Adolescent males may be aware that their female counterparts have been socialized into a love ethic. They also may understand the pressure many of them feel to have a boyfriend. A classic male line shows how males understand female thinking about sex and love: "If you really loved me, you would have sex with me." The female adolescent who says, "If you really loved me, you would not put so much pressure on me," reflects her insight about male sexual motivation.

Some experts on adolescent sexuality believe that we are moving toward a new norm suggesting that sexual intercourse is acceptable, but mainly within the boundary of a loving and affectionate relationship (Dreyer, 1982). As part of this new norm, promiscuity, exploitation, and unprotected sexual intercourse are more often perceived as unacceptable by adolescents. One variation of the new norm is that intercourse is acceptable in a nonlove relationship, but physical or emotional exploitation of the partner is not (Cassell, 1984). The new norm suggests that the double standard that previously existed does not operate as it once did. That is, physical and emotional exploitation of adolescent females by males is not as strong today as in prior decades.

Other experts on adolescent sexuality are not so sure that the new norm has arrived (Gordon & Gilgun, 1987; Morrison, 1985). They argue that remnants of the double standard are still flourishing. In most investigations, about twice as many boys as girls report having positive feelings about sexual intercourse. Females are more likely to report guilt, fear, and hurt. Adolescent males feel considerable pressure from their peers to have experienced sexual intercourse and to be sexually active. As one young adolescent recently remarked, "Look, I feel a lot of pressure from my buddies to go for the score." Further evidence for males' physical and emotional exploitation of females was found in a survey of 432 14-to-18-year-olds (Goodchilds & Zellman, 1984). Both male and female adolescents accepted the right of the male adolescent to be sexually aggressive but left matters up to the female to set the limits for the male's sexual overtures. Another attitude related to the double standard was the belief that females should not plan ahead to have sexual intercourse but should be swept up in the passion of the moment, not taking contraceptive precautions. Unfortunately, although we may have chipped away at some parts of the sexual double standard, other aspects still remain.

Biological Processes, Physical Development, and Perceptual Development

Homosexual Attitudes and Behavior

Both the early (Kinsey) and more recent (Hunt) surveys indicate that about 4 percent of males and 3 percent of females are exclusively homosexual (Hunt, 1974; Kinsey, Pomeroy, & Martin, 1948). Although the incidence of homosexual behavior does not seem to have increased, attitudes toward homosexuality were becoming more permissive, at least until recently. In 1986, the Gallup poll began to detect a shift in attitudes brought about by public awareness of AIDS (acquired immune deficiency syndrome). For example, in 1985, slightly more than 40 percent of Americans believed that "homosexual relations between consenting adults should be legal"; by 1986, the figure had dropped to just above 30 percent (Gallup Report, 1987). Individuals who have negative attitudes toward homosexuals also are likely to favor severe controls for AIDS, such as excluding AIDS carriers from the workplace and schools (Pryor & others, 1989).

Why are some individuals homosexual whereas others are heterosexual? Speculation about this question has been extensive, but no firm answers are available. Homosexual and heterosexual males and females have similar physiological responses during sexual arousal and seem to be aroused by the same types of tactile stimulation. Investigators find that, in terms of a wide range of attitudes, behaviors, and adjustments, no differences between homosexuals and heterosexuals are present (Bell, Weinberg, & Mammersmith, 1981). Recognizing that homosexuality is not a form of mental illness, the American Psychiatric Association discontinued its classification of homosexuality as a disorder, except in those cases where the individuals themselves consider the sexual orientation to be abnormal.

An individual's sexual orientation—heterosexual or homosexual—is most likely determined by a combination of genetic, hormonal, and environmental factors (Bodde, 1989; McWhirter, Reinisch, & Sanders, 1990; Money, 1987). Most experts on homosexuality believe that no one factor alone causes homosexuality and that the relative weight of each factor may vary from one individual to the next. In truth, no one knows *exactly* what causes an individual to become a homosexual. Scientists have a clearer picture of what does *not* cause homosexuality. For example, children raised by gay or lesbian parents or couples are no more likely to be homosexual than are children raised by heterosexual parents. There also is no evidence that male homosexuality is caused by a dominant mother or a weak father, or that female homosexuality is caused by girls choosing male role models. Among the biological factors believed to be involved in homosexuality are prenatal hormone conditions (Ellis & Ames, 1987). In the second to fifth months after conception, exposure to hormone levels characteristic of females is speculated to cause an individual (male or female) to become attracted to males. If this "prenatal critical period hypothesis" turns out to be correct, it would explain why researchers and clinicians have found it difficult to modify a homosexual orientation.

Adolescence may play an important role in the development of homosexuality. In one investigation, participation in homosexual behavior and sexual arousal by same-sex peers in adolescence was strongly related to an adult homosexual orientation (Bell & others, 1981). When interest in the same sex is intense and compelling, an adolescent often experiences severe conflict (Boxer, 1988; Irvin, 1988). The American culture stigmatizes homosexuality; negative labels, such as "fag" and "queer," are given to male homosexuals, and "lessie" and "dyke" to female homosexuals. The sexual socialization of adolescent homosexuals becomes a process of learning to hide (Herdt, 1988). Some gay males wait out their entire adolescence, hoping that heterosexual feelings will develop. Many female adolescent homosexuals have similar experiences. Many adult females who identify themselves as homosexuals considered themselves predominantly heterosexual during adolescence (Bell & others, 1981).

Sexually Transmitted Diseases

Tammy, age 15, has just finished listening to a lecture in her health class. We overhear her talking to one of her girlfriends as she walks down the school corridor. "That was a disgusting lecture. I can't believe all the diseases you can get by having sex. I think she was probably trying to scare us. She spent a lot of time talking about AIDS, which I've heard that normal people don't get. Right? I've heard that only homosexuals and drug addicts get AIDS, and I've also heard that gonorrhea and most other sexual diseases can be cured, so what's the big deal if you get something like that?" Tammy's view of sexually transmitted diseases (formerly called venereal disease, or VD) is common among adolescents. Teenagers tend to believe that sexually transmitted diseases always happen to someone else, can be easily cured without any harm done, and are too disgusting for a nice young person to even hear about, let alone get. This view is wrong. Adolescents who are having sex *do* run the risk of getting sexually transmitted diseases. Sexually transmitted diseases are fairly common among today's adolescents.

Chlamydia

Sexually transmitted diseases are primarily transmitted through sexual intercourse, although they can be transmitted orally. **Chlamydia** *is a sexually transmitted disease named for the bacteria that cause it.* Chlamydia affects as many as 10 percent of all college males and females. Males experience a burning sensation during urination and a mucoid discharge. Females experience painful urination or a vaginal discharge. These signs often mimic gonorrhea. However, when penicillin is prescribed for gonorrhealike symptoms, the problem does not go away as it would if gonorrhea were the culprit. If left untreated, the disease can affect the entire reproductive tract. This can lead to problems left by scar tissue, which can prevent the female from becoming pregnant. Effective drugs are available to treat this common sexually transmitted disease.

Herpes Simplex Virus II

An alarming increase in another sexually transmitted disease, herpes simplex virus II, has occurred in recent years. **Herpes simplex virus II** *is a sexually transmitted disease whose symptoms include irregular cycles of sores and blisters in the genital area.* Although this disease is more common among young adults (estimates range as high as 1 in 5 sexually active adults), as many as 1 in 35 adolescents have genital herpes (Oppenheimer, 1982). The herpes virus is potentially dangerous. If babies are exposed to the active virus during birth, they are vulnerable to brain damage or even death, and women with herpes are eight times more likely than unaffected women to develop cervical cancer (Harvard Medical School Newsletter, 1981). At present, herpes is incurable.

Syphilis

Sexual problems have plagued human beings throughout history. Hippocrates wrote about syphilis in 460 B.C. The first major recorded epidemic of syphilis appeared in Naples, Italy, 2 years after Columbus' first return. It is believed that millions of people died of the disease, which is sexually transmitted through intercourse, kissing, or intimate body contact. The cause of syphilis is a tiny bacterium that requires warm, moist surfaces to penetrate the body. It was not until 400 years after the Italian outbreak that penicillin, a successful treatment for syphilis was discovered.

AIDS

Today, we harbor the same fear of sexually transmitted disease as in Columbus' time, but, instead of syphilis, the fear is of AIDS, a major sexually related problem that has generated considerable fear in today's world (Boyer & Hein, 1991; Rotheram-Borus & Koopman, 1991). **AIDS (acquired immune deficiency syndrome)** *is a virus that destroys the body's immune system. Consequently, many germs that usually do not harm someone with a normal immune system produce devastating results and even death.*

In 1981, when AIDS was first recognized in the United States, there were fewer than 60 reported cases. In 1990, according to Dr. Frank Press, president of the National Academy of Sciences, we began losing as many Americans each year to AIDS as died in the Vietnam War, almost 60,000 people. According to federal health officials, 1 to 1½ million Americans are now asymptomatic carriers of AIDS—those who are infected with the virus and presumably capable of infecting others but who show no clinical symptoms of AIDS. In 1989, the first attempt to assess AIDS among college students was made. Testing of 16,861 students found 30 students infected with the virus (American College Health Association, 1989). If the 12.5 million students attending college were infected at the same rate, 25,000 students would have the AIDS virus.

The AIDS epidemic has led to an increased awareness of the importance of sex education in adolescence.

T A B L E 6 . 4
Understanding AIDS: What's Risky, What's Not

The AIDS virus is not transmitted like colds or the flu, but by an exchange of infected blood, semen, or vaginal fluids. This usually occurs during sexual intercourse, in the sharing of drug needles, or to babies infected before or during birth.

You won't get AIDS from:
—Everyday contact with individuals around you in school or the workplace, at parties, in child-care centers, or in stores
—Swimming in a pool, even if someone in the pool has the AIDS virus
—A mosquito bite or from bedbugs, lice, flies, or other insects
—Saliva, sweat, tears, urine, or a bowel movement
—A kiss
—Clothes, telephones, or toilet seats
—Using a glass or eating utensils that someone else has used
—Being on a bus, train, or crowded elevator with an individual who is infected with the virus or who has AIDS

Blood donations and transfusions:
—You will not come into contact with the AIDS virus by donating blood at a blood bank.
—The risk of getting AIDS from a blood transfusion has been greatly reduced. Donors are screened for risk factors, and donated blood is tested.

Risky behavior includes:
—Having a number of sexual partners
—Sharing drug needles and syringes
—Engaging in anal sex with or without a condom
—Performing vaginal or oral sex with someone who shoots drugs or engages in anal sex
—Engaging in sex with someone you don't know well or with someone who has several sexual partners
—Engaging in unprotected sex (without a condom) with an infected individual

Safe behavior includes:
—Not having sex
—Having sex with one mutually faithful, uninfected partner
—Not shooting drugs

Source: United States Government education pamphlet: *America Responds to AIDS,* 1988.

Experts say that AIDS can be transmitted only through sexual contact, shared needles, or blood transfusion. Although 90 percent of all AIDS cases continue to occur among homosexual males and intravenous drug users, a disproportionate increase among females who are heterosexual partners of bisexual males or of intravenous drug users has been recently noted. This increase suggests the risk of AIDS may be increasing among heterosexual individuals who have multiple sexual partners (Corless & Pittman-Lindeman, 1989; Hein, 1990). Table 6.4 describes what's risky and what's not regarding AIDS.

Evidence that the AIDS epidemic has begun to reduce promiscuous behavior in both homosexual and heterosexual individuals is appearing. In one investigation, it was found that single heterosexual males decreased their number of sexual partners from 2.8 to 1.8 from 1984 to 1986 (Winkelstein & others, 1987). In an investigation of 5,000 homosexual males, the percentage who said they were either celibate or monogamous increased from 14 to 39 percent between 1984 and 1986 (Fineberg, 1988). Although the figures in the latter study are encouraging, virtually all of the homosexual males knew condoms reduce the risk of contracting AIDS, yet 60 percent did not use them.

Adolescent Pregnancy

Angela is 15 years old and pregnant. She reflects, "I'm 3 months pregnant. This could ruin my whole life. I've made all of these plans for the future and now they are down the drain. I don't have anybody to talk to about my problem. I can't talk to my parents. There is no way they can understand." Pregnant adolescents were once practically invisible and unmentionable, but yesterday's secret has become today's national dilemma.

They are of different ethnic groups and from different places, but their circumstances have a distressing sameness. Each year more than 1 million American teenagers become pregnant, four out of five of them unmarried. Like Angela, many become pregnant in their early or middle adolescent years, 30,000 of them under the age of 15. In all, this means that 1 of every 10 adolescent females in the United States becomes pregnant each year, with 8 of the 10 pregnancies unintended (National Research Council, 1987). As one 17-year-old Los Angeles mother of a 1-year-old boy said, "We are children having children." The only bright spot in the adolescent pregnancy statistics is that the adolescent pregnancy rate, after increasing during the 1970s, has leveled off and may even be beginning to decline (National Research Council, 1987).

The adolescent pregnancy rate in the United States is the highest of any in the Western world. It is more than twice the rate in England, France, or Canada; almost three times the rate in Sweden; and seven times the rate in the Netherlands (Alan Guttmacher Institute, 1981; Jones & others, 1985) (see figure 6.10). Although American adolescents are no more sexually active than their counterparts in these other nations, they are many times more likely to become pregnant.

Adolescent pregnancy is a complex American problem, one that strikes many nerves. The subject of adolescent pregnancy touches on many explosive social issues: the battle over abortion rights, contraceptives and the delicate question of whether adolescents should have easy access to them, and the perennially touchy subject of sex education in the public schools (Hofferth, 1990).

Dramatic changes involving sexual attitudes and social morals have swept through the American culture in the last 3 decades. Adolescents actually gave birth at a higher rate in 1957 than they do today, but that was a time of early marriage, with almost 25 percent of 18- and 19-year-olds married. The overwhelming majority of births to adolescent mothers in the 1950s occurred within a marriage and mainly involved females 17 years of age and older. Two or three decades ago, if an unwed adolescent girl became pregnant, in most instances her parents swiftly married her off in a shotgun wedding. If marriage was impractical, the girl would discreetly disappear, the child would be put up for adoption, and the predicament would never be discussed again. Abortion was not an option for most adolescent females until 1973, when the Supreme Court ruled it could not be outlawed.

In today's world of adolescent pregnancies, a different scenario unfolds. If the girl does not choose to have an abortion (45 percent of pregnant adolescent girls do), she usually keeps the baby and raises it without the traditional involvement of marriage. With the stigma of illegitimacy largely absent, girls are less likely to give up their babies for adoption. Fewer than 5 percent do, compared with about 35 percent in the early 1960s. However, although the stigma of illegitimacy has waned, the lives of most pregnant teenagers are anything but rosy.

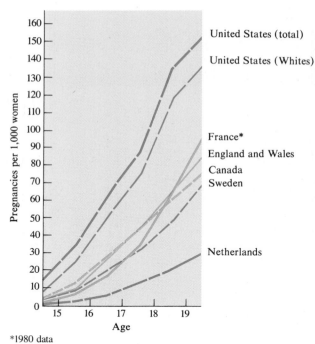

*1980 data

Note: pregnancies are defined here as births plus abortions; age is the age at outcome.

Figure 6.10
Pregnancy Rates per 1,000 Women, 1981

The consequences of our nation's high adolescent pregnancy rate are of great concern. Pregnancy in adolescence increases the health risks of both the child and the mother (Dryfoos, 1990; Osofsky, 1990). Infants born to adolescent mothers are more likely to have low birth weights (a prominent cause of infant mortality), as well as neurological problems and childhood illnesses (Furstenberg, Brooks-Gunn, & Chase-Lansdale, 1989). Adolescent mothers often drop out of school, fail to gain employment, and become dependent on welfare. Although many adolescent mothers resume their education later in life, they generally do not catch up with women who postpone childbearing. In the National Longitudinal Survey of Work Experience of Youth, it was found that only half of the women 20 to 26 years old who first gave birth at age 17 had completed high school by their twenties. The percentage was even lower for those who gave birth at a younger age (Mott & Marsiglio, 1985) (see table 6.5). By contrast, among females who waited until age 20 to have a baby, more than 90 percent had obtained a high school education. Among the younger adolescent mothers, almost half had obtained a General Equivalency Diploma (GED), which does not often open up good employment opportunities.

These educational deficits have negative consequences for the young women themselves and for their children (Kenney, 1987; Scott-Jones & White, 1990). Adolescent parents are more likely than those who delay childbearing to have low-paying, low-status jobs or to be unemployed. The mean family income of White females who give birth before age 17 is about half that of families in which the mother delays birth until her mid- or late twenties.

Serious, extensive efforts need to be developed to help pregnant adolescents and young mothers enhance their educational and occupational opportunities. Adolescent mothers also need extensive help in obtaining competent day care and in planning for the future (Edelman, 1987; Furstenberg, 1991; Furstenberg, Brooks-Gunn, & Morgan, 1987; Paikoff & Brooks-Gunn, 1991). Experts recommend that, to reduce the high rate of teen pregnancy, adoles-

196

TABLE 6.5
Percentages of Young Mothers Completing High School (1983), According to Age at First Birth

Age at first birth	High school completion (%)		
	Diploma	*GED*	*Total*
15	24	21	45
16	28	21	49
17	38	15	53
18	52	10	62
19	68	9	77
Total: ages 15 to 19	86	4	90

From Frank L. Mott and William Marsiglio, "Early Childbearing and Completion of High School" in *Family Planning Perspectives,* September/October 1985. Copyright © 1985 Alan Guttmacher Institute.

cents need improved sex-education and family-planning information, greater access to contraception, and broad community involvement and support (Conger, 1988; Rosenbaum & Kandel, 1990; Treboux & Busch-Rossnagel, 1991; Wallace & Vienonen, 1989). Another very important consideration, especially for young adolescents, is abstention, which is increasingly being included as a theme in sex education classes.

As indicated earlier, adolescent pregnancy is not a major problem in many European countries, especially Holland and the Scandinavian countries. To learn more about adolescent sexual orientation in Holland and Sweden, turn to Cultural Worlds of Development 6.1.

Some Adolescent Problems and Disturbances

In addition to the increase in adolescent pregnancy, other problems that may arise in adolescence are drug abuse, suicide, and eating disorders, each of which we will discuss in turn.

Drugs

The 1960s and 1970s were a time of marked increases in the use of illicit drugs. During the social and political unrest of those years, many youth turned to marijuana, stimulants, and hallucinogens. Increases in alcohol consumption by adolescents also were noted (Robinson & Greene, 1988). More precise data about drug use by adolescents have been collected in recent years. Each year since 1975, Lloyd Johnston, Patrick O'Malley, and Gerald Bachman (1988, 1989, 1990), working at the Institute of Social Research at the University of Michigan, have carefully monitored drug use by America's high school seniors in a wide range of public and private high schools. From time to time, they also sample the drug use of younger adolescents and adults as well.

An encouraging finding from the most recent survey (conducted in 1989) of 16,300 high school seniors is the continued gradual decrease in the use of illicit drugs (Johnston, O'Malley, & Bachman, 1990). Nonetheless, the United States still has the highest rate of drug use among the world's industrialized nations. In 1989, 51 percent of the nation's high school seniors tried an illicit drug other than marijuana. A special concern is the use of alcohol and cocaine by adolescents.

Adolescent Sexual Orientation in Holland and Sweden

In Holland and Sweden, as well as in other European countries, sex does not carry the mystery and conflict it does in American society. Holland does not have a mandated sex-education program, but adolescents can obtain contraceptive counseling at government-sponsored clinics for a small fee. The Dutch media also have played an important role in educating the public about sex through frequent broadcasts focused on birth control, abortion, and related matters. Most Dutch adolescents do not consider having sex without birth control.

Swedish adolescents are sexually active at an earlier age than American adolescents, and they are exposed to even more explicit sex on television. However, the Swedish National Board of Education has developed a curriculum that ensures that every child in the country, beginning at age 7, will experience a thorough grounding in reproductive biology and, by the ages of 10 or 12, will have been introduced to information about various forms of contraceptives. Teachers are expected to handle the subject of sex whenever it becomes relevant, regardless of the subject they are teaching. The idea is to dedramatize and demystify sex so that familiarity will make individuals less vulnerable to unwanted pregnancy and sexually transmitted diseases (Wallis, 1985). American society is not nearly so open about sex education.

In the United States, we mystify and dramatize sex; in Sweden, sex is dedramatized and demystified.

Alcohol

Some mornings, 15-year-old Annie was too drunk to go to school. Other days, she'd stop for a couple of beers or a screwdriver on the way to school. She was tall, blonde, and good looking, and no one who sold her liquor, even at 8:00 in the morning, questioned her age. Where did she get her money? She got it from baby-sitting and from what her mother gave her to buy lunch. Annie used to be a cheerleader, but no longer; she was kicked off the squad for missing practice so often. Soon, she and several of her peers were drinking almost every morning. Sometimes, they skipped school and went to the woods to drink. Annie's whole life began to revolve around her drinking. This routine went on for 2 years. After a while, Annie's parents discovered her problem. Even though they punished her, it did not stop her drinking. Finally, this year, Annie started dating a boy she really liked and who would not put up with her drinking. She agreed to go to Alcoholics Anonymous and has just successfully completed treatment. She has stopped drinking for 4 consecutive months now, and she hopes that her abstinence will continue.

Alcohol is the drug most widely used by adolescents in our society. For them, it has produced many enjoyable moments and many sad ones as well. Alcoholism is the third-leading killer in the United States, with more than 13 million people classified as alcoholics, many of whom established their drinking habits during adolescence. Each year, approximately 25,000 people are killed

What is the pattern of alcohol consumption among adolescents?

and 1.5 million injured by drunk drivers. In 65 percent of the aggressive male acts against females, the offender is under the influence of alcohol (Goodman & others, 1986). In numerous instances of drunk driving and assaults on females, the offenders are adolescents.

How extensive is alcohol use by adolescents? Although the use of marijuana and other drugs among adolescents has declined recently, adolescents do not seem to be drinking more to offset their reduced intake of other drugs. Alcohol use by high school seniors has gradually declined. Monthly use declined from 72 percent in 1980 to 60 percent in 1989. The prevalence of drinking five or more drinks in a row in a two-week interval fell from 41 percent in 1983 to 33 percent in 1989. There remains a substantial gender difference in heavy adolescent drinking: 28 percent for females versus 46 percent for males in 1986, although this difference diminished gradually during the 1980s. However, data from college students show little drop in alcohol use and an increase in heavy drinking: 45 percent in 1986, up 2 percent from the previous year. Heavy drinking at parties among college males is common and is becoming more common (Johnston, O'Malley, & Bachman, 1988, 1990).

Cocaine

Did you know that cocaine was once an ingredient in Coca-Cola? Of course, it has long since been removed from the soft drink. *Cocaine* comes from the coca plant, native to Bolivia and Peru. For many years, Bolivians and Peruvians chewed the plant to increase their stamina. Today, cocaine is usually snorted, smoked, or injected in the form of crystals or powder. The effect is a rush of euphoric feelings, which eventually wear off, followed by depressive feelings, lethargy, insomnia, and irritability.

Cocaine is a highly controversial drug. Users claim it is exciting, makes them feel good, and increases their confidence. It is clear, however, that cocaine has potent cardiovascular effects and is potentially addictive. The recent death of sports star Len Bias demonstrates how lethal cocaine can be. When the drug's effects are extreme, it can produce a heart attack, stroke, or brain seizure. The increase in cocaine-related deaths is traced to very pure or tainted forms of the drug.

Cocaine use, which remained at peak levels throughout much of the 1980s, began an important decline in 1987 that continued through 1989 in high school and college students (Johnston, O'Malley, & Bachman, 1990). Among high school seniors, the proportion of cocaine users fell by more than half from 1986 to 1989, from 6.2 percent to 2.8 percent. An even larger proportional drop in use was observed among college students over the same time interval—from 7 percent to 2.8 percent. A growing proportion of high school seniors and college students are reaching the conclusion that cocaine use holds considerable, unpredictable risk.

The Roles of Parents, Peers, and Schools in Drug Use

Most adolescents become drug users at a point in their development, whether their use is limited to alcohol, caffeine, and cigarettes or is extended to marijuana, cocaine, and hard drugs. A special concern occurs when adolescents use drugs as a way of coping with stress, a practice that can interfere with their development of competent coping and decision-making skills. Researchers have found that, when drug use occurs initially in childhood or in early adolescence, it has more detrimental, long-term effects on the development of responsible, competent behavior than when drug use occurs initially in late adolescence (Newcomb & Bentler, 1989). By using drugs to cope with stress, young adolescents often enter adult roles of marriage and work prematurely without adequate socioemotional growth, and they experience greater failure in adult roles (Gabrielli, 1990; Moos, Finney, & Cronkite, 1990).

A special concern in the use of drugs by adolescents is the roles parents, peers, and schools play in preventing and reducing drug use (Brook & Brook, in press; Brook & others, 1990; Cohen, Brook, & Kandel, 1991; Dielman, Shope, & Butchart, 1990; Kandel, 1991). Families play an important role in adolescent drug use. In one recent longitudinal investigation, boys' poor self-control at age 4 was related to their drug use in adolescence, and permissive parenting in the families of girls at age 4 was related to their drug use in adolescence (Block & Block, 1988). In another recent investigation, social support during adolescence substantially reduced drug use (Newcomb & Bentler, 1988). In this study, social support included good relationships with parents, other adults, siblings, and peers. Another researcher found that the greatest use of drugs by adolescents takes place when both the adolescent's parents take drugs (such as tranquilizers, amphetamines, alcohol, or nicotine) and the adolescent's peers take drugs (Kandel, 1974).

Schools frequently are the place where peers initiate and maintain drug use (Dryfoos, 1990). Schools can play an important role in preventing or reducing drug use; there are few other settings where the adolescent population congregates on such a frequent basis. Although most schools have established policies on drug use, some have gone further and developed drug prevention or intervention programs (Bailey, 1989; Minuchin & Shapiro, 1983). The most promising school programs have been those involving comprehensive long-term approaches, not only providing specific information and services, but also dealing with the social organization of the school as a whole. Programs that have emphasized detection, discipline, and scare tactics have been the least effective in preventing or reducing drug use by adolescents.

Suicide

Suicide is a common problem in our society. Its rate has tripled during the past 30 years in the United States; each year, about 25,000 people take their own lives. Beginning at about the age of 15, the rate of suicide begins to rise rapidly. Suicide accounts for about 12 percent of the mortality in the adolescent and young adult age group (Brent, 1989). Males are about three times as likely to commit suicide as females; this may be because of their more active methods for attempting suicide—shooting, for example. By contrast, females are more likely to use passive methods, such as sleeping pills, which are less likely to produce death. Although males commit suicide more frequently, females attempt it more frequently (Maltsberger, 1988).

There is no easy path leading out of life, and few are the easy ones that lie within it.

—Walter Savage Landor

Estimates indicate that, for every successful suicide in the general population, 6 to 10 attempts are made. For adolescents, the figure is as high as 50 attempts for every life taken. As many as two in every three college students has thought about suicide on at least one occasion; their methods range from overdosing on drugs to crashing into the White House in an airplane.

Why do adolescents attempt suicide? There is no simple answer to this important question (Cole, 1991). It is helpful to think of suicide in terms of proximal and distal factors. Proximal, or immediate, factors can trigger a suicide attempt. Highly stressful circumstances, such as the loss of a boyfriend or girlfriend, poor grades at school, or an unwanted pregnancy, can trigger a suicide attempt. Drugs also have been involved more often in recent suicide attempts than in attempts in the past (Rich, Young, & Fowler, 1986).

Distal, or earlier, experiences often are involved in suicide attempts as well. A longstanding history of family instability and unhappiness may be present (Shapiro & Freedman, 1989). Just as a lack of affection and emotional support, high control, and pressure for achievement by parents during childhood are related to adolescent depression, so are such combinations of family experiences likely to show up as distal factors in suicide attempts. Lack of supportive friendships also may be present (Rubenstein & others, 1989). In an investigation of suicide among gifted women, previous suicide attempts, anxiety, conspicuous instability in work and in relationships, depression, or alcoholism also were present in the women's lives (Tomlinson-Keasey, Warren, & Elliott, 1986). These factors are similar to those found to predict suicide among gifted men (Shneidman, 1971).

Just as genetic factors are associated with depression, so are they associated with suicide. The closer the genetic relationship a person has to someone who has committed suicide, the more likely that person is to commit suicide (Wender & others, 1986). Table 6.6 provides valuable information about what to do and what not to do when you suspect someone is contemplating suicide.

Eating Disorders

Fifteen-year-old Jane gradually eliminated foods from her diet to the point where she subsisted by eating *only* applesauce and eggnog. She spent hours observing her own body, wrapping her fingers around her waist to see if it was getting any thinner. She fantasized about becoming a beautiful fashion model who would wear designer bathing suits. Even when she reached 85 pounds,

TABLE 6.6
What to Do and What Not to Do When You
Suspect Someone Might Commit Suicide

What to do

1. Calmly ask direct, straightforward questions: "Are you thinking about hurting yourself?"
2. Assess the seriousness of the suicidal intent by asking questions about feelings, important relationships, whom else the person has talked with, and the amount of thought given to the means to be used. If a gun, pills, rope, or other means has been obtained and a precise plan developed, the situation is dangerous. Stay with the person until help arrives.
3. Be a good listener and be very supportive without being falsely reassuring.
4. Try to persuade the person to obtain professional help and assist him or her in getting it.

What not to do

1. Do not ignore the warning signs.
2. Do not refuse to talk about suicide if a person approaches you about the topic.
3. Do not react with horror, disapproval, or repulsion.
4. Do not give false reassurances by saying such things as "Everything is going to be OK." Also do not give simple answers or platitudes such as "You have everything to be thankful for."
5. Do not abandon the person after the crisis has passed or after professional help has commenced.

From Center for Early Adolescence, University of North Carolina at Chapel Hill, Carrboro, NC. Reprinted by permission.

Jane still felt fat. She continued to lose weight, eventually emaciating herself. She was hospitalized and treated for **anorexia nervosa,** *an eating disorder that involves the relentless pursuit of thinness through starvation.* Eventually, anorexia nervosa can lead to death, as it did for popular singer Karen Carpenter (Casper, 1989; Schlundt & Johnson, 1990).

Anorexia nervosa afflicts primarily females during adolescence and early adulthood (only about 5 percent of anorexics are male). Most individuals with this disorder are White and from well-educated middle- and upper-income families. Although anorexics avoid eating, they have an intense interest in food; they cook for others, they talk about food, and they insist on watching others eat. Anorexics have a distorted body image, perceiving themselves as beautiful even when they have become skeletal. As self-starvation continues and the fat content of the body drops to a bare minimum, menstruation usually stops and behavior often becomes hyperactive (Polivy & Thomsen, 1987).

Numerous causes of anorexia nervosa have been proposed. They include societal, psychological, and physiological factors (Attie & Brooks-Gunn, in press; Brumberg, 1988; Fisher & Brone, 1991; Litt, 1991; Stern & others, 1989). The societal factor most often held responsible is the current fashion of thinness. Psychological factors include a motivation for attention, a desire for individuality, a denial of sexuality, and a way of coping with overcontrolling parents. Anorexics sometimes have families that place high demands for achievement on them. Unable to meet their parents' high standards, anorexics feel unable to control their own lives. By limiting their food intake, anorexics gain a sense of self-control. Physiological causes focus on the hypothalamus, which becomes abnormal in a number of ways when an individual becomes anorexic (Brumberg, 1988). At this time, however, we are not exactly certain what causes anorexia nervosa.

Bulimia *is an eating disorder that involves a binge-and-purge sequence on a regular basis.* Bulimics binge on large amounts of food and then purge by self-induced vomiting or the use of a laxative. The binges sometimes alternate with fasting; at other times, they alternate with normal eating behavior. Like anorexia nervosa, bulimia is primarily a female disorder, and it has become prevalent among college women (Leon, 1991). Some estimates suggest that one in two college women binge and purge at least some of the time. However, recent estimates suggest that true bulimics—those who binge and purge on a regular basis—make up less than 2 percent of the college female population (Stunkard, 1987). Whereas anorexics can control their eating, bulimics cannot. Depression is a common characteristic of bulimics (Levy, Dixon, & Stern, 1989). Many of the same causes proposed for anorexia nervosa are offered for bulimia.

The Interrelation of Problems and Programs That Prevent or Reduce Adolescent Problems

So far, we have described some of the major problems adolescents are at risk for developing. In later chapters, we will discuss others—for example, in chapter 14, school dropouts, and in chapter 17, delinquency. In many instances, adolescents have more than one problem. Researchers are increasingly finding that problem behaviors in adolescence are interrelated. For example, heavy substance abuse is related to early sexual activity, lower grades, dropping out of school, and delinquency. Early initiation of sexual activity is associated with the use of cigarettes and alcohol, the use of marijuana and other illicit drugs, lower grades, dropping out of school, and delinquency. Delinquency is related to early sexual activity, early pregnancy, substance abuse, and dropping out of school. As many as 10 percent of the adolescent population in the United States have serious multiple-problem behaviors (adolescents who have dropped out of school or are behind in their grade level, are users of heavy drugs, regularly use cigarettes and marijuana, and are sexually active but do not use contraception). Many, but not all, of these very high risk youth "do it all." Another 15 percent of adolescents participate in many of these behaviors but with slightly lower frequency and less deleterious consequences. This group of high-risk youths often engage in two to three problem behaviors (Dryfoos, 1990; Scales, 1990).

In addition to understanding that many adolescents engage in multiple problem behaviors, it also is important to develop programs that reduce adolescent problems. In a recent review of the programs that have been successful in preventing or reducing adolescent problems, adolescence researcher Joy Dryfoos (1990) described the common components in these successful programs:

1. *Intensive individualized attention.* In successful programs, high-risk children are attached to a responsible adult, who gives the child attention and deals with the child's specific needs. This theme occurs in a number of programs. In a successful substance abuse program, a student assistance counselor is available full-time for individual counseling and referral for treatment. In a successful delinquency program, a family worker gives extensive care to predelinquents and the families to help them change their lives to avoid repeated delinquent acts.

2. *Communitywide multiagency collaborative approaches.* The basic philosophy of communitywide programs is that a number of programs and services must be in place. In one successful

substance abuse program, a communitywide health promotion campaign uses local media and community education in concert with a substance abuse curriculum in the schools. In one successful delinquency program, a neighborhood development approach involves local residents in neighborhood councils, which work with the schools, police, courts, gang leaders, and media.

3. *Early identification and intervention.* Reaching children and their families before children develop problems, or at the beginning of their problems, is a successful strategy. One preschool program serves as an excellent model for the prevention of delinquency, pregnancy, substance abuse, and dropping out of school. Operated by the High Scope Foundation in Ypsilanti, Michigan, the Perry Preschool has had a long-term positive impact on its students (Berrueta-Clement & others, 1986). This enrichment program, directed by David Weikart, serves disadvantaged Black American children. They attend a high-quality two-year preschool program and receive weekly home visits from program personnel. Based on official police records, by age 19, individuals who had attended the Perry Preschool program were less likely to have been arrested and committed fewer adult offenses than a control group. The Perry Preschool students also were less likely to drop out of school, and teachers rated their social behavior more competent than a control group that did not receive the enriched preschool experience.

Stereotyping Adolescents and Today's Youth

Have the problems of adolescents been overdramatized? Are many adolescents unfortunately stereotyped? What is the nature of today's youth, especially compared to a decade or two ago? Let's examine these questions.

Stereotyping Adolescents

It is easy to stereotype a person, groups of people, or classes of people. A **stereotype** *is a broad category that reflects our impressions and beliefs about people. All stereotypes refer to an image of what the typical member of a particular group is like.* We live in a complex world and want to simplify this complexity. Stereotyping people is one way we do this. We simply assign a label to a group of people—for example, "Youths are promiscuous." Then we have much less to consider when we think about this set of people. Once we assign the labels, though, it is difficult to abandon them, even in the face of contradictory evidence.

Stereotypes about adolescents are plentiful: "They say they want a job, but when they get one, they don't want to work"; "They are all lazy"; "They are all sex fiends"; "They are all into drugs, every last one of them"; "Kids today don't have the moral fiber of my generation"; "The problems with adolescents today is that they all have it too easy"; "They are a bunch of egotistical, smart-alecks"; and so it goes.

Two studies illustrate just how widespread the stereotyping of adolescents is. In the first study, pollster Daniel Yankelovich (1974) compared the attitudes of adolescents with those of their parents about different values, lifestyles, and codes of personal conduct. There was little or no difference between the attitudes of the adolescents and their parents toward self-control, hard work, saving money, competition, compromise, legal authority, and private property. There was a substantial difference, however, between the adolescents and their parents when their attitudes toward religion were sampled (89 percent of the parents said that religion was important to them, compared to only 66 percent of the adolescents). Note, though, that a majority of the adolescents still subscribed to the belief that religion is important.

A second study, which documents the stereotypical view of adolescence as highly stressful and disturbed, was conducted by adolescence researcher Daniel Offer and his colleagues (1988). The self-images of adolescents around the world were sampled—in the United States, Australia, Bangladesh, Hungary, Israel, Italy, Japan, Taiwan, Turkey, and West Germany. A healthy self-image characterized at least 73 percent of the adolescents studied. They appeared to be moving toward adulthood with a healthy integration of previous experiences, self-confidence, and optimism about the future. Although there were some differences among the adolescents, they were happy most of the time, they enjoyed life, they perceived themselves as able to exercise self-control, they valued work and school, they expressed confidence about their sexual selves, they expressed positive feelings toward their families, and they felt they had the capability to cope with life's stresses: not exactly a storm and stress portrayal of adolescence.

Beginning with G. Stanley Hall's (1904) portrayal of adolescence as a period of storm and stress, for much of this century in the United States and other Western cultures, adolescence has unfortunately been perceived as a problematic period of the human life cycle that youths, their families, and society had to endure. As we just saw in two studies, however, a large majority of adolescents do not seem to be nearly as disturbed and troubled as the popular stereotype of adolescence suggests. According to adolescence researchers Shirley Feldman and Glen Elliott (1990), public attitudes about adolescence emerge from a combination of personal experience and media portrayals, neither of which produce an objective picture of how normal adolescents develop. Some of the readiness to assume the worst about adolescents likely involves the short memories of adults. Many adults measure their current perceptions of adolescents by their memories of their own adolescence. Adults may portray today's adolescents as more troubled, less respectful, more self-centered, more assertive, and more adventurous than they were.

However, in matters of taste and manners, the young people of every generation have seemed radical, unnerving, and different from adults— different in how they look, in how they behave, in the music they enjoy, in their hairstyles, and in the clothing they choose. It is an enormous error, though, to confuse adolescents' enthusiasm for trying on new identities and enjoying moderate amounts of outrageous behavior with hostility toward parental and societal standards. Acting-out and boundary-testing are time-honored ways in which adolescents move toward accepting, rather than rejecting, parental values.

Stereotypes of adolescents are also generated by media portrayals (Condry, 1989; Feldman & Elliott, 1990). The media often present sensational and "newsworthy" material, which means that they are far more likely to focus on troubled adolescents than on normal adolescents. The impact of such media coverage conveys the impression that a majority of young people engage in deviant behaviors, when, in fact, only a small minority recurrently do. As we will see next in our consideration of today's adolescents, not only do the messages of the media convey an image of adolescents as highly troubled, but the messages to adolescents from both adults and the media are often ambivalent.

Today's Youth

What is the current status of adolescents compared to the status of their counterparts earlier in history? Do adults have idealized images of adolescents and does society communicate ambivalent messages to young people? How complex is adolescent development today? We will consider each of these questions.

The Current Status of Adolescents

Today's adolescents face demands and expectations, as well as risks and temptations, that appear to be more numerous and complex than those faced by adolescents only a generation ago (Feldman & Elliott, 1990). Nonetheless, contrary to the popular stereotype of adolescents as highly stressed and incompetent, the vast majority of adolescents successfully negotiate the path from childhood to adulthood (Offer & Church, 1991a,b). By some criteria, today's adolescents are doing better than their counterparts from a decade or two earlier. Today, more adolescents complete high school, especially Black American adolescents. In the past few years, accidents and homicides have declined somewhat, as have drug use, juvenile delinquency, and adolescent pregnancy rates. The majority of adolescents today have positive self-conceptions and positive relationships with others. As indicated earlier, such contemporary findings do not reveal a portrayal of adolescence as a highly disturbed, overly stressful time period in the life cycle. Rather, the majority of adolescents find the transition from childhood to adulthood to be a time of physical, cognitive, and social development that provides considerable challenge, opportunities, and growth.

Although the majority of adolescents experience the transition from childhood to adulthood more positively than is portrayed by many adults and the media, too many adolescents today are not provided with adequate opportunities and support to become competent adults. In many ways, today's adolescents are presented with a less stable environment than adolescents of a decade or two ago. High divorce rates, high adolescent pregnancy rates, and increased geographic mobility of families contribute to this lack of stability in adolescents' lives. Today's adolescents are exposed to a complex menu of life-style options through the media, and, although the adolescent drug rate is beginning to show signs of decline, the rate of adolescent drug use in the United States is higher than that of any other country in the industrialized Western world. Many of today's adolescents face these temptations, as well as sexual activity, at increasingly young ages.

Our discussion underscores an important point about adolescents: They do not make up a homogeneous group. The majority of adolescents negotiate the lengthy path to adult maturity successfully, but too large a group does not. Ethnic, cultural, gender, socioeconomic, age, and life-style differences influence the actual life trajectory of every adolescent (Busch-Rossnagel & Zayas, 1991; Gibbs, 1991; Spencer, 1991).

Different portrayals of adolescence emerge, depending on the particular group of adolescents being described. As we will see next, some of the problems faced by today's adolescents involve adults' idealized images of what adolescents should be and society's ambivalent messages to adolescents.

Idealized Images of Adolescents and Society's Ambivalent Messages

Feldman and Elliott (1990) recently described how our society seems to be uncertain about what adolescence should be or should not be. The following examples illustrate how adults' idealized images of adolescents and society's ambivalent messages to adolescents may contribute to adolescent problems:

- Many adults treasure the independence of youth yet insist that adolescents do not have the maturity to make autonomous, competent decisions about their lives. Some of the ambiguity in messages about adult status and maturity that society communicates to adolescents appears in the form of laws dictating that they cannot drive until they are 16, vote until they are 18, or drink until age 21, yet, in some states, 14-year-olds now have the legal right to choose the parent with whom they want to live after a parental divorce and to override parental wishes about such medical matters as abortion and psychiatric care.

- Society's sexual messages to adolescents are especially ambiguous. Adolescents are somehow supposed to be sexually naive but become sexually knowledgeable. The message to many adolescents is this: You can experiment with sex and "sow your wild oats" but be sure to maintain high standards of maturity and safety. Adolescents must negotiate this formidable task in a society that cannot agree on how much and what kind of explicit sex education adolescents should be given. This same society sanctions alluring messages about the power and attractiveness of sexuality in the media.

- Laws prohibit adolescents from using alcohol, tobacco, or other drugs and adults decry the high level of drug use by adolescents, yet many of the same adults who stereotype and criticize adolescents for their drug use are themselves drug abusers and heavy cigarette smokers.

- Society promotes education and the development of knowledge as essential to success as an adult, yet adolescents frequently observe the rewards society doles out to individuals who develop their athletic skills and business acumen. As adolescents interact with adults who do not value the process of learning, adolescents may attach more importance to simply attaining a diploma than the process of getting one.

We have seen that understanding the current status of adolescents requires the consideration of their heterogeneity and that many adults have idealized images of adolescents and communicate ambivalent messages to adolescents. To further understand today's adolescents, we must turn our attention to the recognition of the complexity of adolescent development.

The Complexity of Adolescent Development

As researchers more carefully examine the lives of adolescents, they are recognizing that a single developmental model may not accurately characterize all adolescents (Dornbusch, Petersen, & Hetherington, 1991; Feldman & Elliott, 1990). The most widely described general model of adolescent development states that adolescence is a transition from childhood to adulthood during which individuals explore alternatives and experiment with choices as part of developing an identity. Although this model may accurately fit many White middle-class adolescents, it is less well suited to adolescents from low-income families, school dropouts, and unemployed adolescents. For many of these youths, development often is more chaotic and restricted. For them, social and racial barriers too frequently signal the presence of discrimination and prejudice (Brookins, 1991).

At this point, we have discussed a number of ideas about puberty, adolescent sexuality, adolescent problems and disturbances, stereotyping adolescents, and today's youth. A summary of these ideas is presented in concept table 6.2. In the next section of the book, we will turn our attention to children's learning, cognition, and language development, beginning with chapter 7, Learning and Motivation.

Increasingly, as researchers carefully examine adolescents' lives, they recognize the complexity of adolescent development. Because of this complexity, no single model fits all adolescents. Too often, today's young people receive ambivalent messages about such topics as sexuality, drugs, and learning.

CONCEPT TABLE 6.2
Puberty, Sexuality, Adolescent Problems and Disturbances, Stereotyping Adolescents, and Today's Youth

Concept	Processes/related ideas	Characteristics/description
Puberty	Pubertal change	Puberty is a period of rapid skeletal and sexual maturation that occurs mainly in early adolescence. Testosterone plays an important role in male pubertal development, estradiol in female pubertal development. The growth spurt occurs about 2 years later for boys than for girls, with 12½ the average age of onset for boys, 10½ for girls. Individual maturation in pubertal change is extensive.
	Psychological accompaniments of physical change	Adolescents show a heightened interest in their body image. Early maturation favors boys, at least during adolescence. As adults, though, late-maturing boys achieve more successful identities than early-maturing boys. The results are more mixed for girls. Some researchers now question whether puberty's effects are as strong as once believed. Of special concern is the health care of early- and late-maturing adolescents.
Sexuality	Heterosexual attitudes and behavior	In the twentieth century, there has been a major increase in the number of adolescents reporting intercourse. The number of females reporting intercourse has increased more rapidly than the proportion of males. National data indicate that, by age 18, 44 percent of females and 64 percent of males are sexually experienced. Inner-city adolescents have even higher incidences. As we develop our sexual attitudes, we follow certain sexual scripts, which are different for males and females.
	Homosexual attitudes and behavior	Rates of homosexuality have remained constant in the twentieth century. Homosexuality is no longer classified as a disorder. Until recently, acceptance of homosexuality was increasing but, in concert with the AIDS epidemic, acceptance of homosexuality has decreased. No definitive conclusions about the cause of homosexuality have been reached.
	Sexually transmitted diseases	Any adolescent who has sex runs the risk of getting a sexually transmitted disease (formerly called venereal disease), although many adolescents underestimate their own risk. Among the sexually transmitted diseases adolescents may get are chlamydia, herpes, and AIDS.
	AIDS	Acquired immune deficiency syndrome is caused by a virus that destroys the body's immune system. AIDS can only be transmitted through sexual contact, shared needles, or blood transfusion.
	Adolescent pregnancy	More than 1 million American adolescents become pregnant each year. Eight of 10 adolescent pregnancies are unintended. Our nation's adolescent pregnancy rate is the highest in the Western world. Dramatic changes have swept through the American culture in the past 3 decades regarding adolescent sexuality and pregnancy. The consequences of adolescent pregnancy include health risks for the mother and the offspring. Adolescent mothers often drop out of school, fail to gain employment, and become dependent on welfare. Experts are calling for increased sex education and family planning, access to contraceptive methods, and broad community involvement and support.

Concept	Processes/related ideas	Characteristics/description
Adolescent problems and disturbances	Drugs and alcohol	The United States has the highest adolescent drug use rate of any industrialized nation. The 1960s and 1970s were a time of marked increase in adolescent drug use. Since the mid-1980s, there has been a slight overall downturn in drug use among adolescents. Alcohol is the drug most widely used by adolescents; alcohol abuse by adolescents is a major problem. Heavy drinking is common. Cocaine is a highly controversial drug. Its use by high school seniors dropped off for the first time in 8 years in 1987, a trend that has continued. Parents, peers, and schools play important roles in adolescent drug use.
	Suicide	The rate of suicide has increased. The suicide rate increases dramatically at about the age of 15. Both proximal and distal factors are involved in suicide's causes.
	Eating disorders	Anorexia nervosa and bulimia increasingly have become problems for adolescent females. Societal, psychological, and physiological causes of these disorders have been proposed.
	Interrelation of problems and programs that prevent or reduce adolescent problems	Very high risk youth have multiple problem behaviors—they make up as many as 10 percent of adolescents. They include adolescents who have been arrested or have committed serious offenses, have dropped out of school or are behind their grade level, are heavy drug users, drink heavily, regularly use cigarettes and marijuana, and are sexually active but do not use contraception. High-risk youths include as many as 15 percent of adolescents who participate in these behaviors but with slightly lower frequency and less deleterious consequences. Researchers are increasingly finding that problem behaviors in adolescence are interrelated. Dryfoos found a number of common components in programs designed to prevent or reduce adolescent problems; they include the importance of providing individual attention to high-risk children, the need to develop communitywide intervention, and early identification and intervention.
Stereotyping adolescents	Its nature	A stereotype is a broad category reflecting our impressions about people. Many stereotypes about adolescents are inaccurate. Stereotypes about adolescence often arise from a blend of personal experiences and media portrayals.
Today's youth	The current status of adolescents	The majority of adolescents today successfully negotiate the path from childhood to adulthood. By some criteria, today's adolescents also are doing better than their counterparts from a decade or two earlier. However, too many of today's adolescents are not provided with adequate opportunities and support to become competent adults. In many ways, today's adolescents are presented with a less stable environment. It is important to view adolescents as a heterogeneous group because a different portrayal emerges depending on the particular set of adolescents being described.
	Idealized images of adolescents and society's ambivalent messages	Our society seems to be uncertain about what adolescents should be. There are many areas, such as independence, sexuality, laws and values, and education, in which adults entertain idealized images of adolescents but communicate ambivalent messages that may contribute to adolescents' problems.
	The complexity of adolescent development and sociocultural contexts	As researchers carefully examine adolescents' lives, they recognize the complexity of adolescent development. Because of this complexity, no single developmental model fits all adolescents.

Summary

I. Physical Development in Early Childhood

The average child grows 2½ inches in height and gains between 5 and 7 pounds a year during early childhood. Growth patterns vary individually, though. By age 5, the brain has reached nine tenths of its size. Some of its increased size during early childhood is due to increases in the number and size of nerve endings, some to myelination. Increasing brain maturation contributes to improved cognitive abilities. Both gross and fine motor skills improve considerably in early childhood. Young children's lives are extremely active, more active than at any other point in the human life cycle. At one time, all children were taught to be right-handed. In today's world, the strategy is to let children use the hand they favor. Both genetic and environmental explanations of handedness have been given.

II. Physical Development in Middle and Late Childhood

During the elementary school years, children grow an average of 2 to 3 inches a year. Muscle mass and strength gradually increase. Legs lengthen and trunks slim down as "baby fat" decreases. Growth is slow and consistent. Children's motor development becomes much smoother and more coordinated. Children gain greater control over their bodies and can sit and attend for longer frames of time. However, their lives should be activity oriented and very active. Increased myelination of the central nervous system is reflected in improved fine motor skills. Boys usually have better gross motor skills; girls have better fine motor skills.

III. Children's Health and Illness

Only recently have researchers applied a developmental perspective to children's health. Children's health care involves their motor, cognitive, and social development. One death of every three in the world is the death of a child under 5. Every week, more than a quarter of a million children die in developing countries. The most frequent cause of children's death is diarrhea. Oral rehydration therapy can be used to prevent diarrhea from leading to death. Most child malnutrition and death could be prevented by parental actions that are affordable and based on knowledge available today. The United States has a relatively low rate of child deaths compared to other countries, although the Scandinavian countries have the lowest rates. The disorders most likely to be fatal for American children in the preschool years are birth defects, cancer, and heart disease.

IV. Nutrition and Exercise

Energy needs increase as children go through the childhood years. Energy requirements vary according to basal metabolism, rate of growth, and activity. Many parents are raising children on diets that are too high in fat and sugar content. Children's diets should include well-balanced proportions of fats, carbohydrates, protein, vitamins, and minerals. Every indication suggests that our nation's children are not getting enough exercise. Television viewing, parents as poor role models for children's exercise, and the lack of adequate physical education classes in schools may be to blame.

V. Pubertal Change

Puberty is a period of rapid skeletal and sexual maturation that occurs mainly in early adolescence. Testosterone plays an important role in male pubertal development, estradiol in female pubertal development. The growth spurt occurs about 2 years later for boys than for girls, with 12½ the average age of onset for boys, 10½ for girls. Individual maturation in pubertal change is extensive.

VI. Psychological Accompaniments of Physical Change

Adolescents show a heightened interest in their body image. Early maturation favors boys, at least during adolescence. As adults, though, late-maturing boys achieve more successful identities than early-maturing boys. The results are more mixed for girls. Some researchers now question whether puberty's effects are as strong as once believed. Of special concern is the health care of early- and late-maturing adolescents.

VII. Heterosexual and Homosexual Attitudes and Behavior

In the twentieth century, there has been a major increase in the number of adolescents reporting intercourse. The proportion of females reporting intercourse has increased more rapidly than the proportion of males. National data indicate that, by age 18, 44 percent of females and 64 percent of males are sexually experienced. Inner-city adolescents have even higher incidences. As we develop our sexual identities, we follow certain sexual scripts, which are different for males and females. Rates of homosexuality have remained constant in the twentieth century. Homosexuality is no longer classified as a disorder. Until recently, acceptance of homosexuality was increasing but, in concert with the AIDS epidemic, acceptance of homosexuality has decreased. No definitive conclusions about the cause of homosexuality have been reached.

VIII. Sexually Transmitted Diseases and Adolescent Pregnancy

Any adolescent who has sex runs that risk of getting a sexually transmitted disease, although many adolescents underestimate their own risk. Among the sexually transmitted diseases adolescents may get are chlamydia, herpes, and AIDS. Acquired immune deficiency syndrome is caused by a virus that destroys the body's immune system. AIDS can only be transmitted through sexual contact, shared needles, or blood transfusion. More than 1 million American adolescents become pregnant each year. Eight of 10 adolescent pregnancies are unintended. Our nation's adolescent pregnancy rate is the highest in the Western world. Dramatic changes have swept through the American culture in the past 3 decades regarding adolescent sexuality and pregnancy. The consequences of adolescent pregnancy include health risks for the mother and the offspring. Adolescent mothers often drop out of school, fail to gain employment, and become dependent on welfare. Experts are calling for increased sex education and family planning, access to contraceptive methods, and broad community involvement and support.

IX. Drugs, Alcohol, Suicide, and Eating Disorders

The United States has the highest adolescent drug use rate of any industrialized nation. The 1960s and 1970s were a time of marked increase in adolescent drug use. Since the mid-1980s, there has been a slight downturn in drug use among adolescents. Alcohol is the drug most widely used by adolescents; alcohol abuse by adolescents is a major problem. Heavy drinking is common. Cocaine is a highly controversial drug. Its use by high school seniors dropped off for the first time in 8 years in 1987, a trend that has continued. Parents, peers, and schools play important roles in adolescent drug use. The rate of suicide has increased; the suicide rate increases dramatically at about the age of 15. Both proximal and distal factors are involved in suicide's causes. Anorexia nervosa and bulimia have become increasing problems for adolescents. Societal, psychological, and physiological causes of these disorders have been proposed.

X. Interrelation of Problems and Programs That Prevent or Reduce Adolescent Problems

Very high risk youth have multiple problems—they make up as many as 10 percent of adolescents. They include adolescents who have been arrested or have committed serious offenses, have dropped out of school or are behind in grade level, are users of heavy drugs, drink heavily, regularly use cigarettes and marijuana, and are sexually active but do not use contraception. High-risk youth include as many as 15 percent of adolescents who participate in these behaviors but with slightly lower frequency and less deleterious consequences. Researchers are increasingly finding that problem behaviors are interrelated. Dryfoos found a number of common components in programs designed to prevent or reduce adolescent problems; they include the importance of providing individual attention to high-risk children, the need to develop communitywide intervention, and early identification and intervention.

XI. Stereotyping Adolescents and Today's Youth

A stereotype is a broad category that reflects our impressions about people. Many stereotypes about adolescence are inaccurate. Stereotypes about adolescence often arise from a blend of personal experiences and media portrayals. The majority of adolescents today successfully negotiate the path from childhood to adulthood. By some criteria, today's adolescents are doing better than their counterparts from a decade or two earlier. However, too many of today's adolescents are not provided adequate opportunities and support to become competent adults. In many ways, today's adolescents are presented with a less stable environment than a decade or two ago. It is important to view adolescents as a heterogeneous group because a different portrayal of adolescence emerges depending on the set of adolescents being described. Our society seems uncertain about what adolescents should be or should not be. There are many areas, such as independence, sexuality, laws and values, and education, in which adults entertain idealized images of adolescents but communicate ambivalent messages that may contribute to adolescents' problems. As researchers carefully examine adolescents' lives, they recognize the complexity of adolescent development. Because of this complexity, no single developmental model fits all adolescents.

Key Terms

myelination 169
Denver Developmental
  Screening Test 171
oral rehydration therapy
  (ORT) 176
basal metabolism rate
  (BMR) 177
menarche 181
puberty 183
testosterone 183

estradiol 183
sexual script 190
chlamydia 192
herpes simplex virus II 192
AIDS (acquired immune
  deficiency syndrome) 193
anorexia nervosa 202
bulimia 203
stereotype 204

Suggested Readings

Bancroft, J., & Reinisch, J. M. (Eds.). (1990). *Adolescence and puberty*. New York: Oxford University Press. This excellent, up-to-date source about the nature of adolescent sexuality includes chapters about cross-cultural aspects of adolescent sexual activity, the biological basis of sexuality, trends in adolescent sexual behavior, and contraception.

Dryfoos, J. G. (1990). *Adolescents at risk: Prevalence and prevention*. New York: Oxford University Press. This is an outstanding contribution to our understanding of problems and disturbances. Dryfoos describes the common components of successful prevention and intervention efforts.

Feldman, S. S. & Elliott, G. R. (1990). Progress and promise of research on normal adolescent development. In S. S. Feldman & G. Elliott (Eds.), *At the threshold: The developing adolescent*. Cambridge, MA: Harvard University Press. The Carnegie Corporation of New York commissioned this book in an effort to pinpoint major gaps in knowledge about normal adolescent development. In this concluding chapter, Shirley Feldman and Glen Elliott pull together significant themes in adolescent development, especially highlighting areas that need further research attention.

Grant, J. P. (1990). *The state of the world's children*. New York: UNICEF and Oxford University Press. This book provides an analysis of children's illness, health, and death in more than 100 countries around the world. Detailed charts and tables about death rates and nutrition are included, as are ways to reduce the child death rate and malnutrition.

Journal of School Health. This journal includes a number of articles about children's health, nutrition, and exercise. Leaf through the issues of the past several years to get a feel for the types of interventions being used in school settings to improve children's health.

Lerner, R. M., & Foch, T. T. (Eds.). (1987). *Biological-psychological interaction in early adolescence*. Hillsdale, NJ: Erlbaum. This book includes articles on a wide range of topics related to pubertal changes and their effects on development.

McAnarney, E. R. (1988). Early adolescent motherhood: Crisis in the making? In M. D. Levine & E. R. McAnarney (Eds.), *Early adolescent transitions*. Lexington, MA: D. C. Heath. Recent information about adolescent mothers, including potential intervention strategies, is provided.

Paikoff, R. L., & Brooks-Gunn, J. (1990). Physiological processes: What role do they play during the transition to adolescence? In R. Montemayor, G. R. Adams, & T. P. Gulotta (Eds.), *From childhood to adolescence: A transitional period*. Newbury Park, CA: Sage. Different models for interpreting puberty's effects on adolescent development are presented and evaluated, along with an up-to-date research overview of what is known about pubertal changes and psychological development.

LEARNING, COGNITION, AND LANGUAGE DEVELOPMENT

LEARNING IS AN

ORNAMENT IN PROSPERITY,

A REFUGE IN ADVERSITY.

—Aristotle

CHAPTER

7

LEARNING AND MOTIVATION

The Nature of Learning and Motivation
Learning
Classical Conditioning
    How Classical Conditioning Works
    Classical Conditioning with Children
    Evaluating Classical Conditioning
    Perspective on Child Development 7.1: Fear,
        Excitement, and Salivation
Operant Conditioning
    What Is Operant Conditioning?
    The Flow of Events
    Arrangements of Reinforcements
    Perspective on Child Development 7.2: The Role
        of Immediate and Delayed Consequences in
        Developing Self-control
    Punishment
    Applications of Operant Conditioning
    Perspective on Child Development 7.3: Assertive
        Discipline in Classrooms: Panacea or
        Problem?
Habituation
Imitation and Cognitive Learning
    Bandura's Concept of Imitation
    Infant Imitation
    Behavior, Person (Cognition), and Environment
Motivation
    Some Ideas About the "Whys" of Children's
        Behavior
    Achievement
    Cultural Worlds of Development 7.1:
        Comparisons of Children's Math
        Achievement in Japan, China, and the United
        States
Summary
Key Terms
Suggested Readings

Cora is in the fifth grade and enjoying her school year immensely. Her teacher, Ms. Greene, is energetic and uses a variety of teaching techniques each school day. The children seem to like the variation and richness of her teaching style. As we eavesdrop on the class one Tuesday morning, we see Cora begin her day's schoolwork by taking out a notebook and writing for 15 minutes. The class has a standing assignment to begin each day by writing a journal entry of what they did in their free time the day before. Ms. Greene feels that the assignment helps settle the children down immediately, motivates them to reflect on their experiences, and lets them practice writing everyday. The teacher observes Cora finish, praises her in front of the class ("I'm happy to see you complete your writing assignment for today, Cora. Good job!"), and records a check next to Cora's name on a large class roster prominently displayed in front of the room. Ms. Greene does this, in turn, for each child who finishes. Each child who completes the writing assignment for every school day of the month is promised a spaghetti dinner at Ms. Greene's house.

Later in the day, we observe Ms. Greene instructing the children in mathematics. She shows the children, step by step, how to complete long division problems, such as 21 divided into 446 and 18 divided into 3,641, emphasizing the testing of multiples, bringing intermediate products down, keeping columns in line, and recording remainders correctly (for example, for the first problem, the answer is 21 R. 5). As she works each example problem, she asks the children to copy her work from the chalkboard and to study the steps. She answers several questions the children have and then gives them several problems to try on their own. Cora works diligently and, since her penmanship isn't especially strong, she devotes attention to the mechanics of aligning columns and writing intermediate products and answers in the right places.

This example illustrates two important concepts in learning that are pervasive in the lives of children throughout the world—reinforcement (or reward) and imitation. **Reinforcement (reward)** *is a consequence that increases the probability that a behavior will recur.* When Cora and her classmates complete their daily journal entries, Ms. Greene provides immediate but modest verbal reinforcement with a concrete record or symbolic token (the check marks) that subsequently is converted into a large concrete reward (the spaghetti dinner). The larger reward is given only after a substantial period of time so that the children learn to delay gratification. In her math instruction, Ms. Greene demonstrates, or models, some techniques for completing a basic task in mathematics. In this situation, the children learn through imitation of an expert model (Ms. Greene) and practice the imitated behaviors. **Imitation (modeling)** *takes place when children learn new behaviors by watching someone else perform the behaviors.* We will have much more to say about these two powerful learning processes—reinforcement and imitation—later in the chapter.

This chapter is about children's learning and motivation—the hows and whys of children's behavior. Among the questions we will evaluate are the following: What are learning and motivation? What are the ways children learn? What are some ways we can motivate children? What is the nature of children's achievement motivation?

The Nature of Learning and Motivation

The term *learning* is used extensively in our everyday conversation. As a result, most of us have fairly rich ideas about what it means to learn and we can call to mind a number of concrete experiences to illustrate actual cases of learning. We might associate learning with what takes place in school, with the conscious efforts of a parent to "teach" a child something, with the outcome of a child exploring a new place or a new object, with the practice of a physical or athletic skill, and so forth. Although many of these examples may involve learning, psychologists try to be more formal and precise about the definition of learning: learning occurs only when certain features of situations are evident.

One feature that shows evidence of learning is *change*. When a parent shows a child how to hold a spoon, when a teacher shows a child how to use a computer keyboard, or when a child attempts to head a soccer ball, the child probably does not perform these feats appropriately at first—for example, holding the spoon backwards, stroking the keys of the keyboard randomly, or missing the soccer ball or striking it with the face. Later however, the child does complete these behaviors appropriately—in effect, changing from not being able to respond correctly to being able to do so.

A second feature that shows evidence of learning is the *relative permanence* of the change in responding. Consider the examples given. We can presume that most children will continue to hold spoons, stroke keyboards, and head soccer balls correctly for a considerable time to come, once they have mastered these feats. These actions have become relatively permanent in the children's repertoire of behavior and skills.

A third feature of learning is the central role of *experience*. Roughly speaking, experience is the opportunity to practice or repeatedly observe events and actions. The infant may repeatedly try to grasp the spoon, the child may practice at the keyboard, and the soccer novice will repeatedly try to head the ball accurately. The practice may be combined with time spent observing skilled adults doing these things.

To summarize, then, **learning** *is defined as a relatively permanent change in behavior that occurs through experience.* This definition helps us distinguish between behaviors that the child acquires through learning and behaviors that originate primarily in another way. For example, if a child is physically ill, drugged, or injured, she may talk and act in unusual and distinct ways that never occurred before and never occur in normal states. Ordinarily, we would not say that the child has learned new behaviors as a result of the illness, drug state, or injury. However, we might waive this disclaimer for a child whose "distressed" condition lasts for a long time, because, then, the behaviors may be practiced to the extent that they become relatively permanent. Another example is that many behaviors develop in children through maturational processes primarily and only secondarily through learning processes. For example, children learn to walk and talk, and adolescents experience intense

Experience is the only teacher.

—Ralph Waldo Emerson

interest in members of the opposite sex. These behaviors are heavily influenced by biological processes. A child learns to walk and talk as part of the natural process of maturation, although practice helps shape these behaviors. An adolescent's interest in members of the opposite sex is largely caused by the physical and hormonal changes occurring at the same time.

Motivation *involves the question of "why" individuals behave, think, and feel the way they do. Two important dimensions of the "whys" of motivation are the activation and direction of behavior.* Why is a child hungry? Why does a child study so hard? Why is a child going to a party? First, when children are motivated, they do something. Their behavior is activated, or energized. If children are hungry, they might go to the refrigerator for a snack. If they are motivated to get a good grade on a test, they might study hard. Second, when children are motivated, their behavior is directed. Why does one child behave one way when there are several options available? For example, if a father reprimands his children for failing to clean their rooms before going out to play, one child might seem to ignore the reprimand, another child might hurry to clean the room before departing, and a third child might start a verbal argument. Motivation, thus, involves an attempt to explain how children direct their behavior or, put another way, motivation involves an attempt to explain the specific behaviors they select in certain situations but not others. To summarize, motivation focuses on the question of "why" children behave, think, and feel the way they do, with special consideration of the activation and direction of their behaviors.

How are learning and motivation connected? The answer is at once simple and complicated. The simple answer is that learning and motivation are inextricably linked—much (but not all) learning occurs in the presence of forces that activate and direct behavior—in other words, factors that motivate the learning. Conversely, much of human motivation is learned—we were not born predisposed to act a particular way; we acquire motivation through learning. The more complicated answer is that we are not always sure how learning and motivation are related. For example, sometimes we cannot decide whether or not a particular learned behavior requires a motivational push or pull to take place. For example, did a child learn in a class out of a strong need for achievement or out of a strong affinity for the teacher?

Learning

What are the major ways in which children learn? In this section, we will discuss the major, traditional forms of learning that psychologists have used to describe a wide range of changes. These include classical conditioning, operant conditioning, habituation, imitation, and cognitive learning. There are other forms of learning, some of which are described in the chapters on cognitive development and Piaget's theory (chapter 8), information processing (chapter 9), and language (chapter 10). The forms of learning described here are especially useful when the change in question involves an easily observed behavior that is shaped by experiences and is relatively easy to define (for example, smiling, crying, hitting). Other behaviors, which involve a considerable amount of mental activity and organization (for instance, talking) and biological supports, are best described by other forms of learning.

Classical Conditioning

It is a nice spring day. A father takes his baby out for a walk. The baby reaches over to touch a pink flower and is badly stung by a bumblebee sitting on the petals. The next day, the baby's mother brings home some pink flowers. She removes a flower from the arrangement and takes it to her baby to smell. The baby cries loudly as soon as she sees the pink flower. The baby's panic at the sight of the pink flower illustrates the learning process of **classical conditioning,** *in which a neutral stimulus acquires the ability to produce a response originally produced by another stimulus.*

How Classical Conditioning Works

In the early 1900s, Russian physiologist Ivan Pavlov investigated the way the body digests food. As part of his experimentation on digestion, he routinely placed meat powder in a dog's mouth, causing the dog to salivate. Pavlov began to notice that the meat powder was not the only stimulus that caused the dog to salivate. The dog salivated in response to a number of stimuli associated with the food, such as the sight of the food dish, the sight of the individual who brought the food into the room, and the sound of the door closing when the food arrived. Pavlov recognized that the dog's association of these sights and sounds with the food was an important type of learning that came to be called classical conditioning.

Pavlov set aside his work on digestion and extensively studied the association of various stimuli with food. He wanted to know *why* the dog salivated to various sights and sounds before eating the meat powder. Pavlov observed that the dog's behavior included both learned and unlearned components. The "unlearned" part of classical conditioning is based on the fact that some stimuli automatically produce certain responses apart from any prior learning; in other words, they are inborn, or innate. **Reflexes** *are automatic stimulus-response connections.* They include salivation in response to food, nausea in response to bad food, shivering in response to low temperature, coughing in response to the throat being clogged, pupil constriction in response to light, and withdrawal in response to blows or burns. An **unconditioned stimulus (UCS)** *is a stimulus that produces a response without prior learning;* food was the UCS in Pavlov's experiments. An **unconditioned response (UCR)** *is an unlearned response that is automatically associated with the UCS.* In Pavlov's experiments, the saliva that flowed from the dog's mouth in response to the food was the UCR. In the case of the baby and the flower, the baby's learning and experience did not cause her to cry when the bee stung her. Her crying was unlearned and occurred automatically. The bee's sting was the UCS and the crying was the UCR.

In classical conditioning, the **conditioned stimulus (CS)** *is a previously neutral stimulus that eventually elicits the conditioned response after being paired with the unconditioned stimulus.* The **conditioned response (CR)** *is the learned response to the conditioned stimulus that occurs after CS-UCS pairing* (Pavlov, 1927). In studying a dog's response to various stimuli associated with meat powder, Pavlov rang a bell before giving the meat powder to the dog. Until then, ringing the bell did not have a particular effect on the dog, except perhaps to wake it from a nap; the bell was a neutral stimulus. However, the dog began to associate the sound of the bell with the food and salivated when

If a bee stings this young girl while she is holding a pink flower, how would classical conditioning explain her panic at the sight of pink flowers in the future?

Cartoon by John Chase.

(a)

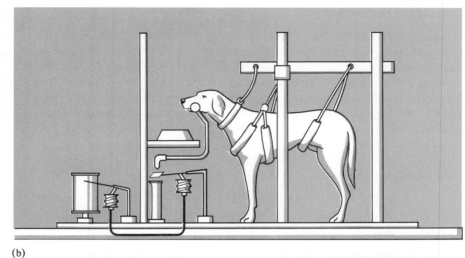
(b)

(c)

Figure 7.1
Pavlov's Experimentation
(a) Surgical preparation for studying the salivary reflex: When the dog salivated, the saliva collected in a glass funnel attached to the dog's cheek. This way, the strength of the salivary response could be measured precisely. (b) Pavlov used this experimental apparatus to examine classical conditioning. (c) Pavlov (the white-bearded gentleman in the center) is shown demonstrating the nature of classical conditioning to students at the Military Medical Academy in the Soviet Union.

the bell was sounded. The bell had become a conditioned (learned) stimulus (CS) and the salivation a conditioned response (CR). Before conditioning (or learning), the bell and the food were not related. After their association, however, the conditioned stimulus (the bell) produced a conditioned response (salivation). Figure 7.1 shows Pavlov's laboratory setting for studying classical conditioning and Pavlov demonstrating the procedure of classical conditioning. A summary of how classical conditioning works is shown in figure 7.2.

Classical Conditioning with Children

Since Pavlov's experiments, children have been conditioned to respond to the sound of a buzzer, a glimpse of light, or the touch of a hand. Classical conditioning has a great deal of survival value for children. Because of classical conditioning, children jerk their hands away before they are burned by fire and they move out of the way of a rapidly approaching truck before it hits them. Classical conditioning is at work in words that serve as important sig-

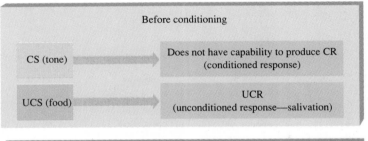

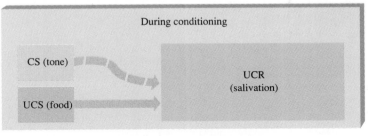

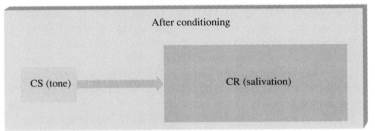

Figure 7.2
Classical Conditioning
At the start of conditioning, the UCS will evoke the UCR, but the CS does not have this capacity. During conditioning, the CS and UCS are paired so that the CS comes to elicit the response. The key learning ingredient is the association of the UCS and CS.

nals. A boy walks into an abandoned house with a friend and yells, "Snake!" His friend bolts out the door. An adolescent imagines a peaceful, tranquil scene—an abandoned beach with waves lapping onto the sand—and relaxes as if she were actually lying on the beach.

Phobias *are irrational fears.* Classical conditioning provides an explanation of these and other fears. Behaviorist John Watson conducted an investigation to demonstrate classical conditioning's role in phobias. A little boy named Albert was shown a white laboratory rat to see if he was afraid of it. He was not. As Albert played with the rat, a loud noise was sounded behind his head. As you might imagine, the noise caused little Albert to cry. After only seven pairings of the loud noise with the white rat, Albert began to fear the rat even when the noise was not sounded. Albert's fear was generalized to a rabbit, a dog, and a sealskin coat (see figure 7.3). Today, we could not ethically conduct such an experiment. Especially noteworthy is the fact that Watson did not remove Albert's fear of rats, so, presumably, this phobia remained with him after the experiment. Many of our fears—fear of the dentist from a painful experience, fear of driving from being in an automobile accident, fear of heights from falling off a high chair when we were infants, and fear of dogs from being bitten, for example—can be learned through classical conditioning.

■ *Critical Thinking*
Examine your life for a moment. If you are like most people, you will have at least one fear that comes to mind. How did you develop the fear? Do you think it was classically conditioned?

Figure 7.3

Little Albert's Generalized Fear
In 1920, 9-month-old little Albert was conditioned to fear a white rat by pairing the rat with a loud noise. When little Albert was subsequently placed with other stimuli similar to the white rat, such as the rabbit shown here, he was afraid of them too. This illustrates the principles of stimulus generalization in classical conditioning.

Photo courtesy of Professor Benjamin Harris, Univ. of Wisconsin.

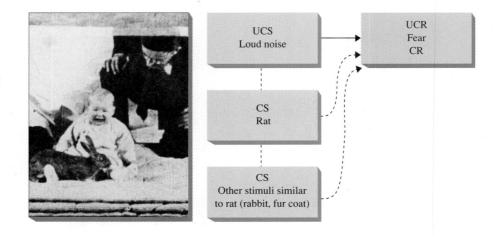

If we can produce fears by classical conditioning, we should be able to eliminate them. **Counterconditioning** *is a classical conditioning procedure for weakening a CR by associating the stimuli with a new response incompatible with the CR.* Though Watson did not eliminate little Albert's fear of white rats, an associate of Watson's, Mary Cover Jones (1924), did eliminate the fears of a 3-year-old boy named Peter. Peter had many of the same fears as Albert; however, Peter's fears were not produced by Jones. Among Peter's fears were white rats, fur coats, frogs, fish, and mechanical toys. To eliminate these fears, a rabbit was brought into Peter's view but kept far enough away that it would not upset him. At the same time the rabbit was brought into view, Peter was fed crackers and milk. On each successive day, the rabbit was moved closer to Peter as he ate crackers and milk. Eventually, Peter reached the point at which he could eat the food with one hand and pet the rabbit with the other.

Some of the behaviors we associate with health problems or mental disturbances can involve classical conditioning. Certain physical complaints—asthma, headaches, ulcers, and high blood pressure, for example—may partly be the products of classical conditioning. We usually say that such health problems are caused by stress, but often what has happened is that certain stimuli, such as a teacher's critical attitude or fighting by parents, are conditioned stimuli for children's physiological responses. Over time, the frequent presence of the physiological responses may produce health disorders.

Evaluating Classical Conditioning

Pavlov described all learning in terms of classical conditioning. In reality, children learn in many ways. Still, classical conditioning helps children learn about their environment and has been successful in eliminating children's fears. However, a view that describes children as *responding* to the environment fails to capture the *active* nature of children and their influence on the environment. More about the role of classical conditioning in children's everyday lives appears in Perspective on Child Development 7.1. Next, we will study a major form of learning that places more emphasis on children's activity in the environment—operant conditioning.

Learning, Cognition, and Language Development

Fear, Excitement, and Salivation

Martha, a third grader, is accompanying her mother on a business errand. The two are walking down a hall in their town's City-County Building. As they pass an office, a clerk inside suddenly opens the door, and Martha notices a pale green wall and smells the strong odor of an alcohol-based disinfectant (someone inside is wiping off his desk top with a cleaning solution). Suddenly, Martha is overcome with apprehension, her heart rate increases, and her palms begin to sweat. On further investigation, we discover that Martha had a serious illness when she was 5 and spent a number of painful and uncomfortable days in a hospital bed. Guess what color the hospital walls were. What do you suppose was a frequent odor in the hospital environment?

Jim, a seventh grader, is taking a leisurely bath. He is lying on his back—relaxing, listening to rock music on his shower radio, and generally unconcerned with anything going on around him. A few minutes go by before he remembers to take his wristwatch off—it isn't water resistant—and he reaches over for a bar of soap to begin washing himself. The song on the radio has a momentary silence, followed by the unmistakable sound of a handgun being fired. Jim becomes excited, crouches, and begins a motion resembling the block-start dive at the outset of a swimming race. Jim is a competitive swimmer who has participated in the sport for 6 years. What cues might have triggered this highly trained response in him—the water, the pistol firing, taking off his wristwatch, or a combination of them?

Sally, like many 4-year-olds, is a junk-a-holic. Just name a sweet or a candy, and Sally would be happy to consume a truckload of it. As she watches the world go by in the front seat of her father's car one day, Sally spies a candy sign on the window of a convenience store. Her eyes grow big, she begins to salivate, and she beckons her father to head to the store.

In each anecdote described, see if you can offer a plausible analysis of the four key elements of the classical conditioning paradigm—the UCS, CS, UCR, and CR. If you can, chances are you grasp the essence of classical conditioning.

Operant Conditioning

Classical conditioning excels at explaining how neutral stimuli become associated with unlearned, involuntary responses, but it does not do as well in explaining voluntary behaviors, such as studying hard for a test, learning to play ping-pong, or memorizing a song. Operant conditioning is usually better than classical conditioning at explaining *voluntary* behavior.

What Is Operant Conditioning?

The concept of operant conditioning was developed by American psychologist B. F. Skinner (1938). **Operant conditioning** *(or instrumental conditioning) is a form of learning in which the consequences of behavior produce changes in the probability of the behavior's occurrence.* In operant conditioning, an organism acts, or *operates,* on the environment to produce a change in the probability of the behavior's occurrence; Skinner chose the term *operants* to describe the responses that are actively emitted because of the consequences for the organism. The consequences are *contingent,* or dependent, on the organism's behavior. For example, a simple operant might be the pressing of a lever that leads to the delivery of food (the consequence); the delivery of food is contingent on pressing the lever.

We have mentioned one main difference between classical and operant conditioning—that classical conditioning is better at explaining involuntary responses, whereas operant conditioning is better at explaining voluntary responses. A second difference is that the stimuli which govern behavior in classical conditioning precede the behavior; the stimuli that govern behavior in operant conditioning *follow* the behavior. For example, if we teach a dog a

Learning and Motivation

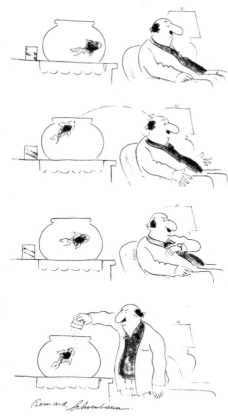

Drawing by Bernard Schoenbaum; © 1987 The
New Yorker Magazine, Inc.

trick, such as learning to roll over and "play dead," in classical conditioning we would present the conditioned stimulus (such as the sound of a bell paired with meat [UCS]) before the dog performed the trick. In operant conditioning, we would present the rewarding stimulus (meat or a pat on the head, for example) *after* the dog performed the trick.

Earlier we indicated that Skinner described operant conditioning as a form of learning in which the consequences of behavior lead to changes in the probability of that behavior's occurrence. The consequences—rewards or punishments—are contingent on the organism's behavior. **Reinforcement** *(or reward) is a consequence that increases the probability a behavior will occur.* By contrast, **punishment** *is a consequence that decreases the probability a behavior will occur.* For example, if an adult smiles at a child, and the adult and child continue talking for some time, the smile reinforced the child's talking. However, if an adult meets a child and frowns at the child, and the child quickly leaves the situation, then the frown punished the child's talking with the adult.

Reinforcement can be complex. Usually we think of reinforcement as positive, but it can also be negative. In **positive reinforcement,** *the frequency of a response increases because it is followed by a pleasant stimulus, as in the example of the smile increasing talking.* By contrast, in **negative reinforcement,** *the frequency of a response increases because the response either removes an unpleasant stimulus or lets the child avoid the stimulus.* For example, a boy's mother nags at him to clean his room. She keeps nagging. Finally, the son gets tired of the nagging and cleans his room. The child's response (cleaning his room) removed the unpleasant stimulus (nagging). Taking an aspirin works the same way: Taking aspirin is reinforced when this behavior is followed by a reduction in pain.

Another way to remember the distinction between positive and negative reinforcement is that, in positive reinforcement, something is *added,* or obtained. In negative reinforcement, something is *subtracted,* avoided, or escaped. For example, if a child receives a sweater from her parents for getting a good grade in a class, something has been added to increase the child's achievement behavior. Consider the situation, however, in which a child's parents criticize him for not studying hard enough. As the child studies harder, they stop criticizing him—their criticism has been subtracted.

Negative reinforcement and punishment are easily confused because they both involve aversive or unpleasant stimuli, such as a slap in the face. To keep them straight, remember that negative reinforcement *increases* the probability a response will occur, whereas punishment *decreases* the probability a response will occur. An overview of the distinctions between positive reinforcement, negative reinforcement, and punishment is presented in table 7.1.

The Flow of Events

Operant psychologists often chart the course of behavioral change in individuals by dividing their observations into three categories: baseline, conditioning, and extinction. The **baseline** *is a measure of how often a behavior occurs before an attempt is made to change the behavior.* For example, suppose we wish to follow the progress of an unruly child, Richard, who rarely stays on task in school. We create an observational sampling procedure by which we observe and record how many times Richard stays in his seat and focuses on his assigned work. For example, we might record how many blocks of time (perhaps in 5-minute intervals) he is on task during 2 designated hours of the school day for a continuous week. We discover, at most, one such interval each day and record it on a chart (see figure 7.4).

Learning, Cognition, and Language Development

TABLE 7.1
Positive Reinforcement, Negative Reinforcement, and Punishment

Process	Type of stimulus	Effect on response
Positive reinforcement	Pleasant	Increases
Negative reinforcement	Aversive	Increases
Punishment	Aversive	Decreases

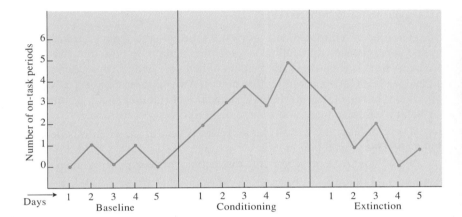

Figure 7.4
Baseline, Conditioning, and Extinction of Richard's On-Task Behavior

After the baseline has been established, a period of conditioning takes place. **Conditioning** *is the institution of a program to change an individual's undesirable behavior.* For example, in Richard's case, everyone is instructed to ignore Richard when he is out of his seat. When he is at his seat working, the teacher praises him and the other children smile at him. We record the number of blocks of time Richard is on task as before, using the sampling scheme for the next continuous week. We discover that he has from two to five such intervals per day during the week (see figure 7.4).

Finally, **extinction,** *a decrease in the tendency to perform a response brought about by unreinforced consequences of that response,* is instituted. In Richard's case, this means that the teacher and other students in the class treat him just as they did in the baseline period. There is no praise from the teacher or smiling faces from the students when Richard is on task. We repeat the recording procedure for another week and discover that Richard is on task from zero to three such intervals on any given day (see figure 7.4).

What have we learned about Richard? We objectively documented that he had a low level of academic behavior at the start of the procedure. Then, when we introduced two reinforcers—teacher's praise and classmates' smiles—Richard's academic behavior increased measurably over the week. These reinforcers were effective in changing Richard's academic behavior. Finally, when we withdrew the reinforcers, Richard's academic behavior gradually decreased, although not to the same low level as before the conditioning.

Learning and Motivation

By using this procedure, it is possible to follow the effects of particular reinforcing events on behavior change. Notice that we chart the behavior change over time in an individual child, that we make our observational scheme as simple and objective as possible, and that we focus on easily observable behaviors such as whether or not a child is sitting at his seat focusing on his schoolwork. These are the hallmarks of operant methodology. They have proven to be powerful observational tools and insightful logical devices for explaining behavior change. In practice, operant experiments are often more complex. There may be several different conditioning phases in which slightly different consequences (contingencies) are used to change behavior, observers might be asked to record the occurrences of several different aspects of behavior at the same time, and the procedure is often tried with a number of subjects at about the same time. However, the complexity does not alter the power of this type of design—only the amount of work the investigators must do to collect, record, and analyze the information.

Arrangements of Reinforcements

Our definition of reinforcement was rather simple—a behavior is strengthened by the consequences that follow it. Notwithstanding, it turns out that there are many details about the arrangement of behavior and its consequences that influence the effectiveness of reinforcement. Among these details are the considerations of time interval, shaping, schedules of reinforcement, primary and secondary reinforcement, and the child's reinforcement history.

Time Interval

As with classical conditioning, learning is more efficient in operant conditioning when the interval between the stimulus and the response is brief. As a rule, learning is more likely when the interval is on the order of seconds rather than minutes or hours. An especially important distinction to remember is that learning is more efficient under *immediate* rather than delayed consequences. Information about the importance of this distinction in children's everyday lives is presented in Perspective on Child Development 7.2.

Shaping

A child who enters a new learning situation may not have the slightest inclination to behave in a way that is appropriate for the setting. On the first day of school, she may walk around the room and talk incessantly, not realizing that, generally, one of the first requirements in school is to sit quietly at one's desk. A boy whose mother asks him for some help baking a cake hasn't the slightest inkling of what to do first. An autistic child initially does not speak at all. In each case, *shaping* is required to develop the desired response. **Shaping** *is the process of rewarding approximations of desired behavior.* The child may gradually learn to sit quietly at her desk by first being reinforced for a distantly related response, such as approaching the desk to sit down, and then a closer response, such as sitting down for a moment, and so on, until the final behavior appears. The boy's mother may first reward him for selecting a baking utensil, then for mixing some ingredients, and so on, until the boy has mastered all the components of the task. A therapist may first reward an autistic child for uttering a sound faintly resembling speech, then for a word, for a phrase, and finally for whole sentences (Lovaas, 1977).

The Role of Immediate and Delayed Consequences in Developing Self-control

A 15-year-old girl is overheard making the following comments during the course of a week:

> "That double-dutch chocolate dessert is just too good to pass up."
> "I know I should exercise more, but I guess I'm just too lazy to get started."
> "I've got an important paper due tomorrow morning. Why am I sitting here watching television?"

Like most people, self-control problems have cropped up in this young girl's life. Such individuals are often described as not having enough "willpower." Actually, many of these situations reflect a conflict between the immediate and delayed consequences of behavior involving various combinations of reinforcers and punishers (Martin & Pear, 1988).

Immediate Small Reinforcers Versus Delayed Strong Punishers. One reason obesity is a major problem for children and adults is that eating is a behavior with immediate positive consequences—food tastes very good and quickly provides a pleasurable feeling. Although the potential delayed consequences of overeating are negative (obesity and other health risks), the immediate consequences are hard to resist. Adolescents who smoke and drink face a similar problem with immediate reinforcement and delayed punishment. The immediate consequences of smoking are reinforcing for most smokers (a powerful combination of positive reinforcement, such as tension relief, and negative reinforcement, such as removal of nicotine cravings). The punishing aspects of smoking are primarily long-term, including shortness of breath, sore throat, coughing, emphysema, heart disease, and cancer. The immediate pleasurable consequences of drinking override the delayed consequences of a hangover or even alcoholism.

Immediate Small Reinforcers Versus Delayed Stronger Reinforcers. Children also face self-control problems brought about by the choice of obtaining a small immediate reinforcer or waiting for a delayed but much higher valued reinforcer. For example, children can spend their money now on candy, trinkets, and inexpensive items or save their money to buy a more expensive item such as a tape player. Also, children can play around now and enjoy themselves, which produces immediate small reinforcers, or they can study hard over a long period of time, which can produce delayed stronger reinforcers such as good grades and better jobs.

Immediate Punishers Versus Delayed Reinforcers. Why are some children so reluctant to take up a new sport? to try a new dance step? to go to a social gathering? to do something different? One reason is that learning new skills often involves minor punishing consequences such as initially looking stupid, not knowing what to do, and having to put up with sarcastic comments from onlookers. In such circumstances, reinforcing consequences are often delayed. For example, it takes a long time to become a good basketball player or musician.

Immediate Weak Punishers Versus Strong Delayed Punishers. Why do so many children want to postpone such activities as going to the dentist, scheduling minor surgery, or paying a library fine? In this kind of self-control problem, if children act immediately, they experience a weak punisher—it hurts to get teeth drilled, it is painful to have minor surgery, and it is not very pleasurable when a library fine has to be paid. However, the delayed consequences can even be more punishing—their teeth can fall out, eventually they might need major surgery, and a bigger library fine might be levied. All too often, though, immediate consequences win out in these self-control situations.

Schedules of Reinforcement

Schedules of reinforcement *are schedules of partial reinforcement, with rules that determine the occasion when a response will be reinforced. These schedules are based on time (interval schedule) and frequency of the specific behaviors (ratio schedule).*

First, let's examine an example of an interval schedule. Consider the example given of Richard, the unruly elementary school child. The teacher decides that she would like Richard to be cooperative throughout the day, but it is difficult to pay attention to him continuously, given her other responsibilities. Instead of praising Richard each time he is sitting at his seat, she arranges to praise him every other hour (9 A.M., 11 A.M., 1 P.M., 3 P.M.) if she has seen him engaged in work for an agreed-upon period of time (for example,

5 minutes) just before the hour in question. She institutes a reward schedule throughout the week, using this same schedule each day.

To illustrate a ratio schedule, we can modify the example. Suppose the teacher finds the reinforcement schedule to be ineffective. Richard does not respond. In fact, his behavior may actually deteriorate in the face of infrequent attention from the teacher. The teacher decides that her initial intuition is still correct. It would be advantageous not to reinforce Richard every time he is on task academically—with the goal being to extend the length and frequency of his on-task behavior throughout the day. Thus, she tries another reinforcement schedule. She decides that she will keep track of each on-task period that Richard displays, but she will only reinforce him after he has displayed three on-task periods—each 5 minutes long. In effect, Richard will receive reinforcement for each set of three behaviors he displays. As before, the reward schedule is instituted each day throughout the week.

Both of these schedules are *intermittent*—that is, the teacher has chosen to reward the child on an occasional, as opposed to continuous, basis. **Partial reinforcement (intermittent reinforcement)** *is a schedule of reinforcement in which responses are not reinforced every time they occur.* The usual technique in operant conditioning is to start off conditioning by shaping a behavior, then reinforcing the behavior continuously, and finally adopting an intermittent schedule. Often, but not always, an intermittent schedule of reinforcement will produce a more stable and long-lasting behavioral change.

Primary and Secondary Reinforcement

Positive reinforcement can be classified as primary reinforcement or secondary reinforcement, distinguishing between the inborn, unlearned aspects and the learned aspects of behavior. **Primary reinforcement** *involves the use of reinforcers that are innately satisfying—that is, they do not take any learning on the organism's part to make them pleasurable.* Food, water, and sexual satisfaction are primary reinforcers.

Secondary reinforcement *acquires its positive value through experience; secondary reinforcers are learned, or conditional, reinforcers.* Hundreds of secondary reinforcers characterize our lives. For example, secondary reinforcers include such social situations as getting a pat on the back, being praised, and making eye contact. One popular story in psychology focuses on the use of eye contact as a secondary reinforcer to shape the behavior of a university professor, an expert on operant conditioning. Some students decided to train the professor to lecture from one corner of the classroom. Using eye contact, they began reinforcing successive approximations to the desired response. Each time the professor moved toward the appropriate corner, the students looked at him. If he moved in another direction, they looked away. By gradually rewarding successive approximations to the desired response, the students were able to get the professor to deliver his lecture from one corner of the classroom. The professor denied that this shaping ever took place, but the story provides an excellent example of how secondary reinforcers can be used to shape behavior in real-life circumstances (Chance, 1979).

Another example can help you understand the importance of secondary reinforcement in our everyday lives. When a student is given $25 for an *A* on her report card, the $25 is a secondary reinforcer. It is not innate, and it increases the likelihood the student will work to get another *A* in the future. Money is often referred to as a *token reinforcer*. When an object can be exchanged for another reinforcer, the object may have reinforcing value itself. Gift certificates and poker chips are token reinforcers.

The Child's Reinforcement History

Another consideration in the reinforcement of learning is the child's reinforcement history. Each child has a unique history of previous reinforcement; an event that is reinforcing for one child may not be reinforcing for another. A child who works to learn a response for the reward of a toy may not work for the reward of new clothes or social praise. Some children are more likely to learn a response when the event that follows the response is social in nature—for example, verbal praise and social attention. Other children are more likely to work for material rewards such as toys, candies, and treats.

One way to find out what is the most effective reinforcing event for a child is by rating the value of various objects. For example, in one investigation, a technique was developed to determine which of two objects children preferred (Witryol, 1971). The objects were drawn from toys, edibles, and other attractive objects, and all possible pairs were presented to the children. From the pattern of preferences that emerged, a hierarchy of incentive values for the items was developed. For example, most children preferred a piece of bubble gum to a marble and a marble to a paper clip. Other objects shown to the children included a penny, a toy cow, a piece of candy, and a metal washer.

Punishment

Earlier in the chapter, we indicated that *punishment* decreases the probability a behavior will occur. That is, if a punishing stimulus follows a behavior, the behavior is less likely to recur. The use of punishment is pervasive in our world. Consider Mark, who asks Valerie for a date and hears, "Are you kidding? Me go out with you?!" Mark does not ask Valerie out again. Also consider a 1-year-old whose mother spanks him for playing with an electrical socket. After the spanking, the infant does not go near the socket again. For ethical reasons, psychologists do not spank infants to see whether such a stimulus decreases behavior. However, a number of laboratory experiments on punishment have been conducted with animals, and some modified versions of punishment experiments with animals have been conducted with humans.

Psychologists have made recommendations on the effective use of punishment and on decisions about when it might be called for in human behavior. First, punishment may lead to escape or avoidance. Second, when a response is successfully reduced or eliminated by punishment and no appropriate alternative behavior is strengthened, other undesirable behaviors may take the place of the punished behavior. Third, a person who administers punishment is serving as an aggressive model, possibly inadvertently modeling how to

It is not the whip that makes men, but the lure of things that are worthy to be loved.

—Woodrow Wilson

behave in an aggressive, punishing manner. Fourth, desirable behaviors may be eliminated along with undesirable ones. For example, a child may stop interacting with other children altogether when he is slapped for biting another child. Because punishment has so many side effects, are there circumstances when it is called for? There may be some circumstances when punishment is beneficial. For example, when positive reinforcement has not been found to work, punishment can be considered, and, when the behavior that is being punished is considered more destructive than the punishment itself, the process may be justified. For example, some children engage in behavior that is very dangerous to their well-being, such as head banging. In such cases, the use of punishment, even electric shock, may reduce the injurious behavior. Nonetheless, as punishment is reduced, it is always wise to reinforce an alternative behavior so that undesirable behavior does not replace the punished response.

Most childrearing experts in the United States today do not advocate the physical punishment of children, but the United States does not have a law that prohibits parents from spanking their children. However, in 1979, a law was passed in Sweden that specifically forbids parents from using physical punishment, including spanking and slapping, when disciplining their children (Ziegert, 1983). The physical punishment of children is treated as an offense, just like any other attack on a person. Sweden is the only industrial country in the world to pass such a law, which is especially designed to curb child abuse.

Could the United States pass this type of law? Probably not at this point in time, because fewer Americans would probably be in favor of the law than Swedes were in 1979. Many Americans would also probably view such a law as totalitarian, and the law would likely stimulate protest from civil libertarians and others. An important factor in Sweden's ability to pass the "anti-spanking" law is its attitude toward laws. The United States enforces laws through punishment. However, Sweden takes a softer approach to its laws, encouraging respect for laws through education designed to change attitudes and behavior.

When people, often teachers or doctors, suspect that a parent has spanked a child, they frequently report the incident because they know that the state will try to provide the parent with emotional and educational support rather than assessing a fine or sending the parent to jail. Accompanying the anti-spanking law was a parenting guide—*Can One Manage to Raise Children Without Spanking or Slapping?*—that was widely available at day-care centers, preschool programs, physicians' offices, and other similar locations. The publication includes advice about why physical punishment is not a good strategy for disciplining children, along with specific information about better ways to handle children's problems.

Parents and educators have been especially concerned about the issue of whether punishment should be used as part of teachers' efforts to manage a classroom effectively. Recently, the strongest controversy has brewed over a concept called Assertive Discipline. To learn more about this controversy, turn to Perspective on Child Development 7.3 on page 234.

■ *Critical Thinking*
Are there circumstances when children deserve to be spanked, or should parents never spank their children? Explain your answer.

Learning, Cognition, and Language Development

Applications of Operant Conditioning

A preschool child repeatedly throws down his glasses and breaks them. A young girl feels depressed. An adolescent mother lacks appropriate parenting skills. Operant conditioning has helped individuals such as these adapt more effectively and cope with their problems.

Behavior modification *is the application of operant conditioning principles to changing human behavior; its main goal is to replace unacceptable responses with acceptable, adaptive ones.* Consequences for behavior are established to ensure that acceptable responses are reinforced and unacceptable ones are not. Advocates of behavior modification believe that many emotional and behavioral problems are caused by inadequate (or inappropriate) response consequences.

The child who throws down his glasses and breaks them may be receiving too much attention from his teacher and peers for his behavior; thus, an unacceptable behavior is unwittingly reinforced. In this instance, the parents and teachers would be instructed to remove their attention from the destructive behavior and transfer it to more constructive behavior such as working quietly and playing cooperatively with peers (Harris, Wolf, & Baer, 1964).

Consider another circumstance. Barbara and her parents were on a collision course. Things got so bad that her parents decided to see a clinical psychologist. The psychologist, who had a behavioral orientation, talked with each family member, trying to get them to pinpoint the problem. The psychologist got the family to sign a behavioral contract that spelled out what everyone needed to do to reduce the conflict. Barbara agreed to: (1) be home before 11 P.M. on weeknights, (2) look for a part-time job so she could begin to pay for some of her activities; and (3) refrain from calling her parents insulting names. Her parents agreed to: (1) talk to Barbara in a low tone of voice if they were angry, rather than yell, (2) refrain from criticizing teenagers, especially Barbara's friends, and (3) give Barbara a small sum of money each week for gas, makeup, and socializing, but only until she obtained a job.

Behavior modification is not only effective in therapy, but it has also been applied to the world of computers to promote better instruction. Some years ago, Skinner developed a machine to assist teachers with their instruction of students. The teaching machine engaged students in a learning activity, paced the material at the students' own rate, tested the students' knowledge of the material, and provided immediate feedback about correct and incorrect answers. Skinner hoped that the machine would revolutionize learning in schools, but the revolution never took place.

Today, the idea behind Skinner's teaching machine has been applied to computers, which assist teachers in the instruction of students. Research comparisons of computer-assisted instruction with traditional teacher-based instruction suggest that, in some areas, such as drill and practice on math problems, computer-assisted instruction produces superior results (Kulik, Kulik, & Gangert-Drowns, 1985; Mandell & Mandell, 1989).

At this point, we have discussed a number of ideas about the nature of learning and motivation, classical conditioning, and operant conditioning. A

Computer-assisted learning has benefited from Skinner's concept of operant conditioning. Originally, Skinner's ideas were applied to the development of teaching machines. Today, computers engage students in learning activity, pacing the material at students' own rate; they test the students' knowledge of the material; and they give immediate feedback about correct and incorrect answers.

Assertive Discipline in Classrooms: Panacea or Problem?

Assertive Discipline was introduced by Lee Canter and Marlene Canter (1976) as a take-charge approach that sets limits on student behavior, provides negative consequences for inappropriate behavior, and supplies positive reinforcement for appropriate behavior. In Assertive Discipline, teachers are not to allow students to interfere with teaching for any reason. According to the Assertive Discipline approach, teachers have three choices: They can be hostile, nonassertive, or assertive. In this approach, they should be assertive. The advocates of Assertive Discipline argue that this approach is needed because children today are more difficult to control than were children in the past. The Canters and their followers claim that Assertive Discipline reduces discipline problems in classrooms by 80 percent. Apparently, the technique has experienced meteoric growth. According to advertising materials disseminated by the Canters, more than 500,000 teachers have been trained in Assertive Discipline strategies in "countless" workshops in "thousands" of schools.

The Canters' advertising materials contain other "evidence" of the dramatic success of Assertive Discipline:

- Ninety-two percent of the teachers feel more confident in their ability to handle disruptive behavior effectively.
- Eighty-eight percent of the educators are more successful in dealing with the parents of students with behavior problems.
- Seventy-one percent of the teachers feel more confident in their ability to work with their principals on discipline problems.
- Eighty-eight percent of the teachers report they enjoy teaching more after learning the Assertive Discipline methods.

How valid are these claims for Assertive Discipline? The percentages are reported with no sources, and no methods of data collection are documented. In a critical review and analysis of the Assertive Discipline approach, it was concluded that there has been a surprising lack of research investigation of this widely used program (Render, Padilla, & Krank, 1989). The research data that are available do not provide strong empirical support of Assertive Discipline. Much of it is based on perceptions of teachers, students, parents, and administrators rather than on controlled, empirical investigations. For example, Assertive Discipline has not yet been studied systematically, especially in a controlled way that compares its effectiveness with that of other discipline strategies or classroom management practices.

What are some of the criticisms of Assertive Discipline? They include:

- Assertive Discipline focuses more on the teacher's needs than the child's needs. The teacher "owns" the classroom.
- Students' reasons for lack of compliance are not considered important and can be dismissed or ignored.
- There is an implicit and sometimes stated assumption that children and their parents are "problems."
- Cooperative and collaborative approaches to conflict resolution are dismissed.
- Individual differences and variations in children are not taken into account. Children are treated as a mass of incorrigible, unruly entities to be impersonally controlled.

summary of these ideas is presented in concept table 7.1 on page 236. Now we will turn our attention to some other important aspects of learning, beginning with the concept of habituation.

Habituation

If a stimulus—a sight or sound—is presented to an infant several times in a row, the infant usually pays less attention to it each time, suggesting that the infant has become bored with the stimulus. This is the process of **habituation,** *the repeated presentation of a stimulus, which causes reduced attention to the stimulus* (Kaplan, Rudy, & Werner, 1989; Tamis-LeMonda & Bornstein, 1989). **Dishabituation** *is an infant's renewed interest in a stimulus.* Among

We are in truth, more than half what we are by imitation.

—Lord Chesterfield

Learning, Cognition, and Language Development

Critics also point out that, too often, teachers and administrators tend to react enthusiastically to Assertive Discipline techniques without asking certain questions (Render, Padilla, & Krank, 1989):

- What guarantee is there that the rules made by one teacher are rational rules?
- Does a school system wish to encourage its students to conform unthinkingly to rules on the sole basis that they were established by an authority figure?
- What will be the long-term effects of Assertive Discipline on staff and students? That is, will Assertive Discipline be healthy and humanizing or harmful and destructive?
- Will Assertive Discipline foster the development of individuals who participate in a society that wants its citizens to govern themselves democratically?

One of education's most important goals should be to produce self-disciplined, responsible individuals who do not comply blindly with the demands of an authority figure. Although Assertive Discipline may be an effective management strategy in some classrooms that are unruly and out of control, most experts on education and child development believe classrooms should be characterized by shared governance, compassion, understanding, negotiation, opportunities for questioning, and choice from an array of logical and rational situations (Glasser, 1990).

One of education's most important goals should be to produce individuals who are self-disciplined and responsible but who do not blindly comply to the demands of authority figures. Most education experts believe that classrooms should be characterized by shared governance, compassion, understanding, negotiation, opportunities for questioning, and choices from an array of logical and rational situations.

the measures researchers use to study whether habituation is occurring are sucking behavior (sucking behavior stops when a young infant attends to a novel object), heart and respiration rates, and the length of time the infant looks at an object. Newborn infants can habituate to repetitive stimulation in virtually every stimulus modality—vision, audition, touch, and so on (Rovee-Collier, 1987). However, habituation becomes more acute during the first 3 months of life. The extensive assessment of habituation in recent years has resulted in its use as a measure of an infant's maturity and well-being. Infants who have brain damage or have suffered birth traumas, such as lack of oxygen, do not habituate well and later may have developmental and learning problems.

A knowledge of habituation and dishabituation can benefit parent-infant interaction. Infants respond to changes in stimulation. If a parent repeats a

The Nature of Learning and Motivation, Classical Conditioning, and Operant Conditioning

Concept	Processes/related ideas	Characteristics/description
The nature of learning and motivation	Learning	Learning is a relatively permanent change in behavior that occurs through experience.
	Motivation	Motivation involves the question of "why" children behave, think, and feel the way they do, with special consideration of the activation and direction of their behaviors.
Classical conditioning	How classical conditioning works	Pavlov discovered that organisms learn the association between an unconditioned stimulus (UCS) and a conditioned stimulus (CS). The UCS automatically produces the unconditioned response (UCR). After conditioning (CS-UCS pairing), the CS elicits the conditioned response (CR) by itself.
	Classical conditioning with children	Classical conditioning has survival value for children, for example, when they develop a fear of hazardous conditions. Irrational fears are explained by classical conditioning. Counterconditioning has been used to eliminate children's fears.
	Evaluating classical conditioning	Classical conditioning is important in explaining how some learning occurs, but it is not the predominant way children learn because it misses the active nature of the child.
Operant conditioning	What is operant conditioning?	Operant conditioning is a form of learning (also called instrumental conditioning) in which the consequences of behavior produce changes in the probability of the behavior's occurrence. Operant conditioning focuses on what happens after a response is made, classical conditioning on what occurs before a response is made. The key connection in classical conditioning is between two stimuli, in operant conditioning between the organism's response and its consequences. Operant conditioning mainly involves voluntary behavior, classical conditioning involuntary behavior. Distinctions in operant conditioning are made between positive reinforcement, negative reinforcement, and punishment.
	The flow of events	Researchers often set up experiments on operant conditioning by establishing a baseline, then instituting conditioning, and finally setting up extinction of the learned behavior.
	Arrangements of reinforcements	These include timing of reinforcement, shaping, schedules of reinforcement, primary and secondary reinforcement, and the child's reinforcement history.
	Punishment	Reasoning is often more effective than high-intensity punishment. Experts recommend that alternatives to punishment be explored before punishment is used.
	Applications of operant conditioning	Behavior modification is the application of operant conditioning principles to changing human behavior; its main goal is to replace unacceptable responses with acceptable, adaptive ones.

stimulation often, the infant's response will decrease to the point that the infant no longer responds to the parent. In parent-infant interaction, it is important for parents to do novel things and to repeat them often until the infant stops responding. The wise parent senses when the infant shows an interest and realizes that many repetitions of the stimulus may be necessary for the infant to process the information. The parent stops or changes behaviors when the infant redirects her attention (Rosenblith & Sims-Knight, 1985).

 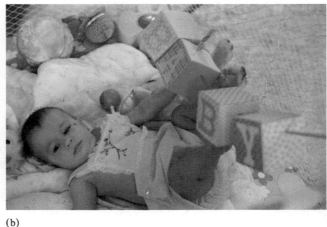

(a)   (b)

Imitation and Cognitive Learning

When children learn, they often cognitively represent or transform their experiences. In Skinner's operant view and Pavlov's classical conditioning view, no room is given to the possibility that cognitive factors, such as memory, thinking, planning, and expectations, might be important in learning. Skinnerians point out that they do not deny the existence of thinking, but, since they cannot observe thinking, they do not believe it is an important factor in the scientific study of learning. Many contemporary learning experts, though, advocate the importance of cognitive factors in learning. Albert Bandura has been a pioneer in promoting the role of cognition in learning. First we will describe his important thoughts and research on imitation and then turn to the fascinating issue of whether infants can imitate an adult's behavior. Finally, we will describe Bandura's recently developed cognitive social learning model.

Bandura's Concept of Imitation

Would it make sense to teach a 15-year-old boy how to drive by either classical conditioning or operant conditioning procedures? Driving a car is a voluntary behavior, so classical conditioning doesn't really apply. In terms of operant conditioning, we would ask him to drive down the road and then reward his positive behaviors. Not many of us would want to be on the road, though, when some of his disastrous mistakes occur. Albert Bandura (1971, 1986, 1989) believes that, if we learned only in such a trial-and-error fashion, it would be exceedingly tedious and, at times, hazardous. Instead, many of our complex behaviors are due to our exposure to competent models who display appropriate behavior in solving problems and in coping with their world.

Recall from our description earlier in the chapter that *imitation,* or modeling, occurs when children learn new behaviors by watching someone else perform the behaviors. The capacity to learn behavior patterns by observation eliminates tedious trial-and-error learning. In many instances, imitation takes less time than operant conditioning.

The following experiment by Bandura (1965) illustrates how observational learning can occur by watching a model who is neither reinforced nor punished. The only requirement for learning is that the individual be connected with the model in time and space. The experiment also illustrates an

Habituation is a common occurrence in an infant's perceptual world. (a) The infant is attending to the blocks hanging overhead. (b) The infant has become bored with the blocks and looks away from them. Habituation is similar to getting bored with a stimulus.

Figure 7.5
Bandura's Experiment on Imitation and Aggression
In the frames on the left, an adult model aggressively attacks a Bobo doll. In the frames on the right, the preschool-aged girl who has observed the adult model's aggressive actions follows suit.

The FAR SIDE cartoon by Gary Larson is reprinted by permission of Chronicle Features, San Francisco, CA.

important distinction between learning and performance. An equal number of boys and girls of nursery school age watched one of three films in which an individual beat up an adult-sized plastic Bobo doll (see figure 7.5). In the first film, the aggressor was rewarded with candy, soft drinks, and praise for aggressive behavior; in the second film, the aggressor was criticized and spanked for the aggressive behavior; and, in the third film, there were no consequences to the aggressor for the behavior. Subsequently, each child was left alone in a room filled with toys, including a Bobo doll. The child's behavior was observed through a one-way mirror. As shown in figure 7.6, children who watched the aggressor be reinforced or suffer no consequences for aggressive behavior imitated the aggressive behavior more than the children who watched the aggressor be punished. As might be expected, boys were more aggressive than girls. The important point about these results is that observational learning occurred just as extensively when modeled aggressive behavior was not reinforced as when it was reinforced.

A second important point focuses on the distinction between learning and performance. Just because an organism does not *perform* a response does not mean it did not *learn* the response. When the children in Bandura's study were offered rewards (in the form of stickers or fruit juice) for imitating the model, the differences in the children's imitative behavior in the three conditions were eliminated. In this experiment, all of the children *learned* about the model's behavior, but some children did not *perform* the behavior until presented with reinforcement. Bandura believes that, when an individual observes behavior but makes no observable response, the individual still may have acquired the modeled response in cognitive form.

Since his early experiments, Bandura (1986, 1989) has focused on some of the specific processes that influence an observer's behavior following exposure to a model. One of these is *attention*. Before individuals can reproduce a model's actions, they must attend to what the model is doing or saying. You may not hear what a friend says if the stereo is blaring or you might miss your teacher's analysis of a problem if you are admiring someone sitting in the next row. Attention to a model is influenced by a host of characteristics. For example, warm, powerful, atypical individuals command more attention than do cold, weak, typical individuals.

The next consideration is the individual's *retention*. To reproduce a model's actions, you must code the information and keep it in memory so that it can be retrieved. A simple verbal description or a vivid image of what the model did assists retention.

Another process involved in observational learning is *motor reproduction*. Individuals may attend to a model and code in memory what they have seen, but, because of limitations in motor development, they may not be able to reproduce the model's action. A 13-year-old may see Chris Evert hit a great two-handed backhand or Michael Jordan do a reverse two-handed dunk but be unable to reproduce the pro's actions.

A final process in Bandura's conception of observational learning involves *reinforcement* or *incentive conditions*. On many occasions, we may attend to what a model says or does, retain the information in memory, and possess the motor capabilities to perform the action but we may fail to repeat the behavior because adequate reinforcement is not present. This was demonstrated in Bandura's study (1965) when the children who had seen a model punished for aggression reproduced the model's aggression only when they were offered an incentive to do so. A summary of Bandura's model of observational learning is shown in figure 7.7.

Learning, Cognition, and Language Development

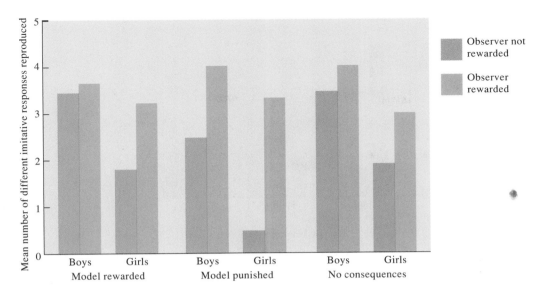

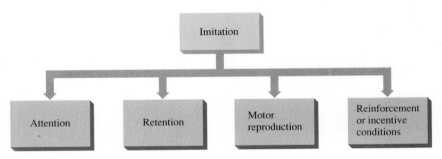

Figure 7.6
The Results of Bandura's Experiment on Observational Learning and Aggression
Children who watched an aggressor be reinforced or experience no consequences for aggressive behavior imitated the aggressive behavior more than did children who saw the aggressor punished, and the boys were more aggressive than the girls. When the children were offered rewards for imitating the aggressive model's behavior, even the children who had seen the model punished demonstrated they had learned the model's aggressive behavior.

Figure 7.7
Bandura's Model of the Processes Involved in Imitation
Bandura argues that observational learning consists of four main processes: attention, retention, motor reproduction, and reinforcement or incentive conditions. Consider a circumstance involving a child learning to ski. The child needs to attend to the instructor's words and demonstrations. The child also must remember what the instructor did and the instructor's tips for avoiding disaster. The child also needs the abilities to reproduce what the instructor has demonstrated. Praise from the instructor after the child has completed a few moves on the slopes should improve the child's motivation to continue skiing.

Infant Imitation

Bandura views imitation as an information-processing activity. As a child observes, information about the world is transformed into cognitive representations that serve as guides to action. An interesting question is whether young infants can engage in imitation. Can a young infant imitate someone else's emotional expressions? If adults smile, will the baby follow with a smile? If adults protrude their lower lips, wrinkle their foreheads, and frown, will the baby show a saddened look? If adults open their mouths, widen their eyes, and raise their eyebrows as though startled, will the baby follow suit? Can infants only 1 day old do these things?

Children need models more than they need critics.

—Joseph Joubert

Learning and Motivation

Figure 7.8
Imitation of Adults' Emotional Facial Expressions by 36-Hour-Old Newborns
The graph shows the mean proportion of trials during which newborn mouth movements followed a model's facial expression. Mouth movements included widened lips (happy), pouting lips (sad), and wide-open mouth (surprised) (Field, 1982).

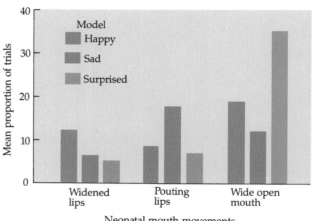

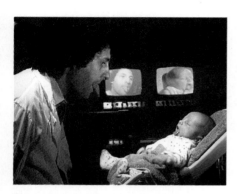

Shown here is infant development researcher Andrew Meltzoff displaying tongue protrusion, prompting an infant to imitate his behavior. Researchers have demonstrated that infants can imitate adults' behavior far earlier than traditionally believed.

Look only on the motive, not the deed.
—William Butler Yeats

Infancy researcher Tiffany Field and her colleagues (1982) explored these questions with newborns only 36 hours after their birth. The model held the newborns' heads upright, with the model's and the newborns' faces separated by 10 inches. The newborns' facial expressions were recorded by an observer who stood behind the model. The observer could not see which facial expressions the model was showing. The model expressed one of three emotions: happiness, sadness, or surprise. As shown in figure 7.8, infants were most likely to imitate the model's display of surprise by widely opening their mouths. When the infants observed a happy mood, they frequently widened their lips. When the model expressed sadness, the infants followed with lips that reflected pouting. Other research supports the belief that young infants can imitate an adult's emotional expressions.

Infant development researcher Andrew Meltzoff (1988, 1990) has conducted numerous studies of infants' imitative abilities. He believes that infants' imitative abilities are biologically based because infants can imitate a facial expression within the first few days after birth, before they have had the opportunity to observe social agents in their environment engage in tongue protrusion and other behaviors. He also believes that infants' imitative abilities are not like the ethologists' concept of a hard-wired, reflexive, innate releasing mechanism, but rather these abilities involve flexibility, adaptability, and intermodal perception. In Meltzoff's observations of infants in the first 72 hours of life, the infants gradually displayed a full imitative response of an adult's facial expressions, such as tongue protrusion or a wide opening of the mouth. Initially, a young infant may only get its tongue to the edge of its lips, but, after a number of attempts and observations of adult behavior, the infant displays a more full-blown response.

Meltzoff also has studied *deferred imitation,* which is the imitation that occurs after a time delay of hours or days. In one recent investigation, Meltzoff (1988) demonstrated that 9-month-old infants can imitate actions they saw performed 24 hours earlier. Each action consisted of an unusual gesture—for example, pushing a recessed button in a box (which produced a beeping sound). Piaget believed that deferred imitation does not occur until about 18 months of age; Meltzoff's research suggests that it occurs much earlier in infant development.

Learning, Cognition, and Language Development

Behavior, Person (Cognition), and Environment

Bandura's (1986, 1989) most recent model of social learning involves behavior, the person, and the environment. As shown in figure 7.9, behavior, environment, and personal or cognitive factors operate interactively. Behavior can influence cognition and vice versa, the child's cognitive activities can influence the environment, environmental influences can change the child's thought processes, and so on.

Let's consider how Bandura's model might work in the case of students' behavior. As students diligently study and get good grades, their behavior produces positive thoughts about their abilities. As part of their effort to make good grades, they plan a number of strategies to make studying more efficient. In these ways, their behavior has influenced their thoughts, and their thoughts have influenced their behavior. At the beginning of the school year, their counselor made a special effort to involve them in a study-skills program. Their success has stimulated the school to expand the program. In these ways, the environment influenced the behavior, and the behavior influenced the environment. The expectations of the school's counselor and principal that the program would work made it possible in the first place. The program's success has spurred expectations that this type of program could work in other schools. In these ways, cognition changed the environment, and the environment changed cognition. Expectations are important in Bandura's model. In this example, we focused on students' achievement behavior. Achievement will be one of the most important topics in our discussion of children's motivation.

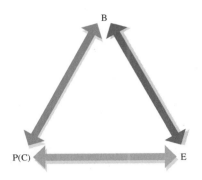

Figure 7.9
Bandura's Model of the Reciprocal Influence of Behavior, Personal and Cognitive Factors, and Environment
P(C) stands for personal and cognitive factors, B for behavior, and E for environment. The arrows reflect how relations between these factors are reciprocal rather than unidirectional. Examples of personal factors include intelligence, skills, and self-control.

Motivation

Remember from our description early in the chapter that *motivation* focuses on the question of "why" children behave the way they do, with special consideration of the activation and direction of their behaviors. First, we will consider some ideas about the "whys" of children's behavior and, second, we will extensively discuss an important dimension of children's lives—their achievement motivation.

Some Ideas About the "Whys" of Children's Behavior

Thirteen-year-old Ann has already made $3,000 this year mowing lawns and doing cleanup work. Fourteen-year-old Richard has already gone steady with four different girls. What motivated Ann to work so hard and make so much money? What motivated Richard to go with so many girls? Psychologists have offered a number of ideas to account for the reasons children behave the way they do.

Biological motives are patterns built into a child's central nervous system at birth. Put another way, all human beings inherit these patterns because they are human. Humans are born with **fixed-action patterns,** *a series of biologically based responses chained together in a stereotyped fashion.* In contrast to reflexes, which are usually simple responses triggered by specific events, fixed-action patterns are more complex. Some examples include moving away from someone when they get too close; holding and exploring a soft, graspable object such as a human body or terry cloth doll; and ending a fight with someone by turning away and falling to the ground. These examples illustrate, respectively, instinctual behavior related to personal space, touch, and retreat from aggression. Notice that, for each example, there are many different events that could trigger the behaviors; notice also that the behaviors themselves consist of several different actions.

Another type of biological motive is drive. A **drive** *is an aroused state that occurs because of a physiological need.* A **need** *is a deprivation that energizes the drive to eliminate or reduce the deprivation.* A child has needs for water and food, for example. The need for food arouses the child's hunger drive. This motivates the child to do something—ask his parents to take him out for a hamburger, perhaps—to reduce the drive and satisfy the need. As a drive becomes stronger, the child is motivated to reduce it. This explanation is known as *drive-reduction theory.*

An important concept in motivation, and one that is important in understanding drives, is **homeostasis,** *the body's tendency to maintain a balanced equilibrium, or steady state.* Literally hundreds of biological states in children's bodies must be maintained within a certain range: temperature, blood-sugar level, potassium and sodium levels, oxygen level, and so on. When a child dives into an icy swimming pool, her body heats up. When children walk out of an air-conditioned room into the heat of a summer day, their bodies begin to cool down. These changes occur automatically in an attempt to restore the children's bodies to their optimal state of functioning.

Homeostasis is used to explain both physiological imbalances and psychological imbalances. For example, if children have not been around friends for a long time, they may be motivated to seek their company. If children have not studied hard for a test in some months, they may be aroused to put in considerably more study time. The concepts of drive and homeostasis have played important roles in understanding children's motivation.

Psychologists became disenchanted with drive-reduction theory as a comprehensive theory of motivation when it became apparent that children and adults are not always motivated to reduce a need. In the 1950s, experiments began to show that, in many instances, individuals are motivated to seek stimulation (Butler, 1953). R. W. White (1959) said that, rather than always being motivated to reduce biological needs, children have **competence motivation** *(also called mastery or effectance motivation), which is the motivation to deal effectively with the environment, to do well what they attempt, to process information efficiently, and to make the world a better place.* White said we do these things not because they fulfill biological needs but because we have an intrinsic (internal) motivation to interact effectively with our environment. Closely related to this idea is the motivation for achievement, which we will discuss later in this section.

In recent years, there has been a flourish of interest in children's motivation for competence (Harter, 1980; MacTurk & others, 1987; Phillips, 1991; Schunk, 1990). Why has competence motivation generated this interest among developmentalists? One attraction is that the concept pulls together many different aspects of children's development under a single theme. Another attraction is that findings indicate that the assessment of competence motivation in infancy may provide a better basis for predicting later competence than do scores on developmental tests (Messer, Yarrow, & Vietze, 1982). Also, researchers are beginning to show that intervention programs with developmentally delayed children are especially beneficial when children are given the opportunity to become effective agents—that is, when they are given the opportunity for self-determination and self-responsibility in effectively interacting and controlling the environment (Brinker & Lewis, 1982).

Learning, Cognition, and Language Development

As psychologists came to recognize the importance of competence motivation and the environment's role in motivation, they began to describe a number of learned motives in humans. These include the motivation for achievement, the motivation for power, the motivation for affiliation, the motivation for identity, and the motivation for self-actualization. As we will see next, self-actualization is viewed as the highest form of motivation in one well-known theory of motivation.

Is getting an *A* in school more important to a child than eating? If the girl of an adolescent boy's dreams told him that he was marvelous, would that motivate him to throw himself in front of a car for her safety? According to Abraham Maslow (1954, 1971), our "basic" needs must be satisfied before our "higher" needs. The **hierarchy of motives** *is Maslow's concept that all individuals have five main needs, which must be satisfied in the following sequence: physiological, safety, love and belongingness, self-esteem, and self-actualization* (see figure 7.10). Based on Maslow's hierarchy of motives, people need to eat before they can achieve, and they need to satisfy their safety needs before their love needs.

It is the need for self-actualization that Maslow has described in the greatest detail. **Self-actualization,** *the highest and most elusive of Maslow's needs, is the motivation to develop one's full potential as a human being.* According to Maslow, self-actualization is possible only after the other needs in the hierarchy are met. Maslow cautions that most individuals stop maturing after they have developed a high level of self-esteem and, thus, do not become self-actualized. Many of Maslow's writings focus on how individuals can reach the elusive motivational state of self-actualization. Among the goals of reaching self-actualization are finding self-fulfillment and peace with one's life, realizing one's full potential, and feeling content with that. Self-actualized individuals have an open manner; are not defensive; love themselves; feel no need to manipulate others or be aggressive toward them; act in ways to promote moral and ethical principles in society; and are creative, curious, and spontaneous in interchanges with others.

The idea that humans have a hierarchy of motives is an appealing one. Maslow's theory stimulates us to think about the ordering of the motives in children's lives. Not everyone agrees on the order in which children satisfy their needs, though. In some instances, the order may be different than Maslow envisioned.

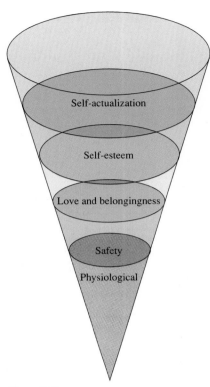

Figure 7.10
Maslow's Hierarchy of Motives
According to Maslow, all individuals have five hierarchically arranged needs, or motives, which must be satisfied in the following order: physiological, safety, love and belongingness, self-esteem, and self-actualization.

Achievement

Children are motivated to do well at what they attempt, to gain mastery over the world in which they live, to explore unknown environments with enthusiasm and curiosity, and to achieve the heights of success. When Vince Lombardi was coach of the Green Bay Packers, in his customary intense manner, he said, "Winning isn't everything, it is the *only* thing."

Children live in an achievement-oriented world, with standards that tell them success is important. These standards suggest that success requires a competitive spirit, a desire to win, a motivation to do well, and the wherewithal to cope with adversity and persist until obstacles are overcome. Some developmentalists, though, believe we are a nation of hurried, wired people who are raising our children to become the same way—too uptight about success and failure and far too worried about what we accomplish in comparison to others (Elkind, 1981). It was in the 1950s that an interest in the need for achievement began to flourish.

Need for Achievement

Think about yourself and your friends for a moment. Are you more achievement oriented than they are, or are you less so? If we were to ask you and your friends to tell stories about achievement-related themes, could we accurately determine which of you is the most achievement oriented?

Some individuals are highly motivated to succeed and expend a lot of effort striving to excel. Other individuals are not as motivated and don't work as hard to achieve success. These two types of individuals vary in their **achievement motivation** *(or need for achievement), the desire to accomplish something, to reach a standard of excellence, to expend effort to excel.* Borrowing from Henry Murray's (1938) theory and measurement of personality, psychologist David McClelland (1955) assessed achievement by showing individuals ambiguous pictures that were likely to stimulate achievement-related responses. The individuals were asked to tell a story about each picture, and their comments were scored according to how strongly they reflected achievement.

A host of studies have correlated achievement-related responses with different aspects of individuals' experiences and behavior. The findings are diverse, but they suggest that achievement-oriented individuals have a stronger hope for success than a fear of failure, they are moderate rather than high or low risk-takers, and they persist in solving difficult problems for appropriate lengths of time (Atkinson & Raynor, 1974). Early research indicated that independence training by parents promotes children's achievement, but more recent research reveals that parents, to increase achievement, need to set high standards for achievement, model achievement-oriented behavior, and reward their children for their achievements (Huston-Stein & Higgens-Trenk, 1978).

Intrinsic and Extrinsic Motivation

As part of their interest in achievement motivation, psychologists have focused on the internal and external factors that contribute to such motivation. Achievement motivation—whether in school, at work, or in sports—can be divided into two main types: **intrinsic motivation,** *the internal desire to be competent and to do something for its own sake,* and **extrinsic motivation,** *which is influenced by external rewards and punishments.* If you work hard in college because a personal standard of excellence is important to you, intrinsic motivation is involved. However, if you work hard in college because you know it will bring you a higher-paying job when you graduate, extrinsic motivation is at work.

An important consideration in extrinsic motivation is whether or not to offer children an incentive (Ames & Ames, 1989; Gottfried, Gottfried, & Bathurst, 1988; Rotter, 1989). If a child is not doing competent work, is bored, or has a negative attitude, it may be worthwhile to consider incentives to improve the child's motivation. However, there are times when external rewards can get in the way of motivation. In one investigation, children with a strong interest in art spent more time in a drawing activity when they expected no reward than when they knew they would be rewarded (Lepper, Greene, & Nisbett, 1973) (see figure 7.11).

Intrinsic motivation implies that internal motivation should be promoted and external factors deemphasized. In this way, children learn to attribute to themselves the cause of their success and failure, and especially the amount of effort they expend. In reality, however, achievement is motivated by both internal and external factors; children are never divorced from their external

The reward of a thing well done is to have done it.

—Ralph Waldo Emerson

Learning, Cognition, and Language Development

environment. Some of the most achievement-oriented children are those who have both a high personal standard for achievement and a highly competitive nature. In one investigation, low-achieving boys and girls who engaged in individual goal setting and who were given comparative information about peers worked more math problems and got more of them correct than did their counterparts who experienced either condition alone (Schunk, 1983). Other research suggests that social comparison by itself is not a wise strategy (Nicholls, 1984). The argument is that social comparison puts children in an ego-involved, threatening, self-focused state rather than in a task-involved, effortful, strategy-focused state.

Another important consideration is the role the child's home environment plays in promoting intrinsic motivation (Gottfried, 1990). In a recent investigation, Adele and Allen Gottfried (1989) found that a greater variety of home experiences, the parental encouragement of competence and curiosity, and a home emphasis on academically related behaviors are related to children's intrinsic motivation for achievement.

Attribution and Achievement

Attribution theorists argue that people want to know the causes of behavior because that knowledge will help them cope more effectively with the situations that confront them. **Attribution theory** *states that individuals are motivated to discover the underlying causes of behavior as part of their interest in making sense out of the behavior.* In a way, attribution theorists say people are much like intuitive scientists, seeking the reasons that something happens (Weiner, 1979).

The reasons people behave the way they do can be classified in various ways, but one basic distinction stands out above all the others: the difference between internal causes, such as a child's personality traits or motives, and external factors, which are environmental, situational factors (Heider, 1958). If children do not do well on a test, do they attribute it to having a bad teacher who made the test too difficult (external cause) or to the fact that they did not study hard enough (internal cause)? If children believe their poor performance is the teacher's fault (she gives unfair tests, for example), they do not feel as bad as when they believe their poor performance is due to their lack of study. As can be seen, the concepts of intrinsic and extrinsic motivation are closely related to attribution theory's emphasis on children's analysis of internal and external causes of behavior.

An extremely important aspect of internal causes of achievement is *effort*. Unlike many causes of success, effort is under the child's control and amenable to change (Jagacinski & Nicholls, 1990, Schunk, 1990). The importance of effort in achievement is recognized by most children. In one recent study, third- to sixth-grade students felt that effort was the most effective strategy for good school performance (Skinner, Wellborn, & Connell, 1990). In another study, achieving students were more likely than underachieving students to believe effort determined their performance (Carr, Borkowski, & Maxwell, 1991).

Mastery Orientation Versus Helpless Orientation

Closely related to an emphasis on intrinsic motivation, attributions of internal causes of behavior, and the importance of effort in achievement is a mastery orientation (Nelson-Legall, 1990). Developmental psychologists Valanne Henderson and Carol Dweck (1990) have found that children and adolescents show two distinct responses to difficult or challenging circumstances. The

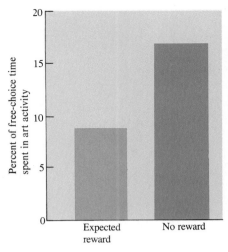

Figure 7.11
Intrinsic Motivation and Drawing Activity
Students with an initial high interest in art spent more time in art activity when no reward was mentioned than when they expected a reward for their participation.

■ *Critical Thinking*
Examine your achievement situations in college during this year. What kind of attributions have you made about the causes of your behavior? Are they more externalized or more internalized?

Learning and Motivation

245

helpless orientation *describes children who seem trapped by the experience of difficulty. They attribute their difficulty to a lack of ability.* They frequently say such things as "I'm not very good at this," even though they may have demonstrated their ability earlier through numerous successes. Once they view their behavior as failure, they often feel anxious about the situation and their performance worsens even further. The **mastery orientation** *describes children who are task oriented. Instead of focusing on their ability, they become concerned about their learning strategies.* Mastery-oriented children often instruct themselves to pay attention, to think carefully, and to remember strategies that have worked for them in previous situations. They frequently report feeling challenged and excited by difficult tasks rather than threatened by them.

What psychological factors have been found to undergird the mastery and helpless achievement orientations? In one recent investigation, students were followed over the first few months of the seventh grade, their first year of junior high school (Henderson & Dweck, 1990). Students who believed that their intelligence is malleable and who had confidence in their abilities earned significantly higher grades than their counterparts who believed their intelligence is fixed and who did not have much confidence in their abilities. Students who believed that their intelligence is fixed also had higher levels of anxiety than students who believed it is changeable. Apparently, then, the way students think about their intelligence and their confidence in their abilities may affect their ability and desire to master academic material. Believing that learning new material increases one's intelligence may actually promote academic mastery.

In summary, we have seen that a number of psychological and motivational factors influence an adolescent's achievement. Especially important in the adolescent's ability to adapt to new academic and social pressures are achievement motivation, internal attributions of effort, intrinsic motivation, and a mastery achievement orientation. Next, we will examine the role of ethnicity in adolescents' achievement.

Ethnicity and Achievement

Too often, the results of research on ethnic minority groups have been interpreted as "deficient" by middle-class White standards. Rather than characterizing individuals as *culturally different,* many conclusions characterize the cultural distinctiveness of Blacks, Hispanics, Asian Americans, and Native Americans as deficient in some way (Jones, 1990; Ramirez, 1990; Sue, 1990; Sue & Okazaki, 1990).

Much of the research on the achievement of minority-group children is plagued by a failure to consider the factor of socioeconomic status (determined by a combination of education, occupation, and income). In many instances, when ethnicity *and* socioeconomic status (also called social class) are investigated in the same study, social class is a far better predictor of achievement orientation than is race. Middle-class individuals fare better than their lower-class counterparts in a variety of achievement-oriented circumstances—expectations for success, achievement aspirations, and recognition of the importance of effort, for example (McAdoo & McAdoo, 1985).

Educational psychologist Sandra Graham has conducted a number of investigations that reveal not only stronger social class than ethnic differences, but also the importance of studying minority-group motivation in the context of general motivational theory (Graham, 1986, 1987, 1990). Her inquiries focus on the causes Blacks give for their achievement orientation—why they

Learning, Cognition, and Language Development

Many Asian American children are very successful in academic settings and have strong achievement orientations. However, large numbers of Asian American refugee children, especially those from Indochina, live in low-income surroundings and share the problems of other children of poverty. It is important to keep in mind that every ethnic group is diverse.

succeed or fail, for example. She is struck by how consistently middle-class Black children do not fit the stereotypes of either deviant or special populations. They, like their middle-class White counterparts, have high expectations and understand that failure is often due to lack of effort rather than to luck.

It is always important to keep in mind the diversity that exists within an ethnic group (Phinney, 1991; Slaughter-DeFoe & others, 1990). Consider Asian American children. Many Asian American children fit the "whiz kid, super-achiever" image, but there are still many Asian American children who are struggling just to learn English. The whiz kid image fits many of the children of Asian immigrant families who arrived in the United States in the late 1960s and early 1970s. Many of these immigrants came from Hong Kong, South Korea, India, and the Philippines. The image also fits many of the more than 100,000 Indochinese (primarily Vietnamese) immigrants who arrived in the United States after the end of the Vietnam War in 1975. Both groups included mostly middle- to upper-income professional people who were reasonably well educated and who passed along a strong interest in education and a strong work ethic to their children. For thousands of Asian Americans, including a high percentage of the 600,000 Indochinese refugees who fled Vietnam, Laos, and Cambodia in the late 1970s, the problems are legion. Many in this wave of refugees lived in poor surroundings in their homelands. They came to the United States with few skills and little education, they speak little English, and they have a difficult time finding decent jobs. They often share housing with relatives. Adjusting to school is difficult for their children; some drop out, and some are attracted to gangs and drugs. Better school systems use a variety of techniques to help these Asian Americans, including English as a Second Language classes and a range of social services.

American children are more achievement oriented than children in many other countries. However, there has recently been concern about the achievement most American children display in comparison with children in other countries with strong educational orientations—Japan, China, and Russia, for example. To learn more about the achievement orientation of American children compared to Japanese and Chinese children, turn to Cultural Worlds of Development 7.1

At this point, we have discussed a number of ideas about habituation, imitation and cognitive learning, motivation, and achievement. A summary of these ideas is presented in concept table 7.2. In the next chapter, we will turn our attention to children's cognitive development, devoting considerable time to the ideas of Jean Piaget.

Learning and Motivation

Comparisons of Children's Math Achievement in Japan, China, and the United States

Harold Stevenson and his colleagues (Chen & Stevenson, 1989; Stevenson, Stigler, & Lee, 1986; Stevenson & others, 1990) have conducted extensive investigations of children's math achievement in the first and fifth grades in Japan, China, and the United States. The stimulation for this research comes from the poor performance of American students on tests of mathematics and science in comparison to students in other countries. For example, in a recent cross-national study of math achievement, American eighth- and twelfth-grade students were below the international average in problem solving, geometry, algebra, calculus, and other areas of math (Garden, 1987; McKnight & others, 1987). In contrast, Japanese eighth graders had the highest average scores of children from 20 countries, and, in the twelfth grade, Japanese students were second only to Chinese students in Hong Kong. Why are Chinese and Japanese students consistently among the top achievers in international comparisons and American students among the lowest achievers?

Japanese children consistently outperform American children in math. What factors are likely to be responsible for their superior performance?

The amount of time spent in school and math classes is probably an important factor. The Japanese school year consists of 240 days of instruction and each school week is 5½ days long. The American school year consists of 178 days of instruction and each school week is 5 days long. In the fifth grade, Japanese children are in school an average of 37.3 hours per week, American children only 30.4 hours. Observations in the children's classrooms reveal that Japanese teachers spend far more time teaching math than do American teachers; approximately one fourth of total classroom time in the first grade is spent in math instruction in Japan, only approximately one tenth in the United States. Observations also indicate that the Japanese children attend more efficiently to what the teacher says than American children do. Japanese children also spend far more time doing homework than American children—on weekends, 66 minutes versus 18 minutes, respectively.

In another recent investigation, it was revealed that Chinese children are assigned more homework and spend more time on homework than Japanese children, who, in turn, are assigned more homework and spend more time on homework than American children (Chen & Stevenson, 1989). Chinese children have more positive attitudes about homework than Japanese children, who in turn have more positive attitudes about homework than American children.

In their most recent investigation, Stevenson and his colleagues (1990) gave special attention to the family's role in comparisons of children's math achievement in Japan, China, and the United States. Background information about children's everyday lives indicated much greater attention to academic activities among Chinese and Japanese than among American children. Children's academic achievement did not appear to be a central concern to American mothers, whereas Japanese and Chinese mothers viewed this as their child's most important pursuit. When the children entered elementary school, Chinese and Japanese parents provided much greater assistance to their children's academic activities than did American parents. Chinese and Japanese mothers had higher standards for their children's achievement than did American mothers. American mothers, though, were more likely than Chinese and Japanese mothers to overestimate their children's abilities and to express greater satisfaction with their accomplishments. Chinese and Japanese mothers stressed the importance of hard work as a basis for children's achievement, whereas American mothers gave more emphasis to innate ability than did Chinese and Japanese mothers.

In sum, the poor performance of American children in math achievement is due to a number of factors related to cultural dimensions of achievement orientation. Stevenson and his colleagues believe that good teaching, interested parents, and hard work could go a long way in enhancing American children's math achievement.

Habituation, Imitation and Cognitive Learning, Motivation, and Achievement

Concept	Processes/related ideas	Characteristics/description
Habituation	Its nature	Habituation is the repeated presentation of a stimulus, causing reduced attention to the stimulus. If a different stimulus is presented and the infant pays attention to it, dishabituation is occurring. Newborn infants can habituate, although habituation becomes more acute over the first 3 months of infancy.
Imitation and cognitive learning	Bandura's concept of imitation	Imitation, also called modeling, occurs when children learn new behaviors by watching someone else perform the behaviors. Bandura believes imitation involves attention, retention, motor reproduction, and reinforcement or incentive conditions.
	Infant imitation	Infants can imitate facial expressions in the first few days of life. Meltzoff has demonstrated that deferred imitation occurs at about 9 months of age, much earlier than Piaget believed.
	Cognitive learning	Many psychologists recognize the importance of studying how cognitive factors mediate environment-behavior connections. Bandura's contemporary model emphasizes reciprocal connections between behavior, person (cognition), and environment.
Motivation	Biological motives	Fixed-action patterns and drive-reduction theory have been proposed as explanations for children's biological motives. Homeostasis is an important concept in drive-reduction theory and in understanding motivation. It describes the motivation for equilibrium.
	Competence motivation	As psychologists recognized there was more to motivation than drive reduction, they turned to the concept of competence motivation, first described by White. Also called mastery motivation, this involves the motivation to deal effectively with the environment.
Achievement	Learned motives	Interest in competence motivation and the environment's role in motivation led to the description of learned motives, including achievement, power, affiliation, identity, and self-actualization.
	Hierarchy of motives	Maslow believed that some motives need to be satisfied before others; self-actualization is given special importance.
	Need for achievement	McClelland argued that we can measure individual differences in achievement motivation. The need for achievement is the motivation to overcome obstacles, the desire for success, and the effort expended to seek out difficult tasks and to do them well. Achievement motivation is associated with a number of aspects of children's experiences and behavior.
	Intrinsic and extrinsic motivation	Intrinsic motivation involves an underlying need for competence and self-determination; extrinsic motivation involves external factors in the environment, especially rewards. Many of the most achievement-oriented children have both a high personal standard of achievement and a highly competitive nature. Social comparison by itself is not a wise strategy.
	Attribution and achievement	Attribution theory states that individuals are motivated to discover the underlying causes of behavior as part of their interest in making sense out of behavior. A basic distinction in attribution theory emphasizes internal and external causes of behavior.

Concept	Processes/related ideas	Characteristics/description
	Mastery orientation vs. helpless orientation	The helpless orientation describes children who seem trapped by the experience of difficulty. They attribute their difficulty to lack of ability. The mastery orientation describes children who remain extremely task oriented. Instead of focusing on their ability, they become concerned about their learning strategies, often instructing themselves to pay attention, to think carefully, and to remember strategies that have worked in previous situations. They frequently report feeling challenged and excited by difficult tasks rather than being threatened by them. Students who believe that their intelligence is malleable and who have confidence in their abilities make better grades than their counterparts who believe their intelligence is fixed and who have low confidence in their abilities.
	Ethnicity and achievement	A special concern is the achievement of children from ethnic minority groups. When ethnicity and social class are investigated, social class is usually a better predictor of achievement than is ethnicity.

Summary

I. The Nature of Learning and Motivation

Learning is a relatively permanent change in behavior that occurs through experience. Motivation involves the question of "why" children behave, think, and feel the way they do, with special consideration of the activation and direction of their behaviors.

II. Classical Conditioning

Pavlov discovered that organisms learn the association between an unconditioned stimulus (UCS) and a conditioned stimulus (CS). The UCS automatically produces the unconditioned response (UCR). After conditioning (CS-UCS pairing), the CS elicits the conditioned response (CR) by itself. Classical conditioning has survival value for children, for example, when they develop a fear of hazardous conditions. Irrational fears have been explained by classical conditioning. Counterconditioning has been used to alleviate children's fears. Classical conditioning is important in explaining how some learning occurs, but it is not the predominant way children learn because it misses the child's active nature.

III. What Is Operant Conditioning?

Operant conditioning (also called instrumental conditioning) is a form of learning in which the consequences of behavior produce changes in the probability of the behavior's occurrence. Operant conditioning focuses on what happens after a response is made, classical conditioning on what occurs before a response is made. The key connection in classical conditioning is between two stimuli; in operant conditioning, the connection is between the organism's response and its consequences. Operant conditioning involves mainly voluntary behavior, classical conditioning involuntary behavior. Distinctions in operant conditioning are made between positive reinforcement, negative reinforcement, and punishment.

IV. Arrangements of Reinforcements and Punishment, and Applications of Operant Conditioning

Researchers often set up experiments on operant conditioning by establishing a baseline, then instituting conditioning, and finally setting up extinction of the learned behavior. Arrangements of reinforcements include the timing of reinforcement, shaping, schedules of reinforcement, primary and secondary reinforcement, and the child's reinforcement history. Reasoning is often more effective than high-intensity punishment. Experts recommend that alternatives to punishment be explored before punishment is used. Behavior modification is the application of operant conditioning principles to changing human behavior; its main goal is to replace unacceptable responses with acceptable, adaptive ones.

V. Habituation

Habituation occurs when repeated presentation of a stimulus causes reduced attention to the stimulus. If a different stimulus is presented and the infant pays attention to it, dishabituation has occurred. Newborn infants can habituate, although habituation becomes more acute over the first 3 months of life.

VI. Imitation and Cognitive Learning

Imitation, also called modeling, occurs when children learn new behaviors by watching someone else perform the behaviors. Bandura believes that imitation involves attention, retention, motor reproduction, and incentive or reinforcement conditions. Infants can imitate the facial expressions of adults in the first few days of life. Meltzoff has demonstrated that deferred imitation occurs at about 9 months of age, much earlier than Piaget believed. Many psychologists recognize the importance of studying how cognitive factors mediate environment-behavior connections. Bandura's contemporary model emphasizes reciprocal connections between behavior, person (cognition), and environment.

VII. Motivation

Understanding motivation involves knowledge of biological motives, competence motivation, learned motives, and the hierarchy of motives. Fixed-action patterns and drive-reduction theory have been proposed as explanations for children's biological motives. Homeostasis is an important concept in drive-reduction theory and in understanding children's motivation. It describes the motivation for a balanced equilibrium. As psychologists recognized there was more to motivation than drive reduction, they turned to the concept of competence motivation, first described by White. Also called mastery motivation, this involves the motivation to deal effectively with the environment. Interest in competence motivation and the environment's role in motivation led to the description of learned motives, including achievement, power, affiliation, identity, and self-actualization. Maslow described the hierarchy of motives—the idea that some motives need to be satisfied prior to others. Self-actualization is given special importance in his view.

VIII. Achievement

McClelland argued that we can measure individual differences in achievement motivation. The need for achievement is the motivation to overcome obstacles, the desire for success, and the effort expended to seek out difficult tasks and to do them well. Achievement motivation is associated with a number of aspects of children's experiences and behaviors. Intrinsic motivation involves an underlying need for competence and self-determination; extrinsic motivation involves external factors in the environment, especially rewards. Many of the most achievement-oriented children have both a high personal standard for success and a highly competitive nature. Social comparison by itself is not a wise strategy. Attribution theory states that individuals are motivated to discover the underlying causes of behavior as part of their interest in making sense of the behavior. A basic distinction in attribution theory emphasizes internal and external causes of behavior. The helpless orientation describes children who seem trapped by the experience of difficulty. They attribute their difficulty to lack of ability. The mastery orientation describes children who remain extremely task oriented. Instead of focusing on their ability, they become concerned about their learning strategies, often instructing themselves to pay attention, to think carefully, and to remember strategies that have worked in previous situations. They frequently report feeling challenged and excited by difficult tasks rather than threatened by them. Students who believe that their intelligence is malleable and who have confidence in their abilities make better grades than their counterparts who believe that intelligence is fixed and who have low confidence in their abilities. A special concern is the achievement of children from ethnic minority groups. When ethnicity and social class are investigated, social class is usually a better predictor of achievement than is ethnicity.

Key Terms

reinforcement
  (reward) 218
imitation (modeling) 218
learning 219
motivation 220
classical conditioning 221
reflexes 221
unconditioned stimulus
  (UCS) 221
unconditioned response
  (UCR) 221
conditioned stimulus
  (CS) 221
conditioned response
  (CR) 221
phobias 223
counterconditioning 224
operant conditioning 225
reinforcement 226
punishment 226
positive reinforcement 226
negative reinforcement 226
baseline 226
conditioning 227
extinction 227
shaping 228

schedules of
  reinforcement 229
partial reinforcement
  (intermittent
  reinforcement) 230
primary reinforcement 230
secondary
  reinforcement 230
behavior modification 233
habituation 234
dishabituation 234
fixed-action patterns 241
drive 242
need 242
homeostasis 242
competence motivation 242
hierarchy of motives 243
self-actualization 243
achievement
  motivation 244
intrinsic motivation 244
extrinsic motivation 244
attribution theory 245
helpless orientation 246
mastery orientation 246

Suggested Readings

Axelrod, S., & Apsche, J. (Eds.). (1983). *The effects of punishment on human behavior.* New York: Academic Press. This authoritative volume tells how punishment can be used effectively to control behavior. Considerable detail about reducing the negative side effects of punishment and a full consideration of the ethical issues involved in the use of punishment are included.

Becker, W. C. (1986). *Applied psychology for teachers.* Chicago: SRA. This behaviorally oriented book includes detailed information about the use of behavior modification in classrooms.

Henderson, V. L., & Dweck, C. S. (1990). Motivation and achievement. In S. S. Feldman & G. R. Elliott (Eds.), *At the threshold: The developing adolescent.* Cambridge, MA: Harvard University Press. Henderson and Dweck present their model of achievement, which places a strong emphasis on mastery motivation.

McAdoo, H. P., & McAdoo, J. L. (1985). *Black children: Social, educational, and parental environments.* Beverly Hills, CA: Sage. This book provides a contemporary look at the nature of achievement orientation in Black children. Included are chapters written by leading experts in the field of minority-group motivation.

Skinner, B. F. (1960). *Walden two.* New York: Macmillan. Skinner once entertained the possibility of a career as a writer. In this interesting and provocative book, he outlines his ideas on how a more complete understanding of the principles of instrumental conditioning can lead to a happier life. Critics argue that his approach is far too manipulative.

CHAPTER

8

COGNITIVE DEVELOPMENT AND PIAGET'S THEORY

Jean Piaget and His Place in Developmental
   Psychology
Cognitive Developmental Theory and Processes
      Cognitive Developmental Theory
      Cognitive Processes
Sensorimotor Thought
      The Substages of Sensorimotor Thought
      Object Permanence
      A New Perspective on Cognitive Development
            in Infancy
Preoperational Thought
      The Nature of Preoperational Thought
      The Substages of Preoperational Thought
      *Perspective on Child Development 8.1: Where
            Pelicans Kiss Seals, Cars Float on Clouds,
            and Humans Are Tadpoles*
Concrete Operational Thought
      *Perspective on Child Development 8.2: Piglet,
            Pooh, and Piaget*
      Conservation
      Classification
      Application of Piaget's Ideas to Education
Formal Operational Thought
      Characteristics of Formal Operational Thought
      Formal Operational Thought and Language
      Adolescent Egocentrism
      Early and Late Formal Operational Thought
      Variations in Adolescent Cognition
      Beyond Formal Operational Thought
Piagetian Contributions and Criticisms
Vygotsky's Theory of Cognitive Development
      Zone of Proximal Development
      Language and Thought
      *Cultural Worlds of Development 8.1: Culture,
            Schooling, and Cognitive Development*
      Culture and Society
      *Cultural Worlds of Development 8.2: Cultural
            Similarities and Variations Among Thinking
            Apprenticeships*
Summary
Key Terms
Suggested Readings

Matthew is 1 year old. He has already seen over 1,000 flash cards with pictures of shells, flowers, insects, flags, countries, and words on them. His mother, Billie, has made almost 10,000 of the 11-inch-square cards for Matthew and his 4-year-old brother, Mark. Billie has religiously followed the regimen recommended by Glenn Doman, the director of the Philadelphia Institute for the Achievement of Human Potential and the author of *How to Teach Your Baby to Read.* Using his methods, which she learned in a course called "How to Multiply Your Baby's Intelligence," Billie is teaching Matthew Japanese and even a little math. Mark is learning geography, natural science, engineering, and fine arts as well.

Parents using the card approach print one word on each card using a bright red felt-tipped pen. The parent repeatedly shows the card to the infant while saying the word aloud. The first word usually is *mommy* and then *daddy,* the baby's name, parts of the body, and all the things the infant can touch. The infant is lavishly praised when he recognizes the word. The idea is to imprint the large red words in the infant's memory so that, in time, he accumulates an impressive vocabulary and begins to read. The parent continues to feed the infant with all manner of information in small, assimilable bits, just as Billie has done with her two boys.

With this method, the child should be reading by 2 years of age, and by 4 or 5 should have begun mastering some math and be able to play the violin, not to mention the vast knowledge of the world he should be able to display because of a monumental vocabulary. Maybe the SAT or ACT test you labored through on your way to college might have been conquered at the age of 6 if your parents had only been enrolled in the "How to Multiply Your Baby's Intelligence" course and had made 10,000 flash cards for you.

Is this the best way for an infant to learn? A number of developmentalists believe Doman's "better baby institute" is a money-making scheme and is not based on sound scientific evidence. They believe that we should not be

These infants and toddlers are being taught in the manner recommended by Glenn Doman, which emphasizes the acceleration of learning to read by intensely exposing children to flash cards with many different words on them. Most developmental psychologists believe there is something fundamentally wrong with Doman's approach. They believe that, rather than pouring information into children's minds in the way Doman advises, children should be permitted to explore their environment spontaneously and to construct their knowledge independently.

trying to accelerate infants' learning so dramatically. Rather than parents' pouring information into infants' minds, infants should be permitted more time to explore the environment spontaneously and to construct their knowledge. Jean Piaget called "What should we do to foster cognitive development?" the American question, because it was asked of him so often when he lectured to American audiences. Developmentalists worry that children exposed to Doman's methods will burn out on learning. It is more important to provide a rich and emotionally supportive atmosphere for learning.

We will spend most of this chapter examining Piaget's theory of cognitive development. Piaget's four main stages of cognitive development will be examined in depth, applications of his theory to education will be presented, and contributions and criticisms of his theory will be outlined. Then we will consider a provocative theory of children's cognitive development that has recently been given a great deal of attention, that of Russian psychologist Lev Vygotsky.

Jean Piaget and His Place in Developmental Psychology

In discussing Sigmund Freud's contribution to psychology, Edwin Boring (1950) remarked that it is not likely the history of experimental psychology can be written in the next three centuries without mention of Freud's name and still claim to be a general history of psychology. Indeed, the best criterion of greatness may be posthumous fame. Four decades after Boring published his book, it seems likely that his judgment was accurate—Freud is still a dominating presence in psychology. However, Jean Piaget's contribution to developmental psychology may be as important as Freud's contribution to personality and abnormal behavior. Piaget's death was a rather recent event (he died in 1980), so it may be too early to judge, but Piaget's contributions will be strongly felt for the foreseeable future. He truly is a giant in the field of developmental psychology.

Shortly after Piaget's death, John Flavell (1980), a leading Piagetian scholar, described what we owe Piaget:

> First, we owe him a host of insightful concepts of enduring power and fascination . . . concepts of object permanence, conservation, assimilation, accommodation, and decentration, for example. Second, we owe him a vast conceptual framework that has highlighted key issues and problems in human cognitive development. This framework is the now-familiar vision of the developing child, who, through its own active and creative commerce with its environment, builds an orderly succession of cognitive structures enroute to intellectual maturity. These two debts add up to a third, more general one: We owe him the present field of cognitive development. . . . Our task is now to extend and go beyond what he began so well. (p. 1)

Jean Piaget

Cognitive Developmental Theory and Processes

What is the basic nature of cognitive developmental theory? How does it differ from the learning perspective described in chapter 7? What cognitive processes are responsible for changes in a child's development? What stages of cognitive development do children move through?

Cognitive Developmental Theory

Cognitive developmental theory emphasizes the developing child's rational thinking and stages of thought. Environmental experiences are important in the cognitive developmental view, but, from Piaget's perspective, they are mainly the "food" for children's cognitive machinery. In the cognitive learning perspective described in chapter 7, cognitive processes were seen as important mediators in linking environmental experiences to children's behavior. In Piaget's view, thoughts are more than mediators of environment-behavior connections. Rather, thoughts are the central focus of development, the primary determinants of children's actions.

Cognitive Processes

Remember from our discussion of theories in chapter 2 that Piaget emphasized the processes of adaptation (assimilation, accommodation) and organization in children's cognitive development. We will review those concepts and explore another important cognitive process—equilibration.

If children are to develop normally, they have to interact effectively with their environment. **Adaptation** *is Piaget's concept of the child's effective interaction with the environment. For Piaget, the interaction is cognitive and involves assimilation and accommodation, which usually work together.* Remember from chapter 2 that assimilation occurs when children incorporate new information into their existing knowledge. Recall also that accommodation occurs when children adjust to new information. An example may help clarify these terms. Suppose that a 16-year-old girl wants to learn how to type. Her parents buy her a typewriter for her birthday. She has never had the opportunity to use a typewriter. From experience and observation, however, she realizes that a typewriter is to be placed on a table, that it has keys to be punched, and that paper must be inserted into it. Since she realizes each of these things, she sets the typewriter on the table, inserts the paper, and begins to punch the keys—incorporating her behavior into a conceptual framework that already exists (assimilation). As she begins to strike some of the keys, however, she makes several mistakes, she begins to type more slowly. Soon she realizes that she needs someone to help her learn to type efficiently or she will have to take a typing class at her high school. These adjustments show her awareness of the need to alter her concept of typing (accommodation).

We also indicated in chapter 2 that assimilation and accommodation operate even in very young infants' lives. Newborns reflexively suck everything that touches their lips (assimilation), but, after several months of experience, they construct a different understanding of the world. Some objects, such as fingers and the mother's breast, can be sucked; others, such as fuzzy blankets, should not be sucked (accommodation).

Piaget also emphasized that, to make sense out of their world, children cognitively organize their experiences. **Organization** *is Piaget's concept of grouping isolated behaviors into a higher-order, more smoothly functioning cognitive system. Every level of thought is organized.* Continual refinement of this organization is an inherent part of development. A boy who has only a vague idea about how to use a hammer may also have a vague idea about how to use other tools. After learning how to use each one, he must interrelate these uses, or organize his knowledge, if he is to become skilled in using tools. In the same way, children continually integrate and coordinate the many other branches of knowledge that often develop independently. Organization occurs within stages of development as well as across them.

Equilibration *is a mechanism in Piaget's theory invoked to explain how children shift from one stage of thought to the next. The shift occurs as children experience cognitive conflict or a disequilibrium in trying to understand the world. Eventually, the child resolves the conflict and reaches a balance, or equilibrium, of thought.* Piaget believed there is considerable movement between states of cognitive equilibrium and disequilibrium as assimilation and accommodation work in concert to produce cognitive change. For example, if a child believes that an amount of liquid changes simply because it is poured into a container with a different shape, she might be puzzled by such issues as where the "extra" liquid came from and whether there is actually more liquid to drink. The child will eventually resolve these puzzles as her thought becomes more advanced. In the everyday world, the child is constantly faced with such counterexamples and inconsistencies. Let's now look in a detailed way at Piaget's stages of thought.

Sensorimotor Thought

Poet Nora Perry asked, "Who knows the thoughts of the child?" As much as anyone, Piaget knew. Through careful, inquisitive interviews and observations of his own three children—Laurent, Lucienne, and Jacqueline—Piaget changed our perceptions of the way infants think about their world. Two of the most important features of sensorimotor thought involve the child's coordination of sensation and action and the nonsymbolic aspects of the period.

The sensorimotor stage lasts from birth to about 2 years of age, corresponding to the period known as infancy. During this time, infants develop the ability to organize and coordinate their sensations and perceptions with their physical movements and actions. This coordination of sensation with action is the source of the term *sensorimotor*. The stage begins with the newborn, who has little more than reflexes to coordinate senses with actions. The stage ends with the 2-year-old, who has complex sensorimotor patterns and is beginning to adopt a primitive symbol system. For example, a 2-year-old can imagine looking at a toy and manipulating it with her hands before she actually does so. The child can also use simple sentences—for example, "Mommy, jump"—to represent a sensorimotor event that has just occurred.

Think about your dog or cat and the kind of intelligence the animal possesses. Although many of us brag about the intelligence of our pets, realistically we know that their cognitive abilities are limited. Piaget would argue that their abilities are limited in a specific way: They are bound up with the animal's behavior. They are not reflective or contemplative abilities, and they do not provide for conscious thinking about things that are not perceptually available. In a word, these abilities are not symbolic.

Think about your own cognition when you are engaged in behavior that is well practiced—such as driving home from work or mowing your lawn. There is a kind of intelligence in such behavior. You show tremendous physical coordination and timing and must continuously monitor perceptual information. You also must make many small adjustments and compensations, even some low-level decisions (for example, to change lanes in preparation for an upcoming turn or to stop when the light turns yellow). Yet, while accomplishing all of these complex behaviors, you may have been thinking about entirely different things (problems at work or with a personal relationship), and your subsequent ability to remember these behaviors probably is quite meager. Piaget would argue that the intelligence you use in such well-practiced behaviors is similar to that of your dog or cat—it is a nonsymbolic sensorimotor

We are born capable of learning.
—Jean-Jacques Rousseau

intelligence. Nonsymbolic, sensorimotor intelligence is what Piaget claimed for the very young infant, up until about 1½ years or so. Thus, the most critical aspect of Piaget's sensorimotor stage is that it is nonsymbolic throughout most of its duration (Flavell, 1985; Piaget, 1970).

Additional arguments for the nonsymbolic nature of thought in early infancy concern the solving of problems through internal reflection or insight. Problem solving occurs quite early in life, perhaps by 12 months of age, however, Piaget claimed that, until about 1½ to 2 years of age, this problem solving is of the trial-and-error variety, devoid of an internal, symbolic component. For example, one of Piaget's daughters insightfully discovered how to get a matchbox open; looking at the slightly open matchbox, she began opening and closing her mouth. Only after making a few such movements did she reach for the matchbox and pull out its drawer with her hands. Piaget interpreted the moving-mouth behavior as reflecting internal, symbolic operations, which emerge only at the end of the sensorimotor stage.

The Substages of Sensorimotor Thought

The sensorimotor stage is divided into six substages, which describe qualitative changes in sensorimotor organization. Within a given substage, there may be different schemes—sucking, rooting, and blinking in Substage 1, for example. The term **scheme** *refers to the basic unit of an organized pattern of sensorimotor functioning.* In Substage 1, schemes are basically reflexive. From substage to substage, the organization of the schemes changes. The six substages of sensorimotor development are (1) simple reflexes; (2) first habits and primary circular reactions; (3) secondary circular reactions; (4) coordination of secondary, circular reactions; (5) tertiary circular reactions, novelty, and curiosity; and (6) internalization of schemes.

Simple reflexes *is Piaget's first sensorimotor substage, which corresponds to the first month after birth. In this substage, the basic means of coordinating sensation and action is through reflexive behaviors, such as rooting and sucking, which the infant has at birth.* In Substage 1, the infant exercises these reflexes. More important, the infant develops an ability to produce behaviors that resemble reflexes in the absence of obvious reflexive stimuli. A newborn may suck when a bottle or nipple is only nearby, for example. When the baby was just born, the bottle or nipple would have produced the sucking pattern only when placed directly in the newborn's mouth or touched to the lips. Reflexlike actions in the absence of a triggering stimulus is evidence that the infant is initiating action and is actively structuring experiences in the first month of life.

First habits and primary circular reactions *is Piaget's second sensorimotor substage, which develops between 1 and 4 months of age. In this substage, infants learn to coordinate sensation and types of schemes or structures—that is, habits and primary circular reactions.* A *habit* is a scheme based on a simple reflex, such as sucking, that has become completely divorced from its eliciting stimulus. For example, an infant in Substage 1 might suck when orally stimulated by a bottle or when visually shown the bottle, but an infant in Substage 2 might exercise the sucking scheme even when no bottle is present.

Primary circular reactions *are schemes based on the infant's attempt to reproduce an interesting or pleasurable event that initially occurred by chance.* In a popular Piagetian example, a child accidentally sucks his fingers when they are placed near his mouth; later, he searches for his fingers to suck them again, but the fingers do not cooperate in the search because the infant cannot coordinate visual and manual actions. Habits and circular reactions are stereotyped in that the infant repeats them the same way each time. The infant's own body remains the center of attention; there is no outward pull by environmental events.

Secondary circular reactions *is Piaget's third sensorimotor substage, which develops between 4 and 8 months of age. In this substage, infants become more object oriented or focused on the world, moving beyond preoccupation with the self in sensorimotor interactions.* The chance shaking of a rattle, for example, may fascinate the infant, and the infant will repeat this action for the sake of experiencing fascination. The infant imitates some simple actions of others, such as the baby talk or burbling of adults, and some physical gestures. However, these imitations are limited to actions the infant is already able to produce. Although directed toward objects in the world, the infant's schemes lack an intentional, goal-directed quality.

Coordination of secondary circular reactions *is Piaget's fourth sensorimotor substage, which develops between 8 and 12 months of age. In this substage, several significant changes take place involving the coordination of schemes and intentionality.* Infants readily combine and recombine previously learned schemes in a *coordinated* way. They may look at an object and grasp it simultaneously or visually inspect a toy, such as a rattle, and finger it simultaneously in obvious tactile exploration. Actions are even more outwardly directed than before. Related to this coordination is the second achievement— the development of *intentionality,* the separation of means and goals in accomplishing simple feats. For example, infants might manipulate a stick (the means) to bring a desired toy within reach (the goal). They may knock over one block in order to reach another to play with.

Tertiary circular reactions, novelty, and curiosity *is Piaget's fifth sensorimotor substage, which develops between 12 and 18 months of age. In this substage, infants become intrigued by the variety of properties that objects possess and by the multiplicity of things they can make happen to objects.* A block can be made to fall, spin, hit another object, slide across the ground, and so on. **Tertiary circular reactions** *are schemes in which the infant purposely explores new possibilities with objects, continually changing what is done to them and exploring the results.* Piaget said that this stage marks the developmental starting point for human curiosity and interest in novelty. Previous circular reactions have been devoted exclusively to reproducing former events, with the exception of imitation of novel acts, which occurs as early as Substage 4. The tertiary circular act is the first to be concerned with novelty.

Internalization of schemes *is Piaget's sixth sensorimotor substage, which develops between 18 and 24 months of age. In this substage, infants' mental functioning shifts from a purely sensorimotor plane to a symbolic plane, and they develop the ability to use primitive symbols.* According to Piaget, a *symbol* is an internalized sensory image or word that represents an event.

(a) (b) (c)

(d) (e) (f)

Figure 8.1
Piaget's Sensorimotor Substages
(a) In Substage 1, the infant practices the reflexive behavior of sucking. (b) In Substage 2, the infant practices the sucking reflex when no bottle is present. (c) In Substage 3, the infant becomes more object oriented. (d) In Substage 4, the infant begins to coordinate action. (e) In Substage 5, the infant becomes intrigued by an object's variety of properties. (f) In Substage 6, the infant's functioning shifts to a symbolic plane.

There was a child who went forth every
  day
And the first object he looked upon,
that object he became.
And that object became part of him for
the day, or a certain
part of the day, or for many years,
or stretching cycles of years.

—Walt Whitman

Primitive symbols permit the infant to think about concrete events without directly acting them out or perceiving them. Moreover, symbols allow the infant to manipulate and transform the represented events in simple ways. In the Piagetian example mentioned earlier, Piaget's young daughter saw a matchbox being opened and closed; sometime later, she mimicked the event by opening and closing her mouth. This was an obvious expression of her image of the event. In another example, a child opened a door slowly to avoid disturbing a piece of paper lying on the floor on the other side. The child had an image of the unseen paper and what would happen to it if the door opened quickly. Developmentalists have debated whether 2-year-olds really have such representations of action sequences at their command, however (Corrigan, 1981). A summary of Piaget's sensorimotor substages is shown in figure 8.1.

Object Permanence

Imagine what thought would be like if you could not distinguish between yourself and your world. Your thought would be chaotic, disorganized, and unpredictable. This is what the mental life of the newborn is like, according to Piaget. There is no self–world differentiation and no sense of object permanence (Piaget, 1952b). By the end of the sensorimotor period, however, both are present.

Object permanence *is the Piagetian term for one of an infant's most important accomplishments: understanding that objects and events continue to exist even when they cannot directly be seen, heard, or touched.*

Learning, Cognition, and Language Development

TABLE 8.1
The Six Substages of Object Permanence

Sensorimotor stage	Behavior
Substage 1	There is no apparent object permanence. When a spot of light moves across the visual field, an infant follows it but quickly ignores its disappearance.
Substage 2	A primitive form of object permanence develops. Given the same experience, the infant looks briefly at the spot where the light disappeared, with an expression of passive expectancy.
Substage 3	The infant's sense of object permanence undergoes further development. With the newfound ability to coordinate simple schemes, the infant shows clear patterns of searching for a missing object, with sustained visual and manual examination of the spot where the object apparently disappeared.
Substage 4	The infant actively searches for a missing object in the spot where it disappeared, with new actions to achieve the goal of searching effectively. For example, if an attractive toy has been hidden behind a screen, the child may look at the screen and try to push it away with a hand. If the screen is too heavy to move or is permanently fixed, the child readily substitutes a secondary scheme—for example, crawling around it or kicking it. These new actions signal that the infant's belief in the continued existence of the missing object is strengthening.
Substage 5	The infant now is able to track an object that disappears and reappears in several locations in rapid succession. For example, a toy may be hidden under different boxes in succession in front of the infant, who succeeds in finding it. The infant is apparently able to hold an image of the missing object in mind longer than before.
Substage 6	The infant can search for a missing object that disappeared and reappeared in several locations in succession, as before. In addition, the infant searches in the appropriate place even when the object has been hidden from view as it is being moved. This activity indicates that the infant is able to "imagine"' the missing object and to follow the image from one location to the next.

Figure 8.2
Object Permanence
Piaget thought that object permanence was one of infancy's landmark cognitive accomplishments. For this 5-month-old boy, ''out-of-sight'' is literally out of mind. The infant looks at the toy monkey (top), but, when his view of the toy is blocked (bottom), he does not search for it. Eventually, he will search for the hidden toy monkey, reflecting the presence of object permanence.

The principal way that object permanence is studied is by watching infants' reactions when an attractive object or event disappears (see figure 8.2). If they show no reaction, it is assumed they believe the object no longer exists. By contrast, if they are surprised at the disappearance and search for the object, it is assumed they believe it continues to exist. According to Piaget, object permanence develops in a series of substages that corresponds to the six substages of sensorimotor development. Table 8.1 shows how the six substages of object permanence reflect Piaget's substages of sensorimotor development.

Cognitive Development and Piaget's Theory

263

Ability to organize and coordinate sensations with physical movements	Is nonsymbolic through most of its duration
Consists of six substages of cognitive development	Object permanence develops

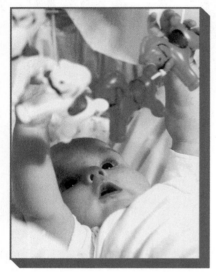

Figure 8.3
Piaget's Description of the Main Characteristics of Sensorimotor Thought

Although Piaget's stage sequence is the best summary of what might happen as an infant fathoms the permanence of things in the world, some contradictory findings have emerged. Piaget's stages broadly describe the interesting changes reasonably well, but an infant's life is not neatly packaged into distinct organizations, as Piaget believed. Some of Piaget's explanations for the causes of change are debated.

For example, Piaget claimed that certain processes are crucial in stage transitions. The data do not always support his explanations, however. According to Piaget, the critical requirement for an infant to progress into sensorimotor Substage 4 is the coordination of vision and the sense of touch, or hand-eye coordination. Another important feature in the progress into Substage 4 is an infant's inclination to search for an object hidden in a familiar location rather than looking for the object in a new location. The **A$\overline{\text{B}}$ error** *is the Piagetian object permanence concept in which an infant progressing into Substage 4 makes frequent mistakes, selecting the familiar hiding place (A) rather than new hiding places ($\overline{B}$).* Researchers have found, however, that the A$\overline{\text{B}}$ error does not show up consistently (Corrigan, 1981; Harris, 1975; Sophian, 1985). There is also accumulating evidence that A$\overline{\text{B}}$ errors are sensitive to the delay between hiding an object at $\overline{B}$ and the infant's attempt to find it (Diamond, 1985). Thus, the A$\overline{\text{B}}$ error might be partly due to the failure of memory.

At this point, we have discussed a number of characteristics of Piaget's stage of sensorimotor thought. To help you remember Piaget's description of the main characteristics of sensorimotor thought, turn to figure 8.3.

A New Perspective on Cognitive Development in Infancy

In the past decade, a new understanding of infants' cognitive development has been taking place. For many years, Piaget's ideas were so widely known and respected that, to many psychologists, one aspect of development seemed certain: Human infants go through a long, protracted period during which they cannot think (Mandler, 1990, 1991). They can learn to recognize things and smile at them, to crawl, and to manipulate objects, but they do not yet have concepts and ideas. Piaget believed that only near the end of the sensorimotor stage of development, at about 1½ to 2 years of age, do infants learn how to represent the world in a symbolic, conceptual manner.

Piaget constructed his view of infancy mainly by observing the development of his own three children. Very few laboratory techniques were available at the time. Recently, however, sophisticated experimental techniques have been devised to study infants, and a large number of research studies on infant cognitive development have accumulated. Much of the new research suggests that Piaget's theory of sensorimotor development will have to be modified substantially.

Piaget's theory of sensorimotor development has been attacked from two sources. First, extensive research in the area of infant perceptual development suggests that a stable and differentiated perceptual world is established much earlier in infancy than Piaget envisioned. Second, researchers recently have found that memory and other forms of symbolic activity occur by at least the second half of the first year.

Perceptual Development

In chapter 5, we described research on infants' perceptual development, indicating that a number of theorists, such as Eleanor Gibson (1989), Elizabeth Spelke (1988), and Tom Bower (1989), believe that infants' perceptual abilities are highly developed very early in development. For example, Spelke has demonstrated that infants as young as 4 months of age have intermodal perception—the ability to coordinate information from two or more sensory modalities, such as vision and audition. Other research by Spelke (1988) and by Renée Baillargeon (1987, 1991) document that infants as young as 4 months expect objects to be substantial—in the sense that the objects cannot move through other objects; neither can other objects move through them—and permanent, in the sense that the objects are assumed to continue to exist when hidden. In sum, the perceptual development researchers believe that infants see objects as bounded, unitary, solid, and separate from their background, possibly at birth or shortly thereafter, but definitely by 3 to 4 months of age. Young infants still have much to learn about objects, but the world appears both stable and orderly to them and, thus, capable of being conceptualized.

Conceptual Development

It is more difficult to study what infants are thinking about than what they see. Still, researchers have devised ways to assess whether or not infants are thinking. One strategy is to look for symbolic activity, such as using a gesture to refer to something. Piaget (1952) used this strategy to document infants' motor recognition. For example, he observed his 6-month-old daughter make a gesture when she saw a familiar toy in a new location. She was used to kicking at the toy in her crib. When she saw it across the room, she made a brief kicking motion. However, Piaget did not consider this to be true symbolic activity because it was a motor movement, not a purely mental act. Nonetheless, Piaget suggested that his daughter was referring to, or classifying, the toy through her actions (Mandler, 1990). In a similar way, infants whose parents use sign language have been observed to start using conventional signs at about 6 to 7 months of age (Bonvillian, Orlansky, & Novack, 1983).

Another type of evidence for conceptual functioning is the recall of absent objects or events. Piaget considered recall to be evidence of conceptual representation. Imagery or other symbolic means must be involved. We usually associate recall with the verbal re-creation of the past, and, as Piaget observed, this does not usually take place until about 18 months of age or older. However, recall does not have to be verbal, as we will see next.

To demonstrate recall, a researcher needs to see a baby do something such as find a hidden object after a delay or imitate a previously observed event. Remember from our discussion of infant imitation in chapter 7 that Andrew Meltzoff (1988) showed that 9-month-old infants can imitate actions they saw performed 24 hours earlier. This is approximately 9 months earlier than Piaget believed possible. In another recent experiment, by Baillargeon and others (1989), 8-month-olds searched for an object behind a screen 70 seconds after the object was hidden. In yet another experiment, Baillargeon and others (1985) found that 4-to-5-month-olds can recall an object's location 8 to 12 seconds later. These performances of infants 9 months of age and younger reflect a representational ability that cannot be attributed to sensorimotor schemes.

In summary, the recent research on infants' perceptual and conceptual development suggests that infants have more sophisticated perceptual abilities and can begin to think earlier than Piaget envisioned. These researchers believe that infants either are born with or acquire these abilities early in their development (Mandler, 1990).

Preoperational Thought

The cognitive world of the preschool child is creative, free, and fanciful. In their art, suns sometimes show up as green and skies as yellow. Cars float on clouds, pelicans kiss seals, and people look like tadpoles. The imagination of preschool children works overtime and their mental grasp of the world improves. When Piaget described the preschool child's cognition as *preoperational,* what did he mean?

The Nature of Preoperational Thought

Since this stage of thought is called *preoperational,* it would seem that not much of importance occurs until full-fledged operational thought appears. Not so. The preoperational stage stretches from approximately the age of 2 to the age of 7. It is a time when stable concepts are formed, mental reasoning emerges, egocentrism begins strongly and then weakens, and magical beliefs are constructed. Preoperational thought is anything but a convenient waiting period for concrete operational thought, although the label *preoperational* emphasizes that the child at this stage does not yet think in an operational way.

What are operations? **Operations** *are internalized sets of actions that allow the child to do mentally what before was done physically.* Operations are highly organized and conform to certain rules and principles of logic. The operations appear in one form in concrete operational thought and in another form in formal operational thought. Thought in the preoperational stage is still flawed and not well organized. Preoperational thought is the beginning of the ability to reconstruct at the level of thought what has been established in behavior. Preoperational thought also involves a transition from primitive to more sophisticated use of symbols.

The Substages of Preoperational Thought

Preoperational thought can be subdivided into two substages: the symbolic function substage and the intuitive thought substage.

Symbolic Function Substage

The **symbolic function substage** *is the first substage of preoperational thought, occurring roughly between the ages of 2 and 4. In this substage, the young child gains the ability to mentally represent an object that is not present.* The ability to engage in such symbolic thought is called symbolic function, and it vastly expands the child's mental world. Young children use scribbled designs to represent people, houses, cars, clouds, and so on. More on young children's

"Mrs. Hammond! I'd know you anywhere from little Billy's portrait of you."

Learning, Cognition, and Language Development

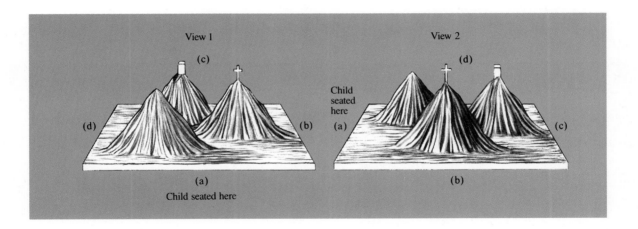

scribbles and art appears in Perspective on Child Development 8.1. Other examples of symbolism in early childhood are the prevalence of pretend play (to be discussed in chapter 13) and language (to be discussed in chapter 10). In sum, the ability to think symbolically and represent the world mentally predominates in this early substage of preoperational thought. However, although young children make distinct progress during this substage, their thought still has several important limitations, two of which are egocentrism and animism.

Egocentrism *is a salient feature of preoperational thought. It is the inability to distinguish between one's own perspective and someone else's perspective.* The following telephone conversation between 4-year-old Mary, who is at home, and her father, who is at work, typifies Mary's egocentric thought:

> *Father:* Mary, is Mommy there?
> *Mary:* (Silently nods)
> *Father:* Mary, may I speak to Mommy?
> *Mary:* (Nods again silently)

Mary's response is egocentric in that she fails to consider her father's perspective before replying. A nonegocentric thinker would have responded verbally.

Piaget and Barbel Inhelder (1969) initially studied young children's egocentrism by devising the three mountains task (see figure 8.4). The child walks around the model of the mountains and becomes familiar with what the mountains look like from different perspectives and can see that there are different objects on the mountains. The child is then seated on one side of the table on which the mountains are placed. The experimenter moves a doll to different locations around the table, at each location asking the child to select, from a series of photos, the one photo that most accurately reflects the view the doll is seeing. Children in the preoperational stage often pick their view from where they are sitting rather than the doll's view. Perspective-taking does not seem to develop uniformly in preschool children, who frequently show perspective skills on some tasks but not others (Shantz, 1983).

Figure 8.4
The Three Mountains Task
View 1 shows the child's perspective from where he or she is sitting. View 2 is an example of the photograph the child would be shown mixed in with others from different perspectives. To correctly identify this view, the child has to take the perspective of a person sitting at spot (b). Invariably, a preschool child who thinks in a preoperational way cannot perform this task. When asked what a view of the mountains looks like from position (b), the child selects a photograph taken from location (a), the child's view at the time.

False would be a picture which insisted on the brutal egocentrism of the child, and ignored the physical beauty which softens it.

—A. A. Milne

Where Pelicans Kiss Seals, Cars Float on Clouds, and Humans Are Tadpoles

At about 3 years of age and sometimes even 2, children's spontaneous scribbles begin to resemble pictures. One 3½-year-old child looked at the scribble he had just drawn and said it was a pelican kissing a seal (figure 8.A). At about 3 to 4 years of age, children begin to create symbols of humans. Invariably, their first symbols look curiously like tadpoles; see the circle and two lines in figure 8.B—the circle represents a head and the two lines are legs.

These observations of children's drawings were made by Denise Wolf, Carol Fucigna, and Howard Gardner at Harvard University. They point out that many people think young children draw a person in this rather odd way because it is the best they can do. Piaget said children intend their drawings to be realistic; they draw what they know rather than what they see, so the tadpole with its strange exemptions of trunk and arms might reflect a child's lack of knowledge of the human body and how its parts fit together. However, children know more about the human body than they are capable of drawing. One 3-year-old child drew a tadpole but described it in complete detail, pointing out where the feet, chin, and neck were. When 3- and 4-year-old children are asked to draw someone playing ball, they produce symbols of humans that include arms, since the task implicitly requires arms.

Possibly because preschool children are not very concerned about reality, their drawings are fanciful and inventive. Suns are blue, skies are yellow, and cars float on clouds in the preschool child's symbolic world. The symbolism is simple but strong, not unlike the abstractions found in some contemporary art. In the elementary school years, the child's symbols become more realistic, neat, and precise. Suns are yellow, skies are blue, and cars are placed on roads (figure 8.C).

A child's ability to represent the world symbolically on paper is related to the development of perceptual motor skills. Once such skills are developed, however, some adult artists revert to the style of young children's drawings. As Picasso commented, "I used to draw like Raphael but it has taken me a whole lifetime to learn to draw like children" (Winner, 1986).

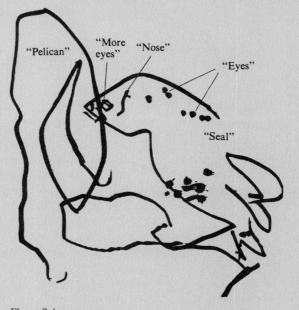

Figure 8.A
A 3½-Year-Old's Symbolic Drawing
Halfway into this drawing, the 3½-year-old artist said it was "a pelican kissing a seal."

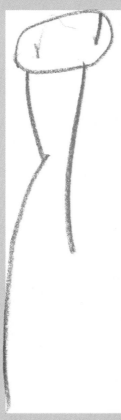

Figure 8.B
A 3-Year-Old's Drawing of a Person
Many 3-year-olds' drawings of people look curiously like tadpoles.

Figure 8.C
An 11-Year-Old's Drawing
An 11-year-old's drawing is neater and more realistic than a 6-year-old's drawing, but it is also less inventive.

Animism, *another facet of preoperational thought, is the belief that in-animate objects have "lifelike" qualities and are capable of action.* A young child might show animism by saying, "That tree pushed the leaf off, and it fell down," or "The sidewalk made me mad; it made me fall down." A young child who uses animism fails to distinguish the appropriate occasions for using human and nonhuman perspectives. Some developmentalists, though, believe that animism represents incomplete knowledge and understanding, not a general conception of the world (Dolgin & Behrend, 1984).

Intuitive Thought Substage

Tommy is 4 years old. Although he is starting to develop his own ideas about the world he lives in, they are still simple and he is not very good at thinking things out. He has difficulty understanding events he knows are taking place but cannot see. He has little control over reality, to which his fantasized thoughts bear little resemblance. He cannot yet reliably answer the question "What if?" For example, he has only a vague idea of what would happen if a car were to hit him. He also has difficulty negotiating traffic because he cannot do the mental calculations necessary to estimate whether an approaching car will hit him when he crosses the road (Goodman, 1979).

The **intuitive thought substage** *is the second substage of preoperational thought, occurring approximately between 4 and 7 years of age. In this substage, children begin to use primitive reasoning and want to know the answers to all sorts of questions.* Piaget called this time period *intuitive* because, on one hand, young children seem sure about their knowledge and understanding yet are unaware of how they know what they know. That is, they say they know something but know it without the use of rational thinking.

An example of young children's reasoning ability is the difficulty they have putting things into their correct classes. Faced with a random collection of objects that can be grouped together on the basis of two or more properties, a preoperational child is seldom capable of using these properties consistently to sort the objects into appropriate categories. Look at the collection of objects in figure 8.5a. You would respond to the direction "Put the things together that you believe belong together" by sorting them by size and shape. Your sorting might look something like that shown in figure 8.5b. In the social realm, a 4-year-old girl might be given the task of dividing her peers into groups according to whether they are friends and whether they are boys or girls. She would be unlikely to arrive at the following classification: friendly boys, friendly girls, unfriendly boys, unfriendly girls. Another example of classification shortcomings involves the preoperational child's understanding of religious concepts (Elkind, 1976). When asked "Can you be a Protestant and an American at the same time?" 6- and 7-year-olds usually say no; 9-year-olds are likely to say yes, understanding that objects can be cross-classified simultaneously.

Many of these examples show a characteristic of preoperational thought called **centration,** *the focusing, or centering, of attention on one characteristic to the exclusion of all others.* Centration is most clearly evidenced in young children's lack of **conservation,** *the idea that an amount stays the same regardless of how its container changes.* To adults, it is obvious that a certain amount of liquid stays the same regardless of a container's shape, but this is not obvious at all to young children; instead, they are struck by the height of the liquid in the container. In the conservation task—Piaget's most famous—a child is presented with two identical beakers, each filled to the same level with liquid (see figure 8.6). The child is asked if these beakers have the same

Learning, Cognition, and Language Development

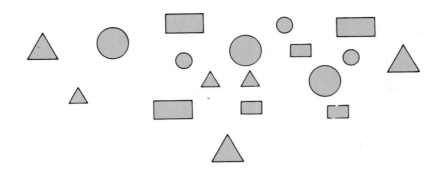

Figure 8.5a
A Random Array of Objects

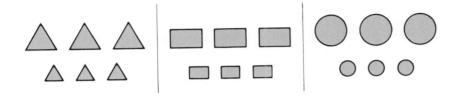

Figure 8.5b
An Ordered Array of Objects

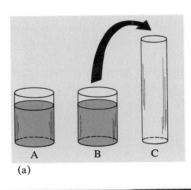 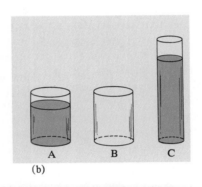

(a)   (b)

Figure 8.6
Piaget's Conservation Task
The beaker test is a well-known Piagetian test to determine whether a child can think operationally—that is, can mentally reverse actions and show conservation of the substance. (a) Two identical beakers are presented to the child. Then, the experimenter pours the liquid from B into C, which is taller and thinner than A or B. (b) The child is asked if these beakers (A and C) have the same amount of liquid. The preoperational child says no. When asked to point to the beaker that has more liquid, the preoperational child points to the tall, thin beaker.

amount of liquid, and she usually says yes. Then, the liquid from one beaker is poured into a third beaker, which is taller and thinner than the first two. The child is then asked if the amount of liquid in the tall, thin beaker is equal to that which remains in one of the original beakers. If the child is less than 7 or 8 years old, she usually says no and justifies her answer in terms of the differing height or width of the beakers. Older children usually answer yes and justify their answers appropriately ("If you poured the milk back, the amount would still be the same"). The older child can mentally reverse actions; the preoperational child cannot.

■ *Critical Thinking*
Is preoperational thought something that develops through maturation, or is it something that can be taught? Explain your answer.

In Piaget's theory, failing the conservation of liquid task is a sign that children are at the preoperational stage of cognitive development, whereas passing this test is a sign that they are at the concrete operational stage. In Piaget's view, preoperational children not only fail to show conservation of liquid but also of number, matter, length, volume, and area (see figure 8.7).

Some developmentalists do not believe Piaget was entirely correct in his estimate of when children's conservation skills emerge. For example, Rochel Gelman (1969; Gelman & Baillargeon, 1983) has shown that, when an experimenter instructs a child to attend to relevant aspects of the conservation task, the child is more likely to conserve. Gelman has also demonstrated that attentional training on one type of task, such as numbers, improves the preschool child's performance on another type of task, such as mass. Thus, Gelman believes that conservation appears earlier than Piaget thought and that the process of attention is especially important in explaining conservation.

Yet another characteristic of preoperational children is that they ask a barrage of questions. Children's earliest questions appear around the age of 3 and, by the age of 5, they have just about exhausted the adults around them with "why" questions. Their questions yield clues about their mental development and reflect intellectual curiosity. These questions signal the emergence of children's interest in reasoning and figuring out why things are the way they are. Some samples of the questions children ask during the questioning period of 4 to 6 years of age are the following (Elkind, 1976):

"What makes you grow up?"
"What makes you stop growing?"
"Why does a lady have to be married to have a baby?"
"Who was the mother when everybody was a baby?"
"Why do leaves fall?"
"Why does the sun shine?"

At this point, we have discussed a number of preoperational thought's characteristics. To help you remember these characteristics, turn to figure 8.8 and read some examples of concepts such as egocentrism and animism; then turn to Perspective on Child Development 8.2, where you will discover how these concepts are included in the story of *Winnie-the-Pooh*. We also have discussed a number of ideas about Piaget and his place in child psychology, cognitive developmental theory, cognitive processes, sensorimotor thought, and preoperational thought. A summary of these ideas is presented in concept table 8.1 on page 276.

Type of conservation	Initial presentation	Manipulation	Preoperational child's answer	

Number

Two identical rows of objects are shown to the child, who agrees they have the same number.

One row is lengthened and the child is asked whether one row now has more objects.

Yes, the longer row.

Matter

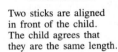

Two identical balls of clay are shown to the child. The child agrees they are equal.

The experimenter changes the shape of one of the balls and asks the child whether they still contain equal amounts of clay.

No, the longer one has more.

Length

Two sticks are aligned in front of the child. The child agrees that they are the same length.

The experimenter moves one stick to the right, then asks the child if they still are equal in length.

No, the one on the top is longer.

Volume

Two balls are placed in two identical glasses with an equal amount of water. The child sees the balls displace equal amounts of water.

The experimenter changes the shape of one of the balls and asks the child if it still will displace the same amount of water.

No, the longer one on the right displaces more.

Area

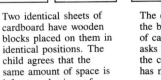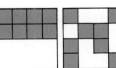

Two identical sheets of cardboard have wooden blocks placed on them in identical positions. The child agrees that the same amount of space is left on each piece of cardboard.

The experimenter scatters the blocks on one piece of cardboard and then asks the child if one of the cardboard pieces has more space covered up.

Yes, the one on the right has more space covered up.

273

Figure 8.8
Preoperational Thought's Characteristics

| More symbolic than sensorimotor thought | Inability to engage in operations; can't mentally reverse actions; lacks conservation skills | Egocentric (inability to distinguish between own perspective and someone else's) | Intuitive rather than logical |

Concrete Operational Thought

Remember that, according to Piaget, concrete operational thought is made up of operations—mental actions or representations that are reversible. In the well-known test of reversibility of thought involving conservation of matter, a child is presented with two identical balls of clay. An experimenter rolls one ball into a long, thin shape; the other remains in its original ball shape. The child is then asked if there is more clay in the ball or in the long, thin piece of clay. By the time children reach the age of 7 or 8, most answer that the amount of clay is the same. To answer this problem correctly, children have to imagine that the clay ball is rolled out into a long, thin strip and then returned to its original round shape—imagination that involves a reversible mental action. Thus, a concrete operation is a reversible mental action on real, concrete objects. Concrete operations allow children to coordinate several characteristics rather than focus on a single property of an object. In the clay example, a preoperational child is likely to focus on height *or* width; a concrete operational child coordinates information about both dimensions. We can get

Learning, Cognition, and Language Development

Piglet, Pooh, and Piaget

According to psychologist Dorothy Singer (1972), if Piaget had opened the pages of *Winnie-the-Pooh*, he would have discovered how A. A. Milne used some of the same concepts he believed were prominent in the preschool child's thought. Milne's psychological insight gives life and meaning to a little story about an imaginary forest peopled with animals from a nursery.

We first meet Edward Bear as he is being dragged down the stairs on the back of his head. "It is, as far as he knows, the only way of coming down the stairs." This example of egocentrism sets the tone for the rest of the book. The narrator tells us that Edward's name is Winnie-the-Pooh. When asked if Winnie is not a girl's name, Christopher replies with a second example of egocentrism. "He's Winnie-ther-Pooh. Don't you know what *ther* means?" Again, this is an example of egocentrism. Christopher knows, so no further explanation is necessary, or forthcoming. Piglet, an egocentric friend of Pooh who is a weak and timid pig, is certain that everyone knows when he is in distress. Pooh is just as egocentric when he tries to read a note. Pooh only recognizes the letter "P" and each "P" convinces him further that "P" means "Pooh," so "it's a very important Missage to me." In a later chapter, Pooh eats a jar of honey that he had intended to give to everyone else on his birthday. In egocentric form, though, Pooh rationalizes his gluttony and decides to give everyone the empty jar: "It's a very nice pot. Everyone could keep things in it."

Milne recognized the pervasiveness of animism in young children's thought. Each of the imaginary characters displays a talent for animism. In the first chapter, Pooh develops an elaborate plan to steal some honey from a bee's hive. He disguises himself as a cloud in a blue sky. He rolls over and over in the mud until he is as dark as a thundercloud, borrows a sky-blue balloon from Christopher, and floats off into the sky, singing as he goes. The singing cloud is an example of animism.

Milne's story of Eeyore's birthday illustrates the principle of conservation. Piglet plans to give Eeyore (the cynical and pessimistic donkey) a large red balloon. On the way, Piglet catches his foot in the rabbit's hole and falls down. When he recovers, he finds out, to his dismay, that the balloon has burst.

How were Piaget's ideas about cognitive development exemplified in A. A. Milne's classic book Winnie-the-Pooh?

All that he has left is a small piece of a damp rag. Nevertheless, Piglet is determined to give a present to Eeyore. When he finally reaches Eeyore, the conversation goes like this:

"Yes, Eeyore, I brought you a balloon."

"*Balloon,*" said Eeyore, . . . "One of those big coloured things you blow up? Gaiety, song-and-dance, here we are and there we are?"

"Yes . . . but I fell down . . . and I burst the balloon."

"My birthday balloon?"

"Yes, Eeyore," said Piglet, sniffing a little. "Here it is. With— many happy returns of the day. . . ."

"My present?"

Piglet nodded again.

"The balloon?"

"Yes."

"Thank you, Piglet," said Eeyore. "You don't mind my asking," he went on, "but what color was this balloon when it—when it *was* a balloon?"

Poor Eeyore cannot understand that red remains red even when the balloon is small and no longer round or full.

Piaget's Place in Developmental Psychology, Cognitive Developmental Theory, Cognitive Processes, Sensorimotor Development, and Preoperational Development

Concept	Processes/related ideas	Characteristics/description
Piaget's place in developmental psychology and cognitive developmental theory	Piaget's giant stature	Piaget's contribution to developmental psychology may be as important as Freud's contribution to personality and abnormal psychology. We owe him the present field of cognitive development.
	Cognitive developmental theory	The developing child's rational thinking and stages of thought are emphasized. Thoughts are the central focus of development, the primary determinants of children's action.
Cognitive processes in Piaget's theory	Adaptation	Piaget developed this concept for the child's effective interaction with the environment. The interaction is a cognitive one that involves assimilation and accommodation.
	Assimilation and accommodation	Assimilation occurs when children incorporate new information into their existing knowledge. Accommodation occurs when children adjust to new information.
	Organization	Organization is Piaget's concept of grouping isolated behaviors into a higher-order, more smoothly functioning cognitive system. Every level of thought is organized.
	Equilibration	Equilibration is a mechanism in Piaget's theory invoked to explain how children shift from one stage of thought to the next. The shift occurs as the child experiences cognitive conflict or a disequilibrium in trying to understand the world. Eventually, the child resolves the conflict and reaches a balance, or equilibrium, of thought. Piaget believed there is considerable movement between states of cognitive equilibrium and disequilibrium as assimilation and accommodation work in concert to produce cognitive change.
Sensorimotor thought	Basic features	The infant is able to organize and coordinate sensations with physical movements. The stage lasts from birth to about 2 years of age and is nonsymbolic through most of its duration.

a better understanding of concrete operational thought by considering further ideas about conservation and the nature of classification.

Conservation

We already have highlighted some of Piaget's basic ideas on conservation in our discussion of preoperational children's failure to answer questions correctly about such circumstances as the beaker task. Remember that conservation involves the recognition that the length, number, mass, quantity, area, weight, and volume of objects and substances do not change by transformations that alter their appearance. An important point that needs to be made about conservation is that children do not conserve all quantities or on all tasks simultaneously. The order of their mastery is number, length, liquid quantity, mass, weight, and volume. **Horizontal décalage** *is Piaget's concept that describes how similar abilities do not appear at the same time within a stage of development.* As we have just seen, during the concrete operational stage,

Concept	Processes/related ideas	Characteristics/description
	Substages of sensorimotor thought	Sensorimotor thought has six substages: simple reflexes; first habits and primary circular reactions; secondary circular reactions; coordination of secondary circular reactions; tertiary circular reactions, novelty, and curiosity; and internalization of schemes.
	Object permanence	Object permanence refers to the ability to understand that objects and events continue to exist even though the infant no longer is in contact with them. Piaget believed that this ability develops over the course of the six substages of sensorimotor thought.
	A new perspective on cognitive development in infancy	In the past decade, a new understanding of infants' cognitive development has been occurring. Piaget's theory has been attacked from two sources. First, extensive research in perceptual development suggests that a stable and differentiated perceptual world is established much earlier than Piaget envisioned. Second, researchers recently have found that memory and other forms of symbolic activity occur by at least the second half of the first year.
Preoperational thought	Its nature	It is the beginning of the ability to reconstruct at the level of thought what has been established in behavior, and a transition from primitive to more sophisticated use of symbols. The child does not yet think in an operational way.
	Symbolic function substage	This substage occurs roughly between 2 and 4 years of age and is characterized by symbolic thought, egocentrism, and animism.
	Intuitive thought substage	This substage stretches from approximately 4 to 7 years of age and is called intuitive because children seem sure about their knowledge, yet they are unaware of how they know what they know. The preoperational child lacks conservation and asks a barrage of questions.

conservation of number usually appears first and conservation of volume last. Also, an 8-year-old child may know that a long stick of clay can be rolled back into a ball but not understand that the ball and the stick weigh the same. At about 9 years of age, the child recognizes that they weigh the same and, eventually, at about 11 to 12 years of age, the child understands that the clay's volume is unchanged by rearranging it. Children initially master tasks in which the dimensions are more salient and visible, only later mastering those not as visually apparent, such as volume.

Classification

Many of the concrete operations identified by Piaget focus on the way children reason about the properties of objects. One important skill that characterizes concrete operational children is the ability to classify or divide things into sets or subsets and to consider their interrelationships. An example of concrete operational classification skills involves a family tree of four generations (Furth

& Wachs, 1975) (figure 8.9). This family tree suggests that the grandfather (A) has three children (B, C, and D), each of whom has two children (E through J), and that one of these children (J) has three children (K, L, and M). A child who comprehends this classification system can move up and down a level (vertically), across a level (horizontally), and up and down and across (obliquely) within the system. The concrete operational child understands that person J can, at the same time, be father, brother, and grandson, for example.

Although concrete operational thought is more advanced than preoperational thought, it has its limitations. Logical reasoning replaces intuitive thought as long as the principles can be applied to specific or *concrete* examples. For example, a concrete operational child cannot imagine the steps necessary to complete an algebraic equation, which is too abstract for thinking at this stage of cognitive development. A summary of the characteristics of concrete operational thought is shown in figure 8.10.

Application of Piaget's Ideas to Education

Piaget was not an educator, but he did provide a sound conceptual framework from which to view educational problems. What are some of the principles in Piaget's theory of cognitive development that can be applied to children's education? David Elkind (1976) describes three. First, the foremost issue in education is *communication*. In Piaget's theory, a child's mind is not a blank slate; to the contrary, the child has a host of ideas about the physical and natural world, but these ideas differ from those of adults. Adults must learn to comprehend what children are saying and to respond in the same mode of discourse that children use. Second, the child is always unlearning and relearning in addition to acquiring knowledge. Children come to school with their own ideas about space, time, causality, quantity, and number. Third, the child is a knowing creature, motivated to acquire knowledge. The best way to nurture this motivation for knowledge is to allow the child to interact spontaneously with the environment; education needs to ensure that it does not dull the child's eagerness to know by providing an overly rigid curriculum that disrupts the child's rhythm and pace of learning.

Formal Operational Thought

Adolescents' developing power of thought opens up new cognitive and social horizons. Their thought becomes more abstract, logical, and idealistic; more capable of examining one's own thoughts, others' thoughts, and what others are thinking about one's self; and more likely to interpret and monitor the social world.

Characteristics of Formal Operational Thought

Piaget believed that formal operational thought comes into play between the ages of 11 and 15. Formal operational thought is more *abstract* than a child's thinking. Adolescents are no longer limited to actual concrete experience as the anchor of thought. Instead, they may conjure up make-believe situations, hypothetical possibilities, or purely abstract propositions and reason about them. Adolescents increasingly think about thought itself. One adolescent pondered, "I began thinking about why I was thinking what I was. Then I began thinking about why I was thinking about why I was thinking about what I was." If this sounds abstract, it is, and it characterizes adolescents' increased interest on thought itself and the abstractness of thought.

Learning, Cognition, and Language Development

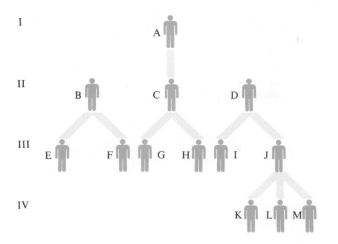

I

II

III

IV

Figure 8.9

A Classification Problem to Demonstrate Concrete Operational Thought
Preoperational children have trouble classifying the members of the four generations in this family tree. Concrete operational children can classify the members vertically, horizontally, and obliquely (up and down and across).

| Can use operations, mentally reversing action; shows conservation skills | Logical reasoning replaces intuitive reasoning, but only in concrete circumstances | Not abstract (can't imagine steps in algebraic equation, for example) | Classification skills — can divide things into sets and subsets and reason about their inter-relations |

Figure 8.10

Concrete Operational Thought's Characteristics

Accompanying the abstract nature of adolescent thought is the quality of idealism. Adolescents begin to think about ideal characteristics for themselves and others and to compare themselves and others to these ideal standards. In contrast, children think more in terms of what is real and what is limited. During adolescence, thoughts often take fantasy flights into the future. It is not unusual for adolescents to become impatient with these newfound ideal standards and to be perplexed about which of many ideal standards to adopt.

At the same time adolescents think more abstractly and idealistically, they also think more logically. Adolescents begin to think more as a scientist

The error of youth is to believe that intelligence is a substitute for experience, while the error of age is to believe that experience is a substitute for intelligence.

—Slyman Bryson

Cognitive Development and Piaget's Theory

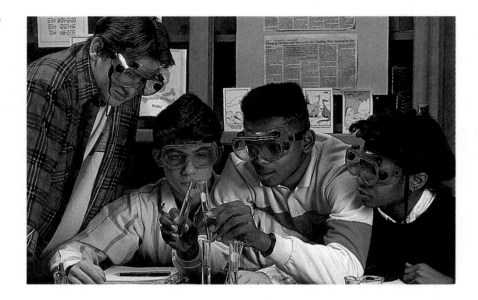

In this chemistry class at a middle school in North Carolina, students are engaging in hypothetical-deductive reasoning to solve problems.

thinks, devising plans to solve problems and systematically testing solutions. This type of problem solving has an imposing name. **Hypothetical-deductive reasoning** *is Piaget's formal operational concept that adolescents have the cognitive ability to develop hypotheses, or best guesses, about ways to solve problems, such as an algebraic equation. They then systematically deduce, or conclude, which is the best path to follow in solving the problem.* By contrast, children are more likely to solve problems in a trial-and-error fashion. An example of a hypothetical-deductive reasoning problem is presented in table 8.2, and a summary of the main features of formal operational thought is shown in figure 8.11.

Formal Operational Thought and Language

As adolescent thought becomes more abstract and logical, language use also changes. This development includes changes in the use of satire and metaphor, in writing skills, and in conversational skills.

A junior high school student is sitting in school making up satirical labels for his teachers. One he calls "the walking wilt Wilkie and his wilking waste." Another he describes as "the magnificent Manifred and his manifest morbidity." The use of nicknames increases during early adolescence, as does their abstractness—"stilt," "spaz," "nerd," and "marshmallow mouth," for example. These examples reflect the aspect of language known as **satire,** *which refers to irony, wit, or derision used to expose folly or wickedness.* Adolescents use and understand satire more than children do (Demorest & others, 1984). The satire of *Mad* magazine, which relies on double meaning, exaggeration, and parody to highlight absurd circumstances and contradictory happenings, finds a more receptive audience among 13-to-14-year-olds than 8-to-9-year-olds.

Another aspect of language that comes into use in adolescence is **metaphor,** *an implied comparison between two ideas that is conveyed by the abstract meaning contained in the words used.* For example, a person's faith and a piece of glass are alike in that they both can be shattered. A runner's performance and a politician's speech are alike in that they both are predictable. Children have a difficult time understanding metaphorical comparisons; adolescents are better able to understand their meaning.

". . . and give me good abstract-reasoning ability, interpersonal skills, cultural perspective, linguistic comprehension, and a high sociodynamic potential."

Drawing by Ed Fisher; © 1981 The New Yorker Magazine, Inc.

An Example of Hypothetical-Deductive Reasoning

A common task for all of us is to determine what can be inferred logically from a statement made by someone else. Young children are often told by teachers that, if they work hard, they will receive good grades. Regardless of the empirical truth of the claim, the children may believe that good grades are the result of hard work and that, if they do not get good grades, they did not work hard enough. (Establishing the direction of the relationship between variables is an important issue.)

Children in the late concrete operational stage, too, are concerned with understanding the relations between their behavior and their teachers' grading practices. However, they are beginning to question the ``truths'' of their childhood. First, they now know that there are four possible combinations if two variables are dichotomized (work hard-not work hard; good grades-not good grades):

Behavior	Consequences
1 Work hard	Good grades
2 Work hard	Not good grades
3 Not work hard	Good grades
4 Not work hard	Not good grades

Two combinations are consistent with the hypothesis that hard work is necessarily related to good grades: (1) students work hard and get good grades and (4) they do not work hard and do not get good grades. When the presumed "cause"' is present, the effect is present; when the cause is absent, the effect is absent. There are also two combinations that do not fit the hypothesis of a direct relation between hard work and good grades: (2) students work hard and do not get good grades and (3) they get good grades without working hard.

An adolescent's notion of possibility allows him or her to take this analysis of combinations one important step further. Each of the four basic combinations of binary variables may be true or it may not. If 1, 2, 3, or 4 is true alone or are true in combination, there are 16 possible patterns of truth values:

1 or 2 or 3 or 4 is true	4 patterns
1-2 or 1-3 or 1-4 or 2-3 or 2-4 or 3-4 are true	6 patterns
1-2-3 or 1-2-4 or 1-3-4 or 2-3-4 are true	4 patterns
All (1-2-3-4) are true	1 pattern
All are false	1 pattern
Total	16 patterns

The list is critically important because each pattern leads to a different conclusion about the possible relation between two variables.

Excerpt from *PIAGET: WITH FEELING* by Philip Cowan, copyright © 1978 by Holt, Rinehart and Winston, Inc., reprinted by permission of the publisher.

Abstract	Idealistic	Logical
Adolescents think more abstractly than children. Formal operational thinkers can solve abstract algebraic equations, for example.	Adolescents often think about what is possible. They think about ideal characteristics of themselves, others, and the world.	Adolescents begin to think more like scientists, devising plans to solve problems and systematically testing solutions. Piaget called this type of logical thinking hypothetical-deductive reasoning.

Figure 8.11
Formal Operational Thought

Think back to when you were a young adolescent—were you intrigued by absurdities and contradictory happenings?

The increased abstractness and logical reasoning of adolescents' cognition can be witnessed in improved writing ability (Scardamalia, Bereiter, & Goelman, 1982). Organizing ideas is critical to good writing. Logical thinking helps writers develop a hierarchical structure, which helps readers understand which ideas are general, which are specific, and which are more important than others. Researchers have discovered that children are poor at organizing their ideas prior to writing and have difficulty detecting the salient points in prose passages (Brown & Smiley, 1977). Although adolescents are not Pulitzer Prize-winning novelists, they are better than children at recognizing the need for making both general and specific points in their writing. The sentences adolescents string together make more sense than those constructed by children, and adolescents are more likely than children to include an introduction, several paragraphs that represent a body, and concluding remarks when writing an essay (Fischer & Lazerson, 1984).

Most adolescents also are better conversationalists than are children. Adolescents are better at letting individuals take turns in discussions instead of everyone talking at once; they are better at using questions to convey commands ("Why is it so noisy in here?"); they are better at using such words as *the* and *a* in ways that enhance understanding ("He is *the* living end! He is not just *a* person); they are better at using polite language in appropriate situations (when a guest comes to the house, for example); and they are better at telling stories that are interesting, jokes that are funny, and lies that convince.

Adolescent Egocentrism

Another characteristic of adolescent thought is adolescent egocentrism. Elkind (1978) believes that **adolescent egocentrism** *has two parts: an imaginary audience and a personal fable.* An **imaginary audience** *is an adolescent's belief that others are as preoccupied with her as she is.* Attention-getting behavior, common in adolescence, reflects egocentrism and the desire to be on-stage, noticed, and visible. Imagine an eighth-grade boy who thinks he is an actor and all others the audience as he stares at the small spot on his trousers. Imagine the seventh-grade girl who thinks that all eyes are riveted on her complexion because of the tiny blemish she has. Current controversy about the nature of egocentrism focuses on whether it emerges because of formal operational thought (Elkind, 1985) or because of perspective-taking and interpersonal understanding (Lapsley, 1989a; Lapsley & Murphy, 1985).

As part of their egocentrism, adolescents believe that others are as preoccupied with them as they themselves are. Adolescent egocentrism reflects the desire to be on-stage, noticed, and visible.

Jennifer talks with her best friend, Anne, about something she has just heard. "Anne, did you hear about Barbara? You know she fools around a lot. Well, the word is that she is pregnant. Can you believe it? That would never happen to me." Later in the conversation, Anne tells Jennifer, "I really like Bob, but sometimes he's a jerk. He just can't understand me. He has no clue about what my personal feelings are." **Personal fable** *refers to adolescents' sense of personal uniqueness and indestructibility.* In their efforts to maintain a sense of uniqueness and indestructibility, adolescents sometimes create fictitious stories, or fables. Imagine a girl who is having difficulty getting a date. She may develop a fictitious account of a handsome young man living in another part of the country who is madly in love with her.

Early and Late Formal Operational Thought

Formal operational thought has been conceptualized as occurring in two phases. In the first phase, the increased ability to think hypothetically produces unconstrained thoughts with unlimited possibilities. This early formal operational thought submerges reality (Broughton, 1983). Reality is overwhelmed. Idealism and possibility dominate. During the middle years of adolescence, an intellectual balance is restored; adolescents test the products of their reasoning against experience and develop a consolidation of formal operational thought.

Piaget's (1952) early writings seemed to indicate that the onset and consolidation of formal operational thought is completed during early adolescence, from about 12 to 15 years of age. Later, Piaget (1972) concluded that formal operational thought is not achieved until later in adolescence, between approximately 15 and 20 years of age.

Piaget's concepts of assimilation and accommodation help us understand the two phases of formal operational thought. Remember that *assimilation* occurs when adolescents incorporate new information into their existing knowledge; *accommodation* occurs when adolescents adjust to new information. During early adolescence, there is an excess of assimilation as the world is perceived too subjectively and idealistically. In the middle years of adolescence, an intellectual balance is restored, as the individual accommodates to the cognitive upheaval that has taken place. In this view, the assimilation of formal operational thought marks the transition to adolescence; accommodation marks a later consolidation of thought (Lapsley, 1989b).

Variations in Adolescent Cognition

Piaget's theory emphasizes universal and consistent patterns of formal operational thought; his theory does not adequately account for the unique differences that characterize the cognitive development of adolescents. These individual variations in adolescents' cognitive development have been documented in a number of investigations (Bart, 1971; Kaufmann & Flaitz, 1987; Neimark, 1982).

Some individuals in early adolescence are formal operational thinkers; others are not. A review of formal operational thought investigations revealed that only about one of every three eighth-grade students is a formal operational thinker (Strahan, 1983). Some investigators have found that formal operational thought increases with age in adolescence (Arlin, 1984; Martorano, 1977); others have not (Strahan, 1987). Many college students and adults do not think in formal operational ways, either. For example, investigators have found that from 17 percent to 67 percent of all college students think in formal operational ways (Elkind, 1961; Tomlinson-Keasey, 1972).

Many young adolescents are at the point of consolidating their concrete operational thought, using it more consistently than in childhood. At the same time, many young adolescents are just beginning to think in a formal operational manner. By late adolescence, many adolescents have begun to consolidate their formal operational thought, using it more consistently, and there often is variation across the content areas of formal operational thought, just as there is in concrete operational thought in childhood. A 14-year-old may reason at the formal operational level when it comes to analyzing algebraic equations but not do so with verbal problem solving or when reasoning about interpersonal relations.

Formal operational thought is more likely to be used in areas in which adolescents have the most experience and knowledge (Carey, 1988; Flavell, 1985). Children and adolescents gradually build up elaborate knowledge through extensive experience and practice in various sports, games, hobbies, and school subjects such as math, English, and science. The development of expertise in different domains of life may make possible high-level, developmentally mature-looking thought. In some instances, the sophisticated reasoning of formal operational thought may be responsible. In other instances, however, the thought may be largely due to the accumulation of knowledge that allows more automatic, memory-based processes to function. Some developmentalists wonder if the acquisition of knowledge accounts for all cognitive growth. Most, however, argue that *both* cognitive changes in such areas as concrete and formal operational thought *and* the development of expertise through experience are at work in understanding the adolescent's cognitive world. More about knowledge's role in the adolescent's thinking appears in the next chapter.

One recent proposal argues that a better understanding of Piaget's theory of formal operational thought can be achieved by considering the distinction between "knowing that" and "knowing how" (Byrnes, 1988a,b). The argument is that reasoning takes place in two basic forms: "knowing that" and "knowing how." "Knowing that" has been called conceptual knowledge or declarative knowledge (Hiebert & LeFevre, 1987; Mandler, 1983). It consists of networks of the core concepts in a given domain, such as biology or physics. "Knowing how" is simply a representation of the steps an individual should follow in order to solve a problem. It has been referred to as procedural knowledge (Anderson, 1990). For example, in the domain of physics, "knowing that" would consist of understanding the relation between the core concepts of "force" and "mass." In contrast, "knowing how" would consist of understanding how to solve introductory physics test problems using formulas and the like.

The argument by James Byrnes (1988a,b) is that Piaget's theory of formal operations can be better understood if it is recast as "knowing that." However, Daniel Keating (1988, 1990b) argues that Piaget's theory is actually about "knowing how," and that considering his view of formal operations in terms of "knowing that" is a misinterpretation. The lively debate about Piaget's theory of formal operations is likely to continue as experts strive to determine exactly what Piaget meant by formal operational thought and to search for the true nature of adolescent cognitive development.

Beyond Formal Operational Thought

Some critics of Piaget's theory argue that specialized thinking about a specific skill represents a higher stage of thought than formal operational thought. Piaget did not believe this was so. For him, the change to reasoning about a special skill (such as the kind of thinking engaged in by a nuclear physicist or medical researcher) is no more than window dressing. A nuclear physicist may think in ways that an adolescent cannot think, but the adolescent and the nuclear physicist differ only in their familiarity with an academic field of inquiry. They differ in the content of their thought, not in the operations they bring to bear on the content (Piaget, 1970).

Some developmentalists believe that the absolute nature of adolescent logic and buoyant optimism diminish in early adulthood. According to Gisela Labouvie-Vief (1982, 1986), a new integration of thought takes place in early adulthood. She thinks the adult years produce pragmatic constraints that require an adaptive strategy of less reliance on logical analysis in solving problems. Commitment, specialization, and channeling energy into finding one's niche in complex social and work systems replace the youth's fascination with idealized logic. If we assume that logical thought and buoyant optimism represent the criteria for cognitive maturity, we would have to admit that the cognitive activity of adults is too concrete and pragmatic. However, from

■ *Critical Thinking*
Other than developing more pragmatic thoughts, can you think of any other ways young adults' thoughts might be different or more advanced than adolescents' thoughts?

Learning, Cognition, and Language Development

Labouvie-Vief's view, the adult's understanding of reality's constraints reflects maturity, not immaturity. Even Piaget (1967) detected that formal operational thought may have its hazards:

> With the advent of formal intelligence, thinking takes wings and it is not surprising that at first this unexpected power is both used and abused. . . . Each new mental ability starts off by incorporating the world in a process of egocentric assimilation. Adolescent egocentricity is manifested by a belief in the omnipotence of reflection, as though the world should submit itself to idealistic schemes rather than to systems of reality. (pp. 63–64)

Our cognitive abilities are very strong in early adulthood, and they do show adaptation to life's pragmatic concerns. Less clear is whether our logical skills actually decline. Competence as a young adult probably requires doses of both logical thinking skills and pragmatic adaptation to reality. For example, when architects design a building, they logically analyze and plan the structure but understand the cost constraints, the environmental concerns, and the time it will take to do the job effectively.

With the ancient is wisdom; *
and in the lengths of days understanding.

Wisdom, like good wine, is a cognitive ability that may get better with age. What is this thing we call wisdom? **Wisdom** *is expert knowledge about the practical aspects of life* (Baltes & Smith, in press; Baltes & others, in press; Kliegl, Smith, & Baltes, 1989). This practical knowledge involves exceptional insight into human development and life matters, good judgment, and an understanding of how to cope with difficult life problems. Thus, wisdom, more than standard conceptions of intelligence, focuses on life's pragmatic concerns and human conditions. This practical knowledge system takes many years to acquire, accumulating through intentional, planned experiences as well as through incidental experiences. Of course, not all older adults solve practical problems in wise ways. In one recent investigation, only 5 percent of adults' responses to life-planning problems were considered wise, and these wise responses were equally distributed across the early, middle, and late adulthood years (Smith & Baltes, in press).

What does the possibility that older adults are as wise or wiser than younger adults mean in terms of the basic issue of intellectual decline in adulthood? Remember that intelligence comes in different forms. In many instances, older adults are not as intelligent as younger adults when speed of processing is involved, and this probably harms their performance on many traditional school-related tasks and standardized intelligence tests. When we consider general knowledge and wisdom, however, that may be an entirely different matter.

Piagetian Contributions and Criticisms

Piaget was a genius when it came to observing children, and his insights are often surprisingly easy to verify. Piaget showed us some important things to look for in development, including the shift from preoperational to concrete operational thought. He also showed us how we must make experiences fit our cognitive framework yet simultaneously adapt our cognitive orientation to experience. Piaget also revealed how cognitive change is likely to occur if the situation is structured to allow gradual movement to the next higher level.

Piaget's view has not gone unquestioned, however. Four findings question the Piagetian approach to cognitive development (Beilin, 1989; Bjorklund, 1989; Case, 1991a,b; Gelman, 1991; Mandler, 1983; Pascual-Leone & Johnson, 1991; Small, 1990; Spelke, 1991; Sugarman, 1989). First, Piaget

Piaget, shown sitting on a bench, was a genius at observing children. By carefully observing and interviewing children, Piaget constructed his comprehensive theory of children's cognitive development.

Cognitive Development and Piaget's Theory

conceived of stages as unitary structures of thought, so his theory assumes that there is a synchrony in development. That is, various aspects of a stage should emerge at about the same time. However, several concrete operational concepts do not appear in synchrony. For example, children do not learn to conserve at the same time they learn to cross-classify. Second, small changes in the procedures involved in a Piagetian task sometimes have significant effects on a child's cognition. Third, in some cases, children who are at one cognitive stage—such as preoperational thought—can be trained to reason at a higher cognitive stage—such as concrete operational thought. This poses a problem for Piaget, who argued that such training works only on a superficial level and is ineffective unless the child is at a transitional point from one stage to the next. Fourth, some cognitive abilities emerge earlier than Piaget believed, and their subsequent development may be more prolonged than he thought. Conservation of number has been demonstrated in children as young as 3 years of age, although Piaget did not believe that it came about until 7 years of age; some aspects of formal operational thought that involve abstract reasoning do not consistently appear as early in adolescence as Piaget believed. In many developing countries, formal operational thought may be a rare occurrence. To read further about the role of culture in children's cognitive development turn to Cultural Worlds of Development 8.1.

Vygotsky's Theory of Cognitive Development

Children's cognitive development does not occur in a social vacuum. Lev Vygotsky, a Russian psychologist, recognized this important point about children's minds more than half a century ago. Vygotsky's theory is increasingly receiving attention as we move toward the close of the twentieth century (Belmont, 1989; Glick, 1991; Moll, 1991; Rogoff, in press; Rogoff & Morelli, 1989). Before we turn to Vygotsky's ideas on language and thought and culture and society, let's examine his important concept called the zone of proximal development.

Zone of Proximal Development

The **zone of proximal development (ZPD)** *is Vygotsky's term for the range of tasks too difficult for children to master alone but that can be mastered with the guidance and assistance of adults or more highly skilled children.* Thus, the lower limit of the ZPD is the level of problem solving reached by a child working independently. The upper limit is the level of additional responsibility the child can accept with the assistance of an able instructor (see figure 8.12). Vygotsky's emphasis on ZPD underscored his belief in the importance of social influences on cognitive development and the role of instruction in children's development. As children experience verbal instruction or demonstration, they organize information into their existing mental structures so they can eventually perform the skill or task without assistance.

The zone of proximal development is conceptualized as a measure of learning potential. IQ or intelligence quotient, also is a measure of learning potential. However, IQ emphasizes that intelligence is a property of the child, whereas ZPD emphasizes that learning is interpersonal, a dynamic social event that depends on a minimum of two minds, one better informed or more drilled than the other. It is inappropriate to say that the child *has* a ZPD; rather, a child *shares* a ZPD with an instructor.

The practical teaching involved in ZPD begins toward the zone's upper limit, where the child is able to reach a goal only through close collaboration with an instructor. With adequate continuing instruction and practice, the child

Upper limit — Level of additional responsibility child can accept with assistance of an able instructor

Zone of proximal development (ZPD)

Lower limit — Tasks too difficult for children to master alone; level of problem solving reached on these tasks by child working alone

Figure 8.12
Vygotsky's Zone of Proximal Development
Vygotsky's zone of proximal development has a lower limit and an upper limit. Tasks in the ZPD are too difficult for the child to perform alone. They require assistance from an adult or a skilled child. As children experience the verbal instruction or demonstration, they organize the information in their existing mental structures so they can eventually perform the skill or task alone.

organizes and masters the behavioral sequences necessary to perform the target skill. As the instruction continues, the performance transfers from the instructor to the child as the teacher gradually reduces the explanations, hints, and demonstrations until the child is able to perform adequately alone. Once the goal is achieved, it may become the foundation for the development of a new ZPD.

Learning by toddlers provides an example of how the zone of proximal development works. Toddlers have to be motivated and must be involved in activities that involve skill at a reasonably high level of difficulty—that is, toward the zone's upper end. The teacher must have the know-how to exercise the target skill at any level required by the activity, and the teacher must be able to locate and stay in the zone. The teacher and the child also must adapt to each other's requirements. The reciprocal relationship between the toddler and the teacher adjusts dynamically as the division of labor is negotiated and aimed at increasing the weaker partner's share of the goal attainment.

Language and Thought

In Vygotsky's view, a child's mental or cognitive structures are made of relations between mental functions. The relation between language and thought is believed to be especially important in this regard (Langer, 1969; Vygotsky, 1962). Vygotsky said that language and thought initially develop independently of each other but eventually merge.

Two principles govern the merging of thought and language. First, all mental functions have external or social origins. Children must use language and communicate with others before they focus inward to their own mental processes. Second, children must communicate externally and use language for a long period of time before the transition from external to internal speech takes place. This transition period occurs between 3 and 7 years of age and involves talking to oneself. After a while, the self-talk becomes second nature to children and they can act without verbalizing. When this occurs, children have internalized their egocentric speech in the form of inner speech, which becomes their thoughts. Vygotsky believed that children who engage in a large

Culture, Schooling, and Cognitive Development

Consider the following conversation between a researcher and an illiterate Kpelle farmer in the West African country of Liberia (Scribner, 1977):

> *Researcher:* All Kpelle men are rice farmers. Mr. Smith is not a rice farmer. Is he a Kpelle man?
> *Kpelle farmer:* I don't know the man. I have not laid eyes on the man myself.

Members of the Kpelle culture who had gone through formal schooling answered the researcher in a logical way, unlike the illiterate Kpelle farmer above.

Piaget may have underestimated the importance of educational experiences in cognitive development. Many of the activities that have been examined in research on Piaget's cognitive developmental theory—such as conservation, classification, and logical reasoning—have been found to relate to children's, adolescents', and adults' experiences of schooling (Cole & Cole, 1989; Farnham-Diggory, 1990; Lave, 1977; Rogoff, 1981, 1990; Rogoff & Morelli, 1989; Sharp, Cole, & Lave, 1979).

Remembering lists of unrelated objects or classifying them is an unusual, rarely practiced activity outside of literate or school-related tasks (Rogoff, 1990; Rogoff & Morelli, 1989). The categories that are viewed as most appropriate in literate situations may not be valued in other circumstances. For example, in one investigation of the Kpelle culture, individuals were asked to sort 20 objects into categories. The subjects classified the objects into functional groups (a knife with an orange, a potato with a hoe, for example) rather than into the categories the experimenter had had in mind (a knife with a hoe, an orange with a potato, for example) (Glick, 1975). When questioned why they had categorized the objects this way, the Kpelle subjects said that any wise man would know to do things this way. When an exasperated experimenter finally asked, "How would a fool do it?" the subjects described the types of categories that were initially anticipated—piles with food in one, tools in another, and so on.

Individuals who have more schooling, such as older children and people in industrialized societies, may excel on cognitive tasks because not only the skills but also the social contexts of testing resemble the activities practiced in school (Rogoff & Morelli, 1989). In contrast with everyday life, where individuals classify and remember things to accomplish a functional goal, in school and on tests, they perform to satisfy an adult's request to do so. Individuals who have gone to school are likely to have had more experience engaging in cognitive processes at the request of an adult without having a clear practical goal (Rogoff & Mistry, in press).

Researchers have investigated whether special training can improve the conservation skills of children who live in cultures in which the concept of conservation is not widely practiced. For example, in one study, brief training in procedures similar to the standard conservation task improved the performance of rural aboriginal Australian children on the standard beaker conservation task (Dasen, Ngini, & Lavallée, 1979). Even with special training, however, the rural aboriginal children lagged behind children from the Australian city of Canberra in the acquisition of conservation by approximately 3 years, indicating that the aboriginal culture does not provide practice that is relevant to the conservation concept.

The ability to think in scientific ways—to develop hypotheses, to systematically evaluate possible solutions, and to deduce a correct answer to a difficult problem—is an important dimension of formal operational thought. The majority of adolescents in the United States do not think in formal operational ways when presented with scientific reasoning problems, but, in developing countries, an even smaller proportion of adolescents and adults do so (Neimark, 1982). In a cross-cultural investigation that included the United States, Germany, Austria, and Italy, only 7 percent of the eighth-grade students tested reasoned in formal operational ways (Karplus, 1981). However, the adolescents in one Italian group did especially well on formal operational tasks. Closer obser-

amount of private speech are more socially competent than those who do not use it extensively. He argued that private speech represents an early transition in becoming more socially communicative.

Vygotsky's theory challenges Piaget's ideas on language and thought. Vygotsky argued that language, even in its earliest forms, is socially based, whereas Piaget emphasized young children's egocentric and nonsocially oriented speech. According to Vygotsky, young children talk to themselves to govern their behavior and to guide themselves (Duncan, 1991). By contrast, Piaget stressed that young children's egocentric speech reflects social and cognitive immaturity.

The age at which children acquire conservation skills is related to the extent the culture provides practice relevant to the concept of conservation. The children shown here live in India and they have extensive experience as potters. They gain an understanding of the concept of conservation of quantity earlier than children the same age who do not have experience manipulating material such as clay (Cole & Cole, 1989).

vation revealed that these adolescents had been with the same outstanding teacher for 3 consecutive years, suggesting the role of education in instilling formal operational thinking.

Education in the logic of science and mathematics is an important cultural experience that promotes the development of formal operational thinking. Thus, cultural experiences play a much stronger role in formal operational thought than Piaget envisioned.

Culture and Society

Many developmentalists who work in the field of culture and development are comfortable with Vygotsky's theory, which focuses on the sociocultural context of development (Pellegrini & others, 1990; Rogoff & Morelli, 1989). Vygotsky's theory offers a portrayal of human development that is inseparable from social and cultural activities. Vygotsky emphasized how the development of higher mental processes, such as memory, attention, and reasoning, involve learning to use the inventions of society such as language, mathematical systems, and memory devices. He also emphasized how children are aided in development by the guidance of individuals who are already skilled in these tools.

Cultural Similarities and Variations Among Thinking Apprenticeships

According to American developmental psychologist Barbara Rogoff (1990), children's cognitive development is an apprenticeship that occurs through participation in social activity, guided by companions who stretch and support children's understanding of and skill in using the "tools" of the culture. Some of the technologies that are important tools for handling information in a culture are (1) language systems that organize categories of reality and structure ways of approaching situations, (2) literate practices to record information and transform it through written exercises, (3) mathematical systems that handle numerical and spatial problems, and (4) memory strategies to preserve information in memory over time. Some of these technologies have material supports such as pencil and paper, word-processing programs, alphabets, calculators, abacus and slide rule, notches on sticks, and knots on ropes. These tools provide a mechanism for transmitting information from one generation to the next.

In presenting her ideas on apprenticeship in thinking, Rogoff draws heavily on Vygotsky's theory. Rogoff argues that guided participation is widely used around the world, but with important variations in activities for and communication with children in different cultures. The most salient differences focus on the goals of development—what lessons are to be learned—and the means available for children either to observe and participate in culturally important activities or to receive instruction outside the context of skilled activity.

The general processes of guided participation appear around the world. Caregivers and children arrange children's activities and revise children's responsibilities as they gain skill and knowledge. With guidance, children participate in cultural activities that socialize them into skilled activities. For

Figure 8.D
Apprenticeship Training in Guatemala
At about 7 years of age, Mayan girls in Guatemala are assisted in beginning to learn to weave a simple belt, with the loom already set up for them. The young girl shown here is American developmental psychologist Barbara Rogoff's daughter, being taught to weave by a Mayan woman.

■ *Critical Thinking*
How are Vygotsky's and Piaget's theories different? Are their implications for education different? Explain.

Vygotsky's emphasis on the role of culture in cognitive development and society contrasts with Piaget's description of the solitary little scientist.

Vygotsky stressed both the institutional and the interpersonal levels of social contexts. At the institutional level, cultural history provides organizations and tools useful to cognitive activity through such institutions as schools and such inventions as the computer and literacy. Institutional interaction gives children broad behavioral and societal norms to guide their lives. The interpersonal level has a more direct influence on a child's mental functioning. According to Vygotsky (1962), skills in mental functioning develop through immediate social interaction. Information about cognitive tools, skills, and interpersonal relations are transmitted through direct interaction with people.

example, Mayan mothers in Guatemala help their daughters learn to weave in a process of guided participation (Rogoff, 1986) (see figure 8.D). In the United States and in many other nations, the development of prominent and creative thinkers is promoted through interaction with a knowledgeable person rather than by studying books or by attending classes and exhibits (John-Steiner, 1985).

Children begin to practice the skills for using cultural tools, such as literacy, even before the children have contact with the technology. For example, most middle-class American parents involve their children in extensive conversation long before they go to kindergarten or elementary school, and they provide their young children with picture books and read stories to them at bedtime as part of their daily routine. Most middle-class American parents embed their children in a way of life in which reading and writing are integral parts of communication, recreation, and livelihood (Cazden, 1988; Rogoff, 1990).

By contrast, consider the practices of two communities whose children have trouble reading (Heath, 1983). Parents in an Appalachian mill town taught their children respect for the written word but did not involve book characters or information in the children's everyday lives. Their children did well in the first several years of learning to read but had difficulty when required to *use* these literate skills to express themselves or interpret text. Children of rural origin in another mill town learned the skillful and creative use of language but were not taught about books or the style of communication and language used in school. These children had difficulty learning to read, which kept them from using their creative skills with language in the school setting. Early childhood in both of these communities did not include school-

Apprenticeship training is an important aspect of children's cognitive development. Through guided participation, children learn about the skills and tools of their culture. For example, with regard to language, most middle-class American parents give their children a number of picture books, which the parents read to and with the children.

style reading and writing in the context of daily life and, not surprisingly, the children experienced difficulties with literacy in school.

In sum, Rogoff argues that guided participation—the participation of children in skilled cultural activities with other people of varying levels of skill and status—is an important aspect of children's cognitive development. Guided participation may be universal, although communities vary in their goals of socialization and in their means of communication.

Through the organization of these social interactional experiences embedded in a cultural backdrop, children's mental development matures. More information about the role of culture in children's cognitive development appears in Cultural Worlds of Development 8.2, where you will read about cultural similarities and variations in children's thinking apprenticeships.

At this point, we have discussed a number of ideas about concrete operational thought, formal operational thought, the contributions and criticisms of Piaget's theory, and Vygotsky's theory of cognitive development. A summary of these ideas is presented in concept table 8.2. In the next chapter, we will turn our attention to another important view of children's cognitive development—information processing.

Concrete Operational Thought, Formal Operational Thought, Piagetian Contributions and Criticisms, and Vygotsky's Theory of Cognitive Development

Concept	Processes/related ideas	Characteristics/description
Concrete operational thought	Its nature	It is made up of operations, mental actions that are reversible. The concrete operational child shows conservation and classification skills. Conservation involves a horizontal décalage. Concrete operational thought is limited by the inability to reason about abstract matters. Piaget's ideas have been widely applied to children's education. Emphasis is on communication and the belief that the child has many ideas about the world, that the child is always learning and unlearning, and that the child is by nature a knowing creature.
Formal operational thought	Its nature	Piaget believed that formal operational thought comes into play between 11 and 15 years of age. Formal operational thought is more abstract, idealistic, and logical than concrete operational thought. Piaget believed that adolescents become capable of using hypothetical-deductive reasoning. Adolescents develop more sophisticated cognitive strategies for handling words and concepts, as well as prose and writing.
	Adolescent egocentrism	Adolescents develop a special type of egocentrism that involves an imaginary audience and a personal fable about being unique and indestructible.
	Early and late formal operational thought and individual variation	Formal operational thought has two phases—an assimilation phase in which reality is overwhelmed (early adolescence) and an accommodation phase in which intellectual balance is restored through a consolidation of formal operational thought (middle years of adolescence). Individual variation in formal operational thought is extensive. Piaget did not give adequate consideration to individual variation. Many young adolescents are not formal operational thinkers but, rather, are consolidating their concrete operational thought.
	Beyond formal operational thought	Many developmentalists believe that Piaget was incorrect in thinking that formal operational thought is the highest form of cognition. They argue that more pragmatic, specialized thought takes place in early adulthood and that wisdom may increase throughout the adult years.
Piagetian contributions and criticisms	Contributions	Piaget was a genius at observing children. He showed us some important things to look for and mapped out some general cognitive changes.
	Criticisms	Criticisms focus on such matters as stages, which are not as unitary as he believed and do not follow the timetable he envisioned.
Vygotsky's theory of cognitive development	Zone of proximal development	ZPD is Vygotsky's term for tasks too difficult for children to master alone but can be mastered with the guidance and assistance of adults or more highly skilled children.
	Language and thought	Language and thought develop independently and then merge. The merging of language and thought takes place between 3 and 7 years of age and involves talking to oneself.
	Culture and society	Vygotsky's theory stresses how the child's mind develops in the context of the sociocultural world. Cognitive skills develop through social interaction embedded in a cultural backdrop.

Summary

I. Piaget's Place in Developmental Psychology and Cognitive Development Theory

Piaget's contribution to developmental psychology may be as important as Freud's contribution to personality and abnormal psychology. We owe him the present field of cognitive development. Cognitive developmental theory emphasizes the developing child's rational thinking and stages of thought. Thoughts are the central focus of development, the primary determinants of children's action.

II. Cognitive Processes in Piaget's Theory

Adaptation is Piaget's concept for the child's effective interaction with the environment. According to Piaget, the interaction is a cognitive one that involves assimilation and accommodation. Assimilation occurs when children incorporate new information into their existing knowledge. Accommodation occurs when children adjust to new information. Organization is Piaget's concept of grouping isolated behaviors into a higher-order, more smoothly functioning cognitive system. Every level of thought is organized. Equilibration is a mechanism in Piaget's theory invoked to explain how children shift from one stage of thought to the next. The shift occurs as the child experiences cognitive conflict or a disequilibrium in trying to understand the world. Eventually, the child resolves the conflict and reaches a balance, or equilibrium, of thought. Piaget believed there is considerable movement between states of cognitive equilibrium and disequilibrium as assimilation and accommodation work in concert to produce cognitive change.

III. Sensorimotor Thought

The basic features of sensorimotor thought involve the infant's ability to organize and coordinate sensations with physical movements. The stage lasts from birth to about 2 years of age and is nonsymbolic through most of its duration. Sensorimotor thought has six substages: simple reflexes; first habits and primary circular reactions; coordination of secondary circular reactions; tertiary circular reactions, novelty, and curiosity; and internalization of schemes. Object permanence refers to the infant's ability to understand that objects and events continue to exist even though the infant is not in contact with them. Piaget believed that this ability develops over the course of the six substages of sensorimotor thought. In the past decade, a new understanding of infants' cognitive development has occurred. Piaget's theory has been attacked from two sources. First, extensive research in perceptual development suggests that a stable and differentiated perceptual world is established much earlier than Piaget envisioned. Second, researchers recently have found that memory and other forms of symbolic activity occur by at least the second half of the first year.

IV. Preoperational Thought

Preoperational thought is the beginning of the ability to reconstruct at the level of thought what has been established in behavior and a transition from primitive to more sophisticated use of symbols. The child does not yet think in an operational way. Operations are internalized sets of actions that allow a child to do mentally what was done physically before. The symbolic function substage occurs roughly between 2 and 4 years of age. The ability to think symbolically and represent the world mentally develops. Thought still has several important limitations, two of which are egocentrism and animism. The intuitive thought substage stretches from approximately 4 to 7 years of age. The substage is called intuitive because, on one hand, children seem very sure of their knowledge, yet on the other hand, they are unaware of how they know what they know. The preoperational child lacks conservation, the idea that an amount stays the same or is conserved regardless of how the shape of the container changes. One of the main reasons young children cannot conserve is the process of centration, or focusing of attention on one characteristic to the exclusion of all others. Gelman believes that conservation occurs earlier than Piaget thought it did and that the process of attention is important in its appearance. The preoperational child also asks a barrage of questions, showing an interest in reasoning and finding out why things are the way they are.

V. Concrete Operational Thought

Concrete operational thought is made up of operations, which are mental actions that are reversible. The concrete operational child shows conservation and classification skills. Conservation involves a horizontal décalage. Concrete operational thought is limited by the inability to reason about abstract matters. Piaget's ideas have been widely applied to children's education. Emphasis is on communication and the belief that the child has many ideas about the world, that the child is always learning and unlearning, and that the child is by nature a knowing creature.

VI. The Nature of Formal Operational Thought and Adolescent Egocentrism

Piaget believed that formal operational thought comes into play between 11 and 15 years of age. Formal operational thought is more abstract, idealistic, and logical than concrete operational thought. Piaget believed that adolescents become capable of using hypothetical-deductive reasoning. Adolescents develop more sophisticated strategies for handling words and concepts, as well as prose and writing. Adolescents also develop a special type of egocentrism that involves an imaginary audience and a personal fable about being unique and indestructible.

VII. Early and Late Formal Operational Thought, Individual Variation, and Beyond Formal Operational Thought

Formal operational thought has two phases—an assimilation phase, in which reality is overwhelmed (early adolescence), and an accommodation phase, in which intellectual balance is restored through a consolidation of formal operational thought (middle years of adolescence). Individual variation in formal operational thought is extensive. Piaget did not give adequate consideration to individual variation. Many young adolescents are not formal operational thinkers but, rather, are consolidating their concrete operational thought. Many developmentalists believe that Piaget was incorrect in thinking that formal-operational thought is the highest form of cognition. They argue that more pragmatic, specialized thought takes place in early adulthood and that wisdom may increase throughout the adult years.

VIII. Piagetian Contributions and Criticisms

Piaget was a genius at observing children and he developed fascinating insights about children's cognition; he showed us some important things to look for in development and mapped out some general cognitive changes in development. Criticisms of Piaget focus on the belief that the stages are not as unitary as he thought, that small changes in procedures affect the child's cognition, that children can sometimes be trained to think at higher stages, that some cognitive skills appear earlier than Piaget thought, and that others are more protracted than he thought. Vygotsky's theory has received increased attention in recent years. Vygotsky emphasized the importance of the zone of proximal development, which has a lower limit and an upper limit. The lower limit is the level of problem solving the child reaches when working independently; the upper level is the additional responsibility the child can accept with the assistance of an able instructor. Vygotsky said that language and thought develop independently, then merge between 3 and 7 years of age, with a key factor being internal speech, or talking to oneself. Vygotsky's theory stresses how the child's mind develops in the sociocultural world. Cognitive skills develop through social interaction embedded in a cultural backdrop.

Key Terms

adaptation 258
organization 258
equilibration 259
scheme 260
simple reflexes 260
first habits and primary circular reactions 260
primary circular reactions 261
secondary circular reactions 261
coordination of secondary circular reactions 261
tertiary circular reactions, novelty, and curiosity 261
tertiary circular reactions 261
internalization of schemes 261
object permanence 262
A$\overline{\text{B}}$ error 264

operations 266
symbolic function substage 266
egocentrism 267
animism 270
intuitive thought substage 270
centration 270
conservation 270
horizontal décalage 276
hypothetical-deductive reasoning 280
satire 280
metaphor 280
adolescent egocentrism 282
imaginary audience 282
personal fable 282
wisdom 285
zone of proximal development (ZPD) 286

Suggested Readings

Cowan, P. A. (1978). *Piaget with feeling: Cognitive, social, and emotional dimensions.* New York: Holt, Rinehart & Winston. Philip Cowan, a clinical psychologist at the University of California, Berkeley, like many clinicians, believes that Piaget has more to tell us about socioemotional development than Piaget himself thought.

Flavell, J. H. (1985). *Cognitive development* (2nd ed.). Englewood Cliffs, NJ: Prentice-Hall. This is an excellent statement of contemporary thinking about children's cognitive development by one of the leading scholars in the field. Although inspired by Piaget's work, the author goes well beyond it, offering new insights, critical evaluations, and reflections about his own research.

Furth, H. G., & Wachs, H. (1975). *Thinking goes to school.* New York: Oxford University Press. This intriguing application of Piaget's ideas to education includes 179 thinking games that can be incorporated into the everyday teaching of children.

Ginsburg, H., & Opper, S. (1988). *Piaget's theory of intellectual development* (3rd ed.). Englewood Cliffs, NJ: Prentice-Hall. This text is one of the best explanations and descriptions of Piaget's theory of development.

Piaget, J. (1987). (H. Feider, Trans.). *Possibility and necessity.* Minneapolis: University of Minnesota Press. Children's understanding of possibility and how they learn to choose among alternatives were of major interest to Piaget late in his life. This book describes a number of problems Piaget devised to assess these possibilities and choices.

Rogoff, B. (1990). *Apprenticeship in thinking: Cognitive development in social context.* New York: Oxford University Press. One of the leading scholars in research on the cultural contexts of cognitive development, Barbara Rogoff describes the important roles that social and cultural interaction play in cognitive development.

CHAPTER

9

INFORMATION PROCESSING

The Nature of Information Processing
    Framework
    Developmental Change
    Perspective on Child Development 9.1: "Ask If
        the Computer Ever Eats Breakfast"
Elementary Cognitive Processes Necessary to Process
  Information
    Attention
    Memory
Higher-Order Cognitive Processes
    Problem Solving
    Cognitive Monitoring
    Critical Thinking
Knowledge and Expertise
    Perspective on Child Development 9.2:
        Information Processing, the Information
        Age, and Children's Education
    Knowledge
    Expertise
    Cultural Worlds of Development 9.1: Cultural
        Literacy
Individual Differences in Information Processing
Summary
Key Terms
Suggested Readings
Answer to Inoperable Tumor Problem

The mind is an enchanting thing.

—Marianne Moore

Sam Winters, a fifth-grade student, leaves his book on the dining room table and goes off to school. It is a popular novel, written for 9-to-12-year-olds, describing how two children strike up a friendship in a rural elementary school in contemporary Maryland. The book is entitled *Bridge to Terabithia;* the author, Katherine Paterson, won a Newbery Award for one of her children's novels in 1981.

Sam's 3-year-old sister Nancy spies the inviting cover of the book shortly after Sam has left, swoops it up, and heads to her room to "read" it. Nancy stares at the book's cover drawing of two children for a while and then turns the book upside down to contemplate what the drawing looks like from that perspective. A few moments later, Nancy is poring over the story. A quick "reader," Nancy finishes the entire 128-page book in about 6 minutes. In that 6 minutes, she studies each of the twelve drawings in the book and thinks to herself what each drawing represents. Nancy also picks out several capital letters she knows (B, A, D, Z, M, N, C, Y) and spots some familiar numbers on different pages (0, 1, 3, 6). She returns the book to the dining room table when she has finished.

Sam comes home from school at noon to have lunch. After wolfing down his hamburger, he decides to spend a little time reading and picks up *Bridge to Terabithia*. He sits quietly for 15 minutes and reads the eight pages of chapter 2, which introduce a new character, Leslie—a bright 11-year-old girl. A few of the words in the chapter are unfamiliar, but Sam gets the idea that Leslie looks like a boy, she says whatever she pleases, and she knows a lot about everything. The other character in the story, Jess, sort of likes her and Sam figures that the rest of the book will be about the two of them.

Nancy, still eating lunch, hollers over to Sam, "Did you finish the book? I did!"

Sam smiles. "You can't read this book, Nancy. You're just a little kid."

Their mother intervenes to prevent a predictable fight. "Well, tell us what you read, Nancy."

"A boy . . . um . . . a girl . . . a little dog house . . . a *B*, a 6."

Sam laughs and Mrs. Winters compliments Nancy for reading so well. After Sam has gone back to school and Nancy is occupied with her crayons and coloring book, Mrs. Winters sits down with *Bridge to Terabithia* to see what she can learn about the novel. She skims the book in 20 minutes, forming a general idea of the plot outline. As she reads, she makes some mental notes about words and concepts she'd discuss at a later time with Sam, because she is fairly certain he doesn't know them. She also considers whether the book is a good selection for Sam. Is the book's difficulty level about right, given her assessment of his reading skills and will Sam assimilate the moral lessons the author is trying to communicate?

When we read, we process information and interpret it; thus, reading serves as a practical and simple example in discussing the topic of information processing in childhood, the focus of this chapter. The study of information processing is concerned with how children analyze the many sources of physical information available to them in the environment and how they make sense of these experiences. When we read, for example, a rich and complex set of visual symbols is available to our senses. The symbols are associated with sounds, the sounds are combined to form words, and the words and larger units that contain them (phrases, sentences, paragraphs) have conventional meanings.

To read effectively, we have to perceive and attend to these symbols. Notice that, whereas Sam and Mrs. Winters attend to words and sentences, Nancy primarily attends to pictures, letters of the alphabet, and printed numbers. Another process in reading is holding the information we attend to in memory while we take in new information. Notice that Mrs. Winters, because she can read much faster than Sam, is able to hold meanings "skimmed" from the entire novel in mind during a 20-minute reading session, whereas Sam holds the meanings from only one chapter in memory.

The study of children's information processing is concerned with basic processes such as perception (which we discussed in chapter 5), attention, memory, and thinking. In this chapter, we will consider these processes and other aspects of information processing, beginning with an overview of information processing. Then follows a description of three major facets of information processing—elementary processes, higher-order processes, and the role of knowledge. Finally, we will discuss individual differences in information processing.

The Nature of Information Processing

Information processing is at once a framework for thinking about children's development and a facet of that development. As a framework, information processing includes certain ideas about how people's minds work and the best methods for studying this. As a facet of development, we can think of the different aspects of information processing that change as children mature. For example, changes in children's attention and memory capabilities are, in effect, changes in information-processing capabilities. In the discussion that follows, we will turn our attention first to information processing as a framework.

Framework

For many experts, the *information-processing approach* is a framework for understanding how children learn and think (Siegler, 1983, 1986; Siegler & Campbell, 1989). It assumes that, to understand children's learning and thinking, we need to analyze the way children take in information (sights, sounds, smells, and so on), how they store the information, and how they evaluate it for some clearly defined purposes and goals. Concepts of learning, if you remember from chapter 7, focus on behaviors and the events in the environment that change these behaviors. Traditional principles of learning do little to explain what is going on in a child's mind, however. Piagetian theory, on the other hand, has quite a lot to say about the child's mind. For example, Piaget described the ways in which a child structures thought at different ages; these are the stage descriptions of sensorimotor, preoperational, concrete, and formal operational thought. The Piagetian description is general; it doesn't tell us much about how the child reads, solves mathematical problems, learns new scientific facts, or composes an essay. It leaves out a lot of important details about how the mind actually works on specific kinds of tasks such as reading, writing, doing arithmetic, and solving a variety of problems. The information-processing framework attempts to correct the shortcomings of traditional

Our life is what our thoughts make it.
—Marcus Aurelius

learning theory and Piagetian ideas about development. It describes mental processes and offers specific details about how these processes work in concrete situations. Where possible, these descriptions include analyses of all the steps needed to complete a task, the specific mental processes needed to complete these steps, and precise mathematical estimates of how "hard" or how "long" the mind has to work to execute these steps. Often, information-processing psychologists try to write computer programs to represent the steps needed to solve problems. Computer "models" of how something is done force scientists to be precise. Computers are basically "dumb" machines. They do only what one tells them to do. If a dumb machine can be made to complete a task, so goes the reasoning, we will have an exhaustive understanding of everything that a person might possibly need to complete the task. In practice, it is not possible to list every step for such complex activities as reading and writing, but we can study particular features of these activities and try to understand them in great detail (Anderson, 1988; Siegler, 1991). To summarize, information processing, as a framework for studying children's development, attempts to be detailed about the mental processes underlying learning and thinking in very specific situations and, where possible, to model the specific steps needed to complete a task using computer programs and mathematical estimates of mental activities.

Let's consider an example of how the information-processing approach differs from the learning and Piagetian approaches. Suppose we observe a third-grade student attempting to perform some subtraction problems—for example, 176 minus 47, 395 minus 46, and 272 minus 34, written out in the usual form:

$$\begin{array}{ccc} 176 & 395 & 272 \\ -47 & -46 & -34 \end{array}$$

The student calculates the answers to be 21, 241, and 132, respectively. It will help you to write out these problems on a piece of paper, calculate the correct answers, and then note the incorrect answers provided by our hypothetical third-grader. Can you figure out the student's errors? Why were these errors made?

Learning theory might explain these mistakes by arguing that the child has not yet learned the correct "behavior" of "borrowing" numbers. There has been insufficient practice, modeling, and/or reinforcement for the child. Piagetian theory would have little to say about these problems. Information-processing theory, on the other hand, would give a detailed description of all the steps needed to solve these arithmetic problems (Brown & Burton, 1978) and predict precisely when a child would and would not have difficulty, based on an explanation of the child's flaws. What are the steps? A partial list includes: (1) recognizing that each is a subtraction problem, (2) understanding which number is to be subtracted from which other number, (3) beginning to subtract the right-most digit on the bottom from the corresponding top digit, (4) realizing that step 3 cannot be done immediately, (5) borrowing 10 from the 10's column, (6) marking the new value of the 10's column, (7) marking 1 to represent the borrowed 10 near the top of the digit's column, (8) performing the new subtraction, (9) repeating the process for the 10's column, and so on.

What are the flaws present in this child's subtraction? There seem to be two "bugs," as they sometimes have been called (Brown & Burton, 1978). First, even though the child may borrow from the 10's column, he still performs the first (digit's column) subtraction incorrectly—ignoring the bor-

Man is but a reed, the weakest in nature; but he is a thinking reed.

—Pascal

Computers have played an important role in the development of the information-processing approach. Often, information-processing psychologists try to write a computer program to represent the steps necessary to solve a particular problem.

Learning, Cognition, and Language Development

rowed number and choosing to subtract the smaller digit's value number on top from the larger one on the bottom. The 10's column subtraction is performed correctly, because the higher and lower numbers are in the locations that the child would expect (top and bottom, respectively). The second "bug" occurs when we move to the 100's column. The child has incorrectly continued to borrow and has reduced the value of the 100's digit, when no borrowing was necessary.

The value of this information-processing analysis, even though it becomes tedious when it is spelled out in such great detail, is that it forces us to consider exactly what the child may be doing and exactly what his procedural "bugs" are. If you know precisely how children think about this task, you have a good beginning point for trying to change and improve their thinking.

Earlier we indicated that an information-processing psychologist may try to write a computer program to represent the steps needed to solve a problem; information-processing psychologists sometimes rely on computers to tell them something about the way children's cognition works (Burns & Parlett, 1991; Redfield & Steuck, 1991). **Artificial intelligence** *is the branch of computer science devoted to creating computers capable of handling complicated tasks that require some "thinking."* Since true "thinking" is usually considered to be a human activity, computer "thought" is dubbed *artificial* when computers play chess, solve math problems, create designs, guide industrial robots, and "see" enemy aircraft approaching (Freedle, 1990; VanLehn, 1991). What is artificial about it? Computers do not have human brains and a central nervous system, so, physically, computers operate differently than people do. Human beings also do not think in a strictly logical fashion; they are intuitive and emotional, even when working on the logical problems of physics and math. As you might be aware, debate rages as to whether computers will ever achieve the powers of human thought (Dreyfus & Dreyfus, 1986). Some computer scientists feel that the best computers already have accomplished this goal. Critics argue that the highest forms of human intelligence have not been created and simply cannot be modeled in a machine. More about this fascinating issue appears in Perspective on Child Development 9.1.

Developmental Change

In general, then, what aspects of information processing change as children mature? How can these changes be described? There are two equally good answers. One is of the "life just is not simple" variety; that is, there are no compelling general changes. The nature of information processing is such that, to understand how younger children differ from older children, we have to examine specific processes (such as attention and memory) and tasks (such as reading, writing, and communicating), observing how children differ on each of them. Much of the remainder of this chapter details this answer, process by process.

You might have anticipated the second answer. It is exactly the opposite of the first. Information processing is complicated, but there are some general features of it that readily distinguish the ways children at different ages perform a variety of mental processes and tasks. It is possible, then, to offer a modest and general description of developmental changes in information processing without getting bogged down in details. What are these general features? Three important ones are processing speed, processing capacity, and automaticity, each of which we will consider in turn.

"Ask If the Computer Ever Eats Breakfast"

Without trying to settle the computer-human debate, Richard Lehrer and Steven Yussen (1988) conducted an investigation with children and adults to discover what ideas these everyday "experts" have about the similarities and differences between human thought/intelligence and the everyday intelligence present in typical computers. Children in the third, fifth, eighth, eleventh, and twelfth grades and university students were asked to respond to a series of questions, such as the following: What is intelligence? Are computers and people intelligent in the same way, or are they different? Do computers think about what they are doing—for example, whether or not they are solving a problem correctly, as people do? Do computers have many different feelings, as people do, such as happy, sad, excited, tired, bored? What question might you ask that you would be sure to get a different answer from a person and from a computer?

The elementary school children in this study frequently cited physical differences between people and computers. For example, their responses included: "Computers can't see!" "Ask if it ever eats breakfast. A computer will have to say no, but a person will have to say yes," and "Ask if it swims."

Although these children generally regarded computers as nonfeeling things, they did believe that computers could feel certain emotions, such as "excited" and "tired." The children explained that a computer might get excited if it figured out a hard problem and tired if it was on for a long time.

The adolescents and adults were more likely to distinguish between computers and humans on the basis of internal, mental properties. For example, they frequently mentioned the extraordinary speed and memory capacities of computers (for example, "Computers can do things much faster than people," and "if you gave it a problem like 3,688 times 4,266, a computer could get it right"). They also commented on the computer's lack of flexibility in problem solving and the stereotyped responses it would give in response to a question. They also strongly stated that a computer could not experience any type of emotion.

The differences between natural and artificial intelligence and thought, then, are interpreted in different ways depending on age, although there is not necessarily any one correct set of ideas about this distinction. Rather, this concept changes with development and experience.

Processing Speed

Many things children do are constrained by how much time is available (Geary & Brown, 1991). A child is told to finish writing a letter in 5 minutes so the family can leave. A phone message must be written down before it is forgotten. The teacher gives children 5 minutes to finish a series of arithmetic problems. There is abundant evidence that the speed with which such tasks is completed improves dramatically across the childhood years (Kail, 1988; Stigler, Nusbaum, & Chalip, 1988). In fact, it is difficult to find any cognitive tasks for which there is *not* some striking developmental change. The causes of the change are not always clear, however. Is a 7-year-old slower to write down a phone message than a 13-year-old because of limitations in the physical act of writing or because of other, more mental limitations such as the time needed to think of how to spell words correctly or to summarize a message briefly? Are such differences readily overcome by concentrated practice or will such age differences persist despite practice, suggesting some maturational, central nervous system differences in maturity?

In one recent study, evidence that processing speed continues to improve in early adolescence was found (Hale, 1990). Ten-year-olds were approximately 1.8 times slower in processing information than young adults on such tasks as reaction time, letter matching, mental rotation, and abstract matching. Twelve-year-olds were approximately 1.5 times slower than young adults, but 15-year-olds processed information on the tasks as fast as the young adults.

Processing Capacity

Information-processing capacity can be viewed as a type of mental energy needed to perform mental work. Our difficulty in dividing attention between two things at once is attributed to our limits on capacity. So also is the trouble we have performing complex tasks (such as mentally working complicated arithmetic problems). Although capacity is believed to be limited at all ages, there is no generally accepted measure of a child's capacity; thus, the findings are ambiguous. For example, it is possible that capacity does not change with age but that young children must spend more capacity on lower-level processes (such as identifying stimuli), leaving less capacity for higher-level processes (such as dividing attention or performing complex computations).

Automaticity

Automaticity *is the ability to process information with little or no effort*. Consider a bright 4-year-old, who picks up some crayons and quickly labels them— yellow, green, brown, blue, and red. An able 10-year-old zips through a practice list of single-digit addition problems (for instance, 5 + 8) with little conscious effort. An adult picks up a newspaper and quickly reads a lead paragraph that reveals the results of an important basketball game held the previous evening. Each of these examples illustrates relatively automatic information processing. By comparison, imagine a 4-year-old trying to sound out the words in a primer, a 10-year-old doing long division with three-to-five-digit numbers, or an adult trying to decipher the meaning of a lead news paragraph in a foreign language studied years ago in high school. These activities require considerable mental processing and effort. Although automatic processing can probably be performed at the same time the individual is completing another (parallel) activity, effortful tasks such as these demand single-minded direction and focus. For any given task, such as calculating, reading, or writing, children's automaticity—the ability to perform automatically with little or no effort—improves dramatically as children get older (Brown & others, 1983; Keating, 1990b; Siegler, 1986). Automaticity is linked to speed and processing capacity; as an activity is completed faster, it requires less processing capacity. As processing capacity increases, it becomes easier to complete tasks that were previously considered to be difficult.

Among the developmental changes in information processing are those involving processing speed, processing capacity, and automaticity. This adolescent studying for a test can process information faster, has more processing capacity, and processes information more automatically than when she was a child.

Elementary Cognitive Processes Necessary to Process Information

What are the elementary processes necessary for children to process information about their world? They are attention and memory, each of which we will consider in turn.

Attention

"Pay attention" is a phrase children hear all of the time. Just what is attention? **Attention** *is the concentration and focusing of mental effort. Attention also is both selective and shifting.* For example, when children take a test, they must attend to it. This implies that they have the ability to focus their mental effort on certain stimuli (the test questions) while excluding other stimuli, an important aspect of attention called *selectivity*. When selective attention fails children, they have difficulty ignoring information that is irrelevant to their interests or goals (Posner & Rothbart, 1989). For example, if a

This young boy's attention is riveted on the dandelion he has just picked; so is the dog's attention. Preschool children are able to attend for longer periods of time than infants are.

television set or stereo is blaring while a child is studying, the child may have difficulty concentrating.

Not only is attention selective, but it is also *shiftable.* If a teacher asks students to pay attention to a certain question and they do so, their behavior indicates they can shift the focus of their mental effort from one stimulus to another. If the telephone rings while an adolescent is studying, the adolescent may shift attention from studying to the telephone. An external stimulus is not necessary to elicit an attention shift. At any moment children may be able to shift their attention from one topic to another virtually at will. They might think about the last time they played basketball, then think about the last time they played soccer, then think about the upcoming baseball game, and so on.

How does attention develop in children? Remember from chapter 7 that attention was discussed in the context of habituation, which is something like being bored in the sense that infants become disinterested in a stimulus and no longer attend to it. The importance of these aspects of attention in infancy for later development was underscored by research indicating that both decrement and recovery of attention—when measured in the first 6 months of life—were associated with higher intelligence toward the end of the preschool years (Bornstein & Sigman, 1986). Although the infant's attention has important implications for cognitive development in the preschool years, significant changes in a child's ability to pay attention take place during this time (Pillow, 1988; Ruff & Lawson, 1990). The toddler wanders around, shifting attention from one activity to another, usually seeming to spend little time focused on any one object or event. By comparison, the preschool child might be observed watching television for a half hour.

The changes in ability to pay attention continue beyond the preschool years into the elementary school years. In the classroom, children are able to observe the teacher for extended periods of time, and they can pour over their books in long hours of independent study. These demands on attention exceed what was required of the preschooler, who is generally free to move about in

Learning, Cognition, and Language Development

Figure 9.1
A Sample of the Stimuli in Vurpillot's Study: Two Identical Houses and Two Different Houses
In Vurpillot's experiment, children were shown these two pairs of houses. In the top pair, the houses are different from each other; in the bottom pair, they are the same. To determine that the top two are different and the bottom two are the same, children have to scan the pictures systematically, comparing them feature by feature. Observations of 6- and 9-year-old children's eye movements indicated they systematically scanned the features of the houses, but observations of 4-year-old children's eye movements indicated they did not.

various play activities. These apparent changes in attention have a dramatic influence on children's learning (Stevenson, 1972).

The development of the strategic use of attention is aptly shown in a study of visual scanning (Vurpillot, 1968). Children were shown two similar pictures and asked to judge whether the two were identical (see figure 9.1). To perform well on this task, the children had to scan the pictures systematically, comparing them feature by feature. Observations of 6- and 9-year-old children's eye-movement patterns suggested they were systematically scanning the pictures, but observations of 4-year-old children suggested they were not.

One deficit in attention during the preschool years concerns the dimensions that stand out, or are *salient,* compared with those that are relevant to solving a problem or performing well on a task. For example, a problem might have a flashy, attractive clown that presents the directions for solving the problem. Preschool children are influenced strongly by the features of the task that stand out—such as the flashy, attractive clown. After the age of 6 or 7, children attend more efficiently to the dimensions of the task that are relevant—such as the directions for solving a problem. Developmentalists believe that this change reflects a shift to cognitive control of attention so that children act less precipitously and reflect more (Paris & Lindauer, 1982).

Memory

There are few moments when children's lives are not steeped in memory. Memory is at work with each step children take, each thought they think, and each word they utter. **Memory** *is the retention of information over time. It is central to mental life and to information processing.* To successfully learn and reason, children need to hold on to information and to retrieve the information they have tucked away. Two important memory systems are short-term memory and long-term memory. **Short-term memory** *is a limited-capacity memory system in which information is retained for as long as 30 seconds, unless the information is rehearsed, in which case it can be retained longer.* **Long-term memory** *is a relatively permanent memory system, which holds huge amounts of information for a long period of time.*

Short-Term Memory

As a child listens to instructions from her mother, to directions from a teacher, or to a story on television, the information she encounters lasts for a short while in her memory. For this information to last longer, it has to be elaborated or transformed in order to move into long-term memory, which may last for years. A child's short-term memory is severely limited, as is the short-term memory of an adult. Only a handful of "bits" of information can be handled. Many years ago, cognitive scientist George Miller (1956) suggested that memory's limit is seven plus or minus two bits of information. If too much information is encountered, some of the information circulating in short-term memory is displaced and may be lost forever.

One way to illustrate this is to present a list of items to children to remember, perhaps the most common method for studying short-term memory in psychology (Case, 1985). A task that has been used in this manner is the memory span task. If you have taken an IQ test, you probably were exposed to one of these tasks. A short list of stimuli—usually digits—are presented at a rapid pace (for example, one per second). Then you are asked to repeat the digits. Research with the memory span task suggests that short-term memory increases during early childhood. For example, in one investigation, memory span increased from about two digits in 2-to-3-year-old children to about five digits in 7-year-old children; however, between 7 and 13 years of age, memory span increased only by one and one half digits (Dempster, 1981) (see figure 9.2). Keep in mind, though, that memory is affected by individual differences, which is why IQ and various aptitude tests are used.

Why are there age differences in memory span? Rehearsal of information seems important—older children rehearse the digits more than younger children do. Also important are the speed and efficiency of information processing, especially the speed with which memory items can be identified. For example, in one investigation, children were tested on their speed of repeating auditorially presented words (Case, Kurland, & Goldberg, 1982). Speed of repetition strongly predicted memory span using these same words. When speed of repetition was controlled, the 6-year-olds' memory spans were equal to those of young adults.

Long-Term Memory

Remember that long-term memory retains information indefinitely—it can be used over and over again. Is the same pattern of developmental change found for short-term memory also found for long-term memory? Long-term memory

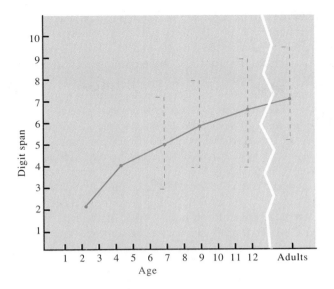

Figure 9.2
Changes in Children's Memory Span
Memory span increased from about two digits in 2-to-3-year-old children to about five digits in 7-year-old children. Between 7 and 13 years of age, memory span increased by only 1½ digits. The solid line represents developmental differences and the dashed lines represent individual differences (Dempster, 1981).

shows a different developmental pattern: Long-term memory increases with age during middle and late childhood; long-term memory depends on the activities individuals engage in when learning and remembering information (Siegler & Campbell, 1989).

Strategies *are cognitive processes that do not occur automatically but require work and effort. They are under the learner's conscious control and can be used to improve memory.* Four important strategies that improve children's memory are rehearsal, organization, elaboration, and imagery.

Rehearsal *is extended repetition of material after it has been presented.* If someone tells a child to remember a phone number, how might the child remember it more effectively? A classic study by John Flavell and his colleagues (Flavell, Beach, & Chinsky, 1966) illustrates the importance of rehearsal and developmental changes in its use. Children from 5 to 10 years old were given the task of remembering the names of a set of two to five pictures for 15 seconds. The novel feature of the experiment was that the experimenter was a trained lip-reader. Some of the children made lip movements showing rehearsal of names and pictures. The percentage of children making lip movements increased with age—10 percent of the 5-year-olds, 60 percent of the 7-year-olds, and 85 percent of the 10-year-olds. In a later study of 6-year-olds, the research team found that children who rehearsed showed better recall than those who did not. When nonrehearsers were taught to rehearse, their performance rivaled that of the spontaneous rehearsers (Keeney, Cannizzo, & Flavell, 1967). More recent investigations make the interesting point that rudimentary, rehearsallike processes begin to appear at very young ages (DeLoache, Cassidy, & Brown, 1985; Wellman, Ritter, & Flavell, 1985). In one study, 3- and 4-year-old children watched a toy dog being hidden under one of three cups. Instructed to remember where the dog was hidden, the children looked at, pointed to, and touched the appropriate cup (Wellman, Ritter, & Flavell, 1985).

Organization *is the grouping or arranging of items into categories.* The use of organization improves long-term memory. Children show increased organization in middle and late childhood. In one investigation, children were presented with a circular array of pictures from four categories: clothing, furniture, animals, and vehicles (Moely & others, 1969). The children were told

My thoughts are my company; I can bring them together, select them, detain them, dismiss them.

—Walter Savage Landor

Figure 9.3
The Keyword Method
To help children remember the state capitals, the keyword method was used. A special component of the keyword method is the use of mental imagery, which was stimulated by presenting the children with a vivid visual image, such as two apples being married. The strategy is to help the children associate *apple* with Annapolis and *marry* with Maryland (Levin, 1980).

to study the pictures so that later they could say their names back to the experimenter. They also were told they could move the pictures around to remember them better. The 10- and 11-year-olds performed such groupings; the younger children did not. When younger children were put through a brief training procedure that encouraged grouping, they were able to follow this strategy, and their memory for the pictures improved.

Elaboration *is the use of more extensive processing of information, often in the form of association.* For example, children's understanding of the concept of *travel* will be enhanced if they can come up with examples of different ways they have traveled—such as by car, by boat, or by plane—rather than simply memorizing the definition of the word *travel*. Thinking of examples of a concept is a good way to understand it. Self-reference is another effective way to elaborate information. For example, if the word *win* is on a list of words to remember, children might think of the last time they won a bicycle race with a friend, or, if the word *cook* appears, they might imagine the last time their father cooked dinner. In general, elaboration is an excellent way to remember (Schacter & McGlynn, 1989).

One reason that elaboration enhances memory is that it adds to the *distinctiveness* of the memory code (Ellis, 1987). To remember a piece of information, such as a name, an experience, or a fact about geography, a child needs to search for the code that contains this information among the mass of codes in the child's long-term memory. The search process is easier if the code is somehow unique. The situation is like a child searching for a friend in a crowded park. If the child's friend has a highly distinctive appearance, the child will more easily find the friend in the park. Similarly, highly distinctive memory codes are more easily differentiated from other memory codes.

Developmental psychologists have found that, as children get older, they are more likely to use elaborative strategies (without being instructed to do so). There are especially impressive increases in the use of elaboration from late childhood to late adolescence (Schneider & Pressley, 1989). However, elementary-school-aged children benefit considerably from instruction on using elaboration in remembering information (Rohwer & Bean, 1973).

Imagine walking up the sidewalk to your house, opening the door, and going inside. What do you see when you are standing inside the door? Now mentally walk through the house to a room in the back and form a picture of what this room is like. Now picture your bedroom in the house. Where is your bed in relation to the door? Imagining these things is reasonably easy for most adults and children. **Imagery** *refers to sensations without the presence of an external stimulus* (Paivio, 1986). Imagery is another strategy that enables children to improve their memory. The **keyword method** *is a powerful imagery strategy that uses vivid imagery of important words, or keywords, to improve memory.* This method has been used to practical advantage by teaching children how to master new information rapidly such as foreign vocabulary words, the states and capitals of the United States, and the names of Presidents of the United States. For example, in teaching children that Annapolis is the capital of Maryland, instructors taught the children the keywords for the states, such that when a state was given (*Maryland*), the children could supply the keyword (*marry*) (Levin, 1980). Then, children were given the reverse type of keyword practice with the capitals. That is, they had to respond with the capital (*Annapolis*) when given a keyword (*apple*). Finally, an illustration was provided (see figure 9.3). The keyword strategy's use of vivid mental imagery, such as the image in figure 9.3, was effective in increasing children's memory

Learning, Cognition, and Language Development

CONCEPT TABLE 9.1
The Nature of Information Processing and the Elementary Cognitive Processes Necessary to Process Information

Concept	Processes/related ideas	Characteristics/description
The nature of information processing	Framework	The information-processing approach attempts to be very detailed about the mental processes underlying learning and thinking in specific situations and, where possible, to model the specific steps needed to complete a task using computer programs and mathematical estimates of mental activities.
	Development	The information-processing approach emphasizes that, with age, children's processing speed, processing capacity, and automaticity increase.
Elementary cognitive processes necessary to process information	Attention	Attention is the concentration and focusing of mental effort. Attention is both selective and shifting. In infancy, attention is often studied through habituation experiments. Children's attention increases dramatically in the preschool years and becomes even more efficient in the elementary school years. During the elementary school years, scanning of visual patterns and attention to relevant dimensions of problems increase.
	Memory	Memory is the retention of information over time. Two important memory systems are short-term memory and long-term memory. Short-term memory is a limited-capacity memory system in which information is retained for as long as 30 seconds, unless the information is rehearsed, in which case it can be retained longer. Long-term memory is a relatively permanent memory system, which holds huge amounts of information for a long period of time. There is evidence that short-term memory improves the most during the preschool years, long-term memory the most during the elementary school years.
	Memory strategies	Memory strategies are cognitive processes that do not occur automatically but require work and effort. They are under the learner's control and can be used to improve memory. Four important strategies are rehearsal, organization, elaboration, and imagery. As children get older, they become more likely to use these strategies without being instructed to do so, but instructions to children to use the strategies usually improve their memory.

of state capitals. Developmentalists today encourage the use of imagery in our nation's schools, believing it helps increase children's memory (McDaniel & Pressley, 1987).

In one recent study, four aspects of visual imagery—image generation, maintenance, scanning, and rotation—were studied in 5-, 8-, and 14-year-old children (Kosslyn & others, 1990). There was no evidence that the younger children used fewer processing components to carry out these imagery tasks, although the younger children were relatively poor at scanning, rotating, and generating images, but relatively good at maintaining images. The observed age differences document that imagery is not a single ability, even in young children.

At this point, we have discussed a number of ideas about the nature of the information-processing approach and about the elementary processes of attention and memory. A summary of these ideas appears in concept table 9.1.

Higher-Order Cognitive Processes

The use of attention and memory may occur rather quickly as children examine information or attempt to complete a task. Children may devote little effort and complete the new activity quickly. By contrast, a variety of activities usually occur over an extended period of time and require the mobilization of considerable cognitive resources on the part of children. When children read or write, for example, the activity usually extends over a period of time, and, when children encounter a difficulty or lapse of attention, they must overcome the temporary impasse and get back on track. Three themes in children's information processing illuminate the ability to guide and take control of activity: problem solving, cognitive monitoring, and critical thinking.

Problem Solving

Problem solving *is an attempt to find an appropriate way of attaining a goal when the goal is not readily available.* We face many problems in our everyday lives—trying to figure out why our car won't start, planning how to get enough money to buy a stereo, or estimating our chances of winning the lottery. Children also face many problems in their everyday lives—working a jigsaw puzzle, doing math homework, or getting some money that is out of reach, for example.

With children, a common research tactic has been to formulate a problem that requires them to apply some newly learned academic skills in a practical context. Word problems in mathematics have been a popular topic of study (Carpenter, Moser, & Romberg, 1982; Hiebert & Wearne, 1988). For example, consider the following word problems.

1. Marie has 9 fish. Her sister Jill has 14 fish. How many more fish does Jill have than Marie?
2. Fred has 8 pieces of candy. How many more pieces does he have to put with them so he has 13 altogether?
3. There are 5 jars of paint. Three jars are red and the rest are blue. How many blue jars of paint are there?

Try to solve the following problem. If a human being has an inoperable stomach tumor, how can the tumor be removed by rays that destroy organic tissue (at sufficient intensity) without destroying the healthy tissue surrounding the tumor (Duncker, 1945)? The question has been posed to many generations of college students to study how they proceed to think through alternative solutions (the answer to the tumor problem appears at the end of the chapter).

How do children and adults solve these and other problems? What accounts for change in problem-solving ability as children mature? There seem to be at least four important parts involved—problem finding and goal setting, planning the approach, monitoring progress, and checking solutions.

First, we have to figure out precisely what the problem is and set one or more goals. This has sometimes been referred to as *problem finding and goal setting.* The examples of problems given earlier are reasonably well defined. The creators of these problems have taken pains to set up the context and to tell us what they want us to find. In everyday problem solving, however, we often have to find out what the problem is and what we have to do to solve it. For example, if a child is asked to clean her room, she must first figure out what must be done. What must the room look like when she is finished and what currently is out of order?

Once the problem and goal have been defined, a second step is to *plan the approach* to solving the problem. Planning may involve isolating the correct pieces to the puzzle and working out the general pattern to solve the problem with these pieces. For example, in Duncker's tumor-removal problem, the student would have to isolate these crucial elements: A tumor is to be destroyed with an intense ray, the tumor is in the stomach, and no tissue around the tumor can be destroyed. The plan then becomes to devise ways to focus the ray intensely on the tumor but not anywhere else. By brainstorming and calling on popular knowledge about technology and physics, a number of ideas may be tried and discarded as impractical, until a single elegant solution suggests itself. With arithmetic word problems, a similar phenomenon of planning may occur for younger children. In the third word problem, for example, the child must recognize that there are five jars of paint, three of a certain color and the remaining ones of a different color. The plan is to figure out how many remaining ones there are.

A third step is to *monitor the progress* of the problem-solving activity. Basically, this involves taking stock of how the solution process is faring, which is a kind of self-assessment in midstream. As ideas for solving the tumor problem come forth, for example, the student may stop to ponder whether a given idea is an improvement over the preceding one and whether he is still keeping the correct problem elements and goal in mind. As another example, younger children working out the arithmetic problems may wonder if they are proceeding smoothly. There are several common approaches taken by first and second graders to solve these problems. Some count on their fingers, some rely on number facts in their heads, and some use counting props made available by the experimenter. The monitoring activity, then, may consist of children's self-assessments of the viability of the counting technique they have chosen.

The fourth step is to *check solutions*. Whereas monitoring focuses on the progress of problem-solving efforts, this final step occurs when individuals feel they have completed their tasks. In the tumor problem, the student may compare the final solution offered against the initial criteria that had to be met, against the solutions that other classmates have thought up, or against published accounts of its ideal solution. Children solving the arithmetic problems may recheck their adding and subtracting or check the internal consistency of answers (for example, by seeing in the third problem if the number of jars of blue paint computed yields five when added to the three jars of red paint). Children writing essays usually need to revise their writing. In one recent study, 12-year-olds were much better than 10-year-olds at skillfully revising problematic texts (Beal, 1990b).

Cognitive Monitoring

Cognitive monitoring *is the process of taking stock of what you are currently doing, what you will do next, and how effectively the mental activity is unfolding.* When children engage in an activity like reading, writing, or solving a math problem, they are repeatedly called on to take stock of what they are doing and what they plan to do next (Baker & Brown, 1984; Beal & Bonitabitus, 1991; Brown & Palincsar, 1989; Lawton, Turner, & Paris, 1991). For example, when children begin to solve a math problem—especially one that might take a while to finish—they must figure out what kind of problem they are working on and what would be a good approach to solving it. Once they undertake a problem solution, it is helpful to check on whether the solution seems to be working or whether another approach would be better.

The source of much cognitive monitoring for young children is other people—especially parents and teachers. Adults provide a lot of guidance and direction for children's activities, and they tell children what specific strategies to use to complete various cognitive tasks (Wertsch, 1985; Yussen, 1985). They suggest when children should start an activity, they intervene at points when they think children might encounter difficulty (to explain difficult words, how to get started writing on a topic, how to look at math problems, or how to study), and they check children's progress and understanding (giving oral spelling quizzes, asking for explanations, or holding discussions). An important aspect of children's progress in cognitive monitoring as they mature, then, is their abilities to take control of their own cognitive activities and to develop the knowledge base to permit significant, strategic performances.

Instructional programs in reading comprehension (Brown & Palincsar, 1984, 1989), writing (Scardamalia, Bereiter, & Steinbach, 1984), and mathematics (Schoenfeld, 1985) have been designed to foster the development of cognitive monitoring (Collins, Brown, & Newman, 1989; Glaser, 1989). Developmental psychologists Ann Brown and Annemarie Palincsar's program for reading comprehension is an excellent example of a cognitive monitoring instructional program. Students in the program acquire specific knowledge and also learn strategies for monitoring their understanding. **Reciprocal teaching** *is an instructional procedure used by Brown and Palincsar to develop cognitive monitoring; it requires that students take turns in leading a study group in the use of strategies for comprehending and remembering text content.* The instruction involves a small group of students, often working with an adult leader, actively discussing a short text, with the goal of *summarizing* it, asking *questions* to promote understanding, offering *clarifying* statements for difficult or confusing words and ideas, and *predicting* what will come next. The procedure actively involves children, it teaches them some techniques to reflect about their own understanding, and the group interaction is highly motivating and engaging.

Critical Thinking

Much of the knowledge children are exposed to in the course of their education passes through their minds like grains of sand washed through a sieve. Children need to do more than just memorize or passively absorb new information. They must learn how to think critically. Currently, a number of psychologists and educators are studying children's critical thinking skills (Ennis, 1991; Jones, Idol, & Brandt, 1991), although it is not a new idea. Educator John Dewey (1933) was working with a similar concept when he contrasted "reflective thinking" with "nonreflective thinking" in the use of formulas or rules to achieve goals. So was Gestalt psychologist Max Wertheimer (1945) when he distinguished between "productive thinking" and "blind induction." Although today's definitions vary, they all have in common the notion that **critical thinking** *involves grasping the deeper meaning of problems, keeping an open mind about different approaches and perspectives, and thinking reflectively rather than accepting statements and carrying out procedures without significant understanding and evaluation.* Another, often implicit assumption is that critical thinking is an important aspect of everyday reasoning (Galotti, 1989a). Critical thinking can and should be used not just in the classroom, but outside it as well.

How can we cultivate the ability to think critically and clearly in children? According to a leading cognitive psychologist, Robert J. Sternberg (1987), we need to teach children to use the right thinking processes, to de-

Learning, Cognition, and Language Development

velop problem-solving strategies, to improve their mental representation, to expand their knowledge base, and to become motivated to use their newly learned thinking skills.

To think critically—or to solve any problem or learn any new knowledge—children need to take an active role in learning. This means that children need to call on a variety of active thinking processes, such as:

- Listening carefully
- Identifying or formulating questions
- Organizing their thoughts
- Noting similarities and differences
- Deducing (reasoning from the general to the specific)
- Distinguishing between logically valid and invalid inferences

Children also need to learn how to ask questions of clarification, such as "What is the main point?" "What do you mean by that?" and "Why?"

Good thinkers use more than just the right thinking processes. They also know how to combine them into workable strategies for solving problems. Rarely can a problem be solved by a single type of thought process used in isolation. Children need to learn how to combine thinking processes to master a new task. Critical thinking involves combining thought processes in a way that makes sense, not just by jumbling them together.

Children need to learn to see things from multiple points of view. Unless children can interpret information from more than one point of view, they may rely on an inadequate set of information. If children are not encouraged to seek alternative explanations and interpretations of problems and issues, their conclusions may be based solely on their own expectations, prejudices, stereotypes, and personal experiences, which may lead to erroneous conclusions.

It is important to keep in mind that thinking does not occur in the absence of knowledge. Children need *something* to think *about*. It is a mistake, however, to concentrate only on information to the exclusion of thinking skills, because children simply would become individuals who have a lot of knowledge but are unable to evaluate and apply it. It is equally a mistake to concentrate only on thinking skills, because children would become individuals who know how to think but have nothing to think about.

Finally, all of the thinking skills children could possibly master would be irrelevant if they were not actually put to use. Critical thinking is both a matter for academic study *and* a part of living. Children need to be motivated to put their critical thinking skills to practical use.

So far, we have learned a great deal about how children process information about their world. We have studied how children attend to information, how they perceive it and retain it over time, how they solve problems, how they engage in cognitive monitoring, and how they develop critical thinking skills. In our discussion of critical thinking skills, we examined some ways in which critical thinking could be encouraged in schools. To read further about how information processing might be applied to children's education, turn to Perspective on Child Development 9.2.

Knowledge and Expertise

As we study changes in children's information-processing skills, it does not take long to realize that specific processes, such as memory, depend on what children already know. It seems obvious that most of what children try to remember and understand in everyday activities depends on the children's

■ *Critical Thinking*
Imagine that you have been asked to develop an information-processing-based curriculum for first-grade students. What would the curriculum be like?

Information Processing, the Information Age, and Children's Education

When you were in elementary school, did any teacher at any time work with you on improving your memory strategies? Did any of your teachers work with you on your reading skills after the first and second grade? Did any of your teachers discuss with you ways in which imagery could be used to enhance your processing of information? If you are like most individuals, you spent little or no time in elementary school on improving these important processes involved in our everyday encounters with the world.

Why is it important to have an educational goal of improving the information-processing skills of children? Think for a moment about yourself and the skills necessary for you to be successful in adapting to your environment and for improving your chances of getting a good job and having a successful career. To an extent, knowledge itself is important; more precisely, content knowledge in certain areas is important. For example, if you plan to become a chemical engineer, a knowledge of chemistry is required. Our schools have done a much better job of imparting knowledge than in instructing students how to process information.

Another important situation in your life where instruction in information processing would have helped you tremendously was when you took the SAT or ACT test. SAT cram courses are popping up all over the United States, in part because schools have not done a good job of developing information-processing skills. For example, is speed of processing information important on the SAT? Most of you probably felt you did not have as much time as you would have liked to handle difficult questions. Are memory strategies important on the SAT? You had to read paragraphs and hold a considerable amount of information in your mind to answer some of the questions. You certainly had to remember how to solve a number of math problems. Didn't you also have to remember the definitions of a large number of vocabulary words, and what about problem solving, inferencing, and understanding? Remember the difficult verbal problems you had to answer and the inferences you had to make when reasoning was required?

The story of information processing is one of attention, perception, memory (especially the control processes in memory), and thinking. These information-processing skills become even more crucial in education when we consider that we are now in the midst of a transition from an industrial to a postindustrial information society, with approximately 65 to 70 percent of all workers involved in service industries. The information revolution in our society has placed strains on workers who are called on daily to process huge amounts of information rapidly, to have efficient memories, to attend to relevant details, to reason logically about difficult issues, and to make inferences about information that may be unclear. Students graduate from high school, college, or postgraduate work and move into jobs requiring information-processing skills, yet they have had little or no instruction in improving these skills.

At this time, there is no specified curriculum of information processing that can be taught in a stepwise, developmental fashion to our nation's children. We also do not have the trained personnel for this instruction. Further, some information-processing experts believe that such processes as attention and memory cannot be trained in a general way. Rather, they argue that information processing is domain, or content specific; for example, we should work on improving information-processing skills that are specific to math or to history. They do believe, though, that an infusion of the information-processing approach into all parts of the curriculum would greatly benefit children (Dillon & Sternberg, 1988; Ennis, 1990; McPeck, 1990; Stankov, 1991).

Researchers are beginning to study the importance of information-processing skills for school learning. Ellen Gagne (1985) provided a menu of information-processing skills that need to be given attention when instructing children in specific content areas—reading, writing, math, and science, for example. Her review concludes that sucessful students—those who get better grades and higher achievement test scores—are better at such information-processing skills as focusing attention, elaborating and organizing information, and monitoring their study strategies. As yet, though, we do not know the extent to which these information-processing skills can be taught. Nonetheless, in one investigation, Gagne and her colleagues (1984) demonstrated that children can be taught effective ways to elaborate information so that it can be remembered more efficiently. Elaboration refers to more extensive processing. Getting children to think of examples of a concept is a good way to improve their memory of the concept; so is getting them to think about how the concept relates to themselves. Other experts in cognitive psychology also believe that information-processing skills can be taught. For example, Joan Baron and R. J. Sternberg (1987) believe we need to teach children to think in less irrational ways; children need to be more critical of the first ideas that pop into their minds. They should be taught to think longer about problems and to search in more organized ways for evidence to support their views.

knowledge about people, places, and things (Neisser, 1982; Wilkening & Anderson, 1991). If a child makes a trip to a toy store, her ability to recount what she saw is largely governed by what the child knows about toy stores and the things found there, for example. With little knowledge about what is usually found in a toy store, the child would have a much harder time recounting what was there. Although prior knowledge proves helpful in this way, it can also be distorting. For example, in an investigation by Ann Brown and her colleagues (1977), third-, fifth-, and seventh-grade children heard the following story with either George or Galen as the main character.

The Fugitive

Galen (George) was alone. He knew they would soon be here. They were not far behind him when he left the village, hungry and cold. He dared not stop for food or shelter for fear of falling into the hands of his pursuers. There were many of them; they were strong and he was weak. Galen (George) could hear the noise as the uniformed band beat its way through the trees not far behind him. The sense of their presence was everywhere. His spine tingled with fear. Eagerly he awaited darkness. In darkness he would find safety.

Children who heard the story about Galen immediately assumed that the vignette was about a popular character in the television show "Planet of the Apes." In recalling the story later, they inferred that the character was an ape, that the pursuers were apes, that his "fur" tingled, and that the pursuers made their way using trees rather than walking among them. Those who read about George had no such "intrusions" in their memories.

As we evaluate the contribution of knowledge to children's information processing, in succeeding sections we will explore the different kinds of knowledge children acquire, how the knowledge is put to use, and how experts differ from novices in the kind of knowledge they have and the way they use it.

Knowledge

Among the most important aspects of understanding how knowledge is involved in the child's cognitive activities are concepts, semantic networks, schemas, and metacognitive knowledge, each of which we will consider in turn.

Knowledge is power.

—Francis Bacon

Concepts

In everyday learning and thinking, children use many simple concepts to understand the world. Words for ordinary objects, people, and places—such as *house, man,* and *street*—stand for simple ideas and concepts that are the building blocks for children's thoughts. A **concept** *is a category used to group objects, events, and characteristics on the basis of common properties.* Why are concepts important? Concepts allow children to relate experiences and objects. For example, New York, California, and Texas are states. Without the concept of "state," children would be unable to compare these states. Without concepts, each object in a child's world would be unique. Generalization would be impossible.

Semantic Networks

Semantic networks *are the organized stores of general information in memory.* Simple concepts are often organized into rich patterns in memory. These semantic networks gradually grow in size and complexity as children develop. As children become older, the increased size and complexity of semantic networks help them connect many ideas quickly and have all of these ideas in

Drawing by Koren; © 1986 The New Yorker Magazine, Inc.

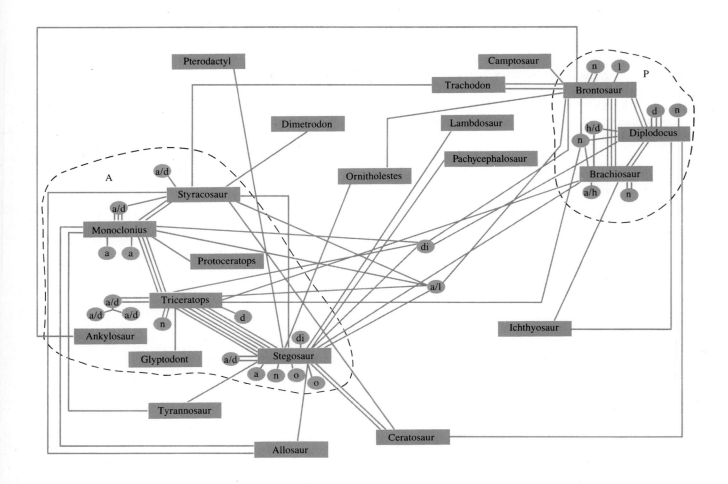

Figure 9.4
A 4-Year-Old Expert's Semantic Network of Dinosaurs

hand to accomplish whatever task is necessary. A good example of a semantic network is provided by an investigation of a 4-year-old dinosaur "expert" (Chi & Koeske, 1983). Like many children his age, this young boy enjoyed hearing stories about dinosaurs and examining picture books of dinosaurs. Unlike most children his age, however, he was able to name at least 46 dinosaurs and could identify at least one, and often many, features of each (for example, whether it ate plants or flew). The researchers carefully mapped out what the child knew about each dinosaur and how directly each dinosaur name was linked in the child's mind to other dinosaur names. Figure 9.4 shows a complete mapping of the boy's semantic dinosaur network. It represents visually how the dinosaurs were linked and the particular features associated with each dinosaur in the child's mind. Although the figure is complicated, some simple points can be learned from it. Each line represents a link, each circled letter represents a dinosaur attribute, and the individual dinosaur names/concepts are included in the boxes. Notice, first, that some dinosaurs are not linked to many others. This is true of Dimetrodon and Pterodactyl. We would not expect these dinosaurs to be as easily remembered or used compared with others. Notice, second, that, among the dinosaurs that are linked, some have more links (for example, Styracosaur has more links than Ornitholestes). Notice, third, that some dinosaurs are more centrally located in a network than those surrounding them. We would expect dinosaur names with more links and a more central location in the network to be more salient in the child's mind when he thinks about dinosaurs.

You may be somewhat intimidated by this young child's knowledge. You can get a good personal understanding of semantic networks by creating your own mapping of a domain of concepts familiar to you. Perhaps try one of these domains: "foods I like to eat," "games I know," or "places I visit."

Schema

Long-term memory has been compared to a library. A library stores books, just as children's long-term memory stores information. Children retrieve the information as they do when they locate and check out a book. The process of retrieving information is not as precise as the library analogy suggests, however. When children search through their long-term memory store, they don't always find *exactly* the "book" they want, or they might find the book they want but discover that only several pages of the book are intact. Children have to *reconstruct* the rest. When children reconstruct information, they often fit it into information that already exists in their mind. A **schema** *is information—concepts, events, and knowledge—that already exists in an individual's mind. A schema influences how a child interprets new information.* Schemas come from prior encounters with the environment and influence the way children encode, make inferences about, and retrieve information. Children have schemas for stories, scenes, spatial layouts (a bathroom or a park, for example), and common events (such as going to a restaurant, playing with toys, or practicing the piano).

Simple stories have structure; after reading or hearing about enough stories, children develop a strong expectation about what kind of information will be contained in a story. That expectation is a story schema.

Children frequently hear and tell stories, and, as they develop the ability to read, they are exposed to many kinds of stories in print. Simple stories have a structure; after hearing enough stories, children develop a strong expectation about what kind of information will be contained in a story. This expectation is a *story schema*. For example, a story tells about what happens in a particular place and circumstance. This context is called the setting. A story also has at least one main character, the protagonist, who attempts to achieve a purposeful goal for a clear reason. The protagonist's actions are usually captured in one or more episodes of a story, which can be further broken down, depicting a fairly simple, one-episode story (see figure 9.5).

A decade of research has shown that children at a very young age are able to use structures like these to fill in missing information, remember better, and tell relatively coherent stories (Ackerman, 1988; Buss & others, 1983; Rahman & Bisanz, 1986; Stein & Glenn, 1979; Yussen & others, 1988). Changes occur throughout the childhood years, however, in children's abilities to identify salient events in stories, to unscramble mixed-up stories, and to keep multiple plot lines straight in their minds when facing more complex stories involving several episodes and more than one major character.

A **script** *is a schema for an event* (Schank & Abelson, 1977). Children's first scripts appear very early in development, perhaps as early as the first year of life. Children clearly have scripts by the time they enter school (Firush & Cobb, 1989; Flannagan & Tate, 1989; Furman & Walden, 1989, 1990). As children develop, their scripts become less crude and more sophisticated. For example, a 4-year-old's script for a restaurant might include information only about sitting down and eating food. By middle and late childhood, the child adds information to the restaurant script about the types of people who serve food, about paying the cashier, and so on.

Figure 9.5
"Albert, the Fish," a Representative Story

Setting	1 Once there was a big gray fish named Albert.
	2 He lived in a pond near the edge of a forest.
Initiating event	3 One day Albert was swimming around the pond.
	4 Then he spotted a big juicy worm on top of the water.
Internal response	5 Albert knew how delicious worms tasted.
	6 He wanted to eat that one for his dinner.
Attempt	7 So he swam very close to the worm.
	8 Then he bit into him.
Consequence	9 Suddenly, Albert was pulled through the water into a boat.
	10 He had been caught by a fisherman.
Reaction	11 Albert felt sad.
	12 He wished he had been more careful.

Metacognitive Knowledge

Metacognitive knowledge *is the segment of acquired world knowledge that involves cognitive matters.* It is the knowledge children have accumulated through experience and stored in long-term memory that concern the human mind and its workings. According to one of the leading cognitive developmentalists, John Flavell (1985), metacognitive knowledge can be subdivided roughly into knowledge about *persons* (oneself as well as all human beings), *tasks,* and *strategies.*

Metacognitive knowledge about persons includes such insights as the following (Yussen & Levy, 1975):

1. People, including myself, have limits to the amount of information they can process. It is not possible to deal with all of the information that comes my way. If I worry too much about this, I will feel the stress of information overload.
2. I am better at doing some things than at other things (for example, I am better at reading than arithmetic, and better at verbalizing than imaging events).
3. I can handle information better in some states (for example, when I am relaxed, rested, or happy) than in others (for example, when I am anxious, tired, or sad).

Metacognitive knowledge about *tasks* includes such insights as the following:

1. Some conditions always make it harder or easier to solve a problem or complete a task. For example, the more time available to solve a problem, the better I do. The fewer number of items to be processed (that is, attended to, remembered, perceived, and so on), the easier it is for me to do.
2. Some tasks are harder than others. It is easier to understand what someone says than to explain the same message to someone else. It is easier to read something than to explain the main ideas contained in the reading. Tests of recall (for example, retrieving previously learned information, as on an essay test) are more

difficult than tests of recognition (for example, merely identifying or "recognizing," previously learned items, as on a multiple-choice test).

3. I cannot complete some tasks. For example, the tasks might require knowledge I do not have and cannot obtain, or the tasks might require a highly developed skill that I have not yet mastered (a different language, use of a tool, or social skills).

Metacognitive knowledge about *strategies* includes such insights as the following:

1. Some cognitive steps will be useful across a wide range of cognitive tasks (remembering, communicating, reading, and so on). Among these are some steps we discussed in the section on problem solving (establishing goals, planning one's approach, and monitoring the progress one is making).

2. Particular cognitive tasks require specific strategies in addition to the general steps if a person is to maximize performance. Thus, to remember something, the strategies of imaging, rehearsal, organization, and elaboration are often very helpful. However, to communicate adequately, it may be more important to state the message in several different ways to the listener and to focus on the listener's signals of comprehension or miscomprehension.

3. A third type of metacognitive knowledge about strategies is the all-important understanding that some strategies are more effective with a particular task than are others. For example, it is generally easier to master a lengthy list of names using the imagery keyword method than to rehearse the names by simple repetition (Levin, 1980). It also is more effective to study for a test by focusing only on the material to be included on it than by reviewing everything covered in the course.

Information Processing 319

Many developmentalists believe that metacognitive knowledge is beneficial in school learning and, that, if students (especially younger ones) are deficient in metacognitive knowledge, this knowledge can possibly be taught to them (Flavell, 1985). Several researchers have developed school programs to impart metacognitive knowledge to children in the areas of reading comprehension, writing, and mathematics. The research we discussed earlier pertaining to the importance of cognitive monitoring in reading comprehension is an excellent example of how metacognitive knowledge can be taught to children (Brown & Palincsar, 1984, 1989).

Earlier, we also addressed the possibility of applying the information-processing approach to children's education. Some educators believe that a broad base of knowledge, or cultural literacy, is sorely lacking in our nation's children. To learn more about a provocative new concern pertaining to improving children's broad-based knowledge, turn to Cultural Worlds of Development 9.1.

Expertise

What is an expert? An **expert** *is someone who has a great deal of knowledge about a domain of human interest and a great deal of experience performing tasks typical of that domain.* These individuals are recognized by others in their field as having reached the highest levels of knowledge and performance. Examples of experts are easy to offer. Any list would include, but not be limited to, exceptional athletes, talented musicians, acclaimed artists, highly esteemed professionals in medicine and law, highly skilled manual tradespeople, and chess masters. Experts are often contrasted with novices, who are just beginning to learn in the domain (Harnishfeger & Cassel, 1991; Metz, 1991). A great deal of research has been done in the past 2 decades to characterize the differences between experts and others. Most of this work is with adults, a result of the limited time children have had to become expert at anything. Our survey of the topic considers why an understanding of expertise is important in the study of children's information processing, some of the differences between experts and others, and implications for learning and instruction.

Developmental Implications of Expertise

In some ways, young children are universal novices. They perform almost any cognitive task with very little of the knowledge and experience of adults. Adults are not always experts, but neither are they rank novices, at reading, writing,

■ *Critical Thinking*
Should a national literacy test be developed and given to all school children? Explain your answer.

Although in some ways children are universal novices, one can find children with high levels of skill in chess.

Cultural Literacy

We are in the midst of an era of educational reform across the country. State after state is implementing legislated changes at all levels of schooling to try to improve public education. The list of concerns is legion (Bernstein, 1988). Some worry that not enough students are taking mathematics and science classes in high school, with the consequence that our country will compete poorly with Japan and Western Europe in future high-technology industries. Others worry that we are not teaching children to read and write very effectively anymore. Undergirding specific curriculum concerns such as these is a basic sense of uneasiness about the quality of people entering the teaching profession. Add to this list a provocative new concern popularized by English professor E. D. Hirsch of the University of Virginia in his book *Cultural Literacy* (1987). Hirsch's idea is receiving a great deal of attention among members of the educational community.

To have some appreciation of Hirsch's concerns, try a little test on yourself. Following is a list of words and terms. Read each one and see if you can silently identify its basic meaning. For example, define it, give an example, or explain its significance, even in a crude way.

1066	mainspring	Zurich	golden fleece
burgher	golden rule	nicotine	probate court

These words were selected at random from several thousand included in a glossary in Hirsch's book that runs over 60 pages in length. It is a provisional list defining what Hirsch calls the knowledge that every literate adult should learn in school in order to function well in our contemporary society. It includes terms drawn from history, literature, government, science, mathematics, art, geography and other areas of knowledge.

Simplifying the argument somewhat, here are Hirsch's bold claims.

1. To be a full participant in our modern democratic society, it is necessary to be literate.
2. Stripped of its subtleties, the core of adult literacy is having a broad and wide-ranging base of knowledge.

3. The knowledge he has in mind is *schematic*. It needn't be detailed or complete. If you know that nicotine is an ingredient in cigarettes or that Zurich is a city in Switzerland, that is sufficient.
4. American schools used to make students learn more schematic knowledge. The curriculum had substance and factual content. Recently, it has slipped, with faddish concerns about "process," "thinking skills," and "developmental curricula."
5. We need to reform the American school curriculum, starting at the beginning of elementary school, so that more content is present, specifically of the sort outlined in his glossary.
6. To guarantee that recommendation 5 is taken seriously, school systems ought to begin immediately creating tests to see whether children's knowledge bases are improving.

What do you think of Hirsch's ideas? Do they make sense to you? Do you accept his arguments? You may be faced with the consequences of their adoption. Few educators could or would want to argue against the notion that the accumulation of a broad base of knowledge is important. As we have seen throughout this chapter, children's general knowledge has repercussions on the success of their learning and with the later success the children have as adults. However, should we be content with "shallow" knowledge of the sort that would be encouraged by a test such as his, and should everyone be expected to be a broad, Renaissance collector of information? Do we, in our specialized society, need to tolerate otherwise well-educated people becoming narrowly "expert"? Also, how will we ever resolve the perpetually thorny issue of who defines what's asked on such tests and whose consensus defines what constitutes contemporary cultural literacy? Shouldn't we also be concerned about improving children's information-processing skills?

solving mathematics problems, following travel directions, and so on. However, young children are almost always novices at these tasks. There are exceptions, of course; we can find children with high levels of skill in chess, handling an abacus, and dinosaur identification, for example, but our interest in these forms of childhood expertise is partly a result of the novelty and rarity with which it occurs. If we were to study such forms of childhood expertise carefully, we would probably conclude that the children are not really experts at all. Our 4-year-old dinosaur "expert" is certainly a wonder, but he hardly has the knowledge of paleontologists—among whom the real dinosaur experts would be found.

It is wise, then, not to make children experts. This is not a feat we're likely to manage with any great success. The attraction, instead, is to understand what an expert does, how the expert got to that level of functioning, and the stages or landmarks that led to the high level of functioning. With this knowledge in hand, we can have realistic goals about fostering high levels of competence in children and of cultivating expertise in children who seem to have interest and potential in particular fields.

Differences Between Experts and Novices

How do experts and novices differ in the way they approach tasks in a particular domain? One difference concerns initial *planning time* (Berg & Sansone, 1991; Friedman, 1991; Hudson & Fivush, 1991; Trabasso, 1991). Present a problem to an expert and the expert spends more time, relative to the total time needed to complete the task, than a novice or less experienced person would in thinking about how to solve the problem or complete the task. Expert writers spend a great deal of time thinking about what they want to communicate, how to communicate it, and what the parts or units of their written product will look like. Expert computer programmers spend a considerable amount of time describing to themselves what their finished program will accomplish and the form their program will take. Expert athletes spend a great deal of effort planning their approach to conditioning, polishing skills, and choosing competition. Novices, on the other hand, leap right in. They may not have the skill to plan effectively or they may not realize the value of initial planning. The experts' emphasis on planning often surprises people, because a common stereotype of experts is that they know how to do everything in their domain of expertise with relatively little effort.

In fact, if a task is straightforward and not a "problem" to solve, experts are extremely fast. Their performances seem *automatic* and *effortless*. Having planned an essay, an expert writer may dash off pages of print in just several hours. Having planned a computer program, a programmer writes code at a speed that dazzles beginners. Having prepared physically and mentally for a match, an expert tennis player serves, volleys, and returns ground strokes with speed and grace. The contrasting performance of a novice is one of sluggish fits and starts, conscious thought about what to do, and great effort.

Another feature of expert performance is the tendency to see what might be called the *underlying structure* of the task and to ignore surface details. Faced with creating a political speech, an expert writer will set aside the fact that the speech must be 10 pages long and must cover certain current issues. These are less important than to communicate the message, the perspective, and the leadership qualities that the candidate wants to project to a particular audience. These goals define the underlying structure of the writing task. A novice is more likely to focus on the length and topics to be covered; these will be sufficiently challenging, although ultimately not what writing a speech is principally about.

A final characteristic is the tendency of an expert to use **heuristics,** *strategies or rules of thumb that suggest a solution to a problem but do not guarantee it will work,* and intuition to complete tasks rather than formal rules and principles (Yaniv & Shatz, 1990). In school, we are taught to do things according to formal rules and guidelines. To write a good essay, we need a central thesis and supporting arguments. To do well on an exam, we should review all the material likely to be on a test and distribute our study time over a reasonable period of days and hours. To perform well in an athletic contest, we must remember the fundamentals of the game and concentrate on doing things simply and cleanly. Rules such as these serve most of us, who are not experts, quite well most of the time. Novices also need rules to perform tasks with a degree of proficiency. However, experts often throw rules and principles out the window when they are functioning at their highest form. They rely, instead, on their own informal rules and intuition. Have you ever read a political essay by Mike Royko? His form is usually meandering, with a tone of outrage and disbelief, in the form of a story. Have you ever watched a chess match among masters? What is the player thinking while waiting to make a move? The chess master isn't computing all possible moves, as is commonly thought. Usually he comes up with one or two likely moves very quickly and intuitively (based on experience and a fantastic memory of similar game situations faced before) and spends the rest of the time making sure these are not going to cause trouble later (in other words, backtracking).

Expertise, Learning, and Instruction

Experts are made, not born. It takes a long time and a lot of practice to reach high levels of expertise in most fields of human endeavor. Cognitive scientist Herbert Simon has estimated that world-class athletes, for example, are the product of 10 or more years of continuous training for the equivalent of about 8 hours a day. Experts in academic and creative walks of life may likely require much more time than this.

There are no shortcuts. One simply cannot emulate the characteristics of experts (spending more time planning, looking for underlying structure, and functioning intuitively) and expect to mimic their levels of performance. If an area of human endeavor holds some appeal to a child, the best advice to the child is to learn patiently, to acquire more knowledge and experience, and to practice the skills of the discipline.

Experts must be sought out as teachers, because they have insight into what was required to reach high levels of accomplishment. Although instruction in school is a good starting point to build toward an expert level in a domain, school is limited. Usually, expert levels are achieved at a later point in a person's life. If we take Simon's estimate to heart, we see, for example, that, in 12 years of public school, there is simply not sufficient time for most children to focus on a single area of endeavor for the number of hours necessary to reach a true expert level. The exceptions to this, of course, are some areas of athletics (swimming and gymnastics), in which learning and practice begin very early; relative "youth" is a necessity for speed, strength, and agility; and students manage to cram in 3 to 5 hours of practice per day.

Individual Differences in Information Processing

Virtually all teachers are aware that the children in their classrooms vary in their ability to process information—some may attend efficiently to the teacher's instructions, others may rarely listen to what the teacher says; some students may be able to remember efficiently, others not so well; some students seem to process information rapidly, others more slowly; some students are impulsive in solving problems, others are more reflective; and some students focus on the details or elements of information, others on the gist or the overall picture of the information. Researchers who have studied individual differences in information processing have primarily focused on **cognitive styles,** *the general, usually consistent ways individuals process information. Cognitive style is determined not only by an individual's attention to a task, organi-*

According to our discussion of the differences between novices and experts, how might this gymnastics expert differ from novices in gymnastics?

As many men, so many minds; every one his own way.

—Terence

■ *Critical Thinking*
What is your cognitive style of information processing? Are there ways that you could improve your style of processing information?

Information Processing   323

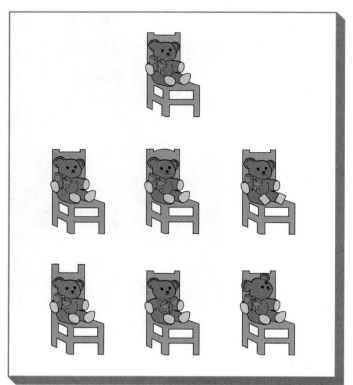

Figure 9.6
Two Sample Items from the Matching Familiar Figures Test
The child is asked to find the object in the six items at the bottom of each card that is identical to the object at the top of the card.

zational skills, and cognitive strategies, but by the person's personality and motivation as well. The type of cognitive style that has received the most attention is impulsivity versus reflection.

Impulsivity *is a cognitive style in which individuals act before they think, usually making rapid scans of information and, if fine discriminations of information are required, making errors.* **Reflection** *is cognitive style in which individuals think before they act, usually scanning information carefully and slowly and, if fine discriminations of information are required, making few errors* (Entwistle, 1981). Impulsive students usually finish objective tests quickly, whereas reflective students are still contemplating their answers when the exam period is almost over. The test most often used to measure individual differences in impulsivity/reflection is the Matching Familiar Figures Test (Kagan, 1965) (see figure 9.6). On this test, children are presented a series of pictures in which they must select the one picture of the six at the bottom that exactly matches the picture at the top. Impulsive children scan the six options quickly, making a choice that often is inaccurate. By contrast, reflective children carefully examine the six pictures, slowly making a choice that often is correct.

Much learning that takes place in classrooms requires reflection rather than impulsivity. To do well on school tasks, children must carefully examine the details of information, reflect on what the best answer is, and evaluate their errors after they have failed at a task (Pascual-Leone & Shafrir, 1991; Shafrir, 1991; Siegel, 1991). Researchers have trained impulsive children to become

Learning, Cognition, and Language Development

more reflective by improving their scanning strategies, teaching them to take more time, and instructing them to talk to themselves to control their behavior (Egeland, 1974; Meichenbaum & Goodman, 1971). Even with reflection training, though, impulsive children rarely attain a competence level of careful examination of information that characterizes their reflective counterparts, and no long-term benefits of reflection training have been demonstrated. Also, it is important to keep in mind that not all cognitive tasks require extensive examination of the fine details of information. Sometimes a quick scan of information is all that is needed to discover the information one needs. If a child wakes up in the morning, looks out the window, and sees it is raining, she does not have to reflect at length when she looks in her closet to determine what type of coat she will wear to school. She only has to quickly pick out her raincoat.

The ability to process information rapidly is often an important ability in our society. We usually do not have unlimited amounts of time to perform what is requested of us, either in school or at work. Consider the exams that children and college students take in classes, as well as standardized national tests of achievement and ability. Most tests have time limits. Consider also the jobs that employees are given to do. A supervisor may want an information-processing task finished in 15 minutes, not 1 or 2 hours. In one investigation, the speed of decoding information significantly differentiated college students who did extremely well on the verbal portion of the SAT, college students who did not do well on the verbal portion of the SAT, young adults not in a university, 10-year-old children, and mildly retarded school children (Hunt, 1978). The high-verbal SAT college students were the most rapid processors of information, the mildly retarded school children the slowest. Apparently, some individuals, such as the talented college students who did well on the verbal part of the SAT, do not fit neatly into the impulsive or the reflective category. These individuals may work rapidly *and* accurately. By contrast, other individuals may work slowly *and* inaccurately.

Most information-processing psychologists have not been interested in individual differences. Rather, they are interested in capturing the *typical* way people process information rather than the *variations* in how they process information (Siegler & Campbell, 1989). Also, most information-processing psychologists view the concept of cognitive style as too global and general, believing that more precise cognitive processes, such as specific attentional, memory, and thinking strategies, are the keys to understanding children's cognition (Ackerman, Sternberg, & Glaser, 1989). In one recent investigation that combined an emphasis on individual differences and specificity of cognitive processes, Robert Siegler (in press) found that, in math classes, "not so good" students, who would normally be called "impulsive," had a memory system in which they set very low standards for retrieving information (answers to a math problem), whereas "perfectionist" students, who would normally be called "reflective," had a memory system with high standards for retrieving answers to math problems.

At this point, we have discussed a number of ideas about higher-order cognitive processes, knowledge and expertise, and individual differences in information processing. A summary of these ideas is presented in concept table 9.2. In the next chapter, we will turn our attention to another important area of children's development—language.

Higher-Order Cognitive Processes, Knowledge and Expertise, and
Individual Differences in Information Processing

Concept	Processes/related ideas	Characteristics/description
Higher-order cognitive processes	Problem solving	Problem solving is an attempt to find an appropriate way of attaining a goal when the goal is not readily available. The components of problem solving include: problem finding and goal setting, planning the approach to the problem, monitoring the progress on the problem, and checking solutions.
	Cognitive monitoring	Cognitive monitoring is the process of taking stock of what one is currently doing, what will be done next, and how effectively the mental activity is unfolding. The source of much cognitive monitoring in young children is other people. With development through the elementary school years, greater independence in cognitive monitoring is usually achieved. Instructional programs in reading comprehension, writing, and mathematics have been designed to foster the development of cognitive monitoring in children. Reciprocal teaching is an instructional procedure used by Brown and Palincsar to develop children's cognitive monitoring.
	Critical thinking	Critical thinking refers to grasping the deeper meaning of problems, keeping an open mind about different approaches and perspectives, and thinking reflectively rather than accepting statements and carrying out procedures without significant understanding and evaluation. To cultivate critical thinking in children, we need to teach them to use the right thinking processes, to develop problem-solving strategies, to improve their mental representation, to expand their knowledge base, and to become motivated to use their newly developed thinking skills.
Knowledge and expertise	Knowledge	Among the most important aspects of understanding how knowledge is involved in the child's cognitive activities are concepts (categories used to group objects, events, and characteristics on the basis of common properties), semantic networks (organized stores of general information in memory), a schema (information that already exists in an individual's mind that influences how the individual interprets new information), and metacognitive knowledge (the segment of acquired knowledge that involves cognitive matters, especially the way the human mind works). Metacognitive knowledge can be subdivided into knowledge about persons, tasks, and strategies.
	Expertise	Expertise is a highly developed knowledge base coupled with a considerable amount of experience in a domain, which permits individuals to perform at very effective levels. Experts are the best at what they do. They differ from novices in several ways: they plan more, their performances are often automatic and effortless, they search for underlying structure in cognitive tasks, and they use heuristics and intuition.
Individual differences in information processing	Their nature	Researchers who have studied individual differences in information processing have primarily focused on cognitive styles—the general, usually consistent ways individuals process information. Cognitive styles are not only determined by individuals' attention to the task, organizational skills, and cognitive strategies, but by personality and motivation as well. The type of cognitive style that has received the most attention is impulsivity versus reflection. Most information-processing psychologists have been interested in the typical way people process information rather than in variations in the way they process information. Many information-processing psychologists also believe that the concept of cognitive style is too global.

Summary

I. The Nature of Information Processing

The information-processing approach attempts to be very detailed about the mental processes underlying learning and thinking in specific situations and, where possible, to model the specific steps needed to complete a task, using computer programs and mathematical estimates of mental activities. The information-processing approach emphasizes that, with age, children's processing speed, processing capacity, and automaticity increase.

II. Attention

Attention is the concentration and focusing of mental effort. Attention is both selective and shifting. In infancy, attention is often studied through habituation experiments. Children's attention increases dramatically in the preschool years and becomes even more efficient in the elementary school years. During the elementary school years, scanning of visual patterns and attention to relevant dimensions of problems increase.

III. Memory

Memory is the retention of information over time. Two important memory systems are short-term memory and long-term memory. Short-term memory is a limited-capacity memory system in which information is retained for as long as 30 seconds, unless the information is rehearsed, in which case it can be retained longer. Long-term memory is a relatively permanent memory system, which holds huge amounts of information for a long period of time. There is evidence that short-term memory improves the most during the preschool years; long-term memory improves the most during the elementary school years.

IV. Memory Strategies

Memory strategies are cognitive processes that do not occur automatically but require work and effort. They are under the learner's control and can be used to improve memory. Four important strategies are rehearsal, organization, elaboration, and imagery. As children get older, they are more likely to use these strategies without being instructed to do so, but instructions to use the strategies usually improve children's memory.

V. Problem Solving

Problem solving is an attempt to find an appropriate way of attaining a goal when the goal is not readily available. The components of problem solving include: problem finding and goal setting, planning the approach to the problem, monitoring the progress on the problem, and checking solutions.

VI. Cognitive Monitoring

Cognitive monitoring is the process of taking stock of what one is currently doing, what one will do next, and how effectively the mental activity is unfolding. The source of much cognitive monitoring in young children is other people. With development through the elementary school years, greater independence in cognitive monitoring is usually achieved. Instructional programs in reading comprehension, writing, and mathematics have been designed to foster the development of cognitive monitoring in children. Reciprocal teaching is an instructional program used by Brown and Palincsar to develop children's cognitive monitoring.

VII. Critical Thinking

Critical thinking refers to grasping the deeper meaning of problems, keeping an open mind about different approaches and perspectives, and thinking reflectively rather than accepting statements and carrying out procedures without significant understanding and evaluation. To cultivate critical thinking in children, we need to teach children to use the right thinking processes, to develop problem-solving strategies, to improve their mental representation, to expand their knowledge base, and to become motivated to use their newly developed thinking skills.

VIII. Knowledge

Among the most important aspects of understanding how knowledge is involved in the child's cognitive activities are concepts (categories used to group objects, events, and characteristics on the basis of common properties), semantic networks (organized stores of general information in memory), a schema (information that already exists in an individual's mind that influences how the individual interprets new information), and metacognitive knowledge (the segment of acquired knowledge that involves cognitive matters, especially the way the human mind works). Metacognitive knowledge can be subdivided into knowledge about persons, tasks, and strategies.

IX. Expertise

Expertise is a highly developed knowledge base coupled with a considerable amount of experience in a domain, which permits individuals to perform at very effective levels. Experts are the best at what they do. They differ from novices in several ways: they plan more, their performance is often automatic and effortless, they search for underlying structure in cognitive tasks, and they use heuristics and intuition.

X. Individual Differences in Information Processing

Researchers who have studied individual differences in information processing have primarily focused on cognitive styles—the general, usually consistent ways individuals process information. Cognitive styles are not only determined by individuals' attention to the task, organizational skills, and cognitive strategies, but by personality and motivation as well. The type of cognitive style that has received the most attention is impulsivity versus reflection. Most information-processing psychologists have been interested in the typical way people process information rather than in variations in the way they process information. Many information-processing psychologists also believe that the concept of cognitive style is too global.

Key Terms

artificial intelligence 301
automaticity 303
attention 303
memory 306
short-term memory 306
long-term memory 306
strategies 307
rehearsal 307
organization 307
elaboration 308
imagery 308
keyword method 308
problem solving 310
cognitive monitoring 311

reciprocal teaching 312
critical thinking 312
concept 315
semantic networks 315
schema 317
script 317
metacognitive
 knowledge 318
expert 320
heuristics 322
cognitive styles 323
impulsivity 324
reflection 324

Suggested Readings

Ackerman, P. L., Sternberg, R. J., & Glaser, R. (Eds.). (1989). *Learning and individual differences*. New York: W. H. Freeman. This text is a modern treatment of individual differences in cognitive styles and information processing.

Baron, J. B., & Sternberg, R. J. (Eds.). (1987). *Teaching thinking skills: Theory and practice*. New York: W. H. Freeman. Ten eminent psychologists, educators, and philosophers describe ways to improve critical thinking skills and offer various strategies and exercises for children and adults.

Brown, A. L., & Palincsar, A. M. (1989). Guided, cooperative learning and individual knowledge acquisition. In L. B. Resnick (Ed.), *Knowing and learning: Essays in honor of Robert Glaser*. Hillsdale, NJ: Erlbaum. This is a detailed presentation of Brown and Palincsar's provocative ideas about teaching cognitive monitoring skills to children.

Hirsch, E. D. (1987). *Cultural literacy: What every American needs to know*. Boston: Houghton Mifflin. In this easy-to-read and engaging critique of school practices, Hirsch reviews schema theory from a broad perspective, considers the nature of national culture, and concludes with arguments supporting the adoption of a national test for literacy.

Schneider, W., & Pressley, M. (1989). *Memory development between 2 and 20*. New York: Springer-Verlag. Two leading researchers provide up-to-date, detailed analyses and insightful information about the nature and development of children's memory.

Answer to Inoperable Tumor Problem

The solution is to isolate the tumor tissue and focus several rays (that is, of a laser beam) on it through an optical arrangement that guarantees the rays are intensely focused only on one spot. The rays must be too diffuse to harm the surrounding tissue.

CHAPTER

10

LANGUAGE DEVELOPMENT

What Is Language?
Language's Rule Systems
   Phonology
   Morphology
   Syntax
   Semantics
   Pragmatics
Language's Biological and Sociocultural/
   Environmental Heritages
   Biological Influences
   Perspective on Child Development 10.1: Genie,
      Modern-Day Wild Child
   Sociocultural and Environmental Influences
   Cultural Worlds of Development 10.1: Mother-
      Child Interaction in an Inner-City Housing
      Project
   Perspective on Child Development 10.2: Picture
      Books, First Words, and Labeling
The Role of Cognition in Language
How Language Develops
   Language Development in Infancy
   Language Development in Early Childhood
   Language Development in Middle and Late
      Childhood
Summary
Key Terms
Suggested Readings

Y ou are an intelligent young girl who has been captured by a group of some rather bizarre creatures, members of a highly advanced species who interact with all sorts of complex devices, drape unusual garments all over themselves, frequently emit long sequences of sound, and in general behave in complex and mysterious ways. You have no idea where these creatures came from or what they want with you. On the bright side, they appear to be friendly, even affectionate, and give you plenty of good food, including lots of chocolate, which you love. However, they won't let you go, and they insist that you play a weird game they have invented.

They started the game one day at your snack time. You expected some fruit, and one of your captors came with a banana. However, instead of giving the banana to you, he placed it where you could see it but could not get to it. Then he gave you a small, plastic, pink square and a small board. Not knowing what else to do, you took the pink square and placed it on the board. It stuck in place. Your captor then made some very strange excited sounds and gave you the banana.

Your captors repeated this game again and again. After a time, they started using other fruits as well as bananas. It soon became obvious that, for you to get different fruits, you had to put certain pieces of plastic on the board. For example, to get an apple, you had to put a blue triangle on the board. If you put the pink square on the board, your captors made some of their very strange sounds, but the apple stayed where it was—out of reach.

Various chips for different foods was only the start of the complexity that followed. Before long, getting some food depended not only on you sticking the corresponding chip on the board; in addition, you had to put a special chip above it. This chip was a funny-looking, six-sided thing. Order was important. If you put the six-sided shape below the chip instead of above it, you did not get your food.

After a while, the captors taught you a plastic "name" for yourself, as well as a name for each of them and for each of your fellow prisoners. If you wanted one of your captors to give you an apple, you had to put his plastic name at the top of the board, put the six-sided chip below it, put the blue-triangle chip (for apple) below that, and, finally, put your own plastic name at the bottom. So much work, just for an apple?

Later, your captors taught you ways of asking and answering questions and of making strange deals. For example, one of your captors wrote to you on the board, "If you pick up the apple, you will get some chocolate; if you pick up the banana, you will get no chocolate." You picked up the apple, and sure enough, they gave you chocolate.

What could this game be about? Who are these creatures and why are they interested in you? These creatures are psychologists who are studying language. You are one of their nonhuman subjects, a chimpanzee named Sarah. They are interested in you because they want to find out if nonhuman species can learn simple languages.

In this chapter, we will tell the elegant story of children's language development. Among the questions we will explore are the following: What is language? What are language's rule systems? What is language's biological heritage (including the question of whether chimpanzees can learn language)?

What is language's environmental heritage? What is cognition's role in language? What is the course of children's language development? How should reading be taught to children? What issues are involved in bilingualism?

What Is Language?

Every human society has language. There are thousands of human languages, and they differ so dramatically that many individuals despair of ever mastering more than one. However, all human languages have some things in common. What are the characteristics that all human languages share?

Language has been defined by one expert as a sequence of words (Miller, 1981). This definition describes language as having two characteristics—the presence of words and sequencing. It might seem obvious that all languages have *words,* but think for a minute about what words are. We produce and perceive words every day—yet words have an almost magical property: They stand for, or symbolize, things. We use words to refer to objects, people, actions, events, and even abstract ideas. What a word refers to is arbitrary in the sense that it is based on convention; a word symbolizes something commonly agreed on by a group of language users. To understand this point, consider the fact that different languages have different names for the same thing. What we call a *house* is called *casa* in Spanish and *maison* in French. Since different languages have different words, we are forced to conclude that words are linked arbitrarily and by convention to their referents.

Although words are important in language, the mere presence of words is not enough to make a language. Sequencing of the words also is required. Can you imagine a language with only one-word utterances? A 13-month-old infant may use one-word utterances, but, as we will see later in the chapter, experts argue that the infant has whole sentences in mind when uttering a single word.

Why is sequencing important for language? The answer leads us to a third characteristic of language—**infinite generativity,** *an individual's ability to generate an infinite number of meaningful sentences using a finite set of words and rules, which makes language a highly creative enterprise.* It is possible for us to say things never said before by anyone else.

Yet another characteristic of language is **displacement,** *the use of language to communicate information about another place and time,* although we also use language to describe what is currently happening in our immediate environment. Anyone hooked on reading light fiction can attest to the power of displacement in language. However, reading light fiction is just one example of how language gives secondhand experience. Consider the everyday experience of being told what happened elsewhere or what someone else said. Language not only contributes to the transmission of knowledge from one individual to another but also from one generation to the next (Brown, 1986).

A final, very important aspect of language is that it is characterized by rule systems. Thus, we can define **language** *as a system of symbols and sequence of words, used to communicate with others, that involves infinite generativity, displacement, and rule systems.* Let's now examine these important rule systems.

The maker of a sentence launches out into the infinite and builds a road into chaos and old night, and is followed by those who hear him with something of wild, creative delight.

—Ralph Waldo Emerson

Language's Rule Systems

When nineteenth-century American writer Ralph Waldo Emerson said, "The world was built in order and the atoms march in tune," he must have had

Figure 10.1
Language's Rule Systems

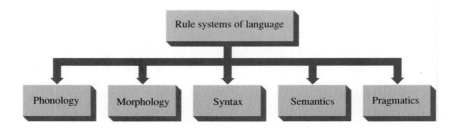

language in mind. The truly elegant system of language is highly ordered and organized. What is this order and organization like? The order and organization of language involve five rule systems: phonology, morphology, syntax, semantics, and pragmatics (see figure 10.1).

Phonology

Language is made up of basic sounds, or *phonemes*. In the English language, there are approximately 36 phonemes. **Phonology** *is the study of a language's sound system.* Phonological rules ensure that certain sound sequences occur (for example, *sp, ba,* or *ar*) and others do not (for example, *zx* or *qp*). A good example of a phoneme in the English language is /k/, the sound represented by the letter *k* in the word *ski* and the letter *c* in the word *cat.* Although the /k/ sound is slightly different in these two words, the variation is not distinguished and the /k/ sound is described as a single phoneme. In some languages, such as Arabic, this kind of variation is represented by separate phonemes.

Imagine what language would be like if there were no phonology. Each word in the language would have to be represented by a signal—a sound, for example—that differed from the signals of all other words. The obvious consequence is that the number of words could be no larger than the number of different signals that an individual could efficiently produce and perceive. We do not know precisely what that number is, but we do know that it is very small, especially in the case of speech, in contrast to the tens or even hundreds of thousands of words that commonly constitute a language.

What phonology does is to provide a basis for constructing a large and expandable set of words—all that are or ever will be—out of two to three dozen signal elements. We do not need five hundred thousand. All we need is two to three dozen.

Morphology

Morphology *refers to the rules for combining morphemes; a* morpheme *is the smallest string of sounds that gives meaning to what we say and hear.* Every word in the English language is made up of one or more morphemes. Some words consist of a single morpheme (for example, *help*), whereas others are made up of more than one morpheme (for example, *helper,* which has two morphemes, *help + er,* with the morpheme *er* meaning "one who"—in this case "one who helps"). However, not all morphemes are words (for example, *pre-, -tion,* and *-ing*). Just as the rules that govern phonemes ensure that certain sound sequences occur, the rules that govern morphemes ensure that certain strings of sounds occur in meaningful sequences. For example, we would not reorder *helper* to *erhelp.*

Learning, Cognition, and Language Development

Syntax

Syntax *involves the way words are combined to form acceptable phrases and sentences.* Because you and I share the same syntactic understanding of sentence structure, if I say to you, "Bob slugged Tom" and "Bob was slugged by Tom," you know who did the slugging and who was slugged in each case. You also understand that the sentence "You didn't stay, did you?" is a grammatical sentence but that "You didn't stay, didn't you?" is unacceptable and ambiguous.

A concept closely related to syntax is **grammar,** *the formal description of syntactical rules.* In elementary school and high school, most of us learned rules about sentence structure. Linguists devise rules of grammar that are similar to those you learned in school but are much more complex and powerful. Many contemporary linguists distinguish between the "surface" and "deep" structure of a sentence. **Surface structure** *is the actual order of words in a sentence.* **Deep structure** *is the syntactic relation of the words in a sentence.* By applying syntactic rules in different ways, one sentence can have two very different deep structures. For example, consider this sentence: "Mrs. Smith found drunk on her lawn." Was Mrs. Smith drunk or did she find a drunk on the lawn? Either interpretation fits the sentence, depending on the deep structure applied.

Semantics

Semantics *refers to the meaning of words and sentences.* Every word has a set of semantic features. Girl and woman, for example, share the same semantic features as the words female and human but differ in regard to age. Words have semantic restrictions on how they can be used in sentences. The sentence "The bicycle talked the boy into buying a candy bar" is syntactically correct but semantically incorrect. The sentence violates our semantic knowledge—bicycles do not talk.

Pragmatics

A final set of language rules involves **pragmatics,** *the use of appropriate conversation.* The domain of pragmatics is broad, covering such circumstances as: (a) taking turns in discussions instead of everyone talking at once; (b) using questions to convey commands ("Why is it so noisy in here?" "What is this, Grand Central Station?"); (c) using words like *the* and *a* in a way that enhances understanding ("I read *a* book last night. *The* plot was boring."); (d) using polite language in appropriate situations (for example, when talking to one's teacher); and (e) telling stories that are interesting, jokes that are funny, and lies that convince.

Pragmatic rules can be complex and differ from one culture to another (Becker, 1990). If you were to study the Japanese language, you would come face to face with countless pragmatic rules about conversing with individuals of various social levels and with various relationships to you. Some of these pragmatic rules concern the ways of saying thank you (see figure 10.2). Indeed, the pragmatics of saying thank you are complex even in our own culture. Preschoolers' use of this term varies with sex, socioeconomic status, and the age of the individual they are addressing. Through pragmatics, children learn to convey meaning with words, phrases, and sentences. Pragmatics helps children communicate more smoothly with others (Anderson, 1989; Gleason, 1988; Gleason, Hay, & Cain, 1989; Pan, Rollins, & Snow, 1991).

"If you don't mind my asking, how much does a sentence diagrammer pull down a year?"

© Bob Thaves.

The adjective is the banana peel of the parts of speech.

—Clifton Fadiman

A person gets from a symbol the meaning he puts into it, and what is one man's comfort and inspiration is another's jest and scorn.

—Justice Robert Jackson

Words not only affect us temporarily; they change us, they socialize us and they unsocialize us.

—David Riesman

Figure 10.2
Saying "Thank You" in Japanese

Expression	Context
Dōmo	Used with a social "inferior" who has served you in some way (e.g., a servant who has brought some tea)
Arigatō	A more formal expression used in similar situations as *Dōmo* (tourists are advised to use this word after being served in a store or shop)
Dōmo arigatō	Used with a social "equal" who has done a small favor for you (e.g., held open a door)
Arigatō gozaimasu	Used with a social "superior" in a polite or a formal situation (e.g., a "greeter" in a department store might say this as you leave the store with packages)
Dōmo arigatō gozaimasu	Used with a "superior" in a very formal situation (e.g., your boss has just given you a gift)

Is this ability to generate rule systems for language and then use them to create an almost infinite number of words the product of biology and evolution, or is it learned?

Language's Biological and Sociocultural/Environmental Heritages

In 1882, 2-year-old Helen Keller was left deaf, blind, and mute by a severe illness. By the time she was 7 years old, she had learned to fear the world she could not see or hear. Alexander Graham Bell suggested to her parents that they hire a tutor named Anne Sullivan to help Helen overcome her fears (figure 10.3). By using sign language, Anne was able to teach Helen a great deal about language. Helen Keller became an honors graduate of Radcliffe College and had this to say: "Whatever the process, the result is wonderful. Gradually from naming an object we advance step by step until we have traversed the vast distance between our first stammered syllable and the sweep of thought in a line of Shakespeare."

What is the process of learning language? Helen Keller had the benefit of a marvelous teacher, which suggests that experience is important in learning language. However, might there have been biological explanations for her language capabilities?

Biological Influences

How strongly is language influenced by biological evolution? Are children biologically prewired to learn langauge? What is the brain's role in language? Do animals have language? Is there a critical period for learning language? We will consider each of these questions in turn.

Biological Evolution

A number of experts on language stress its biological basis (Chomsky, 1957; Maratsos, 1989; Miller, 1981; Studdert-Kennedy, 1991). They believe that

Figure 10.3
Anne Sullivan Teaching Helen Keller About Language

Learning, Cognition, and Language Development

human infants are not unlike newborn birds, who come into the world biologically prepared to sing the song of their species. These language experts believe that biological evolution shaped humans into linguistic creatures. In terms of biological evolution, the brain, nervous system, and vocal system changed over hundreds of thousands of years. Prior to *Homo sapiens,* the physical equipment to produce language did not exist; *Homo sapiens* went beyond the groans and shrieks of their predecessors to develop abstract speech. Estimates vary as to how long ago humans acquired language—from about 20,000 to 70,000 years ago. In evolutionary time, then, language is a very recent acquisition.

Biological Prewiring—LAD

Linguist Noam Chomsky (1957) believes that humans are biologically prewired to learn language at a certain time and in a certain way. He also has said that children are born into the world with a **Language Acquisition Device (LAD),** *a biological prewiring that enables children to detect certain language categories, such as phonology, syntax, and semantics. LAD is an innate grammatical ability that underlies all human languages.*

The Brain's Role in Language

Another aspect of biology's role in language involves the accumulating evidence that language processing is controlled in the brain's left hemisphere (Gazzaniga, 1986; Sperry, 1974). Studies of language in brain-damaged individuals have pinpointed two areas of the left hemisphere that are especially critical. In 1861, a patient of Paul Broca, a French surgeon and anthropologist, received an injury to the left side of his brain. The patient became known as Tan, because that was the only word he could speak after his brain injury. Tan suffered from **aphasia,** *a language disorder, resulting from brain damage, that involves a loss of the ability to articulate ideas in any form.* Tan died several days after Broca evaluated him, and an autopsy revealed the location of the injury. Today, we refer to the part of the brain in which Broca's patient was injured as **Broca's area,** *an area of the left frontal lobe of the brain that directs the muscle movements involved in speech production.* Another place in the brain where an injury can seriously impair language is **Wernicke's area,** *an area of the brain's left hemisphere involved in language comprehension.* Individuals with damage to Wernicke's area often babble words in a meaningless way (Geschwind, 1979). The locations of Broca's area and Wernicke's area are shown in figure 10.4.

Although the brain's left hemisphere is especially important in language, keep in mind that, in most activities, there is an interplay between the brain's two hemispheres (Efron, in press; Heller, 1990; Hellige, 1990). For example, in reading, the left hemisphere comprehends syntax and grammar, which the right hemisphere does not. However, the right hemisphere is better at understanding a story's intonation and emotion.

Do Animals Have Language?

The role of language in human evolution has stimulated psychologists to think about the possibility that animals have language. No one doubts that animals of many species have wondrous and ingenious communication systems and that their communication is adaptive in signaling danger, food, and sex. Indeed, some of these communication systems are complex. For example, the female of one firefly species has learned to imitate the flashing signal of another species to lure the aliens into her territory. Then she eats them. However, is this

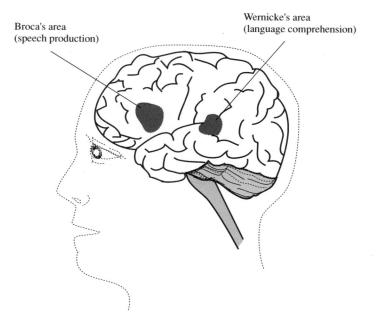

Figure 10.4
Broca's Area and Wernicke's Area
Damage to Broca's area causes problems in speech production, whereas damage to Wernicke's area causes problems in language comprehension. These areas are in the left hemisphere of the brain.

Broca's area
(speech production)

Wernicke's area
(language comprehension)

language in the human sense? What about animals higher on the evolutionary scale, such as apes? Is ape communication similar to human language? Can we teach language to them? Consider the efforts to teach language to a chimp named Washoe, who was adopted when she was about 10 months old (Gardner & Gardner, 1971). Because apes do not have the physical equipment to speak, the trainers tried to teach Washoe the American Sign Language, the sign language of the deaf. Daily routine events, such as meals, washing, household chores, play with toys, and car rides to interesting places provided many opportunities for the use of sign language. In 2 years, Washoe learned 38 different signs and, by the age of 5, had acquired a vocabulary of 160 signs. Washoe learned how to put signs together in such combinations as "you drink" and "you me tickle" (see figure 10.5). Most of her sign combinations resembled those of her human companions, but Washoe also combined signs in novel ways: She called her refrigerator the "open food drink" and her toilet chair the "dirty good," even though her companions referred to these as the "cold box" and the "potty chair." The Gardners have replicated the Washoe study with four additional chimpanzees, Moja, Pili, Tatu, and Dar (Gardner, Gardner, & Van Cantfort, 1989), and a number of other efforts to teach language to chimps have had similar results (Premack, 1986).

The debate about language in chimpanzees focuses on two key issues. First, can apes understand the meaning of symbols—that is, can they comprehend that one thing stands for another? Second, can apes learn syntax—that is, can they learn systems of rules that give human language its creative productivity? The first of these issues seems to have been settled recently. Sue Savage-Rumbaugh and Duane Rumbaugh have studied two chimps named Sherman and Austin, discovering strong evidence that their subjects understand symbols (see figure 10.6). For example, if Sherman or Austin is sitting in a room, and a symbol for an object is displayed on a screen, the chimp will go into another room, find the object, and bring it back. If the object is not there, the chimp will come back empty-handed (Cowley, 1988). Austin can play a game in which one chimp points to a symbol for food, the other chimp selects the food from a tray, then they both eat it. These observations are clear evidence that chimps can understand symbols (Rumbaugh & others, 1991; Savage-Rumbaugh, 1991).

Figure 10.5
Washoe Using the American Sign "Sweet" for Lollipop
Washoe learned 160 signs by the age of 5 and learned how to put signs together in novel ways, such as "you me tickle."

There still is no strong evidence that chimps can learn syntax, though. Other animals possibly can, however. Animal researcher Ron Schusterman has worked with a sea lion named Rocky, teaching him to follow commands such as "ball fetch" and "disc ball fetch." The first command means that Rocky should take a disc to a ball in his tank. The second command means that Rocky should take the ball to the disc. Although Rocky and other sea lions make some errors in decoding these complex commands, they perform much better than chance, indicating they have learned the rules linking the ordering of symbols to abstract meanings. Such rules are either syntax or something close to it. Animals can communicate with each other and can be trained to manipulate languagelike symbols. Whether animals, such as dolphins, can learn language with all the characteristics of human language is doubtful.

Figure 10.6
The Rumbaughs with Chimp Austin
Sue Savage-Rumbaugh and Duane Rumbaugh are shown with their chimpanzee Austin. A keyboard is reflected in the glass, and Austin is using a joystick to select words at the Rumbaughs' laboratory at Georgia State University.

Is There a Critical Period for Learning Language?

If you have listened to former secretary of state Henry Kissinger speak, you have some evidence for the belief that a critical period for learning language exists. If an individual over 12 years of age emigrates to a country and then starts to learn its language, the individual probably will speak the language with a foreign accent the rest of his life. Such was the case with Kissinger. If an individual emigrates as a young child, however, her accent goes away as she learns the new language (Asher & Garcia, 1969). Similarly, speaking like a native New Yorker is less related to how long you have lived in the city than to the age at which you moved there. Speaking with a New York "dialect" is more likely if you moved there before the age of 12. Apparently, puberty marks the close of a critical period for acquiring the phonological rules of languages and dialects.

The experiences of a modern-day wild child named Genie raises further interest in the idea of whether a critical time period for acquiring language exists. To learn more about Genie, turn to Perspective on Child Development 10.1.

Such findings confirm the belief that language must be triggered to be learned and that the optimal time for that triggering is during the early years of childhood. Biology's role in language is powerful, but even the most heavily inherited aspects of human development require an environment for their expression.

Genie, Modern-Day Wild Child

Genie was found in 1970 in California (see figure 10.A). At the time, she was 13 years old and had been reared by a partially blind mother and a violent father. She was discovered because her mother applied for assistance at a public welfare office. At the time, Genie could not speak and could not stand erect. She had lived in almost total isolation during her childhood years. Naked and restrained by a harness that her father had fashioned, she was left to sit on her potty seat day after day. She could move only her hands and feet and had virtually nothing to do every day of her life. At night, she was placed in a kind of straitjacket and caged in a crib with wire mesh sides and an overhead cover. She was fed, although sparingly. When she made a noise, her father beat her. He never spoke to her with words but growled and made barking sounds toward her.

Genie underwent extensive rehabilitation and training over a number of years (Curtiss, 1977). During her therapy, she learned to walk with a jerky motion and was toilet trained. She learned to recognize many words and to speak. At first she spoke in one-word utterances and eventually began to string together two-word utterances. She began to create some two-word sequences on her own, such as "big teeth," "little marble," and "two hand." Later she was able to put together three words—"small two cup," for example.

Unlike normal children, however, Genie never learned how to ask questions and she never understood grammar. Even 4 years later, after she began to put words together, her speech sounded like a garbled telegram. Genie never understood the

Figure 10.A
An Artist's Drawing of Modern-Day Wild Child Genie
Illustration by Roger Burkhart.

differences between pronouns and between passive and active verbs. As an adult, she continues to speak in short, mangled sentences, such as "father hit leg," "big wood," and "Genie hurt."

Sociocultural and Environmental Influences

In 1799, a nude boy was observed running through the woods of France. The boy was captured when he was approximately 11 years old. It was believed he had lived in the wild for at least 6 years. He was called the Wild Boy of Aveyron (Lane, 1976). When the boy was found, he made no effort to communicate. Even after a number of years, he could not communicate effectively. His social isolation likely contributed to his language inadequacies, just as Genie's social isolation did. We do not learn language in a social vacuum. Most of us are bathed in language from a very early age. We need this early exposure to language to acquire competent language skills (Rogoff, 1990; Schegloff, 1989; Snow, 1989).

Cultural Change and the Sociocultural Context of Language

In our discussion of biological evolution, we indicated that, prior to *Homo sapiens,* the physical equipment to produce speech did not exist. Anthropologists speculate about the social conditions that led to the development of language. Social forces may have pushed humans to develop abstract reasoning

Learning, Cognition, and Language Development

and to create an economical system for communicating with others (Crick, 1977). For example, humans probably developed complex plans and strategies for obtaining food and finding shelter, and they may have been motivated to develop language to reach a higher level of competence.

The sociocultural context continues to play an important role in children's language today. In chapter 8, we discussed Vygotsky's view of development, which emphasizes the important role of adults or more highly skilled children in a child's development. Middle-class American parents impart the skills for the use of cultural tools, such as literacy, to their children very early in life (Rogoff, 1990). These parents also involve their children in extensive conversation long before they go to kindergarten or elementary school, and they provide their young children with picture books and read stories to them at bedtime as part of their daily routine. Middle-class American parents embed their children in a way of life in which reading and writing are integral parts of communication, recreation, and livelihood. However, as discussed in Cultural Worlds of Development 10.1, children who grow up in the slum areas of large cities are usually not exposed to the guided participation in language that their middle-class counterparts are.

American psychologist Jerome Bruner (1983, 1989) also believes that the sociocultural context is extremely important in understanding children's language development. Like Vygotsky, Bruner stresses the role of parents and teachers in constructing a child's communication environment. **Language Acquisition Support System (LASS)** *is Bruner's concept that describes the behaviors of a language-skilled individual, especially a parent, in structuring and supporting the child's development of language.* Bruner's concept has much in common with Vygotsky's zone of proximal development, which was discussed in chapter 8. Thus, language development requires social involvement as well as a child's natural propensity to learn language (Furrow & Moore, 1991; Hoff-Ginsberg, 1991; Lock, 1991; Rogoff, 1990). In this view, the Language Acquisition Device (LAD), developed by Chomsky (1957) to account for the complexity and speed of young children's understanding of grammar, interacts with the Language Acquisition Support System (LASS) to make the language system function (see figure 10.7).

Social Supports for Language

What are some of the social supports that provide infants and children with a rich language learning environment? They include the parental simplification and framing of language through motherese, recasting, echoing, expanding, labeling, modeling, and corrective feedback.

One intriguing element of the environment in a young child's language acquisition is called **motherese,** *the way mothers and other adults often talk to babies in a higher-than-normal frequency and greater-than-normal pitch and with simple words and sentences.* It is hard to talk in motherese when not in the presence of a baby, but, as soon as you start talking to a baby, you immediately shift into motherese. Much of this is automatic and something most parents are not aware that they are doing. Motherese has the important functions of capturing the infant's attention and maintaining communication (Snow, 1989). When parents are asked why they use motherese, they point out that it is designed to teach their baby to talk. Older peers also talk motherese to infants (Dunn & Kendrick, 1982).

Other than motherese, are there other strategies adults use to enhance the child's acquisition of language? Four candidates are recasting, echoing, expanding, and labeling. **Recasting** *is phrasing the same or a similar meaning*

Mother-Child Interaction in an Inner-City Housing Project

Some young children are brought up in the blighted urban areas of high-rise housing projects. Many of them are the children of single mothers. The small apartments and public housing rules discourage extended families. High-rise buildings frequently eliminate the possibility of free play outside by young children.

Young mothers isolated in these small apartments with their young children are often separated from family members by the expense and trouble of cross-town public transportation. The mothers watch television, talk on the phone, or perform household and caregiving chores. Playmates for their children are scarce. So are toys. Visits to the grocery store, the welfare office, and the laundromat may represent the only breaks in daily apartment routines. So may the usually traumatic visits to the health clinic.

One mother agreed to let researcher Shirley Heath (in press) tape-record her interactions with her children over a 2-year period and to write notes about her activities with them. Within 500 hours of tape and more than 1,000 lines of notes, the mother initiated talk with her three preschool children on only 18 occasions (other than giving them a brief directive or asking a quick question). Few of the mother's conversations involved either planning or executing actions with or for her children.

When children are brought up in the blighted urban areas of high-rise housing projects, often they cannot engage in free play outside and their conversations with adults are minimal and do not involve cognitive and social skills training.

Heath (1989) points out that the lack of family and community supports is widespread in urban housing projects, especially among Black Americans. The deteriorating, impoverished conditions of these inner-city areas severely impede the ability of young children to develop the cognitive and social skills they need to function competently.

---

of a sentence in a different way, perhaps turning it into a question. For example, if a child says, "The dog was barking," the adult can respond by asking, "When was the dog barking?" The effects of recasting fit with suggestions that "following in order to lead" helps a child learn language. That is, letting a child initially indicate an interest and then proceeding to elaborate that interest—commenting, demonstrating, and explaining—may enhance communication and help language acquisition. In contrast, an overly active, directive approach to communicating with the child may be harmful (Rice, 1989). **Echoing** *is repeating what the child says to you, especially if it is an incomplete phrase or sentence.* **Expanding** *is restating what the child has said in a linguistically sophisticated form.* **Labeling** *is identifying the names of objects.* Young children are forever being asked to identify the names of objects. Roger Brown (1986) identified this as the great word game and claimed that much of the early vocabulary acquired by children is motivated by this adult pressure to identify the words associated with objects. Information about picture books, first words, and labeling is presented in Perspective on Child Development 10.2.

Parents and teachers also contribute to children's language development through their roles as language models and through corrective feedback to children (Bohannon, MacWhinney, & Snow, 1990). Children who are slow in developing language skills can be helped if parents use carefully selected lists

■ *Critical Thinking*

What should be the nature of parents' responses to children's grammatical mistakes in conversation? Should parents allow the mistakes to continue and assume that their young children will grow out of them, or should they closely monitor their children's grammar and correct mistakes whenever they hear them? Explain your answer.

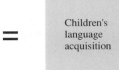

| Language Acquisition Device (LAD) Biological prewiring for language | $\times$ | Language Acquisition Support System (LASS) Sociocultural structuring and support | $=$ | Children's language acquisition |

Figure 10.7
An Interactionist View of Language: Chomsky's LAD and Bruner's LASS
In the interactionist view, language acquisition involves the child's natural propensity to learn language (described by Chomsky as the Language Acquisition Device [LAD]) and social involvement (described by Bruner as the Language Acquisition Support System [LASS]).

of words and grammatical constructions of speech to the children (Whitehurst & Valdez-Menchaca, 1988). Parents also shape children's grammatical utterances by correcting their grammatical errors (Bohannon & Stanowicz, 1988; Penner, 1987). Nonetheless, a number of experts on language believe that imitation and reinforcement facilitate language but are not absolutely necessary for its acquisition (de Villiers, 1988; de Villiers & de Villiers, 1978).

The Behavioral View

Behaviorists view language as just another behavior, like sitting, walking, or running. They argue that children's language is acquired through the learning processes of reinforcement (Skinner, 1957) and imitation (Bandura, 1977). However, many of the sentences children produce are novel in the sense that they have not previously heard them. For example, children might hear the sentence "The plate fell on the floor" and then say, "My mirror fell on the blanket," after they drop the mirror on the blanket. The behavioral mechanisms of reinforcement (smiles, hugs, pats on the back, corrective feedback) and imitation (modeling of words and syntax) cannot completely explain this utterance.

While spending long hours observing parents and their young children, American pioneer in language research Roger Brown (1973) searched for evidence that parents reinforce their children for speaking grammatically. He found that parents sometimes smiled and praised their children for sentences they liked, but that they also reinforced sentences that were ungrammatical. Brown concluded that no evidence exists to document that reinforcement is responsible for language's rule systems. However, recently, some researchers

Picture Books, First Words, and Labeling

Anat Ninio and Jerome Bruner (1978) took a close look at the subtle interplay between a mother and her infant son as the two performed the great word game in its quintessential setting—reading picture books and playing with objects. The mother and child were part of a longitudinal study that covered the period of 8 to 18 months in the child's life. The child was firstborn, and his parents were White, English, and middle class. Labeling was part of the filmed play activity captured in the videotape records, made every 2 to 3 weeks in the infant's home.

The investigators uncovered some remarkable findings. Chief among these was the ritualized nature of mother-child labeling activity. The labeling of pictures was a highly structured activity that obeyed clear rules and had the texture of a dialogue. A number of scholars have described such conversations as having fairly tight patterns in ascribing roles, turn taking, imitating, and responding (Bruner, 1983; Snow, 1989). So did the labeling activity. Each time the mother and child interacted over a picture name, for example, they took about the same number of turns, which lasted about the same length of time. The linguistic forms of the mother's utterances in book reading were very limited. She made repeated use of four key types of statements: (1) "Look!" (to get the child's attention); (2) "What's that?"; (3) "It's an X!" (labeling the picture for the child); and (4) "Yes!" (giving the child feedback on his utterance). These types of statements accounted for virtually all of the language the mother directed toward the child while reading books during the entire period of the study, and they obeyed some simple rules of occurrence. For example, the attention getter "Look!" always preceded the query "What's that?" or the labeling phrase "It's an X!" Similarly, the query always preceded the labeling phrase.

At the outset of the study, of course, few of the child's verbal responses to the mother's queries were distinguishable words. At best, the child produced consistent babble. By the end of the period, however, words were present. Associated

Mothers and children often play the great word game involving mother-child labeling. In this game, mother and child take about the same number of turns, lasting about the same length of time.

with this change, the mother dropped the question "What's that?" from the ritual, since the child now could produce a word for the picture.

Summarizing the key points of the study, in the authors' own words:

> The book reading dialogue seems . . . to be a format well suited to the teaching of labeling. It has few elements and strict ordering rules between them. It is flexible in the sense of accepting a great variety of responses by the child. It is highly repetitive. Not only do the fixed elements ["Look," "What's that?" and "It's a (label)"] appear over and over again, with minimal changes in the wording, but the variable elements, the labels themselves, appear repeatedly as well. (Ninio & Bruner, 1978, p. 12)

have found evidence that many parents provide more corrective feedback for children's ungrammatical utterances than Brown originally thought (Penner, 1987).

Famous American linguist Noam Chomsky (1957, 1986) believes that the behavioral view of language is wrong. Chomsky says that children do learn the language of their sociocultural world, but the speed at which they acquire words and grammar cannot be explained by learning principles such as reinforcement and imitation. Remember that Chomsky says that children come into the world equipped with a biologically prewired Language Acquisition Device, which is much like a biological machine with switches. According to

Chomsky, all that is needed to turn on the switches of the biological machine is for the child to hear a particular language spoken.

As can be seen, the question of how children acquire language has met with spirited debate. Basically, the debate is another version of the pervasive nature-nurture controversy, which was first introduced in chapter 1 and which we have frequently visited throughout this book. How do children acquire language? Their biological foundations prepare them to learn language as they and their caregivers interact socially. As in other areas of children's development, once again we find biology and experience interacting and working together.

At this point, we have discussed a number of ideas about what language is, language's rule systems, and the biological and sociocultural environmental heritages of language. A summary of these ideas is presented in concept table 10.1.

The Role of Cognition in Language

Noam Chomsky's idea of the young language learner as richly endowed with prewired equipment is widely accepted today, but there is a question about the type of equipment the child possesses. Is the equipment specifically linguistic, like Chomsky's Language Acquisition Device, or is it more cognitive, being derived from humans' generally high level of intelligence (Maratsos, 1983)? The basic claim of the cognitive theorists is that a child's growing intelligence and desire to express meanings, together with language input from parents, "drive" the acquisition of language (Markman, 1989; Waxman & Kosowski, 1990). Thus, the cognitive view's focus is on the semantic and pragmatic levels of language rather than on the syntactic, morphological, and phonological levels.

Language is the dress of thought.

—Samuel Johnson

One type of evidence for the cognitive view is that children's early utterances seem to indicate knowledge of semantic categories, such as agent and action, rather than linguistic categories such as noun and verb (Bowerman, 1989). In support of this view, children can tell that semantically deviant sentences are wrong before they can tell syntactically deviant sentences are wrong (Washburn & Hakes, 1985). This implies that a 5-year-old might detect the unacceptability of the sentence "The bicycle talked to the boy" (semantically deviant), yet fail to reject the sentences "The boy ride the bicycle" and "What you are doing today?" (syntactically deviant).

Evidence that cognition is important for language comes from studies of deaf children. On a variety of thinking and problem-solving skills, deaf children perform at the same level as children of the same age who have no hearing problems. Some of the deaf children in these studies do not even have command of written or sign language (Furth, 1973).

Another argument for a cognitive theory of language concerns what we know about how language evolved. Since a spoken language leaves no physical trace, the age of human language is difficult to determine. According to some estimates, however, language evolved as recently as 10,000 to 100,000 years ago (Swadesh, 1971)—quite recent in evolutionary time—perhaps too recent for a large amount of purely linguistic machinery to have evolved in the brain. From an evolutionary perspective, cognition is much older than human language. For example, tool-making activity—a clear sign of high intellectual functioning—is at least 2 million years old (Miller, 1981). Considerations such as these favor the view that language is at least partly a product of cognition, not being solely determined by specific linguistic abilities.

What Is Language, Language's Rule Systems, and Language's Biological and Sociocultural/Environmental Heritages

Concept	Processes/related ideas	Characteristics/description
What is language?	Its nature	Language is a system of symbols and sequence of words, used to communicate with others, that involves infinite generativity, displacement, and rule systems.
Language's rule systems	Phonology	Phonology governs the sequencing of phonemes (basic sounds that differ in their distinctive features).
	Morphology	Morphology governs the sequencing of morphemes (the smallest units of language that carry meaning).
	Syntax	Syntax governs the ordering of words within sentences or phrases. These rules apply to deep and surface structures.
	Semantics	Semantics places restrictions on how words must be used to make meaningful sentences.
	Pragmatics	Pragmatics facilitates good communication and good social relations among language users.
Biological influences	Biological evolution	The fact that biological evolution shaped humans into linguistic creatures is undeniable.
	Biological prewiring—LAD	Linguist Noam Chomsky believes that humans are prewired to learn language. He said children are born with a Language Acquisition Device (LAD), a biological prewiring that enables a child to detect certain language categories. LAD is an innate grammatical ability.
	The brain's role in language	The brain's left hemisphere plays an important role in language. Damage to Broca's area affects speech production, whereas damage to Wernicke's area affects language comprehension. Although the left hemisphere has a powerful influence on language, keep in mind that, in most activities, there is an interplay between the brain's two hemispheres.
	Do animals have language?	Animals can communicate and chimpanzees can be taught to use symbols. Whether animals have all of the properties of human language is debated.
	Is there a critical period for learning language?	The experiences of Genie and other children suggest that the early years of childhood are a critical time for learning language. If exposure to language does not occur before puberty, lifelong deficits in grammar occur.
Cultural, environmental, and behavioral influences	Cultural change and the sociocultural context of language	Sociocultural conditions may have pushed humans to develop abstract reasoning and to create an economical system for communicating with others. Bruner believes that the Language Acquisition Support System (LASS) plays an important role in structuring and supporting children's language. Among the social supports that contribute to children's language are parental simplification and framing of language through motherese, recasting, echoing, expanding, labeling, modeling, and corrective feedback.
	The behavioral view	Behaviorists view language as just another behavior, like sitting, walking, or running. They argue that children's language is acquired through reinforcement and imitation. Chomsky believes that the behavioral view is wrong. An interactionist view emphasizes the contributions of both biology and experience in language—that is, children are biologically prepared to learn language as they and their caregivers interact.

How Language Develops

In the thirteenth century, the Holy Roman Emperor Frederick II had a cruel idea. He wanted to know what language children would speak if no one talked to them. He selected several newborns and threatened their caregivers with death if they ever talked to the infants. Frederick never found out what language the children spoke because they all died. As we move toward the twenty-first century, we are still curious about infants' development of language, although our experiments and observations are, to say the least, far more humane than the evil Frederick's.

Language Development in Infancy

When does an infant utter her first word? The event usually occurs at about 10 to 13 months of age, though some infants wait longer. Many parents view the onset of language development as coincident with this first word, but some significant accomplishments are attained earlier. Before babies say words, they babble, emitting such vocalizations as "goo-goo" and "ga-ga." Babbling starts at about 3 to 6 months of age. The start is determined by biological maturation, not reinforcement or the ability to hear (Locke & others, 1991). Even deaf babies babble for a time (Lenneberg, Rebelsky, & Nichols, 1965). Babbling exercises the baby's vocal apparatus and facilitates the development of articulation skills that are useful in later speech (Clark & Clark, 1977). The purpose of a baby's earliest communication, however, is to attract attention from parents and others in the environment. Infants engage the attention of others by making or breaking eye contact, by vocalizing sounds, and by performing manual actions such as pointing. All of those behaviors involve pragmatics.

A child's first words include those that name important people (*dada*), familiar animals (*kittie*), vehicles (*car*), toys (*ball*), food (*milk*), body parts (*eye*), clothes (*hat*), household items (*clock*), or greeting terms (*bye*). These were the first words of babies 50 years ago and they are the first words of babies today (Clark, 1983). At times, it is hard to tell what these one-word utterances mean. One possibility is that they stand for an entire sentence in the infant's mind. Because of limited cognitive or linguistic skills, possibly only one word comes out instead of the whole sentence. The **holophrase hypothesis** *is the theory that a single word is used to imply a complete sentence; it is characteristic of an infant's first words.*

Children sometimes overextend or underextend the meanings of the words they use. **Overextension** *is the tendency of children to misuse words by extending one word's meaning to include objects that are not related to or are inappropriate for the word's meaning.* For example, when children learn to say the word *dada* for "father," they often apply the word beyond the individual it was intended to represent, using it for other men, strangers, or boys. With time, such overextensions decrease and eventually disappear. **Underextension** *occurs when children fail to use a noun to name a relevant event or object.* For example, children may learn to use the word *boy* to describe a 5-year-old neighbor but not apply the word to a male infant or a 9-year-old male.

By the time children are 18 to 24 months of age, they usually have begun to utter two-word statements. During this two-word stage, they quickly grasp the importance of expressing concepts and the role that language plays in communicating with others. To convey meaning with two-word utterances, the child

Around the world, young children learn to speak in two-word utterances, in most cases at about 18 to 24 months of age.

relies heavily on gesture, tone, and context. The wealth of meaning children can communicate with a two-word utterance includes:

Identification: See doggie.
Location: Book there.
Repetition: More milk.
Nonexistence: Allgone thing.
Negation: Not wolf.
Possession: My candy.
Attribution: Big car.
Agent-action: Mama walk.
Action-direct-object: Hit you.
Action-indirect-object: Give papa.
Action-instrument: Cut knife.
Question: Where ball? (Slobin, 1972)

One of the most striking aspects of this list is that it is used by children all over the world. The examples are taken from utterances in English, German, Russian, Finnish, Turkish, Samoan, and Luo.

Telegraphic speech *is the use of short, precise words to communicate; it is characteristic of young children's two-word utterances.* When we write telegrams, we try to be terse, excluding any unnecessary words. As indicated in the examples of telegraphic speech from children from around the world, articles, auxiliary verbs, and other connectives usually are omitted. Of course, telegraphic speech is not limited to two-word utterances. "Mommy give ice cream" and "Mommy give Tommy ice cream" also are examples of telegraphic speech.

In expanding this concept of classifying children's language development in terms of number of utterances, Roger Brown (1973) has proposed that **mean length of utterance** (MLU), *an index of language development based on the number of words per sentence a child produces in a sample of about 50 to 100 sentences,* is a good index of language maturity. Brown identified five stages based on MLU:

Stage	MLU
1	1 + to 2.0
2	2.5
3	3.0
4	3.5
5	4.0

The first stage begins when a child generates sentences consisting of more than one word, such as the examples of two-word utterances mentioned earlier. The 1 + designation suggests that the average number of words in each utterance is greater than one but not yet two, because some of the child's utterances are still holophrases. This stage continues until the child averages two words per utterance. Subsequent stages are marked by increments of .5 in mean length of utterance.

Brown's stages are important for several reasons. First, children who vary in chronological age as much as one half to three fourths of a year still have similar speech patterns. Second, children with similar mean lengths of utterance seem to have similar rule systems that characterize their language. In some ways, then, MLU is a better indicator of language development than is chronological age. Figure 10.8 shows the individual variation in chronological age that characterizes children's MLU.

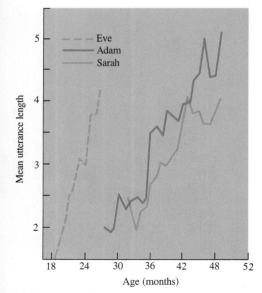

Figure 10.8

An Examination of MLU in Three Children Shown here is the average length of utterances generated by three children ranging in age from 1½ to just over 4 years.

Learning, Cognition, and Language Development

Language Development in Early Childhood

Young children's understanding sometimes gets way ahead of their speech. One 3-year-old, laughing with delight as an abrupt summer breeze stirred his hair and tickled his skin, commented, "It did winding me!" Adults would be understandably perplexed if a young child ventured, "Anything is not to break, only plates and glasses," when she meant, "Nothing is breaking except plates and glasses." Many of the oddities of young children's language sound like mistakes to adult listeners. From the children's point of view, however, they are not mistakes; they represent the way young children perceive and understand their world at that point in their development. Among the important issues in language during the early childhood years are those involving developmental changes in language's rule systems and the role of early childhood education in literacy.

Changes in Rule Systems

What kinds of changes occur in language development during early childhood? Language continues to obey certain principles, following the rules of phonology, morphology, syntax, semantics, and pragmatics.

Regarding phonology, some preschool children have difficulty speaking in consonant clusters (for example, *str* as in *string*). Pronouncing some of the more difficult phonemes—*r,* for example—is still problematic and can continue to be a problem in the elementary school years. Also, some of the phonological rules for pronouncing word endings (in the past tense, for example) are not mastered until children are 6 to 8 years of age.

Regarding morphology, as children move beyond two-word utterances, there is clear evidence that they know morphological rules. Children begin using the plural and possessive forms of nouns (*dogs* and *dog's*); putting appropriate endings on verbs (*s* when the subject is third-person singular, *ed* for the past tense, and *ing* for the present progressive tense); and using prepositions (*in* and *on*), articles (*a* and *the*), and various forms of the verb *to be* ("I was going to the store"). Some of the best evidence for morphological rules appears in the form of *overgeneralizations* of these rules. Have you ever heard a preschool child say "foots" instead of "feet" or "goed" instead of "went"? If you do not remember having heard such things, talk to some parents who have young children or to the young children themselves. You will hear some interesting errors in the use of morphological rule endings.

In a classic experiment, children's language researcher Jean Berko (1958) presented preschool and first-grade children with cards such as the one shown in figure 10.9. Children were asked to look at the card while the experimenter read the words on it aloud. Then the children were asked to supply the missing word. This might sound easy, but Berko was interested not just in the children's ability to recall the right word but their ability to say it "correctly" (with the ending that was dictated by morphological rules). *Wugs* would be the correct response for the card in figure 10.9. Although the children were not perfectly accurate, they were much better than chance would dictate. Moreover, they demonstrated their knowledge of morphological rules not only with the plural forms of nouns ("There are two wugs") but also with possessive forms of nouns and with the third-person singular and past-tense forms of verbs. What makes Berko's study impressive is that most of the words were fictional; they were created especially for the experiment. Thus, the children could not base their responses on remembering past instances of hearing the words. It seems, instead, that they were forced to rely on *rules*. Their performance suggested that they did so successfully.

This is a wug.

Now there is another one. There are two of them. There are two _____.

Figure 10.9

Stimuli in Berko's Study of Young Children's Understanding of Morphological Rules
In Jean Berko's (1958) study, young children were presented cards such as this one with a "wug" on it. Then the children were asked to supply the missing word and say it correctly. "Wugs" is the correct response here.

"No, Timmy, not 'I *sawed* the chair.' It's 'I *saw* the chair' or 'I *have seen* the chair.'"

© BERNHARDT.

Similar evidence that children learn and actively apply rules can be found at the level of syntax. After advancing beyond two-word utterances, the child speaks word sequences that show a growing mastery of complex rules for how words should be ordered. Consider the case of *wh*-questions: "Where is Daddy going?" and "What is that boy doing?" for example. To ask these questions properly, the child has to know two important differences between *wh*-questions and simple affirmative statements (for instance, "Daddy is going to work" and "That boy is waiting on the school bus"). First, a *wh*- word must be added at the beginning of the sentence. Second, the auxiliary verb must be "inverted"—that is, exchanged with the subject of the sentence. Young children learn quite early where to put the *wh*- word, but they take much longer to learn the auxiliary-inversion rule. Thus, it is common to hear preschool children asking such questions as "Where daddy is going?" and "What that boy is doing?"

As children move into the elementary school years, they become skilled at using syntactical rules to construct lengthy and complex sentences. Sentences such as "The man who fixed the house went home" and "I don't want you to use my bike" are impressive demonstrations of how the child can use syntax to combine ideas into a single sentence. Just how a young child achieves the mastery of such complex rules, while at the same time she may be struggling with relatively simple arithmetic rules, is a mystery we have yet to solve.

Regarding semantics, as children move beyond the two-word stage, their knowledge of meanings also rapidly advances. The speaking vocabulary of a 6-year-old child ranges from 8,000 to 14,000 words (Carey, 1977). Assuming that word learning began when the child was 12 months old, this translates into a rate for new word meanings of five to eight words a day between the ages of 1 and 6. After 5 years of word learning, the 6-year-old child does not slow down. According to some estimates, the average child of this age is moving along at the awe-inspiring rate of 22 words a day (Miller, 1981). How would you fare if you were given the task of learning 22 new words every day? It is truly miraculous how quickly children learn language.

Although there are many differences between a 2-year-old's language and a 6-year-old's language, none are more important than those pertaining to pragmatics—that is, rules of conversation. A 6-year-old is simply a much better conversationalist than a 2-year-old. What are some of the improvements in pragmatics that are made in the preschool years? At about 3 years of age, children improve in their ability to talk about things that are not physically present; that is, they improve their command of the characteristic of language known as *displacement*. One way displacement is revealed is in games of pretend. Although a 2-year-old might know the word *table,* he is unlikely to use this word to refer to an imaginary table that he pretends is standing in front of him. A child over 3 probably has this ability, though, even if she does not always use it. There are large individual differences in preschoolers' talk about imaginary people and things.

Somewhat later in the preschool years—at about 4 years of age—children develop a remarkable sensitivity to the needs of others in conversation (Gleason, 1988). One way in which they show such sensitivity is their use of the articles *the* and *an* (or *a*). When adults tell a story or describe an event, they generally use *an* (or *a*) when they first refer to an animal or an object, and then use *the* when referring to it later (for example, "Two boys were walking through the jungle when *a* fierce lion appeared. *The* lion lunged at one boy while the other ran for cover"). Even 3-year-olds follow part of this rule (they consistently use the word *the* when referring to previously men-

As children develop, they become much better conversationalists. At about 4 years of age, children become more sensitive to the needs of others in conversation.

Learning, Cognition, and Language Development

tioned things). However, using the word *a* when something is initially mentioned develops more slowly. Although 5-year-old children follow this rule on some occasions, they fail to follow it on others.

Another pragmatic ability that appears around 4 to 5 years of age involves speech style. As adults, we have the ability to change our speech style in accordance with social situations and persons with whom we are speaking. An obvious example is that adults speak in a simpler way to a 2-year-old child than to an older child or to an adult. Interestingly, even 4-year-old children speak differently to a 2-year-old than to a same-aged peer (they "talk down" to the 2-year-old using shorter utterance lengths). They also speak differently to an adult than to a same-aged peer, using more polite and formal language with the adult (Shatz & Gelman, 1973).

Literacy and Early Childhood Education

The concern about our nation's **literacy,** *the ability to read and write,* has led to a careful examination of preschool and kindergarten children's experiences, with the hope that children will develop a positive orientation toward reading and writing early in life (Dickinson & Moreton, 1991; Early Childhood and Literacy Development Committee, 1986; Liberg, 1990; Linden & Whimbey, 1990). Literacy begins in infancy. Reading and writing skills in young children should build on their existing understanding of oral and written language. Learning should occur in a supportive environment, one in which children can generate a positive perception of themselves and develop a positive attitude toward reading and writing (Beals & De Temple, 1991; Bloome, 1989; Garton & Pratt, 1989).

Unfortunately, in the push to develop a nation of literate people by emphasizing the early development of reading and writing skills, some dangers have emerged (Early Childhood and Literacy Development Committee, 1986). Too many preschool children are being subjected to rigid, formal prereading programs with expectations and experiences that are too advanced for children of their levels of development. Too little attention is being given to the individual development of young children's learning styles and skills. Too little attention is given to reading for pleasure, which may keep children from associating reading with enjoyment. The pressure to achieve high scores on standardized tests, which often are inappropriate for preschool children, has resulted in a curriculum that is too advanced and too intense. Such programs frequently restrict curiosity, critical thinking, and creative expression.

What should a literacy program for preschool children be like? Instruction should be built on what children already know about oral language, reading, and writing. All young children should experience feelings of success and pride in their early reading and writing exercises. Teachers need to help them perceive themselves as people who can enjoy exploring oral and written language. Reading should be integrated into the broad communication process, which includes speaking, listening, and writing, as well as other communication systems such as art, math, and music. Children's early writing attempts should be encouraged without concern for the proper formation of letters or correct conventional spelling (figure 10.10). Children should be encouraged to take risks in reading and writing, and errors should be viewed as a natural part of the child's growth. Teachers and parents should regularly take time to read to children from a wide variety of poetry, fiction, and nonfiction. Teachers and parents should present models for young children to emulate by using language appropriately, listening and responding to children's

■ *Critical Thinking*
Assume that you have been hired as a consultant to an early childhood education program. Many of the parents want their children to learn to read early and want reading to be a main focus of the program. How would you handle the pushy parents?

In a real sense, the writer writes to teach himself, to understand himself, to satisfy himself.

—Alfred Kazin

Figure 10.10
A 4-Year-Old's Written Version of
The Three Bears
Young children's early writing attempts
should be encouraged without concern for
the proper formation of letters or correct
conventional spelling. Children should be
encouraged to take risks in writing.

talk, and engaging in their own reading and writing. Children also should be encouraged to be active participants in the learning process rather than passive recipients of knowledge. This can be accomplished by using activities that stimulate their experimentation with talking, listening, writing, and reading.

Language Development in Middle and Late Childhood

As children develop during middle and late childhood, changes in their vocabulary and grammar take place. Reading assumes a prominent role in their language world. An increasingly important consideration is bilingualism. We will consider each of these aspects of children's language development in turn.

Vocabulary and Grammar

During middle and late childhood, a change occurs in the way children think about words. They become less tied to the actions and perceptual dimensions associated with words, and they become more analytical in their approach to words. For example, when asked to say the first thing that comes to mind when they hear a word, such as *dog,* preschool children often respond with a word related to the immediate context of a dog. A child might associate *dog* with a word that indicates its appearance (*black, big*) or to an action associated with it (*bark, sit*). Older children more frequently respond to *dog* by associating it with an appropriate category (*animal*) or to information that intelligently expands the context (*cat, veterinarian*) (Holzman, 1983). The increasing ability of elementary school children to analyze words helps them understand words that have no direct relation to their personal experiences. This allows children to add more abstract words to their vocabulary. For example, *precious stones* can be understood by understanding the common characteristics of *diamonds* and *emeralds.* Also, children's increasing analytic abilities allow them to distinguish between such similar words as *cousin* and *nephew* or *city, village,* and *suburb.*

Children make similar advances in grammar. The elementary school child's improvement in logical reasoning and analytical skills helps in the understanding of such constructions as the appropriate use of comparatives (*shorter, deeper*) and subjectives ("If you were president, . . ."). By the end of the elementary school years, children can usually apply many of the appropriate rules of grammar (de Villiers & de Villiers, 1978).

Reading

Reading becomes a special skill during the elementary school years. Not being a competent reader places children at a substantial disadvantage in relation to their peers.

In the history of learning-to-read techniques, three approaches have dominated: the ABC method, the whole-word method, and the phonics method. The **ABC method** *is a learning-to-read technique that emphasizes memorizing the names and letters of the alphabet.* The **whole-word method** *is a learning-to-read technique that emphasizes learning direct associations between whole words and their meanings.* The **phonics method** *is a learning-to-read technique that emphasizes the sounds that letters make when in words (such sounds can differ from the names of these letters, as when the sound of the letter* C *is not found in* cat). The ABC method is in ill repute today. Because of the imperfect relationship between the names of letters and their sounds in words, the technique is regarded as ineffective, if not harmful, in teaching children to read. Despite its poor reputation, the ABC method was

Reading becomes a special skill during the elementary school years. A special concern of our nation is the improvement of the reading skills of children from low-income, ethnic minority backgrounds.

the technique that taught many children in past generations to read successfully. Disputes in recent years have centered on the merits of the whole-word and phonics methods (Goswami & Bryant, 1990). Although some research has been done comparing these two techniques, the findings have not been conclusive (Carbo, 1987). However, there is evidence that drill practice with the sounds made by letters in words (part of some phonics methods) improves reading ability (Williams, 1979). Many current techniques of reading instruction incorporate components of both wholeword and phonics (Karlin & Karlin, 1987).

Reading is more than the sum of whole-word and phonics methods. Information-processing skills are also involved in successful reading (Hall, 1989; Rieben & Perfetti, 1991). When children read, they process information and interpret it, so reading serves as a practical example to illustrate the approach of information processing we have talked about at various other times in this book. Remember that information processing is concerned with how children analyze the many different sources of information available to them in the environment and how they make sense of those experiences. When children read, for example, a rich and complex set of visual symbols is available to their senses. The symbols are associated with sounds, the sounds are combined to form words, and the words and large units that contain them (phrases, sentences, paragraphs) have conventional meanings. To read effectively, chil-

354   Learning, Cognition, and Language Development

Reading is more than the sum of whole-word and phonics methods. Information-processing skills are involved in successful reading. When children read, they process information and interpret it.

dren must perceive and attend to words and sentences. They must also hold information in memory while processing new information. A number of information-processing skills, then, are involved in children's ability to read effectively.

Bilingualism

Octavio's Mexican parents moved to the United States 1 year before Octavio was born. They do not speak English fluently and have always spoken to Octavio in Spanish. At 6 years of age, Octavio has just entered the first grade at an elementary school in San Antonio, Texas, and he speaks no English. What is the best way to teach Octavio? How much easier would elementary school be for Octavio if his parents had been able to speak to him in Spanish *and* English when he was an infant?

Well over 6 million children in the United States come from homes in which English is not the primary language. Often, like Octavio, they live in a community in which non-English language is the main means of communication. These children face a more difficult task than most of us: They must master the native tongue of their family to communicate effectively at home and they must also master English to make their way in the larger society. The number of bilingual children is expanding at such a rapid rate in our country (some experts predict a tripling of their number early in the twenty-first century) that they constitute an important subgroup of language learners that society must deal with. Although the education of such children in the public schools has a long history, only recently has a national policy evolved to guarantee a high-quality language experience for them.

Bilingual education *refers to programs for students with limited proficiency in English that instruct students in their own language part of the time while they learn English.* The rationale for bilingual education was provided by the United States Commission on Civil Rights (1975): Lack of English proficiency is the main reason language minority students do poorly in school;

A difficult task faced by the more than 6 million children who come from homes in which the primary language is not English is to master both their native tongue, spoken at home, and English to make their way in the larger society.

bilingual education should keep students from falling far behind in a subject while they are learning English. Bilingual programs vary extensively in content and quality. At a minimum, they include English instruction as a second language for students with limited English proficiency. Bilingual programs often include some instruction in Spanish as well. The largest number of bilingual programs in the United States are in Spanish, so our examples refer to Spanish, although the principles also apply to bilingual programs in other languages. Bilingual programs differ in the extent to which the Hispanic culture is taught to all students, and some bilingual programs teach Spanish to all students, regardless of whether their primary language is Spanish.

Most bilingual education programs are simply transitional programs developed to support students in Spanish until they can understand English well enough to function in the regular classroom, which is taught in English. A typical bilingual program begins teaching students with limited English proficiency in their primary language in kindergarten and then changes to English-only classes at the end of the first or second grade (Slavin, 1988).

Research evaluation of bilingualism has led to the conclusion that bilingualism does not interfere with performance in either language (Hakuta & Garcia, 1989). There is no evidence that the native language should be eliminated as early as possible because it might interfere with learning a second language. Instead, higher degrees of bilingualism are associated with cognitive flexibility and improved concept formation (Diaz, 1983). These findings are based primarily on research in additive bilingual settings—that is, in settings where the second language is added as an enrichment to the native language and not at its expense. Causal relations between bilingualism and cognitive or language competence are difficult to establish, but, in general,

Learning, Cognition, and Language Development

positive outcomes are often noted in communities where bilingualism is not socially stigmatized.

Increasingly, researchers are recognizing the complexity of bilingualism's effects (Fillmore, 1989). For example, as indicated earlier, the nature of bilingualism programs varies enormously—some are of excellent quality; others are of poor quality. Some teachers in bilingual education programs are completely bilingual; others are not. Some programs begin in kindergarten, others in elementary school. Some programs end in the first or second grade; others continue through the fifth or sixth grade. Some include instruction in the Hispanic culture; others focus only on language instruction. Some researchers select outcome measures that include only proficiency in English; others focus on cognitive variables such as cognitive flexibility and concept formation; and still others include more social variables such as integration into the school, self-esteem, and attitude toward school. In sum, there is more to understanding the effects of bilingual education than simple language proficiency (Hakuta & Garcia, 1989).

One final point about bilingualism deserves attention. The United States is one of the few countries in the world in which most students graduate from high school knowing only their own language. For example, in the Soviet Union, schools have 10 grades, called forms, which correspond roughly to the 12 grades in American schools. Children begin school at age 7. In the third form, Russian students begin learning English. Because of the emphasis on teaching English in their schools, most Soviet citizens today under the age of 35 speak at least some English (Cameron, 1988).

At this point, we have discussed a number of ideas about the role of cognition in language and the development of language. A summary of these ideas is presented in concept table 10.2. In the next chapter, we will turn our attention to another important aspect of children's development—intelligence.

■ *Critical Thinking*
Assume that you have taken a position as a director of bilingual education in a large school system in a major U.S. city. What social policy on bilingual education would you urge the school board to adopt? Explain your answer.

CONCEPT TABLE 10.2
The Role of Cognition in Language and How Language Develops

Concept	Processes/related ideas	Characteristics/description
The role of cognition	Its nature	Although children have prewired machinery for language, the cognitive view emphasizes that at least some of it is cognitive rather than strictly linguistic.
Language development in infancy and early childhood	Infancy	Vocalization begins with babbling at about 3 to 6 months of age. A baby's earliest communication skills are pragmatic. One-word utterances occur at about 10 to 13 months; the holophrase hypothesis has been applied to this. By 18 to 24 months, most infants have begun to use two-word utterances. Language at this point is referred to as telegraphic. Brown developed the idea of mean length of utterance (MLU). Five stages of MLU have been identified, providing a valuable indicator of language maturity.
	Early childhood	Advances in phonology, morphology, syntax, semantics, and pragmatics continue in early childhood. There has been increased interest in teaching young children reading and writing skills. Unfortunately, this has led to some dangers, with too many preschool children subjected to rigid, intense programs too advanced for their development. Young children need to develop positive feelings about their reading and writing skills through a supportive environment. Children should be active participants and be immersed in a wide range of interesting and enjoyable listening, talking, writing, and reading experiences.
Language development in middle and late childhood	Vocabulary and grammar	In middle and late childhood, children become more analytical and logical in their approach to words and grammar.
	Reading	In the history of learning to read, three techniques dominate: ABC, whole-word, and phonics. Current strategies often focus on a combination of the whole-word and phonics methods. However, reading is much more than the sum of these approaches. Understanding how reading works requires consideration of information processing.
	Bilingualism	This has become a major issue in our nation's schools, with debate raging over the best way to conduct bilingual education. No negative effects of bilingualism have been found, and bilingual education is often associated with positive outcomes, although causal relations are difficult to establish. Increasingly, researchers are recognizing the complexity of bilingual education.

Summary

I. What Is Language?
Language is a system of symbols and sequence of words, used to communicate with others, that involves infinite generativity, displacement, and rule systems.

II. Language's Rule Systems
Phonology governs the sequencing of phonemes (basic sounds that differ in their distinctive features). Morphology governs the sequencing of morphemes (the smallest units of language that carry meaning).

Syntax governs the ordering of words within sentences or phrases (these rules apply to deep and surface structures). Semantics places restrictions on how words must be used to make meaningful sentences. Pragmatics facilitates good communication and good social relations among language users.

III. Biological Evolution, Biological Prewiring—LAD, and the Brain's Role in Language
The fact that biological evolution shaped humans into linguistic creatures is undeniable. Linguist Noam

Chomsky believes that humans are prewired to learn language. He said children are born with a Language Acquisition Device (LAD), a biological prewiring that enables the child to detect certain language categories. LAD is an innate grammatical ability. The brain's left hemisphere plays an important role in language. Damage to Broca's area affects speech production, whereas damage to Wernicke's area affects language comprehension. Although the left hemisphere has a powerful influence on language, keep in mind that, in most activities, there is interplay between the brain's two hemispheres.

IV. Do Animals Have Language? Is There a Critical Period for Learning Language?

Animals can communicate and chimpanzees have been taught to use symbols. Whether animals have all of the properties of human language is debated. The experiences of Genie and other children suggest that the early years of childhood are a critical time for learning language. If exposure to language does not occur before puberty, lifelong deficits in grammar occur.

V. Cultural Change and the Cultural Context of Language

Sociocultural conditions may have pushed humans to develop abstract reasoning and to create an economical system for communicating with others. Bruner believes that the Language Acquisition Support System (LASS) plays an important role in structuring and supporting children's language. Among the social supports that contribute to children's language are parental simplification and framing of language through motherese, recasting, echoing, expanding, labeling, modeling, and corrective feedback.

VI. The Behavioral View

Behaviorists view language as just another behavior, like sitting, walking, or running. They argue that children's language is acquired through reinforcement and imitation. Chomsky believes that the behavioral view is wrong. An interactionist view emphasizes the contributions of both biology and experience in language—that is, children are biologically prepared to learn language as they and their caregivers interact.

VII. The Role of Cognition in Language

Although children have prewired machinery for language, the cognitive view emphasizes that at least some of it is cognitive rather than strictly linguistic.

VIII. Language Development in Infancy

Vocalization begins with babbling at about 3 to 6 months of age. A baby's earliest communication skills are pragmatic. One-word utterances occur at about 10 to 13 months; the holophrase hypothesis has been applied to this. By 18 to 24 months, most infants have begun to use two-word utterances. Language at this point is called telegraphic. Brown developed the idea of mean length of utterance (MLU). Five stages of MLU have been identified, providing a valuable indicator of language maturity.

IX. Language Development in Early Childhood

Advances in phonology, morphology, syntax, semantics, and pragmatics continue in early childhood. There has been increased interest in teaching young children reading and writing skills. Unfortunately, this had led to some dangers, with too many preschool children subjected to rigid, intense programs too advanced for their development. Young children need to develop positive feelings about their reading and writing skills through a supportive environment. Children should be active participants and be immersed in a wide range of enjoyable listening, talking, writing, and reading experiences.

X. Language Development in Middle and Late Childhood

In middle and late childhood, children become more analytical and logical in their approach to words and grammar. In the history of learning to read, three techniques dominate—ABC, whole-word, and phonics. Current strategies often focus on a combination of the whole-word and phonics methods. However, reading is much more than the sum of these approaches. Understanding how reading works requires a consideration of information processing. Bilingualism has become a major issue in our nation's schools, with debate raging over the best way to conduct bilingual education. No negative effects of bilingual education have been found, and bilingual education is often associated with positive outcomes, although causal relations are difficult to establish. Increasingly, researchers are recognizing the complexity of bilingual education.

Key Terms

infinite generativity 333
displacement 333
language 333
phonology 334
morphology 334
syntax 335
grammar 335
surface structure 335
deep structure 335
semantics 335
pragmatics 335
Language Acquisition
  Device (LAD) 337
aphasia 337
Broca's area 337
Wernicke's area 337
Language Acquisition
  Support System
  (LASS) 341

motherese 341
recasting 341
echoing 342
expanding 342
labeling 342
holophrase hypothesis 347
overextension 347
underextension 347
telegraphic speech 348
mean length of utterance
  (MLU) 348
literacy 351
ABC method 353
whole-word method 353
phonics method 353
bilingual education 355

Suggested Readings

Bloome, D. (Ed.). (1989). *Classrooms and literacy.* Norwood, NJ: Ablex. This book includes extensive discussion of how education should be improved to increase the literacy of children. A number of experts discuss programs to improve children's reading and writing skills.

Bruner, J. (1983). *Child talk.* New York: W. W. Norton. This is a fascinating view of children's language development by one of the leading cognitive theorists.

Curtiss, S. (1977). *Genie.* New York: Academic Press. Susan Curtiss tells the remarkable story of Genie, a modern-day wild child and her ordeal of trying to acquire language.

Hakuta, K., & Garcia, E. E. (1989). Bilingualism and education. *American Psychologist, 44,* 374–379. An up-to-date review of research and policy on bilingual education is provided.

Kessel, F. (Ed.). (1988). *The development of language and language researchers.* Hillsdale, NJ: Erlbaum. A number of chapters by experts on language development are presented, including a chapter by Gleason on language and socialization and Winner and Gardner on creating a world with words.

Premack, D. (1986). *Gavagai! The future history of the ape language controversy.* Cambridge, MA: MIT Press. Premack describes the fascinating ape language controversy and predicts its future directions.

CHAPTER

11

INTELLIGENCE

What Is Intelligence?
How Tests Are Constructed and Evaluated
    Reliability
    Validity
    Standardization
The Measurement and Nature of Children's
  Intelligence
    Alfred Binet and the Binet Tests
    The Wechsler Scales
    Does Intelligence Have a Single Nature?
Infant Intelligence and the Stability of Intelligence
    Infant Intelligence Tests
    The Stability of Intelligence
    Use of Information-Processing Tasks in Infancy to
        Predict Intelligence
Controversies and Issues in Intelligence
    The Heredity-Environment Controversy
    Culture and Ethnicity
    Cultural Worlds of Development 11.1: Larry P.,
        Intelligent but Not on Intelligence Tests
    Knowledge Versus Process in Intelligence
    The Use and Misuse of Intelligence Tests
The Extremes of Intelligence
    Mental Retardation
    Giftedness
    Creativity
    Perspective on Child Development 11.1: The
        Snowflake Model of Creativity and Its
        Application to Education
Summary
Key Terms
Suggested Readings

CHILDREN ARE REMARKABLE FOR THEIR INTELLIGENCE AND ARDOR, FOR THEIR CURIOSITY, THEIR INTOLERANCE OF SHAMS, THE CLARITY OF THEIR VISION.

—Aldous Huxley

I nformation about children's intelligence and intelligence tests frequently makes the news. The following two stories appeared in the *Los Angeles Times:*

> IQ testing that leads to the placement of an unusually large number of black children in so-called mentally retarded classes has been ruled unconstitutional by a federal judge. On behalf of five black children, Chief District Court Judge Robert Peckham said the use of standardized IQ tests to place children in educable mentally retarded (EMR) classes violated recently enacted federal laws and the state and federal constitutions. . . . Peckham said the history of IQ testing and special education in California "revealed an unlawful discriminatory intent . . . not necessarily to hurt black children, but it was an intent to assign a grossly disproportionate number of black children to the special, inferior and dead-end EMR classes." (October 18, 1979)

> A controversial Escondido sperm bank for superbrains has produced its first baby—a healthy, nine-pound girl born to a woman identified only as a small-town resident in "a sparsely populated state." . . . Founded by inventor Robert K. Graham of Escondido in 1979, the facility contains sperm donated by at least three Nobel Prize winners, plus other prominent researchers. . . . The sperm bank was founded to breed children of higher intelligence. The goal has been denounced by many critics, who say that a child's intelligence is not determined so much by his genes as by his upbringing and environment. (May 25, 1982)

As you might expect, these stories sparked impassioned debate (Kail & Pellegrino, 1985). Some arguments focus on the ethical and moral implications of selective breeding of bright children and selective placement of children in special classes. Other arguments concern the statistical basis of conclusions of intelligence tests, such as whether the tests are really biased if the data are analyzed properly. What you hear *less* often but should hear *more* often is a discussion of the construct of intelligence itself (Sternberg, 1990). That is, what is intelligence? How should it be conceptualized?

What Is Intelligence?

Intelligence is a possession most of us value highly, yet it is an abstract concept with few agreed-upon referents (Thorndike, 1990). We all would agree on referents for such characteristics as children's height, weight, and age, but there is less certainty about the referents for a child's size. Size is more *abstract* than height or weight. Also, size is more difficult to measure directly. We can only estimate size from a set of empirical measures of height and weight. Measuring intelligence is much the same as measuring size, though intelligence is *much more* abstract. That is, we believe children's intelligence exists, but we do not measure their intelligence directly. We cannot peel back a child's scalp and observe her intellectual processes in action. We can only study those intellectual processes *indirectly,* by evaluating the intelligent acts that children generate. For the most part, psychologists have relied on intelligence tests to provide an estimate of children's intellectual processes.

Throughout much of the history of Western civilization, intelligence has been described in terms of knowledge and reasoning (Kail & Pellegrino, 1985). Today, most of us view intelligence in a similar light. In one investigation, individuals were asked to judge which of 250 behaviors were typical of an intelligent individual (Sternberg & others, 1981). Both experts (psychologists researching intelligence) and lay individuals (people of various backgrounds and education) judged the behaviors similarly. The two groups agreed that intelligence can be divided into two main categories. The first is *verbal ability,* reflected in such behaviors as "displays a good vocabulary," "reads with high comprehension," "is knowledgeable about a particular field of knowledge," and "displays curiosity." The second is *problem-solving skills,* reflected in such behaviors as "reasons logically and well," "is able to apply knowledge to problems at hand," and "makes good decisions."

Thus, the primary components of intelligence are close to the mental processes we discussed in the chapters on language, cognitive development, and information processing. The differences in how we discussed language, cognition, and information processing and how we will discuss intelligence lie in the concepts of individual differences and measurement. **Individual differences** *are the stable, consistent ways in which children are different from each other.* The history of the study of intelligence has focused extensively on individual differences. We can talk about individual differences in personality or in any other domain of development, but it is in the area of intelligence that the most attention is given to individual differences. For example, an intelligence test tells us whether a child can reason better than most others who have taken the test. **Psychometrics** *is the field that involves the assessment of individual differences.* We will examine several of the most widely used tests to assess children's intelligence, but first we need to know something very important in psychometrics—how tests are constructed and evaluated.

How Tests Are Constructed and Evaluated

Any good test must meet three criteria—it must be reliable, it must be valid, and it must be standardized. We will examine each of these three criteria in turn.

Reliability

If a test that measures a child's characteristic is a stable and consistent test, the child's scores should not significantly fluctuate because of chance factors, such as how much sleep the child got the night before the test, who the examiner is, the temperature in the room where the child takes the test, and so on. **Reliability** *is the extent to which a test yields a consistent, reproducible measure of a child's performance.*

Reliability can be measured in several ways. **Test-retest reliability** *involves giving a child the same test on two different occasions.* Thus, if we were to give an intelligence test to a group of elementary school children today and then give them the same test in 6 months, the test would be considered reliable if those who score high on the test today also score high on the test in 6 months. One negative aspect of assessing test-retest reliability is that children sometimes do better the second time they take a test because they are familiar with it.

What a piece of work is a man! How noble in reason! how infinite in faculty! in form, in moving, how express and admirable! in action how like an angel! in apprehension how like a god!

—William Shakespeare

A second method of measuring reliability is to give alternate forms of a test on two different occasions. The test items on the two forms are similar but not identical. This strategy eliminates the chance of children doing better because they are familiar with the items, but it does not eliminate a child's familiarity with the procedures and strategies involved in the testing.

A third method of measuring reliability is to determine a test's **split-half reliability,** *in which test items are divided into halves, such as into groups of only the odd-numbered items or the even-numbered items. The items are different, and the two scores are compared to determine how consistently a child performed.* When split-half reliability is high, we say the test is *internally consistent.* For example, if we were to give an intelligence test that includes vocabulary items on one half and logical reasoning items on the second half of the test, we would expect the total scores of the children taking the test to be similar to their scores on each half of the test.

Validity

A test may consistently measure an attribute, such as intelligence, but this consistency does not ensure that it measures the attribute we want it to measure (Wiley, 1990). A test of children's intelligence might actually measure something else, such as children's anxiety. The test might consistently measure how anxious children are and, thus, have high reliability but not measure children's intelligence, which it purports to measure. **Validity** *is the extent to which a test measures what it is intended to measure.*

Like reliability, there are a number of ways to measure validity. One method is to assess a test's **content validity,** *which refers to the test's ability to give a broad picture of what is to be measured.* For example, a final test in a high school class, if it covers an entire textbook, should sample items from each of the chapters rather than just two or three chapters. If an intelligence test purports to measure both children's verbal ability and problem-solving ability, the items should include a liberal sampling of items that reflects both of these domains. The test would not have high content validity if it asked children to define several vocabulary words but did not require them to reason logically in solving a number of problems.

One of the most important methods of measuring validity is to check a test's **criterion validity,** *which is the test's ability to predict other measures, or criteria, of an attribute.* For example, a psychologist might validate an intelligence test by investigating how well it predicts children's grades in school. The grades in school are a criterion for measuring intelligence. When the scores on the two measures substantially overlap, we say the test has high criterion validity. We might give the children a second intelligence test, get their teacher's perceptions of their intelligence, and observe their behavior in problem-solving situations as other ways of establishing an intelligence test's criterion validity.

Criterion validity can follow one of two courses, concurrent or predictive. **Concurrent validity** *is the relation of a test's scores to a criterion that is presently available* (*concurrent*). For example, a test might assess children's intelligence. Concurrent validity might be established by analyzing how the scores on the intelligence test correspond to the children's grades in school at that time. **Predictive validity** *is the relation of a test's scores to an individual's performance at a point in the future.* For example, scores on an intelligence test might be used to predict whether a child will be successful in college. The SAT test is used for a similar purpose. Individuals take the test and then, later, are evaluated to see if the test actually predicted their performance.

Learning, Cognition, and Language Development

Figure 11.1
Test Construction and Evaluation

Standardization

Good tests are not only reliable and valid, but they are standardized as well. **Standardization** *involves developing uniform procedures for administering and scoring a test, and it also involves developing norms for the test.* Uniform testing procedures require that a testing environment be as similar as possible for all children. The test directions and the amount of time allowed to complete the test should be the same, for example. **Norms** *are established standards of performance for a test.* Norms are developed by giving a test to a large group of children representative of the population for whom the test is intended. This allows the test constructor to determine the normal distribution of the test scores. Norms inform us which scores should be considered high, low, or average. For example, if a child scores 120 on an intelligence test, that number alone has little meaning. The score takes on meaning when we compare it with other children's scores. If only 20 percent of the children in the standardized group scored above 120, then we can interpret the child's score as high rather than low or average. Many tests of intelligence have been designed for children from diverse groups. So that the tests are applicable to such different groups, many of them have norms—that is, established standards of performance for children of different ages, social classes, and races. Figure 11.1 summarizes the main points of our discussion of test construction and evaluation.

No man is smart, except by comparison with others who know less.

—Edgar Watson Howe

Alfred Binet (1857–1911) constructed the first intelligence test.

The Measurement and Nature of Children's Intelligence

Earlier we indicated that often intelligence is defined in terms of verbal ability and problem-solving skills. We also indicated that intelligence is an abstract concept that is difficult to define. Whereas many psychologists and lay people equate intelligence with verbal ability and problem-solving skills, others prefer to define it as a child's ability to learn from and adapt to the experiences of everyday life. If we were to settle on a definition of children's intelligence based on these criteria, it would be that **intelligence** *is verbal ability, problem-solving skills, and the ability to learn from and adapt to the experiences of everyday life.*

Keep in mind, however, that, although we can provide a general definition of intelligence, the way intelligence is behaviorally displayed may vary across cultures (Lonner, 1990). For example, in most Western cultures, individuals are considered intelligent if they are both smart (have considerable knowledge and can solve verbal problems) and fast (can process information quickly). However, individuals in the Buganda culture in Uganda believe that intelligent individuals are those who are wise, who are slow in thought, and who say the socially correct thing (Wober, 1974). Thus, we cannot always transport a concept (such as intelligence) from one culture to another and assume its behavioral indicators will always be the same. To do so is methodologically unsound, ethnocentric, and often culturally insensitive. As we further discuss the most widely used intelligence tests for children and the nature of intelligence, you will discover that experts still debate what intelligence is.

Alfred Binet and the Binet Tests

In 1904, the French Ministry of Education asked psychologist Alfred Binet to devise a method that would determine which students did not profit from typical school instruction. School officials wanted to reduce overcrowding by placing those who did not benefit from regular classroom teaching in special schools. Binet and his student Theophile Simon developed an intelligence test, the 1905 Scale, to meet this request. The test consisted of 30 items ranging from the ability to touch one's nose or ear when asked to the ability to draw designs from memory and define abstract concepts.

Binet also developed the concept of **mental age (MA),** *which is a child's level of mental development relative to others.* Binet reasoned that a mentally retarded child performs like a normal child of a younger age. He developed norms for intelligence by testing 50 nonretarded children from 3 to 11 years of age. Children suspected of mental retardation were given the test, and their performance was compared with normal children of the same chronological age. Average mental age scores (MA) correspond to chronological age (CA), which is age from birth. A bright child has an MA above CA; a dull child has an MA below CA.

The term **intelligence quotient (IQ)** *was devised in 1912 by William Stern. IQ consists of a child's mental age divided by chronological age, multiplied by 100:*

$$IQ = \frac{MA}{CA} \times 100$$

If mental age is the same as chronological age, then the child's IQ is 100; if mental age is above chronological age, the IQ is more than 100; if mental age

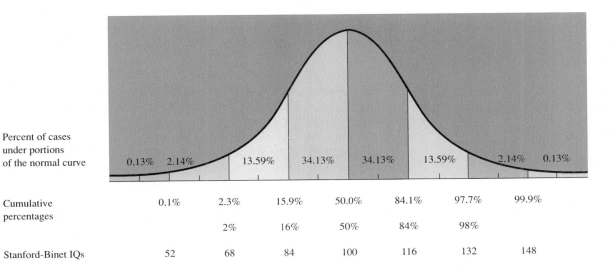

Percent of cases under portions of the normal curve	0.13%	2.14%	13.59%	34.13%	34.13%	13.59%	2.14%	0.13%
Cumulative percentages	0.1%	2.3%	15.9%	50.0%	84.1%	97.7%	99.9%	
		2%	16%	50%	84%	98%		
Stanford-Binet IQs	52	68	84	100	116	132	148	

is below chronological age, the IQ is less than 100. Scores noticeably above 100 are considered above average; those noticeably below are considered below average. For example, a 6-year-old child with a mental age of 8 would have an IQ of 133, whereas a 6-year-old child with a mental age of 5 would have an IQ of 83.

Over the years, extensive effort has been expended to standardize the Stanford-Binet test, which has been given to thousands of children and adults selected at random from different parts of the United States. By administering the test to large numbers of individuals and recording the results, it has been found that intelligence measured by the Stanford-Binet approximates a normal distribution (see figure 11.2). A **normal distribution** *is a symmetrical configuration of scores with a majority of cases falling in the middle of the possible range of scores and few scores appearing toward the extremes of the range.*

The Binet test has been revised many times to incorporate advances in the understanding of intelligence and intelligence testing. The many revisions are called the Stanford-Binet tests (Stanford University is where the revisions were done). Many of the revisions were carried out by Lewis Terman, who applied Stern's IQ concept to the test, developed extensive norms, and provided clear, detailed instructions for each problem on the test.

The current Stanford-Binet is given to individuals from the age of 2 through adulthood. It includes a wide variety of items, some requiring verbal responses, others nonverbal responses. For example, items that characterize a 6-year-old's performance on the test include the verbal ability to define at least six words, such as *orange* and *envelope,* and the nonverbal ability to trace a path through a maze. Items that reflect an average adult's intelligence include defining such words as *disproportionate* and *regard,* explaining a proverb, and comparing idleness and laziness.

The fourth edition of the Stanford-Binet was published in 1985 (Thorndike, Hagan, & Sattler, 1985). One important addition to this version is the analysis of the individuals' responses in terms of four content areas: verbal reasoning, quantitative reasoning, abstract/visual reasoning, and short-term memory (Keith & others, 1988). A general composite score also is obtained to reflect overall intelligence. The Stanford-Binet continues to be one of the most widely used individual tests of intelligence.

Figure 11.2
The Normal Curve and Stanford-Binet IQ Scores
The distribution of IQ scores approximates a normal curve. Most of the population falls in the middle range of scores. Notice that extremely high and extremely low scores are very rare. Slightly more than two thirds of the scores fall between 84 and 116. Only about 1 in 50 individuals has an IQ of more than 132 and only about 1 in 50 individuals has an IQ of less than 68.

The Wechsler Scales

Besides the Stanford-Binet, the other most widely used individual intelligence tests are the Wechsler scales, developed by David Wechsler. They include the Wechsler Adult Intelligence Scale-Revised (WAIS-R); the Wechsler Intelligence Scale for Children-Revised (WISC-R), for use with children between the ages of 6 and 16; and the Wechsler Preschool and Primary Scale of Intelligence (WPPSI), for use with children from the ages of 4 to 6½ (Wechsler, 1949, 1955, 1967, 1974, 1981).

The items on the Wechsler scales are grouped according to 11 subscales, 6 of which are verbal and 5 are nonverbal. This allows examiners to obtain separate verbal and nonverbal IQ scores and to see quickly the areas of mental performance in which tested individuals are below average, average, or above average. The inclusion of a number of nonverbal subscales makes the Wechsler test more representative of verbal *and* nonverbal intelligence; the Binet test includes some nonverbal items but not as many as the Wechsler scales, which also provide an overall IQ score. Several of the subscales of the WISC-R are shown in figure 11.3.

Does Intelligence Have a Single Nature?

Is it more appropriate to think of a child's intelligence as a general ability or as a number of specific abilities? Psychologists were debating the nature of the components of intelligence long before David Wechsler analyzed intelligence in terms of general and specific abilities (giving a child an overall IQ but also providing information about specific subcomponents of intelligence).

Early Factor Approaches

Charles Spearman (1927) proposed that intelligence has two factors. **Two-factor theory** *is Spearman's theory that children have both general intelligence, which he called* g, *and a number of specific types of intelligence, which he called* s. Spearman believed that these two factors account for a child's performance on an intelligence test.

However, some factor approaches abandoned the idea of general intelligence and searched for specific factors only. **Multiple-factor theory** *is L. L. Thurstone's (1938) theory that intelligence consists of seven primary abilities: verbal comprehension, number ability, word fluency, spatial visualization, associative memory, reasoning, and perceptual speed.*

Gardner's Seven Frames of Mind

A more recent attempt to classify intelligence, developed by Howard Gardner (1983, 1989), includes seven components, which he calls *frames of mind,* although they are not the same as Thurstone's seven factors. For example, the talents of Larry Bird and Ludwig von Beethoven reflect the diversity of Gardner's concept of intelligence. Bird and Beethoven are two different types of individuals, with different types of abilities. Bird, the 6'9" superstar of the Boston Celtics, springs into motion. Grabbing a rebound off the defensive board, he quickly moves across two thirds of the 94-foot basketball court, all the while processing the whereabouts of his five opponents and four teammates. As the crowd screams, Bird calmly looks left, finesses his way past a defender, and whirls a behind-the-back pass to a fast-breaking teammate, who dunks the ball for two points. Is there specific intelligence in Bird's movement and perception of the basketball court's spatial layout? Now we turn the clock back

200 years. A tiny boy just 4 years old is standing on a footstool in front of a piano keyboard, practicing. At the age of 6, the boy is given the honor of playing concertos and trios at a concert. Beethoven's musical genius was evident at a young age. Did Beethoven have a specific type of intelligence, one we might call musical intelligence?

Gardner argues that Bird's talent reflects his movement intelligence and his ability to analyze the world spatially, and that Beethoven's talent reflects his musical intelligence. Beyond these three forms of intelligence, Gardner believes there are four other main forms of intelligence: verbal intelligence, mathematical intelligence, insightful skills for analyzing ourselves, and insightful skills for analyzing others.

Gardner believes that each of the seven intelligences can be destroyed by brain damage, that each involves unique cognitive skills, and that each shows up in exaggerated fashion in both the gifted and *idiots savants* (individuals who are mentally retarded but who have unbelievable skill in a particular domain, such as drawing, music, or computing).

Gardner is especially interested in musical intelligence, particularly when it is exhibited at an early age. He points out that musically inclined preschool children not only have the remarkable ability to learn musical patterns easily, but that they rarely forget them. He recounts a story about Stravinsky, who, as an adult, could still remember the musical patterns of the tuba, drums, and piccolos of the fife-and-drum band that marched outside his window when he was a young child.

To measure musical intelligence in young children, Gardner might ask a child to listen to a melody and then ask the child to recreate the tune on some bells he provides. He believes that such evaluations can be used to develop a profile of a child's intelligence. He also believes that it is during this early time in life that parents can make an important difference in how a child's intelligence develops.

Critics of Gardner's approach point out that there are geniuses in many domains other than music. There are outstanding chess players, prize-fighters, writers, politicians, physicians, lawyers, preachers, and poets, for example, yet we do not refer to chess intelligence, prize-fighter intelligence, and so on.

Gardner proposed that there are seven frames of mind, one of those being musical intelligence, especially when it is exhibited at an early age.

Sternberg's Triarchic Theory of Intelligence

Robert J. Sternberg recalls being terrified of taking IQ tests as a child. He says he literally froze when the time came to take such tests. When Sternberg was in the sixth grade, he was sent to take an IQ test with the fifth graders and still talks about how humiliating the experience was. Sternberg became so fascinated by IQ tests that he devised his own at the age of 13 and began assessing the abilities of his classmates until the school psychologist found out and scolded him. Recently, Sternberg (1986, 1989, 1990) developed a theory which states that intelligence has three factors. **Triarchic theory** *is Sternberg's theory that intelligence consists of componential intelligence, experiential intelligence, and contextual intelligence.* Consider, Ann, who scores high on traditional intelligence tests, such as the Stanford-Binet, and is a star analytical thinker. Consider Todd, who does not have the best test scores but has an insightful and creative mind. Consider Art, a street-smart child who has learned to deal in practical ways with his world, although his scores on traditional IQ tests are low.

Sternberg calls Ann's analytical thinking and abstract reasoning *componential intelligence;* it is the closest to what we call intelligence in this chapter and what is commonly measured by intelligence tests. Sternberg calls Todd's

Robert Sternberg developed the triarchic theory of intelligence, which states that intelligence has three basic forms: componential, experiential, and contextual.

Figure 11.3

Subtests of the WISC-R and Examples of Each Subtest

Verbal subtests

General information
The individual is asked a number of general information questions about experiences that are considered normal for individuals in our society.
  For example, "How many wings does a bird have?"

Similarities
The individual must think logically and abstractly to answer a number of questions about how things are similar.
  For example, "In what way are boats and trains the same?"

Arithmetic reasoning
Problems measure the individual's ability to do arithmetic mentally and include addition, subtraction, multiplication, and division.
  For example, "If two buttons cost 14¢, what will be the cost of a dozen buttons?"

Vocabulary
To evaluate word knowledge, the individual is asked to define a number of words. This subtest measures a number of cognitive functions, including concept formation, memory, and language.
  For example, "What does the word biography mean?"

Comprehension
This subtest is designed to measure the individual's judgment and common sense.
  For example, "What is the advantage of keeping money in the bank?"

Digit span
This subtest primarily measures attention and short-term memory. The individual is required to repeat numbers forward and backward.
  For example, "I am going to say some numbers and I want you to repeat them backward: 4 7 5 2 8."

Performance subtests

Picture completion
A number of drawings are shown, each with a significant part missing. Within a period of several seconds, the individual must differentiate essential from nonessential parts of the picture and identify which part is missing. This subtest evaluates visual alertness and the ability to organize information visually.
  For example, "I am going to show you a picture with an important part missing. Tell me what is missing."

Picture arrangement
A series of pictures out of sequence are shown to the individual, who is asked to place them in their proper order to tell an appropriate story. This subtest evaluates how individuals integrate information to make it logical and meaningful.
  For example, "The pictures below need to be placed in an appropriate order to tell a meaningful story."

Object assembly
The individual is asked to assemble pieces into something. This subtest measures visual-motor coordination and perceptual organization.
   For example, "When these pieces are put together correctly, they make something. Put them together as quickly as you can."

Block design
The individual must assemble a set of multi-colored blocks to match designs that the examiner shows. Visual-motor coordination, perceptual organization, and the ability to visualize spatially are measured.
   For example, "Use the four blocks on the left to make the pattern on the right."

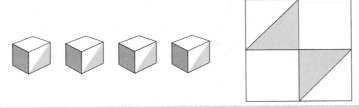

Coding
This subtest evaluates how quickly and accurately an individual can link code symbols and digits. The subtest assesses visual-motor coordination and speed of thought.
   For example, "As quickly as you can, transfer the appropriate code symbols to the blank spaces."

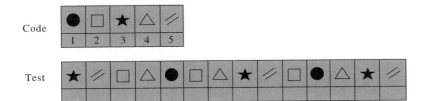

insightful and creative thinking *experiential intelligence* and Art's street smarts and practical know-how *contextual intelligence* (see figure 11.4).

   In Sternberg's view, the basic unit of intelligence is a *component,* simply defined as a basic unit of information processing. Sternberg believes that such components include the ability to acquire or store information, to retain or retrieve information, to transfer information, to plan, to make decisions, to solve problems, and to translate thought into performance.

   The second part of Sternberg's model focuses on experience. According to Sternberg, intellectual individuals have the ability to solve new problems quickly, but they also learn how to solve familiar problems in an automatic, rote way so that their minds are free to handle other problems that require insight and creativity.

Intelligence

(a)

(b)

(c)

Figure 11.4

Sternberg's Triarchic Model of Intelligence
(a) Componential intelligence is the closest to what is commonly measured on intelligence tests and is reflected in the ability to process information as we learn how to use a computer. (b) Experiential intelligence involves creativity and insight. (c) Contextual intelligence refers to practical knowledge, such as knowing how to get along with other people.

■ *Critical Thinking*
We have examined a number of the components of intelligence. What do you believe are the basic components of intelligence? How would you find out empirically if your theory is accurate?

The third part of Sternberg's model involves practical intelligence—such as how to get out of trouble, how to replace a fuse, and how to get along with people. Sternberg describes this practical, or contextual, intelligence as all of the important information about getting along in the real world that you are not taught in school. He believes that contextual intelligence is sometimes more important than the "book knowledge" that is taught in school.

Why Are There So Many Different Theories of the Components of Intelligence?

As we discussed different approaches to intelligence, you probably noticed that theorists often disagree about the definition of intelligence. Two reasons explain this disagreement (Kail & Pellegrino, 1985). First, the same data can be analyzed in many ways. Different apparent solutions, which produce different psychological interpretations, can be obtained from the same data. Second, the data obtained in separate studies differ. The critical data for interpretations of whether intelligence is a general ability or a cluster of specific abilities involve correlations (recall our discussion of this in chapter 1). The pattern of correlations depends on the group tested (school children, armed service recruits, or criminals, for example), the total number of tests administered, and the specific tests that are included in the battery (Meehl, 1990). The outcome of such studies is that the abilities thought to make up the core of intelligence may vary across investigations. Despite these inconsistencies, evidence suggests that intelligence is *both* a general ability and a number of specific abilities.

Infant Intelligence and the Stability of Intelligence

Many standardized intelligence tests do not assess infant intelligence. Intelligence tests that have been created for infants are often called *developmental scales*. What are these tests like? Can we predict a child's or an adolescent's intelligence from the individual's scores on an infant intelligence test? How much do intelligence test scores change as children grow and develop?

"You're wise, but you lack tree smarts."

Infant Intelligence Tests

In chapter 4, we discussed the Brazelton Neonatal Behavioral Assessment Scale, which is widely used to evaluate newborns. Developmentalists want to know how development proceeds during the course of infancy as well. If an infant advances at an especially slow rate, then enrichment may be necessary. If an infant develops at an advanced pace, parents may be advised to provide toys that stimulate cognitive growth in slightly older infants.

The infant testing movement grew out of the tradition of IQ testing with older children. However, the measures that assess infants are necessarily less verbal than IQ tests that assess the intelligence of older children. The infant developmental scales contain far more items related to perceptual motor development. They also include measures of social interaction.

The most important early contributor to the developmental testing of infants was Arnold Gesell (1934). He developed a measure that served as a clinical tool to help sort out potentially normal babies from abnormal ones. This was especially useful to adoption agencies, which had large numbers of babies awaiting placement. Gesell's examination was used widely for many years and still is frequently employed by pediatricians in their assessment of normal and abnormal infants. The current version of the Gesell test has four categories of behavior: motor, language, adaptive, and personal-social. The **developmental quotient (DQ)** *is an overall developmental score that combines subscores in the motor, language, adaptive, and personal-social domains in the Gesell assessment of infants.* Overall scores on such tests as the Gesell do not correlate highly with IQ scores obtained later in childhood. This is not surprising, since the nature of the items on the developmental scales are considerably less verbal than the items on intelligence tests given to older children.

The **Bayley Scales of Infant Development,** *developed by Nancy Bayley (1969), are widely used in the assessment of infant development. The current version has three components: a Mental scale, a Motor scale, and an Infant*

Behavior Profile. Unlike Gesell, whose scales were clinically motivated, Bayley wanted to develop scales that could document infant behavior and predict later development. The early version of the Bayley scales covered only the first year of development; in the 1950s, the scales were extended to assess older infants.

According to the Bayley scales, at approximately 6 months of age an average baby should be able to:

1. Accept a second cube—the baby holds the first cube, while the examiner places the second cube within easy reach of the infant
2. Grasp the edge of a piece of paper when it is presented
3. Vocalize pleasure and displeasure
4. Persistently reach for objects placed just out of immediate reach
5. Turn his or her head after a spoon the experimenter suddenly drops on the floor
6. Approach a mirror when the examiner places it in front of the infant

At approximately 12 months of age, an average baby should be able to:

1. Inhibit behavior when commanded to do so—for example, when the infant puts a block in his or her mouth and the examiner says, "No, no," the infant should cease the activity
2. Repeat an action if he or she is laughed at
3. Imitate words the experimenter says, such as *mama* and *dada*
4. Imitate the experimenter's actions—for example, if the experimenter rattles a spoon in a cup, the infant should imitate this action
5. Respond to simple requests, such as "take a drink"

The Stability of Intelligence

In one study conducted by Nancy Bayley, no relation was found between the Bayley scales and intelligence as measured by the Stanford-Binet at the ages of 6 and 7 (Bayley, 1943). Another investigation found correlations of only .01 between intelligence measured at 3 months and at 5 years of age and .05 between measurements at 1 year and at 5 years (Anderson, 1939). These findings indicate virtually no relationship between infant development scales and intelligence at 5 years of age. Again, it should be remembered that one of the reasons for this finding is that the components of intelligence tested in infancy are not the same as the components of intelligence tested at the age of 5.

There is a strong relation between IQ scores obtained at the ages of 6, 8, and 9 and IQ scores obtained at the age of 10. For example, in one study, the correlation between IQ at the age of 8 and IQ at the age of 10 was .88. The correlation between IQ at the age of 9 and IQ at the age of 10 was .90. These figures show a very high relation between IQ scores obtained in these years. The correlation of IQ in the preadolescent years and IQ at the age of 18 is slightly less but still statistically significant. For example, the correlation between IQ at the age of 10 and IQ at the age of 18 was .70 in one study (Honzik, MacFarlane, & Allen, 1948).

What has been said so far about the stability of intelligence has been based on measures of groups of individuals. The stability of intelligence also can be evaluated through studies of individuals. As we will see next, there can be considerable variability in an individual's scores on IQ tests.

The Mental Scale of the Bayley test includes assessment of an infant's auditory and visual attention to objects.

Let's look at an example of the absence of a relation between intelligence in infancy and intelligence in later years for two children in the same family. The first child learned to speak at a very early age. She displayed the characteristics of an extravert, and her advanced motor coordination was indicated by her ability to walk at a very early age. The second child learned speech very late, saying very few words until she was 2½ years old. Both children were given standardized tests of intelligence during infancy and then later, during the elementary school years. In the earlier test, the first child's scores were higher than her sister's. In the later test, their scores were reversed. What are some of the possible reasons for the reversal in the IQ scores of the two girls? When the second child did begin to speak, she did so prolifically, and the complexity of her language increased rapidly, undoubtedly as a result of her biological readiness to talk. Her sensorimotor coordination had never been as competent as the first child's, perhaps also accounting in part for her lower scores on the infant intelligence tests. The parents recognized that they had initially given the first child extensive amounts of their time. They were not able to give the second child as much of their time, but, when the second child was about 3 years old, they made every opportunity to involve her in physical and academic activities. They put her in a Montessori preschool program, gave her dancing and swimming lessons, and frequently invited other children of her age in to play with her. There may have been other reasons as well for the changes in scores, but these demonstrate that infant intelligence tests may not be good predictors of intelligence in later years.

Can you predict what a child's IQ will be when she is 10 or 18 years old from her scores on an IQ test administered when she is 2, 3, and 4 years old? IQ tests still do not provide very reliable predictions of this sort. Based on statistical techniques, IQ scores obtained at 2 and 3 years of age are related to the IQ scores of the same individuals even at 10 and 18 years, although they are not very strongly related. IQ scores obtained at the age of 4 are much better at predicting IQ at the age of 10 than at the age of 18 (Honzik, MacFarlane, & Allen, 1948).

Robert McCall and his associates (1973) studied 140 children between the ages of 2½ and 17. They found that the average range of IQ scores was more than 28 points. The scores of one out of three children changed by as much as 30 points and one out of seven by as much as 40 points. These data suggest that intelligence test scores can fluctuate dramatically across the childhood years and that intelligence is not as stable as the original intelligence theorists envisioned.

Use of Information-Processing Tasks in Infancy to Predict Intelligence

The explosion of interest in infant development has produced many new measures, especially tasks that evaluate the way infants process information (Ensher & Meller, 1989; Fagan & Knevel, 1989; Gottfried & Bathurst, 1989; Rose, 1989). Evidence is accumulating that measures of habituation and dishabituation predict intelligence in childhood (Bornstein, 1989; Bornstein & Sigman, 1986; Sigman & others, 1989). Quicker decays or less cumulative looking in the habituation situation and greater amounts of looking in the dishabituation situation reflect more efficient information processing. Both types of attention—decrement and recovery—when measured in the first 6 months of infancy, are related to higher IQ scores on standardized intelligence tests given at various times between infancy and adolescence. In sum, more precise assessment of infant cognition with information-processing tasks involving attention has led to the conclusion that continuity between infant and childhood intelligence is greater than was previously believed (Bornstein & Krasnegor, 1989).

What can we conclude about the nature of stability and change in childhood intelligence? Children are adaptive beings. They have the capacity for intellectual change but they do not become entirely new intelligent beings. In a sense, children's intelligence changes but has connections to earlier points in development—amid intellectual changes is some underlying coherence and continuity.

At this point, we have discussed many ideas about the nature of intelligence, test construction, and intelligence tests. A summary of these ideas is presented in concept table 11.1. Now we will turn our attention to some controversies and issues in intelligence.

Controversies and Issues in Intelligence

Intelligence has been one of psychology's concepts that seems to attract controversy. Among the most controversial issues of intelligence are those related to hereditary-environmental determination, cultural and ethnic differences, whether intelligence is knowledge or process, and the use and misuse of intelligence tests, each of which we will discuss in turn.

CONCEPT TABLE 11.1
Intelligence, Test Construction, and Intelligence Tests

Concept	Processes/related ideas	Characteristics/description
What is intelligence?	Its nature	Intelligence is an abstract concept that is measured indirectly. Psychologists rely on intelligence tests to estimate intellectual processes. Verbal ability and problem-solving skills are included in a definition of intelligence. Some psychologists believe intelligence includes an ability to learn from and adapt to everyday life. Extensive effort is given to assessing individual differences in intelligence. This is called psychometrics.
How tests are constructed and evaluated	Reliability	Reliability is the consistency with which a test measures performance. Three forms of reliability are test-retest, alternate forms, and split-half.
	Validity	Validity is the extent to which a test measures what it is intended to measure. Two methods of assessing validity are by determining content validity and criterion validity.
	Standardization	Standardization involves uniform procedures for administering and scoring a test; it also involves norms.
The measurement and nature of intelligence	Alfred Binet and the Binet tests	Alfred Binet developed the first intelligence test, known as the 1905 Scale. He developed the concept of mental age, whereas William Stern developed the concept of IQ. The Binet has been standardized and revised a number of times. The many revisions are called the Stanford-Binet tests. The test approximates a normal distribution. The current test is given to individuals from the age of 2 through adulthood.
	The Wechsler scales	Besides the Binet, the Wechsler scales are the most widely used intelligence tests. They include the WAIS-R, the WISC-R, and the WPPSI. These tests provide an overall IQ, verbal and performance IQ, and information about subtests.
	Does intelligence have a single nature?	Psychologists debate whether intelligence is a general ability or a number of specific abilities. Spearman's two-factor theory and Thurstone's multiple-factor theory state that a number of specific factors are involved. Current thinking suggests that Spearman's conceptualization of intelligence as both a set of specific abilities and a general ability was right. Gardner's seven frames of mind and Sternberg's triarchic theory—componential, experiential, and contextual intelligence—are contemporary efforts to determine the components of intelligence.
Infant intelligence and the stability of intelligence	Infant intelligence tests	Many standardized intelligence tests do not assess infant intelligence. Intelligence tests designed to assess infant intelligence are often referred to as developmental scales, the most widely used being the Bayley scales. Gesell was an important early contributor to the developmental testing of infants. The developmental quotient (DQ) is an overall score in the Gesell assessment of infants.
	Stability of intelligence	Although intelligence is more stable across the childhood years than are many attributes, many children's scores on intelligence tests fluctuate considerably.
	Use of information-processing tasks in infancy to predict intelligence	Recently, developmentalists have found that information-processing tasks that involve attention—especially habituation and dishabituation—are related to scores on standardized tests in childhood.

These children of migrant workers are growing up in a life of poverty. Their impoverished experiences and the extensive amount of time they spend in the fields may restrict their educational opportunities. Such environmental experiences likely contribute to lower scores on intelligence tests by children from low-income families.

The Heredity-Environment Controversy

The heredity-environment controversy in intelligence was introduced in chapter 2. We will review that controversy here and discuss additional information about the complexity of environmental influences.

Arthur Jensen (1969) sparked a lively and, at times, hostile debate when he presented his thesis that intelligence is primarily inherited. Jensen believes that environment and culture play only a minimal role in intelligence. In one of his most provocative statements, Jensen claimed that clear-cut genetic differences are present in the average intelligence of races, nationalities, and social classes. When Jensen first stated in the *Harvard Educational Review* in 1969 that lower intelligence probably was the reason that Blacks do not perform as well in school as Whites, he was called naive and racist. He received hate mail by the bushel and police escorted him to his classes at the University of California at Berkeley.

Jensen examined a number of studies of intelligence, many of which involved comparisons of identical and fraternal twins. Remember that identical twins have identical genetic endowments, so, if intelligence is genetically determined, said Jensen, their IQs should be similar. Fraternal twins and ordinary siblings are less similar genetically, so their IQs should be less similar. Jensen found support for his argument in these studies. Investigations of identical twins produced an average correlation of .82, a very high positive association. Investigations of fraternal twins produced an average correlation of .50, a moderately high positive correlation. Note the difference of .32, which is substantial. To show that genetic factors are more important than environmental factors, Jensen compared identical twins reared together with those reared apart. The correlation for those reared together was .89, and for those reared apart it was .78, a difference of .11. Jensen argued that, if environmental factors are more important than genetic factors, siblings reared apart, who experienced different environments, should have IQs that differed more than .11. Jensen places heredity's influence on intelligence at about 80 percent.

The consensus of today's experts on intelligence is that its genetic determination is not as strong as Jensen envisions. Their estimates fall more in the range of 50 percent genetic determination, 50 percent environmental determination (Plomin, 1989; Plomin, DeFries, & McClearn, in press). For most individuals, this means that modification of environmental conditions can change their IQ scores considerably (Weinberg, 1989). It also means that programs designed to enrich an individual's environment can have a considerable impact, improving school achievement and the acquisition of skills needed for employability. Although genetic endowment may always influence individuals' intellectual ability, the environments and opportunities we provide children and adults do make a difference.

Consider the following environmental circumstance of a family living in a house in a low-income area of a large city. The parents can barely pay the monthly mortgage, and the electric company has threatened to turn off the electricity. There are seven children in the family, ranging in age from 2 to 16. Neither of the parents has completed high school. The father works as a brick-layer when he can find a job and the mother irons clothes in a laundry. The parents want their children to have more opportunities than they had, but, so far, their children have experienced a life of social disadvantage. Keep in mind, though, that environmental effects are *complex* and that being "poor" or "disadvantaged" does not automatically equal "doomed." In this example of an impoverished family, there are both positive and negative potential influences on the children. On one hand, the children are growing up in an intact family, where they are encouraged to finish school, and their parents provide a model of the work ethic. On the other hand, the children experience few opportunities to develop their intellectual abilities. In wealthy families, children may have many more opportunities to develop their intellectual abilities through access to excellent schools, books, travel, and tutoring, but they may become spoiled because they are given everything and fail to develop a strong motivation to learn and achieve.

Increasingly, researchers have become interested in manipulating the environment early in children's lives when the children are at risk for impoverished intelligence. The emphasis is on *prevention* rather than remediation (Garwood & others, 1989; Heinicke, Beckwith, & Thompson, 1988). Many low-income parents have difficulty providing an adequate environment for their children's intellectual needs. Successful programs have included training parents to be more sensitive caregivers, training parents to teach their children more effectively, and providing support services such as educational day care (Ramey, 1989; Ramey & Landesman, in press).

In a program conducted in North Carolina by Craig Ramey and his associates, pregnant women with IQs averaging 80 were recruited for an intervention study. After their babies were born, half of the infants were cared for during the day at an educational day-care center and half were reared at home by their mothers. Both groups of children were given medical care and dietary supplements, and their families were given social services if they requested them.

At the age of 3, the children who attended the educational day-care center had significantly higher IQs than the home-reared children. This difference seemed to be due to a decline in the IQs of the home-reared children during the 12-to-18-month period. At the age of 5, 39 percent of the home-reared children had IQs below 85 but only 11 percent of the educational day-care children had IQs this low.

A recent review of family intervention studies suggests that intervention is more likely to be successful if the number of contacts between an intervenor and family is approximately 11 or more, if contacts begin shortly after birth, and if they extend over a period of at least 3 months (Heinicke, Beckwith, & Thompson, 1988). Although 11 sessions is a somewhat arbitrary number, it does reflect that a certain duration of contact is necessary for the success of the intervention.

One of the most challenging circumstances in the area of intelligence is how best to help parents in high-risk families provide a more enriched environment for their children. The research by Craig Ramey and his associates in North Carolina suggests that educational day care, medical care, and dietary supplements are likely to benefit the offspring of pregnant women with low IQs.

Culture and Ethnicity

Are there cultural and ethnic differences in intelligence? Are standard intelligence tests biased, and, if so, can we develop culture-fair tests? We will consider each of these questions in turn.

Cultural and Ethnic Comparisons

There are cultural and ethnic differences in performance on intelligence tests. For example, in the United States, children in Black and Hispanic families score below children from White families on standardized intelligence tests. The most interest has focused on Black-White comparisons. On the average, Black American school children score 10 to 15 points lower on standardized intelligence tests than do White American school children (Anastasi, 1988). Keep in mind, though, that we are talking about average scores. Many Black American children score higher than many White American children. Estimates indicate that 15 to 25 percent of Black American school children score higher than half of all White school children.

Jewish child

Chinese child

Black American child

Puerto Rican child

What are some of the strengths and weaknesses of these children's intelligence?

Many research investigations that compare Black American and White American children do not take into account the diversity that exists within these groups (Jones, 1990; McLoyd, 1990; Spencer, 1990). Critics argue that, when ethnic groups are compared, researchers often document the way an ethnic group, especially Black American or Hispanic American, *does not* behave rather than how it *does* behave (McLoyd, 1990). Further, the critics stress that studies of ethnic groups often fail to examine the underlying processes or mechanisms that explain behavioral outcomes. Such research has the unfortunate result of fostering ethnic-group stereotypes and ignoring ethnic-group diversity. Consequently, we know little about individual differences among Black American children.

Although the greatest interest has been in Black-White comparisons, patterns of intelligence in Jewish, Chinese, Black, and Puerto Rican children suggest some strengths and weaknesses in children from different ethnic backgrounds (Lesser, Fifer, & Clark, 1965). Jewish children scored higher on verbal abilities, lower on numerical and spatial abilities; Chinese children scored higher on numerical and spatial abilities, lower on verbal abilities; Black children rated higher on verbal abilities, lower on reasoning and numerical abilities; and Puerto Rican children scored higher on spatial and reasoning abilities, lower on verbal abilities.

How extensively are ethnic differences in intelligence influenced by heredity and environment? The consensus is that the available data do not support a genetic interpretation. For example, in recent decades, as Black Americans have experienced improved social, economic, and educational opportunities, the gap between White and Black children on standardized intelligence tests has begun to diminish (Jones, 1984). Also, when children from disadvantaged Black American families are adopted by more-advantaged middle-class families, their scores on intelligence tests more closely resemble the national averages for middle-class than for lower-class children (Scarr, 1989; Scarr & Weinberg, 1976).

Learning, Cognition, and Language Development

T A B L E 11.1 The Chitling Intelligence Test	

1. A "gas head" is a person who has a:
   (a) fast-moving car
   (b) stable of "lace"
   (c) "process"
   (d) habit of stealing cars
   (e) long jail record for arson
2. "Bo Diddley" is a:
   (a) game for children
   (b) down-home cheap wine
   (c) down-home singer
   (d) new dance
   (e) Moejoe call
3. If a pimp is uptight with a woman who gets state aid, what does he mean when he talks about "Mother's day"?
   (a) second Sunday in May
   (b) third Sunday in June
   (c) first of every month
   (d) none of these
   (e) first and fifteenth of every month
	4. A "handkerchief head" is:
	   (a) a cool cat
	   (b) a porter
	   (c) an Uncle Tom
	   (d) a hoddi
	   (e) a preacher
	5. If a man is called a "blood," then he is a:
	   (a) fighter
	   (b) Mexican-American
	   (c) Negro
	   (d) hungry hemophile
	   (e) red man, or Indian
	6. Cheap chitlings (not the kind you purchase at a frozen-food counter) will taste rubbery unless they are cooked long enough. How soon can you quit cooking them to eat and enjoy them?
	   (a) 45 minutes
	   (b) 2 hours
	   (c) 24 hours
	   (d) 1 week (on a low flame)
	   (e) 1 hour

Answers: 1. c, 2. c, 3. e, 4. c, 5. c, 6. c	

Source: Adrian Dove, 1968.

Cultural Bias and Culture-Fair Tests

Many of the early intelligence tests were culturally biased, favoring urban over rural individuals, middle-class over lower-class people, and Whites over Blacks. The norms for the early intelligence tests were based almost entirely on American White, middle-class standards (Miller-Jones, 1989, 1991). For example, one item on an early test asked what should be done if you find a 3-year-old child in the street. The correct answer was "call the police." Children from impoverished inner-city families might not choose this answer if the police force was perceived as unfriendly, and rural children might not choose it, since they may not have police nearby. Such items clearly do not measure the knowledge necessary to adapt to one's environment or to be "intelligent" in an inner-city neighborhood or in rural America (Scarr, 1984a).

Even if the content of the test items is made appropriate, another problem may exist with intelligence tests. Since many of the questions are verbal, minority groups may encounter problems understanding the language of the questions (Gibbs & Huang, 1989). Minority groups often speak a language that is very different from standard English. Consequently, they may be at a disadvantage when they take intelligence tests oriented toward middle-class White children. Cultural bias is dramatically underscored by such tests as the one shown in table 11.1. The items in this test were developed to reduce the cultural disadvantage Black American children might experience on traditional intelligence tests. More information about cultural bias in intelligence testing appears in Cultural Worlds of Development 11.1, where you will read about a widely publicized case involving the use of an intelligence test to classify a 6-year-old Black boy as mentally retarded.

Larry P., Intelligent but Not on Intelligence Tests

Larry P. is Black American and comes from a low-income background. When he was 6 years old, he was placed in a class for the educable mentally retarded (EMR), primarily because of his very low score of 64 on an intelligence test.

Is there a possibility that the intelligence test Larry was given was culturally biased? Psychologists still debate the issue of bias. The controversy has been the target of a major class action challenging the use of standardized IQ tests to place Black elementary school students in classes for the educable mentally retarded. The initial lawsuit, filed on behalf of Larry P., claimed that the IQ test he took underestimated his learning ability. The lawyers for Larry P. argued that IQ tests place too much emphasis on verbal skills and fail to account for the background of Black children. Therefore, it was argued, Larry was incorrectly labeled mentally retarded and may forever be saddled with the stigma of being called retarded.

As part of the lengthy court battle involving Larry P., six Black EMR students were retested by members of the Bay Area Association of Black Psychologists in California. The psychologists made sure that they established good rapport with the students and made special efforts to overcome the students' defeatism and distraction. The psychologists rewarded certain items in terms more consistent with the children's social background and recognized nonstandard answers that showed a logical, intelligent approach to problems. The

retesting produced scores of 79 to 104—17 to 38 points higher than the scores the students received when initially tested by school psychologists. The retest scores were above the ceiling for placement in an EMR class.

In Larry's case, it was ruled that IQ tests are biased and their use discriminates against Blacks and other ethnic minorities. The ruling continued the moratorium on the use of IQ tests in decisions about placement of a child in an EMR class. During the Larry P. trial, it was revealed that 66 percent of elementary school students in EMR classes in San Francisco were Black, whereas Blacks made up only 28.5 percent of the San Francisco school population.

What was the state's argument for using intelligence tests as part of the criteria for placing children in EMR classes? At one point, the state suggested that, because Blacks tend to be poor and poor pregnant women tend to suffer from inadequate nutrition, it is possible that the brain development of many Black children is retarded by their mother's poor diets during pregnancy. However, from the beginning of the trial, a basic point made by the state was that Blacks are genetically inferior to Whites intellectually.

The decision in favor of Larry P. was upheld by a three-judge appeals panel in 1984, but, in another court case, *Pase v. Hannon* in Illinois, it was ruled that IQ tests are not culturally biased.

Cultural bias is also dramatically underscored in the life of Gregory Ochoa. When Gregory was a high school student, he and his classmates were given an IQ test. School authorities informed them the test would allow the school to place them in classes appropriate for their skills. Gregory looked at the test questions and didn't understand many of the words. Spanish was spoken at his home, and his English was not very good. Several weeks later, Gregory was placed in a "special" class. Many of the other students in the class had last names like Ramirez and Gonzales. The special class was for mentally retarded students. Gregory lost interest in school and dropped out, eventually joining the Navy, where he took high school courses and earned enough credits to attend college. He graduated from San Jose City College as an honor student, continued his education, and wound up as a professor of social work at the University of Washington in Seattle.

Culture-fair tests *are tests of intelligence that attempt to reduce cultural bias.* Two types of culture-fair tests have been devised. The first includes items that are familiar to individuals from all socioeconomic and ethnic backgrounds, or items that at least are familiar to the individuals taking the test. For example, a child might be asked how a bird and a dog are different, on the assumption that virtually all children have been exposed to dogs and birds.

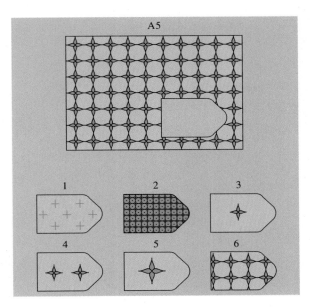

Figure 11.5
Sample Item from the Raven Progressive Matrices Test
Individuals are presented with a matrix arrangement of symbols, such as the one at the top of this figure, and must then complete the matrix by selecting the appropriate missing symbol from a group of symbols.

The second type of culture-fair test has all the verbal items removed. Figure 11.5 shows a sample item from the Raven Progressive Matrices Test, which exemplifies this approach. Even though such tests are designed to be culture-fair, individuals with more education score higher on them than do those with less education.

One test that takes into account the socioeconomic background of children is the SOMPA, which stands for System of Multicultural Pluralistic Assessment (Mercer & Lewis, 1978). This test can be given to children from 5 to 11 years of age. SOMPA was designed for children from low-income families. Instead of relying on a single test, SOMPA is based on information about four different areas of a child's life: (1) verbal and nonverbal intelligence in the traditional intelligence test mold, assessed by the WISC-R; (2) social and economic background of the family, obtained through a 1-hour parent interview; (3) social adjustment to school, evaluated by an adaptive behavior inventory completed by parents; and (4) physical health, determined by a medical examination.

The Kaufman Assessment Battery for Children (K-ABC) has been trumpeted as an improvement over past culture-fair tests (Kaufman & Kaufman, 1983). It can be given to children from 2½ to 12½ years of age. This test is standardized on a more representative sample, which includes more minority and handicapped children, than are most tests. The intelligence portion focuses less on language than the Stanford-Binet, and the test includes an achievement section with subtests for arithmetic and reading (figure 11.6 shows a sample item from the K-ABC). Nonetheless, like other culture-fair tests, the K-ABC has its detractors. On our three main criteria for evaluating tests, the K-ABC fares better on reliability and standardization, but not as well on validity (Sax, 1989).

These attempts to produce culture-fair tests remind us that traditional intelligence tests are probably culturally biased, yet the effort to develop a truly culture-fair test has not yielded a satisfactory alternative. Constructing a culture-fair intelligence test, one that rules out the role of experience emanating from socioeconomic and ethnic background, has been difficult and may

Figure 11.6

Sample Arithmetic Item from the K-ABC
On this item, a child is asked to determine how much the child's admission price is if adults have to pay 75¢ and the children's price is one third of the adult price.

(a)

(b)

Figure 11.7

Iatmul and Caroline Islander Intelligence
(a) The intelligence of the Iatmul people of Papua, New Guinea, involves the ability to remember the names of many clans.
(b) The Caroline Islands number 680 in the Pacific Ocean east of the Philippines. The intelligence of their inhabitants includes the ability to navigate by the stars.

be impossible. Consider, for example, that the intelligence of the Iatmul people of Papua, New Guinea, involves the ability to remember the names of 10,000 to 20,000 clans; by contrast, the intelligence of islanders in the widely dispersed Caroline Islands involves the talent of navigating by the stars (see figure 11.7).

Knowledge Versus Process in Intelligence

The information-processing approach we discussed in chapter 9 raises two interesting questions about children's intelligence: What are children's fundamental information-processing abilities? How do these develop?

Few of us would deny that changes in both processing and knowledge occur as we develop. However, a consensus does not exist on something more fundamental. We accumulate knowledge as we grow from infancy to adulthood, but what may be growing is simply a reserve of processing capacity. That is, your greater processing capacity as an adult than as a child might be what allows you to learn more. By contrast, possibly your greater processing capacity as an adult is a consequence of your greater knowledge, which allows you to process information more effectively. It is not easy to choose between these two possibilities, and the issue has been called the great *structure-process dilemma* of intelligence (Keil, 1984). That is, what are the mechanisms of intelligence and how do they develop? Does information-processing ability change, does knowledge and expertise change, or both?

To make the structure-process dilemma more concrete, consider a simple computer metaphor. Suppose we have two computers, each of which is capable of solving multiplication problems (for example, 13 × 24 or 45 × 21), but one computer works faster than the other. What is the explanation? One possibility is that the faster computer has a greater capacity—that is, core memory—in which to do mental work. This greater core memory, which psychologists refer to as *working memory,* might allow the computer to work on two or more components of a problem at once. Another explanation is that the faster computer might have a greater store of relevant knowledge. Perhaps it

Learning, Cognition, and Language Development

has in its data bank (long-term memory) a complete multiplication table up to 99 × 99. The slower computer might have a table up to 12 × 12 (as do most humans). The faster computer need not be fundamentally faster—its subroutines may be relatively slow, but it is able to perform the multiplication task because of knowledge, not because of processing capacity.

Explaining intelligence is similar to explaining the difference between the fast and slow computers—is processing or knowledge responsible for how intelligence changes with age? Based on research on memory, it seems likely that the answer is both (Zembar & Naus, 1985). If so, the essential task in explaining intelligence becomes one of determining the ways that processing and knowledge interact in the course of intellectual development.

The modern information-processing approach does not argue that knowledge is unimportant. Rather, many information-processing psychologists believe that attention should be given to the knowledge base generated by intellectual processes.

The Use and Misuse of Intelligence Tests

Psychological tests are tools. Like all tools, their effectiveness depends on the knowledge, skill, and integrity of the user. A hammer can be used to build a beautiful kitchen cabinet or it can be used as a weapon of assault. Like a hammer, intelligence tests can be used for positive purposes or they can be badly abused. It is important for both test constructors and test examiners to be familiar with the current state of scientific knowledge about intelligence and intelligence tests (Anastasi, 1988).

Even though they have limitations, intelligence tests are among psychology's most widely used tools. To be effective, though, intelligence tests must be viewed realistically. They should not be thought of as unchanging indicators of intelligence. They also should be used in conjunction with other information about people and should not be relied on as the sole indicator of intelligence. For example, an intelligence test should not be used as the sole indicator of whether a child should be placed in a special education or gifted class. The child's developmental history, medical background, performance in school, social competencies, cultural background, and family experiences should be taken into account too.

The single number provided by many IQ tests can easily lead to stereotypes and expectations about a child. Many people do not know how to interpret the results of an intelligence test, and sweeping generalizations about a child often are made on the basis of an IQ score. For example, imagine that you are a teacher in the teacher's lounge on the day after school has started in the fall. You mention a student—Johnny Jones—and a fellow teacher remarks that she had Johnny in class last year; she comments that he was a real dunce and points out that his IQ is 78. You cannot help but remember this information, and it may lead to thoughts that Johnny Jones is not very bright and it is useless to spend much time teaching him. In this way, IQ scores are misused, stereotypes are formed, and negative expectations are developed (Rosenthal & Jacobsen, 1968).

We also have a tendency in our culture to consider intelligence or a high IQ as the ultimate human value. It is important to keep in mind that our value as humans includes other matters—consideration of others, positive close relationships, and competence in social situations, for example. The verbal and problem-solving skills measured on traditional intelligence tests are only one part of human competence.

■ *Critical Thinking*
How close are Piaget's view of intelligence and the intelligence test approach to intelligence? Explain your answer.

Almost all the joyful things of life are outside the measure of IQ tests.
—Madeleine L'Engle

TABLE 11.2
The Classifications of Mental Retardation

Level of functioning	IQ range	% of all mentally retarded individuals
Mild retardation	50-55 to approximately 70	80
Moderate retardation	35-40 to 50-55	12
Severe retardation	20-25 to 35-40	7
Profound retardation	Below 20-25	1

Despite their limitations, when used judiciously by a competent examiner, intelligence tests provide valuable information about individuals. There are not many alternatives to intelligence tests. Subjective judgments about individuals simply reintroduce the biases the tests were designed to eliminate.

The Extremes of Intelligence

Atypical children have always been of interest to developmentalists. Intellectual atypicality has intrigued many psychologists and drawn them to study the mentally retarded, the gifted, and the creative.

Mental Retardation

The most distinctive feature of mental retardation is inadequate intellectual functioning. Long before formal tests were introduced to assess intelligence, the mentally retarded were identified by a lack of age-appropriate skills in learning and caring for oneself. With the development of intelligence tests, more emphasis was placed on IQ as an indicator of mental retardation. It is not unusual, however, to find two retarded individuals with the same low IQ, one of whom is married, employed, and involved in the community and the other requiring constant supervision in an institution. These differences in social competence led developmentalists to include deficits in adaptive behavior in their definition of mental retardation. **Mental retardation** *is a condition of limited mental ability in which individuals have a low IQ, usually below 70 on a traditional test of intelligence, and have difficulty adapting to everyday life.* About 5 million Americans fit this definition of mental retardation.

The classifications of mental retardation, the IQs associated with them, and the percentage of individuals in each category are presented in table 11.2. Although classified as mentally retarded, *mildly mentally retarded individuals* (IQ 50–55 to approximately 70) can still learn to read and write. With proper education and training, as adults they can adjust socially, master simple academic and occupational skills, and become self-supporting citizens. As adults, *moderately mentally retarded individuals* (IQ 35–40 to 50–55), with proper education and training, can achieve partial independence in daily self-care, acceptable behavior, and economic usefulness in a family or other sheltered setting. *Severely mentally retarded individuals* (IQ 20–25 to 35–40), with proper education and training, can develop limited personal hygiene and

Learning, Cognition, and Language Development

self-help skills, but their motor and speech development are impaired and they require a great deal of care. Many can learn to perform simple occupational tasks under supervision. *Profoundly mentally retarded individuals* (IQ below 20–25) are extremely deficient in adaptive behavior and can master only the simplest of tasks. Speech impairment is often severe, and these individuals need to remain in custodial care all of their lives.

What causes mental retardation? The causes are divided into two categories: organic and cultural-familial. **Organic retardation** *is mental retardation caused by a genetic disorder or brain damage;* organic *refers to the tissues or organs of the body, so there is some physical damage in organic retardation.* Down's syndrome, a form of mental retardation (see figure 11.8), occurs when an extra chromosome is present in a child's genetic make-up. It is not known why the extra chromosome is present, but it may involve the health or age of the mother's ovum or father's sperm. Although those who suffer organic retardation are found across the spectrum of IQ distribution, most have IQs between 0 and 50. **Cultural-familial retardation** *is mental retardation in which there is no evidence of organic brain damage; individuals' IQs range from 50 to 70.* Psychologists seek the cause of this type of retardation in impoverished environments. Even with organic retardation, though, it is wise to think about the contributions of genetic-environment interaction. Parents with low IQs not only may be more likely to transmit genes for low intelligence to their offspring but also tend to provide them with a less enriched environment (Landesman, in press; Landesman & Ramey, 1989).

Giftedness

Conventional wisdom has identified some individuals in all cultures and historical periods as exceptional because they have had talents not evident in the majority of the people. Children who are **gifted** *have above-average intelligence (an IQ of 120 or higher), a superior talent for something, or both.* Most school systems emphasize intellectual superiority and academic aptitude when selecting children for gifted programs, rarely considering competence and potential in the visual and performing arts (arts, drama, dance), psychomotor abilities (tennis, golf, basketball), or other special aptitudes (Reis, 1989).

A classic study of the gifted was begun by Lewis Terman (1925) more than 60 years ago. Terman studied approximately 1,500 children whose Stanford-Binet IQs averaged 150. His goal was to follow these children through their adult lives—the study will not be complete until the year 2010. The accomplishments of the 1,500 children in Terman's study are remarkable. Of the 800 males, 78 have obtained Ph.D.s (they include two past presidents of the American Psychological Association), 48 have earned M.D.s, and 85 have been granted law degrees. Nearly all of these figures are 10 to 30 times greater than found among 800 men of the same age chosen randomly from the overall population. The children in Terman's study were also rated as better adjusted and more popular than average children (Wallach & Kogan, 1965). These findings challenge the commonly held belief that the intellectually gifted are disturbed emotionally or maladjusted socially, a belief based on some striking instances of mental disturbance among the gifted. Sir Isaac Newton, Vincent van Gogh, Leonardo da Vinci, Socrates, and Edgar Allan Poe all had emotional problems. These are the exception rather than the rule, however; no relation between giftedness and mental disturbance in general has been found.

Figure 11.8
A Down Syndrome Child
What causes a child to develop Down syndrome? In which major classification of mental retardation does the condition fall?

There is hardly anybody good for everything, and there is scarcely anybody who is absolutely good for nothing.
—Lord Chesterfield

■ *Critical Thinking*
What should be the criteria for placing a child in a gifted program?

Each of us would like to be talented, and, if each of us were to have children, we would like to be able to develop the talents of our children. Some children become extraordinarily gifted, reaching the status of "star." Becoming a "star" takes years of special tutelage with remarkable coaches; extensive support by parents; and day after day, week after week, month after month, and year after year of practice.

Creativity involves thinking about something in novel and unusual ways and coming up with unique solutions to problems. Creativity is enhanced when children have the time and independence to entertain a wide range of possible solutions in an enjoyable setting.

A number of recent studies support Terman's conclusion that the gifted tend to be more mature and have fewer emotional problems than do others (Janos & Robinson, 1985).

Creativity

Most of us would like to be both gifted and creative. Why was Thomas Edison able to invent so many things? Was he simply more intelligent than most individuals? Did he spend long hours toiling away in private? Surprisingly, when Edison was a young boy, his teacher told him he was too dumb to learn anything. Other examples of famous individuals whose creative genius went unnoticed when they were young include Walt Disney, who was fired from a newspaper job because he did not have any good ideas; Enrico Caruso, whose music teacher told him that his voice was terrible; and Winston Churchill, who failed a year of secondary school.

Creativity *is the ability to think about something in a novel and unusual way and to come up with unique solutions to problems.* When individuals in the arts and sciences who fit the description of "creative" are asked what enables them to produce their creative works, they say they generate large amounts of associative content when solving problems, and they have the time and independence to entertain a wide range of possible solutions in an enjoyable setting. How strongly is creativity related to intelligence? A certain level of intelligence is required to be creative in most fields, but many highly intelligent individuals (as measured by IQ tests) are not very creative (Wakefield, 1991).

Edison, Disney, Caruso, and Churchill were intelligent and creative individuals, but experts believe that intelligence and creativity are not the same thing (Winner, 1989). One common distinction between intelligence and creativity involves the thinking process. **Convergent thinking** *produces one correct answer and is characteristic of the kind of thinking required on standardized intelligence tests,* whereas **divergent thinking** *produces many different answers to the same question and is more characteristic of creativity* (Guilford, 1967; Runcor, 1991) (see figure 11.9). For example, the following intellectual

Learning, Cognition, and Language Development

1. Sketches: Add just enough detail to the circle below to make a recognizable object (two examples of acceptable responses are shown).

2. Word fluency: Write as many words as you can think of with the first and last letters R_____M ("rim" would be one).

3. Name grouping: Classify the following six names in as many different ways as you can (a person might group 1, 3, and 4 together because each has two syllables).

    1. GERTRUDE 2. BILL
    3. ALEX   4. CARRIE
    5. BELLE   6. DON

4. Making objects: Using two or more of the forms shown below, make a face. Now make a lamp (examples of good responses are shown).

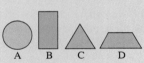

A   B   C   D   Face   Lamp

problem-solving tasks characteristic of intelligence test items has one correct answer and, thus, requires convergent thinking: "How many quarters will you get in return for 60 dimes?" However, the following question, an example of an item used to assess creative thinking, has many possible answers: "What images does 'sitting alone in a dark room' make you think of?" (Barron, 1989). Answering "the sound of a violin with no strings" and "patience" are considered creative answers, whereas "a person in a crowd" or "insomnia" are considered common and, thus, not very creative, responses.

Some experts remain skeptical that we will ever fully understand the creative process. Others believe that a psychology of creativity is in reach. Most experts agree, however, that the concept of creativity as spontaneously bubbling up from a magical well is a myth. Momentary flashes of insight, accompanied by images, make up only a small part of the creative process. At the heart of the creative process are ability and experience that shape an individual's intentional and sustained effort, often over the course of a lifetime. Based on his research on creativity and analysis of the literature, Daniel Perkins (1984; Perkins & Gardner, 1989) has developed a model that takes into account the complexity of the creative process. An overview of Perkins' model and its application to children's education is presented in Perspective on Child Development 11.1. As we learn more about creativity, we come to understand how important it is as a human resource and as truly one of life's wondrous gifts.

The artist finds a greater pleasure in painting than in having completed the picture.

—Seneca

The Snowflake Model of Creativity and Its Application to Education

Daniel Perkins (1984) describes his view as the *snowflake model of creativity.* Like the six sides of a snowflake, each with its own complex structure, Perkins' model consists of six characteristics common to highly creative individuals (see figure 11.A). Children and adults who are creative may not have all six characteristics, but the more they have, the more creative they tend to be, says Perkins.

First, creative thinking involves aesthetics as much as practical standards. Aesthetics involves beauty. Outside of literature and the arts, conventional schooling pays little attention to the aesthetics of human inquiry. For example, the beauty of scientific theories, mathematical systems, and historical syntheses is rarely addressed by teachers, and how often do teachers comment on the aesthetics of students' work in math and science?

Second, creative thinking involves an ability to excel in finding problems. Creative individuals spend an unusual amount of time thinking about problems. They also explore a number of options in solving a particular problem before choosing a solution to pursue. Creative individuals value good questions because they can produce discoveries and creative answers. A student once asked Nobel laureate Linus Pauling how he came up with good ideas. Pauling said he developed a lot of ideas and threw away the bad ones. Most assignments in school are so narrow that students have little opportunity to generate, or even select among, different ideas, according to Perkins.

Third, creative thinking involves mental mobility, which allows individuals to find new perspectives and approaches to problems. One example of mental mobility is being able to think in terms of opposites and contraries while seeking a new solution. According to Perkins, most problems students work on in school are convergent, not divergent. For the most part, the learning problems students face in school lack the elbow room for exercising mental mobility.

Fourth, creative thinking involves the willingness to take risks. Accompanying risk is the acceptance of failure as part of the creative quest and the ability to learn from failures. Creative geniuses don't always produce masterpieces. For example, Picasso produced more than 20,000 works of art, but much of it was mediocre. The more children produce, the better is their chance of creating something unique. According to Perkins, most schools do not challenge students to take the risks necessary to think creatively and to produce creative work.

Fifth, creative thinking involves objectivity. The popular image of creative individuals usually highlights their subjective, personal insights and commitments; however, without some objectivity and feedback from others, they would create a private world that is distant from reality and could not be shared or appreciated by others. Creative individuals not only criticize their own work but they also seek criticism from others. Schools typically do highlight objectivity, although usually not in the arts.

Sixth, creative thinking involves inner motivation. Creative individuals are motivated to produce something for its own sake, not for school grades or for money. Their catalyst is the challenge, enjoyment, and satisfaction of the work itself. Researchers have found that individuals ranging from preschool children through adults are more creative when they are internally rather than externally motivated. Work evaluation, competition for prizes, and supervision tend to undermine internal motivation and diminish creativity (Amabile & Hennessey, 1988).

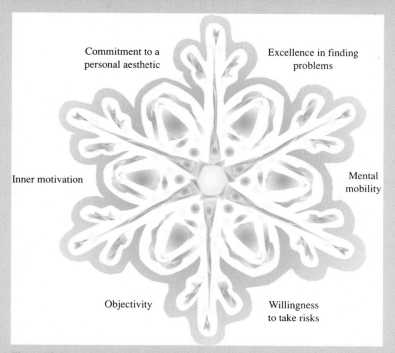

Figure 11.A
Snowflake Model of Creativity
Like a snowflake, Perkins' model of creativity has six parts: commitment to a
personal aesthetic, excellence in finding problems, mental mobility, willingness
to take risks, objectivity, and inner motivation.

CONCEPT TABLE 11.2
Controversies and Issues in Intelligence and the Extremes of Intelligence

Concept	Processes/related ideas	Characteristics/description
Controversies and issues	The heredity-environment controversy	In the late 1960s, Jensen argued that intelligence is approximately 80 percent hereditary and that genetic differences exist in the average intelligence of ethnic groups and social classes. Intelligence is influenced by heredity, but not as strongly as Jensen believed. The environments we provide children do make a difference.
	Culture and ethnicity	There are cultural and ethnic differences on intelligence tests, but the evidence suggests they are not genetically based. In recent decades, as Blacks have experienced more opportunities, the gap in Black-White intelligence test scores has diminished. Ethnic research needs to increase its emphasis on diversity within an ethnic group and the processes that explain ethnic differences rather than focusing solely on behavioral outcomes in comparisons of ethnic groups. Early intelligence tests favored White, middle-class, urban individuals. Current tests try to reduce this bias. Culture-fair tests are alternatives to traditional tests; most psychologists believe that they cannot completely replace the traditional tests.
	Knowledge versus process in intelligence	The mechanisms of intelligence and its development are both those of changing information-processing abilities and changing expertise and knowledge. Sternberg's triarchic model includes an emphasis on both information-processing and knowledge. He believes intelligence comes in three forms: componential, experiential, and contextual.
	The use and misuse of intelligence tests	Despite limitations, when used by a judicious examiner, tests are valuable tools for determining individual differences in children's intelligence. The tests should be used with other information about children. IQ scores can produce unfortunate stereotypes and expectations. Ability tests can help divide children into homogeneous groups. However, periodic testing should be done. Intelligence or a high IQ is not necessarily the ultimate human value.
The extremes of intelligence	Mental retardation	A mentally retarded child has a low IQ, usually below 70 on a traditional IQ test, and has difficulty adapting to everyday life. Classifications of mental retardation have been made. The two main types of retardation are organic and cultural-familial.
	Giftedness and creativity	A gifted child has above-average intelligence (an IQ of 120 or more) and/or superior talent for something. Creativity is the ability to think about something in a novel or unusual way and to come up with unique solutions to problems.

At this point, we have discussed a number of ideas about controversies and issues in intelligence and about the extremes of intelligence. A summary of these ideas is presented in concept table 11.2. This chapter concludes the section of the book on learning, cognition, and language development. In the next section, we will turn our attention to children's social and personality development, beginning with a discussion of the important role of families in children's lives.

Summary

I. What Is Intelligence?

Intelligence is an abstract concept that is measured indirectly; psychologists rely on intelligence tests to estimate intellectual processes. Verbal ability and problem-solving skills are described by both experts and lay people as components of intelligence. Some psychologists believe that the definition of intelligence should include the ability to learn and adapt to experiences in everyday life. Extensive effort has been given to assessing individual differences in intelligence. This field is called psychometrics.

II. How Tests Are Constructed and Evaluated

Three important aspects of test construction are reliability, validity, and standardization. Reliability refers to the consistency with which a test measures performance. Three measures of a test's reliability are test-retest, alternate forms, and split-half. Validity is the extent to which a test measures what it is intended to measure. Two main types of validity are content validity and criterion validity. Standardization focuses on the development of uniform procedures for administering and scoring a test and norms.

III. The Measurement and Nature of Children's Intelligence

Alfred Binet developed the first intelligence test, known as the 1905 Scale. He developed the concept of mental age; William Stern developed the concept of IQ. The Binet has been standardized and revised a number of times. The many revisions are called the Stanford-Binet tests. The test approximates a normal distribution. The current test is given to individuals from the age of 2 through adulthood. Besides the Binet, the Wechsler scales are the most widely used intelligence tests. They include the WAIS-R, the WISC-R, and the WPPSI. These tests provide an overall IQ, verbal and performance IQ, and information about subtests. Psychologists debate whether intelligence is a general ability or a number of specific abilities. Spearman's two-factor theory and Thurstone's multiple-factor theory state that a number of specific factors are involved. Current thinking suggests that Spearman's conceptualization of intelligence as both a general ability and a set of specific factors is right. Gardner's seven frames of mind and Sternberg's triarchic theory—componential, experiential, and contextual intelligence—are contemporary efforts to determine the components of intelligence.

IV. Infant Intelligence and the Stability of Intelligence

Many standardized tests do not assess infant intelligence. Tests designed to assess infant intelligence are often referred to as developmental scales; the most widely used is the Bayley scales. Gesell was an important early contributor to the developmental testing of infants. The developmental quotient (DQ) is an overall score in the Gesell assessment of infants. Although intelligence is more stable across the childhood years than many attributes, many children's scores on intelligence tests fluctuate considerably. Recently, developmentalists have found that information-processing tasks that involve attention—especially habituation and dishabituation—are related to scores on standardized tests in childhood.

V. The Heredity-Environment Controversy

In the late 1960s, Jensen argued that intelligence is approximately 80 percent hereditary and that genetic differences exist in the average intelligence of ethnic groups and social classes. Intelligence is influenced by heredity, but not as strongly as Jensen believed. The environments we provide children do make a difference.

VI. Culture and Ethnicity

There are cultural and ethnic differences on intelligence tests, but the evidence suggests they are not genetically based. In recent decades, as Black Americans have experienced more opportunities, the gap in Black-White intelligence test scores has diminished. Ethnic research needs to increase its emphasis on diversity within ethnic groups and on the processes that explain ethnic differences rather than focusing solely on behavioral outcomes in comparing ethnic groups. Early intelligence tests favored White, middle-class, urban individuals. Current tests try to reduce this bias. Culture-fair tests are alternatives to traditional tests; most psychologists believe they cannot completely replace the traditional tests.

VII. Knowledge Versus Process

The mechanisms of intelligence and its development are both those of changing information-processing abilities and changing expertise and knowledge. Sternberg's triarchic model includes an emphasis on both information processing and knowledge. He believes that intelligence comes in three forms: componential, experiential, and contextual.

VIII. The Use and Misuse of Intelligence Tests

Despite limitations, when used by a judicious examiner, tests are valuable tools for determining individual differences in children's intelligence. The tests should be used in conjunction with other information about a child. IQ scores can produce unfortunate stereotypes and expectations. Ability tests can help divide children into homogeneous groups; however, periodic testing should be done. Intelligence or a high IQ is not necessarily the ultimate human value.

IX. The Extremes of Intelligence

A mentally retarded child has a low IQ, usually below 70 on a traditional IQ test, and has difficulty adapting to everyday life. Classifications of retardation exist. The two main classes of retardation are organic and cultural-familial. A gifted child has well-above-average intelligence (an IQ of 120 or above), a superior talent for something, or both. Creativity is the ability to think about something in a novel and unusual way and to come up with unique solutions to problems.

Key Terms

individual differences 365
psychometrics 365
reliability 365
test-retest reliability 365
split-half reliability 366
validity 366
content validity 366
criterion validity 366
concurrent validity 366
predictive validity 366
standardization 367
norms 367
intelligence 368
mental age (MA) 368
intelligence quotient
 (IQ) 368
normal distribution 369

two-factor theory 370
multiple-factor theory 370
triarchic theory 371
developmental quotient
 (DQ) 375
Bayley Scales of Infant
 Development 375
culture-fair tests 384
mental retardation 388
organic retardation 389
cultural-familial
 retardation 389
gifted 389
creativity 390
convergent thinking 390
divergent thinking 390

Suggested Readings

Gardner, H., & Perkins, D. P. (Eds.). (1989). *Art, mind, and education.* Ithaca, NY: The University of Illinois Press. Extensive, valuable information is provided about enhancing the creative thinking of children.

Horowitz, F. D., & O'Brien, M. (Eds.). (1985). *The gifted and the talented.* Washington, DC: American Psychological Association. This volume pulls together what we currently know about the gifted and the talented. Experts have contributed chapters on the nature of the gifted and the diverse topics involved.

Kail, R., & Pellegrino, J. W. (1985). *Human intelligence.* New York: W. H. Freeman. This book brings together a number of different perspectives on human intelligence; it includes separate chapters on the psychometric and information-processing approaches.

Sattler, J. M. (1982). *Assessment of children's intelligence and special abilities.* Boston: Allyn & Bacon. Extensive information is provided about the measurement of children's intelligence, both for normal children and for those from special populations, such as the mentally retarded.

Sax, G. (1989). *Principles of educational and psychological measurement* (3rd ed.). Belmont, CA: Wadsworth. This book includes information about many intelligence tests, cultural bias, and the extremes of intelligence.

SOCIAL AND PERSONALITY DEVELOPMENT

IT IS NOT ENOUGH FOR

PARENTS TO UNDERSTAND

CHILDREN. THEY MUST

ACCORD CHILDREN THE

PRIVILEGE OF

UNDERSTANDING THEM.

—Milton Sapirstein

Family Processes
    Transition to Parenthood
    Reciprocal Socialization
    The Family As a System
Attachment
    What Is Attachment?
    Individual Differences
    Attachment, Temperament, and the Wider
        Social World
The Father's Role
Day Care
    Cultural Worlds of Development 12.1: Child-Care
        Policies Around the World
    Perspective on Child Development 12.1: What Is
        Quality Day Care?
Parenting Styles
    The Nature of Parenting Styles
    Adapting Parenting to Developmental Changes in
        the Child
    Perspective on Child Development 12.2: A Primer
        for Competent Parenting
    Cultural, Social Class, and Ethnic Variations in
        Families
    Child Abuse
    Cultural Worlds of Development 12.2: Black
        American and Mexican Family Orientations
Sibling Relationships and Birth Order
Family Processes in Adolescence
    Autonomy and Attachment
    Parent-Adolescent Conflict
    The Maturation of the Adolescent and Parents
The Changing Family in a Changing Society
    Working Parents
    The Effects of Divorce on Children
    Stepfamilies
Summary
Key Terms
Suggested Readings

The beast and the bird their common charge attend the mothers nurse it, and the sires defend; the young dismissed, to wander earth or air, their stops the instinct, and there the care. A longer care man's helpless kind demands, that longer care contracts more lasting bonds.

—Alexander Pope

The newborns of some species function independently in the world. Other species are not so independent. At birth, an opossum is still considered fetal and is capable of finding its way around only in its mother's pouch, where it attaches itself to her nipple and continues to develop. This protective environment is similar to the uterus. By contrast, a wildebeest must be able to run with the herd moments after birth. The newborn wildebeest's behavior is far more adultlike than the opossum's, although the wildebeest also must obtain food through suckling. The maturation of a human infant lies somewhere between these two extremes. Much learning and development must take place before the infant can sustain itself (Maccoby, 1980) (see figure 12.1).

Because it cannot sustain itself, a human infant requires extensive care. What kind of care is needed and how does the infant begin the road to social maturity? As part of our discussion of family processes, we will discuss the transition to parenthood and the importance of attachment in a child's development. Researchers are intensely exploring the nature of infant attachment, raising and evaluating a number of exciting questions such as these: Is a secure attachment to a caregiver necessary for a child's competent social development? What role does an infant's temperament play in the attachment process? What is the father's role in infant attachment? How does day care influence attachment?

Beyond the attachment process, we will explore some parenting styles and the nature of sibling relations. In keeping with the developmental theme of this text, we will then turn our attention to family processes in adolescence. As we move toward the end of the twentieth century, more children are experiencing socialization in a greater variety of family structures than at any point in history. To conclude the chapter, we will consider children's development in the changing American family, giving special attention to children's lives in latchkey, divorced, and stepparent families.

Family Processes

Most of us began our lives in families and spent thousands of hours during our childhood interacting with our parents. Some of you already are parents; others of you may become parents. What is the transition to parenthood like? What is the nature of family processes?

Transition to Parenthood

When people become parents through pregnancy, adoption, or stepparenting, they face disequilibrium and must adapt. Parents want to develop a strong attachment with their infant, but they still want to maintain a strong attachment to their spouse and friends and possibly continue their careers. Parents ask themselves how this new being will change their lives. A baby places new

(a)

(b)

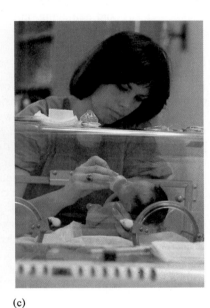

(c)

Figure 12.1
Variations in the Dependency of Newborns in Various Species
(a) The newborn opossum is fetal, capable of finding its way around only in its mother's pouch, where it attaches itself to her nipple and continues to develop. (b) By contrast, the wildebeest runs with the herd moments after birth. (c) The human newborn's maturation lies somewhere between that of the opossum and the wildebeest.

restrictions on partners; no longer will they be able to rush out to a movie on a moment's notice, and money will not be readily available for vacations and other luxuries. Dual-career parents ask, "Will day care harm the baby? Will we be able to find responsible baby-sitters?"

The excitement and joy that accompany the birth of a healthy baby are often followed by "postpartum blues" in mothers—a depressed state that lasts as long as 9 months into the infant's first year (Fleming & others, 1988; Osofsky, 1989). The early months of the baby's physical demands may bring not only the joy of intimacy but also the sorrow of exhaustion. Pregnancy and childbirth are demanding physical events that require recovery time for the mother.

Many fathers are not sensitive to these extreme demands placed on the mother. Busy trying to make enough money to pay the bills, some fathers may not be at home much of the time. A father's ability to sense and adapt to the stress placed on his wife during the first year of the infant's life has important implications for the success of the marriage and the family.

Becoming a parent is both wonderful and stressful. In a longitudinal investigation of couples from late pregnancy until 3½ years after their babies were born, Carolyn and Phillip Cowan (Cowan, 1988; Cowan & Cowan, 1989) found that the couples enjoyed more positive marital relations before the birth than after. Still, almost one third showed an increase in marital satisfaction. Some couples said that the baby had both brought them closer together *and* moved them further apart. They commented that being parents enhanced their sense of themselves and gave them a new, more stable identity as a couple. Babies opened the men up to a concern with intimate relationships, and the demands of juggling work and family roles stimulated the women to manage family tasks more efficiently and pay attention to their personal growth.

At a point during the early years of a child's life, parents face the difficult task of juggling their roles as parents and self-actualizing adults. Until recently in our culture, nurturing children and having a career were thought to be incompatible. Fortunately, we have come to recognize that the balance between caring and achieving, nurturing and working—although difficult to manage—can be accomplished.

Reciprocal Socialization

For many years, socialization between parents and children was viewed as a one-way process: Children were considered to be the products of their parents' socialization techniques. Today, however, we view parent-child interaction as reciprocal. **Reciprocal socialization** *is the view that socialization is bidirectional; children socialize parents just as parents socialize children.* For example, the interaction of mothers and their infants is symbolized as a dance or dialogue in which successive actions of the partners are closely coordinated. This coordinated dance or dialogue can assume the form of mutual synchrony (each person's behavior depends on the partner's previous behavior), or it can be reciprocal in a more precise sense; the actions of the partners can be matched, as when one partner imitates the other or when there is mutual smiling (Cohn & Tronick, 1988).

When reciprocal socialization has been investigated in infancy, mutual gaze or eye contact has been found to play an important role in early social interaction (Fogel, Toda, & Kawai, 1988). In one investigation, the mother and infant engaged in a variety of behaviors while they looked at each other; by contrast, when they looked away from each other, the rate of such behaviors dropped considerably (Stern & others, 1977). In sum, the behaviors of mothers and infants involve substantial interconnection and synchronization.

Scaffolding *is a term used to describe an important caregiver's role in early parent-child interaction. Through their attention and choice of behaviors, caregivers provide a framework around which they and their infants interact. One function of scaffolding is to introduce infants to social rules, especially turn taking* (Bruner, 1989; Lyons, 1991). For example, in the game peek-a-boo, mothers initially cover their babies, then remove the covering, and finally register "surprise" at the reappearance. As infants become more skilled at peek-a-boo, they do the covering and uncovering. Infant researcher Tiffany Field (1987) observed that, in addition to peek-a-boo, pat-a-cake and so big are other caregiver-infant games that involve scaffolding and its turn-taking sequences (see figure 12.2). In one recent investigation, infants who had more extensive scaffolding experiences with their parents, especially in the form of turn taking, were more likely to engage in turn taking as they interacted with their peers (Vandell & Wilson, 1988).

Social and Personality Development

(a)

(b)

(c)

The Family As a System

As a social system, the family can be thought of as a constellation of subsystems defined in terms of generation, gender, and role. Divisions of labor among family members define particular subunits, and attachments define others. Each family member is a participant in several subsystems—some dyadic (involving two people), some polyadic (involving more than two people). The father and child represent one dyadic subsystem, the mother and father another; the mother-father-child represent one polyadic subsystem, the mother and two siblings another (Belsky, Rovine, & Fish, 1989).

An organizational scheme that highlights the reciprocal influences of family members and family subsystems is shown in figure 12.3 (Belsky, 1981). As the arrows in the figure show, marital relations, parenting, and infant/child behavior can have both direct and indirect effects on each other. An example of a direct effect is the influence of the parent's behavior on the child; an example of an indirect effect is how the relationship between the spouses mediates the way a parent acts toward the child. For example, marital conflict might reduce the efficiency of parenting, in which case marital conflict would be an indirect effect on the child's behavior. In the family system, the infant's most important experiences involve the process of attachment.

Attachment

A small curly-haired girl named Danielle, age 11 months, begins to whimper. After a few seconds, she begins to wail. The psychologist observing Danielle is conducting a research study on the nature of attachment between infants and their mothers. The psychologist is watching Danielle cry. Subsequently, the mother reenters the room, and Danielle's crying ceases. Quickly, Danielle crawls over to where her mother is seated and reaches out to be held. This scenario is one of the main ways that psychologists study the nature of attachment during infancy.

Figure 12.2
Caregiver-Infant Games That Involve Scaffolding
(a) Pat-a-cake, (b) peek-a-boo, and (c) so-big are excellent games for parents to play with their infants. Through such games, children learn social rules, especially turn-taking.

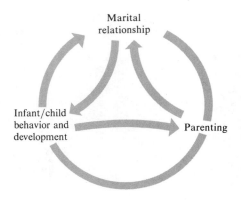

Figure 12.3
The Family As a System of Interacting Individuals: Direct and Indirect Effects
Jay Belsky developed this model to describe how family interaction patterns can have both direct and indirect effects. For example, parents' behavior can have a direct effect on the infant's or child's behavior, or their marital relationship can have indirect effects on the infant's or child's development by influencing parenting behavior.

Figure 12.4
Harlow's Classic "Contact Comfort" Study
Regardless of whether they were fed by a wire mother or by a cloth mother, the infant monkeys overwhelmingly preferred to be in contact with the cloth mother, demonstrating the importance of contact comfort in attachment.

What Is Attachment?

In everyday language, attachment refers to a relationship between two individuals in which each individual feels strongly about the other and does a number of things to continue the relationship. Many pairs of people are attached: relatives, lovers, a teacher and a student. In the language of developmental psychology, though, attachment is often restricted to a relationship between particular social figures and to a particular phenomenon thought to reflect unique characteristics of the relationship. The developmental period is infancy, the social figures are the infant and one or more adult caregivers, and the phenomenon in question is a bond (Bowlby, 1969, 1989). To summarize, **attachment** *is a close emotional bond between an infant and a caregiver.*

There is no shortage of theories about infant attachment. Freud believed that infants become attached to the person or object that provides oral satisfaction; for most infants, this is the mother, since she is most likely to feed the infant.

However, is feeding as important as Freud thought? A classic study by Harry Harlow and Robert Zimmerman (1959) suggests that the answer is no. These researchers evaluated whether feeding or contact comfort was more important to infant attachment. Infant monkeys were removed from their mothers at birth and reared for 6 months by surrogate (substitute) "mothers." As shown in figure 12.4, one of the mothers was made of wire, the other of cloth. Half of the infant monkeys were fed by the wire mother, half by the cloth mother. Periodically, the amount of time the infant monkeys spent with either the wire or the cloth monkey was computed. Regardless of whether they were fed by the wire or the cloth mother, the infant monkeys spent far more time with the cloth mother. This study clearly demonstrated that feeding is not the crucial element in the attachment process and that contact comfort is important.

Most toddlers develop a strong attachment to a favorite soft toy or a particular blanket. Toddlers may carry the toy or blanket with them everywhere they go, just as Linus does in the "Peanuts" cartoon strip, or they may run for the toy or blanket only in moments of crisis, such as after an argument or a fall. By the time they have outgrown the security object, all that may be left is a small fragment of the blanket, or an animal that is hardly recognizable, having had a couple of new faces and all its seams resewn half a dozen times. If parents try to replace the security object with something newer, the toddler will resist. There is nothing abnormal about a toddler carrying around a security blanket. Children know that the blanket or teddy bear is not their mother, and yet they react affectively to these objects and derive comfort from them as if they were their mother. Eventually, they abandon the security object as they grow up and become more sure of themselves.

Might familiarity breed attachment? The famous study by ethologist Konrad Lorenz (1965) suggests that the answer is yes. Remember from our description of this study in chapter 2 that newborn goslings became attached to "father" Lorenz rather than to their mother because he was the first moving object they saw. The time period during which familiarity is important for goslings is the first 36 hours after birth; for human beings, it is more on the order of the first year of life.

Erik Erikson (1968) believes that the first year of life is the key time frame for the development of attachment. Recall his proposal—also discussed in chapter 2—that the first year of life represents the stage of trust versus mistrust. A sense of trust requires a feeling of physical comfort and a minimal amount of fear and apprehension about the future. Trust in infancy sets the stage for a lifelong expectation that the world will be a good and pleasant place to be. Erikson also believes that responsive, sensitive parenting contributes to an infant's sense of trust.

The ethological perspective of British psychiatrist John Bowlby (1969, 1989) also stresses the importance of attachment in the first year of life and the responsiveness of the caregiver. Bowlby believes that an infant and its mother instinctively form an attachment. He argues that the newborn is biologically equipped to elicit the mother's attachment behavior. The baby cries, clings, coos, and smiles. Later, the infant crawls, walks, and follows the mother. The infant's goal is to keep the mother nearby. Research on attachment supports Bowlby's view that, at about 6 to 7 months of age, the infant's attachment to the caregiver intensifies (Sroufe, 1985).

Individual Differences

Although attachment to a caregiver intensifies midway through the first year, isn't it likely that some babies have a more positive attachment experience than others? Mary Ainsworth (1979) thinks so and says that, in **secure attachment,** *infants use the caregiver, usually the mother, as a secure base from which to explore the environment. Ainsworth believes that secure attachment in the first year of life provides an important foundation for psychological development later in life.* The caregiver's sensitivity to the infant's signals increases secure attachment. The securely attached infant moves freely away from the mother but processes her location through periodic glances. The securely attached infant responds positively to being picked up by others and, when put back down, freely moves away to play. An insecurely attached infant, by contrast, avoids the mother or is ambivalent toward her, fears strangers, and is upset by minor, everyday separations.

Ainsworth believes that insecurely attached infants can be classified as either anxious-avoidant or anxious-resistant, making three main attachment categories: secure (type B), anxious-avoidant (type A), and anxious-resistant (type C). **Type B babies** *use the caregiver as a secure base from which to explore the environment.* **Type A babies** *exhibit insecurity by avoiding the mother (for example, ignoring her, averting her gaze, and failing to seek proximity).* **Type C babies** *exhibit insecurity by resisting the mother (for example, clinging to her but at the same time fighting against the closeness, perhaps by kicking and pushing away).*

Why are some infants securely attached and others insecurely attached? Following Bowlby's lead, Ainsworth believes that attachment security depends on how sensitive and responsive a caregiver is to an infant's signals. For example, infants who are securely attached are more likely to have mothers who are more sensitive, accepting, and expressive of affection toward them than those who are insecurely attached (Pederson & others, 1989).

Soft toys or a blanket are common attachment objects of toddlers. Most toddlers eventually abandon their security object as they grow up and become more sure of themselves.

A child forsaken, waking suddenly,
Whose gaze affeard on all things round
*   doth rove,*
And seeth only that it cannot see
The meeting eyes of love.

—George Eliot

The attachment theorists argue that early experiences play an important role in a child's later social development. For example, Bowlby and Ainsworth argue that a secure attachment to the caregiver in infancy is related to the development of social competence during the childhood years.

If early attachment to a caregiver is important, it should relate to a child's social behavior later in development. Research by Alan Sroufe (1985, in press) documents this connection. In one investigation, infants who were securely attached to their mothers early in infancy were less frustrated and happier at 2 years of age than their insecurely attached counterparts (Matas, Arend, & Sroufe, 1978). In another longitudinal investigation, securely attached infants were more socially competent and had better grades in the third grade (Egeland, 1989).

Attachment, Temperament, and the Wider Social World

Not all developmentalists believe that a secure attachment in infancy is the only path to competence in life. Indeed, some developmentalists believe that too much emphasis is placed on the importance of the attachment bond in infancy. Jerome Kagan (1987a, 1989), for example, believes that infants are highly resilient and adaptive; he argues that they are evolutionarily equipped to stay on a positive developmental course even in the face of wide variations in parenting. Kagan and others stress that genetic and temperament characteristics play more important roles in a child's social competence than the attachment theorists, such as Bowlby, Ainsworth, and Sroufe, are willing to acknowledge (Fish, 1989; Fox & others, 1989). For example, infants may have inherited a low tolerance for stress; this, rather than an insecure attachment bond, may be responsible for their inability to get along with peers.

Another criticism of the attachment theory is that it ignores the diversity of social agents and social contexts that exist in an infant's world. Experiences with both the mother and the father, changing gender roles, day care, the mother's employment, peer experiences, socioeconomic status, and cultural values are not considered adequately in the attachment concept (Lamb & others, 1984; Thompson, 1991). In all of these perspectives, the importance of social relationships with parents is recognized; their differences lie in the criticalness of the attachment bond. Keep in mind that there is currently a great deal of controversy surrounding the concept of secure attachment. Some experts argue for its primacy in influencing a child's competent development, and others argue that it is given too much weight.

Social and Personality Development

The Father's Role

A father gently cuddles his infant son, softly stroking his forehead. Another father dresses his infant daughter as he readies her for her daily trip to a day-care center. How common are these circumstances in the lives of fathers and their infants? Has the father's role changed dramatically?

The father's role has undergone major changes (Bronstein, 1988; Lamb, 1986, 1987; Pleck, 1984). During the colonial period in American history, fathers were mainly responsible for moral teaching. Fathers provided moral guidance and values, especially through religion. With the Industrial Revolution, the father's role changed; he gained the responsibility as the breadwinner, a role that continued through the Great Depression. By the end of World War II, another role for fathers emerged, that of a gender role model. Although being a breadwinner and moral guardian continued to be important father roles, attention shifted to his role as a male, especially for sons. Then, in the 1970s, the current interest in the father as an active, nurturant, caregiving parent emerged. Rather than being responsible only for the discipline and control of older children and for providing the family's economic base, the father now is being evaluated in terms of his active, nurturant involvement with his children (McBride, 1991).

Are fathers more actively involved with their children than they were 10 to 20 years ago? Few data document changes in the father's involvement from one point in history to another. However, in one investigation, fathers' involvement in 1975 and 1981 was compared (Juster, 1985). In 1981, fathers spent about one fourth more time in direct interaction with the child than in 1975. Mothers increased their direct interaction about 7 percent over this time period, but fathers—although increasing their direct interaction—still were far below mothers in this regard. In this study, the fathers' involvement was about one third that of the mothers, both in 1975 and in 1981. If the mother is employed, does the father increase his involvement with his children? Only slightly. In sum, the father's active involvement with the child has increased somewhat, although this involvement does not approach the mother's, even when she is employed. Although fathers are spending more time with their infants and children, the evidence so far indicates that more time does not necessarily mean quality time. In one recent investigation, there was no relation between the amount of time fathers spent with their 5-year-old children and the quality of fathering (Grossman, Pollack, & Golding, 1988).

Can fathers take care of infants as competently as mothers can? Observations of fathers and their infants suggest that fathers have the ability to act sensitively and responsively with their infants (Parke & Sawin, 1980). Probably the strongest evidence of the placticity of male caregiving abilities is derived from information about male primates who are notoriously low in their interest in offspring but are forced to live with infants whose female caregivers are absent. Under these circumstances, the adult male competently rears the infants. Remember, however, that, although fathers can be active, nurturant, involved caregivers with their infants, most of the time they choose not to follow this pattern.

Do fathers behave differently toward infants than mothers do? Whereas maternal interactions usually center around child-care activities—feeding, changing diapers, bathing—paternal interactions are more likely to include play. Fathers engage in more rough-and-tumble play, bouncing the infant, throwing him up in the air, tickling him, and so on (Lamb, 1986). Mothers do play with infants, but their play is less physical and arousing than that of fathers.

■ *Critical Thinking*
The father's role has changed considerably in the twentieth century. What do you think the father's role in child development will be in the twenty-first century?

The current image of the father as an active, nurturant, caregiving parent emerged in the 1970s.

All men know their children mean more than life.

—Euripides

The father's role in China has been slow to change. Traditionally, in China, the father has been expected to be strict, the mother kind. The father is characterized as a stern disciplinarian to be feared and respected. The notion of the strict father has ancient roots. The Chinese character for father (fu) evolved from a primitive character representing a hand holding a cane, which symbolizes authority. However, the twentieth century has witnessed a decline in the father's authority. Younger fathers are more inclined to allow their children to express their opinions and be more independent. Influenced to a degree by the increased employment of mothers, Chinese fathers are becoming more involved in caring for their children. In some instances, intergenerational tension has developed between fathers and sons, as younger generations have begun to behave in less traditional ways (Ho, 1987).

In many European countries, mothers or fathers are given paid maternity or paternity leave for up to 9 months.

In stressful circumstances, do infants prefer their mother or father? In one investigation, twenty 12-month-olds were observed interacting with their parents (Lamb, 1977). With both parents present, the infants preferred neither their mother nor their father. The same was true when the infants were alone with the mother or the father. However, the entrance of a stranger, combined with boredom and fatigue, produced a shift in the infants' social behavior toward the mother. In stressful circumstances, then, infants show a stronger attachment to the mother.

Might the nature of parent-infant interaction be different in families that adopt nontraditional gender roles? This question was investigated by Michael Lamb and his colleagues (1982). They studied Swedish families in which the fathers were the primary caregivers of their firstborn, 8-month-old infants. The mothers were working full time. In all observations, the mothers were more likely to discipline, hold, soothe, kiss, and talk to the infants than were the fathers. These mothers and fathers dealt with their infants differently, along the lines of American fathers and mothers following traditional gender roles. Having fathers assume the primary caregiving role did not seem to alter substantially the way they interacted with their infants. This may be because of biological reasons or because of deeply ingrained socialization patterns in cultures.

In Sweden, mothers or fathers are given paid maternity or paternity leave for up to 9 months. Sweden and many other European countries have well-developed child-care policies. To learn about these policies, turn to Cultural Worlds of Development 12.1. In Sweden, day care for infants under 1 year of age is usually not a major concern because one parent is on paid leave for child care. As we will see, since the United States does not have a policy of paid leave for child care, day care in the United States has become a major national concern.

Day Care

Each weekday at 8:00 A.M., Ellen Smith takes her 1-year-old daughter Tanya to the day-care center at Brookhaven College in Dallas. Then Mrs. Smith goes to work and returns in the afternoon to take Tanya home. After 3 years, Mrs. Smith reports that her daughter is adventuresome and interacts confidently with peers and adults. Mrs. Smith believes that day care has been a wonderful way to raise Tanya.

In Los Angeles, however, day care has been a series of horror stories for Barbara Jones. After 2 years of unpleasant experiences with sitters, day-care centers, and day-care homes, Mrs. Jones has quit her job as a successful real estate agent to stay home and take care of her 2½-year-old daughter Gretchen. "I didn't want to sacrifice my baby for my job," said Mrs. Jones, who was unable to find good substitute care in day-care homes. When she put Gretchen into a day-care center, she said that she felt her daughter was being treated like a piece of merchandise—dropped off and picked up.

Many parents worry whether day care will adversely affect their children. They fear that day care will reduce their infants' emotional attachment to them, retard the infants' cognitive development, fail to teach them how to control anger, and allow them to be unduly influenced by their peers. How extensive is day care? Are the worries of these parents justified?

In the 1990s, far more young children are in day care than at any other time in history; about 2 million children currently receive formal, licensed day care, and more than 5 million children attend kindergarten. Also, uncounted

Social and Personality Development

Child-Care Policies Around the World

Sheila Kamerman (1989) recently surveyed the nature of child-care policies around the world, giving special attention to European countries. Maternity and paternity policies for working parents include paid, job-protected leaves, which sometimes are supplemented by additional unpaid, job-protected leaves. Child-care policy packages also often include full health insurance. An effective child-care policy is designed to get an infant off to a competent start in life and to protect maternal health while maintaining income. More than 100 countries around the world have such child-care policies, including all of Europe, Canada, Israel, and many developing countries (Kamerman & Kahn, 1988). Infants are assured of at least 2 to 3 months of maternal/paternal care and, in most European countries, 5 to 6 months.

The maternity policy as now implemented in several countries involves a paid maternity leave that begins 2 to 6 weeks prior to expected childbirth and lasts from 8 to 20 or even 24 weeks after birth. This traditional maternal policy stems from an effort to protect the health of pregnant working women, new mothers, and their infants. Only since the 1960s has the maternity policy's link with employment become strong. A second child-care policy emphasizes the importance of parenting and recognizes the potential of fathers as well as mothers to care for infants. In Sweden, a parent insurance benefit provides protection to new mothers before birth and for 6 to 12 weeks after birth but then allows fathers to participate in the postchildbirth leave. Approximately one fourth of all Swedish fathers take at least part of the postchildbirth leave, in addition to the 2 weeks' paid leave all fathers are entitled to at the time of childbirth. In a typical pattern in Sweden, a working mother might take off 3 months, after which she and her husband might share child care between them, each working half-time for 6 months. In addition, Swedish parents have the option of taking an unpaid but fully protected job leave until their child is 18 months old and to work a 6-hour day (without additional pay) from the end of the parental leave until their child is 8 years old. In table 12.A on page 412, maternity/paternity leave provisions in various Western countries are shown.

In sum, almost all the industrialized countries, except the United States, have recognized the importance of developing maternity/paternity policies that allow working parents some time off after childbirth to recover physically, to adapt to parenting, and to improve the well-being of the infant—without losing employment or income.

---

millions of children are cared for by unlicensed baby-sitters. Day care clearly has become a basic need of the American family (Caldwell, 1991; Phillips, 1989).

The type of day care that young children receive varies extensively. Many day-care centers house large groups of children and have elaborate facilities. Some are commercial operations; others are nonprofit centers run by churches, civic groups, and employers. Home care frequently is provided in private homes, at times by child-care professionals, at others by mothers who want to earn extra money (Lombardi, 1991).

The quality of care children experience in day care also varies extensively. Some caregivers have no training; others have extensive training. Some day-care centers have a low caregiver-child ratio; others have a high caregiver-child ratio. Some experts recently have argued that the quality of day care most children receive in the United States is poor. Infant researcher Jay Belsky (1989) believes not only that the quality of day care children experience is generally poor, but he also thinks this translates into negative developmental outcomes for children. Belsky concludes that extensive day-care experience during the first 12 months of life—as typically experienced in the United States—is associated with insecure attachment, as well as increased aggression, noncompliance, and possibly social withdrawal during the preschool and early elementary school years.

A recent study by Deborah Vandell and Mary Anne Corasaniti (1988) supports Belsky's beliefs. They found that extensive day care in the first year

TABLE 12.A
Maternity/Paternity Leave Provisions in Various Western Countries

Country/date	Duration of paid leave	Available to fathers	Supplementary unpaid or paid leave
Benefit level 100% of earnings[a]			
Norway, 1984	4 months	Yes	Yes
Austria, 1987	16 weeks		10 months at lower level[b]
F. R. Germany, 1987	14 weeks[c]	Yes	1 year at flat rate[d]
Portugal, 1984	3 months		Yes
Netherlands, 1984	12 weeks[c]		
Benefit level 90% of earnings			
Sweden, 1987	9 months plus 3 months at flat rate	Yes	Up to 18 months; 6-hour work day, up to 8 years
Denmark, 1987	24 weeks	Yes	Yes
France, 1987	16 weeks[c]		Up to 2 years
United Kingdom, 1987	6 weeks + 12 weeks at flat rate		Maternity leave
Benefit level 80% of earnings			
Finland, 1987	11 months	Yes	Yes
Italy, 1984	5 months[e]		Yes
Belgium, 1984	14 weeks		
Ireland, 1982	14 weeks		
Benefit level 75% of earnings			
Spain, 1982	14 weeks		
Israel, 1984	12 weeks		
Canada, 1984	17 weeks, 15 paid		
Benefit level 50% of earnings			
Greece, 1982	12 weeks		

[a]Up to maximum covered under Social Security
[b]Plus 2 years for low-income single mothers if they cannot find child care
[c]6 weeks must be taken before expected birth; in other countries, this time is voluntary
[d]Last 6 months available only on an income-tested basis
[e]100% paid for first 4 weeks; 2 months leave before birth mandated

of an infant's life is associated with long-term negative outcomes. In contrast to children who began full-time day care later, children who began full-time day care (defined as more than 30 hours per week) as infants were rated by parents and teachers as being less compliant and as having poorer peer relations. In the first grade, they received lower grades and had poorer work habits.

Belsky's conclusions about day care are controversial. Other respected researchers have arrived at a different conclusion; their review of the day-care research suggests no ill effects of day care (Clarke-Stewart, 1989; Scarr, 1984b, 1991; Scarr, Lande, & McCartney, 1989).

What can we conclude? Does day care have adverse effects on children's development? Trying to combine the results into an overall conclusion about day-care effects is a problem because of the different types of day care children experience and the different measures used to assess the outcome. Belsky's analysis does suggest, however, that parents should be very careful about the quality of day care they select for their infants, especially those 1 year of age or less. Even Belsky agrees, though, that day care itself is not the culprit; rather, it is the quality of day care that is problematic in this country. Belsky acknowledges that no evidence exists to show that children in high-quality day care are at risk in any way (Belsky, 1989; Doll, 1988).

What constitutes a high-quality day-care program for infants? The demonstration program developed by Jerome Kagan and his colleagues (1978) at Harvard University is exemplary. The day-care center included a pediatrician, a nonteaching director, and an infant-teacher ratio of 3 to 1. Teachers' aides assisted at the center. The teachers and aides were trained to smile frequently, to talk with the infants, and to provide them with a safe environment that included many stimulating toys. No adverse effects of day care were observed in this project. More information about what to look for in a high-quality day-care center is presented in Perspective on Child Development 12.1. Using such criteria, Carolee Howes (1988) discovered that children who enter low-quality child care as infants are the least likely to be socially competent in early childhood (less compliant, less self-controlled, less task oriented, more hostile, and having more problems in peer interaction).

Edward Zigler (1987, 1991) recently proposed a solution to the day-care needs of families. Zigler says that we should not think of school as an institution but, rather, as a building owned by tax-paying parents who need day care for their children. Part of the school building would be for teaching and part would be for child care and supervision. This system could provide parents with competent developmental child-care services. Zigler believes it should be available to every child over the age of 3. He does not think children should start formal schooling at age 3; they would be in the schools only for day care. At the age of 5, children would start kindergarten, but only for half days. If the child has a parent at home, the child would spend the remainder of the day at home. If the parents are working, the child would spend the second half of the day in the day-care part of the school. For children aged 6 to 12, after-school and vacation care would be available to those who need it.

Zigler does not believe that teachers should provide day care; they are trained as educators and are too expensive. What we need, he says, is a child development associate, someone who is trained to work with children, someone we can afford to pay. This is a large vision, one that involves a structural change in society and a new face for our school system. Zigler believes that a bill legislating such experimental schools will soon be introduced in Congress. As Zigler remembers, between the fall of 1964 and the summer of 1965, we managed to put 560,000 children into Head Start, an educational program for impoverished children. He believes we can do the same thing with day care (Trotter, 1987). Despite the efforts of Zigler and others, the child-care bills currently being introduced in Congress do not adequately address the quality of child care and the low pay of child-care workers (DeAngelis, 1990).

At this point, we have discussed a number of ideas about family processes, attachment, the father's role, and day care. A summary of these ideas is presented in concept table 12.1. Now we will turn our attention to the different types of parenting styles to which children are exposed.

■ *Critical Thinking*
Of the criteria listed in Perspective on Child Development 12.1, which do you believe would be the most important if your own children were going to day care? Are there criteria not listed in the box that you believe should be considered?

We have all the knowledge necessary to provide absolutely first-rate child care in the United States. What is missing is the commitment and the will.

—Edward Zigler

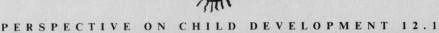

What Is Quality Day Care?

What constitutes quality child care? The following recommendations were made by the National Association for the Education of Young Children (1986). They are based on a consensus arrived at by experts in early childhood education and child development. It is especially important for parents to meet the adults who will care for their children—they are responsible for every aspect of the program's operation.

1. *The Adult Caregivers*
   - The adults should enjoy and understand how infants and young children grow.
   - There should be enough adults to work with a group and to care for the individual needs of children. More specifically, there should be no more than four infants for each adult caregiver, no more than eight 2-to-3-year-old children for each caregiver, and no more than ten 4-to-5-year-old children for each adult caregiver.
   - They observe and record each child's progress and development.
2. *The Program Activities and Equipment*
   - The environment fosters the growth and development of young children working and playing together.
   - A good center provides appropriate and sufficient equipment and play materials and makes them readily available.

- Infants and children are helped to increase their language skills and to expand their understanding of the world.
3. *Relation of Staff to Families and the Community*
   - A good program considers and supports the needs of the entire family. Parents should be welcome to observe, discuss policies, make suggestions, and work in the activities of the center.
   - The staff members in a good center are aware of and contribute to community resources. The staff should share information about community recreational and learning opportunities with families.
4. *The Facility and the Program Should Be Designed to Meet the Varied Demands of Infants and Young Children, Their Families, and the Staff*
   - The health of children, staff, and parents is protected and promoted. The staff should be alert to the health of each child.
   - The facility should be safe for children and adults.
   - The environment should be spacious to accommodate a variety of activities and equipment. More specifically, there should be a minimum of 35 square feet of usable playroom floor space indoors per child and 75 square feet of play space outdoors per child.

These young children are at a day-care center while their parents are at work. Day care has become a basic need of the American family. What are some variations in the type of day care children can experience?

414

Family Processes, Attachment, the Father's Role, and Day Care

Concept	Processes/related ideas	Characteristics/description
Family processes	Transition to parenthood	It produces a disequilibrium, requiring considerable adaptation. Becoming a parent is both wonderful and stressful.
	Reciprocal socialization	Children socialize their parents just as parents socialize their children. Scaffolding, synchronization, and mutual regulation are important dimensions of reciprocal socialization.
	The family as a system	The family is a system of interacting individuals with different subsystems, some dyadic, others polyadic. Belsky's model describes direct and indirect effects.
Attachment	What is attachment?	Attachment is a relationship between two people in which each person feels strongly about the other and does a number of things to ensure the relationship's continuation. In infancy, attachment refers to the bond between caregiver and infant. Feeding is not the critical element in attachment, although contact comfort, familiarity, and trust are important. Bowlby's ethological theory stresses that the mother and infant instinctively trigger attachment. Attachment to the caregiver intensifies at about 6 to 7 months.
	Individual differences	Ainsworth believes that individual differences in attachment can be classified into secure, avoidant, and resistant categories. Ainsworth believes that securely attached babies have sensitive and responsive caregivers. In some investigations, secure attachment is related to social competence later in childhood.
	Attachment, temperament, and the wider social world	Some developmentalists believe that too much emphasis is placed on the role of attachment; they believe that genetics and temperament, on the one hand, and the diversity of social agents and contexts, on the other, deserve more credit.
The father's role	Its nature	Over time, the father's role in the child's development has evolved from moral teacher to breadwinner to gender role model to active, nurturant caregiver.
	Father-child interaction and attachment	Fathers have increased their interaction with their children, but they still lag far behind mothers, even when mothers are employed. Fathers can act sensitively to the infant's signals, but most of the time they do not. The mother's role in the infant's development is primarily caregiving. That of the father involves playful interaction. Infants generally prefer their mother under stressful circumstances. Even in nontraditional families, as when the father is the main caregiver, the behaviors of mothers and fathers follow traditional gender lines.
Day care	Its nature	Day care has become a basic need of the American family; more children are in day care today than at any other time in history.
	Quality of care and effects on development	The quality of day care is uneven. Belsky concluded that most day care is inadequate and that extensive day care in the first 12 months of an infant's life has negative developmental outcomes. Other experts disagree with Belsky. Day care remains a controversial topic. Quality day care can be achieved and it seems to have few adverse effects on children.

Parenting Styles

Parents want their children to grow into socially mature individuals, and they may feel frustrated in trying to discover the best way to accomplish this. Developmentalists have long searched for the ingredients of parenting that promote competent social development in children. For example, in the 1930s, John Watson argued that parents are too affectionate with their children. In the 1950s, a distinction was made between physical and psychological discipline, with psychological discipline, especially reasoning, emphasized as the best way to rear a child. In the 1970s and beyond, the dimensions of competent parenting have become more precise.

Especially widespread is the view of Diana Baumrind (1971, 1991, in press), who believes that parents should be neither punitive nor aloof but, instead, should develop rules for their children and be affectionate with them. She emphasizes three types of parenting that are associated with different aspects of a child's social behavior: authoritarian, authoritative, and laissez-faire (permissive). More recently, developmentalists have argued that permissive parenting comes in two forms: permissive-indulgent and permissive-indifferent. What are these forms of parenting like?

The Nature of Parenting Styles

Authoritarian parenting *is a restrictive, punitive style that exhorts a child to follow a parent's directions and to respect work and effort. An authoritarian parent places firm limits and controls on a child with little verbal exchange allowed. Authoritarian parenting is associated with children's social incompetence.* For example, an authoritarian parent might say, "You do it my way or else. There will be no discussion!" Children of authoritarian parents often are anxious about social comparison, fail to initiate activity, and have poor communication skills.

Authoritative parenting *encourages children to be independent but still places limits and controls on their actions. Extensive verbal give-and-take is allowed and parents are warm and nurturant toward children. Authoritative parenting is associated with children's social competence.* An authoritative parent might put her arm around the child in a comforting way and say, "You know you should not have done that; let's talk about how you can handle the situation better next time." Children whose parents are authoritative are socially competent, self-reliant, and socially responsible.

Permissive parenting comes in two forms: permissive-indifferent and permissive-indulgent (Maccoby & Martin, 1983). **Permissive-indifferent parenting** *is a style in which the parent is very uninvolved in the child's life; it is associated with children's social incompetence, especially a lack of self-control.* This parent cannot answer the question "It is 10 P.M.; do you know where your child is?" Children have a strong need for their parents to care about them; children whose parents are permissive-indifferent develop the sense that other aspects of the parents' lives are more important than they are. Children whose parents are permissive-indifferent are socially incompetent—they show poor self-control and do not handle independence well.

Permissive-indulgent parenting *is a style of parenting in which parents are highly involved with their children but place few demands or controls on them. Permissive-indulgent parenting is associated with children's social incompetence, especially a lack of self-control.* They let their children do what they want, and the result is the children never learn to control their own behavior and always expect to get their way. Some parents deliberately rear their

Reprinted by permission of Jerry Marcus.

"Are you going to believe me, your own flesh and blood, or some stranger you married?"

children in this way because they believe the combination of warm involvement with few restraints will produce a creative, confident child. One boy whose parents deliberately reared him in a permissive-indulgent manner moved his parents out of their bedroom suite and took it over for himself. He is 18 years old and has not learned to control his behavior; when he can't get something he wants, he still throws temper tantrums. As you might expect, he is not very popular with his peers. Children whose parents are permissive-indulgent never learn respect for others and have difficulty controlling their behavior.

The four classifications of parenting just discussed involve combinations of acceptance and responsiveness on the one hand, and demand and control on the other. How these dimensions combine to produce authoritarian, authoritative, permissive-indifferent, and permissive-indulgent parenting is shown in figure 12.5. Further advice for parents that dovetails with the concept of authoritative parenting is discussed in Perspective on Child Development 12.2.

Adapting Parenting to Developmental Changes in the Child

Parents need to adapt their behavior toward the child based on the child's developmental maturity. Parents should not treat a 5-year-old the same as a 2-year-old. The 5-year-old and 2-year-old have different needs and abilities. In the first year, parent-child interaction moves from a heavy focus on routine caretaking—feeding, changing diapers, bathing, and soothing—to later include more noncaretaking activities, such as play and visual-vocal exchanges. During the child's second and third years, parents often handle disciplinary matters by physical manipulation: They carry the child away from a mischievous activity to the place they want the child to go; they put fragile and dangerous objects out of reach; they sometimes spank. As the child grows older, however, parents increasingly turn to reasoning, moral exhortation, and giving or withholding special privileges. As children move toward the elementary school years, parents show them less physical affection (Maccoby, 1984).

417

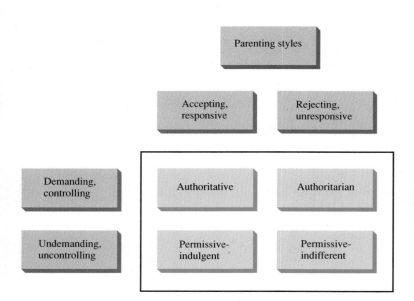

Classifications of Parenting Styles
The four types of parenting styles
(authoritarian, authoritative, permissive-
indulgent, and permissive-indifferent)
involve the dimensions of acceptance and
responsiveness on the one hand and
demand and control on the other.

Parent-child interactions during early childhood focus on such matters as modesty, bedtime regularities, control of temper, fighting with siblings and peers, eating behavior and manners, autonomy in dressing, and attention seeking. Although some of these issues—fighting and reaction to discipline, for example—are carried forward into the elementary school years, many new issues appear by the age of 7 (Maccoby, 1984). These include whether children should be made to perform chores and, if so, whether they should be paid for them, how to help children learn to entertain themselves rather than relying on parents for everything, and how to monitor children's lives outside the family in school and peer settings.

As children move into the middle and late childhood years, parents spend considerably less time with them. In one investigation, parents spent less than half as much time with their children aged 5 to 12 in caregiving, instruction, reading, talking, and playing as when the children were younger (Hill & Stafford, 1980). This drop in parent-child interaction may be even more extensive in families with little parental education. Although parents spend less time with their children in middle and late childhood than in early childhood, parents continue to be extremely important socializing agents in their children's lives. Children also must learn to relate to adults outside the family on a regular basis—adults who interact with the child much differently than parents. During middle and late childhood, interactions with adults outside the family involve more formal control and achievement orientation.

Discipline during middle and late childhood is often easier for parents than it was during early childhood; it may also be easier than during adolescence. In middle and late childhood, children's cognitive development has matured to the point where it is possible for parents to reason with them about resisting deviation and controlling their behavior. By adolescence, children's reasoning has become more sophisticated and they may be less likely to accept parental discipline. Adolescents also push more strongly for independence, which contributes to parenting difficulties. Parents of elementary school children use less physical discipline than do parents of preschool children. By contrast, parents of elementary school children are more likely to use deprivation of privileges, appeals directed at the child's self-esteem, comments designed to increase the child's sense of guilt, and statements indicating to the child that she is responsible for her actions.

A Primer for Competent Parenting

In the 1980s, the Missouri Department of Education hired Michael Meyerhoff and Burton White to design a model parent-education program and help set it up in four school districts across the state: one urban, one suburban, one small town, and one rural town. The families cover a wide range of social and economic backgrounds. The services include get-togethers—at which 10 to 20 parents meet with a parent educator at the resource center—and individual home visits by a parent educator. Services begin during the final 3 months of pregnancy and continue until the child's third birthday, with increasing emphasis on private visits after the child is 6 years old. The average amount of contact with the families is once a month for an hour and a half.

During group and private sessions, parents are given basic information about what kinds of parenting practices are likely to help or hinder their children's progress. Table 12.B shows the do's and don'ts told to parents, advice that makes sense and is likely to promote the child's competence (Meyerhoff & White, 1986; White, 1988).

Parenting practices play an important role in young children's development. What were the characteristics of competent parents found by Meyeroff and White?

TABLE 12.B
A Primer for Competent Parenting

Things to do:	Things not to do:
Provide children with the maximum opportunity for exploration and investigation.	Don't confine your children regularly for long periods of time.
Be available to act as your children's personal consultant as much as possible. You don't have to hover, but be around to provide attention and support as needed.	Don't allow them to concentrate their energies on you so much that independent exploration and investigation are excluded.
Respond to your children promptly and favorably as often as you can, providing appropriate enthusiasm and encouragement.	Don't ignore attention getting to the point where children have to throw a tantrum to gain your interest.
Set limits—do not give in to unreasonable requests or permit unacceptable behavior to continue.	Don't worry that your children won't love you if you say "no" on occasion.
Talk to your children often. Make an effort to understand what they are trying to do and concentrate on what they see as important.	Don't try to win all the arguments, especially during the second half of the second year when most children are passing through a normal period of negativism.
Use words they understand but also add new words and related ideas.	Don't be overprotective.
Provide new learning opportunities. Having children accompany you to the supermarket or allowing them to bake cookies with you is more enriching than sitting them down and conducting a flash card session.	Don't bore your child if you can avoid it. Don't worry about when children learn to count or say the alphabet.
Give your children a chance to direct some of your shared activities from time to time.	Don't worry if they are slow to talk, as long as they seem to understand more and more language as time goes by.
Try to help your children be as spontaneous emotionally as your own behavior patterns will allow.	Don't try to force toilet training; it will be easier when they are 2.
Encourage your child's pretend activities, especially those in which they act out adult roles.	Don't spoil your children, giving them the notion that the world was made just for them.

During middle and late childhood, some control is transferred from parent to child, although the process is gradual and involves *coregulation* rather than control by either the child or the parent alone (Maccoby, 1984). The major shift to autonomy does not occur until about the age of 12 or later. During middle and late childhood, parents continue to exercise general supervision and exert control while children are allowed to engage in moment-to-moment self-regulation. This coregulation process is a transition period between the strong parental control of early childhood and the increased relinquishment of general supervision of adolescence.

During this coregulation, parents should:

■ Monitor, guide, and support children at a distance
■ Effectively use the times when they have direct contact with the child
■ Strengthen in their children the ability to monitor their own behavior, to adopt appropriate standards of conduct, to avoid hazardous risks, and to sense when parental support and contact are appropriate

To be a competent parent, further adaptation is required as children become adolescents, which will be discussed later in the chapter. As we will see next, however, other important aspects of understanding parenting are cultural, social class, and ethnic variations in families.

Cultural, Social Class, and Ethnic Variations in Families

Cultures vary on a number of issues involving families, such as what the father's role in the family should be, the extent to which support systems are available to families, and how children should be disciplined. Although there are cross-cultural variations in parenting (Whiting & Edwards, 1988), in one study of parenting behavior in 186 cultures around the world, the most common pattern was a warm and controlling style, one that was neither permissive nor restrictive (Rohner & Rohner, 1981). The investigators commented that the majority of cultures have discovered, over many centuries, a "truth" that has only recently emerged from research in the Western world—namely, that children's healthy social development is most effectively promoted by love and at least some moderate parental control.

In America and most Western cultures, social class differences in childrearing have been found. Working-class and low-income parents often place a high value on external characteristics, such as obedience and neatness, whereas middle-class families often place a high value on internal characteristics, such as self-control and delay of gratification. Not only are there social class differences in childrearing values but also in parenting behaviors. Middle-class parents are more likely to explain things, give verbal praise, use reasoning to accompany their discipline, and ask their children questions. By contrast, parents in low-income and working-class households are more likely to discipline their children with physical punishment and criticism (Heath, 1983; Kohn, 1977).

Ethnic minority families differ from White American families in their size, structure, composition, reliance on kinship networks, and levels of income and education (Spencer, 1991; Spencer & Dornbusch, 1990). Large and extended families are more common among ethnic minority groups than among White Americans (Wilson, 1989; Wilson & others, 1991). For example, more than 30 percent of Hispanic American families consist of five or more individuals, compared to the general population (Keefe & Padilla, 1987; Rogler, Cortes, & Malgady, 1991). Black American and Hispanic American children interact more with grandparents, aunts, uncles, cousins, and distant relatives than do White American children.

Single-parent families are more common among Black Americans and Hispanic Americans than among White Americans. In comparison with two-parent households, single parents often have less time, money, and energy. This shortage of resources may prompt them to encourage their adolescents to gain early autonomy (Spencer & Dornbusch, 1990).

Ethnic minority parents are less well educated and engage in less joint decision making than do White American parents. Also, ethnic minority children are more likely to come from low-income families than are White American children (Committee for Economic Development, 1987; McLoyd, in press). Although impoverished families often raise competent youths, poor parents may have a diminished capacity for supportive and involved parenting (McLoyd, in press).

Some aspects of home life can help protect ethnic minority children from social patterns of injustice (Spencer & Dornbusch, 1990). The community and family can filter out destructive racist messages, parents can provide alternative frames of reference than those presented by the majority, and parents can provide competent role models and encouragement (Bowman & Howard, 1985; Jones, 1990). Also, the extended family system in many ethnic minority families provides an important buffer against stress. To read further about the extended family system in Black American and Hispanic American families, turn to Cultural Worlds of Development 12.2.

Child Abuse

Unfortunately, parental hostility toward children in some families escalates to the point where one or both parents abuse the children. Child abuse is an increasing problem in the United States. Estimates of its incidence vary, but some authorities say that as many as 500,000 children are physically abused every year. Laws in many states now require doctors and teachers to report suspected cases of child abuse, yet many cases go unreported, especially those of battered infants (Fontana, 1988; Hutchings, 1988).

Child abuse is such a disturbing circumstance that many people have difficulty understanding or sympathizing with parents who abuse or neglect their children (Crittenden, 1988a,b). Our response is often outrage and anger directed at the parent. This outrage focuses our attention on parents as bad, sick, monstrous, sadistic individuals who cause their children to suffer. Experts on child abuse believe that this view is too simple and deflects attention away from the social context of the abuse and parents' coping skills. It is especially important to recognize that child abuse is a diverse condition, that it is usually mild to moderate in severity, and that it is only partially caused by individual personality characteristics of parents (Cicchetti, 1991; Emery, 1989; Haugard & Emery, in press).

The Multifaceted Nature of Child Maltreatment

Whereas the public and many professionals use the term *child abuse* to refer to both abuse and neglect, developmentalists increasingly are using the term *child maltreatment* (Crittenden & Partridge, 1991). This term reduces the emotional impact of the term *abuse* and acknowledges that maltreatment includes several different conditions. Among the different types of maltreatment are physical and sexual abuse; fostering delinquency; lack of supervision; medical, educational, and nutritional neglect; and drug or alcohol abuse (Garbarino, 1989). In one large survey, approximately 20 percent of the reported

Black American and Mexican Family Orientations

In the 1985 Children's Defense Fund Study, "Black and White Children in America: Key Facts" (Edelman, 1987), Black American children were 3 times as likely as White American children to be poor, live with a parent who has separated from a spouse, or die of child abuse; 5 times as likely to be dependent on welfare; and 12 times as likely to live with a parent who never married. Nonetheless, it is important to keep in mind that millions of Black American families are not on welfare; have children who stay in school and out of trouble; and, if they experience difficult times, find a way to cope with and overcome their problems. In 1967, Martin Luther King, Jr., reflected on the Black American family and gave the following caution. As public awareness of the predicament of the Black family increases, there will be danger and opportunity. The opportunity will be to deal fully rather than haphazardly with the problem as a whole, as a social catastrophe brought on by many years of oppression. The danger is that the problems will be attributed to innate Black weaknesses and used to justify further neglect and to rationalize continued oppression. In today's world, Dr. King's words still ring true.

The Black cultural tradition of an extended family household—in which one or several grandparents, uncles, aunts, siblings, or cousins either live together or provide support—has helped many Black parents cope with adverse social conditions such as economic impoverishment (Harrison & others, 1990; McAdoo, 1988; Wilson & others, 1991). The extended family tradition can be traced to the African heritage of many Black Americans, in which a newly married couple does not move away from relatives. Instead, the extended family assists its members with basic family functions. Researchers have found that the extended Black family does help reduce the stress of poverty and single parenting through emotional support, the sharing of income and economic responsibility, and surrogate parenting (Allen & Majidi-Ahi, 1989; McAdoo, 1988; Wilson, 1989). The presence of grandmothers in the households of many Black adolescents and their infants has been an important support system both for the mothers and their infants (Stevens, 1984).

Although Black children are more likely than White children to be poor and live with a parent who has been separated from a spouse, it is important to keep in mind that millions of Black American families are not on welfare, have children who stay in school and out of trouble, and, if they experience difficult times, find a way to cope with and overcome their problems.

Active and involved extended family support systems also help parents of other ethnic groups cope with poverty and its related stress (Keefe & Padilla, 1987; Marín & Marín, 1991). A basic value in Mexico is represented by the saying "As long as our family stays together, we are strong." Mexican children are brought up to stay close to their families, often playing with siblings rather than with schoolmates or neighborhood children, as American children usually do. Unlike the father in many American families, the Mexican father is the undisputed authority on all family matters and is usually obeyed without question. The mother is revered as the primary source of affection and care. This emphasis on family attachment leads the Mexican to say, "I will achieve mainly because of my family, and for my family, rather than myself." By contrast, the self-reliant American would say, "I will achieve mainly because of my ability and initiative and for myself rather than for my family." Unlike most Americans, families in Mexico tend to stretch out in a network of relatives that often runs to scores of individuals.

---

cases involved abuse alone, 46 percent neglect alone, 23 percent both abuse and neglect, and 11 percent sexual abuse (American Association for Protecting Children, 1986). Abused children are more likely to be angry or wary than neglected children, who tend to be passive (Lynch & Roberts, 1982).

Severity of Abuse

The concern about child abuse began with the identification of the "battered child syndrome" and has retained the characteristic of severe, brutal injury

Hispanic American children often grow up in families with a network of relatives that runs into scores of individuals.

Both cultures—Mexican and American—have undergone considerable change in recent decades. Whether Mexican children will gradually take on the characteristics of American children, or whether American children will shift closer to Mexican children, is difficult to predict. The cultures of both countries will probably move to a new order more in keeping with future demands, retaining some common features of the old while establishing new priorities and values (Holtzmann, 1982).

for several reasons. First, the media tend to underscore the most bizarre and vicious incidents. Second, much of the funding for child-abuse prevention, identification, and treatment depends on the public's perception of the horror of child abuse and the medical professions' lobby for funds to investigate and treat abused children and their parents. The emphasis is often on the worst cases. These horrific cases do exist, and are indeed terrible, but they make up only a small minority of abused children. Less than 1 percent of abused children die, and another 11 percent suffer life-threatening, disabling injuries

(American Association for Protecting Children, 1986). By contrast, almost 90 percent suffer temporary physical injuries. These milder injuries, though, are likely to be experienced repeatedly in the context of daily hostile family exchanges. Similarly, neglected children, who suffer no physical injuries, often experience extensive, long-term psychological harm.

The Cultural Context of Maltreatment

The extensive violence of the American culture is reflected in the occurrence of violence in the family. A regular diet of violence appears on television screens, and parents often resort to power assertion as a disciplinary technique. In China, where physical punishment is rarely used to discipline children, the incidence of child abuse is reported to be very low. In the United States, many abusing parents report that they do not have sufficient resources or help from others. This may be a realistic evaluation of the situation experienced by many low-income families, who do not have adequate preventive and supportive services (Rodriguez-Haynes & Crittenden, 1988; Trickett & others, 1991).

Community support systems are especially important in alleviating stressful family situations, thereby preventing child abuse. An investigation of the support systems in 58 counties in New York State revealed a relation between the incidence of child abuse and the absence of support systems available to the family. Both family resources—relatives and friends, for example—and such formal community support systems as crisis centers and child abuse counseling were associated with a reduction in child abuse (Garbarino, 1976).

Family Influences

To understand abuse in the family, the interaction of all family members needs to be considered, regardless of who actually performs the violent acts against the child (Daro, 1988). For example, even though the father may be the one who physically abuses the child, contributions by the mother, the child, and siblings also should be evaluated. Many parents who abuse their children come from families in which physical punishment was used. These parents view physical punishment as a legitimate way of controlling the child's behavior, and physical punishment may be a part of this sanctioning. Children themselves may unwittingly contribute to child abuse: An unattractive child may receive more physical punishment than an attractive child, and a child from an unwanted pregnancy may be especially vulnerable to abuse (Harter, Alexander, & Neimeyer, 1988). Husband-wife violence and financial problems may result in displaced aggression toward a defenseless child. Displaced aggression is commonly involved in child abuse.

As they are developing, most children not only interact with parents but also with siblings. Next, we will examine the influence of siblings on children's development.

Sibling Relationships and Birth Order

Sandra describes to her mother what happened in a conflict with her sister:

> We had just come home from the ball game. I sat down on the sofa next to the light so I could read. Sally [the sister] said, "Get up. I was sitting there first. I just got up for a second to get a drink." I told her I was not going to get up and that I didn't see her name on the chair. I got mad and started pushing her. Her drink spilled all over her. Then she got really mad; she shoved me against the wall, hitting and clawing at me. I managed to grab a handful of hair.

At this point, Sally comes into the room and begins to tell her side of the story. Sandra interrupts, "Mother, you always take her side." Sound familiar? Any of you who have grown up with siblings (brothers or sisters) probably have a rich memory of aggressive, hostile interchanges, but sibling relationships have many pleasant, caring moments as well. Children's sibling relationships include helping, sharing, teaching, fighting, and playing. Children can act as emotional supports, rivals, and communication partners (Stocker & Dunn, 1991; Vandell, 1987; Zukow, 1989). More than 80 percent of American children have one or more siblings. Because there are so many possible sibling combinations, it is difficult to generalize about sibling influences. Among the factors to be considered are the number of siblings, the ages of siblings, birth order, age spacing, the sex of siblings, and whether sibling relationships are different from parent-child relationships.

Is sibling interaction different from parent-child interaction? There is some evidence that it is. Observations indicate that children interact more positively and in more varied ways with their parents than with their siblings (Baskett & Johnston, 1982). Children also follow their parents' dictates more than those of their siblings, and they behave more negatively and punitively with their siblings than with their parents.

In some instances, siblings may be stronger socializing influences on the child than parents are (Cicirelli, 1977). Someone close in age to the child—such as a sibling—may be able to understand the child's problems and be able to communicate more effectively than parents can. In dealing with peers, coping with difficult teachers, and discussing taboo subjects, such as sex, siblings may be more influential in the socialization process than parents.

Birth order is a special interest of sibling researchers. When differences in siblings are found, they usually are explained by variations in their interactions with parents and siblings and are associated with the unique experiences of being in a particular position in the family (McCartney & others, 1991; Musun-Miller, 1991). This is especially true in the case of the firstborn child. The oldest child is the only one who does not have to share parents' love and affection—until another sibling comes along. An infant requires more attention than an older child; this means that the firstborn sibling now gets less attention than before the newborn arrived. Does this result in conflict between parents and the firstborn? In one research study, mothers became more negative, coercive, and restraining and played less with the firstborn following the birth of a second child (Dunn & Kendrick, 1982). Even though a new infant requires more attention from parents than does an older child, an especially intense relationship seems to be maintained between parents and firstborns throughout the life cycle. Parents have higher expectations for their firstborn, put more pressure for achievement and responsibility on them, and interfere more with their activities than they do with later-born children (Rothbart, 1971).

Birth order also is associated with variations in sibling relationships. The oldest sibling is expected to exercise self-control and show responsibility in interacting with younger siblings. When the oldest sibling is jealous or hostile, parents often protect the younger siblings. The oldest sibling is more dominant, competent, and powerful than the younger siblings; the oldest sibling also is expected to assist and teach younger siblings. Indeed, researchers have shown that older siblings are both more antagonistic—hitting, kicking, biting—and more nurturant toward their younger siblings than vice versa (Abramovitch & others, 1986). There also is something unique about same-sex sibling relationships. Aggression, dominance, and cheating occur more in same-sex relationships than in opposite-sex sibling relationships (Minnett, Vandell, & Santrock, 1983).

Big sisters are the crab grass in the lawn of life.

—Charles Schulz

More than 80 percent of American children have siblings. Children's sibling relationships include helping, sharing, teaching, fighting, and playing.

425

Given the variations in the family dynamics involved in birth order, it is not surprising that firstborns and later-borns have different characteristics. Firstborn children are more adult oriented, more helpful, more conforming, and more anxious than their siblings. Parental demands and high standards established for firstborns result in these children excelling in academic and professional endeavors. Firstborns are overrepresented in *Who's Who* and as Rhodes scholars, for example. However, some of the same pressures placed on firstborns for high achievement may be the reason they also have more guilt, more anxiety, greater difficulty in coping with stressful situations, and a higher probability of being admitted to child guidance clinics.

What is an only child like? The popular conception of an only child is a "spoiled brat," with such undesirable characteristics as dependency, lack of self-control, and self-centered behavior. However, researchers present a more positive portrayal of the only child, who often is achievement oriented and displays a desirable personality, especially in comparison with later-borns and children from large families (Falbo & Polit, 1986).

So far our consideration of birth order effects would seem to indicate that they are strong predictors of behavior. However, an increasing number of family researchers believe that birth order has been overdramatized and given undeserved status. The critics argue that, when all of the factors that influence behavior are considered—heredity, temperament, parent-child interaction, peer influences, school influences, and so on—birth order shows little ability to predict behavior. Although birth order may not be a good predictor of behavior, sibling relationships and interaction are important dimensions of family processes.

Family Processes in Adolescence

Earlier in the chapter, we discussed how parents spend less time with their children during middle and late childhood than in early childhood, how discipline involves an increased use of reasoning and deprivation of privileges, and how there is a gradual transfer of control from parents to children but still within the boundary of coregulation. What are some of the most important issues and questions that need to be raised about family relationships in adolescence? They include: What is the nature of autonomy and attachment in adolescence? How extensive is parent-adolescent conflict and how does it influence the adolescent's development? Do maturation of the adolescent and maturation of parents contribute to understanding parent-adolescent relationships?

Autonomy and Attachment

The adolescent's push for autonomy and a sense of responsibility puzzles and angers many parents. Parents see their teenager slipping from their grasp. They may have an urge to take stronger control as the adolescent seeks autonomy and responsibility. Heated emotional exchanges may ensue, with either side calling names, making threats, and doing whatever seems necessary to gain control. Parents may seem frustrated because they *expect* their teenager to heed their advice, to want to spend time with the family, and to grow up to do what is right. Most parents anticipate that their teenager will have some difficulty adjusting to the changes that adolescence brings, but few parents can imagine and predict just how strong an adolescent's desires will be to spend

When I was a boy of 14, my father was so ignorant I could hardly stand to have the man around. But when I got to be 21, I was astonished at how much he had learnt in 7 years.

—Mark Twain

time with peers and how much adolescents want to show that it is they—not their parents—who are responsible for their successes and failures.

Expectations for adolescents' autonomy sometimes vary from one culture to another. For example, Western adolescents expect to achieve autonomy earlier than Eastern adolescents. In one recent study of 200 10th- and 11th-grade students, Hong Kong youths expected to achieve autonomy earlier than their American-born Caucasian counterparts in the United States (Feldman & Rosenthal, 1990b). Chinese youth who reside in the United States and Australia have later expectations for autonomy than their Western counterparts (Feldman & Rosenthal, 1990a). With such cultural variations in mind, let's examine more closely what autonomy is.

The ability to attain autonomy and gain control over one's behavior in adolescence is acquired through appropriate adult reactions to the adolescent's desire for control. At the onset of adolescence, the average individual does not have the knowledge to make appropriate or mature decisions in all areas of life. As the adolescent pushes for autonomy, the wise adult relinquishes control in those areas in which the adolescent can make reasonable decisions and continues to guide the adolescent to make reasonable decisions in areas in which the adolescent's knowledge is more limited. Gradually, adolescents acquire the ability to make mature decisions on their own.

However, adolescents do not simply move away from parental influence into a decision-making process all their own. There is continued connectedness to parents as adolescents move toward and gain autonomy. In the past decade, developmentalists have begun to explore the role of secure attachment and related concepts, such as connectedness to parents, in adolescent development (Fisher & Jenkins, 1991; Hill & Holmbeck, 1986; Santrock, 1990a). They believe that attachment to parents in adolescence may facilitate adolescents' social competence and well-being, as reflected in such characteristics as self-esteem, emotional adjustment, and physical health (Armsden & Greenberg, 1987; Kobak & Sceery, 1988; Papini, Roggman, & Anderson, 1990). For example, adolescents who have secure relationships with their parents have higher self-esteem and better emotional well-being (Armsden & Greenberg, 1987). In contrast, emotional detachment from parents is associated with greater feelings of parental rejection and a lower sense of one's own social and romantic attractiveness (Ryan & Lynch, 1989). Thus, attachment to parents during adolescence may serve the adaptive function of providing a secure base from which adolescents can explore and master new environments and a widening social world in a psychologically healthy manner. Secure attachment to parents may buffer adolescents from the anxiety and potential depression or emotional distress associated with the transition from childhood to adulthood. In one recent study, when young adolescents had a secure attachment to their parents, they perceived their family as cohesive and reported little social anxiety or feelings of depression (Papini, Roggman, & Anderson, 1990).

Secure attachment and connectedness to parents promotes competent peer relations and positive close relationships outside of the family. In one investigation, attachment to parents and peers was assessed (Armsden & Greenberg, 1984). Adolescents who were securely attached to parents also were securely attached to peers; those who were insecurely attached to parents also were more likely to be insecurely attached to peers. In another investigation, college students who were securely attached to their parents as young children were more likely to have securely attached relationships with friends, dates, and spouses than were their insecurely attached counterparts (Hazan & Shaver, 1987). In yet another investigation, older adolescents who had an ambivalent attachment history with their parents reported greater jealousy, conflict, and dependency along with less satisfaction in their relationship with their best friend than did their securely attached counterparts (Fisher, 1990). There are times when adolescents reject this closeness as they try to assert their own ability to make decisions, develop an identity, and identify with peers. For the most part, however, parent-adolescent and adolescent-peer relationships are coordinated and connected, not uncoordinated and disconnected.

Parent-Adolescent Conflict

Although attachment and connectedness to parents remains strong during adolescence, the attachment and connectedness are not always smooth. Early adolescence is a time when conflict with parents escalates beyond childhood levels (Montemayor & Flannery, 1991; Montemayor & Hanson, 1985; Steinberg, 1987, 1990b, 1991). This increase may be due to a number of factors: the biological changes of puberty, cognitive changes involving increased idealism and logical reasoning, social changes focused on independence and identity, maturational changes in parents, and violated expectations on the part of parents and adolescents. Adolescents compare their parents to an ideal standard and then criticize the flaws. A 13-year-old girl tells her mother, "That is the tackiest-looking dress I have ever seen. Nobody would be caught dead wearing that." Adolescents demand logical explanations for comments and discipline. A 14-year-old boy tells his mother, "What do you mean I have to be home at 10 P.M. because it's the way we do things around here? Why do we do things around here that way? It doesn't make sense to me."

Many parents see their adolescent changing from a compliant child to someone who is noncompliant, oppositional, and resistant to parental standards. When this happens, parents tend to clamp down and put more pressure on the adolescent to conform to parental standards (Collins, 1989, 1990). Parents often expect their adolescents to become mature adults overnight instead of understanding that the journey takes 10 to 15 years. Parents who recognize that this transition takes time handle their youth more competently and calmly than those who demand immediate conformity to adult standards. The opposite tactic—letting adolescents do as they please without supervision—also is unwise.

Although conflict with parents does increase in early adolescence, it does not reach the tumultuous proportions G. Stanley Hall envisioned at the beginning of the twentieth century. Rather, much of the conflict involves the everyday events of family life such as keeping a bedroom clean, dressing neatly, getting home by a certain time, and not talking forever on the phone. The conflicts rarely involve major dilemmas such as drugs and delinquency.

It is not unusual to talk to parents of young adolescents and hear them ask "Is it ever going to get better?" Things usually do get better as adolescents move from early to late adolescence. Conflict between parents usually escalates during early adolescence, remains somewhat stable during the high school years, and then lessens as the adolescent reaches 17 to 20 years of age. Parent-adolescent relationships become more positive if adolescents go away to college than if they stay at home and go to college (Sullivan & Sullivan, 1980).

The everyday conflicts that characterize parent-adolescent relationships may serve a positive developmental function (Blos, 1989; Hill, 1983). These minor disputes and negotiations facilitate the adolescent's transition from being dependent on parents to becoming autonomous. For example, in one investigation, adolescents who expressed disagreement with parents explored identity development more actively than adolescents who did not express disagreement with their parents (Carlson, Cooper, & Hsu, 1990; Cooper & others, 1982).

As suggested earlier, one way for parents to cope with the adolescent's push for independence and identity is to recognize that adolescence is a 10-to-15-year transition period rather than an overnight accomplishment. Recognizing that conflict and negotiation can serve a positive developmental function can tone down parental hostility too. Understanding parent-adolescent conflict, though, is not simple.

In sum, the old model of parent-adolescent relationships suggested that, as adolescents mature, they detach themselves from parents and move into a world of autonomy apart from parents. The old model also suggested that parent-adolescent conflict is intense and stressful throughout adolescence. The new model emphasizes that parents serve as important attachment figures and support systems as adolescents explore a wider, more complex social world. The new model also emphasizes that, in the majority of families, parent-adolescent conflict is moderate rather than severe, and that everyday negotiations and minor disputes are normal and can serve the positive developmental function of helping the adolescent make the transition from childhood dependency to adult independence (see figure 12.6).

The Maturation of the Adolescent and Parents

Physical, cognitive, and social changes in the adolescent's development influence the nature of parent-adolescent relationships. Parental changes also influence the nature of these relationships. Among the changes in the adolescent are puberty; expanded logical reasoning and increased idealistic and egocentric thought; violated expectations; changes in schooling, peers, friendship, and dating; and movement toward independence. Several recent investigations have shown that conflict between parents and adolescents, especially between mothers and sons, during the apex of pubertal growth, is the most stressful (Hill & others, 1985; Steinberg, 1981, 1988a).

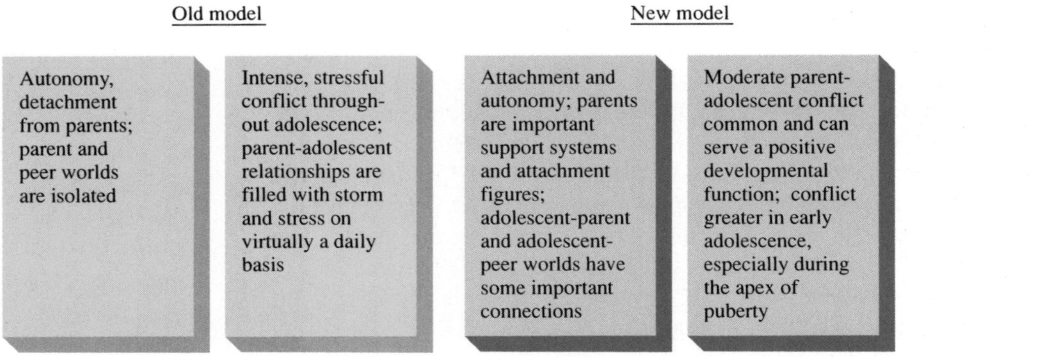

Old model
New model
Autonomy, detachment from parents; parent and peer worlds are isolated
Intense, stressful conflict throughout adolescence; parent-adolescent relationships are filled with storm and stress on virtually a daily basis
Attachment and autonomy; parents are important support systems and attachment figures; adolescent-parent and adolescent-peer worlds have some important connections
Moderate parent-adolescent conflict common and can serve a positive developmental function; conflict greater in early adolescence, especially during the apex of puberty

Figure 12.6
The Old and New Models of Parent-Adolescent Relationships

Parental changes include those involving marital dissatisfaction, economic burdens, career reevaluation and time perspective, and health and body concerns (Silverberg & Steinberg, 1990b). Marital dissatisfaction is greater when the offspring is an adolescent rather than a child or an adult. A greater economic burden is placed on parents during the rearing of their adolescents. Parents may reevaluate their occupational achievement, deciding whether they have met their youthful aspirations for success. Parents may look to the future and think about how much time they have remaining to accomplish what they want. Adolescents, however, look to the future with unbounded optimism, sensing that they have an unlimited amount of time to accomplish what they desire. Health concerns and an interest in body integrity and sexual attractiveness become prominent themes of adolescents' parents. Even when their body and sexual attractiveness are not deteriorating, many parents of adolescents perceive that they are. By contrast, adolescents are beginning to reach the peak of their physical attractiveness, strength, and health. Although both adolescents and their parents show a heightened preoccupation with their bodies, the adolescent's outcome probably is more positive.

1980
1988
Percentage of children under 18 living with a single parent
60
50
40
30
20
10
0
46%
54%
15%
19%
21%
30%
Black
White
Hispanic

Figure 12.7
Percentage of Children Under 18 Living with One Parent (1980 and 1988)
The percentage of children under 18 living with one parent increased from 20 percent in 1980 to 24 percent in 1988. The figures in this graph reveal the breakdown of single parents in Black, White, and Hispanic families. Note the substantially higher percentage of Black and Hispanic single-parent families.

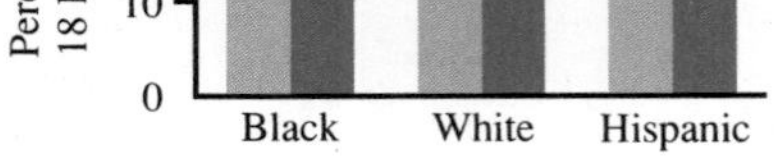

The Changing Family in a Changing Society

Children are growing up in a greater variety of family structures than ever before. Many mothers spend the greatest part of their day away from their children, even their infants. More than one of every two mothers with a child under the age of 5 is in the labor force; as is more than two of every three with a child from 6 to 17. Also, the increasing number of children growing up in single-parent families is staggering. As shown in figure 12.7, a substantial increase in the number of children under the age of 18 living in single-parent families occurred between 1980 and 1988. Also note that a much higher percentage of Black American families are single-parent families than White American or Hispanic American families, and if current trends continue, by the year 2000, one in every four children will have lived a portion of their lives in a stepparent family.

Working Parents

Because household operations have become more efficient and family size has decreased in America, it is not certain that children with mothers working outside the home actually receive less attention than children in the past, whose mothers were not employed. Outside employment—at least for mothers with school-aged children—may simply be filling time previously taken up by added household burdens and more children. It also cannot be assumed that, if the mother did not go to work, the child would benefit from the time freed by streamlined household operations and smaller families. Mothering does not always have a positive effect on children. The educated, nonworking mother may overinvest her energies in her children, fostering an excess of worry and discouraging the child's independence. In such situations, the mother may inject more parenting than the child can profitably handle.

Although some investigators have found associations between parental work status and children's behavior or well-being, the majority of researchers have not (Armistead, Wierson, & Forehand, 1990; Bird & Kemerait, 1990; Galambos & Maggs, 1990; Keith & others, 1990; Orthner, 1990). As Lois Hoffman (1979, 1989) comments, maternal employment is a part of modern life. It is not an aberrant aspect of it, but a response to other social changes that meets the needs the previous family ideal of a full-time mother and home-maker cannot. Not only does it meet the parent's needs, but, in many ways, it may be a pattern better suited to socializing children for the adult roles they will occupy. This is especially true for daughters, but it is also true for sons. The broader range of emotions and skills that each parent presents is more consistent with this adult role. Just as his father shares the breadwinning role and the childrearing role with his mother, so the son, too, will be more likely to share these roles. The rigid gender role stereotyping perpetuated by the divisions of labor in the traditional family is not appropriate for the demands children of either sex will have made on them as adults. The needs of the growing child require the mother to loosen her hold on the child, and this task may be easier for the working woman, whose job is an additional source of identity and self-esteem.

The mother's working outside the home does not necessarily have neg-ative outcomes for her child. However, a certain set of children from working-mother families deserve further scrutiny: latchkey children. These children typically do not see their parents from the time they leave for school in the morning until about 6:00 or 7:00 P.M. They are called latchkey children be-cause they are given the key to their home, take the key to school, and then use it to let themselves into the home while their parents are still at work. Latchkey children are largely unsupervised for 2 to 4 hours a day during each school week. During the summer months, they may be unsupervised for entire days, 5 days a week.

Thomas and Lynette Long (1983) interviewed more than 1,500 latchkey children. They concluded that a slight majority of these children had had neg-ative latchkey experiences. Some latchkey children may grow up too fast, hur-ried by the responsibilities placed on them (Elkind, 1981). How do latchkey children handle the lack of limits and structure during the latchkey hours? Without limits and parental supervision, latchkey children find their way into trouble more easily, possibly stealing, vandalizing, or abusing a sibling. The Longs point out that 90 percent of the juvenile delinquents in Montgomery County, Maryland, are latchkey children. Joan Lipsitz (1983), in testifying before the Select Committee on Children, Youth, and Families, called the lack of adult supervision of children in the after-school hours one of today's major problems. Lipsitz calls it the "three-to-six o'clock problem" because it is during this time that the Center for Early Adolescence in North Carolina, of which Lipsitz is director, experiences a peak of referrals for clinical help. In a 1987 national poll, teachers called the latchkey children phenomenon the number one reason that children have problems in school (Harris, 1987).

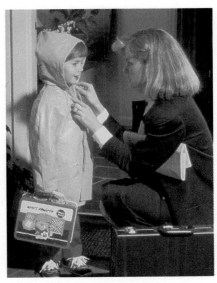

What issues do women face as they combine career and family?

Although latchkey children may be vulnerable to problems, the experiences of latchkey children vary enormously, as do the experiences of all children with working mothers. Parents need to give special attention to the ways in which their latchkey children's lives can be effectively monitored. Variations in latchkey experiences suggest that parental monitoring and authoritative parenting help the child cope more effectively with latchkey experiences, especially in resisting peer pressure (Belle & others, 1991; Galambos & Maggs, 1989; Steinberg, 1986). The degree of developmental risk to latchkey children remains undetermined. One positive sign is that researchers are beginning to conduct more fine-grained analyses of children's latchkey experiences to determine which aspects of latchkey circumstances are the most detrimental (Rodman, Pratto, & Nelson, 1988; Steinberg, 1988b).

Another aspect of the influence of working parents on children's development is geographical relocations, which are a fact of life for many American families. The U.S. Census Bureau estimates that 17 percent of the population change residences yearly (U.S. Bureau of the Census, 1986). This figure does not include multiple moves within the same year, so it may even underestimate the population's mobility. The majority of these moves are made because of job demands. Moving can be especially stressful for children and adolescents, disrupting friendship ties and adolescent activities (Brown & Orthner, 1990). The sources of support to which children and their parents turn, such as extended family members and friends, are often unavailable to recently moved families.

Although relocations are often stressful for all individuals involved, they may be especially stressful for adolescents because of their developing sense of identity and the importance of peer relations in their lives. In one recent study, geographical relocation was detrimental to the well-being of 12-to-14-year-old females but not to their male counterparts (Brown & Orthner, 1990). The adolescent girls' life satisfaction was negatively related both to recent moves and to a high number of moves in their history; a history of frequent moves was also associated with the girls' depression. However, the immediate negative effects on the girls disappeared over time. The researchers concluded that female adolescents may require more time to adapt to family relocations. Male adolescents may use sports and other activities in their new locale to ease the effects of relocation.

Other aspects of how working parents influence children's development involve unemployment and economic distress. Unemployment rates and economic distress in the past decade reached levels unknown since the Great Depression. Plant closings, layoffs, and demotions are facts of life for many contemporary parents. What effects do they have on families and adolescents' development? During the Great Depression, unemployment dramatically increased parental stress and undermined the school achievement and health of children and adolescents (Angell, 1936; Elder, 1974). One recent investigation studied the effects of the interactions of work status, family integration, and sex of young adolescents on parent-adolescent decision making (Flanagan, 1990a,b). *Deprived* families reported a layoff or demotion but no recovery 2 years later. *Recovery* families reported similar work losses but reemployment 2 years later. *Nondeprived* families reported stable employment across the 2-year period. Young adolescents in deprived families reported the highest conflict with parents. Adolescents in recovery families reported high conflict when parents were unemployed but lower levels when parents were reemployed. In sum, unemployment increases the stress of parents and has negative effects on children's development (Orthner, 1990).

Social and Personality Development

The Effects of Divorce on Children

Early studies of the effects of divorce on children followed a father-absent tradition, in which children from father-absent and father-present families were compared, and differences in their development were attributed to the absence of the father. However, family structure (such as father present, divorced, and widowed) is only one of many factors that influence a child's adjustment. The contemporary approach advocates evaluating the strengths and weaknesses of the child prior to divorce, the nature of events surrounding the divorce itself, and postdivorce family functioning. Support systems (baby-sitters, relatives, day care), an ongoing, positive relationship between the custodial parent and the ex-spouse, authoritative parenting, financial stability, and the child's competencies at the time of the divorce are related to the child's adjustment (Block, Block, & Gjerde, 1986; Camara, Brennan, & Resnick, 1991; Chase-Landsdale & Hetherington, in press; Cherlin & others, 1991; Guidubaldi & Perry, 1985; Hetherington, 1991; Hetherington & Clingempeel, in press; Hetherington, Cox, & Cox, 1982; Santrock, 1990b,c; Santrock & Warshak, 1986; Wallerstein & Kelly, 1980).

Many separations and divorces are highly emotional affairs that immerse the child in conflict (Buchanan, 1991; Parish, 1988; Parish & Osterberg, 1985). Conflict is a critical aspect of family functioning that seems to outweigh the influence of family structure on the child's development. Children in divorced families low in conflict function better than children in intact, never-divorced families high in conflict, for example (Rutter, 1983; Wallerstein, Corbin, & Lewis, 1988). Although escape from conflict may be a positive benefit for children, in the year immediately following the divorce, the conflict does not decline but, instead, increases. At this time, children—especially boys—in divorced families show more adjustment problems than children in homes with both parents present. During the first year after the divorce, the child often experiences a poor quality of parenting; parents seem preoccupied with their own needs and adjustment—experiencing anger, depression, confusion, and emotional instability—which inhibits their ability to respond sensitively to the child's needs. During the second year after the divorce, parents are more effective in their childrearing duties, especially with daughters (Hetherington, Cox, & Cox, 1982).

Recent evaluations by Mavis Hetherington and her colleagues (Hetherington, 1989, 1991; Hetherington & Clingempeel, in press; Hetherington, Hagan, & Anderson, 1989) of children 6 years after the divorce of their parents found that living in nonremarried mother-custody homes has long-term negative effects on boys, with negative outcomes appearing consistently from preschool to adolescence. In contrast, most girls from these families recovered from divorce early in their lives. However, although the preadolescent girls in divorced families adapted reasonably well, at the onset of adolescence, these girls engaged in frequent conflict with their mothers, behaved in noncompliant ways, had lower self-esteem, and experienced more problems in heterosexual reactions.

The sex of the child and the sex of the custodial parent are important considerations in evaluating the effects of divorce on children. One research study directly compared children living in father-custody and mother-custody families (Santrock & Warshak, 1979, 1986). On a number of measures, including videotaped observations of parent-child interaction, children living with the same-sex parent were more socially competent—happier, more independent, and more mature—and had higher self-esteem than children living with the opposite-sex parent. Other research has supported these findings (Camara & Resnick, 1987; Furstenberg, 1988).

■ *Critical Thinking*
Imagine you are a judge in a custodial dispute. What are some of the key factors you will consider in awarding custody?

Support systems are especially important for low-income divorced families. The extended family and community services may play a critical role in the functioning of low-income divorced families. These support systems may be crucial for low-income divorced families with infants and young children, because the majority of these parents must work full-time but still may not be able to make ends meet (Wilson, 1989).

The age of the child at the time of the divorce also needs to be considered. Young children's responses to divorce are mediated by their limited cognitive and social competencies, their dependency on their parents, and their restriction to the home or inferior day care (Hetherington, Hagan, & Anderson, 1989). During the interval immediately following divorce, young children less accurately appraise the divorce situation. These young children may blame themselves for the divorce, may fear abandonment by both parents, and may misperceive and be confused by what is happening (Wallerstein, Corbin, & Lewis, 1988).

The cognitive immaturity that creates extensive anxiety for children who are young at the time of their parents' divorce may benefit the children over time. Ten years after the divorce of their parents, adolescents have few memories of their own earlier fears and suffering or of their parents' conflict (Wallerstein, Corbin, & Lewis, 1988). Nonetheless, approximately one third of these children continue to express anger about not being able to grow up in an intact, never-divorced family. Those who were adolescents at the time of their parents' divorce are more likely to remember the conflict and stress surrounding the divorce 10 years later in their early adult years. They, too, express disappointment at not being able to grow up in an intact family and wonder if their life would have been better if they had been able to do so. In one recent study, adolescents who experienced the divorce of their parents during adolescence were more likely to have drug problems than either adolescents whose parents were divorced when the adolescents were children or adolescents living in continuously married families (Needle, Su, & Doherty, 1990).

In sum, large numbers of children are growing up in divorced families. Most children initially experience considerable stress when their parents divorce, and they are at risk for developing problem behaviors. However, divorce also can remove children from marriages in which there is a great deal of conflict. Many children emerge from divorce as competent individuals. In recent years, researchers have moved away from the view that single-parent families are atypical or pathological, focusing more on the diversity of children's responses to divorce and the factors that facilitate or disrupt the development and adjustment of children in these family circumstances (Hetherington, 1991; Hetherington, Hagan, & Anderson, 1989).

Stepfamilies

The number of remarriages involving children has steadily grown in recent years, although both the rate of increase in divorce and stepfamilies slowed in the 1980s. Stepfather families, in which a woman has custody of children from a previous marriage, make up 70 percent of stepfamilies. Stepmother families make up almost 20 percent of stepfamilies, and a small minority are blended, with both partners bringing children from a previous marriage. A substantial percentage of stepfamilies produce children of their own.

Research on stepfamilies has lagged behind research on divorced families, but recently a number of investigators have turned their attention to this increasingly common family structure (Bray, 1988; Bray & others, 1991; Hetherington & Clingempeel, in press; Hetherington, Hagan, & Anderson, 1989; Pasley & Ihinger-Tallman, 1987; Santrock & Sitterle, 1987; Santrock, Sitterle, & Warshak, 1988). Following remarriage of their parents, children of all ages show a resurgence of behavior problems. Eventually, younger children seem to form an attachment to a stepparent and accept the stepparenting role. However, the developmental tasks facing adolescents make them especially vulnerable to the entrance of a stepparent. At the time that they are searching for an identity and exploring sexual and other close relationships outside the family, a nonbiological parent may increase the stress associated with these important tasks.

Following the remarriage of the custodial parent, an emotional upheaval usually occurs in girls, and problems in boys often intensify. Over time, preadolescent boys seem to improve more than girls in stepfather families. Sons who frequently are involved in conflicted or coercive relations with their custodial mothers probably have much to gain from living with a warm, supportive stepfather. In contrast, daughters who have a close relationship with their custodial mothers and considerable independence frequently find a stepfather both disruptive and constraining.

Children's relationships with their biological parents are more positive than with their stepparents, regardless of whether a stepmother or a stepfather family is involved. However, stepfathers are often distant and disengaged from their stepchildren. As a rule, the more complex the stepfamily, the more difficult the child's adjustment. Families in which both parents bring children from a previous marriage have the highest level of behavioral problems.

In sum, as with divorce, entrance into a stepfamily involves a disequilibrium in children's and adolescents' lives. Most children and adolescents experience their parents' remarriage as stressful. Remarrriage, though, can remove children and adolescents from stressful single-parent circumstances and provide additional resources for children and adolescents. Many children and adolescents emerge from their remarried family as competent individuals. As with divorced families, it is important to consider the complexity of stepfamilies, the diversity of possible outcomes, and the factors that facilitate children's and adolescents' adjustment in stepfamilies (Hetherington & Clingempeel, in press; Santrock, Sitterle, & Warshak, 1988).

At this point, we have discussed a number of ideas about parenting styles, sibling relationships and birth order, family processes in adolescence, and the changing family in a changing society. A summary of these ideas is presented in concept table 12.2. In the next chapter, we will turn our attention to other important aspects of children's social worlds—their peer relations, their play, and the role of television in their lives.

Parenting Styles, Sibling Relationships and Birth Order, Family Processes in Adolescence, and the Changing Family in a Changing Society

Concept	Processes/related ideas	Characteristics/description
Parenting styles	Their nature	Authoritarian, authoritative, permissive-indulgent, and permissive-indifferent are four main categories of parenting. Authoritative parenting is associated with children's social competence more than the other styles.
	Adapting parenting to developmental changes in the child	Parents need to adapt their interaction strategies as the child grows older, using less physical manipulation and more reasoning in the process. Parents spend less time with children during middle and late childhood, including less time in caregiving, instruction, reading, talking, and playing. Nonetheless, parents still are powerful and important socializing agents in this period. New parent-child issues emerge, and discipline changes. Control becomes more coregulatory.
	Cultural, social class, and ethnic variations in families	Authoritative parenting is the most common childrearing pattern around the world. Ethnic minority families differ from White American families in their size, structure, composition, reliance on kinship networks, and levels of income and education. Working-class and low-income parents place a higher value on external characteristics, middle-class parents place a higher value on internal characteristics, and these social classes vary in their childrearing patterns.
	Child abuse	Child abuse is an increasing problem in the United States. Child abuse is a multifaceted problem. Increasingly, developmentalists use the term *maltreatment* rather than *abuse* or *neglect*. Understanding child maltreatment requires information about the cultural context and family influences.
Sibling relationships and birth order	Sibling relationships	More than 80 percent of American children have one or more siblings. Siblings interact with each other in more negative, less positive, and less varied ways than parents and children interact. In some cases, siblings are stronger socializing influences than parents.
	Birth order	The relationship of the firstborn child and parents seems to be especially close and demanding, which may account for the greater achievement orientation and anxiety in firstborn children. Some critics argue that birth order is not a good predictor of behavior.

Concept	Processes/related ideas	Characteristics/description
Family processes in adolescence	Autonomy and attachment	Many parents have a difficult time handling the adolescent's push for autonomy, even though this push is one of the hallmarks of adolescent development. Adolescents do not simply move into a world isolated from parents; attachment to parents increases the probability that the adolescent will be socially competent and explore a widening social world in healthy ways.
	Parent-adolescent conflict	Conflict with parents seems to increase in early adolescence. Such conflict usually is moderate. The increase in conflict probably serves the positive developmental function of promoting autonomy and identity.
	The maturation of the adolescent and parents	Physical, cognitive, and social changes in the adolescent's development influence parent-adolescent relationships. Parental changes—marital dissatisfaction, economic burdens, career reevaluation and time perspective, and health and body concerns—also influence parent-adolescent relationships.
The changing family in a changing society	Working parents	A mother's working full-time can have both positive and negative effects on the child. There is no indication that long-term effects are negative overall. Latchkey children may become vulnerable when they are not monitored by adults in the after-school hours. Relocation may have a more adverse effect on adolescents than on children, but research on this issue is sparse. Parental unemployment has a detrimental effect on adolescent development.
	Effects of divorce on children	The early father-absent tradition has been supplanted by an emphasis on the complexity of the divorced family, pre- and postdivorce family functioning, and varied responses to divorce. Among the factors that influence the child's adjustment in divorced families are conflict, time since divorce, sex of the child, sex of the custodial parent, parenting competence, and the availability and use of support systems.
	Stepfamilies	Just as divorce produces disequilibrium and stress for children, so does the entrance of a stepparent. Over time, preadolescent boys seem to improve more than girls in stepfather families. Adolescence appears to be an especially difficult time for adjustment to the entrance of a stepparent. Children's relationships with biological parents are consistently better than with stepparents and children's adjustment is adversely affected the more complex the stepfamily becomes.

Summary

I. Family Processes

The transition to parenthood produces a disequilibrium, requiring considerable adaptation. Becoming a parent is both wonderful *and* stressful. The concept of reciprocal socialization states that children socialize parents, just as parents socialize children. Scaffolding, synchronization, and mutual regulation are important dimensions of reciprocal socialization. The family is a system of interacting individuals with different subsystems—some dyadic, others polyadic. Belsky's model describes direct and indirect effects.

II. What Is Attachment?

Attachment is a relationship between two people in which each person feels strongly about the other and does a number of things to ensure the relationship's continuation. In infancy, attachment refers to the bond between the caregiver and the infant. Feeding is not the critical element in attachment, although contact comfort, familiarity, and trust are important. Bowlby's ethological theory stresses that the mother and infant instinctively trigger attachment. Attachment to the caregiver intensifies at about 6 to 7 months.

III. Individual Differences in Attachment, Temperament, and the Wider Social World

Ainsworth believes that individual differences in attachment can be classified into secure, avoidant, and resistant categories. Ainsworth believes that securely attached babies have sensitive and responsive caregivers. In some investigations, secure attachment is related to social competence later in childhood. Some developmentalists believe that the role of attachment is emphasized too much; they believe that genetics and temperament, on the one hand, and the diversity of social agents and contexts, on the other, deserve more credit.

IV. The Father's Role

Over time, the father's role has evolved from moral teacher to breadwinner to gender role model to active, nurturant caregiver. Fathers have increased their interaction with their children, but fathers still lag far behind mothers, even when the mother is employed. Fathers can act sensitively to the infant's signals, but most of the time they do not. The mother's role in the infant's development is primarily caregiving, and that of the father involves playful interaction. Infants generally prefer their mother under stressful circumstances. Even in nontraditional families, as when the father is the primary caregiver, the behaviors of mothers and fathers follow traditional gender lines.

V. Day Care

Day care has become a basic need of the American family. More children are in day care today than at any other time in history. The quality of day care is uneven. Belsky contends that most day care is inadequate and that extensive day care in the first 12 months of the infant's life has negative developmental outcomes. Other experts disagree with Belsky. Day care remains a controversial topic. High-quality day care can be achieved and it seems to have little adverse effect on children.

VI. The Nature of Parenting Styles and Adapting Parenting to Developmental Changes in the Child

Authoritarian, authoritative, permissive-indulgent, and permissive-indifferent are four main categories of parenting. Authoritative parenting is associated with children's social competence more than with the other styles. Parents need to adapt their interaction strategies as the child grows older, using less physical manipulation and more reasoning in the process. Parents spend less time with children during middle and late childhood, including less time in caregiving, instruction, reading, talking, and playing. Nonetheless, parents still are powerful and important socialization agents in this period. New parent-child issues emerge, and discipline changes. Control becomes more coregulatory.

VII. Cultural, Social Class, and Ethnic Variations in Families

Authoritative parenting is the most common childrearing pattern around the world. Ethnic minority families differ from White American families in their size, structure, composition, reliance on kinship networks, and levels of income and education. Working-class and low-income parents place a higher value on external characteristics, middle-class parents place a higher value on internal characteristics, and these social classes vary in their childrearing patterns.

VIII. Child Abuse

Child abuse is an increasing problem in the United States. Child abuse is a multifaceted problem. Developmentalists increasingly use the term *maltreatment* rather than *abuse* or *neglect*. Understanding child maltreatment requires information about the cultural context and family influences.

IX. Sibling Relationships and Birth Order

More than 80 percent of American children have one or more siblings. Siblings interact with each other in more negative, less positive, and less varied ways than parents and children interact. In some cases, siblings are stronger socializing influences than children. The relationship of firstborn children and parents seems to be especially close and demanding, which may account for the greater achievement orientation and anxiety of firstborn children. Some critics argue that birth order is not a good predictor of behavior.

X. Parent-Adolescent Relationships

Many parents have a difficult time handling the adolescent's push for autonomy, even though this push is one of the hallmarks of adolescent development. Adolescents do not simply move into a peer world isolated from parents. Attachment to parents increases the likelihood the adolescent will be socially competent and explore a widening social world in healthy ways. Conflict with parents usually increases in early adolescence. This conflict often is of the moderate variety. The increase in conflict probably serves a positive developmental function of promoting autonomy and identity. Physical, cognitive, and social changes in the adolescent's development influence parent-adolescent relationships. Parental changes—marital dissatisfaction, economic burdens, career reevaluation and time perspective, and health and body concerns—also influence parent-adolescent relationships.

XI. Working Parents

A mother's working full-time can have both positive and negative effects on the child. There is no indication that long-term effects are negative overall. Latchkey children may become vulnerable when they are not monitored by adults in the after-school hours. Relocation may have a more adverse effect on adolescents than on children, but research on this issue is sparse. Parental unemployment has a detrimental effect on adolescent development.

XII. Effects of Divorce on Children and Stepfamilies

The early father-absent tradition has been supplanted by an emphasis on the complexity of the divorced family, pre- and postdivorce family functioning, and varied responses to divorce. Among the factors that influence the child's adjustment in divorced families are conflict, time since divorce, sex of the child, sex of the parent, parenting competence, and the availability and use of support systems. Just as divorce produces disequilibrium and stress for children, so does the entrance of a stepparent. Over time, preadolescent boys seem to improve more than girls in stepfather families. Adolescence appears to be an especially difficult time for adjustment to the entrance of a stepparent. Children's relationships with biological parents are consistently better than with stepparents and children's adjustment is adversely affected the more complex the stepfamily becomes.

Key Terms

reciprocal socialization 404
scaffolding 404
attachment 406
secure attachment 407
type B babies 407
type A babies 407
type C babies 407

authoritarian parenting 416
authoritative parenting 416
permissive-indifferent parenting 416
permissive-indulgent parenting 416

Suggested Readings

Hetherington, E. M., Hagan, M. S., & Anderson, E. R. (1989). Family transitions: A child's perspective. *American Psychologist, 44,* 303–312. Hetherington is a leading researcher in the investigation of the effects of divorce on children's development. In this article, she and her colleagues review the recent literature on divorce, giving special attention to transitions in divorced and stepparent families.

Lamb, M. E. (1987). *The father's role: Cross-cultural perspectives.* Hillsdale, NJ: Erlbaum. Intriguing descriptions of the father's role in different cultures are provided. Includes information about English, American, Israeli, Italian, Chinese, Swedish, and Aka pygmy fathers.

Lande, J. S., Scarr, S., & Gunzenhauser, N. (Eds.). (1989). *Caring for children: Challenge to America.* Hillsdale, NJ: Erlbaum. This up-to-date treatment of child care includes chapters on child care in European countries, child care in Black families, licensing of child-care facilities, and the future directions of child care in the United States.

Sroufe, L. A., & Fleeson, J. (1986). Attachment and the construction of relationships. In W. Hartup and Z. Rubin (Eds.), *Relationships and development.* Hillsdale, NJ: Erlbaum. Sroufe and Fleeson offer insight into the importance of attachment in our development of relationships.

Steinberg, L. D., & Levine, A. (1990). *You and your adolescent: A parent's guide for ages 10 to 20.* New York: Columbia University Press. Steinberg and Levine describe the nature of parent-adolescent relationships and give valuable suggestions for improving parent-adolescent relationships.

White, B. L. (1988). *Educating the infant and toddler.* Lexington, MA: Lexington Books. Burton White provides a number of wise suggestions for competent ways to rear infants and young children.

Peers
    Peer Group Functions
    The Distinct but Coordinated Worlds of Parent-
        Child and Peer Relations
    The Developmental Course of Peer Relations in
        Childhood
    Peer Popularity, Rejection, and Neglect
    Social Cognition
    Friends
    Peer Relations in Adolescence
    *Cultural Worlds of Development 13.1: Ethnic
        Minority Adolescents' Peer Relations*
Play
    Play's Functions
    Parten's Classic Study of Play
    Types of Play
    *Perspective on Child Development 13.1:
        Superhero Play*
    The Sociocultural Contexts of Play
Media Influences
    Television
    *Cultural Worlds of Development 13.2: Sesame
        Street Around the World*
    Computers and Children
Summary
Key Terms
Suggested Readings

A MAN'S GROWTH IS SEEN IN THE SUCCESSIVE CHOIRS OF HIS FRIENDS.

—Ralph Waldo Emerson

"Y ou jerk, what are you trying to do to me?" Jess yelled at his teacher. "I got no use for this school and people like you. Leave me alone and quit hassling me."

Jess is 10 years old and has already had more than his share of confrontations with society. He has been arrested three times for stealing and has been suspended from school twice. He also has a great deal of difficulty getting along with people in social circumstances. He especially has difficulty with authority figures. No longer able to cope with his outbursts in class, his teacher recommends that he be suspended from school once again; however, the principal knows of a different kind of school she thinks might help Jess.

Jess is transferred to the Manville School, a clinic in the Judge Baker Guidance Center in Boston for learning disabled and emotionally disturbed children 7 to 15 years of age. Like many other students at the Manville School, Jess has shown considerable difficulty in interpersonal relationships. Peer relationships become a crucial aspect of development during the elementary school years, so Robert Selman has designed a peer therapy program at the Manville School to help students like Jess improve their peer relations in classroom settings, group activities, and sports (Selman, Newberger, & Jacquette, 1977). The staff at the Manville School has been trained to help peers support and encourage one another in such group settings.

Structured programs at the Manville School are designed to help the children assist each other in such areas as cooperation, trust, leadership, and conformity. Four school activities were developed to improve students' social reasoning skills in these areas. First, there is a weekly peer problem-solving session in the classroom, in which the peers work cooperatively to plan activities and relate problems. At the end of each week, the peers evaluate their effectiveness in making improvements in such areas as cooperation and conflict resolution. Second, class members, numbering from six to eight students, plan a series of weekly field trips—for example, going to the movies or visiting historical sites. Although the counselor provides some assistance, peer decision making dominates. When each activity is completed, the students discuss how things went and what might have been done to improve social relations with each other on the outings. Third, Selman recognizes that there are times when students have to get away from settings where intense frustration occurs. When students find themselves in a highly frustrating situation (for example, angry enough to strike out at a classmate), they are allowed to leave the room and go to a private "time-out" area of the school to regain composure. In time-out, students also are given the opportunity to discuss the problems with a counselor who has been trained to help children or adolescents improve their social reasoning skills. Fourth, during social studies and current events discussion sessions, the students evaluate a number of moral and societal issues that incorporate the thinking of such theorists as Lawrence Kohlberg.

In this chapter, we will turn our attention to some important aspects of children's socialization outside of the family, describing the nature of children's peer relations, play, and the influence of the media, especially television and computers.

Social and Personality Development

Peers are children who are about the same age or maturity level. From the peer group, children receive feedback about their abilities and they learn about a world outside of their family.

Peers

As children grow older, peer relations consume increasing amounts of their time. What is the function of a child's peer group? Although children spend increasingly more time with peers as they become older, are there ways in which family and peer relations are coordinated? What is the developmental course of peer relations in childhood? Why are some children popular, rejected, or neglected? What is the role of cognition in peer relations? What is the nature of friendship and of peer relations in adolescence? We will consider each of these questions in turn.

Peer Group Functions

Peers *are children of about the same age or maturity level.* Same-age peer interaction fills a unique role in our culture (Hartup, 1976). Age grading would occur even if schools were not age graded and children were left alone to determine the composition of their own societies. One of the most important functions of the peer group is to provide a source of information and comparison about the world outside the family. Children receive feedback about their abilities from their peer group. Children evaluate what they do in terms of whether it is better than, as good as, or worse than what other children do. It is hard to do this at home because siblings are usually older or younger (Berndt & Ladd, 1989).

Are peers necessary for development? When peer monkeys who have been reared together are separated, they become depressed and less advanced socially (Suomi, Harlow, & Domek, 1970). The human development literature contains a classic example of the importance of peers in social development. Anna Freud (Freud & Dann, 1951) studied six children from different families who banded together after their parents were killed in World War II. Intensive peer attachment was observed; the children formed a tightly knit group, dependent on one another and aloof with outsiders. Even though deprived of parental care, they became neither delinquent nor psychotic.

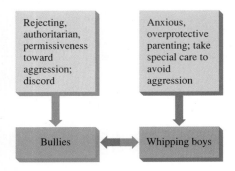

Rejecting, authoritarian, permissiveness toward aggression; discord	Anxious, overprotective parenting; take special care to avoid aggression
↓	↓
Bullies ↔	Whipping boys

Figure 13.1
Peer Aggression: The Influence of the Relationship Histories of Each Peer

Thus, good peer relations may be necessary for normal social development. Social isolation, or the inability to "plug in" to a social network, is linked with many problems and disturbances, ranging from delinquency and problem drinking to depression (Cairns & Cairns, 1989; Dishion, Andrews, & Crosby, 1991; Dishion & Skinner, 1989). In one investigation, poor peer relations in childhood was associated with a tendency to drop out of school and delinquent behavior in adolescence (Roff, Sells, & Golden, 1972). In another investigation, harmonious peer relations in adolescence was related to positive mental health at midlife (Hightower, 1990).

The Distinct but Coordinated Worlds of Parent-Child and Peer Relations

What are some similarities and differences between peer and parent-child relationships? Children touch, smile, frown, and vocalize when they interact with both parents and other children. However, rough-and-tumble play occurs mainly with other children, not with adults, and, in times of stress, children usually move toward their parents rather than toward their peers.

The worlds of parent-child and peer relations are distinct, but they are coordinated too. Some developmentalists believe that secure attachment to parents promotes healthy peer relations (Ainsworth, 1979; Hazen & others, 1991; Sroufe, in press). However, as we discussed in chapter 12, others believe the route to competency, including positive peer relations, is not always through secure attachment (Kagan, 1987a). Nonetheless, the data are consistent with the theory that children's relationships with their parents serve as emotional bases for exploring and enjoying peer relations (Hart, Ladd, & Burleson, 1990; Hartup, 1989, Pettit, Dodge, & Brown, 1988; Youngblade & Belsky, 1991).

One investigation revealed how the relationship history of each peer helps predict the nature of the interaction in a peer group (Olweus, 1980) (see figure 13.1). In this study, some boys were highly aggressive and other boys were the recipients of aggression throughout the preschool years. The "bullies" as well as the "whipping boys" had distinctive relationship histories. The bullies' parents treated them with rejection, had an authoritarian orientation, and were permissive toward aggression; the bullies' families also were characterized by discord. By contrast, the whipping boys' parents were anxious and overprotective, taking special care to have their sons avoid aggression. The well-adjusted boys in the study were not as involved in aggressive interchanges. Their parents did not sanction aggression; their responsive involvement with their children promoted the development of self-assertion as an adaptive pattern (Olweus, 1989).

Parents also may model or coach their children in the ways of relating to peers. In one investigation, parents indicated they recommended specific strategies to their children regarding peer relations (Rubin & Sloman, 1984). For example, parents told their children how to mediate disputes or how to become less shy with others. They also encouraged them to be tolerant and to resist peer pressure.

A key aspect of peer relations can be traced to basic life-style decisions by parents (Cooper & Ayers-Lopez, 1985). Parents' choices of neighborhoods, churches, schools, and their own friends influence the pool from which their children might select possible friends. For example, the chosen schools can lead to specific grouping policies, as well as particular academic and extra-curricular activities. In turn, such factors affect which students their children meet, their purpose in interacting, and eventually who become friends. For example, classrooms in which teachers encourage more cooperative peer interchanges have fewer isolates.

Social and Personality Development

The Developmental Course of Peer Relations in Childhood

Although we generally think of peer relations as assuming an important role in early childhood, some researchers believe that the quality of peer interaction in infancy provides valuable information about social development (Hay, 1985; Mueller, 1985; Vandell, 1985). For example, in one investigation, positive affect in infant peer relations was related to easy access to peer play groups and to peer popularity in early childhood (Howes, 1985). As increasing numbers of children attend day care, peer interaction in infancy takes on a more important developmental role.

The frequency of peer interaction, both positive and negative, picks up considerably during early childhood (Hartup, 1983). Although aggressive interaction and rough-and-tumble play increase, the *proportion* of aggressive exchanges to friendly exchanges decreases. Children tend to abandon their immature and inefficient social exchanges with age and acquire more mature ways of relating to peers.

Children spend an increasing amount of time in peer interaction during middle and late childhood and adolescence. In one investigation, children interacted with peers 10 percent of their day at age 2, 20 percent at age 4, and more than 40 percent between the ages of 7 and 11. In a typical school day, episodes with peers totaled 299 times per day (Barker & Wright, 1951).

Peer Popularity, Rejection, and Neglect

Children often think, "What can I do to get all of the kids at school to like me?" or "What's wrong with me? Something must be wrong or I would be more popular." What makes a child popular with peers? Children who give out the most reinforcements are often popular. So is a child who listens carefully to other children and maintains open lines of communication. Being themselves, being happy, showing enthusiasm and concern for others, and being self-confident but not conceited are characteristics that serve children well in their quest for peer popularity (Hartup, 1983). In one recent study, popular children were more likely to communicate clearly with their peers, to elicit their peers' attention, and to maintain conversation with peers more than were unpopular children (Kennedy, 1990).

Recently, developmentalists have distinguished between two types of children who are not popular with their peers: those who are neglected and those who are rejected (Asher & Parker, in press; Coie & Koeppl, 1990; Gest, Bermann, & Hartup, 1991; Parker & Asher, 1987; Parkhurst & others, 1991). **Neglected children** *receive little attention from their peers but they are not necessarily disliked.* **Rejected children** *are disliked by their peers. They are more likely to be disruptive and aggressive than are neglected children.* Rejected children often have more serious adjustment problems later in life than do neglected children (Dodge & others, 1986; Kupersmidt, Coie, & Dodge, 1990; Kupersmidt & Coie, 1990). For example, in one recent study, 112 fifth-grade boys were evaluated over a period of 7 years until the end of high school (Kupersmidt & Coie, 1990). The key factor in predicting whether rejected children would engage in delinquent behavior or drop out of school later during adolescence was their aggression toward peers in elementary school.

How can neglected and rejected children be trained to interact more effectively with their peers? The goal of training programs with neglected children is often to help them attract attention from their peers in positive ways and to hold their attention by asking questions, by listening in a warm and friendly way, and by saying things about themselves that relate to the other children's interests. They also are taught to enter groups more assertively (Duck, 1988).

Training programs with rejected children try to help them listen to other children and "hear what they say" rather than dominate peer interactions. Rejected children are trained to join other children's play without trying to change what is taking place in the peer group.

Children may need to be persuaded that these strategies work effectively and are satisfying. In some programs, the children are shown videotapes of other children behaving and acting in appropriate ways, and the children who watch the tapes are then asked to comment on and draw lessons from what they have seen. In other training programs, popular children are taught to be more accepting of rejected or neglected children.

One issue in improving a rejected child's peer relations is whether to focus initially on training the rejected child's prosocial skills (better empathy, careful listening, improved communication skills, and so on) or to specifically reduce the frequency of the rejected child's aggressive, disruptive behavior and improve the child's self-control (Coie & Koeppl, 1990). On the one hand, children who acquire the skills to relate to their peers more effectively likely will find themselves resorting less often to aggressive solutions in peer interaction. On the other hand, acquiring positive status with peers may take time, so it may be hard for peers to change their opinion if a child still frequently engages in aggressive behavior. Further, aggression often leads to reinforcement. In these latter instances, then, it may be necessary to eliminate or significantly reduce the child's aggressive actions before prosocial strategies can be taught effectively. To reduce the rejected child's aggressive behavior, training programs often try to get the child to try out self-control skills. At present, no consensus has been reached on which of these strategies is best in the initial training of rejected children to interact more effectively with their peers. Which strategy—prosocial skills training or reducing aggression/improving self-control—is most effective may vary depending on the particular problems of the rejected child. Rejected children who are highly aggressive likely will require some initial reduction of their aggressive behavior, whereas those who show low levels of aggression may benefit immediately from prosocial skills training. It is important to keep in mind that rejected children are a heterogeneous group—some are highly aggressive, others show much less aggression. Next, we will turn our attention to the role of social cognition in understanding peer relations. As part of this discussion, we will consider further ideas about reducing the aggression of children in their peer encounters.

Social Cognition

How might children's thoughts contribute to their peer relations? Three possibilities are through their perspective-taking ability, social information-processing skills, and social knowledge.

Perspective taking *involves the ability to take another's point of view.* As children enter the elementary school years, both their peer interaction and perspective-taking ability increase. Reciprocity is especially important in peer interchanges at this point in development—playing games, functioning in groups, and cultivating friendships, for example. One of the important skills that helps elementary school children improve their peer relations is com-

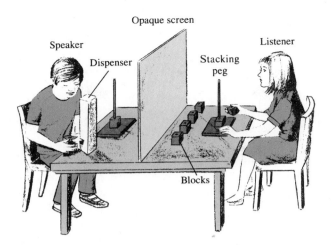

Speaker

Opaque screen

Dispenser

Stacking peg

Listener

Blocks

munication effectiveness. In one investigation, the communication exchanges among peers at kindergarten, first-, third-, and fifth-grade levels were evaluated (Krauss & Glucksberg, 1969). Children were asked to tell a peer about a new set of block designs. The peer sat behind a screen with blocks similar to those the subject communicated to her (see figure 13.2). The kindergarten children made numerous errors in telling the peer how to duplicate the novel block stack. The older children were much more efficient in communicating to a peer how to construct the novel block stack, especially the fifth graders. They were sensitive to the communication demands of the task and were far superior at perspective taking and figuring out how they had to talk for the peer to understand them. During elementary school, children also become more efficient at understanding complex messages, so the listening skills of the peer in this experiment probably helped the communicating peer as well. Other researchers have documented the link between perspective-taking skills and the quality of peer relations, especially in the elementary school years (LeMare & Rubin, 1987).

Of special interest is how children process information about peer relations. For example, a boy accidentally trips and knocks a peer's soft drink out of his hand. The peer misinterprets the encounter as hostile, which leads him to retaliate aggressively against the boy. Through repeated encounters of this kind, other peers come to perceive the aggressive boys as habitually acting inappropriately. Peer relations researcher Kenneth Dodge (1983) argues that children go through five steps in processing information about their social world: decoding social cues, interpreting, searching for a response, selecting an optimal response, and enacting. Dodge has found that aggressive boys are more likely to perceive another child's actions as hostile when the child's intention is ambiguous, and when aggressive boys search for clues to determine a peer's intention, they respond more rapidly, less efficiently, and less reflectively than nonaggressive children. These are among the social cognitive factors believed to be involved in the nature of children's conflicts (Dodge & Feldman, 1990; Shantz, 1988).

Social knowledge also is involved in children's ability to get along with peers. An important part of children's social life involves choosing which goals to pursue in poorly defined or ambiguous situations. Social relationship goals are also important, such as how to initiate and maintain a social bond. Children need to know what scripts to follow to get children to be their friends.

For example, as part of the script for getting friends, it helps to know that saying nice things, regardless of what the peer does or says, will make the peer like the child more.

From a social cognitive perspective, children who are maladjusted do not have adequate social cognitive skills to interact skillfully with others (Kelly & de Armas, 1989; Rabiner & others, 1991; Weissberg, Caplan, & Sivo, 1989). One investigation explored the possibility that maladjusted children do not have the social cognitive skills necessary for positive social interaction (Asarnow & Callan, 1985). Boys with and without peer adjustment difficulties were identified, and their social cognitive skills were assessed. Boys without peer adjustment problems generated more alternative solutions to problems, proposed more assertive and mature solutions, gave less intense aggressive solutions, showed more adaptive planning, and evaluated physically aggressive responses less positively than did the boys with peer adjustment problems.

The world of peers is one of varying acquaintances; children interact with some children they barely know and with others they know well for hours every day. It is to the latter type—friends—that we now turn.

Friends

"My best friend is nice. She is honest and I can trust her. I can tell her my innermost secrets and know that nobody else will find out about them. I have other friends, but she is my best friend. We consider each other's feelings and don't want to hurt each other. We help each other out when we have problems. We make up funny names for people and laugh ourselves silly. We make lists of which boys we think are the ugliest, which are the biggest jerks, and so on. Some of these things we share with other friends; some we don't." This is a description of a friendship by a 10-year-old girl. It reflects the belief that children are interested in specific peers—not just any peers. They want to share concerns, interests, information, and secrets with them.

Hold a true friend with both hands.
—Nigerian proverb

Why are children's friendships important? They serve six functions: companionship, stimulation, physical support, ego support, social comparison, and intimacy/affection (Gottman & Parker, 1987; Parker & Gottman, 1989). Friendship provides children with a familiar companion and playmate, someone who is willing to spend time with them and to join in collaborative activities. Friendship also provides children with stimulating information, excitement, and amusement. Friendship gives children physical support by providing time, resources, and assistance. In offering ego support, friendship provides the expectation of support, encouragement, and feedback that helps children maintain an impression of themselves as competent, attractive, and worthwhile individuals. Concerning social comparison, friendship provides information about where the child stands vis-à-vis others and whether the child is doing OK. Friendship also provides children with intimacy and affection through a warm, close, trusting relationship with another individual, in which self-disclosure takes place (see figure 13.3).

Although friendships exist in early childhood, they become more predominant during middle and late childhood. Robert Selman (1980) proposed a developmental model that highlights the changing faces of friendship. Friendship often begins at about 3 to 4 years of age with momentary friendships. At this age, children recognize and name as friends children who live nearby or those who are brought to play with them. This type of friendship is unstable and changes according to circumstances. Preschool children often value friends for what they have—toys, candy, or similar material possessions that might bring pleasure. One young child's description of a friend typifies this early period: "He lives in a big house and has a big dog."

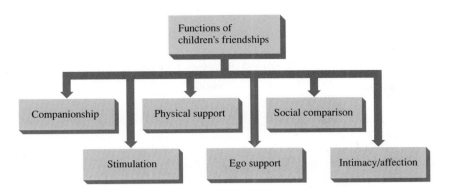

Figure 13.3
Functions of Children's Friendships

At about 4 years of age, the idea that "a friend has things I want" becomes transformed into the idea that "a friend has personal resources or abilities that can be useful." Until about 7 years of age, children look to friends for assistance but do not develop the reciprocal idea of helping a friend in return. Young children may admire a friend's toughness or skills, but they make little assessment of the friend's character and they are relatively unaware of rights or ideas of cooperation.

Between the ages of 6 and 12, children develop more knowledge about give-and-take and cooperation, appreciating that friends do things for one another. In the elementary school years, children have some idea that being a friend creates obligations such as loyalty. For example, one 9-year-old said, "You are my friend so you shouldn't talk behind my back." Still, in the 6-to-12-year age period, most children do not understand that cooperation between friends is mutually beneficial; in this age period, friendship often means a selfish way of getting someone else to help the child.

At about 9 years of age, many children can begin to see things from their friend's point of view and realize that joint ventures can have mutual benefits for the child and a friend. Friends now share secrets, are more open and genuine with each other, show more loyalty, and are more likely to engage in self-sacrifice. They begin to understand that intimacy and mutual understanding are important aspects of friendship. Nonetheless, between 9 and 12 years of age, children are possessive about their best friends, not readily accepting that best friends can also have other very good friends. In this age period, children value loyalty and commitment only to themselves.

From about 12 years of age on, adolescents know that friends have independent needs and other friends that may be equally special. They also realize that attraction to other friends does not necessarily detract from their friendship with those individuals. The beginnings of adultlike friendships occur: Character is now an important dimension of friendship and friends are now liked because they have the capacity for intimacy, have interests similar to those of the adolescent, and have attractive personal qualities. As we will see next, intimacy is an extremely important aspect of friendship, especially among adolescents.

Two of friendship's most common characteristics are intimacy and similarity. **Intimacy in friendships** *is defined as self-disclosure and the sharing of private thoughts.* Research reveals that intimate friendships may not appear until early adolescence (Berndt, 1982; Berndt & Park, 1991; Berndt & Perry, 1990; Buhrmester, 1989). Also, throughout childhood, friends are more similar than dissimilar in terms of age, sex, race, and many other factors. Friends often have similar attitudes toward school, similar educational aspirations, and closely aligned achievement orientations. Friends like the same music, the same kind of clothes, and the same kind of leisure activities.

Peer Relations in Adolescence

Imagine you are back in junior or senior high school, especially during one of your good times. Peers, friends, cliques, dates, parties, and clubs probably come to mind. Adolescents spend huge chunks of time with peers, more than in middle and late childhood. Among the important issues and questions to be asked about peer relations in adolescents are the following: What is the nature of peer pressure and conformity? How important are cliques in adolescence? How do children and adolescent groups differ? What is the nature of dating in adolescence?

Peer Pressure and Conformity

Consider the following statement made by an adolescent girl:

> Peer pressure is extremely influential in my life. I have never had very many friends, and I spend quite a bit of time alone. The friends I have are older. . . . The closest friend I have had is a lot like me in that we are both sad and depressed a lot. I began to act even more depressed than before when I was with her. I would call her up and try to act even more depressed than I was because that is what I thought she liked. In that relationship, I felt pressure to be like her. . . .

During adolescence, especially early adolescence, we conformed more to peer standards than we did in childhood. Investigators have found that, around the eighth and ninth grades, conformity to peers—especially to their antisocial standards—peaks (Berndt, 1979; Berndt & Perry, 1990). At this point in development, an adolescent is most likely to go along with a peer to steal hubcaps off a car, draw grafitti on a wall, or steal cosmetics from a store counter.

Most adolescents conform to the mainstream standards of their peers. However, the rebellious or anticonformist adolescent reacts counter to the mainstream peer group's expectations, deliberately moving away from the actions or beliefs they advocate. Two contemporary versions of anticonformist teenagers are the (a) "skinheads" and (b) punks.

(a)

(b)

Cliques and Crowds

Most peer group relationships in adolescence can be categorized in one of three ways: the crowd, the clique, or individual friendships. The **crowd** *is the largest and least personal of adolescent groups.* Members of the crowd meet because of their mutual interest in activities, not because they are mutually attracted to each other. **Cliques** *are smaller, involve greater intimacy among members, and have more group cohesion than crowds.*

Allegiance to cliques, clubs, organizations, and teams exerts powerful control over the lives of many adolescents. Group identity often overrides personal identity. The leader of a group may place a member in a position of considerable moral conflict by asking, in effect, "What's more important, our code or your parents'?" or "Are you looking out for yourself, or the members of the group?" Such labels as "brother" and "sister" sometimes are adopted and used in the members' conversations with each other. These labels symbolize the bond between the members and suggest the high status of group membership.

One of the most widely cited studies of adolescent cliques and crowds is that of James Coleman (1961). Students from 10 high schools were asked to identify the leading crowds in their schools. They also were asked to identify the students who were the most outstanding in athletics, popularity, and various school activities. Regardless of the school sampled, the leading crowds were composed of athletes and popular girls. Much less power in the leading crowd was attributed to bright students. Coleman's finding that being an athlete contributes to popularity for adolescent boys was reconfirmed in a more recent investigation (Eitzen, 1975).

Peer relations play important roles in an adolescent's life. During adolescence, heterosexual cliques become much more common than in childhood.

Think about your high school years. What were the cliques, and which one were you in? Although the names of cliques change, we could go to almost any high school in the United States and find three to six well-defined cliques or crowds. In one recent investigation, six peer group structures emerged: populars, unpopulars, jocks, brains, druggies, and average students (Brown & Mounts, 1989). The proportion of students placed in these cliques was much lower in multiethnic schools because of the additional existence of ethnically based crowds.

A recent investigation revealed that clique membership is associated with the adolescent's self-esteem (Brown & Lohr, 1987). Cliques included jocks (athletically oriented), populars (well-known students who lead social activities), normals (middle-of-the-road students who make up the masses), druggies or toughs (known for illicit drug use or other delinquent activities), and nobodies (low in social skills or intellectual abilities). The self-esteem of the jocks and the populars was highest, whereas that of the nobodies was lowest. One group of adolescents not in a clique had self-esteem equivalent to that of the jocks and the populars; this group was the independents, who indicated that clique membership was not important to them. Keep in mind that these data are correlational; self-esteem could increase an adolescent's probability of becoming a clique member, just as clique membership could increase the adolescent's self-esteem.

Adolescent Groups Versus Children Groups

Children groups differ from adolescent groups in several important ways. The members of children groups often are friends or neighborhood acquaintances, and their groups usually are not as formalized as many adolescent groups. During the adolescent years, groups tend to include a broader array of members. In other words, adolescents other than friends or neighborhood acquaintances often are members of adolescent groups. Try to recall the student council, honor society, or football team at your junior high school. If you were a member of any of these organizations, you probably remember that they were made up of many people you had not met before and that they were a more heterogeneous group than your childhood peer groups. For example, peer groups in adolescence are more likely to have a mixture of individuals from different ethnic groups than are peer groups in childhood. To read further about ethnic minority adolescents' peer groups, turn to Cultural Worlds of Development 13.1. Also, in adolescent peer groups, rules and regulations are usually defined more precisely than in children's peer groups. For example, captains or leaders are often formally elected or appointed in adolescent peer groups.

A well-known observational study by Dexter Dunphy (1963) supports the notion that opposite-sex participation in groups increases during adolescence. In late childhood, boys and girls participate in small, same-sex cliques. As they move into the early adolescent years, the same-sex cliques begin to interact with each other. Gradually, the leaders and high-status members form further cliques based on heterosexual relationships. Eventually, the newly created heterosexual cliques replace the same-sex cliques. The heterosexual cliques interact with each other in large crowd activities, too—at dances and athletic events, for example. In late adolescence, the crowd begins to dissolve as couples develop more serious relationships and make long-range plans that may include engagement and marriage.

Social and Personality Development

Ethnic Minority Adolescents' Peer Relations

As ethnic minority children move into adolescence and enter schools with more heterogeneous school populations, they become more aware of their ethnic minority status. In many schools, peer groups are strongly segregated according to social class and ethnicity. In schools with large numbers of middle- and lower-class students, middle-class students often assume the leadership roles in formal organizations such as student council, the honor society, and fraternity-sorority groups. Athletic teams are one type of adolescent group in which Black adolescents and adolescents from low-income families have been able to gain parity or even surpass adolescents from middle- and upper-income families in achieving status.

Ethnic minority adolescents, especially immigrants, may turn to their peer group more than White adolescents do (Spencer & Dornbusch, 1990). This is especially true when ethnic minority parents have not been very successful in their careers or when the adolescent loses the ability to speak the ethnic minority group's language. The desire to be accepted by peers is especially strong among refugee adolescents, whose greatest threat is not the stress of belonging to two cultures but the stress of belonging to none (Lee, 1988).

For many ethnic minority youths, especially immigrants, peers from their own ethnic group provide a crucial sense of family within the majority culture. Peer groups may form to oppose those of the majority group and to provide adaptive supports that reduce feelings of isolation.

Adolescent peer relations take place in diverse settings—at school, in the neighborhood, and in the community. Ethnic minority adolescents often have two sets of peer relationships—one at school, the other in the community. Community peers are more likely to be from their own ethnic group in their immediate neighborhood. Sometimes they go to the same church and participate in activities together such as Black History Week, Chinese New Year's, or Cinco de Mayo

Festival. Because ethnic-group adolescents usually have two sets of peers and friends, researchers asking about their peers and friends should focus on relationships both at school and in the neighborhood and community. Ethnic minority adolescents who are social isolates at school may be sociometric stars in their segregated neighborhood. Also, because adolescents are more mobile than children, inquiries should be made about the scope of their social networks (Gibbs & Huang, 1989).

In one recent investigation, the school and neighborhood friendship patterns of 292 Black and White adolescents who attended an integrated junior high school were studied (DuBois & Hirsch, 1990). Most students reported having an other-ethnic school friend, but only 28 percent of the students saw such a friend frequently outside of school. Reports of an interethnic school friendship that extended to nonschool settings were more common among Black adolescents than White adolescents and among adolescents who lived in an integrated rather than a segregated neighborhood. Black adolescents were more likely than White adolescents to have extensive neighborhood friendship networks, but Black adolescents said they talked with fewer friends during the school day.

A special interest is the degree of peer support for an ethnic minority adolescent's achievement orientation. Some researchers argue that peers often dissuade Black adolescents from doing well in school (Fordham & Ogbu, 1986; Fuller, 1984). However, in one recent investigation, peer support of achievement was relatively high among Asian American adolescents, moderate among Black American and Hispanic American adolescents, and relatively low among Anglo American adolescents (Brown & others, 1990). Possibly the low peer support of achievement among Anglo American adolescents is due to their strong individual, competitive, and social comparison orientation.

As boys and girls move into adolescence, they become more aware of their ethnic background. Although ethnic minority adolescents may have trouble joining peer groups in predominantly White schools, it is important to keep in mind that peer relations take place in many settings other than the school, such as in the neighborhood and in the community.

Most adolescents spend a lot of time thinking about dating, and some adolescents spend a lot of time on dates. Female adolescents bring a stronger desire for intimacy and personality exploration to dating than do male adolescents.

■ *Critical Thinking*

Earlier in this chapter, we discussed the distinct but coordinated worlds of parent-child and peer relations. How might adolescent dating be distinct but coordinated with parent-adolescent relations?

And that park grew up with me; That small world widened as I learned its secret boundaries, as I discovered new refuges in the woods and jungles: hidden homes and lairs for the multitudes of imagination, for cowboys and Indians, and the tall-terrible half-people who rode on nightmares through my bedroom. But it was not the only world—that world of rockery, gravel path, playbank, bowling green, bandstands, reservoir, dahlia garden, where an ancient keeper named Smoky, was the whiskered snake in the grass one must keep off. There was another world where with my friends I used to dawdle on half holidays along the bent and Devon-facing seashore, hoping for gold watches or the skull of a sheep or a message in a bottle to be washed up by the tide.

—Dylan Thomas

Dating

Dating takes on added importance during adolescence. As Dick Cavett (1974) remembers, the thought of an upcoming dance or sock hop was absolute agony: "I knew I'd never get a date. There seemed to be only this limited set of girls I could and should be seen with, and they were all taken by the jocks." Adolescents spend considerable time either dating or thinking about dating, which has gone far beyond its original courtship function to a form of recreation, a source of status and achievement, and a setting for learning about close relationships. One function of dating, though, continues to be mate selection.

Most girls in the United States begin dating at the age of 14, whereas most boys begin sometime between the ages of 14 and 15 (Douvan & Adelson, 1966; Sorenson, 1973). The majority of adolescents have their first date between the ages of 12 and 16. Fewer than 10 percent have a first date before the age of 10, and by the age of 16, more than 90 percent have had at least one date. More than 50 percent of high school students average one or more dates per week (Dickinson, 1975). About 15 percent date less than once per month, and about three of every four students have gone steady at least once by the end of high school.

Female adolescents bring a stronger desire for intimacy and personality exploration to dating than do male adolescents (Duck, 1975). Adolescent dating is a context in which gender-related role expectations intensify. Males feel pressured to perform in "masculine" ways and females feel pressured to perform in "feminine" ways. Especially in early adolescence, when pubertal changes are occurring, the adolescent male wants to show that he is the very best male possible, and the adolescent female wants to show that she is the very best female possible.

At this point, we have discussed a number of ideas about peer relations. A summary of these ideas is presented in concept table 13.1. Now we will turn our attention to the world of children's play.

Play

An extensive amount of peer interaction during childhood involves play; however, social play is but one type. **Play** *is a pleasurable activity that is engaged in for its own sake.* Our coverage of play includes its functions, Parten's classic study of play, the types of play, and the sociocultural contexts of play.

Play's Functions

Play is essential to a young child's health. As today's children move into the twenty-first century and continue to experience pressure in their lives, play becomes even more crucial. Play increases affiliation with peers, releases tension, advances cognitive development, increases exploration, and provides a safe haven in which to engage in potentially dangerous behavior. Play increases the probability that children will converse and interact with each other. During this interaction, children practice the roles they will assume later in life.

According to Freud and Erikson, play is an especially useful form of human adjustment, helping the child master anxieties and conflicts. Because tensions are relieved in play, the child can cope with life's problems. Play permits the child to work off excess physical energy and to release pent-up tensions. **Play therapy** *allows children to work off frustrations and is a medium*

Peers

Concept	Processes/related ideas	Characteristics/description
Peer group functions	Their nature	Peers are children of about the same age or maturity level. Peers are powerful social agents. Peers provide a source of information and comparison about the world outside of the family.
The worlds of parent-child and peer relations	Distinctness	Rough-and-tumble play occurs mainly with peers. In times of stress, children generally seek out their parents.
	Coordination	Children touch, smile, and vocalize when they interact with parents and peers. Healthy family relations usually promote healthy peer relations. Parents also may model or coach their children in ways of relating to peers, and parents' choices of neighborhoods, churches, schools, and their own friends influence the pool from which their children might select possible friends.
The developmental course of peer relations in childhood	Infancy	Some researchers believe that the quality of social interaction with peers in infancy provides valuable information about social development. As increasing numbers of children attend day care, infant peer interaction has increased.
	Childhood	The frequency of peer interaction, both positive and negative, increases during the preschool years, and children spend even more time with peers in the elementary and secondary school years.
Peer popularity, rejection, and neglect	Their nature	Listening skills and effective communication, being yourself, being happy, showing enthusiasm and concern for others, and indicating self-confidence but not conceit are predictors of peer popularity. Rejected children are at risk for adjustment problems; the risk status of neglected children is less clear. Of special interest is the improvement of the peer relations of neglected and rejected children. One issue involving rejected children is whether to initially train their prosocial skills or to reduce their aggressive behavior and improve their self-control. It is important to remember that rejected children reflect a heterogeneous group.
Social cognition	Its nature	Perspective taking, information-processing skills, and social knowledge are important dimensions of social cognition in peer relations.
Friendships	Functions and characteristics	Children's friendships serve six functions: companionship, stimulation, physical support, ego support, social comparison, and intimacy/affection. Intimacy and similarity are two common characteristics of friendships.
Peer relations in adolescence	Peer pressure and conformity	The pressure to conform to peers is strong during adolescence, especially during the eighth and ninth grades.
	Cliques and crowds	There usually are three to six well-defined cliques in every secondary school. Membership in certain cliques—especially jocks and populars—is associated with increased self-esteem. Independents also show high self-esteem.
	Adolescent groups versus children groups	Children groups are less formal, less heterogeneous, and less heterosexual than adolescent groups.
	Dating	Dating can be a form of mate selection, a type of recreation, a source of status, and achievement, and a setting for learning about close relationships. Most adolescents are involved in dating. Adolescent females appear to be more interested in intimacy and personality exploration than adolescent males are.

Play is pleasurable activity that is engaged in for its own sake. Both Piaget and Vygotsky believed that play is an excellent setting for advancing young children's cognitive development.

through which therapists can analyze children's conflicts and ways of coping with them. Children may feel less threatened and be more likely to express their true feelings in the context of play.

Piaget (1962) saw play as a medium that advances children's cognitive development. At the same time, he said that children's cognitive development *constrains* the way they play. Play permits children to practice their competencies and acquired skills in a relaxed, pleasurable way. Piaget believed that cognitive structures need to be exercised, and play provides the perfect setting for this exercise. For example, children who have just learned to add or multiply begin to play with numbers in different ways as they perfect these operations, laughing as they do so.

Vygotsky (1962), whose developmental theory was discussed in chapter 8, also believed that play is an excellent setting for cognitive development. He was especially interested in the symbolic and make-believe aspects of play, as when a child substitutes a stick for a horse and rides the stick as if it were a horse (Smolucha, 1989). For young children, the imaginary situation is real. Parents should encourage such imaginary play because it advances the child's cognitive development, especially creative thought (Arman-Nolley, 1989).

Daniel Berlyne (1960) described play as exciting and pleasurable in itself because it satisfies the exploratory drive each of us possesses. This drive involves curiosity and a desire for information about something new or unusual. Play is a means whereby children can safely explore and seek out new information—something they might not otherwise do. Play encourages this exploratory behavior by offering children the possibilities of novelty, complexity, uncertainty, surprise, and incongruity.

Parten's Classic Study of Play

Many years ago, Mildred Parten (1932) developed one of the most elaborate attempts to categorize children's play. Based on observations of children in free play at nursery school, Parten arrived at the following play categories:

1. **Unoccupied play** *occurs when the child is not engaging in play as it is commonly understood and may stand in one spot, look around the room, or perform random movements that do not seem to have a goal.* In most nursery schools, unoccupied play is less frequent than other forms.

2. **Solitary play** *occurs when the child plays alone.* In this type of play, children seem engrossed in what they are doing and do not care much about what others are doing. Two- and three-year-olds engage more frequently in solitary play than older preschoolers do.

3. **Onlooker play** *occurs when the child watches other children play.* The child may talk with other children and ask questions but does not enter into their play behavior. The child's active interest in other children's play distinguishes onlooker play from unoccupied play.

4. **Parallel play** *occurs when the child plays separately from others, but with toys like those the others are using or in a manner that mimics their play.* Young preschool children engage in this type of play more often than do older preschool children, but even older preschool children engage in parallel play quite often.

5. **Associative play** *occurs when play involves social interaction with little or no organization.* In this type of play, children seem to be more interested in each other than in the tasks they are performing. Borrowing or lending toys and following or leading one another in line are examples of associative play.

6. **Cooperative play** *involves social interaction in a group with a sense of group identity and organized activity.* Children's formal games, competition aimed at winning, and groups formed by the teacher for doing things together are examples of cooperative play. Cooperative play is the prototype for the games of middle childhood. Little cooperative play is seen in the preschool years.

Parten's research on play was conducted more than half a century ago. To determine whether her findings were out of date, Keith Barnes (1971) used Parten's categories of play to observe a group of preschoolers. He found that children in the 1970s did not engage in as much associative and cooperative play as children did in the 1930s. These changes in play probably occurred because children became more passive as a consequence of heavy television viewing and because toys were more abundant and attractive in 1971 than in the 1930s. The developmental changes that were observed by Parten also were observed by Barnes. That is, 3-year-old children engaged in solitary play and parallel play more than 5-year-old children did, and 5-year-old children engaged in cooperative and associative play more than other types of play. Today, solitary play may be more natural, and parents may encourage children to play by themselves more than parents did years ago.

Types of Play

Parten's categories represent one way of thinking about the different types of play. However, today, researchers and practitioners who are involved with children's play believe there are other types of play that are important in children's development (Rogers & Sawyers, 1988). Whereas Parten's categories emphasize the role of play in the child's social world, the contemporary perspective on play emphasizes both the cognitive and social aspects of play. Among the most widely studied types of children's play today are sensorimotor and practice play, pretense/symbolic play, social play, constructive play, and games (Bergin, 1988).

Sensorimotor and Practice Play

Sensorimotor play *is behavior engaged in by infants to derive pleasure from exercising their existing sensorimotor schemas.* The development of sensorimotor play follows Piaget's description of sensorimotor thought, which we discussed in chapter 8. Infants initially engage in exploratory and playful visual and motor transactions in the second quarter of the first year of life. By 9 months of age, infants have begun to select novel objects for exploration and play, especially those that are responsive such as toys that make noise or bounce. At 12 months of age, infants enjoy making things work and exploring cause-and-effect. At this point in development, children like toys that perform when they act on them. In the second year, infants begin to understand the social meaning of objects and their play reflects this awareness. Two-year-olds may distinguish between exploratory play that is interesting but not humorous and "playful" play, which has incongruous and humorous dimensions (McGhee, 1984). For example, a 2-year-old might "drink" from a shoe or call a dog a "cow." When 2-year-olds find these deliberate incongruities funny, they are beginning to show evidence of symbolic play and the ability to play with ideas.

Practice play *involves the repetition of behavior when new skills are being learned or when physical or mental mastery and coordination of skills is required for games or sports.* Sensorimotor play, which often involves practice play, is confined to infancy, whereas practice play can be engaged in throughout life. During the preschool years, children often engage in play that involves practicing various skills. Estimates indicate that practice play constitutes about one third of the preschool child's play activities but less than one sixth of the elementary school child's play activities (Rubin, Fein, & Vandenberg, 1983). Practice play contributes to the development of coordinated motor skills that will be needed later for game playing. Although practice play declines in the elementary school years, such practice play activities as running, jumping, sliding, twirling, and throwing balls or other objects can be observed on the playgrounds at elementary schools. Although these activities appear similar to the earlier practice play of the preschool years, much of the practice play in the elementary school years is ends rather than means related. That is, elementary school children often engage in practice play for the purpose of improving the motor skills needed to compete in games or sports.

Pretense/Symbolic Play

Pretense/symbolic play *occurs when the child transforms the physical environment into a symbol* (DeHart & Smith, 1991; Fein, 1986; Howes, Unger, & Seidner, 1989; Rogers & Sawyers, 1988). Between 9 and 30 months of age, children increase their use of objects in symbolic play. They learn to transform objects, substituting them for other objects and acting toward them as if they were these other objects. For example, a preschool child might treat a table as if it were a car and say, "I'm fixing the car," as he grabs one of the table's legs.

Many experts on play consider the preschool years the "golden age" of symbolic/pretense play that is dramatic or sociodramatic in nature (Bergin, 1988; Singer & Singer, 1988). This type of make-believe play often appears at about 18 months of age, reaches a peak at 4 to 5 years of age, then gradually declines. In the early elementary school years, children's interests often shift to games.

Catherine Garvey (1977) has spent many years observing young children's play. She indicates that three elements are found in almost all of the pretend play she has observed: props, plot, and roles. Children use objects as

I imagine, therefore I am free.

—Lawrence Durrell

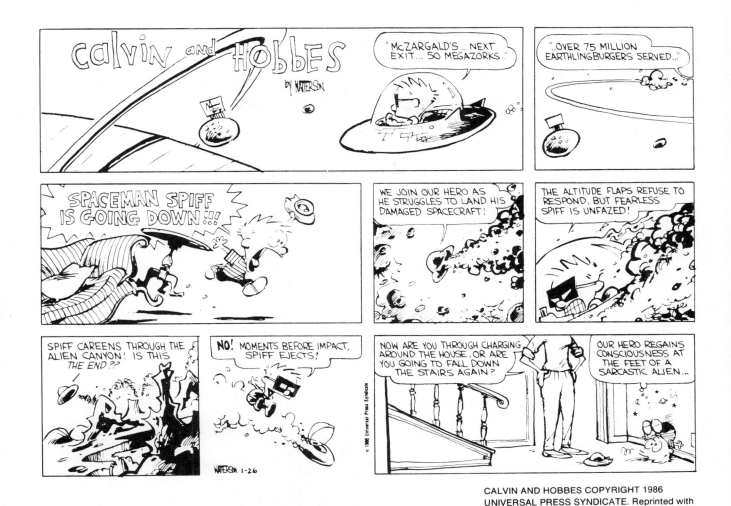

props in their pretend play. Children can pretend to drink from a real cup or from a seashell. They even can create a make-believe cup from thin air, if nothing else is available. Most pretend play also has a story line, though the *plot* may be quite simple. Pretend play themes often reflect what children see going on in their lives, as when they play family, school, or doctor. Fantasy play can take its theme from a story children have heard, or a show they have seen. In pretend play, children try out many different *roles.* Some roles, like mother or teacher, are derived from reality. Other roles, such as cowgirls or Superman, come from fantasy. More about superhero play appears in Perspective on Child Development 13.1.

Social Play

Social play *is play that involves social interaction with peers.* Parten's categories, which were described earlier, are oriented toward social play. Social play with peers increases dramatically in the preschool years. In addition to general social play with peers and group pretense or sociodramatic play, another form of social play is rough-and-tumble play. The movement patterns of rough-and-tumble play are often similar to those of hostile behavior (running, chasing, wrestling, jumping, falling, hitting), but in rough-and-tumble play these behaviors are accompanied by such signals as laughter, exaggerated movement, and open rather than closed hands, which indicate that this is play.

Superhero Play

Jonathan runs into the classroom, charges over to the block cabinet, and selects a long, thin board. He shoves it under his sweater, takes a fighting stance, and announces, "I have the power." He laughingly advances toward his playmates, who run from him, leaping, shouting, and giggling.

Another day of superhero play has begun. Superhero play is a common occurrence in young children's lives and there is little doubt that they find it exhilarating. Marilyn Kostelnik, Alice Whiren, and Laura Stein (1988) recently described why children find superhero play attractive and how it relates to their development.

Superhero characters have been endowed with powers and qualities that embody the best of human nature. Consider Superman, Wonder Woman, Princess Leia, and He-Man. These superheroes and superheroines

- Are unquestionably good, being wise, fearless, clever, and strong
- Possess powers children wished they had themselves; superheroes have amazing speed, strength, or endurance and can fly, swim under water for miles, or change the shape of their bodies
- Solve every problem and overcome all obstacles and their solutions are always accepted
- Are in control—no one tells them what to do
- Know what is right—they rarely, if ever, make a mistake
- Receive praise and recognition from powerful adults; everyone wants to be their friend

Children have little power in the world because it is dominated by adults, yet, through their play, children can take on powerful roles that allow them to dominate villains or experience circumstances that entail no real risk. Feelings of fear and vulnerability can be overcome and transformed through playful shows of courage, strength, and wisdom. Superhero play also provides children the opportunity to pretend to be someone they admire and would like to resemble. Because superheroes are all good and antiheroes are all bad, children have clear, precise models for imitation. Finally, as with all other forms of dramatic play, through superhero play, children improve their language skills, problem-solving abilities, and cooperation.

How can teachers and parents help children make superhero play a constructive experience? They can

- Help children recognize the humane characteristics of superheroes they admire—for example, a teacher might say, "Barbara, you must have felt as helpful as Wonder Woman when you carried the chairs over to the table"

- Discuss real heroes and heroines with children; introduce children to such people as Martin Luther King, Jr., and Helen Keller
- Help children understand what happens when play goes awry; children often are surprised when one of them is injured or frightened during play—the teacher might say, "Jane did not know you were playing," or "That was a real hit, not a pretend hit"
- Make it clear that aggression is unacceptable; children's aggressive acts need to be stopped, and adults need to make it clear that aggression will not be tolerated

In summary, superhero play is a specialized form of dramatic pretense play that is considerably appealing to young children. Although superhero play should not be actively promoted, when carefully monitored and directed, superhero play can have positive benefits.

Shown here is a preschool "superhero" at play.

Constructive Play

Constructive play *combines sensorimotor and practice repetitive activity with the symbolic representation of ideas. Constructive play occurs when children engage in self-regulated creation or construction of a product or problem solution.* Constructive play increases in the preschool years as symbolic play increases and sensorimotor play decreases. In the preschool years, some practice play is replaced by constructive play. For example, instead of moving their fingers around in finger paint (practice play), children are now more likely to draw the outline of a house or a person in the paint (constructive play). Some researchers have found that constructive play is the most common type of play in the preschool years (Hetherington, Cox, & Cox, 1979; Rubin, Maioni, & Hornung, 1976). Constructive play is also frequently a form of play in the elementary school years, both in and out of the classroom. Constructive play is one of the few playlike activities allowed in work-centered classrooms. For example, having children create a skit about a social studies topic involves constructive play. Whether such activities are considered play by children usually depends on whether they get to choose whether to do it (thus, it is play) or whether the teacher imposes it (it is not play), and also whether it is enjoyable (it is play) or not (it is not play) (King, 1982).

Constructive play may also be used in the elementary school years to foster academic skill learning, thinking skills, and problem solving. Many educators plan classroom activities that include humor, that encourage playing with ideas, and that promote creativity (Bergin, 1988). Educators also often support the performance of plays, the writing of imaginative stories, the expression of artistic abilities, and the playful exploration of computers and other technological equipment. Distinctions between work and play frequently become blurred in the elementary school classroom.

Games

Games *are activities engaged in for pleasure that include rules and often competition with one or more individuals.* Preschool children may participate in social game play that involves simple rules of reciprocity and turn taking, but games take on a much more salient role in the lives of elementary school children. In one investigation, the highest incidence of game playing occurred between 10 and 12 years of age (Eiferman, 1971). After children reach the age of 12, games decline in popularity, often being replaced by practice play, conversations, and organized sports (Bergin, 1988).

In the elementary years, games feature the meaningfulness of a challenge (Eiferman, 1971). This challenge is present if two or more children have the skills required to play and understand the rules of the game. Among the types of games children engage in are steady or constant games, such as tag, which are played consistently; recurrent or cyclical games, such as marbles or hopscotch, which seem to follow cycles of popularity and decline; sporadic games, which are rarely played; and one-time games, such as hula hoop contests, which rise once to popularity and then disappear.

In sum, play is a multidimensional, complex concept. It ranges from an infant's simple exercise of a newfound sensorimotor talent to a preschool child's mastery of a motor skill to an older child's participation in organized games. An overview of the different forms of play described by contemporary play theorists and researchers is presented in figure 13.4.

You are troubled at seeing him spend his early years in doing nothing. What! Is it nothing to be happy? Is it nothing to skip, to play, to run about all day long? Never in his life will he be so busy as now.

—Jean-Jacques Rousseau

■ *Critical Thinking*
Are elementary schools too work centered? Should constructive play be used more extensively in the education of elementary school children? Explain your answer.

Sensorimotor/ practice play	Pretense/ symbolic play	Social play	Constructive play	Games
Sensorimotor play is behavior infants engage in to derive pleasure from exercising their existing sensorimotor schemas. Sensorimotor play begins in the second quarter of the first year of life. Sensorimotor play is practice play. Practice play involves the repetition of behavior when new skills are being learned or when physical or mental mastery and coordination of skills are required for games or sports. Sensorimotor play is confined to infancy, whereas practice play continues through life.	Pretense/symbolic play occurs when the child transforms the environment into a symbol. Between 9 and 30 months, children increase their use of objects in symbolic play. Many experts consider the preschool years the "golden years" of pretense/symbolic play that is dramatic or sociodramatic in nature. This type of play peaks at about 4 to 5 years of age, then gradually declines.	Social play involves social interaction with peers. Parten's categories are oriented toward social rather than cognitive play. Social play with peers increases dramatically in the preschool years. In addition to general social play with peers, a specific form of social play is rough-and-tumble play. Group pretense or sociodramatic play also is social play.	Constructive play combines sensorimotor/practice repetitive activity with symbolic representation of objects and ideas. Constructive play occurs when children engage in self-regulated creation or construction of a product or a problem solution. Constructive play increases in the preschool years as symbolic play increases and sensorimotor play decreases. Constructive play is one of the most frequent types of play in the preschool and elementary school years.	Games are activities engaged in for pleasure that include rules and often competition with other individuals. Preschool children may begin to participate in social game play that involves simple rules of reciprocity and turn-taking, but games take on a more salient role in children's lives in the elementary school years.

Figure 13.4
Types of Play

The Sociocultural Contexts of Play

American children's freewheeling play once took place in rural fields and city streets, using equipment largely made by children themselves. Today, play is becoming confined to backyards, basements, playrooms, and bedrooms and derives much of its content from video games, television dramas, and Saturday morning cartoons (Sutton-Smith, 1985). Modern children spend a large part of their lives alone with their toys, which was inconceivable several centuries earlier. Childhood was once part of collective village life. Children did not play separately but joined adults in seasonal festivals that intruded on the work world with regularity and boisterousness (see figure 13.5).

One of the most widely debated issues in the sociocultural contexts of play is whether children from low socioeconomic groups and traditional, non-Western societies have underdeveloped skills in the imaginative and socio-dramatic aspects of pretense play (Johnson, Christie, & Yawkey, 1987). Some researchers believe there are developmental deficiencies in the imaginative and

Social and Personality Development

Figure 13.5
Children's Games by Pieter Breughel, 1560
How might the play of today's children differ
from that of children in collective village
life?

sociodramatic play of children from low socioeconomic groups and traditional, non-Western societies, whereas others believe that many methodological shortcomings in this research cloud the results. For example, many of these studies do not adequately measure socioeconomic status, do not systematically measure classroom and school variables, and in some cases do not use statistical analysis (McLoyd, 1982).

Some children may be capable of high-level imaginative play but require adult prompting and encouragement to overcome their initial shyness (Johnson, Christie, & Yawkey, 1987). Before expecting high-level play from children, teachers should determine if the children have had adequate time to become familiar with the materials and routines in their day-care center or preschool classroom. This familiarity is especially important for children whose main language is not English or for any child who comes from a home environment that is in marked contrast with the school environment.

The form and content of children's play are influenced by cultural and socioeconomic factors. The typical day-care or preschool environment is designed for middle-class children. Play experts recommend that children from low-income backgrounds be given considerable time to adapt to these new surroundings, and they also recommend that educators be ready to modify the environment to accommodate the diverse backgrounds of children. The need for adaptation was underscored in an observation of a group of young Navajo children (Curry, 1971). These children were familiar with the props available for dramatic play in the housekeeping corner of their middle-class-oriented preschool center. Teachers reported that the Navajo children would not engage in dramatic play. Many of the Navajo children came from homes with no running water and the cooking was performed over an open fire. The Navajo children did not use the domestic corner because it was set up for free play. One day—not by teacher design—the toys were left against the wall after cleaning, which prompted the Navajo children to engage vigorously in sociodramatic play. Why? Because the props were in the position they were familiar with in their circular homes.

We have seen that play is diverse and complex and that it is essential to the child's healthy development. We have also seen that the child's sociocultural world influences the nature of play. One of the main changes in children's

"Mrs. Horton, could you stop by school today?"

© Martha F. Campbell.

Television is a medium of entertainment which permits millions of people to listen to the same joke at the same time, and yet remain lonesome.

—T. S. Eliot

sociocultural worlds in the twentieth century has been the introduction of television, which influences play, because it both competes for the child's time and stimulates or implants ideas for play themes and content. Next, we will study not only television's influence on children's development, but also the influence of other media, especially computers.

Media Influences

In the twentieth century, media influences on children's development have increased. Media are forms of mass communication, such as television, newspapers, magazines, movies, and computers. In this section, we will consider two powerful media in children's lives today—television and computers.

Television

Few developments in society over the past 35 years have had a greater impact on children than television has. Many children spend more time in front of the television set than they do with their parents. Although it is only one mass medium that affects children's behavior, television is the most influential. The persuasive capabilities of television are staggering; the 20,000 hours of television watched by the time the average American adolescent graduates from high school are greater than the number of hours spent in the classroom.

Television's Many Roles

Television can have a negative influence on children's development by taking them away from homework, making them passive learners, teaching them stereotypes, providing them with violent models of aggression, and presenting them with unrealistic views of the world. However, television can also have a positive influence on children's development by presenting motivating educational programs, increasing children's information about the world beyond their immediate environment, and providing models of prosocial behavior (Esty & Fisch, 1991).

Television has been called many things, not all of them good. Depending on one's point of view, it may be a "window on the world," the "one-eyed monster," or the "boob tube." Television has been attacked as one of the reasons that scores on national achievement tests in reading and mathematics are lower now than in the past. Television, it is claimed, attracts children away from books and schoolwork. In one study, children who read printed materials, such as books, watched television less than those who did not read (Huston, Seigle, & Bremer, 1983). Furthermore, critics argue that television trains children to become passive learners; rarely, if ever, does television require active responses from the observer.

Television also is said to deceive; that is, it teaches children that problems are resolved easily and that everything always comes out right in the end. For example, TV detectives usually take only 30 to 60 minutes to sort through a complex array of clues to reveal a killer—and they *always* find the killer. Violence is a way of life on many shows. It is all right for police to use violence and to break moral codes in their fight against evildoers. The lasting results of violence are rarely brought home to the viewer. A person who is injured on TV suffers for only a few seconds; in real life, the person might need months or years to recover, or might not recover at all. One out of every two first-grade children says that the adults on television are like adults in real life (Lyle & Hoffman, 1972).

A special concern is how ethnic minorities are portrayed on television. Ethnic minorities have historically been underrepresented and misrepresented on television. Ethnic minority characters—whether Black, Asian, Hispanic, or Native American—have traditionally been presented as less dignified and less positive than White characters (Condry, 1989). In one recent investigation, character portrayals of ethnic minorities were examined during heavy children's viewing hours (weekdays 4–6 P.M. and 7–11 P.M.) (Williams & Condry, 1989). The percentage of White characters far exceeded the actual percentage of Whites in the United States; the percentage of Black, Asian, and Hispanic characters fell short of the population statistics. Hispanic characters were especially underrepresented—only 0.6 percent of the characters were Hispanic, although the Hispanic population in the United States is 6.4 percent of the total. Minorities tended to hold lower-status jobs and were more likely than Whites to be cast as criminals or victims.

There are some positive aspects to television's influence on children, however. For one, television presents children with a world that is different from the one in which they live. It exposes children to a wider variety of viewpoints and information than they might get from only their parents, teachers, and peers. Also, some television programs have educational and developmental benefits. One of television's major programming attempts to educate children is *Sesame Street,* which is designed to teach both cognitive and social skills. The program began in 1969 and is still going strong.

Sesame Street demonstrates that education and entertainment can work well together. Through *Sesame Street,* children experience a world of learning that is both exciting and entertaining. *Sesame Street* also follows the principle that teaching can be accomplished both directly and indirectly. Using the direct way, a teacher might tell children exactly what they are going to be taught and then teach them. However, in real life, social skills are often communicated in indirect ways. Rather than merely telling children, "You should cooperate with others," TV can show children so that they can figure out what it means to be cooperative and what the advantages are. More about *Sesame Street* appears in Cultural Worlds of Development 13.2.

The Cosby Show *is an excellent example how television can present positive models for ethnic minority children.*

Amount of Television Children Watch

Just how much television do young children watch? They watch a lot, and they seem to be watching more all the time. In the 1950s, 3-year-old children watched television for less than 1 hour a day; 5-year-olds watched just over 2 hours a day. In the 1970s, however, preschool children watched television for an average of 4 hours a day; elementary school children watched for as long as 6 hours a day (Friedrich & Stein, 1973). In the 1980s, children averaged 11 to 28 hours of television per week (Huston, Watkins, & Kunkel, 1989), which is more than for any other activity except sleep. Of special concern is the extent to which children are exposed to violence and aggression on television. Up to 80 percent of the prime time shows include violent acts, including beatings, shootings, and stabbings. The frequency of violence increases on the Saturday morning cartoon shows, which average more than 25 violent acts per hour.

Effects of Television on Aggression and Prosocial Behavior

What are the effects of television violence on children's aggression? Does television merely stimulate a child to go out and buy a Star Wars ray gun, or can it trigger an attack on a playmate? When the child grows up, can television violence increase the likelihood he will violently attack someone?

465

Sesame Street Around the World

Street first appeared in 1969, the creators of
no idea that this "street" would lead to loca-
tant as Kuwait, Israel, Latin America, and the
s. In the 20 years since *Sesame Street* first aired
nited States, the show has been televised in 84 coun-
hirteen foreign language versions of the show have been
ced. Following is a sampling of *Sesame Street* produc-
s in various countries:

Plaza Sesamo, Latin America   The show is seen in 17
South and Central American countries, as well as in
Puerto Rico. The diversity of cultures and life-styles in
Latin America is given special emphasis.

Rechov Sumsum, Israel   The setting represents a typical
Israeli neighborhood, with old houses next to modern
apartment buildings. The show's puppet characters include Kippy, a full-size pink porcupine that is naive,
friendly, and opinionated. Moishe Oofnick is a shaggy
grouch. Reflecting the diversity of Israel's population,
the cast includes people from different ethnic and religious backgrounds who live in harmony.

Sesamstraat, The Netherlands   Children are familiar-
ized with the concept of school and any anxieties they
might have about school are dispelled. Some segments
encourage children to discuss their fears openly. Other
segments show interactions between disabled and non-
disabled children. One of the puppets is Pino, a 7-foot-
tall blue bird that is eager to learn.

*Shown here is Don Pimpón of Spain's
"Barrio Sesamo."*

Barrio Sesamo, Spain   The bakery is *Barrio Sesamo*'s
central meeting place. The residents include two full-
size puppets. Espinete, a special friend of the children,
is a hedgehog that tries to get the cast members to play
games whenever possible. Don Pimpon is a shaggy old
codger, at times a bit absent-minded, who has traveled
extensively and entertains with stories of his adven-
tures (Corwin, 1989).

In one longitudinal investigation, the amount of violence viewed on television at age 8 was significantly related to the seriousness of criminal acts
performed as an adult (Huesmann, 1986). In another investigation, long-term
exposure to television violence was significantly related to the likelihood of
aggression in 1,565 12-to-17-year-old boys (Belson, 1978). Boys who watched
the most aggression on television were the most likely to commit a violent
crime, swear, be aggressive in sports, threaten violence toward another boy,
write slogans on walls, or break windows. These investigations are *correlational,* so we cannot conclude from them that television violence causes children to be more aggressive, only that watching television violence is *associated
with* aggressive behavior. In one experiment, children were randomly assigned
to one of two groups: One watched television shows taken directly from violent
Saturday morning cartoon offerings on 11 different days; the second group
watched television cartoon shows with all of the violence removed (Steur, Applefield, & Smith, 1971). The children were then observed during play at their
preschool. The preschool children who saw the TV cartoon shows with vio-

lence kicked, choked, and pushed their playmates more than the preschool children who watched nonviolent TV cartoon shows did. Because children were randomly assigned to the two conditions (TV cartoons with violence versus no violence), we can conclude that exposure to TV violence *caused* the increased aggression in children in this investigation.

Whereas some critics have argued that the effects of television violence do not warrant the conclusion that TV violence causes aggression (Freedman, 1984), others have concluded that TV violence can induce aggressive or antisocial behavior in children (Condry, 1989; Huston, Watkins, & Kunkel, 1989; Liebert & Spratkin, 1988). Of course, television is not the *only* cause of aggression. There is no *one,* single cause of any social behavior. Aggression, like all other social behaviors, is multiply determined.

Children need to be taught critical viewing skills to counter the adverse effects of television violence. In one investigation, elementary school children were randomly assigned to either an experimental or a control group (Huesmann & others, 1983). In the experimental group, children assisted in making a film to help children who had been fooled or harmed by television. The children also composed essays that focused on how television is not like real life and why it is bad to imitate TV violence or watch too much television. In the control group, children received no training in critical viewing skills. The children who were trained in critical viewing skills developed more negative attitudes about TV violence and reduced their aggressive behavior.

Television can also teach children that it is better to behave in positive, prosocial ways than in negative, antisocial ways. Television researcher Aimee Leifer (1973) demonstrated that television is associated with prosocial behavior in young children; she selected a number of *Sesame Street* episodes that reflected positive social interchanges. She was especially interested in situations that taught children how to use their social skills. For example, in one interchange, two men were fighting over the amount of space available to them; they gradually began to cooperate and to share the space. Children who watched these episodes copied these behaviors and, in later social situations, they applied the prosocial lessons they had learned.

Parents' Role in Children's Television Viewing

How much do parents take an active role in discussing television with their children? For the most part, parents do not discuss the content of television shows with their children (Leiffer, Gordon, & Graves, 1974). Parents need to be especially sensitive to young children's viewing habits because the age period of 2½ to 6 is when long-term television-viewing habits begin to be established (Murphy, Talley, & Huston, 1991). Children from lower socioeconomic status families watch television more than children from higher socioeconomic status families (Huston, Seigle, & Bremer, 1983). Also, children who live in families involved in high conflict watch more television than children who live in families low in conflict (Price & Feshbach, 1982). In one recent investigation (Tangney, in press), the children of parents who showed more empathy and sensitivity toward them preferred less fantasy fare on television. In dysfunctional families, children may use the lower developmental level of fantasy-oriented children's programs to escape from the taxing, stressful circumstances of their home environment.

Parents can make television a more positive influence in children's lives. The following guidelines developed by Dorothy and Jerome Singer (1987) can go a long way in reducing television's negative effects and improving its role as a positive influence in children's development.

1. Develop good viewing habits early in the child's life.
2. Encourage planned viewing of specific programs rather than random viewing. Be active with young children between planned programs.
3. Look for children's programs that feature children in the child's age group.
4. Make sure that television is not used as a substitute for participating in other activities.
5. Develop discussions about sensitive television themes with children. Give them the opportunity to ask questions about the programs.
6. Balance reading and television activities. Children can "follow up" interesting television programs by checking out the library books for which some programs are adapted and by pursuing additional stories by the authors of those books.
7. Help children develop a balanced viewing schedule of education, action, comedy, fine arts, fantasy, sports, and so on.
8. Point out positive examples that show how various ethnic and cultural groups contribute to making a better society.
9. Point out positive examples of females performing competently both in professions and at home.

Computers and Children

At mid-twentieth century, commercial television had barely made its debut and IBM had yet to bring its first computer to market. Now as we move toward the close of the twentieth century, both television *and* computers are important influences in children's lives. For some, the computer is a positive tool with the power to transform our schools and revolutionize children's learning. For others, the computer is a menacing force, more likely to undermine than to improve children's education. Let's examine some of the possible positive and negative influences of computers in children's lives.

Positive Influences of Computers on Children

Among the potential positive influences of computers on children's development are those involving the computer as a personal tutor, as a medium for experiential learning, and as a multipurpose tool, as well as motivational and social effects (Lepper & Gurtner, 1989).

Computer-assisted instruction *is a method of education that uses the computer as a tutor to individualize instruction. The concept behind computer-assisted instruction is to use the computer to present information, give students practice, assess their level of understanding, and provide additional instruction if needed.* Computer-assisted instruction requires the active participation of the student; it is patient and nonjudgmental in giving immediate feedback to students. Over the past 2 decades, more than 200 research studies involving computer-assisted instruction have been conducted. In general, the effects of computer-assisted instruction are positive (Steinberg, 1990a). More precisely, the effects are more positive with programs involving tutorials rather than drill and practice, with younger rather than older students, and with children of lower ability than with average or general populations (Lepper & Gurtner, 1989).

The influence of computer use on children's learning, motivation, and social behavior continues to be a source of debate and controversy.

A second important influence of the computer in children's lives is its role in experiential learning. Some experts view the computer as an excellent medium for open-ended, exploratory, and experiential learning. The most widely studied activity has been the use of the Logo computing language, especially its simplified "turtle graphics" programming environment, as a way to improve children's planning and problem-solving abilities (Papert, 1980). Logo involves children in active experimentation with "turtle graphics." The research on the effects of Logo are mixed. The early studies of Logo essentially found no benefits for children's learning; however, more recent studies have been supportive of Logo. In recent studies, more favorable adult-child ratios are present, prepared support materials and explicit task requirements are included, younger children are studied, and a wider array of dependent variable measures are used (such as creativity, cognitive monitoring, and solution checking).

A third important influence of the computer in children's lives is its function as a multipurpose tool in helping children achieve academic goals and become more creative. The computer is especially helpful in improving children's writing and communication skills (Collins, 1986). Word-processing programs diminish the drudgery of writing, increasing the probability that children will edit and revise their work. Programs that assist students in outlining a paper may help them organize their thoughts before they write.

Several other themes appear in the discussion of the computer's positive influence on children's development. For one, computer adherents argue that the computer makes learning more intrinsically motivating (Lepper, 1985). Computer enthusiasts also argue that the computer can make learning more fun, and lessons can often be embedded in instructional "games" or puzzles that encourage children's curiosity and sense of challenge. Some computer adherents also argue that increased computer use in schools will lead to increased cooperation and collaboration on the part of students, as well as increased intellectual discussion among students. If the computer does increase students' interest, it may free teachers to spend more time working with students individually. Finally, computer adherents hope that the computer can increase the equality of educational opportunity (Becker & Sterling, 1987). Since the computer allows students to work at their own pace, it may help students who do not normally succeed in school. The computer's fairness and impartiality should minimize any adverse influences of teacher prejudice and stereotyping.

Negative Influences of Computers on Children

Among the potential negative influences of computers on children's development are the regimentation and dehumanization of the classroom, unwarranted "shaping" of the curriculum, and the generalization and limitations of computer-based teaching (Lepper & Gurtner, 1989).

Skeptics worry that, rather than increased individualization of instruction, computers will bring a much greater regimentation and homogenization of classroom learning experiences. Whereas some students may prefer to work autonomously and may learn most effectively when they are allowed to progress on their own, other students may rely on social interaction with and guidance by the teacher for effective learning. Some computer skeptics also worry that the computer will ultimately increase inequality, rather than equality, in educational outcomes (Malcom, 1988). School funding in middle-class neighborhoods is usually better than in low-income areas, and the homes of children in middle-class neighborhoods are more likely to have computers than are those in low-income neighborhoods. Thus, an increasing emphasis on computer literacy may be inequitable for children from low-income backgrounds because they have likely had less opportunities to use computers. Some critics also worry about the dehumanization of the classroom. They argue that school is a social world as well as a cognitive, learning world. From this perspective, children plugged into a computer all day long have little opportunity to engage in social interaction.

A further concern is that computers may inadvertently and inappropriately shape the curriculum. Some subjects, such as mathematics and science, seem to be more easily and successfully adapted to computers than are such subjects as art and literature. Consequently, there is concern that the computer may eventually shape the curriculum exclusively in the direction of science and math because these areas are more easily computerized.

Yet another issue is the transfer of learning and motivation to domains outside the computer. If the instructional effectiveness and motivational appeal of computer-based education depends on the use of impressive technical devices, such as color, animation, and sound effects, how effectively will student learning or motivation transfer to other contexts without these technical supports? Will children provided with the editorial assistance of the computer still learn the basic skills needed to progress to more complex forms of creative writing later in their careers? Will children using computers in math gain the proficiency to deal with more complicated math in the future or will their ability to solve complex conceptual problems without the computer have atrophied? Presently, we do not know the answers to these important questions about the computer's role in children's development.

At this point, we have discussed a number of ideas about play and about media influences on children's development. A summary of these ideas is presented in concept table 13.2. In our discussion of children and computers, we addressed a number of aspects of the computer's role in children's education. In the next chapter, we will study further the important role of school in children's development.

■ *Critical Thinking*
In our discussion of television, we mentioned ways that parents could effectively monitor children's television viewing. What roles can parents play in their children's use of computers?

Concept Table 13.2
Play and Media Influences

Concept	Processes/related ideas	Characteristics/description
Play	Play's functions	They include affiliation with peers, tension release, advances in cognitive development, exploration, and provision of a safe haven in which to engage in potentially dangerous activities.
	Parten's classic study of play	Parten examined the categories of unoccupied, solitary, onlooker, parallel, associative, and cooperative play. Three-year-old children engage in more solitary play and parallel play than 5-year-old children, whereas 5-year-old children engage in cooperative and associative play more than other types of play.
	Types of play	The contemporary perspective emphasizes both the cognitive and social aspects of play. Among the most widely studied aspects of children's play today are sensorimotor and practice play, pretense/symbolic play, social play, constructive play, and games.
	The sociocultural contexts of play	Modern children spend a large part of their lives with toys, and play is increasingly confined to backyards, basements, playrooms, and bedrooms rather than occurring in rural fields and city streets. A widely debated issue is whether children from low socioeconomic and traditional, non-Western societies have underdeveloped skills in the imaginative and sociodramatic aspects of pretense play. The form and content of children's play are influenced by cultural and socioeconomic factors.
Media influences	Television	Although television can have a negative influence on children's development by taking them away from homework, making them passive learners, teaching them stereotypes, providing them with violent models of aggression, and presenting them with unrealistic views of the world, television can also have a positive influence by presenting motivating educational programs, increasing children's information about the world beyond their immediate environment, and providing models of prosocial behavior. Children watch huge amounts of television, with preschool children watching an average of 4 hours a day. Up to 80 percent of the prime time shows have violent episodes. Television violence is not the only cause of children's aggression, but most experts conclude that it can induce aggression and antisocial behavior in children. Prosocial behavior on television is associated with increased positive behavior by children. Parents rarely discuss television's contents with their children. Television-viewing habits are often formed in the early childhood years.
	Computers and children	Among the potential positive effects of computers on children's development are those involving the computer as a personal tutor (computer-assisted instruction), as a medium for experiential learning, and as a multipurpose tool, as well as the motivational and social aspects of computers. Among the potential negative effects of computers on children's development are the regimentation and dehumanization of the classroom, unwarranted ''shaping'' of the curriculum, and the generalization and limitations of computer-based teaching.

Summary

I. Peer Group Functions and the Distinct but Coordinated Worlds of Parent-Child and Peer Relations

Peers are children of about the same age or maturity level. Peers are powerful social agents. Peers provide a source of information and comparison about the world outside of the family. The distinctness of parent and peer worlds involves rough-and-tumble play occurring mainly with peers, but in times of stress children generally seek out their parents. The coordinated worlds of parents and peers include similar behaviors: Children touch, smile, and vocalize when they interact with parents and peers. Healthy family relations usually promote healthy peer relations. Parents also may model or coach their children in ways of relating to peers. Parents' choice of neighborhoods, churches, schools, and their own friends influence the pool from which their children might select possible friends.

II. The Developmental Course of Peer Relations in Childhood

Some researchers believe that the quality of social interaction with peers in infancy provides valuable information about social development. As increasing numbers of children attend day care, infant peer interaction has increased. The frequency of peer interaction, both positive and negative, increases during the preschool years, and children spend even more time with peers in the elementary and secondary school years.

III. Peer Popularity, Rejection, and Neglect; Social Cognition; and Friendships

Listening skills and effective communication, being yourself, being happy, showing enthusiasm and concern for others, and indicating self-confidence but not conceit are predictors of peer popularity. Rejected children are at risk for adjustment problems; the risk for neglected children is less clear. Of special interest is the improvement of the peer relations of neglected and rejected children. One issue involving rejected children is whether to initially train their prosocial skills or to reduce their aggressive behavior and improve their self-control. It is important to remember that rejected children reflect a heterogeneous group. Perspective taking, information-processing skills, and social knowledge are important dimensions of social cognition in peer relations. Children's friendships serve six functions: companionship, stimulation, physical support, ego support, social comparison, and intimacy/ affection. Intimacy and similarity are two common characteristics of friendships.

IV. Peer Relations in Adolescence

The pressure to conform to peers is strong during adolescence, especially during the eighth and ninth grades. There usually are three to six well-defined cliques in every secondary school. Membership in certain cliques—especially jocks and populars—is associated with increased self-esteem. Independents also show high self-esteem. Children groups are less formal, less heterogeneous, and less heterosexual than adolescent groups. Dating can be a form of mate selection, a type of recreation, a source of status and achievement, and a setting for learning about close relationships. Most adolescents are involved in dating. Adolescent females are more interested in intimacy and personality exploration than adolescent males are.

V. Play's Functions and Parten's Classic Study of Play

Play's functions include affiliation with peers, tension release, advances in cognitive development, exploration, and the provision of a safe haven in which to engage in potentially dangerous activities. Parten examined the categories of unoccupied, solitary, onlooker, parallel, associative, and cooperative play. Three-year-old children engage in more solitary and parallel play than 5-year-old children, whereas 5-year-old children engage in cooperative and associative play more than other types of play.

VI. Types of Play and the Sociocultural Contexts of Play

The contemporary perspective emphasizes both the cognitive and the social aspects of play. Among the most widely studied aspects of children's play today are sensorimotor and practice play, pretense/symbolic play, social play, constructive play, and games. Modern children spend a large part of their lives with toys, and play is increasingly confined to backyards, basements, playrooms, and bedrooms rather than occurring in rural fields and city streets. A widely debated issue is whether children from low socioeconomic and traditional, non-Western societies have underdeveloped skills in the imaginative and sociodramatic aspects of pretense play. The form and content of children's play are influenced by cultural and socioeconomic factors.

VII. Television

Although television can have a negative influence on children's development by taking them away from homework, making them passive learners, teaching them stereotypes, providing them with violent models of aggressive behavior, and presenting them with unrealistic views of the world, television can also have a positive influence by presenting motivating educational programs, increasing children's information about the world beyond their immediate environment, and providing models of prosocial behavior. Children watch huge amounts of television, with preschool children watching an average of 4 hours a day. Up to 80 percent of the prime time shows have violent episodes. Television violence is not the only cause of children's aggression, but most experts conclude it can induce aggression and antisocial behavior in children. Prosocial behavior on television is associated with increased positive behavior by children. Parents rarely discuss television's content with their children. Television-viewing habits are often formed in the early childhood years.

VIII. Computers and Children

Among the potential positive effects of computers on children's development are those involving the computer as a personal tutor (computer-assisted instruction), as a medium for experiential learning, and as a multipurpose tool, as well as the motivational and social aspects of computers. Among the potential negative effects of computers on children's development are the regimentation and dehumanization of the classroom, unwarranted "shaping" of the curriculum, and the generalization and limitations of computer-based teaching.

Key Terms

peers 443
neglected children 445
rejected children 445
perspective taking 446
intimacy in friendships 449
crowd 451
cliques 451
play 454
play therapy 454
unoccupied play 456
solitary play 457
onlooker play 457
parallel play 457
associative play 457
cooperative play 457
sensorimotor play 458
practice play 458
pretense/symbolic play 458
social play 458
constructive play 461
games 461
computer-assisted
instruction 469

Suggested Readings

Bloch, M. N., & Pellegrini, A. D. (Eds.). (1989). *The ecological context of play.* Norwood, NJ: Ablex. This book focuses on the sociocultural contexts of play, including information about the role of play in different cultures and socioeconomic contexts.

Hartup, W. W. (1983). The peer system. In P. H. Mussen (Ed.), *Handbook of child psychology* (4th ed., Vol. 4). New York: Wiley. This is a detailed look at the development of peer relations by one of the leading experts in the field.

Lepper, M. R., & Gurtner, J. (1989). Children and computers: Approaching the twenty-first century. *American Psychologist, 44,* 170–178. This article provides an excellent, well-balanced treatment of the computer's role in children's development.

Liebert, R. M., & Spratkin, J. N. (1988). *The early window: Effects of television on children and youth* (3rd ed.). Elmsford, NY: Pergamon. This updated account of theory and research addresses the effects of television on children's development.

Rogers, C. R., & Sawyers, J. K. (1988). *Play in the lives of children.* Washington, DC: National Association for the Education of Young Children. This book includes a wealth of material on various types of play. Especially valuable are the examples of play in the lives of children.

CHAPTER

14

■

SCHOOLS

The Nature of Children's Schooling
    Do Schools Make a Difference?
    Functions of Children's Schools
    Schools' Changing Social Developmental Contexts
Early Childhood Education
    Child-Centered Kindergarten
    Developmentally Appropriate and Inappropriate
        Practices in the Education of Young Children
    Does It Matter If Children Attend Preschool
        Before Kindergarten?
    The Effects of Early Childhood Education
    Cultural Worlds of Development 14.1: Early
        Childhood Education in Japan
    Education for Disadvantaged Young Children
The Transition to Elementary School
Schools, Classrooms, and Teachers
    School Size and Classroom Size
    Classroom Structure and Climate
    Teachers
Social Class and Ethnicity in Schools
    Social Class
    Ethnicity
    Cultural Worlds of Development 14.2: The
        Jigsaw Classroom
The Nature of Adolescents' Schooling
    The Transition to Middle or Junior High School
    High School Dropouts
    Perspective on Child Development 14.1: Beyond
        the Zoo
    Cultural Worlds of Development 14.3: Helping
        Hispanic Youths Stay in School and Go to
        College
    Part-Time Work and School
Educating Children with Special Needs
    Handicapped Children
    Learning Disabilities
Summary
Key Terms
Suggested Readings

Amy began attending a Montessori school when she was 3 years old, over a year ago. Her mother was interested in a preschool program that involved academic instruction rather than play. Amy's mother talked to a number of mothers in her neighborhood, read extensively about different approaches to early childhood education, and visited eight preschool programs to observe a typical day and talk with teachers before making her decision about which school would be best for Amy.

Montessori schools are patterned after the educational philosophy of Maria Montessori, an Italian physician-turned-educator, who crafted a revolutionary approach to young children's education at the beginning of the twentieth century. Her work began with a group of mentally retarded children in Rome. She was successful in teaching them to read, write, and pass examinations designed for normal children. Some time later, she turned her attention to poor children from the slums of Rome and had similar success in teaching them. Her approach has since been adopted extensively in private nursery schools in the United States.

The **Montessori approach** *is a philosophy of education in which children are given considerable freedom and spontaneity in choosing activities. The teacher acts as a facilitator rather than a director of learning and allows the child to work independently to complete tasks in a prescribed manner. The teacher can offer assistance if asked by the child.* Some developmentalists favor the Montessori approach, but others believe it neglects children's social development. For example, although Montessori schools foster the development of children's independence and cognitive skills, the schools deemphasize verbal interaction between the teacher and child. Montessori's critics also argue that imaginative play and peer interaction are restricted. Later in this chapter, other preschool education programs will be described. Keep the Montessori approach in mind so that you can compare its focus with that of other approaches.

Our coverage of the role of schools in children's development examines the following questions: What is the nature of children's schooling? What is the nature of early childhood education? What is the transition to elementary school like? How do various characteristics of classrooms and teachers influence children's development? What roles do social class and ethnicity play in children's schooling? What is the nature of adolescents' schooling? How should children with special needs be educated? We will consider each of these questions in turn.

The Nature of Children's Schooling

Three questions arise pertaining to the nature of children's schooling: Do schools make a difference in child development? What is the function of schools? What is the nature of changing social developmental contexts in schools?

Do Schools Make a Difference?

It is justifiable to be concerned about the impact of schools on children and adolescents because of the degree of influence schools have in their lives. By the time students graduate from high school, they have accumulated more than 10,000 hours in the classroom. School influences are more powerful today than in past generations because more individuals are in school longer. For example, in 1900, 11.4 percent of all 14-to-17-year-olds were in school. Today, 94 percent of the children in that age group are in school.

Children spend many years in schools as members of a small society in which there are tasks to be accomplished; there are people to socialize and to be socialized by; and there are rules that define and limit behavior, feelings, and attitudes. Children's experiences in this society are likely to have a strong influence in such areas as identity development, belief in one's competence, images of life and career possibilities, social relationships, standards of right and wrong, and conceptions of how a social system beyond the family functions, not to mention the influence of schooling on learning and the development of knowledge.

It may seem odd even to question whether school has any effect, given the incredible number of hours children spend at school and the diversity of socialization activities taking place there. The issue has been raised, however, and evaluated from two points of view: (1) Is there a difference between the cognitive performances of those who have gone to school and those who have not? (2) Can schools override the negative effects of poverty? Concerning the first question, there is evidence that schooled children do perform differently than the unschooled on a variety of cognitive tasks (Cole & Cole, 1989; Farnham-Diggory, 1990; Rogoff, 1990; Wagner & Stevenson, 1982). However, we do not yet have a very complete picture of how schooling affects social development. Research on the second question, regarding poverty, has been extraordinarily controversial. The disagreement is rooted in the work of sociologists James Coleman and Christopher Jencks (Coleman & others, 1966; Jencks & others, 1972). In such investigations, the characteristics of schools are compared with family and economic factors as predictors of school achievement and success. Both Coleman and Jencks argue that the evidence shows that schools have little impact on the cognitive development of poverty-stricken students.

Coleman and Jencks are not without their critics, however, who fault them on a variety of issues, including the methods they used in collecting their data. One of the most serious criticisms leveled at them is that their analysis is too global, that it was conducted at the level of the school as a whole rather than at the more fine-grained level of everyday happenings in classrooms. In their study of achievement in school and after, the dissenters have compared the effectiveness of schools and classrooms and arrived at exactly the opposite conclusion from Coleman and Jencks' (Brookover & others, 1979; Edmonds, 1979; Klitgaard & Hall, 1975; Rutter & others, 1979). These researchers identified an important idea that we will carry through the remainder of this chapter: Academic and social patterns are intricately interwoven. In these studies, schools that produced high achievement in lower-income students were identified not only by particular types of curriculum and time involved in teaching, but by many features of the climate of the school such as the nature of the teachers' expectations and the patterns of interaction between teachers and students. In other words, various aspects of the school as a social system contributed to the achievement of students in the school.

The back-to-basics movement became very popular in children's education in the 1980s. The back-to-basics approach is still the dominant form of education, although a number of educators and child developmentalists believe that a more comprehensive approach that takes into consideration both social and cognitive development should characterize children's education.

In the first place God made idiots. This was for practice. Then he made school boards.

—Mark Twain

Additional research focusing on whether schools make a difference in a student's achievement suggests that this question cannot be appropriately addressed unless the extensive variation in schooling is considered. Schools vary even among similar neighborhoods serving similar populations, and they may differ on such dimensions as whether they are integrated or segregated, coed or single sex, parochial or secular, rural or urban, and large or small. Schools are also different in terms of their social climates, educational ideologies, and concepts of what constitutes the best way to promote the child's development.

Functions of Children's Schools

What should the functions of school be? In the 1980s, the back-to-basics movement gained momentum. The **back-to-basics movement** *stresses that the function of schools should be the rigorous training of intellectual skills through such subjects as English, math, and science.* Advocates of the back-to-basics movement point to the excessive fluff in elementary and secondary school curricula, with too many alternative subjects that do not give students a basic education in intellectual subjects. Back-to-basics advocates also believe that schools should be in the business of imparting knowledge to children and should not be as concerned about their social and emotional lives. Critics of the fluff in schools also sometimes argue that the school day should be longer and that the school year should be extended into the summer months.

The back-to-basics advocates want students to have more homework, more tests, and more discipline. They usually believe that children should be behind their desks and not roaming around the room. Teachers should be at the head of the classroom, drilling knowledge into children's minds. Much of the current back-to-basics emphasis is a reaction against the trend toward open education in the 1970s. Based on the British educational system, the open education approach allowed children to learn and develop at their own pace within a highly structured classroom. However, too many school systems that implemented open education in the United States thought that it meant tearing down classroom walls and letting children do whatever they wanted. Because open education was incorrectly applied in American schools, there was a strong backlash against it (Kantrowitz & Wingert, 1989).

Social and Personality Development

At the same time, parents, too, were demanding more from their elementary schools. By the mid-1980s, the majority of 3- and 4-year-old children were attending preschool, and their parents expected these classroom veterans to be reading by the second semester of kindergarten. However, the truth is that many 5-year-old children are not ready for reading—or most of the other demanding academic tasks that are more easily learned by older children—no matter how many years of school they have completed (Elkind, 1988). Thus, as we approach the end of the twentieth century, preschool and kindergarten programs are becoming downward extensions of traditional elementary school education. Many educators and psychologists also worry that, in the push for back-to-basics, more discipline, more homework, and more tests, elementary and secondary schools are becoming pressure cookers for students (Beane, 1990; Duke & Canady, 1991; Glasser, 1990; Perkinson, 1991).

The debate about the function of schools produces shifts of emphasis much like a swinging pendulum, moving toward basic skills and intellectual development at one point in time and toward options and comprehensive training for life in intellectual and social development at another, and so on back and forth (Cross, 1984). In the 1980s, the pendulum swung strongly in the direction of back-to-basics, but today a number of experts on education and child development are trying to push the pendulum toward a more comprehensive education that includes social as well as cognitive development. These experts also believe that the back-to-basics movement has increased the stress in children's lives and does not give adequate attention to individual variations among children.

What does education often do? It makes a straight-cut ditch of a free, meandering brook.

—Henry David Thoreau

Schools' Changing Social Developmental Contexts

Social contexts differ at the preschool, elementary, and secondary levels. The preschool setting is a protected environment, whose boundary is the classroom. In this limited social setting, preschool children interact with one or two teachers, usually female, who are powerful figures in the young child's life.

The preschool child also interacts with peers in a dyadic relationship or in small groups. Preschool children have little concept of the classroom as an organized social system, although they are learning how to make and maintain social contacts and communicate their needs. The preschool serves to modify some patterns of behavior developed through family experiences. Greater self-control may be required in the preschool than earlier in development.

The classroom is still the major context for the elementary school child, although it is more likely to be experienced as a social unit than is the preschool classroom. The network of social expression also is more complex. Teachers and peers have a prominent influence on children during the elementary school years. The teacher symbolizes authority, which establishes the climate of the classroom, the conditions of social interaction, and the nature of group functioning. Peer groups become more salient, with increased interest in friendship, belonging, and status. Peer groups also become learning communities in which social roles and standards related to work and achievement are formed.

As children move into middle or junior high schools, the school environment increases in scope and complexity. The social field is the school as a whole rather than the classroom. Adolescents interact socially with many different teachers and peers from a range of social and ethnic backgrounds. Students are often exposed to a greater mix of male and female teachers, and their social behavior is heavily weighted toward peers, extracurricular activities, clubs, and the community. The student in secondary school is usually aware of the school as a social system and may be motivated to conform and adapt to the system or challenge it (Minuchin & Shapiro, 1983).

Early Childhood Education

With an increased understanding of how young children develop and learn has come a greater emphasis on young children's education. We will explore the following questions about early childhood education: What is child-centered kindergarten? What are developmentally appropriate and inappropriate practices in programs for young children? Does it matter if children attend preschool before kindergarten? What are the effects of early childhood education? What is the nature of education for disadvantaged young children?

Child-Centered Kindergarten

Kindergarten programs vary a great deal. The Montessori approach described at the beginning of the chapter is one variation. Some approaches place more emphasis on young children's social development, others on their cognitive development. Some experts on early childhood education believe that the curricula of too many of today's kindergarten and preschool programs place too much emphasis on achievement and success, putting pressure on young children too early in their development (Bredekamp & Shepard, 1989; Burts & others, in press; Charlesworth, 1989; Elkind, 1987, 1988; Moyer, Egertson, & Isenberg, 1987). Placing such heavy emphasis on success is not what kindergartens were originally intended to do. In the 1840s, Friedrich Froebel's concern for high-quality education for young children led to the founding of kindergarten, literally "a garden for children." The founder of kindergarten understood that, like growing plants, children require careful nurturing. Unfortunately, too many of today's kindergartens have forgotten the importance of careful nurturing for our nation's young children.

Social and Personality Development

In a child-centered kindergarten, education involves the whole child and includes firsthand experiences with people and materials, such as the art experience of these children in an Oakland, California, kindergarten.

In **child-centered kindergarten,** *education involves the whole child and includes concern for the child's physical, cognitive, and social development. Instruction is organized around the child's needs, interests, and learning styles. The process of learning, rather than the finished product, is emphasized.* Each child follows a unique developmental pattern, and young children learn best through firsthand experiences with people and materials, and play is extremely important in the child's total development. *Experimenting, exploring, discovering, trying out, restructuring, speaking,* and *listening* are all words that describe excellent kindergarten programs. Such programs are closely attuned to the developmental status of 4- and 5-year-old children. They are based on a state of *being,* not on a state of *becoming* (Ballenger, 1983).

Developmentally Appropriate and Inappropriate Practices in the Education of Young Children

It is time for number games in a kindergarten class at the Greenbrook School in South Brunswick, New Jersey. With little prodding from the teacher, twenty-three 5- and 6-year-old children pick up geometric puzzles, playing cards, and counting equipment from the shelves lining the room. At one round table, some young children fit together brightly colored shapes. One girl forms a hexagon out of triangles. Other children gather around her to count how many parts are needed to make the whole. After about half an hour, the children prepare for story time. They put away their counting equipment and sit in a circle around one young girl, who holds up a giant book about a character named Mrs. Wishywashy, who insists on giving farm animals a bath. The children recite the whimsical lines, clearly enjoying one of their favorite stories. The hallway outside the kindergarten is lined with drawings depicting the children's interpretations of the book. After the first reading, volunteers act out various parts of the book. There is not one bored face in the room (Kantrowitz & Wingert, 1989).

This is not reading, writing, and arithmetic the way most people remember it. A growing number of educators and psychologists believe that preschool and young elementary school children learn best through active,

Children have to be educated, but they also have to be left to educate themselves.

—Ernest Dimnet

hands-on teaching methods such as games and dramatic play. They know that children develop at varying rates and that schools need to allow for these individual differences. They also believe that schools should focus on improving children's social development as well as their cognitive development. Educators refer to this type of schooling as **developmentally appropriate practice,** *which is education based on knowledge of the typical development of children within an age span (age appropriateness) as well as the uniqueness of the child (individual appropriateness).* Developmentally appropriate practice contrasts with developmentally inappropriate practice, which ignores the concrete, hands-on approach to learning. Direct teaching largely through abstract, paper-and-pencil activities presented to large groups of young children is believed to be developmentally inappropriate.

One of the most comprehensive documents addressing the issue of developmentally appropriate practice in early childhood programs is the position statement by the National Association for the Education of Young Children (NAEYC) (Bredekamp, 1987; NAEYC, 1991). This document represents the expertise of many of the foremost experts in the field of early childhood education. By turning to table 14.1, you can examine some of the NAEYC recommendations for developmentally appropriate practice.

A special worry of early childhood educators is that the back-to-basics movement and its emphasis on academic rigor, which has characterized recent educational reform, is filtering down to kindergarten. Another worry is that many parents want their children to go to school earlier than kindergarten for the purpose of getting a "head start" in achievement.

Does It Matter If Children Attend Preschool Before Kindergarten?

According to child developmental education expert David Elkind (1987, 1988), parents who are exceptionally competent and dedicated and who have both the time and the energy can provide the basic ingredients of early childhood education in their home. If parents have the competence and resources to provide young children with a variety of learning experiences and exposure to other children and adults (possibly through neighborhood play groups), along with opportunities for extensive play, then home schooling may sufficiently educate young children. However, if parents do not have the commitment, time, energy, and resources to provide young children with an environment that approximates a good early childhood education program, then it *does* matter whether a child attends preschool. In this case, the issue is not whether preschool is important, but whether home schooling can duplicate what a competent preschool program can offer.

We should always keep in mind the unfortunate idea of early childhood education as an early start to ensure the participants will finish early or on top in an educational race. Elkind (1988) points out that perhaps the choice of the phrase "head start" for the education of disadvantaged children was a mistake. "Head Start" does not imply a race. Not surprisingly, when middle-class parents heard that low-income children were getting a "head start," they wanted a "head start" for their own young children. In some instances, starting children in formal academic training too early can produce more harm than good. In Denmark, where reading instruction follows a language experience approach and formal instruction is delayed until the age of 7, illiteracy is virtually nonexistent. By contrast, in France, where state-mandated formal instruction in reading begins at age 5, 30 percent of the children have reading problems. Education should not be stressful for young children. Early childhood education should not be solely an academic prep school.

TABLE 14.1

Developmentally Appropriate and Inappropriate Practice in Early Childhood Education: Recommendations by the National Association for the Education of Young Children

Component	Appropriate practice	Inappropriate practice
Curriculum goals	Experiences are provided in all developmental areas—physical, cognitive, social, and emotional. Individual differences are expected, accepted, and used to design appropriate activities. Interactions and activities are designed to develop children's self-esteem and positive feelings toward learning.	Experiences are narrowly focused on cognitive development without recognition that all areas of children's development are interrelated. Children are only evaluated against group norms and all are expected to perform the same tasks and achieve the same narrowly defined skills. Children's worth is measured by how well they conform to rigid expectations and perform on standardized tests.
Teaching strategies	Teachers prepare the environment for children to learn through active exploration and interaction with adults, other children, and materials. Children select many of their own activities from among a variety the teacher prepares. Children are expected to be mentally and physically active. Children work individually or in small, informal groups most of the time. Children are provided with concrete learning activities that include materials relevant to their own life experiences. Teachers move among groups and individuals to facilitate children's involvement with materials by asking questions, offering suggestions, or adding more complex materials or ideas to a situation. Teachers accept that there is often more than one right answer or one right way to do something. Teachers recognize that children learn from self-directed problem solving and experimentation.	Teachers use highly structured, teacher-directed lessons almost exclusively. The teacher directs all activity, deciding what children will do and when. Children are expected to sit down, be quiet, and listen, or do paper-and-pencil tasks for long periods of time. A major portion of time is spent passively sitting, watching, and listening. Large group, teacher-directed instruction is used most of the time. Workbooks, ditto sheets, flashcards, and other similarly structured abstract materials dominate the curriculum. Teachers dominate the environment by talking to the whole group most of the time and telling children what to do. Children are expected to respond correctly with one right answer. Rote memorization and drill are emphasized.

T A B L E   1 4 . 1
Continued

Component	Appropriate practice	Inappropriate practice
Guidance of socioemotional development	Teachers enhance children's self-control by using positive guidance techniques such as modeling and encouraging expected behavior, redirecting children to a more acceptable activity, and setting clear limits. Children are provided many opportunities to develop social skills such as cooperating, helping, negotiating, and talking with the person involved to solve interpersonal problems.	Teachers spend considerable time enforcing rules, punishing unacceptable behavior, demeaning children who misbehave, making children sit and be quiet, or refereeing disagreements. Children work individually at desks and tables most of the time or listen to teacher directions to the total group.
Language development and literacy	Children are provided many opportunities to see how reading and writing are useful before they are instructed in letter names, sounds, and word identification. Basic skills develop when they are meaningful to children. An abundance of these activities is provided to develop language and literacy: listening to and reading stories and poems, taking field trips, dictating stories, participating in dramatic play, talking informally with other children and adults, and experimenting with writing.	Reading and writing instruction stresses isolated skill development such as recognizing single letters, reading the alphabet, singing the alphabet song, coloring within predefined lines, or being instructed in correct formation of letters on a printed line.
Cognitive development	Children develop an understanding of concepts about themselves, others, and the world around them through observing, interacting with people and real objects, and seeking solutions to concrete problems. Learning about math, science, social studies, health, and other content areas is integrated through meaningful activities.	Instruction stresses isolated skill development through memorization. Children's cognitive development is seen as fragmented in such content areas as math or science, and times are set aside for each of these.

TABLE 14.1
Continued

Component	Appropriate practice	Inappropriate practice
Physical development	Children have daily opportunities to use large muscles, including running, jumping, and balancing. Outdoor activity is planned daily so children can freely express themselves. Children have daily opportunities to develop small muscle skills through play activities such as puzzles, painting, and cutting.	Opportunity for large muscle activity is limited. Outdoor time is limited because it is viewed as interfering with instructional time, rather than an integral part of children's learning environment. Small motor activity is limited to writing with pencils, coloring predrawn forms, or engaging in similar structured lessons.
Aesthetic development	Children have daily opportunities for aesthetic expression and appreciation through art and music. A variety of art media is available.	Art and music are given limited attention. Art consists of coloring predrawn forms or following adult-prescribed directions.
Motivation	Children's natural curiosity and desire to make sense of their world are used to motivate them to become involved in learning.	Children are required to participate in all activities to obtain the teacher's approval, to obtain extrinsic rewards such as stickers or privileges, or to avoid punishment.

Note: Other areas in which the NAEYC has made recommendations for appropriate practice are parent-teacher relations, the assessment of children, program entry, teacher qualifications, and staffing.

Preschool is rapidly becoming a norm in early childhood education. Twenty-three states already have legislation pending to provide schooling for 4-year-old children, and there already are many private preschool programs. The increase in public preschools underscores the growing belief that early childhood education should be a legitimate component of public education. There are dangers, though. According to Elkind (1988), early childhood education is not well understood by many high-level educational administrators. The danger is that public preschool education for 4-year-old children will become little more than a downward extension of traditional elementary education. This is already occurring in preschool programs in which testing, workbooks, and group drill are imposed on 4- and 5-year-old children.

Elkind believes that early childhood education should become a part of public education but on its own terms. Early childhood education has its own curriculum, its own methods of evaluation and classroom management, and its own teacher-training programs. There is some overlap of early childhood curricula, evaluation, classroom management, and teacher training with the upper levels of schooling, but they certainly are not identical.

The little ones leaped, and shouted, and Laugh'd and all the hills echoed.

—William Blake

■ *Critical Thinking*
Most of you went to a preschool or kindergarten. Can you remember what it was like? In what ways could the kindergarten you attended have been improved? How can we make our nation's preschool education programs better?

Researchers are already beginning to document some of the stress that increased academic pressure can bring to young children (Burts, Charlesworth, & Fleege, 1991; Burts & others, in press; Charlesworth & others, in press). In one recent investigation, Diane Burts and her colleagues (1989) compared developmentally appropriate instructional practices with developmentally inappropriate techniques, observing the frequencies of stress behaviors in young children. The children in the developmentally inappropriate classrooms exhibited more stress behaviors than the children in the developmentally appropriate classrooms. In another recent investigation, children in a high academically oriented early childhood education program were compared with children in a low academically oriented early childhood education program (Hirsch-Pasek & others, 1989). No benefits appeared for the children in the high academically oriented early childhood education program, and there were some possible harmful effects: higher test anxiety, less creativity, and a less positive attitude toward school.

One of the concerns of Americans is that our school children fare poorly when their achievement test scores in math and science are compared with the test scores of school children from many other industrialized nations, especially such Asian nations as Japan and China (McKnight & others, 1987). Many Americans attribute higher achievement scores to a rigid system that sets young children in a lock-step march from cradle to college. In fact, the early years of Japanese schooling are anything but a boot camp. To read further about the nature of early childhood education in Japan, turn to Cultural Worlds of Development 14.1.

The Effects of Early Childhood Education

Because kindergarten and preschool programs are diverse, it is difficult to make overall conclusions about their effects on children's development. Nonetheless, in one review of early childhood education's influence (Clarke-Stewart & Fein, 1983), it was concluded that children who attend preschool or kindergarten:

- Interact more with peers, both positively and negatively
- Are less cooperative with and responsive to adults than home-reared children
- Are more socially competent and mature in that they are more confident, extraverted, assertive, self-sufficient, independent, verbally expressive, knowledgeable about the social world, comfortable in social and stressful circumstances, and better adjusted when they go to school (exhibiting more task persistence, leadership, and goal direction, for example)
- Are less socially competent in that they are less polite, less compliant to teacher demands, louder, and more aggressive and bossy, especially if the school or family supports such behavior

In sum, early childhood education generally has a positive effect on children's development, since the behaviors just mentioned—although at times negative—seem to be in the direction of developmental maturity in that they increase as the child ages through the preschool years.

Social and Personality Development

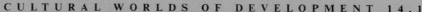
Early Childhood Education in Japan

In the midst of low academic achievement by American children, many Americans are turning to Japan, a country of high academic achievement and economic success, for possible answers. However, the answers being provided by Japanese preschools are not the ones Americans expected to find. In most Japanese preschools, there is surprisingly little emphasis on academic instruction. In one recent investigation, 300 Japanese and 210 American preschool teachers, child development specialists, and parents were asked about various aspects of early childhood education (Tobin, Wu, & Davidson, 1989). Only 2 percent of the Japanese respondents listed "to give children a good start academically" as one of their top three reasons for a society to have preschools. In contrast, over half the American respondents chose this as one of the top three reasons. To prepare children for successful careers in first grade and beyond, Japanese schools do not teach reading, writing, and mathematics, but more fundamental pre-academic skills such as persistence, concentration, and the ability to function as a member of a group. The vast majority of young Japanese children are taught to read at home by their parents.

In a recent comparison of Japanese and American preschool education, 61 percent of the Japanese respondents chose "providing children with a group experience" as the single most important reason for a society to have preschools (Tobin, Wu, & Davidson, 1989). Ninety-one percent of the Japanese made this one of their top three choices. Americans did not give group experience as high a priority, although 62 percent of the more individually oriented Americans listed group experience as one of their top three choices. An emphasis on the importance of the group appears not only in Japanese early childhood education, but also in elementary school education.

Lessons in living and working together grow naturally out of the Japanese culture. In many Japanese kindergartens, children wear the same type of uniform, including caps that are of different colors to indicate the classrooms to which they belong. They keep identical sets of equipment in identical drawers and shelves. This is not intended to turn the young children into robots, as some Americans have observed, but to impress on them that other people just like themselves have needs and desires that are equally important (Hendry, 1986).

As in America, there is diversity in Japanese early childhood education. Some Japanese kindergartens have specific aims such as early musical training or the practice of Montessori skills (Hendry, 1986). In large cities, some kindergartens are attached to universities, where there also are elementary and secondary schools. Some parents believe that if their young children attend the university-based programs, they will increase their chances of eventually being admitted to top-rated schools and universities. At the same time, the overintellectualization of some Japanese kindergartens has led to the introduction of free play as a specialty in several, more progressive programs.

Two Japanese preschool girls are the last to arrive at their kindergarten. In Japanese kindergartens, leaving one's shoes outside the door is common practice. Notice the identical uniforms worn by the Japanese kindergarten girls.

In Japan, teaching cooperation and group experiences is viewed as an extremely important goal of early childhood education.

Education for Disadvantaged Young Children

For many years, children from low-income families did not receive any education before they entered the first grade. In the 1960s, an effort was made to break the cycle of poverty and poor education for young children in the United States through compensatory education. **Project Head Start** *is a compensatory education program designed to give children from low-income families the opportunity to acquire the skills and experiences important for success in school.* Project Head Start began in the summer of 1965, funded by the Economic Opportunity Act, and it continues to serve disadvantaged children.

Project Head Start consists of many different types of preschool programs in different parts of the country. Initially, little effort was made to find out whether some programs worked better than others, but it became apparent that some programs did work better than others. **Project Follow Through** *was implemented in 1967 as an adjunct to Project Head Start. In Project Follow Through, different types of educational programs were devised to determine which were the most effective. In the Follow Through programs, the enriched planned variation was carried through the first few years of elementary school.* Were some Follow Through programs more effective than others? Many of the variations were able to produce the desired effects on children. For example, children in academically oriented, direct-instruction approaches did better on achievement tests and were more persistent on tasks than were children in the other approaches. Children in affective education approaches were absent from school less often and showed more independence than children in other approaches. Thus, Project Follow Through was important in demonstrating that variation in early childhood education does have significant effects in a wide range of social and cognitive areas (Stallings, 1975).

The effects of early childhood compensatory education continue to be studied, and recent evaluations support its positive influence on both the cognitive and social worlds of disadvantaged young children (Haskins, 1989; Kagan, 1988a; Lee, Brooks-Gunn, & Schnur, 1988; Raver & Zigler, 1991;

These preschool children are attending a Head Start program, a national effort to provide children from low-income families the opportunity to experience an enriched environment.

Schweinhart, 1991). Of special interest are the long-term effects such intervention might produce. Model preschool programs lead to lower rates of placement in special education, of dropping out of school, of grade retention, of delinquency, and of the use of welfare programs. Such programs might also lead to higher rates of high school graduation and employment. For every dollar invested in high-quality, model preschool programs, taxpayers receive about $1.50 in return by the time the participants reach the age of 20 (Darlington, 1991; Haskins, 1989). The benefits include savings on public school education (such as special-education services), tax payments on additional earnings, reduced welfare payments, and savings in juvenile justice system costs. Predicted benefits over a lifetime are much greater to the taxpayer, a return of $5.73 on every dollar invested.

One long-term investigation of early childhood education was conducted by Irving Lazar, Richard Darlington, and their colleagues (1982). They pooled their resources into what they called a consortium for longitudinal studies, developed to share information about the long-term effects of preschool programs so that better designs and methods could be created. At the time the data from 11 different early education studies were analyzed together, the children ranged in age from 9 to 19 years. The early education models varied substantially, but all were carefully planned and executed by experts in early childhood education. Outcome measures included indicators of school competence (such as special education and grade retention), abilities (as measured by standardized intelligence and achievement tests), attitudes and values, and impact on the family. The results indicated substantial benefits of competent preschool education with low-income children on all four dimensions investigated. In sum, there is ample evidence that well-designed and well-implemented early childhood education programs with low-income children are successful (Haskins, 1989; Kagan, 1988a).

At this point, we have discussed a number of ideas about children's education and early childhood education. A summary of these ideas is presented in concept table 14.1. Next, we will turn our attention to the transition to elementary school.

The Transition to Elementary School

For most children, entering the first grade signals a change from being a "homechild" to being a "schoolchild"—new roles and obligations are being experienced. Children take up a new role (being a student), interact and develop relationships with new significant others, adopt new reference groups, and develop new standards by which to judge themselves. School provides children with a rich source of new ideas to shape their sense of self.

A special concern about children's early school experiences is emerging. Evidence is mounting that early schooling proceeds mainly on the basis of negative feedback. For example, children's self-esteem in the latter part of elementary school is lower than it is in the earlier part, and older children rate themselves as less smart, less good, and less hard-working than do younger ones (Blumenfeld & others, 1981). In one recent investigation, the first year of school was identified as a period of considerable importance in shaping achievement, especially for ethnic minority children (Alexander & Entwisle, 1988). Black and White children began school with similar achievement test scores, but, by the end of the first year, Black children's performance lagged noticeably behind that of the White children, and the gap widened over the second year of schooling. The grades that the teachers gave to Black children

Knowledge which is acquired under compulsion obtains no hold on the mind.

—Plato

The Nature of Children's Schooling and Early Childhood Education

Concept	Processes/related ideas	Characteristics/description
The nature of children's schooling	Do schools make a difference?	Some sociologists have argued that schools have little impact on children's development, but, when researchers have conducted more precise, observational studies of what goes on in schools and classrooms, the effects of schooling have become more apparent.
	Functions of children's schools	In the 1980s, the back-to-basics movement gained momentum. The back-to-basics movement emphasizes rigorous academic training. This movement especially opposed the misapplied open education orientation that became popular in the 1970s. A special worry is that early childhood education is becoming a downward extension of back-to-basics elementary and secondary education. Many experts on education and child development believe the back-to-basics movement has increased the stress in children's lives and does not adequately address individual variation in children. They also believe education should be more comprehensive, focusing on social as well as cognitive development.
	Schools' changing social developmental contexts	Social contexts differ at the preschool, elementary, and secondary levels, becoming much more expansive for adolescents.
Early childhood education	Child-centered kindergarten	It involves education of the whole child, with emphasis on individual variation, the process of learning, and the importance of play in development.
	Developmentally appropriate and inappropriate practices in the education of young children	Developmentally appropriate practice is based on knowledge of the typical development of children within an age span (age appropriateness) as well as the uniqueness of the child (individual appropriateness). Developmentally appropriate practice contrasts with developmentally inappropriate practice, which ignores the concrete, hands-on approach to learning. Direct teaching largely through abstract, paper-and-pencil activities presented to large groups of young children is believed to be developmentally inappropriate. The National Association for the Education of Young Children has been a strong proponent of developmentally appropriate practice and has developed extensive recommendations for its implementation.
	Does it matter if children attend preschool before kindergarten?	Parents can educate their young children just as effectively as schools can. However, many parents do not have the commitment, time, energy, and resources needed to provide young children with an environment that approaches a competent early childhood education program. Too often, parents see education as a race and preschool as a chance to get ahead in the race. However, education is not a race and it should not be stressful for young children. Public preschools are appearing in many states. A concern is that they should not become merely simple versions of elementary school. Early childhood education has some issues that overlap with upper levels of schooling, but in many ways the agenda of early childhood education is different.
	How does early childhood education influence children's development?	It is difficult to evaluate, but the effects overall seem to be positive. However, outcome measures reveal areas in which social competence is more positive, others in which it is less competent.
	Education for disadvantaged young children	Compensatory education has tried to break through the poverty cycle with such programs as Head Start and Follow Through. Long-term studies reveal that model preschool programs have positive effects on development.

in the first two grades of school also were lower than those they gave to White children.

In school, as well as out of school, children's learning, like children's development, is *integrated* (NAEYC, 1988). One of the main pressures on elementary teachers has been the need to "cover the curriculum." Frequently, teachers have tried to do so by tightly scheduling discrete time segments for each subject. This approach ignores the fact that children often do not need to distinguish learning by subject area. For example, they advance their knowledge of reading and writing when they work on social studies projects; they learn mathematical concepts through music and physical education (Katz & Chard, 1989; Van Deusen-Henkel & Argondizza, 1987). A curriculum can be facilitated by providing learning areas in which children plan and select their activities. For example, the classroom may include a fully equipped publishing center, complete with materials for writing, illustrating, typing, and binding student-made books; a science area with animals and plants for observation and books to study; and other similar areas (Van Deusen-Henkel & Argondizza, 1987). In this type of classroom, children learn reading as they discover information about science; they learn writing as they work together on interesting projects. Such classrooms also provide opportunities for spontaneous play, recognizing that elementary school children continue to learn in all areas through unstructured play, either alone or with other children.

Education experts Lillian Katz and Sylvia Chard (1989) recently described two elementary school classrooms. In one, children spent an entire morning making identical pictures of traffic lights. The teacher made no attempt to get the children to relate the pictures to anything else the class was doing. In the other class, children were investigating a school bus. They wrote to the district and asked if they could have a bus parked at their school for a few days. They studied the bus, discovered the functions of its parts, and discussed traffic rules. Then, in the classroom, they built their own bus out of cardboard. The children had fun, but they also practiced writing, problem solving, and even some arithmetic. When the class had their parents' night, the teacher was ready with reports on how each child was doing. However, all the parents wanted to see was the bus because their children had been coming home and talking about it for weeks. Many contemporary education experts believe that this is the kind of education all children deserve. That is, they believe that children should be taught through concrete, hands-on experience.

Children in the early elementary school years learn best through concrete, hands-on experience. For example, 6-year-olds can easily understand addition and subtraction if they have actual objects to count instead of a series of numbers written on a chalkboard. For the child shown here, the numbers don't seem so abstract and forbidding when he counts colored balls.

■ *Critical Thinking*
Why does early elementary school involve so much negative feedback? What aspects of our culture and the nature of education are responsible?

Schools, Classrooms, and Teachers

Schools, classrooms, and teachers vary on many dimensions, among them school size and classroom size, classroom structure and climate, and teacher traits. We will consider each of these in turn.

School Size and Classroom Size

A number of factors led to the increased size of schools in the United States: increasing urban enrollments, decreasing budgets, and an educational rationale of increased academic stimulation in consolidated institutions (Conant, 1959; Minuchin & Shapiro, 1983). However, is bigger really better? No systematic relation between school size and academic achievement has been found, but more prosocial and possibly less antisocial behavior take place in small schools (Rutter & others, 1979). For secondary schools, the upper limit has been set at various levels between 500 and 1,000 students (Garbarino, 1980b).

Large schools may not provide a personalized climate that allows for an effective system of social control. Students may feel alienated and not take responsibility for their conduct. This may be especially true for unsuccessful students who do not identify with their school and who become members of oppositional peer groups. The responsiveness of the school may mediate the impact of school size on adolescent behavior. For example, in one investigation, low responsive schools (that is, schools that offer few rewards for desirable behavior) had higher crime rates than did high responsive schools (McPartland & McDill, 1976). Even though school responsiveness may mediate conduct, small schools may be more flexible and responsive than larger schools.

Besides the belief that smaller schools provide children and adolescents with a better education, there also is a belief that smaller classes are better than larger classes. Traditional schools in the United States have about 30 to 35 students. An analysis of a large number of investigations revealed that, as class size increases, achievement decreases (Glass & Smith, 1978). The researchers concluded that a pupil who would score at about the 63rd percentile on a national test when taught individually would score at about the 37th percentile when taught in a class of 40 students. They also concluded that being taught in a class of 20 students rather than in a class of 40 students is an advantage of about 10 percentile points on national achievement tests. These researchers also found that the greatest gains in achievement occurred among students who were taught in classes of 15 students or less. In classes of 20 to 40 students, class size had a less dramatic influence on students' achievement. Although this research has been criticized on methodological grounds, other researchers have reanalyzed the data using different techniques and have arrived at the same conclusions (Hedges & Stock, 1983).

Unfortunately, to maximize each child's learning potential, classes must be so small that few schools can afford to staff and house them (Klein, 1985; Slavin, 1989a). Although a class size of 15 students or less is not feasible for all subjects, one alternative is to allocate a larger portion of resources to the grade levels or subjects that seem the most critical. For example, some schools are beginning to reduce class size in core academic subjects, such as math, English, and science, while increasing class size in elective subjects.

Classroom Structure and Climate

The most widely debated issue in classroom structure and climate in recent years has focused on open versus traditional classrooms. The open versus traditional classroom concept is multidimensional. Open classrooms, or open schools, have such characteristics as the following:

- Free choice by students of activities they will participate in
- Space flexibility
- Varied, enriched learning materials
- Emphasis on individual and small-group instruction
- The teacher is more a facilitator than a director of learning
- Students learn to assume responsibility for their learning
- Multi-age grouping of children
- Team teaching
- Classrooms without walls in which the physical nature of the school is more open

Overall, researchers have found that open classrooms are associated with lower language achievement but improved attitudes toward school (Giaconia & Hedges, 1982).

Beyond the overall effects of open versus traditional classrooms, it is important to evaluate how specific dimensions of open classrooms are related to specific dimensions of a child's development. In this regard, researchers have found that individualized instruction (adjusting rate, methods, materials, small-group methods) and the role of the child (the degree of activity in learning) are associated with positive effects on the child's self-concept (Giaconia & Hedges, 1982).

The characteristics of the child also need to be considered when evaluating the effects of classroom structure and climate (Linney & Seidman, 1989). For example, some children may benefit from structure more than others. **Aptitude-treatment interaction (ATI)** *stresses the importance of both children's aptitudes or characteristics and the treatments or experiences they are given in classrooms. Aptitude refers to such characteristics as the academic potential and personality characteristics on which students differ; treatment refers to educational techniques, such as structured versus flexible classrooms* (Cronbach & Snow, 1977). Researchers have found that children's achievement level (aptitude) interacts with classroom structure (treatment) to produce the best learning (Peterson, 1977). For example, students who are highly achievement oriented usually do well in a flexible classroom and enjoy it; low-achievement-oriented students usually fare worse and dislike such flexibility. The reverse often appears in structured classrooms.

Teachers

Almost everyone's life is affected in one way or another by teachers. You were probably influenced by teachers as you grew up; you may become a teacher yourself or work with teachers through counseling or psychological services; and you may one day have children whose education will be guided by many teachers through the years. You can probably remember several of your teachers vividly. Perhaps one never smiled, another required you to memorize everything in sight, and yet another always appeared happy and vibrant and encouraged verbal interaction. Psychologists and educators have tried to create a profile of a good teacher's personality traits, but the complexity of personality, education, learning, and individual differences makes the task difficult (Sadker & Sadker, 1991). Nonetheless, some teacher traits are associated with positive student outcomes more than others; enthusiasm, ability to plan, poise, adaptability, warmth, flexibility, and awareness of individual differences are a few (Gage, 1965).

Erik Erikson (1968) believes that good teachers should be able to produce a sense of industry, rather than inferiority, in their students. Good teachers are trusted and respected by the community and know how to alternate work and play, study and games, says Erikson. They know how to recognize special efforts and to encourage special abilities. They also know how to create a setting in which children feel good about themselves and how to handle children to whom school is not important. In Erikson's (1968) words, children should be "mildly but firmly coerced into the adventure of finding out that one can learn to accomplish things which one would never have thought of by oneself" (p. 127).

The whole art of teaching is only the art of awakening the natural curiosity of young minds.

—Anatole France

Social Class and Ethnicity in Schools

Sometimes it seems as though the major function of schools has been to train children to contribute to a middle-class society. Politicians who vote on school funding have been from middle-class or elite backgrounds, school board members have often been from middle-class backgrounds, and principals and teachers also have had middle-class upbringing. Critics argue that schools have not done a good job of educating lower-class and ethnic minority children to overcome the barriers that block the enhancement of their position (Glasser, 1990; Huang & Gibbs, 1989).

Social Class

In *Dark Ghetto,* Kenneth Clark (1965) described the ways in which lower- and middle-class children are treated differently in school. According to Clark's observations, teachers in middle-class schools spend more time teaching students and evaluate students' work more than twice as much as teachers in low-income schools. He observed that teachers in low-income schools made three times as many negative comments to students as teachers did in middle-class schools, who made more positive than negative comments to students. The following observations vividly describe a school in a large urban slum area:

> It is 2 P.M., beginning of the sixth-period class, and Warren Benson, a young teacher, looks around the room. Eight students are present out of thirty. "Where is everybody?" he demands. "They don't like your class," a girl volunteers. Three girls saunter in. Cora, who is playing a cassette recorder, bumps over to her desk in time with the music. She lowers the volume. "Don't mark us down late," she shouts. "We was right here."
> . . . Here you find students from poverty homes, students who can't read, students with drug problems, students wanting to drop out. . . .

Teachers' expectations for children from low-income families are lower than for children from middle-income families (Entwisle, 1990). A teacher who knows that a child comes from a lower-class background may spend less time trying to help the child solve a problem and may anticipate that the child will get into trouble. The teacher may believe that the parents in low-income families are not interested in helping the child, so she may make fewer efforts to communicate with them. However, there is evidence that teachers of lower-class origin may have different attitudes toward lower-class students than teachers of middle-class origin (Gottlieb, 1966). Perhaps because they have experienced many inequities themselves, teachers of lower-class origin may be more empathetic to the problems that lower-class children encounter. When asked to list the most outstanding characteristics of their lower-class students, middle-class teachers checked lazy, rebellious, and fun-loving; lower-class teachers checked happy, cooperative, energetic, and ambitious. The teachers with lower-class backgrounds perceived the lower-class children's behaviors as adaptive; the middle-class teachers viewed the same behaviors as falling short of middle-class standards.

Ethnicity

Children from lower-class backgrounds are not the only students who have difficulties in school; so have children from various ethnic backgrounds (Tharp, 1989). In his famous speech "I Have a Dream," Martin Luther King, Jr., said, "I have a dream that my four little children will one day live in a nation where

they will not be judged by the color of their skin but by the content of their character." In most American schools, Blacks, Mexicans, Puerto Ricans, Native Americans, Japanese, and Asian Indians are minorities, and many teachers have been ignorant of the different cultural meanings non-Anglo children have learned in their community (Huang & Gibbs, 1989). The social and academic development of children from minority groups depends on teacher expectations; the teacher's experience in working with children from different backgrounds; the curriculum; the presence of role models in the schools for minority students; the quality of relations between school personnel and parents from different ethnic, economic, and educational backgrounds; and the relations between the school and the community (Minuchin & Shapiro, 1983).

American anthropologist John Ogbu (1974, 1986, 1989) proposed a controversial view that ethnic minority children are placed in a position of subordination and exploitation in the American educational system. He believes that ethnic minority children, especially Black and Hispanic Americans, have inferior educational opportunities, are exposed to teachers and administrators who have low academic expectations for them, and encounter negative stereotypes about ethnic minority groups. Ogbu states that ethnic minority opposition to the middle-class, White educational system stems from a lack of trust because of years of discrimination and oppression. Says Ogbu, it makes little sense to do well academically if occupational opportunities are often closed to ethnic minority young adults.

Some critics argue that one of the main functions of schools has been to train children to contribute to a middle-class, White society. These critics argue that schools have not done a competent job of educating low-income, ethnic minority children.

Completing high school, or even college, does not always bring the same job opportunities for many ethnic minority youth as for White youth (Entwisle, 1990). In terms of earnings and employment rates, Black American high school graduates do not do as well as their White counterparts. Giving up in school because of a perceived lack of reward involving inadequate job opportunities characterizes many Hispanic American youths as well (Gibson & Ogbu, 1991).

According to American educational psychologist Margaret Beale Spencer and sociologist Sanford Dornbusch (1990), a form of institutional racism prevails in many American schools. That is, well-meaning teachers, acting out of misguided liberalism, often fail to challenge ethnic minority students. Knowing the handicaps these children face, some teachers accept a low level of performance from them, substituting warmth and affection for academic challenge and high standards of performance. Ethnic minority students, like their White counterparts, learn best when teachers combine warmth with challenging standards.

Do teachers have lower academic expectations for minority children? The evidence indicates that teachers look for and reward achievement-oriented behavior in White students more often than in Black students (Scott-Jones & Clark, 1986). When teachers praise Black students for their academic performance, the praise is often qualified: "This is a good paper. It is better than yesterday's." Also, teachers have been found to criticize gifted Black students more than gifted White students, possibly because they do not expect intellectual competence in Black students (Baron, Tom, & Cooper, 1985).

One of the largest efforts to study ethnicity in schools has focused on desegregation through busing (Bell, 1980). Desegregation attempts to improve the proportions of minority-group and White student populations in schools. Efforts to improve this ratio have often involved busing students, usually minority-group students, from their home neighborhoods to more distant schools. The underlying belief is that bringing different groups together will reduce stereotyped attitudes and improve intergroup relations. However, busing tells us nothing about what goes on inside the school once students get there. Minority-group adolescents bused to a predominantly White school are often resegregated in the classroom through seating patterns, ability grouping, and tracking systems. Overall, the findings pertaining to desegregation through busing have shown dismal results (Minuchin & Shapiro, 1983).

Improvements in interracial relations among children in schools depend on what happens after students arrive at the school. In one comprehensive national investigation of factors that contribute to positive interracial relations, more than 5,000 fifth-grade students and more than 400 tenth-grade students were evaluated (Forehand, Ragosta, & Rock, 1976). Multiethnic curricula, projects focused on racial issues, mixed work groups, and supportive teachers and principals led to improved interracial relations.

When the schools of Austin, Texas, were desegregated through extensive busing, the outcome was increased racial tension among Blacks, Mexican Americans, and Whites, producing violence in the schools. The superintendent consulted with Eliot Aronson, a prominent social psychologist, who was at the University of Texas at Austin at the time. Aronson thought it was more important to prevent racial hostility than to control it. This led him to observe a number of elementary school classrooms in Austin. What he saw was fierce competition between persons of unequal status. To learn how Aronson proposed to reduce the tension and fierce competition, turn to Cultural Worlds of Development 14.2.

The Jigsaw Classroom

Aronson stressed that the reward structure of elementary school classrooms needed to be changed from a setting of unequal competition to one of cooperation among equals, without making any curriculum changes. To accomplish this, he put together the *jigsaw classroom*. How might this work? Consider a class of 30 students, some White, some Black, some Hispanic. The lesson to be learned in the class focuses on the life of Joseph Pulitzer. The class might be broken up into five groups of six students each, with the groups being as equal as possible in terms of ethnic composition and academic achievement level. The lesson about Pulitzer's life could be divided into six parts, with one part given to each member of each six-person group. The parts might be paragraphs from Pulitzer's biography, such as how the Pulitzer family came to the United States, Pulitzer's childhood, his early work, and so on. The components are like parts of a jigsaw puzzle. They have to be put together to form the complete puzzle.

All students in each group are given an allotted time to study their parts. Then the groups meet and each member tries to teach a part to her group. After an hour or so, each member is tested on the entire life of Pulitzer, with each member receiving an individual rather than a group score. Each student, therefore, must learn the entire lesson; learning depends on the cooperation and effort of the other members. Aronson (1986) believes that this type of learning increases the students' interdependence through cooperatively reaching the same goal.

The strategy of emphasizing cooperation rather than competition and the jigsaw classroom have been widely used in classrooms in the United States. A number of research studies reveal that this type of cooperative learning is associated with increased self-esteem, better academic performance, friendships among classmates, and improved interethnic perceptions (Aronson, 1986; Slavin, 1987, 1989b).

The jigsaw classroom and cooperative learning have become popular methods of teaching. What are their strengths and weaknesses?

Although the cooperative classroom strategy has many merits, it may have a built-in difficulty that restricts its effectiveness. Academic achievement is as much an individual as a team "sport" (Brown, 1986). It is individuals, not groups, who enter college, take jobs, and follow careers. Parents with advantaged children in the jigsaw classroom might react with increased ethnic hostility when their children bring home lower grades than they had been used to getting before the jigsaw classroom was introduced. A child may tell his father, "The teacher is getting us to teach each other. In my group, we have a kid named Carlos, who can barely speak English." Although the jigsaw classroom can be an important strategy for reducing interracial hostility, caution needs to be exercised in its use because of the unequal status of the participants and the individual nature of achievement.

The Nature of Adolescents' Schooling

Three special concerns about adolescents' schooling are the transition to middle or junior high school, high school dropouts and noncollege youth, and the ability of adolescents to juggle part-time work and school, each of which we will consider in turn.

In youth we learn, in age we understand.
—Marie Ebner-von Eschenbach

The Transition to Middle or Junior High School

The emergence of junior high schools in the 1920s and 1930s was justified on the basis of physical, cognitive, and social changes that characterize early adolescence, as well as the need for more schools for the growing student population. Old high schools became junior high schools and new, regional high

The transition from elementary to middle or junior high school occurs at the same time a number of other changes take place in development. Biological, cognitive, and social changes converge with this schooling transition to make it a time of considerable adaptation.

schools were built. In most systems, the ninth grade remained a part of the high school in content, although physically separated from it in a 6-3-3 system. Gradually, the ninth grade has been restored to the high school as many school systems have developed middle schools that include the seventh and eighth grades, or sixth, seventh, and eighth grades. The creation of middle schools has been influenced by the earlier onset of puberty in recent decades.

One worry of educators and psychologists is that junior high and middle schools have simply become watered-down versions of high schools, mimicking their curricular and extracurricular schedules (Entwisle, 1990; Hill, 1980). The critics argue that unique curricular and extracurricular activities reflecting a wide range of individual differences in biological and psychological development in early adolescence should be incorporated into our junior high and middle schools. The critics also stress that many high schools foster passivity rather than autonomy and that schools should create a variety of pathways for students to achieve an identity.

The transition to middle school or junior high school from elementary school interests developmentalists because, even though it is a normative experience for most children, the transition can be stressful. The transition takes place at a time when simultaneous changes are occurring, including changes in the individual, the family, and the school (Eccles & Midgley, 1990; Hawkins & Berndt, 1985; Hirsch, 1989; Simmons & Blyth, 1987). These changes include puberty and related concerns about body image, the emergence of at least some aspects of formal operational thought, and increased responsibility and independence in association with decreased dependency on parents. The changes also include movement from a small, contained classroom structure to a larger, more impersonal school structure, from one teacher to many

Social and Personality Development

teachers, and from a small, homogeneous set of peers to a larger, more heterogeneous set of peers. Increased focus on achievement and its assessment also occurs. This list includes a number of negative, stressful features, but the transition can also have positive aspects. Students are more likely to feel grown up, have more subjects from which to select, have more opportunities to spend time with peers and more opportunities to locate compatible friends, enjoy increased independence from direct parental monitoring, and be more challenged intellectually by academic work (Hawkins & Berndt, 1985).

When students make the transition from elementary school to middle school or junior high school, they experience the **top-dog phenomenon,** *the circumstance of moving from the top position (in elementary school, the oldest, biggest, and most powerful students in the school) to the lowest position (in middle or junior high school, the youngest, smallest, and least powerful students in the school).* Researchers who have charted the transition from elementary to middle or junior high school find that the first year of middle school or junior high school can be difficult for many students (Hawkins & Berndt, 1985; Hirsch & Rapkin, 1987; Simmons & Blyth, 1987). For example, in one investigation of the transition from sixth grade in an elementary school to the seventh grade in a junior high school, adolescents' perceptions of the quality of school life plunged in the seventh grade (Hirsch & Rapkin, 1987). In the seventh grade, students were less satisfied with school, were less committed to school, and liked their teachers less. This drop in school satisfaction occurred regardless of how academically competent the students were.

What kind of experiences might ease the transition from elementary school to middle or junior high school? Schools that provide more support, less anonymity, more stability, and less complexity improve student adjustment during the transition from elementary school to middle or junior high school (Fenzel, Blyth, & Simmons, 1991). For example, in one investigation, 101 students were studied at three times: spring of the sixth grade (pretransition), fall of the seventh grade (early transition), and spring of the seventh grade (late transition) (Hawkins & Berndt, 1985). Two schools were sampled—one a traditional junior high school, the other a junior high in which the students were grouped into small teams (100 students, four teachers). The students' adjustment was assessed through self-reports, peer ratings, and teacher ratings. Adjustment dropped during the posttransition. For example, the self-esteem of students was lower in the seventh grade than in the sixth grade. More teacher support was reported by students in the team-oriented junior high school, and students with greater friendship contact and higher quality of friendship had a more positive perception of themselves and of their junior high school. These data indicate that a supportive, more intimate school environment and friendship can ease the students' stressful school transitions.

What makes a successful middle school? Joan Lipsitz (1984) and her colleagues searched the nation for the best middle schools, making extensive contacts and observations. Based on the recommendations of education experts and observations in schools in different parts of the United States, four middle schools were chosen for their outstanding ability to educate young adolescents. What were these middle schools like? The most striking feature was their willingness and ability to adapt all school practices to their students' individual differences in physical, cognitive, and social development. The schools took seriously the knowledge we have developed about young adolescents. This seriousness was reflected in the schools' decisions about various aspects of school life. For example, one middle school fought to keep its schedule of minicourses on Friday so that every student could be with friends and pursue

As shown in this situation of an eighth-grade boy teasing a seventh-grade boy, the transition from elementary to middle school can be difficult. Elementary school children move from being the ''top dog'' to being the ''underdog.''

personal interests. Two other middle schools expended considerable energy on a complex school organization so that small groups of students worked with small groups of teachers who could vary the tone and pace of the school day, depending on students' needs. Another middle school developed an advisory scheme so that each student had daily contact with an adult who was willing to listen to, explain things to, comfort, and prod the adolescent. Such school policies reflect thoughtfulness and personal concern about individuals who have compelling developmental needs. Another aspect of the effective middle schools was that, early in their existence, they emphasized the importance of creating an environment that was positive for the adolescent's social and emotional development. This goal was established not only because such environments contribute to academic excellence, but also because social and emotional development are intrinsically valued as important in adolescents' schooling. More information about competent schools for young adolescents is presented in Perspective on Child Development 14.1.

Recognizing that the vast majority of middle schools do not approach the excellent schools described by Joan Lipsitz (1984), in 1989 the Carnegie Corporation issued an extremely negative evaluation of our nation's middle schools. The report, "Turning Points: Preparing American Youth for the 21st Century," concluded that most young adolescents attend massive, impersonal schools, learn from seemingly irrelevant curricula, trust few adults in school, and lack access to health care and counseling. The Carnegie report recommended the following:

- Develop smaller "communities" or "houses" to lessen the impersonal nature of large middle schools.
- Lower student-to-counselor ratios from several hundred to 1 to 10 to 1.
- Involve parents and community leaders in schools.
- Develop a curriculum that produces students who are literate; who understand the sciences; and who have a sense of health, ethics, and citizenship.
- Have teachers team teach in more flexibly designed curriculum blocks that integrate several disciplines instead of presenting students with disconnected, rigidly separated 50-minute segments.
- Boost students' health and fitness with more in-school programs and help students who need public health care to get it.

Many of these same recommendations were echoed in a report from the National Governor's Association (America in Transition, 1989), which stated that the structure of middle school education in America neglects the basic developmental needs of young adolescents. Many educators and psychologists strongly support these recommendations (Entwisle, 1990). The Edna McConnell Clark Foundation's Program for Disadvantaged Youth is an example of a multiyear, multisite effort designed to implement many of the proposals for middle school improvement. The foundation has engaged the Center for Early Adolescence at the University of North Carolina to guide five urban school districts in their middle school reform (Scales, 1990). In sum, middle schools throughout the nation need a major redesign if they are to be effective in educating adolescents for becoming competent adults in the twenty-first century.

High School Dropouts

For many decades, dropping out of high school has been viewed as a serious educational and societal problem. By leaving high school before graduating,

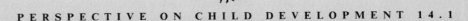
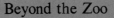

Beyond the Zoo

When teachers complain about young adolescents, animal imagery is pervasive: "This school is a zoo," "Those students are like animals," "It is a jungle in the classroom." In schools that seem like zoos, students usually do not learn effectively and often are not very happy. Consider these vignettes about ineffective middle schools:

A teacher sits in the back of the room, her legs up on her desk, asking students questions from the textbook. The students, bored and listless, sit in straight rows facing no one in the front of the room, answering laconically to a blank blackboard. When the principal enters the room, the teacher lowers her legs to the floor. Nothing else changes.

A teacher drills students for a seemingly endless amount of time on prime numbers. After the lesson, not one of them can say why it is important to learn prime numbers.

A visitor asks a teacher if hers is an eighth-grade class. "It's called eighth grade," she answers archly, "but we know it's really kindergarten—right, class?"

In a predominantly Hispanic school, only the one adult hired as a bilingual teacher speaks Spanish.

In a biracial school, the principal and the guidance counselor cite test scores with pride. They are asked if the difference between the test scores of black and white students is narrowing. "Oh, that's an interesting question!" the guidance counselor says in surprise. The principal agrees. It has never been asked by or of them before.

A teacher in a social studies class squelches several imaginative questions, exclaiming, "You're always asking 'what if' questions. Stop asking 'what if'!" When a visitor asks who will become president if the president-elect dies before the electoral college meets, the teacher explodes: "You're as bad as they are! That's another 'what if' question!" (Lipsitz, 1984, pp. 169–170)

By contrast, consider the following circumstances in effective middle schools:

Everything is peaceful. There are open cubbies instead of locked lockers. There is no theft. Students walk quietly in the corridor. "Why?" they are asked. "So as not to disturb the media center," they answer, which is self-evident to them but not the visitor who is left wondering. . . . When asked, "Do you like this school?" (They) answer: "No, we don't like it. We love it!" (Lipsitz, 1984, p. 27)

When asked how the school feels, one student answered, "It feels smart. We're smart. Look at our test scores." Comments from one of the parents of a student at the school are revealing: "My child would have been a dropout. In elementary school, his teacher said to me: 'That child isn't going to give you anything but heartaches.' He had perfect attendance here. He didn't want to miss a day. Summer vacation was too long and boring. Now he's majoring in communications at the University of Texas. He got here and all of a sudden someone cared for him. I had been getting notes about Roger every other day, with threats about expulsion. Here, the first note said: 'It's just a joy to have him in the classroom.' " (Lipsitz, 1984, p. 84)

The humane environment that encourages teachers' growth . . . is translated by the teachers . . . into a humane environment that encourages students' growth. The school feels cold when one first enters. It has the institutional feeling of any large school building with metal lockers and impersonal halls. Then one opens the door to a team area, and it is filled with energy, movement, productivity, doing. There is a lot of informal relating among students and between students and teachers. Visible from one vantage point are students working on written projects, putting the last touches on posters, watching a film, and working independently from reading kits. . . . Most know what they are doing, can say why it is important, and go back to work immediately after being interrupted. (Lipsitz, 1984, p. 109)

Authors' Week is yet another special activity built into the school's curriculum that entices students to consider themselves in relation to the rich variety of making and doing in people's lives. Based on student interest, availability, and diversity, authors are invited . . . to discuss their craft. Students sign up to meet with individual authors. They must have read one individual book by the author. . . . Students prepare questions for their sessions with the authors. . . . Sometimes, an author stays several days to work with a group of students on his or her manuscript. (Lipsitz, 1984, p. 141)

These excerpts about a variety of schools in different areas of the United States reveal the great diversity among schools for adolescents. They also tell us that, despite the ineffectiveness of many schools for adolescents, others are very effective. Secondary schools can be breeding grounds for competent academic *and* social development.

---

many dropouts take with them educational deficiencies that severely curtail their economic and social well-being throughout their adult lives (Rumberger, 1987). We will study the scope of this problem, the causes of dropping out, and some ways to reduce dropout rates.

Despite the overall decline in high school dropout rates, a major concern remains the higher dropout rate of ethnic minority students and low-income students, especially in large cities (Carrasquillo, 1991; Dryfoos, 1990; Eccles,

Among the reasons students drop out of school are school-related matters, such as not liking school or being expelled; economic problems; and personal circumstances, such as pregnancy. Overall, males are more likely to drop out than females.

1991; McCall, 1991). Although the dropout rates of most ethnic minority students have been declining, they remain substantially above those of White students. Thirty-five percent of 20-to-21-year-old Hispanic Americans, 18 percent of 20-to-21-year-old Black Americans, and 14 percent of 20-to-21-year-old White Americans have dropped out of school. Among Hispanic American youths in 1989, Mexican Americans had the highest dropout rate (57 percent) (American Council on Education, 1991). Dropout rates are extremely high for Native Americans—less than 10 percent graduate from high school (LaFromboise & Low, 1989). In some inner-city areas, the dropout rate for ethnic minority students is especially high, reaching more than 50 percent in Chicago, for example (Hahn, 1987). Hispanic American dropout rates actually increased from 1985 to 1989 (American Council on Education, 1991). Although the dropout rate of Black Americans has improved considerably in recent years, it still remains above that of White students.

Students drop out of school for many reasons—school-related, economic, family, peer-related, and personal (Bachman, 1991; Goertz, Ekstrom, & Rock, 1991; McCall, 1991). School-related problems are consistently associated with dropping out of school (O'Sullivan, 1990). In one investigation, almost 50 percent of the dropouts cited school-related reasons for leaving, such as not liking school, being suspended, or being expelled (Rumberger, 1983). Twenty percent of the dropouts (but 40 percent of the Hispanic American students) cited economic reasons for dropping out. Many of these students quit school and go to work to help support their families. Socioeconomic status is the main factor in family background that is strongly related to dropping out of school—students from low-income families are more likely to drop out than are those from middle-income families. Many school dropouts have friends who also are school dropouts. In the study cited earlier, one third of the girls dropped out for personal reasons, such as pregnancy or marriage (Rumberger, 1983). However, overall males are more likely to drop out than females.

To help reduce the dropout rate, community institutions, especially schools, need to break down the barriers between work and school (Scales, 1990; Spencer & Dornbusch, 1990). Many youths step off the education ladder long before reaching the level of a professional career, often with nowhere to step next, and are left to their own devices to search for work. These youths need more assistance than they are now receiving. The following are some approaches worth considering (William T. Grant Foundation, 1988):

- Monitored work experiences, such as through cooperative education, apprenticeships, internships, preemployment training, and youth-operated enterprises
- Community and neighborhood services, including voluntary service and youth-guided services
- Redirected vocational education, the principal thrust of which should not be preparation for specific jobs but the acquisition of basic skills needed for a wide range of jobs
- Guarantees of continuing education, employment, or training, especially in conjunction with mentor programs
- Career information and counseling to expose youth to job opportunities and career options as well as to successful role models
- School volunteer programs, not only for tutoring but to provide access to adult friends and mentors

For more information about improving our nation's education of minority-group students, turn to Cultural Worlds of Development 14.3.

Helping Hispanic Youths Stay in School and Go to College

The Hispanic population in the United States is increasing more rapidly than any other ethnic minority. Educators are increasingly interested in helping Hispanic adolescents stay in school and succeed in the courses needed for educational and occupational success. As colleges compete to recruit seniors from the small pool of college-eligible and college-ready Hispanics, it is apparent that the pool itself needs to be greatly expanded. In 1989, only 16 percent of Hispanic Americans aged 18 to 24 were enrolled in college (compared to 23 percent of Black Americans and 32 percent of White Americans) (American Council on Education, 1991). Gloria De Necochea (1988) recently described seven strategies to help keep Hispanic adolescents in school and get them ready to go to college:

1. Identify students early for a college preparatory curriculum. As early as the sixth grade, both students and parents need to know about the college preparatory curriculum and the long-term consequences of choices.
2. Give more attention to math and science. Mathematics and science are critical for both college admissions and a range of career options, but these subjects pose big barriers for Hispanic students. Success can be increased by teaching the complex academic language necessary to tackle these subjects effectively. This is especially important in grades seven through nine, where the gatekeeping course for future scientific and technical courses—algebra—is taught.

3. Increase school participation. Counselors and teachers can make college-related information more visible throughout the school. Precollege clubs can be developed. Administrators can invite college representatives, alumni, and individuals in various careers to address students. Critical thinking skills can be stressed. Teachers also can occasionally tailor the structure of exams to be more like the SAT and the ACT.
4. Expose students to the world of college. College recruiters, faculty, and financial-aid officers are important role models and sources of current information. Visits to colleges enable youths to gain firsthand knowledge about campus life (Justiz & Rendon, 1989).
5. Increase workshops. Study skills, assertiveness training, and survival tips can be taught. College-related topics, such as "How to choose a college" and "What to say to college admissions officers," should be offered during the senior year.
6. Involve parents. Invitations to all activities should be bilingual and mailed home well in advance of the event. To increase attendance, students can provide child care. Parents should be encouraged to come to workshops and to participate in planning activities.
7. Organize outside support. Better coordination between community organizations and schools could provide a central source for descriptions of available programs at the school and in the community.

These Hispanic youth leaders, participating in a mock legislation session, are positive examples of the increased concern for helping Hispanic youth stay in school and go to college.

Part-Time Work and School

In 1940, only 1 of 25 tenth-grade males attended school while working part-time. In the 1970s, the number had increased to more than 1 of every 4, and, in the 1980s, 3 of 4 combined school and part-time work. Adolescents also are working longer hours now than in the past. For example, the number of 14- and 15-year-olds who work more than 14 hours per week has increased substantially since 1960. A similar picture emerges for 16-year-olds. In 1960, 44 percent of the 16-year-old males who attended school worked more than 14 hours a week, but, by the 1980s, the figure had increased to more than 60 percent.

What kinds of jobs are adolescents working at today? About 17 percent who work do so in restaurants, waiting on customers, cleaning up, and so on. Other adolescents work in retail stores as cashiers or salespeople (about 20 percent), in offices as clerical assistants (about 10 percent), or as unskilled laborers (about 10 percent) (Cole, 1981).

Do male and female adolescents take the same type of jobs and are they paid equally? Some jobs are held almost exclusively by male adolescents—busboy, gardener, manual laborer, and newspaper carrier—whereas other jobs are held almost exclusively by female adolescents—baby-sitter and maid. Male adolescents generally work longer hours and are paid more per hour than female adolescents (Helson, Elliott, & Leigh, 1989).

Does work have benefits for adolescents? In some cases, yes; in others, no. Ellen Greenberger and Laurence Steinberg (1981) examined the work experiences of students in four California high schools. Their findings disproved some common myths. For example, generally it is assumed that adolescents get extensive on-the-job training when they are hired for work; the reality is that they get little training at all. Also, it is assumed that youths, through work experiences, learn to get along better with adults. However, the adolescents in this study reported that they rarely felt close to the adults with whom they worked. The work experiences of the adolescents did help them understand how the business world works, how to get and keep a job, and how to manage money. Working also helps adolescents learn to budget their time, to take pride in their accomplishments, and to evaluate their goals. However, working adolescents often have to give up sports, social affairs with peers, and sometimes sleep, and they have to balance the demands of work, school, family, and peers. Greenberger and Steinberg asked students about their grade-point averages, school attendance, satisfaction from school, and the number of hours spent studying and participating in extracurricular activities since they began working. They found that working adolescents have lower grade-point averages than nonworking adolescents. More than one of four students reported that their grades dropped when they began working; only one of nine said that their grades improved. However, it was not just working that affected adolescents' grades: more important was *how long* they worked. Tenth-graders who worked more than 14 hours a week suffered a drop in grades. Eleventh-graders worked up to 20 hours a week before their grades dropped. When adolescents work more than 20 hours per week, they have little time to study for tests and to complete homework assignments.

Educating Children with Special Needs

A final consideration in our discussion of schools is the education of children with special needs. First, we will examine the scope and education of handi-

What are the effects of working and going to school on an adolescent's grades and integration into school activities?

capped children, second, children with a learning disability, and, third, children with attention-deficit hyperactivity disorder.

Handicapped Children

The elementary school years are a time when handicapped children become more sensitive about their differentness and how it is perceived by others. One 6-year-old girl came home from school and asked, "Am I disabled or handicapped?" Another articulate 6-year-old girl described in detail how her premature birth was the cause of her cerebral palsy: "I was a teensy-weensy baby. They put me in an incubator and I almost died." Later, when asked about being teased by her classmates because she could not walk, she replied, "I hate their guts, but if I said anything the teacher would get mad at me." A 7-year-old handicapped boy commented about how he had successfully completed a rocket-making course during the summer; he was the youngest and the most knowledgeable child in the class: "For the first time, some kids really liked me" (Howard, 1982). Life is not always fair, especially for handicapped children. As evidenced by the comments of the handicapped children just mentioned, adjusting to the world of peers and school often is painful and difficult.

An estimated 10 to 15 percent of the United States population of children between the ages of 5 and 18 are handicapped (see table 14.2). The estimates range from the 0.1 percent who are visually impaired to the 3 to 4 percent who have speech handicaps. Estimates vary because of problems in classification and testing. Experts sometimes differ in how they define the various categories of handicapped children, and different tests may be used by different school systems or psychologists to assess whether a child is handicapped.

Public Law 94–142 *(PL 94–142) is the federal government's mandate to all states to provide a free, appropriate education for all children.* This law, also called the Education for All Handicapped Children Act, was passed

Estimates of the Percentage and Number of Handicapped Children in the United States

Handicap	% of population	Number of children, ages 5 to 18
Visual impairment (includes blindness)	0.1	55,000
Hearing impairment (includes deafness)	0.5-0.7	275,000-385,000
Speech handicap	3.0-4.0	1,650,000-2,200,000
Orthopedic and health impairments	0.5	275,000
Emotional disturbance	2.0-3.0	1,100,000-1,650,000
Mental retardation (both educable and trainable)	2.0-3.0	1,100,000-1,650,000
Learning disabilities	2.0-3.0	1,100,000-1,650,000
Multiple handicaps	0.5-0.7	275,000-385,000
Total	10.6-15.0	5,830,000-8,250,000

Reprinted by permission of Merrill, an imprint of Macmillan Publishing Company from *The Exceptional Student in the Regular Classroom*, 3d edition, by Bill R. Gearheart and Mel W. Weishahn. Copyright © 1984 by Merrill Publishing.

by Congress in 1975. A key provision of the bill was the development of an individualized education program for each identified handicapped child. Another provision of Public Law 94–142 is to provide the *least restrictive environment* for the education of handicapped children. Each state must ensure that all handicapped students are educated with students who are not handicapped. Special education classes, separate schooling, or other removal of handicapped children from the regular education environment should occur only when the nature or severity of the handicap is such that an education in regular classes with the use of supplementary aids and services cannot be satisfactorily achieved (Gaylord-Ross, 1989; Lipsky & Gartner, 1989).

Mainstreaming *occurs when handicapped children attend regular school classes with nonhandicapped children.* In this way, handicapped children enter the "mainstream" of education in the school and are not separated from nonhandicapped students. However, even under PL 94–142, which emphasizes mainstreaming, certain types of handicapped children, such as those with hearing impairments, usually spend part of each day in separate classes taught by specially trained teachers. The results of mainstreaming have met with mixed results. In some schools, teachers assign children to environments that are not the best contexts for learning (Brady & others, 1988). Some people believe that mainstreaming means there will be a number of profoundly retarded, drugged children sitting in classrooms in dazed, unresponsive states. Others believe that including handicapped children in regular classrooms will detract from the quality of the education given to nonhandicapped children. The picture is not as bleak as some of these criticisms suggest. Virtually all profoundly retarded children are institutionalized and will never be schooled in public classrooms. Only the mildly retarded are mainstreamed. Mainstreaming makes children and teachers become more aware of the special needs of handicapped people.

In practice, mainstreaming has not been the simple solution its architects hoped for. Many handicapped children require extensive and expensive services to help them become effective learners in regular classrooms. As school systems have become increasingly strapped financially, many services for handicapped children have been cut back. Some teachers, already burdened with heavy course loads and time demands, have felt overwhelmed by the added requirement of developing special teaching arrangements for handicapped children, and the social interaction of handicapped and nonhandicapped children has not always gone smoothly in mainstreamed classrooms (Gallagher, Trohanis, & Clifford, 1989).

The hope that mainstreaming would be a positive solution for all handicapped children needs to be balanced with the reality of each handicapped child's life and special needs. The specially tailored education program should meet with the acceptance of parents and counselors, educational authorities, and, when feasible, the children themselves (Hallahan & others, 1988; Kusche, 1991).

Is there a disadvantage to referring to these children as handicapped or disabled? Children who are labeled as handicapped or disabled may feel permanently stigmatized and rejected, and they may be denied opportunities for full development. Children labeled as handicapped or disabled may be assigned to inferior educational programs or placed in institutions without the legal protection given to "normal" individuals. Paradoxically, however, if handicapped or disabled children are not labeled, they may not be able to take advantage of the special programs designed to help them (Hobbs, 1975; Horne, 1988).

There are no quick fixes for the education of handicapped children. Although progress has been made in recent years to provide supportive instruction for handicapped children, increasing effort needs to be devoted to developing the skills of handicapped children (Hynd & Obrzut, 1986). Handicapped children have a strong will to survive, to grow, and to learn. They deserve our very best educational efforts (Wood, 1988).

Public Law 94-142 mandates a free, appropriate education for all children. A key provision of the bill was the development of an individualized education program for each identified handicapped child. Among the important issues involved in the education of handicapped children are mainstreaming and labeling.

Learning Disabilities

Paula doesn't like kindergarten and can't seem to remember the names of her teacher or classmates. Bobby's third-grade teacher complains that his spelling is awful and that he is always reversing letters. Ten-year-old Tim hates to read. He says it is too hard for him and the words just don't make any sense. Each of these children is learning disabled. Children with **learning disabilities** *(1) are of normal or higher intelligence, (2) have difficulties in several academic areas but usually do not show deficits in others, and (3) are not suffering from some other conditions or disorders that could explain their learning problems* (Reid, 1988). The breadth of definitions of learning disabilities has generated controversy about just what learning disabilities are (Chalfant, 1989; Siegel & Ryan, 1989; Silver, 1989).

Within the global concept of learning disabilities fall problems in listening, thinking, memory, reading, writing, spelling, and math. Attention deficits involving an inability to sit still, pay attention, and concentrate also are classified under learning disabilities. Estimates of the number of learning-disabled children in the United States are as broad as the definition, ranging from 1 to 30 percent (Lerner, 1988). The U.S. Department of Education puts the number of identified learning-disabled children between the ages of 3 and 21 at approximately 2 million.

Improving the lives of learning-disabled children will come from (1) recognizing the complex, multifaceted nature of learning disabilities (considering their biological, cognitive, and social aspects) and (2) becoming more precise in our analysis of the learning environments in which learning-disabled children participate (Lerner, 1989). The following discussion of one subtype of learning disability, attention-deficit hyperactivity disorder, exemplifies the consideration of this complexity and precision.

Matthew failed the first grade. His handwriting was messy. He did not know the alphabet and never attended very well to the lessons the teacher taught. Matthew is almost always in motion; he can't sit still for more than a few minutes at a time, and his mother describes him as very fidgety. Matthew has **attention-deficit hyperactivity disorder,** *the technical term for what is commonly called hyperactivity. This disorder is characterized by a short attention span, high distractibility, and high levels of physical activity* (Barkeley, in press; Silver, 1987). In short, these children do not pay attention and have difficulty concentrating on what they are doing (Loge & Schatz, 1991; Pierce, 1991). Estimates of the number of children with attention-deficit hyperactivity disorder vary from less than 1 percent to 5 percent of the U.S. population. Although young children or even infants show characteristics of this disorder, the vast majority of hyperactive children are identified in the first three grades of elementary school, when teachers recognize that these children have great difficulty paying attention, sitting still, and concentrating on their schoolwork.

What makes hyperactive children so impulsive, distractible, and excitable? Possible causes include heredity, prenatal damage, diet, family dynamics, and the physical environment. As we saw in chapter 3, the influence of heredity on temperament is increasingly being considered, with activity level as one aspect of temperament that differentiates one child from another very early in development. Approximately four times as many boys as girls are hyperactive. This sex difference may be due to differences in the brains of boys and girls determined by genes on the Y chromosome. The prenatal hazards we discussed in chapter 4 also may produce hyperactive behavior. Excessive drinking by women during pregnancy is associated with poor attention and concentration by their offspring at 4 years of age, for example (Streissguth & others, 1984). With regard to diet, severe vitamin deficiencies can lead to attentional problems. Vitamin B deficiencies are of special concern. High levels of caffeine and sugar intake by pregnant women also may contribute to off-springs' attentional problems.

The social and physical environments in which children live also contribute to attentional problems (Henker & Whalen, 1989). Children with attention-deficit hyperactivity disorder are more likely to come from families who move frequently and who are more concerned with controlling the child's behavior than with improving the child's academic work (Lambert & Hartsough, 1984). Hyperactive children are more likely to misbehave when they are in exciting but unstructured circumstances (such as a typical birthday party) or in circumstances with many behavioral demands (such as a typical school classroom). Lead poisoning also can produce attentional problems and hyperactive behavior.

Children with attention-deficit hyperactivity disorder may continue to have problems in adolescence, although, by that time, the attentional problem is usually less severe. Even in adulthood, approximately one third to one half continue to be troubled by attentional difficulties (Weiss & Hechtman, 1986).

A wide range of psychotherapies and drug therapy have been used to improve the lives of hyperactive children. For unknown reasons, some drugs that stimulate the brains and behaviors of adults have a quieting effect on the brains and behaviors of children. The drugs most widely prescribed for hyperactive children are amphetamines, especially Ritalin. Amphetamines work effectively for some hyperactive children, but not for all (Batshaw & Perret, 1986; Buhrmester & MacDonald, 1991; MacDonald & others, 1991). As many as 20 percent of the hyperactive children treated with Ritalin do not respond to it. Even when Ritalin works, it is also important to consider the social world of the hyperactive child. The teacher is especially important in this social world, helping monitor the child's academic and social behavior to determine whether the drug works and whether the prescribed dosage is correct.

At this point, we have discussed a number of ideas about the transition to elementary school; schools, classrooms, and teachers; social class and ethnicity in schools; the nature of adolescents' schooling; and the education of children with special needs. A summary of these ideas is presented in concept table 14.2. In the next chapter, we will turn our attention to the development of the self, social competence, and identity.

The Transition to Elementary School; Schools, Classrooms, and Teachers; Social Class and Ethnicity in Schools; the Nature of Adolescents' Schooling; and the Education of Children with Special Needs

Concept	Processes/related ideas	Characteristics/description
The transition to elementary school	Its nature	A special concern is that early elementary school education proceeds mainly on the basis of negative feedback to children. The curriculum in elementary schools should be integrated. Many educators and psychologists believe that children should be taught through concrete, hands-on experience in the early elementary school years.
Schools, classrooms, and teachers	School size and classroom size	Smaller is usually better when school size and classroom size are at issue. Recommended maximum secondary school size ranges from 500 to 1,000 children. Most class sizes are 30 to 35 students, but a class size of 15 or less benefits student learning.
	Classroom structure and climate	The open classroom concept is multidimensional. Specific dimensions of open and traditional classrooms need to be considered, as well as specific outcomes. Overall, open classrooms are associated with lower language achievement but improved school attitudes. Individualized instruction and the role of the child are associated with positive self-concept. Aptitude-treatment interaction also needs to be considered.
	Teachers	Teacher characteristics involve many different dimensions, and coming up with a profile of a competent teacher of children is difficult. Erikson believes that a good teacher creates a sense of industry rather than inferiority.
Social class and ethnicity in schools	Social class	Schools have a strong middle-class orientation. Teachers have lower expectations for children from low-income backgrounds, although teachers from these backgrounds perceive these students' behavior as more adaptive than do teachers from other backgrounds.
	Ethnicity	Many teachers have been ignorant of the different cultural meanings non–Anglo children have learned in their communities. John Ogbu proposed a controversial view that ethnic minority children are placed in a position of subordination and exploitation in the American educational system. Some experts believe that a form of institutional racism exists in some schools because teachers fail to academically challenge ethnic minority children. Teachers have lower expectations for ethnic minority children. Desegregation through busing has shown virtually no benefits in reducing racial tension. What is important to study is what goes on at school after children arrive. Multiethnic curricula, supportive teachers and administrators, and cooperative learning benefit students from ethnic minority backgrounds.

Concept	Processes/related ideas	Characteristics/description
The nature of adolescents' schooling	Transition to middle or junior high school	The emergence of junior highs in the 1920s and 1930s was justified on the basis of physical, cognitive, and social changes in early adolescence and the need for more schools in response to a growing student population. Middle schools have become more popular in recent years and coincide with puberty's earlier arrival. The transition to middle or junior high school coincides with many social, familial, and individual changes in the adolescent's life. The transition involves moving from the top-dog to the lowest position. Successful schools for young adolescents take individual differences in development seriously, show a deep concern for what is known about early adolescence, and emphasize social and emotional development as much as intellectual development. In 1989, the Carnegie Corporation recommended a major redesign of middle schools.
	High school dropouts	Dropping out has been a serious problem for decades. Many dropouts have educational deficiencies that curtail their economic and social well-being for much of their adult life. Some progress has been made in that dropout rates for most ethnic minority groups have declined in recent decades, although dropout rates for inner-city, low-income minorities, Hispanic Americans, and Native Americans are still precariously high. Dropping out of school is associated with demographic, family-related, peer-related, school-related, economic, and individual factors. Reducing the dropout rate and improving the lives of noncollege youth could be accomplished by strengthening schools and bridging the gap between school and work.
	Part-time work and school	There has been a tremendous increase in the number of adolescents who work part-time and go to school, which has both advantages and disadvantages. When adolescents work too many hours per week, their grades suffer and they are less integrated in the school.
Educating children with special needs	Handicapped children	Approximately 10 to 15 percent of children in the United States are estimated to be handicapped. Public Law 94–142 ordered a free, appropriate education for every handicapped child. The law emphasizes an individually tailored education program for every child and the provision of a least restrictive environment, which has led to extensive mainstreaming of handicapped children into the regular classroom. Mainstreaming has been a controversial topic. Another issue is the labeling of handicapped children and its benefits and drawbacks.
	Learning disabilities	Such children have normal or above-normal intelligence, have difficulties in some areas but not others, and do not suffer from any other disorder that could explain their learning problems. Learning disabilities are complex and multifaceted and require precise analysis.
	Attention-deficit hyperactivity disorder	The technical term for hyperactivity, this disorder is characterized by a short attention span, distractibility, and high levels of physical activity. Possible causes include heredity, prenatal damage, diet, family dynamics, and the physical environment. Amphetamines have been used with some success in treatment, but they do not work for all hyperactive children.

Summary

I. Do Schools Make a Difference?

Some sociologists have argued that schools have little impact on children's development; however, when researchers conduct more precise, observational studies of what goes on in schools and classrooms, the effects of schooling become more apparent.

II. Functions of Children's Schools and Schools' Changing Social Developmental Contexts

In the 1980s, the back-to-basics movement gained momentum. The back-to-basics movement emphasizes rigorous academic training. It especially opposes the misapplied open education orientation that became popular in the 1970s. A special worry is that early childhood education is becoming a downward extension of back-to-basics elementary and secondary education. Many experts on education and child development believe that the back-to-basics movement has increased the stress in children's lives and does not adequately address individual variations among children. They also believe that education should be more comprehensive, focusing on social as well as cognitive development. The social context differs at the preschool, elementary, and secondary levels, becoming much more expansive for adolescents.

III. Child-Centered Kindergarten, and Developmentally Appropriate and Inappropriate Practices in the Education of Young Children

Child-centered kindergarten involves education of the whole child, with emphasis on individual variation, the process of learning, and the importance of play in development. Developmentally appropriate practice is based on knowledge of the typical development of children within an age span (age appropriateness) as well as the uniqueness of the child (individual appropriateness). Developmentally appropriate practice contrasts with developmentally inappropriate practice, which ignores the concrete, hands-on approach to learning. Direct teaching largely through abstract, paper-and-pencil activities presented to large groups of young children is believed to be developmentally inappropriate. The National Association for the Education of Young Children has been a strong proponent of developmentally appropriate practice and has developed extensive recommendations for its implementation.

IV. Does It Matter If Children Attend Preschool Before Kindergarten?

Parents can educate their young children just as effectively as schools can. However, many parents do not have the commitment, time, energy, and resources needed to provide young children with an environment that approaches a competent early childhood education program. Too often, parents see education as a race and preschool as a chance to get ahead in the race. However, education should not be a race and it should not be stressful for young children. Public preschools are appearing in many states. They should not become simple versions of traditional elementary schools. Early childhood education has some issues that overlap with upper levels of schooling, but, in many ways, the agenda of early childhood education is different.

V. The Influence of Early Childhood Education and Education for Disadvantaged Young Children

The effects of early childhood education on children's development are difficult to evaluate, but overall they seem to be positive. However, although outcome measures reveal areas in which social competence is more positive for children who have experienced early childhood education, in other areas there is less social competence. Compensatory education has tried to break through the poverty cycle with such programs as Head Start and Follow Through. Long-term studies reveal that model preschool programs have positive effects on disadvantaged children's development.

VI. The Transition to Elementary School

A special concern is that early elementary school education proceeds mainly on the basis of negative feedback to children. The curriculum in elementary schools should be integrated. Many educators and child developmentalists believe that children should be taught through concrete, hands-on experience in the early elementary school years.

VII. Schools, Classrooms, and Teachers

Smaller is usually better when school size and classroom size are at issue. Recommended maximum secondary school size ranges from 500 to 1,000 students. Most class sizes are 30 to 35 students, but a class size of 15 or less benefits student learning. The open classroom concept is multidimensional. Specific dimensions of open and traditional classrooms need to be considered, as well as specific outcomes. Overall, open classrooms are associated with lower language achievement but improved school attitudes. Individualized instruction and the role of the child are associated with positive self-concept. Aptitude-treatment interaction also needs to be considered. Teacher characteristics involve many different dimensions, and coming up with a profile of a competent teacher of children is difficult. Erikson believes that a good teacher creates a sense of industry rather than inferiority.

VIII. Social Class and Ethnicity in Schools

Schools have a strong middle-class orientation. Teachers have lower expectations for children from low-income backgrounds, although teachers from these backgrounds perceive these students' behaviors as more adaptive. Many teachers have been ignorant of the different cultural meanings non–Anglo children have learned in their communities. John Ogbu proposed a controversial view that ethnic minority children are placed in a position of subordination and exploitation in the American educational system. Some experts believe that a form of institutional racism exists in some schools because teachers fail to academically challenge ethnic minority children. Teachers have lower expectations for ethnic minority children. Desegregation through busing has shown virtually no benefits in reducing racial tension. What is important to study is what goes on at school after children arrive. Multiethnic curricula, supportive teachers and administrators, and cooperative learning benefit students from ethnic minority backgrounds.

IX. Transition to Middle or Junior High School

The emergence of junior highs in the 1920s and 1930s was justified on the basis of physical, cognitive, and social changes in early adolescence and the need for more schools in response to a growing population. Middle schools have become more popular in recent years and coincide with puberty's earlier arrival. The transition to middle or junior high school coincides with many social, familial, and individual changes in the adolescent's life. The transition involves moving from the top-dog to the lowest position. Successful schools for young adolescents take individual differences in development seriously, show a deep concern for what is known about early adolescence, and emphasize social and emotional development as much as intellectual development. In 1989, the Carnegie Corporation recommended a major redesign of middle schools.

X. High School Dropouts, Noncollege Youth, and Part-time Work and School

Dropping out has been a serious problem for decades. Many dropouts have educational deficiencies that curtail their economic and social well-being for much of their adult life. Some progress has been made in that dropout rates for most ethnic minority groups have declined in recent decades, although dropout rates for inner-city, low-income ethnic minorities, Hispanic Americans, and Native Americans are still precariously high. Dropping out of school is associated with demographic, family-related, peer-related, school-related, economic, and individual factors. Reducing the dropout rate and improving the lives of noncollege youth could be accomplished by strengthening the schools and bridging the gap between school and work. There has been a tremendous increase in the number of adolescents who work part-time and go to school, which has both advantages and disadvantages. When adolescents work too many hours per week, their grades suffer and they are less integrated in the school.

XI. Educating Children with Special Needs

An estimated 10 to 15 percent of children in the United States are handicapped. Public Law 94–142 ordered a free, appropriate education for every handicapped child. The law emphasizes an individually tailored program for every child and provision of a least restrictive environment, which has led to extensive mainstreaming of handicapped children into the regular classroom. Mainstreaming has been a controversial topic. Another issue is the labeling of handicapped children and its benefits and drawbacks. Children with learning disabilities have normal or above-normal intelligence, have difficulties in some areas but not in others, and do not suffer from any other disorder that could explain their learning problems. Learning disabilities are complex and multifaceted and require precise analysis. Attention-deficit hyperactivity disorder is the technical term for hyperactivity. This disorder is characterized by a short attention span, distractibility, and high levels of physical activity. Possible causes include heredity, prenatal damage, diet, family dynamics, and the physical environment. Amphetamines have been used with some success in treatment, but they do not work for all hyperactive children.

Key Terms

Montessori approach 476
back-to-basics
  movement 478
child-centered
  kindergarten 481
developmentally
  appropriate practice 482
Project Head Start 488
Project Follow
  Through 488

aptitude-treatment
  interaction (ATI) 493
top-dog phenomenon 499
Public Law 94–142 505
mainstreaming 506
learning disabilities 508
attention-deficit
  hyperactivity disorder 508

Suggested Readings

Lipsitz, J. (1984). *Successful schools for young adolescents.* New Brunswick, NJ: Transaction. This is important reading for anyone interested in better schools for young adolescents; it is filled with rich examples of adolescents in schools.

Minuchin, P. P., & Shapiro, E. K. (1983). The school as a context for social development. In P. H. Mussen (Ed.), *Handbook of child psychology* (4th ed., Vol. 4). New York: Wiley. This authoritative review of the role of the school in the adolescent's development by two leading educators covers most of the topics in this chapter.

Phi Delta Kappan. Leaf through the 1980s issues of this leading educational journal to get a feel for the controversial, widely debated ideas in secondary education.

Review of Educational Research. This journal publishes reviews of educational research. By leafing through the issues of the past several years, you will come across research summaries with references to many of the topics in this chapter.

William T. Grant Foundation Commission on Work, Family, and Citizenship (1988). *The forgotten half: Non-college-bound youth in America.* New York: William T. Grant Foundation. This excellent report on the status of non-college-bound youth in America calls attention to ways our society can help these individuals make the school-to-work transition more effectively.

Young Children, published by the National Association for the Education of Young Children, Washington, DC. This journal includes a variety of articles about young children's physical, cognitive, and social development. Special attention is given to how various aspects of development can be fostered in our nation's preschool and kindergarten programs. Look through the issues of the past 5 years to get a feel for the important concerns in this area.

CHAPTER

15

THE SELF, SOCIAL COMPETENCE, AND IDENTITY

The Self
    Self-understanding
    Self-esteem
    Cultural Worlds of Development 15.1: Ethnicity,
        Self, and Self-esteem
Social Competence
    What is Social Competence?
    Measuring Social Competence
Identity
    Erikson's Ideas on Identity
    Some Contemporary Thoughts on Identity
    The Four Statuses of Identity
    Developmental Changes
    Perspective on Child Development 15.1: Hitler,
        Luther, and Gandhi—the Development of
        Their Identities
    Family Influences on Identity
    Cultural and Ethnic Aspects of Identity
    Cultural Worlds of Development 15.2: The
        Development of Identity in Native American
        Adolescents
    Gender and Identity
Summary
Key Terms
Suggested Readings

WHEN I SAY "I", I MEAN A THING ABSOLUTELY UNIQUE NOT TO BE CONFUSED WITH ANY OTHER.

—Ugo Betti

W ho are you when you say "I"? Who are your best friends when they say "I"? If you look in the mirror, you see a face, one that always looks back at you. When your best friends look in the mirror, they see faces that are very different from yours. When each of us looks in the mirror, we see someone "absolutely unique not to be confused with any other," as Italian playwright Ugo Betti's words so vividly describe. "I" means a unique individual, as each of us is, was, and will be, and "I" means a physical person, the someone whose skin, stature, and shape you see in the mirror.

Beyond the self's uniqueness and physical nature lie other important dimensions—those that are psychological and social in nature. As you look in the mirror, you see the color of your skin. Each of us has an ethnic identity, a psychological part of our self that goes beyond the mere tone of our skin. You might also see a learned individual in the mirror, one who possibly has become more educated than prior generations in your family. You might also see someone who is at ease in social situations and has developed positive close relationships with others. These are some of the most important characteristics of the self—its unique nature, its physical nature, its cognitive nature, and its social nature.

In thinking about what "I" means, would you have described yourself differently when you were a child or an adolescent than you do at this point in your life cycle? Probably so. Wasn't there a point early in your existence when you didn't even distinguish between yourself and others? When did you begin to recognize this self-identity? Didn't you become much more acutely conscious of who you are, what you are all about as a person, and where you are headed in life during your adolescent years?

This chapter is about the self and its development and about what it takes to be socially competent—as an infant, as a child, and as an adolescent. Among the important concepts to be evaluated are the self, social competence, and identity. Why are these concepts together in the same chapter? Each of these concepts attempts to look at children and adolescents in a global way. They strive to portray children as complete entities; each child has only one mind and one body, only one set of behaviors, thoughts, and feelings. The concepts we will discuss in this chapter are integrative—they attempt to synthesize the many dimensions of children, which is not an easy task. As you will see, there is not always agreement on what the integration and synthesis should be. Some critics, especially those of a behavioral persuasion, believe it does not make sense to study children in such a global manner. Their strategy is to focus on the pieces of the child, the fine-grained aspects of a child's makeup. In recent years, however, there has been increased acceptance of conceptualizing and measuring both molar and molecular—broad and fine-grained—dimensions of children's development.

The Self

In chapter 2, we described Carl Rogers' humanistic theory, which stresses the importance of the self in understanding children's development. We examined

Rogers' ideas about self-concept, the overall perception of one's self. In recent years, child developmentalists have given special attention to two aspects of the child's self or self-conceptions: self-understanding and self-esteem.

Self-understanding

What is self-understanding? When do children initially develop a self-understanding? How does self-understanding develop during the childhood and adolescent years? What is the role of perspective taking in self-understanding? We will examine each of these questions.

What Is Self-understanding?

Self-understanding *is a child's cognitive representation of the self, the substance and content of the child's self conceptions* (Damon & Hart, 1988). For example, an 11-year-old boy understands that he is a student, a boy, a football player, a family member, a video game lover, and a rock music fan. A 13-year-old girl understands that she is a middle school student, in the midst of puberty, a girl, a cheerleader, a student council member, and a movie fan. A child's self-understanding is based, in part, on the various roles and membership categories that define who children are (Harter, 1988, 1990a,b). Though not the whole of personal identity, self-understanding provides its rational underpinnings (Damon & Hart, 1988).

Infancy—the Development of Self-recognition

Infants cannot verbally express their views on the nature of the self. They also cannot understand the complex instructions required to engage in a child developmentalist's tasks. Given these restrictions, how can researchers study infants' self-understanding? They test infants' *visual self-recognition* by presenting them with images of themselves in mirrors, pictures, and other visual media. For example, let's examine how the mirror technique works. An infant's mother puts a dot of rouge on the infant's nose. An observer watches to see how often the infant touches its nose. Next, the infant is placed in front of a mirror, and observers detect whether nose touching increases. In two separate investigations, in the second half of the second year of life, infants recognized their own images in the mirror and coordinated the images they saw with the actions of touching their own bodies (Amsterdam, 1968; Lewis & Brooks-Gunn, 1979) (see figure 15.1). In sum, human infants initially develop a sense of rudimentary self-understanding called self-recognition at approximately 18 months of age (Lewis & others, 1989).

Early Childhood

Because children can verbally communicate their ideas, research on self-understanding in childhood is not limited to visual self-recognition, as it is during infancy. Mainly through interviews, researchers have probed children's conceptions of many aspects of self-understanding, including mind and body, self in relation to others, and pride and shame in self. In early childhood, children usually conceive of the self in physical terms. Most young children conceive of the self as part of the body, which usually means the head. Young children generally confuse self, mind, and body (Broughton, 1978). Because the self is a body part, it can be described along many material dimensions, such as size, shape, and color. Young children distinguish themselves from others through many different physical and material attributes. Says 4-year-old Sandra, "I'm different from Jennifer because I have brown hair and she

Know thyself, for once we know ourselves, we may learn how to care for ourselves, but otherwise we never shall.

—Socrates

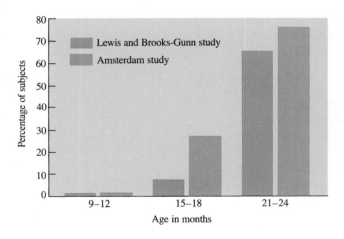

Figure 15.1
Development of Self-recognition in Infancy
The graph gives the findings of two studies
in which infants of different ages showed
recognition of rouge by touching, wiping, or
verbally referring to it. Notice that self-
recognition did not occur extensively until
the second half of the second year of life.

has blonde hair." Says 4-year-old Ralph, "I am different from Hank because I am taller and I am different from my sister because I have a bicycle."

Researchers also believe that the *active dimension* is a central component of the self in early childhood (Keller, Ford, & Meacham, 1978; Mohr, 1978). If we define the category "physical" broadly enough, we can include physical actions as well as body image and material possessions. For example, preschool children often describe themselves in terms of activities such as play. In sum, in early childhood, children often describe themselves in terms of a physical self or an active self.

Middle and Late Childhood

In middle and late childhood, self-understanding increasingly shifts from defining oneself through external characteristics to defining oneself through internal characteristics. Also, elementary-school-aged children are more likely to define themselves in terms of social characteristics and social comparison.

In middle and late childhood, children not only recognize differences between inner and outer states, but they are also more likely to include subjective inner states in their definition of self. For example, in one investigation, second-grade children were much more likely than younger children to name psychological characteristics (such as preferences or personality traits) in their self-definition and less likely to name physical characteristics (such as eye color or possessions) (Aboud & Skerry, 1983). For example, 8-year-old Todd includes in his self-description, "I am smart and I am popular." Ten-year-old Tina says about herself, "I am pretty good about not worrying most of the time. I used to lose my temper but I'm better about that now. I also feel proud when I do well in school."

In addition to the increase of psychological characteristics in self-definition during the elementary school years, the *social aspects* of the self also increase at this point in development. In one investigation, elementary school children included references to social groups in their self-descriptions (Livesly & Bromley, 1973). For example, some children referred to themselves as Girl Scouts, as Catholics, or as someone who has two close friends.

Children's self-understanding in the elementary school years also includes increasing reference to *social comparison*. At this point in development, children are more likely to distinguish themselves from others in comparative rather than in absolute terms. That is, elementary-school-aged children are no longer as likely to think about what I do or do not do, but are more likely to think about what I can do *in comparison with others*. This developmental shift provides an increased tendency of establishing one's differences as an individual apart from others. In a series of studies, Diane Ruble (1983) investigated children's use of social comparison in their self-evaluations. Children were given a difficult task and then offered feedback on their performance, as well as information about the performances of other children their age. The children were then asked for self-evaluations. Children younger than 7 made virtually no reference to the information about other children's performances. However, many children older than 7 included socially comparative information in their self-descriptions.

Adolescence

The development of self-understanding in adolescence is complex and involves a number of aspects of the self. Compared with that of children, adolescents' self-understanding is more abstract, more idealistic, more differentiated, more self-contradictory, more self-conscious, more self-protective, and more integrated, and it involves increased recognition of unconscious influences on the self. We will consider each of these dimensions of adolescents' development of self-understanding.

Remember from our discussion of Piaget's theory of cognitive development in chapters 2 and 8 that many adolescents begin to think in more *abstract* and *idealistic* ways. When asked to describe themselves, adolescents are more likely than children to use abstract and idealistic labels. Consider 14-year-old Laurie's abstract descriptions of herself: "I am a human being. I am indecisive. I don't know who I am." Also consider her idealistic descriptions of herself: "I am a naturally sensitive person who really cares about people's feelings. I think I am pretty good-looking most of the time." Of course, not all adolescents describe themselves in idealistic ways, but most adolescents increasingly distinguish between the real self and the ideal self. For example, Laurie's friend Jane says, "I think I am pretty ugly. I sure wish I could look like Brooke Shields."

Adolescents' self-understanding becomes *increasingly differentiated*. Adolescents are more likely than children to describe the self with contextual or situational variations. For example, 15-year-old Amy describes herself with one set of characteristics in her relationship with her family and another set of characteristics in her relationship with peers and friends. Yet another set of characteristics appears in her description of her romantic relationship. In sum, adolescents are more likely than children to understand that one possesses different selves depending on one's role or the particular context (Harter, 1990a,b).

Self-understanding in adolescence also involves more *contradictions within the self*. In one investigation, Susan Harter (1986) asked seventh-, ninth-, and eleventh-graders to describe themselves. She found that there was a dramatic increase between the seventh and ninth grades in the number of contradictory terms used to describe oneself (moody *and* understanding, ugly *and* attractive, bored *and* inquisitive, caring *and* uncaring, introverted *and* fun-loving, and so on). The contradictory self-descriptions declined in the eleventh grade, but were still higher than in the seventh grade. Adolescents develop the cognitive ability to detect these inconsistencies in the self as they strive to construct a general theory of the self or of one's personality (Damon, 1991).

Adolescents' self-understanding becomes more *self-conscious* and *preoccupied*. Adolescents are more likely than children to be preoccupied with their self-understanding. As part of their self-conscious and preoccupied self-exploration, adolescents become more introspective. However, the introspection is not always done in social isolation. Sometimes adolescents turn to their friends for support and self-clarification, obtaining their friends' opinions of an emerging self-definition. As one researcher on self-development commented, adolescents' friends are often the main source of reflected self-appraisals, becoming the social mirror in which adolescents anxiously stare (Rosenberg, 1979). This self-consciousness and self-preoccupation reflect the concept of adolescent egocentrism, which we discussed in chapter 8.

Adolescents' self-understanding includes more *mechanisms to protect the self* (Harter, 1988, 1990a,b). Although adolescents often display a sense of confusion and conflict stimulated by introspective efforts to understand the self, they also call on mechanisms designed to protect and enhance the self. In protecting the self, adolescents are prone to denying their negative characteristics. For example, in Harter's investigation of adolescent self-understanding, positive self-descriptions, such as attractive, fun-loving, sensitive, affectionate, and inquisitive, were more likely to be placed at the core of the self, indicating more importance, whereas negative self-descriptions, such as ugly, mediocre, depressed, selfish, and nervous, were more likely to be located at the periphery of the self, indicating less importance (Harter, 1986). The tendency of adolescents to protect themselves fits with our earlier description of adolescents' tendency to describe themselves in idealistic ways.

Adolescents' self-understanding includes greater recognition that the self includes *unconscious,* as well as conscious, components, a recognition that is not likely to occur until late adolescence (Selman, 1980). That is, older adolescents are more likely than younger adolescents to believe that certain aspects of their mental experience may be beyond their own awareness or control.

Finally, adolescents' self-understanding becomes more *integrative,* with the disparate parts of the self more systematically pieced together, especially in late adolescence. Older adolescents are more likely to detect inconsistencies in their earlier self-description as they attempt to construct a general theory of self, an integrated sense of identity (Harter, 1986; Selman, 1980).

At this point, we have discussed a number of developmental sequences in self-understanding. A summary of these developmental sequences is presented in figure 15.2.

Further Developmental Considerations in Self-understanding

In the developmental sequence of self-understanding just outlined, we presented the emergence of various self-dimensions. It is important to keep in mind that just because a particular dimension of the self is listed in a particular period that the dimension does not occur exclusively in that period. For example, early childhood is described as the time period for the emergence of a physical and active self; however, many elementary school children also describe themselves in terms of physical characteristics and various activities. We described middle and late childhood as the time period when the internal self, social self, and social comparative self become more prominent. These characteristics of the self also are very important in adolescent self-understanding and, in many cases, are more prevalent in adolescent self-description than in children's self-description. However, these characteristics were placed in the middle and late childhood period because that is the time when many developmentalists believe they emerge to become important self-dimensions.

■ *Critical Thinking*
Think about your development of self-understanding when you were an adolescent. Can you think of other aspects of the development of self-understanding in adolescence than those we have discussed?

Social and Personality Development

Age period	Aspect of self-understanding	Description
Infancy	Self-recognition	At approximately 18 months, infants develop a sense of self-recognition.
Early childhood	Physical self, active self	Young children often describe themselves in physical or active terms.
Middle and late childhood	Internal self, social self, and social comparative self	Elementary-school-aged children increasingly define themselves with internal, psychological characteristics. They also are more likely to define themselves in terms of social characteristics and social comparison.
Adolescence	Abstract, idealistic, differentiated, self-contradictory, self-conscious, unconscious self, and self-protective	Self-understanding in adolescence is complex. Self-understanding is more abstract, more idealistic, more self-contradictory, differentiated, more self-conscious, and more self-protective. Especially in late adolescence, self-understanding involves recognition of unconscious influences and is more integrative.

The Role of Perspective Taking in Self-understanding

Many child developmentalists believe that perspective taking plays an important role in self-understanding. As you learned in chapter 13, perspective taking is the ability to assume another person's perspective and understand his or her thoughts and feelings. Robert Selman (1980) has proposed a developmental theory of perspective taking that has been given considerable attention. He believes that perspective taking involves a series of five stages, ranging from 3 years of age through adolescence (see table 15.1). These stages begin with the egocentric viewpoint in early childhood and end with in-depth perspective taking in adolescence.

To study children's perspective taking, Selman interviews individual children, asking them to comment on such dilemmas as the following:

Holly is an 8-year-old girl who likes to climb trees. She is the best tree climber in the neighborhood. One day while climbing down from a tall tree, she falls, . . . but does not hurt herself. Her father sees her fall. He is upset and asks her to promise not to climb trees anymore. Holly promises.

Figure 15.2
Developmental Sequence of Self-understanding

TABLE 15.1
Selman's Stages of Perspective Taking

Perspective taking stage	Age	Description
0 Egocentric viewpoint	3-6	Child has a sense of differentiation of self and other but fails to distinguish between the social perspective (thoughts, feelings) of other and self. Child can label other's overt feelings but does not see the cause-and-effect relation of reasons to social actions.
1 Social-informational perspective taking	6-8	Child is aware that other has a social perspective based on other's own reasoning, which may or may not be similar to child's. However, child tends to focus on one perspective rather than coordinating viewpoints.
2 Self-reflective perspective taking	8-10	Child is conscious that each individual is aware of the other's perspective and that this awareness influences self and other's view of each other. Putting self in other's place is a way of judging other's intentions, purposes, and actions. Child can form a coordinated chain of perspectives but cannot yet abstract from this process to the level of simultaneous mutuality.
3 Mutual perspective taking	10-12	Child realizes that both self and other can view each other mutually and simultaneously as subjects. Child can step outside the two-person dyad and view the interaction from a third-person perspective.
4 Social and conventional system perspective taking	12-15	Person realizes mutual perspective taking does not always lead to complete understanding. Social conventions are seen as necessary because they are understood by all members of the group (the generalized other), regardless of their position, role, or experience.

From R. L. Selman, "Social-Cognitive Understanding" in T. Lickona (Ed.). *Moral Development and Behavior,* 1976; reprinted by permission of the editor.

Later that day, Holly and her friends meet Shawn. Shawn's kitten is caught in a tree and can't get down. Something has to be done right away or the kitten may fall. Holly is the only one who climbs trees well enough to reach the kitten and get it down but she remembers her promise to her father. (Selman, 1976, p. 302)

Subsequently, Selman asks each child a series of questions about the dilemma, such as:

- Does Holly know how Shawn feels about the kitten?
- How will Holly's father feel if he finds out she climbed the tree?
- What does Holly think her father will do if he finds out she climbed the tree?
- What would you do in this situation?

By analyzing children's responses to these dilemmas, Selman (1980) concluded that children's perspective taking follows the developmental sequence described in table 15.1

Children's perspective taking not only can increase their self-understanding, but it can also improve their peer group status and the quality of their friendships. For example, one investigation found that the most popular children in the third and eighth grades had competent perspective-taking skills (Kurdek & Krile, 1982). Children who are competent at perspective taking are better at understanding the needs of their companions, so they likely can

Social and Personality Development

communicate more effectively with them (Hudson, Forman, & Brion-Meisels, 1982).

At this point, we have studied a number of developmental changes in self-understanding. Remember from our introduction to the self that self-conception not only involves self-understanding but also self-esteem.

Self-esteem

Among the questions we will explore regarding children's self-esteem are the following: What is self-esteem? How is self-esteem measured? How do parent-child relationships contribute to children's self-esteem? How is group identity involved in children's self-esteem? How can children's self-esteem be enhanced? We will consider each of these questions in turn.

What Is Self-esteem?

It is difficult to make people miserable when they feel worthy of themselves.
—Abraham Lincoln

Self-esteem *is the evaluative and affective dimension of self-concept. Self-esteem also is referred to as self-worth or self-image.* That is, a child may perceive that she is not merely a student, but a *good* student. Another child may perceive that he is not merely a basketball player, but a *good* basketball player. These self-evaluations often stimulate an emotional reaction. The good student feels proud that she just received an *A* on an exam; the good basketball player feels elated that he scored the winning basket in last night's game. Of course, not all self-evaluations are positive. A child may feel sad that she is not a good student. Another child may feel ashamed that he is a poor reader. These are all evaluative judgments regarding the child's self-esteem.

Until recently, theorists and researchers conceptualized self-esteem as a general, global judgment about the self. However, children make evaluative judgments about many different aspects of their lives. For example, they perceive that they are good or bad in physical skills, good or bad in cognitive skills, and good or bad in social skills. As we will see next, interest in the domain-specific aspects of self-esteem has led to the development of new measures of self-esteem.

Measuring Self-esteem

Although it is recognized that all children evaluate their self-worth, psychologists have had a difficult time trying to measure self-worth or self-esteem (Wylie, 1979; Yardley, 1987). One method that has been used frequently is the Piers-Harris Scale (Piers & Harris, 1964), which consists of 80 items designed to measure a child's overall self-esteem. School psychologists often use this scale with children who have been referred to them for evaluation. By responding yes or no to such items as "I have good ideas," children reveal whether they have high or low self-esteem.

However, as indicated, a child's self-esteem may vary according to different skill domains or areas of competence. The scales developed by Susan Harter have been welcome additions to the assessment of self-esteem or self-worth. The Self-perception Profile for Children taps five specific domains (scholastic competence, athletic competence, social acceptance, physical appearance, and behavioral conduct), plus general self-worth (Harter, 1985). The Self-perception Profile for Children is a revision of the original instrument, the Perceived Competence Scale for Children (Harter, 1982). Harter's scale does an excellent job of separating children's feelings of self-worth in different skill areas, and, when general self-worth is assessed, questions focus on overall perceptions of self-esteem rather than specific skill domains. Many

The Self, Social Competence, and Identity

developmentalists believe that the differentiated assessment of self-esteem in various skill domains, as well as the independent assessment of general self-worth, provides a richer picture than those measures that yield only a single self-worth score.

The Self-perception Profile for Children is designed to be used with third-grade through sixth-grade children. Harter also has developed separate scales for younger children and for adolescents, recognizing important developmental changes in self-perceptions. The Pictorial Scale for Perceived Competence and Social Acceptance (Harter & Pike, 1984) taps four domains: cognitive competence, physical competence, maternal acceptance, and peer acceptance. This measure has two versions, one for preschool/kindergarten children and one for first and second graders. Harter (1989) also developed the Self-perception Profile for Adolescents, which taps eight domains (scholastic competence, athletic competence, social acceptance, physical appearance, behavioral conduct, close friendship, romantic appeal, and job competence)—plus global self-worth. Thus, the adolescent version has three skill domains not present in the children's version—job competence, romantic appeal, and close friendship.

Some assessment experts believe that a combination of several methods should be used to measure children's self-esteem. In addition to self-report scales, ratings of a child's self-esteem by others and observations of the child's behavior in various settings may provide a more comprehensive portrait of self-esteem. Children's facial expressions and the extent to which they congratulate or condemn themselves are also good indicators of self-esteem. For example, children who rarely smile or act happy reveal something about their self-esteem. By turning to figure 15.3, you can examine the behavioral categories that were used to measure self-esteem in one investigation (Savin-Williams & Demo, 1983).

Parent-Child Relationships and Self-esteem

In the most extensive investigation of parent-child relationships and self-esteem, a measure of self-esteem was given to elementary school boys, and the boys and their mothers were interviewed about their family relationships (Coopersmith, 1967). Based on these assessments, the following parenting attributes were associated with boys' high self-esteem:

- Expression of affection
- Concern about the child's problems
- Harmony in the home
- Participation in joint family activities
- Availability to give competent, organized help to the boys when they need it
- Setting clear and fair rules
- Abiding by these rules
- Allowing the children freedom within well-prescribed limits

■ *Critical Thinking*
Other than the parenting attributes described by Coopersmith, can you think of other ways children's self-esteem can be improved?

Remember that these findings are correlational, and so, we cannot say that these parenting attributes *cause* children's high self-esteem. Such factors as parental acceptance and allowing children freedom within well-prescribed limits probably are important determinants of children's self-esteem, but we still must say that *they are related to* rather than *they cause* children's self-esteem, based on the available research data.

Positive indicators

1. Gives others directives or commands
2. Voice quality is appropriate for situation
3. Expresses opinions
4. Sits with others during social activities
5. Works cooperatively in a group
6. Faces others when speaking or being spoken to
7. Maintains eye contact during conversation
8. Initiates friendly contact with others
9. Maintains comfortable space between self and others
10. Little hesitation in speech, speaks fluently

Negative indicators

1. Puts down others by teasing, name calling, or gossiping
2. Gestures are dramatic or out of context
3. Inappropriate touching or avoids physical contact
4. Gives excuses for failures
5. Glances around to monitor others
6. Brags excessively about achievements, skills, appearance
7. Verbally puts self down; self-depreciation
8. Speaks too loudly, abruptly, or in a dogmatic tone
9. Does not express views or opinions, especially when asked
10. Assumes a submissive stance

Group Identity and Self-esteem

Children's group identity is also related to their self-esteem. **Social identity theory** *is social psychologist Henry Tajfel's (1978) theory that, when individuals are assigned to a group, they invariably think of that group as an ingroup for them. This occurs because individuals want to have a positive self-image.* According to Tajfel, self-image consists of both a personal identity and many different social identities. Tajfel argues that individuals can improve their self-image by enhancing either their personal or their social identity. Tajfel believes that social identity is especially important. When children or adults compare the social identity of their group with the social identity of another group, they often maximize the distinctions between the two groups. For example, think of an adolescent's identity with the school's football or basketball team. When the school's teams win, students' self-images are enhanced, regardless of whether they play on the teams or not. Why? Because they have a social identity with the school and the school's teams.

As children and adults strive to promote their social identities, it is not long before proud, self-congratulatory remarks are interspersed with nasty comments about the opposing group(s). In a capsule, the theme becomes, "My group is good and I am good. Your group is bad and you are bad." So it goes with the sexes, ethnic groups, teams, social classes, religions, and countless other groups, all seeking to improve their respective self-images through social identity with the group and comparison of the group with other groups. These comparisons can easily lead to competition, conflict, and even a perception that discrimination against other groups is legitimate.

Tajfel showed that it does not take much to get children or adults to think in terms of "we" and "they," or in-group and out-group. He assigned children to two groups based on a trivial task. For example, one individual was assigned to one group because she overestimated the number of dots on a screen

The Self, Social Competence, and Identity

527

and another individual was assigned to another group because he underestimated the number. Once assigned to the two groups, the members were asked to award amounts of money to pairs of other subjects. Those eligible to receive the money were anonymous except for their membership in one of the two groups Tajfel created. Invariably, the children acted favorably toward (awarded money to) members of their own group. It is no wonder, then, that, if we favor our own group based on such trivial criteria, we will show intense in-group favoritism when differences are not as trivial (Rappaport, Bornstein, & Erev, 1989).

Closely related to group identity and self-esteem is **ethnocentrism,** *the tendency to favor one's own group over other groups.* Ethnocentrism's positive side appears in the sense of in-group pride that fulfills our strong urge to attain and maintain a positive self-image. In-group pride has mushroomed as we approach the end of the twentieth century. Children observe and listen to their parents speak about Black pride, Hispanic pride, Native American pride, Irish pride, Italian pride, and so on. Unfortunately, sometimes prejudice develops. **Prejudice** *is an unjustified negative attitude toward an individual because of that person's membership in a group.* People can be prejudiced against groups of people made up of a particular ethnic group, sex, age, religion, or other detectable difference (Devine, 1989; Schaller & Maass, 1989).

Also related to group identity and self-esteem is the self-esteem of various ethnic minority groups. To learn more about self-esteem in ethnic-minority-group children, turn to Cultural Worlds of Development 15.1.

Increasing Children's Self-esteem

Social support in the form of approval and confirmation from others is a powerful influence on children's self-esteem (Harter, 1990b). Some children with low self-esteem come from conflicted families or conditions in which they experienced abuse or neglect—situations in which support is unavailable. In some cases, alternative forms of support can be implemented, either informally through the encouragement of a teacher, coach, or other significant adult, or more formally, through such programs as Big Brothers and Big Sisters.

According to Susan Harter (1990b), identifying a child's sources of self-esteem—that is, competence in domains important to the self—as well as social support, is critical to improving the child's self-esteem. Harter points out that the self-esteem enhancement programs of the 1960s, in which self-esteem itself was the target and children were encouraged to believe that they should feel good about themselves, were ineffective. Rather, Harter believes that intervention must take place at the level of the *causes* of self-esteem if a major impact on improving children's self-esteem is to result.

Children have the highest levels of self-esteem when they perform competently in domains that are important to the self. Therefore, programs that encourage children and adolescents to identify and value areas of competence should be implemented. One strategy is to encourage our society and school systems to recognize the benefits of competence in areas other than academic performance. However, in contrast, another strategy is to understand that education is the primary means of achieving success and to provide children and adolescents who have poor academic skills and low self-esteem better support and more individualized attention in schools. The inspiration of Hispanic high school teacher Jaime Escalante, documented in the movie *Stand and Deliver,* reflects this latter strategy. Escalante was a high school teacher in California who spent many evenings and weekends tutoring Hispanic students in math in addition to effectively teaching math in the classroom. Escalante's com-

Ethnicity, Self, and Self-esteem

Many of the early attempts to assess the nature of self-esteem in various ethnic groups compared Black and White individuals (Clark & Clark, 1939; Coopersmith, 1967; Deutsch, 1967). The early reports indicated that Black individuals, especially Black children, have less self-esteem than White individuals. However, more recent research suggests that Black American, Mexican American, and Puerto Rican American children and adults report equal if not higher self-esteem than children and adults from other ethnic groups, such as Anglo American children and adults (Allen & Majidi-Ahi, 1989; Powell & Fuller, 1972).

A generation of ethnic awareness and pride appears to have advanced the self-esteem of ethnic minority groups (Garbarino, 1985). Ethnic pride based on success within a subgroup has both costs and benefits for individuals. An obvious benefit is that their cultural roles are more clearly defined by the subgroup (such as Black American, Mexican American, or Native American) and that they know what they must do to become competent people in the subculture. In these usually tight-knit neighborhoods, there is a feeling of closeness and support among neighbors. Thus, individuals from the ethnic group can obtain help and learn strategies for coping with problems, which makes developing a positive sense of self somewhat easier. An ethnic-group individual gains a sense of rootedness and acceptance.

However, there is no indication that the distribution of self-acceptance in a group is related to the social prestige of the group in American society at large (Rosenberg, 1965). Thus, there may be a negative reality in the social environment beyond the ethnic-group neighborhood with which individuals must eventually come to terms if they are to succeed in the larger society. The ethnic-group neighborhood's beliefs, values, morals, and behaviors may not be accepted by the society as a whole, which can impede the development of social competence in the mainstream of society.

A discussion of ethnicity and self-esteem raises the fundamental question of "What kind of people does the world need?" (Garbarino, 1980a, 1985). There is a growing recognition of the need for individuals to develop more harmonious, cooperative relationships if the quality of life on this planet is to be enhanced. Such a society needs persons to define themselves in new ways that deemphasize competition, achievement, and materialism in favor of cooperation, connectedness with others, empathy, and spiritual development. We need to ask whether we are socializing children to develop the kind of self that is needed to create a competent, caring, sustainable society.

mitment and motivation were transferred to the Hispanic high school students, many of whom obtained college scholarships and passed advanced placement tests in calculus. Insisting that high school and college athletes maintain a respectable grade point average is a policy that endorses the importance of academic achievement and competence in other domains, as is the requirement that students maintain respectable grades to participate in job programs (Harter, 1990b).

At this point, we have discussed a number of ideas about the self. A summary of these ideas is presented in concept table 15.1. Next, we will turn our attention to the nature of children's social competence.

Social Competence

What is social competence? How can we assess children's social competence? These are among the questions we will attempt to answer in this section.

What Is Social Competence?

Virtually every parent wants to rear a son or daughter to become socially competent. What does this mean? Social competence has been defined in ways that reflect the varying perspectives of social theorists (Dodge & others, 1986). Among the definitions of social competence are "effective response of the in-

Concept	Processes/related ideas	Characteristics/description
Self-understanding	What is it?	It is a child's cognitive representation of self, the substance and content of the child's self-conceptions. Self-understanding provides the rational underpinnings of personal identity.
	Infancy—the development of self-recognition	Infants initially develop a rudimentary form of self-understanding—self-recognition—at approximately 18 months of age.
	Early childhood	The physical and active self becomes a part of self-understanding as young children often describe themselves in physical or active terms.
	Middle and late childhood	The internal self, the social self, and the socially comparative self become more prominent in self-understanding. Elementary-school-aged children increasingly describe themselves with internal, psychological characteristics. They also are more likely to define themselves in terms of social characteristics and social comparison.
	Adolescence	Self-understanding in adolescence is complex. Self-understanding is more abstract, idealistic, differentiated, self-contradictory, self-conscious, and self-protective. Especially in late adolescence, self-understanding involves the recognition of unconscious influences and is more integrative.
	Further developmental considerations	Once the characteristics emerge as a part of self-understanding, they continue to be part of self-understanding, although they may wax and wane in varying degrees as development proceeds. For example, although the internal self is described as becoming more prominent in middle and late childhood, the internal self continues to be an integral part of self-understanding in adolescence. The physical self continues to be a part of self-description in adolescence, but it is often less central in self-description than in early childhood.
	Perspective taking	It is the ability to assume another person's perspective and understand his or her thoughts and feelings. Selman proposed a developmental theory of perspective taking with five stages, ranging from 3 years of age through adolescence, beginning with the egocentric viewpoint in early childhood and ending with the in-depth perspective taking of adolescence.

dividual to life situations" (Goldfried & d'Zurilla, 1969), "capacity to interact with the environment" (White, 1959), and "able to make use of environmental and personal resources to achieve a developmental outcome" (Waters & Sroufe, 1983). Even Socrates defined social competence: "those who manage well the circumstances they encounter daily." Most of these definitions overlap, but we will adopt Everett Waters and Alan Sroufe's definition: **Social competence** *is the ability to use resources within oneself and in the environment to achieve positive developmental outcomes.*

Resources within the child range from specific skills and abilities to general concepts such as self-esteem. Delay of gratification, adaptation, flexibility, and self-control are important strengths of the socially competent child. The

Concept	Processes/related ideas	Characteristics/description
Self-esteem	What is it?	It is the evaluative and affective dimension of self-concept. Self-esteem is also referred to as self-worth or self-image. Until recently, self-esteem was described in global terms. Today, domain-specific aspects of self-esteem are also considered.
	Measuring self-esteem	Measuring self-esteem is a difficult task. Harter's measures have been appealing to many developmentalists because they provide a differentiated assessment of self-esteem in various skill domains, as well as an independent assessment of general self-worth. Some assessment experts believe several methods should be used to measure self-esteem, including observations of a child's behavior.
	Parent-child relationships and self-esteem	In Coopersmith's study, children's self-esteem was associated with such parenting attributes as parental acceptance and allowing children freedom within well-prescribed limits. It is important to remember that these associations are correlational.
	Group identity and self-esteem	Social identity theory is Tajfel's theory that, when individuals are assigned to a group, they invariably think of the group as an in-group for them. This occurs because they want to have a positive self-image. Tajfel believes self-image consists of a personal *and* many different social identities related to group membership and identity. Group identity often leads to competitiveness, and sometimes conflict, between groups. Closely related to group identity and self-esteem is ethnocentrism, the tendency to favor one's own group over other groups. The positive side of ethnocentrism is the sense of in-group pride, but sometimes a negative side—prejudice—develops. A special concern is the self-esteem of ethnic minority children.
	Improving children's self-esteem	Social support in the form of approval and confirmation from others is a powerful influence on children's self-esteem. Identifying the sources of self-esteem is critical to improving a child's self-esteem. Programs that encourage children and adolescents to identify and value areas of competence should be implemented. One strategy is to emphasize the positive benefits of competence in areas other than academic achievement; another strategy is to recognize that academic achievement is the route to success and high self-esteem. Some programs emphasize competence in academic achievement and other domains as well.

motivation to do something well also is an important aspect of being socially competent, especially in the achievement-oriented American society. Socially competent children also develop a good understanding of themselves, develop appropriate perspective-taking skills, and have a positive self-worth.

Resources in the environment are those things that can support or develop the child's ability to coordinate affect, cognition, and behavior, both in the service of short-term adaptation and in long-term developmental progress. In infancy, adult social agents clearly are important environmental resources. In early childhood and beyond, play and peer relations become more important. From early childhood on, the range of potential resources expands.

The perspective of Martin Ford (1986), like that of Waters and Sroufe, also emphasizes that children's social competence involves both individual and social goals. Thus, social competence is not solely a property of an individual or of the social world. Rather, the most socially competent children accomplish both self-assertive (individual) and integrative (social) goals. Ford believes that social competence consists of four defining issues, each of which has a self-assertive and an integrative goal (see figure 15.4). The four defining issues are identity, control, social comparison, and resource distribution.

Regarding identity, the self-assertive task is to develop and express one's individuality. Examples of this type of social competence might be a unique behavioral style or an unusual pattern of interests. The self-assertive child or adolescent also may reveal a strongly endorsed set of social values and a clear, stable set of self-conceptions. The self-assertive nature of the child or adolescent would not depend on other individuals or social groups for self-definition. The integrative aspect of identity development is belongingness. It involves efforts to create, maintain, or enhance the identity of the social units of which the child or adolescent is a part. The units might be small and intimate, as in one's family or close friendships, or large, abstract units such as ethnic groups. Ford believes that the emphasis should be on active engagement of the social environment to create situations that enhance the self-assertive and belongingness aspects of identity.

Regarding control, self-determination is the self-assertive goal, social responsibility the integrative goal. Children and adolescents who are making progress in self-determination are beginning to establish and maintain personal control over their life circumstances and regain control when it is lost. Social responsibility is attained by accepting legitimate and necessary types of social control. The control is exercised, to a degree, through the broad rules of society, such as the prohibition of certain immoral or illegal actions (for instance, violence and theft), and through the regulation of conduct in social contexts such as the classroom and the neighborhood. Social control also is developed through formal obligations to personal roles, such as being a student and later being an employee, and it is established by informal obligations involving social contracts with friends, relatives, and others. Thus, social responsibility occurs when duties are upheld, commitments are kept, and roles are fulfilled. Social responsibility also is reflected in such characteristics as dependability, trustworthiness, and integrity.

The third issue in Ford's model of social competence is social comparison. When children or adolescents compare themselves with others, the self-assertive consequence is the sense that they are better or higher on a relevant dimension than the other person or reference group. Since superiority is relative rather than absolute, self-assertiveness occurs most often in competitive situations. In these situations, a high social status is achieved through active engagement of the social world rather than through social assignment or social accident. Superiority also is revealed through commerce with peers, since individuals who are dissimilar, such as adults, usually do not provide the best basis for meaningful comparison. The integrative aspect involved in this part of social competence is equity, an important interest of group leaders, such as teachers, parents, and employers, who need to be concerned about demands for fair, unbiased treatment. Equity can occur in relationships with siblings, peers, and friends, where powerful norms about sharing and fairness are important in maintaining the positive quality of the relationships. Equity also may be demonstrated in relationships with dissimilar others, such as children who are disadvantaged (those who have less money, lower intelligence, and so on).

Defining issue	Type of goal	
	Self-assertive goals	Integrative goals
Identity	Individuality	Belongingness
Control	Self-determination	Social responsibility
Social comparison	Superiority	Equity
Resource distribution	Resource acquisition	Resource provision

Figure 15.4
Ford's Model of Social Competence

The final issue in Ford's model of social competence is resource allocation. Children and adolescents need to be competent at resource allocation. Alternatively, resource provision may be needed to improve the functioning of other individuals and social groups. Such resources might involve goods and possessions, such as food, clothing, or money. The resources might also pertain to assistance, advice, or cognitive validation. Since social resources usually are distributed in friendships and social support networks developed through mutual give-and-take, resource acquisition and provision often can be attained in the same contexts. Indeed, the child's or adolescent's unwillingness to provide resources reciprocally to others may make it difficult for the child or adolescent to acquire resources.

In sum, Ford argues that children and adolescents who maintain and promote the functioning of themselves and others are more socially competent than those who do not. Again, we underscore the importance of viewing social competence in terms of both internal, self, self-assertive dimensions and external, social, environmental dimensions. Both Ford's and Waters and Sroufe's models capture this dual nature of social competence.

Measuring Social Competence

In describing the important features of assessing social competence, Waters and Sroufe (1983) point out four considerations: (1) broadband versus narrow assessments; (2) real behavior versus laboratory tasks; (3) assessments emphasizing the coordination of affect, cognition, and behavior; and (4) challenging, or taxing, behavioral and integrative/adaptive capacity.

It is important to assess both the global and the more fine-grained aspects of children's social behavior. Waters and Sroufe (1983) argue that, at least initially, it would be wise to understand broadly what a child's social competence is like. For example, in studying toddler problem solving, the focus might be on enthusiasm, persistence, flexibility, and enjoyment in dealing with the problem rather than the part of the problem first addressed, the tool used first, or even the time required to solve the problem. In the attachment literature, researchers have often assessed the infant's tendency to stay close to its mother in terms of specific discrete behaviors. Often, counts of touching the mother, looking at her, and the like are selected for measurement. However, such measures tend to be more situation-specific than broad-based. An alternative approach is to select more broadly defined measures of proximity-seeking or contact-maintaining behaviors. Assessments of this nature usually do not involve frequency counts of behaviors but, rather, rating scales. Thus, in assessing attachment, Ainsworth, Sroufe, Waters, Main, and others have begun to use ratings of secure and insecure attachment rather than frequency counts of proximity seeking in their attempts to accurately capture the nature of social competence in infants. Keep in mind, however, that in our assessment of the child's development it is wise to consider both fine-grained, behavioral measures of the child and the more broadly based measures Waters and Sroufe recommend (Maccoby & Martin, 1983).

A second issue in assessment focuses on whether we should be studying social competence through specific tasks in controlled laboratory contexts or by designing more naturalistic and ecologically valid measures. Advantages and disadvantages are associated with both choices. Developmental psychologists interested in assessing social competence are likely to find themselves going into and out of laboratory situations. However, Waters and Sroufe (1983) argue that, early in the development of assessment devices for measuring social competence, it is especially important to conduct ecologically valid assessments in real-life circumstances. They reason that laboratory measures often evaluate a narrow dimension of social competence, whereas real-life, naturalistic assessments typically are more broadly based, which fits with their first assessment recommendation.

A third assessment issue in social competence focuses on the evaluation of how children coordinate affect, cognition, and behavior. Waters and Sroufe believe that information about early social behavior (social attachment, problem solving, peer interaction, and self/behavior relationships) suggests that psychologists should be studying how affect, cognition, and behavior are coordinated. Assessing the coordination of these three dimensions rather than each dimension alone fits nicely with the belief that broad-based measures of social competence are needed. This also meshes with the belief that the affective world of children is important, as are their cognitive and behavioral worlds. Cognition and behavior are obviously important dimensions of the child's development, but, in isolation, they may not effectively reflect social competence. Social competence clearly is linked to motivation and control, and, in circumstances where these are relevant, affect often is involved and frequently arises from either success or failure.

Waters and Sroufe also believe that the assessment of social competence needs to include measures that plug into the child's integrative/adaptive capacity in dealing with critical events or transactions in his or her world. Even within the range of typical behaviors, there are circumstances that challenge or tax the child's integrative capacity: for example, temperature change, sustained face-to-face interaction, response to separation and union, exploration of new environments, responses to success and failure, and sustained social play.

As you have just learned, identity is one of the four key ingredients in Ford's model of social competence. Next, we will consider the nature of identity in much greater detail, focusing heavily on Erik Erikson's view that identity becomes an issue of special importance in the adolescent years.

Identity

By far the most comprehensive and provocative story of identity development has been told by Erik Erikson. As you may remember from chapter 2, identity versus identity confusion is the fifth stage in Erikson's eight stages of the life cycle, occurring at about the same time as adolescence. It is a time of interest in finding out who one is, what one is all about, and where one is headed in life. Our further consideration of identity involves continued discussion of Erikson's ideas, Marcia's four statuses of identity, developmental changes, family influences, culture and ethnicity, and gender, each of which we will examine in turn.

Erikson's Ideas on Identity

Erikson (1968) believes that adolescents enter a **psychological moratorium,** *the long gap or transition between childhood security and adult autonomy during which adolescents explore and examine different identities.* Numerous identities can be drawn from the surrounding culture. As adolescents explore the culture's identity files, they experiment with various roles. A youth who successfully copes with these conflicting identities emerges with a new sense of self that is both refreshing and acceptable. Adolescents who do not successfully resolve this identity crisis suffer what Erikson calls identity confusion. This confusion takes one of two courses: Individuals may withdraw, isolating themselves from peers and family, or they may lose their identity in the crowd.

Two core ingredients of Erikson's ideas on identity are personality and role experimentation. As indicated earlier, Erikson believes that adolescents face an overwhelming number of choices and, at a point during youth, enter a period of psychological moratorium. During this moratorium, they try out different roles and personalities before they reach a stable sense of self. They may be argumentative one moment, cooperative the next. They may dress neatly one day, sloppily the next day. They may like a particular friend one week, despise the friend the next week. This personality experimentation is a deliberate effort on the part of adolescents to find out where they fit in the world.

As they gradually come to realize that they will be responsible for themselves and their own lives, adolescents search for what those lives are going to be. Many parents and other adults, accustomed to having children go along with what they say, may be bewildered or incensed by the wisecracks, the rebelliousness, and the rapid mood changes that accompany adolescence. It is important for adults to give adolescents the time and opportunities to explore roles and personalities. In turn, most adolescents eventually discard undesirable roles.

There are literally hundreds of roles for adolescents to try out, and probably just as many ways to pursue each role. Erikson believes that, by late adolescence, vocational roles are central to identity's development, especially in

"Who are you?" said the Caterpillar. Alice replied, rather shyly, "I—I hardly know, Sir, just at present—at least I know who I was when I got up this morning, but I must have changed several times since then."

—Lewis Carroll

■ *Critical Thinking*

Is identity development more difficult for adolescents today than it was 50 years ago? Explain your answer.

One of adolescence's most important tasks is the development of identity—of finding out who one is, what one is all about, and where one is headed in life. What is important about identity in adolescence, especially late adolescence, is that, for the first time, physical development, cognitive development, and social development advance to the point at which the individual can sort through and synthesize childhood identities and identifications to construct a viable pathway to adult maturity.

The thoughts of youth are I thoughts.

—Henry Wadsworth

Explore thyself. Herein are demanded the eye and the nerve.

—Henry David Thoreau

a highly technological society such as the United States. Youths who have been well trained to enter a workforce that offers the potential of reasonably high self-esteem will experience the least stress during the development of identity. Some youths have rejected jobs offering good pay and traditionally high social status, choosing instead to work in situations that allow them to be more genuinely helpful to their fellow humans, such as in the Peace Corps, in mental health clinics, or in schools for children from low-income backgrounds. Some youths prefer unemployment to the prospect of working at a job they feel they would be unable to perform well or at which they would feel useless. To Erikson, this attitude reflects the desire to achieve a meaningful identity through being true to oneself, rather than burying one's identity in that of the larger society. More information about Erikson's ideas on identity development appears in Perspective on Child Development 15.1, where you can read about his analysis of the identity development of some famous individuals.

Some Contemporary Thoughts on Identity

Contemporary views of identity development suggest several important considerations. First, identity development is a lengthy process, in many instances a more gradual, less cataclysmic transition than Erikson implies (Baumeister, 1991). Second, as we just indicated, identity development is extraordinarily complex (Marcia, 1980, 1987, 1989). Identity formation neither begins nor ends with adolescence. It begins with the appearance of attachment, the development of a sense of self, and the emergence of independence in infancy and reaches its final phase with a life review and integration in old age. What is important about identity development in adolescence, especially late adolescence, is that, for the first time, physical development, cognitive development, and social development advance to the point at which the individual can sort through and synthesize childhood identities and identifications to construct a viable path toward adult maturity. Resolution of the identity issue at adolescence does not mean that identity will be stable through the remainder of life, however; an individual who develops a healthy identity is flexible and adaptive, open to changes in society, in relationships, and in careers. This openness assures numerous reorganizations of identity's contents throughout the identity-achieved individual's life.

Identity formation does not happen neatly, and it usually does not happen cataclysmically. At the bare minimum, it involves commitment to a vocational direction, an ideological stance, and a sexual orientation. Synthesizing the identity components can be a long process, with many negations and affirmations of various roles and faces. Identity development occurs in bits and pieces. Decisions are not made once and for all, but must be made again and again. The decisions may seem trivial at the time: whom to date, whether to break up, whether to have intercourse, whether to take drugs, whether to go to college or finish high school and get a job, which major to choose, whether to study or to play, whether to be politically active, and so on. Over the years of adolescence, the decisions begin to form a core of what the individual is all about as a human being—his or her identity.

The Four Statuses of Identity

Canadian psychologist James Marcia (1966, 1980, 1991) analyzed Erikson's theory of identity development and concluded that four identity statuses, or modes of resolution, appear in the theory: identity diffusion, identity foreclo-

Social and Personality Development

sure, identity moratorium, and identity achievement. The extent of an adolescent's crisis and commitment is used to classify the individual according to one of the four identity statuses. **Crisis** *is defined as a period of identity development during which the adolescent is choosing among meaningful alternatives.* Most researchers now use the term *exploration* rather than *crisis,* although, in the spirit of Marcia's original formulation, we will use the term *crisis.* **Commitment** *is the part of identity development in which adolescents show a personal investment in what they are going to do.*

Identity diffusion *is the term Marcia uses to describe adolescents who have not yet experienced a crisis (that is, they have not yet explored meaningful alternatives) or made any commitments.* Not only are they undecided about occupational and ideological choices, they are also likely to show little interest in such matters. **Identity foreclosure** *is the term Marcia uses to describe adolescents who have made a commitment but have not experienced a crisis.* This occurs most often when parents hand down commitments to their adolescents, more often than not in an authoritarian manner. In these circumstances, adolescents have not had an adequate opportunity to explore different approaches, ideologies, and vocations on their own. **Identity moratorium** *is the term Marcia uses to describe adolescents who are in the midst of a crisis, but their commitments either are absent or are only vaguely defined.* **Identity achievement** *is Marcia's term for adolescents who have undergone a crisis and have made a commitment.* Marcia's four statuses of identity are summarized in figure 15.5.

The identity status approach has come under sharp criticism by some researchers and theoreticians (Blasi, 1988; Cote & Levine, 1988a,b, 1989; Lapsley & Power, 1988). They believe that the identity status approach distorts and trivializes Erikson's notions of crisis and commitment. For example, concerning crisis, Erikson emphasized youths' questioning the perceptions and expectations of one's culture and developing an autonomous position with regard to one's society. In the identity status approach, these complex questions are dealt with by simply evaluating whether a youth has thought about certain issues and has considered alternatives. Erikson's idea of commitment loses the meaning of investing one's self in certain lifelong projects and is interpreted simply as having made a firm decision or not. Others still believe that the identity status approach is a valuable contribution to understanding identity (Archer, 1989; Marcia, 1989; Waterman, 1989).

Developmental Changes

Early adolescents are primarily in Marcia's identity diffusion or moratorium status. At least three aspects of the young adolescent's development are important in identity formation (Marcia, 1987). Young adolescents must establish confidence in parental support, develop a sense of industry, and gain a self-reflective perspective on their future.

Some researchers believe that the most important identity changes take place in youth rather than earlier in adolescence. For example, Alan Waterman (1985, 1989) has found that, from the years preceding high school through the last few years of college, the number of individuals who are identity achieved increases, along with a decrease in those who are identity diffused. College juniors and seniors are more likely to be identity achieved than college freshmen or high school students. Many young adolescents are identity diffused. These developmental changes are especially true for vocational choice. For religious beliefs and political ideology, fewer college students have reached the identity achieved status, with a substantial number characterized by foreclosure and

In the beginning was alpha and the end is omega, but somewhere in between occurred delta, which is nothing less than the arrival of man himself into the daylight of . . . being himself and not being himself, of being at home and being a stranger.

—Walker Percy

Hitler, Luther, and Gandhi—the Development of Their Identities

Erik Erikson is a master at analyzing famous individuals' lives and discovering historical clues about their identity formation. Erikson also developed ideas for his view of identity development by analyzing the developmental history of clients in his clinical practice. Erikson (1968) believes that an individual's developmental history must be carefully scrutinized and analyzed to obtain clues about identity. He also believes that the best clues to understanding the world's history appear in the composite of individual life cycles. In the excerpts that follow, Erikson analyzes the lives of Adolf Hitler, Martin Luther, and Mahatma Gandhi.

About Hitler, Erikson (1962) commented:

I will not go into the symbolism of Hitler's urge to build except to say that his shiftless and brutal father had consistently denied the mother a steady residence: one must read how Adolf took care of his mother when she wasted away from breast cancer to get an inkling of this young man's desperate urge to cure. But it would take a very extensive analysis, indeed, to indicate in what way a single boy can daydream his way into history and emerge a sinister genius, and how a whole nation becomes ready to accept the emotive power of that genius as a hope of fulfillment for its national aspirations and as a warrant for national criminality. . . .

The memoirs of young Hitler's friend indicate an almost pitiful fear on the part of the future dictator that he might be nothing. He had to challenge this possibility by being deliberately and totally anonymous; and only out of this self-chosen nothingness could he become everything. (pp. 108–109)

Although the identity crisis of Adolf Hitler led him to politics in a pathological effort to create a world order, the identity crisis of Martin Luther in a different era led him to theology in an attempt to deal systematically with human nothingness, or lack of identity:

In confession, for example, he was so meticulous in the attempt to be truthful that he spelled out every intention as well as every deed; he splintered relatively acceptable purities into smaller and smaller impurities; he reported temptations in historical sequence, starting back in childhood; and after having confessed for hours, would ask for special appointments in order to correct previous statements. In doing this, he was obviously both exceedingly compulsive and, at least unconsciously, rebellious. . . .

At this point, we must note a characteristic of great young rebels: their inner split between the temptation to surrender and the need to dominate. A great young rebel is torn between, on the one hand, tendencies to give in and fantasies of defeat (Luther used to resign himself to an early death at times of impending success), and the absolute need, on the other hand, to take the lead, not only over himself but over all the forces and people who impinge on him. (Erikson, 1968, pp. 155–157)

In his Pulitzer Prize-winning novel on Mahatma Gandhi's life, Erikson (1969) describes the personality formation of Gandhi during his youth:

Straight and yet not stiff; shy and yet not withdrawn; intelligent and yet not bookish; willful and yet not stubborn; sensual and yet not soft. . . . We must try to reflect on the relation of such a youth to his father, because the Mahatma places service to the father and the crushing guilt of failing in such service in the center of his adolescent turbulence. Some historians and political scientists seem to find it easy to interpret this account in psychoanalytic terms; I do not. For the question is not how a particular version of the oedipal complex "causes" a man to be both great and neurotic in a particular way, but rather how such a young person . . . manages the complexes which constrict other men. (p. 113)

In these passages, the workings of an insightful, sensitive mind is shown looking for a historical perspective on personality development. Through analysis of the lives of such famous people as Hitler, Luther, and Gandhi and through the thousands of youth he has talked with personally, Erikson has pieced together a descriptive picture of identity development.

diffusion. Thus, the timing of identity may depend on the particular role involved, and many college students are still wrestling with ideological commitments (Arehart & Smith, 1990; Harter, 1990a).

Many identity status researchers believe that individuals who develop positive identities follow a common pattern called "MAMA" (*m*oratorium–*a*chiever–*m*oratorium–*a*chiever) cycles (Archer, 1989; Marcia, 1991). These cycles may be repeated throughout life (Francis, Fraser, & Marcia, 1989). Personal, family, and societal changes are inevitable and, as they occur, the flexibility and skill required to explore new alternatives and develop new commitments likely facilitate an individual's coping skills.

(a)

(b)

(a) Hitler is in the center of the top row in this elementary school photo. In Erikson's analysis, what are some important experiences that contributed to Hitler's identity development? (b) What did Erikson believe were some of the key ingredients in Mahatma Gandhi's development of identity?

Family Influences on Identity

Parents are important figures in adolescents' development of identity. In studies that relate identity development to parenting styles, democratic parents, who encourage adolescents to participate in family decision making, foster identity achievement. Autocratic parents, who control the adolescent's behavior without giving the adolescent an opportunity to express an opinion, encourage identity foreclosure. Permissive parents, who provide little guidance to adolescents and allow them to make their own decisions, promote identity diffusion (Bernard, 1981; Enright & others, 1980; Marcia, 1980).

The Self, Social Competence, and Identity

Figure 15.5
Four Statuses of Identity

	Identity status (position on occupation and ideology)			
	Identity moratorium	Identity foreclosure	Identity diffusion	Identity achievement
Crisis	Present	Absent	Absent	Present
Commitment	Absent	Present	Absent	Present

In addition to studying parenting styles, researchers also have examined the role of individuality and connectedness in the development of identity. Developmentalist Catherine Cooper and her colleagues (Carlson, Cooper, & Hsu, 1990; Cooper & Carlson, 1991; Cooper & Grotevant, 1989; Grotevant & Cooper, 1985) believe that the presence of a family atmosphere that promotes both individuality and connectedness is important in adolescent identity development. **Individuality** *consists of two dimensions: self-assertion—the ability to have and communicate a point of view—and separateness—the use of communication patterns to express how one differs from others.* **Connectedness** *also consists of two dimensions: mutuality—sensitivity to and respect for others' views—and permeability—openness to others' views.* In general, Cooper's research reveals that identity formation is enhanced by family relationships that are both individualized, which encourages adolescents to develop their own point of view, and connected, which provides a secure base from which to explore the widening social worlds of adolescence.

Stuart Hauser and his colleagues (1990, 1991; Hauser & others, 1984) have also illuminated the family processes that promote adolescents' identity development. They have found that parents who use *enabling* behaviors (such as explaining, accepting, and giving empathy) facilitate the adolescent identity development more than parents who use *constraining* behaviors (such as judging and devaluing). In sum, family interaction styles that give adolescents the right to question and to be different, within a context of support and mutuality, foster healthy patterns of identity development (Harter, 1990b).

An adolescent's positive development of identity is related both to connectedness with parents and to individuation.

Cultural and Ethnic Aspects of Identity

Erikson is especially sensitive to the role of culture in identity development. He points out that, throughout the world, ethnic minority groups have struggled to maintain their cultural identities while blending into a dominant culture (Erikson, 1968). Erikson says that this struggle for an inclusive identity, or identity within a larger culture, has been the driving force in the founding of churches, empires, and revolutions throughout history.

For ethnic minority individuals, adolescence is often a special juncture in their development (Spencer, 1991; Spencer & Dornbusch, 1990). Although children are aware of some ethnic and cultural differences, most ethnic minority individuals first consciously confront their ethnicity in adolescence. In contrast to children, adolescents have the ability to interpret ethnic and cultural information, to reflect on the past, and to speculate about the future (Harter, 1990a). As they mature cognitively, ethnic minority adolescents become acutely aware of the evaluations of their ethnic group by the majority White culture (Comer, 1988; Ogbu, 1989). As one researcher commented, a young Black American child may learn that Black is beautiful but conclude as an adolescent that White is powerful (Semaj, 1985).

Ethnic minority youths' awareness of negative appraisals, conflicting values, and restricted occupational opportunities can influence life choices and plans for the future (Spencer & Dornbusch, 1990). As one ethnic minority youth stated, "The future seems shut off, closed. Why dream? You can't reach your dreams. Why set goals? At least if you don't set any goals, you don't fail."

For many ethnic minority youths, a lack of successful ethnic minority role models with whom to identify is a special concern (Jackson & others, 1991). The problem is especially acute for inner-city ethnic minority youths. Because of the lack of adult ethnic minority role models, some ethnic minority youths may conform to middle-class White values and identify with successful White role models. However, for many adolescents, their ethnicity and skin color constrain their acceptance by the White culture. Thus, many ethnic minority adolescents have a difficult task: negotiating two value systems—that of their own ethnic group and that of the White society. Some adolescents reject the mainstream, foregoing the rewards controlled by White Americans; others adopt the values and standards of the majority White culture; yet others take the difficult path of biculturality.

In one recent investigation, ethnic identity exploration was higher among ethnic minority than White American college students (Phinney & Alipuria, 1990). In this same investigation, ethnic minority college students who had thought about and resolved issues involving their ethnicity had higher self-esteem than their ethnic minority counterparts who had not. In another investigation, the ethnic identity development of Asian American, Black American, Hispanic American, and White American tenth-grade students in Los Angeles was studied (Phinney, 1989). Adolescents from each of the three ethnic minority groups faced a similar need to deal with their ethnic-group identification in a predominately White American culture. In some instances, the adolescents from the three ethnic minority groups perceived different issues to be important in their resolution of ethnic identity. For Asian American adolescents, pressures to achieve academically and concerns about quotas that make it difficult to get into good colleges were salient issues. Many Black American adolescent females discussed their realization that White American standards of beauty (especially hair and skin color) did not apply to them; Black American adolescent males were concerned with possible job discrimination and the need to distinguish themselves from a negative societal image of Black male adolescents. For Hispanic American adolescents, prejudice was a recurrent theme, as was conflicting values between their Hispanic cultural heritage and the majority culture. To read further about identity development in ethnic minority youths, turn to Cultural Worlds of Development 15.2.

The Development of Identity in Native American Adolescents

Substandard living conditions, poverty, and chronic unemployment place many Native American youths at risk for school failure and poor health, which can contribute to problems in developing a positive identity (LaFromboise & Low, 1989; Spencer & Markstrom-Adams, 1990). A special concern is the negative image of Native Americans that has been perpetuated for centuries in the majority White American culture. To consider further the development of identity in Native American youths, let's examine the experiences of a Hopi Indian boy.

The Hopi Indians are a quiet, thoughtful people, who go to great lengths not to offend anyone. In a pueblo north of Albuquerque, a 12-year-old boy speaks: "I've been living in Albuquerque for a year. The Anglos I've met, they're different. I don't know why. In school, I drew a picture of my father's horse. One of the other kids wouldn't believe that it was ours. He said, 'You don't really own that horse.' I said, 'It's a horse my father rides, and I feed it every morning.' He said, 'How come?' I said, 'My uncle and my father are good riders, and I'm pretty good.' He said, 'I can ride a horse better than you, and I'd rather be a pilot.' I told him I never thought of being a pilot."

The 12-year-old Indian boy continues, "Anglo kids, they won't let you get away with anything. Tell them something, and fast as lightning and loud as thunder, they'll say, 'I'm better than you, so there!' My father says it's always been like that."

Native American adolescents are not really angry or envious of White adolescents. Maybe they are in awe of their future power; maybe they fear it. White adolescents can't keep from wondering if, in some way, they have missed out on something and may end up "losing" (Coles, 1986).

Like children and adolescents from other ethnic minority groups, Native American youths often are confronted with conflicting values and expectations—those of the larger society and those of their ethnic group—from which they must choose an identity (Spencer & Markstrom-Adams, 1990). Tribal spirituality continues to be an important aspect of Native American culture. Native American children and adolescents are expected to participate in ceremonies related to these spiritual practices, which may violate attendance policies of Anglo-operated schools (LaFromboise & Low, 1989). The Native American youths' task of sorting through the values and expectations of the larger society and the Native American culture and then arriving at a coherent identity is a formidable one. If Native American youths develop an identity that includes many ingredients of the larger culture, they risk being rejected by their tribal members. Many Native American adolescents oscillate between an identity with the larger Anglo society and an identity with a tribe.

The following words of a Native American vividly capture some important aspects of Native American youths' search for an identity:

Rivers flow.
The sea sings.
Oceans roar.
Tides rise.
Who am I?

A small pebble
On a giant shore;
Who am I
To ask who I am?
Isn't it enough to be?

Gender and Identity

In Erikson's (1968) classic presentation of identity development, the division of labor between the genders was reflected in his assertion that males' aspirations were mainly oriented toward career and ideological commitments, whereas females' were centered around marriage and childrearing. In the 1960s and 1970s, researchers found support for Erikson's assertion about gender differences in identity. For example, vocational concerns were more central to the identity of males, affiliative concerns more important in the identity of females (LaVoie, 1976). However, in the past decade, as females have developed stronger vocational interests, gender differences are turning into gender similarities (Archer, 1991; Waterman, 1985).

The Native American adolescent's quest for identity involves a cultural meshing of tribal customs and the technological, educational demands of modern society.

Some investigators believe that the order of stages proposed by Erikson is different for females and males. One view is that, for males, identity formation precedes the stage of intimacy, whereas, for females, intimacy precedes identity (Douvan & Adelson, 1966). These ideas are consistent with the belief that relationships and emotional bonds are more important concerns of females, whereas autonomy and achievement are more important concerns of males (Gilligan, 1990). In one study, the development of a clear sense of self by adolescent girls was related to their concerns about care and response in relationships (Rogers, 1987). In another investigation, a strong sense of self in college women was associated with their ability to solve problems of care in relationships while staying connected with both self and others (Skoe & Marcia, 1988).

CONCEPT TABLE 15.2
Social Competence and Identity

Concept	Processes/related ideas	Characteristics/description
Social competence	What is it?	Social competence has been defined in various ways. Both the definitions of Waters and Sroufe and of Ford emphasize its internal, self, self-assertive dimensions and its external, social, environmental dimensions. Waters and Sroufe emphasize the use of personal and environmental resources. Ford emphasizes four issues—identity, control, social comparison, and resource distribution—and their self-assertive and integrative components.
	Measurement	Measurement should include broadband and narrow assessments; real-world behavior and laboratory tasks; coordination of affect, cognition, and behavior; and taxing behavioral and integrative/adaptive capacity.
Erikson's ideas on identity	Their nature	Erikson argues that identity versus identity confusion is the fifth stage in the human life cycle, occurring at about the time of adolescence, a time when individuals enter a psychological moratorium between the security of childhood and the autonomy of adulthood. Personality exploration and the exploration of roles are two important ingredients of identity development. In technological societies, such as the United States, the vocational role is especially important.
	Some contemporary thoughts about identity	Identity development is a lengthy process, in many cases more gradual than Erikson implied. Identity development is extraordinarily complex. Identity development is done in bits and pieces. For the first time in development, individuals during adolescence are physically, cognitively, and socially mature enough to synthesize their lives and pursue a viable path toward adult maturity.
	The four statuses of identity	Marcia proposed four identity statuses—identity diffusion, identity foreclosure, identity moratorium, and identity achievement—that are based on crisis (exploration) and commitment. Some experts believe that the identity status approach oversimplifies Erikson's ideas.
	Developmental changes	Some experts believe that the main identity changes take place in youth rather than earlier in adolescence. College juniors and seniors are more likely to be identity achieved than freshmen or high school students, although many college students are still wrestling with ideological commitments. Individuals often follow "moratorium-achievement-moratorium-achievement" cycles throughout life.

The task of identity exploration may be more complex for females than males in that females may try to establish identities in more domains than males. In today's world, the options for females have increased, and thus may at times be confusing and conflicting, especially for females who hope to successfully integrate family and career roles (Archer, 1989; Gilligan, 1990; Marcia, 1989).

At this point, we have discussed a number of ideas about social competence and identity. A summary of these ideas is presented in concept table 15.2. In the next chapter, we will turn our attention exclusively to children's gender.

Concept	Processes/related ideas	Characteristics/description
	Family influences	Parents are important figures in adolescents' identity development. Democratic parenting facilitates identity development in adolescence; autocratic and permissive parenting do not. Cooper and her colleagues have shown that both individuality and connectedness in family relations are important contributors to adolescent identity development. Hauser has shown that enabling behaviors promote identity development more than constraining behaviors.
	Cultural and ethnic aspects of identity	Erikson is especially sensitive to the role of culture in identity development, underscoring how, throughout the world, ethnic minority groups have struggled to maintain their cultural identities while blending into dominant cultures. Adolescence is often a special juncture in the identity development of ethnic minority individuals because for the first time they consciously confront their ethnic identity. Although children are aware of some ethnic and cultural differences, most individuals first consciously confront their ethnicity in adolescence. A problem for many ethnic minority youths is the lack of successful ethnic minority role models with whom to identify.
	Identity and gender	Erikson's classical theory argued that gender differences in identity development exist, with adolescent males having a stronger interest in vocational roles, adolescent females a stronger interest in marriage and family roles. More recent studies have revealed that, as females have developed stronger vocational interests, gender differences in identity have turned into similarities. However, others argue that relationships and emotional bonds are more central to the identity development of females than of males and that female identity development is more complex than male identity development.

Summary

I. The Nature of Self-understanding and Infant Self-recognition

Self-understanding is the child's cognitive representation of self, the substance and content of the child's self-conceptions. Self-understanding provides the rational underpinnings of personal identity. Infants initially develop a rudimentary form of self-understanding—self-recognition—at approximately 18 months of age.

II. Development of Self-understanding in Early Childhood and Middle and Late Childhood

In early childhood, the physical and active self becomes a part of self-understanding, as many young children describe themselves in physical or active terms. In middle and late childhood, the internal self, the social self, and the socially comparative self become more prominent in self-understanding. Elementary-school-aged children increasingly describe themselves with internal, psychological characteristics. They also are more likely to define themselves in terms of social characteristics and social comparison.

III. Self-understanding in Adolescence and Further Developmental Considerations

Self-understanding in adolescence is complex. Self-understanding is more abstract, idealistic, differentiated, self-contradictory, self-conscious, and self-protective than in childhood. Especially in late adolescence, self-understanding involves recognition of unconscious influences and is more integrative. Once the characteristics emerge as part of self-understanding, they continue to be a part of self-understanding, although they may wax and wane to varying degrees as development proceeds. For example, although the internal self is described as becoming more prominent in middle and late childhood, the internal self continues to be an integral part of self-understanding in adolescence. The physical self continues to be a part of self-description in adolescence as well, but it often is less central in self-description than in early childhood.

IV. Perspective Taking

Perspective taking is the ability to assume another person's perspective and understand his or her thoughts and feelings. Selman proposed a developmental theory of perspective taking with five stages, ranging from 3 years of age through adolescence, beginning with the egocentric viewpoint in early childhood and ending with the in-depth perspective taking of adolescence.

V. The Nature of Self-esteem and Its Measurement

Self-esteem is the evaluative and affective dimension of self-concept. Self-esteem is also referred to as self-worth or self-image. Until recently, self-esteem was described in global terms. Today, domain-specific aspects of self-esteem are also considered. Measuring self-esteem is a difficult task. Harter's measures have been appealing to many developmentalists because they provide a differentiated assessment of self-esteem in various skill domains, as well as an independent assessment of general self-worth. Some assessment experts believe several methods should be used to measure self-esteem, including observations of a child's behavior.

VI. Self-esteem: Parent-Child Relationships, Group Identity, and Improving Children's Self-esteem

In Coopersmith's study, children's self-esteem was associated with such parenting attributes as parental acceptance and allowing children freedom within well-prescribed limits. It is important to remember that these associations are correlational. Social identity theory is Tajfel's theory that, when individuals are assigned to a group, they invariably think of the group as an in-group for them. This occurs because they want to have a positive self-image. Tajfel believes self-image consists of a personal *and* many different social identities related to group membership and identity.

Group identity often leads to competition, and sometimes conflict, between groups. Closely related to group identity and self-esteem is ethnocentrism, the tendency to favor one's own group over other groups. The positive side of ethnocentrism is a sense of in-group pride, but sometimes a negative side—prejudice—develops. A special concern is the self-esteem of ethnic minority children. Social support in the form of approval and confirmation from others is a powerful influence on adolescents' self-esteem. Both adult and peer support are important in increasing adolescent self-esteem. Identifying the sources of self-esteem is critical to improving adolescent self-esteem. Programs that encourage adolescents to identify and value areas of competence should be implemented. One strategy is to emphasize the positive benefits of competence in areas other than academic achievement; another strategy is to recognize that academic achievement is the route to success and high self-esteem. Some programs emphasize competence in academic achievement and other domains as well.

VII. Social Competence

Social competence has been defined in various ways. Both the definitions of Waters and Sroufe and of Ford emphasize its internal, self, self-assertive dimensions, and its external, social, environmental dimensions. Waters and Sroufe emphasize the use of personal and environmental resources to increase social competence. Ford emphasizes four issues—identity, control, social comparison, and resource distribution—and their self-assertive and integrative components. The measurement of social competence should include broadband and narrow assessments; real-world behavior and laboratory tasks; coordination of affect, cognition, and behavior; and taxing behavioral and integrative/adaptive capacity.

VIII. Erikson's Ideas on Identity

Erikson argues that identity versus identity confusion is the fifth stage in the human life cycle, occurring at about the time of adolescence, when individuals enter a psychological moratorium between the security of childhood and the autonomy of adulthood. Personality exploration and the exploration of roles are two important ingredients of identity development. In technological societies, such as the United States, the vocational role is especially important.

IX. Some Contemporary Thoughts on Identity

Identity development is a lengthy process, in many cases being more gradual than Erikson implied. Identity development is extraordinarily complex and is done in bits and pieces. For the first time in their development, individuals during adolescence are physically, cognitively, and socially mature enough to synthesize their lives and pursue a viable path toward adult maturity.

X. The Four Statuses of Identity, Developmental Changes, and Family Influences on Identity

Marcia proposed four identity statuses—identity diffusion, identity foreclosure, identity moratorium, and identity achievement—that are based on crisis (exploration) and commitment. Some experts believe that the identity status approach oversimplifies Erikson's ideas. Some experts believe that the main identity changes take place in youth rather than earlier in adolescence. College juniors and seniors are more likely to be identity achieved than freshmen or high school students, although many college students are still wrestling with ideological commitments. Individuals often follow "moratorium-achievement-moratorium-achievement" cycles throughout life. Parents are important figures in adolescents' identity development. Democratic parenting facilitates adolescents' identity development; autocratic and permissive parenting do not. Cooper has shown that both individuality and connectedness in family relations are important contributors to adolescent identity development. Hauser has shown that enabling behaviors promote identity development more than constraining behaviors.

XI. Cultural and Ethnic Aspects of Identity and Identity and Gender

Erikson is especially sensitive to the role of culture in identity development, underscoring how, throughout the world, ethnic minority groups have struggled to maintain their cultural identities while blending into majority cultures. Adolescence is often a special juncture in the identity development of ethnic minority individuals because for the first time they consciously confront their ethnic identity. Although children are aware of some ethnic and cultural differences, most individuals first consciously confront their ethnicity in adolescence. A problem for many ethnic minority youths is a lack of successful ethnic minority role models with whom to identify. Erikson's classical theory argued that gender differences in identity development exist, with adolescent males having a stronger interest in vocational roles, adolescent females a stronger interest in marriage and family roles. More recent studies have revealed that, as females have developed stronger vocational interests, gender differences in identity have turned into similarities. However, others argue that relationships and emotional bonds are more central to the identity development of females than of males and that female identity development is more complex than male identity development.

Key Terms

self-understanding 519
self-esteem 525
social identity theory 527
ethnocentrism 528
prejudice 528
social competence 530
psychological
  moratorium 535

crisis 537
commitment 537
identity diffusion 537
identity foreclosure 537
identity moratorium 537
identity achievement 537
individuality 540
connectedness 540

Suggested Readings

Damon, W., & Hart, D. (1988). *Self-understanding in childhood and adolescence*. New York: Cambridge University Press. An extensive description of the development of self-understanding is provided, including Damon and Hart's integrative, developmental model of self-understanding.

Erikson, E. H. (1969). *Gandhi's truth*. New York: W. W. Norton. In this Pulitzer Prize–winning novel, Erikson weaves an insightful picture of Gandhi's development of identity.

Ford, M., & Ford, D. (Eds.). (1987). *Humans as self-constructing living systems*. Hillsdale, NJ: Erlbaum. This book provides an extensive interpretation of social competence, including Martin Ford's model of social competence in terms of self-assertive and integrative criteria.

Harter, S. (1990). Self and identity development. In S. S. Feldman & G. R. Elliott (Eds.), *At the threshold: The developing adolescent*. Cambridge, MA: Harvard University Press. This is an excellent overview of contemporary theory and research on the nature of self and identity development in adolescence by one of the leading researchers in the area of self-understanding.

Lapsley, D. K., & Power, F. C. (1988). *Self, ego, and identity*. New York: Springer-Verlag. This is an up-to-date, authoritative treatment of the issues involved in the nature of the self and identity by leading scholars.

Selman, R. L. (1980). *The growth of interpersonal understanding*. New York: Academic Press. Considerable detail about Selman's developmental theory of perspective taking and self-development is provided. The book includes information about clinical implications for helping children with problems.

CHAPTER

16

∎

GENDER

What Is Gender?
What Are the Biological, Social, and Cognitive
  Influences on Gender?
    Biological Influences
    Social Influences
    Cognitive Influences
    Perspective on Child Development 16.1: How
       Good Are Girls at Wudgemaking if the
       Wudgemaker Is He?
Gender Stereotypes, Similarities and Differences, and
  Achievement
    Gender Role Stereotyping
    Gender Similarities and Differences
    Achievement
Gender Role Classification—Masculinity, Femininity,
  and Androgyny
    Cultural Worlds of Development 16.1: Gender
      Roles in Egypt, China, and the Soviet Union
The Feminist Perspective on Gender
Gender and Social Policy
    Gender Role Stereotypes and the Media
    Gender and Education
    Gender and Child Care
Ethnicity and Gender
    Ethnic Minority Females
    Ethnic Minority Males
Summary
Key Terms
Suggested Readings

IT IS FATAL TO BE MAN OR WOMAN PURE AND SIMPLE; ONE MUST BE WOMAN-MANLY OR MAN-WOMANLY.

—Virginia Woolf

The year is 1957 and the conversation is with 16-year-old Mary Smith. "What are your plans when you finish high school?" Mary replies, "I am going steady with someone I really love and we plan to get married in the summer after I finish high school. I'm a sophomore and he is a junior so he is going to get a job for a year before we get married. I would like to have a baby about a year after we are married. I can't wait. Marrying Tom and having a baby are all I can think about. We plan to set up housekeeping and I will stay home with the baby. We want to live here and have no plans to leave."

"What do you think the man's role and the woman's role should be in a relationship?" Mary responds, "Well, I think a man should be dominant and be the provider. He should make most of the decisions but he should allow the woman to make everyday decisions about the home and children. A man should be good to a woman but she should try to please him the best she can. It's been that way with my parents and I think it works out best that way."

The year is now 1992 and the conversation is with 16-year-old Tracy McKinley. "What are your plans when you finish high school?" Tracy replies, "I plan to go to college. Right now I'm looking seriously at several large universities in the West and the Northeast. I want to be an electrical engineer or a computer analyst. I probably will go to graduate school after college. Marriage and a family aren't in my plans. I imagine I might get married when I'm about 30 years old, but that definitely would be the earliest. If I have children, I want to continue my career with as little interruption as possible."

"What do you think the man's role and the women's role should be in a relationship?" Tracy responds. "I think they should be equal. Completely equal, no ifs, ands, or buts. Why should it be any different? I'm a human being, so are all other females, and so are all other males. I know there still are some girls who want a male to be macho and dominant. I just don't understand that. It doesn't make sense. Those girls must not have thought very much about what life is all about. Sure, I want to date guys that are handsome and strong, but I expect them to be extremely nice, warm, and caring toward me at the same time. At my high school, there are a few guys that fit this description, but they are the exception rather than the rule. My mother tells me that, in her day, there were even fewer. Some guys have trouble handling my assertiveness. They want a girl who builds up their ego. Hey, my ego needs building up, too, and it is important to me to stand up for my rights. Still, I can be feminine and affectionate toward the right guy, if he is what I want."

How the gender times have changed. The Tracy McKinleys were few and far between in 1957. The Mary Smiths are still around in the 1990s but their ranks are dramatically reduced. This chapter is about gender, about children's worlds as female and male. Among the questions we will explore are the following: What is gender? What are the biological, social, and cognitive influences on gender? Are there many gender differences or are most of what we often consider differences actually stereotypes? How can gender roles be classified? What is the feminist perspective on gender? What gender issues are involved in social policy? What is the role of gender in ethnicity? We will consider each of these questions in turn.

What Is Gender?

Nowhere in children's social development have more sweeping changes occurred in recent years than in the area of gender. What exactly do we mean by gender? Whereas the term *sex* refers to the biological dimension of being male or female, **gender** *refers to the social dimension of being male or female.* Few aspects of children's development are more central to their identity and to their social relationships than is gender. Two aspects of gender bear special mention—gender identity and gender role. **Gender identity** *is the sense of being male or female, which most children acquire by the time they are 3 years old.* For example, a 3-year-old girl is aware she is a girl and a 3-year-old boy knows he is a boy. **Gender role** *is a set of expectations that prescribes how females or males should think, act, and feel.* For example, does the society in which children live prescribe that boys should be assertive and that girls should be considerate of others?

What Are the Biological, Social, and Cognitive Influences on Gender?

How strong is biology's influence on gender? How extensively do children's social experiences shape their gender development? How do cognitive factors influence gender development? We will explore the answers to each of these questions in turn.

Biological Influences

One of Freud's basic assumptions is that human behavior and history are directly related to the reproductive processes. From this assumption arises the belief that sexuality is essentially unlearned and instinctual. Erikson (1968) extended this argument, claiming that the psychological differences between males and females stem from anatomical differences. Erikson argued that—because of genital structure—males are more intrusive and aggressive, females more inclusive and passive. Erikson's belief has become known as "anatomy is destiny." Critics of the anatomy-is-destiny view believe that Erikson has not given experience adequate importance. They argue that males and females are more free to choose their gender role than Erikson would allow. In response to the critics, Erikson has modified his view, saying that females in today's world are transcending their biological heritage and correcting society's overemphasis on male intrusiveness.

Biology's influence on gender roles also involves sex hormones, which you learned about in chapter 3. These are among the most powerful and subtle chemicals in nature. Remember that these hormones are controlled by the brain's master gland, the pituitary. In females, hormones from the pituitary carry messages to the ovaries and produce the hormone estrogen. In males, the pituitary messages travel to the testes, where the sex hormone androgen is manufactured.

The secretion of androgen from the testes of the young male fetus (or the absence of androgen in the female) completely controls sexual development in the womb. If enough androgen is produced, as happens with a normally developing boy, male organs and genitals develop. **Hermaphrodites** *are individuals whose genitals become intermediate between male and female because of a hormonal imbalance (as in the developing male with insufficient androgen, or a female exposed to an excess of androgen).* When genetically female infants are born with masculine-looking genitals, surgery is usually performed so that a female genital/female genetic match is achieved. Until they reach puberty, these females often behave in a more aggressive, "tomboyish" manner than most girls. They also dress and play in ways that are considered to be more characteristic of boys than girls (Ehrhardt, 1987; Money, 1987).

Is the behavior of these surgically corrected females due to their prenatal hormones, or is their behavior due to their social experiences? Experiments with various animal species—rats, monkeys, and many others—reveal that, when male hormones are injected into female embryos, the females later display a more masculine appearance and behave in a more masculine way (Hines, 1982). However, hormonal control over behavior is usually less dominant in humans than in animals. Since androgenized girls look more "masculine," people may react to them as if they were boys. The biological appearance of sex has social consequences for gender.

No one argues about the presence of genetic, biochemical, and anatomical differences between the sexes. Even child developmentalists with a strong environmental orientation acknowledge that boys and girls are treated differently because of their physical differences and their different roles in reproduction. The importance of biological factors is not at issue. What is at issue is the directness or indirectness of their effects on social behavior (Huston, 1983). For example, if a high androgen level directly influences the central nervous system, which, in turn, increases activity level, then the biological effect on behavior is direct. By contrast, if a child's high level of androgen produces strong muscle development, which, in turn, causes others to expect the child to be a good athlete and, in turn, leads the child to participate in sports, then the biological effect on behavior is indirect.

Although virtually everyone thinks that children's behavior as males or females is due to an interaction of biological and environmental factors, an interactionist position means different things to different people (Bancroft & Reinisch, 1990; Hinde, 1989a; Maccoby, 1987b; Money, 1987). For some, it suggests that certain environmental conditions are required before preprogrammed dispositions appear. For others, it suggests that a particular environment will have different effects depending on the child's predispositions. For still others, it means that children shape their environments, including their interpersonal environment, and vice versa. The processes of influence and counterinfluence unfold over time. Throughout development, males and females actively construct their own versions of acceptable masculine and feminine behavior patterns.

Social Influences

In our culture, adults discriminate between the sexes shortly after the infant's birth. The "pink and blue" treatment may be applied to boys and girls even before they leave the hospital. Soon afterward, differences in hairstyles, clothes, and toys become obvious. Adults and peers reward these differences throughout development, and boys and girls learn gender roles through imitation or observational learning by watching what other people say and do. In recent years, however, the idea that parents are the critical socialization agents in gender role development has come under fire (Huston, 1983; Huston & Alvarez, 1990). Parents are only one of many sources from which a child learns gender roles. Culture, schools, peers, the media, and other family members are others. However, it is important to guard against swinging too far in this direction of thought, because—especially in the early years of development—parents are important influences on gender development.

Theory	Processes		Outcome
Freud's identification theory	Sexual attraction to opposite-sex parent at 3 to 5 years of age	Anxiety about sexual attraction and subsequent identification with same-sex parent at 5 to 6 years of age	Gender behavior similar to same-sex parent
Social learning theory	Rewards and punishments of gender-appropriate and inappropriate behavior by adults and peers	Observation and imitation of models' masculine and feminine behavior	Gender behavior

Identification and Social Learning Theories

Two prominent theories address the way children acquire masculine and feminine attitudes and behaviors from their parents. **Identification theory** *stems from Freud's view that preschool children develop a sexual attraction to the opposite-sex parent, then, at 5 to 6 years of age, renounce this attraction because of anxious feelings, subsequently identifying with the same-sex parent and unconsciously adopting the same-sex parent's characteristics.* Today, however, many child developmentalists do not believe gender development proceeds on the basis of identification, at least in terms of Freud's emphasis on childhood sexual attraction. Children become gender-typed much earlier than 5 to 6 years of age, and they become masculine or feminine even when the same-sex parent is not present in the family.

The **social learning view of gender** *emphasizes that children's gender development occurs through observation and imitation of gender behavior as well as through the rewards and punishments children experience for gender-appropriate and gender-inappropriate behavior.* Unlike identification theory, social learning theory argues that sexual attraction to parents is not involved in gender development. (A comparison of identification and social learning views is presented in figure 16.1) Parents often use rewards and punishments to teach their daughters to be feminine ("Karen, you are being a good girl when you play gently with your doll") and masculine ("Keith, a boy as big as you is not supposed to cry"). Peers also extensively reward and punish gender behavior. At home, at school, in the neighborhood, and in watching television, children are widely exposed to a myriad of models who display masculine and feminine behavior. Critics of the social learning view argue that gender development is not acquired as passively as the theory proposes. Later in the chapter, we will discuss the cognitive views of gender development, which stress that children actively construct their gender world.

Figure 16.1
A Comparison of Identification and Social Learning Views of Gender Development

Children need models rather than critics.
—Joseph Joubert

Parents influence their children's gender development by action and by example.

Parental Influences

Parents, by action and by example, influence their children's gender development. Both mothers and fathers are psychologically important in children's gender development. Mothers are more consistently given responsibility for nurturance and physical care; fathers are more likely to engage in playful interaction and be responsible for ensuring that boys and girls conform to existing cultural norms. Whether or not they have more influence on them, fathers are more involved in socializing their sons than their daughters (Lamb, 1986). Fathers seem to play an especially important part in gender role development—they are more likely to act differently toward sons and daughters than mothers are (Huston, 1983).

Many parents encourage boys and girls to engage in different types of play and activities (Lewis, 1987). Girls are more likely to be given dolls to play with during childhood and, when old enough, are more likely to be assigned baby-sitting duties. Girls are encouraged to be more nurturant and emotional than boys, and fathers are more likely to engage in aggressive play with their sons than with their daughters. As adolescents increase in age, parents permit boys more freedom than girls, allowing them to be away from home and stay out later without supervision. Parents who place severe restrictions on their adolescent sons often disrupt the adolescents' development (Baumrind, 1989).

Peer Influences

Parents provide the earliest discrimination of gender roles in development, but, before long, peers join the societal process of responding to and modeling masculine and feminine behavior. Children who play in gender-appropriate activities tend to be rewarded for doing so by their peers. Those who play in cross-sexed activities tend to be criticized by their peers or left to play alone. Children show a clear preference for being with and liking same-sex peers (Maccoby, 1989; Maccoby & Jacklin, in press), and this tendency usually becomes stronger during the middle and late childhood years (Hayden-Thomson, Rubin, & Hymel, 1987). After extensive observations of elementary school playgrounds, two researchers characterized the play settings as "gender school," pointing out that boys teach one another the required masculine behavior and enforce it strictly (Luria & Herzog, 1985). Girls also pass on the female culture and congregate mainly with one another. Individual girls can join boys' activities without losing their status in the girls' groups, but the reverse is not true for boys, reflecting our society's greater gender-typing pressure on boys.

Peer demands for conformity to gender roles become especially intense during early adolescence. Although there is greater social mixing of males and females during early adolescence than in childhood, in both formal groups and in dating, peer pressure is strong for the adolescent boy to be the very best male possible and for the adolescent girl to be the very best female possible.

School and Teacher Influences

In a recent Gallup poll, 80 percent of the respondents agreed that the federal government should promote educational programs intended to reduce such social problems as poverty and unequal educational opportunities for minorities and females (Gallup & Clark, 1987). Discriminatory treatment involving gender affects people at all levels of ability, but, in many cases, the stereotypically lower-valued group (by race, and so on) is treated similarly to the lower-valued ability group. For example, girls with strong math abilities (a stereo-

As reflected in this tug-of-war battle between boys and girls, the playground in elementary school is like "gender school." Elementary school children show a clear preference for being with and liking same-sex peers.

typically lower-valued group) frequently are given fewer quality instructional interactions from teachers than are their male counterparts (Eccles, MacIver, & Lange, 1986; Eccles & Midgley, 1990), and minority females are given fewer teacher interactions than other females, who are given fewer than Black males, who are given fewer than White males (Sadker, Sadker, & Klein, 1986). In one study, researchers were trained in an observation system to collect data in more than a hundred fourth-, sixth-, and eighth-grade classrooms (Sadker & Sadker, 1986). At all three grade levels, the male students were involved in more interactions than the female students, and the males received more attention from teachers. Male students also were given more remediation, more criticism, and more praise than female students.

Historically, education in the United States has been male defined rather than gender balanced. In many instances, traditional male activities, especially White male activities, have been the educational norm. Although girls mature earlier, are ready for verbal and math training at a younger age, and have control of small-motor skills earlier than boys, educational curricula have been constructed mainly to mirror male development. Decisions about the grade in which students should read *Huckleberry Finn,* do long division, or begin to write essays are based primarily on male developmental patterns. Some experts believe that this state of educational affairs means that some girls may become bored or give up, with most girls learning simply to hold back and be quiet (Shakeshaft, 1986).

Three trends in gender equity education research have been identified (Klein, 1988). First, there is a trend toward greater investigation of subtle discrimination and stereotyping. Much of the gender equity research and initial gender equity policies in the 1970s focused on identifying and putting an end to overt discrimination and stereotyping. In 1981, it was noted that, although some progress toward equity had been made in some areas of overt sex discrimination, such as athletics and college admissions, many subtle types of sex discrimination and stereotyping, such as bias in classroom interactions, still remained. Gender equity researchers are now calling attention to sex discrimination and stereotyping in less visible problem areas such as home economics, foreign languages, visual arts, and sex education (Klein, in press; Spencer, 1986).

A second trend in gender equity education research is a shift toward male- and female-valued educational outcome goals. In addition to assisting females in achieving parity with males, researchers and policymakers are focusing more on the development of skills associated with females (Belenky & others, 1986). For example, placing more value on such skills as writing and human relations, areas in which females excel, can change the content covered in many standardized academic achievement tests. This type of change could improve females' achievement test scores, self-esteem, and job prospects.

A third trend in gender equity education research is an increased emphasis on gender equity outcomes. Much of the initial gender equity education research focused on identifying inequities or problems. Once researchers understand how far we are from attaining gender equity goals, they can emphasize the effectiveness of various gender equity solutions in reaching these goals. For example, researchers have found that girls' participation and achievement in mathematics become more equal to boys' through the use of multiple strategies that include anxiety reduction, "hands on" math instructional experiences, career awareness activities, "girl-friendly" classrooms, and role models (Eccles, MacIver, & Lange, 1986; Eccles & Midgley, 1990; Stage & others, 1985).

A special concern is that most middle and junior high schools consist of independent, masculine learning environments, which appear better suited to the learning style of the average adolescent boy than to that of the average adolescent girl (Huston & Alvarez, 1990). Middle and junior high schools provide a more impersonal environment than elementary schools, which meshes better with the autonomous orientation of male adolescents than the relationship, connectedness orientation of female adolescents.

Media Influences

As we have described, children encounter masculine and feminine roles in their everyday interactions with parents, peers, and teachers. The messages carried by the media about what is appropriate or inappropriate for males and for females are important influences on gender development as well.

The world of television is highly gender stereotyped and conveys clear messages about the relative power and importance of females and males (Condry, 1989; Huston & Alvarez, 1990). Males are overrepresented and females are underrepresented—on virtually every type of program, males outnumber females by approximately 2 or 3 to 1 (Williams & others, 1986). Men and women usually engage in gender-typed occupational and family roles. In the 1970s, female characters appeared more often than males in the contexts of the home, romance, and physical appearance; males appeared more frequently than females in the contexts of work, cars, and sports. By the mid-1980s, whenever females were portrayed outside the home it was almost as likely to be in nontraditional roles (for example, as a police officer or an attorney) as in traditional roles (for example, as a secretary or nurse). Men continued to be shown almost entirely in traditionally male occupations. One analysis revealed that women were shown as sexual objects (that is, in scanty clothing or engaged in sexually provocative behavior) in 35 percent of the commercial television programs in 1985 (Williams & others, 1986). Such portrayals are even more frequent on music videos. Male characters are portrayed more often than female characters as aggressive, dominant, competent, autonomous, and active, whereas female characters are more often portrayed as passive.

Early adolescence may be a period of heightened sensitivity to television messages about gender roles (Huston & Alvarez, 1990). Young adolescents view programs designed for adults that include messages about gender-appropriate behavior, especially in heterosexual relationships. Cognitively, adolescents engage in more idealistic thoughts than do children, and television has its share of idealized characters with whom adolescents can identify and imitate—highly appealing models who are young, glamorous, and successful (Durkin, 1985).

Researchers who have studied early adolescent television viewing have found that it influences early adolescents' gender role attitudes and behavior (Morgan, 1982, 1987). The researchers adopt the assumption that television carries sexist messages and that, the more one is exposed, the more stereotyped messages are likely to be received. In one investigation of eighth-grade boys and girls, heavy television viewing predicted an increased tendency to endorse traditional gender-role divisions of labor with respect to household chores (Morgan, 1987).

If television can communicate sexist messages and influence children's gender behavior, might nonstereotyped gender messages on television reduce sexist behavior? One major effort to reduce gender role stereotypes was the television series *Freestyle* (Williams, LaRose, & Frost, 1981). The series was designed to counteract the effects of career and ethnic stereotypes on the career interests of 9-to-12-year-olds. The series was somewhat successful in countering gender stereotypes, and girls who saw the series said they would participate in athletics and engage in mechanical activities more than did their counterparts who did not watch the series (Johnston & Ettema, 1982). The producers of the series hoped it would encourage girls to show a stronger interest in math and science careers, but research revealed that it did not.

Gender role stereotyping also appears in the print media. In magazines, for example, women are more likely to appear in advertisements for beauty products, cleaning products, and home appliances, whereas men are more likely to appear in advertisements for cars, liquor, and travel. As with television programs, although females are being portrayed as more competent in advertisements than they have been in the past, advertisers have not yet given them equal status with men.

So far, in our discussion of gender, we have seen that both biological and social factors play important roles in children's gender development. Recently, many child developmentalists have also recognized the important role that cognitive factors play.

Cognitive Influences

What is the cognitive developmental view of gender? What is the gender schema theory of gender development? What role does language play in gender development? We will consider each of these questions in turn.

Cognitive Developmental Theory

In the **cognitive developmental theory of gender,** *children's gender-typing occurs after they have developed a concept of gender. Once they begin to consistently conceive of themselves as male or female, children often organize their world on the basis of gender.* Based on Piaget's cognitive developmental theory, and initially developed by psychologist Lawrence Kohlberg (1966), cognitive developmental theory of gender argues that gender development proceeds in the following fashion. A young girl decides, "I am a girl. I want to do girl things;

Childhood decides.

—Jean-Paul Sartre

therefore, the opportunity to do girl things is rewarding." Having acquired the ability to categorize, children strive toward consistency in using categories and in their behavior. As children's cognitive development matures, so does their understanding of gender. Two-year-olds can apply the labels of "boy" and "girl" correctly to themselves and others, and their concept of gender is simple and concrete. Preschool children rely on physical features, such as dress and hairstyle, to decide who falls into which categories; "girls" are people with long hair, whereas "boys" are people who never wear dresses. Many preschool children believe that people can change their gender at will by getting a haircut or a new outfit. They do not yet have the cognitive machinery to think of gender as adults do. According to Kohlberg, all the reinforcement in the world won't modify that fact. However, by the concrete operational stage (the third stage in Piaget's theory, entered at 6 to 7 years of age), children understand gender constancy—that a male is still a male regardless of whether he wears pants or a skirt, or his hair short or long. When their concept of gender constancy is clearly established, children are then motivated to become competent, or "proper," boys or girls. Consequently, they find female or male activities rewarding and imitate the behavior of same-sex models.

Gender Schema Theory

A **schema** *is a cognitive structure, a network of associations that organizes and guides an individual's perceptions.* A **gender schema** *organizes the world in terms of female and male.* Thus, **gender schema theory** *argues that children's attention and behavior are guided by an internal motivation to conform to gender-based, sociocultural standards and stereotypes* (Bem, 1981; Levy, 1991; Levy & Carter, 1989; Liben & Signorella, 1987; Martin 1989; Martin & Halverson, 1981, 1987; Martin & Rose, 1991; Murphy & Carter, 1991; Yekel, Bigler, & Liben, 1991). Gender schema theory suggests that gender-typing occurs when individuals are ready to encode and organize information along the lines of what is considered appropriate or typical for males and females in a society. Whereas Kohlberg's cognitive developmental theory argues that the attainment of a particular cognitive prerequisite—gender constancy—is necessary for gender-typing, gender schema theory states that a general readiness to respond to and categorize information on the basis of culturally defined gender roles is the key ingredient that fuels children's gender-typing activities. A comparison of the cognitive developmental and gender schema theories of gender development is presented in figure 16.2.

Although researchers have shown that the appearance of gender constancy in children is related to their level of cognitive development, especially to their acquisition of conservation skills (which supports the cognitive developmental theory of gender) (Emmerich & others, 1977; Serbin & Sprafkin, 1986), they also have shown that pre-gender-constant young children have more gender role knowledge than the cognitive developmental theory of gender would predict (which supports gender schema theory) (Carter & Levy, 1988; Carter & Taylor, in press). Today, gender schema theorists acknowledge that gender constancy is one important aspect of gender role development but stress that other cognitive factors—such as gender schemas—are also very important (Levy & Carter, 1989).

For an example of a gender schema's influence on adolescents, consider a 17-year-old high school student deciding which hobby to try from among the many available possibilities. The student could ask about how expensive each possibility is, whether it can be done in cold weather, whether it can be done during the school week, whether it will interfere with studying, and so

■ *Critical Thinking*
How do the cognitive theories of gender differ from the social learning theory of gender discussed earlier in the chapter?

Social and Personality Development

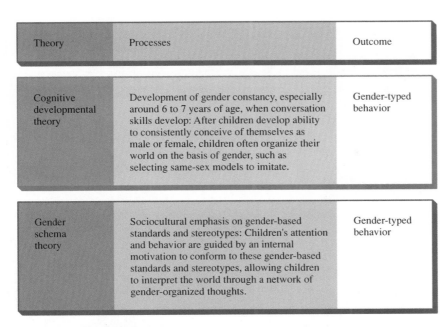

Theory	Processes	Outcome
Cognitive developmental theory	Development of gender constancy, especially around 6 to 7 years of age, when conversation skills develop: After children develop ability to consistently conceive of themselves as male or female, children often organize their world on the basis of gender, such as selecting same-sex models to imitate.	Gender-typed behavior
Gender schema theory	Sociocultural emphasis on gender-based standards and stereotypes: Children's attention and behavior are guided by an internal motivation to conform to these gender-based standards and stereotypes, allowing children to interpret the world through a network of gender-organized thoughts.	Gender-typed behavior

Figure 16.2
A Comparison of Cognitive Developmental and Gender Schema Theories of Gender Development

on. However, the adolescent also is likely to look at the hobby through the lens of gender and ask: For which sex is the hobby? What sex am I? Do they match? If so, I will consider the hobby further. If not, I will reject it. The student may not be consciously aware of her gender schema's influence on the decision of which hobby to pursue. Indeed, in many of our everyday encounters, we are not consciously aware of how gender schemas affect our behavior. In sum, the gender schema approach emphasizes the active cognitive construction of gender but also accepts that societies determine which schemas are important and the associations that are involved (Lorber & Farrell, 1991).

The Role of Language in Gender Development

Gender is present in the language children use and encounter. In fact, the language that children hear most of the time is sexist. That is, the English language contains sex bias, especially through the use of *he* and *man* to refer to everyone (Leinbach & Hurt, 1989; O'Donnel, 1989). For example, in one

How Good Are Girls at Wudgemaking If the Wudgemaker Is *He?*

In one investigation, the following description of a fictitious gender-neutral occupation—wudgemaker—was read to third- and fifth-grade children, with repeated references to *he, they, he or she,* or *she* (Hyde, 1984):

> Few people have heard of a job in factories, being a wudgemaker. Wudges are made of oddly shaped plastic and are an important part of video games. The wudgemaker works from a plan or pattern posted at eye level as *he or she* puts together the pieces at a table while *he or she* is sitting down. Eleven plastic pieces must be snapped together. Some of the pieces are tiny, so that *he or she* must have good coordination in *his or her* fingers. Once all eleven pieces are put together, *he or she* must test out the wudge to make sure that all of the moving pieces move properly. The wudgemaker is well paid, and must be a high school graduate, but *he or she* does not have to have gone to college to get the job. (Hyde, 1984, p. 702)

One fourth of the children were read the story with *he* as the pronoun, one fourth with *they,* one fourth with *he or she* (as shown), and one fourth with *she.* The children were asked to rate how well women could do the job of wudgemaking and also how well they thought men could perform the job. As shown in figure 16.A, ratings of how well women could make wudges were influenced by the pronoun used; women's competence was rated lowest when *he* was used, intermediate when *they* and *he or she* were used, and highest when *she* was used. This suggests that the use of *he,* compared with other pronouns, influences children's conceptions of how competent males and females are in our society.

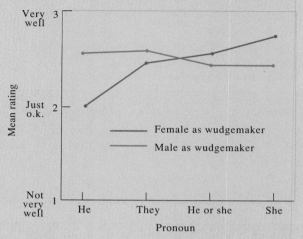

Figure 16.A

Children's Mean Ratings of Women and Men As Wudgemakers
Elementary school children's ratings of women's competence were lowest when the pronoun *he* was used, intermediate when *they* or *he or she* was used, and highest when *she* was used.

recent investigation, mothers and their 1-to-3-year-old children looked at popular children's books, such as *The Three Bears,* together (DeLoache, Cassidy, & Carpenter, 1987). The mothers almost always referred to the three bears as boys: The mothers referred to 95 percent of all characters of indeterminate gender as males. More about children's experiences with sexist language appears in Perspective on Child Development 16.1.

At this point, we have discussed a number of ideas about what gender is and about the biological, social, and cognitive influences on gender. A summary of these ideas is presented in concept table 16.1. Now we will turn our attention to gender stereotyping and the similarities and differences between boys and girls.

Gender Stereotypes, Similarities and Differences, and Achievement

How pervasive is gender role stereotyping? What are the real differences between boys and girls? What is gender's role in achievement? We will consider each of these questions in turn.

The Nature of Gender and Biological, Cognitive, and Social Influences on Gender

Concept	Processes/related ideas	Characteristics/description
What is gender?	Gender, gender identity, and gender roles	Whereas *sex* refers to the biological dimension of being male or female, *gender* refers to the social dimension of being male or female. Gender identity is the sense of being male or female, which most children acquire by 3 years of age. A gender role is a set of expectations that prescribes how females or males should think, act, and feel.
Biological influences	Their nature	Freud's and Erikson's theories promote the idea that anatomy is destiny. Hormones influence gender development, although not as pervasively as in animals. Hermaphrodites are individuals whose genitals become intermediate between male and female because of a hormonal imbalance. Today's child developmentalists are all interactionists when biological and environmental influences on gender are considered. However, interaction means different things to different people.
Social influences	Identification and social learning theories	Identification theory stems from Freud's view that a preschool child develops a sexual attraction to the opposite-sex parent, then, by 5 to 6 years of age, renounces this attraction because of anxious feelings, subsequently identifying with the same-sex parent and unconsciously adopting that parent's characteristics. This theory is not widely accepted by child developmentalists today. The social learning view states that gender development occurs through observation and imitation of gender behavior, and through rewards and punishments for gender-appropriate and gender-inappropriate behavior.
	Parents	Parents, by action and example, influence gender role development. Mothers and fathers often play different roles—mothers more nurturant and responsible for physical care, fathers more playful and demanding. Fathers are more likely than mothers to act differently toward sons and daughters.
	Peer influences	Peers are especially adept at rewarding gender-appropriate behavior. Strong same-sex preference is shown in elementary school; in adolescence, more cross-sex mixing occurs, as sexuality and dating become more prominent interests. Peer demands for conforming to gender become intense during early adolescence.
	School and teacher influences	Historically, in the United States, education has been male defined rather than gender balanced. Males receive more attention and teacher interaction in schools. Current trends focus on the investigation of subtle sex discrimination and stereotyping, male- and female-valued educational goals, and increased emphasis on gender equity outcomes. A special concern is that most middle and junior high schools are better suited to the learning styles of males than females because they are more impersonal and encourage independence more than elementary schools.
	The media	Despite improvements, television and advertising still portray males as more competent than females. Early adolescence may be a period of heightened sensitivity to television messages about gender roles, especially gender-appropriate behavior in heterosexual relationships.

CONCEPT TABLE 16.1

(continued)

Concept	Processes/related ideas	Characteristics/description
Cognitive influences	Cognitive developmental theory	Children's gender-typing occurs after they have developed a concept of gender. Once children consistently think of themselves as male or female, they organize their world on the basis of gender, such as selecting same-sex models to imitate. Kohlberg initially developed this theory of gender, believing that gender constancy is achieved in concert with the development of conservation skills at about 6 to 7 years of age.
	Gender schema theory	Gender schema theory states that children's attention and behavior are guided by an internal motivation to conform to gender-based, sociocultural standards and stereotypes. Rather than emphasizing gender constancy as the sole prerequisite for gender-typing, as cognitive developmental theory does, gender schema theory stresses the child's general readiness to respond to and categorize information on the basis of culturally defined gender roles as the key ingredient that fuels children's gender-typing activities. Researchers have found that conservation skills and the child's cognitive developmental level are related to gender-typed behavior (which supports cognitive developmental theory), but that pre-gender-constant young children have more gender role knowledge than cognitive developmental theory would predict (which supports gender schema theory).
	The role of language	Gender is present in the language children use and encounter. The language children hear most of the time is sexist.

What are little boys made of?
Frogs and snails.
And puppy dogs' tails.

What are little girls made of?
Sugar and spice
And all that's nice.

—J. O. Halliwell

Gender Role Stereotyping

Gender role stereotypes *are broad categories that reflect our impressions and beliefs about females and males.* All stereotypes, whether they are based on gender, ethnicity, or other groupings, refer to an image of a typical member of a particular social category. The world is extremely complex. Every day we are confronted with thousands of stimuli. The use of stereotypes is one way we simplify this complexity. If we assign a label to someone (such as the quality of softness), we then have much less to consider when we think about the individual. However, once labels are assigned, they are remarkably difficult to abandon, even in the face of contradictory evidence.

Many stereotypes are so general that they are ambiguous. Consider the stereotypes for "masculine" and "feminine." Diverse behaviors can be called on to support each stereotype, such as scoring a touchdown or growing facial hair for "masculine" and playing with dolls or wearing lipstick for "feminine." Stereotypes may be modified in the face of cultural change. At one point in history, muscular development may be thought of as masculine; at another point, "masculine" may be a more lithe, slender physique. The behaviors popularly agreed upon as reflecting a stereotype also may fluctuate according to socioeconomic circumstances. For example, a lower socioeconomic group might be more likely than higher socioeconomic groups to include "rough and tough" as part of a masculine stereotype.

Even though the behaviors that are supposed to fit a stereotype often do not, the label itself can have significant consequences for an individual. Labeling a male "feminine" and a female "masculine" can produce significant social reactions to the individuals in terms of their status and acceptance in groups, for example (Mischel, 1970).

How widespread is feminine and masculine stereotyping? According to a far-ranging study of college students in 30 countries, stereotyping of females and males is pervasive (Williams & Best, 1982). Males were widely believed to be dominant, independent, aggressive, achievement oriented, and enduring, whereas females were widely believed to be nurturant, affiliative, less esteemed, and more helpful in times of distress.

In a more recent investigation, women and men who lived in more highly developed countries perceived themselves to be more similar to one another than did women and men who lived in less-developed countries (Williams & Best, 1989). In the more highly developed countries, women are more likely to attend college and be gainfully employed. Thus, as gender equality increases, stereotypes, as well as actual behavioral differences, between women and men may diminish. In this investigation, women were more likely to perceive similarity between the sexes than men were (Williams & Best, 1989), and the sexes were perceived similarly more often in Christian than in Muslim societies. Next, we will go beyond stereotyping and examine the behavioral similarities and differences between the sexes.

Gender Similarities and Differences

There is a growing consensus in gender research that differences between the sexes have often been exaggerated (Hyde, 1981, in press). You might remember our discussion of reducing sexist research in psychology in chapter 1. In the research literature, it is not unusual to find statements such as the following: "Whereas only 32 percent of the women were found to . . . , fully 37 percent of the men were . . . " This difference of 5 percent likely is a very small difference and may or may not even be statistically significant or capable of being replicated (Denmark & Paludi, in press). Also, when statements are made about female-male comparisons, such as "males outperform females in math," this does not mean all females versus all males. Rather, it usually means that the average math achievement scores for males at certain ages is higher than the average math achievement scores for females. The math achievement scores of females and males overlap considerably, so that, although an *average* difference may favor males, many females have higher math achievement than many males. Further, there is a tendency to think of differences between females and males as biologically based. Remember that, when differences occur, they may be socioculturally based.

Let's now examine some of the differences between the sexes, keeping in mind that (1) the differences are averages, not all females versus all males; (2) even when differences are reported, there is considerable overlap between the sexes; and (3) the differences may be due primarily to biological factors, sociocultural factors, or both. First, we will examine physical and biological differences, then turn to cognitive and social differences.

Females are more resistant to disease and less likely to die than males at any particular point in the life cycle, and females are less likely to develop physical or mental disorders than males. Estrogen strengthens the immune system, making females more resistant to infection, for example. Female hormones also signal the liver to produce more "good" cholesterol, which makes their blood vessels more elastic than males'. Testosterone triggers the production of low-density lipoprotein, which clogs blood vessels; thus, males have twice the risk of coronary disease as females. Higher levels of stress hormones cause faster blood clotting in males, but also higher blood pressure than in females. Women have about twice the body fat of men, most concentrated around breasts and hips. In men, fat is more likely to go to the abdomen. Males grow an average of 10 percent taller than females; male hormones promote the growth of long bones, whereas female hormones stop such growth at puberty. In sum, there are many physical differences between females and males, but are there as many cognitive differences?

In a classic review of gender differences in 1974, Eleanor Maccoby and Carol Jacklin (1974) concluded that males have better math skills and better visuospatial ability (the kind of skills an architect needs to design a building's angles and dimensions), whereas females have better verbal abilities. Recently, Maccoby (1987a) revised her conclusion about several gender dimensions. She commented that the accumulation of research evidence now indicates that the verbal differences between males and females have virtually disappeared, but the math and visuospatial differences are still present.

A number of gender researchers point out that there are more cognitive similarities than differences between females and males. They also believe that the differences that do exist, such as the math and visuospatial differences, have been exaggerated. Males do outperform females in math, but only for a certain portion of the population—the gifted (Hyde, in press; Linn & Hyde, 1991). Further, males do not always outperform females on all visuospatial tasks—consistent differences occur only in the ability to rotate objects mentally (Linn & Petersen, 1986). Keep in mind also that a considerable overlap exists between females and males, even when differences are reported. Figure 16.3 shows the small average difference on visuospatial tasks that favors males, but it also clearly reveals the substantial overlap in the visuospatial abilities of females and males. Combined with the recent information about convergence in the verbal abilities of males and females (females used to have higher scores on the verbal section of the SAT, but now there are no differences, for example), we can conclude that there are no cognitive differences between females and males in many areas, they are disappearing in other areas, and they are small when they do exist.

The most consistent gender difference in social behavior is that males are more active and more aggressive than females (Maccoby, 1987b; Maccoby & Jacklin, 1974). The difference in aggression appears in children's development, often as early as at 2 years of age. With regard to emotions, males and females do not experience different emotions, but, frequently, males and females differ in how they express their emotions and in which emotions they feel free to express in public (Doyle & Paludi, 1991). Females grow up to smile more and "read" emotions better than males (Malatesta, 1990), and, by elementary school, girls show more helping and caregiving behavior (Zahn-Waxler, 1990). However, in cultures where both boys and girls care for younger siblings, boys and girls show similar nurturant behavior (Whiting, 1989). Girls also have a wider social network than boys do (Zahn-Waxler, 1990). As we will see next, one area in the study of gender that has received considerable attention is achievement.

Achievement

For some areas of achievement, gender differences are so large that they can best be described as nonoverlapping. For example, all major league baseball players are male and 96 percent of all registered nurses are female. In contrast, many measures of achievement-related behaviors yield no gender differences (for example, girls show just as much persistence at tasks as boys

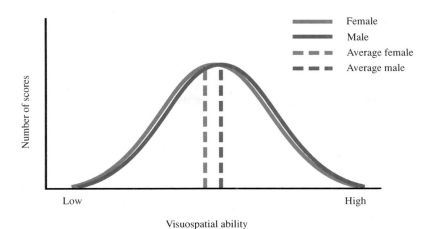

Figure 16.3
Visuospatial Ability of Males and Females
Notice that, although an average male's
visuospatial ability is higher than an
average female's, the overlap between the
sexes is substantial. Not all males have
better visuospatial ability than all females—
the substantial overlap indicates that,
although the average score of males is
higher, many females outperform many
males on such tasks.

do), and the question of whether males and females differ in their expectations for success at various achievement tasks is not yet settled (Eccles, 1987).

Because females are often stereotyped as less competent than males, the incorporation of gender role stereotypes into a child's self-concept could lead girls to have less confidence than boys in their general intellectual abilities. This could lead girls to have lower expectations for success at difficult academic and vocational activities. It also could lead girls to expect to have to work harder to achieve success at these activities than boys expect to have to work. Evidence supports these predictions (Eccles, Harold-Goldsmith, & Miller, 1989). Either of these beliefs could keep girls from selecting demanding educational or vocational options, especially if girls perceive these options as unimportant or uninteresting.

Gender roles also could produce different expectations of success, depending on the gender stereotyping of the activity. Both educational programs and vocational options are gender stereotyped in our culture. Many high-level professions, especially those that are math-related and scientific/technical, are thought to be male activities. In contrast, teaching below the college level, working in clerical and related support jobs, and excelling in language-related courses are thought to be female activities by both children and adults (Eccles, 1987; Eccles & Hoffman, 1984; Huston, 1983). Incorporating these beliefs into girls' self-concepts could cause them to have lower expectations for success in male-typed activities and higher expectations for success in female-typed activities. This pattern could lead girls to select female-typed activities over male-typed activities. Some support for this perspective has been found (Eccles, 1987). At times, though, researchers have found no gender differences in achievement expectations.

An intriguing view of gender roles and achievement argues that, on the basis of an instrumental-achievement (male) versus expressive-affiliation (female) dichotomy, we might expect male superiority in achievement patterns. This is not always the case. In an investigation by Lloyd Lueptow (1984), the adolescent girls had both higher levels of motivation and higher levels of academic achievement than did the adolescent boys. It may be that achievement is a stronger component of the female gender role than the male gender role, or it may be that a distinction is necessary between achievement based on excellence and accomplishment (a stronger focus of females) and achievement based on assertion and aggressive competition (a stronger focus of males). That is, females may be stronger achievers, males stronger competitors. Since researchers often have neglected this distinction, it may be that the achievement orientation of females has been underestimated.

Some of the brightest and most gifted girls do not have achievement and career aspirations that match their talents. Gender researchers hope that gender role stereotypes that prevent girls from developing a more positive orientation toward math and science can be eliminated.

A special concern is that some of the brightest and most gifted girls do not have achievement and career aspirations that match their talents. In one investigation, high-achieving girls had much lower expectations for success than high-achieving boys (Stipek & Hoffman, 1980). In the gifted research program at Johns Hopkins University, many mathematically precocious girls did select scientific and medical careers, although only 46 percent aspired to a full-time career, compared with 98 percent of the boys (Fox, Brody, & Tobin, 1979).

To help talented girls redirect their paths, some high schools are using programs developed by colleges and universities. Project CHOICE (Creating Her Options In Career Education) was designed by Case Western University to detect barriers in reaching one's potential. Gifted eleventh-grade females receive individualized counseling that includes interviews with female role models, referral to appropriate occupational groups, and information about career workshops. A program at the University of Nebraska (Kerr, 1983) was successful in encouraging talented female high school students to pursue more prestigious careers. This was accomplished by individualized counseling and participation in a "Perfect Future Day," in which girls shared career fantasies and discussed barriers that might impede their fantasies. Internal and external constraints were evaluated, gender role stereotypes were discouraged, and high aspirations were applauded. Although these programs have shown short-term success in redirecting the career paths of high-ability females, in some instances, the benefits fade over time—6 months or more, for example. It is important to be concerned about improving the awareness of career alternatives for all girls, however, and not just those of high ability.

Parents also play an important role in their sons' and daughters' career development. In one recent study, 1,500 mothers and their young adolescent sons and daughters were studied to determine the role of maternal expectations, advice, and provision of opportunities in their sons' and daughters' occupational aspirations (Eccles & Harold, 1991; Harold & Eccles, 1990). Mothers were more likely to encourage their sons to consider the military, to expect their sons to go into the military right after high school, and to discuss with their sons the education needed for and likely income of various jobs. Expecting marriage right after high school and discussing the problems of combining work and family were more common to daughters. Also, mothers were more worried that their daughters would not have a happy marriage, and they were more likely to want their sons to have a job that would support a family. Further information in this study indicated that mothers worked more with boys on computers; they also more often provided boys with computers, software, and programs. The mothers also bought more math or science books and games for boys and more often enrolled boys in computer classes. Boys were provided more sports opportunities, whereas girls were given more opportunities in music, art, and dance. Mothers said boys have more talent in math and are better suited for careers involving math, although they believed that girls have more talent in English and are better suited for English-related careers. In sum, there were differences in the kinds of advice and opportunities the mothers provided and in their expectations for and ability assessments of their sons and daughters. The maternal advice, provision of opportunities, expectations, and ability assessments were associated with adolescents' occupational aspirations in this study. More often, mothers tended to provide math or science books to daughters who aspired to male-typed occupations (nontraditional girls) than to daughters who aspired to female-typed jobs (traditional girls). Mothers talked more about the importance of looking good to their daughters who aspired to more female-typed occupations than to their daughters who aspired to male-typed jobs. They also expected daughters who aspired to more female-typed occupations to be more likely to get married right after high school than their nontraditional counterparts. Further, several of the mothers' and adolescent daughters' family/work role values were related. For example, the mothers' belief that it was better for the man to be a breadwinner and the woman to take care of the family was related to the adolescents' belief. The mothers' belief that working mothers can establish just as warm and secure a relationship with their children as nonworking mothers was related to their adolescents' belief that it is all right for mothers to have full-time careers. Nontraditional girls were more likely to endorse the belief that women are better wives and mothers if they have paid jobs. In sum, this research study documented that parental socialization practices in the form of provision of opportunities, expectations, and beliefs are important sources of adolescent females' and males' occupational aspirations (Harold & Eccles, 1990).

Now that we have considered gender role stereotyping, the similarities and differences between boys and girls, and achievement, we will turn our attention to the ways in which gender roles are classified.

Gender Role Classification— Masculinity, Femininity, and Androgyny

Not long ago, it was accepted that boys should grow up to be masculine and that girls should grow up to be feminine, that boys are made of frogs and snails and puppy dogs' tails and that girls are made of sugar and spice and all that's nice. Today, diversity characterizes gender roles and the feedback individuals receive from their culture. A girl's mother might promote femininity, whereas her teachers at school might encourage her assertiveness.

In the past, a well-adjusted male was expected to be independent, aggressive, and power oriented. A well-adjusted female was expected to be dependent, nurturant, and uninterested in power. Further, masculine characteristics were considered to be healthy and good by society; female characteristics were undesirable. A classic study in the early 1970s summarized the traits and behaviors that college students believed were characteristic of males and females (Broverman & others, 1972). The traits clustered into two groups, labeled "instrumental" and "expressive." The instrumental traits paralleled the male's purposeful, competent entry into the outside world to gain goods for his family; the expressive traits paralleled the female's responsibility to be warm and emotional in the home. Such stereotypes are more harmful to females than to males because the characteristics assigned to males are more valued by society than those assigned to women. Such beliefs and stereotypes have led to the negative treatment of women because of their gender, or what is called *sexism*. Females receive less attention in schools; are less visible in leading roles on television; are rarely depicted as competent, dominant characters in children's books; are paid less than males even when they have more education; and are underrepresented in decision-making roles throughout our society, from corporate executive suites to Congress.

In the 1970s, as both males and females became dissatisfied with the burdens imposed by their strictly stereotyped roles, they began to explore the alternatives to "masculinity" and "femininity." Instead of thinking of masculinity and femininity as a continuum, with more of one meaning less of the other, it was proposed that individuals could show both expressive and instrumental traits. This thinking led to the development of the concept of

(a)

(b)

Androgyny consists of (a) self-assertive characteristics, such as those shown by this young girl's independence, competitiveness, and individualism and (b) integrative characteristics, such as those shown by these young boys' sympathy, affection, and understanding.

■ *Critical Thinking*

Should parents try to instill a particular gender role orientation in their child, or should they allow the child to choose his or her gender role? Explain.

androgyny, *the presence of desirable masculine and feminine characteristics in one individual* (Bem, 1977; Spence & Helmreich, 1978). An androgynous individual might be a male who is assertive (masculine) and nurturant (feminine) or a female who is dominant (masculine) and sensitive to others' feelings (feminine).

Measures have been developed to assess androgyny. One of the most widely used gender measures is the Bem sex-role inventory, constructed by a leading early proponent of androgyny, Sandra Bem. To see what the items on Bem's measure are like, turn to table 16.1. Based on individuals' responses to the items in the Bem sex-role inventory, they are classified as having one of four gender role orientations: masculine, feminine, androgynous, or undifferentiated (see figure 16.4). Recently the Children's Sex Role Inventory, the children's version of the adult Bem measure, was constructed (Boldizar, 1991). An androgynous individual is simply a male or female who has a high degree of both feminine (expressive) and masculine (instrumental) traits. An undifferentiated individual is neither high on masculine nor high on feminine traits. Androgynous individuals are described as more flexible and more mentally healthy than either masculine or feminine individuals, and those who are undifferentiated are the least competent. To a degree, though, the context influences which gender role is most adaptive. In close relationships, a feminine or androgynous gender role may be more desirable because of the expressive nature of close relationships. However, a masculine or androgynous gender role may be more desirable in academic and work settings because of the in-

TABLE 16.1
The Bem Sex-Role Inventory: Are You Androgynous?

To find out whether you score as androgynous, first rate yourself on each item, on a scale from 1 (never or almost never true) to 7 (always or almost always true).

1. self-reliant	17. loyal	32. compassionate	47. gullible
2. yielding	18. unpredictable	33. sincere	48. inefficient
3. helpful	19. forceful	34. self-sufficient	49. acts as a leader
4. defends own beliefs	20. feminine	35. eager to soothe hurt	50. childlike
5. cheerful	21. reliable	feelings	51. adaptable
6. moody	22. analytical	36. conceited	52. individualistic
7. independent	23. sympathetic	37. dominant	53. does not use harsh
8. shy	24. jealous	38. soft-spoken	language
9. conscientious	25. has leadership abilities	39. likable	54. unsystematic
10. athletic	26. sensitive to the needs of	40. masculine	55. competitive
11. affectionate	others	41. warm	56. love children
12. theatrical	27. truthful	42. solemn	57. tactful
13. assertive	28. willing to take risks	43. willing to take a stand	58. ambitious
14. flatterable	29. understanding	44. tender	59. gentle
15. happy	30. secretive	45. friendly	60. conventional
16. strong personality	31. makes decisions easily	46. aggressive	

Scoring
(a) Add your ratings for items 1, 4, 7, 10, 13, 16, 19, 22, 25, 28, 31, 34, 37, 40, 43, 46, 49, 52, 55, and 58. Divide the total by 20. That is your masculinity score.
(b) Add your ratings for items 2, 5, 8, 11, 14, 17, 20, 23, 26, 29, 32, 35, 38, 41, 44, 47, 50, 53, 56, and 59. Divide the total by 20. That is your femininity score.
(c) If your masculinity score is above 4.9 (the approximate median for the masculinity scale) and your femininity score is above 4.9 (the approximate femininity median), then you would be classified as androgynous on Bem's scale.

From Janet S. Hyde, *Half the Human Experience: The Psychology of Women,* 3d ed. Copyright © 1985 D. C. Heath and Company, Lexington, MA. Reprinted by permission.

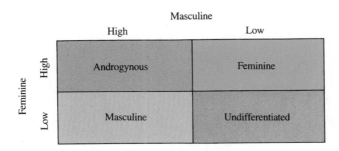

Figure 16.4
Categories Used in Androgyny Scales

strumental nature of these settings. The culture in which individuals live also plays an important role in determining what is adaptive. On the one hand, increasing numbers of children in the United States and other modernized countries, such as Sweden, are being raised to behave in androgynous ways. On the other hand, traditional gender roles continue to dominate the cultures of many countries around the world. To read about the traditional gender role practices in Egypt, China, and the Soviet Union, turn to Cultural Worlds of Development 16.1.

Although androgyny is an improvement over the perspective that femininity and masculinity are at opposite ends of gender, it has turned out to be less of a panacea than many of its early proponents envisioned (Doyle & Paludi, 1991). Some theorists, such as Joe Pleck (1979), believe that the concept of

CULTURAL WORLDS OF DEVELOPMENT 16.1

Gender Roles in Egypt, China, and the Soviet Union

In recent decades, roles assumed by males and females in the United States have become increasingly similar—that is, androgynous. In many countries, though, gender roles have remained more gender specific. Egypt is one example of such a country. The division of labor between Egyptian men and women is dramatic: Egyptian men are socialized to work in the public sphere, women in the private world of home and childrearing. The Islamic religion dictates that the man's duty is to provide for his family, the woman's duty to care for her family and household (Dickersheid & others, 1988). Any deviations from this traditional gender role orientation are severely disapproved.

It is not just Egypt that socializes males and females to behave, think, and feel in strongly gender-specific ways. In the People's Republic of China, the female's status has historically been lower than the male's. The teachings of the fifth century B.C. Chinese philosopher Confucius were used to enforce the image of female inferiority. Beginning with the Chinese revolution in 1949, economic freedom for women and more equal status in marital relationships were instituted.

However, even with the sanctions of a socialist government, the old patriarchal traditions of male supremacy in China have not been completely uprooted. Chinese women still make considerably less money than Chinese men in comparable positions, and, in rural China, a tradition of male supremacy still governs women's lives.

The Soviet Union is another country in which a socialist government improved the status of women, but, as in China, women still do not have the same status as men. Only 25 percent of the Communist party, the ruling political body, is made up of women, and, as in the United States, women with careers are also primarily responsible for household care and childrearing.

In sum, although in the United States, Sweden, other Western countries, China, and the Soviet Union women have made considerable strides, complete equality has still not been reached. In many other cultures, such as Egypt and other predominately Muslim countries, gender-specific behavior is pronounced and females are not given access to high-status positions.

In Egypt near the Aswan Dam, women are returning from the Nile River, where they have filled their water jugs. How might gender role socialization for girls in Egypt compare to that in the United States?

570

androgyny should be replaced with the concept of *gender role transcendence*. Thus, rather than merging their gender roles, women and men should transcend prescribed gender role characteristics and stereotypes. However, both concepts of androgyny and gender role transcendence draw attention away from women's needs and the power imbalance between women and men in most cultures (Hare-Mustin & Maracek, 1988). As we will see next, a major focus of the feminist agenda is to reduce the power imbalance between girls and boys, women and men.

The Feminist Perspective on Gender

Many feminist scholars believe that much of psychology's history portrays human behavior with a "male dominant theme" (Boles, 1991; DeFour & Paludi, in press; Denmark & Paludi, in press). They also believe that sexism is still rampant in society. As leading feminist scholar Jean Baker Miller (1986) wrote in *Toward a New Psychology of Women,*

> In the last decade it has become clearer that if women are trying to define and create a full personhood, we are engaged in a huge undertaking. We see that this attempt means building a new way of living which encompasses all realms of life, from global economic, social and political levels to the most intimate personal relationships. (p. xi)

Feminist scholars are developing new perspectives that focus on girls' and women's life experiences and development. These perspectives include an emphasis on girls and women as authorities about their own experiences. As Harvard psychologist Carol Gilligan (1990) advocates, they focus on listening to girls' and women's voices, on girls' and women's ways of knowing (Belenky & others, 1986), on women's career and family roles (Baruch, Biener, & Barnett, 1987), on the abuse of women and rape (McBride, 1990; Russo, 1990), and on girls' and women's experiences of connectedness and self-determination (Brown & Gilligan, 1990; Chodorow, 1989; Gilligan, Brown, & Rogers, 1990; Josselson, 1987; Lerner, 1989; Miller, 1986).

Miller (1976, 1986) has been an important voice in stimulating the examination of psychological issues from a female perspective. She believes that the study of female psychological development opens up paths to a better understanding of all psychological development. She also concludes that researchers who examine what females have been doing in life will find that a large part of it has been active participation in the development of others. In Miller's view, females usually try to interact with others in ways that will foster the others' development along many dimensions—emotionally, intellectually, and socially. Many females are very competent at building other people's strengths, resources, and well-being.

Many feminist thinkers believe it is important for females not only to maintain their competency in relationships but to balance this other-oriented competence with an increased motivation for self-determination. Many women came from a position in which their lives were extensively determined by others as they grew up in a male-dominated culture, which dictated what females should be like. Miller believes that, through increased self-determination, coupled with already developed relationship skills, many females will discover the route to a deserved status of greater power in the American culture. As fem-

Yes, I am wise but it is wisdom for the pain. Yes, I've paid the price but look how much I've gained. If I have to I can do anything. I am strong. I am invincible, I am woman.

—Helen Reddy

Jean Baker Miller has made important contributions to the view that a woman's sense of self is often organized around being able to make and then maintain affiliations and relationships.

Reprinted by permission of UFS, Inc.

inist scholar Harriet Lerner (1989) concludes in her book *The Dance of Intimacy,* it is important for females to bring to their relationships nothing less than a strong, assertive, independent, and authentic self. She believes that competent relationships are those in which the separate "I-ness" of every individual can be appreciated and enhanced while each remains emotionally connected to the significant other.

Feminists also believe that social policy regarding children's gender must be scrutinized carefully. Next, we will discuss some of the areas in which social policy and children's gender should be examined.

Gender and Social Policy

Many gender-related research findings have implications for public policy regarding children. Among such areas of gender-related research are gender role stereotypes and the media, education, and child care (Jacklin, 1989).

Gender Role Stereotypes and the Media

An extensive amount of information about children is brought to parents by the media. However, the media can misinform parents. For example, in the early 1980s, a series of articles on gender differences in math were published, causing a stir in the media (Benbow & Stanley, 1980, 1982, 1983). In each of the articles, boys were reported as scoring higher in math than girls. What was especially important about these results is that the authors speculated about the biological causes of their findings. As these speculations became exaggerated in the popular media, the biological causes became the overriding message of the studies, whereas the sociocultural factors were overlooked.

Might media reports of biologically based gender differences in math ability influence parents' attitudes toward boys' and girls' math abilities? In one investigation, parents who were aware of media reports of biological gender differences in math ability were compared with those who were not aware of them (Eccles & Jacobs, 1986). The uninformed mothers believed that the math ability of their sons and daughters was equivalent, whereas mothers who knew about the findings felt that math was much more difficult for their daughters than for their sons. Thus, the media campaign had a direct influence on parental attitudes toward gender-related aspects of math ability, which was clearly deleterious for girls. As the mothers came to believe that math was much more difficult for girls than for boys, their daughters became less likely to take additional math courses (Jacklin, 1989). These gender expectations for math not only are present in the United States but in many other countries as well. For example, in one recent investigation, children and their mothers tended to believe that boys were better at math and girls were better at reading as early as the first grade in the United States, Japan, and Taiwan (Lummis & Stevenson, 1990).

Gender and Education

According to psychologist Carol Jacklin (1989), many teachers and parents are not aware of the powerful gender expectations they communicate to children. Nationally organized groups, such as the Parent Teacher Association (PTA), could alert parents to the findings of such researchers as Jacqueline Eccles and her colleagues (1983), but currently they do not.

Gender and Child Care

Gender roles and the division of labor are important factors in gender differences. If interacting with infants and children stimulates nurturance in caregivers—and there is considerable evidence that it does—then, according to Jacklin (1989), we should be rethinking who does the child care in our society. Currently women and girls do most of this care and men and boys may even be discouraged from doing it. Why should nurturance be encouraged in only one sex? According to Jacklin, nurturance may be an antidote for violence.

In sum, changes are needed in the way the media, teachers and parents, and society view gender roles (see figure 16.5). Next, we will see that, in addition to social policy issues involving children's gender, another important aspect of children's and adult's gender is the way gender roles are prescribed in various ethnic minority groups.

Ethnicity and Gender

Are gender-related attitudes and behavior similar across ethnic groups? All ethnic minority females are females and all ethnic minority males are males, so there are many similarities in the gender-related attitudes of females and of males across different ethnic minority groups. Nevertheless, the varied ethnic and cultural experiences of Black American, Hispanic American, Asian American, and Native American females and males need to be considered in

■ *Critical Thinking*
Other than through the Parent Teacher Association, how can parents' gender expectations about math be modified?

Figure 16.5
**Three Important Social Policy Issues
Involving Children's Gender Development**

The media can misinform parents about children's gender development, as exemplified in the exaggeration of biological explanations of gender differences in math.

Teachers communicate gender expectations to children. So do parents. Many teachers and parents are not aware of how strongly they communicate gender expectations.

Currently, girls and women do most of the child care in our society, and boys and men may even be discouraged from it. Might increased child care, especially nurturing infants and young children, reduce male aggression?

understanding their gender-related attitudes and behavior, because, in some instances, even small differences can be important (Swanson & Cunningham, 1991; Walsh, Katz, & Downey, 1991). For example, the socialization of males and females in other cultures who subsequently migrate to America often reflects a stronger gap between the status of males and females than is experienced in America. Keeping in mind that there are many similarities among the females in all ethnic minority groups and among the males in all ethnic minority groups, we will first examine females from particular ethnic minority groups, and then discuss males from specific ethnic minority groups.

Ethnic Minority Females

Let's now consider the behavior and psychological orientations of females from four ethnic minority groups, beginning with Black American females. In turn, we will study Asian American, Hispanic American, and Native American females.

Researchers in psychology have only begun to focus on the behavior of Black American females. For too long, Black females have served only as a comparison group for White American females on a few psychological dimensions, or they have served as the subjects in studies in which the primary research interest related to poverty, unwed motherhood, and so on (Hall, Evans, & Selice, 1989). This narrow research approach could be viewed as attributing no personal characteristics to Black females beyond the labels given to them by society. The nature and focus of psychological research on Black American females has begun to change—to some extent, paralleling societal changes (Hall, Evans, & Selice, 1989). In the past decade, more individualized, positive dimensions of Black females have been studied, such as self-esteem, achievement, motivation, and self-control. In the 1980s, psychological studies of Black females began to shift away from studies focused only on the problems of Black females and toward research on the positive aspects of being a Black female in a pluralistic society.

Black American females, as well as other ethnic minority females, have experienced the double jeopardy of racism and sexism. The ingenuity and perseverance shown by ethnic minority females as they have survived and grown against the odds are remarkable. For example, in 1986, 499 Black American women earned doctoral degrees. This represents only 2 percent of the Ph.D.'s awarded (compared with the 6.4 percent of the general population represented by Black females). However, the positive side of these figures is that the Ph.D.'s earned by Black women in 1986 was almost a 16 percent increase over the number earned in 1977. Despite such gains, our society needs to make a strong commitment to providing Black, and other ethnic minority, females with the opportunities they deserve.

Asian American females often are expected to carry out domestic duties; to marry; to become obedient helpers of their mothers-in-law; and to bear children, especially males (Sue, 1989). In China, the mother's responsibility for the emotional nurturance and well-being of the family and for raising children derives from Confucian ethics (Huang & Ying, 1989). As China has become modernized, however, these roles have become less rigid. Similarly, in acculturated Chinese families in the United States, only derivatives of these rigidly defined roles remain. For example, many Chinese American females are not entirely relegated to subservient roles.

Traditionally, in Mexican families, women have assumed the expressive role of homemaker and caretaker of children. This continues to be the norm, although less so than in the past (Ramirez, 1989). Historically, the Mexican female's role has been one of self-denial, her needs subordinate to those of other family members. Joint decision making and greater equality between males' and females' roles are becoming more characteristic of Mexican American families (Ramirez & Arce, 1981). Of special significance is the increased frequency of Mexican American women's employment outside the home, which, in many instances, has enhanced their status in the family and in decision making (Baca Zinn, 1977).

For Native Americans, the amount of social and governing influence exhibited by women depends on the tribe (LaFromboise & Low, 1989). For example, in the traditional matriarchal Navaho family, an older woman might live with her husband, her unmarried children, her married daughter, and the daughter's husband and children (Ryan, 1980). In patriarchal tribes, women function as the central "core" of the family, maintaining primary responsibility for the welfare of the children. Many grandmothers and aunts, as well as mothers, provide child care. As with other ethnic minority females, Native Americans who have moved to urban areas experience the cultural conflict between their traditional ethnic values and the values of the American society.

Ethnic Minority Males

Just as ethnic minority females have experienced considerable discrimination and have had to develop coping strategies in the face of adversity, so have ethnic minority males. As with ethnic minority females, we will discuss Black American males, Asian American males, Hispanic American males, and Native American males.

Some statistics portray the difficulties many Black American males have faced. Black males of all ages are three times as likely as White males to live below the poverty line. Black males are twice as likely to die between the ages of 20 and 44 than White males. Black male heads of household earn 70 percent of the income of their White male counterparts. Although they make up only 6.3 percent of the U.S. population, Black males comprise 42 percent of all jail inmates and more than 50 percent of the men executed for any reason in the past 50 years. However, such statistics do not tell the complete picture (Evans & Whitfield, 1988). The sociocultural aspects of historical discrimination against an ethnic minority group must be taken into account to understand these figures. Just as with Black American females, researchers are beginning to focus on some of the more positive dimensions of Black American males. For example, researchers are finding that many Black males are especially efficient at the use of body language in communication, the decoding of nonverbal cues, multilingual/multicultural expression, and improvised problem solving.

Asian cultural values are reflected in traditional patriarchal Chinese and Japanese families (Sue, 1989). The father's behavior in relation to other family members is generally dignified, authoritative, remote, and aloof. Sons are generally valued over daughters, and first-born sons have an especially high status. As with Asian American females, the acculturation experienced by Asian American males has eroded some of the rigid gender roles that characterized Asian families in the past. Fathers still are often the figurative heads of families, especially when dealing with the public, but, in private, many have relinquished some of their decision-making power to their wives (Huang & Ying, 1989).

In Mexican families, men have traditionally assumed the instrumental role of provider and protector of the family (Ramirez, 1989). The concept of *machismo*—being macho—continues to influence the role of the male and the patriarchical orientation of Mexican American families, though less so than in the past. Traditionally, this orientation has required males to be forceful and strong and to withhold affectionate emotions. Ideally, it involves a strong sense of personal honor, family, loyalty, and care for children; however, it also has included exaggerated masculinity and aggression (Trankina, 1983). The concepts of machismo and absolute patriarchy currently are diminishing in influence, although adolescent males are still given much more freedom than adolescent females in Mexican American families.

Some Native American tribes are also patriarchal, with the male as the head of the family and primary decision maker. In some tribes, though, child care is shared by men. For example, Mescalero Apache men take responsibility for the children when they are not working away from the family (Ryan, 1980). Autonomy is highly valued among the boys in many Native American tribes, and they operate semi-independently at an early age (LaFromboise & Low, 1989). As with Native American females, increased movement to urban areas has led to modifications in the values and traditions of some Native American males.

At this point, we have discussed a number of ideas about gender stereotypes, similarities and differences, and achievement; gender role classification; the feminist perspective on gender; gender and social policy; and ethnicity and gender. A summary of these ideas is presented in concept table 16.2. In the next chapter, we will turn our attention to another important facet of children's development—their moral development. As part of our discussion of moral development, we will examine Carol Gilligan's ideas on connectedness and relationships in greater detail.

Social and Personality Development

CONCEPT TABLE 16.2

Gender Stereotyping, Similarities and Differences, and Achievement; Gender Role Classification; the Feminist Perspective on Gender; Gender and Social Policy with Children; and Ethnicity and Gender

Concept	Processes/related ideas	Characteristics/description
Gender stereotypes, similarities and differences, and achievement	Stereotypes	Gender role stereotypes are broad categories that reflect our impressions and beliefs about males and females. These stereotypes are widespread around the world, especially emphasizing the male's power and the female's nurturance. However, in more highly developed countries, females and males are more likely to be perceived as more similar.
	Similarities and differences	Many gender researchers believe that a number of differences between females and males have been exaggerated. In considering differences, it is important to recognize that the differences are averages; there is considerable overlap between the sexes; and the differences may be due primarily to biological factors, sociocultural factors, or both. There are a number of physical differences between the sexes, but cognitive differences are either small or nonexistent. At the level of the gifted, the average male outperforms the average female in math achievement. In terms of social behavior, males are more aggressive and active than females, but females are usually more adept at "reading" emotions, show more helping behavior, and have a wider social network than males. Overall, though, there are more similarities than differences between females and males.
	Achievement	Although the answer to the question of whether males and females differ in their expectations for success is not yet settled, some of the brightest and most gifted girls do not have achievement and career aspirations that match their talents. An often neglected distinction by researchers is that females may be more achievement oriented, males more competitive and assertive. Parents often have different expectations for, give different advice to, and provide different opportunities in career development to their sons and daughters.
How can gender roles be classified?	The past	In the past, a well-adjusted male was supposed to show instrumental traits, a well-adjusted female expressive traits. Masculine traits were more valued by society. Sexism was widespread.
	Androgyny	In the 1970s, alternatives to traditional masculinity and femininity were explored. It was proposed that individuals could show both expressive and instrumental traits. This thinking led to the development of the concept of androgyny, the presence of desirable masculine and feminine traits in one individual. Gender role measures often categorize individuals as masculine, feminine, androgynous, or undifferentiated. Androgynous individuals are often flexible and mentally healthy, although the particular context and the individual's culture also determine the adaptiveness of a gender role orientation. One alternative to androgyny is gender role transcendence, but, like androgyny, it diverts attention away from the imbalance of power between females and males.
The feminist perspective on gender	Its nature	Feminist scholars are developing new perspectives that focus on girls' and women's experiences and development. Girls' and women's strengths have been especially important in relationships and connections with others. A special emphasis is that, while staying emotionally connected to significant others, females can enhance their psychological well-being by developing stronger self-determination.

Concept	Processes/related ideas	Characteristics/description
Gender and social policy with children	Its nature	Many gender-related findings have implications for social policy regarding children. Three areas are gender role stereotypes and the media, education, and child care. Changes are needed in the way the media, teachers and parents, and society view gender roles.
Ethnicity and gender	Similarities and differences	There are many similarities among the females in various ethnic minority groups and among the males in different ethnic minority groups, but even small differences can sometimes be important.
	Ethnic minority females	Researchers in psychology have only begun to focus on female behavior in specific ethnic groups in a positive way. Many ethnic minority females have experienced the double jeopardy of racism and sexism. In many instances, Asian American, Hispanic American, and Native American females have lived in patriarchal, male-dominated families, although gender roles have become less rigid in these ethnic groups in recent years.
	Ethnic minority males	Just as ethnic minority females have experienced considerable discrimination and have had to develop coping strategies in the face of adversity, so have ethnic minority males. Just as with Black American females, researchers are beginning to focus more on the positive dimensions of Black American males. A patriarchal, male-dominant orientation has characterized many ethnic minority groups, such as Asian American, Hispanic American, and Native American, although females are gaining greater decision-making power in these cultures, especially those who develop careers and work outside of the home.

Summary

I. What Is Gender?

Whereas *sex* refers to the biological dimension of being male or female, *gender* refers to the social dimension of being male or female. Gender identity is the sense of being male or female, which most children acquire by 3 years of age. A gender role is a set of expectations that prescribes how females or males should think, act, and feel.

II. Biological Influences

Freud's and Erikson's theories promote the idea that anatomy is destiny. Hormones influence gender development, although often not as pervasively as in animals. Hermaphrodites are individuals whose genitals become intermediate between male and female because of a hormonal imbalance. Today's child developmentalists are all interactionists when biological and environmental influences on gender are considered. However, interaction means different things to different people.

III. Identification and Social Learning Theories of Gender

Identification theory stems from Freud's view that the preschool child develops a sexual attraction to the opposite-sex parent, then, by 5 to 6 years of age, renounces this attraction because of anxious feelings, subsequently identifying with the same-sex parent and unconsciously adopting that parent's characteristics. This theory is not widely accepted by child developmentalists today. Social learning theory states that gender development occurs through observation and imitation of gender behavior, and through rewards and punishments for gender-appropriate and gender-inappropriate behavior.

IV. Parental and Peer Influences on Gender

Parents, by action and by example, influence gender development. Mothers and fathers often play different roles—mothers more nurturant and responsible for physical care, fathers more playful and demanding. Fathers are more likely than mothers to act differently toward sons and daughters. Peers are especially adept at rewarding gender-appropriate behavior. Strong same-sex preference is shown in elementary school. In adolescence, more cross-sex mixing occurs, as sexuality and dating become more prominent interests. Peer demands for conforming to gender become intense during early adolescence.

V. School, Teacher, and Media Influences on Gender

Historically, in the United States, education has been male defined rather than gender balanced. Males receive more attention and teacher interaction in schools. Current trends focus on subtle sex discrimination and stereotyping, male- and female-valued educational goals, and sex-equity outcomes. A special concern is that most middle and junior high schools are better suited to the learning styles of males than of females because the schools are more impersonal than elementary schools and they encourage independence more. Despite improvements, television and advertising still portray males as more competent than females. Early adolescence may be a period of heightened sensitivity to television messages about gender roles, especially gender-appropriate behavior in heterosexual relationships.

VI. Cognitive Developmental Theory of Gender

Gender-typing occurs after children have developed a concept of gender. Once children consistently think of themselves as male or female, they often organize their world on the basis of gender, such as electing to imitate same-sex parents. Kohlberg initially developed this theory of gender, believing that gender constancy is achieved in concert with the development of conservation skills at 6 to 7 years of age.

VII. Gender Schema Theory and the Role of Language in Gender Development

Gender schema theory states that children's attention and behavior are guided by an internal motivation to conform to gender-based, sociocultural standards and stereotypes. Rather than emphasizing gender constancy as the sole prerequisite for gender-typing, as does cognitive developmental theory, gender schema theory stresses the child's general readiness to respond to and categorize information on the basis of culturally defined gender as the key ingredient that fuels children's gender-typing activities. Researchers have found that conservation skills and the child's cognitive developmental level are related to gender-typed behavior (which supports cognitive developmental theory) but that pre-gender-constant young children have more gender role knowledge than cognitive developmental theory would predict (which supports gender schema theory). Gender is present in the language children use and encounter. The language children hear most of the time is sexist.

VIII. Gender Stereotypes, Similarities and Differences, and Achievement

Gender role stereotypes are broad categories that reflect our impressions and beliefs about males and females. These stereotypes are widespread around the world, especially emphasizing the male's power and the female's nurturance. However, in more highly developed countries, females and males are more likely to be perceived as similar. Many gender researchers believe that a number of differences between females and males have been exaggerated. In considering differences, it is important to recognize that the differences are averages; there is considerable overlap between the sexes; and the differences may be due primarily to biological factors, sociocultural factors, or both. There are a number of physical differences between females and males, but cognitive differences are either small or nonexistent. At the level of the gifted, the average male outperforms the average female in math achievement. In terms of social behavior, males are more aggressive and active than females, but females are usually more adept at "reading" emotions, show more helping behavior, and have a wider social network than males. Overall, though, there are more similarities than differences between females and males. Although the answer to the question of whether males and females differ in their achievement expectations has not been settled, some of the brightest and most gifted girls do not have achievement and career aspirations that match their talents. An often neglected distinction by researchers is that females may be more achievement oriented, males more competitive and assertive. Parents often have different expectations for, give different advice to, and provide different opportunities in career development to their sons and daughters.

IX. How Can Gender Roles Be Classified?

In the past, a well-adjusted male was supposed to show instrumental traits, a well-adjusted female expressive traits. Masculine traits were more valued by society. Sexism was widespread. In the 1970s, alternatives to traditional masculinity and femininity were explored. It was proposed that individuals could show both expressive and instrumental traits. This thinking led to the development of the concept of androgyny, the presence of desirable masculine and feminine traits in one individual. Gender role measures often categorize individuals as masculine, feminine, androgynous, or undifferentiated. Androgynous individuals are often flexible and mentally healthy, although the particular context and the individual's culture also determine the adaptiveness of a gender role orientation. One alternative to androgyny is gender role transcendence, but, like androgyny, it draws attention from the imbalance of power between females and males.

X. The Feminist Perspective on Gender and Social Policy with Children

Feminist scholars are developing new perspectives that focus on girls' and women's experiences and development. Girls' and women's strengths have been especially important in relationships and connections with others. A special emphasis is that, while staying emotionally connected to significant others, females can enhance their psychological well-being by developing stronger self-determination. Many gender-related findings have important implications for social policy regarding children. Three areas are gender role stereotypes and the media, education, and child care. Changes are needed in the way the media, teachers and parents, and society view gender roles.

XI. Gender and Ethnicity

There are many similarities among the females in various ethnic minority groups and among the males in different ethnic minority groups, but even small differences are sometimes significant. Researchers in psychology have only begun to focus on female behavior in ethnic groups in a positive way. Many ethnic minority females have experienced the double jeopardy of racism and sexism. In many instances, Asian American, Hispanic American, and Native American females have lived in patriarchal, male-dominated families, although gender roles have become less rigid in these ethnic groups in recent years. Just as ethnic minority females have experienced considerable discrimination and have had to develop coping strategies in the face of adversity, so have ethnic minority males. Just as with Black American females, researchers are beginning to focus more on the positive dimensions of Black American males. A patriarchal, male-dominant orientation has characterized many ethnic minority groups, such as Asian American, Hispanic American, and Native American, although females are gaining greater decision-making power in these cultures, especially those who develop careers and work outside of the home.

Key Terms

gender 551
gender identity 551
gender role 551
hermaphrodites 551
identification theory 553
social learning view of
  gender 553

cognitive developmental
  theory of gender 557
schema 558
gender schema 558
gender schema theory 558
gender role stereotypes 562
androgyny 568

Suggested Readings

Huston, A. C. (1983). Sex-typing. In P. H. Mussen (Ed.), *Handbook of child psychology* (4th ed., Vol. 4). New York: Wiley. This is a lengthy, comprehensive review of what is known about gender role development.

Hyde, J. S. (1985). *Half the human experience* (3rd ed.). Lexington, MA: D. C. Heath. This book is an excellent overview of female gender role development.

Jacklin, C. N. (1989). Female and male: Issues of gender. *American Psychologist, 44,* 127–133. Gender expert Carol Nagy Jacklin describes a number of contemporary issues involving gender, including gender differences and public policy considerations.

Levy, G. D., & Carter, D. B. (1989). Gender schema, gender constancy, and gender-role knowledge: The role of cognitive factors in preschoolers' gender-role stereotype attributions. *Developmental Psychology, 25,* 444–449. The contemporary perspective of gender schema theory is competently presented.

Reinisch, J. M., Rosenblum, L. A., & Sanders, S. A. (Eds.). (1987). *Masculinity/femininity.* New York: Oxford University Press. This outstanding collection of articles by leading experts, such as Eleanor Maccoby, John Money, and Jacqueline Eccles, includes a special section of papers on the development of gender roles.

Sex Roles. This journal is devoted solely to articles about gender. Go to a library and leaf through the issues of the past several years to discover the concerns that researchers are currently studying.

CHAPTER

17

MORAL
DEVELOPMENT

What Is Moral Development?
Moral Thoughts
    Piaget's Ideas About Moral Development
    Kohlberg's Ideas About Moral Development
    Influences on the Kohlberg Stages
    Kohlberg's Critics
    *Perspective on Child Development 17.1: Amy
        Says They Should Just Talk It Out and
        Find Some Other Way to Make Money*
    *Cultural Worlds of Development 17.1: Cultural
        Variations in Children's Moral Development*
Moral Behavior
    Reinforcement, Punishment, and Imitation
    Resistance to Temptation and Self-control
    Cognitive Social Learning Theory
Moral Feelings
    Psychoanalytic Theory
    Childrearing Techniques and Moral Development
    Empathy
    The Contemporary Perspective on the Role of
        Emotions in Moral Development
Altruism
Moral Education
    The Hidden Curriculum
    Direct and Indirect Moral Education
    Damon's Comprehensive Approach to Moral
        Education
Juvenile Delinquency
    *Perspective on Child Development 17.2: Frog
        and Dolores*
Summary
Key Terms
Suggested Readings

Can children understand such concepts as discrimination, economic inequality, affirmative action, and comparable worth? Probably not if we use these terms, but might we be able to construct circumstances involving these terms that they are able to understand? Phyllis Katz (1987) asked elementary-school-aged children to pretend that they had taken a long ride on a spaceship to a make-believe planet called Pax. She asked for their opinions about various situations in which they found themselves. The situations involved conflict, socioeconomic inequality, and civil-political rights. For example, included in the conflict items was the question of what a teacher should do when two students were tied for a prize or when they have been fighting. The economic equality dilemmas included a proposed field trip that not all students could afford, a comparable worth situation in which janitors were paid more than teachers, and an employment situation that discriminated against those with dots on their noses instead of stripes. The rights items dealt with minority rights and freedom of the press.

The elementary school children did indeed recognize injustice and often came up with interesting solutions to problems. For example, all but two children believed that teachers should earn as much as janitors—the holdouts said teachers should make less because they stay in one room or because cleaning toilets is more disgusting and, therefore, deserves higher wages. Children were especially responsive to the economic inequality items. All but one thought that not giving a job to a qualified applicant who had different physical characteristics (a striped rather than a dotted nose) was unfair. The majority recommended an affirmative action solution—giving the job to the one from the discriminated minority. None of the children verbalized the concept of freedom of the press or seemed to understand that a newspaper has the right to criticize a mayor in print without being punished. What are our schools teaching children about democracy? Some of the courses of action suggested were intriguing. Several argued that the reporters should be jailed. One child said that, if she were the mayor being criticized, she would worry, make speeches, and say, "I didn't do anything wrong," not unlike what American presidents have done in recent years. Another said that the mayor should not put the newspaper people out of work because that might make them print more bad things. "Make them write comics instead," he said. The children believed that poverty exists on Earth but mainly in Africa, big cities, or Vietnam. War was mentioned as the biggest problem on Earth, although children were not certain where it is presently occurring. Other problems mentioned were crime, hatred, school, smog, meanness, and Delta Airlines (the questions were asked in the summer of 1986, just after a Delta Airlines crash killed hundreds of passengers). Overall, the types of rules the children believed a society should abide by were quite sensible—almost all included the need for equitable sharing of resources and work and prohibitions against aggression.

This chapter is about such matters as equitable sharing, helping, rules and regulations, moral dilemmas, values, and self-control. Among the questions we will examine are the following: What is moral development? What is the nature of children's moral thoughts, moral behavior, moral feelings, and altruism? Should children be morally educated and, if so, what should that education be like? What is the nature of juvenile delinquency?

What Is Moral Development?

Moral development is one of the oldest topics of interest to those who are curious about human nature. In prescientific periods, philosophers and theologians heatedly debated children's moral status at birth, which they felt had important implications for how children should be reared. Today, people are hardly neutral about moral development; most have very strong opinions about acceptable and unacceptable behavior, ethical and unethical conduct, and the ways in which acceptable and ethical behaviors are to be fostered in children.

Moral development *concerns rules and conventions about what people* should *do in their interactions with other people.* In studying these rules, developmentalists examine three domains. First, how do children *reason* or *think* about rules for ethical conduct? For example, consider cheating. A child can be presented with a story in which someone has a conflict about whether or not to cheat in a particular situation, such as when taking a test in school. The child is asked to decide what is appropriate for the character to do and why. The focus is placed on the reasoning children use to justify their moral decisions.

Second, how do children actually *behave* in moral circumstances? In our example of cheating, emphasis is on observing the child's cheating and the environmental circumstances that produced and maintain the cheating. Children might be presented with some toys and asked to select which one they believe is the most attractive. Then, the experimenter tells the young child that the particular toy selected is someone else's and is not to be played with. Observations of different conditions under which the child deviates from the prohibition or resists temptation are conducted.

Third, how does the child *feel* about the moral matters? In the example of cheating, does the child feel enough guilt to resist temptation? If children cheat, do feelings of guilt after the transgression keep them from cheating the next time they face temptation?

Moral Thoughts

How do children think about the standards of right and wrong? Piaget had some thoughts about this question and so did Lawrence Kohlberg.

Piaget's Ideas About Moral Development

Interest in how children think about moral issues was stimulated by Piaget (1932), who extensively observed and interviewed children from the ages of 4 to 12. Piaget watched children play marbles to learn how they used and thought about the game's rules. He also asked children questions about ethical issues—theft, lies, punishment, and justice, for example. Piaget concluded that children think in two distinct ways about morality, depending on their developmental maturity. **Heteronomous morality** *is the first stage of moral development in Piaget's theory, occurring from 4 to 7 years of age. Justice and rules are conceived of as unchangeable properties of the world, removed from the control of people.* **Autonomous morality** *is the second stage of moral*

Piaget observed and interviewed children from the ages of 4 to 12. Through these observations, Piaget learned how children use and think about rules and regulations.

development in Piaget's theory, displayed by older children (about 10 years of age and older). The child becomes aware that rules and laws are created by people and that, in judging an action, one should consider the actor's intentions as well as the consequences. Children 7 to 10 years of age are in a transition between the two stages, evidencing some features of both.

Let's consider Piaget's two stages of moral development further. A heteronomous thinker judges the rightness or goodness of behavior by considering the consequences of the behavior, not the intentions of the actor. For example, the heteronomous thinker says that breaking 12 cups accidently is worse than breaking 1 cup intentionally while trying to steal a cookie. For the moral autonomist, the reverse is true. The actor's intentions assume paramount importance. The heteronomous thinker also believes that rules are unchangeable and are handed down by all-powerful authorities. When Piaget suggested to a group of young children that new rules be introduced into the game of marbles, they resisted. They insisted that the rules had always been the same and could not be altered. By contrast, older children—who are moral autonomists—accept change and recognize that rules are merely convenient, socially agreed-upon conventions, subject to change by consensus.

The heteronomous thinker also believes in **immanent justice,** *Piaget's concept that, if a rule is broken, punishment will be meted out immediately.* The young child somehow believes that the violation is connected automatically to the punishment. Thus, young children often look around worriedly after committing a transgression, expecting inevitable punishment. Older children, who are moral autonomists, recognize that punishment is socially mediated and occurs only if a relevant person witnesses the wrongdoing and that, even then, punishment is not inevitable.

Piaget argued that, as children develop, they become more sophisticated in thinking about social matters, especially about the possibilities and conditions of cooperation. Piaget believed that this social understanding comes about through the mutual give-and-take of peer relations. In the peer group, where others have power and status similar to the individual, plans are negotiated and coordinated, and disagreements are reasoned about and eventually settled. Parent-child relations, in which parents have the power and children do not, are less likely to advance moral reasoning because rules are often handed down in an authoritarian way.

Remember that Piaget believed that adolescents usually become formal operational thinkers. Thus, they are no longer tied to immediate and concrete phenomena but are more logical, abstract, and deductive reasoners. Formal operational thinkers frequently compare the real to the ideal; create contrary-to-fact propositions; are cognitively capable of relating the distant past to the present; understand their roles in society, in history, and in the universe; and can conceptualize their own thoughts and think about their mental constructs as objects. For example, it usually is not until about the age of 11 or 12 that boys and girls spontaneously introduce concepts of belief, intelligence, and faith into their definitions of their religious identities.

Kohlberg's Ideas About Moral Development

The most provocative view of moral development in recent years was crafted by Lawrence Kohlberg (Kohlberg, 1958, 1976, 1986). Kohlberg believed that moral development is based primarily on moral reasoning and unfolds in a series of stages. He arrived at his view after about 20 years of using a unique interview with children. In the interview, children are presented with a series of stories in which characters face moral dilemmas. The following is the most popular of the Kohlberg dilemmas:

> In Europe a woman was near death from a special kind of cancer. There was one drug that the doctors thought might save her. It was a form of radium that a druggist in the same town had recently discovered. The drug was expensive to make, but the druggist was charging ten times what the drug cost him to make. He paid $200 for the radium and charged $2,000 for a small dose of the drug. The sick woman's husband, Heinz, went to everyone he knew to borrow the money, but he could only get together $1,000 which is half of what it cost. He told the druggist that his wife was dying and asked him to sell it cheaper or let him pay later. But the druggist said, "No, I discovered the drug, and I am going to make money from it," So Heinz got desperate and broke into the man's store to steal the drug for his wife. (Kohlberg, 1969, p. 379)

This story is one of 11 Kohlberg devised to investigate the nature of moral thought. After reading the story, interviewees answer a series of questions about the moral dilemma. Should Heinz have stolen the drug? Was stealing it right or wrong? Why? Is it a husband's duty to steal the drug for his wife if he can get it no other way? Would a good husband steal? Did the druggist have the right to charge that much when there was no law setting a limit on the price? Why?

Based on the answers interviewees gave for this and other moral dilemmas, Kohlberg believed that three levels of moral development exist, each of which is characterized by two stages. A key concept in understanding moral development, especially Kohlberg's theory, is **internalization,** *the developmental change from behavior that is externally controlled to behavior that is controlled by internal, self-generated standards and principles.* As children develop, their moral thoughts become more internalized. Let's look further at Kohlberg's three levels of development.

1. Kohlberg's Level 1: preconventional reasoning. **Preconventional reasoning** *is the lowest level in Kohlberg's theory of moral development. At this level, the child shows no internalization of moral values—moral reasoning is controlled by external rewards and punishments.*
   - Stage 1. **Punishment and obedience orientation** *is the first stage in Kohlberg's theory of moral development. At this stage, moral thinking is based on punishment.* Children obey because adults tell them to obey.
   - Stage 2. **Individualism and purpose** *is the second stage in Kohlberg's theory of moral development. At this stage, moral thinking is based on rewards and self-interest.* Children obey when they want to obey and when it is in their best interest to obey. What is right is what feels good and what is rewarding.
2. Kohlberg's Level 2: conventional reasoning. **Conventional reasoning** *is the second, or intermediate, level in Kohlberg's theory of moral development. At this level, children's internalization is intermediate. The child abides by certain standards (internal), but they are the standards of others (external), such as parents or the laws of society.*
   - Stage 3. **Interpersonal norms** *is the third stage in Kohlberg's theory of moral development. At this stage, children value*

trust, caring, and loyalty to others as the basis of moral judgments. Children often adopt their parents' moral standards at this stage, seeking to be thought of by their parents as a "good girl" or a "good boy."

- Stage 4. **Social system morality** *is the fourth stage in Kohlberg's theory of moral development. At this stage, moral judgments are based on understanding the social order, law, justice, duty.* For example, an individual might say that it is always wrong to steal because laws that have been developed are for the good of society.

3. Kohlberg's Level 3: postconventional reasoning. **Postconventional reasoning** *is the highest level in Kohlberg's theory of moral development. At this level, morality is completely internalized and not based on others' standards.* The person recognizes alternative moral courses, explores the options, and then decides on a personal moral code.

- Stage 5. **Community rights versus individual rights** *is the fifth stage in Kohlberg's theory of moral development. At this stage, the person understands that values and laws are relative and that standards may vary from one person to another.* The person recognizes that laws are important for society but knows that laws can be changed. The person believes that some values, such as liberty, are more important than the law.
- Stage 6. **Universal ethical principles** *is the sixth and highest stage in Kohlberg's theory of moral development. At this stage, one has developed a moral standard based on universal human rights.* When faced with a conflict between law and conscience, the person will follow conscience, even though the decision might involve personal risk.

Some of the responses to the dilemma of Heinz and the druggist are given in figure 17.1, which should provide you with a better understanding of the reasoning that occurs at the six stages in Kohlberg's theory. Notice that whether Heinz steals the drug is not the important issue in Kohlberg's cognitive developmental theory. What is crucial is how the person reasons about the moral dilemma.

Kohlberg believed that these levels and stages occur in a sequence and are age related: Before age 9, most children reason about moral dilemmas in a preconventional way; by early adolescence, they reason in more conventional ways; and, by early adulthood, a small number of people reason in postconventional ways. In a 20-year longitudinal investigation, the uses of Stages 1 and 2 decreased. Stage 4, which did not appear at all in the moral reasoning of the 10-year-olds, was reflected in 62 percent of the moral thinking of the 36-year-olds. Stage 5 did not appear until the age of 20 to 22 and never characterized more than 10 percent of the individuals. Thus, the moral stages appeared somewhat later than Kohlberg initially envisioned, and the higher stages, especially Stage 6, were extremely elusive (Colby & others, 1983). Recently, Stage 6 was removed from the Kohlberg scoring manual but is still considered to be theoretically important in the Kohlberg scheme of moral development.

Influences on the Kohlberg Stages

Kohlberg believed that children's moral orientation unfolds as a consequence of their cognitive development. Children construct their moral thoughts as they pass from one stage to the next rather than passively accepting a cultural

Stage description	Examples of moral reasoning that support Heinz's theft of the drug	Examples of moral reasoning that indicate Heinz should not steal the drug
Preconventional reasoning		
Stage 1: Avoid punishment	Heinz should not let his wife die; if he does, he will be in big trouble.	Heinz might get caught and sent to jail.
Stage 2: Seek rewards	If Heinz gets caught, he could give the drug back and maybe they would not give him a long jail sentence.	The druggist is a businessman and needs to make money.
Conventional reasoning		
Stage 3: Gain approval/ avoid disapproval especially with family	Heinz was only doing something that a good husband would do; it shows how much he loves his wife.	If his wife dies, he can't be blamed for it; it is the druggist's fault. He is the selfish one.
Stage 4: Conformity to society's rules	If you did nothing, you would be letting your wife die; it is your responsibility if she dies. You have to steal it with the idea of paying the druggist later.	It is always wrong to steal; Heinz will always feel guilty if he steals the drug.
Postconventional reasoning		
Stage 5: Principles accepted by the community	The law was not set up for these circumstances; taking the drug is not really right, but Heinz is justified in doing it.	You can't really blame someone for stealing, but extreme circumstances don't really justify taking the law into your own hands. You might lose respect for yourself if you let your emotions take over; you have to think about the long term.
Stage 6: Individualized conscience	By stealing the drug, you would have lived up to society's rules, but you would have let down your conscience.	Heinz is faced with the decision of whether to consider other people who need the drug as badly as his wife. He needs to act by considering the value of all the lives involved.

norm of morality. Investigators have sought to understand the factors that influence children's movement through the moral stages, among them modeling, cognitive conflict, peer relations, and perspective-taking opportunities.

Several investigators have attempted to advance individuals' levels of moral development by having a model present arguments that reflect moral thinking one stage above the individuals' established levels. These studies are based on the cognitive developmental concepts of equilibrium and conflict (Walker & Taylor, 1991b). By presenting moral information slightly beyond the children's cognitive level, a disequilibrium is created that motivates them to restructure their moral thought. The resolution of the disequilibrium and conflict should be toward increased competence, but the data are mixed. In one of the pioneer studies on this topic, Eliot Turiel (1966) discovered that children prefer a moral judgment stage one stage above their current stage over two stages above it. However, in the study, they chose one stage below their stage more often than one stage above it. Apparently, the children were motivated more by security needs than by the need to reorganize their thought to a higher level. Other studies indicate children prefer a more advanced stage over a less advanced stage (Rest, Turiel, & Kohlberg, 1969).

Since the early studies of stage modeling, a number of investigations have attempted to determine more precisely the effectiveness of various forms of stage modeling and argument (Lapsley & Quintana, 1985). The upshot of these studies is that virtually any plus-stage discussion format, for any length

Figure 17.1

Moral Reasoning at Kohlberg's Stages in Response to the "Heinz and the Druggist" Story

Both Piaget and Kohlberg believed that peer relations are a critical part of the social stimulation that challenges children to advance their moral reasoning. The mutual give-and-take of peer relations provides children with role-taking opportunities that give children a sense that rules are generated democratically.

of time, seems to promote more advanced moral reasoning. For example, in one investigation (Walker, 1982), exposure to plus-two stage reasoning (arguments two stages above the child's current stage of moral thought) was just as effective in advancing moral thought as plus-one stage reasoning. Exposure to plus-two stage reasoning did not produce more plus-two stage reasoning but rather, like exposure to plus-one stage reasoning, increased the likelihood that the child would reason one stage above her current stage. Other research has found that exposure to reasoning only one third of a stage higher than the individual's current level of moral thought advances that person's moral thought (Berkowitz & Gibbs, 1983). In sum, current research on modeling and cognitive conflict reveals that moral thought can be moved to a higher level through exposure to models or discussion that is more advanced than the child's level.

Kohlberg believed that peer interaction is a critical part of the social stimulation that challenges children to change their moral orientation. Whereas adults characteristically impose rules and regulations on children, the mutual give-and-take in peer interaction provides children with an opportunity to take the perspective of another person and to generate rules democratically. Kohlberg stressed that perspective-taking opportunities can, in principle, be engendered by any peer group encounter. Although Kohlberg believed that such perspective-taking opportunities are ideal for moral development, he also believed that certain types of parent-child experiences can induce the child to think at more advanced levels of moral thinking. In particular, parents who allow or encourage conversation about value-laden issues promote more advanced moral thought in their children; however, many parents do not systematically provide their children with such perspective-taking opportunities. Nonetheless, in one recent study, children's moral development was related to their parents' discussion style, which involved questioning and supportive interaction (Walker & Taylor, 1991a).

Kohlberg's Critics

Kohlberg's provocative theory of moral development has not gone unchallenged (Kurtines & Gewirtz, in press; Puka, in press). The criticisms involve the link between moral thought and moral behavior, the quality of the research, gender and the care perspective, and cultural bias.

■ *Critical Thinking*
Are parents more important in children's moral development than Kohlberg envisioned? Explain your answer.

Moral Thought and Moral Behavior

Critics argue that Kohlberg places too much emphasis on how people morally *think* and not enough on how they morally *behave*. Moral reasons can sometimes be a shelter for immoral behavior. Bank embezzlers and presidents address the loftiest of moral virtues when analyzing moral dilemmas but their own behavior may be immoral. No one wants a nation of cheaters and thieves who can reason at the postconventional level. The cheaters and thieves may know what is right yet do what is wrong.

Assessment of Moral Reasoning

Some developmentalists believe more attention should be paid to the way in which moral development is assessed. For example, James Rest (1976, 1983, 1986) points out that alternative methods should be used to collect information about moral thinking instead of relying on a single method that requires children to reason about hypothetical moral dilemmas. Rest also says that Kohlberg's stories are extremely difficult to score. To help remedy this problem, Rest developed his own measure of moral development, called the Defining Issues Test (DIT).

The DIT attempts to determine which moral issues individuals feel are more crucial in a given situation by presenting them with a series of dilemmas and a list of definitions of the major issues involved (Kohlberg's procedure does not make use of such a list). In the dilemma of Heinz and the druggist, children might be asked whether a community's laws should be upheld or whether Heinz should be willing to risk being injured or caught as a burglar. They might also be asked to list the most important values that govern human interaction. They are given six stories and asked to rate the importance of each issue involved in deciding what ought to be done. Then they are asked to list what they believe are the four most important issues. Rest argues that this method provides a more valid and reliable way to assess moral thinking than Kohlberg's method.

Researchers also have found that the hypothetical moral dilemmas posed in Kohlberg's stories do not match the moral dilemmas many children and adults face in their everyday lives (Walker, de Vries, & Trevethan, 1987; Yussen, 1977). Most of Kohlberg's stories focus on the family and authority. However, when one researcher invited adolescents to write stories about their own moral dilemmas, they generated dilemmas that were broader in scope, focusing on friends, acquaintances, and other issues, as well as family and authority (Yussen, 1977). As shown in table 17.1, the issue that concerned adolescents more than any other was interpersonal relationships.

Gender and the Care Perspective

Another criticism of Kohlberg's view is that it does not adequately reflect relationships and concern for others. The **justice perspective** *is a moral perspective that focuses on the rights of the individual; individuals stand alone and independently make moral decisions.* Kohlberg's theory is a justice perspective. By contrast, the **care perspective** *is a moral perspective developed by Carol Gilligan (1982) that views people in terms of their connectedness with others and focuses on interpersonal communication, relationships with others, and concern for others.* According to Gilligan, Kohlberg greatly underplayed the care perspective in moral development. She believes this may have happened because he was a male, most of his research was with males rather than females, and he used male responses as a model for his theory.

There is nothing so bad it can masquerade as moral.

—Walter Lippman

Moral Development   591

TABLE 17.1
The Subjects of Moral Dilemma Stories Generated by Adolescents

Story subject	Grade 7	Grade 9	Grade 12
Alcohol	2%	0%	5%
Civil rights	0	6	7
Drugs	7	10	5
Interpersonal relations	38	24	35
Physical safety	22	8	3
Sexual relations	2	20	10
Smoking	7	2	0
Stealing	9	2	0
Working	2	2	15
Other	11	26	20

From Steven R. Yussen, "Characteristics of Moral Dilemmas Written by Adolescents" in *Developmental Psychology,* 13:162–163. Copyright 1977 by the American Psychological Association. Reprinted by permission of the author.

Carol Gilligan interviewed students about the importance of relationships in a female's development. According to Gilligan, the sense of relationships and connectedness is at the heart of female development.

Amy Says They Should Just Talk It Out and Find Some Other Way to Make Money

The main character in Kohlberg's most widely used dilemma is a male, Heinz. Females may have a difficult time identifying with him. Some of Kohlberg's dilemmas are gender neutral, but one concerns the captain of a company of Marines, which is highly masculine. The subjects in Kohlberg's original research were all males. Going beyond her critique of Kohlberg's failure to consider females, Gilligan (1982) argues that an important voice is not present in his view. Following are two excerpts from children's responses to the story of Heinz and the druggist, one from 11-year-old Jake, the other from 11-year-old Amy. Jake's comments:

> For one thing, human life is worth more than money, and if the druggist only makes $1,000, he is still going to live, but if Heinz doesn't steal the drug, his wife is going to die. (*Why is life worth more than money?*) Because the druggist can get $1,000 later from rich people with cancer, but Heinz can't get his wife again. (Gilligan, 1982, p. 26)

Amy's comments:

> I think there might be other ways besides stealing it, like if he could borrow the money or make a loan or something, but he really shouldn't steal the drug—but his wife shouldn't die either. (*Why shouldn't he steal the drug?*) If he stole the drug, he might save his wife then, but if he did, he might have to go to jail, and then his wife might get sicker again, and he couldn't get more of the drug, and it might not be good. So, they should really just talk it out and find some other way to make the money. (Gilligan, 1982, p. 28)

Jake's comments are a mixture of Kohlberg's Stages 3 and 4, but they also include some of the components of a mature, Level 3 moral thinker. Amy, by contrast, does not fit into Kohlberg's scoring system as well. Jake sees the problem as one of rules and balancing the rights of people. However, Amy views the problem as involving relationships: the druggist's failure to live up to his relationship to the needy woman, the need to maintain the relationship between Heinz and his wife, and the hope that a bad relationship between Heinz and the druggist can be avoided. Amy concludes that the characters should talk it out and try to repair their relationships.

Gilligan argues that moral development has three basic levels. She calls Level I *preconventional morality,* which reflects a concern for self and survival. Level II, *conventional morality,* shows a concern for being responsible and caring for others. Level III, *postconventional morality,* shows a concern for self and others as interdependent. Gilligan believes Kohlberg underemphasized the care perspective in the moral development of both males and females and that the highest level of morality for both sexes involves a search for moral equality between oneself and others. To read further about Gilligan's ideas on moral development, turn to Perspective on Child Development 17.1.

Recently, Gilligan has conducted extensive interviews with girls from 6 to 18 years of age (Brown & Gilligan, 1990; Gilligan, 1990; Gilligan, Brown, & Rogers, 1990). She and her colleagues report that girls consistently reveal detailed knowledge about human relationships, based on listening and watching what happens between people. According to Gilligan, girls have the ability to sensitively pick up different rhythms in relationships and often are able to follow the pathways of feelings.

Gilligan also believes that girls reach a critical juncture in their development when they reach adolescence. Gilligan says that, in early adolescence, (usually around 11 to 12 years of age), girls become aware that their intense interest in intimacy is not prized by the male-dominated culture, even though society values women as caring and altruistic. The dilemma, says Gilligan, is that girls are presented with a choice that makes them appear either selfish (if they become independent and self-sufficient) or selfless (if they remain responsive to others). Gilligan states that, as girls experience this dilemma during early adolescence, they increasingly "silence" their distinctive voice. They

Carol Gilligan believes that Kohlberg's theory does not place enough emphasis on the importance of caring and relationships in development. According to Gilligan, the American culture has promoted the care perspective in the socialization of females but not of males.

Moral Development

become less confident and more tentative in offering their opinions, which often persists into adulthood. Some researchers believe that this self-doubt and ambivalence too often translates into depression and eating disorders among adolescent girls.

Researchers have found support for Gilligan's claim that females' and males' moral reasoning often center around different concerns and issues (Bussey & Maughan, 1982; Galotti, 1989b; Galotti, Kozberg, & Appleman, in press; Galotti, Kozberg, & Farmer, 1990; Hanson & Mullis, 1985; Lyons, 1983; Scheidel & Marcia, 1985; Yussen, 1977). However, one of Gilligan's initial claims—that traditional Kohlbergian measures of moral development are biased against females—has been extensively disputed. For example, most research studies using the Kohlberg stories and scoring system do not find gender differences (Thoma, 1986; Walker, 1984, 1991a,b). Thus, the strongest support for Gilligan's claims comes from studies that focus more strongly on items and scoring systems pertaining to close relationships, pathways of feelings, sensitive listening, and the rhythm of interpersonal behavior (Galotti, Kozberg, & Farmer, 1990).

Although females often articulate a care perspective and males a justice perspective, the gender difference is not absolute and the two orientations are not mutually exclusive (Gilligan & Attanucci, 1988; Lyons, 1983, 1990; Rothbart, Hanley, & Albert, 1986). For example, in one study, 53 of 80 females and males showed either a care or a justice perspective, but 27 subjects used both orientations, with neither predominating (Gilligan & Attanucci, 1988).

Revisionists such as Gilligan say that their work provides a way to liberate females and transform a society that has far too long discriminated against females. They also say that, if females' approach to life is acknowledged as authentic, they will no longer have to act like men. The revisionists state that females' sensitivity in relationships is a special gift in our culture. Influenced by Gilligan's and other feminists' thinking, some schools are beginning to incorporate the feminine voice into their curricula. For example, at the Emma Willard School in Troy, New York, the entire curriculum has been revamped to emphasize cooperation rather than competition and to encourage girls to analyze and express ideas from their own perspective rather than responding in stereotyped or conformist ways.

Culture and Moral Development

■ *Critical Thinking*
Can you think of some ways that children's moral development might vary across cultures, other than those variations described in this text?

Yet another criticism of Kohlberg's view is that it is culturally biased (Bronstein & Paludi, 1988; Snarey & Keljo, 1991). In a review of research on moral development in 27 countries, it was concluded that moral reasoning is more culture specific than Kohlberg envisioned and that Kohlberg's scoring system does not recognize higher-level moral reasoning in certain cultural groups (Snarey, 1987). Examples of higher-level moral reasoning that would not be recognized as such by Kohlberg's system are the values related to communal equity and collective happiness in Israel, the unity and sacredness of all life forms in India, and the relation of the individual to the community in New Guinea. These examples of moral reasoning would not be scored at the highest level in Kohlberg's system because they do not emphasize the individual's rights and abstract principles of justice. In one recent study, the moral development of 20 adolescent Buddhist monks in Nepal was assessed (Huebner, Garrod, & Snarey, 1990). The issue of justice, a basic theme in Kohlberg's theory, was not of paramount importance in the monks' moral views, and their concerns about the prevention of suffering and the role of compassion were not captured by Kohlberg's theory. More about cultural variations in adolescents' moral

Cultural Variations in Children's Moral Development

Cultural meaning systems vary around the world, and these systems shape children's morality (Damon, 1988). Consider a comparison of American and Asian Indian children (Shweder, Mahapatra, & Miller, 1987). Like people in many other non-Western societies, Indians view moral rules as part of the natural world order. This means that Indians do not distinguish between physical, moral, and social regulation, as Americans do. For example, in India, violations of food taboos and marital restrictions can be just as serious as acts intended to cause harm to others. In India, social rules are seen as inevitable, much like the law of gravity.

As shown in table 17.A, there is some but not much overlap in the moral concerns of children in Indian and American cultures. For Americans accustomed to viewing morality as a freely chosen social contract, Indian beliefs pose a different world view, one that is not easy to reconcile with such treasured ideas as the autonomy of an individualized conscience.

The interviews of Richard Shweder and his colleagues (1987) with Indian and with American children reveal sharp cultural differences in what people judge to be right and wrong. For example, Indian and American children disagree about eating beef. On the other hand, there are areas of overlap between the children in the two cultures. For example, both think that breaking promises and ignoring beggars is wrong.

According to developmentalist William Damon (1988), where culturally specific practices take on profound moral and religious importance, as in India, the moral development of children focuses extensively on their adherence to custom and convention. In contrast, Western moral doctrine tends to elevate abstract principles, such as justice and welfare, to a higher moral status than customs or conventions. As in India, socialization practices in many third-world countries actively instill in children a great respect for their culture's traditional codes and practices (Edwards, 1987).

TABLE 17.A
Agreement/Disagreement Between American and Indian Hindu Brahman Children About Right and Wrong

Agreement	Disagreement
American and Brahman children think it is right: ■ Men holding hands *American and Brahman children think it is wrong:* ■ Ignoring a beggar ■ Destroying another's picture ■ Kicking a harmless animal ■ Stealing flowers	*American children think it is right; Brahman children think it is wrong:* ■ Addressing one's father by his first name ■ Eating beef ■ Cutting one's hair and eating chicken after father's death *American children think it is wrong; Brahman children think it is right:* ■ Hitting an errant child with a cane ■ Eating with one's hands ■ Father opening a son's letter

From R. Shweder, et al., "Culture and Moral Development" in J. Kagan and S. Lamb, editors, The Emergency in Morality in Young Children. Copyright © 1987 The University of Chicago Press, Chicago, IL. Reprinted by permission.

thought appears in Cultural Worlds of Development 17.1. In sum, moral reasoning is shaped more by the values and beliefs of a culture than Kohlberg acknowledged.

Moral Behavior

What are the basic processes that behaviorists believe are responsible for children's moral behavior? What is the nature of resistance to temptation and self-control? How do cognitive social learning theorists view children's moral development? We will explore each of these questions in turn.

Reinforcement, Punishment, and Imitation

The study of moral behavior has been influenced primarily by social learning theory. The familiar processes of reinforcement, punishment, and imitation have been invoked to explain how and why children learn certain responses and why their responses differ from one another; the general conclusions to be drawn are the same as elsewhere. When children are reinforced for behavior that is consistent with laws and social conventions, they are likely to repeat that behavior. When provided with models who behave "morally," children are likely to adopt their actions. Finally, when children are punished for "immoral" or unacceptable behaviors, those behaviors can be eliminated, but at the expense of sanctioning punishment by its very use and of causing emotional side effects for the child.

To these general conclusions are added some qualifiers. The effectiveness of reward and punishment depends on the consistency with which they are administered and the schedule (for example, continuous, partial) that is adopted. The effectiveness of modeling depends on the characteristics of the model (esteem, power) and the presence of symbolic codes to enhance retention of the modeled behavior.

What kind of adult moral models are children being exposed to in our society? Do such models usually do what they say? There is evidence that the adult models children are exposed to often display a double standard, with their moral thinking not always corresponding to their actions. A poll of 24,000 Americans sampled their views on a wide variety of moral issues. Eight detailed scenarios of everyday moral problems were developed to test moral decision making. A summary of the responses to these moral dilemmas is shown in table 17.2. Consider the example of whether the person queried would knowingly buy a stolen color television set. More than 20 percent of the respondents said they would, even though 87 percent said that such an act is probably morally wrong. Further, approximately 31 percent of the adults said that, if they knew they would not get caught, they would be more likely to buy the stolen television. Although moral thought is a very important dimension of moral development, these data glaringly point out that what people believe about right and wrong does not always predict how they will act in moral situations.

In addition to emphasizing the role of reinforcement, punishment, and imitation in determining moral behavior, behaviorists make a strong claim that moral behavior is situationally dependent. That is, from the behavioral perspective, children do not consistently display moral behavior in different situations. In a classic investigation of moral behavior, one of the most extensive ever conducted, Hugh Hartshorne and Mark May (1928–1930) observed the moral responses of 11,000 children who were given the opportunity to lie, cheat, and steal in a variety of circumstances—at home, at school, at social events, and in athletics. A completely honest or a completely dishonest child was difficult to find. Situation-specific behavior was the rule. Children were more likely to cheat when their friends put pressure on them to do so and when the chance of being caught was slim. Other analyses of the consistency of moral behavior suggest that, although moral behavior is influenced by situational determinants, some children are more likely to cheat, lie, and steal than others (Burton, 1984).

	% who said yes or probably	% who said it is or probably is unethical	% who would or probably would be more likely to if sure they wouldn't get caught

T A B L E 1 7 . 2
Adults As Moral Models for Children

	% who said yes or probably	% who said it is or probably is unethical	% who would or probably would be more likely to if sure they wouldn't get caught
Would you drive away after scratching a car without telling the owner?	44	89	52
Would you cover for a friend's secret affair?	41	66	33
Would you cheat on your spouse?	37	68	42
Would you keep $10 extra change at a local supermarket?	26	85	33
Would you knowingly buy a stolen color television set?	22	87	31
Would you try to keep your neighborhood segregated?	13	81	8
Would you drive while drunk?	11	90	24
Would you accept praise for another's work?	4	96	8

Resistance to Temptation and Self-control

A key ingredient of moral development from the social learning perspective is a child's ability to resist temptation and to develop self-control (Bandura, 1986; Mischel, 1987). When pressures mount for children to cheat, lie, or steal, it is important to ask whether they have developed the ability to control themselves and to resist such temptations.

Developmentalists have invented a number of ways to investigate such temptations. In one procedure, children are shown attractive toys and told that the toys belong to someone else, who has requested that they not be touched. Children then experience social influence, perhaps in the form of a discussion of virtues about respecting other people's property or in the form of a model resisting or giving in to the temptation to play with prohibited objects. Children are left alone in the room to amuse themselves when the experimenter departs (under a pretext), announcing that he or she will return in 10 to 15 minutes. The experimenter than watches through a one-way mirror to see whether children resist or give in to the temptation to play with the toys.

There has been considerable interest in examining the effects of punishment on children's ability to resist temptation (Parke, 1972, 1977). For the most part, offering children cognitive rationales enhances most forms of punishment, such as reasons a child should not play with a forbidden toy. Cognitive rationales have been more effective in getting children to resist temptation over a period of time than have strategies that do not use reasoning, such as when parents place children in their rooms without explaining the consequences for others of the children's deviant behavior.

The ability to resist temptation is closely tied to delay of gratification. Self-control is involved in both the ability to resist temptation and the ability to delay gratification. In the case of resisting temptation, children must overcome their impulses to get something that is desired but is known to be prohibitive. Similarly, children must show a sense of patience and self-control in delaying gratification for a desirable future reward rather than succumbing to the immediate pressure of pursuing a smaller reward.

Considerable research has been conducted on children's self-control. Walter Mischel (1974, 1987) believes that self-control is strongly influenced by cognitive factors. Researchers have shown that children can instruct themselves to be more patient and, in the process, show more self-control. In one investigation, preschool children were asked to perform a very dull task (Mischel & Patterson, 1976). Close by was a very enticing talking mechanical clown that tried to persuade the children to play with it. The children who had been trained to say to themselves, "I'm not going to look at Mr. Clown when Mr. Clown says to look at him" were more likely to control their behavior and continue working on the dull task than children who were not given the self-instructional strategy.

Interest in the cognitive factors in resistance to temptation, delay of gratification, and self-control reflects the increasing interest among social learning theorists in the ways in which such cognitions mediate the link between environmental experiences and moral behavior. Next, we will examine a view that captures this cognitive trend.

Cognitive Social Learning Theory

The **cognitive social learning theory of morality** *emphasizes a distinction between a child's* moral competence—*the ability to produce moral behaviors—and* moral performance—*those behaviors in specific situations* (Mischel & Mischel, 1975). Moral competence, or acquisition of moral knowledge, depends primarily on cognitive-sensory processes; it is the outgrowth of these processes. Competencies include what children are capable of doing, what they know, their skills, their awareness of moral rules and regulations, and their cognitive ability to construct behaviors. Children's moral performance, or behavior, however, is determined by their motivation and the rewards and incentives to act in a specific moral way. Albert Bandura (1991) also believes that moral development is best understood by considering a combination of social and cognitive factors, especially those involving self-control.

In general, social learning theorists have been critical of Kohlberg's theory of moral development. Among other reasons, they believe he placed too little emphasis on moral behavior and the situational determinants of morality. However, although Kohlberg argued that moral judgment is an important determinant of moral behavior, he, like the Mischels, stressed that an individual's interpretation of both the moral and factual aspects of a situation leads to a moral decision (Kohlberg & Candee, 1979). For example, Kohlberg mentioned that "extra-moral" factors, such as the desire to avoid embarrassment, may cause children to avoid doing what they believe to be morally right. In sum, according to both the Mischels and Kohlberg, moral action is influenced by a complex of factors. Overall, the findings are mixed with regard to the association of moral thought and behavior (Arnold, 1989), although in one investigation with college students, individuals with both high-principled moral reasoning and high ego strength were less likely to cheat in a resistance-to-temptation situation than were their low-principled and low-ego-strength counterparts (Hess, Lonky, & Roodin, 1985).

At this point, we have discussed a number of ideas about what moral development is, moral thoughts, and moral behavior. A summary of these ideas is presented in concept table 17.1. In the next section, we will turn our attention to moral feelings.

CONCEPT TABLE 17.1
The Nature of Moral Development, Moral Thought, and Moral Behavior

Concept	Processes/related ideas	Characteristics/description
What is moral development?	Its nature	Moral development concerns rules and regulations about what people should do in their interactions with others. Developmentalists study how children think, behave, and feel about such rules and regulations.
Moral thought	Piaget's theory	It distinguishes between the heteronomous morality of younger children and the autonomous morality of older children. Piaget's ideas on formal operational thought have implications for understanding adolescents' moral development.
	Kohlberg's theory	Kohlberg developed a provocative view of the development of moral reasoning. He argued that moral development consists of three levels—preconventional, conventional, and postconventional—and six stages (two at each level). Increased internalization characterizes movement to Levels 2 and 3. Kohlberg's longitudinal data show a relation of the stages to age, although the highest two stages, especially Stage 6, rarely appear.
	Influences on the Kohlberg stages	Influences include cognitive development, imitation and cognitive conflict, peer relations, and perspective taking.
	Kohlberg's critics	Criticisms involve an overemphasis on cognitive and underemphasis on behavior, the quality of the research, inadequate consideration of the care perspective, and an underestimation of the role of culture. Carol Gilligan advocates a stronger care perspective (which views people in terms of their connectedness to others and interpersonal communication). Gilligan also believes that early adolescence is a critical juncture in the development of a moral voice for females. Researchers have found support for Gilligan's claim that females' and males' moral reasoning often center around different concerns, although gender differences in Kohlberg's stages have not been found consistently. Studies that focus more extensively on the items pertaining to close relationships, and use scoring systems that emphasize connectedness, support Gilligan's claims.
Moral behavior	Reinforcement, punishment, and imitation	Behaviorists argue that children's moral behavior is determined by the processes of reinforcement, punishment, and imitation. Situational variability in morality is stressed.
	Resistance to temptation and self-control	Behaviorists who study children's moral behavior often examine resistance to temptation and the development of self-control. The use of cognitive rationales has improved children's ability to resist temptation. Children's self-control is also influenced by cognitive factors, such as self-instruction.
	Cognitive social learning theory	It emphasizes a distinction between moral competence—the ability to produce moral behaviors—and moral performance—those behaviors in specific situations. In general, social learning theorists have been critical of Kohlberg's theory, believing he placed too little emphasis on moral behavior and its situational variability.

Moral Feelings

Among the ideas formulated about the development of children's moral feelings have been the concepts developed by psychoanalytic theorists, the role of childrearing techniques, the nature of empathy, and the role of emotions in moral development.

Psychoanalytic Theory

What is moral is what you feel good after and what is immoral is what you feel bad after.

—Ernest Hemingway

In chapter 2, we extensively discussed Sigmund Freud's psychoanalytic theory, which describes the *superego* as one of the three main structures of personality (the id and ego are the other two). In Freud's classical psychoanalytic theory, a child's superego—the moral branch of personality—develops as the child resolves the Oedipal conflict and identifies with the same-sex parent in the early childhood years. One reason children resolve the Oedipal conflict is to alleviate the fears of losing their parents' love and of being punished for their unacceptable sexual wishes toward the opposite-sex parent. To reduce anxiety, avoid punishment, and maintain parental affection, children form a superego by identifying with the same-sex parent. Through this identification, children internalize the parent's standards of right and wrong that reflect societal prohibitions. Also, the child turns inward the hostility that was previously aimed externally at the same-sex parent. This inwardly directed hostility is then experienced self-punitively (and unconsciously) as guilt. In the psychoanalytic account of moral development, self-punitiveness of guilt keeps children from committing transgressions. That is, children conform to societal standards to avoid guilt.

In Freud's view, the superego consists of two main components, ego-ideal and conscience, which promote children's development of moral feelings. The **ego-ideal** *is the component of the superego that involves ideal standards approved of by parents,* whereas **conscience** *is the component of the superego that involves prohibitions disapproved of by parents.* A child's ego-ideal rewards the child by conveying a sense of pride and personal value when the child acts according to moral standards. The conscience punishes the child for acting immorally by making the child feel guilty and worthless. In this way, self-control replaces parental control.

■ *Critical Thinking*
How would you assess children's feelings of guilt? Describe the kind of measure(s) you would use.

Childrearing Techniques and Moral Development

In Freud's psychoanalytic theory, the aspects of childrearing that encourage moral development are practices that instill the fears of punishment and of losing parental love. Child developmentalists who have studied childrearing techniques and moral development have focused on parents' discipline. These discipline techniques include love withdrawal, power assertion, and induction (Hoffman, 1970). Love withdrawal comes closest to the psychoanalytic emphasis on fear of punishment and of losing parental love. **Love withdrawal** *is a discipline technique in which a parent removes attention or love from the child,* as when the parent refuses to talk to the child or states a dislike for the child. For example, the parent might say, "I'm going to leave you if you do that again," or "I don't like you when you do that." **Power assertion** *is a discipline technique in which a parent attempts to gain control over the child or the child's resources.* Examples include spanking, threatening, or removing privileges. **Induction** *is the discipline technique in which a parent uses reason and explanation of the consequences for others of the child's actions.* Examples of induction include, "Don't hit him. He was only trying to help," and "Why are you yelling at her? She didn't mean to trip you."

Social and Personality Development

In most instances, induction is the discipline technique preferred over power assertion or love withdrawal. Why might induction advance moral development more effectively than the other two discipline techniques?

Moral development theorist and researcher Martin Hoffman (1970) believes that any discipline produces arousal on the child's part. Love withdrawal and power assertion are likely to evoke a very high level of arousal, with love withdrawal generating considerable anxiety and power assertion considerable hostility. Induction is more likely to produce a moderate level of arousal in children, a level that permits them to attend to the cognitive rationales parents offer. When a parent uses power assertion and love withdrawal, the child may be so aroused that, even if the parent gives accompanying explanations about the consequences for others of the child's actions, the child may not attend to them. Power assertion presents parents as weak models of self-control—as individuals who cannot control their feelings. Accordingly, children may imitate this model of poor self-control when they face stressful circumstances. The use of induction, however, focuses the child's attention on the action's consequences for others, not on the child's own shortcomings. For these reasons, Hoffman (1988) believes that parents should use induction to encourage children's moral development. In research on parenting techniques, induction is more positively related to moral development than is love withdrawal or power assertion, although the findings vary according to children's developmental level and socioeconomic status. Induction works better with elementary-school-aged children than with preschool children (Brody & Shaffer, 1982) and better with middle-class than lower-class children (Hoffman, 1970). Older children are probably better able to understand the reasons given to them and are better at perspective taking. Some theorists believe that the internalization of society's moral standards is more likely among middle-class than lower-class individuals because internalization is more rewarding in the middle-class culture (Kohn, 1977).

Empathy

Positive feelings, such as empathy, contribute to the child's moral development. Feeling **empathy** *means reacting to another's feelings with an emotional response that is similar to the other's response* (Damon, 1988).

Although empathy is experienced as an emotional state, it often has a cognitive component—the ability to discern another's inner psychological states, or what we have previously called *perspective taking* (Eisenberg & others, 1991). Infants have the capacity for some purely empathic responses, but, for effective moral action, children need to learn to identify a wide range of emotional states in others and to anticipate what kinds of action will improve another person's emotional state.

What are the main milestones in children's development of empathy? According to a recent analysis by child developmentalist William Damon (1988), changes in empathy take place in early infancy, at 1 to 2 years in age, in early childhood, and at 10 to 12 years of age. **Global empathy** *is the young infant's empathic response in which clear boundaries between the feelings and needs of the self and those of another have not yet been established* (Hoffman, 1983). For example, one 11-month-old infant fought off her own tears, sucked her thumb, and buried her head in her mother's lap after she had seen another child fall and hurt himself. Not all infants cry every time someone else is hurt, though. Many times, an infant will stare at another's pain with curiosity. Although global empathy is observed in some infants, it does not consistently characterize all infants' behavior.

Between 1 and 2 years of age, the infant's undifferentiated feelings of discomfort at another's distress grow into more genuine feelings of concern. The infant realizes that others are independent persons in their own right, with their own unhappy feelings. The infant may sense that these unhappy feelings in others need attention and relief, but the infant cannot translate this realization into effective behavior. For example, toddlers may offer a beloved blanket or doll for comfort to an unhappy-looking adult.

In the early childhood years, children become aware that every person's perspective is unique and that someone else may have a reaction to a situation that is different from their own. Such awareness permits the child to respond more appropriately to another's distress. For example, at the age of 6, a child may realize that, in some instances, an unhappy person may best be left alone rather than helped, or the child may learn to wait for just the right time to give comfort. In sum, at this point, children make more objective assessments of others' distress and needs.

Toward the end of the elementary schools years, at about 10 to 12 years of age, children develop empathy for people who live in unfortunate circumstances. Children's concerns are no longer limited to the feelings of particular persons in situations the child observes directly. Instead, children expand their concerns to the general problems of people in unfortunate situations—the poor, the handicapped, and the socially outcast, for example. This newfound sensitivity may lead to altruistic behavior by the older elementary school child and later, in adolescence, give a humanitarian flavor to the adolescent's development of ideological and political views. A summary of Damon's description of empathy development is shown in figure 17.2.

Although everyone may be capable of responding with empathy, not all individuals do. There is considerable variation in individual empathic behavior. For example, in older children and adolescents, empathic dysfunctions can contribute to antisocial behavior. Some delinquents convicted of violent crimes show a lack of feeling for their victims' distress. A 13-year-old boy convicted of violently mugging a number of elderly people, when asked about the pain he had caused for one blind woman, said, "What do I care? I'm not her" (Damon, 1988).

Age period	Nature of empathy
Early infancy	Characterized by global empathy, the young infant's empathic response does not distinguish between feelings and needs of self and others.
1 to 2 years of age	Undifferentiated feelings of discomfort at another's distress grow into more genuine feelings of concern, but infants cannot translate realization of others' unhappy feelings into effective action.
Early childhood	Children become aware that every person's perspective is unique and that someone else may have a different reaction to a situation. This awareness allows the child to respond more appropriately to another person's distress.
10 to 12 years of age	Children develop an emergent orientation of empathy for people who live in unfortunate circumstances—the poor, the handicapped, and the socially outcast. In adolescence, this newfound sensitivity may give a humanitarian flavor to the individual's ideological and political views.

Figure 17.2
Damon's Description of Developmental Changes in Empathy

Not only is there individual variation in adolescents' empathy and concern about the welfare of others, but sociohistorical influences also may be involved. Over the past 2 decades, adolescents have shown an increased concern for personal well-being and a decreased concern for the welfare of others, especially for the disadvantaged (Astin, Green, & Korn, 1987; Conger, 1981, 1988). As shown in figure 17.3, today's college freshmen are more strongly motivated to be well-off financially and less motivated to develop a meaningful philosophy of life than were their counterparts 20 or even 10 years ago. Among high school seniors, increasing numbers are motivated by the opportunity to make a considerable amount of money (Bachman, Johnston, & O'Malley, 1987).

However, two values that increased during the 1960s continue to characterize today's youth: self-fulfillment and self-expression (Conger, 1981, 1988). As part of their motivation for self-fulfillment, many adolescents show great interest in their physical health and well-being. Greater self-fulfillment and self-expression can be laudable goals, but, if they become the only goals, self-destruction, loneliness, or alienation may result. Young people also need

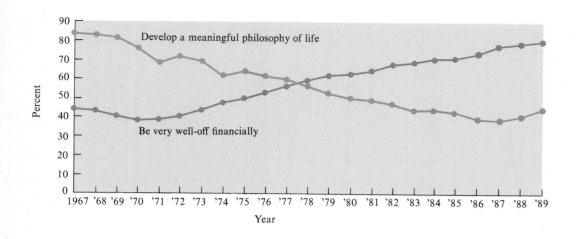

Figure 17.3
Changing Freshman Goals, 1967–1989

to develop a corresponding sense of commitment to others' welfare. Encouraging adolescents to have a strong commitment to others, in concert with an interest in self-fulfillment, is a major task for our nation at the close of the twentieth century.

The Contemporary Perspective on the Role of Emotions in Moral Development

We have seen that classical psychoanalytic theory emphasizes the power of unconscious guilt in moral development but that other theorists, such as Hoffman and Damon, emphasize the role of empathy. Today, many child developmentalists believe that both positive feelings, such as empathy, sympathy, admiration, and self-esteem, and negative feelings, such as anger, outrage, shame, and guilt, contribute to children's moral development (Damon, 1988). When strongly experienced, these emotions influence children to act in accord with standards of right and wrong. Such emotions as empathy, shame, guilt, and anxiety over other people's violations of standards are present early in development and undergo developmental change throughout childhood and beyond (Damon, 1988). These emotions provide a natural base for children's acquisition of moral values, both orienting children toward moral events and motivating them to pay close attention to such events. However, moral emotions do not operate in a vacuum to build a child's moral awareness, and they are not sufficient in themselves to generate moral responsivity. They do not give the "substance" of moral regulation—the rules, values, and standards of behavior that children need to understand and act on. Moral emotions are inextricably interwoven with the cognitive and social aspects of children's development. The web of feeling, cognition, and social behavior is also experienced in altruism—the aspect of children's moral development we will discuss next.

Altruism

Altruism *is an unselfish interest in helping someone.* Human acts of altruism are plentiful—the hardworking laborer who places $5 in a Salvation Army kettle; rock concerts to feed the hungry, help farmers, and fund AIDS research; and the child who takes in a wounded cat and cares for it. How do psychologists account for such acts of altruism?

Social and Personality Development

Reciprocity and exchange are involved in altruism. Reciprocity is found throughout the human world. Not only is it the highest moral principle in Christianity but it is also present in every widely practiced religion in the world—Judaism, Hinduism, Buddhism, and Islam. Reciprocity encourages children to do unto others as they would have others do unto them. Human sentiments are wrapped up in this reciprocity. Trust is probably the most important principle over the long run in altruism. Guilt surfaces if the child does not reciprocate, and anger may result if someone else does not reciprocate. Not all altruism is motivated by reciprocity and exchange, but self-other interactions and relationships help us understand altruism's nature. The circumstances most likely to involve altruism are empathic emotion for an individual in need or a close relationship between benefactor and recipient (Batson, 1989).

In addition to presenting a developmental sequence of children's empathy, which we discussed earlier, Damon (1988) has also described a developmental sequence of children's altruism, especially of sharing. Most sharing during the first 3 years of life is done for nonempathic reasons, such as for the fun of the social play ritual or out of mere imitation. Then, at about 4 years of age, a combination of empathic awareness and adult encouragement produces a sense of obligation on the part of the child to share with others. This obligation forces the child to share, even though the child may not perceive this as the best way to have fun. Most 4-year-olds are not selfless saints, however. Children believe they have an obligation to share but do not necessarily think they should be as generous to others as they are to themselves. Neither do their actions always support their beliefs, especially when the object of contention is a coveted one. What is important developmentally is that the child has developed an internal belief that sharing is an obligatory part of a social relationship and that this involves a question of right and wrong. However, a preschool child's sense of reciprocity does not constitute a moral duty but, rather, a pragmatic means of getting one's way. Despite their shortcomings, these ideas about justice formed in early childhood set the stage for giant strides that children make in the years that follow.

By the start of the elementary school years, children genuinely begin to express more objective ideas about fairness. These notions about fairness have been used throughout history to distribute goods and to resolve conflicts. They involve the principles of equality, merit, and benevolence. *Equality* means that everyone is treated the same. *Merit* means giving extra rewards for hard work, a talented performance, or other laudatory behavior. *Benevolence* means giving special consideration to individuals in a disadvantaged condition. Equality is the first of these principles used regularly by elementary school children. It is common to hear 6-year-old children use the word "fair" as synonymous with "equal" or "same." By the mid- to late-elementary-school years, children also believe that equity means special treatment for those who deserve it—the principles of merit and benevolence.

Missing from the factors that guide children's altruism is one that many adults might expect to be the most influential of all: the motivation to obey adult authority figures. Surprisingly, a number of studies have shown that adult authority has only a small influence on children's sharing. For example, when child developmentalist Nancy Eisenberg (1982) asked children to explain their own altruistic acts, they mainly gave empathic and pragmatic reasons for their spontaneous acts of sharing. Not one of the children referred to the demands of adult authority. Parental advice and prodding certainly foster standards of sharing, but the give-and-take of peer requests and arguments provide the most immediate stimulation of sharing. Parents may set examples that children carry

Every man takes care that his neighbor shall not cheat him. But a day comes when he begins to care that he does not cheat his neighbor. Then all goes well.

—Ralph Waldo Emerson

into peer interaction and communication, but parents are not present during all of their children's peer exchanges. The day-to-day construction of fairness standards is done by children in collaboration and negotiation with each other. Over the course of many years and thousands of encounters, children's understanding of altruism deepens. With this conceptual elaboration that involves such notions as equality, merit, benevolence, and compromise come a greater consistency and generosity in children's sharing behavior (Damon, 1988).

Moral Education

Without civic morality communities perish; without personal morality their survival has no value.

—Bertrand Russell

The moral education of children has become a widely discussed topic. Many parents worry that their children are growing up without traditional values. Teachers complain that many of their students are unethical. Among the questions about moral education we will examine are the following: What is the hidden curriculum? What is the nature of direct moral education versus indirect moral education? What is values clarification? What is cognitive moral education? How should we foster children's moral growth?

The Hidden Curriculum

The **hidden curriculum** *is the pervasive moral atmosphere that characterizes schools. This atmosphere includes school and classroom rules, attitudes toward academics and extracurricular activities, the moral orientation of teachers and school administrators, and text materials.* More than half a century ago, educator John Dewey (1933) recognized that, whether or not they offer specific programs in moral education, schools provide moral education through the hidden curriculum. Schools, like families, are settings for moral development. Teachers serve as models of ethical or unethical behavior. Classroom rules and peer relations at school transmit attitudes about cheating, lying, stealing, and consideration of others, and the school administration, through its rules and regulations, represents a value system to children.

Direct and Indirect Moral Education

The approaches to moral education can be classified as either direct or indirect (Benninga, 1988). **Direct moral education** *involves either emphasizing values or character traits during specified time slots or integrating those values or traits throughout the curriculum.* **Indirect moral education** *involves encouraging children to define their own and others' values and helping them define the moral perspectives that support those values.*

In the direct moral education approach, instruction in specified moral concepts can assume the form of example and definition, class discussions and role playing, or rewarding students for proper behavior (Jensen & Knight, 1981). The use of McGuffey Readers during the early part of the twentieth century exemplifies the direct approach. The stories and poems in the readers taught moral behavior and character in addition to academics. A number of contemporary educators advocate a direct approach to moral education. Former U.S. Secretary of Education William Bennett (1986) wrote:

> If a college is really interested in teaching its students a clear lesson in moral responsibility, it should tell the truth about drugs in a straightforward way. This summer our college presidents should send every student a letter saying

Many years ago, educator John Dewey (1933) recognized that, whether or not they offer specific programs in moral education, schools provide moral education through a hidden curriculum. For example, classroom rules and peer relations at school transmit attitudes about cheating, lying, stealing, and consideration of others.

Social and Personality Development

they will not tolerate drugs on campus—period. The letter should then spell out precisely what the college's policy will be toward students who use drugs. Being simple and straightforward about moral responsibility is not the same as being simplistic and unsophisticated.

Bennett also believes that every elementary and secondary school should have a discipline code, making clear to adolescents and parents what the school expects of them. Then the school should enforce the code.

The most widely adopted indirect approaches to moral education are values clarification and cognitive moral education. We will consider each of these in turn.

Values Clarification

Values clarification *is an indirect moral education approach that focuses on helping students clarify what their lives are for and what is worth working for.* In values clarification, students are asked questions or presented with dilemmas and expected to respond, either individually or in small groups. The intent is to help students define their own values and to become aware of others' values (Nucci & Weber, 1991).

In the following example of values clarification, students are asked to select from among 10 people the 6 who will be admitted to a fallout shelter during World War III:

> Suppose you are a government decision maker in Washington, DC, when World War III breaks out. A fallout shelter under your administration in a remote Montana highland contains only enough space, air, food, and water for 6 people for 3 months, but 10 people wish to be admitted. The 10 have agreed by radio contact that, for the survival of the human race, you must decide which 6 of them shall be saved. You have exactly 30 minutes to make up your mind before Washington goes up in smoke. These are your choices:
> 1. A 16-year-old girl of questionable IQ, who is a high school dropout and pregnant
> 2. A policeman with a gun (which cannot be taken from him), thrown off the force recently for brutality
> 3. A clergyman, 75
> 4. A woman physician, 36, known to be a confirmed racist
> 5. A male violinist, 46, who served 7 years for pushing narcotics
> 6. A 20-year-old Black militant with no special skills
> 7. A former prostitute, female, 39
> 8. An architect who is a male homosexual
> 9. A 26-year-old law student
> 10. The law student's 25-year-old wife, who spent the past 9 months in a mental hospital and is still heavily sedated; they refuse to be separated

In this exercise, no answers are considered right or wrong. The clarification of values is left up to individual students. Advocates of the values clarification approach argue that it is value free, but critics argue that, because of its controversial content, it offends community standards (Eger, 1981). Critics also say that, because of its relativistic nature, values clarification undermines accepted values and fails to stress truth and right behavior (Oser, 1986).

Cognitive Moral Education

Like values clarification, cognitive moral education also challenges direct moral instruction. **Cognitive moral education** *is an indirect moral education approach that emphasizes that children adopt such values as democracy and* *justice as their moral reasoning is developed.* In this approach, students' moral standards are allowed to develop through their attention to environmental settings and exercises that encourage more advanced moral thinking. Thus, in contrast to values clarification, cognitive moral education is not value free. Such values as democracy and justice are emphasized. The advocates of cognitive moral education argue that when moral standards are imposed—as in the direct instruction approach—children can never completely integrate and fully understand moral principles. Only through participation and discussion can children learn to apply the rules and principles of cooperation, trust, community, and self-reliance.

Lawrence Kohlberg's theory of moral development has extensively influenced the cognitive moral education approach. Contrary to what some critics say, Kohlberg's theory is not completely relativistic and it is not completely morally neutral. It treats higher-level moral thinking as better than lower-level moral thinking, and it stresses that higher-level thinking can be stimulated through focused discussion of moral dilemmas (Higgins, 1991; Power, 1991). Also, in the 1980s, Kohlberg (1981, 1986) revised his views on moral education by placing more emphasis on the school's moral atmosphere, as John Dewey did many years ago.

Damon's Comprehensive Approach to Moral Education

Damon (1988) believes that moral education should follow from what we know about the nature of children's moral development. Based on scientific studies and observations of children's moral development, Damon believes that the following six principles should serve as a foundation for the development of moral education programs:

1. Children experience classic moral issues facing humans everywhere simply by participating in social relationships: issues of fairness, honesty, responsibility, kindness, and obedience, for example. Thus, children's moral awareness develops within their normal social experiences. Their moral awareness may need to be guided, informed, and enhanced, but it does not need to be imposed directly in a punitive, authoritarian manner.
2. Children's moral awareness is shaped and supported by natural emotional reactions to observations and events, which begin as early as infancy. Such emotional reactions as empathy support moral compassion and altruism. Such reactions as shame, guilt, and fear support obedience and rule adoption. Children's love and attachment feelings for parents provide an affective foundation for children's developing respect for authority.
3. Interactions with parents, teachers, and other adults introduce children to important social standards and rules. These interactions produce knowledge and respect for the social order, including its principles of organization and legitimate authority. Authoritative adult-child (for example, parent-child or teacher-child) relationships, in which extensive verbal give-and-take and nonpunitive adult control that justifies demands are present, yield the most positive results for children's moral judgment and behavior.

William Damon has presented a number of insightful ideas about children's moral development and moral education.

Social and Personality Development

4. Peer relations introduce children to the norms of direct reciprocity and to the standards for sharing, cooperation, and fairness. Through peer relations, children learn about mutuality, equality, and perspective taking, which promote the development of altruism.

5. Broad variations in social experiences can produce broad differences in moral orientation among children. One such variation is the different roles and expectations that girls and boys experience, especially in traditional social environments. As we learned earlier in our discussion of Carol Gilligan's ideas, the moral development of girls is oriented more toward relationships and care, whereas the moral development of boys is oriented more toward the individual and justice. There is reason to believe that such orientations can be socially transformed as cultures change. According to Damon, there should be an increased emphasis on learning the principles of care *and* justice by both boys and girls.

6. Moral development in schools is determined by the same cognitive and social processes that apply to moral development in other settings. This means that children acquire moral values by actively participating in adult-child and peer relationships that support, enhance, and guide their natural moral tendencies. According to Damon, children's morality is not enhanced by lessons or lectures in which children are passive recipients of information or, even worse, are captive and recalcitrant audiences. Further, the quality of social interaction in a school setting communicates a moral message that is more enduring than direct, declarative statements and lectures by teachers. To receive a competent moral education in a democratic society, children need to experience egalitarian interactions that reflect democratic values—among them, equality, fairness, and responsibility.

Damon (1988) argues that, for teachers and parents to contribute positively to a child's moral development, they need to practice *respectful engagement* with the child. Children need adult guidance, but, for the guidance to register, children need to be productively engaged and their own initiatives and reactions must be respected.

Damon recognizes that parents alone, or schools alone, are not completely responsible for children's moral development. Children's moral education occurs both in and out of school through their interactions with parents, peers, and teachers and through their experiences with society's standards. These interactions are not value free, and, although there is some disagreement about exactly what should be communicated to children in the course of moral education, there also is more agreement than is commonly acknowledged. There are some fundamental values that are shared widely enough for them to be transmitted without hesitation to children; no one wants children to follow a path of dishonesty, drug abuse, or cruel antisocial behavior. All of us want children to endorse justice, abide by legitimate authority, consider the needs of others, and be responsible citizens in a democratic society.

Damon's approach stands in contrast to the permissive approach, which assumes children's moral growth is enhanced when they are left alone. It also stands in contrast to the indoctrinational approach of direct moral education

It is easy to perform a good action, but not easy to acquire a selected habit of performing such actions.

—Aristotle

that children can learn moral values by passively listening to the demands of authority figures. Damon's ideas have much in common with cognitive moral education, but they go beyond the traditional views of cognitive moral education, which focus almost exclusively on the role of schools, peers, and cognition in moral development. Damon's view is more comprehensive than the traditional cognitive moral education views, because it recognizes the importance of emotions, parent-child relations, and culture in moral development, integrating them with the influence of schools, peers, and cognition in a meaningful way.

Juvenile Delinquency

Arnie is 13 years old. His history includes a string of thefts and physical assaults. The first theft occurred when Arnie was 8; he stole a Sony Walkman from an electronics store. The first physical assult took place a year later when he shoved his 7-year-old brother up against a wall, bloodied his face, and then threatened to kill him with a butcher knife. Recently, the thefts and physical assaults have increased. In the past week, he stole a television set and struck his mother repeatedly, threatening to kill her. He also broke some neighborhood street lights and threatened some youths with a wrench and hammer. Arnie's father left home when Arnie was 3 years old. Until his father left, his parents argued extensively and his father often beat up his mother. Arnie's mother indicates that, when Arnie was younger, she was able to control his behavior, but, in the past several years, she has not been able to enforce any sanctions on his antisocial behavior. Because of Arnie's volatility and dangerous behavior, he was placed in a group home with other juvenile delinquents.

The label **juvenile delinquent** *is applied to a child or an adolescent who breaks the law or engages in behavior that is considered illegal.* Like other categories of disturbance, juvenile delinquency is a broad concept; legal infractions range from littering to murder. Because an adolescent technically becomes a juvenile delinquent only after being judged guilty of a crime by a court of law, official records do not accurately reflect the number of illegal acts juvenile delinquents commit. Nevertheless, there is every indication that, in the past 10 to 15 years, juvenile delinquency has increased in relation to the number of crimes committed by adults. Estimates regarding the number of juvenile delinquents in the United States are sketchy, but FBI statistics indicate that at least 2 percent of all youths are involved in juvenile court cases. The number of girls found guilty of juvenile delinquency has increased substantially in recent years. Delinquency rates among Blacks, other minority groups, and the lower class are especially high in proportion to the overall population of these groups. However, such groups have little influence over the judicial decision-making process in the United States and, therefore, may be judged delinquent more readily than their White, middle-class counterparts (Gold, 1987; Polier, 1989).

What causes delinquency? Many causes have been proposed, including heredity, identity problems, community influences, and family experiences (Kennedy, 1991). Erik Erikson (1968), for example, believes that adolescents whose development has restricted them from acceptable social roles or has made them feel that they cannot measure up to the demands placed on them may choose a negative identity. The adolescent with a negative identity may find support for his delinquent image among peers, reinforcing the negative identity. According to Erikson, delinquency is an attempt to establish an identity, although it is a negative identity.

Although delinquency is less exclusively a lower-class phenomenon than it was in the past, some characteristics of the lower-class culture may promote delinquency (Simons & Gray, 1989). The norms of many lower-class peer groups and gangs are antisocial or counterproductive to the goals and norms of society at large. Getting into or staying out of trouble becomes a prominent feature of life for some adolescents in low-income neighborhoods. Adolescents from low-income backgrounds may sense that they can gain attention and status by performing antisocial actions. Being "tough" and "masculine" are high-status traits for lower-class boys, and these traits often are measured by one's success in performing and getting away with delinquent acts. A community with a high crime rate also provides adolescents with many models who engage in criminal activities. These communities may be characterized by poverty, unemployment, and feelings of alienation toward the middle class. High-quality schooling, educational funding, and organized neighborhood activities may be lacking in these communities (Chesney-Lind, 1989).

Weak family support systems are also associated with delinquency. Parents of delinquents are less skilled in discouraging antisocial behavior and in encouraging skilled behavior than are parents of nondelinquents. Parental monitoring of adolescents is especially important in determining whether an adolescent becomes a delinquent (Dishion, Patterson, & Skinner, 1989; Patterson & Grimaldi, 1991; Patterson, DeBaryshe, & Ramsey, 1989). "It's 10 P.M.; do you know where your children are?" seems to be an important question for parents to be able to answer affirmatively. Family discord and inconsistent and inappropriate discipline are also associated with delinquency.

A special concern in delinquency has surfaced recently: escalating gang violence, which is being waged on a level more lethal than ever before. Knives and clubs have been replaced by grenades and automatic weapons, frequently purchased with money made from selling drugs. The lure of gang membership is powerful, especially for children and adolescents who are disconnected from family, school, work, and the community. Children as young as 9 cling to the fringes of neighborhood gangs, eager to prove themselves worthy of membership by the age of 12. Once children become members of a gang, it is difficult to get them to leave. Recommendations for the prevention of gang violence

Moral Development

involve identifying disconnected children in elementary schools and initiating counseling with the children and their families (Calhoun, 1988). More about life in gangs and an effort in Detroit, Michigan, that has made a difference in reducing gang participation appears in Perspective on Child Development 17.2.

A large book could be filled just with brief descriptions of the varied attempts to reduce delinquency. These attempts include forms of individual and group psychotherapy, family therapy, behavior modification, recreation, vocational training, alternative schools, survival camping and wilderness canoeing, incarceration and probation, "Big Brothers" and "Big Sisters," community organizations, and Bible reading (Gold & Petronio, 1980). However, we know surprisingly little about what actually does help reduce delinquency, and, in many instances, prevention and intervention have not been successful (Leitenberg, 1986; Lundman, 1984; Rabkin, 1987).

Although few successful models of delinquency prevention and intervention have been identified, there are a number of points that many experts on delinquency agree should be examined more closely because they are likely candidates for better prevention and intervention (Dryfoos, 1990):

1. Programs should be broader than focusing only on delinquency (O'Donnell, Manos, & Chesney-Lind, 1987). For example, it is virtually impossible to improve delinquency prevention without considering the quality of education available to high-risk children.

2. Programs must have multiple components, because no one component has been found to be the "magic bullet" that decreases delinquency.

3. Programs should begin early in a child's development to prevent learning and conduct problems (Berrueta-Clement & others, 1986).

4. Schools play an important role. Schools with strong governance, fair discipline policies, student participation in decision making, and high investment in school outcomes by both students and staff are important candidates for improving the school's role in curbing delinquency (Hawkins & Lam, 1986; Hawkins & Lishner, 1987).

5. Efforts should often be directed at institutional rather than individual change. Especially important is upgrading the quality of education for disadvantaged children.

6. Although point 5 is accurate, researchers have found that intensive individual attention and personalized planning are important factors in working with children at high risk for becoming delinquent.

7. Program benefits often "wash out" after the program stops. Thus, maintenance programs and continued effort are usually necessary.

In her recent review of delinquency prevention, Joy Dryfoos (1990) also outlined what has *not* worked in preventing or reducing delinquency: preventive casework, group counseling, pharmacological interventions (except for extremely violent behavior), work experience, vocational education, "scaring straight" efforts, and the juvenile justice system. Current school practices that are ineffective in reducing delinquency include suspension, detention, expulsion, security guards, and corporal punishment.

Social and Personality Development

Frog and Dolores

He goes by the name of Frog. He is the cocky prince of the barrio in East Los Angeles. He has street smarts. Frog happily smiles as he talks about raking in $200 a week selling crack cocaine. He proudly details his newly acquired membership in a violent street gang, the Crips. Frog brags about using his drug money to rent a convertible on weekends, even though, at less than 5 feet in height, he can barely see over the dashboard. Frog is 13 years old.

With the advent of crack, juvenile arrests in New York City tripled from 1983 to 1987 and almost quadrupled in the same time frame in Washington, DC. Adults who founded the crack trade recognized early on that young adolescents do not run the risk of the mandatory jail sentence that courts hand out to adults. Being a lookout is the entry-level position for 9- and 10-year-olds. They can make as much as $100 a day warning dealers that police are in the area. The next step up the ladder is runner, a job that can pay as much as $300 a day. A runner transports drugs to the dealers on the street from makeshift factories, where cocaine powder is cooked into rock-hard crack. At the next level, an older adolescent can reach the status of dealer; in a hot market such as New York City, a dealer can make over $1,000 a day.

The escalating drug-related gang violence is difficult to either contain or reduce. Police crackdowns across the country seem to have a minimal impact. In a recent weekend-long raid of drug-dealing gangs in Los Angeles, police arrested 1,453 people, including 315 adolescents; half had to be released for lack of evidence. The Los Angeles County juvenile facilities are designed to house 1,317. Today, more than 2,000 adolescents are crammed into their facilities.

Counselors, school officials, and community workers report that it is extremely difficult to turn around the lives of children and adolescents involved in drug-related gang violence. When impoverished children can make $100 a day, it is hard to wean them from gangs. Federal budgets for training and employment programs, which provide crucial assistance to disadvantaged youth, have been reduced dramatically.

In Detroit, Michigan, Dolores Bennett, though, has made a difference. For 25 years, she has worked long hours trying to find things to keep children from low-income families busy. Her activities have led to the creation of neighborhood sports teams, fairs and picnics, and an informal job-referral service for the children in her neighborhood. She also holds many casual get-togethers for the youths in her small, tidy yellow frame house. The youths talk openly and freely about their problems and their hopes, knowing that Dolores will listen. Dolores says that she has found being a volunteer to be a priceless job. On the mantel in her living room are hundreds of pictures of children and adolescents she has worked with. She points out that most of them did not have someone in their homes who would listen to them and give them love. Our nation needs more Dolores Bennetts.

Dolores Bennett, a volunteer in a low-income area of Detroit, Michigan, talks with two of her "children."

CONCEPT TABLE 17.2
Moral Feelings, Altruism, Moral Education, and Juvenile Delinquency

Concept	Processes/related ideas	Characteristics/description
Moral feelings	Psychoanalytic theory	The superego is one of the three main structures of personality. The child's superego—the moral branch of personality—develops as the child resolves the Oedipal confict and identifies with the same-sex parent in the early childhood years. Through identification, children internalize a parent's standards of right and wrong. Children conform to societal standards to avoid guilt. The superego consists of two main components: ego-ideal and conscience.
	Childrearing techniques and moral development	The focus is on parents' discipline, which includes love withdrawal, power assertion, and induction. Love withdrawal and power assertion have been ineffective in promoting children's moral growth, but induction has been effective, especially with older, middle-class children.
	Empathy	Feeling empathy means reacting to another's feelings with an emotional response that is similar to the other's response. Empathy often has a cognitive component—perspective taking. Developmental changes in empathy include: global empathy in early infancy, more genuine feelings of concern at 1 to 2 years of age, awareness of each person's uniqueness and more appropriate empathy in early childhood, and empathy for people who live in unfortunate circumstances in late childhood. Individual variation and sociohistorical changes are involved in empathy.
	The contemporary perspective on the role of emotions in moral development	Both positive feelings—such as empathy, sympathy, admiration, and self-esteem—and negative feelings—such as anger, outrage, shame and guilt—contribute to children's moral development. When strongly experienced, these emotions influence children to act in accord with moral standards. Moral emotions do not operate in a vacuum—they are interwoven with the cognitive and social aspects of moral development.
Altruism	Its nature	Altruism is an unselfish interest in helping someone. Reciprocity and exchange are involved in altruism. Damon described a developmental sequence of altruism, especially sharing: At 0 to 3 years, sharing is done for nonempathic reasons; at about 4 years of age, the combination of empathic awareness and adult encouragement produces a sense of obligation to share; in the early elementary years, children genuinely begin to show more objective ideas about fairness, at which time the principle of equality is understood; in the middle to late elementary years, the principles of merit and benevolence are understood.

At this point, we have discussed a number of ideas about moral feelings, altruism, moral education, and delinquency. A summary of these ideas is presented in concept table 17.2.

You have arrived at the end of this book, although there is one additional section for you to read. Following this chapter is a brief epilogue that describes the importance of children to any society.

Concept	Processes/related ideas	Characteristics/description
Moral education	Hidden curriculum	The hidden curriculum is the pervasive moral atmosphere that characterizes any school, regardless of whether there is a specific moral curriculum.
	Direct and indirect moral education	Direct moral education involves either emphasizing values or character traits during specified time slots or integrating them throughout the curriculum. Indirect moral education involves encouraging children to define their own and others' values and helping them define the moral perspectives that support those values. The two main indirect moral education approaches are values clarification and cognitive moral education. Values clarification is a moral education approach that focuses on helping students clarify what their lives are for and what is worth working for. Cognitive moral education emphasizes that such values as democracy and justice will be adopted through the development of students' moral reasoning. Kohlberg's theory has extensively influenced the cognitive moral education approach.
	Damon's comprehensive approach to moral education	Damon believes moral education should follow from what we know about the nature of children's moral development. The approach emphasizes that children's moral awareness develops within normal social experiences; that children need to be guided but not directly taught moral values in an authoritarian manner; that moral awareness is shaped by emotional reactions such as empathy; that interactions with parents and other adults introduce children to important social standards (authoritative parenting is preferred); that peer relations introduce children to sharing, cooperation, and fairness; that principles of care and justice should be part of the culture's experiences for boys and girls; and that moral development in the schools is determined by the same cognitive and social processes that apply to moral development in other settings. Moral education should involve active participation by the child, not passive reception of rules. Children need to experience egalitarian interactions that reflect democratic values. Adults should practice respectful engagement in interacting with children.
Juvenile delinquency	Its nature	A juvenile delinquent is a child or an adolescent who breaks the law or engages in illegal conduct. Heredity, identity problems; community influences, and family experiences have been proposed as delinquency's causes. Parents' failure to discourage antisocial behavior and encourage skilled behavior, as well as parents' lack of monitoring of the adolescents' whereabouts, are related to delinquency. Successful programs do not focus on delinquency alone (rather, they include other components such as education), have multiple components but no one component as a "magic bullet," begin early in a child's development, often involve schools, focus on institutions, emphasize giving individual attention to delinquents, and include maintenance.

Summary

I. What Is Moral Development?

Moral development concerns rules and regulations about what people should do in their interactions with others. Developmentalists study how children think, behave, and feel about such rules and regulations.

II. Piaget's Theory and Kohlberg's Theory

Piaget distinguished between the heteronomous morality of young children and the autonomous morality of older children. Piaget's ideas on formal operational thought have implications for understanding adolescents' moral development. Kohlberg developed a provocative theory of the development of moral reasoning. He argued that moral development consists of three levels—preconventional, conventional, and postconventional—and six stages (two at each level). Increased internalization characterizes movement to Levels 2 and 3. Kohlberg's longitudinal data show a relation of the stages to age, although the highest two stages, especially Stage 6, rarely appear.

III. Influences on the Kohlberg Stages and Criticisms of Kohlberg's Theory

Influences include cognitive development, imitation and cognitive conflict, peer relations, and perspective taking. Criticisms include an overemphasis on cognition and an underemphasis on behavior, the quality of the research, an inadequate consideration of gender and the care perspective, and an underestimation of the role of culture. Carol Gilligan advocates a stronger care perspective (which views people in terms of their connectedness to others and interpersonal communication). Gilligan also believes that early adolescence is a critical juncture in the development of a moral voice for females. Researchers have found support for Gilligan's claim that females' and males' moral reasoning often center around different concerns, although gender differences in Kohlberg's stages have not been found consistently. Studies that focus more extensively on items pertaining to close relationships, and that use scoring systems that emphasize connectedness, support Gilligan's claims.

IV. Moral Behavior

Behaviorists argue that children's moral behavior is determined by the processes of reinforcement, punishment, and imitation. Situational variability is stressed by the behaviorists. Behaviorists who study children's moral behavior often examine resistance to temptation and self-control. The use of cognitive rationales improves children's ability to resist temptation. Children's self-control is also influenced by cognitive factors, such as self-instruction. Cognitive social learning theory emphasizes a distinction between moral competence—the ability to produce moral behavior—and moral performance—those behaviors in specific situations. In general, social learning theorists have been critical of Kohlberg's theory, believing he placed too little emphasis on moral behavior and its situational variability.

V. Moral Feelings—Psychoanalytic Theory and Childrearing Techniques

In psychoanalytic theory, the superego is one of the three main structures of personality. The child's superego—the moral branch of personality—develops as the child resolves the Oedipal conflict and identifies with the same-sex parent in the early childhood years. Through identification, children internalize a parent's standards of right and wrong. Children conform to societal standards to avoid guilt. The superego consists of two main components—ego-ideal and conscience. In the study of childrearing techniques and moral development, the focus is on parents' discipline, which includes love withdrawal, power assertion, and induction. Love withdrawal and power assertion have been ineffective in promoting children's moral growth, whereas induction has been effective, especially with older, middle-class children.

VI. Empathy and the Contemporary Perspective on the Role of Emotions in Moral Development

Feeling empathy means reacting to another's feelings with an emotional response that is similar to the other's response. Empathy often has a cognitive component—perspective taking. Developmental changes in empathy include: global empathy in early infancy; more genuine feelings of concern at 1 to 2 years of age; awareness of each person's uniqueness and more appropriate empathy in early childhood; and, in late childhood, empathy for people who live in unfortunate circumstances. Individual variation and sociohistorical changes are involved in empathy. The contemporary perspective on emotions emphasizes that both positive feelings—such as empathy, sympathy, admiration, and self-esteem—and negative feelings—such as anger, outrage, shame, and guilt—contribute to children's moral development. When strongly experienced, these emotions influence children to act in accord with moral standards. Moral emotions do not operate in a vacuum; they are interwoven with the cognitive and social aspects of moral development.

VII. Altruism

Altruism is an unselfish interest in helping someone. Reciprocity and exchange are involved in altruism. Damon described a developmental sequence of altruism, especially sharing: At 0 to 3 years, sharing is done for nonempathic reasons; at about 4 years of age, the combination of empathic awareness and adult encouragement produces a sense of obligation to share; in the early elementary school years, children genuinely begin to show more objective ideas about fairness, at which time the principle of equality is understood; in the middle to late elementary school years, the principles of merit and benevolence are understood.

VIII. Moral Education—the Hidden Curriculum, Direct and Indirect Moral Education, and Values Clarification

The hidden curriculum is the pervasive moral atmosphere that characterizes any school, regardless of whether there is a specific moral curriculum. Direct moral education involves either emphasizing values or character traits during specified time slots or integrating them throughout the curriculum. Indirect moral education involves encouraging children to define their own and others' values and helping them define the moral perspectives that support those values. The two main indirect moral education approaches are values clarification and cognitive moral education. Values clarification is a moral education approach that focuses on helping students clarify what their lives are for and what is worth working for.

IX. Cognitive Moral Education and Damon's Comprehensive Approach to Moral Education

Cognitive moral education emphasizes that such values as democracy and justice will be adopted through the development of students' moral reasoning. Kohlberg's theory has extensively influenced the cognitive moral education approach. Damon believes moral education should follow from what we know about the nature of children's moral development. He emphasizes that children's moral awareness develops within normal social experiences; that children need to be guided but not directly taught moral values in an authoritarian manner; that moral awareness is shaped by such emotional reactions as empathy; that interactions with parents and other adults introduce children to important social standards (authoritative parenting is preferred); that peer relations introduce children to sharing, cooperation, and fairness; that principles of care and justice should be part of the culture's experiences for boys and girls; and that moral development in the schools is determined by the same cognitive and social processes that apply to moral development in other settings. Moral education should involve active participation by the child, not passive reception of rules. Children need to experience egalitarian interactions that reflect democratic values. Adults should practice respectful engagement in interacting with children.

X. Juvenile Delinquency

A juvenile delinquent is a child or an adolescent who breaks the law or engages in illegal conduct. Heredity, identity problems, community influences, and family experiences have been proposed as delinquency's causes. Parents' failure to discourage antisocial behavior and encourage skilled behavior, as well as parents' lack of monitoring of adolescents' whereabouts, are related to delinquency. Successful programs do not focus on delinquency alone (rather, they include other components such as education), have multiple components but no one component as a "magic bullet," begin early in a child's development, often involve schools, focus on institutions, emphasize giving individual attention to delinquents, and include maintenance.

Key Terms

moral development 585
heteronomous morality 585
autonomous morality 585
immanent justice 586
internalization 587
preconventional
    reasoning 587
punishment and obedience
    orientation 587
individualism and
    purpose 587
conventional reasoning 587
interpersonal norms 587
social system morality 588
postconventional
    reasoning 588
community rights versus
    individual rights 588
universal ethical
    principles 588
justice perspective 591
care perspective 591
cognitive social learning
    theory of morality 598
ego-ideal 600
conscience 600
love withdrawal 600
power assertion 600
induction 600
empathy 601
global empathy 602
altruism 604
hidden curriculum 606
direct moral education 606
indirect moral
    education 606
values clarification 607
cognitive moral
    education 607
juvenile delinquent 610

Suggested Readings

Damon, W. (1988). *The moral child*. New York: Free Press. Damon presents his intelligent views on the nature of children's moral development, including some excellent ideas about moral education.

Gilligan, C. (1982). *In a different voice*. Cambridge, MA: Harvard University Press. This book advances Gilligan's provocative view that a care perspective is underrepresented in Kohlberg's theory and research.

Lickona, T. (Ed.). (1976). *Moral development and behavior*. New York: Holt, Rinehart & Winston. Contemporary essays outline the major theories, research findings, and educational implications of moral development. Included are essays by Kohlberg, Hoffman, Mischel, Aronfreed, Bronfenbrenner, and Rest.

Modgil, S., & Modgil, C. (Eds.). (1986). *Lawrence Kohlberg*. Philadelphia: Falmer. A number of experts evaluate Kohlberg's theory of moral development. The book includes a concluding chapter by Kohlberg.

Quay, H. C. (Ed.). (1987). *Handbook of juvenile delinquency*. New York: Wiley. This collection of articles by leading experts explores the many dimensions of delinquency.

618

EPILOGUE

Children: The Future of Society

We have arrived at the end of this book. I hope you can look back and say that you learned a lot about children, not only other children, but yourself as a child and how your childhood contributed to who you are today. The insightful words of philosopher Sören Kierkegaard capture the importance of looking back to understand ourselves: "Life is lived forward but understood backwards." I also hope that those of you who become the parents of children or who work with children in some capacity—whether as a teacher, counselor, or community leader—feel that you have a better grasp of what children's development is all about.

As the twenty-first century approaches, the well-being of children is one of America's foremost concerns. We all cherish the future of our children, because they are the future of any society. Children who do not reach their potential, who are destined to make fewer contributions to society than society needs, and who do not take their place as productive adults diminish the power of that society's future.

Future generations depend on our ability to face our children. At some point in our adult lives, each one of us needs to examine the shape of our life and ask whether we have met the responsibility of competently and caringly carving out a better world for our children. Twenty-one centuries ago, Roman poet and philosopher Lucretius described one of adult life's richest meanings: grasping that the generations of living things pass in a short while and, like runners, pass on the torch of life. More than twenty centuries later, American writer James Agee captured yet another of life's richest meanings: In every child who is born the potentiality of the human race is born again.

John W. Santrock

GLOSSARY

A

ABC method A learning-to-read technique that emphasizes memorizing the names and letters of the alphabet. 353

AB̄ error The Piagetian object permanence concept in which an infant progressing into Substage 4 makes frequent mistakes, selecting the familiar hiding place (A) rather than new hiding places (B̄). 264

accommodation Piagetian concept of adjustment to new information. 58

achievement motivation The desire to accomplish something, to reach a standard of excellence, to expend effort to excel. 244

activity level The tempo and vigor of movement. 99

adaptation Piaget's concept of children's effective interaction with the environment. The interaction is cognitive and involves assimilation and accommodation, which usually work together. 258

adolescence The developmental period of transition from childhood to early adulthood, entered at approximately 10 to 12 years of age and ending at 18 to 22 years of age. 18

adolescent egocentrism A characteristic of adolescence composed of an imaginary audience and a personal fable. 282

adoption study A study in which investigators seek to discover whether the behavior and psychological characteristics of adopted children are more like their adoptive parents, who provide a home environment, or their biological parents, who contributed their heredity. 95

afterbirth The third birth stage, when the placenta, umbilical cord, and other membranes are detached and expelled. 124

AIDS (acquired immune deficiency syndrome) A virus that destroys the body's immune

system. Consequently, germs that usually do not harm someone with a normal immune system produce devastating results and death. 193

altruism An unselfish interest in helping someone. 604

amniocentesis A prenatal medical procedure in which a sample of amniotic fluid is withdrawn by syringe and tested to discover if the fetus is suffering from any chromosomal or metabolic disorders. It is performed in the 12th to 16th week of pregnancy. 92

amnion A bag or envelope that contains a clear fluid in which the developing embryo floats. The amnion is an important life-support system. It provides an environment that is temperature and humidity controlled, as well as shock-proof. 110

anal stage The second Freudian stage of development, occurring between 1½ and 3 years of age, in which the child's greatest pleasure involves the anus or the eliminative functions associated with it. 50

androgyny The presence of desirable masculine and feminine characteristics in one individual. 568

animism A facet of preoperational thought, the belief that inanimate objects have lifelike qualities and are capable of action. 270

anorexia nervosa An eating disorder that involves the relentless pursuit of thinness through starvation. 202

anoxia The insufficient availability of oxygen to the infant. 124

Apgar scale A widely used method to assess the health of newborns at 1 and 5 minutes after birth. The Apgar scale evaluates

infants' heart rate, respiratory effort, muscle tone, body color, and reflex irritability. 129

aphasia A language disorder, resulting from brain damage, that involves a loss of the ability to articulate ideas in any form. 337

applied research The study of issues that have direct practical significance, often with the intent of changing human behavior. 35

aptitude-treatment interaction (ATI) ATI stresses the importance of both children's aptitudes or characteristics and the treatments or experiences they are given in classrooms. "Aptitude" refers to such characteristics as the academic potential and personality characteristics on which students differ; "treatment" refers to educational techniques, such as structured versus flexible classrooms. 493

artificial intelligence The branch of computer science devoted to creating computers capable of handling complicated tasks that require "thinking." 301

assimilation Piagetian concept of the incorporation of new information into existing knowledge. 58

associative play Play that involves social interaction, with little or no organization. 457

attachment A close emotional bond between an infant and a caregiver. 406

attention The concentration and focusing of mental effort. 303

attention-deficit hyperactivity disorder Hyperactivity, characterized by a short attention span, high distractibility, and high levels of physical activity. 508

attribution theory The theory that individuals are motivated to discover the underlying causes of behavior as part of their interest in making sense out of the behavior. 245

authoritarian parenting A restrictive, punitive parenting style that exhorts a child to follow a parent's directions and to respect work and effort. An authoritarian parent places firm limits and controls on a child, with little verbal exchange allowed. Authoritarian parenting is associated with children's social incompetence. 416

authoritative parenting A parenting style that encourages children to be independent but places limits and controls on their actions. Extensive verbal give-and-take is allowed, and parents are warm and nurturant. Authoritative parenting is associated with children's social competence. 416

automaticity The ability to process information with little or no effort. 303

autonomous morality The second stage of moral development in Piaget's theory, displayed by older children (about 10 years of age and older). The child becomes aware that rules and laws are created by people and that, in judging an action, one should consider the actor's intentions as well as the consequences. 587

autonomy versus shame and doubt Erikson's second stage of development, occurring in late infancy and toddlerhood (1–3 years). 53

B

back-to-basics movement The idea that the function of schools should be rigorous training of intellectual skills through such subjects as English, math, and science. 478

basal metabolism rate The minimum amount of energy a person uses in a resting state. 177

baseline A measure of how often a behavior occurs before an attempt is made to change the behavior. 226

basic research The study of issues to obtain knowledge for its own sake rather than for practical application, also called pure research. 35

Bayley Scales of Infant Development An instrument, developed by Nancy Bayley, to be used in the assessment of infant development. The current version has three components: a mental scale, a motor scale, and an infant behavior profile. 375

behavior genetics The degree and nature of behavior's hereditary basis. 95

behavior modification The application of operant conditioning principles to changing human behavior; its main goal is to replace unacceptable responses with acceptable, adaptive ones. 233

behaviorism The developmental theory that emphasizes the scientific study of observable behavioral responses and their environmental determinants. 65

bilingual education Programs for students with limited proficiency in English that instruct students in their own language part of the time while they learn English. 355

biological processes Changes in an individual's physical nature. 17

blastocyst The inner layer of cells that develops during the germinal period. These cells later develop into the embryo. 109

bonding Close contact, especially physical, between parents and their newborn in the period shortly after birth. 132

Brazelton Neonatal Behavioral Assessment Scale A test, given several days after birth, to assess newborns' neurological development, reflexes, and reactions to people. 130

Brazelton training A method of using the Brazelton scale to show parents how their newborn responds to people. 130

breech position The baby's position in the uterus that causes the buttocks to be the first part to emerge from the vagina. 124

Broca's area An area of the left frontal lobe of the brain that directs the muscle movement involved in language comprehension. 337

bulimia An eating disorder that involves a binge-and-purge sequence on a regular basis. 203

C

canalization The process by which characteristics take a narrow path or developmental course. Apparently, preservative forces help protect a person from environmental extremes. 94

care perspective The moral perspective, developed by Carol Gilligan, that views people in terms of their connectedness to others and focuses on interpersonal communication, relationships with others, and concern for others. 591

case study An in-depth look at an individual; it is used mainly by clinical psychologists when the unique aspects of a person's life cannot be duplicated, either for practical or ethical reasons. 27

centration The focusing of attention on one characteristic to the exclusion of all others. 270

cephalocaudal pattern The sequence in which the greatest growth occurs at the top—the head—with growth in size, weight, and feature differentiation gradually working down from top to bottom. 146

cesarean section The surgical removal of the baby from the uterus. 124

child-centered kindergarten The education of the whole child, including concern for the child's physical, cognitive, and social development. Instruction is organized around the child's needs, interests, and learning style. The process of learning, rather than the finished product, is emphasized. 481

chlamydia A sexually transmitted disease named for the bacteria that cause it. 192

chorionic villus test A prenatal medical procedure in which a small sample of the placenta is removed at a certain point in the pregnancy from the 8th through the 11th week. 92

chromosomes Threadlike structures that come in 23 pairs, one member of each pair coming from each parent. Chromosomes contain the genetic substance DNA. 87

chronosystem In Bronfenbrenner's ecological system, the patterning of environmental events and transitions over the life course. 75

classical conditioning A neutral stimulus acquires the ability to produce a response originally produced by another stimulus. 221

cliques Small adolescent groups that involve greater intimacy among members and more group cohesion than crowds. 451

cognitive developmental theory of gender In this view, children's gender-typing occurs after they have developed a concept of gender. Once they begin to consistently conceive of themselves as male or female, children often organize their world on the basis of gender. 557

cognitive monitoring The process of taking stock of what you are currently doing, what you will do next, and how effectively the mental activity is unfolding. 311

cognitive moral education An indirect moral education approach that emphasizes that children adopt such values as democracy and justice as their moral reasoning is developed. 607

cognitive processes Changes in an individual's thought, intelligence, and language. 17

cognitive social learning theory of morality The theory that distinguishes between a child's moral competence—the ability to produce moral behaviors—and moral performance—those behaviors in specific situations. 598

cognitive styles The general, usually consistent ways individuals process information. Cognitive style is determined not only by an individual's attention to a task, organizational skills, and cognitive strategies, but by the person's personality and motivation as well. 323

cohort effects Effects due to a subject's time of birth or generation but not actually to age. 34

commitment The part of identity development in which adolescents show a personal investment in what they are going to do. 537

community rights versus individual rights The fifth stage in Kohlberg's theory of moral development. Children understand that values and laws are relative and that standards vary from one person to another. 588

competence motivation (mastery or effectance motivation) The motivation to deal effectively with the environment, to do well what is attempted, to process information effectively, and to make the world a better place. 242

computer-assisted instruction A method of education that uses the computer as a tutor to individualize instruction: to present information, give students practice, assess their level of understanding, and provide additional instruction if needed. 469

concept A category used to group objects, events, and characteristics on the basis of common properties. 315

concrete operational stage The third Piagetian developmental stage, which lasts from 7 to 11 years of age. Children can perform operations, and logical reasoning replaces intuitive thought as long as reasoning can be applied to specific or concrete examples. 59

concurrent validity The relation of a test's scores to a criterion that is presently available (concurrent). 366

conditioned response (CR) The learned response to the conditioned stimulus that occurs after CS-UCS pairing. 221

conditioned stimulus (CS) A previously neutral stimulus that eventually elicits the conditioned response after being paired with the unconditioned stimulus. 221

conditioning Instituting a program to change an individual's undesirable behavior. 227

connectedness An important element in adolescent identity development. It consists of two dimensions: mutuality (sensitivity to and respect for others' views) and permeability (openness to others' views). 540

conscience The component of the superego that involves behaviors disapproved of by parents. 600

conservation The idea that an amount stays the same regardless of how its container changes. 270

constructive play Play that combines sensorimotor and practice repetitive activity with the symbolic representation of ideas. Constructive play occurs when children engage in self-regulated creation

or construction of a product or problem solution. 461

constructivist view Piaget's view that the main perceptual abilities are completely uncoordinated at birth and that infants do not have intermodal perception. Infant perception involves a representation of the world that builds up as the infant constructs an image of experiences. 160

content validity A form of validity; a test's ability to give a broad picture of what is to be measured. 366

continuity of development The view that development involves gradual, cumulative change from conception to death. 21

conventional reasoning The second, or intermediate, level in Kohlberg's theory of moral development. Children's internalization is intermediate. They abide by certain standards (internal), but they are the standards of others (external), such as parents or the laws of society. 587

convergent thinking Thinking that produces one correct answer and is characteristic of the kind of thinking required on standardized intelligence tests. 390

cooperative play Play that involves social interaction in a group, with a sense of group identity and organized activity. 457

coordination of secondary circular reactions Piaget's fourth sensorimotor substage, which develops between 8 and 12 months of age. In this substage, several significant changes take place involving the coordination of schemes and intentionality. 261

correlation coefficient A number based on statistical analysis used to describe the degree of association between two variables. 30

correlational strategy A way to describe the relation between two or more events or characteristics. This is useful strategy because, the more strongly events are correlated, the more we can predict one from the other. 30

counterconditioning A classical conditioning procedure for weakening a CR by associating the stimuli with a new response incompatible with the CR. 224

creativity The ability to think about something in a novel and unusual way and to come up with unique solutions to problems. 390

crisis A period of identity development during which adolescents choose among meaningful alternatives. 537

criterion validity A form of validity; a test's ability to predict other measures, or criteria, of an attribute. 366

critical period A fixed time period very early in development during which certain behaviors optimally emerge. 71

critical thinking Grasping the deeper meaning of problems, keeping an open mind about different approaches and perspectives, and thinking reflectively rather than accepting statements and carrying out procedures without significant understanding and evaluations. 312

cross-sectional approach A research strategy in which individuals of different ages are compared all at one time. 32

crowd The largest and least personal of adolescent groups. 451

cultural-familial retardation Mental retardation in which there is no evidence of organic brain damage; individuals' IQs range from 50 to 70. 389

culture The behavior patterns, beliefs, and all other products of a group that are passed from generation to generation. 72

culture-fair tests Intelligence tests that attempt to reduce cultural bias. 384

D

deep structure The syntactic relation among the words in a sentence. 335

defense mechanisms The psychoanalytic term for an unconscious method through which the ego distorts reality, thereby protecting it from anxiety. 48

Denver Developmental Screening Test A widely used test to measure young children's motor development. It is especially helpful in assessing developmental delay in motor skills and can be used with children from birth through 6 years of age. 171

dependent variable The factor measured in an experiment; it may change because of the manipulation of the independent variable. The label "dependent" is used because this variable depends on what happens to the subjects in the experiment. 31

developmentally appropriate practice Education based on knowledge of the typical development of children within an age span (age appropriateness) and the uniqueness of each child (individual appropriateness). 482

development The pattern of movement or change that begins at conception and continues through the life cycle. 17

developmental quotient (DQ) An overall developmental score that combines subscores in the motor, language, adaptive, and personal-social domains in the Gesell assessment of infants. 375

difficult child A child who tends to react negatively and cry frequently, who engages in irregular daily routines, and who is slow to accept new experiences. 99

direct moral education An educational approach that involves either emphasizing values or character traits during specified time slots or integrating those values or traits throughout the curriculum. 606

direct perception view The view that infants are born with intermodal perception abilities that enable them to display intermodal perception early in infancy. Infants have to attend only to the appropriate sensory information; they do not have to build up an internal representation of the information through months of sensory experiences. 160

discontinuity of development The view that development involves distinct stages in the life span. 22

dishabituation An infant's renewed interest in a stimulus. 234

displacement The psychoanalytic defense mechanism that occurs when an individual shifts feelings from one object to another, more acceptable object. 49

displacement The use of language to communicate information about another place and time. 333

divergent thinking Thinking that produces many answers to a question and is characteristic of creativity. 390

DNA A complex molecule that contains genetic information. 87

dominant-recessive genes principle If one gene of a pair is dominant and one is recessive (goes back or recedes), the dominant gene exerts its effect, overriding the potential influence of the recessive gene. A recessive gene exerts its influence only if both genes in a pair are recessive. 91

Down syndrome The most common genetically transmitted form of mental retardation, which is caused by the presence of an extra (47th) chromosome. 90

drive An aroused state that occurs because of a physiological need. 242

E

early childhood The developmental period that extends from the end of infancy to about 5 or 6 years, sometimes called the preschool years. 18

easy child A child who is generally in a positive mood, who quickly establishes regular routines in infancy, and who adapts easily to new experiences. 99

echoing Repeating what someone says, especially if it is an incomplete phrase or sentence. 342

ecological theory Bronfenbrenner's sociocultural view of development, which consists of five environmental systems, ranging from the fine-grained inputs of

direct interactions with social agents to the broad-based inputs of culture. 72

ectoderm The outermost layer of the cells, which becomes the nervous system, sensory receptors (ear, nose, and eyes, for example), and skin parts (hair and nails, for example). 109

ego The Freudian structure of personality that deals with the demands of reality. The ego is called the executive branch of personality because it makes rational decisions. 48

ego-ideal The component of the superego that involves ideal standards approved of by parents. 600

egocentrism A salient feature of preoperational thought, the inability to distinguish between one's own and someone else's perspective. 267

elaboration The extensive processing of information, often in the form of association. 308

embryonic period The period of prenatal development that occurs 2 to 8 weeks after conception. During the embryonic period, the rate of cell differentiation intensifies, support systems for the cells form, and organs appear. 109

emic approach A way to describe behavior in one culture or ethnic group in terms that are meaningful and important to the people in that culture or ethnic group, without regard to other cultures or ethnic groups. 28

emotionality The tendency to be distressed. 99

empathy Reacting to another's feelings with an emotional response that is similar to the other's response. 601

endoderm The inner layer of cells that develops into digestive and respiratory systems. 109

epigenetic principle Erikson's term for the process that guides development through the life cycle. It states that anything which grows has a blueprint, each part having a special time of ascendency, until all of the parts have arisen to form a functioning whole. 52

equilibration A mechanism in Piaget's theory invoked to explain how children shift from one stage of thought to the next. The shift occurs as children experience cognitive conflict or a disequilibrium in trying to understand the world. Eventually, they resolve the conflict and reach an equilibrium of thought. 259

erogenous zone Freud's concept of the parts of the body that have especially strong pleasure-giving qualities at each stage of development. 50

estradiol A hormone associated with breast, uterine, and skeletal development in girls. 183

ethnicity A dimension of culture based on cultural heritage, nationality characteristics, religion, and language. 72

ethnocentrism The tendency to favor one's own group over other groups. 528

ethology The theory that behavior is strongly influenced by biology, is tied to evolution, and is characterized by critical or sensitive periods. 70

etic approach A way to describe behavior so that generalizations can be made across cultures. 28

exosystem In Bronfenbrenner's ecological system, the exosystem is involved when experiences in social settings in which an individual does not have an active role influence what that person experiences in an immediate context. 72

expanding Restating what someone has said in a linguistically sophisticated form. 342

experimental strategy A strategy that allows precise determination of behavior's causes. Psychologists accomplish this task by performing an experiment, a study done in a carefully regulated setting in which one or more of the factors believed to influence the behavior being studied is manipulated and all others are held constant. 31

expert Someone who has a great deal of knowledge about a domain of human interest and a great deal of experience performing tasks typical of that domain. 320

extinction A decrease in the tendency to perform a response brought about by unreinforced consequences of that response. 227

extrinsic motivation Motivation influenced by external rewards and punishments. 244

F

fetal alcohol syndrome (FAS) A cluster of abnormalities that appears in the offspring of mothers who drink alcohol heavily during pregnancy. 118

fetal period The prenatal period of development that begins 2 months after conception and lasts for 7 months on the average. 111

fine motor skills Motor skills that involve finely tuned movements, such as finger dexterity. 147

first habits and primary circular reactions Piaget's second sensorimotor substage, which develops between 1 and 4 months of age. Infants learn to coordinate sensation and types of schemes or structures—that is, habits and primary circular reactions. 260

fixation The psychoanalytic defense mechanism that occurs when an individual remains locked into an earlier developmental stage because needs are under- or overgratified. 50

fixed-action patterns A series of biologically based responses chained together in a stereotyped fashion. 241

formal operational stage The fourth and final Piagetian developmental stage, which appears between the ages of 11 and 15. Individuals move beyond the world of concrete experiences and think in abstract and more logical terms. 59

fraternal twins (dyzygotic twins) Twins who develop from separate eggs, making them genetically less similar than identical twins. 95

G

games Activities engaged in for pleasure that include rules and often competition. 461

gametes Human reproduction cells created in the testes of males and the ovaries of females. 87

gender The social dimension of being male or female. 551

gender identity The sense of being male or female, which most children acquire by the time they are 3 years old. 551

gender role stereotypes Broad categories that reflect our impressions and beliefs about females and males. 562

gender role A set of expectations that prescribes how females or males should think, act, and feel. 551

gender schema theory The theory that children's attention and behavior are guided by an internal motivation to conform to gender-based, sociocultural standards and stereotypes. 558

gender schema A cognitive structure that organizes the world in terms of female and male. 558

generativity versus stagnation Erikson's seventh developmental stage, which individuals experience during middle adulthood. 54

genes Units of hereditary information on the DNA "staircase." Genes act like a blueprint for cells to reproduce themselves and manufacture the proteins that maintain life. 87

genetic epistemology A term, used by Baldwin, that refers to the study of how children's knowledge changes over the course of their development. 12

genital stage The fifth and final Freudian stage of development, occurring from puberty on. The genital stage is a time of sexual reawakening; the source of sexual pleasure now becomes someone outside of the family. 51

genotype A person's genetic heritage; the actual genetic material. 93

germinal period The period of prenatal development that takes place in the first 2 weeks after conception. It includes the creation of the zygote, continued cell division, and the attachment of the zygote to the uterine wall. 108

gifted Having above-average intelligence (an IQ of 120 or higher), a superior talent for something, or both. 389

global empathy A young infant's empathic response in which clear boundaries between the feelings and needs of the self and those of another have not yet been established. 602

grammar The formal description of syntactical rules. 335

grasping reflex A neonatal reflex that occurs when something touches an infant's palms. The infant responds by grasping tightly. 139

gross motor skills Motor skills that involve large muscle activities, such as walking. 147

H

habituation The repeated presentation of a stimulus, which causes reduced attention to the stimulus. 234

helpless orientation A description of children who seem trapped by the experience of difficulty. They attribute their difficulty to a lack of ability. 246

hermaphrodites Individuals whose genitals become intermediate between male and female because of a hormonal imbalance (as in a developing male with insufficient androgen or a female exposed to an excess of androgen). 551

herpes simplex virus II A virus that causes a sexually transmitted disease whose symptoms include irregular cycles of sores and blisters in the genital area. 192

heteronomous morality The first stage of moral development in Piaget's theory, occurring from 4 to 7 years of age. Justice and rules are conceived of as unchangeable properties of the world, removed from the control of people. 585

heuristics Strategies that suggest a solution to a problem but do not guarantee it will work. 322

hidden curriculum The pervasive moral atmosphere that characterizes schools. This atmosphere includes school and classroom rules, attitudes toward academics and extracurricular activities, the moral orientation of teachers and school administrators, and the text materials. 606

hierarchy of motives Maslow's concept that all individuals have five main needs, which must be satisfied in the following sequence: physiological, safety, love and belongingness, self-esteem, and self-actualization. 243

holophrase hypothesis The theory that a single word is used to imply a complete sentence; it is characteristic of an infant's first words. 347

homeostasis The body's tendency to maintain equilibrium. 242

horizontal décalage Piaget's concept that describes how similar abilities do not appear at the same time within a stage of development. 276

humanistic theories The developmental theories that are the most widely known phenomenological approaches to understanding personality. Humanistic theories stress children's capacity for personal growth, freedom to choose one's destiny, and positive qualities. 67

hypotheses Assumptions that can be tested to determine their accuracy. 24

hypothetical-deductive reasoning Piaget's formal operational concept that adolescents have the cognitive ability to develop hypotheses about ways to solve problems. They then systematically deduce which is the best path to follow in solving the problem. 280

I

id The Freudian structure of personality that consists of instincts, which are an individual's reservoir of psychic energy. 48

identical twins (monozygotic twins) Twins who develop from a single fertilized egg, which splits into two genetically identical replicas, each of which becomes a person. 95

identification theory A theory that stems from Freud's view that preschool children develop a sexual attraction to the opposite-sex parent, then, at 5 to 6 years of age, renounce this attraction because of anxious feelings, subsequently identifying with the same-sex parent and unconsciously adopting the same-sex parent's characteristics. 553

identity achievement Marcia's term for adolescents who have undergone a crisis and have made a commitment. 537

identity diffusion Marcia's term for adolescents who have not yet experienced a crisis or made any commitments. 537

identity foreclosure Marcia's term for adolescents who have made a commitment but have not experienced a crisis. 537

identity moratorium Marcia's term for adolescents who are in the midst of a crisis, but their commitments are either absent or only vaguely defined. 537

identity versus identity confusion Erikson's fifth developmental stage, which individuals experience during the adolescent years. At this time, individuals are faced with finding out who they are, what they are all about, and where they are going in life. 54

imagery Sensations without the presence of an external stimulus. 308

imaginary audience An adolescent's belief that others are as preoccupied with her as she is. 282

imitation (modeling) A form of learning in which children acquire new behaviors by watching someone else perform the behaviors. 218

immanent justice Piaget's concept that, if a rule is broken, punishment will be meted out immediately. 586

implantation The attachment of the zygote to the uterine wall, which takes place about 10 days after conception. 109

imprinting The ethological concept of rapid, innate learning within a limited critical period of time, which involves attachment to the first moving object seen. 70

impulsivity A cognitive style in which individuals act before they think, usually making rapid scans of information and, if fine discriminations of information are required, making errors. 324

in vitro fertilization Conception outside the body. 88

independent variable The manipulated, influential, experimental factor in an experiment. The label "independent" is used because this variable can be changed independently. 31

indirect moral education An educational approach that involves encouraging children to define their own and others' values and helping them define the moral perspectives that support those values. 606

individual differences The stable, consistent ways in which children are different from each other. 365

individualism and purpose The second stage in Kohlberg's theory of moral development. Moral thinking is based on rewards and self-interest. 587

individuality An important element in adolescent identity development. It consists of two dimensions: self-assertion (the ability to have and communicate a point of view) and separateness (the use of communication patterns to express how one differs from others). 540

induction A discipline technique in which a parent uses reason and explanation of the consequences for others of a child's actions. 600

industry versus inferiority Erikson's fourth developmental stage, occurring

approximately in the elementary school years. 54

infancy The developmental period that extends from birth to 18 or 24 months. 18

infertility The inability to conceive a child after 12 months of regular intercourse without contraception. 89

infinite generativity An individual's ability to generate an infinite number of meaningful sentences using a finite set of words and rules, which makes language a highly creative enterprise. 333

information processing A model of cognition concerned with how individuals process information about their world—how information enters the mind, how it is stored and transformed, and how it is retrieved to perform such complex activities as problem solving and reasoning. 59

initiative versus guilt Erikson's third stage of development, occurring during the preschool years. 53

innate goodness view The idea, presented by Swiss-born philosopher Jean-Jacques Rousseau, that children are inherently good. 10

integrity versus despair Erikson's eighth and final developmental stage, which individuals experience during late adulthood. 54

intelligence Verbal ability, problem-solving skills, and ability to learn from and adapt to the experiences of everyday life. 368

intelligence quotient (IQ) Devised in 1912 by William Stern, IQ consists of mental age divided by chronological age, multiplied by 100. 368

intermodal perception The ability to relate and integrate information about two or more sensory modalities, such as vision and hearing. 160

internalization The developmental change from behavior that is externally controlled to behavior that is controlled by internal, self-generated standards and principles. 587

internalization of schemes Piaget's sixth sensorimotor substage, which develops between 18 and 24 months of age. In this substage, infants' mental functioning shifts from a purely sensorimotor plane to a symbolic plane, and they develop the ability to use primitive symbols. 261

interpersonal norms The third stage in Kohlberg's theory of moral development. Children value trust, caring, and loyalty to others as the bases of moral judgments. 587

intimacy in friendships Self-disclosure and the sharing of private thoughts. 449

intimacy versus isolation Erikson's sixth developmental stage, which individuals experience during early adulthood years.

At this time, individuals face the developmental task of forming intimate relationships with others. 54

intrinsic motivation The internal desire to be competent and to do something for its own sake. 244

intuitive thought substage The second substage of preoperational thought, occurring approximately between 4 and 7 years of age. Children begin to use primitive reasoning and want to know the answers to all sorts of questions. 270

J

justice perspective A moral perspective that focuses on the rights of the individual; individuals independently make moral decisions. 591

juvenile delinquent A child or an adolescent who breaks the law or engages in illegal behavior. 610

K

keyword method A powerful strategy that uses vivid imagery of important words, or keywords, to improve memory. 308

Klinefelter syndrome A genetic disorder in which males have an extra X chromosome, making them XXY instead of just XY. 90

L

labeling Identifying the names of objects. 342

laboratory A controlled setting in which many of the complex factors of the "real world" are removed. 25

Lamaze method A form of prepared or natural childbirth developed by Fernand Lamaze, a pioneering French obstetrician. Widely accepted in the medical profession, it involves helping pregnant women cope actively with the pain of childbirth to avoid or reduce medication. 123

language A system of symbols and sequence of words, used to communicate with others, that involve infinite generativity, displacement, and rule systems. 333

Language Acquisition Device (LAD) A biological prewiring that enables children to detect certain language categories, such as phonology, syntax, and semantics. LAD is an innate grammatical ability that underlies all human languages. 337

Language Acquisition Support System (LASS) Bruner's concept that describes the behaviors of a language-skilled individual in structuring and supporting a child's development of language. 341

latency stage The fourth Freudian stage of development, which occurs between approximately 6 years of age and puberty; the child represses all interest in sexuality and develops social and intellectual skills. 51

learning A relatively permanent change in behavior that occurs through experience. 219

learning disabilities Children with learning disabilities are of normal or higher intelligence, have difficulties in several academic areas but usually do not show deficits in others, and are not suffering from other conditions or disorders that could explain their learning problems. 508

Leboyer method A birth process, developed by French obstetrician Frederick Leboyer, that intends to make birth less stressful for infants. Leboyer's procedure is referred to as "birth without violence." 123

literacy The ability to read and write. 351

long-term memory A relatively permanent memory system, which holds huge amounts of information for a long time. 306

longitudinal approach A research strategy in which the same individuals are studied over a period of time, usually several years or more. 33

love withdrawal A discipline technique in which a parent removes attention or love from a child. 600

low-birthweight infants Infants born after a regular period of gestation (the length of time between conception and birth) of 38 to 42 weeks but who weigh less than 5½ pounds. 125

M

macrosystem In Bronfenbrenner's ecological system, the culture in which individuals live. 72

mainstreaming Integrating handicapped children into regular school classes with nonhandicapped children. 506

marasmus A wasting away of body tissues in an infant's first year, caused by a severe protein-calorie deficiency. 152

mastery orientation A description of children who are task oriented. Instead of focusing on their ability, they become concerned about their learning strategies. 246

maturation The orderly sequence of changes dictated by a genetic blueprint. 20

Maximally Discriminative Facial Movement Coding System (MAX) Izard's system of coding infants' facial expressions related to emotions. Using MAX, coders watch slow-motion and stop-action videotapes of infants' facial reactions to stimuli. 142

mean length of utterance (MLU) An index of language development based on the number of words per sentence a child produces in a sample of about 50 to 100 sentences. 348

meiosis The process of cell division in which each pair of chromosomes in a cell separates, with one member of each pair going into each gamete. 87

memory The retention of information over time. It is central to mental life and to information processing. 306

menarche First menstruation. 181

mental age (MA) A child's level of mental development relative to others. 368

mental retardation A condition of limited mental ability in which individuals have a low IQ, usually below 70 on a traditional test of intelligence, and have difficulty adapting to everyday life. 388

mesoderm The middle layer of cells, which becomes the circulatory system, bones, muscles, excretory system, and reproductive system. 109

mesosystem In Bronfenbrenner's ecological system, the mesosystem involves relations between microsystems. 72

metacognitive knowledge The segment of acquired world knowledge that involves cognitive matters. 318

metaphor An implied comparison of two ideas that is conveyed by the abstract meaning contained in the words used. 280

microsystem In Bronfenbrenner's ecological theory, the setting in which an individual lives, including the person's family, peers, school, and neighborhood. 72

middle and late childhood The developmental period that extends from about 6 to 11 years of age, approximately corresponding to the elementary school years, sometimes called the elementary school years. 18

Montessori approach A philosophy of education in which children are given considerable freedom and spontaneity in choosing activities. The teacher acts as a facilitator rather than a director of learning and allows children to work independently to complete tasks in a prescribed manner. The teacher can offer assistance if asked by the children. 476

moral development Rules and conventions about what people should do in their interactions with other people. 585

Moro reflex A neonatal startle response that occurs in reaction to a sudden, intense noise or movement. When startled, the newborn arches its back, throws its head back, and flings out its arms and legs. Then, the newborn rapidly closes its arms and legs to the center of its body. 139

morphology The rules for combining morphemes; a morpheme is the smallest string of sounds that gives meaning to what we say and hear. 334

motherese The way mothers and other adults often talk to babies at a higher-than-normal frequency and greater-than-normal pitch and with simple words and sentences. 341

motivation "Why" individuals behave, think, and feel the way they do. Two important dimensions of motivation are the activation and direction of behavior. 220

multiple-factor theory Thurstone's theory that intelligence consists of seven primary abilities: verbal comprehension, number ability, word fluency, spatial visualization, associative memory, reasoning, and perceptual speed. 370

myelination A process in which nerve cells are insulated with a layer of fat cells, which increases the speed at which information travels through the nervous system. 169

N

natural selection The evolutionary process that favors individuals within a species that are best adapted to survive and reproduce. 85

naturalistic observation Observation of behavior in a real-world setting, in which scientists make no effort to manipulate or control the situation. 26

nature-nurture controversy "Nature" refers to an organism's biological inheritance, "nurture" to environmental experiences. The "nature" proponents claim biological inheritance is the most important influence on development; the "nurture" proponents claim that environmental experiences are the most important. 20

need A deprivation that energizes the drive to eliminate or reduce the deprivation. 242

negative reinforcement The frequency of a response increases because the response either removes an unpleasant stimulus or allows one to avoid the stimulus. 226

neglected children Children who receive little attention from their peers but who are not necessarily disliked. 445

neo-ethological theory Hinde's view that emphasizes sensitive rather than critical periods of development, social development and relationships, and the application of ethological theory to human development. 71

nonnutritive sucking Sucking behavior unrelated to the infant's feeding. 141

normal distribution A symmetrical configuration of scores, with a majority of cases falling in the middle of the possible range of scores and few scores appearing toward the extremes of the range. 369

norms Established standards of performance for a test. 367

O

object permanence The Piagetian term for one of an infant's most important accomplishments: understanding that objects and events continue to exist even when they cannot directly be seen, heard, or touched. 262

Oedipus complex The Freudian concept that young children develop an intense desire to replace the parent of the same sex and enjoy the affections of the opposite-sex parent. 50

onlooker play Play that occurs when a child watches other children play. 457

operant conditioning A form of learning in which the consequences of behavior lead to changes in the probability of that behavior's occurrence. 65, 225

operations Internalized sets of actions that allow children to do mentally what before was done physically. 266

oral rehydration therapy (ORT) A treatment involving a range of techniques designed to prevent dehydration during episodes of diarrhea by giving children fluids by mouth. 176

oral stage The first Freudian stage of development, occurring during the first 18 months of life, in which the infant's pleasure centers around the mouth. 50

organic retardation Mental retardation caused by a genetic disorder or brain damage; "organic" refers to the tissues or organs of the body, so there is some physical damage in organic retardation. 389

organization The arranging of items into categories. 307

organization Piaget's concept of grouping isolated behaviors into a high-order, smoothly functioning cognitive system. Every level of thought is organized. 258

organogenesis The process of organ formation that takes place during the first 2 months of prenatal development. 110

original sin view The idea, especially advocated during the Middle Ages, that children are basically bad and born into the world as evil beings. 9

overextension Children's tendency to misuse words by extending one word's meaning to include objects that are not related to or are inappropriate for the word's meaning. 347

oxytocin A hormone that stimulates and regulates the rhythmicity of uterine contractions. It has been widely used as a drug to speed delivery. Controversy surrounds its use. 125

P

parallel play Play that occurs separately from other children, but with toys like those the others are using or in a manner that mimics their play. 457

partial reinforcement (intermittent reinforcement) A schedule of reinforcement in which responses are not reinforced every time they occur. 230

peers Children of about the same age or maturity level. 443

perception The interpretation of what is sensed. 155

permissive-indulgent parenting A parenting style in which parents are highly involved with their children but place few demands or controls on them. Permissive-indulgent parenting is associated with children's social incompetence, especially a lack of self-control. 416

permissive-indifferent parenting A parenting style in which parents are very uninvolved in a child's life; it is associated with children's social incompetence, especially lack of self-control. 416

personal fable An adolescent's sense of personal uniqueness and indestructibility. 282

perspective taking Taking another's point of view. 446

phallic stage The third Freudian stage of development, which occurs between the ages of 3 and 6; its name comes from the Latin word *phallus*, which means "penis." During the phallic stage, pleasure focuses on the genitals, as the child discovers that self-manipulation is enjoyable. 50

phenomenological theories Developmental theories that stress the importance of children's perceptions of themselves and their environment. 67

phenotype The way an individual's genotype is expressed in observed and measurable characteristics. 93

phenylketonuria (PKU) A genetic disorder in which an individual cannot properly metabolize protein. PKU is now easily detected but, if left untreated, results in mental retardation and hyperactivity. 90

phobias Irrational fears. 223

phonics method A learning-to-read technique that emphasizes the sounds that letters make when in words (such sounds can differ from the names of the letters, as when the sound of the letter *c* is not found in *cat*). 353

phonology The study of a language's sound system. 334

placenta A life-support system that consists of a disk-shaped group of tissues in which small blood vessels from the mother and the offspring intertwine but do not join. 110

play Pleasurable activity engaged in for its own sake. 454

play therapy Therapy that allows children to work off frustrations and a medium through which therapists can analyze children's conflicts and ways of coping with them. Children may feel less threatened and be more likely to express their true feelings in the context of play. 454

pleasure principle The Freudian concept that the id always seeks pleasure and avoids pain. 48

polygenic inheritance A genetic principle that describes the interaction of many genes to produce a particular characteristic. 93

positive reinforcement The frequency of a response increases because it is followed by a pleasant stimulus. 226

postconventional reasoning The highest level in Kohlberg's theory of moral development. Morality is completely internalized. 588

power assertion A discipline technique in which a parent attempts to gain control over a child or a child's resources. 600

practice play Play that involves the repetition of behavior when new skills are being learned or when physical or mental mastery and coordination of skills are required for games or sports. 458

pragmatics The use of appropriate conversation. 335

precipitate A form of delivery that takes place too rapidly; the baby squeezes through the birth canal in less than 10 minutes. 124

preconventional reasoning The lowest level in Kohlberg's theory of moral development. The child shows no internalization of moral values—moral reasoning is controlled by external rewards and punishments. 587

predictive validity The relation of a test's scores to an individual's performance in the future. 366

prejudice An unjustified negative attitude toward an individual because of that person's membership in a group. 528

prenatal period The time from conception to birth. 18

preoperational stage The second Piagetian developmental stage, which lasts from 2 to 7 years of age. Children begin to represent the world with words, images, and drawings. 59

pretense/symbolic play Play that occurs when a child transforms the physical environment into a symbol. 458

preterm infant An infant born prior to 38 weeks after conception. 125

primary circular reactions Schemes based on the infant's attempt to reproduce an interesting or pleasurable event that initially occurred by chance. 261

primary reinforcement Reinforcers that are innately satisfying—that is, they do not take any learning on the organism's part to make them pleasurable. 230

problem solving Attempting to find an appropriate way of attaining a goal when the goal is not readily available. 310

Project Follow Through A program implemented in 1967 as an adjunct to Project Head Start. In the Follow Through programs, the enriched planned variation was carried through the first few years of elementary school. 488

Project Head Start A compensatory education program designed to give children from low-income families the opportunity to acquire the skills and experiences important for success in school. 488

projection The psychoanalytic defense mechanism used to attribute one's own shortcomings, problems, and faults to others. 49

proximodistal pattern The sequence in which growth starts at the center of the body and moves toward the extremities. 146

psychological moratorium The long gap or transition between childhood security and adult autonomy during which adolescents explore and examine various identities. 535

psychometrics The field that involves the assessment of individual differences. 365

puberty A period of rapid skeletal and sexual maturation that occurs mainly in early adolescence. 183

Public Law 94–142 The federal government's mandate to all states to provide a free, appropriate education for all children. 505

punishment A consequence that decreases the probability a behavior will occur. 65, 226

punishment and obedience orientation The first stage in Kohlberg's theory of moral development. Moral thinking is based on punishment. 587

Q

questionnaire A method of obtaining information. It is similar to a highly structured interview except that respondents read the questions and mark their answers on paper rather than respond verbally to an interviewer. 27

R

random assignment The assignment of research subjects to experimental and control conditions by chance, thus reducing the likelihood that the results of

the experiment will be due to preexisting differences between the groups. 31

reaction formation The psychoanalytic defense mechanism that expresses an unacceptable impulse by transforming it into its opposite. 49

reaction range The range of phenotypes for each genotype, suggesting the importance of an environment's restrictiveness or enrichment. 94

reality principle The Freudian concept that the ego tries to bring individuals pleasure within the boundaries of reality. 48

recasting Phrasing the same or a similar meaning of a sentence in a different way, perhaps turning it into a question. 341

reciprocal socialization The view that socialization is bidirectional; children socialize parents just as parents socialize children. 404

reciprocal teaching An instructional procedure used by Brown and Palincsar to develop cognitive monitoring; it requires that students take turns leading a study group in the use of strategies for comprehending and remembering text content. 312

reflection A cognitive style in which individuals think before they act, usually scanning information carefully and slowly and, if fine discriminations of information are required, making few errors. 324

reflexes Automatic stimulus-response connections. 221

reflexive smile A smile that does not occur in response to external stimuli. It happens during the first month after birth, usually during irregular patterns of sleep, not when the infant is in an alert state. 141

regression The psychoanalytic defense mechanism that occurs when individuals behave in a way that characterizes a previous developmental level. 49

rehearsal The extended repetition of material after it has been presented. 307

reinforcement (reward) A consequence that increases the probability a behavior will occur. 65, 218, 226

rejected children Children who are disliked by their peers. They are more likely to be disruptive and aggressive than are neglected children. 445

reliability The extent to which a test yields a consistent, reproducible measure of performance. 365

REM (rapid eye movement) sleep A recurring sleep stage during which vivid dreams commonly occur among children and adults. 145

repression The most powerful and pervasive defense mechanism, according to Freud; it works to push unacceptable id impulses out of awareness and into the unconscious mind. 49

reproduction The process that occurs when a female gamete (ovum) is fertilized by a male gamete (sperm). 88

rooting reflex A newborn's built-in reaction that occurs when the infant's cheek is stroked or the side of its mouth is touched. In response, the infant turns its head toward the side that was touched in an apparent effort to find something to suck. 139

S

satire Irony, wit, or derision used to expose folly or wickedness. 280

scaffolding An important caregiver's role in early parent-child interaction. Through their attention and choice of behaviors, caregivers provide a framework around which they interact with infants. 404

schedules of reinforcement Schedules of partial reinforcement, with rules that determine the occasion when a response will be reinforced. These schedules are based on time interval schedule and frequency of the specific behaviors (ratio schedule). 229

schema A cognitive structure or network of associations that organizes and guides an individual's perceptions. 558

schema Information—concepts, events, and knowledge—that already exists in an individual's mind. A schema influences how a child interprets new information. 317

scheme The basic unit of an organized pattern of sensorimotor functioning. 260

scientific method An approach that can be used to discover accurate information about behavior and development and that includes the following steps: identify and analyze the problem, collect data, draw conclusions, and revise theories. 24

script A schema for events. 317

secondary circular reactions Piaget's third sensorimotor substage, which develops between 4 and 8 months of age. Infants become more object oriented or focused on the world, moving beyond preoccupation with the self in sensorimotor interactions. 261

secondary reinforcement Reinforcement that acquires positive value through experience; secondary reinforcers are learned, or conditional, reinforcers. 230

secure attachment The infant uses a caregiver as a secure base from which to explore the environment. Ainsworth believes that secure attachment in the first year of life provides an important foundation for psychological development later in life. 407

self-actualization The highest and most elusive of Maslow's needs: the motivation to develop one's full potential as a human being. 243

self-concept A central theme in Rogers' and other humanistic views; refers to individuals' overall perceptions of their abilities, behavior, and personality. 68

self-esteem The evaluative and affective dimension of self-concept. 525

self-understanding A child's cognitive representation of the self, the substance and content of the child's self-conceptions. 519

semantic networks Organized stores of general information in memory. 315

semantics The meaning of words and sentences. 335

sensation Information that contacts the sensory receptors (eyes, ears, tongue, nostrils, and skin). 155

sensitive period The ethological concept that describes a more flexible band of time for behavior to emerge than does the concept of a critical period. 71

sensorimotor play Behavior engaged in by infants to derive pleasure from exercising their sensorimotor schemas. 458

sensorimotor stage The first Piagetian developmental stage, which lasts from birth to about 2 years of age. Infants construct an understanding of the world by coordinating sensory experiences (such as seeing and hearing) with motor actions. 59

sequential approach A research strategy that combines cross-sectional and longitudinal designs. In most instances, this approach starts with a cross-sectional study that includes individuals of different ages. A number of months or years after the initial assessments, the same individuals are tested again (the longitudinal aspect of the design). At this time, a new group of subjects is assessed at each age level. 34

sexual script A stereotyped pattern of role prescriptions for how individuals should behave sexually. 190

shaping Rewarding approximations of desired behavior. 228

short-term memory A limited-capacity memory system in which information is retained for as long as 30 seconds, unless the information is rehearsed, in which case it can be retained longer. 306

sickle-cell anemia A genetic disorder that affects the red blood cells and occurs most often in Black individuals. 90

simple reflexes Piaget's first sensorimotor substage, which corresponds to the first month after birth. The basic means of coordinating sensation and action is

through reflexive behaviors, such as rooting and sucking, which infants have at birth. 260

slow-to-warm-up child A child who has a low activity level, is somewhat negative, shows low adaptability, and displays a low intensity of mood. 99

sociability The tendency to prefer the company of others to being alone. 99

social competence The ability to use resources within oneself and in the environment to achieve positive developmental outcomes. 530

social identity theory Social psychologist Henry Tajfel's theory that, when individuals are assigned to a group, they invariably think of that group as an in-group for them, because individuals want to have a positive self-image. 527

social learning theory The view of psychologists who emphasize behavior, environment, and cognition as the key factors in development. 65

social learning view of gender The idea that children's gender development occurs through observation and imitation of gender behavior, as well as through the rewards and punishments children experience for gender-appropriate and gender-inappropriate behavior. 553

social play Play that involves social interaction with peers. 458

social policy A national government's course of action designed to influence the welfare of its citizens. 13

social processes Changes in an individual's relationships with other people, emotions, and personality. 17

social smile A smile in response to an external stimulus, which, early in development, typically is in response to a face. 141

social system morality The fourth stage in Kohlberg's theory of moral development. Moral judgments are based on understanding the social order, law, justice, and duty. 588

solitary play Play when a child is alone. 457

split-half reliability A form of reliability in which test items are divided into halves, such as into groups of only the odd-numbered items. The items are different, and the two scores are compared to determine how consistently a child performed. 366

stability-change issue This issue addresses whether development is best described by stability or by change. It involves the degree to which we become older renditions of our early experience or whether we can develop into someone different from who we were at an earlier point in development. 22

standardization The development of uniform procedures for administering and scoring a test. It also involves the development of norms for the test. 367

standardized tests Tests that require people to answer a series of written or oral questions. They have two distinct features. First, psychologists usually total an individual's score to yield a single score, or set of scores, that reflects something about the individual. Second, psychologists compare the individual's score to the scores of a large group of similar people to determine how the individual responded relative to others. 27

stereotype A broad category that reflects our impressions and beliefs about people. All stereotypes refer to an image of the typical member of a particular group. 204

strategies Cognitive processes that do not occur automatically but require work and effort. They are under a learner's conscious control and can be used to improve memory. 307

sublimation The psychoanalytic defense mechanism that causes a socially useful course of action to replace a distasteful one. 49

sucking reflex Newborns' built-in reaction of automatically sucking an object placed in the mouth. The sucking reflex enables them to get nourishment before they have associated a nipple with food. 139

superego The Freudian structure of personality that is the moral branch. The superego takes into account whether something is right or wrong. 48

surface structure The order of words in a sentence. 335

symbolic function substage The first substage of preoperational thought, occurring roughly between the ages of 2 and 4. In this substage, the young child gains the ability to represent mentally an object that is not present. 266

syntax The way words are combined to form acceptable phrases and sentences. 335

T

tabula rasa **view** The idea, proposed by English philosopher John Locke, that children are not innately bad but instead are like a "blank tablet." 10

telegraphic speech The use of short, precise words to communicate; it is characteristic of young children's two-word utterances. 348

temperament An individual's behavioral style and characteristic way of responding. 97

teratogen From the Greek word *tera,* meaning "monster," any agent that causes a birth defect. The field of study that investigates the causes of birth defects is called teratology. 113

tertiary circular reactions Schemes in which the infant purposely explores new possibilities with objects, continually changing what is done to them and exploring the results. 261

tertiary circular reactions, novelty, and curiosity Piaget's fifth sensorimotor substage, which develops between 12 and 18 months of age. Infants become intrigued by the variety of properties that objects possess and by the multiplicity of things they can make happen to objects. 261

test-retest reliability A form of reliability in which a child is given the same test on two different occasions. 365

testosterone A hormone associated with the development of genitals, an increase in height, and a change in voice in boys. 183

theory A coherent set of ideas that helps explain data and make predictions. 24

top-dog phenomenon The circumstance of moving from the top position (in elementary school, the oldest, biggest, and most powerful students in the school) to the lowest position (in middle or junior high school, the youngest, smallest, and least powerful students in the school). 499

triarchic theory Sternberg's theory that intelligence consists of componential intelligence, experiential intelligence, and contextual intelligence. 371

trophoblast The outer layer of cells, which develops during the germinal period. It later provides nutrition and support for the embryo. 109

trust versus mistrust Erikson's first psychosocial stage, which is experienced in the first year of life. A sense of trust requires a feeling of physical comfort and a minimal amount of fear and apprehension about the future. 52

Turner syndrome A genetic disorder in which females are missing an X chromosome, making them XO instead of XX. 91

twin study A study in which the behavior of identical twins is compared with the behavior of fraternal twins. 95

two-factor theory Spearman's theory that children have both general intelligence, called *g,* and a number of specific types of intelligence, called *s.* 370

Type A babies Infants who exhibit insecurity by avoiding a caregiver—for example, by failing to seek proximity. 407

Type B babies Infants who use a caregiver as a secure base from which to explore the environment. 407

Type C babies Infants who exhibit insecurity by resisting a caregiver—for example, clinging but at the same time fighting against closeness. 407

U

ultrasound sonography A medical procedure in which high-frequency sound waves are directed into a pregnant woman's abdomen. 92

umbilical cord A life-support system, containing two arteries and one vein, that connects the baby to the placenta. 110

unconditional positive regard Rogers' concept of accepting, valuing, and being positive toward another person regardless of that person's behavior. 68

unconditioned response (UCR) An unlearned response automatically associated with the UCS. 221

unconditioned stimulus (UCS) A stimulus that produces a response without prior learning. 221

underextension A child's failure to use a noun to name a relevant event or object. 347

universal ethical principles The sixth and highest stage in Kohlberg's theory of moral development. Individuals develop a moral standard based on universal human rights. 588

unoccupied play Play that occurs when a child is not engaging in play as it is commonly understood; the child may stand in one spot, look around the room, or perform random movements that do not seem to have a goal. 456

V

validity The extent to which a test measures what it is intended to measure. 366

values clarification An indirect moral education approach that focuses on helping students clarify what their lives are for and what is worth working for. 607

W

Wernicke's area An area of the brain's left hemisphere involved in language comprehension. 337

whole-word method A learning-to-read technique that emphasizes learning direct associations between whole words and their meanings. 353

wisdom Expert knowledge about the practical aspects of life. 285

X

XYY syndrome A genetic disorder in which males have an extra Y chromosome. 91

Z

zone of proximal development (ZPD) Vygotsky's term for the range of tasks too difficult for children to master alone but that can be mastered with the guidance and assistance of adults or more highly skilled children. 286

zygote A single cell formed through fertilization. 88

REFERENCES

A

Aboud, F., & Skerry, S. (1983). Self and ethnic concepts in relation to ethnic constancy. *Canadian Journal of Behavioral Science, 15,* 3–34.

Abramovitch, R., Corter, C., Pepler, D. J., & Stanhope, L. (1986). Sibling and peer interaction: A final follow-up and comparison. *Child Development, 47,* 217–229.

Achenbach, T. M., Phares, V., Howell, V. A., & Nurcombe, B. (1990). Seven-year outcome of the Vermont Intervention Program for Low-Birthweight Infants. *Child Development, 61,* 1672–1681.

Ackerman, B. P. (1988). Thematic influences on children's judgments about story accuracy. *Child Development, 59,* 918–938.

Ackerman, P. L., Sternberg, R. J., & Glaser, R. (Eds.). (1989). *Learning and individual differences.* New York: W. H. Freeman.

Acredolo, L. P., & Hake, J. L. (1982). Infant perception. In B. B. Wolman (Ed.), *Handbook of developmental psychology.* Englewood Cliffs, NJ: Prentice-Hall.

Adams, G. R. (1991). Physical attractiveness and adolescent development. In R. M. Lerner, A. C. Petersen, & J. Brooks-Gunn (Eds.), *Encyclopedia of adolescence* (Vol. 2). New York: Garland.

Adams, G. R., Abraham, K. G., & Markstrom, C. A. (1987). The relations among identity development, self-consciousness, and self-focusing during middle and late adolescence. *Developmental Psychology, 23,* 292–297.

Adler, T. (1991, January). Seeing double? Controversial twins study is widely reported, debated. *APA Monitor, 22,* 1, 8.

Ainsworth, M. D. S. (1979). Infant-mother attachment. *American Psychologist, 34,* 932–937.

Alan Guttmacher Institute (1981). *Teenage pregnancy: The problem that has not gone away.* New York: Alan Guttmacher Institute.

Alexander, K. L., & Entwisle, D. R. (1988). Achievement in the first two years of school: Patterns and processes. *Monographs of the Society for Research in Child Development, 53* (2, Serial No. 218).

Allen, L., & Majidi-Ahi, S. (1989). Black American adolescents. In J. T. Gibbs & L. N. Huang (Eds.), *Children of color.* San Francisco: Jossey-Bass.

Allen, L., & Santrock, J. W. (in press). *Psychology: The contexts of behavior.* Dubuque, IA: Wm. C. Brown.

Amabile, T. M., & Hennessey, B. A. (1988). The motivation for creativity in children. In A. K. Boggiano & T. Pittman (Eds.), *Achievement motivation: A social-developmental perspective.* New York: Cambridge University Press.

American Association for Protecting Children (1986). *Highlights of official child neglect and abuse reporting: 1984.* Denver: American Humane Association.

American College Health Association (1989, May). *Survey of AIDS on American college and university campuses.* Washington, DC: American College Health Association.

American Council on Education (1991, January). *Graduation rates for ethnic minority students.* Washington, DC: American Council on Education.

America in transition (1989). Washington, DC: National Governors' Association Task Force on Children.

American Psychological Association (1989, January). *APA research review finds no evidence of 'post abortion syndrome,' but research studies on psychological effects of abortion inconclusive.* Washington, DC: American Psychological Association.

Ames, C., & Ames, R. (Eds.). (1989). *Research on motivation in education* Vol. 3. *Goals and cognitions.* San Diego: Academic Press.

Amsterdam, B. K. (1968). *Mirror behavior in children under two years of age.* Unpublished doctoral dissertation, University of North Carolina, Chapel Hill.

Anastasi, A. (1988). *Psychological testing* (6th ed.). New York: Macmillan.

Anderson, J. R. (1988). Cognitive principles in the design of computer tutors. In P. E. Morris (Ed.), *Modelling cognition.* New York: Wiley.

Anderson, J. R. (1990). *Cognitive psychology and its implications* (3rd ed.). New York: W. H. Freeman.

Anderson, L. D. (1939). The predictive value of infant tests in relation to intelligence at 5 years. *Child Development, 10,* 202–212.

Anderson, L. W. (1989, April). *The impact of sex and age on the resolutions of preschool children's conversational disagreements.* Paper presented at the Society for Research in Child Development meeting, Kansas City.

Angell, R. C. (1936). *The family encounters the depression.* New York: Scribner's.

Archer, S. L. (1989). Gender differences in identity development: Issues of process, domain, and timing. *Journal of Adolescence, 12,* 117–138.

Archer, S. L. (1989). The status of identity: Reflections on the need for intervention. *Journal of Adolescence, 12,* 345–359.

Archer, S. L. (1991). Identity development, gender differences in. In R. M. Lerner, A. C. Petersen, & J. Brooks-Gunn (Eds.), *Encyclopedia of adolescence* (Vol. 1). New York: Garland.

Arehart, D. M., & Smith, P. H. (1990). Identity in adolescence: Influences on dysfunction and psychosocial task issues. *Journal of Youth and Adolescence, 19,* 63–72.

Aries, P. (1962). *Centuries of childhood* (R. Baldrick, Trans.). New York: Knopf.

Arlin, P. K. (1984). *Arlin Test of Formal Reasoning.* East Aurora, NY: Slosson Educational Publications.

Arman-Nolley, S. (1989, April). *Vygotsky's perspective on development of creativity and imagination.* Paper presented at the Society for Research on Child Development meeting, Kansas City.

Armistead, L., Wierson, M., & Forehand, R. (1990). Adolescents and maternal employment: Is it harmful for an adolescent to have an employed mother? *Journal of Early Adolescence, 10,* 260–278.

Armsden, G., & Greenberg, M. T. (1984). *The inventory of parent and peer attachment: Individual differences and their relationship to psychological well-being in adolescence.* Unpublished manuscript, University of Washington.

Armsden, G., & Greenberg, M. T. (1987). The inventory of parent and peer attachment: Individual differences and their relationship to psychological well-being in adolescence. *Journal of Youth and Adolescence, 16,* 427–454.

Arnold, M. L. (1989, April). *Moral cognition and conduct: A quantitative review of the literature.* Paper presented at the Society for Research in Child Development meeting, Kansas City.

Aronson, E. (1986, August). *Teaching students things they think they already know about: The case of prejudice and desegregation.* Paper presented at the meeting of the American Psychological Association, Washington, DC.

Asarnow, J. R., & Callan, J. W. (1985). Boys with peer adjustment problems: Social cognitive processes. *Journal of Consulting and Clinical Psychology, 53,* 80–87.

Asher, J. (1987, April). Born to be shy? *Psychology Today,* pp. 56–64.

Asher, J., & Garcia, R. (1969). The optimal age to learn a foreign language. *Modern Language Journal, 53,* 334–341.

Asher, S. R., & Parker, J. G. (in press). The significance of peer relationship problems in childhood. In B. H. Schneider, G. Attili, J. Nadel, & R. P. Weisberg (Eds.), *Social competence in developmental perspective.* Amsterdam: Kluwer.

Astin, A. W., Green, K. C., & Korn, W. S. (1987). *The American freshman: Twenty year trends.* Los Angeles: UCLA Higher Education Research Institute.

Atkinson, J. W., & Raynor, I. O. (1974). *Motivation and achievement.* New York: Wiley.

Attie, I., & Brooks-Gunn, J. (in press). The emergence of eating disorders and eating problems in adolescence: A developmental perspective. *Journal of Child Psychology and Psychiatry, and Allied Disciplines.*

B

Baca Zinn, M. (1977, April). *Urban kinship and midwest Chicano families: Review and reformulation.* Paper presented at the meeting of the Western Social Science meeting, Los Angeles.

Bachman, J. G. (1991). Dropouts, school. In R. M. Lerner, A. C. Petersen, & J. Brooks-Gunn (Eds.), *Encyclopedia of adolescence* (Vol. 1). New York: Garland.

Bachman, J. G., Johnston, L. P., & O'Malley, P. M. (1987). *Monitoring the future.* Ann Arbor: University of Michigan, Institute of Social Research.

Baer, D. M. (1989, April). *Behavior analysis of human development.* Paper presented at the Society for Research in Child Development meeting, Kansas City.

Bahrick, L. E. (1988). Intermodal learning in infancy: Learning on the basis of two kinds of invariant relations in audible and visible events. *Child Development, 59,* 197–209.

Bailey, G. W. (1989). Current perspectives on substance abuse in youth. *Journal of the American Academy of Child and Adolescent Psychiatry, 28,* 151–162.

Baillargeon, R. (1987). Object permanence in 3.5- and 4.5-month-old infants. *Developmental Psychology, 23,* 655–664.

Baillargeon, R. (1991, April). *Infants' reasoning about collision events.* Paper presented at the Society for Research in Child Development meeting, Seattle.

Baillargeon, R., DeVos, J., & Graber, M. (1989). Location memory in 8-month-old infants in a nonsearch AB task: Further evidence. *Cognitive Development, 4,* 345–367.

Baillargeon, R., Spelke, E. S., & Wasserman, S. (1985). Object permanence in five-month-old infants. *Cognition, 20,* 191–208.

Bakeman, R., & Brown, J. V. (1980). Early interaction: Consequences for social and mental development at three years. *Child Development, 51,* 437–447.

Baker, L., & Brown, A. L. (1984). Metacognitive skills and reading. In P. D. Pearson (Ed.), *Handbook of reading research, Part 2.* New York: Longman.

Ballenger, M. (1983). Reading in the kindergarten: Comment. *Childhood Education, 59,* 187.

Baltes, P. B., & Smith, J. (in press). Toward a psychology of wisdom and its ontogenesis. In R. J. Sternberg (Ed.), *Wisdom: Its nature, origins, and development.* New York: Cambridge University Press.

Baltes, P B., Smith, J., Staudinger, U. M., & Sowarka, D. (in press). Wisdom: One facet of successful aging? In M. Perlmutter (Ed.), *Late-life potential.* Washington, DC: Gerontological Association of America.

Bancroft, J. (1990). The impact of sociocultural influences on adolescent sexual development: Further considerations. In J. Bancroft & J. M. Reinisch (Eds.), *Adolescence and puberty.* New York: Oxford University Press.

Bancroft, J., & Reinisch, J. M. (1990). *Adolescence and puberty.* New York: Oxford University Press.

Bandura, A. (1965). Influence of models' reinforcement contingencies on the acquisition of imitative responses. *Journal of Personality and Social Psychology, 1,* 589–595.

Bandura, A. (1971). *Social learning theory.* New York: General Learning Press.

Bandura, A. (1977). *Social learning theory.* Englewood Cliffs, NJ: Prentice-Hall.

Bandura, A. (1986). *Social foundations of thought and action: A social cognitive theory.* Englewood Cliffs, NJ: Prentice-Hall.

Bandura, A. (1989). Social cognitive theory. In R. Vasta (Ed.), *Six theories of child development.* Greenwich, CT: JAI.

Bandura, A. (1991). Social cognitive theory of moral thought and action. In W. M. Kurtines & J. Gewirtz (Eds.), *Moral behavior and development: Advances in theory, research, and application.* Hillsdale, NJ: Erlbaum.

Banks, M. S., & Salapatek, P. (1983). Infant visual perception. In P. H. Mussen (Ed.), *Handbook of child psychology* (4th ed., Vol. 2). New York: Wiley.

Barkeley, R. (in press). Attention deficit disorders: History, definition, diagnosis. In M. Lewis & S. Miller (Eds.), *Handbook of developmental psychopathology*. New York: Plenum.

Barker, R., & Wright, H. F. (1951). *One boy's day*. New York: Harper & Row.

Barnes, K. E. (1971). Preschool play norms: A replication. *Developmental Psychology, 4,* 99–103

Baron, J. B., & Sternberg, R. J. (Eds.). (1987). *Teaching thinking skills*. New York: W. H. Freeman.

Baron, R., Tom, D., & Cooper, H. (1985). Social class, race, and teacher expectations. In J. Dusek & G. Joseph (Eds.), *Teacher expectancies*. Hillsdale, NJ: Erlbaum.

Barr, R. G., Desilets, J., & Rotman, A. (1991, April). *Parsing the normal crying curve: Is it really the evening fussing curve?* Paper presented at the Society for Research in Child Development meeting, Seattle.

Barrett, D. E., Radke-Yarrow, M., & Klein, R. E. (1982). Chronic malnutrition and child behavior: Effects of calorie supplementation on social and emotional functioning at school age. *Developmental Psychology, 18,* 541–556.

Barrett, K. C., & Campos, J. J. (1987). A functionalist approach to emotions. In J. D. Osofsky (Ed.), *Handbook of infant development*. New York: Wiley.

Barron, F. (1989, April). The birth of a notion: Exercises to tap your creative potential, *Omni*, pp. 112–119.

Bart, W. M. (1971). The factor structure of formal operations. *The British Journal of Educational Psychology, 41,* 40–77.

Baruch, G. K., Biener, L., & Barnett, R. C. (1987). Women and gender in research on work and family. *American Psychologist, 42,* 130–136.

Baskett, L. M., & Johnston, S. M. (1982). The young child's interaction with parents versus siblings. *Child Development, 53,* 643–650.

Batshaw, M. L., & Perret, Y. M. (1986). *Children with handicaps*. Baltimore: Brookes.

Batson, C. D. (1989). Personal values, moral principles, and the three path model of prosocial motivation. In N. Eisenberg & J. Reykowski (Eds.), *Social and moral values*. Hillsdale, NJ: Erlbaum.

Baumeister, R. F. (1991). Identity crisis. In R. M. Lerner, A. C. Petersen, & J. Brooks-Gunn (Eds.), *Encyclopedia of adolescence* (Vol. 1). New York: Garland.

Baumrind, D. (1971). Current patterns of parental authority. *Developmental Psychology Monographs, 4* (1, Pt. 2).

Baumrind, D. (1991). Parenting styles and adolescent development. In J. Brooks-Gunn, R. Lerner, & A. C. Petersen (Eds.), *The encyclopedia of adolescence*. New York: Garland.

Baumrind, D. (in press). Effective parenting during the early adolescent transition. In P. A. Cowan & E. M. Hetherington (Eds.), *Advances in family research* (Vol. 2). Hillsdale, NJ: Erlbaum.

Bayley, N. (1943). Mental growth during the first three years. In R. G. Barker, J. S. Kounin, & H. F. Wright (Eds.), *Child behavior and development*. New York: McGraw-Hill.

Bayley, N. (1969). *Manual for the Bayley Scales of infant development*. New York: Psychological Corp.

Bayley, N. (1970). Development of mental abilities. In P. H. Mussen (Ed.), *Manual of child psychology* (3rd ed., Vol. 1). New York: Wiley.

Beal, C. R. (1990a). Development of knowledge about the role of inference in text comprehension. *Child Development, 61,* 1011–1023.

Beal, C. R. (1990b). The development of text evaluation and revision skills. *Child Development, 61,* 247–258.

Beal, C. R., & Bonitabitus, G. J. (1991, April). *Children's developing ability to identify alternative interpretations in narratives: The role of text structure*. Paper presented at the Society for Research in Child Development meeting, Seattle.

Beals, D. E., & De Temple, J. (1991, April). *Reading, reporting, and repast: Three R's for co-constructing language and literacy skills*. Paper presented at the Society for Research in Child Development meeting, Seattle.

Beane, J. A. (1990, May). Rethinking the middle school curriculum. *Middle School Journal, 21,* 1–5.

Becker, H. J., & Sterling, C. W. (1987). Equity in school computer use: National data and neglected considerations. *Journal of Educational Computing Research, 3,* 289–311.

Becker, J. A. (1990). Processes in the acquisition of pragmatic competence. In G. Conti-Ramsden & C. E. Snow (Eds.), *Children's language* (Vol. 7). Hillsdale, NJ: Erlbaum.

Beckwith, L., & Howard, J. (1991, April). *Development of toddlers exposed prenatally to PCP and cocaine*. Paper presented at the Society for Research in Child Development meeting, Seattle.

Behnke, M., & Eyler, F. D. (1991, April). *Issues in perinatal cocaine abuse research: The interface between medicine and child development*. Paper presented at the Society for Research in Child Development meeting, Seattle.

Beilin, H. (1989). Piagetian theory. In R. Vasta (Ed.), *Six theories of child development: Revised formulations and current issues*. Greenwich, CT: JAI.

Belenky, M. F., Clinchy, B. M., Goldberger, N. R., & Tarule, J. M. (1986). *Women's ways of knowing: The development of self, voice and mind*. New York: Basic.

Bell, A. P., Weinberg, M. S., & Mammersmith, S. K. (1981). *Sexual preference: Its development in men and women*. New York: Simon & Schuster.

Bell, D. (Ed.). (1980). *Shades of Brown: New perspectives on school desegregation*. New York: Teachers College Press.

Bell, S. M., & Ainsworth, M. D. S. (1972). Infant crying and maternal responsiveness. *Child Development, 43,* 1171–1190.

Bell-Scott, P., & Taylor, R. L. (1989). Introduction: The multiple ecologies of black adolescent development. *Journal of Adolescent Research, 4,* 117–118.

Belle, D., Burr, R., Shadmon, O., Woodbury, A., Heffernan, M., & Ozer, D. (1991, April). *Unsupervised after-school time, social support, and children's well-being*. Paper presented at the Society for Research in Child Development meeting, Seattle.

Bellinger, D., Leviton, A., Waternaux, C., Needleman, H., & Rabinowitz, M. (1987). Longitudinal analysis of prenatal and postnatal lead exposure and early cognitive development. *New England Journal of Medicine, 316,* 1037–1043.

Belmont, J. M. (1989). Cognitive strategies and strategic learning: The socio-instructional approach. *American Psychologist, 44,* 142–148.

Belsky, J. (1981). Early human experience: A family perspective. *Developmental Psychology, 17,* 3–23.

Belsky, J. (1989). Infant-parent attachment and day care: In defense of the strange situation. In J. S. Lande, S. Scarr, & N. Gunzenhauser (Eds.), *Caring for children: Challenge to America*. Hillsdale, NJ: Erlbaum.

Belsky, J., Rovine, M., & Fish, M. (1989). The developing family system. In M. R. Gunnar & E. Thelen (Eds.), *Systems and development: The Minnesota Symposia on Child Psychology Series* (Vol. 22). Hillsdale, NJ: Erlbaum.

Belson, W. (1978). *Television violence and the adolescent boy*. London: Saxon House.

Bem, S. L. (1977). On the utility of alternative procedures for assessing psychological androgyny. *Journal of Consulting and Clinical Psychology, 45,* 196–205.

Bem, S. L. (1981). Gender schema theory: A cognitive account of sex-typing. *Psychological Review, 88,* 354–364.

Benbow, C. P., & Stanley, J. C. (1980). Sex differences in mathematics ability: Fact or artifact? *Science, 210,* 1262–1264.

Benbow, C. P., & Stanley, J. C. (1982). Consequences in high school and college of sex differences in mathematical reasoning ability: A longitudinal perspective. *American Educational Research Journal, 19,* 598–622.

Benbow, C. P., & Stanley, J. C. (1983). Sex differences in mathematical reasoning ability: More facts. *Science, 222,* 1029–1031.

Bennett, W. J. (1986). *First lessons: A report on elementary education in America.* Washington, DC: U.S. Government Printing Office.

Benninga, J. S. (1988, February). An emerging synthesis in moral education. *Phi Delta Kappan,* pp. 415–418.

Berensen, G. (1989, February). *The Bogalusa heart study.* Paper presented at the science forum, American Heart Association, Monterey.

Berg, C. A., & Sansone, C. (1991, April). *To plan or not to plan?* Paper presented at the Society for Research in Child Development meeting, Seattle.

Berg, W. K., & Berg, K. M. (1987). Psychophysiological development in infancy: State, startle, & attention. In J. D. Osofsky (Ed.), *Handbook of infant development* (2nd ed.). New York: Wiley.

Bergen, D. (1988). Stages of play development. In D. Bergen (Ed.), *Play as a medium for learning and development.* Portsmouth, NH: Heinemann.

Berko, J. (1958). The child's learning of English morphology. *Word, 14,* 150–177.

Berkowitz, M., & Gibbs, J. (1983). Measuring the developmental features of moral discussion. *Merrill-Palmer Quarterly, 29,* 399–410.

Berlyne, D. E. (1960). *Conflict, arousal, and curiosity.* New York: McGraw-Hill.

Bernard, H. S. (1981). Identity formation in late adolescence: A review of some empirical findings. *Adolescence, 16,* 349–358.

Berndt, T. J. (1979). Developmental changes in conformity to peers and parents. *Developmental Psychology, 15,* 608–616.

Berndt, T. J. (1982). The features and effects of friendships in early adolescence. *Child Development, 53,* 1447–1460.

Berndt, T. J., & Ladd, G. W. (Eds.). (1989). *Peer relationships in child development.* New York: Wiley.

Berndt, T. J., & Park, K. (1991, April). *How friends influence adolescents' adjustment to school.* Paper presented at the Society for Research in Child Development meeting, Seattle.

Berndt, T. J., & Perry, T. B. (1990). Distinctive features and effects of early adolescent friendships. In R. Montemayor (Ed.), *Advances in adolescent research.* Greenwich, CT: JAI.

Bernstein, A. (1988). Cultural literacy: Process and content. *Change, 20,* 4.

Berrueta-Clement, J., Schweinhart, L., Barnett, W., & Weikart, D. (1986). The effects of early educational intervention on crime and delinquency in adolescence and early adulthood. In J. Burchard & S. Burchard (Eds.), *Prevention of delinquent behavior.* Newbury Park, CA: Sage.

Berry, J. W. (1969). On cross-cultural comparability. *International Journal of Psychology, 4,* 119–128.

Berry, J. W. (1980). Introduction to methodology. In H. C. Triandis & J. W. Berry (Eds.), *Handbook of cross-cultural psychology: Methodology* (Vol. 2). Boston: Allyn & Bacon.

Berry, J. W., Poortinga, Y. H., Segall, M. H., & Dasen, P. R. (in press). *Cross-cultural psychology: Theory, method, and applications.* Cambridge, England: Cambridge University Press.

Bijou, S. W. (1989). Behavior analysis. In R. Vasta (Ed.), *Six theories of child development: Revised formulations and current issues.* Greenwich, CT: JAI.

Bird, G. W., & Kemerait, L. N. (1990). Stress among early adolescents in two-earner families. *Journal of Early Adolescence, 10,* 344–365.

Bjorklund, D. F. (1989). *Children's thinking.* Belmont, CA: Brooks/Cole.

Blasi, A. (1988). Identity and the development of the self. In D. Lapsley & F. C. Power (Eds.), *Self, ego, and identity: Integrative approaches.* New York: Springer-Verlag.

Block, J., & Block, J. H. (1988). Longitudinally foretelling drug usage in adolescence: Early childhood personality and environmental precursors. *Child Development, 59,* 336–355.

Block, J. H., Block, J., & Gjerde, P. F. (1986). The personality of children prior to divorce. *Child Development, 57,* 827–840.

Bloome, D. (Ed.). (1989). *Classrooms and literacy.* Norwood, NJ: Ablex.

Blos, P. (1989). The inner world of the adolescent. In A. H. Esman (Ed.), *International annals of adolescent psychiatry.* Chicago: University of Chicago Press.

Blumenfeld, P. C., Pintrich, P. R., Wessles, K., & Meece, J. (1981, April). *Age and sex differences in the impact of classroom experiences on self-perceptions.* Paper presented at the Society for Research in Child Development meeting, Boston.

Blyth, D. A., Bulcroft, R., & Simmons, R. G. (1981, August). *The impact of puberty on adolescents: A longitudinal study.* Paper presented at the meeting of the American Psychological Association, Los Angeles.

Bodde, T. (1989). *Why is my child gay?* Washington, DC: Federation of Parents FLAG.

Bohannon, J. N. III, & Stanowicz, L. (1988). The issue of negative evidence. Adult responses to children's language errors. *Developmental Psychology, 24,* 684–689.

Bohannon, J. N. III, MacWhinney, B., & Snow, C. (1990). No negative evidence revisited: Beyond learnability or who has to prove what to whom. *Developmental Psychology, 26,* 221–226.

Boldizar, J. P. (1991). Assessing sex typing and androgyny in children: The Children's Sex Role Inventory. *Developmental Psychology, 27,* 505–515.

Boles, J. K. (Ed.). (1991). *American feminism.* Newbury Park, CA: Sage.

Bonvillian, J. D., Orlansky, M. D., & Novack, L. L. (1983). Developmental milestones: Sign language and motor development. *Child Development 54,* 1435–1445.

Boring, E. G. (1950). *A history of experimental psychology.* New York: Appleton-Century-Crofts.

Bornstein, M. H. (1989). Stability in early mental development. In M. H. Bornstein & N. A. Krasnegor (Eds.), *Stability and continuity in mental development.* Hillsdale, NJ: Erlbaum.

Bornstein, M. H. (Ed.). (1987). *Sensitive periods in development.* Hillsdale, NJ: Erlbaum.

Bornstein, M. H., & Krasnegor, N. A. (1989). *Stability and continuity in mental development.* Hillsdale, NJ: Erlbaum.

Bornstein, M. H., & Sigman, M. D. (1986). Continuity in mental development from infancy. *Child Development, 57,* 251–274.

Borstelmann, L. J. (1983). Children before psychology: Ideas about children from antiquity to the late 1800s. In P. H. Mussen (Ed.), *Handbook of child psychology* (4th ed., Vol. 1). New York: Wiley.

References

Bouchard, T. J., Heston, L., Eckert, E., Keyes, M., & Resnick, S. (1981). The Minnesota study of twins reared apart: Project description and sample results in the developmental domain. *Twin Research, 3,* 227–233.

Bower, B. (1985). The left hand of math and verbal talent. *Science News, 127,* 263.

Bower, T. G. R. (1989). *The rational infant.* San Francisco: W. H. Freeman.

Bower, T. G. R. (1990, February). [Personal communication.] Program in psychology and human development, University of Texas at Dallas.

Bower, T. G. R. (1991, April). [Personal communication.] Program in Psychology and Human Development, University of Texas at Dallas.

Bowerman, M. (1989). Learning a semantic system: What role do cognitive predispositions play? In M. L. Rice & R. L. Schiefelbusch (Eds.), *The teachability of language.* Baltimore: Paul Brooks.

Bowlby, J. (1969). *Attachment and loss* (Vol. 1). London: Hogarth.

Bowlby, J. (1989). *Secure attachment.* New York: Basic.

Bowman, P. J., & Howard, C. (1985). Race-related socialization, motivation, and academic achievement: A study of Black youths in three-generation families. *Journal of the American Academy of Child Psychiatry, 24,* 134–141.

Boxer, A. M. (1988, August). *Developmental continuities of gay and lesbian youth.* Paper presented at the meeting of the American Psychological Association, Atlanta.

Boyer, C. B., & Hein, K. (1991). AIDS and HIV infection in adolescents: The role of education and antibody testing. In R. M. Lerner, A. C. Petersen, & J. Brooks-Gunn (Eds.), *Encyclopedia of adolescence* (Vol. 1). New York: Garland.

Brackbill, Y. (1979). Obstetric medication and infant behavior. In J. D. Osofsky (Ed.), *Handbook of infant development.* New York: Wiley.

Bracken, M. B., Eskenazi, B., Sachse, K., McSharry, J., Hellenbrand, K., & Leo-Summers, L. (1990). Association of cocaine use with sperm concentration, motility, and morphology. *Fertility and Sterility, 53,* 315–322.

Brady, M. P., Swank, P. R., Taylor, R. D., & Freiberg, H. J. (1988). Teacher-student interactions in middle school mainstreamed classes: Differences with special and regular students. *Journal of Educational Research, 81,* 332–340.

Bray, J. H. (1988). The effects of early remarriage on children's development: Preliminary analyses of the developmental issues in stepfamily research project. In E. M. Hetherington & J. D. Arasteh (Eds.), *Impact of divorce, single-parenting, and stepparenting on children.* Hillsdale, NJ: Erlbaum.

Bray, J. H., Berger, S., Pacey, K., & Boethel, C. (1991, April). *Longitudinal predictors of children's adjustment to divorce and remarriage.* Paper presented at the Society for Research in Child Development meeting, Seattle.

Brazelton, T. B. (1956). Sucking in infancy. *Pediatrics, 17,* 400–404.

Brazelton, T. B. (1973). *Neonatal Behavioral Assessment Scale.* London: Heinemann.

Brazelton, T. B. (1984). *Neonatal Behavioral Assessment Scale* (2nd ed.). Philadelphia: Lippincott.

Brazelton, T. B. (1987, August). *Opportunities for intervention with infants at risk.* Paper presented at the meeting of the American Psychological Association, New York City.

Brazelton, T. B. (1989). Observations of the neonate. In C. Rovee-Collier & L. P. Lipsitt (Eds.), *Advances in infancy* (Vol. 6). Norwood, NJ: Ablex.

Brazelton, T. B., Nugent, J. K., & Lester, B. M. (1987). Neonatal Behavioral Assessment Scale. In J. D. Osofsky (Ed.), *Handbook of infant development* (2nd ed.). New York: Wiley.

Bredekamp, S. (1987). *Developmentally appropriate practice in early childhood programs serving children from birth through age 8.* Washington, DC: NAEYC.

Bredekamp, S., & Shepard, L. (1989). How to best protect children from inappropriate school expectations, practices, and policies. *Young Children, 44,* 14–24.

Brent, D. A. (1989). Suicide and suicidal behavior in children and adolescents. *Pediatrics in Review, 10,* 269–275.

Bretherton, I., Fritz, J., Zahn-Waxler, C., & Ridgeway, D. (1986). Learning to talk about emotions. *Child Development, 57,* 529–548.

Brinker, R. P., & Lewis, M. (1982). Discovering the competent handicapped infant: A process approach to assessment and intervention. *Topics in Early Childhood Special Education, 2,* 121–151.

Brislin, R. W. (1990). Applied cross-cultural psychology: An introduction. In R. W. Brislin (Ed.), *Applied cross-cultural psychology.* Newbury Park, CA: Sage.

Brody, G. H., & Shaffer, D. R. (1982). Contributions of parents and peers to children's moral socialization. *Developmental Review, 2,* 31–75.

Brodzinsky, D. M., Schechter, D. E., Braff, A. M., & Singer, L. M. (1984). Psychological and academic adjustment in adopted children. *Journal of Consulting and Clinical Psychology, 52,* 582–590.

Bronfenbrenner, U. (1970). *Two worlds of childhood: U.S. and U.S.S.R.* Newbury Park, CA: Sage.

Bronfenbrenner, U. (1979). Contexts of child rearing: Problems and prospects. *American Psychologist, 34,* 844–850.

Bronfenbrenner, U. (1986). Ecology of the family as a context for human development: Research perspectives. *Developmental Psychology, 22,* 723–742.

Bronfenbrenner, U. (1989, April). *The developing ecology of human development.* Paper presented at the Society for Research in Child Development meeting, Kansas City.

Bronstein, P. A. (1988). Marital and parenting roles in transition. In P. Bronstein & C. P. Cowen (Eds.), *Contemporary fatherhood.* New York: Wiley.

Bronstein, P. A., & Paludi, M. (1988). The introductory course from a broader perspective. In P. A. Bronstein & K. Quina (Eds.), *Teaching a psychology of people.* Washington, DC: American Psychological Association.

Bronstein, P. A., & Quina, K. (Eds.). (1988). *Teaching a psychology of people.* Washington, DC: American Psychological Association.

Brook, D. W., & Brook, J. S. (in press). Family processes associated with alcohol and drug use and abuse. In E. Kaufman & P. Kaufman (Eds.), *Family therapy of drug and alcohol abuse: Ten years later.* New York: Gardner.

Brook, J. S., Brook, D. W., Gordon, A. S., Whiteman, M., & Cohen, P. (1990). The psychological etiology of adolescent drug use: A family interactional approach. *Genetic, Social, and General Psychology Monographs, 116,* 110–267.

Brookins, G. K. (1991). Socialization of African-American adolescents. In R. M. Lerner, A. C. Petersen, & J. Brooks-Gunn (Eds.), *Encyclopedia of adolescence* (Vol. 2). New York: Garland.

Brookover, W., Beady, C., Flood, P., Schweitzer, J., & Wisenbaker, J. (1979). *School social systems and student achievement: Schools can make a difference.* New York: Praeger.

Brooks-Gunn, J. (1988). Antecedents and consequences of variations in girls' maturational timing. In M. D. Levine & E. R. McAnarney (Eds.), *Early adolescent transitions.* Lexington, MA: Lexington.

Brooks-Gunn, J. (1991). Maturational timing variations in adolescent girls, antecedents of. In R. M. Lerner, A. C. Petersen, & J. Brooks-Gunn (Eds.), *Encyclopedia of adolescence*. New York: Garland.

Brooks-Gunn, J., & Reiter, E. O. (1990). The role of pubertal processes. In S. S. Feldman & G. R. Elliott (Eds.), *At the threshold: The developing adolescent*. Cambridge, MA: Harvard University Press.

Brooks-Gunn, J., & Warren, M. P. (1989a, April). *How important are pubertal and social events for different problem behaviors and contexts?* Paper presented at the Society for Research in Child Development meeting, Kansas City.

Brooks-Gunn, J., & Warren, M. P. (1989b). The psychological significance of secondary sexual characteristics in 9- to 11-year-old girls. *Child Development, 59*, 161–169.

Broughton, J. M. (1983). The cognitive developmental theory of self and identity. In B. Lee & G. Noam (Eds.), *Developmental approaches to self*. New York: Plenum.

Broughton, J. M. (1978). Development of concepts of self, mind, reality, and knowledge. In W. Damon (Ed.), *Social cognition*. San Francisco: Jossey-Bass.

Broverman, I., Vogel, S., Boverman, D., Clarkson, F., & Rosenkranz, P. (1972). Sex-role stereotypes: A current appraisal. *Journal of Social Issues, 28*, 59–78.

Brown, A. C., & Orthner, D. K. (1990). Relocation and personal well-being among early adolescents. *Journal of Early Adolescence, 10*, 366–381.

Brown, A. L., & Palincsar, A. M. (1984). Reciprocal teaching of comprehension-fostering and monitoring activities. *Cognition and Instruction, 1*, 175–177.

Brown, A. L., & Palincsar, A. M. (1989). Guided, cooperative learning and individual knowledge acquisition. In L. B. Resnick (Ed.), *Knowing and learning: Essays in honor of Robert Glaser*. Hillsdale, NJ: Erlbaum.

Brown, A. L., & Smiley, S. S. (1977). Rating the importance of structural units of prose passages: A problem of metacognitive development. *Child Development, 48*, 1–8.

Brown, A. L., Bransford, J. D., Ferrara, R. A., & Campione, J. C. (1983). Learning, remembering, and understanding. In P. H. Mussen (Ed.), *Handbook of child psychology* (4th ed., Vol. 3). New York: Wiley.

Brown, A. L., Smiley, S. S., Day, J. D., Townsend, M. A. R., & Lawton, S. C. (1977). Intrusion of a thematic idea in children's comprehension and retention of stories. *Child Development, 48*, 1454–1466.

Brown, B. B., & Lohr, M. J. (1987). Peer group affiliation and adolescent self-esteem: An integration of ego identity and symbolic interaction theories. *Journal of Personality and Social Psychology, 52*, 47–55.

Brown, B. B., & Mounts, N. (1989, April). *Peer group structures in single versus multiethnic high schools*. Paper presented at the Society for Research in Child Development meeting, Kansas City.

Brown, B. B., Steinberg, L., Mounts, N., & Philipp, M. (1990, March). *The comparative influence of peers and parents on high school achievement: Ethnic differences*. Paper presented at the meeting of the Society for Research on Adolescence, Atlanta.

Brown, J. L. (1964). States in newborn infants. *Merrill-Palmer Quarterly, 10*, 313–327.

Brown, J. L., & Pizer, H. F. (1987). *Living hungry in America*. New York: Macmillan.

Brown, J. S., & Burton, R. B. (1978). Diagnostic models for procedural bugs in basic mathematical skills. *Cognitive Science, 2*, 155–192.

Brown, L. M., & Gilligan, C. (1990, March). *The psychology of women and the development of girls*. Paper presented at the meeting of the Society for Research on Adolescence, Atlanta.

Brown, R. (1973). *A first language: The early stages*. Cambridge, MA: Harvard University Press.

Brown, R. (1986). *Social psychology* (2nd ed.). New York: Free Press.

Brumberg, J. J. (1988). *Fasting girls*. Cambridge, MA: Harvard University Press.

Bruner, J. S. (1983). *Child talk*. New York: W. W. Norton.

Bruner, J. S. (1989, April). *The state of developmental psychology*. Paper presented at the Society for Research in Child Development meeting, Kansas City.

Bruner, J. S. (1991, April). *Social-cultural determinants of concept of mind*. Paper presented at the Society for Research in Child Development meeting, Seattle.

Buchanan, C. M. (1991, April). *Variation in adjustment to divorce: The role of feeling caught in the middle between parents*. Paper presented at the Society for Research in Child Development meeting, Seattle.

Buhrmester, D. (1989). *Changes in friendship, interpersonal competence, and social adaptation during early adolescence*. Unpublished manuscript, Department of Psychology, UCLA.

Buhrmester, D., & MacDonald, V. (1991, April). *The effects of hyperactivity and stimulant medication on prosocial behavior*. Paper presented at the Society for Research in Child Development meeting, Seattle.

Burns, H. L., & Parlett, J. W. (1991). The evolution of intelligent tutoring systems: Dimensions of design. In H. Burns, J. W. Parlett, & C. L. Redfield (Eds.), *Intelligent tutoring systems: Evolutions in design*. Hillsdale, NJ: Erlbaum.

Burtchaell, J. (in press). University policy on experimental use of aborted fetal tissue. *IRB, A Review of Human Subjects*.

Burton, R. V. (1984). A paradox in theories and research in moral development. In W. M. Kurtines & J. L. Gewirtz (Eds.), *Morality, moral behavior, and moral development*. New York: Wiley.

Burts, D. C., Charlesworth, R., & Fleege, P. O. (1991, April). *Achievement of kindergarten children in developmentally appropriate and developmentally inappropriate classrooms*. Paper presented at the Society for Research in Child Development meeting, Seattle.

Burts, D. C., Hart, C. H., Charlesworth, R., Fleege, P. O., Mosley, J., & Thomasson, R. (in press). Observed activities and stress behaviors of children in developmentally appropriate and inappropriate kindergarten classrooms. *Early Childhood Research Quarterly*.

Burts, D. C., Hart, C. H., Charlesworth, R., Hernandez, S., Kirk, L., & Mosley, J. (1989, March). *A comparison of the frequencies of stress behaviors observed in kindergarten children in classrooms with developmentally appropriate vs. developmentally inappropriate instructional practices*. Paper presented at the annual meeting of the American Educational Research Association, San Francisco.

Busch-Rossnagel, N. A., & Zayas, L. H. (1991). Hispanic adolescents. In R. M. Lerner, A. C. Petersen, & J. Brooks-Gunn (Eds.), *Encyclopedia of adolescence* (Vol. 1). New York: Garland.

Buss, A. H., & Plomin, R. (1984). *A temperament theory of personality development*. New York: Wiley-Interscience.

Buss, A. H., & Plomin, R. (1987). Commentary. In H. H. Goldsmith, A. H. Buss, R. Plomin, M. K. Rothbart, A. Thomas, A. Chess, R. R. Hinde, & R. B. McCall (Eds.), Roundtable: What is temperament? Four approaches. *Child Development, 58*, 505–529.

Buss, R. R., Yussen, S. R., Mathews, S. R., Miller, G. E., & Rembold, K. L. (1983). Development of children's use of a story schema to retrieve information. *Developmental Psychology, 19,* 22–28.

Bussey, K., & Maughan, B. (1982). Gender differences in moral reasoning. *Journal of Personality and Social Psychology, 42,* 701–706.

Butler, R. A. (1953). Discrimination learning by rhesus monkeys to visual-exploration motivation. *Journal of Comparative and Physiological Psychology, 46,* 95–98.

Byer, C. O., & Shainberg, L. W. (1991). *Dimensions of human sexuality* (3rd ed.). Dubuque, IA: William C. Brown.

Byrnes, J. P. (1988a). Formal operations: A systematic reformulation. *Developmental Review, 8,* 66–87.

Byrnes, J. P. (1988b). What's left is closer to right. *Developmental Review, 8,* 385–392.

C

Cairns, R. B. (1983). The emergence of developmental psychology. In P. H. Mussen (Ed.), *Handbook of child psychology* (4th ed., Vol. 1). New York: Wiley.

Cairns, R. B. (1991). Multiple metaphors for a singular idea. *Developmental Psychology, 27,* 23–236.

Cairns, R. B., & Cairns, B. D. (1989, April). *Risks and lifelines in adolescence.* Paper presented at the Society for Research in Child Development meeting, Kansas City.

Cairns, R. B., & Cairns, B. D. (in press). Social cognition and social networks. A developmental perspective. In D. Pepler & K. Rubin (Eds.), *Aggression in childhood.* Hillsdale, NJ: Erlbaum.

Caldwell, B. (1964). The effects of infant care. In M. Hoffman & L. Hoffman (Eds.), *Review of child development research* (Vol. 1). New York: Russell Sage.

Caldwell, B. (1991, October). *Impact on the child.* Paper presented at the symposium on day care for children, Arlington, VA.

Calhoun, J. A. (1988, March). *Gang violence.* Testimony to the House Select Committee on Children, Youth, and Families, Washington, DC.

Camara, K. A., & Resnick, G. (1988). Interparental conflict and cooperation: Factors moderating children's postdivorce adjustment. In E. M. Hetherington & J. D. Arasteh (Eds.), *Impact of divorce, single-parenting, and stepparenting on children.* Hillsdale, NJ: Erlbaum.

Camara, K. A., Brennan, K., & Resnick, G. (1991, April). *Emerging family cultures in single- and two-parent households:*

Relationships to the social and academic functioning of children. Paper presented at the Society for Research in Child Development meeting, Seattle.

Cameron, D. (1988, February). Soviet schools. *NEA Today,* p. 15.

Campos, J. J., Langer, A., & Krowitz, A. (1970). Cardiac responses on the visual cliff in prelocomotor human infants. *Science, 170,* 196–197.

Canter, L., & Canter, M. (1976). *Assertive Discipline: A take charge approach for today.* Santa Monica, CA: Lee Canter & Associates.

Carbo, M. (1987). Reading styles research: "What works" isn't always phonics. *Phi Delta Kappan,* pp. 431–435.

Carey, S. (1977). The child as word learner. In M. Halle, J. Bresman, & G. A. Miller (Eds.), *Linguistic theory and psychological reality.* Cambridge, MA: MIT Press.

Carey, S. (1988). Are children fundamentally different kinds of thinkers and learners than adults? In K. Richardson & S. Sheldon (Eds.), *Cognitive development to adolescence.* Hillsdale, NJ: Erlbaum.

Carlson, C., Cooper, C., & Hsu, J. (1990, March). *Predicting school achievement in early adolescence: The role of family process.* Paper presented at the meeting of the Society for Research in Adolescence, Atlanta.

Carnegie Corporation (1989). *Turning points: Preparing American youth for the 21st century.* New York: Carnegie Corporation.

Carpenter, T. P., Moser, J. M., & Romberg, T. A. (Eds.). (1982). *Addition and subtraction: A cognitive perspective.* Hillsdale, NJ: Erlbaum.

Carr, M., Borkowski, J. G., & Maxwell, S. E. (1991). Motivational components of underachievement. *Developmental Psychology, 27,* 108–118.

Carrasquillo, A. L. (1991). *Hispanic children and youth in the United States.* New York: Garland.

Carskadon, M. A., & Dement, W. C. (1989). Normal human sleep: An overview. In M. H. Kryger, T. Roth, & W. C. Dement (Eds.), *Principles and practices of sleep medicine.* San Diego: Harcourt Brace Jovanovich.

Carter, D. B., & Levy, G. D. (1988). Cognitive aspects of children's early sex-role development: The influence of gender schemas on preschoolers' memories and preference for sex-typed toys and activities. *Child Development, 59,* 782–793.

Carter, D. B., & Taylor, R. D. (in press). The development of children's awareness and understanding of flexibility in sex-role stereotypes: Implications for preferences, attitude, and behavior. *Sex Roles.*

Carter-Saltzman, L. (1980). Biological and sociocultural effects on handedness: Comparison between biological and adoptive families. *Science, 209,* 1263–1265.

Case, R. (1985). *Intellectual development: A systematic reinterpretation.* New York: Academic Press.

Case, R. (1991a). Advantages and disadvantages of the neo-Piagetian position. In R. Case (Ed.), *The mind's staircase.* Hillsdale, NJ: Erlbaum.

Case, R. (1991b). General and specific: Views of the mind, its structure, and development. In R. Case (Ed.), *The mind's staircase.* Hillsdale, NJ: Erlbaum.

Case, R., Kurland, D. M., & Goldberg, J. (1982). Operational efficiency and the growth of short-term memory span. *Journal of Experimental Child Psychology, 33,* 386–404.

Casper, R. C. (1989). Psychodynamic psychotherapy in acute anorexia nervosa and acute bulimia nervosa. In A. H. Esman (Ed.), *International annals of adolescent psychiatry.* Chicago: University of Chicago Press.

Cassell, C. (1984). *Swept away: Why women fear their own sexuality.* New York: Simon & Schuster.

Castelle, K. (1988). *In the child's best interest: A primer on the U.N. convention on the rights of the child.* East Greenwich, RI: Foster Parents Plan International.

Cavett, D. (1974). *Cavett.* San Diego: Harcourt Brace Jovanovich.

Cazden, C. B. (1988). *Classroom discourse.* Portsmouth, NH: Heinemann.

Ceci, S. J. (1991, April). *Intellectual development in context.* Paper presented at the Society for Research in Child Development meeting, Seattle.

Chalfant, J. C. (1989). Learning disabilities: Policy issues and promising approaches. *American Psychologist, 44,* 392–398.

Chance, P. (1979). *Learning and behavior.* Belmont, CA: Wadsworth.

Charlesworth, R. (1989). "Behind" before they start? *Young Children, 44,* 5–13.

Charlesworth, R., Hart, C. H., Burts, D. C., & Hernandez, S. (in press). Kindergarten teachers' beliefs and practices. *Early Child Development and Care.*

Chase-Lansdale, P. L., & Hetherington, E. M. (in press). The impact of divorce on life-span development: Short and long-term effects. In P. B. Baltes, D. L. Featherman, & R. M. Lerner (Eds.), *Life-span development and behavior.* Hillsdale, NJ: Erlbaum.

Chasnoff, I. J. (1991, April). *Cocaine versus tobacco: Impact on infant and child outcome.* Paper presented at the Society for Research in Child Development meeting, Seattle.

Chasnoff, I. J., Griffith, D. R., MacGregor, S., Dirkes, K., & Burns, K. A. (1989). Temporal patterns of cocaine use in pregnancy. *Journal of the American Medical Association, 261,* 1741–1744.

Chen, C., & Stevenson, H. W. (1989). Homework: A cross-cultural examination. *Child Development, 60,* 551–561.

Cherlin, A. J., Chase-Lansdale, P. L., Furstenberg, F. F., Kiernan, K., & Robins, P. K. (1991, April). *The effects of divorce on children's emotional adjustment: Two prospective studies.* Paper presented at the Society for Research in Child Development meeting, Seattle.

Chesney-Lind, M. (1989). Girls' crime and woman's place: Toward a feminist model of female delinquency. *Crime and Delinquency, 35,* 5–30.

Chess, S., & Thomas, A. (1977). Temperamental individuality from childhood to adolescence. *Journal of Child Psychiatry, 16,* 218–226.

Chi, M. T. H., & Koeske, R. D. (1983). Network representation of a child's dinosaur knowledge. *Developmental Psychology, 19,* 29–39.

Children's Defense Fund. (1990). *Children 1990.* Washington, DC: Children's Defense Fund.

Chodorow, N. (1978). *The reproduction of mothering.* Berkeley: University of California Press.

Chodorow, N. (1989). *Feminism and psychoanalytic theory.* New Haven, CT: Yale University Press.

Chomsky, N. (1957). *Syntactic structures.* The Hague: Mouton.

Chomsky, N. (1986). *Knowledge of language.* New York: Praeger.

Cicchetti, D. (1991, April). *Developmental theory: Lessons from the study of risk and psychopathology.* Invited address presented at the Society for Research in Child Development meeting, Seattle.

Cicirelli, V. (1977). Family structure and interaction: Sibling effects on socialization. In M. McMillan & M. Sergio (Eds.), *Child psychiatry: Treatment and research.* New York: Brunner/Mazel.

Clark, E. V. (1983). Meanings and concepts. In P. H. Mussen (Ed.), *Handbook of child psychology* (4th ed., Vol. 4). New York: Wiley.

Clark, H. H., & Clark, E. V. (1977). *Psychology and language.* New York: Harcourt Brace Jovanovich.

Clark, K. (1965). *Dark ghetto.* New York: Harper.

Clark, S. D., Zabin, L. S., & Hardy, J. B. (1984). Sex, contraception, and parenthood: Experience and attitudes among urban black young men. *Family Planning Perspectives, 16,* 77–82.

Clarke-Stewart, K. A. (1989). Infant day care: Maligned or malignant? *American Psychologist, 44,* 266–273.

Clarke-Stewart, K. A., & Fein, G. G. (1983). Early childhood programs. In P. H. Mussen (Ed.), *Handbook of child psychology* (4th ed., Vol. 2). New York: Wiley.

Cohen, C. P., & Naimark, H. (1991). United Nations convention on the rights of the child: Individual rights concepts and their significance for social scientists. *American Psychologist, 46,* 60–65.

Cohen, P., Brook, J. S., & Kandel, D. B. (1991). Drug use, predictors and correlates of. In R. M. Lerner, A. C. Petersen, & J. Brooks-Gunn (Eds.), *Encyclopedia of adolescence* (Vol. 1). New York: Garland.

Cohen, P., Velez, C. N., Brooks, J., & Smith, J. (1989). Mechanism of the relation between perinatal problems, early childhood illness, and psychopathology in late childhood and adolescence. *Child Development, 60,* 701–709.

Cohn, J. F., & Tronick, E. Z. (1988). Mother-infant face-to-face interaction. Influence is bidirectional and unrelated to periodic cycles in either partner's behavior. *Developmental Psychology, 24,* 396–397.

Coie, J. D., & Koeppl, G. K. (1990). Adapting intervention to the problems of aggressive and disruptive rejected children. In S. R. Asher & J. D. Coie (Eds.), *Peer rejection in childhood.* New York: Cambridge University Press.

Colby, A., Kohlberg, L., Gibbs, J., & Lieberman, M. (1983). A longitudinal study of moral judgment. *Monographs of the Society for Research in Child Development* (Serial No. 201).

Cole, D. A. (1991). Suicide, adolescent. In R. M. Lerner, A. C. Petersen, & J. Brooks-Gunn (Eds.), *Encyclopedia of adolescence* (Vol. 2). New York: Garland.

Cole, M., & Cole, S. R. (1989). *The development of children.* New York: Scientific American.

Cole, S. (1981). *Working kids on working.* New York: Lothrop, Lee, & Shephard.

Coleman, J. S., Campbell, E. Q., Hobson, C. J., McPartland, J., Mood, A. M., Weinfeld, F. D., & York, R. L. (1966). *Equality of educational opportunity.* Washington, DC: U.S. Government Printing Office.

Coleman, J. S. (1961). *The adolescent society.* New York: Free Press.

Coles, C. D., Platzman, K. A., & Smith, I. E. (1991, April). *Substance abuse and neonates: Alcohol and cocaine effects.* Paper presented at the Society for Research in Child Development meeting, Seattle.

Coles, R. (1970). *Erik Erikson: The growth of his work.* Boston: Little, Brown.

Coles, R. (1986). *The political life of children.* Boston: Little, Brown.

Coll, C. T. G. (1990). Developmental outcome of minority infants: A process-oriented look at our beginnings. *Child Development, 61,* 270–289.

Collins, A. (1986). Teaching reading and writing with personal computers. In J. Oransanu (Ed.), *A decade of reading research: Implications for practice.* Hillsdale, NJ: Erlbaum.

Collins, A., Brown, J. S., & Newman, S. E. (1989). Cognitive apprenticeship: Teaching the craft of reading, writing, and mathematics. In L. B. Resnick (Ed.), *Knowing and learning: Essays in honor of Robert Glaser.* Hillsdale, NJ: Erlbaum.

Collins, W. A. (1989, April). *Parents' relational cognitions and developmental changes in relationships during adolescence.* Paper presented at the Society for Research in Child Development meeting, Kansas City.

Collins, W. A. (1990). Parent-child relationships in the transition to adolescence: Continuity and change in interaction, affect, and cognition. In R. Montemayor, G. R. Adams, & T. P. Gulotta (Eds.), *From childhood to adolescence: A transitional period?* Newbury Park, CA: Sage.

Colombo, J., Moss, M., & Horowitz, F. D. (in press). Neonatal state profiles: Reliability and short-term prediction of neurobehavioral status. *Child Development.*

Comer, J. P. (1988). Educating poor minority children. *Scientific American, 259,* 42–48.

Committee for Economic Development (1987). *Children in need: Investment strategies for the educationally disadvantaged.* Washington, DC: Committee for Economic Development.

Conant, J. B. (1959). *The American high school today.* New York: McGraw-Hill.

Condry, J. C. (1989). *The psychology of television*. Hillsdale, NJ: Erlbaum.

Conger, J. J. (1981). Freedom and commitment: Families, youth, and social change. *American Psychologist, 36,* 1475–1484.

Conger, J. J. (1988). Hostages to the future: Youth, values, and the public interest. *American Psychologist, 43,* 291–300.

Coons, S., & Guilleminault, C. (1984). Development of consolidated sleep and wakeful periods in relation to the day/night cycle of infancy. *Developmental Medicine and Child Neurology, 26,* 169–176.

Cooper, C. R., & Ayers-Lopez, S. (1985). Family and peer systems in early adolescence: New models of the role of relationships in development. *Journal of Early Adolescence, 5,* 9–22.

Cooper, C. R., & Carlson, C. (1991, April). *Continuity and change in adolescents' family communication: Developmental, gender, and ethnic perspectives.* Paper presented at the Society for Research in Child Development meeting, Seattle.

Cooper, C. R., & Grotevant, H. D. (1989, April). *Individuality and connectedness in the family and adolescents' self and relational competence.* Paper presented at the Society for Research in Child Development meeting, Kansas City.

Cooper, C. R., Grotevant, H. D., Moore, M. S., & Condon, S. M. (1982, August). *Family support and conflict: Both foster adolescent identity and role taking.* Paper presented at the meeting of the American Psychological Association, Washington, DC.

Coopersmith, S. (1967). *The antecedents of self-esteem.* San Francisco: W. H. Freeman.

Corless, I. B., & Pittman-Lindeman, M. (1989). *AIDS: Principles, practices, and politics.* New York: Hemisphere.

Corrigan, R. (1981). The effects of task and practice on search for invisibly displaced objects. *Developmental Review, 1,* 1–17.

Corser, J., Stevenson, H. W., & Lee, S. (1989, April). *Education for excellence: The Asian experience.* Paper presented at the Society for Research in Child Development meeting, Kansas City.

Corwin, V. (1989, March). *Sesame Street* abroad. *Sesame Street Magazine Parent's Guide,* pp. 24, 26.

Cote, J. E., & Levine, C. (1988a). A critical examination of the ego identity status paradigm. *Developmental Review, 8,* 147–184.

Cote, J. E., & Levine, C. (1988b). On critiquing the identity status paradigm: A rejoinder to Waterman. *Developmental Review, 8,* 209–218.

Cote, J. E., & Levine, C. (1989). *An empirical investigation of the validity of the ego status paradigm.* Unpublished manuscript, University of Western Ontario.

Cowan, P. A. (1988). Becoming a father: A time of change, an opportunity for development. In P. Bronstein & C. P. Cowan (Eds.), *Fatherhood today.* New York: Wiley.

Cowan, P. A., & Cowan, C. P. (1989, April). *From parent adaptation in pregnancy to child adaptation in kindergarten.* Paper presented at the Society for Research in Child Development meeting, Kansas City.

Cowley, G. (1988, May 23). The wisdom of animals. *Newsweek,* pp. 52–58.

Crick, M. (1977). *Explorations in language and meaning: Toward a scientific anthropology.* New York: Halstead.

Crisafi, M. A., & Driscoll, J. M. (1991, April). *Developmental outcome in very low birth-weight infants at three years of age.* Paper presented at the Society for Research in Child Development meeting, Seattle.

Crittenden, P. (1988a). Family and dyadic patterns of functioning in maltreating families. In K. Browne, C. Davies, & P. Stratton (Eds.), *Early prediction and prevention of child abuse.* New York: Wiley.

Crittenden, P. (1988b). Relationships at risk. In J. Belsky & T. Nezworski (Eds.), *The clinical implications for attachment.* Hillsdale, NJ: Erlbaum.

Crittenden, P., & Partridge, M. (1991, April). *Maltreating couples' representations of attachment.* Paper presented at the Society for Research in Child Development meeting, Seattle.

Cronbach, L. J., & Snow, R. E. (1977). *Aptitudes and instructional methods.* New York: Irvington.

Cross, K. P. (1984, November). The rising tide of school reform reports. *Phi Delta Kappan,* pp. 167–172.

Curry, N. E. (1971). Consideration of current basic issues in play. In N. E. Curry & S. Arnaud (Eds.), *Play: The child strives toward self-regulation.* Washington, DC: NAEYC.

Curtiss, S. (1977). *Genie.* New York: Academic Press.

D

Damon, W. (1988). *The moral child.* New York: Free Press.

Damon, W. (1991). Self-concept, adolescent. In R. M. Lerner, A. C. Petersen, & J. Brooks-Gunn (Eds.), *Encyclopedia of adolescence* (Vol. 2). New York: Garland.

Damon, W., & Hart, D. (1988). *Self-understanding in childhood and adolescence.* New York: Cambridge University Press.

Darling, C. A., Kallen, D. J., & VanDusen, J. E. (1984). Sex in transition, 1900–1984. *Journal of Youth and Adolescence, 13,* 385–399.

Darlington, R. B. (1991). The long-term effects of model preschool programs. In L. Okagaki & R. J. Sternberg (Eds.), *Directors of development: Influences on the development of children's thinking.* Hillsdale, NJ: Erlbaum.

Daro, D. (1988). *Confronting child abuse.* New York: Free Press.

Darwin, C. (1859). *On the origin of species.* London: John Murray.

Dasen, P. R., Ngini, L., & Lavalée, M. (1979). Cross-cultural training studies of concrete operations. In L. H. Eckenberger, W. J. Lonner, & Y. H. Poortinga (Eds.), *Cross-cultural contributions to psychology.* Amsterdam, Holland: Swets & Zeilinger.

Day, N. (1991, April). *Effects of alcohol and marijuana on growth and development.* Paper presented at the Society for Research in Child Development meeting, Seattle.

DeAngelis, T. (1990, June). House child-care bill ignores quality issue. *APA Monitor,* p. 21.

DeCasper, A. J., & Spence, M. J. (1986). Prenatal maternal speech influences newborn's perception of speech sounds. *Infant Behavior and Development, 9,* 133–150.

Dedrick, C., Dedrick, R., Plunkett, J., Berlin, M., & Meisels, S. (1991, April). *Persistence of effects of prematurity in the second year of life: Maternal behavior and infant security.* Paper presented at the Society for Research in Child Development meeting, Seattle.

DeFour, D. C., & Paludi, M. A. (in press). Integrating scholarship on ethnicity into the psychology of women course. *Teaching of Psychology.*

DeHart, G., & Smith, B. (1991, April). *The role of age and gender composition in sibling pretend play.* Paper presented at the Society for Research in Child Development meeting, Seattle.

DeLoache, J. S., Cassidy, D. J., & Brown, A. L. (1985). Precursors of mnemonic strategies in very young children's memory. *Child Development, 56,* 125–137.

DeLoache, J. S., Cassidy, D. J., & Carpenter, C. J. (1987). The Three Bears are all boys: Mothers' gender labeling of neutral picture book characters. *Sex Roles, 17,* 163–178.

Demorest, A., Meyer, C., Phelps, E., Gardner, H., & Winner, E. (1984). Words speak louder than actions: Understanding deliberately false remarks. *Child Development, 55,* 1527–1534.

Dempster, F. N. (1981). Memory span: Sources of individual and developmental differences. *Psychological Bulletin, 89,* 63–100.

De Necochea, G. (1988, May). Expanding the Hispanic college pool. *Change.* pp. 61–62.

Denmark, F. L., & Paludi, M. A. (Eds.). (in press). *Handbook on the psychology of women.* Westport, CT: Greenwood.

Denmark, F. L., Russo, N. F., Frieze, I. H., & Sechzur, J. (1988). Guidelines for avoiding sexism in psychological research: A report of the Ad Hoc Committee on Nonsexist Research. *American Psychologist, 43,* 582–585.

Deutsch, M. (Ed.). (1967). *The disadvantaged child: Selected papers of Martin Deutsch and his associates.* New York: Basic.

de Villiers, J. (1988). Faith, doubt, and meaning. In F. S. Kessel (Ed.), *The development of language and language researchers.* Hillsdale, NJ: Erlbaum.

de Villiers, J., & de Villiers, P. A. (1978). *Language acquisition.* Cambridge, MA: Harvard University Press.

Devine, P. G. (1989). Stereotypes and prejudice: Their automatic and controlled components. *Journal of Personality and Social Psychology, 56,* 5–18.

Dewey, J. (1933). *How we think: A restatement of the relation of reflective thinking to the educative process.* Lexington, MA: D. C. Heath.

Diamond, A. (1985). Development of the ability to use recall to guide action, as indicated by infants' performance on AB. *Child Development, 56,* 868–883.

Diaz, R. M. (1983). Thought and two languages: The impact of bilingualism on cognitive development. *Review of Research in Education, 10,* 23–54.

Dickerscheid, J. D., Schwarz, P. M., Noir, S., & El-Taliawy, T. (1988). Gender concept development of preschool-aged children in the United States and Egypt. *Sex Roles, 18,* 669–677.

Dickinson, D. K., & Moreton, J. (1991, April). *Predicting specific kindergarten literacy skills from three-year-olds' preschool experiences.* Paper presented at the Society for Research in Child Development meeting, Seattle.

Dickinson, G. E. (1975). Dating behavior of black and white adolescents before and after desegregation. *Journal of Marriage and the Family, 37,* 602–608.

Dielman, T. E., Shope, J. T., & Butchart, A. T. (1990, March). *Peer, family, and intrapersonal predictors of adolescent alcohol use and misuse.* Paper presented at the meeting of the Society for Research in Adolescence, Atlanta.

Dillon, R. F., & Sternberg, R. J. (Eds.). (1988). *Cognition and instruction.* San Diego: Academic Press.

Dishion, T. J., & Skinner, M. S. (1989, April). *A process model for the role of peer relations in adolescent social adjustment.* Paper presented at the Society for Research in Child Development meeting, Kansas City.

Dishion, T. J., Andrews, D. W., & Crosby, L. (1991, April). *From family to friends: Microsocial processes relating the two spheres.* Paper presented at the Society for Research in Child Development meeting, Seattle.

Dishion, T. J., Patterson, G. R., & Skinner, M. L. (1989, April). *Parent monitoring and peer relations in the drift to deviant peers.* Paper presented at the Society for Research in Child Development meeting, Kansas City.

Dixon, S. D. (1991, April). *Infants exposed perinatally to cocaine or methaamphetamine demonstrate behavioral and neurophysiologic changes.* Paper presented at the Society for Research in Child Development meeting, Seattle.

Dodge, K. A. (1983). Behavioral antecedents of peer social status. *Child Development, 54,* 1386–1399.

Dodge, K. A., & Feldman, E. (1990). Issues in social cognition and sociometric status. In S. R. Asher & J. D. Coie (Eds.), *Peer rejection in childhood.* New York: Cambridge University Press.

Dodge, K. A., Pettit, G. S., McClaskey, C. L., & Brown, M. M. (1986). Social competence in children. *Monographs of the Society for Research in Child Development, 51* (2, Serial No. 213).

Dolgin, K. G., & Behrend, D. A. (1984). Children's knowledge about animates and inanimates. *Child Development, 55,* 1646–1650.

Doll, G. (1988, Spring). Day care. *Vanderbilt Magazine,* p. 29.

Dornbusch, S. M., Petersen, A. C., & Hetherington, E. M. (1991). Projecting the future of research on adolescence. *Journal of Research on Adolescence, 1,* 7–18.

Douvan, E., & Adelson, J. (1966). *The adolescent experience.* New York: Wiley.

Downey, A. M., Frank, G. C., Webber, L. S., Harsha, D. W., Virgilio, S. J., Franklin, F. A., & Berenson, G. S. (1987). Implementation of "Heart Smart": A cardiovascular school health promotion program. *Journal of School Health, 57,* 98–104.

Doyle, J. A., & Paludi, M. A. (1991). *Sex and gender* (2nd ed.). Dubuque, IA: Wm. C. Brown.

Dreyer, P. H. (1982). Sexuality during adolescence. In B. B. Wolman (Ed.), *Handbook of developmental psychology.* Englewood Cliffs, NJ: Prentice-Hall.

Dreyfus, H. L., & Dreyfus, S. E. (1986). *Mind over machine.* New York: Free Press.

Dryfoos, J. G. (1990). *Adolescents at risk: Prevalence and prevention.* New York: Oxford University Press.

DuBois, D. L., & Hirsch, B. J. (1990). School and neighborhood friendship patterns of Blacks and Whites in early adolescence. *Child Development, 61,* 524–536.

Duck, S. W. (1975). Personality similarity and friendship choices by adolescents. *European Journal of Social Psychology, 5,* 351–365.

Duck, S. W. (1988). Child and adolescent friendships. In P. Marsh (Ed.), *Eye to eye: How people interact.* Topsfield, MA: Salem House.

Duke, D. L., & Canady, R. L. (1991). *School policy.* New York: McGraw-Hill.

Duncan, R. M. (1991, April). *An examination of Vygotsky's theory of children's private speech.* Paper presented at the Society for Research in Child Development meeting, Seattle.

Duncker, K. (1945). On problem solving. *Psychological Monographs, 58* (Whole No. 270).

Dunn, J., & Kendrick, C. (1982). *Siblings.* Cambridge, MA: Harvard University Press.

Dunphy, D. C. (1963). The social structure of urban adolescent peer groups. *Society, 26,* 230–246.

Durkin, K. (1985). Television and sex-role acquisition: 1. Content. *British Journal of Social Psychology, 24,* 101–113.

E

Early Childhood and Literacy Development Committee of the International Reading Association (1986). Literacy development and pre-first grade. *Young Children, 41,* 10–13.

Eccles, J. S. (1987). Gender roles and achievement patterns: An expectancy value perspective. In J. M. Reinisch, L. A. Rosenblum, & S. A. Sanders (Eds.), *Masculinity/femininity: Basic perspectives*. New York: Oxford University Press.

Eccles, J. S. (1991). Academic achievement. In R. M. Lerner, A. C. Petersen, & J. Brooks-Gunn (Eds.), *Encyclopedia of adolescence* (Vol. 1). New York: Garland.

Eccles, J. S., & Harold, R. (1991, April). *Influences on, and consequences of, parents' beliefs regarding their children's abilities and interests*. Paper presented at the Society for Research in Child Development meeting, Seattle.

Eccles, J. S., & Hoffman, L. W. (1984). Sex roles, socialization, and occupational behavior. In H. W. Stevenson & A. E. Siegel (Eds.), *Research in child development and public policy* (Vol. 1). Chicago: University of Chicago Press.

Eccles, J. S., & Jacobs, J. E. (1986). Social forces shape math attitudes and performance. *Signs, 11,* 367–389.

Eccles, J. S., & Midgley, C. (1990). Changes in academic motivation and self-perception during early adolescence. In R. Montemayor, G. R. Adams, & T. P. Gullotta (Eds.), *From childhood to adolescence: A transitional period?* Newbury Park, CA: Sage.

Eccles, J. S., Harold-Goldsmith, R., & Miller, C. R. (1989, April). *Parents' stereotypic beliefs about gender differences in adolescence*. Paper presented at the Society for Research in Child Development meeting, Kansas City.

Eccles, J. S., MacIver, D., & Lange, L. (1986). *Classroom practices and motivation to study math*. Paper presented at the annual meeting of the American Educational Research Association, San Francisco.

Edelman, M. W. (1987). *Families in peril: An agenda for social change*. New York: Alan Guttmacher Institute.

Edmonds, R. (1979). Some schools work and more can. *Social Policy, 9,* 28–32.

Edwards, C. P. (1987). Culture and the construction of moral values. In J. Kagan & S. Lamb (Eds.), *The emergence of morality in young children*. Chicago: University of Chicago Press.

Efron, R. (in press). *The decline and fall of hemispheric specialization*. Hillsdale, NJ: Erlbaum.

Egeland, B. (1974). Training impulsive children in the use of more efficient scanning techniques. *Child Development, 45,* 165–171.

Egeland, B. (1989, January). *Secure attachment in infancy and competence in the third grade*. Paper presented at the meeting of the American Association for the Advancement of Science, San Francisco.

Eger, M. (1981). The conflict in moral education: An informal case study. *Public Interest, 63,* 62–80.

Ehrhardt, A. A. (1987). A transactional perspective on the development of gender differences. In J. M. Reinisch, L. A. Rosenblum, & S. A. Sanders (Eds.), *Masculinity/femininity: Basic perspectives*. New York: Oxford University Press.

Eiferman, R. R. (1971). Social play in childhood. In R. E. Herron & B. Sutton-Smith (Eds.), *Child's play*. New York: Wiley.

Eisenberg, N. (Ed.). (1982). *The development of prosocial behavior*. New York: Wiley.

Eisenberg, N., Shea, C. I., Carolo, G., & Knight, G. P. (1991). Empathy-related responding and cognition: A chicken and egg dilemma. In W. M. Kurtines & J. Gewirtz (Eds.), *Moral behavior and development* (Vol. 2). Hillsdale, NJ: Erlbaum.

Eitzen, D. S. (1975). Athletics in the status system of male adolescents. A replication of Coleman's *The Adolescent Society*. *Adolescence, 10,* 267–276.

Elder, G. H. (1974). *Children of the Great Depression*. Chicago: University of Chicago Press.

Elder, G. H., & Caspi, A. (in press). Studying lives in a changing society. In A. I. Rabin, R. A. Zucker, R. Emmons, & S. Franck, (Eds.), *Studying lives and persons*. New York: Springer.

Elder, G. H., Caspi, A., & Downey, G. (1986). Problem behavior and family relationships: A multigenerational analysis. In A. Sorensen, F. Weinert, & L. Sherrod (Eds.), *Human development and the life course*. Hillsdale: NJ: Erlbaum.

Elkind, D. (1961). Quantity conceptions in junior and senior high school students. *Child Development, 32,* 551–560.

Elkind, D. (1976). *Child development and education*. New York: Oxford University Press.

Elkind, D. (1978). Understanding the young adolescent. *Adolescence, 13,* 127–134.

Elkind, D. (1981). *The hurried child*. Reading, MA: Addison-Wesley.

Elkind, D. (1985). Egocentrism redux. *Developmental Review, 5,* 218–226.

Elkind, D. (1987). *Miseducation: Preschoolers at risk*. New York: Knopf.

Elkind, D. (1988, January). Educating the very young: A call for clear thinking. *NEA Today,* pp. 22–27.

Ellis, H. C. (1987). Recent developments in human memory. In V. P. Makosky (Ed.), *The G. Stanley Hall Lecture Series*. Washington, DC: American Psychological Association.

Ellis, L., & Ames, M. A. (1987). Neurohormonal functioning and sexual orientation: A theory of homosexuality-heterosexuality. *Psychological Bulletin, 101,* 233–258.

Emde, R. N., Gaensbauer, T. G., & Harmon, R. J. (1976). Emotional expression in infancy: A biobehavioral study. *Psychological Issues: Monograph Series, 10* (37).

Emery, R. E. (1989). Family violence. *American Psychologist, 44,* 321–328.

Emmerich, W., Goodman, K. S., Kirsch, B., & Sharabany, R. (1977). Evidence for a transitional phase in the development of gender constancy. *Child Development, 48,* 930–936.

Engle, P. L. (1991, April). *The effects of nutritional supplementation on cognitive functioning of preschoolers in Guatemala*. Paper presented at the Society for Research in Child Development meeting, Seattle.

Enkin, M. W. (1989). Cesarean section: Why do the rates differ? *Birth, 16,* 207–208.

Ennis, R. H. (1990). The extent to which critical thinking is subject-specific: Further clarification. *Educational Leadership, 19,* 13–16.

Ennis, R. H. (1991). Critical thinking: Literature review and needed research. In L. Idol & B. F. Jones (Eds.), *Educational values and cognitive instruction*. Hillsdale, NJ: Erlbaum.

Enright, R. D., Lapsley, D. K., Dricas, A. S., & Fehr, L. A. (1980). Parental influence on the development of adolescent autonomy and identity. *Journal of Youth and Adolescence, 9,* 529–546.

Ensher, G., & Miller, P. (1989, April). *The Syracuse Scales of Infant Development and Home Observation: A standardized measure for high risk and handicapped babies, birth to 12 months*. Paper presented at the Society for Research in Child Development meeting, Kansas City.

Entwisle, D. R. (1990). Schools and the adolescent. In S. S. Feldman & G. R. Elliott (Eds.), *At the threshold: The developing adolescent*. Cambridge, MA: Harvard University Press.

Entwistle, N. (1981). *Styles of learning and teaching*. New York: Wiley.

Erikson, E. H. (1950). *Childhood and society*. New York: W. W. Norton.

Erikson, E. H. (1962). *Young man Luther*. New York: W. W. Norton.

Erikson, E. H. (1968). *Identity: Youth and crisis*. New York: W. W. Norton.

Erikson, E. H. (1969). *Gandhi's truth*. New York: W. W. Norton.

Esty, E. T., & Fisch, S. M. (1991, April). *SQUARE ONE TV: Using television to enhance children's problem solving*. Paper presented at the Society for Research in Child Development meeting, Seattle.

Etzel, R. (1988, October). *Children of smokers*. Paper presented at the American Academy of Pediatrics meeting, New Orleans.

Evans, B. J., & Whitfield, J. R. (Eds.). (1988). *Black males in the United States: An annotated bibliography from 1967 to 1987*. Washington, DC: American Psychological Association.

Eyler, F. D., Behnke, M. L., & Stewart, N. J. (1990). *Issues in identification and follow-up of cocaine-exposed neonates*. Unpublished manuscript, University of Florida, Gainesville.

F

Fagan, J. F., & Knevel, C. R. (1989, April). *The prediction of above average intelligence from infancy*. Paper presented at the Society for Research in Child Development meeting, Kansas City.

Falbo, T., & Polit, D. F. (1986). A quantitative review of the only-child literature. Research evidence and theory development. *Psychological Bulletin, 100,* 176–189.

Fantz, R. L. (1983). Pattern vision in newborn infants. *Science, 140,* 296–297.

Farmer, J. E., Peterson, L., & Kashani, J. H. (1989, April). *Injury risk, parent and child psychopathology*. Paper presented at the Society for Research in Child Development meeting, Kansas City.

Farnham-Diggory, S. (1990). *Schooling*. Cambridge, MA: Harvard University Press.

Fein, G. G. (1986). Pretend play. In D. Görlitz & J. F. Wohlwill (Eds.), *Curiosity, imagination, and play*. Hillsdale, NJ: Erlbaum.

Feldman, S. S., & Elliott, G. R. (1990). Progress and promise of research on normal adolescent development. In S. S. Feldman & G. Elliott (Eds.), *At the threshold: The developing adolescent*. Cambridge, MA: Harvard University Press.

Feldman, S. S., & Rosenthal, D. A. (1990a). The acculturation of autonomy expectations in Chinese high schoolers residing in two Western nations. *International Journal of Psychology, 25,* 259–281.

Feldman, S. S., & Rosenthal, D. A. (1990b). *The influence of family variables and adolescents' values on age expectations of behavioral autonomy: A cross-cultural study of Hong Kong, Australian, and American youth*. Unpublished manuscript, Stanford Center for the Study of Families.

Fenzel, L. M., Blyth, D. A., & Simmons, R. G. (1991). School transitions, secondary. In R. M. Lerner, A. C. Petersen, & J. Brooks-Gunn (Eds.), *Encyclopedia of adolescence* (Vol. 2). New York: Garland.

Ferber, R. (1989). Sleeplessness in the child. In M. H. Kryger, T. Roth, & W. C. Dement (Eds.), *Principles and practices of sleep medicine*. San Diego: Harcourt Brace Jovanovich.

Ferguson, D. M., Harwood, L. J., & Shannon, F. T. (1987). Breast feeding and subsequent social adjustment in six-to-eight-year-old children. *Journal of Child Psychology and Psychiatry, 28,* 378–386.

Field, T. (1987, January). [Interview.] *Psychology Today*, p. 31.

Field, T. M. (1979). Visual and cardiac responses to animate and inanimate faces by young term and preterm infants. *Child Development, 50,* 188–194.

Field, T. M. (1990). Alleviating stress in newborn infants in the intensive care unit. In B. M. Lester & E. Z. Tronick (Eds.), *Stimulation and the preterm infant: The limits of plasticity*. Philadelphia: W. B. Saunders.

Field, T. M. (1991). Reducing stress in child and psychiatric patients by massage and relaxation therapy. In T. M. Field, P. M. McCabe, & N. Schneiderman (Eds.), *Stress and coping in infancy and childhood* (Vol. 4). Hillsdale, NJ: Erlbaum.

Field, T. M., Scafidi, F., & Schanberg, S. (1987). Massage of preterm newborns to improve growth and development. *Pediatric Nursing, 13,* 385–387.

Field, T. M., Woodson, R., Greenberg, R., & Cohen, D. (1982). Discrimination and imitation of facial expressions by neonates. *Science, 218,* 179–181.

Fillmore, L. W. (1989). Teachability and second language acquisition. In M. L. Rice & R. L. Schiefelbusch (Eds.), *The teachability of language*. Baltimore: Paul Brooks.

Fincher, J. (1982). Before their time. *Science*.

Fineberg, H. V. (1988). Education to prevent AIDS: Prospects and obstacles. *Science, 239,* 592–596.

Firush, R., & Cobb, P. A. (1989, April). *Developing scripts*. Paper presented at the Society for Research in Child Development meeting, Kansas City.

Fischer, K. W., & Lazerson, A. (1984). *Human development*. San Francisco: W. H. Freeman.

Fish, M. (1989, April) *Temperament and attachment of separation intolerance at three years*. Paper presented at the Society for Research in Child Development meeting, Kansas City.

Fisher, C. B., & Brone, R. J. (1991). Eating disorders in adolescence. In R. M. Lerner, A. C. Petersen, & J. Brooks-Gunn (Eds.), *Encyclopedia of adolescence* (Vol. 1). New York: Garland.

Fisher, D. (1990, March). *Effects of attachment on adolescents' friendships*. Paper presented at the meeting of the Society for Research in Adolescence, Atlanta.

Fisher, D. A., & Jenkins, V. Y. (1991, April). *Attachment in adolescence: Relationship quality and conflict resolution*. Paper presented at the Society for Research in Child Development meeting, Seattle.

Flanagan, C. A. (1990a). Change in family work status: Effects on parent-adolescent decision making. *Child Development, 61,* 163–177.

Flanagan, C. A. (1990b). Families and schools in hard times. In V. C. McLoyd & C. A. Flanagan (Eds.), *Economic stress: Effects on family life and child development*. San Francisco: Jossey-Bass.

Flannagan, D. A., & Tate, C. S. (1989, April). *The effects of children's script knowledge on their communication and recall of scenes*. Paper presented at the Society for Research in Child Development meeting, Kansas City.

Flavell, J. H. (1980, Fall). A tribute to Piaget. *Society for Research in Child Development Newsletter*, p. 1.

Flavell, J. H. (1985). *Cognitive development* (2nd ed.). Englewood Cliffs, NJ: Prentice-Hall.

Flavell, J. H., Beach, D. R., & Chinsky, J. M. (1966). Spontaneous verbal rehearsal in a memory task as a function of age. *Child Development, 37,* 283–299.

Fleming, A. S., Ruble, D. N., Flett, G. L., & Shaul, D. L. (1988). Postpartum adjustment in first-time mothers: Relations between mood, maternal attitudes, and mother-infant interactions. *Developmental Psychology, 24,* 71–81.

Fogel, A., Toda, S., & Kawai, M. (1988). Mother-infant face-to-face interaction in Japan and the United States: A laboratory comparison using 3-month-old infants. *Developmental Psychology, 24,* 398–406.

Fontana, V. J. (1988, February). Detection and management of child sexual abuse. *Medical Aspects of Human Sexuality,* pp. 126–142.

Ford, M. E. (1986). A living systems conceptualization of social intelligence: Outcomes, processes, and developmental change. In R. J. Steinberg (Ed.), *Advances in the psychology of human intelligence* (Vol. 3). Hillsdale, NJ: Erlbaum.

Fordham, S., & Ogbu, J. U. (1986). Black students' school success: Coping with the burden of "acting white." *Urban Review, 18,* 176–206.

Forehand, G., Ragosta, J., & Rock, D. (1976). *Conditions and processes of effective school desegregation.* Princeton, NJ: Educational Testing Service.

Forrest, J. D. (1990). Cultural influences on adolescents' reproductive behavior. In J. Bancroft & J. M. Reinisch (Eds.), *Adolescence and puberty.* New York: Oxford University Press.

Forsyth, B. W. C., Leventhal, J. M., & McCarthy, P. L. (1985). Mothers' perceptions of feeding and crying behaviors. *American Journal of Diseases of Children, 139,* 269–272.

Fox, L. H., Brody, L., & Tobin, D. (1979). *Women and mathematics.* Baltimore: Intellectually Gifted Study Group, Johns Hopkins University.

Fox, N. A., Sutton, B., Aaron, N., & Luebering, A. (1989, April). *Infant temperament and attachment: A new look at an old issue.* Paper presented at the Society for Research in Child Development meeting, Kansas City.

Francis, J., Fraser, G., & Marcia, J. E. (1989). *Cognitive and experimental factors in Moratorium-Achievement (MAMA) cycles.* Unpublished manuscript, Department of Psychology, Simon Fraser University, Burnaby, British Columbia.

Freedle, R. (Ed.). (1990). *Artificial intelligence and the future of testing.* Hillsdale, NJ: Erlbaum.

Freedman, D. G. (1971). Genetic influences on development of behavior. In G. B. A. Stoelinga & J. J. Van Der Werff Ten Bosch (Eds.), *Normal and abnormal development of behavior.* Leiden: Leiden University Press.

Freedman, D. G., & Freedman, N. (1969). Behavioral differences between Chinese-American and European-American newborns. *Nature, 224,* 1127.

Freedman, J. L. (1984). Effects of television violence on aggressiveness. *Psychological Bulletin, 96,* 227–246.

Freud, A., & Dann, S. (1951). Instinctual anxiety during puberty. In A. Freud (Ed.), *The ego and its mechanisms of defense.* New York: International Universities Press.

Freud, S. (1917). *A general introduction to psychoanalysis.* New York: Washington Square.

Fried, P., & O'Connell, C. (1991, April). *Marijuana and tobacco as prenatal correlates of child behavior: Follow-up to school age.* Paper presented at the Society for Research in Child Development meeting, Seattle.

Fried, P. A., & Watkinson, B. (1990). 36- and 48-month neurobehavioral follow-up of children prenatally exposed to marijuana, cigarettes, and alcohol. *Developmental and Behavioral Pediatrics, 11,* 49–58.

Fried, P. A., Watkinson, B., & Dillon, R. F. (1987). Neonatal neurological status in a low-risk population after prenatal exposure to cigarettes, marijuana, and alcohol. *Journal of Developmental and Behavioral Pediatrics, 8,* 318–326.

Friedman, S. L. (1991, April). *Development and change in planning skills: An overview.* Paper presented at the Society for Research in Child Development meeting, Seattle.

Friedrich, L. K., & Stein, A. H. (1973). Aggressive and prosocial TV programs and the natural behavior of preschool children. *Monographs of the Society for Research in Child Development, 38* (4, Serial No. 151).

Frisch, R. E. (1991). Puberty and body fat. In R. M. Lerner, A. C. Petersen, & J. Brooks-Gunn (Eds.), *Encyclopedia of adolescence.* New York: Garland.

Frost, J. L., & Wortham, S. C. (1988, July). The evolution of American playgrounds. *Young Children,* 19–28.

Fuller, M. (1984). Black girls in a London comprehensive school. In M. Hammersley & P. Woods (Eds.), *Life in school: The sociology of pop culture.* New York: Open University Press.

Furman, L. N., & Walden, T. A. (1989, April). *The effect of script knowledge on children's communicative interactions.* Paper presented at the Society for Research in Child Development meeting, Kansas City.

Furman, L. N., & Walden, T. A. (1990). Effect of script knowledge on preschool children's communicative interactions. *Developmental Psychology, 26,* 227–233.

Furrow, D., & Moore, C. (1991, April). *Mothers' feedback to children's utterances: The role of context.* Paper presented at the Society for Research in Child Development meeting, Seattle.

Furstenberg, F. F. (1988). Child care after divorce and remarriage. In E. M. Hetherington & J. D. Arasteh (Eds.), *Impact of divorce, single-parenting, and stepparenting on children.* Hillsdale, NJ: Erlbaum.

Furstenberg, F. F. (1991). Pregnancy and childbearing: Effects on teen mothers. In R. M. Lerner, A. C. Petersen, & J. Brooks-Gunn (Eds.), *Encyclopedia of adolescence* (Vol. 2). New York: Garland.

Furstenberg, F. F., Brooks-Gunn, J., & Chase-Lansdale, L. (1989). Teenaged pregnancy and childbearing. *American Psychologist, 44,* 313–320.

Furstenberg, J. J., Brooks-Gunn, J., & Morgan, S. P. (1987). Adolescent mothers in later life. New York: Cambridge University Press.

Furth, H. G. (1973). *Deafness and learning: A psychosocial approach.* Belmont, CA: Wadsworth.

Furth, H. G., & Wachs, H. (1975). *Thinking goes to school.* New York: Oxford University Press.

G

Gabrielli, W. (1990, June). *Alcoholism from a biological perspective.* Paper presented at the meeting of the American Psychological Society, Dallas.

Gage, N. L. (1965). Desirable behaviors of teachers. *Urban Education, 1,* 85–96.

Gagne, E. D. (1985). *The cognitive psychology of school learning.* Boston: Little, Brown.

Gagne, E. D., Weidemann, C., Bell, M. S., & Ander, T. D. (1984). Training thirteen-year-olds to elaborate while studying text. *Human Learning: Journal of Practical Research and Application, 3,* 281–294.

Gagnon, J. H., & Simon, W. (1973). *Sexual conduct.* New York: Aldine.

Galambos, N. L., & Maggs, J. L. (1989, April). *The after-school ecology of young adolescents and self-reported behavior.* Paper presented at the Society for Research in Child Development meeting, Kansas City.

Galambos, N. L., & Maggs, J. L. (1990). Putting mothers' work-related stress in perspective. *Journal of Early Adolescence, 10,* 313–328.

Gallagher, J. J. (1989). Children and social policy: Section introduction. *American Psychologist, 44,* 386.

Gallagher, J. J., Trohanis, P. L., & Clifford, R. M. (1989). *Policy implementation and PL 99-457.* Baltimore, MD: Brookes.

Gallup, A. M., & Clark, D. L. (1987). The 19th annual Gallup poll of the public's attitude toward the public schools. *Phi Delta Kappan,* pp. 17–30.

Gallup Report (1987). Legalized gay relations. *Gallup Report,* No. 254, 25.

Galotti, K. M. (1989a). Approaches to studying formal and everyday reasoning. *Psychological Bulletin, 105,* 331–351.

Galotti, K. M. (1989b). Gender differences in self-reported moral reasoning: A review and new evidence. *Journal of Youth and Adolescence, 18,* 475–488.

Galotti, K. M., Kozberg, S. F., & Appleman, D. (in press). Younger and older adolescents' thinking about commitments. *Journal of Experimental Child Psychology.*

Galotti, K. M., Kozberg, S. F., & Farmer, M. C. (1990, March). *Gender and developmental differences in adolescents' conceptions of moral reasoning.* Paper presented at the meeting of the Society for Research in Adolescence, Atlanta.

Garbarino, J. (1976). The ecological correlates of child abuse: The impact of socioeconomic stress on mothers. *Child Development, 47,* 178–185.

Garbarino, J. (1980a). The issue is human quality: In praise of children. *Children and Youth Services Review, 1,* 353–377.

Garbarino, J. (1980b). Some thoughts on school size and its effects on adolescent development. *Journal of Youth and Adolescence, 9,* 19–31.

Garbarino, J. (1985). *Adolescent development: An ecological perspective.* Columbus, OH: Merrill.

Garbarino, J. (1989). *The psychologically battered child.* San Francisco: Jossey-Bass.

Garden, R. A. (1987). The second IEA mathematics study. *Comparative Education Review, 31,* 47–68.

Gardner, B. T., & Gardner, R. A. (1971). Two-way communication with an infant chimpanzee. In A. Schrier & F. Stollnitz (Eds.), *Behavior of nonhuman primates* (Vol. 4). New York: Academic Press.

Gardner, H. (1983). *Frames of mind.* New York: Basic.

Gardner, H. (1989). Beyond a modular view of mind. In W. Damon (Ed.), *Child development today and tomorrow.* San Francisco: Jossey-Bass.

Gardner, R. A., Gardner, B. T., & Van Cantfort, T. E. (1989). *Teaching sign language to chimpanzees.* Albany: State University of New York Press.

Garelik, G. (1985, October). Are the progeny prodigies? *Discoverer, 6,* 45–47, 78–84.

Garrison, W. T., & McQuiston, S. (1989). *Chronic illness during childhood and adolescence.* Newbury Park, CA: Sage.

Garton, A. F., & Pratt, C. (1989). *Learning to be literate.* New York: Basil Blackwell.

Garvey, C. (1977). *Play.* Cambridge, MA: Harvard University Press.

Garwood, S. G., Phillips, D., Hartman, A., & Zigler, E. F. (1989). As the pendulum swings: Federal agency programs for children. *American Psychologist, 44,* 434–440.

Gaylord-Ross, R. (Ed.). (1989). *Integration strategies for students with handicaps.* Baltimore: Brookes.

Gazzaniga, M. S. (1986). *The social brain.* New York: Plenum.

Geary, D. C., & Brown, S. C. (1991). Cognitive addition: Strategy choice and speed-of-processing differences in gifted, normal, and mathematically disabled children. *Developmental Psychology, 27,* 398–406.

Gelman, R. (1969). Conservation acquisition: A problem of learning to attend to relevant attributes. *Journal of Experimental Child Psychology, 7,* 67–87.

Gelman, R. (1991). Epigenetic foundations of knowledge structures: Initial and transcendent constructions. In S. Carey & R. Gelman (Eds.), *The epigenesis of mind: Essays on biology and cognition.* Hillsdale, NJ: Erlbaum.

Gelman, R., & Baillargeon, R. (1983). A review of some Piagetian concepts. In P. H. Mussen (Ed.), *Handbook of child psychology* (4th ed., Vol. 3). New York: Wiley.

Geschwind, N. (1979, September). Specializations of the human brain. *Scientific American,* pp. 180–199.

Gesell, A. L. (1928). *Infancy and human growth.* New York: Macmillan.

Gesell, A. L. (1934). *An atlas of infant behavior.* New Haven, CT: Yale University Press.

Gest, S., Berman, S., & Hartup, W. W. (1991, April). *Social affiliations and social reputations of popular, average, and rejected children.* Paper presented at the Society for Research in Child Development meeting, Seattle.

Gewirtz, J. (1977). Maternal responding and the conditioning of infant crying: Directions of influence within the attachment-acquisition process. In B. C. Etzel, J. M. LeBlanc, & D. M. Baer (Eds.), *New developments in behavioral research.* Hillsdale, NJ: Erlbaum.

Giaconia, R. M., & Hedges, L. V. (1982). Identifying features of effective open education. *Review of Educational Research, 52,* 579–602.

Gibbs, J. T. (1989). Black American adolescents. In J. T. Gibbs, & L. N. Huang (Eds.), *Children of color.* San Francisco: Jossey-Bass.

Gibbs, J. T. (1991). Black adolescents at risk: Approaches to prevention. In R. M. Lerner, A. C. Petersen, & J. Brooks-Gunn (Eds.), *Encyclopedia of adolescence* (Vol. 1). New York: Garland.

Gibbs, J. T., & Huang, L. N. (1989). A conceptual framework for assessing and treating minority youth. In J. T. Gibbs & L. N. Huang (Eds.), *Children of color.* San Francisco: Jossey-Bass.

Gibson, E. J. (1969). *The principles of perceptual learning and development.* New York: Appleton-Century-Crofts.

Gibson, E. J. (1989). Exploratory behavior in the development of perceiving, acting, and the acquiring of knowledge. *Annual Review of Psychology, 39.* Palo Alto, CA: Annual Reviews.

Gibson, E. J., & Spelke, E. S. (1983). The development of perception. In P. H. Mussen (Ed.), *Handbook of child psychology* (4th ed., Vol. 3). New York: Wiley.

Gibson, E. J., & Walk, R. D. (1960). The "visual cliff." *Scientific American, 202,* 64–71.

Gibson, M. A., & Ogbu, J. U. (1991). *Minority status and schooling.* New York: Garland.

Gilgun, J. F. (1984). Sexual abuse of the young female in life course perspective. *Dissertations Abstracts International, 45,* 3058.

Gilligan, C. (1982). *In a different voice.* Cambridge, MA: Harvard University Press.

Gilligan, C. (1990). Teaching Shakespeare's sister. In C. Gilligan, N. Lyons, & T. Hanmer (Eds.), *Making connections: The relational worlds of adolescent girls at Emma Willard School.* Cambridge, MA: Harvard University Press.

Gilligan, C. (1991, April). Discussant, *Psychology and the good: How should "we" talk about development?* Symposium at the Society for Research in Child Development meeting, Seattle.

Gilligan, C., & Attanucci, J. (1988). Two moral orientations. In C. Gilligan, J. V. Ward, J. M. Taylor, & B. Bardige (Eds.), *Mapping the moral domain* (pp. 73–86). Cambridge, MA: Harvard University Press.

Gilligan, C., Brown, L. M., & Rogers, A. G. (1990). Psyche embedded: A place for body, relationships, and culture in personality theory. In A. I. Rabin, R. A. Zucker, R. Emmons, & S. Frank (Eds.), *Studying lives and persons.* New York: Springer.

Glaser, R. (1989). The reemergence of learning theory within instructional research. *American Psychologist, 45,* 29–39.

Glass, G. V., & Smith, M. L. (1978, September). *Meta-analysis of research on the relationship of class size and achievement.* San Francisco: Far West Educational Laboratory.

Glasser, W. (1990). The quality school. *Phi Delta Kappan,* pp. 424–435.

Gleason, J. B. (1988). Language and socialization. In F. Kessel (Ed.), *The development of language and language researchers.* Hillsdale, NJ: Erlbaum.

Gleason, J. B., Hay, D., & Cain, L. (1989). Social and affective determinants of language acquisition. In M. L. Rice & R. L. Schiefelbusch (Eds.), *The teachability of language.* Baltimore: Paul Brooks.

Glick, J. (1975). Cognitive development in cross-cultural perspective. In F. Horowitz (Ed.), *Review of child development research* (Vol. 4). Chicago: University of Chicago Press.

Glick, J. (1991, April). *The uses and abuses of Vygotsky.* Paper presented at the Society for Research in Child Development meeting, Seattle.

Goertz, M. E., Ekstrom, R. B., & Rock, D. (1991). Dropouts, high school: Issues of race and sex. In R. M. Lerner, A. C. Petersen, & J. Brooks-Gunn (Eds.), *Encyclopedia of adolescence* (Vol. 1). New York: Garland.

Gold, M. (1987). Social ecology. In H. C. Quay (Ed.), *Handbook of juvenile delinquency.* New York: Wiley.

Gold, M., & Petronio, R. J. (1980). Delinquent behavior in adolescence. In J. Adelson (Ed.), *Handbook of adolescent psychology.* New York: Wiley.

Goldfried, M. R., & d'Zurilla, T. J. (1969). A behavioral-analytic model for assessing competence. In C. D. Speilberger (Ed.), *Current topics in clinical and community psychology* (Vol. 1). New York: Academic Press.

Goldman-Rakic, P. S., Isseroff, A., Schwartz, M. L., & Bugbee, N. M. (1983). The neurobiology of cognitive development. In P. H. Mussen (Ed.), *Handbook of child psychology* (4th ed., Vol. 2). New York: Wiley.

Goldsmith, H. H. (1988, August). *Does early temperament predict late development?* Paper presented at the meeting of the American Psychological Association, Atlanta.

Goldsmith, H. H., & Gottesman, I. I. (1981). Origins of variation in behavioral style: A longitudinal study of temperament in young twins. *Child Development, 52,* 91–103.

Goldsmith, H. H., Rothbart, M. K., Crowley, J. M., Harmon-Losova, S. G., & Bowden, L. M. (1991, April). *Behavioral assessment of early temperament in the laboratory.* Paper presented at the Society for Research in Child Development meeting, Seattle.

Goodchilds, J. D., & Zellman, G. L. (1984). Sexual signalling and sexual aggression in adolescent relationship. In N. M. Malamuth & E. D. Donnerstein (Eds.), *Pornography and sexual aggression.* New York: Academic Press.

Goodman, R. A., Mercy, J. A., Loya, F., Rosenberg, M. L., Smith, J. C., Allen, N. H., Vargas, L., & Kolts, R. (1986). Alcohol use and interpersonal violence: Alcohol detected in homicide victims. *American Journal of Public Health, 76,* 144–149.

Goodman, S. (1979). *You and your child: From birth to adolescence.* Chicago: Rand McNally.

Gordon, D. (1991, April). *Supportive policies for children of color: Strategies for the year 2000 and beyond.* Keynote address at the SRCD pre-conference on ethnicity and diversity, Seattle.

Gordon, S., & Gilgun, J. F. (1987). Adolescent sexuality. In V. B. Van Hasselt & M. Hersen (Eds.), *Handbook of adolescent psychology.* New York: Pergamon.

Gorman, K., & Pollitt, E. (1991, April). *The effects of early supplementary feeding on cognitive outcomes in adolescence in rural Guatemala.* Paper presented at the Society for Research in Child Development meeting, Seattle.

Goswami, U., & Bryant, P. (1990). *Phonological skills and learning to read.* Hillsdale, NJ: Erlbaum.

Gotowiec, A., & Ames, E. W. (1989, April). *Crying and behavioral state organization in six- to eight-week-old infants.* Paper presented at the Society for Research in Child Development meeting, Kansas City.

Gottfried, A. E. (1990). Academic intrinsic motivation on young elementary school children. *Journal of Educational Psychology, 82,* 525–538.

Gottfried, A. E., & Gottfried, A. W. (1989, April). *Home environment and children's academic intrinsic motivation: A longitudinal study.* Paper presented at the Society for Child Development meeting, Kansas City.

Gottfried, A. E., Gottfried, A. W., & Bathurst, K. (1988). Maternal employment, family environment, and children's development: Infancy through the school years. In A. E. Gottfried & A. W. Gottfried (Eds.), *Maternal employment and children's development: Longitudinal research.* New York: Plenum.

Gottfried, A. W., & Bathurst, K. (1989, April). *Infant predictors of IQ and achievement: A comparative analysis.* Paper presented at the Society for Research in Child Development meeting, Kansas City.

Gottlieb, D. (1966). Teaching and students: The views of Negro and white teachers. *Sociology of Education, 37,* 345–353.

Gottlieb, G. (1991a). Epigenetic systems view of human development. *Developmental Psychology, 27,* 33–34.

Gottlieb, G. (1991b). Experiential canalization of behavioral development theory. *Developmental Psychology, 27,* 4–13.

Gottman, J. M., & Parker, J. G. (Eds.). (1987). *Conversations of friends.* New York: Cambridge University Press.

Graham, S. (1986, August). *Can attribution theory tell us something about motivation in blacks?* Paper presented at the meeting of the American Psychological Association, Washington, DC.

Graham, S. (1987, August). *Developing relations between attributions, affect, and intended social behavior.* Paper presented at the meeting of the American Psychological Association, New York.

Graham, S. (1990). Motivation in Afro-Americans. In G. L. Berry & J. K. Asamen (Eds.), *Black students: Psychosocial issues and academic achievement.* Newbury Park, CA: Sage.

Grant, J. P. (1990). *The state of the world's children.* New York: UNICEF and Oxford University Press.

Greenberger, E., & Steinberg, L. D. (1981). *Project for the study of adolescent work: Final report.* Report prepared for the National Institute of Education, U.S. Department of Education, Washington, DC.

Greene, B. (1988, May). The children's hour. *Esquire,* pp. 47–49.

Grossman, F. K., Pollack, W. S., & Golding, E. (1988). Fathers and children: Predicting the quality and quantity of fathering. *Developmental Psychology, 24,* 82–91.

Grotevant, H. D., & Cooper, C. R. (1985). Patterns of interaction in family relationships and the development of identity exploration in adolescence. *Child Development, 56,* 415–428.

Guidubaldi, J., & Perry, J. D. (1985). Divorce and mental health sequelae for children: A two-year follow-up of a nationwide sample. *Journal of the American Academy of Child Psychiatry, 24,* 531–537.

Guilford, J. P. (1967). *The structure of intellect.* New York: McGraw-Hill.

Gunnar, M. R., Malone, S., & Fisch, R. O. (1987). The psychobiology of stress and coping in the human neonate: Studies of the adrenocortical activity in response to stress in the first week of life. In T. Field, P. McCabe, & N. Scheiderman (Eds.), *Stress and coping*. Hillsdale, NJ: Erlbaum.

Gustafson, G. E., & Green, J. A. (1989). On the importance of fundamental frequency and other acoustic features in cry perception and infant development. *Child Development, 60,* 772–780.

Gustafson, G. E., & Green, J. A. (1991, April). *Infant crying as a moving target*. Paper presented at the Society for Research in Child Development meeting, Seattle.

H

Hahn, A. (1987, December). Reaching out to America's dropouts: What to do? *Phi Delta Kappan,* pp. 256–263.

Haith, M. H. (1991, April). *Setting a path for the '90s: Some goals and challenges in infant sensory and perceptual development*. Paper presented at the Society for Research in Child Development meeting, Seattle.

Hakuta, K., & Garcia, E. E. (1989). Bilingualism and education. *American Psychologist, 44,* 374–379.

Hale, S. (1990). A global developmental trend in cognitive processing speed. *Child Development, 61,* 653–663.

Hall, C. C. I., Evans, B. J., & Selice, S. (Eds.). (1989). *Black females in the United States*. Washington, DC: American Psychological Association.

Hall, W. S. (1989). Reading comprehension. *American Psychologist, 44,* 157–161.

Hallahan, D. P., Kauffman, J. M., Lloyd, J. W., & McKinney, J. D. (1988). Questions about the regular education initiative. *Journal of Learning Disabilities, 21,* 3–5.

Hans, S. (1989, April). *Infant behavioral effects of prenatal exposure to methadone*. Paper presented at the Society for Research in Child Development meeting, Kansas City.

Hanson, R. A., & Mullis, R. L. (1985). Age and gender differences in empathy and moral reasoning among adolescents. *Child Study Journal, 15,* 181–188.

Hardyck, C., & Petrinovich, L. F. (1977). Left-handedness. *Psychological Bulletin, 84,* 385–404.

Hare-Mustin, R., & Marecek, J. (1988). The meaning of difference: Gender theory, postmodernism, and psychology. *American Psychologist, 43,* 455–464.

Harlow, H. F., & Zimmerman, R. R. (1959). Affectional responses in the infant monkey. *Science, 130,* 421–432.

Harnishfeger, K. K., & Cassel, W. S. (1991, April). *Children's memory and knowledge base: When motivation is not an issue*. Paper presented at the Society for Research in Child Development meeting, Seattle.

Harold, R. D., & Eccles, J. S. (1990, March). *Maternal expectations, advice, and provision of opportunities: Their relationships to boys' and girls' occupational aspirations*. Paper presented at the meeting of the Society for Research in Adolescence, Atlanta.

Harris, L. (1987, September 3). The latchkey child phenomena. *Dallas Morning News*.

Harris, P. L. (1975). Development of search and object permanence during infancy. *Psychological Bulletin, 82,* 332–344.

Harris, R. F., Wolf, N. M., & Baer, D. M. (1964). Effects of adult social reinforcement on child behavior. *Young Children, 20,* 8–17.

Harrison, A. O., Wilson, M. N., Pine, C., Chan, S. Q., & Buriel, R. (1990). Family ecologies of ethnic minority children. *Child Development, 61,* 347–362.

Hart, G. H., Ladd, G. W., & Burleson, B. R. (1990). Children's expectations of the outcomes of social strategies: Relations with sociometric status and maternal disciplinary styles. *Child Development, 61,* 127–137.

Hart, P. D. (1987, June). *KidsPac poll on qualities for the next president*. Cambridge, MA: KidsPac.

Hart, S. N. (1991). From property to person status: Historical perspectives on children's rights. *American Psychologist, 46,* 53–59.

Harter, S. (1980). A model of intrinsic motivation in children: Individual differences and developmental change. In W. A. Collins (Ed.), *Minnesota Symposium on Child Psychology* (Vol. 14). Hillsdale, NJ: Erlbaum.

Harter, S. (1982). The Perceived Competence Scale for Children. *Child Development, 53,* 87–97.

Harter, S. (1985). *Self-perception Profile for Children*. Denver: Department of Psychology, University of Denver.

Harter, S. (1986). Processes underlying the construction, maintenance, and enhancement of the self-concept in children. In J. Suls & A. Greenwald (Eds.), *Psychological perspectives on the self* (Vol. 3). Hillsdale, NJ: Erlbaum.

Harter, S. (1988). Developmental processes in the construction of self. In T. D. Yawkey & J. E. Johnson (Eds.), *Integrative processes and socialization: Early to middle childhood*. Hillsdale, NJ: Erlbaum.

Harter, S. (1989). *Self-perception Profile for Adolescents*. Denver: Department of Psychology, University of Denver.

Harter, S. (1990a). Processes underlying adolescent self-concept formation. In R. Montemayor, G. R. Adams, & T. P. Gullotta (Eds.), *From childhood to adolescence: A transitional period?* Newbury Park, CA: Sage.

Harter, S. (1990b). Self and identity development. In S. S. Feldman & G. R. Elliott (Eds.), *At the threshold: The developing adolescent*. Cambridge, MA: Harvard University Press.

Harter, S., & Pike, R. (1984). The pictorial scale of perceived competence and social acceptance for young children. *Child Development, 55,* 1969–1982.

Harter, S., Alexander, P. C., & Neimeyer, R. A. (1988). Long-term effects of incestuous child abuse in college women: Social adjustment, social cognition, and family characteristics. *Journal of Consulting and Clinical Psychology, 56,* 5–8.

Hartshorne, H., & May, M. S. (1928–1930). *Moral studies in the nature of character: Studies in deceit* (Vol. 1); *Studies in self-control* (Vol. 2); *Studies in the organization of character* (Vol. 3). New York: Macmillan.

Hartup, W. W. (1976). Peer interaction and the development of the individual child. In E. Schopler & R. J. Reichler (Eds.), *Psychopathology and child development*. New York: Plenum.

Hartup, W. W. (1983). The peer system. In P. H. Mussen (Ed.), *Handbook of child psychology* (4th ed., Vol. 4). New York: Wiley.

Hartup, W. W. (1989). Social relationships and their developmental significance. *American Psychologist, 44,* 120–126.

Harvard Medical School Newsletter (1981, April). Cambridge, MA: Harvard Medical School.

Haskins, R. (1989). Beyond metaphor: The efficacy of early childhood education. *American Psychologist, 44,* 274–282.

Haugard, J. J., & Emery, R. E. (in press). Methodological issues in child sex abuse research. *Child Abuse and Neglect*.

Hauser, S. T. (1991, April). *Antecedents of young adult ego development: The contributions of adolescent and parent ego development*. Paper presented at the Society for Research in Child Development meeting, Seattle.

Hauser, S. T., & Bowlds, M. K. (1990). Stress, coping, and adaptation. In S. S. Feldman & G. R. Elliott (Eds.), *At the threshold: The developing adolescent.* Cambridge, MA: Harvard University Press.

Hauser, S. T., Powers, S. I., Noam, G. G., Jacobson, A. M., Weisse, B., & Follansbee, D. J. (1984). Familial contexts of adolescent ego development. *Child Development, 55*, 195–213.

Havighurst, R. J. (1987). Adolescent culture and subculture. In V. B. Van Hasselt & M. Hersen (Eds.), *Handbook of adolescent psychology.* New York: Pergamon.

Hawkins, D., & Lam, T. (1986). Teacher practices, social development and delinquency. In J. Burchard & S. Burchard (Eds.), *Prevention of delinquent behavior.* Newbury Park, CA: Sage.

Hawkins, D., & Lishner, D. (1987). School and delinquency. In E. Johnson (Ed.), *Handbook on crime and delinquency prevention.* Westport, CT: Greenwood.

Hawkins, J. A., & Berndt, T. J. (1985, April). *Adjustment following the transition to junior high school.* Paper presented at the Society for Research in Child Development meeting, Toronto.

Hay, D. F. (1985, April). *The search for general principles in social life: Some lessons from young peers.* Paper presented at the Society for Research in Child Development meeting, Toronto.

Hayden-Thomson, L., Rubin, K. M., & Hymel, S. (1987). Sex preferences in sociometric choices. *Developmental Psychology, 23*, 558–562.

Haywood, H. C., & Brooks, P. (1991). Theory development and curriculum development in cognitive education. In M. Schwebel, C. A. Maher, & N. S. Fagley (Eds.), *Promoting cognitive growth over the life span.* Hillsdale, NJ: Erlbaum.

Hazan, C., & Shaver, P. (1987). Romantic love conceptualized as an attachment process. *Journal of Personality and Social Psychology, 51*, 511–524.

Hazen, N., Bohman, T., Burton, H., DeSantis, R., Matula, K., & Kemple, K. (1991, April). *From family to peer: Family influences on peer relations from early childhood through adolescence.* Paper presented at the Society for Research in Child Development meeting, Seattle.

Heath, S. B. (1983). *Ways with words.* Cambridge, England: Cambridge University Press.

Heath, S. B. (1989). Oral and literate traditions among Black Americans living in poverty. *American Psychologist, 44*, 367–373.

Heath, S. B. (in press). The children of Trackton's children: Spoken and written language in social change. In J. Stigler, G. Herdt, & R. A. Shweder (Eds.), *Cultural psychology: The Chicago symposia.* New York: Cambridge University Press.

Hedges, L. V., & Stock, W. (1983, Spring). The effects of class size: An examination of rival hypotheses. *American Educational Research Journal*, 63–85.

Heider, F. (1958). *The psychology of interpersonal relations.* New York: Wiley.

Hein, K. (1990). AIDS in adolescence. *Journal of Adolescent Health Care, 10*, 10–35.

Heinicke, C. M., Beckwith, L., & Thompson, A. (1988). Early intervention in the family system: A framework and review. *Infant Mental Health Journal, 9*, 2.

Heller, W. (1990, May/June). Of one mind: Second thoughts about the brain's dual nature. *The Sciences*, 38–44.

Hellige, J. B. (1990). Hemispheric asymmetry. *Annual Review of Psychology, 41*. Palo Alto, CA: Annual Reviews.

Helson, R., Elliot, T., & Leigh, J. (1989). Adolescent antecedents of women's work patterns. In D. Stern & D. Eichorn (Eds.), *Adolescence and work.* Hillsdale, NJ: Erlbaum.

Henderson, V. L., & Dweck, C. S. (1990). Motivation and achievement. In S. S. Feldman & G. R. Elliott (Eds.), *At the threshold: The developing adolescent.* Cambridge, MA: Harvard University Press.

Hendry, J. (1986). *Becoming Japanese: The world of the preschool child.* Honolulu: University of Hawaii Press.

Henker, B., & Whalen, C. K. (1989). Hyperactivity and attention deficits. *American Psychologist, 44*, 216–223.

Herdt, G. H. (1988, August). *Coming out processes as an anthropological rite of passage.* Paper presented at the meeting of the American Psychological Association, Atlanta.

Hess, L., Lonky, E., & Roodin, P. A. (1985, April). *The relationship of moral reasoning and ego strength to cheating behavior.* Paper presented at the Society for Research in Child Development meeting, Toronto.

Hetherington, E. M. (1989). Coping with family transitions: Winners, losers, and survivors. *Child Development, 60*, 1–14.

Hetherington, E. M. (1991). The role of individual differences and family relationships in coping with divorce and remarriage. In P. A. Cowan & E. M. Hetherington (Eds.), *Family transitions.* Hillsdale, NJ: Erlbaum.

Hetherington, E. M., & Baltes, P. B. (1989). Child psychology and life-span development. In E. M. Hetherington, R. M. Lerner, & M. Perlmutter (Eds.), *Child development in a life-span perspective.* Hillsdale, NJ: Erlbaum.

Hetherington, E. M., & Clingempeel, W. G. (in press). Coping with marital transitions: A family systems perspective. *Monographs of the Society for Research in Child Development.*

Hetherington, E. M., Cox, M., & Cox, R. (1979). Play and social interaction in children following divorce. *Journal of Social Issues, 35*, 26–49.

Hetherington, E. M., Cox, M., & Cox, R. (1982). Effects of divorce on children and parents. In M. E. Lamb (Ed.), *Nontraditional families.* Hillsdale, NJ: Erlbaum.

Hetherington, E. M., Hagan, M. S., & Anderson, E. R. (1989). Family transitions: A child's perspective. *American Psychologist, 44*, 303–312.

Hiebert, J., & LeFevre, P. (Eds.). (1987). *Conceptual and procedural knowledge: The case of mathematics.* Hillsdale, NJ: Erlbaum.

Hiebert, J., & Wearne, D. (1988). Instruction and cognitive change in mathematics. *Educational Psychologist, 23*, 105–118.

Higgins, A. (1991). Lawrence Kohlberg: The vocation of an educator, part II. In W. M. Kurtines & J. Gewirtz (Eds.), *Moral behavior and development* (Vol. 1). Hillsdale, NJ: Erlbaum.

Hightower, E. (1990). Adolescent interpersonal and familial precursors of positive mental health at midlife. *Journal of Youth and Adolescence, 19*, 257–275.

Hill, C. R., & Stafford, F. P. (1980). Parental care of children: Time diary estimate of quantity, predictability, and variety. *Journal of Human Resources, 15*, 219–239.

Hill, J. P. (1980). The early adolescent and the family. In M. Johnson (Ed.), *The 79th yearbook of the National Society for the Study of Education.* Chicago: University of Chicago Press.

Hill, J. P. (1983, April). *Early adolescence: A research agenda.* Paper presented at the biennial meeting of the Society for Research in Child Development, Detroit.

Hill, J. P., & Holmbeck, G. N. (1986). Attachment and autonomy during adolescence. In *Annals of child development.* Greenwich, CT: JAI.

Hill, J. P., Holmbeck, G. N., Marlow, L., Green, T. M., & Lynch, M. E. (1985). Pubertal status and parent-child relations in families of seventh-grade boys. *Journal of Early Adolescence, 5*, 31–44.

Hinde, R. A., & Gorebel, J. (1989). The problem of aggression. In J. Gorebel & R. A. Hinde (Eds.), *Aggression and war: Their biological bases.* New York: Cambridge.

Hinde, R. A. (1983). Ethology and child development. In P. H. Mussen (Ed.), *Handbook of child psychology* (4th ed., Vol. 2). New York: Wiley.

Hinde, R. A (1989a, April). *Differential treatment of particular characteristics in boys and girls.* Paper presented at the Society for Research in Child Development meeting, Kansas City.

Hinde, R. A. (1989b). Ethological and relationship approaches. In R. Vasta (Ed.), *Six theories of child development: Revised formulations and current issues.* Greenwich, CT: JAI.

Hines, M. (1982). Prenatal gonadal hormones and sex differences in human behavior. *Psychological Bulletin, 92,* 56–80.

Hirsch, B. J., & Rapkin, B. D. (1987). The transition to junior high school: A longitudinal study of self-esteem, psychological symptomatology, school life, and social support. *Child Development, 58,* 1235–1243.

Hirsch, B. J. (1989, April). *School transitions and psychological well-being in adolescence: Comparative longitudinal analyses.* Paper presented at the Society for Research in Child Development meeting, Kansas City.

Hirsch, E. D. (1987). *Cultural literacy: What every American needs to know.* Boston: Houghton Mifflin.

Hirsch-Pasek, K., Hyson, M., Rescorla, L., & Cone, J. (1989, April). *Hurrying children: How does it affect their academic, social, creative, and emotional development?* Paper presented at the Society for Research in Child Development meeting, Kansas City.

Ho, D. Y. F. (1987). Fatherhood in Chinese culture. In M. E. Lamb (Ed.), *The father's role: Cross-cultural perspectives.* Hillsdale, NJ: Erlbaum.

Hobbs, N. (Ed.). (1975). *Issues in the classification of children* (Vol. 1). San Francisco: Jossey-Bass.

Hoff-Ginsberg, E. (1991, April). *Why and how some mothers talk more to their children than other mothers.* Paper presented at the Society for Research in Child Development meeting, Seattle.

Hofferth, S. L. (1990). Trends in adolescent sexual activity, contraception, and pregnancy in the United States. In J. Bancroft & J. M. Reinisch (Eds.), *Adolescence and puberty.* New York: Oxford University Press.

Hoffereth, S. L., & Brayfield, A. (1991, April). *Child care in the United States: 1990.* Paper presented at the Society for Research in Child Development meeting, Seattle.

Hofferth, S. L., & Hayes, C. D. (Eds.). (1987). *Risking the future: Adolescent sexuality, pregnancy, and childbearing* (Vol. 2). Washington, DC: National Academy Press.

Hoffman, L. (1991, April). Discussant, *Current research on parents' work and children's behavior.* Symposium at the Society for Research in Child Development meeting, Seattle.

Hoffman, L. W. (1979). Maternal employment: 1979. *American Psychologist, 34,* 859–865.

Hoffman, L. W. (1989). Effects of maternal employment in two-parent families. *American Psychologist, 44,* 283–293.

Hoffman, M. L. (1970). Moral development. In P. H. Mussen (Ed.), *Manual of child psychology* (3rd ed., Vol. 2). New York: Wiley.

Hoffman, M. L. (1983). Empathy, guilt, and social cognition. In W. F. Overton (Ed.), *The relationship between social and cognitive development.* Hillsdale, NJ: Erlbaum.

Hoffman, M. L. (1988). Moral development. In M. H. Bornstein & M. E. Lamb (Eds.), *Developmental psychology: An advanced textbook* (2nd ed.). Hillsdale, NJ: Erlbaum.

Hofstede, G. (1980). *Culture's consequences: International differences in work-related values.* Newbury Park, CA: Sage.

Holmes, D. L., Reich, J. N., & Gyurke, J. S. (1989). The development of high-risk infants in low-risk families. In F. J. Morrison, C. Lord, & D. P. Keating (Eds.), *Psychological development in infancy.* San Diego: Academic Press.

Holtzmann, W. H. (1982). Cross-cultural comparisons of personality development in Mexico and the United States. In D. A. Wagner & H. W. Stevenson (Eds.), *Cultural perspectives on child development.* New York: W. H. Freeman.

Holzman, M. (1983). *The language of children: Development in home and school.* Englewood Cliffs, NJ: Prentice-Hall.

Honzik, M. P., MacFarlane, J. W., & Allen, L. (1948). The stability of mental test performance between two and eighteen years. *Journal of Experimental Education, 17,* 309–324.

Hood, K. E. (1991). Menstrual cycle. In R. M. Lerner, A. C. Petersen, & J. Brooks-Gunn (Eds.), *Encyclopedia of adolescence.* New York: Garland.

Hopwood, N. J., Kelsch, R. P., Hale, P. M., Mendes, T. M., Foster, C. M., & Beitens, I. Z. (1990). The onset of puberty: Biological and environmental factors. In J. Bancroft & J. M. Reinisch (Eds.), *Adolescence and puberty.* New York: Oxford University Press.

Horne, M. D. (1988). Handicapped, disabled, or exceptional: Terminological issues. *Psychology in the Schools, 25,* 419–421.

Horney, K. (1967). *Feminine psychology.* New York: W. W. Norton.

Horowitz, F. D., & O'Brien, M. (1989). In the interest of the nation: A reflective essay on the state of knowledge and the challenges before us. *American Psychologist, 44,* 441–445.

Howes, C. (1985, April). *Predicting preschool sociometric status from toddler peer interaction.* Paper presented at the Society for Research in Child Development meeting, Toronto.

Howes, C. (1988, April). *Can the age of entry and the quality of infant child care predict behaviors in kindergarten?* Paper presented at the International Conference on Infant Studies, Washington, DC.

Howes, C., Unger, O., & Seidner, L. B. (1989). Social pretend play in toddlers: Parallels with social play and solitary pretend. *Child Development, 60,* 77–84.

Huang, L. N., & Gibbs, J. T. (1989). Future directions: Implications for research, training, and practice. In J. T. Gibbs & L. N. Huang (Eds.), *Children of color.* San Francisco: Jossey-Bass.

Huang, L. N., & Ying, Y. (1989). Japanese children and adolescents. In J. T. Gibbs & L. N. Huang (Eds.), *Children of color.* San Francisco: Jossey-Bass.

Hudson, J. A., & Fivush, R. (1991, April). *Planning in the preschool years: The emergence of plans from general event knowledge.* Paper presented at the Society for Research in Child Development meeting, Seattle.

Hudson, L. M., Forman, E. R., & Brion-Meisels, S. (1982). Role-taking as a predictor of prosocial behavior in cross-age tutors. *Child Development, 53,* 1320–1329.

Huebner, A. M., Garrod, A. C., & Snarey, J. (1990, March). *Moral development in Tibetan Buddhist monks: A cross-cultural study of adolescents and young adults in Nepal.* Paper presented at the meeting of the Society for Research in Adolescence, Atlanta.

Huesmann, L. R. (1986). Psychological processes promoting the relation between exposure to media violence and aggressive behavior by the viewer. *Journal of Social Issues, 42,* 125–139.

Huesmann, L. R., Eron, L. D., Klein, R., Brice, P., & Fischer, P. (1983). Mitigating the imitation of aggressive behaviors by changing children's attitudes about media violence. *Journal of Personality and Social Psychology, 44,* 899–910.

Hui, C. H., & Villareal, M. J. (1989). Individualism-collectivism and psychological needs. *Journal of Cross-Cultural Psychology, 20,* 310–323.

Hunt, E. (1978). Mechanics of verbal ability. *Psychological Review, 85,* 109–130.

Hunt, J. V., & Cooper, B. A. (1989). Determining the risk for high-risk preterm infants. In M. Bornstein & N. A. Krasnegor (Eds.), *Stability and continuity in mental development.* Hillsdale, NJ: Erlbaum.

Hunt, M. (1974). *Sexual behavior in the 1970s.* Chicago: Playboy Press.

Huston, A. C. (1983). Sex-typing. In P. H. Mussen (Ed.), *Handbook of child psychology* (4th ed., Vol. 4). New York: Wiley.

Huston, A. C., & Alvarez, M. (1990). The socialization context of gender role development in early adolescence. In R. Montemayor, G. R. Adams, & T. P. Gulotta (Eds.), *From childhood to adolescence: A transitional period?* Newbury Park, CA: Sage.

Huston, A. C., Seigle, J., & Bremer, M. (1983, April). *Family environment and television use by preschool children.* Paper presented at the Society for Research in Child Development meeting, Detroit.

Huston, A. C., Watkins, B. A., & Kunkel, D. (1989). Public policy and children's television. *American Psychologist, 44,* 424–433.

Huston-Stein, A., & Higgens-Trenk, A. (1978). Development of females from childhood through adulthood: Career and feminine role orientations. In P. Baltes (Ed.), *Life-span development and behavior* (Vol. 1). New York: Academic Press.

Hutchings, D. E., & Fifer, W. P. (1986). Neurobehavioral effects in human and animal offspring following prenatal exposure to methadone. In E. P. Riley & C. V. Vorhees (Eds.), *Handbook of behavioral teratology.* New York: Plenum.

Hutchings, N. (Ed.). (1988). *The violent family.* New York: Human Sciences Press.

Hyde, J. S. (1981). How large are cognitive gender differences? A meta-analysis using w^2 and *d. American Psychologist, 36,* 892–901.

Hyde, J. S. (1984). Children's understanding of sexist language. *Developmental Psychology, 20,* 697–706.

Hyde, J. S. (1985). *Half the human experience* (3rd ed.). Lexington, MA: D. C. Heath.

Hyde, J. S. (in press). Meta-analysis and the psychology of women. In F. L. Denmark & M. A. Paludi (Eds.), *Handbook on the psychology of women.* Dubuque, IA: Wm. C. Brown.

Hynd, G. W., & Obrzut, J. E. (1986). Exceptionality: Historical antecedents and present positions. In R. T. Brown & C. R. Reynolds (Eds.), *Psychological perspectives on childhood exceptionality: A handbook.* New York: Wiley.

I

Inoff-Germain, G., Arnold, G. S., Nottlemann, E. D., Susman, E. J., Cutler, G. B., & Chrousos, G. P. (1988). Relations between hormone levels and observational measures of aggressive behavior of young adolescents in family interactions. *Developmental Psychology, 24,* 129–139.

Irvin, F. S. (1988, August). *Clinical perspectives on resilience among gay and lesbian youth.* Paper presented at the annual meeting of the American Psychological Association, Atlanta.

Izard, C. E. (1982). *Measuring emotions in infants and young children.* New York: Cambridge University Press.

Izard, C. E., & Malatesta, C. Z. (1987). Differential emotions theory of early emotional development. In J. D. Osofsky (Ed.), *Handbook of infant development.* New York: Wiley.

J

Jacklin, C. N. (1989). Female and male: Issues of gender. *American Psychologist, 44,* 127–133.

Jackson, J. S., McCullough, W. R., Gurin, G., & Broman, C. L. (1991). Race identity. In J. S. Jackson (Ed.), *Life in Black America.* Newbury Park, CA: Sage.

Jacobson, J. L., Jacobson, S. W., Fein, G. G., Schwartz, P. M., & Dowler, J. K. (1984). Prenatal exposure to an environmental toxin: A test of the multiple effects model. *Developmental Psychology, 20,* 523–532.

Jagacinski, C. M., & Nicholls, J. G. (1990). Reducing effort to protect perceived ability: "They'd do it but I wouldn't." *Journal of Educational Psychology, 82,* 15–21.

James, W. (1890). *The principles of psychology.* New York: Dover.

Janos, P. M., & Robinson, N. M. (1985). Psychosocial development in intellectually gifted children. In F. D. Horowitz & M. O'Brien (Eds.), *The gifted and the talented.* Washington, DC: American Psychological Association.

Javernik, E. (1988, January). Johnny's not jumping: Can we help obese children? *Young Children,* 18–23.

Jeans, P. C., Smith, M. B., & Stearns, G. (1955). Incidence of prematurity in relation to maternal nutrition. *Journal of the American Dietary Association, 31,* 576–581.

Jencks, C. S., Smith, M., Acland, H., Bane, M. J., Cohen, D., Gintis, H., Heyns, B., & Michelson, S. (1972). *Inequality: A reassessment of the effects of family and schooling in America.* New York: Basic.

Jensen, A. R. (1969). How much can we boost IQ and scholastic achievement? *Harvard Educational Review, 39,* 1–123.

Jensen, L. C., & Knight, R. S. (1981). *Moral education: Historical perspectives.* Washington, DC: University Press of America.

Jessor, L., & Jessor, R. (1975). Transition from virginity to nonvirginity among youth: A social-psychological study over time. *Developmental Psychology, 11,* 473–484.

John-Steiner, V. (1985). *Notebooks of the mind: Explorations of thinking.* Albuquerque: University of New Mexico Press.

Johnson, J. E., Christie, J. F., & Yawkey, T. D. (1987). *Play and early childhood development.* Glenview, IL: Scott, Foresman.

Johnston, J., & Ettema, J. S. (1982). *Positive images: Breaking stereotypes with children's television.* Newbury Park, CA: Sage.

Johnston, L. D., O'Malley, P. M., & Bachman, J. G. (1988). *Illicit drug use, smoking, and drinking by America's high school students, college students, and young adults, 1975–1987.* Washington, DC: National Institute of Drug Abuse.

Johnston, L. D., O'Malley, P. M., & Bachman, J. G. (1989, February 24). *Teen drug use continues decline.* News Release, Institute for Social Research, University of Michigan, Ann Arbor.

Johnston, L. D., O'Malley, P. M., & Bachman, J. G. (1990, February 13). *Drug use continues to decline.* News Release, Institute for Social Research, University of Michigan, Ann Arbor.

Jones, B. F., Idol, L., & Brandt, R. S. (1991). Dimensions of thinking. In B. F. Jones & L. Idol (Eds.), *Dimensions of thinking and cognitive instruction.* Hillsdale, NJ: Erlbaum.

Jones, E. R., Forrest, J. D., Goldman, N., Henshaw, S. K., Lincoln, R., Rosoff, J. I., Westoff, C. G., & Wulf, D. (1985). Teenage pregnancy in developed countries: Determinants and policy implications. *Family Planning Perspectives, 17*, 53–63.

Jones, J. M. (1990, August). *Psychological approaches to race: What have they been and what should they be?* Paper presented at the meeting of the American Psychological Association, Boston.

Jones, L. V. (1984). White-Black achievement differences: The narrowing gap. *American Psychologist, 39*, 1207–1213.

Jones, M. C. (1924). A laboratory study of fear: The case of Peter. *Journal of Genetic Psychology, 31*, 308–315.

Jones, M. C. (1965). Psychological correlates of somatic development. *Child Development, 36*, 899–911.

Josselson, R. (1987). *Finding herself.* San Francisco: Jossey-Bass.

Juster, F. T. (1985). A note on recent changes in time use. In F. T. Juster & F. Stafford (Eds.), *Time, goods, and well-being.* Ann Arbor, MI: Institute for Social Research.

Justiz, M. J., & Rendon, L. I. (1989). Hispanic students. In M. L. Upcraft & J. N. Gardner (Eds.), *The freshman experience.* San Francisco: Jossey-Bass.

K

Kagan, J. (1965). Impulsive and reflective children: Significance of conceptual tempo. In J. D. Krumboltz (Ed.), *Learning and the educational process.* Chicago: Rand McNally.

Kagan, J. (1984). *The nature of the child.* New York: Basic.

Kagan, J. (1987a). Perspectives on infancy. In J. D. Osofsky (Ed.), *Handbook on infant development* (2nd ed.). New York: Wiley.

Kagan, J. (1987b, April). *Temperamental bases for reactions to uncertainty.* Paper presented at the Society for Research in Child Development meeting, Baltimore.

Kagan, J. (1988b, August). *The idea of temperament categories.* Paper presented at the meeting of the American Psychological Association, Atlanta.

Kagan, J. (1989). *Unstable ideas: Temperament, cognition, and self.* Cambridge, MA: Harvard University Press.

Kagan, J. (1991). On cognitive development. In M. Schwebel, C. A. Maher, & N. S.

Fagley (Eds.), *Promoting cognitive growth over the life span.* Hillsdale, NJ: Erlbaum.

Kagan, J. (in press). Inhibited and uninhibited types of children. *Child Development.*

Kagan, J., Kearsley, R. B., & Zelazo, P. R. (1978). *Infancy.* Cambridge, MA: Harvard University Press.

Kagan, J., Rosman, B. L., Day, D., Albert, J., & Phillips, W. (1964). Information processing in the child: Significance of analytic and reflective attitudes. *Psychological Monographs* (Whole No. 578).

Kagan, S. L. (1988a, January). Current reforms in early childhood education: Are we addressing the issues? *Young Children, 43*, 27–38.

Kagitcibasi, C. (1988). Diversity of socialization and social change. In P. R. Dasen, J. W. Berry, & N. Sartorious (Eds.), *Health and cross-cultural psychology: Toward applications.* Newbury Park, CA: Sage.

Kagitcibasi, C., & Berry, J. W. (1989). Cross-cultural psychology: Current research and trends. *Annual Review of Psychology, 40.* Palo Alto, CA: Annual Reviews.

Kail, R. (1988). Reply to Stigler, Nusbaum, and Chalip. *Child Development, 59*, 1154–1157.

Kail, R., & Pellegrino, J. W. (1985). *Human intelligence.* New York: W. H. Freeman.

Kamerman, S. B. (1989). Child care, women, work, and the family: An international overview of child care services and related policies. In J. S. Lande, S. Scarr, & N. Gunzenhauser (Eds.), *Caring for children: Challenge to America.* Hillsdale, NJ: Erlbaum.

Kamerman, S B., & Kahn, A. J. (1988). Social policy and children in the United States and Europe. In J. L. Palmer, T. Smeeding, & B.B. Torrey (Eds.), *The vulnerable America's young and old in the industrialized world.* Washington, DC: Urban Institute.

Kandel, D. B. (1974). The role of parents and peers in marijuana use. *Journal of Social Issues, 30*, 107–135.

Kandel, D. B. (1991). Drug use, epidemiology and developmental stages of involvement. In R. M. Lerner, A. C. Petersen, & J. Brooks-Gunn (Eds.), *Encyclopedia of adolescence* (Vol. 1). New York: Garland.

Kantrowitz, B., & Wingert, P. (1989, April 17). How kids learn. *Newsweek*, pp. 4–10.

Kaplan, P. S., Rudy, J. W., & Werner, J. S. (1989). Habituation, sensitization, and infant visual attention. In C. Rovee-

Collier & L. P. Lipsitt (Eds.), *Advances in infancy research.* Norwood, NJ: Ablex.

Karlin, R., & Karlin, A. R. (1987). *Teaching elementary reading.* San Diego: Harcourt Brace Jovanovich.

Karplus, R. (1981). Education and formal operational thought—A modest proposal. In I. Siegel, D. Brodzinsky, & R. Golinkoff (Eds.), *Piagetian theory and research: New directions and applications.* Hillsdale, NJ: Erlbaum.

Katz, L. G. & Chard, S. C. (1989). *Engaging children's minds: The project approach.* Norwood, NJ: Ablex.

Katz, P. A. (1987, August). *Children and social issues.* Paper presented at the meeting of the American Psychological Association, New York.

Kaufman, A. S., & Kaufman, N. L. (1983). *Kaufman assessment battery for children: Interpretive manual.* Circle Pines, MN: American Guidance Series.

Kaufmann, A. S., & Flaitz, J. (1987). Intellectual growth. In V. B. Van Hasselt & M. Hersen (Eds.), *Handbook of adolescent psychology.* New York: Pergamon.

Kearns, D. T. (1988b, April). An education recovery plan for America. *Phi Delta Kappan*, pp. 565–570.

Keating, D. P. (1988a). Byrnes' reformulation of Piaget's formal operations: Is what's left what's right? *Developmental Review, 8*, 376–384.

Keating, D. P. (1990a). Adolescent thinking. In S. S. Feldman & G. R. Elliott (Eds.), *At the threshold: The developing adolescent.* Cambridge, MA: Harvard University Press.

Keating, D. P. (1990b). Structuralism, deconstruction, reconstruction: The limits of reasoning. In W. F. Overton (Ed.), *Reasoning, necessity, and logic: Developmental perspectives.* Hillsdale, NJ: Erlbaum.

Keefe, S. E., & Padilla, A. M. (1987). *Chicano ethnicity.* Albuquerque: University of New Mexico Press.

Keeney, T. J., Cannizzo, S. R., & Flavell, J. H. (1967). Spontaneous and induced verbal rehearsal in a recall task. *Child Development, 38*, 953–966.

Keil, F. C. (1984). Mechanisms in cognitive development and the structure of knowledge. In R. J. Sternberg (Ed.), *Mechanisms of cognitive development.* New York: W. H. Freeman.

Keith, J. G., Nelson, C. S., Schlabach, J. H., & Thompson, C. J. (1990). The relationship between parental employment and three measures of early adolescent responsibility. *Journal of Early Adolescence, 10*, 399–415.

Keith, T. Z., Cool, V. A., Novak, C. G., White, L. J., & Pottebaum, S. M. (1988). Confirmatory factor analysis of the Stanford-Binet fourth edition. *Journal of Educational Psychology, 26,* 253–274.

Keller, A., Ford, L., & Meacham, J. (1978). Dimensions of self-concept in preschool children. *Developmental Psychology, 14,* 483–489.

Kelly, J. A., & de Armas, A. (1989). Social relationships in adolescence: Skill development and training. In J. Worell & F. Danner (Eds.), *The adolescent as decision-maker.* San Diego: Academic Press.

Kennedy, J. H. (1990). Determinants of peer social status: Contributions of physical appearance, reputation, and behavior. *Journal of Youth and Adolescence, 19,* 233–244.

Kennedy, R. E. (1991). Delinquency. In R. M. Lerner, A. C. Petersen, & J. Brooks-Gunn (Eds.), *Encyclopedia of adolescence* (Vol. 1). New York: Garland.

Kenney, A. M. (1987, June). Teen pregnancy: An issue for schools. *Phi Delta Kappan,* pp. 728–736.

Kerr, B. A. (1983). Raising the career aspirations of gifted girls. *Vocational Guidance Quarterly, 32,* 37–43.

Kessen, W., Haith, M. M., & Salapatek, P. (1970). Human infancy. In P. H. Mussen (Ed.), *Manual of child psychology* (3rd ed., Vol. 1). New York: Wiley.

King, N. (1982). School uses of materials traditionally associated with children's play. *Theory and Research in Social Education, 10,* 17–27.

Kinsey, A. C., Pomeroy, W. B., & Martin, E. E. (1948). *Sexual behavior in the human male.* Philadelphia: W. B. Saunders.

Klahr, D. (1989). Information-processing approaches. In R. Vasta (Ed.), *Six theories of child development: Revised formulations and current issues.* Greenwich, CT: JAI.

Klein, K. (1985, April). The research on class size. *Phi Delta Kappan,* pp. 578–580.

Klein, S. S. (1988). Using sex equity research to improve education policies. *Theory into Practice, 27,* 152–160.

Klein, S. S. (in press). Sex equity and gender equity. *Educational Leadership.*

Kliegl, R., Smith, J., & Baltes, P. B. (1989). Testing-the-limits and the study of age differences in cognitive plasticity of a mnemonic skill. *Developmental Psychology, 25,* 247–256.

Klitgaard, R. E., & Hall, G. R. (1975). Are there unusually effective schools? *Journal of Human Resources, 10,* 90–106.

Kobak, R. R., & Sceery, A. (1988). Attachment in late adolescence: Working models, affect regulation, and representations of self and others. *Child Development, 59,* 135–146.

Koff, E., & Riordan, J. (1991). Menarche and body image. In R. M. Lerner, A. C. Petersen, & J. Brooks-Gunn, (Eds.), *Encyclopedia of adolescence.* New York: Garland.

Kohlberg, L. (1958). *The development of modes of moral thinking and choice in the years 10 to 16.* Unpublished doctoral dissertation. University of Chicago.

Kohlberg, L. (1966). A cognitive-developmental analysis of children's sex-role concepts and attitudes. In E. E. Maccoby (Ed.), *The development of sex differences.* Palo Alto, CA: Stanford University Press.

Kohlberg, L. (1969). Stage and sequence: The cognitive-developmental approach to socialization. In D. A. Goslin (Ed.), *Handbook of socialization theory and research.* Chicago: Rand McNally.

Kohlberg, L. (1976). Moral stages and moralization: The cognitive-developmental approach. In T. Lickona (Ed.), *Moral development and behavior.* New York: Holt, Rinehart & Winston.

Kohlberg, L. (1981). *The philosophy of moral development.* New York: Harper & Row.

Kohlberg, L. (1986). A current statement on some theoretical issues. In S. Modgil & C. Modgil (Eds.), *Lawrence Kohlberg.* Philadelphia: Falmer.

Kohlberg, L., & Candee, D. (1979). *Relationships between moral judgment and moral action.* Unpublished manuscript, Harvard University.

Kohn, M. L. (1977). *Class and conformity: A study in values* (2nd ed.). Chicago: University of Chicago Press.

Kopp, C. B. (1983). Risk factors in development. In P. H. Mussen (Ed.), *Handbook of child psychology* (4th ed., Vol. 2). New York: Wiley.

Kopp, C. B. (1987). Developmental risk: Historical reflections. In J. D. Osofsky (Ed.), *Handbook of infant development* (2nd ed.). New York: Wiley.

Kopp, C. B., & Kaler, S. R. (1989). Risk in infancy: Origins and implications. *American Psychologist, 44,* 224–230.

Korner, A. F. (1990). Infant stimulation: Issues of theory and research. In B. M. Lester & E. Z. Tronick (Eds.), *Stimulation and the preterm infant: The limits of plasticity.* Philadelphia: W. B. Saunders.

Kosslyn, S. M., Margolis, J. A., Barrett, A. M., Goldknopf, E. J., & Day, P. F. (1990). Age differences in imagery abilities. *Child Development, 61,* 995–1010.

Kostelnik, M. J., Whiren, A. P., & Stein, L. C. (1988). Living with He-Man: Managing superhero fantasy play. *Young Children, 41,* 3–9.

Krauss, R. A., & Glucksberg, S. (1969). The development of communication: Competence as a function of age. *Child Development, 40,* 255–266.

Kuhn, D. (1991). Education for thinking: What can psychology contribute? In M. Schwebel, C. A. Maher, & N. S. Fagley, (Eds.), *Promoting cognitive growth over the life span.* Hillsdale, NJ: Erlbaum.

Kulik, J. A., Kulik, C. C., & Gangert-Drowns, R. L. (1985). Effectiveness of computer-based education in elementary schools. *Computers in Human Behavior, 1,* 59–74.

Kulin, H. E. (1991). Puberty, hypothalamic-pituitary changes of. In R. M. Lerner, A. C. Petersen, & J. Brooks-Gunn (Eds.), *Encyclopedia of adolescence.* (Vol. 2). New York: Garland.

Kupersmidt, J. B., & Coie, J. D. (1990). Preadolescent peer status, aggression, and school adjustment as predictors of externalizing problems in adolescence. *Child Development, 61,* 1350–1362.

Kupersmidt, J. B., Coie, J. D., & Dodge, K. A. (1990). Predicting disorder from peer social problems. In S. R. Asher & J. D. Coie (Eds.), *Peer rejection in childhood.* New York: Cambridge University Press.

Kurdek, L. A., & Krile, D. (1982). A developmental analysis of the relation between peer acceptance and both interpersonal understanding and perceived social self-competence. *Child Development, 53,* 1485–1491.

Kurtines, W. M., & Gewirtz, J. (Eds.). (in press). *Moral behavior and development: Advances in theory, research, and application.* Hillsdale, NJ: Erlbaum.

Kusche, C. A. (1991, April). *Improving classroom behavior and emotional understanding in special needs children: The effects of the PATHS curriculum.* Paper presented at the Society for Research in Child Development meeting, Seattle.

L

Labouvie-Vief, G. (1982). Dynamic development and mature autonomy: A theoretical prologue. *Human Development, 25,* 161–191.

Labouvie-Vief, G. (1986, August). *Modes of knowing and life-span cognition.* Paper presented at the annual meeting of the American Psychological Association, Washington, DC.

LaFromboise, T. D., & Low, K. G. (1989). American Indian children and adolescents. In J. T. Gibbs & L. N. Huang (Eds.), *Children of color*. San Francisco: Jossey-Bass.

Lamb, M. E. (1977). The development of mother-infant and father-infant attachments in the second year of life. *Developmental Psychology, 13*, 637–648.

Lamb, M. E. (1986). *The father's role: Applied perspectives*. New York: Wiley.

Lamb, M. E., Frodi, A. M., Hwang, C. P., Frodi, M., & Steinberg, J. (1982). Mother- and father-infant interaction involving play and holding in traditional and nontraditional Swedish families. *Developmental Psychology, 18*, 215–221.

Lamb, M. E., Thompson, R. A., Gardner, W. R., Charnov, E. L., & Estes, D. P. (1984). Security of infantile attachment as assessed in the "strange situation": Its study and biological interpretation. *The Behavioral and Brain Sciences, 7*, 121–171.

Lambert, N. M., & Hartsough, C. S. (1984). Contribution of predispositional factors to the diagnosis of hyperactivity. *American Journal of Orthopsychiatry, 54*, 97–109.

Landesman, S. L. (in press). Stage (and re-staging) the trio of service, evaluation, and research. *American Journal of Mental Retardation*.

Landesman, S. L., & Ramey, C. T. (1989). Developmental psychology and mental retardation: Integrating scientific principles with treatment practices. *American Psychologist, 44*, 409–415.

Landesman-Dwyer, S., & Sackett, G. P. (1983, April). *Prenatal nicotine exposure and sleep-wake patterns in infancy*. Paper presented at the Society for Research in Child Development meeting, Detroit.

Lane, H. (1976). *The wild boy of Aveyron*. Cambridge, MA: Harvard University Press.

Langer, J. (1969). *Theories of development*. New York: Holt, Rinehart & Winston.

Lapsley, D. K. (1989a). The adolescent egocentrism theory and the "new look" at the imaginary audience and personal fable. In R. M. Lerner, A. C. Petersen, & J. Brooks-Gunn (Eds.), *The encyclopedia of adolescence*. New York: Garland.

Lapsley, D. K. (1989b). Continuity and discontinuity in adolescent social cognitive development. In R. Montemayor, G. Adams, & T. Gullota (Eds.), *Advances in adolescence research* (Vol. 2). Orlando, FL: Academic Press.

Lapsley, D. K., & Murphy, M. N. (1985). Another look at the theoretical assumptions of adolescent egocentrism. *Developmental Review, 5*, 201–217.

Lapsley, D. K., & Power, F. C. (Eds.). (1988). *Self, ego, and identity*. New York: Springer-Verlag.

Lapsley, D. K., & Quintana, S. M. (1985). Recent approaches in children's elementary moral and social education. *Elementary School Guidance and Counseling Journal, 19*, 246–251.

Laval, R. A., Gomez, E. A., & Ruiz, P. (1989). A language minority: Hispanic Americans and mental health care. In D. R. Atkinson, G. Morten, & D. W. Sue (Eds.), *Counseling American minorities*. Dubuque, IA: Wm. C. Brown.

Lave, J. (1977). Tailor-made experiments and evaluating the intellectual consequences of apprenticeship training. *The Quarterly Newsletter of the Institute for Comparative Human Development, 1*, 1–3.

LaVoie, J. (1976). Ego identity formation in middle adolescence. *Journal of Youth and Adolescence, 5*, 371–385.

Lawton, T. A., Turner, J. C., & Paris, S. G. (1991, April). *Comprehension and metacognition of beginning readers*. Paper presented at the Society for Research in Child Development meeting, Seattle.

Lazar, I., Darlington, R., & collaborators. (1982). Lasting effects of early education: A report from the consortium for longitudinal studies. *Monographs of the Society for Research in Child Development, 47*.

Leboyer, F. (1975). *Birth without violence*. New York: Knopf.

Lee, E. (1988). Cultural factors in working with Southeast Asian refugee adolescents. *Journal of Adolescence, 2*, 167–179.

Lee, V. E., Brooks-Gunn, J., & Schnur, E. (1988). Does Head Start work? A 1-year follow-up comparison of disadvantaged children attending Head Start, no preschool, and other preschool programs. *Developmental Psychology, 24*, 210–222.

Lehrer, R., & Yussen, S. R. (1988, April). *Conceptions of computer and human intelligence*. Paper presented at the meeting of the American Educational Research Association, New Orleans.

Leiffer, A. D. (1973). *Television and the development of social behavior*. Paper presented at the meeting of the International Society for the Study of Behavioral Development, Ann Arbor.

Leiffer, A. D., Gordon, N. J., & Graves, S. B. (1974). Children's television: More than entertainment. *Harvard Educational Review, 44*, 213–245.

Leinbach, J. D., & Hurt, B. (1989, April). *Bears are for boys: "Metaphorical"*

associations in the young child's gender schema. Paper presented at the Society for Research in Child Development meeting, Kansas City.

Leitenberg, H. (1986). Primary prevention in delinquency. In J. Burchard & S. Burchard (Eds.), *Prevention of delinquent behavior*. Newbury Park, CA: Sage.

LeMare, L. J., & Rubin, K. H. (1987). Perspective taking and peer interaction: Structural and developmental analyses. *Child Development, 58*, 306–315.

Lenneberg, E. H., Rebelsky, F. G., & Nichols, I. A. (1965). The vocalization of infants born to deaf and hearing parents. *Human Development, 8*, 23–37.

Leon, G. R. (1991). Bulimia nervosa. In R. M. Lerner, A. C. Peterson, & J. Brooks-Gunn (Eds.), *Encyclopedia of adolescence* (Vol. 1). New York: Garland.

Lepper, M., Greene, D., & Nisbett, R. R. (1973). Undermining children's intrinsic interest with extrinsic rewards. *Journal of Personality and Social Psychology, 28*, 129–137.

Lepper, M. R. (1985). Microcomputers in education: Motivational and social issues. *American Psychologist, 40*, 1–18.

Lepper, M. R., & Gurtner, J. (1989). Children and computers: Approaching the twenty-first century. *American Psychologist, 44*, 170–178.

Lerner, H. G. (1989). *The dance of intimacy*. New York: Harper & Row.

Lerner, J. W. (1989). Educational interventions in learning disabilities. *Journal of the American Academy of Child and Adolescent Psychiatry, 28*, 326–331.

Lerner, R. M. (1991). Changing organism-context relations as the basic process of development: A developmental-contextual perspective. *Developmental Psychology, 27*, 27–32.

Lerner, R. M., & Karabenick, S. A. (1974). Physical attractiveness, body attitudes, and self-concept in late adolescence. *Journal of Youth and Adolescence, 3*, 307–316.

Lerner, R. M., Petersen, A. C., & Brooks-Gunn, J. (Eds.). (1991). *Encyclopedia of adolescence*. New York: Garland.

Lesser, G., Fifer, G., & Clark, D. (1965). Mental abilities of children from different social classes and cultural groups. *Monographs of the Society for Research in Child Development, 30* (4, Whole No. 102).

Lester, B. M. (1991, April). *Neurobehavioral syndromes in cocaine-exposed newborn infants.* Paper presented at the Society for Research in Child Development meeting, Seattle.

Lester, B. M., & Boukydis, C. F. Z. (1991, April). *Infant cry characteristics and maternal cry perception: Is a 'good fit' for good development?* Paper presented at the Society for Research in Child Development meeting, Seattle.

Lester, B. M., & Tronick, E. Z. (1990a). Introduction. In B. M. Lester & E. Z. Tronick (Eds.), *Stimulation and the preterm infant: The limits of plasticity.* Philadelphia: W. B. Saunders.

Lester, B. M., & Tronick, E. Z. (1990b). Preface. In B. M. Lester & E. Z. Tronick (Eds.), *Stimulation and the preterm infant: The limits of plasticity.* Philadelphia: W. B. Saunders.

Lester, B. M., Boukydis, C. F., McGrath, M., Censullo, M., Zahr, L., & Brazelton, T. B. (1990). Behavioral and psychophysiologic assessment of the newborn. In B. M. Lester & E. Z. Tronick (Eds.), *Stimulation and the preterm infant: The limits of plasticity.* Philadelphia: W. B. Saunders.

Levin, J. (1980). *The mnemonic '80s: Keywords in the classroom.* Theoretical paper No. 86. Wisconsin Research and Development Center for Individualized Schooling, Madison.

Levy, A. B., Dixon, K. N., & Stern, S. L. (1989). How are depression and bulimia related? *American Journal of Psychiatry, 146,* 162–169.

Levy, G. D. (1991, April). *Effects of gender constancy, figure's sex and size on preschoolers' gender constancy: Sometimes big girls do cry.* Paper presented at the Society for Research in Child Development meeting, Seattle.

Levy, G. D., & Carter, D. B. (1989). Gender schema, gender constancy, and gender-role knowledge: The roles of cognitive factors in preschoolers' gender-role stereotype attributions. *Developmental Psychology, 25,* 444–449.

Lewin, T. (1987, August 16). The new debate over life, death. *Dallas Morning News.*

Lewis, M. (1987). Early sex-role behavior and school age adjustment. In J. M. Reinisch, L. A. Rosenblum, & S. A. Sanders (Eds.), *Masculinity/femininity: Basic perspectives.* New York: Oxford University Press.

Lewis, M. (1989). What do we mean when we say emotional development? In L. Cirillo, B. Kaplan, & S. Wapner (Eds.), *Emotions in ideal human development.* Hillsdale, NJ: Erlbaum.

Lewis, M., & Brooks-Gunn, J. (1979). *Social cognition and the acquisition of the self.* New York: Plenum.

Lewis, M., Sullivan, M. W., Sanger, C., & Weiss, M. (1989). Self-development and self-conscious emotions. *Child Development, 60,* 146–156.

Lewis, V. G., Money, J., & Bobrow, N. A. (1977). Idiopathic pubertal delay beyond the age of fifteen: Psychological study of twelve boys. *Adolescence, 12,* 1–11.

Lewkowicz, D. J. (1988). Sensory dominance in infants: 1. Six-month-old infants' response to auditory-visual compounds. *Developmental Psychology, 24,* 155–171.

Liben, L. S., & Signorella, M. L. (Eds.). (1987). *Children's gender schemata: New directions in child development.* San Francisco: Jossey-Bass.

Liberg, C. (1990). "I am not guessing!": Children's achievement in early literacy. In G. Conti-Ramsden & C. E. Snow (Eds.), *Children's language* (Vol. 7). Hillsdale, NJ: Erlbaum.

Liebert, R. M., & Spratkin, J. N. (1988). *The early window: Effects of television on children and youth* (3rd ed.). Elmsford, NY: Pergamon.

Lifshitz, F., Pugliese, M. T., Moses, N., & Weyman-Daum, M. (1987). Parental health beliefs as a cause of non-organic failure to thrive. *Pediatrics, 80,* 175–182.

Linden, M. J., Whimbey, A. (1990). *Why Johnny can't write: How to improve writing skills.* Hillsdale, NJ: Erlbaum.

Linn, M. C., & Hyde, J. S. (1991). Cognitive and psychosocial gender differences, trends in. In R. M. Lerner, A. C. Petersen, & J. Brooks-Gunn (Eds.), *Encyclopedia of adolescence* (Vol. 1). New York: Garland.

Linn, M. C., & Peterson, A. C. (1986). A meta-analysis of gender differences in spatial ability: Implications for mathematics and science achievement. In J. S. Hyde & M. C. Linn (Eds.), *The psychology of gender: Advances through meta-analysis.* Baltimore: Johns Hopkins University Press.

Linney, J. A., & Seidman, E. (1989). The future of schooling. *American Psychologist, 44,* 336–340.

Lipsitt, L. P., Reilly, B. M., Butcher, M. J., & Greenwood, M. M. (1976). The stability and interrelationships of newborn sucking and heart rate. *Developmental Psychology, 9,* 305–310.

Lipsitz, J. (1983, October). *Making it the hard way: Adolescents in the 1980s.* Testimony prepared for the Crisis Intervention Task Force, House Select Committee on Children, Youth, and Families, Washington, DC.

Lipsitz, J. (1984). *Successful schools for young adolescents.* New Brunswick, NJ: Transaction.

Lipsky, D. K., & Gartner, A. (1989). *Beyond separate education.* Baltimore: Brookes.

Litt, I. F. (1991). Eating disorders, medical complications of. In R. M. Lerner, A. C. Petersen, & J. Brooks-Gunn (Eds.), *Encyclopedia of adolescence* (Vol. 1). New York: Garland.

Little, B. B., Snell, L. M., Klein, V. R., & Gilstrap, L. C. (1989). Cocaine abuse during pregnancy: Maternal and fetal implications. *Obstetrics and Gynecology, 73,* 157–160.

Lively, W., & Bromley, D. (1973). *Person perception in childhood and adolescence.* New York: Wiley.

Lock, A. (1991). The role of social interaction in early language development. In N. A. Krasnegor, D. M. Rumbaugh, M. Studdert-Kennedy, & R. L. Schiefelbusch (Eds.), *Biological and behavioral determinants of language development.* Hillsdale, NJ: Erlbaum.

Locke, J. L., Bekken, K. E., Wein, D., & Ruzecki, V. (1991, April). *Neuropsychology of babbling: Laterality effects in the production of rhythmic manual activity.* Paper presented at the Society for Research in Child Development meeting, Seattle.

Loge, D. V., & Schatz, J. (1991, April). *Social interactions of children with Attention Deficit Disorder: The role of emotions and self-control.* Paper presented at the Society for Research in Child Development meeting, Seattle.

Lombardi, J. (1991, October). *Type and availability of day care for children in America.* Paper presented at the symposium on day care for children, Arlington, VA.

Long, T., & Long, L. (1983). *Latchkey children.* New York: Penguin.

Longabaugh, R. (1980). The systematic observation of behavior in naturalistic settings. In H. C. Triandis & J. W. Berry (Eds.), *Handbook of cross-cultural psychology: Methodology* (Vol. 2). Boston: Allyn & Bacon.

Lonner, W. J. (1988). *The introductory psychology text and cross-cultural psychology. A survey of cross-cultural psychologists.* Bellingham, WA: Center for Cross-Cultural Research, Western Washington University.

Lonner, W. J. (1990). An overview of cross-cultural testing and assessment. In R. W. Brislin (Ed.), *Applied cross-cultural psychology.* Newbury Park, CA: Sage.

Looney, J. G., & Blotcky, M. J. (1989). Adolescent psychological development revisited. In A. H. Esman (Ed.), *International annals of adolescent psychiatry.* Chicago: University of Chicago Press.

Lorber, J., & Farrell, S. A. (Eds.). (1991). *The social construction of gender.* Newbury Park, CA: Sage.

Lorden, R. B., & Falkenberg, S. D. (1988, August). *Applications of cognitive research to improvement of classroom teaching and learning.* Paper presented at the meeting of the American Psychological Association, Atlanta.

Lorenz, K. Z. (1965). *Evolution and the modification of behavior.* Chicago: University of Chicago Press.

Louv, R. (1990). *Childhood's future.* Boston: Houghton Mifflin.

Lovaas, O. I. (1977). *The autistic child: Language development through behavior modification.* New York: Halstead.

Lozoff, B. (1989). Nutrition and behavior. *American Psychologist, 44,* 231–236.

Lueptow, L. (1984). *Adolescent sex roles and social change.* New York: Columbia University Press.

Lummis, M., & Stevenson, H. W. (1990). Gender differences in beliefs and achievement: A cross-cultural study. *Developmental Psychology, 26,* 254–263.

Lundman, R. (1984). *Prevention and control of juvenile delinquency.* New York: Oxford University Press.

Luria, A., & Herzog, E. (1985, April). *Gender segregation across and within settings.* Paper presented at the Society for Research in Child Development meeting, Toronto.

Lyle, J., & Hoffman, H. R. (1972). Children's use of television and other media. In E. A. Rubenstein, G. A. Comstock, & J. P. Murray (Eds.), *Television and social behavior* (Vol. 4). Washington, DC: U.S. Government Printing Office.

Lynch, M. A., & Roberts, J. (1982). *The consequences of child abuse.* New York: Academic Press.

Lyons, J. M. (1991, April). *The influence of parental scaffolding on the development of coping skills in clinically distressed and nondistressed children.* Paper presented at the Society for Research in Child Development meeting, Seattle.

Lyons, N. P. (1983). Two perspectives: On self, relationships, and morality. *Harvard Educational Review, 53,* 125–145.

Lyons, N. P. (1990). Listening to voices we have not heard. In C. Gilligan, N. P. Lyons, & T. J. Hanmer (Eds.), *Making connections.* Cambridge, MA: Harvard University Press.

M

Maccoby, E. E. (1980). *Social development.* San Diego: Harcourt Brace Jovanovich.

Maccoby, E. E. (1984). Middle childhood in the context of the family. In *Development during middle childhood.* Washington, DC: National Academy Press.

Maccoby, E. E. (1987a, November). Interview with Elizabeth Hall: All in the family. *Psychology Today,* pp. 54–60.

Maccoby, E. E. (1987b). The varied meanings of "masculine" and "feminine." In J. M. Reinisch, L. A. Rosenblum, & S. A. Sanders (Eds.), *Masculinity/ femininity: Basic perspectives.* New York: Oxford University Press.

Maccoby, E. E. (1989, August). *Gender and relationships: A developmental account.* Paper presented at the meeting of the American Psychological Association, New Orleans.

Maccoby, E. E., & Jacklin, C. N. (1974). *The psychology of sex differences.* Palo Alto, CA: Stanford University Press.

Maccoby, E. E., & Jacklin, C. N. (in press). Gender segregation in childhood. In H. Reese (Ed.), *Advances in child development and behavior* (Vol. 20). New York: Academic Press.

Maccoby, E. E., & Martin, J. A. (1983). Socialization in the context of the family: Parent-child interaction. In P. H. Mussen (Ed.), *Handbook of child psychology* (4th ed., Vol. 4). New York: Wiley.

MacDonald, K. B., Cluff, C., Kosmos, J., & Jones, C. (1991, April). *The effects of hyperactivity and stimulant medication on prosocial behavior.* Paper presented at the Society for Research in Child Development meeting, Seattle.

MacFarlane, J. A. (1975). Olfaction in the development of social preferences in the human neonate. In *Parent-infant interaction.* Ciba Foundation Symposium, 33. Amsterdam: Elsevier.

MacTurk, R. H., McCarthy, M. E., Vietze, P. M., & Yarrow, L. J. (1987). Sequential analysis of mastery behavior in 6- and 12-month-old infants. *Developmental Psychology, 23,* 199–203.

Maddux, J. E., Roberts, M. C., Sledden, E. A., & Wright, L. (1986). Developmental issues in child health psychology. *American Psychologist, 41,* 24–34.

Malatesta, C. (1990, May 28). Commentary. *Newsweek,* p. 61.

Malcom, S. M. (1988). Technology in 2020: Educating a diverse population. In R. S. Nickerson & P. P. Zodhiates (Eds.), *Technology in education: Looking toward 2020.* Hillsdale, NJ: Erlbaum.

Malina, R. M. (1990). Physical growth and performance during the transitional years (9–16). In R. Montemayor, G. R. Adams, & T. P. Gulotta (Eds.), *From childhood to adolescence: A transitional period?* Newbury Park, CA: Sage.

Malina, R. M. (1991). Growth spurt, adolescent. II. In R. M. Lerner, A. C. Petersen, & J. Brooks-Gunn (Eds.), *Encyclopedia of adolescence* (Vol. 1). New York: Garland.

Malinowski, B. (1927). *Sex and repression in savage society.* New York: Meridian.

Maltsberger, J. T. (1988). *Suicide risk.* New York: Human Sciences Press.

Mandell, C. J., & Mandell, S. L. (1989). *Computers in education today.* St. Paul, MN: West.

Mandler, J. (1991, April). *The foundation of symbolic thought in infancy.* Paper presented at the Society for Research in Child Development meeting, Seattle.

Mandler, J. M. (1983). Representation. In P. H. Mussen (Ed.), *Handbook of child psychology* (4th ed., Vol. 3). New York: Wiley.

Mandler, J. M. (1990). A new perspective on cognitive development in infancy. *American Scientist, 78,* 236–243.

Maratsos, M. P. (1983). Some current issues in the study of the acquisition of grammar. In P. H. Mussen (Ed.), *Handbook of child psychology* (4th ed., Vol. 3). New York: Wiley.

Maratsos, M. P. (1989). Innateness and plasticity in language acquisition. In M. L. Rice & R. L. Schiefelbusch (Eds.), *The teachability of language.* Baltimore: Paul Brooks.

Marcia, J. (1966). Identity six years after: A follow-up study. *Journal of Youth and Adolescence, 5,* 145–160.

Marcia, J. (1980). Ego identity development. In J. Adelson (Ed.), *Handbook of adolescent psychology.* New York: Wiley.

Marcia, J. (1987). The identity status approach to the study of ego identity development. In T. Honess & K. Yardley (Eds.), *Self and identity: Perspectives across the lifespan.* London: Routledge & Kegan Paul.

Marcia, J. (1989). Identity and intervention. *Journal of Adolescence, 12,* 401–410.

Marcia, J. E. (1991). Identity and self-development. In R. M. Lerner, A. C. Petersen, & J. Brooks-Gunn (Eds.), *Encyclopedia of adolescence* (Vol. 1). New York: Garland.

Marieskind, H. I. (1989). Cesarean section in the United States: Has it changed since 1979? *Birth, 16,* 196–202.

Marín, G., & Marín, B. V. (1991). *Research with Hispanic populations.* Newbury Park, CA: Sage.

Markman, E. M. (1989). *Categorization and naming in children: Problems of induction.* Cambridge, MA: MIT Press.

Marquis, K. S., & Detweiler, R. A. (1985). Does adopted mean different? An attributional analysis. *Journal of Personality and Social Psychology, 48,* 1054–1066.

Martin, C. L. (1989, April). *Beyond knowledge-based conceptions of gender schematic processing.* Paper presented at the Society for Research in Child Development meeting, Kansas City.

Martin, C. L., & Halverson, C. F. (1981). A schematic processing model of sex-typing and stereotyping in children. *Child Development, 52,* 1119–1132.

Martin, C. L., & Halverson, C. F. (1987). The role of cognition in sex role acquisition. In D. B. Carter (Ed.), *Current conceptions of sex roles and sex-typing: Theory and research.* New York: Praeger.

Martin, C. L., Rose, H. A. (1991, April). *Children's gender-based distinctive theories.* Paper presented at the Society for Research in Child Development meeting, Seattle.

Martin, G., & Pear, J. (1988). *Behavior modification: What is it and how to do it* (3rd ed.). Englewood Cliffs, NJ: Prentice-Hall.

Martorano, S. (1977). A developmental analysis of performance on Piaget's formal operations tasks. *Developmental Psychology, 13,* 666–672.

Maslow, A. H. (1954). *Motivation and personality.* New York: Harper & Row.

Maslow, A. H. (1971). *The farther reaches of human nature.* New York: Viking.

Matas, L., Arend, R. A., & Sroufe, L. A. (1978). Continuity in adaptation: Quality of attachment and later competence. *Child Development, 49,* 547–556.

Matheny, A. P., Dolan, R. S., & Wilson, R. S. (1976). Relation between twins' similarity: Testing an assumption. *Behavior Genetics, 6,* 343–351.

McAdoo, H. P., & McAdoo, J. L. (Eds.). (1985). *Black children: Social, educational, and parental environments.* Beverly Hills: Sage.

McAdoo, H. P. (Ed.). (1988). *Black families.* Newbury Park, CA: Sage.

McBride, A. B. (1990). Mental health effects of women's multiple roles. *American Psychologist, 45,* 381–384.

McBride, B. A. (1991, April). *Variations in father involvement with preschool-aged children.* Paper presented at the Society for Research in Child Development meeting, Seattle.

McCall, R. B. (1991). Underachievers and dropouts. In R. M. Lerner, A. C. Petersen, & J. Brooks-Gunn (Eds.), *Encyclopedia of adolescence* (Vol. 2). New York: Garland.

McCall, R. B., Applebaum, M. I., & Hogarty, P. S. (1973). Developmental changes in mental performance. *Monographs of the Society for Research in Child Development, 38* (Serial No. 150).

McCarley, R. W. (1989). The biology of dreaming sleep. In M. H. Kryger, T. Roth, & W. C. Dement (Eds.), *Principles and practices of sleep medicine.* San Diego: Harcourt Brace Jovanovich.

McCartney, K., Robeson, W. W., Jordon, E., & Mouradian, V. (1991, April). *Mothers' language with first- and second-born children: A within-family study.* Paper presented at the Society for Research in Child Development meeting, Seattle.

McClelland, D. C. (1955). Some social consequences of achievement motivation. In M. R. Jones (Ed.), *Nebraska Symposium on Motivation.* Lincoln: University of Nebraska Press.

McDaniel, M. A., & Pressley, M. (1987). *Imagery and related mnemonic process.* New York: Springer-Verlag.

McGhee, P. E. (1984). Play, incongruity, and humor. In T. Yawkey & A. D. Pellegrini (Eds.), *Child's play: Developmental and applied.* Hillsdale, NJ: Erlbaum.

McGue, M., & Bouchard, T. J. (1989). Genetic and environmental determinants of information processing and special mental abilities. In R. J. Sternberg (Ed.), *Advances in the psychology of human intelligence.* Hillsdale, NJ: Erlbaum.

McHugh, M., Koeske, R., & Frieze, I. H. (1986). Issues to consider in conducting nonsexist psychological research: A guide for researchers. *American Psychologist, 41,* 879–890.

McKnight, C. C., Crosswhite, F. J., Dossey, J. A., Kifer, E., Swafford, J. O., Travers, K. J., & Cooney, T. J. (1987). *The underachieving curriculum: Assessing U.S. school mathematics from an international perspective.* Champaign, IL: Stipes.

McLoyd, V. C. (1982). Social class differences in sociodramatic play: A critical review. *Developmental Review, 2,* 1–30.

McLoyd, V. C. (1990). Minority children: An introduction to the special issue. *Child Development, 61,* 263–266.

McLoyd, V. C. (in press). The declining fortunes of Black children: Psychological distress, parenting, and socioemotional development in the context of economic hardship. *Child Development.*

McLoyd, V. C., & Wilson, L. (in press). Maternal behavior, social support, and economic conditions as predictors of psychological distress in children. In V. C. McLoyd & C. Flanagan (Eds.), *New directions for child development: Economic stress.* San Francisco: Jossey-Bass.

McPartland, J. M., & McDill, E. L. (1976). *The unique role of schools in the causes of youthful crime.* Baltimore: Johns Hopkins University Press.

McPeck, J. E. (1990). Critical thinking and subject specificity: A reply to Ennis. *Educational Leadership, 19,* 10–12.

McWhirter, D. P., Reinisch, J. M., & Sanders, S. A. (1990). *Homosexuality/heterosexuality.* New York: Oxford University Press.

Meehl, P. (1990). Why summaries of research on a psychological theory are often uninterpretable. In R. E. Snow & D. E. Wiley (Eds.), *Improving inquiry in social science.* Hillsdale, NJ: Erlbaum.

Meichenbaum, D. H., & Goodman, J. (1971). Training impulsive children to talk to themselves: A means of developing self-control. *Journal of Abnormal Psychology, 77,* 115–126.

Meilman, P. W. (1979). Cross-sectional age changes in ego identity status during adolescence. *Developmental Psychology, 15,* 230–231.

Melton, G. B. (1991). Socialization in the global community: Respect for the dignity of children. *American Psychologist, 46,* 66–71.

Meltzoff, A. N. (1988). Infant imitation and memory: Nine-month-olds in immediate and deferred tests. *Child Development, 59,* 217–225.

Meltzoff, A. N. (1990, June). *Infant imitation.* Invited address at the University of Texas at Dallas.

Mercer, J. R., & Lewis, J. F. (1978). *System of multicultural pluralistic assessment.* New York: Psychological Corp.

Meredith, H. V. (1978). Research between 1960 and 1970 on the standing height of young children in different parts of the world. In H. W. Reece & L. P. Lipsitt (Eds.), *Advances in child development and behavior* (Vol. 12). New York: Academic Press.

Messer, D. J., Yarrow, L. J., & Vietze, P. M. (1982, August). *Mastery in infancy and competence in early childhood.* Paper presented at the meeting of the American Psychological Association, Washington, DC.

Metz, K. E. (1991, April). *Reflection on the methodology of microgenetic analysis: View from a study of novices learning physics.* Paper presented at the Society for Research in Child Development meeting, Seattle.

Meyerhoff, M. K., & White, B. L. (1986, September). Making the grade as parents. *Psychology Today*, pp. 38–45.

Michel, G. L. (1981). Right-handedness: A consequence of infant supine head-orientation preference? *Science, 212,* 685–687.

Miller, C. A. (1987). A review of maternity care programs in Western Europe. *Family Planning Perspectives, 19,* 207–211.

Miller, G. (1981). *Language and speech.* New York: W. H. Freeman.

Miller, G. (1989). Foreward. In J. T. Gibbs & L. N. Huang (Eds.), *Children of color.* San Francisco: Jossey-Bass.

Miller, G. A. (1956). The magical number seven, plus or minus two: Some limits on our capacity for information processing. *Psychological Review, 63,* 81–97.

Miller, G. A. (1981). *Language and speech.* New York: W. H. Freeman.

Miller, J. B. (1976). *Toward a new psychology of women.* Boston: Beacon.

Miller, J. B. (1986). *Toward a new psychology of women* (2nd ed.). Boston: Beacon.

Miller-Jones, D. (1989). Culture and testing. *American Psychologist, 44,* 360–366.

Miller-Jones, D. (1991). Informal reasoning in inner-city children. In J. Voss, D. Perkins, & J. Segal (Eds.), *Informal reasoning and education.* Hillsdale, NJ: Erlbaum.

Minnett, A. M., Vandell, D. L., & Santrock, J. W. (1983). The effects of sibling status on sibling interaction: Influence of birth order, age spacing, sex of the child, and sex of the sibling. *Child Development, 54,* 1064–1072.

Minuchin, P. P., & Shapiro, E. K. (1983). The school as a context for social development. In P. H. Mussen (Ed.), *Handbook of child psychology* (4th ed., Vol. 4). New York: Wiley.

Mischel, W. (1970). Sex-typing and socialization. In P. H. Mussen (Ed.), *Manual of child psychology* (3rd ed., Vol. 2). New York: Wiley.

Mischel, W. (1973). Toward a cognitive social learning reconceptualization of personality. *Psychological Review, 80,* 252–283.

Mischel, W. (1974). Process in delay of gratification. In L. Berkowitz (Ed.), *Advances in experimental social psychology* (Vol. 7). New York: Academic Press.

Mischel, W. (1984). Convergences and challenges in the search for consistency. *American Psychologist, 39,* 351–364.

Mischel, W. (1987). *Personality* (4th ed.). New York: Holt, Rinehart & Winston.

Mischel, W., & Mischel, H. (1975, April). *A cognitive social-learning analysis of moral development.* Paper presented at the Society for Research in Child Development meeting, Denver.

Mischel, W., & Patterson, C. J. (1976). Substantive and structural elements of effective plans for self-control. *Journal of Social and Personality Psychology, 34,* 942–950.

Moely, B. E., Olson, F. A., Halwes, T. G., & Flavell, J. H. (1969). Production deficiency in young children's clustered recall. *Developmental Psychology, 1,* 26–34.

Mohr, D. (1978). Development of attributes of personal identity. *Developmental Psychology, 4,* 427–428.

Moll, I. (1991, April). *The material and the social in Vygotsky's theory of cognitive development.* Paper presented at the Society for Research in Child Development meeting, Seattle.

Money, J. (1987). Sin, sickness, or status? Homosexual gender identity and psychoneuroendocrinology. *American Psychologist, 42,* 384–389.

Montemayor, R., & Flannery, D. J. (1991). Parent-adolescent relations in middle and late adolescence. In R. M. Lerner, A. C. Petersen, & J. Brooks-Gunn (Eds.), *Encyclopedia of adolescence* (Vol. 2). New York: Garland.

Montemayor, R., & Hanson, E. (1985). A naturalistic view of conflict between adolescents and their parents and siblings. *Journal of Early Adolescence, 5,* 23–30.

Montemayor, R., Adams, G. R., & Gulotta, T. P. (Eds.). (1990). *From childhood to adolescence: A transitional period.* Newbury Park, CA: Sage.

Moos, R. H., Finney, J. W., & Cronkite, R. C. (1990). *Alcoholism treatment: Contexts, process, and outcome.* New York: Oxford University Press.

Morgan, M. (1982). Television and adolescents' sex-role stereotypes: A longitudinal study. *Journal of Personality and Social Psychology, 43,* 947–955.

Morgan, M. (1987). Television, sex-role attitudes, and sex-role behavior. *Journal of Early Adolescence, 7,* 269–282.

Morrison, D. M. (1985). Adolescent contraceptive behavior: A review. *Psychological Bulletin, 98,* 538–568.

Morrongiello, B. A., Fenwick, K. D., & Chance, G. (1990). Sound localization acuity in very young infants: An observer-based testing procedure. *Developmental Psychology, 26,* 75–84.

Mott, F. L., & Mariglio, W. (1985, September/October). Early childbearing and completion of high school. *Family Planning Perspectives,* p. 234.

Moyer, J., Egertson, H., & Isenberg, J. (1987). The child-centered kindergarten. *Childhood Education, 63,* 235–242.

Mueller, E. (1985, April). *Early peer relations: Ten years of research.* Symposium presented at the Society for Research in Child Development meeting, Toronto.

Munroe, R. L., & Munroe, R. H. (1975). *Cross-cultural human development.* Monterey, CA: Brooks/Cole.

Murphy, K. C., Talley, J. A., & Huston, A. C. (1991, April). *Family ecology and young children's viewing of television designed for children.* Paper presented at the Society for Research in Child Development meeting, Seattle.

Murphy, M. P., & Carter, D. B. (1991, April). *Familial characteristics and the development of gender schemas.* Paper presented at the Society for Research in Child Development meeting, Seattle.

Murray, H. A. (1938). *Explorations in personality.* New York: Oxford University Press.

Musun-Miller, L. (1991, April). *Children's birth order as a mediator in responses by mothers and siblings.* Paper presented at the Society for Research in Child Development meeting, Seattle.

N

NAEYC. (1988). NAEYC position statement on developmentally appropriate practices in the primary grades, serving 5- through 8-year-olds. *Young Children, 43,* 64–83.

NAEYC. (1991). Position statement: Guidelines for appropriate curriculum content and assessment in programs serving children ages 3 through 8. *Young Children, 46,* 21–39.

National Association for the Education of Young Children (1986). *How to choose a good early childhood program.* Washington, DC: NAEYC.

National Research Council (1987). *Risking the future: Adolescent sexuality, pregnancy, and childbearing.* Washington, DC: National Academy Press.

Needle, R. H., Su, S. S., & Doherty, W. J. (1990). Divorce, remarriage, and adolescent substance use: A prospective longitudinal study. *Journal of Marriage and the Family, 52,* 157–175.

Neimark, E. D. (1982). Adolescent thought: Transition to formal operations. In B. B. Wolman (Ed.), *Handbook of developmental psychology*. Englewood Cliffs, NJ: Prentice-Hall.

Neisser, U. (1982). *Memory observed.* New York: W. H. Freeman.

Nelson-Legall, S. (1990). Academic achievement orientation and help-seeking behavior in early adolescent girls. *Journal of Early Adolescence, 10,* 176–190.

Newcomb, M. D., & Bentler, P. M. (1989). Substance use and abuse among children and teenagers. *American Psychologist, 44,* 242–248.

Nicholls, J. G. (1984). Conceptions of ability and achievement motivation. In R. E. Ames & C. Ames (Eds.), *Motivation in education.* New York: Academic Press.

Nichtern, S. (1989). Introduction: The world within the adolescent. In A. H. Esman (Ed.), *International annals of adolescent psychiatry.* Chicago: University of Chicago Press.

Nicolopoulou, A., & Cole, M. (1991, April). *Taking culture seriously.* Paper presented at the Society for Research in Child Development meeting, Seattle.

Ninio, A., & Bruner, J. (1978). The achievement and antecedent of labeling. *Journal of Child Language, 5,* 1–15.

Nitz, V., & Lerner, J. V. (1991). Temperament during adolescence. In R. M. Lerner, A. C. Petersen, & J. Brooks-Gunn (Eds.), *Encyclopedia of adolescence* (Vol. 2). New York: Garland.

Nix, D., & Spiro, R. (1991). *Cognition, education, and multimedia.* Hillsdale, NJ: Erlbaum.

Nottelman, E. D., Inoff-Germain, G., Susman, E. J., & Chrousos, G. P. (1990). Hormones and behavior at puberty. In J. Bancroft & J. M. Reinisch (Eds.), *Adolescence and puberty.* New York: Oxford University Press.

Nottelmann, E. D., Susman, E. J., Blue, J. H., Inoff-Germain, G., Dorn, L. D., Loriaux, D. L., Cutler, G. B., & Chrousos, G. P. (1987). Gonadal and adrenal hormone correlates of adjustment in early adolescence. In R. M. Lerner & T. T. Foch (Eds.), *Biological-psychological interactions in early adolescence.* Hillsdale, NJ: Erlbaum.

Novick, B. (1989). Pediatric AIDS: A medical overview. In J. M. Seibert & R. A. Olson (Eds.), *Children, adolescents, and AIDS.* Lincoln: University of Nebraska Press.

Nucci, L., & Weber, E. K. (1991). The domain approach to values education: From theory to practice. In W. M. Kurtines & J. Gewirtz (Eds.), *Moral behavior and development* (Vol. 3). Hillsdale, NJ: Erlbaum.

O

O'Donnel, B. (1989, April). *Altering children's gender stereotypes about adult occupations with nonsexist books.* Paper presented at the Society for Research in Child Development meeting, Kansas City.

O'Donnell, C., Manos, M., & Chesney-Lind, M. (1987). Diversion and neighborhood delinquency programs in open settings. In E. Morris & C. Braukmann (Eds.), *Behavioral approaches to crime and delinquency.* New York: Plenum.

O'Sullivan, R. G. (1990). Validating a method to identify at-risk middle school students for participation in a dropout prevention program. *Journal of Early Adolescence, 10,* 209–220.

Offer, D., & Church, R. B. (1991a). Generation gap. In R. M. Lerner, A. C. Petersen, & J. Brooks-Gunn (Eds.), *Encyclopedia of adolescence* (Vol. 1). New York: Garland.

Offer, D., & Church, R. B. (1991b). Turmoil, adolescent. In R. M. Lerner, A. C. Petersen, & J. Brooks-Gunn (Eds.), *Encyclopedia of adolescence* (Vol. 2). New York: Garland.

Offer, D., Ostrov, E., Howard, K. I., & Atkinson, R. (1988). *The teenage world: Adolescents' self-image in ten countries.* New York: Plenum.

Ogbu, J. U. (1974). *The next generation: An ethnography of education in an urban neighborhood.* New York: Academic Press.

Ogbu, J. U. (1986). The consequences of the American caste system. In U. Neisser (Ed.), *The school achievement of minority children: New perspectives.* Hillsdale, NJ: Erlbaum.

Ogbu, J. U. (1989, April). *Academic socialization of Black children: An inoculation against future failure?* Paper presented at the Society for Research in Child Development meeting, Kansas City.

Olmedo, E. L., & Walker, V. R. (Eds.). (1991). *Hispanics in the United States.* Washington, DC: American Psychological Association.

Olweus, D. (1980). Bullying among schoolboys. In R. Barnen (Ed.), *Children and violence.* Stockholm: Adaemic Litteratur.

Olweus, D. (1989, April). *Peer relationships problems: Conceptual issues and a successful intervention program against bully/victim problems.* Paper presented at the Society for Research in Child Development meeting, Kansas City.

Oppenheimer, M. (1982, October). What you should know about herpes. *Seventeen Magazine,* pp. 154–155, 170.

Orthner, D. K. (1990). Parental work and early adolescence: Issues for research and practice. *Journal of Early Adolescence, 10,* 246–259.

Oser, F. K. (1986). Moral education and values education: The discourse perspective. In M. C. Wittrock (Ed.), *Handbook of research on teaching.* New York: Macmillan.

Osofsky, J. D. (1989, April). *Affective relationships in adolescent mothers and their infants.* Paper presented at the Society for Research in Child Development meeting, Kansas City.

Osofsky, J. D. (1990, Winter). Risk and protective factors for teenage mothers and their infants. *SRCD Newsletter,* pp. 1–2.

Ostrov, E., Offer, D., Howard, K. I., Kaufman, B., & Meyer, H. (1985). Adolescent sexual behavior. *Medical Aspects of Human Sexuality, 19,* 28, 30–31, 34–36.

Ottinger, D. R., & Simmons, J. E. (1964). Behavior of human neonates and prenatal maternal anxiety. *Psychological Reports, 14,* 391–394.

P

Paikoff, R. L., & Brooks-Gunn, J. (1990). Physiological processes: What role do they play during the transition to adolescence? In R. Montemayor, G. R. Adams, & T. P. Gulotta (Eds.), *From childhood to adolescence: A transitional period.* Newbury Park, CA: Sage.

Paikoff, R. L., & Brooks-Gunn, J. (1991). Pregnancy, interventions to prevent. In R. M. Lerner, A. C. Petersen, & J. Brooks-Gunn (Eds.), *Encyclopedia of adolescence* (Vol. 2). New York: Garland.

Paikoff, R. L., Buchanan, C. M., & Brooks-Gunn, J. (1991). Hormone-behavior links at puberty, methodological links in the study of. In R. M. Lerner, A. C. Petersen, & J. Brooks-Gunn (Eds.), *Encyclopedia of adolescence.* New York: Garland.

Paivio, A. (1986). *Mental representations: A dual coding approach.* New York: Oxford University Press.

Pan, B. A., Rollins, P. R., & Snow, C. E. (1991, April). *Pragmatic development and its relationship to morphosyntactic indices.* Paper presented at the Society for Research in Child Development meeting, Seattle.

Papert, S. (1980). *Mindstorms: Children, computers, and powerful ideas.* New York: Basic.

Papini, D. R., Roggman, L. A., & Anderson, J. (1990, March). *Early adolescent perceptions of attachment to mother and* *father: A test of the emotional distancing hypothesis.* Paper presented at the meeting of the Society for Research in Adolescence, Atlanta.

Parcel, G. S., Simons-Morton, G. G., O'Hara, N. M., Baranowski, T., Kolbe, L. J., & Bee, D. E. (1987). School promotion of healthful diet and exercise behavior: An integration of organizational change and social learning theory interventions. *Journal of School Health, 57,* 150–156.

Parcel, G. S., Tiernan, K., Nadar, P. R., & Gottlob, D. (1979). Health education and kindergarten children. *Journal of School Health, 49,* 129–131.

Paris, S. G., & Lindauer, B. K. (1982). The development of cognitive skills during childhood. In B. B. Wolman (Ed.), *Handbook of developmental psychology.* Englewood Cliffs, NJ: Prentice-Hall.

Parish, T. S., & Osterberg, J. (1985). Evaluations of self, parents, and family: Variations caused by family structure and personal stress. *Journal of Psychology, 119,* 231–233.

Parish, T. S. (1988). Evaluations of family as a function of one's family structure and sex. *Perceptual and Motor Skills, 66,* 25–26.

Parke, R. D. (1972). Some effects of punishment on children's behavior. In W. W. Hartup (Ed.), *The young child* (Vol. 2). Washington, DC: NAEYC.

Parke, R. D. (1977). Some effects of punishment on children's behavior—Revisited. In E. M. Hetherington & R. D. Parke (Eds.), *Readings in contemporary child psychology.* New York: McGraw-Hill.

Parke, R. D., & Sawin, D. B. (1980). The family in early infancy. In F. Pedersen (Ed.), *The father-infant relationship: Observational studies in family context.* New York: Praeger.

Parker, J. G., & Asher, S. R. (1987). Peer relations and later personal adjustment: Are low accepted children at risk? *Psychological Bulletin, 102,* 357–389.

Parker, J. G., & Gottman, J. M. (1989). Social and emotional development in a relational context: Friendship interaction from early childhood to adolescence. In T. J. Berndt & G. W. Ladd (Eds.), *Peer relations in child development.* New York: Wiley.

Parkhurst, J. T., Roedel, T. D., Bendixen, L. D., & Potenza, M. T. (1991, April). *Subgroups of rejected middle school students: Their behavioral characteristics, friendships, social concerns.* Paper presented at the Society for Research in Child Development meeting, Seattle.

Parmalee, A., Wenner, W., & Schulz, H. (1964). Infant sleep patterns from birth to 16 weeks of age. *Journal of Pediatrics, 65,* 572–576.

Parmalee, A. H. (1986). Children's illnesses: Their beneficial effects on behavioral development. *Child Development, 57,* 1–10.

Parten, M. (1932). Social play among preschool children. *Journal of Abnormal and Social Psychology, 27,* 243–269.

Pascual-Leone, J., & Johnson, J. (1991). The psychological unit and its role in task analysis: A reinterpretation of object permanence. In M. Chandler & M. Chapman (Eds.), *Criteria for competence.* Hillsdale, NJ: Erlbaum.

Pascual-Leone, J., & Shafrir, U. (1991, April). *The development of post-failure reflectivity.* Paper presented at the Society for Child Development meeting, Seattle.

Pasley, K., & Ihinger-Tallman, M. (Eds.). (1987). *Remarriage and stepparenting.* New York: Guilford.

Patterson, G. R. (1986). Performance models for antisocial boys. *American Psychologist, 41,* 432–444.

Patterson, G. R. (1991, April). *Which parenting skills are necessary for what?* Paper presented at the Society for Research in Child Development meeting, Seattle.

Patterson, G. R., Capaldi, D., & Bank, L. (1991). An early starter model for predicting delinquency. In D. Pepler & K. Rubin (Eds.), *The development and treatment of childhood aggression.* Hillsdale, NJ: Erlbaum.

Patterson, G. R., DeBaryshe, B. D., & Ramsey, E. (1989). A developmental perspective on antisocial behavior. *American Psychologist, 44,* 329–335.

Patterson, G. R., & Grimaldi, D. M. (1991). Antisocial parents: Unskilled and vulnerable during family transitions. In P. A. Cowan & E. M. Hetherington (Eds.), *Family transitions.* Hillsdale, NJ: Erlbaum.

Pavlov, I. P. (1927). *Conditioned reflexes* (F. V. Anrep, Trans. and Ed.). New York: Dover.

Pederson, D. R., Moran, G., Sitko, C., Campbell, K., Ghesquire, K., & Acton, H. (1989, April). *Maternal sensitivity and the security of infant-mother attachment.* Paper presented at the Society for Research in Child Development meeting, Kansas City.

Pellegrini, A. D., Perlmutter, J. C., Galda, L., & Brody, G. H. (1990). Joint reading between Black Head Start children and their mothers. *Child Development, 61,* 443–453.

Penner, S. G. (1987). Parental responses to grammatical and ungrammatical child utterances. *Child Development, 58,* 376–384.

Perkins, D. N. (1984, September). Creativity by design. *Educational Leadership,* 18–25.

Perkins, D. P., & Gardner, H. (1989). *Why "Zero"? A brief introduction to Project Zero.* In H. Gardner & D. P. Perkins (Eds.), *Art, mind, and education.* Ithaca, NY: The University of Illinois Press.

Perkinson, H. J. (1991). *The imperfect panacea: American faith in education, 1865–1990* (3rd ed.). New York: McGraw-Hill.

Peskin, H. (1967). Pubertal onset and ego functioning. *Journal of Abnormal Psychology, 72,* 1–15.

Petersen, A. C. (1979, January). Can puberty come any faster? *Psychology Today,* pp. 45–56.

Peterson, L. M., Widmayer, S. M., Bacon, K. L., Burns, W. J., & Calderon, A. E. (1991, April). *Developmental outcome of HIV positive infants.* Paper presented at the Society for Research in Child Development meeting, Seattle.

Peterson, P. L. (1977). Interactive effects of student anxiety, achievement orientation, and teacher behavior on student achievement and attitude. *Journal of Educational Psychology, 69,* 779–792.

Pettit, G. S., Dodge, K. A., & Brown, M. M. (1988). Early family experience, social problem solving patterns, and children's social competence. *Child Development, 59,* 107–120.

Phillips, D. (1989). Future directions and needs for child care in the United States. In J. S. Lande, S. Scarr, & N. Gunzenhauser (Eds.), *Caring for children: Challenge to America.* Hillsdale, NJ: Erlbaum.

Phillips, D. (1991, April). *The developmental course of perceived competence and incompetence among competent children.* Paper presented at the Society for Research in Child Development meeting, Seattle.

Phinney, J. (1991, April). *Research with ethnic minority adolescents.* Paper presented at the Society for Research in Child Development meeting, Seattle.

Phinney, J. S. (1989). Stages of identity development in minority group adolescents. *Journal of Early Adolescence, 9,* 34–49.

Phinney, J. S., & Alipuria, L. L. (1990). Ethnic identity in college students from four ethnic groups. *Journal of Adolescence, 13,* 171–183.

Piaget, J. (1932). *The moral judgment of the child.* New York: Harcourt Brace Jovanovich.

Piaget, J. (1952a). Jean Piaget. In C. A. Murchison (Ed.), *A history of psychology in autobiography* (Vol. 4). Worcester, MA: Clark University Press.

Piaget, J. (1952b). *The origins of intelligence in children* (M. Cook, Trans.). New York: International Universities Press.

Piaget, J. (1954). *The construction of reality in the child.* New York: Basic.

Piaget, J. (1962). *Play, dreams, and imitation in childhood.* New York: W. W. Norton.

Piaget, J. (1967). The mental development of the child. In D. Elkind (Ed.), *Six psychological studies by Piaget.* New York: Random House.

Piaget, J. (1970). Piaget's theory. In P. H. Mussen (Ed.), *Manual of child psychology* (3rd ed., Vol. 1). New York: Wiley.

Piaget, J. (1972). Intellectual evolution from adolescence to adulthood. *Human Development, 15,* 1–12.

Piaget, J., & Inhelder, B. (1969). *The child's conception of space* (F. J. Langdon & J. L. Lunzer, Trans.). New York: W. W. Norton. (Original work published 1948)

Pierce, E. W. (1991, April). *Impulsivity as a component of behavior problems in preschool boys.* Paper presented at the Society for Research in Child Development meeting, Seattle.

Piers, E. V., & Harris, D. V. (1964). Age and other correlates of self-concept in children. *Journal of Educational Psychology, 55,* 91–95.

Pillow, B. H. (1988). Young children's understanding of attentional limits. *Child Development, 49,* 38–46.

Pipes, P. (1988a). Nutrition during infancy. In S. R. Williams & B. S. Worthington-Roberts (Eds.), *Nutrition through the life cycle.* St. Louis: Times Mirror/Mosby.

Pipes, P. (1988b). Nutrition in childhood. In S. R. Williams & B. S. Worthington (Eds.), *Nutrition throughout the life cycle.* St. Louis: Times Mirror/Mosby.

Pleck, J. H. (1979). Men's family work: Three perspectives and some new data. *Family Coordinator, 28,* 481–488.

Pleck, J. H. (1984). *Working wives and family well-being.* Beverly Hills: Sage.

Plomin, R. (1989). Environment and genes: Determinants of behavior. *American Psychologist, 44,* 105–111.

Plomin, R. (1991, April). *The nature of nurture: Genetic influence on "environmental" measures.* Paper presented at the Society for Research in Child Development meeting, Seattle.

Plomin, R., & Thompson, L. (1987). Life-span developmental behavior genetics. In P. B. Baltes, D. L. Featherman, & R. M. Lerner (Eds.), *Life-span development and behavior* (Vol. 7). Hillsdale, NJ: Erlbaum.

Plomin, R., DeFries, J. C., & McClearn, G. E. (in press). *Behavioral genetics: A primer.* New York: W. H. Freeman.

Polier, J. W. (1989). *Juvenile justice in double jeopardy.* Hillsdale, NJ: Erlbaum.

Polivy, J., & Thomsen, L. (1987). Eating, dieting, and body image. In E. A. Blechman & K. D. Brownell (Eds.), *Handbook of behavioral medicine for women.* Elmsford, NY: Pergamon.

Porter, F. L., Porges, S. W., & Marshall, R. E. (1988). Newborn pain cries and vagal tone: Parallel changes in response to circumcision. *Child Development, 59,* 495–515.

Posner, M., & Rothbart, M. (1989, August). *Attention: Normal and pathological development.* Paper presented at the meeting of the American Psychological Association, New Orleans.

Powell, G. J., & Fuller, M. (1972). The variables for positive self-concept among young Southern Black adolescents. *Journal of the National Medical Association, 43,* 72–79.

Power, C. (1991). Lawrence Kohlberg: The vocation of an educator, part I. In W. M. Kurtines & J. Gewirtz (Eds.), *Moral behavior and development* (Vol. 1). Hillsdale, NJ: Erlbaum.

Premack, D. (1986). *Gavagai! The future history of the ape language controversy.* Cambridge, MA: MIT Press.

Price, J., & Feshbach, S. (1982, August). *Emotional adjustment correlates of television viewing in children.* Paper presented at the meeting of the American Psychological Association, Washington, DC.

Pryor, J. B., Reeder, G. D., Vinaco, R., & Kott, T. L. (1989). The instrumental and symbolic functions of attitudes toward persons with AIDS. *Journal of Applied Social Psychology, 19,* 377–404.

Puffer, J. C. (1987, September). *Risky sports for young children.* Paper presented at the annual meeting of the American Academy of Family Physicians, San Francisco.

Puka, B. (in press). Toward the redevelopment of Kohlberg's theory: Preserving essential structure, removing controversial content. In W. M. Kurtines & J. Gewirtz (Eds.), *Moral behavior and development: Advances in theory, research, and application.* Hillsdale, NJ: Erlbaum.

Quina, K. (1986). *Teaching research methods: A multidimensional feminist curricular transformation plan.* Wellesley College Center for Research on Women. Working Paper No. 164.

Rabin, D. S., & Chrousos, G. P. (1991). Androgens, gonadal. In R. M. Lerner, A. C. Petersen, & J. Brooks-Gunn (Eds.), *Encyclopedia of adolescence* (Vol. 1). New York: Garland.

Rabiner, D. L., Gordon, L., Klumb, D., & Thompson, L. B. (1991, April). *Social problem solving deficiencies in rejected children: Motivational factors and skill deficits.* Paper presented at the Society for Research in Child Development meeting, Seattle.

Rabkin, J. (1987). *Epidemiology of adolescent violence: Risk factors, career patterns, and intervention programs.* Paper presented at the conference on adolescent violence, Stanford University.

Rahman, T., & Bisanz, G. L. (1986). Reading ability and use of a story schema in recalling and reconstructing information. *Journal of Educational Psychology, 5,* 323–333.

Ramey, C. T. (1989, April). *Parent-child intellectual similarities in natural and altered ecologies.* Paper presented at the Society for Research in Child Development meeting, Kansas City.

Ramey, C. T., & Landesman, S. L. (in press). Intensive educational intervention for children in poverty. *Intelligence.*

Ramirez, M. (1990). *Psychotherapy and counseling with minorities.* Riverside, NJ: Pergamon.

Ramirez, O. (1989). Mexican American children and adolescents. In J. T. Gibbs & L. N. Huang (Eds.), *Children of color.* San Francisco: Jossey-Bass.

Ramirez, O., & Arce, C. Y. (1981). The contemporary Chicano family: An empirically based review. In A. Baron (Ed.), *Explorations in Chicano psychology.* New York: Praeger.

Ramsay, D. S. (1980). Onset of unimanual handedness in infants. *Infant Behavior and Development, 3,* 377–385.

Rappaport, A., Bornstein, G., & Erev, I. (1989). Intergroup competition for public goods: Effects of unequal resources and relative group size. *Journal of Personality and Social Psychology, 5,* 748–756.

Raver, C. C., & Zigler, E. F. (1991). Three steps forward, two steps back: Head Start and the measurement of social competence. *Young Children, 46,* 3–9.

Redfield, C. L., & Steuck, K. (1991). The future of intelligent tutoring systems. In H. Burns, J. W. Parlett, & C. L. Redfield (Eds.), *Intelligent tutoring systems: Evolutions in design.* Hillsdale, NJ: Erlbaum.

Reid, D. K. (1988). *Teaching the learning disabled.* Boston, MA: Allyn & Bacon.

Reilly, R. (1988, August 15). Here no one is spared. *Sports Illustrated,* pp. 70–77.

Reis, S. M. (1989). Reflections on policy affecting the education of gifted and talented students. *American Psychologist, 44,* 399–408.

Render, G. F., Padilla, J. N. M., & Krank, H. M. (1989). Assertive discipline: A critical review and analysis. *Teachers College Record, 90,* 610–630.

Rest, J. R. (1976). New approaches in the assessment of moral judgment. In T. Lickona (Ed.), *Moral development and behavior.* New York: Holt, Rinehart & Winston.

Rest, J. R. (1983). Morality. In P. H. Mussen (Ed.), *Handbook of child psychology* (4th ed., Vol. 3). New York: Wiley.

Rest, J. R. (1986). *Moral development: Advances in theory and research.* New York: Praeger.

Rest, J. R., Turiel, E., & Kohlberg, L. (1969). Relations between level of moral judgment and preference and comprehension of the moral judgments of others. *Journal of Personality, 37,* 225–252.

Rice, M. L. (1989). Children's language acquisition. *American Psychologist, 44,* 149–156.

Rich, C. L., Young, D., & Fowler, R. C. (1986). San Diego suicide study. *Archives of General Psychiatry, 43,* 577–582.

Rieben, L., & Perfetti, C. A. (1991). *Learning to read: Basic research and its implications.* Hillsdale, NJ: Erlbaum.

Risser, W. L. (1989). Exercise for children. *Pediatrics in Review, 10,* 131–140.

Robinson, D. P., & Greene, J. W. (1988). The adolescent alcohol and drug problem: A practical approach. *Pediatric Nursing, 14,* 305–310.

Rode, S. S., Chang, P., Fisch, R. O., & Sroufe, L. A. (1981). Attachment patterns of infants separated at birth. *Developmental Psychology, 17,* 188–191.

Rodman, H., Pratto, D. J., & Nelson, R. S. (1988). Toward a definition of self-care children: A commentary on Steinberg (1986). *Developmental Psychology, 24,* 292–294.

Rodriguez-Haynes, M., & Crittenden, P. (1988). *Ethnic differences among abusing, neglecting, and nonmaltreating families.* Paper presented at the Southeastern Conference on Human Development, Charleston.

Roff, M., Sells, S. B., & Golden, M. W. (1972). *Social adjustment and personality development in children.* Minneapolis: University of Minnesota Press.

Roffwarg, H. P. (1966, March 29). Ontogenetic development of the human sleep-dream cycle. *Science, 154,* 604–619.

Rogers, A. (1987). *Questions of gender differences: Ego development and moral voice in adolescence.* Unpublished manuscript, Dept. of Education, Harvard University.

Rogers, C. R. (1961). *On becoming a person.* Boston: Houghton Mifflin.

Rogers, C. R. (1974). In retrospect: Forty-six years. *American Psychologist, 29,* 115–123.

Rogers, C. S., & Sawyers, J. K. (1988). *Play in the lives of children.* Washington, DC: NAEYC.

Rogers, C. S., & Sawyers, J. K. (1988). *Play in the lives of children.* Washington, DC: NAEYC.

Rogler, L. H., Cortes, D. E., & Malgady, R. G. (1991). Acculturation and mental health status among Hispanics: Convergence and new directions for research. *American Psychologist, 46,* 585–597.

Rogoff, B. (1981). Schooling and the development of cognitive skills. In H. C. Triandis & W. Lonner (Eds.), *Handbook of cross-cultural psychology* (Vol. 3). Boston: Allyn & Bacon.

Rogoff, B. (1990). *Apprenticeship in thinking.* New York: Oxford University Press.

Rogoff, B. (in press). Peer influences on cognitive development: Piagetian versus Vygotskian perspectives. In M. H. Bornstein & J. S. Bruner (Eds.), *Interaction in human development.* Hillsdale, NJ: Erlbaum.

Rogoff, B., & Mistry, J. J. (in press). The social and motivational context of children's memory skills. In R. Fivish & J. Hudson (Eds.), *What young children remember and why.* Cambridge, England: Cambridge University Press.

Rogoff, B., & Morelli, G. (1989). Perspectives on children's development from cultural psychology. *American Psychologist, 44,* 343–348.

Rohner, R. P., & Rohner, E. C. (1981). Parental acceptance-rejection and parental control: Cross-cultural codes. *Ethnology, 20,* 245–260.

Rohwer, W. D., & Bean, J. P. (1973). Sentence effects and noun-pair learning: A developmental interaction during adolescence. *Journal of Experimental Child Psychology, 15,* 521–533.

Rose, R. J., Koskenvuo, M., Kaprio, J., Sarna, S., & Langinvainio, H. (1988). Shared genes, shared experiences, and similarity of personality: Data from 14,228 adult Finnish co-twins. *Journal of Personality and Social Psychology, 54,* 161–171.

Rose, S. A. (1989). Measuring infant intelligence: New perspectives. In M. H. Bornstein & N. A. Krasnegor (Eds.), *Stability and continuity in mental development.* Hillsdale, NJ: Erlbaum.

Rose, S. A., & Ruff, H. A. (1987). Cross-modal abilities in human infants. In J. D. Osofsky (Ed.), *Handbook of infant development* (2nd ed.). New York: Wiley.

Rose, S. A., Feldman, J. F., McCarton, C. M., & Wolfson, J. (1988). Information processing in seven-month-old infants as a function of risk status. *Child Development, 59,* 489–603.

Rosenbaum, E., & Kandel, D. B. (1990). Early onset of adolescent sexual behavior and drug involvement. *Journal of Marriage and the Family, 52,* 783–798.

Rosenberg, M. (1965). *Society and the adolescent self-image.* Princeton, NJ: Princeton University Press.

Rosenberg, M. (1979). *Conceiving the self.* New York: Basic.

Rosenblith, J. F., & Sims-Knight, J. E. (1985). *In the beginning: Development in the first two years.* Monterey, CA: Brooks/Cole.

Rosenthal, R., & Jacobsen, L. (1968). *Pygmalian in the classroom.* New York: Holt, Rinehart & Winston.

Rothbart, M. K. (in press). Temperament and the development of inhibited approach. *Child Development.*

Rothbart, M. K., Hanley, D., & Albert, M. (1986). Gender differences in moral reasoning. *Sex Roles, 15,* 645–653.

Rothbart, M. L. K. (1971). Birth order and mother-child interaction. *Dissertation Abstracts, 27,* 45–57.

Rotheram-Borus, M. J., & Koopman, C. (1991). AIDS and adolescents. In R. M. Lerner, A. C. Petersen, & J. Brooks-Gunn (Eds.), *Encyclopedia of adolescence* (Vol. 1). New York: Garland.

Rotter, J. B. (1989, August). *Internal versus external locus of control of reinforcement: A case history of a variable.* Paper presented at the meeting of the American Psychological Association, New Orleans.

Rovee-Collier, C. (1987). Learning and memory in children. In J. D. Osofsky (Ed.), *Handbook of infant development* (2nd ed.). New York: Wiley.

Rowe, D. C., & Rodgers, J. E. (1989). Behavioral genetics, adolescent deviance, and "d" contributions and issues. In G. R. Adams, R. Montemayor, & T. P. Gulotta (Eds.), *Biology of adolescent behavior and development.* Newbury Park, CA: Sage.

Rubin, K. H., Maioni, T. L., & Hornung, M. (1976). Free play behaviors in middle and lower social class preschoolers: Parten and Piaget revisited. *Child Development, 47,* 414–419.

Rubin, K. N., Fein, G. G., & Vandenberg, B. (1983). Play. In P. H. Mussen (Ed.), *Handbook of child psychology* (4th ed., Vol. 4). New York: Wiley.

Rubin, Z., & Sloman, J. (1984). How parents influence their children's friendships. In M. Lewis (Ed.), *Beyond the dyad.* New York: Plenum.

Ruble, D. (1983). The development of social comparison processes and their role in achievement-related self-socialization. In E. Higgins, D. Ruble, & W. Hartup (Eds.), *Social cognitive development: A social-cultural perspective.* New York: Cambridge University Press.

Ruebenstein, J., Heeren, T., Housman, D., Rubin, C., & Stechler, G. (1989). Suicidal behavior in "normal" adolescents: Risk and protective factors. *American Journal of Orthopsychiatry, 59,* 59–71.

Ruff, H. A., & Lawson, K. R. (1990). Development of sustained, focused attention in young children during free play. *Developmental Psychology, 26,* 85–93.

Rumbaugh, D. M., Hopkins, W. D., Washburn, D. A., & Savage-Rumbaugh, E. S. (1991). Comparative perspectives of brain, cognition, and language. In N. A. Krasnegor, D. M. Rumbaugh, M. Studdert-Kennedy, & R. L. Schiefelbusch (Eds.), *Biological and behavioral determinants of language development.* Hillsdale, NJ: Erlbaum.

Rumberger, R. W. (1983). Dropping out of high school: The influence of race, sex, and family background. *American Educational Research Journal, 20,* 199–220.

Rumberger, R. W. (1987). High school dropouts: A review of the issues and evidence. *Review of Educational Research, 57,* 101–121.

Runco, M. A. (1991). *Divergent thinking.* Norwood, NJ: Ablex.

Russo, N. F. (1990). Overview: Forging research priorities for women's mental health. *American Psychologist, 45,* 368–374.

Rutter, M., Maughan, B., Mortimore, P., & Ouston, J. (1979). *Fifteen thousand hours: Secondary schools and their effects on children.* Cambridge, MA: Harvard University Press.

Rutter, M. (1983, April). *Influences from family and school.* Paper presented at the meeting of the Society for Research in Child Development, Detroit.

Ryan, R. A. (1980). Strengths of the American Indian family: State of the art. In F. Hoffman (Ed.), *The American Indian family: Strengths and stresses.* Isleta, NM: American Indian Social Research and Development Association.

Ryan, R. M., & Lynch, J. H. (1989). Emotional autonomy versus detachment: Revisiting the vicissitudes of adolescence and young adulthood. *Child Development, 60,* 340–356.

S

Sachdev, P. (1988). Abortion trends: An international review. In P. Sachdev (Ed.), *International handbook on abortion.* New York: Greenwood.

Sadker, M., & Sadker, D. (1986, March). Sexism in the classroom: From grade school to graduate school. *Phi Delta Kappan,* pp. 512–515.

Sadker, M., Sadker, D., & Klein, S. S. (1986). Abolishing misperceptions about sex equity in education. *Theory into Practice, 25,* 219–226.

Sadker, M. P., & Sadker, D. M. (1991). *Teachers, schools, and society* (2nd ed.). New York: McGraw-Hill.

Sagan, C. (1980). *Cosmos.* New York: Random House.

St. James-Roberts, I., Bowyer, J., & Hurry, J. (1991, April). *Delineating "problem" infant crying: Findings in community and referred infants, using tape recordings, diaries, and direct questionnaires.* Paper presented at the Society for Research in Child Development meeting, Seattle.

Santrock, J. W. (1990a). *Adolescence* (4th ed.). Dubuque, IA: Wm. C. Brown.

Santrock, J. W. (1990b). The changing tapestry of children's family worlds. *Contemporary Psychology, 35,* 692–693.

Santrock, J. W. (1990c). Children of divorce: A concise eclectic review. *Contemporary Psychology, 35,* 559–560.

Santrock, J. W. (1992). *Life-span development* (4th ed.). Dubuque, IA: Wm. C. Brown.

Santrock, J. W., & Bartlett, J. C. (1986). *Developmental psychology.* Dubuque, IA: Wm. C. Brown.

Santrock, J. W., & Sitterle, K. A. (1987). Parent-child relationships in stepmother families. In K. Pasley & M. Ihinger-Tallman (Eds.), *Remarriage and stepparenting.* New York: Guilford.

Santrock, J. W., & Warshak, R. A. (1979). Father custody and social development in boys and girls. *Journal of Social Issues, 35,* 112–125.

Santrock, J. W., & Warshak, R. A. (1986). Development, relationships, and legal/clinical considerations in father custody families. In M. E. Lamb (Ed.), *The father's role: Applied perspectives.* New York: Wiley.

Santrock, J. W., Sitterle, K. A., & Warshak, R. A. (1988). Parent-child relationships in stepfather families. In P. Bronstein & C. Cowan (Eds.), *The father's role today: Men's changing roles in the family.* New York: Wiley.

Savage-Rumbaugh, E. S. (1991). Language learning in the Bonobo: How and why they learn. In N. A. Krasnegor, D. M. Rumbaugh, M. Studdert-Kennedy, & R. L. Schiefelbusch (Eds.), *Biological and behavioral determinants of language development.* Hillsdale, NJ: Erlbaum.

Savin-Williams, R. C., & Demo, D. H. (1983). Conceiving or misconceiving the self: Issues in adolescent self-esteem. *Journal of Early Adolescence, 3,* 121–140.

Sax, G. (1989). *Principles of educational and psychological measurement* (3rd ed.). Belmont, CA: Wadsworth.

Scales, P. (1990). Developing capable young people: An alternative strategy for prevention programs. *Journal of Early Adolescence, 10,* 420–438.

Scardamalia, M., Bereiter, C., & Goelman, H. (1982). The role of production factors in writing ability. In M. Nystrand (Ed.), *What writers know: The language, process, and structure of written discourse.* New York: Academic Press.

Scardamalia, M., Bereiter, C., & Steinbach, R. (1984). Teachability of reflective processes in written composition. *Cognitive Science, 8,* 173–190.

Scarr, S. (1984a, May). [Interview.] *Psychology Today,* pp. 59–63.

Scarr, S. (1984b). *Mother care/other care.* New York: Basic.

Scarr, S. (1989, April). *Transracial adoption.* Discussion at the Society for Research in Child Development meeting, Kansas City.

Scarr, S. (1991a, April). *Developmental theories for the 1990s*. Presidential address, Society for Research in Child Development meeting, Seattle.

Scarr, S. (1991b, October). *A study of the quality of day care in three states*. Paper presented at the symposium on day care for children, Arlington, VA.

Scarr, S., & Kidd, K. K. (1983). Developmental behavior genetics. In P. H. Mussen (Ed.), *Handbook of child psychology* (4th ed., Vol. 2). New York: Wiley.

Scarr, S., & Weinberg, R. A. (1976). IQ test performance of black children adopted by white families. *American Psychologist, 31*, 726–739.

Scarr, S., & Weinberg, R. A. (1980). Calling all camps! The war is over. *American Sociological Review, 45*, 859–865.

Scarr, S., & Weinberg, R. A. (1983). The Minnesota adoption studies: Genetic differences and malleability. *Child Development, 54*, 253–259.

Scarr, S., Lande, J. S., & McCartney, K. (1989). Child care and the family: Complements and interactions. In J. S. Lande, S. Scarr, & N. Gunzenhauser, (Eds.), *Caring for children: Challenge to America*, Hillsdale, NJ: Erlbaum.

Schacter, D. L., & McGlynn, S. M. (1989). Implicit memory: Effects of elaboration depend on unitization. *American Journal of Psychology, 102*, 151–181.

Schaie, K. W. (1973). Methodological problems in descriptive developmental research on adulthood and aging. In J. R. Nesselroade & H. W. Reese (Eds.), *Life-span developmental psychology: Methodological issues*. New York: Academic Press.

Schaie, K. W. (1989). Introduction. In K. W. Schaie & C. Schooler (Eds.), *Social structure and aging: Psychological processes*. Hillsdale, NJ: Erlbaum.

Schaller, M., & Maass, A. (1989). Illusory correlation and social categorization: Toward an integration of motivational and cognitive factors in stereotype formation. *Journal of Personality and Social Psychology, 56*, 709–721.

Schank, R., & Abelson, R. (1977). *Scripts, plans, goals, and understanding*. Hillsdale, NJ: Erlbaum.

Schegloff, E. A. (1989). Reflections on language, development, and the interactional character of talk-in-interaction. In M. H. Bornstein & J. S. Bruner (Eds.), *Interaction in human development*. Hillsdale, NJ: Erlbaum.

Scheidel, D. G., & Marcia, J. E. (1985). Ego identity, intimacy, sex-role orientation, and gender. *Developmental Psychology, 21*, 149–160.

Schlundt, D. G., & Johnson, W. G. (1990). *Assessment and treatment of anorexia nervosa and bulimia nervosa*. Needham Heights, MA: Allyn & Bacon.

Schneider, W., & Pressley, M. (1989). *Memory development between 2 and 20*. New York: Springer-Verlag.

Schoenfeld, A. H. (1985). *Mathematical problem solving*. Orlando, FL: Academic Press.

Schrag, S. G., & Dixon, R. L. (1985). Occupational exposure associated with male reproductive dysfunction. *Annual Review of Pharmacology and Toxicology, 25*, 467–592.

Schunk, D. H. (1983). Developing children's self-efficacy and skills: The roles of social comparative information and goal-setting. *Contemporary Educational Psychology, 8*, 76–86.

Schunk, D. H. (1990). Introduction to the special section on motivation and efficacy. *Journal of Educational Psychology, 82*, 3–6.

Schwartz, B. (1990). The creation and destruction of value. *American Psychologist, 45*, 7–15.

Schwartz, D., & Mayaux, M. J. (1982). Female fecundity as a function of age: Results of artificial insemination in nullparous women with azoospermic husbands. *New England Journal of Medicine, 306*, 304–406.

Schweinhart, L. J. (1991, April). *The High Scope/Perry preschool study, similar studies, and their implications for public policy in the United States*. Paper presented at the Society for Research in Child Development meeting, Seattle.

Scott-Jones, D., & Clark, M. L. (1986, March). The school experiences of black girls: The interaction of gender, race, and socioeconomic status. *Phi Delta Kappan*, pp. 520–526.

Scott-Jones, D., & White, A. B. (1990). Correlates of sexual activity in early adolescence. *Journal of Early Adolescence, 10*, 221–238.

Scribner, S. (1977). Modes of thinking and ways of speaking: Culture and logic reconsidered. In P. N. Johnson-Laird & P. C. Wason (Eds.), *Thinking: Readings in cognitive science*. New York: Cambridge University Press.

Segall, M. H., Dasen, P. R., Berry, J. W., & Poortinga, Y. H. (1990). *Human behavior in global perspective*. New York: Pergamon.

Seibert, J. M., & Olson, R. A. (Eds.). (1989). *Children, adolescents, and AIDS*. Lincoln: University of Nebraska Press.

Selman, R. (1976). Social-cognitive understanding: A guide to educational and clinical practice. In T. Lickona (Ed.), *Moral development and behavior: Theory, research, and social issues*. New York: Holt, Rinehart & Winston.

Selman, R. L. (1980). *The growth of interpersonal understanding*. New York: Academic Press.

Selman, R. L., Newberger, C. M., & Jacquette, D. (1977, April). *Observing interpersonal reasoning in a clinic/educational setting: Toward the integration of developmental and clinical child psychology*. Paper presented at the Society for Research in Child Development meeting, New Orleans.

Semaj, L. T. (1985). Afrikanity, cognition, and extended self-identity. In M. B. Spencer, G. K. Brookins, & W. R. Allen (Eds.), *Beginnings: The social and affective development of Black children*. Hillsdale, NJ: Erlbaum.

Senn, M. J. (1975). Insights on the child development movement in the United States. *Monographs of the Society for Research in Child Development, 40*(3–4, Serial No. 161).

Serbin, L. A., & Sprafkin, C. (1986). The salience of gender in the process of sex-typing in three- to seven-year-old children. *Child Development, 57*, 1188–1209.

Sexton, M., & Hebel, J. R. (1984). A clinical trial of change in maternal smoking and its effects on birth weight. *Journal of the American Medical Association, 251*, 911–915.

Shafrir, U. (1991, April). *Diagnosing reflectivity*. Paper presented at the Society for Research in Child Development meeting, Seattle.

Shakeshaft, C. (1986, March). A gender at risk. *Phi Delta Kappan*, pp. 499–503.

Shantz, C. O. (1988). Conflicts between children. *Child Development, 59*, 283–305.

Shantz, C. U. (1983). The development of social cognition. In P. H. Mussen (Ed.), *Handbook of child psychology* (4th ed., Vol. 3). New York: Wiley.

Shapiro, E. R., & Freedman, J. (1989). Family dynamics of adolescent suicide. In A. H. Esman (Ed.), *International annals of adolescent psychiatry*. Chicago: University of Chicago Press.

Sharp, D., Cole, M., & Lave, C. (1979). Education and cognitive development: The evidence from experimental research. *Monographs of the Society for Research in Child Development, 1–2* (Serial No. 178).

Shatz, M., & Gelman, R. (1973). The development of communication skills: Modifications in the speech of young children as a function of the listener.

Monographs of the Society for Research in Child Development, 38 (Serial No. 152).

Shneidman, E. S. (1971). Suicide among the gifted. *Suicide and life-threatening behavior, 1*, 23–45.

Shweder, R., Mahapatra, M., & Miller, J. (1987). Culture and moral development. In J. Kagan & S. Lamb (Eds.), *The emergence of morality in young children.* Chicago: University of Chicago Press.

Siegel, L. (1991, April). *Learning disabilities and post-failure reflectivity.* Paper presented at the Society for Research in Child Development meeting, Seattle.

Siegel, L. S., & Ryan, E. B. (1989). The development of working memory in normally achieving and subtypes of learning disabled children. *Child Development, 69*, 973–980.

Siegler, R. S. (1983). Information processing approaches to development. In P. H. Mussen (Ed.), *Handbook of child psychology* (4th ed., Vol. 1). New York: Wiley.

Siegler, R. S. (1986). *Children's thinking.* Englewood Cliffs, NJ: Prentice-Hall.

Siegler, R. S. (1991, April). *Variation and selection as cognitive transition mechanisms.* Paper presented at the Society for Research in Child Development meeting, Seattle.

Siegler, R. S. (in press). Individual differences in strategy choices: Good students, not-so-good students, and perfectionists. *Child Development.*

Siegler, R. S., & Campbell, J. (1989). Individual differences in children's strategy choices. In P. L. Ackerman, R. J. Sternberg, & R. Glaser (Eds.), *Learning and individual differences.* New York: W. H. Freeman.

Siegler, R. S., & McGilly, K. (in press). Strategy choices in time telling. In I. Levin & D. Zakay (Eds.), *Time and human cognition: A life-span perspective.* New York: Elsevier.

Sigman, M. D., Asarnow, R., Cohen, S., & Parmalee, A. H. (1989, April). *Infant attention as a measure of information processing.* Paper presented at the Society for Research in Child Development meeting, Kansas City.

Silver, L. B. (1987). *Attention deficit disorders.* Summit, NJ: CIBA.

Silver, L. B. (1989). Learning disabilities. *Journal of the American Academy of Child and Adolescent Psychiatry, 28*, 309.

Silverberg, S. B., & Steinberg, L. (1990). Psychological well-being of parents with early adolescent children. *Developmental Psychology, 26*, 658–666.

Simmons, R. G., & Blyth, D. A. (1987). *Moving into adolescence.* Hawthorne, NY: Aldine.

Simons, R. L., & Gray, P. A. (1989). Perceived blocked opportunity as an explanation of delinquency among lower-class black males: A research note. *Journal of Research in Crime and Delinquency, 26*, 90–101.

Singer, D. (1972, June). Piglet, Pooh, & Piaget. *Psychology Today*, pp. 70–74.

Singer, D. G., & Singer, J. L. (1987). Practical suggestions for controlling television. *Journal of Early Adolescence, 7*, 365–369.

Singer, J. L. (1984). *The human personality.* San Diego: Harcourt Brace Jovanovich.

Singer, J. L., & Singer, D. G. (1988). Imaginative play and human development: Schemas, scripts, and possibilities. In D. Bergen (Ed.), *Play as a medium for learning and development.* Portsmouth, NH: Heinemann.

Skinner, B. F. (1938). *The behavior of organisms: An experimental analysis.* New York: Appleton-Century-Crofts.

Skinner, B. F. (1948). *Walden two.* New York: Macmillan.

Skinner, B. F. (1957). *Verbal behavior.* New York: Appleton-Century-Crofts.

Skinner, E. A., Wellborn, J. G., & Connell, J. P. (1990). What it takes to do well in school and whether I've got it: A process model of perceived control and children's engagement and achievement in school. *Journal of Educational Psychology, 82*, 22–32.

Skoe, E. E., & Marcia, J. E. (1988). *Ego identity and care-based moral reasoning in college women.* Unpublished manuscript, Acadia University.

Slaughter-DeFoe, D. T., Nakagawa, K., Takanishi, R., & Johnson, D. J. (1990). Toward cultural/ecological perspectives on schooling and achievement in African- and Asian-American children. *Child Development, 61*, 363–383.

Slavin, R. E. (1987). Developmental and motivational perspectives on cooperative learning: A reconciliation. *Child Development, 58*, 1161–1167.

Slavin, R. E. (1988). *Educational psychology* (2nd ed.). Englewood Cliffs, NJ: Prentice-Hall.

Slavin, R. E. (1989a). Achievement effects of substantial reductions in class size. In R. E. Slavin (Ed.), *School and classroom organization.* Hillsdale, NJ: Erlbaum.

Slavin, R. E. (1989b). Cooperative learning and student achievement. In R. E. Slavin (Ed.), *School and classroom organization.* Hillsdale, NJ: Erlbaum.

Slobin, D. (1972, July). Children and language: They learn the same all around the world. *Psychology Today*, pp. 71–76.

Small, M. (1990). *Cognitive development.* San Diego: Harcourt Brace Jovanovich.

Smith, B. A. Fillion, T. J., & Blass, E. M. (1990). Orally mediated sources of calming in 1- to 3-day-old human infants. *Developmental Psychology, 26*, 731–737.

Smith, J., & Baltes, P. B. (in press). A study of wisdom-related knowledge: Age-cohort differences in response to life-planning problems. *Developmental Psychology.*

Smolucha, F. (1989, April). *Vygotsky's theory of creative imagination and its relevance for research on play.* Paper presented at the Society for Research on Child Development meeting, Kansas City.

Snarey, J. (1987, June). A question of morality. *Psychology Today*, pp. 6–8.

Snarey, J., & Keljo, K. (1991). In a *gemeinschaft* voice: The cross-cultural expansion of moral development theory. In W. M. Kurtines & J. Gewirtz (Eds.), *Moral behavior and development* (Vol. 1). Hillsdale, NJ: Erlbaum.

Snidman, N., & Kagan, J. (1989, April). *Infant predictors of behaviorally inhibited and uninhibited children.* Paper presented at the Society for Research in Child Development meeting, Kansas City.

Snow, C. E. (1989). Understanding social interaction in language interaction: Sentences are not enough. In M. H. Bornstein & J. S. Bruner (Eds.), *Interaction in human development.* Hillsdale, NJ: Erlbaum.

Sophian, C. (1985). Perseveration and infants' search: A comparison of two- and three-location tasks. *Developmental Psychology, 21*, 187–194.

Sorensen, R. C. (1973). *Adolescent sexuality in contemporary America.* New York: World.

Spearman, C. E. (1927). *The abilities of man.* New York: Macmillan.

Spelke, E. S. (1979). Perceiving bimodally specified events in infancy. *Developmental Psychology, 5*, 626–636.

Spelke, E. S. (1988). The origins of physical knowledge. In L. Weiskrantz (Ed.), *Thought without language.* New York: Oxford University Press.

Spelke, E. S. (1991). Physical knowledge in infancy: Reflections on Piaget's theory. In S. Carey & R. Gelman (Eds.), *The epigenesis of mind: Essays on biology and cognition.* Hillsdale, NJ: Erlbaum.

Spence, J. T., & Helmreich, R. (1978). *Masculinity and femininity: Their psychological dimensions.* Austin: University of Texas Press.

Spence, M., & DeCasper, A. J. (1982). *Human fetuses perceive human speech.* Paper presented at the International Conference on Infant Studies, Austin.

Spencer, M. B. (1990). Development of minority children: An introduction. *Child Development, 61,* 267–269.

Spencer, M. B. (1991a). Identity, minority development of. In R. M. Lerner, A. C. Petersen, & J. Brooks-Gunn (Eds.), *Encyclopedia of adolescence* (Vol. 1). New York: Garland.

Spencer, M. B. (1991b, April). *Research methods: Prospects, perils, and "pearls of opportunity."* Paper presented at the Society for Research in Child Development meeting, Seattle.

Spencer, M. B., & Dornbusch, S. M. (1990). Challenges in studying minority youth. In S. S. Feldman & G. R. Elliott (Eds.), *At the threshold: The developing adolescent.* Cambridge, MA: Harvard University Press.

Spencer, M. B., & Markstrom-Adams, C. (1990). Identity processes among racial and ethnic minority children in America. *Child Development, 61,* 290–310.

Spencer, M. L. (1986). Sex equity in bilingual education, English as a second language, and foreign language instruction. *Theory into Practice, 25,* 257–266.

Sperry, R. W. (1974). Lateral specialization in surgically separated hemispheres. In F. O. Schmitt & F. G. Worden (Eds.), *The neurosciences: Third study program.* Cambridge, MA: MIT Press.

Sroufe, L. A. (1985). Attachment classification from the perspective of infant-caregiver relationships and infant temperament. *Child Development, 56,* 1–14.

Sroufe, L. A. (in press). Pathways to adaptation and maladaptation: Psychopathology as developmental deviation. In D. Cicchetti (Ed.), *Developmental psychopathology: Past, present, and future.* Hillsdale, NJ: Erlbaum.

Sroufe, L. A., & Waters, E. (1976). The ontogenesis of smiling and laughter: A perspective on the organization of development in infancy. *Psychological Review, 83,* 173–198.

Stage, E. K., Kreinberg, N., Eccles, J., & Becker, J. R. (1985). Increasing the participation and achievement of girls and women in mathematics, science, and engineering. In S. S. Klein (Ed.), *Handbook for achieving sex equity through education.* Baltimore: Johns Hopkins University Press.

Stallings, J. (1975). Implementation and child effects of teaching practices in Follow Through classrooms. *Monographs of the Society for Research in Child Development, 40* (Serial No. 163).

Stankov, L. (1991). The effects of practice and training on human abilities. In H. A. H. Rowe (Eds.), *Intelligence: Reconceptualization and measurement.* Hillsdale, NJ: Erlbaum.

Stein, N. L., & Glenn, C. G. (1979). An analysis of story comprehension in elementary school children. In R. O. Freedle (Ed.), *Discourse processing: Multidisciplinary perspectives* (pp. 53–120). Norwood, NJ: Ablex.

Steinberg, E. R. (1990a). *Computer-assisted instruction.* Hillsdale, NJ: Erlbaum.

Steinberg, L. (1990b). Autonomy, conflict, and harmony in the family relationship. In S. S. Feldman & G. R. Elliott (Eds.), *At the threshold: The developing adolescent.* Cambridge, MA: Harvard University Press.

Steinberg, L. (1991). Parent-adolescent relations. In R. M. Lerner, A. C. Petersen, & J. Brooks-Gunn (Eds.), *Encyclopedia of adolescence.* New York: Garland.

Steinberg, L. D. (1981). Transformations in family relations at puberty. *Developmental Psychology, 17,* 833–840.

Steinberg, L. D. (1986). Latchkey children and susceptibility to peer pressure: An ecological analysis. *Developmental Psychology, 22,* 433–439.

Steinberg, L. D. (1987). Impact of puberty on family relations: Effects of pubertal status and pubertal timing. *Developmental Psychology, 23,* 451–460.

Steinberg, L. D. (1988a). Reciprocal relation between parent-child distance and pubertal maturation. *Developmental Psychology, 24,* 122–128.

Steinberg, L. D. (1988b). Simple solutions to a complex problem: A response to Rodman, Pratto, and Nelson (1988). *Developmental Psychology, 24,* 295–296.

Steiner, J. E. (1979). Human facial expressions in response to taste and smell stimulation. In H. Reese & L. Lipsitt (Eds.), *Advances in child development and behavior* (Vol. 13). New York: Academic Press.

Stern, D. N., Beebe, B., Jaffe, J., & Bennett, S. L. (1977). The infant's stimulus world during social interaction: A study of caregiver behaviors with particular reference to repetition and timing. In H. R. Schaffer (Ed.), *Studies in mother-infant interaction.* London: Academic Press.

Stern, S. L., Dixon, K. N., Jones, D., Lake, M., Nemzer, E., & Sansone, R. (1989).

Family environment in anorexia nervosa and bulimia. *International Journal of Eating Disorders, 8,* 25–31.

Sternberg, R. J. (1986). *Intelligence applied.* San Diego: Harcourt Brace Jovanovich.

Sternberg, R. J. (1987). Teaching intelligence: The application of cognitive psychology of intellectual skills. In J. B. Baron & R. J. Sternberg (Eds.), *Teaching thinking skills: Theory and practice.* New York: W. H. Freeman.

Sternberg, R. J. (1989). Introduction: In R. J. Sternberg (Ed.), *Advances in the psychology of human intelligence* (Vol. 5). Hillsdale, NJ: Erlbaum.

Sternberg, R. J. (1990, April). *Academic and practical cognition as different aspects of intelligence.* Paper presented at the 12th West Virginia conference on life-span developmental psychology, Morgantown.

Sternberg, R. J., Conway, B. E., Ketron, J. L., & Berstein, M. (1981). People's conceptions of intelligence. *Journal of Personality and Social Psychology, 41,* 37–55.

Steur, F. B., Applefield, J. M., & Smith, R. (1971). Televised aggression and interpersonal aggression of preschool children. *Journal of Experimental Child Psychology, 11,* 442–447.

Stevens, J. H. (1984). Black grandmothers' and Black adolescent mothers' knowledge about parenting. *Developmental Psychology, 20,* 1017–1025.

Stevenson, H. W. (1972). *Children's learning.* New York: Appleton-Century-Crofts.

Stevenson, H. W., Lee, S., Chen, C., Stigler, J., Hsu, C., & Kitamura, G. (1990). Contexts of achievement. *Monograph of the Society for Research in Child Development* (Serial No. 221, Vol. 55, Nos. 1–2).

Stevenson, H. W., Stigler, J. W., & Lee, S. (1986). Achievement in mathematics. In H. W. Stevenson, H. Azuma, & K. Hakuta (Eds.), *Child development and education in Japan.* San Francisco: W. H. Freeman.

Stewart, N. (1990, January 27). *The effects of cocaine use by pregnant mothers on the development of their offspring.* Invited presentation, University of Texas at Dallas.

Stigler, J. W., Nusbaum, H. C., & Chalip, L. (1988). Developmental changes in speed of processing: Central limiting mechanism or skill transfer. *Child Development, 59,* 1144–1153.

Stipek, D. J., & Hoffman, J. M. (1980). Children's achievement-related expectancies as a function of academic performance histories and sex. *Journal of Educational Psychology, 72,* 861–865.

Stocker, C., & Dunn, J. (1991). Sibling relationships in adolescence. In R. M. Lerner, A. C. Petersen, & J. Brooks-Gunn (Eds.), *Encyclopedia of adolescence* (Vol. 2). New York: Garland.

Strahan, D. B. (1983). The emergence of formal operations in adolescence. *Transcendence, 11*, 7–14.

Strahan, D. B. (1987). A developmental analysis of formal reasoning in the middle grades. *Journal of Instructional Psychology, 14*, 67–73.

Streissguth, A. P., Aase, J. M., Clarren, S. K., Randels, S. P., LaDue, R. A., & Smith, D. F. (1991). Fetal alcoholism syndrome in adolescents and adults. *Journal of the American Medical Association, 265*, 1961–1967.

Streissguth, A. P., Carmichael-Olson, H., Sampston, P. D., & Barr, H. M. (1991, April). *Alcohol vs. tobacco as prenatal correlates of child behavior.* Paper presented at the Society for Research in Child Development meeting, Seattle.

Streissguth, A. P., Martin, D. C., Barr, H. M., Sandman, B. M., Kirshner, G. L., & Darby, B. L. (1984). Intrauterine alcohol and nicotine exposure: Attention and reaction time in 4-year-old children. *Developmental Psychology, 20*, 533–541.

Studdert-Kennedy, M. (1991). Language development from an evolutionary perspective. In N. A. Krasnegor, D. M. Rumbaugh, M. Studdert-Kennedy, & R. L. Schiefelbusch (Eds.), *Biological and behavioral determinants of language development*. Hillsdale, NJ: Erlbaum.

Stunkard, A. J. (1987). The regulation of body weight and the treatment of obesity. In H. Weiner & A. Baum (Eds.), *Eating regulation and discontrol*. Hillsdale, NJ: Erlbaum.

Stunkard, A. J. (1989). Perspectives on human obesity. In A. J. Stunkard & A. Baum (Eds.), *Perspectives on behavioral medicine: Eating, sleeping, and sex*. Hillsdale, NJ: Erlbaum.

Sue, D. W. (1989). Ethnic identity: The impact of two cultures on the psychological development of Asians in America. In D. R. Atkinson, G. Morten, & D. W. Sue (Eds.), *Counseling American minorities* (3rd ed.). Dubuque, IA: Wm. C. Brown.

Sue, S. (1990, August). *Ethnicity and culture in psychological research and practice.* Paper presented at the meeting of the American Psychological Association, Boston.

Sue, S., & Okazaki, S. (1990). Asian-American educational achievements. *American Psychologist, 45*, 913–920.

Suen, H. K. (1990). *Principles of test theories*. Hillsdale, NJ: Erlbaum.

Sugarman, S. (1989). *Piaget's construction of the child's reality*. New York: Cambridge University Press.

Sullivan, K., & Sullivan, A. (1980). Adolescent-parent separation. *Developmental Psychology, 16*, 93–99.

Suomi, S. (1987, April). *Individual differences in rhesus monkey behavioral and adrenocortical responses to social challenge: Correlations with measures of heart rate variability.* Paper presented at the Society for Research in Child Development meeting, Baltimore.

Suomi, S. J., Harlow, H. F., & Domek, C. J. (1970). Effect of repetitive infant-infant separations of young monkeys. *Journal of Abnormal Psychology, 76*, 161–172.

Super, C. M., Herrera, M. G., & Mora, J. O. (1991, April). *Cognitive outcomes of the early nutritional intervention in the Bogota study.* Paper presented at the Society for Research in Child Development meeting, Seattle.

Super, C. M., Herrera, M. G., & Mora, J. O. (1990). Long-term effects of food supplementation and psychosocial intervention on the physical growth of Columbian infants at risk of malnutrition. *Child Development, 61*, 29–49.

Susman, E. J., & Dorn, L. D. (1991). Hormones and behavior in adolescence. In R. M. Lerner, A. C. Petersen, & J. Brooks-Gunn (Eds.), *Encyclopedia of adolescence*. New York: Garland.

Sutton-Smith, B. (1985, October). The child at play. *Psychology Today*, pp. 64–65.

Swadesh, M. (1971). *The origin and diversification of language*. Chicago: Aldine-Atherton.

Swanson, D. P., & Cunningham, M. (1991, April). *Issues in gender and racial socialization of African American children.* Paper presented at the Society for Research in Child Development meeting, Seattle.

T

Tajfel, H. (1978). The achievement of group differentiation. In H. Tajfel (Ed.), *Differentiation between social groups: Studies in the social psychology of intergroup relations*. London: Academic Press.

Tamis-LeMonda, C. S., & Bornstein, M. H. (1989). Habituation and maternal encouragement of attention in infancy as predictors of toddler language, play, and representational competence. *Child Development, 60*, 738–751.

Tangney, J. P. (in press). Aspects of the family and children's television viewing content preferences. *Child Development.*

Tanner, J. M. (1978). *Fetus into man: Physical growth from conception into maturity*. Cambridge, MA: Harvard University Press.

Tanner, J. M. (1991). Growth spurt, adolescent. I. In R. M. Lerner, A. C. Petersen, & J. Brooks-Gunn (Eds.), *Encyclopedia of adolescence*. New York: Garland.

Task Force on Pediatric AIDS. (1989). Pediatric AIDS and human immunodeficiency virus infection. *American Psychologist, 44*, 248–264.

Tavris, C., & Wade, C. (1984). *The longest war: Sex differences in perspective* (2nd ed.). San Diego: Harcourt Brace Jovanovich.

Terman, L. (1925). *Genetic studies of genius: Vol. 1. Mental and physical traits of a thousand gifted children*. Stanford, CA: Stanford University Press.

Tharp, R. G. (1989). Psychocultural variables and constants: Effects on teaching and learning in schools. *American Psychologist, 44*, 349–359.

Thoma, S. J. (1986). Estimating gender differences in the comprehension and preference of moral issues. *Developmental Review, 6*, 165–180.

Thomas, A., & Chess, S. (1987). Commentary. In H. H. Goldsmith, A. H. Buss, R. Plomin, M. K. Rothbart, A. Thomas, A. Chess, R. R. Hinde, & R. B. McCall (Eds.), Roundtable: What is temperament? Four approaches. *Child Development, 58*, 505–529.

Thomas, A., & Chess, S. (1991). Temperament in adolescence and its functional significance. In R. M. Lerner, A. C. Petersen, & J. Brooks-Gunn (Eds.), *Encyclopedia of adolescence* (Vol. 2). New York: Garland.

Thompson, R. A. (1991). Construction and reconstruction of early attachments: Taking perspective on attachment theory and research. In D. P. Keating & H. G. Rosen (Eds.), *Constructivist perspectives on atypical development*. Hillsdale, NJ: Erlbaum.

Thorndike, R. L. (1990). Is there any future for intelligence? In R. E. Snow & D. E. Wiley (Eds.), *Improving inquiry in social science*. Hillsdale, NJ: Erlbaum.

Thorndike, R. L., Hagan, E. P., & Sattler, J. M. (1985). *Stanford-Binet* (4th ed.). Chicago: Riverside.

Thorpy, M. J., & Glovinsky, P. B. (1989). Headbanging (*Jactatio capitis nocturna*). In M. H. Kryger, T. Roth, & W. C. Dement (Eds.), *Principles and practices of sleep medicine*. San Diego: Harcourt Brace Jovanovich.

Thurstone, L. L. (1938). *Primary mental abilities*. Chicago: University of Chicago Press.

Timberlake, B., Fox, R. A., Baisch, M. J., & Goldberg, B. D. (1987). Prenatal education for pregnant adolescents. *Journal of School Health, 57*, 105–108.

Tobin, J. J., Wu, D. Y. H., & Davidson, D. H. (1989). *Preschool in three cultures*. New Haven, CT: Yale University Press.

Tomlinson-Keasey, C. (1972). Formal operations in females from 11 to 54 years of age. *Developmental Psychology, 6*, 364.

Tomlinson-Keasey, C., Warren, L. W., & Elliott, J. E. (1986). Suicide among gifted women: A prospective study. *Journal of Abnormal Psychology, 95*, 123–130.

Toth, A. (1991). *The fertility solution*. New York: Atlantic Monthly Press.

Trabasso, T. (1991, April). *The development and use of planning knowledge in narrative production*. Paper presented at the Society for Research in Child Development meeting, Seattle.

Trankina, F. (1983). Clinical issues and techniques in working with Hispanic children and their families. In G. J. Powell, J. Yamamoto, A. Romero, & A. Morales (Eds.), *The psychosocial development of minority group children*. New York: Brunner/Mazel.

Treboux, D. A., & Busch-Rossnagel, N. A. (1991). Sexual behavior, sexual attitudes, and contraceptive use, age differences in adolescent. In R. M. Lerner, A. C. Petersen, & J. Brooks-Gunn (Eds.), *Encyclopedia of adolescence* (Vol. 2). New York: Garland.

Trehub, S. E., Schneider, B. A., Thorpe, L. A., & Judge, P. (1991). Observational measures of auditory sensitivity in early infancy. *Developmental Psychology, 27*, 40–49.

Triandis, H. (1985). Collectivism vs. individualism: A reconceptualization of a basic concept in cross-cultural social psychology. In C. Bagley & G. K. Verman (Eds.), *Personality, cognition, and values*. London: Macmillan.

Trickett, P. K., Aber, J. L., Carlson, V., & Cicchetti, D. (1991). Relationship of socioeconomic status to the etiology and developmental sequelae of physical child abuse. *Developmental Psychology, 27*, 148–158.

Trimble, J. E. (1989). *The enculturation of contemporary psychology*. Paper presented at the meeting of the American Psychological Association, New Orleans.

Trimble, J. E. (in press). Ethnic specification, validation prospects and the future of drug use research. *International Journal of Addiction*.

Trotter, R. J. (1987, December). Project Day-Care. *Psychology Today*, pp. 32–38.

Tucker, L. A. (1987). Television, teenagers, and health. *Journal of Youth and Adolescence, 16*, 415–425.

Tuckman, B. W., & Hinkle, J. S. (1988). An experimental study of the physical and psychological effects of aerobic exercise on school children. In B. G. Melamed, K. A. Matthews, D. K. Routh, B. Stabler, & N. Schneiderman (Eds.), *Child health psychology*. Hillsdale, NJ: Erlbaum.

Turiel, E. (1966). An experimental test of the sequentiality of developmental stages in the child's moral judgments. *Journal of Personality and Social Psychology, 3*, 611–618.

U

U.S. Bureau of the Census (1986). *Geographical mobility: March 1980 to March 1985* (Current Population Reports Series P–20, No. 368). Washington, DC: U.S. Government Printing Office.

U.S. Public Health Service. (1988). *Moratorium on certain fetal tissue research*. Washington, DC: U.S. Government Printing Office.

United States Commission on Civil Rights (1975). *A better chance to learn: Bilingual bicultural education*. Washington, DC: U.S. Government Printing Office.

V

Valsinar, J. (1991, April). Discussant, *Innovative uses of microcomputers in social development research*. Symposium at the Society for Research in Child Development meeting, Seattle.

Van Deusen-Henkel, J., & Argondizza, M. (1987). Early elementary education: Curriculum planning for the primary grades. In *A framework for curriculum design*. Augusta: Division of Curriculum, Maine Department of Educational and Cultural Services.

Vandell, D. L. (1985, April). *Relationship between infant-peer and infant-mother interactions: What we have learned*. Paper presented at the Society for Research in Child Development meeting, Toronto.

Vandell, D. L. (1987). Baby sister/baby brother: Reactions to the birth of a sibling and patterns of early sibling relations. In F. F. Schachter & R. K. Stone (Eds.), *Practical concerns about siblings*. New York: Haworth.

Vandell, D. L., & Corasaniti, M. A. (1988). Variations in early child care: Do they predict subsequent social, emotional, and cognitive differences? *Child Development, 59*, 176–186.

Vandell, D. L., & Wilson, K. S. (1988). Infants' interactions with mother, sibling, and peer: Contrasts and relations between interaction systems. *Child Development, 48*, 176–186.

VanLehn, K. (Ed.). (1991). *Architectures for intelligence*. Hillsdale, NJ: Erlbaum.

Vorhees, C. V., & Mollnow, E. (1987). Behavioral teratogenesis: Long-term influences in behavior from early exposure to environmental agents. In J. D. Osofsky (Ed.), *Handbook of infant development*. New York: Wiley.

Vurpillot, E. (1968). The development of scanning strategies and their relation to visual differentiation. *Journal of Experimental Child Psychology, 6*, 632–650.

Vygotsky, L. S. (1962). *Thought and language*. Cambridge, MA: MIT Press.

W

Waddington, C. H. (1957). *The strategy of the genes*. London: Allen & Son.

Wade, C., & Tavris, C. (1990). *Psychology* (2nd ed.). New York: Harper & Row.

Wagner, D. A., & Stevenson, H. W. (1982). *Cultural perspectives on child development*. San Francisco: W. H. Freeman.

Wahlsten, D. (1991, April). *Molecular biology requires a reformulation of the nature-nurture question in developmental psychology*. Paper presented at the Society for Research in Child Development meeting, Seattle.

Wakefield, J. F. (1991). *Creative thinking: Problem solving skills and the arts orientation*. Norwood, NJ: Ablex.

Walker, E. L. (1970). Relevant psychology is a snark. *American Psychologist, 25*, 1081–1086.

Walker, L. (1982). The sequentiality of Kohlberg's stages of moral development. *Child Development, 53*, 1330–1336.

Walker, L. J. (1984). Sex differences in the development of moral reasoning: A critical review. *Child Development, 51*, 131–139.

Walker, L. J. (1991a). Sex differences in moral development. In W. M. Kurtines & J. Gewirtz (Eds.), *Moral behavior and development* (Vol. 2). Hillsdale, NJ: Erlbaum.

Walker, L. J. (1991b, April). *The validity of an ethic of care.* Paper presented at the Society for Research in Child Development meeting, Seattle.

Walker, L. J., & Taylor, J. H. (1991a). Family interaction and the development of moral reasoning. *Child Development, 62,* 264–283.

Walker, L. J., & Taylor, J. H. (1991b). Stage transitions in moral reasoning: A longitudinal study of developmental processes. *Developmental Psychology, 27,* 330–337.

Walker, L. J., de Vries, B., & Trevethan, S. D. (1987). Moral stages and moral orientation in real-life and hypothetical dilemmas. *Child Development, 58,* 842–858.

Wallace, H. M., & Vienonen, M. (1989). Teenage pregnancy in Sweden and Finland: Implications for the United States. *Journal of Adolescent Health Care, 10,* 231–236.

Wallach, M. A., & Kogan, N. (1965). *Modes of thinking in young children.* New York: Holt, Rinehart & Winston.

Wallerstein, J., Corbin, S. B., & Lewis, J. M. (1988). Children of divorce: A ten-year study. In E. M. Hetherington & J. D. Arasteh (Eds.), *Impact of divorce, single-parenting, and stepparenting on children.* Hillsdale, NJ: Erlbaum.

Wallerstein, J. S., & Kelly, J. B. (1980). *Surviving the breakup: How children actually cope with divorce.* New York: Basic.

Wallis, C. (1985, December 9). Children having children. *Time,* pp. 78–88.

Walsh, P. V., Katz, P. A., & Downey, E. P. (1991, April). *A longitudinal perspective on race and gender socialization in infants and toddlers.* Paper presented at the Society for Research in Child Development meeting, Seattle.

Walton, M. D., & Vallelunga, L. R. (1989, April). *The role of breastfeeding in establishing early mother-infant interactions.* Paper presented at the Society for Research in Child Development meeting, Kansas City.

Warshak, R. A. (1991, January 15). [Personal Communication.] Department of Psychology, University of Texas at Dallas.

Washburn, K. J., & Hakes, D. T. (1985, April). *Changes in children's semantic and syntactic acceptability judgments.* Paper presented at the Society for Research in Child Development meeting, Toronto.

Waterman, A. S. (1985). Identity in the context of adolescent psychology. In A. S. Waterman (Ed.), *Identity in adolescence: Processes and contents.* San Francisco: Jossey-Bass.

Waterman, A. S. (1989). Curricula interventions for identity change: Substantive and ethical considerations. *Journal of Adolescence, 12,* 389–400.

Waterman, A. S., & Waterman, C. K. (1971). A longitudinal study of changes in ego identity status during the freshman year of college. *Developmental Psychology, 5,* 167–173.

Waterman, A. S., & Waterman, C. K. (1972). Relationship between ego identity status and subsequent academic behavior: A test of the predictive validity of Marcia's categorization for identity status. *Developmental Psychology, 6,* 179.

Waters, E., & Sroufe, L. A. (1983). Social competence as a developmental construct. *Developmental Review, 3,* 79–97.

Watson, J. B. (1928). *Psychological care of infant and child.* New York: W. W. Norton.

Waxman, S. R., & Kosowski, T. D. (1990). Nouns mark category relations: Toddlers' and preschoolers' word-learning biases. *Child Development, 61,* 1461–1473.

Wechsler, D. (1949). *Wechsler Intelligence Scale for Children.* New York: Psychological Corp.

Wechsler, D. (1955). *Wechsler Adult Intelligence Scale manual.* New York: Psychological Corp.

Wechsler, D. (1967). *Wechsler Preschool and Primary Scale of Intelligence.* New York: Psychological Corp.

Wechsler, D. (1974). *Wechsler Intelligence Scale for Children—Revised.* New York: Psychological Corp.

Wechsler, D. (1981). *Wechsler Adult Intelligence Scale—Revised.* New York: Psychological Corp.

Wegman, W. E. (1986). Annual summary of vital statistics—1985. *Pediatrics, 78,* 983–984.

Weinberg, R. A. (1989). Intelligence and IQ: Landmark issues and great debates. *American Psychologist, 44,* 98–104.

Weiner, B. (1979). A theory of motivation for some classroom experiences. *Journal of Educational Psychology, 71,* 3–25.

Weiss, G., & Hechtman, L. T. (1986). *Hyperactive children grown up.* New York: Guilford.

Weissberg, R. P., Caplan, M. Z., & Sivo, P. J. (1989). A new conceptual framework for establishing school-based social competence promotion programs. In L. A. Bond, B. E. Compas, & C. Swift (Eds.), *Prevention in the schools.* Menlo Park, CA: Sage.

Wellman, H. M., Ritter, R., & Flavell, J. H. (1985). Deliberate memory behavior in the delayed reactions of very young children. *Developmental Psychology, 11,* 780–787.

Wender, P. H., Kety, S. S., Rosenthal, D., Schulsinger, F., Ortmann, J., & Lunde, I. (1986). Psychiatric disorders in the biological and adoptive families of adopted individuals with affective disorders. *Archives of General Psychiatry, 43,* 923–929.

Werner, E. E. (1979). *Cross-cultural child development: A view from planet earth.* Monterey, CA: Brooks/Cole.

Wertheimer, M. (1945). *Productive thinking.* New York: Harper.

Wertsch, J. V. (1985). Adult-child interaction as a source of self-regulation in children. In S. R. Yussen (Ed.), *The growth of reflection in children.* New York: Academic Press.

Whaley, L. F., & Wong, D. L. (1988). *Essentials of pediatric nursing.* St. Louis: Mosby.

White, B. L. (1988). *Educating the infant and toddler.* Lexington, MA: Lexington.

White, R. W. (1959). Motivation reconsidered: The concept of competence. *Psychological Review, 66,* 297–333.

Whitehurst, G. J., & Valdez-Menchaca, M. C. (1988). What is the role of reinforcement in early language acquisition? *Child Development, 59,* 430–440.

Whiting, B. B. (1989, April). *Culture and interpersonal behavior.* Paper presented at the Society for Research in Child Development meeting, Kansas City.

Whiting, B. B., & Edwards, C. P. (1988). *Children of different worlds.* Cambridge, MA: Harvard University Press.

Whiting, B. B., & Whiting, J. W. M. (1975). *Children of six cultures.* Cambridge, MA: Harvard University Press.

Widmayer, S., & Field, T. M. (1980). Effects of Brazelton demonstrations on early patterns of preterm infants and their teenage mothers. *Infant Behavior and Development, 3,* 79–89.

Wilcox, B. L., & Naimark, H. (1991). The rights of the child: Progress toward human dignity. *American Psychologist, 46,* 49.

Wiley, D. E. (1990). Test validity and invalidity revisited. In R. E. Snow & D. E. Wiley (Eds.), *Improving inquiry in social science*. Hillsdale, NJ: Erlbaum.

Wilkening, F., & Anderson, N. H. (1991). Representation and diagnosis of knowledge structures in developmental psychology. In N. H. Anderson (Ed.), *Contributions to information integration theory* (Vol. 3). Hillsdale, NJ: Erlbaum.

William T. Grant Foundation (1989). *American youth: A statistical snapshot*. Washington, DC: The William T. Grant Foundation Commission on Work, Family, and Citizenship.

Williams, F., LaRose, R., & Frost, F. (1981). *Children, television, and sex-role stereotyping*. New York: Praeger.

Williams, J. (1979). Reading instruction today. *American Psychologist, 34*, 917–922.

Williams, J. E., & Best, D. L. (1982). *Measuring sex stereotypes: A thirty nation study*. Newbury Park, CA: Sage.

Williams, J. E., & Best, D. L. (1989). *Sex and psyche: Self-concept viewed cross-culturally*. Newbury Park, CA: Sage.

Williams, M. F., & Condry, J. C. (1989, April). *Living color: Minority portrayals and cross-racial interactions on television*. Paper presented at the Society for Research in Child Development meeting, Kansas City.

Williams, T. M., Baron, D., Phillips, S., Travis, L., & Jackson, D. (1986, August). *The portrayal of sex roles on Canadian and U.S. television*. Paper presented at the conference of the International Association for Mass Communication Research, New Delhi, India.

Willis, S. L. (1989). Cohort differences in cognitive aging: A sample case. In K. W. Schaie & C. Schooler (Eds.), *Social structure and aging: Psychological processes*. Hillsdale, NJ: Erlbaum.

Willis, S. L., & Schaie, K. W. (1986). Training the elderly on the ability factors of spatial orientation and inductive reasoning. *Psychology and Aging, 1*, 239–247.

Wilson, M., Kohn, L., Hinton, I., Underwood, A., & Do, L. (1991, April). *The context of socialization in diverse Black families*. Paper presented at the Society for Research in Child Development meeting, Seattle.

Wilson, M. N. (1989). Child development in the context of the extended family. *American Psychologist, 44*, 380–385.

Windle, W. F. (1940). *Physiology of the human fetus*. Philadelphia: W. B. Saunders.

Winkelstein, W., Samuel, M., Padian, N. S., & Wiley, J. A. (1987). Selected sexual practices of San Francisco heterosexual men and risk of infection by human immunodeficiency virus. *Journal of the American Medical Association, 257*, 1470.

Winner, E. (1986, August). Where pelicans kiss seals. *Psychology Today*, pp. 24–35.

Winner, E. (1989). Development in the visual arts. In W. Damon (Ed.), *Child development today and tomorrow*. San Francisco: Jossey-Bass.

Witkin, H. A., Mednick, S. A., Schulsinger, R., Bakkestrom, E., Christiansen, K. O., Goodenbough, D. R., Hirchhorn, K., Lunsteen, C., Owen, D. R., Philip, J., Ruben, D. B., & Stocking, M. (1976). Criminality in XYY and XXY men. *Science, 193*, 547–555.

Witryol, S. (1971). Incentives and learning in children. In H. W. Reese (Ed.), *Advances in child development and behavior* (Vol. 6). New York: Academic Press.

Wober, M. (1974). Towards an understanding of the Kiganda concept of intelligence. In J. W. Berry & P. R. Dasen (Eds.), *Culture and cognition*. London: Methuen.

Wong, H. Z. (1982). Asian and Pacific Americans. In L. Snowden (Ed.), *Reaching the underserved: Mental health needs of neglected populations*. Newbury Park, CA: Sage.

Wood, F. H. (1988). Learners at risk. *Teaching Exceptional Children, 20*, 4–9.

Worobey, J., & Belsky, J. (1982). Employing the Brazelton Scale to influence mothering: An experimental comparison of three strategies. *Developmental Psychology, 18*, 736–743.

Worthington-Roberts, B. S. (1988). Lactation and human milk. In S. R. Williams & B. S. Worthington-Roberts (Eds.), *Nutrition through the life cycle*. St. Louis: Times Mirror/Mosby.

Wright, M. R. (1989). Body image satisfaction in adolescent girls and boys. *Journal of Youth and Adolescence, 18*, 71–84.

Wylie, R. (1979). *The self-concept: Theory and research on selected topics*. (Rev. ed., Vol. 2). Lincoln: University of Nebraska Press.

Y

Yaniv, I., & Shatz, M. (1990). Heuristics of reasoning and analogy in children's visual perspective taking. *Child Development, 61*, 1491–1501.

Yankelovich, D. (1974). *The new morality: A profile of American youth in the 1970s*. New York: McGraw-Hill.

Yardley, K. (1987). What do you mean "Who am I?": Exploring the implications of a self-concept measurement with subjects. In K. Yardley & T. Honess (Eds.), *Self and identity: Psychosocial perspectives*. New York: Wiley.

Yekel, C. A., Bigler, R. S., & Liben, L. S. (1991, April). *Children's gender schemata: Occupation, activity, and trait*. Paper presented at the Society for Research in Child Development meeting, Seattle.

Young, K. T. (1990). American conceptions of infant development from 1955 to 1984: What the experts are telling parents. *Child Development, 61*, 17–28.

Youngblade, L., & Belsky, J. (1991, April). *Predicting five-year-olds' relationships with close friends from antecedent parent-child relationships: A soft-modeling approach*. Paper presented at the Society for Research in Child Development meeting, Seattle.

Yussen, S. R. (1977). Characteristics of moral dilemmas written by adolescents. *Developmental Psychology, 13*, 162–163.

Yussen, S. R. (1985). The role of metacognition in contemporary theories of cognitive development. In D. Forrest-Pressley and G. Waller (Eds.), *Contemporary research in cognition and metacognition*. Orlando, FL: Academic Press.

Yussen, S. R., & Levy, V. (1975). Developmental changes in predicting one's own span of short-term memory. *Journal of Experimental Child Psychology, 19*, 502–508.

Yussen, S. R., Mathews, S. R., Huang, S., & Evans, R. (1988). The robustness and temporal course of the story schema's influence on recall. *Journal of Experimental Psychology: Learning, Memory, and Cognition, 14*, 173–179.

Z

Zahn-Waxler, C. (1990, May 28). Commentary. *Newsweek*, p. 61.

Zelnik, M., & Kantner, J. F. (1980). Sexual activity, contraceptive use and pregnancy among metropolitan-area teenagers: 1971–1979. *Family Planning Perspectives, 12*, 230–237.

Zembar, M. J., & Naus, M. J. (1985, April). *The combined effect of knowledge base and mnemonic strategies in children's memory*. Paper presented at the Society for Research in Child Development meeting, Toronto.

Zeskind, P. S., & Marshall, T. R. (1988). The relation between variations in pitch and maternal perception of infant crying. *Child Development, 59,* 193–196.

Ziegert, K. A. (1983). The Swedish prohibition of corporal punishment: A preliminary report. *Journal of Marriage and the Family, 45,* 917–926.

Zigler, E. (1987, April). *Child care for parents who work outside the home: Problems and solutions.* Paper presented at the Society for Research in Child Development meeting, Baltimore.

Zigler, E. (1988). *A solution to the nation's child care crisis: The school of the 21st century.* Unpublished manuscript, Department of Psychology, Yale University.

Zigler, E. F. (1991a, October). *Day care in America: What is needed.* Paper presented at the symposium on day care for children, Arlington, VA.

Zigler, E. F. (1991b, April). Discussant, *Early intervention with premature infants.* Symposium at the Society for Research in Child Development meeting, Seattle.

Zigler, E. F. (1991c, March). *Needs in social policy research.* Invited presentation, Program in Psychology and Human Development, University of Texas at Dallas.

Zukow, P. G. (Ed.). (1989). *Sibling interaction across cultures.* New York: Springer-Verlag.

CREDITS

Illustrations and Text

Chapter 2

Figure 2.1: From *Psychology: A Scientific Study of Human Behavior*, 5th ed. by L. S. Wrightsman, et al. Copyright © 1979 Wadsworth Publishing Co, Pacific Grove, CA 93950. **Figure 2.9:** J. Garbarino, "Sociocultural Risk" from Kopp/Krakow, *The Child*, © 1982 by Addison-Wesley Publishing Co., Inc. Reprinted by permission of Addison-Wesley Publishing Co., Inc. Reading, MA. **Poem, page 48:** From *The Poetry of Robert Frost* edited by Edward Connery Lathem. Copyright 1936 by Robert Frost. Copyright © 1964 by Lesley Frost Ballantine. Copyright © 1969 by Holt, Rinehart and Winston. Reprinted by permission of Henry Holt and Company, Inc; and to the Estate of Robert Frost, by permission of Jonathan Cape, London, England.

Chapter 3

Figure 3.7: From I. Gottesman, "Genetic Aspects of Intellectual Behavior" in *Handbook of Mental Deficiency*, edited by Norman R. Ellis. Copyright © McGraw-Hill Book Company, New York, NY. Reprinted by permission of Norman R. Ellis. **Poem, page 88:** From *Verses From 1929 On* by Ogden Nash. Copyright © 1940 by Ogden Nash. By permission of Little, Brown and Company; Curtis Brown Ltd., New York, NY. **Figure 4.4:** From K. L. Moore, *The Developing Human: Clinically Oriented*, 4th ed. Copyright © 1988 W. B. Saunders Company, Philadelphia, PA. Reprinted by permission of the publisher and author.

Chapter 5

Excerpt, page 144: Reprinted from "States in Newborn Infants" in *Merrill-Palmer Quarterly*, Volume 10, No. 4. (1964), pp. 313–327 by J. L. Brown, by permission of the Wayne State University Press. Copyright © 1964 Wayne State University Press. **Figure 5.2:** From Howard P. Roffwarg, et al., "Ontogenetic Development of the Human Sleep-Dream Cycle" in *Science*, 152:608, 1966. Copyright 1966 by the American Association for the Advancement of Science. Reprinted by permission of the publisher and author. **Figure 5.3:** From L. Patten, *Human Embryology*. Copyright © 1933 McGraw-Hill Book Company, New York, NY. Reprinted by permission of McGraw-Hill, Inc. **Figure 5.5:** J. L. Conel (1939–1963), *Postnatal Development of the Human Cerebral Cortex*, Vols. I-VI. Copyright © Harvard University Press, Cambridge, MA. Reprinted by permission.

Chapter 6

Figure 6.2: left From George H. Lowrey, *Growth and Development of Children*, 7th ed. Copyright © 1978 Year Book Medical Publishers, Chicago, IL. Reprinted by permission. **Figure 6.3:** From Albert Damon, *Human Biology*. Copyright © 1972 W. W. Norton & Company, Inc., New York, NY. **Figure 6.4:** From A. F. Roche, "Secular Trends in Stature, Weight and Maturation" in *Monographs of the Society for Research in Child Development*, 44, ser. no. 179, 1977. Copyright © 1977 The Society for Research in Child Development, Inc., Chicago, IL. Reprinted by permission. **Figure 6.5 (left):** Reproduced with kind permission from J. M. Tanner, R. H. Whitehouse, and M. Takaishi, "Standards from Birth to Maturity for Height, Weight, Height Velocity, and Weight Velocity: British Children 1965" in *Archives of Diseases in Childhood*, 41, 1966. Copyright © 1966 British Medical Association, London, England. **Figure 6.8:** From D. A. Blythe, et al., "The Impact of Puberty on Adolescence: A Longitudinal Study" in *Girls at Puberty* by Jeanne Brooks-Gunn. Copyright © 1981 Plenum Publishing Co., Inc., New York, NY. Reprinted by permission. **Figure 6.9:** Reprinted from *Family Planning Perspectives*, vol. 17, no. 2, March/April 1985. The Alan Guttmacher Institute 1985. **Figure 6.10:** Reprinted from *Family Planning Perspectives*, vol. 17, no. 2, March/April 1985. The Alan Guttmacher Institute 1985.

Chapter 7

Figure 7.1a: From *LEARNING AND BEHAVIOR* by Paul Chance © 1979 by Wadsworth Publishing Company, Inc. Reprinted by permission of the publisher. **Figure 7.1b:** From Benjamin B. Lahey, *Psychology: An Introduction*, 3d ed. Copyright © 1989 Wm. C. Brown Publishers, Dubuque, Iowa. All Rights Reserved. Reprinted by permission. **Figure 7.6:** From Albert Bandura, "Influence of Model's Reinforcement Contingencies on the Acquisition of Imitative Responses" in *Journal of Personality and Social Psychology*, 1:589–595, 1965. Copyright 1965 by the American Psychological Association. Reprinted by permission of the author. **Figure 7.8:** From Tiffany M. Field, "Discrimination and Imitation of Facial Expressions by Neonates" in *Science*, 218(4568):179–181, October 8, 1982. Copyright 1982 by American Association for the Advancement of Science. Reprinted by permission of the publisher and author.

Figure 7.9: Albert Bandura, *Social Foundations of Thought and Action: A Social Cognitive Theory,* © 1986, p. 24. Adapted by permission of Prentice-Hall, Inc., Englewood Cliffs, NJ. **Figure 7.10:** Source: Maslow's Hierarchy of Needs, "A Theory of Human Motivation" in *Motivation and Personality,* 2d ed. Copyright © 1970 by Abraham H. Maslow. **Figure 7.11:** From Mark L. Lepper, et al., "Interests with Extrinsic Rewards" in *Journal of Personality and Social Psychology,* 28:129–137, 1973. Copyright 1973 by the American Psychological Association. Reprinted by permission of the author.

Chapter 8

Excerpt, page 257: From J. H. Flavell, "A Tribute to Piaget" in *Society for Research in Child Development Newsletter,* Fall 1980. Reprinted by permission of The Society for Research in Child Development, Inc., Chicago, IL. **Figure 8a:** Dennie Wolf/Josh Nove. **Figures 8.B & 8.C:** Courtesy of Dr. Ellen Winner, Project Zero.

Chapter 9

Figure 9.1: From Elaine Vurpillot, "The Development of Scanning Strategies and Their Relation to Visual Differentiation" in *Journal of Experimental Psychology,* 6:632–650, 1968. Copyright 1968 by the American Psychological Association. Reprinted by permission. **Figure 9.2:** From Frank N. Dempster, "Memory Span: Sources of Individual and Developmental Differences" in *Psychological Bulletin,* 89:63–100, 1981. Copyright 1981 by the American Psychological Association. Reprinted by permission of the author. **Figure 9.3:** From Joel Levin, et al., "The Keyword Method in the Classroom" in *Elementary School Journal,* 80(4), 1980. Copyright © 1980 The University of Chicago Press, Chicago, IL. Reprinted by permission. **Figure 9.4:** From M. T. H. Chi and R. D. Koeske, "Network Representation of a Child's Dinosaur Knowledge" in *Developmental Psychology,* 19:29–39, 1983. Copyright 1983 by the American Psychological Association. Reprinted by permission of the authors. **Figure 9.5:** From Steve R. Yussen, et al., "The Robustness and Temporal Cause of the Story Schemics Influence on Recall" in *Journal of Experimental Psychology Learning, Memory, and Cognition,* 14:173–179, 1988. Copyright 1988 by the American Psychological Association. Reprinted by permission of the authors. **Figure 9.6:** From J. Kagan, et al., "Conceptual Impulsivity and Inductive Reasoning" in *Child Development,* 37:585, 1966. © 1966 The Society for Research in Child Development, Inc., Chicago, IL. Reprinted by permission.

Chapter 10

Figure 10.8: From R. Brown, et al., "The Child's Grammar from 1–111" in *Minnesota Symposium on Child Psychology,* Vol. 2, edited by J. P. Hill. Copyright © 1969 University of Minnesota Press, Minneapolis, MN. Reprinted by permission. **Figure 10.9:** From J. Berko, "The Child's Learning of English Morphology" in *Word,* 14:361. Copyright © 1958 International Linguistic Association. Reprinted by permission.

Chapter 11

Figure 11.2: From Jerome M. Sattler, *Assessment of Children's Intelligence and Special Abilities,* 2d ed. Copyright © 1982 Allyn & Bacon, Inc., Needham Heights, MA. Reprinted by permission of the author. **Figure 11.5:** Item A5 from Raven's *Standard Progressive Matrices,* reproduced by permission of J. C. Raven Limited.

Chapter 12

Poem, page 402: Excerpt from *The Elder Statesman* by T.S. Eliot. Copyright © 1959 by T.S. Eliot. Renewal copyright © 1987 by Valerie Eliot. Reprinted by permission of Farrar, Straus & Giroux, Inc. Faber & Faber, London, England. **Figure 12.3 left:** From Jay Belsky, "Early Human Experience: A Family Perspective" in *Developmental Psychology,* 17:3–23, 1981. Copyright 1981 by the American Psychological Association. Reprinted by permission of the author.

Chapter 13

Figure 13.2: From R. M. Krauss and S. Glicksberg, "The Development of Communication Competence as a Function of Age" in *Child Development,* 40:255–266, 1969. Copyright © 1969 The Society for Research in Child Development, Inc., Chicago, IL. Reprinted by permission.

Chapter 14

Excerpt, page 501: Published by Transaction Publishers, from *Successful Schools for Young Adolescents,* by Joan Lipsitz. Copyright © 1984 by Transaction Publishers. Reprinted by permission.

Chapter 15

Figure 15.1 left: From M. Lewis and Jeanne Brooks-Gunn, *Social Cognition and the Acquisition of the Self.* Copyright © 1979 Plenum Publishing Corporation, New York, NY. Reprinted by permission of the publisher and authors. **Figure 15.3:** Reprinted from the *Journal of Early Adolescence,* 1983, 3, 121–140. By permission of the Publishers, H.E.L.P. Books, Inc., Tucson, AZ. **Figure 15.4 top:** From Martin Ford, "A Living Systems Conceptualization of Social Intelligence: Outcomes, Processes, and Developmental Change" in *Advances in the Psychology of Human Intelligence,* 3, 1986, edited by R. J. Sternberg. Copyright © 1986 Lawrence Erlbaum Associates, Hillsdale, NJ. Reprinted by permission of the publisher and author.

Chapter 16

Figure 16.A: From Janet S. Hyde, "Children's Understanding of Sexist Language" in *Developmental Psychology,* 20:703, 1984. Copyright 1984 by the American Psychological Association. Reprinted by permission of the author. **Figure 16.3:** From Janet S. Hyde, et al., "Gender Differences in Mathematics Performance" in *Psychological Bulletin,* 107:139–155, 1990. Copyright 1990 by the American Psychological Association. **Lyrics, page 571:** I AM WOMAN. Words by Helen Reddy, Music by Ray Burton © 1971 Irving Music, Inc. and Buggerlugs Music Co. (BMI) Irving Music, Inc. administers for Buggerlugs Music Co. for the world. All Rights Reserved. International Copyright Secured.

Chapter 17

Figure 17.3 (graph): Source: Data from The Higher Education Research Institute, Graduate School of Education, University of California, Los Angeles, 1987.

Photographs

Table of Contents

Page vii left: © Joe Devenney/The Image Bank; **right:** © Elyse Lewin/The Image Bank; **p. viii left:** © Kathleen Loewenberg; **right:** Photograph courtesy of Northern Telecom/Photographer, JoAnn Carney; **p. ix left:** © James G. White Photography; **right:** © Lennart Nilsson, "A Child Is Born," Dell Publishing Company; **p. x left:** © Nick Kelsch, Philadelphia; **right:** © Andy Levin; **p. xi left:** © Lisl Dennis/The Image Bank; **right:** © Suzanne Szasz/Photo Researchers, Inc.; **p. xii left:** © Margaret W. Peterson/The Image Bank; **right:** © Superstock/Four by Five; **p. xiii left:** © Elizabeth Crews/The Image Works; **right:** © Owen Franken/Stock Boston; **p. xiv left:** © Comstock, Inc.; **right:** © Stephen Marks/Stockphotos, Inc.; **p. xv left:** © Melchior DiGiacomo/The Image Bank; **right:** © Whitney Lane/The Image Bank; **p. xvi left:** © Gio Barto/The Image Bank; **right:** © Don Klumpp/The Image Bank

Section Openers

Section 1: © Joe Devenney/The Image Bank; **Section 2:** Photograph Courtesy of Northern Telecom/Photographer, JoAnn Carney; **Section 3:** © Lisl Dennis/The Image Bank; **Section 4:** © Owen Franken/Stock Boston

Chapter 1

Opener: © Elyse Lewin/The Image Bank; **p. 7:** © Paul Conklin/Monkmeyer Press Photo Service; **p. 8:** © Steve Schapiro/Gamma Liason; **1.1A & B:** © Scala/Art Resource, New York; **1.2:** © Herbert Gehr, Life Magazine copyright 1947, Time Warner; **p. 15 top:** Courtesy of Miriam Wright Edelman/The Children's Defense Fund, Photograph by Rick Reinhard; **bottom:** Courtesy of Edward Zigler, Yale University; **p. 16 left:** © Tim Carlson/Stock Boston; **right:** © Sobel/Klonsky/The Image Bank; **1.4 top to bottom:** © Mel Digiacomo/The Image Bank, © Maria Taglienti/The Image Bank, © Suzanne Szasz/Photo Researchers, Inc., © Helena Frost Associates, Ltd., © Landrum Shettles; **p. 21:** © Bob Daemmrich/The Image Works; **1.6A:** © Cary Wolinsky/Stock Boston; **1.6B:** © Carl Glassman/The Image Works; **p. 27:** Reprinted with permission from Psychology Today magazine. © 1985. PT Partners LP. by John Modire.; **p. 28:** © Anthro-Photo; **1.8 left:** © Lorraine Rorke/The Image Works; **right:** © Gary Chapman/The Image Bank; **p. 29 top:** © Anthony Bannister/Animals Animals/Earth Scenes; **bottom:** © Chagran/Anthro-Photo; **p. 36:** © Mitchell Funk/The Image Bank; **p. 37:** Courtesy of Dr. Florence L. Denmark/Photo by Robert Wesner

Chapter 2

Opener: © Kathleen Loewenberg; **p. 47:** © The Bettmann Archive; **p. 52 top:** © Robin Smith/Superstock, Inc.; **bottom:** © The Bettmann Archive; **p. 53 left:** The Bettmann Archive; **p. 53 right:** Courtesy of Nancy Chodorow/Photo by Jean Margolis; **2.2 left top to bottom:** © William Hopkins Photography, © Suzanne Szasz/Photo Researchers, Inc., © Superstock/Four by Five, © Alan Becker/The Image Bank; **right top to bottom:** © Sam Zarember/The Image Bank, © Brett Froomer/The Image Bank, © Alan Carey/The Image Works, © Harold Sund/The Image Bank; **p. 58:** © Yves DeBraine/Black Star; **2.3 left to right:** © Julie O'Neil Photography, © Gale Zucker/Stock Boston, © Liane Enkelis/Stock Boston, © Mary L. Baer/Tom Stack & Associates; **p. 65:** © Joe McNally/Sygma; **p. 66 left:** Reprinted with permission from Psychology Today Magazine Copyright 1986, (PT Partners, L.P.); **right:** Courtesy of Walter Mischel, Columbia University; **2.7:** Museum of Modern Art, New York, Gift of Mrs. Simon Guggenheim.; **p. 68 top:** © The Bettmann Archive; **2.8:** Photo by Nina Leen/LIFE Magazine, Copyright Time, Inc.; **p. 71:** Courtesy of Robert Hinde, MRC Unit on the Development and Integration of Behavior, Cambridge University, Cambridge, England; **p. 72:** Courtesy of Urie Bronfenbrenner, Cornell University; **p. 74 top:** © Gilda Schiff/Photo Researchers, Inc.; **bottom:** © Debra L. Martin/Unicorn Stock Photos

Chapter 3

Opener: © James G. White Photography; **p. 84 (all):** © D. Gorton/Time Magazine; **3.1 left to right:** © NASA/Science Source/Photo Researchers, Inc., © Pat Caufield/Photo Researchers, Inc., © Spencer Grant/Stock Boston, © Miguel Castro/Photo Researchers, Inc., © John P. Kelly/The Image Bank, © Bonnie Rauch/The Image Bank; **3.2:** Regents of the University of California; **3.3 top:** © Frank Pedrick/Light Images; **bottom:** © Elyse Lewin/The Image Bank; **3.4:** © Lennart Nilsson, Albert Bonniers Porlog AB; **3.5:** © Alexander Tsiaras/Science Source/Photo Researchers, Inc; **p. 91:** © Robert McElroy/Woodfin Camp and Associates; **p. 92 top:** © Deni McIntyre/Photo Researchers, Inc.; **bottom:** © Jacques Pavlovsky/Sygma; **3.6 top:** © Tim Davis/Photo Researchers, Inc.; **bottom:** © Sandy Roessler/The Stock Market; **p. 95:** © Porterfield-Chickering/Photo Reseachers, Inc.; **p. 98 (all):** © Enrico Ferorelli; **101 top:** © Nancy Anne Dawe/Creative Communications; **bottom:** © Adrienne T. Gibson/Tom Stack and Associates; **p. 102:** © Alan Oddie/PhotoEdit

Chapter 4

Opener: © Lennart Nilsson, "A Child Is Born," Dell Publishing Company; **4.1, 4.2, 4.3:** © Lennart Nilsson, "Behold Man," Little, Brown and Company 1974; **4.5:** Streissguth, A. P., Clarren, S. K. and Jones, K. L. (1985 July) Natural History of the Fetal Alcohol Syndrome: A ten-year follow-up of eleven patients, Lancet, 2, 85–92; **4.6:** © James Kamp/Black Star; **p. 121:** © Erika Stone; **p. 123:** © Richard Anderson/Anderson Photoimages; **p. 126:** © Charles Gupton/Stock Boston; **p. 129:** © Tiffany Field; **p. 130:** © Comstock, Inc./Tom Grill; **p. 131:** © Roberto Valladares/The Image Bank; **p. 132:** © James G. White Photography

Chapter 5

Opener: © Nick Kelsch, Philadelphia; **p. 140 top row left to right:** © Elizabeth Crews/The Image Works, © James G. White Photography, © Petit Format/Photo Researchers, Inc.; **bottom row left to right:** © Tom Pollak/Monkmeyer Press Photo Service, © Elizabeth Crews/The Image Works, © Comstock, Inc./Stuart Cohen; **5.1 top row left to right:** © Erika Stone, © Erika Stone, © Nancy Anne Dawe/Creative Communications, © Erika Stone; **bottom row left to right:** © Erika Stone, © Nancy Anne Dawe/Creative Communications, ©Erika Stone, © Erika Stone; **5.2 left:** © David

DeLossy/The Image Bank; **right:** Dreamstage Scientific Catalogue. J. Allan Hobson & Hoffman La Roche Inc.; **p. 147:** © Harold Hoffman/Photo Researchers, Inc.; **p. 149:** © Bob Daemmrich/The Image Works; **p. 151 left:** © Joyce Photographics/Photo Researchers, Inc.; **right:** © Mark Antman/The Image Works; **p. 152:** © Will McIntyre/Photo Researchers, Inc.; **p. 153:** © T. Fujihira/Monkmeyer Press Photo Service; **5.6:** © David Linton; **5.7:** © Enrico Ferorelli; **5.8:** © Jean Guichard/Sygma; **p. 159 top:** © Michael Siluk; **bottom:** © Dr. Melanie Spence, University of Texas, Dallas

Chapter 6

Opener: © Andy Levin; **6.1:** © Joe McNally/Sports Illustrated; **p. 170:** © Joe Devenney/The Image Bank; **p. 171 top:** © Nancy Anne Dawe/Creative Communications; **bottom:** © Marc Romanelli/The Image Bank; **p. 173:** © Pat LaCroix/The Image Bank; **p. 175:** © Mel DiGiacomo/The Image Bank; **p. 176:** © William Campbell/Time Magazine; **p. 178:** © Melchior Digicomo/The Image Bank; **p. 180:** © Bob Daemmrich/The Image Works; **6.5:** © Jeff Persons/Stock Boston; **p. 183:** © Guiseppe Molteni/The Image Bank; **p. 188:** © Abigail Heyman; **p. 190:** © Roger Sandler/Black Star; **p. 193:** © James D. Wilson/Woodfin Camp and Associates; **6.10:** © William Hopkins Photography; **p. 198:** © Superstock/Four by Five; **p. 199:** © Alan Carey/The Image Works; **p. 207:** © David R. Frazier/Photo Researchers, Inc.

Chapter 7

Opener: © Jim Tuten/Black Star; **p. 221:** © Whitney Lane/The Image Bank; **7.1 (all):** © The Granger Collection; **7.3:** Courtesy of Benjamin Harris, University of Wisconsin; **7.4:** © Blair Seitz/Photo Researchers, Inc.; **p. 233:** © Frank Pedrich/Light Images; **p. 235:** © Henley and Savage/The Stock Market; **p. 237 left:** © Cleo Freelance Photography; **right:** © Cleo Freelance Photography; **7.5 (all):** © Albert Bandura; **7.7:** © David Brownell/The Image Bank; **p. 240:** © Enrico Ferorelli; **p. 247:** © Andre Gallant/The Image Bank; **p. 248:** © Peter Dublin/Stock Boston

Chapter 8

Opener: © Suzanne Szasz/Photo Researchers, Inc.; **p. 256:** © Jacques Chenet/Woodfin Camp and Associates; **p. 257:** © Yves DeBraine/Black Star; **8.1 top row left to right:** © Cleo Freelance Photography, © C & W Shields, Inc., © Gabor Demjen/Stock Boston; **bottom row left to right:** © Elizabeth Crews/The Image Works, © William Hopkins Photography, © Patricia Agre/Photo Researchers, Inc.; **8.2 (all):** © D. Goodman/Monkmeyer Press Photo Service; **8.3:** © Niki

Mareschal/The Image Bank; **8.6:** © Paul Fusco/Magnum Photos, Inc.; **8.8:** © Owen Franken/Stock Boston; **p. 275:** © Mark M. Walker/Photo Factory; **8.10:** © Richard Hutchings/Photo Researchers, Inc.; **p. 280:** © Will & Deni McIntyre/Photo Researchers, Inc.; **p. 282 top:** © Michael Siluk; **bottom:** © Mimi Forsyth/Monkmeyer Press Photo Service; **8.11:** © Butch Martin/The Image Bank; **p. 285:** © Yves DeBraine/Black Star; **p. 289:** UNICEF/Photo by Sean Sprague; **8.12:** © Alan Becker/The Image Bank; **8.D:** © 1990 Barbara Rogoff/Apprenticeship in Thinking (Oxford University Press); **p. 291:** © Butch Martin/The Image Bank

Chapter 9

Opener: © Margaret W. Peterson/The Image Bank; **p. 300:** © Gabe Palmer/The Stock Market; **p. 303:** © Jeff Persons/Stock Boston; **p. 304:** © Skjold Photographs; **p. 317:** © Suzanne Szasz/Photo Researchers, Inc.; **p. 319:** Courtesy of John Flavell; **p. 320:** © Superstock/Four by Five; **p. 323:** © Bob Daemmrich/Stock Boston

Chapter 10

Opener: © Superstock/Four by Five; **10.2:** © James L. Shaffer; **10.3:** AP/Wide World Photos; **10.5:** From B. T. Gardner, Animal Behavior Research Group, University of Nevada, Reno; **10.6:** Courtesy of Duane M. Rumbaugh, Yerkes Regional Primate Center, Atlanta; **10.7:** © Jeffrey W. Myers/The Stock Market; **p. 342:** © C. Vergara/Photo Researchers, Inc.; **p. 344:** © Margaret W. Peterson/The Image Bank; **p. 348:** © Anthony Bannister/Animals Animals/Earth Scenes; **p. 350:** © Brett Froomer/The Image Bank; **10.10B:** © Larry Voight/Photo Researchers, Inc.; **p. 354:** © H. Anders/The Image Bank; **p. 355:** © Doug Menuez/Stock Boston; **p. 356:** © Blair Seitz/Photo Researchers, Inc.; **p. 357:** © Stephanie Dinkins/Photo Researchers, Inc.

Chapter 11

Opener: © Elizabeth Crews/The Image Works; **11.1:** © Billy E. Barnes/Jeroboam; **p. 368:** Culver Pictures, Inc.; **p. 371 top:** © Mark Antman/The Image Works; **bottom:** Courtesy of Robert J. Sternberg; **11.4A:** © Mel Digiacomo/The Image Works; **11.4B:** © Alan Carey/The Image Works; **11.4C:** © Sumo/The Image Bank; **p. 377:** © Patrick Donehue/Photo Researchers, Inc.; **p. 380:** © Shelly Katz/Black Star; **p. 381:** © David Campbell/Photo Researchers, Inc.; **p. 382 left to right:** © Heinerfield/Finkle/Light Images, © Gwen Berghorn, © Roy King, © Suzanne L. Murphy Photography; **11.7A:** © David Austen/Stock Boston; **11.7B:** © Ben Simmons/The Stock Market; **11.8:** © Jill Connefax/EKM Nepenthe; **p. 390 top:**

© Jean Pierre Horlin/The Image Bank; **bottom:** © Frank Sheman/Stock Boston

Chapter 12

Opener: © Comstock, Inc.; **12.1A:** © Leonard Lee Rue III/Photo Researchers, Inc.; **12.1B:** © Mitch Reardon/Photo Researchers, Inc.; **12.1C:** © Allen Green/Photo Researchers, Inc.; **12.2A:** © James L. Shaffer; **12.2B:** © James G. White Photography; **12.2C:** © James G. White Photography; **12.3:** © James L. Shaffer; **12.4:** © Martin Rogers/Stock Boston; **p. 407:** © James G. White Photography; **p. 408:** © Chris Hackett/The Image Bank; **p. 409:** © Peter Menzel/Stock Boston; **p. 410 top:** © Kathy Tarantola; **bottom:** © Superstock/Four by Five; **p. 414:** © Joseph Schuyler/Stock Boston; **12.5:** © Tim Bieber/The Image Bank; **p. 419:** © Mimi Forsyth/Monkmeyer Press Photo Service; **p. 422:** © Bachmann/The Image Works; **p. 423:** © Bob Daemmrich/The Image Works; **p. 425:** © Dario Perla/International Stock Photography; **p. 427:** © Guido Alberto Rossi/The Image Bank; **p. 431:** © Elyse Lewin/The Image Bank

Chapter 13

Opener: © Stephen Marks/Stockphotos, Inc.; **p. 443:** © Bill Foley/Black Star; **13.1:** © Erik Anderson/Stock Boston; **p. 450 left:** © Mark Richards/SIPA Press; **right:** © Gio Barto/The Image Bank; **p. 451:** © Lanpher Productions, Inc.; **p. 453:** © Jan Doyle; **p. 454:** © Superstock/Four by Five; **p. 456:** © Miro Vintoniv/Stock Boston; **p. 460:** © Bryan Peterson Photography; **13.4 left to right:** © Terje Rakke/The Image Bank, © Maria Taglienti/The Image Bank, © Margaret W. Peterson/The Image Bank, © Elizabeth Crews/The Image Works, © Alvis Upitis/The Image Bank; **13.5:** The Kunsthistorisches Museum, Vienna; **p. 465:** © The Everett Collection, Inc.; **p. 466:** © 1989 Children's Television Workshop (New York, New York). All rights reserved; **p. 467:** © Larry Kolvoord/The Image Works; **p. 469:** © Bob Daemmrich/Stock Boston

Chapter 14

Opener: © Melchior DiGiacomo/The Image Bank; **p. 478:** © Don Klumpp/The Image Bank; **p. 479:** © John Ficara/Woodfin Camp and Associates; **p. 481:** © Lawrence Migdale/Stock Boston; **p. 483 top:** © Elizabeth Crews/The Image Works; **bottom:** © Jeffrey W. Myers/The Stock Market; **p. 484 top:** © Elizabeth Crews/Stock Boston; **middle:** © Elizabeth Crews/The Image Works; **bottom:** © Elisabeth Nichols; **p. 485 top:** © Alan Carey/The Image Works; **middle:** © Gregg Mancuso/The Image Bank; **bottom:** © Francis Wardle; **p. 487 left:** © Robert Wallis/SIPA Press; **right:** © Dr. R.J. Hendry;

p. 488: © Robert Knowles/Black Star; **p. 491:** © Art Kane/The Image Bank; **p. 495:** © Bob Daemmrich/The Image Works; **p. 497:** © James L. Shaffer; **p. 498:** © Bob Daemmrich/The Image Works; **p. 499:** © James G. White; **p. 502:** © Richard Anderson; **p. 503:** © Bob Daemmrich/The Image Works; **p. 505:** © Richard Anderson/Anderson Photoimages; **p. 507 left:** © Will McIntyre/Photo Researchers, Inc.; **right:** © Richard Hutchings/Photo Researchers, Inc.

Chapter 15

Opener: © Whitney Lane/The Image Bank; **15.1:** © D. E. Cox; **15.2 top to bottom:** © Laura Dwight/Black Star, © Superstock/Four by Five, © Romilly Lockyer/The Image Bank, © Gary Cralle/The Image Bank; **15.4:** © Robert Frerck/Odyssey Productions; **p. 536:** © Jeff Persons/Stock Boston; **p. 539 left:** © The Bettmann Archive; **right:** © Paul Popper, Ltd.; **p. 540 bottom:** © Benn Mitchell/The Image Bank; **15.5:** © Richard Hutchings/Photo Researchers, Inc.; **p. 543:** © Bob Daemmrich/The Image Works

Chapter 16

Opener: © Gio Barto/The Image Bank; **16.1:** © Erika Stone; **p. 554:** © Janeart Ltd./The Image Bank; **p. 555:** © Suzanne Szasz/Photo Researchers, Inc.; **16.2:** © Ken Gaghan/Jeroboam; **p. 566:** © Will and Deni McIntyre/Photo Researchers, Inc.; **p. 568 left:** © Lorraine Rorke/The Image Works; **right:** © Jan Doyle Photography; **p. 570:** © Bernard Pierre Wolff/Photo Researchers, Inc.; **16.5 top to bottom:** © Frank S. Balthis/Jeroboam, © Elizabeth Crews/The Image Works, © Rhoda Sidney/Monkmeyer Press Photo Service; **p. 573:** Courtesy of Beacon Press

Chapter 17

Opener: © Don Klumpp/The Image Bank; **p. 585:** © Suzanne Szasz/Photo Researchers, Inc.; **p. 590:** © Richard Choy/Peter Arnold, Inc.; **p. 592 top:** AP/Wide World Photos; **bottom:** © Keith Carter; **p. 593:** © Gabor Demjen/Stock Boston; **p. 601:** © Comstock, Inc.; **17.2 top:** © Ulli Seer/The Image Bank; **bottom:** © Bob Daemmrich/The Image Works; **17.3:** © Steve Proehl/The Image Bank; **p. 606:** © Peter Vandermark/Stock Boston; **p. 608:** © John Foraste/Brown University; **p. 611:** © Barbara Burnes/Photo Researchers, Inc.; **p. 613:** © Andrew Sacks/Time Magazine

Epilogue

Page 618 top: Photograph Courtesy of Northern Telecom/Photographer, JoAnn Carney; **bottom left:** © Nicholas DeSciose/Photo Researchers, Inc.; **bottom right:** © David W. Hamilton/The Image Bank

NAME INDEX

A

Abelson, R., 317
Aboud, F., 520
Abramovitch, R., 425
Achenbach, T. M., 125
Ackerman, B. P., 317
Ackerman, P. L., 325
Acredolo, L. P., 158
Adams, G. R., 185, 186
Adelson, J., 454, 543
Adler, T., 85
Ainsworth, M. D. S., 141, 407, 444
Alan Guttmacher Institute, 195
Albert, M., 594
Alexander, K. L., 489
Alexander, P. C., 424
Alipuria, L. L., 541
Allen, L., 8, 376, 378, 422, 529
Alvarez, M., 552, 556, 557
Amabile, T. M., 392
America in Transition, 500
American Association for Protecting Children, 422, 424
American College Health Association, 193
American Council on Education, 502, 503
Ames, C., 244
Ames, E. W., 141
Ames, M. A., 191
Ames, R., 244
Amsterdam, B. K., 519
Anastasi, A., 381, 387
Anderson, E. R., 433, 434, 435
Anderson, J., 427, 428
Anderson, J. R., 284, 300
Anderson, L. D., 376
Anderson, L. W., 335
Anderson, N. H., 315
Andrews, D. W., 444
Angell, R. C., 432
Applefield, J. M., 466
Appleman, D., 594
Arce, C. Y., 575
Archer, S. L., 537, 538, 542, 544
Arehart, D. M., 538
Arend, R. A., 408
Argondizza, M., 491

Aries, P., 9
Arlin, P. K., 283
Arman-Nolley, S., 456
Armistead, L., 431
Armsden, G. C., 427, 428
Arnold, M. L., 598
Aronson, E., 497
Asarnow, J. R., 448
Asher, J., 101, 339
Asher, S. R., 445
Astin, A. W., 603
Atkinson, J. W., 244
Attanucci, J., 594
Attie, I., 202
Ayers-Lopez, S., 444

B

Baca Zinn, M., 575
Bachman, J. G., 197, 199, 200, 502, 603
Baer, D. M., 63, 233
Bahrick, I. E., 160
Bailey, G. W., 200
Baillargeon, R., 265, 272
Bakeman, R., 132
Baker, L., 311
Ballenger, M., 481
Baltes, P. B., 18, 285
Bancroft, J., 190, 552
Bandura, A., 25, 66, 237, 238, 241, 343, 597, 598
Bank, L., 24
Banks, M. S., 156
Barkeley, R., 508
Barker, R., 445
Barnes, K. E., 457
Barnett, R. C., 571
Baron, J. B., 314
Baron, R., 496
Barr, R. G., 141
Barrett, D. E., 153
Barrett, K. C., 142
Barron, F., 391
Bart, W. M., 283
Bartlett, J. C., 62
Baruch, G. K., 571
Baskett, L. M., 425

Bathurst, K., 244, 378
Batshaw, M. L., 509
Batson, C. D., 605
Baumeister, R. F., 536
Baumrind, D., 416
Bayley, N., 153, 375, 376
Beach, D. R., 307
Beal, C. R., 311
Beals, D. E., 351
Bean, J. P., 308
Beane, J. A., 479
Becker, H. J., 470
Becker, J. A., 335
Beckwith, L., 120, 381
Behnke, M. L., 120
Behrend, D. A., 270
Beilin, H., 62, 285
Belenky, M. F., 556, 571
Bell, A. P., 191, 192
Bell, D., 496
Bell, S. M., 141
Belle, D., 432
Bellinger, D., 119
Bell-Scott, P., 21
Belmont, J. M., 7, 286
Belsky, J., 8, 132, 405, 411, 413, 444
Belson, W., 466
Bem, S. L., 558, 568
Benbow, C. P., 572
Bennett, W. J., 606
Bennings, J. S., 606
Bentler, P. M., 200
Bereiter, C., 282, 312
Berensen, G., 179
Berg, C. A., 322
Berg, K. M., 144
Berg, W. K., 144
Berko, J., 349
Berkowitz, M., 590
Berlyne, D. E., 456
Berman, S., 445
Bernard, H. S., 539
Berndt, T. J., 443, 449, 450, 498, 499
Bernstein, A., 321
Berrueta-Clement, J., 204, 612
Berry, J. W., 28, 74
Best, D. L., 563
Biener, L., 571

Bigler, R. S., 558
Bijou, S. W., 63
Bird, G. W., 431
Bisanz, G. L., 317
Bjorklund, D. F., 285
Blasi, A., 537
Blass, E. M., 158
Block, J. H., 200, 433
Bloome, D., 351
Blos, P., 429
Blotcky, M. J., 47
Blumenfeld, P. C., 489
Blyth, D. A., 186, 498, 499
Bobrow, N. A., 187
Bodde, T., 191
Bohamon, J. N. III, 342, 343
Boldizar, J. P., 568
Boles, J. K., 571
Bonitabitus, G. J., 311
Bonvillian, J. D., 265
Boring, E. G., 257
Borkowski, J. g., 245
Bornstein, G., 528
Bornstein, M. H., 21, 71, 234, 304, 378
Borstelmann, L. J., 9
Bouchard, T. J., 85
Boukydis, C. F. Z., 141
Bowden, L. M., 99
Bower, B., 171
Bower, T. G. R., 155, 161, 265
Bowerman, M., 345
Bowlby, J., 71, 142, 406, 407
Bowman, P. J., 421
Bowyer, J., 141
Boxer, A. M., 191
Boyer, C. B., 193
Brackbill, Y., 125
Bracken, M. B., 89
Brady, M. P., 506
Brandt, R. S., 312
Bray, J. H., 435
Brayfield, A., 8
Brazelton, T. B., 130, 132, 139
Bredekamp, S., 480, 482
Bremer, M., 464, 468
Brennan, K., 433
Brent, D. A., 201
Bretherton, I., 142
Brinker, R. P., 242
Brion-Meisels, S., 525
Brislin, R. W., 28
Brody, G. H., 601
Brody, L., 566
Brodzinsky, D. M., 90
Bromley, D., 520
Brone, R. J., 202
Bronfenbrenner, U., 26, 72, 74
Bronstein, P., 8, 409, 594
Brook, D. W., 200
Brook, J. S., 200
Brookins, G. K., 207
Brookover, W., 477
Brooks, P., 7
Brooks-Gunn, J., 183, 184, 186, 187, 196, 202, 488,
    519
Broughton, J., 283, 519
Broverman, I., 567
Brown, A. C., 432
Brown, A. L., 282, 303, 307, 311, 312, 315, 320
Brown, B. B., 452, 453

Brown, I. M., 9, 571, 593
Brown, J. L., 144, 153
Brown, J. S., 300, 312
Brown, J. V., 132
Brown, L. M., 571, 593
Brown, M. M., 444
Brown, R., 333, 342, 343, 348, 497
Brown, S. C., 302
Brumberg, J. J., 202
Bruner, J. S., 20, 341, 344, 404
Bryant, P., 354
Buchanan, C. M., 184, 433
Buhrmester, D., 449, 509
Buriel, R., 21
Burleson, B. R., 444
Burns, H. L., 301
Burtchaell, J., 114
Burton, R. B., 300
Burton, R. V., 596
Burts, D. C., 480, 486
Busch-Rossnagel, N. A., 197, 206
Buss, R. R., 317
Bussey, K., 594
Butchart, A. T., 200
Butler, R. A., 242
Byer, C. O., 116
Byrnes, J. P., 284

C

Cain, L., 335
Cairnes, B. D., 26, 444
Cairnes, R. B., 10, 11, 26, 95, 444
Caldwell, B., 150, 411
Calhoun, J. A., 612
Callan, J. W., 448
Camara, K. A., 433
Cameron, D., 357
Campbell, J., 299, 307, 325
Campos, J. J., 142, 157
Canady, R. L., 479
Candee, D., 598
Cannizzo, S. R., 307
Canter, L., 234
Canter, M., 234
Capaldi, D., 24
Caplan, M. Z., 448
Carbo, M., 354
Carey, S., 283, 350
Carlson, C., 429, 540
Carpenter, C. J., 560
Carpenter, T. P., 310
Carr, M., 245
Carrasquillo, A. L., 501
Carskadon, M. A., 145
Carter, D. B., 558
Carter-Saltzman, L., 172
Case, R., 285, 306
Casper, R. C., 202
Caspi, A., 75
Cassel, W. S., 320
Cassell, C., 190
Cassidy, D. J., 307, 560
Cavett, D., 454
Cazden, C. B., 291
Ceci, S. J., 20
Chalfant, J. C., 508
Chalip, L., 302

Chan, S. Q., 21
Chance, G., 157
Chance, P., 230
Chard, S. C., 172, 491
Charlesworth, R., 480, 486
Chase-Lansdale, L., 196
Chase-Lansdale, P. L., 433
Chasnoff, I. J., 118, 120
Chen, C., 248
Cherlin, A. J., 433
Chesney-Lind, M., 611, 612
Chess, S., 99
Chi, M. T. H., 316
Children's Defense Fund, 13, 14
Chinsky, J. M., 307
Chodorow, N., 53, 571
Chomsky, N., 336, 337, 341, 344
Christie, J. F., 462, 463
Church, R. B., 206
Cicchetti, D., 421
Cicirelli, V., 425
Clark, D., 382, 554
Clark, E. V., 347
Clark, H. H., 347
Clark, K., 494
Clark, M. L., 496
Clark, S. D., 189
Clarke-Stewart, K., 412, 486
Clifford, R. M., 507
Clingempeel, W. G., 433, 435
Cobb, P. A., 317
Cohen, C. P., 14
Cohen, D., 240
Cohen, P., 126, 200
Cohn, J. F., 404
Coie, J. D., 445, 446
Colby, A., 588
Cole, D. A., 201
Cole, M., 20, 288, 289, 477
Cole, S., 288, 289, 477, 504
Coleman, J. S., 451, 477
Coles, C. D., 118
Coles, R., 46, 542
Coll, C. T. G., 21
Collins, A., 312, 469
Collins, W. A., 428
Colombo, J., 144
Comer, J. P., 541
Committee for Economic Development, 16, 421
Conant, J. B., 491
Condry, J. C., 205, 465, 467, 556
Conger, J. J., 197, 603
Connell, J. P., 245
Coons, S., 144
Cooper, B. A., 125
Cooper, C. R., 429, 444, 540
Cooper, H., 496
Coopersmith, S., 526, 529
Corasaniti, M. A., 411
Corbin, S. B., 433, 434
Corless, I. B., 194
Corrigan, R., 262, 264
Corser, J., 73
Cortes, D. E., 420
Corwin, V., 466
Cote, J. E., 537
Cowan, C. P., 404
Cowan, P. A., 404
Cowley, G., 338
Cox, M., 75, 433, 461

Cox, R., 75, 433, 461
Crick, M., 341
Crisafi, M. A., 125
Crittenden, P., 421, 424
Cronbach, L. J., 493
Cronkite, R. C., 200
Crosby, L., 444
Cross, K. P., 479
Crowley, J. M., 99
Cunningham, M., 574
Curry, N. E., 463
Curtiss, S., 340

D

Damon, W., 519, 521, 595, 601, 602, 604, 605, 606, 608, 609
Dann, S., 443
Darling, C. A., 188, 189
Darlington, R. B., 489
Daro, D., 424
Darwin, C., 85
Dasen, P. R., 288
Davidson, D. H., 487
Day, N., 119
DeAngelis, T., 413
de Armas, A., 448
DeBaryshe, B. D., 24, 611
DeCasper, A. J., 159
Dedrick, C., 125
DeFour, D. C., 9, 571
DeFries, J. C., 97, 380
DeHart, G., 458
DeLoache, J. S., 307, 560
Dement, W. C., 145
Demo, D. H., 526
Demorest, A., 280
Dempster, F. N., 306, 307
De Necochea, G., 503
Denmark, F. L., 37, 563, 571
Desilets, J., 141
De Temple, J., 351
Detweiler, R. A., 90
Deutsch, M., 529
de Villiers, J. G., 343, 353
de Villiers, P. A., 343, 353
Devine, P. G., 528
de Vries, B., 591
Dewey, J., 312, 606
Diamond, A., 264
Diaz, R. M., 356
Dickerscheid, J. D., 570
Dickinson, D. K., 351
Dickinson, G. E., 454
Dielman, T. E., 200
Dillon, R. F., 119, 314
Dishion, T. J., 444, 611
Dixon, K. N., 203
Dixon, R. L., 119
Dixon, S. D., 120
Dodge, K. A., 444, 445, 447, 529
Doherty, W. J., 434
Dolan, R. S., 99
Dolgin, K. G., 270
Doll, G., 413
Domek, C. J., 443

Dorn, L. D., 29, 183
Dornbusch, S. M., 8, 21, 207, 420, 421, 453, 496, 502, 540, 541
Douvan, E., 454, 543
Downey, A. M., 179
Downey, E. P., 574
Downey, G., 75
Doyle, J. A., 8, 35, 564, 569
Dreyer, P. H., 189, 190
Dreyfus, H. L., 301
Dreyfus, S. E., 301
Driscoll, J. M., 125
Dryfoos, J., 196, 200, 203, 501, 612
DuBois, D. L., 453
Duck, S. W., 446, 454
Duke, D. L., 479
Duncan, R. M., 288
Duncker, K., 310
Dunn, J., 341, 425
Dunphy, D. C., 452
Durkin, K., 557
Dweck, C. S., 245, 246
d'Zurilla, T. J., 530

E

Early Childhood Literacy Development Committee of the International Reading Association, 351
Eccles, J. S., 498, 501–502, 555, 556, 565, 566, 567, 573
Edelman, M. W., 14, 128, 196, 422
Edmonds, R., 477
Edwards, C. P., 420, 595
Efron, R., 337
Egeland, B., 325, 408
Eger, M., 607
Egerston, H., 480
Ehrhardt, A. A., 552
Eiferman, R. R., 461
Eisenberg, N., 602, 605
Eitzen, D. S., 451
Ekstrom, R. B., 502
Elder, G. H., 75, 432
Elkind, D., 243, 270, 272, 278, 282, 283, 431, 479, 480, 482, 485
Elliot, T., 504
Elliott, G. R., 205, 206, 207
Elliott, J. E., 201
Ellis, H. C., 308
Ellis, L., 191
Emde, R. N., 141
Emery, R. E., 421
Emmerich, J. W., 558
Engle, P. L., 153
Enkin, M. W., 124
Ennis, R. H., 312, 314
Enright, R. D., 539
Ensher, G., 378
Entwisle, D. R., 7, 489, 494, 496, 498, 500
Entwistle, N., 324
Erev, I., 528
Erikson, E. H., 51, 54, 407, 493, 535, 538, 540, 542, 551, 610
Esty, E. T., 464
Ettema, J. S., 557
Etzel, R., 174
Evans, B. J., 574, 576
Eyler, F. D., 120

F

Fagan, J. F., 378
Falbo, T., 426
Farmer, J. E., 174
Farmer, M. C., 594
Farnham-Diggory, S., 288, 477
Farrell, S. A., 559
Fein, G. G., 458, 486
Feldman, E., 447
Feldman, S. S., 205, 206, 207, 427
Fenwick, K. D., 157
Fenzel, L. M., 499
Ferber, R., 145
Ferguson, D. M., 150
Feshbach, S., 468
Field, T., 126, 127, 129, 132, 240, 404
Fifer, G., 382
Fifer, W. P., 119
Fillion, T. J., 158
Fillmore, L. W., 357
Fincher, J., 108
Fineberg, H. V., 194
Finney, J. W., 200
Firush, R., 317
Fisch, R. O., 158
Fisch, S. M., 464
Fischer, K. W., 282
Fish, M., 405, 408
Fisher, C. B., 202
Fisher, D., 427, 428
Fivush, R., 322
Flaitz, J., 283
Flanagan, C. A., 432
Flannagan, D. A., 317
Flannery, D. J., 428
Flavell, J. H., 257, 260, 283, 307, 318, 320
Fleege, P. O., 486
Fleming, A. S., 403
Fogel, A., 404
Follansbee, D. J., 540
Fontana, V. J., 421
Ford, M. E., 532
Fordham, S., 453
Forehand, G., 496
Forehand, R., 431
Forman, E. R., 525
Forrest, J. D., 188
Forsyth, B. W. C., 150
Fowler, R. C., 201
Fox, L. H., 566
Fox, N. A., 408
Francis, J., 538
Freedle, R., 301
Freedman, D. G., 102
Freedman, J., 201, 467
Freedman, N., 102
Freud, A., 443
Freud, S., 47
Fried, P. A., 118, 119
Friedman, S. L., 322
Friedrich, L. K., 465
Frieze, I. H., 37
Frisch, R. E., 185
Frost, F., 557
Frost, J. L., 174
Fuller, M., 453, 529

Furman, L. N., 317
Furrow, D., 341
Furstenberg, F. F., 196, 433
Furstenberg, J. J., 196
Furth, H. G., 277–278, 345

G

Gabrielli, W., 200
Gaensbauer, T. G., 141
Gage, N. L., 493
Gagne, E. D., 314
Gagnon, J. H., 190
Galambos, N. L., 8, 431, 432
Gallagher, J. J., 13, 507
Gallup, A. M., 554
Gallup Report, 191
Galotti, K. M., 312, 594
Gangert-Drowns, R. L., 233
Garbarino, J., 421, 424, 491, 529
Garcia, E. E., 356, 357
Garcia, R., 339
Garden, R. A., 248
Gardner, B. T., 338
Gardner, H., 370, 391
Gardner, R. A., 338
Garelik, G., 98
Garrison, W. T., 177
Garrod, A. C., 594
Gartner, A., 506
Garton, A. F., 351
Garvey, C., 458
Garwood, S. G., 14, 16, 17, 381
Gaylord-Ross, R., 506
Gazzaniga, M. S., 337
Geary, D. C., 302
Gelman, R., 272, 285, 351
Geschwind, N., 337
Gesell, A. L., 11, 375
Gest, S., 445
Gewirtz, J., 141, 590
Giaconia, R. M., 493
Gibbs, J., 8, 20, 21, 206, 383, 453, 590
Gibson, E. J., 156, 157, 160, 265
Gibson, M. A., 496
Gilgun, J. F., 189, 190
Gilligan, C., 9, 543, 544, 571, 593, 594
Gjerde, P. F., 433
Glaser, R., 312, 325
Glaser, W., 7, 235, 479, 494
Glass, G. V., 492
Gleason, J. B., 335, 350
Glenn, C. G., 317
Glick, J., 286, 288
Glovinsky, P. B., 145
Glucksberg, S., 447
Goelman, H., 282
Goertz, M. E., 502
Gold, M., 610, 612
Goldberg, J., 306
Golden, M. W., 444
Goldfried, M. R., 530
Golding, E., 409
Goldman-Rakic, P. S., 149
Goldsmith, H. H., 99
Goodchilds, J. D., 190
Goodman, J., 325
Goodman, R. A., 199
Goodman, S., 270

Gordon, D., 8
Gordon, N. J., 468
Gordon, S., 190
Gorman, K., 153
Goswami, U., 354
Gotowiec, A., 141
Gottesman, I. I., 99
Gottfried, A. E., 244, 245
Gottfried, A. W., 244, 245, 378
Gottlieb, D., 494
Gottlieb, G., 95
Gottman, J. M., 448
Graham, S., 246
Grant, J. P., 128, 152, 176
Graves, S. B., 468
Gray, P. A., 611
Green, J. A., 141
Green, K. C., 603
Greenberg, M. T., 427, 428
Greenberg, R., 240
Greenberger, E., 504
Greene, B., 183
Greene, D., 244
Greene, J. W., 197
Grimaldi, D. M., 611
Grossman, F. K., 409
Grotevant, H. D., 540
Guidubaldi, J., 433
Guilford, J. P., 390
Guilleminault, C., 144
Gulotta, T. P., 186
Gunnar, M. R., 158, 159
Gurtner, J., 8, 469, 470
Gustafson, G. E., 141
Gyurke, J. S., 125

H

Hagan, E. P., 369
Hagan, M. S., 433, 434, 435
Hahn, A., 502
Haith, M. H., 156
Haith, M. M., 141
Hake, J. L., 158
Hakes, D. T., 345
Hakuta, K., 356, 357
Hale, S., 302
Hall, C. C. I., 574
Hall, G. R., 477
Hall, W. S., 354
Hallahan, D. P., 507
Halverson, C. F., 558
Hanley, D., 594
Hans, S., 119
Hanson, E., 428
Hanson, R. A., 594
Hardy, J. B., 189
Hardyck, C., 172
Hare-Mustin, R., 571
Harlow, H. F., 406, 443
Harmon, R. J., 141
Harmon-Losova, S. G., 99
Harnishfeger, K. K., 320
Harold, R. D., 566, 567
Harold-Goldsmith, R., 565
Harris, D. V., 525
Harris, L., 431
Harris, P. L., 264
Harris, R. F., 233

Harrison, A. O., 21, 422
Hart, D., 519
Hart, G. H., 444
Hart, P. D., 16
Hart, S. N., 14
Harter, S., 242, 424, 519, 521, 522, 525, 526, 528, 529, 538, 540, 541
Hartshorne, H., 596
Hartsough, C. S., 509
Hartup, W. W., 443, 444, 445
Harvard Medical School Newsletter, 192
Harwood, L. J., 150
Haskins, R., 488, 489
Haugard, J. J., 421
Hauser, S. T., 540
Havighurst, R. J., 21
Hawkins, D., 612
Hawkins, J. A., 498, 499
Hay, D., 335, 445
Hayden-Thomson, L., 554
Hayes, C. D., 188
Haywood, H. C., 7
Hazen, N., 444
Heath, S. B., 291, 342, 420
Hebel, J. R., 119
Hechtman, L. T., 509
Hedges, L. V., 492, 493
Heider, F., 245
Hein, K., 193, 194
Heinicke, C. M., 381
Heller, W., 337
Hellige, J. B., 337
Helmreich, R., 568
Helson, R., 504
Henderson, V. L., 245, 246
Hendry, J., 74, 487
Henker, B., 509
Hennessey, B. A., 392
Herdt, G. H., 192
Herrera, M. G., 152, 153
Herzog, E., 554
Hess, L., 598
Hetherington, E. M., 18, 75, 207, 433, 434, 435, 461
Hiebert, J., 284, 310
Higgens-Trenk A., 244
Higgins, A., 608
Hightower, E., 444
Hill, C. R., 418
Hill, J. P., 427, 429, 498
Hinde, R. A., 20, 71, 552
Hines, M., 552
Hinkle, J. S., 179
Hirsch, B. J., 453, 498, 499
Hirsch, E. D., 321
Hirsch-Pasek, K., 486
Ho, D. Y. F., 410
Hobbs, N., 507
Hoffereth, S. L., 8
Hofferth, S. L., 188, 195
Hoff-Ginsberg, E., 341
Hoffman, H. R., 464
Hoffman, J. M., 566
Hoffman, L., 8, 431, 565
Hoffman, M. L., 600, 601, 602
Hofstede, G., 74
Holmbeck, G. N., 427
Holmes, D. L., 125
Holtzmann, W. H., 74, 423
Holzman, M., 353
Honzik, M. P., 376, 378

Hood, K. E., 184
Hopwood, N. J., 103
Horne, M. D., 507
Horney, K., 53
Hornung, M., 461
Horowitz, F. D., 13, 17, 144
Howard, C., 421
Howard, J., 120
Howes, C., 413, 445, 458
Hsu, J., 429, 540
Huang, L. N., 494, 495, 575, 576
Huang, S., 317
Hudson, J. A., 322
Hudson, L. M., 525
Huebner, A. M., 594
Huesmann, L. R., 466, 467
Hui, C. H., 74
Hunt, E., 325
Hunt, J. V., 125
Hunt, M., 191
Hurry, J., 141
Hurt, B., 559
Huston, A. C., 464, 465, 467, 468, 552, 554, 556, 557, 565
Huston-Stein, A., 244
Hutchings, D. E., 119
Hutchings, N., 421
Hyde, J. S., 52, 560, 563, 564
Hymel, S., 554
Hynd, G. W., 507

I

Idol, L., 312
Ihinger-Tallman, M., 435
Inhelder, B., 267
Inoff-Germain, G., 184
Irvin, F. S., 191
Isenberg, J., 480
Izard, C. E., 142

J

Jacklin, C. N., 554, 564, 572, 573
Jackson, J. S., 541
Jacobs, J. E., 573
Jacobsen, L., 387
Jacobson, A. M., 540
Jacobson, J. L., 119
Jacquette, D., 442
Jagacinski, C. M., 245
James, W., 155
Janos, P. M., 390
Javernik, E., 178
Jeans, P. C., 117
Jencks, C. S., 477
Jenkins, V. Y., 427
Jensen, A. R., 97, 380
Jensen, L. C., 606
Jessor, L., 189
Jessor, R., 189
Johnson, J., 285, 462, 463
Johnson, W. G., 202
John-Steiner, V., 291
Johnston, J., 557
Johnston, L. D., 197, 199, 200
Johnston, L. P., 603
Johnston, S. M., 425

Jones, B. F., 312
Jones, E. R., 195
Jones, J. M., 8, 246, 382, 421
Jones, L. V., 382
Jones, M. C., 186, 224
Josselson, R., 571
Juster, F. T., 409
Justiz, M. J., 503

K

Kagan, J., 7, 94, 100, 101, 324, 408, 444
Kagan, S. L., 488, 489
Kagitcibasi, C., 74
Kahn, A. J., 411
Kail, R., 302, 364, 365, 374
Kaler, S. R., 126
Kallen, D. J., 188, 189
Kamerman, S. B., 411
Kandel, D. B., 197, 200
Kantner, J. F., 188
Kantrowitz, B., 478, 481
Kaplan, P. S., 234
Karabenick, S. A., 185
Karlin, A. R., 354
Karlin, R., 354
Karplus, R., 288
Kashani, J. H., 174
Katz, L. G., 172, 491
Katz, P. A., 574, 584
Kaufman, A. S., 385
Kaufman, N. L., 385
Kaufmann, A. S., 283
Kawai, M., 404
Kearns, D. T., 7
Keating, D. P., 284, 303
Keefe, S. E., 420, 422
Keeney, T. J., 307
Keil, F. C., 386
Keith, J. G., 431
Keith, T. Z., 369
Kelio, K., 594
Keller, A., 520
Kelly, J. A., 448
Kelly, J. B., 433
Kemerait, L. N., 431
Kendrick, C., 341, 425
Kennedy, J. H., 445
Kennedy, R. E., 610
Kenney, A. M., 196
Kerr, B. A., 566
Kessen, W., 141
Kidd, K. K., 103, 185
King, N., 461
Kinsey, A. C., 191
Klahr, D., 62
Klein, K., 492
Klein, R. E., 153
Klein, S. S., 555
Kliegl, R., 285
Klitgaard, R. E., 477
Knevel, C. R., 378
Knight, R. S., 606
Kobak, R. R., 427
Koeppl, G. K., 445, 446
Koeske, R., 37
Koeske, R. D., 316
Koff, E., 185
Kogan, N., 389

Kohlberg, L., 557, 586, 587, 589, 598, 608
Kohn, M. L., 420, 601
Koopman, C., 193
Kopp, C. B., 126
Korn, W. S., 603
Korner, A. F., 127
Kosowski, T. D., 345
Kosslyn, S. M., 309
Kostelnik, M. J., 460
Kozberg, S. F., 594
Krank, H. M., 234, 235
Krasnegor, N. A., 21, 378
Krauss, R. A., 447
Krile, D., 524
Krowitz, A., 157
Kuhn, D., 7
Kulik, C. C., 233
Kulik, J. A., 233
Kulin, H. E., 183
Kunkel, D., 465, 467
Kupersmidt, J. B., 445
Kurdek, L. A., 524
Kurland, D. M., 306
Kurtines, W. M., 590
Kusche, C. A., 507

L

LaBouvie-Vief, G., 284
Ladd, G. W., 443, 444
LaFromboise, T. D., 502, 542, 575, 576
Lam, T., 612
Lamb, M. E., 408, 409, 410, 554
Lambert, N. M., 509
Lande, J. S., 8, 412
Landesman, S. L., 381, 389
Lane, H., 340
Lange, L., 555, 556
Langer, A., 157
Langer, J., 287
Lapsley, D. K., 282, 283, 537, 589
LaRose, R., 557
Laval, R. A., 21
Lavalee, M., 288
Lave, C., 288
Lave, J., 288
LaVoie, J., 542
Lawson, K. R., 304
Lawton, T. A., 311
Lazar, I., 489
Lazerson, A., 282
Leboyer, F., 123
Lee, E., 453
Lee, S., 73, 248
Lee, V. E., 488
LeFevre, P., 284
Lehrer, R., 302
Leiffer, A. D., 468
Leigh, J., 504
Leinbach, J. D., 559
Leitenberg, H., 612
LeMare, L. J., 447
Lenneberg, E. H., 347
Leon, G. R., 203
Lepper, M., 244
Lepper, M. R., 8, 469, 470
Lerner, H. G., 572
Lerner, J. V., 100
Lerner, R. M., 95, 185, 186

Lesser, G., 382
Lester, B. M., 127, 129, 141
Leventhal, J. M., 150
Levin, J., 308, 319
Levine, C., 537
Levy, A. B., 203
Levy, G. D., 558
Levy, V., 318
Lewin, T., 114
Lewis, J. F., 385
Lewis, J. M., 433, 434
Lewis, M., 142, 242, 519, 554
Lewis, V. G., 187
Lewkowicz, D. J., 160
Liben, L. S., 558
Liberg, C., 351
Liebert, R. M., 467
Lifshitz, F., 152
Lindauer, B. K., 305
Linden, M. J., 351
Linn, M. C., 564
Linney, J. A., 493
Lipsitt, L. P., 158
Lipsitz, J., 431, 499, 500, 501
Lipsky, D. K., 506
Lishner, D., 612
Litt, I. F., 202
Little, B. B., 120
Livesly, W., 520
Lock, A., 341
Locke, J. L., 347
Loge, D. V., 508
Lohr, M. J., 452
Lombardi, J., 411
Long, L., 431
Long, T., 431
Longabaugh, R., 28
Lonky, E., 598
Lonner, W. J., 28, 74, 368
Looney, J. G., 47
Lorber, J., 559
Lorenz, K. Z., 70, 407
Louv, R., 34
Lovaas, O. I., 228
Low, K. G., 502, 542, 575, 576
Lozoff, B., 150
Lueptow, L., 565
Lummis, M., 573
Lundman, R., 612
Luria, A., 554
Lyle, J., 464
Lynch, J. H., 428
Lynch, M. A., 422
Lyons, J. M., 404
Lyons, N. P., 594

M

Maass, A., 528
McAdoo, H. P., 246, 422
McAdoo, J. L., 246
McBride, A. B., 571
McBride, B. A., 409
McCall, R. B., 378, 502
McCarley, R. W., 145
McCarthy, P. L., 150
McCartney, K., 8, 412, 425
McClearn, G. E., 97, 380
McClelland, D. C., 244

Maccoby, E. E., 132, 402, 416, 417, 418, 420, 534, 552, 554, 564
McDaniel, M. A., 309
McDill, E. L., 492
MacDonald, K. B., 509
MacDonald, V., 509
MacFarlane, J. A., 157
MacFarlane, J. W., 376, 378
McGhee, P. E., 458
McGlynn, S. M., 308
McGue, M., 85
McHugh, M., 37
MacIver, D., 555, 556
McKnight, C. C., 248, 486
McLoyd, V. C., 14, 21, 382, 421, 463
McPartland, J. M., 492
McPeck, J. E., 314
McQuiston, S., 177
MacTurk, R. H., 242
MacWhinney, B., 342
McWhirter, D. P., 191
Maddux, J. E., 174
Maggs, J. L., 8, 431, 432
Mahapatra, M., 595
Maioni, T. L., 461
Majidi-Ahi, S., 422, 529
Malatesta, C., 142, 564
Malcom, S. M., 470
Malgady, R. G., 420
Malina, R. M., 183, 184
Malinowski, B., 52
Malone, S., 158
Maltsberger, J. T., 201
Mammersmith, S. K., 191
Mandell, C. J., 233
Mandell, S. L., 233
Mandler, J. M., 157, 161, 264, 265, 266, 284, 285
Manos, M., 612
Maratsos, M. P., 336, 345
Marcia, J., 536, 537, 538, 539, 543, 544, 594
Marecek, J., 571
Marieskind, H. I., 124
Mariglio, W., 196, 197
Marín, B. V., 8, 422
Marín, G., 8, 422
Markman, E. M., 345
Markstrom-Adams, C., 542
Marquis, K. S., 90
Marshall, R. E., 158
Marshall, T. R., 141
Martin, C. L., 558
Martin, E. E., 191
Martin, G., 229
Martin, J. A., 132, 416, 534
Martorano, S., 283
Maslow, A. H., 243
Matas, L., 408
Matheny, A. P., 99
Mathews, S. R., 317
Maughan, B., 594
Maxwell, S. E., 245
May, M. S., 596
Mayaux, M. J., 117
Meehl, P., 374
Meichenbaum, D. H., 325
Melton, G. B., 14
Meltzoff, A. N., 240, 265
Mercer, J. R., 385
Meredith, H. V., 168
Messer, D. J., 242

Metz, K. E., 320
Meyerhoff, M. K., 419
Michel, G. L., 171
Midgley, C., 498, 555, 556
Miller, C. A., 128
Miller, C. R., 565
Miller, G., 75, 333, 350
Miller, G. A., 306, 336, 345
Miller, J., 571, 595
Miller, P., 378
Miller-Jones, D., 383
Minnett, A. M., 425
Minuchin, P. P., 200, 480, 491, 495, 496
Mischel, H., 598
Mischel, W., 66, 563, 598
Mistry, J. J., 288
Moely, B. E., 307
Mohr, D., 520
Moll, I., 286
Mollnow, E., 119
Money, J., 187, 191, 552
Montemayor, R., 186, 428
Moore, C., 341
Moos, R. H., 200
Mora, J. O., 152, 153
Morelli, G., 20, 286, 288, 289
Moreton, J., 351
Morgan, M., 557
Morgan, S. P., 196
Morrison, D. M., 190
Morrongiello, B. A., 157
Moser, J. M., 310
Moss, M., 144
Mott, F. L., 196, 197
Mounts, N., 452
Moyer, J., 480
Mueller, E., 445
Mullis, R. L., 594
Munroe, R. H., 74
Munroe, R. L., 74
Murphy, K. C., 468
Murphy, M. N., 282
Murphy, M. P., 558
Murray, H. A., 244
Musun-Miller, L., 425

N

Naimark, H., 13, 14
National Association for the Education of Young Children, 414, 482, 491
National Research Council, 188, 189, 195
Naus, M. J., 387
Needle, R. H., 434
Neimark, E. D., 283, 288
Neimeyer, R. A., 424
Neisser, U., 315
Nelson, R. S., 432
Nelson-Legall, S., 245
Newberger, C. M., 442
Newcomb, M. D., 200
Newman, S. E., 312
Ngini, L., 288
Nicholls, J. G., 245
Nichols, I. A., 347
Nichtern, S., 47
Nicolopoulou, A., 20
Ninio, A., 344

Nisbett, R. R., 244
Nitz, V., 100
Nix, D., 8
Noam, G. G., 540
Nottelman, E. D., 29
Nottelmann, E. D., 183, 184
Novack, L. L., 265
Novick, B., 116
Nucci, L., 607
Nusbaum, H. C., 302

O

O'Brien, M., 13, 17
Obrzut, J. E., 507
O'Connell, C., 118
O'Donnel, B., 559
O'Donnell, C., 612
Offer, D., 205, 206
Ogbu, J. U., 453, 495, 496, 541
Okazaki, S., 246
Olmedo, E. L., 8
Olweus, D., 444
O'Malley, P. M., 197, 199, 200, 603
Oppenheimer, M., 192
Orlansky, M. D., 265
Orthner, D. K., 431, 432
Oser, F. K., 607
Osofsky, J. D., 116, 196, 403
Osterberg, J., 433
Ostrov, E., 189
O'Sullivan, R. G., 502
Ottinger, D. R., 118

P

Padilla, A. M., 420, 422
Padilla, J. N. M., 234, 235
Paikoff, R. L., 184, 186, 196
Paivio, A., 308
Palincsar, A. M., 311, 312, 320
Paludi, M. A., 8, 9, 35, 563, 564, 569, 571, 594
Pan, B. A., 335
Papert, S., 469
Papini, D. R., 427, 428
Parcel, G. S., 174, 179
Paris, S. G., 305, 311
Parish, T. S., 433
Park, K., 449
Parke, R. D., 409, 597
Parker, J. G., 445, 448
Parkhurst, J. T., 445
Parlett, J. W., 301
Parmalee, A., 144, 174, 175
Parten, M., 456
Partridge, M., 421
Pascual-Leone, J., 285
Pasley, K., 435
Patterson, C. J., 598
Patterson, G. R., 24, 611
Pavlov, I. P., 221
Pear, J., 229
Pederson, D. R., 407
Pellegrini, A. D., 289
Pellegrino, J. W., 364, 365, 374
Penner, S. G., 343, 344
Perfetti, C. A., 354
Perkins, D. N., 391, 392

Perkins, D. P., 391
Perkinson, H. J., 479
Perret, Y. M., 509
Perry, J. D., 433
Perry, T. B., 449, 450
Peskin, H., 186
Petersen, A. C., 181, 186, 207
Peterson, A. C., 564
Peterson, L., 174
Peterson, L. M., 116
Peterson, P. L., 493
Petrinovich, L. F., 172
Petronio, R. J., 612
Pettit, G. S., 444
Phillips, D., 242, 411
Phinney, J., 247, 541
Piaget, J., 46, 58, 260, 262, 265, 267, 283, 284, 285, 456, 585
Pierce, E. W., 508
Piers, E. V., 525
Pike, R., 526
Pillow, B. H., 304
Pine, C., 21
Pipes, P., 150, 177
Pittman-Lindeman, M., 194
Pizer, H. F., 153
Platzman, K. A., 118
Pleck, J. H., 409, 569
Plomin, R., 22, 97, 99, 100, 102, 380
Polier, J. W., 610
Polit, D. F., 426
Polivy, J., 202
Pollack, W. S., 409
Pollitt, E., 153
Pomeroy, W. B., 191
Porges, S. W., 158
Porter, F. L., 158
Posner, M., 303
Powell, G. J., 529
Power, C., 608
Power, F. C., 537
Powers, S. I., 540
Pratt, C., 351
Pratto, D. J., 432
Premack, D., 338
Pressley, M., 308, 309
Price, J., 468
Pryor, J. B., 191
Puffer, J. C., 181
Puka, B., 590

Q

Quina, K., 8, 37
Quintana, S. M., 589

R

Rabiner, D. L., 448
Rabkin, J., 612
Radke-Yarrow, M., 153
Ragosta, J., 496
Rahman, T., 317
Ramey, C. T., 381, 389
Ramirez, M., 8, 246
Ramirez, O., 575, 576
Ramsay, D. S., 172

Ramsey, E., 24, 611
Rapkin, B. D., 499
Rappaport, A., 528
Raver, C. C., 488
Raynor, I. O., 244
Rebelsky, F. G., 347
Redfield, C. L., 301
Reich, J. N., 125
Reid, D. K., 508
Reilly, R., 166
Reinisch, J. M., 191, 552
Reis, S. M., 389
Render, G. F., 234, 235
Rendon, L. I., 503
Resnick, G., 433
Rest, J. R., 589, 591
Rice, M. L., 342
Rich, C. L., 201
Rieben, L., 354
Riordan, J., 185
Risser, W. L., 181
Ritter, R., 307
Roberts, J., 422
Robinson, D. P., 197
Robinson, N. M., 390
Rock, D., 496, 502
Rode, S. S., 132
Rodgers, J. E., 103
Rodman, H., 432
Rodriguez-Haynes, M., 424
Roff, M., 444
Rogers, A., 9, 543, 571, 593
Rogers, C. R., 68
Rogers, C. S., 457, 458
Roggman, L. A., 427, 428
Rogler, L. H., 420
Rogoff, B., 20, 286, 288, 289, 290, 291, 340, 341, 477
Rohner, E. C., 420
Rohner, R. P., 420
Rohwer, W. D., 308
Rollins, P. R., 335
Romberg, T. A., 310
Roodin, P. A., 598
Rose, H. A., 558
Rose, S. A., 95, 126, 160, 378
Rosenbaum, E., 197
Rosenberg, M., 522, 529
Rosenblith, J. F., 110, 123, 125, 236
Rosenthal, D. A., 427
Rosenthal, R., 387
Rothbart, M., 99, 100, 303, 425, 594
Rotheram-Borus, M. J., 193
Rotman, A., 141
Rotter, J. B., 244
Rovee-Collier, C., 235
Rovine, M., 405
Rowe, D. C., 103
Rubin, K. H., 447, 461
Rubin, K. M., 554
Rubin, K. N., 458
Rubin, Z., 444
Ruble, D., 521
Rudy, J. W., 234
Ruebenstein, J., 201
Ruff, H. A., 160, 304
Rumbaugh, D. M., 338
Rumberger, R. W., 501, 502

Runco, M. A., 390
Russo, N. F., 571
Rutter, M., 433, 477, 491
Ryan, E. B., 508
Ryan, R. A., 575, 576
Ryan, R. M., 428

S

Sachdev, P., 113
Sadker, D., 493, 555
Sadker, M., 493, 555
Sagan, C., 85
St. James-Roberts, 141
Salapatek, P., 141, 156
Sanders, S. A., 191
Sansone, C., 322
Santrock, J. W., 8, 18, 62, 425, 427, 433, 435
Sattler, J. M., 369
Savage-Rumbaugh, E. S., 338
Savin-Williams, R. C., 526
Sawin, D. B., 409
Sawyers, J. K., 457, 458
Sax, G., 385
Scafidi, F., 129
Scales, P., 203, 500, 502
Scardamalia, M., 282, 312
Scarr, S., 8, 22, 94, 96, 102, 103, 185, 382, 383, 412
Sceery, A., 427
Schacter, D. L., 308
Schaie, K. W., 34
Schaller, M., 528
Schanberg, S., 129
Schank, R., 317
Schatz, J., 508
Schegloff, E. A., 340
Scheidel, D. G., 594
Schlundt, D. G., 202
Schneider, W., 308
Schnur, E., 488
Schoenfeld, A. H., 312
Schrag, S. G., 119
Schulz, H., 144
Schunk, D. H., 242, 245
Schwartz, D., 117
Schweinhart, L. J., 489
Scott-Jones, D., 196, 496
Scribner, S., 288
Segall, M. H., 29
Seibert, J. M., 116
Seidman, E., 493
Seidner, L. B., 458
Seigle, J., 464, 468
Selice, S., 574
Sells, S. B., 444
Selman, R. L., 442, 448, 522, 523, 524
Semaj, L. T., 541
Senn, M. J., 11
Serbin, L. A., 558
Sexton, M., 119
Shaffer, D. R., 601
Shafrir, U., 324
Shainberg, L. W., 116
Shakeshaft, C., 555
Shannon, F. T., 150

Shantz, C. O., 447
Shantz, C. U., 267
Shapiro, E. K., 200, 480, 491, 495, 496
Shapiro, E. R., 201
Sharp, D., 288
Shatz, M., 322, 351
Shepard, L., 480
Shneidman, E. S., 201
Shope, J. T., 200
Shweder, R., 595
Siegel, L., 324, 508
Siegler, R. S., 299, 300, 303, 307, 325
Sigman, M. D., 304, 378
Signorella, M. L., 558
Silver, L. B., 508
Silverberg, S. B., 430
Simmons, J. E., 118
Simmons, R. G., 186, 498, 499
Simon, W., 190
Simons, R. L., 611
Sims-Knight, J. E., 110, 123, 125, 236
Singer, D., 275, 458, 468
Singer, J. L., 47, 458, 468
Sitterle, K. A., 435
Sivo, P. J., 448
Skerry, S., 520
Skinner, B. F., 63, 65, 225, 343
Skinner, E. A., 245
Skinner, M. L., 611
Skinner, M. S., 444
Skoe, E. E., 543
Slaughter-DeFoe, D. T., 247
Slavin, R. E., 356, 492, 497
Slobin, D., 348
Sloman, J., 444
Small, M., 285
Smiley, S. S., 282
Smith, B., 158, 458
Smith, I. E., 118
Smith, J., 285
Smith, M. B., 117
Smith, M. L., 492
Smith, P. H., 538
Smith, R., 466
Smolucha, F., 456
Snarey, J., 594
Snidman, N., 101
Snow, C. E., 335, 340, 341, 342, 344
Snow, R. E., 493
Sophian, C., 264
Sorensen, R. C., 454
Spearman, C. E., 370
Spelke, E. S., 160, 265, 285
Spence, J. T., 568
Spence, M., 159
Spencer, M. B., 8, 14, 21, 206, 382, 420, 421, 453, 496, 502, 540, 541, 542
Spencer, M. L., 555
Sperry, R. W., 337
Spiro, R., 8
Sprafkin, C., 558
Spratkin, J. N., 467
Sroufe, L. A., 142, 407, 408, 444, 530, 533, 534
Stafford, F. P., 418
Stage, E. K., 556

Stallings, J., 488
Stankov, L., 314
Stanley, J. C., 572
Stanowicz, L., 343
Stearns, G., 117
Stein, A. H., 465
Stein, L. C., 460
Stein, N. L., 317
Steinbach, R., 312
Steinberg, E. R., 469
Steinberg, L. D., 428, 429, 430, 432, 504
Steiner, J. E., 157, 158
Sterling, C. W., 470
Stern, D. N., 404
Stern, S. L., 202, 203
Sternberg, R. J., 312, 314, 325, 364, 365, 371
Steuck, K., 301
Steur, F. B., 466
Stevens, J. H., 422
Stevenson, H. W., 73, 248, 305, 477, 573
Stewart, N., 120
Stigler, J. W., 248, 302
Stipek, D. J., 566
Stock, W., 492
Stocker, C., 425
Strahan, D. B., 283
Streissguth, A. P., 118, 509
Studdert-Kennedy, M., 336
Stunkard, A. J., 151, 203
Su, S. S., 434
Sue, D. W., 575, 576
Sue, S., 8, 28, 246
Sugarman, S., 285
Sullivan, A., 429
Sullivan, K., 429
Suomi, S., 100, 101, 443
Super, C. M., 152, 153
Susman, E. J., 29, 183
Sutton-Smith, B., 462
Swadesh, M., 345
Swanson, D. P., 574

T

Tajfel, H., 527
Talley, J. A., 468
Tamis-LeMonda, C. S., 234
Tangney, J. P., 468
Tanner, J. M., 169, 184
Task Force on Pediatric AIDS, 116
Tate, C. S., 317
Tavris, C., 35
Taylor, J. H., 589, 590
Taylor, R. D., 558
Taylor, R. L., 21
Terman, L., 389
Tharp, R. G., 494
Thoma, S. J., 594
Thomas, A., 99
Thompson, A., 381
Thompson, L., 100
Thompson, R. A., 408
Thomsen, L., 202

Thorndike, R. L., 364, 369
Thorpy, M. J., 145
Thurstone, L. L., 370
Timberlake, B., 116
Tobin, D., 566
Tobin, J. J., 487
Toda, S., 404
Tom, D., 496
Tomlinson-Keasey, C., 201, 283
Toth, A., 117
Trabasso, T., 322
Trankina, F., 576
Treboux, D. A., 197
Trehub, S. E., 157
Trevethan, S. D., 591
Triandis, H., 74
Trickett, P. K., 424
Trimble, J. E., 21, 28
Trohanis, P. L., 507
Tronick, E. Z., 127, 404
Trotter, R. J., 413
Tucker, L. A., 179
Tuckman, B. W., 179
Turiel, E., 589
Turner, J. C., 311

U

Unger, O., 458
U.S. Bureau of the Census, 432
United States Commission on Civil Rights, 355
U.S. Public Health Service, 114

V

Valdez-Menchaca, M. C., 343
Vallelunga, L. R., 150
Valsinar, J., 8
Van Cantfort, T. E., 338
Vandell, D. L., 404, 411, 425, 445
Vandenberg, B., 458
Van Deusen-Henkel, J., 491
VanDusen, J. E., 188, 189
VanLehn, K., 301
Vienonen, M., 197
Vietze, P. M., 242
Villareal, M. J., 74
Vorhees, C. V., 119
Vurpillot, E., 305
Vygotsky, L. S., 287, 290, 456

W

Wachs, H., 277–278
Waddington, C. H., 94
Wade, C., 35
Wagner, D. A., 477
Wahlsten, D., 102

Wakefield, J. F., 390
Walden, T. A., 317
Walk, R. D., 157
Walker, E. L., 35
Walker, L., 589, 590, 591, 594
Walker, V. R., 8
Wallace, H. M., 197
Wallach, M. A., 389
Wallerstein, J., 433, 434
Wallis, C., 198
Walsh, P. V., 574
Walton, M. D., 150
Warren, L. W., 201
Warren, M. P., 184, 186
Warshak, R. A., 90, 433, 435
Washburn, K. J., 345
Waterman, A. S., 537, 542
Waters, E., 142, 530, 533, 534
Watkins, B. A., 465, 467
Watkinson, B., 118, 119
Watson, J. B., 12, 141, 151
Waxman, S. R., 345
Wearne, D., 310
Weber, E. K., 607
Wechsler, D., 370
Wegman, W. E., 128
Weinberg, M. S., 191
Weinberg, R. A., 96, 102, 380, 382
Weiner, B., 245
Weiss, G., 509
Weissberg, R. P., 448
Weisse, B., 540
Wellborn, J. G., 245
Wellman, H. M., 307
Wender, P. H., 201
Wenner, W., 144
Werner, E. E., 117
Werner, J. S., 234
Wertheimer, M., 312
Wertsch, J. V., 312
Whalen, C. K., 509
Whaley, L. F., 90, 172
Whimbey, A., 351
Whiren, A. P., 460
White, A. B., 196
White, B. L., 145, 147, 419
White, R. W., 242, 530
Whitehurst, G. J., 343
Whitfield, J. R., 576
Whiting, B. B., 28, 73, 420, 564
Whiting, J. W. M., 28
Widmayer, S., 132
Wierson, M., 431
Wilcox, B. L., 13
Wiley, D. E., 366
Wilkening, F., 315
William, J., 354
Williams, F., 557
Williams, J. E., 563
Williams, M. F., 465
Williams, T. M., 556

William T. Grant Foundation, 7, 502
Willis, S. L., 34
Wilson, K. S., 404
Wilson, L., 21
Wilson, M. N., 21, 420, 422, 434
Wilson, R. S., 99
Windle, W. F., 158
Wingert, P., 478, 481
Winkelstein, W., 194
Winner, E., 268, 390
Witkin, H. A., 91
Witryol, S., 231
Wober, M., 368
Wolf, N. M., 233
Wong, D. L., 90, 172
Wong, H. Z., 21
Wood, F. H., 507
Woodson, R., 240
Worobey, J., 132
Wortham, S. C., 174
Worthington-Roberts, B. S., 150
Wright, H. F., 445
Wright, M. R., 185
Wu, D. Y. H., 487
Wylie, R., 525

Y

Yaniv, I., 322
Yankelovich, D., 204
Yardley, K., 525
Yarrow, L. J., 242
Yawkey, T. D., 462, 463
Yekel, C. A., 558
Ying, Y., 575, 576
Young, D., 201
Young, K. T., 151
Youngblade, L., 444
Yussen, S. R., 302, 312, 317, 318, 591, 592, 594

Z

Zabin, L. S., 189
Zahn-Waxler, C., 564
Zayas, L. H., 206
Zellman, G. L., 190
Zelnik, M., 188
Zembar, M. J., 387
Zeskind, P. S., 141
Ziegert, K. A., 232
Zigler, E., 14, 16, 413, 488
Zimmerman, R. R., 406
Zukow, P. G., 425

SUBJECT INDEX

A

ABC method, 353
A$\overline{\text{B}}$ error, 264
Abortion
  adolescent pregnancy and, 195
  ethics of medical use of fetal tissue and, 114
  induced, 112–113, 195
  international trends in, 113
  spontaneous, 112
Abstraction, formal operational thought and, 278–280
Accommodation
  formal operational thought and, 283
  in Piagetian theory, 58
Achievement, gender differences in, 564–567
Achievement motivation, 243–248
Acquired immune deficiency syndrome. See AIDS
Activity level, 99
Adaptation, in Piagetian theory, 258
Adolescence, 18. See also Puberty
  autonomy and attachment in, 426–428
  cognitive variations in, 283–284
  complexity of adolescent development and, 207
  current status of adolescents and, 206
  drugs and, 197–201
  eating disorders during, 201–203
  egocentrism in, 282
  empathy in, 603–604
  family processes in, 426–430
  groups in, 452
  interrelation of problems and programs that prevent or reduce problems in, 203–204
  maturation of adolescents and parents during, 429–430
  parent-adolescent conflict in, 428–429
  peer relations in, 450–454
  pregnancy during, 195–197
  self-understanding in, 521–522
  sexuality during. See Sexuality
  stereotyping, 204–205
  suicide and, 201
  transition to middle or junior high school in, 497–500
Adolescent egocentrism, 282
Adoption, 89–90, 195

Adoption study, 95–96
Afterbirth, 124
Aggression
  child abuse and, 421–424
  effect of television on, 465–467
  gang violence and, 611–612
AIDS (acquired immune deficiency syndrome), 116, 193–194
Alcohol use and abuse
  among adolescents, 198–199
  prenatal development and, 118
Alert activity, in infancy, 144
Alert and focused state, in infancy, 144
Altruism, 604–606
Anal stage, 50
Androgyny, 568–569, 571
Animals, language development in, 337–339
Animism, 270
Anorexia nervosa, 202
Anoxia, 124
Apgar scale, 129
Aphasia, 337
Applied research, 35
Aptitude-treatment interaction, 493
Artificial intelligence, 301
Assertive discipline, in schools, 234
Assimilation, 58, 283
Associative play, 457
Attachment, 405–408, 427–428
Attention, 238, 303–305
Attention-deficit hyperactivity disorder, 508–509
Attribution theory, achievement and, 245
Authoritarian parenting, 416
Authoritative parenting, 416
Automaticity, information processing and, 303
Autonomous morality, 585–586
Autonomy, in adolescence, 426–428
Autonomy versus shame and doubt, 53

B

Babbling, 347
Back-to-basics movement, 478
Basal metabolism rate (BMR), 177
Bayley Scales of Infant Development, 375–376

Behavior genetics, 95–96
Behaviorism, 12, 63, 65. See also Operant conditioning
  evaluation of, 66–67
  language development and, 343–345
Behavior modification, 233
Bem Sex-Role Inventory, 568
Benevolence, altruism and, 605
Bilingualism, 355–357
Birth order, 425–426
Blastocyst, 109
BMR. See Basal metabolism rate
Body image, during puberty, 185
Body mass, puberty and, 185
Bogalusa Heart Study, 179, 180
Bonding, 132
Brain
  in early childhood, 168–169
  in infancy, 148–149
  information-processing theory and, 61
  role in language, 337
Brazelton Neonatal Behavioral Assessment Scale, 130–132, 375
Brazelton training, 130, 132
Breast-feeding, bottle-feeding versus, 150–151
Breech position, 124
Broca's area, 337
Bronfenbrenner's ecological theory, 72–73, 75
Bulimia, 203

C

Canalization, 94
Career counselors, education of, 39
Careers, in child development, 38–39
Caregivers, 174. See also Father; Mother(s); Parent(s)
Care perspective, moral development and, 591, 593
Case study, 27
Centration, 270
Cephalocaudal pattern, 146
Cesarean section, 124
Child abuse, 421–424
Childbirth, 120–132, 403. See also Neonate

Child care, 410–415
  cross-cultural comparisons of, 14
  gender roles and, 573
  international comparison of policies regarding, 411
  quality, 414
  social policy and, 16
Child-centered kindergarten, 480–481
Child development research, 23–38
  basic versus applied, 35
  case studies in, 27
  cohort effects and, 34–35, 36
  correlational, 30–31
  cross-cultural and ethnic minority group, 28–29
  cross-sectional, 32–33
  ethics in, 38
  experimental, 31–32
  interviews and questionnaires in, 26–27
  longitudinal, 33
  modern, 10–13
  multimeasure, multisource, multicontext approach to, 29
  observation in, 25–26
  physiological, 29
  sequential, 34
  sexist, reducing, 35, 37
  standardized tests in, 27–28
  theory and scientific method and, 24–25
  twins studies and, 84–85, 95
Child development theories, 45–79
  behavioral, 63, 65, 66–67
  cognitive, 55, 58–63
  eclectic orientation to, 75–77
  ecological, 72–75
  ethological, 70–72
  phenomenological and humanistic, 67–69
  psychoanalytic, 47–55
  social learning, 65–67
Children's Defense Fund, 14
Children's rights, declaration of, 15
Children's Sex Role Inventory, 568
Child study movement, 11
Chlamydia, 192
Chorionic villus test, 92
Chromosomes, 87
  abnormalities in, 90–91, 119
  X and Y, 88, 90–91
Chronosystem, in ecological theory, 75
Cigarette smoking, prenatal development and, 118–119
Circular reactions, 260–261
Circumcision, pain and, in infancy, 158–159
Classical conditioning, 221–225
Classification, concrete operational thought and, 277–278
Classroom. See also Education; School(s)
  jigsaw, 497
  size of, 492
  structure and climate of, 492–493
Cliques, 451–452
Cocaine use
  among adolescents, 199–200
  prenatal development and, 119, 120
Cognition, 345, 564
Cognitive development, 255–294
  Piagetian theory of, 257–286
  schooling and culture and, 288
  Vygotsky's theory of, 286–291
Cognitive developmental theory, 258, 557–558
Cognitive learning, 237–241
Cognitive monitoring, 311–312

Cognitive moral education, 607–608
Cognitive processes, 17, 258–259. See also
    Intelligence; Intelligence tests; IQ scores;
    Thinking; Thought(s)
  higher-order, 310–313
  information processing and, 303–309
Cognitive social learning theory, 66, 241, 598
Cognitive styles, 323–325
Cognitive theories, 55, 58–63
  developmental, 258, 557–558
  evaluation of, 62–63
  information-processing, 59, 61–62
  of Piaget, 58–59
  social learning, 66, 241, 598
Cohort effects, 34–35, 36
Collectivistic personality orientation, 74
Commitment, identity and, 537
Communication, in education, 278
Community rights, moral development and, 588
Competence, social. See Social competence
Competence motivation, 242–243
Componential intelligence, 371
Comprehensive Child Care bill, 16
Computer(s), 468–470
  human intelligence versus intelligence of, 302
  influences on children, 469–470
  prenatal development and video display
      terminals and, 120
Computer-assisted instruction, 469–470
Computer skills, cohort effects and, 36
Concepts, 315
Conceptual development, in infancy, 265–266
Concrete operational thought, 59, 274, 276–278, 283
Concurrent validity, 366
Conditioned response (CR), 221–222
Conditioned stimulus (CS), 221–222
Conditioning, 227. See also Classical conditioning;
    Operant conditioning
Conformity, peer pressure and, 450
Connectedness, 540. See also Attachment
Conscience, 600. See also Moral development
Conservation, 270, 272, 276
Constraining behaviors, identity and, 540
Constructive play, 461
Constructivist view, 160–161
Contact comfort, attachment and, 406
Content validity, 366
Contextual intelligence, 373
Continuity of development, 20–21
Control
  of self, 229, 597–598
  social competence and, 532
Conventional morality, 593
Conventional reasoning, moral development and, 587–588
Convergent thinking, 390–391
Conversational skills, formal operational thought
    and, 282
Cooperative play, 457
Coordination of secondary circular reactions, 261
Correlational strategy, 30–31
Correlation coefficient, 30–31
Counterconditioning, 224
CR. See Conditioned response
Creativity, 390–394
Crib death, maternal smoking and, 118–119
Crisis, identity and, 537
Criterion validity, 366
Critical period, 71, 339
Critical thinking, 312–313

Cross-cultural research, 28, 29
Cross-sectional approach, 32–33
Crowds, 451
Crying, in infancy, 141
CS. See Conditioned stimulus
Cultural-familial retardation, 389
Culture. See also Ethnic minority groups;
    Sociocultural context
  child abuse and, 424
  cross-cultural comparisons of child care and, 14
  cross-cultural comparisons of prenatal care and, 128
  cultural literacy and, 321
  in ecological theory, 72–73, 75
  family and, 420
  heterogeneity of ethnic and cultural groups and, 21
  identity and, 540–541
  intelligence and, 381–386
  international perspective on abortion trends and, 113
  moral development and, 594–595
  mother-child interaction in inner-city housing
      project and, 342
  personality and, 74
  of play, 462–464
  schooling and cognitive development and, 288
  similarities and variations among thinking
      apprenticeships and, 290–291
  society and, 289–291
  undernutrition in America and, 153
Culture-fair intelligence tests, 384–386
Curriculum, hidden, moral education and, 606

D

Dating, 454
Day care. See Child care
Declaration of Children's Rights, 15
Deep sleep, in infancy, 144
Deep structure, 335
Defense mechanisms, 48–49
Defining Issues Test (DIT), 591
Delivery. See Childbirth
Denver Developmental Screening Test, 171
Dependent variable, 31
Depth perception, in infancy, 157
Developmentally appropriate practice, 482
Developmental quotient (DQ), 375
Developmental scales, 374
Diet. See Eating behavior; Nutrition
Difficult child, 99
Direct moral education, 606–607
Direct perception view, 160, 161
Disadvantaged children, preschool education for, 488–489
Discipline, assertive, 234
Discontinuity of development, 22
Dishabituation, 234–236
Displacement, 49, 333, 350
Disturbed sleep, in infancy, 144
DIT. See Defining Issues Test
Divergent thinking, 390–391
Divorce, effects on children, 433–434
DNA, 87
Dominant-recessive genes principle, 91
Dopamine, in infancy, 149
Down syndrome, 90, 92, 116–117, 389
Drive, 242

Drug(s)
  during childbirth, 125
  for learning disabled children, 509
Drug use and abuse
  among adolescents, 197–201
  maternal, prenatal development and, 118–119
Dyzygotic twins, 95

E

Early childhood, 18
  altruism in, 605
  body growth and change during, 167–168
  brain during, 168–169
  empathy in, 602
  health education for, 174
  language development during, 349–353
  motor development during, 169–172
  self-understanding in, 519–520
Early childhood education, 480. *See also*
    Kindergarten; Preschool(s)
  effects of, 486
  in Japan, 487
  literacy and, 351–353
Easy child, 99
Eating behavior, 151, 178–181
Eating disorders, among adolescents, 201–203
Echoing, 342
Eclectic theoretical orientation, 75–77
Ecological theory, 72–75
Economic distress, 432. *See also* Socioeconomic
    status
Ectoderm, 109
Education. *See also* Instruction; School(s); Teachers
  adolescent pregnancy and, 196
  bilingual, 355–357
  for careers in child development, 39
  cognitive development and, 288
  developmentally appropriate and inappropriate
    practices in, 481–482
  for disadvantaged young children, 488–489
  early childhood, 351–353, 480, 486–487. *See
    also* Kindergarten; Preschool(s)
  gender and, 555–556, 573
  of handicapped children, 504–507
  information processing and information age and,
    314
  of learning disabled children, 508–509
  literacy and, 351–353
  moral, 606–610
  Piagetian theory applied to, 278
Effectance motivation, 242–243
Effort, achievement and, 245
Ego, 47, 48
Egocentrism, 267, 282
Ego-ideal, 600
Elaboration, 308, 314
Electra complex, 52
Elementary schools, 480, 489, 491
Embryonic period, 109–110
Emic approach, 28
Emotion(s)
  in infancy, 142
  maternal, prenatal development and, 117–118
  role in moral development, 600–604
Emotionality, 99
Empathy, 68
  global, 602
  moral development and, 601–604

Enabling behaviors, identity and, 540
Endoderm, 109
Energy needs, 177
Environment
  interaction with heredity, 102–103. *See also*
    Nature-nurture controversy
  least restrictive, 506
  manipulating, intelligence and, 381
Environmental hazards, prenatal development and,
    119–120
Environmental systems, in ecological theory, 72–73,
    75
Epigenetic principle, 52
Equality, altruism and, 605
Equilibration, in Piagetian theory, 259
Erikson's theory, 51–55, 535–536
Erogenous zones, 50
Estradiol, during puberty, 183
Ethics. *See also* Moral development
  in child development research, 38
  medical use of fetal tissue and, 114
Ethnic gloss, 28–29
Ethnicity, in ecological theory, 73, 75
Ethnic minority groups, 8
  achievement and, 246–248
  ethnocentrism and, 528
  family and, 420–421, 422
  gender roles and, 573–576
  heterogeneity of, 21
  high school dropouts among, 501–502, 503
  identity and, 540–541, 542
  intelligence and, 381–386
  peer relations and, 453
  portrayal on television, 465
  prejudice and, 528
  prenatal care and, 128
  research with, 28–29
  schools and, 494–496
  self-esteem and, 529
  transition to elementary schools and, 489, 491
Ethnocentrism, 528
Ethological theories, 70–72
Ethology, 70
Etic approach, 28
Evolution, 85–86, 336–337
Exchange, in altruism, 605
Exercise
  development and, 178–181
  for infants, 149
Exosystem, in ecological theory, 72
Experiential intelligence, 373
Experimental strategy, 31–32
Expertise, 320–323
Extinction, 227
Extrinsic motivation, 244–245

F

Facial expressions, in infancy, 142
Family(ies), 401–439. *See also* Father; Mother-
    child interaction; Sibling relationships
  adolescents and, 426–430
  attachment and, 405–408
  birth order and, 425–426
  changing, 430–435
  child abuse and, 421–424
  cultural, social class, and ethnic variations in,
    420–421, 422
  day care and, 410–415

  exercise and, 181
  father's role in, 409–410
  identity and, 539–540
  parenting styles and, 416–420
  pressures on, 7–8
  reciprocal socialization and, 404
  sibling relationships and, 424–425
  stepfamilies and, 434–435
  as system, 405
  transition to parenthood and, 402–404
Fat, in diet, 177
Father. *See also* Family(ies); Parent(s); Parenting
    styles
  role in family, 409–410
  transition to parenthood and, 403
Fears, irrational, 223
Femininity, 566–567
Feminism, 52–53, 571–572
Fertility, maternal age and, 117
Fertilization, in vitro, 88–89
Fetal alcohol syndrome (FAS), 118
Fetal period, 111–112, 159
Fetal tissue, ethics of medical use of, 114
Fine motor skills, 147–148
  in early childhood, 170–171
  during middle and late childhood, 173
First habits and primary circular reactions, 260
Fixation, 50
Fixed-action patterns, 241–242
Formal operational thought, 59, 278–285
  adolescent egocentrism and, 282
  characteristics of, 278–280
  early and late, 282–283
  language and, 280, 282
  variations in adolescent cognition and, 283–284
Fraternal twins, 95
Freudian theory, 47–51
  defense mechanisms and, 48–49
  evaluation of, 55
  gender-based criticisms of, 52–53
  moral feelings and, 600
  personality development and, 50–51
  personality structure and, 47–48
Friends, 448–450. *See also* Peer relations

G

Games, 461
Gametes, 87–88
Gang violence, 611–612
Gardner's seven frames of mind, 370–371
Gender. *See also* Gender role(s); Gender role
    stereotypes
  achievement and, 564–567
  biological influences on, 551–552
  definition of, 551
  genetic determination of, 88, 90–91
  moral development and, 593–594
  sexist research and, 35, 37, 563
Gender equity education, 555–556
Gender identity, 551
Gender role(s), 8–9, 549–580. *See also* Gender role
    stereotypes
  child care and, 573
  classification of, 567–571
  cognitive influences on, 557–560
  in Egypt, China, and the Soviet Union, 570
  ethnicity and, 573–576
  feminist perspective on, 571–572

identification theory and, 553
identity and, 542–544
parent-infant interaction and, 410
similarities and differences between sexes and, 563–564
social influences on, 552–557
social learning theory and, 553
social policy and, 572–573
transcendence of, 571
Gender role stereotypes, 560, 562–567
achievement and, 565
in media, 572–573
Gender role transcendence, 571
Gender schema theory, 558–559
Gene(s), 87–88, 90–91, 119
Generativity versus stagnation, 54
Genetic counseling, 92
Genetic epistemology, 12
Genetics, 86–103
behavior genetics and, 95–96
canalization and, 94
dominant-recessive genes principle and, 91
gene and chromosomal abnormalities and, 90–91
genes and, 87–88
genetic counseling and, 92
genotype and phenotype and, 93–94
heredity-environment interaction and, 102–103.
See also Nature-nurture controversy
intelligence and, 96, 97
polygenic inheritance and, 93
puberty and, 185
reaction range and, 94
reproduction and, 88–90
temperament and, 97, 99–102
Genital herpes, 116, 192
Genital stage, 51
Genotype, 93, 94
Genuineness, 68
Germinal period, 108–109
Gesell test, 375
Giftedness, 389–390
Global empathy, moral development and, 602
Grammar, 335, 353
Grasping reflex, 139
Gross motor skills, 147–148, 169–170
Group(s), adolescent versus children, 452
Group identity, self-esteem and, 527–528

H

Habituation, 234–236
Handedness, development of, 171–172
Handicapped children, educating, 505–507
Health. See also Illness
adolescent pregnancy and, 196
in developing countries, 176
development and, 174–175
psychological aspects of, 174
in United States, 177
Health care, pubertal timing and, 187
Health education, for preschool children, 174
Hearing, 157, 159
Heart Smart, 179, 180
Helpless orientation, 245–246
Hermaphrodites, 551–552
Heroin, prenatal development and, 119
Herpes simplex virus II, 116, 192
orality, 585

Heuristics, 322–323
Hierarchy of motives, 243
High school dropouts, 500–502
Hinde's neo-ethological theory, 71–72
Holophrase hypothesis, 347
Homeostasis, 242
Homosexuality, 191–192
Horizontal déclage, 276–277
Hormones
gender differences and, 563–564
homosexuality and, 191
during puberty, 183–184
Humanistic theories, 67–69
Hypotheses, 24
Hypothetical-deductive reasoning, 280

I

Id, 47, 48
Identical twins, 84–85, 95
Identification theory, gender roles and, 553
Identity, 535–544
gender, 551
group, self-esteem and, 527–528
social competence and, 532
social identity theory and, 527–528
Identity achievement, 537
Identity diffusion, 537
Identity foreclosure, 537
Identity moratorium, 537
Identity versus identity confusion, 54
Idiots savants, 371
Imaginary audience, 282
Imitation, 218
Bandura's concept of, 237–238
cognitive learning and, 237–241
deferred, 240
infant, 239–240
moral behavior and, 596
Immanent justice, 586
Immunizations, 177
Implantation, 109
Imprinting, 70
Impulsivity, 324
Incentive conditions, imitation and, 238
Independent variable, 31
Indirect moral education, 606, 607–608
Individual differences, 365
in attachment, 407–408
in information processing, 323–325
in intelligence, 365
standardized tests and, 27
Individualistic personality orientation, 74
Individuality, 540, 587
Individual rights, moral development and, 588
Induction, moral development and, 600, 601
Industry versus inferiority, 54
Infant(s), 18. See also Childbirth; Neonate
attachment and, 405–408
brain of, 148–149
care required by, 402
cognitive development in, 264–266
conceptual development in, 265–266
crying and smiling in, 141–142
emotions in, 142
fathers and, 409–410
with genetic disorders, 91
global empathy in, 602
hearing in, 157

imitation by, 239–240
intelligence tests for, 375–376
intermodal perception in, 160–161
language development in, 347–348
low-birthweight, 125–126
mothers and, 410
nutrition of, 149–155
pain perception in, 158–159
perceptual development in, 265
physical growth and motor development of, 145–148, 149
preterm. See Preterm infants
reflexes in, 138–142
self-recognition in, 519
smell in, 157
states of, 144–145
sucking in, 139, 141
taste in, 158
touch in, 158
types A, B, and C, 407
visual perception in, 155–157
Infertility, 89
Infinite generativity, of language, 333
Inflexibly focused state, in infancy, 144
Information age, 8, 314
Information processing, 297–328
about peer relations, 447
elementary cognitive processes necessary for, 303–309
higher-order cognitive processes and, 310–313
individual differences in, 323–325
in infancy, predicting intelligence from, 378
information age and children's education and, 314
knowledge and expertise and, 313, 315–323
learning and Piagetian approaches compared with, 300–301
nature of, 299–303
processing capacity and, 303
speed of, 302, 325
Information-processing theory, 59, 61–63
Initiative versus guilt, 53–54
Innate goodness view, 10
Instruction. See also Education; School(s)
computer-assisted, 469–470
expertise and, 323
Instrumental conditioning. See Operant conditioning
Integrity versus despair, 54
Intelligence, 363–396. See also IQ scores
artificial, 301
componential, 371
components of, reasons for multiple theories of, 374
contextual, 373
creativity and, 390–394
culture and ethnicity and, 381–386
definition of, 364–365, 368
early factor approaches to, 370
experiential, 373
Gardner's seven frames of mind and, 370–371
genetics and, 96, 97, 380–381
giftedness and, 389–390
heredity-environment controversy and, 380–381
of humans versus computers, 302
knowledge versus process in, 386–387
mental retardation and. See mental retardation
movement, 371
multiple-factor theory of, 370
musical, 371
practical, 374
predicting, 378

stability of, 376–378
Sternberg's triarchic theory of, 371, 373–374
two-factor theory of, 370
Intelligence quotient. *See* Intelligence tests; IQ scores
Intermittent reinforcement, 230
Intermodal perception, in infancy, 160–161
Internalization, 261–262, 587
Interpersonal norms, 587–588
Interval schedule of reinforcement, 229–230
Interviews, 26
Intimacy in friendships, 449
Intimacy versus isolation, 54
Intrinsic motivation, 244–245
Intuitive thought substage, 270–272
In vitro fertilization, 88–89
IQ scores, 368–369. *See also* Intelligence
    fetal alcohol syndrome and, 118
    genetics and, 96, 97
    stability of, 376–378
    use and misuse of, 387

J

Jigsaw classroom, 497
Justice perspective, moral development and, 591
Juvenile delinquency, 610–614

K

Kaufman Assessment Battery for Children (K-ABC), 385
Keyword method, memory and, 308–309
"Kilogram kids," 126
Kindergarten. *See also* Early childhood education
    child-centered, 480–481
    impact of preschool attendance on, 482, 485–486
Klinefelter syndrome, 90–91
Knowledge, 315–320, 386–387
Kohlberg's theory of moral development, 586–595

L

Labeling, language development and, 342, 344
Lamaze method, 123
Language. *See also* reading
    bilingualism and, 355–357
    definition of, 333
    development of. *See* Language development
    role in gender development, 559–560
    thought and, 287–288
Language Acquisition Device (LAD), 337, 341
Language Acquisition Support System (LASS), 341
Language development, 331–359
    in animals, 337–339
    biological influences on, 336–339
    in early childhood, 349–353
    in infancy, 347–348
    in middle and late childhood, 353–357
    role of cognition in, 345
    rule systems and, 333–336, 349–351
    sociocultural and environmental influences on, 340–345
Latchkey children, 431–432
Latency stage, 51

Learning, 219–241. *See also* Social learning theory
    classical conditioning and, 221–225
    cognitive, imitation and, 237–241
    expertise and, 323
    habituation and, 234–236
    of language, critical period for, 339
    nature of, 219–220
    operant conditioning and, 65, 225–234
    zone of proximal development and, 286–287
Learning disabilities, 508
    educating children with, 508–509
Learning theory, 300–301. *See also* Social learning theory
Least restrictive environment, 506
Leboyer method, 123
Literacy, 321, 351–353. *See also* Reading
Longitudinal approach, 33
Long-term memory, 306–309
Lorenz's classical ethological theory, 70–72
Love withdrawal, moral development and, 600, 601
Low-birthweight infants, 125–126

M

MA. *See* Mental age
Macrosystem, in ecological theory, 72–73, 75
Mainstreaming, 506–507
Malnutrition, 152–155, 176
MAMA cycles, 538
Marasmus, 152
Marijuana, prenatal development and, 119
Masculinity, 566–567
Mastery motivation, 242–243
Mastery orientation, 245–246
Maternal diseases and conditions, prenatal development and, 115–116
Math achievement, in Japan, China, and the United States, 248
Maturation, 20, 429–430
Maximally Discriminative Facial Movement Coding System (MAX), 142
Mean length of utterance (MLU), 348
Media, 464–470
    computers and, 468–470
    gender roles and, 556–557
    gender role stereotypes in, 572–573
    stereotypes of adolescents in, 205
    television and, 179, 464–468, 556–557
Meiosis, 87–88
Memory, 306–309, 386
Menarche, 181, 185
Mental age (MA), 368
Mental retardation, 90, 92, 116–117, 388–389
Merit, altruism and, 605
Mesoderm, 109
Mesosystem, in ecological theory, 72
Metacognitive knowledge, 318–320
Metaphor, 280
Microsystem, in ecological theory, 72
Middle and late childhood, 18
    altruism in, 605
    empathy in, 602
    friendships in, 448–449
    language development during, 353–357
    motor skills during, 172–173
    self-understanding in, 520–521
    skeletal and muscular systems during, 172
Mild mental retardation, 388
Minnesota Multiphasic Personality Inventory (MMPI), 27–28

Minnesota Study of Twins Reared Apart, 85
Minority groups. *See* Ethnic minority groups
Miscarriage, 112
MLU. *See* Mean length of utterance
MMPI. *See* Minnesota Multiphasic Personality Inventory
Modeling. *See* Imitation
Moderate mental retardation, 388
Monozygotic twins, 84–85, 95
Montessori approach, 476, 480
Moral behavior, 595–598
Moral development, 583–617
    altruism and, 604–606
    assessment of moral reasoning and, 591
    childrearing techniques and, 600–601
    cognitive social learning theory and, 598
    culture and, 594–595
    definition of, 585
    empathy and, 601–604
    gender and care perspective and, 591, 593–594
    juvenile delinquency and, 610–614
    Kohlberg's views on, 586–595
    moral behavior and, 591, 595–598
    moral education and, 606–610
    moral feelings and, 600–604
    moral thought and, 591
    Piaget's views on, 585–586
    psychoanalytic theory and, 600
    self-control and resistance to temptation and, 597–598
Moral education, 606–610
    cognitive, 607–608
    Damon's comprehensive approach to, 608–610
    direct and indirect, 606–608
    hidden curriculum in, 606
    values clarification and, 607
Moral feelings, 600–604
Morality. *See also* Moral development
    autonomous, 585–586
    conventional, 593
    heteronomous, 585
    postconventional, 593
    preconventional, 593
    social system, 588
Moral reasoning, 591
Moral thought, moral behavior and, 591
Moro reflex, 139
Morphemes, 334
Morphology, 334, 349
Mortality
    international comparisons of, 176
    sudden infant death syndrome and, 118–119
Mother(s). *See also* Family(ies); Mother-child interaction; Parent(s); Parenting styles
    age of, fertility and, 117
    age of, prenatal development and, 116–117
    diseases and conditions of, prenatal development and, 115–116
    drug use by, prenatal development and, 118–119
    emotional state and stress of, prenatal development and, 117–118
    international comparisons of prenatal care and, 128
    nutrition of, prenatal development and, 117
    role in family, 410
    transition to parenthood and, 403
    working, 430–432
Mother-child interaction
    in inner-city housing project, 342
    labeling and, 344
Motherese, 341

Motivation, 241–247
 achievement and, 243–248
 children's behavior and, 241–243
 competence (mastery, effectance), 242–243
 intrinsic and extrinsic, 244–245
 nature of, 220
Motor development
 cephalocaudal pattern of, 146
 during early childhood, 169–172
 fine motor skills and, 147–148, 170–171, 173
 gross motor skills and, 147–148, 169–170
 handedness and, 171–172
 during infancy, 146–148
 during middle and late childhood, 172–173
 proximodistal pattern of, 146
Motor reproduction, imitation and, 238
Movement intelligence, 371
Multimeasure, multisource, multicontext research
  approach, 29
Multiple-factor theory, of intelligence, 370
Muscular development, during middle and late
  childhood, 172
Musical intelligence, 371
Myelination, 169

N

National Association for the Education of Young
  Children (NAEYC), 482
Natural selection, 85–86
Nature-nurture controversy, 20, 22, 102–103,
  380–381
Need(s), 242
 hierarchy of, 243
 nutritional. See Nutrition
 of others in conversation, development of
  sensitivity to, 350–351
Negative reinforcement, 228
Neglected children, 445–446
Neo-ethological theory, 71–72
Neonate. See also Childbirth; Infant(s); Preterm
  infants
 bonding and, 132
 low-birthweight, 125–126
 maternal diseases and, 116
 measures of health and responsiveness of,
  129–132
 short-gestation, 126. See also Preterm infants
 visual perception in, 156–157
Neurotransmitters, in infancy, 148–149
Nonnutritive sucking, 141
Norm(s)
 interpersonal, 587–588
 test standardization and, 367
Normal distribution, 369
Nutrition
 development and, 177–178
 eating behavior and, 177–178
 eating disorders and, 201–203
 energy needs and, 177
 in infancy, 149–155
 infant eating behavior and, 151
 maternal, prenatal development and, 117

O

Obedience orientation, moral development and, 587
  ...ence, 262–264
  ...—26

Oedipus complex, 50, 52–53
Onlooker play, 457
Only child, 426
Open education approach, 478
Operant conditioning, 65, 225–234
 applications of, 233
 flow of events in, 226–228
 punishment and, 231–232
 reinforcement and, 228–231
Operation(s), preoperational thought and, 266
Operation PAR (Parental Awareness and
  Responsibility), 120
Oral rehydration therapy (ORT), 176
Oral stage, 50
Organ donations, medical use of fetal tissue and,
  114
Organic retardation, 389
Organization
 memory and, 307–308
 in Piagetian theory, 258
Organogenesis, 110, 114–115
Original sin view, 9–10
ORT. See Oral rehydration therapy
Overextension, 347
Overgeneralizations, 349
Overweight, 178
Ovum, 88
Oxytocin, during childbirth, 125

P

Pain perception, in infancy, 158–159
Parallel play, 457
Parent(s). See also Family(ies); Father; Mother(s);
  Parenting styles
 of adolescent, maturation of, 429–430
 adolescent drug use and, 200
 adoptive, 90
 attachment to. See Attachment
 children's career development and, 566–567
 children's television viewing and, 468
 divorce of, effects on children, 433–434
 gender roles and, 554
 influence of infants on, 102
 language development and, 342–344
 moral development and, 590
 moral education and, 609
 sharing and, 605–606
 working, 430–432
Parenthood, transition to, 402–404
Parenting styles, 416–420
Partial reinforcement, 230
PCBs, prenatal development and, 119
Pediatricians, education of, 39
Peer(s), 200, 443
Peer relations, 443–454
 in adolescence, 450–454
 cliques and crowds and, 451–452
 dating and, 454
 developmental course of, 445
 of ethnic minority adolescents, 453
 friends and, 448–450
 gender roles and, 554
 moral development and, 590
 parent-child relations and, 444
 peer group functions and, 443–444
 peer pressure and conformity and, 450
 play and. See Play

popularity, rejection, and neglect and, 445–446
 sharing and, 605–606
 social cognition and, 446–448
Penis envy, 52
Perception, 155
 auditory, in infancy, 157
 intermodal, in infancy, 160–161
 of odors, in infancy, 157
 of pain, in infancy, 158–159
 of tastes, in infancy, 158
 of touch, in infancy, 158
 visual, in infancy, 155–157
Perceptual development, in infancy, 155–161, 265
Permissive-indifferent parenting, 416
Permissive-indulgent parenting, 416–417
Personal fable, 282
Personality
 culture and, 74
 development of, Freudian theory and, 50–51
 structure of, Freudian theory and, 47–48
Perspective taking
 empathy and, 602
 peer relations and, 446–447
 role in self-understanding, 523–525
Phallic stage, 50
Phenomenological theories, 67–69
Phenotype, 93–94
Phenylketonuria (PKU), 90, 103
Philadelphia Institute for the Achievement of
  Human Potential, 256
Phobias, 223
Phonics method, 353
Phonology, 334, 349
Physical fitness
 classes for infants and, 149
 exercise and, 179–181
Physiological research, 29
Piagetian theory, 58–59, 257–286
 cognitive developmental theory and, 258
 cognitive processes and, 258–259
 concrete operational thought and, 274, 276–278
 contributions and criticisms of, 285–286
 evaluation of, 62–63
 formal operational thought and, 278–285
 information-processing approach compared
  with, 300–301
 moral development and, 585–586
 preoperational thought and, 266–272
 sensorimotor thought and, 259–266
Pictorial Scale for Perceived Competence and Social
  Acceptance, 526
PKU. See Phenylketonuria
Placenta, 110
Play, 454–464
Playgrounds, safety of, 174
Play therapy, 454, 456
Pleasure principle, 48
Pollution, prenatal development and, 119
Polygenic inheritance, 93
Popularity, 445
Positive reinforcement, 228
Postconventional morality, 593
Postconventional reasoning, moral development and,
  588
"Postpartum blues," 403
Power assertion, moral development and, 600, 601
Practical intelligence, 374
Practice play, 458
Pragmatics, 335–336
Precipitate delivery, 124
Preconventional morality, 593

Preconventional reasoning, 587
Predictive validity, 366
Pregnancy. *See also* Prenatal development
  adolescent, 195–197
Prejudice, 528
Prenatal development, 108–120
  course of, 108–112
  drugs and, 118–119, 120
  environmental hazards and, 119–120
  fetal period and, 159
  maternal age and, 116–117
  maternal diseases and conditions and, 115–116
  maternal nutrition and, 117
  miscarriage and abortion and, 112–113
  mother's emotional state and stress and,
    117–118
  teratology and, 113–115
Prenatal period, 18
Preoperational thought, 59, 266–272
Preschool(s). *See also* Early childhood education
  for disadvantaged children, 488–489
  education of, 480
  impact on kindergarten children, 482, 485–486
Preschool children. *See* Early childhood
Pretense/symbolic play, 458–459
Preterm infants, 125–127, 129
Primary circular reactions, 260–261
Primary reinforcement, 230
Print media, 557. *See also* Media
Problem solving, 310–311
Process, knowledge versus, in intelligence, 386–387
Profound mental retardation, 389
Project CHOICE (Creating Her Options in Career
  Education), 566
Project Follow Through, 488
Project Head Start, 488
Projection, 49
Prosocial behavior, effect of television on, 467–468
Prosocial skills, peer relations and, 446
Proximodistal pattern, 146
Psychiatrists, education of, 39
Psychoanalytic theories, 12, 47–55
  of Erikson, 51–55, 535–536
  of Freud, 47–51, 52–53, 600
  moral feelings and, 600
  valuation of, 55
Psychological changes, during puberty, 185–186
Psychological moratorium, 535
Psychometrics, 365
Psychosocial stages, of Erikson, 51–55
Psychotherapy, for learning disabled children, 509
Puberty, 181, 183–187
Public Law 94–142 (PL 94–142), 505–507
Punishment, 65
  moral development and, 587, 596
  operant conditioning and, 228, 231–232
Purpose, moral development and, 587

R

Radiation, prenatal development and, 119
Random assignment, 31
Ratio schedule of reinforcement, 230
Reaction formation, 49
Reaction range, 94
Reading, 353–355
Reality principle, 48
Reasoning, 587–588, 591
Recasting, 341–342
Reciprocal teaching, 312

Reciprocity, in altruism, 605
Reflection, 324
Reflexes, 221
  grasping, 139
  in infancy, 138–142
  Moro, 139
  rooting, 139
  simple, 260
  sucking, 139, 141
Reflexive smile, 141
Regression, 49
Regular sleep, in infancy, 144
Rehearsal, memory and, 307
Reinforcement, 65, 218
  history of, 231
  imitation and, 238
  immediate versus delayed, 228, 229
  moral behavior and, 596
  negative, 228
  operant conditioning and, 226, 228–231
  partial (intermittent), 230
  positive, 228
  primary, 230
  schedules of, 229–230
  secondary, 230–231
  shaping and, 228
  token, 231
Rejected children, 445–446
Reliability, 365–366
REM sleep, in infancy, 145
Repository for Germinal Choice, 97, 98
Repression, 49
Reproduction, genetics and, 88–90
Research. *See* Child development research
  on preterm infants, 126–127
  sexism in, 563
Resource allocation, social competence and, 533
Retention, imitation and, 238
Reward. *See* Reinforcement
Ritalin, 509
Rogers' humanistic approach, 68–69
Roles, gender. *See* Gender role(s)
Rooting reflex, 139
Rubella (German measles), prenatal development
  and, 115–116

S

Safety, of playgrounds, 174
Scaffolding, 404
Schedules of reinforcement, 229–230
Schema, 317, 558
Schemes, 260, 261–262
School(s), 475–513. *See also* Education;
    Kindergarten; Preschool(s); Teachers
  adolescent drug use and, 200–201
  assertive discipline in, 234
  assistance for talented girls in, 566
  changing social developmental contexts of,
    479–480
  child-centered kindergarten and, 480–481
  classroom structure and climate and, 492–493
  computers in, 470
  elementary, 480, 489, 491
  functions of, 478–479
  gender roles and, 554–556
  helping Hispanic youths stay in, 503
  hidden curriculum in, moral development and,
    606
  high school dropouts and, 500–502

  impact on children and adolescents, 477–478
  middle or junior high, 480, 497–500, 501
  Montessori, 476
  part-time work and, 504
  physical fitness and, 179
  school and classroom size and, 491–492
  social class and ethnicity in, 494–496
  teachers and, 493
School counselors, education of, 39
School psychologists, education of, 39
Scientific method, 24
Script, 317
Secondary circular reactions, 261
Secondary reinforcement, 230–231
Secure attachment, 407, 427–428
Self, 518–529
Self-actualization, 243
Self-concept, 68
Self-control
  immediate and delayed consequences and, 229
  moral behavior and, 597–598
Self-esteem, 525–529
  cliques and, 452
  definition of, 525
  ethnicity and, 528, 529
  group identity and, 527–528
  increasing, 528–529
  measuring, 525–526
  parent-child relationships and, 526
Self-perception Profile for Children, 525–526
Self-reference, elaboration and, 308
Self-understanding, 519–525
Semantic networks, 315–317
Semantics, 335, 350
Sensation, 155–161
Sensitive period, 71
Sensorimotor play, 458
Sensorimotor thought, 59, 259–266
Sensory and perceptual development, in infancy,
    155–161, 265
Sequential approach, 34
Sesame Street, 465
Severe mental retardation, 388–389
Sex. *See* Gender; Gender role(s); Gender role
    stereotypes
Sexist research, 35, 37, 563
Sexuality, 187–197
  adolescent pregnancy and, 195–197
  heterosexual behavior and, 188–189
  homosexual attitudes and behavior and,
    191–192
  sexually transmitted diseases and, 192–194
  sexual scripts and, 190
Sexually transmitted diseases, 116, 192–194
Sexual scripts, among adolescents, 190
Shaping, 228
Sharing, altruism and, 605
Short-gestation infant, 126
Short-term memory, 306
Shyness, 101
Sibling relationships, 424–425
Sickle-cell anemia, 90
Simple reflexes, 260
Skeletal development, during middle and late
    childhood, 172
Skinner's behaviorism, 63, 65, 66–67. *See also*
    Operant conditioning
Sleep
  following circumcision, 159
  REM, in infancy, 145
  states of, in infancy, 144

Slow-to-warm-up child, 99
Smell sense, in infancy, 157
Smiling, 141–142
Smoking, prenatal development and, 118–119
Sociability, 99
Social cognition, peer relations and, 446–448
Social competence, 529–535
Social developmental context, of schools, 479–480
Social identity theory, self-esteem and, 527–528
Social influences, on gender roles, 552–557
Socialization, reciprocal, 404
Social knowledge, peer relations and, 447–448
Social learning theory, 65–66
    cognitive, 66, 241, 598
    evaluation of, 66–67
    gender roles and, 553
Social play, 459
Social policy, 13–17, 572–573
Social processes, 17
Social smile, 141–142
Social supports, for language, 341–343
Social system morality, 588
Social workers, education of, 39
Society for Research in Child Development, 11
Sociocultural context, 289–291. *See also* Culture
    ambivalent messages about adolescence and, 206–207
    attachment and, 408
    of play, 462–464
Socioeconomic status
    family and, 420
    high school dropouts and, 502
    juvenile delinquency and, 611
    preterm infants and, 126–127
    schools and, 494
Solitary play, 457
SOMPA (System of Multicultural Pluralistic Assessment), 385
Speech, 348. *See also* Language development
Sperm, 88
Sperm bank, 97, 98
Split-half reliability, 366
Stability-change issue, 22
Sternberg's triarchic theory of intelligence, 371, 373–374
Stimulation, of preterm infants, 127, 129
Story schema, 317
Strategies, memory and, 307
Structure-process dilemma of intelligence, 386–387
Sublimation, 49
Sucking, 139, 141
Sudden infant death syndrome, maternal smoking and, 118–119
Suicide, among adolescents, 201
Superego, 47, 48
Superhero play, 460
Surface structure, 335
Symbolic drawings, 268–269
Symbolic function substage, 266–270
Syntax, 335
Syphilis, 116, 193
System of Multicultural Pluralistic Assessment (SOMPA), 385

T

Tabula rasa view, 10
Taste sense, in infancy, 158
Teachers, 493. *See also* Education; Instruction; School(s)
    expectations for children from low-income families, 494
    expectations for ethnic minority group children, 495, 496
    language development and, 342–343
    moral education and, 609
Teenagers. *See* Adolescence
Telegraphic speech, 348
Television, 464–468
    amount watched by children, 465
    effects on aggression and prosocial behavior, 465–468
    gender roles and, 556–557
    parents' role in children's viewing of, 468
    physical fitness and, 179
    portrayal of ethnic minorities on, 465
    roles of, 464–465
Temperament
    attachment and, 408
    genetics and, 97, 99–102
Temptation, resistance to, moral behavior and, 597–598
Teratology, 113–115
Tertiary circular reactions, novelty, and curiosity, 261
Testosterone
    gender differences and, 563
    during puberty, 183–184
Test-retest reliability, 365–366
Thalidomide, prenatal development and, 118
Theory, 24–25. *See also* Child development theories; *specific theories*
Thinking. *See also* Cognitive development; Thought(s)
    convergent, 390–391
    critical, 312–313
    cultural similarities and variations among thinking apprenticeships and, 290–291
Thought(s). *See also* Cognitive development; Thinking
    concrete operational, 59, 274, 276–278, 283
    formal operational, 59, 278–285
    intuitive thought substage and, 270–272
    language and, 287–288
    moral, moral behavior and, 591
    preoperational, 59, 266–272
    sensorimotor, 59, 259–266
Toddlers. *See* Early childhood
Token reinforcer, 231
Top-dog phenomenon, 499
Touch
    contact comfort and, 406
    sense of, in infancy, 158
Toxic wastes, prenatal development and, 119
Triarchic theory of intelligence, 371, 373–374
Trophoblast, 109
Trust versus mistrust, 52–53
Turner syndrome, 91

Twins
    fraternal (dizygotic), 95
    identical (monozygotic), 84–85, 95
    reared apart, 84–85
Twin studies, 84–85, 95
Two-factor theory, of intelligence, 370
Type A babies, 407
Type B babies, 407
Type C babies, 407

U

Ultrasound sonography, 92
Umbilical cord, 110
Unconditional positive regard, 68
Unconditioned response (UCR), 221
Unconditioned stimulus (UCS), 221
Underextension, 347

V

Vaccinations, 177
Validity, 366
Values clarification, 607
Variables, independent and dependent, 31
Venereal disease (VD), 116, 192–194
Video display terminals, prenatal development and, 120
Visual cliff, 157
Visual perception, in infancy, 155–157
Vocabulary, during middle and late childhood, 353
Vygotsky's theory, 286–291

W

Wechsler Adult Intelligence Scale-Revised (WAIS-R), 370
Wechsler Intelligence Scale for Children-Revised (WISC-R), 370
Wechsler Preschool and Primary Scale of Intelligence (WPPSI), 370
Wernicke's area, 337
Whole-word method, 353
Wild Boy of Aveyron, 340
WISC-R. *See* Wechsler Intelligence Scale for Children-Revised
Wisdom, 285
Work, part-time, school and, 504
Working memory, 386
WPPSI. *See* Wechsler Preschool and Primary Scale of Intelligence
Writing ability, formal operational thought and, 282

Z

Zone of proximal development (ZPD), 286–287
Zygote, 88, 108–109